Principles of Finance

Written for the MBA or undergraduate first course in finance, as well as follow-on courses, this textbook provides a clear, accessible, and thorough explanation of the principles of finance, how they connect to real-world practice, and how they are used to solve problems.

Structured around ten unifying principles representing the core tenets of the science, this book imparts basic financial concepts irrespective of the institutional framework, ensuring that students learn about finance in a way that is applicable both now and into the future.

Pedagogical features include learning objectives and major takeaways, applications in the world of business, numerous worked examples, key equation boxes highlighting the most important financial equations, Quick Check questions with solutions, key finance terms with a detailed glossary, and more than 380 homework problems. Online resources include a solutions manual, a detailed instructor manual to adapt the book to your course, lectures slides, and an 800-question test bank for instructors.

Zvi Bodie is Professor Emeritus at Boston University, where he was the Norman and Adele Barron Professor of Management. He has served on the finance faculty at the Harvard Business School (1992–1994) and MIT Sloan School of Management (2008–2009). Among his many published books and textbooks is the best-selling *Investments* textbook, with Alex Kane and Alan Marcus.

Robert C. Merton is the School of Management Distinguished Professor of Finance at the MIT Sloan School of Management and John and Natty McArthur University Professor Emeritus at Harvard University. Merton received the Alfred Nobel Memorial Prize in Economic Sciences in 1997 for a new method to determine the value of derivatives.

Richard T. Thakor is Associate Professor of Finance at the University of Minnesota, Carlson School of Management. He is a research affiliate at the MIT Laboratory for Financial Engineering (LFE) and at the WFA Center for Finance and Accounting Research (WFA-CFAR) at Washington University in St. Louis. He has published numerous academic articles in top economics, management, and finance journals, and has won multiple teaching awards.

PRINCIPLES OF FINANCE

ZVI BODIE
Boston University

ROBERT C. MERTON
Massachusetts Institute of Technology

RICHARD T. THAKOR
University of Minnesota

Shaftesbury Road, Cambridge CB2 8EA, United Kingdom

One Liberty Plaza, 20th Floor, New York, NY 10006, USA

477 Williamstown Road, Port Melbourne, VIC 3207, Australia

314–321, 3rd Floor, Plot 3, Splendor Forum, Jasola District Centre, New Delhi – 110025, India

103 Penang Road, #05-06/07, Visioncrest Commercial, Singapore 238467

Cambridge University Press is part of Cambridge University Press & Assessment,
a department of the University of Cambridge.

We share the University's mission to contribute to society through the pursuit of
education, learning and research at the highest international levels of excellence.

www.cambridge.org
Information on this title: www.cambridge.org/highereducation/isbn/9781108833813

DOI: 10.1017/9781108982610

© Zvi Bodie, Robert C. Merton, and Richard T. Thakor 2025

This publication is in copyright. Subject to statutory exception and to the provisions of
relevant collective licensing agreements, no reproduction of any part may take place
without the written permission of Cambridge University Press & Assessment.

When citing this work, please include a reference to the DOI 10.1017/9781108982610

First published 2025

A catalogue record for this publication is available from the British Library

A Cataloging-in-Publication data record for this book is available from the Library of Congress

ISBN 978-1-108-83381-3 Hardback
ISBN 978-1-108-98716-5 Paperback

Cambridge University Press & Assessment has no responsibility for the persistence or
accuracy of URLs for external or third-party internet websites referred to in
this publication and does not guarantee that any content on such websites is,
or will remain, accurate or appropriate.

Zvi Bodie: To my wife, Judy Bodie, whose patience and love keep me going.

Robert C. Merton: In memory of Paul Samuelson – mentor, teacher, co-researcher, colleague, and friend.

Richard T. Thakor: To my parents Serry and Anjan, and to my wife Stina, and children Aiden and Lily, whose constant love and support got me to this point and keep me going.

Zvi Bodie: To my wife, Judy Bodie, whose patience and love keep me going.

Robert C. Merton: In memory of Paul Samuelson – mentor, teacher, co-researcher, colleague, and friend.

Richard T. Thakor: To my parents Serry and Anjan, and to my wife Stina, and children Aiden and Lily, whose constant love and support got me to this point and keep me going.

CONTENTS

Detailed Contents		*page* viii
Preface		xvii
About the Authors		xxi
Acknowledgments		xxii
PART I	PRINCIPLES AND CORE CONCEPTS	1
Chapter 1	The Ten Principles of Finance	2
Chapter 2	Basics of Valuation: The Time Value of Money	12
Chapter 3	Personal Finance	55
Chapter 4	Principles of Valuation	75
Chapter 5	Financial Instruments and Rates of Return	102
Chapter 6	Principles of Risk Management	139
Chapter 7	Analyzing Uncertainty: Options	170
Chapter 8	Financial Statements: Analyzing and Forecasting	209
PART II	CORPORATE FINANCE	259
Chapter 9	Company Valuation	260
Chapter 10	Capital Budgeting	288
Chapter 11	Agency Costs and Governance	312
Chapter 12	Payout Policy	333
Chapter 13	Capital Structure	353
Chapter 14	A Unified Approach to the Valuation of Corporate Assets and Capital Structure	405
Chapter 15	Financing over a Firm's Life	439
PART III	ASSET PRICING AND FINANCIAL MARKETS	467
Chapter 16	The Term Structure of Interest Rates	468
Chapter 17	Portfolio Theory	513
Chapter 18	Capital Market Equilibrium	560
Chapter 19	Derivatives	594
Chapter 20	The Financial System and its Functions	634
Answers to Quick Check Questions		660
Glossary		705
Bibliography		722
Index		727

DETAILED CONTENTS

Preface xvii
About the Authors xxi
Acknowledgments xxii

PART I   PRINCIPLES AND CORE CONCEPTS   1

Chapter 1   The Ten Principles of Finance   2

Chapter Overview 2
Learning Objectives 2
Introduction 3
1.1 What Is Finance? 3
1.1.1 Why Study Finance? 4
1.2 Overview of the Financial System 5
1.2.1 The Institutions of the Financial System 5
1.2.2 The Functions of the Financial System 5
1.3 Ten Principles of Finance 6
Conclusion 11
Takeaways 11
Key Terms 11

Chapter 2   Basics of Valuation: The Time Value of Money   12

Chapter Overview 12
Learning Objectives 12
Introduction 13
2.1 Using Timelines to Analyze Cash Flows 14
2.2 Future Value and Compounding 15
2.2.1 Valuing Cash Flows Over Multiple Periods 15
2.2.2 Compound and Simple Interest 16
2.2.3 The Future Value Equation 17
Box 2.1 Calculating Future Values 18
2.2.4 The Frequency of Compounding 21
Box 2.2 Excel in Practice: Using Excel to Calculate the Effective Annual Rate 24
2.2.5 Future Value When Interest Rates Change over Time 24
2.3 Present Value and Discounting 26
2.3.1 Present Value of Multiple Cash Flows in the Future 28
2.3.2 Discounting with Compounding More Frequently Than Annually 30
Box 2.3 Excel in Practice: Using Excel to Calculate Present Values 31
2.3.3 Future Value with Negative Interest Rates 33
2.4 Investment Decisions Using Net Present Value 34
2.5 Valuing Annuities 37
2.5.1 The Future and Present Values of an Annuity 38
2.5.2 The Present Value of Growing Annuities 40
2.6 Valuing Perpetuities 41
2.6.1 Growing Perpetuities 43
2.7 Inflation and Discounted Cash Flow Analysis 44
2.7.1 Inflation and Future Values 45
2.7.2 Inflation and Calculating Present Values 47
2.7.3 Inflation and Investment Decisions 48
Conclusion 49
Takeaways 49
Key Terms 50
Key Equations 50
Problems 51

Chapter 3   Personal Finance   55

Chapter Overview 55
Learning Objectives 55
Equations You Know 55
Introduction 56
Box 3.1 Managing Your Personal Resources: Financial Literacy Is Trending around the World 56
3.1 Financial Decisions and Household Balance Sheets 57
3.1.1 Accounting and Economic Balance Sheets 58
3.2 A Discounted Cash Flow Model of Lifetime Labor and Consumption 59
3.2.1 Saving to Maintain a Constant Standard of Living 59
3.2.2 Using Excel to Plan for the Future 61
3.3 Should You Defer Taxes through Voluntary Retirement Plans? 64
3.4 Should You Invest in a Professional Degree? 64
3.5 Should You Buy or Rent? 66
3.5.1 Present Values of Buying Costs 66
3.5.2 Present Value of Renting Costs 67
3.5.3 The Decision 68
3.5.4 Breakeven Rent 68
3.5.5 Sensitivity Analysis of the Buy versus Rent Decision 68

Conclusion	70	Key Equations	99
Takeaways	70	Problems	100
Key Terms	71		
Key Equations	71		
Problems	71		

Chapter 4 Principles of Valuation — 75

Chapter Overview — 75
Learning Objectives — 75
Equations You Know — 76
Introduction — 76
4.1 The Crucial Role of Market Prices in Asset Valuation — 77
4.2 Value Maximization and Financial Decisions — 78
4.3 The Law of One Price and Arbitrage — 79
4.3.1 Limits to Arbitrage — 79
4.4 How the Law of One Price Determines Financial Asset Prices — 80
4.4.1 When Arbitrage Is Not Possible, There Is Still Dominance — 82
4.5 The Law of One Price and Valuation Models — 82
4.5.1 Choosing Valuation Models — 83
4.5.2 Valuation Using Comparables — 84
4.5.3 Valuation Using the Discounted Cash Flow Model — 85
4.6 Interest Rates and the Law of One Price — 87
4.7 Market Prices and Information — 89
4.7.1 The Efficient Markets Hypothesis — 90
Box 4.1 World of Business: Stock Market Reactions during the COVID-19 Pandemic of 2020 — 90
Box 4.2 World of Business: The Space Shuttle *Challenger* Explosion and Market Efficiency — 93
4.7.2 Valuation and the Efficient Markets Hypothesis — 93
Box 4.3 World of Business: Instantaneous Trading on the News — 94
Box 4.4 Efficient Markets Hypothesis in the Law — 95
4.7.3 The Efficient Markets Hypothesis and Behavioral Finance — 96
4.7.4 Extracting Information from Market Prices — 96
4.8 The Law of One Price and Efficient Markets — 97
Conclusion — 97
Takeaways — 98
Key Terms — 99

Chapter 5 Financial Instruments and Rates of Return — 102

Chapter Overview — 102
Learning Objectives — 102
Introduction — 103
5.1 Financial Markets and Instruments — 103
5.1.1 Debt — 104
5.1.2 Equity — 105
5.1.3 Derivatives — 106
5.2 Financial Market Rates: Interest Rates — 107
5.2.1 How the Time Pattern of Promised Payments Affects Interest Rates — 107
Box 5.1 The History of STRIPS — 111
5.2.2 How the Unit of Account Affects Interest Rates — 111
Box 5.2 World of Business: Series I Saving Bonds — 113
5.2.3 How Default Risk Affects Interest Rates — 113
5.2.4 How Inflation Affects Interest Rates — 115
5.3 Financial Market Rates: Stocks and Equity Funds — 116
5.3.1 Stocks — 117
5.3.2 Market Indexes and Mutual Funds — 118
5.3.3 Exchange-Traded Funds — 119
Box 5.3 Different Stock Market Indexes — 120
5.4 The Fundamental Determinants of Rates of Return — 121
5.4.1 The Expected Productivity of Capital Goods — 121
5.4.2 The Degree of Uncertainty about the Productivity of Capital Goods — 122
5.4.3 Time Preferences of People — 122
5.4.4 Risk Aversion — 122
5.5 History of Stock and Bond Returns — 123
5.5.1 Calculating Historical Rates of Return and Volatility — 123
5.5.2 Historical Equity and Bond Returns across the World — 128
Box 5.4 World of Business: Even Successful Investment Managers Are Not Always Successful — 130
5.6 Monte Carlo Simulation of Future Stock Market Performance — 131
Conclusion — 135
Takeaways — 135
Key Terms — 135
Key Equations — 136
Problems — 137

Chapter 6 Principles of Risk Management 139

Chapter Overview 139
Learning Objectives 139
Equations You Know 139
Introduction 140
6.1 What Is Risk? 140
Box 6.1 Knight's Approach to Risk and Uncertainty 142
6.2 Risk and Financial Decisions 142
6.2.1 Risk and Returns in Financial Investments 143
6.2.2 Valuation and Risk 144
6.2.3 Measuring Financial Risk 145
6.3 Risk Management 149
6.3.1 Risk Identification 149
Box 6.2 Investment Risk Defined by the SEC 151
6.3.2 Risk Assessment 151
6.3.3 Selection of Risk Management Techniques 152
6.3.4 Implementation of Risk Management Techniques 152
6.3.5 Review of Outcomes 153
6.4 The Three Dimensions of Risk Transfer: Diversifying, Hedging, and Insuring 153
6.4.1 Risk Transfer by Diversifying 153
Box 6.3 World of Business: Diversification and Expanding Drug Development 158
6.4.2 Risk Transfer by Hedging 158
6.4.3 Risk Transfer by Insuring 161
6.5 Risk Transfer and Economic Efficiency 162
6.5.1 Improving Welfare through Redistributing Risks 163
6.5.2 Allowing More Investments through Risk Transfer 163
6.6 Risk Management in Practice 164
Conclusion 164
Takeaways 165
Key Terms 166
Key Equations 166
Problems 166

Chapter 7 Analyzing Uncertainty: Options 170

Chapter Overview 170
Learning Objectives 170
Introduction 171
Box 7.1 Options Are Everywhere 172
7.1 How Options Work 174
7.1.1 Put Options 174
7.1.2 Call Options 177
7.2 The Put–Call Parity Relation 180
7.2.1 Payoff Diagrams for Stocks and Riskless Bonds 180
7.2.2 The Relationship between the Payoffs of Options, Stocks, and Bonds 181
7.2.3 Option Prices and the Put–Call Parity 184
7.3 Option Trading in Markets 187
7.4 Investment Strategies with Options 189
7.4.1 Using Options to Modify Payoff Patterns from Stock Exposure 189
7.4.2 Options as Building Blocks to Create Tailored Investment Strategies 192
7.5 Valuing Options: The Black–Scholes–Merton Model 195
7.5.1 The Black–Scholes–Merton Formula 196
7.5.2 Volatility and Option Prices 200
7.5.3 Implied Volatility 202
Conclusion 204
Takeaways 204
Key Terms 204
Key Equations 205
Problems 206

Chapter 8 Financial Statements: Analyzing and Forecasting 209

Chapter Overview 209
Learning Objectives 209
Equations You Know 209
Introduction 210
8.1 Financial Statements 210
8.2 Balance Sheet 211
8.2.1 Assets 213
8.2.2 Liabilities 213
8.3 Income Statement 214
8.3.1 Revenues 214
8.3.2 Expenses 215
Box 8.1 World of Business: Accounting for Employee Stock Options 216
8.4 Statement of Cash Flows 217
8.4.1 Cash Flow from Operating Activities 218
8.4.2 Cash Flow from Investing Activities 219
8.4.3 Cash Flow from Financing Activities 219
8.4.4 Total Change in Cash and Equivalents 219
8.5 Notes to Financial Statements 220
8.6 The Difference between Market Values and Accounting Book Values 221

Conclusion	70
Takeaways	70
Key Terms	71
Key Equations	71
Problems	71

Chapter 4 Principles of Valuation — 75

Chapter Overview		75
Learning Objectives		75
Equations You Know		76
Introduction		76
4.1	The Crucial Role of Market Prices in Asset Valuation	77
4.2	Value Maximization and Financial Decisions	78
4.3	The Law of One Price and Arbitrage	79
4.3.1	Limits to Arbitrage	79
4.4	How the Law of One Price Determines Financial Asset Prices	80
4.4.1	When Arbitrage Is Not Possible, There Is Still Dominance	82
4.5	The Law of One Price and Valuation Models	82
4.5.1	Choosing Valuation Models	83
4.5.2	Valuation Using Comparables	84
4.5.3	Valuation Using the Discounted Cash Flow Model	85
4.6	Interest Rates and the Law of One Price	87
4.7	Market Prices and Information	89
4.7.1	The Efficient Markets Hypothesis	90
Box 4.1 World of Business: Stock Market Reactions during the COVID-19 Pandemic of 2020		90
Box 4.2 World of Business: The Space Shuttle *Challenger* Explosion and Market Efficiency		93
4.7.2	Valuation and the Efficient Markets Hypothesis	93
Box 4.3 World of Business: Instantaneous Trading on the News		94
Box 4.4 Efficient Markets Hypothesis in the Law		95
4.7.3	The Efficient Markets Hypothesis and Behavioral Finance	96
4.7.4	Extracting Information from Market Prices	96
4.8	The Law of One Price and Efficient Markets	97
Conclusion		97
Takeaways		98
Key Terms		99
Key Equations		99
Problems		100

Chapter 5 Financial Instruments and Rates of Return — 102

Chapter Overview		102
Learning Objectives		102
Introduction		103
5.1	Financial Markets and Instruments	103
5.1.1	Debt	104
5.1.2	Equity	105
5.1.3	Derivatives	106
5.2	Financial Market Rates: Interest Rates	107
5.2.1	How the Time Pattern of Promised Payments Affects Interest Rates	107
Box 5.1 The History of STRIPS		111
5.2.2	How the Unit of Account Affects Interest Rates	111
Box 5.2 World of Business: Series I Saving Bonds		113
5.2.3	How Default Risk Affects Interest Rates	113
5.2.4	How Inflation Affects Interest Rates	115
5.3	Financial Market Rates: Stocks and Equity Funds	116
5.3.1	Stocks	117
5.3.2	Market Indexes and Mutual Funds	118
5.3.3	Exchange-Traded Funds	119
Box 5.3 Different Stock Market Indexes		120
5.4	The Fundamental Determinants of Rates of Return	121
5.4.1	The Expected Productivity of Capital Goods	121
5.4.2	The Degree of Uncertainty about the Productivity of Capital Goods	122
5.4.3	Time Preferences of People	122
5.4.4	Risk Aversion	122
5.5	History of Stock and Bond Returns	123
5.5.1	Calculating Historical Rates of Return and Volatility	123
5.5.2	Historical Equity and Bond Returns across the World	128
Box 5.4 World of Business: Even Successful Investment Managers Are Not Always Successful		130
5.6	Monte Carlo Simulation of Future Stock Market Performance	131
Conclusion		135
Takeaways		135
Key Terms		135
Key Equations		136
Problems		137

Chapter 6 Principles of Risk Management 139

Chapter Overview 139
Learning Objectives 139
Equations You Know 139
Introduction 140
6.1 What Is Risk? 140
Box 6.1 Knight's Approach to Risk and Uncertainty 142
6.2 Risk and Financial Decisions 142
6.2.1 Risk and Returns in Financial Investments 143
6.2.2 Valuation and Risk 144
6.2.3 Measuring Financial Risk 145
6.3 Risk Management 149
6.3.1 Risk Identification 149
Box 6.2 Investment Risk Defined by the SEC 151
6.3.2 Risk Assessment 151
6.3.3 Selection of Risk Management Techniques 152
6.3.4 Implementation of Risk Management Techniques 152
6.3.5 Review of Outcomes 153
6.4 The Three Dimensions of Risk Transfer: Diversifying, Hedging, and Insuring 153
6.4.1 Risk Transfer by Diversifying 153
Box 6.3 World of Business: Diversification and Expanding Drug Development 158
6.4.2 Risk Transfer by Hedging 158
6.4.3 Risk Transfer by Insuring 161
6.5 Risk Transfer and Economic Efficiency 162
6.5.1 Improving Welfare through Redistributing Risks 163
6.5.2 Allowing More Investments through Risk Transfer 163
6.6 Risk Management in Practice 164
Conclusion 164
Takeaways 165
Key Terms 166
Key Equations 166
Problems 166

Chapter 7 Analyzing Uncertainty: Options 170

Chapter Overview 170
Learning Objectives 170
Introduction 171
Box 7.1 Options Are Everywhere 172
7.1 How Options Work 174
7.1.1 Put Options 174
7.1.2 Call Options 177
7.2 The Put–Call Parity Relation 180
7.2.1 Payoff Diagrams for Stocks and Riskless Bonds 180
7.2.2 The Relationship between the Payoffs of Options, Stocks, and Bonds 181
7.2.3 Option Prices and the Put-Call Parity 184
7.3 Option Trading in Markets 187
7.4 Investment Strategies with Options 189
7.4.1 Using Options to Modify Payoff Patterns from Stock Exposure 189
7.4.2 Options as Building Blocks to Create Tailored Investment Strategies 192
7.5 Valuing Options: The Black–Scholes–Merton Model 195
7.5.1 The Black-Scholes-Merton Formula 196
7.5.2 Volatility and Option Prices 200
7.5.3 Implied Volatility 202
Conclusion 204
Takeaways 204
Key Terms 204
Key Equations 205
Problems 206

Chapter 8 Financial Statements: Analyzing and Forecasting 209

Chapter Overview 209
Learning Objectives 209
Equations You Know 209
Introduction 210
8.1 Financial Statements 210
8.2 Balance Sheet 211
8.2.1 Assets 213
8.2.2 Liabilities 213
8.3 Income Statement 214
8.3.1 Revenues 214
8.3.2 Expenses 215
Box 8.1 World of Business: Accounting for Employee Stock Options 216
8.4 Statement of Cash Flows 217
8.4.1 Cash Flow from Operating Activities 218
8.4.2 Cash Flow from Investing Activities 219
8.4.3 Cash Flow from Financing Activities 219
8.4.4 Total Change in Cash and Equivalents 219
8.5 Notes to Financial Statements 220
8.6 The Difference between Market Values and Accounting Book Values 221

8.6.1	Why Market and Book Values Differ	221
Box 8.2 World of Business: The Rapid Failure of Silicon Valley Bank		223
8.6.2	Calculating Returns with Market and Book Values	223
8.7	Financial Ratio Analysis	225
8.7.1	Profitability Ratios	225
8.7.2	Turnover Ratios	227
8.7.3	Financial Leverage Ratios	228
8.7.4	Liquidity Ratios	229
8.7.5	Market Value Ratios	230
8.8	Using the Financial Ratios: Information about Performance	235
8.9	Using the Financial Ratios: Market Valuation	237
8.9.1	Valuation Using Comparables	237
8.9.2	Using Ratios to Assess Firm Growth Prospects	239
8.10	Limitations of Financial Ratios	240
8.11	Future Financial Planning and Projections	241
8.11.1	Constructing Pro Forma Financial Statements	242
8.11.2	Working Capital and Liquidity Management	246
Conclusion		248
Takeaways		248
Key Terms		249
Key Equations		250
Problems		252

PART II   CORPORATE FINANCE   259

Chapter 9   Company Valuation   260

Chapter Overview		260
Learning Objectives		260
Equations You Know		260
Introduction		261
9.1	Company Value	261
9.2	Calculating Company Value: Valuation Using Comparables	263
9.3	Calculating Company Value: Discounted Cash Flow Analysis	265
9.3.1	Projecting a Company's Cash Flows	265
9.3.2	Terminal Values and Long-Run Growth Rates	269
Box 9.1 Calculating Cash Flow Growth Rates in Practice		272
9.3.3	Calculating Company Discount Rates	274
9.3.4	Sensitivity Analysis and Valuation Adjustments	277
Box 9.2 Excel in Practice: Sensitivity Analysis		277
9.4	Calculating Equity Value	278

9.4.1	Equity Value Using the Dividend Discount Model	279
9.4.2	Equity Value Using the DCF Method	279
9.4.3	Equity Value Using the Flows to Equity Model	280
Conclusion		282
Takeaways		282
Key Terms		282
Key Equations		283
Problems		284

Chapter 10   Capital Budgeting   288

Chapter Overview		288
Learning Objectives		288
Equations You Know		288
Introduction		289
10.1	Choosing between Investment Projects: Capital Budgeting	289
10.1.1	Where Do Investment Ideas Come From?	290
Box 10.1 World of Business: Microsoft's Expanding Empire Using Acquisitions		290
10.1.2	Evaluating Projects	291
10.2	The Net Present Value Investment Rule	292
10.2.1	Calculating Net Present Value	292
10.2.2	Estimating a Project's Cash Flows	293
10.2.3	Analyzing Cost-Reducing Projects	296
10.2.4	A Project's Cost of Capital	297
10.3	Other Project Decision Criteria: IRR and Payback	298
10.3.1	Internal Rate of Return	298
Box 10.2 Excel in Practice: Calculating NPV and IRR		302
10.3.2	Payback Period	303
Box 10.3 World of Business: Capital Budgeting Decisions in Practice		304
10.4	Inflation and Capital Budgeting	305
Conclusion		306
Takeaways		306
Key Terms		307
Key Equations		307
Problems		307

Chapter 11   Agency Costs and Governance   312

Chapter Overview		312
Learning Objectives		312
Introduction		313
11.1	Organizational Structure of Companies	314
11.1.1	Forms of Business Organization	314

11.1.2	Separation of Ownership and Control	315	Box 12.1 World of Business: Signaling with Dividends	342
11.1.3	Structure of Ownership and Control in Companies	316	12.3.2 Agency Frictions	343
11.2	Agency Problems	319	Box 12.2 World of Business: Global Tech Companies Reduce Cash Using Payout	344
11.2.1	Conflicts with Shareholders and Debtholders	319	12.3.3 Capital Structure Effects	344
11.2.2	Managerial Conflicts of Interest	320	12.3.4 Transaction Costs, Taxes, and Regulations	344
11.2.3	Conflicts of Interest and the Board of Directors	321	Box 12.3 The Legal Landscape of Share Repurchases across the Globe	345
11.3	Corporate Governance and Strategies: Internal Governance	322	12.3.5 Flexibility and Firm Life Cycles	346
11.3.1	Pay and Contracts	322	12.4 Stock Dividends and Splits	346
11.3.2	Shareholder Voting and Board Composition	323	Conclusion	349
11.3.3	Financial Policy	323	Takeaways	349
11.3.4	Voluntary Disclosure	323	Key Terms	350
11.4	Regulation and Market Discipline: External Governance	324	Problems	350

Chapter 12 Payout Policy — 333

11.4.1 Regulation	324	
Box 11.1 World of Business: The Sarbanes–Oxley Act	325	
11.4.2 Market Discipline: Hostile Takeovers	325	
Box 11.2 World of Business: The Hostile Takeover Attempt on Disney	327	
11.4.3 Market Discipline: Activist Shareholders	327	
Box 11.3 World of Business: Activist Investors, Netflix, and Japan	328	
11.5 The Challenge of Multiple Objectives	329	
Box 11.4 World of Business: An Activist Investor Gains Three Seats on Exxon-Mobil's Board	329	
Conclusion	330	
Takeaways	330	
Key Terms	331	
Problems	331	

Chapter 13 Capital Structure — 353

Chapter Overview — 353
Learning Objectives — 353
Equations You Know — 353
Introduction — 355

13.1	Internal and External Financing	356
13.2	Capital Structure and the Modigliani–Miller Propositions (No Frictions)	357
13.2.1	Modigliani–Miller and the Irrelevance of Capital Structure to Firm Value	357
13.2.2	Modigliani–Miller and the Effect of Capital Structure on the Firm's Risk and Cost of Capital	360
13.2.3	Calculating the Cost of Capital	363
13.2.4	Summary of the Implications of the M-M Framework	367
13.3	Capital Structure with Default/Bankruptcy Risk	368
13.3.1	Bankruptcy Risk and the Cost of Debt	369
Box 13.1 World of Business: Bond Ratings		370
13.3.2	Changes in Capital Structure with Default Risk	371
13.4	Capital Structure with Frictions: Taxes	373
13.4.1	Corporate Taxes	374
13.4.2	The After-Tax WACC Method	374
13.4.3	The After-Tax WACC Method with a Changing Capital Structure	379
13.4.4	The Adjusted Present Value Method	382
Box 13.2 Debt and Other Taxes		386
13.4.5	Calculating the Cost of Capital for Projects	387

Chapter Overview — 333
Learning Objectives — 333
Equations You Know — 333
Introduction — 334

12.1	Forms of Payout	334
12.2	Does Payout Policy Matter? Payout in a Frictionless Environment	336
12.2.1	Dividends in a Frictionless Environment	336
12.2.2	Share Repurchases in a Frictionless Environment	338
12.3	How Payout Policy Can Add Value: Payout with Frictions	340
12.3.1	Asymmetric Information and Signaling	340

13.5 Capital Structure with Other Frictions	388
13.5.1 Costs of Financial Distress	389
Box 13.3 World of Business: Toys "R" Us and Direct Costs of Financial Distress	389
13.5.2 Conflicts between Shareholders and Debtholders	391
Box 13.4 World of Business: Petrobras' Capital Structure and Debt Overhang	393
13.5.3 Advantages of Debt	393
13.5.4 Asymmetric Information	393
13.5.5 The Structure of Debt: Maturity and Seniority	395
13.6 Optimal Capital Structure	396
Conclusion	397
Takeaways	398
Key Terms	398
Key Equations	399
Problems	400

Chapter 14 A Unified Approach to the Valuation of Corporate Assets and Capital Structure — 405

Chapter Overview	405
Learning Objectives	405
Equations You Know	406
Introduction	406
14.1 Analyzing Corporate Equity and Debt	407
14.1.1 Equity	408
14.1.2 Debt	410
14.1.3 Determining the Values of Equity and Debt	413
Box 14.1 Applying the BSM Formula to Value Equity in Practice	415
14.2 Corporate Debt Structure	416
14.2.1 Capital Structure and Investment Decisions	416
14.2.2 Multiple Debt Issues: Debt Seniority	418
14.3 Guarantees and Other Securities	422
14.3.1 Credit Guarantees	422
Box 14.2 Government Guarantees	422
14.3.2 Hybrid Securities	424
14.4 Project Valuation Using Real Options	426
14.4.1 Types of Real Options	427
Box 14.3 World of Business: Real Options in Practice	429
14.4.2 Determining the Value of a Real Option	430
14.5 Applications of Real Options outside Firms	432

14.6 The Options-Based Approach versus DCF	433
Conclusion	434
Takeaways	434
Key Terms	435
Key Equations	435
Problems	435

Chapter 15 Financing over a Firm's Life — 439

Chapter Overview	439
Learning Objectives	439
Equations You Know	439
Introduction	440
15.1 Life of a Firm and Financing Sources	441
15.2 Sources of External Private Firm Financing	443
15.2.1 Bank Loans	443
Box 15.1 World of Business: The Banking System	445
15.2.2 Venture Capital	446
Box 15.2 World of Business: *Shark Tank* and Venture Capital	449
15.2.3 Alternative Sources of Financing	449
15.3 Going Public or Staying Private	450
15.3.1 Initial Public Offerings	450
Box 15.3 World of Business: eBay's IPO	453
15.3.2 Going Private and Private Equity	453
15.4 Mergers and Acquisitions	456
Box 15.4 World of Business: Culture and M&As	460
15.5 Bankruptcy and Liquidation	461
Conclusion	462
Takeaways	462
Key Terms	463
Key Equations	463
Problems	464

PART III ASSET PRICING AND FINANCIAL MARKETS — 467

Chapter 16 The Term Structure of Interest Rates — 468

Chapter Overview	468
Learning Objectives	468
Equations You Know	469
Introduction	469
16.1 Interest Rates for Different Borrowing Horizons	470

16.1.1 Certain and Constant Interest Rates	470	17.2.4 Achieving a Target Expected Return or Risk	524
16.1.2 When Interest Rates Differ by Maturity	472	17.2.5 Investing More Than Your Entire Wealth	525
16.2 Determining Interest Rates from Pure Discount Bonds	474	17.3 Portfolios of Multiple Risky Assets	527
		17.3.1 Portfolio Efficiency	527
Box 16.1 The Shape of the Yield Curve and Recessions	479	17.3.2 Portfolios of Two Risky Assets	528
		Box 17.2 The Fallacy of Time Diversification	532
16.3 Coupon Bonds	481	17.3.3 The Optimal Combination of Risky Assets	533
16.3.1 Coupon Payments	481	Box 17.3 Excel in Practice: Portfolio Calculations	538
16.3.2 Prices of Coupon Bonds	482	17.3.4 Selecting a Preferred Portfolio with Risky and Riskless Assets	540
16.3.3 Yields of Coupon Bonds	485		
Box 16.2 Excel in Practice: Calculating YTM	487	17.3.5 Portfolios with Many Risky Assets	545
16.3.4 Other Effects on Bond Yields	491	17.4 Mean-Variance Analysis and Asset Management	546
16.4 Uncertainty in Interest Rates	491		
16.4.1 Uncertainty in Interest Rates and Investments	491	Conclusion	549
16.4.2 Forward Rates of Interest	492	Takeaways	549
16.4.3 Estimating Forward Rates of Interest	493	Key Terms	550
16.5 Measuring Interest Rate Risk	496	Key Equations	550
16.5.1 Duration	496	Problems	551
Box 16.3 Excel in Practice: Calculating Duration	499	17.A.1 The Minimum Variance Portfolio	556
16.5.2 Convexity	501	Box 17.A.1 Excel in Practice: Calculating the Minimum Variance Portfolio	557
16.6 Real versus Nominal Interest Rates	505		
Conclusion	506		
Takeaways	506	**Chapter 18 Capital Market Equilibrium**	**560**
Key Terms	507	Chapter Overview	560
Key Equations	507	Learning Objectives	560
Problems	509	Equations You Know	560
		Introduction	561
Chapter 17 Portfolio Theory	**513**	18.1 The Capital Asset Pricing Model	562
Chapter Overview	513	18.1.1 The Capital Asset Pricing Model in Brief	562
Learning Objectives	513	18.1.2 The Capital Market Line	564
Equations You Know	513	18.1.3 Betas and Expected Returns	566
Introduction	514	18.1.4 The Security Market Line or the Capital Market Line?	571
17.1 The Process of Portfolio Selection by Individuals	515		
17.1.1 Personal Circumstances and Portfolio Selection	515	18.2 Applying the CAPM in Practice	571
17.1.2 Time Horizons	516	18.2.1 Using the CAPM in Portfolio Selection	571
Box 17.1 Computing Life Expectancy	517	18.2.2 Applying the CAPM Using Data	575
17.1.3 Risk Tolerance	518	Box 18.1 Excel in Practice: CAPM Calculations	577
17.2 Forming Portfolios: The Trade-Off between Expected Return and Risk	518	18.3 Calculating Discount Rates Using the CAPM	579
17.2.1 What Is a Riskless Asset?	518	18.3.1 Calculating Cost of Capital	579
17.2.2 What Are Risky Assets?	519	Box 18.2 World of Business: Do You Know Your Cost of Capital?	583
17.2.3 Combining a Riskless Asset and a Single Risky Asset	520	18.3.2 Capital Structure and Betas	584
		18.4 Alternatives to the CAPM	585

13.5	Capital Structure with Other Frictions	388	14.6 The Options-Based Approach versus DCF	433

13.5 Capital Structure with Other Frictions 388
13.5.1 Costs of Financial Distress 389
Box 13.3 World of Business: Toys "R" Us and Direct Costs of Financial Distress 389
13.5.2 Conflicts between Shareholders and Debtholders 391
Box 13.4 World of Business: Petrobras' Capital Structure and Debt Overhang 393
13.5.3 Advantages of Debt 393
13.5.4 Asymmetric Information 393
13.5.5 The Structure of Debt: Maturity and Seniority 395
13.6 Optimal Capital Structure 396
Conclusion 397
Takeaways 398
Key Terms 398
Key Equations 399
Problems 400

Chapter 14 A Unified Approach to the Valuation of Corporate Assets and Capital Structure 405

Chapter Overview 405
Learning Objectives 405
Equations You Know 406
Introduction 406
14.1 Analyzing Corporate Equity and Debt 407
14.1.1 Equity 408
14.1.2 Debt 410
14.1.3 Determining the Values of Equity and Debt 413
Box 14.1 Applying the BSM Formula to Value Equity in Practice 415
14.2 Corporate Debt Structure 416
14.2.1 Capital Structure and Investment Decisions 416
14.2.2 Multiple Debt Issues: Debt Seniority 418
14.3 Guarantees and Other Securities 422
14.3.1 Credit Guarantees 422
Box 14.2 Government Guarantees 422
14.3.2 Hybrid Securities 424
14.4 Project Valuation Using Real Options 426
14.4.1 Types of Real Options 427
Box 14.3 World of Business: Real Options in Practice 429
14.4.2 Determining the Value of a Real Option 430
14.5 Applications of Real Options outside Firms 432

14.6 The Options-Based Approach versus DCF 433
Conclusion 434
Takeaways 434
Key Terms 435
Key Equations 435
Problems 435

Chapter 15 Financing over a Firm's Life 439

Chapter Overview 439
Learning Objectives 439
Equations You Know 439
Introduction 440
15.1 Life of a Firm and Financing Sources 441
15.2 Sources of External Private Firm Financing 443
15.2.1 Bank Loans 443
Box 15.1 World of Business: The Banking System 445
15.2.2 Venture Capital 446
Box 15.2 World of Business: *Shark Tank* and Venture Capital 449
15.2.3 Alternative Sources of Financing 449
15.3 Going Public or Staying Private 450
15.3.1 Initial Public Offerings 450
Box 15.3 World of Business: eBay's IPO 453
15.3.2 Going Private and Private Equity 453
15.4 Mergers and Acquisitions 456
Box 15.4 World of Business: Culture and M&As 460
15.5 Bankruptcy and Liquidation 461
Conclusion 462
Takeaways 462
Key Terms 463
Key Equations 463
Problems 464

PART III ASSET PRICING AND FINANCIAL MARKETS 467

Chapter 16 The Term Structure of Interest Rates 468

Chapter Overview 468
Learning Objectives 468
Equations You Know 469
Introduction 469
16.1 Interest Rates for Different Borrowing Horizons 470

16.1.1 Certain and Constant Interest Rates	470	17.2.4 Achieving a Target Expected Return or Risk	524
16.1.2 When Interest Rates Differ by Maturity	472	17.2.5 Investing More Than Your Entire Wealth	525
16.2 Determining Interest Rates from Pure Discount Bonds	474	17.3 Portfolios of Multiple Risky Assets	527
		17.3.1 Portfolio Efficiency	527
Box 16.1 The Shape of the Yield Curve and Recessions	479	17.3.2 Portfolios of Two Risky Assets	528
		Box 17.2 The Fallacy of Time Diversification	532
16.3 Coupon Bonds	481	17.3.3 The Optimal Combination of Risky Assets	533
16.3.1 Coupon Payments	481	Box 17.3 Excel in Practice: Portfolio Calculations	538
16.3.2 Prices of Coupon Bonds	482	17.3.4 Selecting a Preferred Portfolio with Risky and Riskless Assets	540
16.3.3 Yields of Coupon Bonds	485		
Box 16.2 Excel in Practice: Calculating YTM	487	17.3.5 Portfolios with Many Risky Assets	545
16.3.4 Other Effects on Bond Yields	491	17.4 Mean-Variance Analysis and Asset Management	546
16.4 Uncertainty in Interest Rates	491		
16.4.1 Uncertainty in Interest Rates and Investments	491	Conclusion	549
16.4.2 Forward Rates of Interest	492	Takeaways	549
16.4.3 Estimating Forward Rates of Interest	493	Key Terms	550
16.5 Measuring Interest Rate Risk	496	Key Equations	550
16.5.1 Duration	496	Problems	551
Box 16.3 Excel in Practice: Calculating Duration	499	17.A.1 The Minimum Variance Portfolio	556
16.5.2 Convexity	501	Box 17.A.1 Excel in Practice: Calculating the Minimum Variance Portfolio	557
16.6 Real versus Nominal Interest Rates	505		
Conclusion	506		
Takeaways	506	**Chapter 18 Capital Market Equilibrium**	**560**
Key Terms	507	Chapter Overview	560
Key Equations	507	Learning Objectives	560
Problems	509	Equations You Know	560
		Introduction	561
Chapter 17 Portfolio Theory	**513**	18.1 The Capital Asset Pricing Model	562
Chapter Overview	513	18.1.1 The Capital Asset Pricing Model in Brief	562
Learning Objectives	513	18.1.2 The Capital Market Line	564
Equations You Know	513	18.1.3 Betas and Expected Returns	566
Introduction	514	18.1.4 The Security Market Line or the Capital Market Line?	571
17.1 The Process of Portfolio Selection by Individuals	515		
		18.2 Applying the CAPM in Practice	571
17.1.1 Personal Circumstances and Portfolio Selection	515	18.2.1 Using the CAPM in Portfolio Selection	571
17.1.2 Time Horizons	516	18.2.2 Applying the CAPM Using Data	575
Box 17.1 Computing Life Expectancy	517	Box 18.1 Excel in Practice: CAPM Calculations	577
17.1.3 Risk Tolerance	518	18.3 Calculating Discount Rates Using the CAPM	579
17.2 Forming Portfolios: The Trade-Off between Expected Return and Risk	518	18.3.1 Calculating Cost of Capital	579
17.2.1 What Is a Riskless Asset?	518	Box 18.2 World of Business: Do You Know Your Cost of Capital?	583
17.2.2 What Are Risky Assets?	519	18.3.2 Capital Structure and Betas	584
17.2.3 Combining a Riskless Asset and a Single Risky Asset	520	18.4 Alternatives to the CAPM	585

Conclusion	587
Takeaways	587
Key Terms	588
Key Equations	588
Problems	589

Chapter 19 Derivatives — 594

Chapter Overview	594
Learning Objectives	594
Equations You Know	594
Introduction	595
19.1 Types of Derivative Contracts	596
19.2 Derivative Markets	597
19.3 Options	598
19.4 Futures and Forwards	599
19.4.1 How Futures and Forwards Work	599
19.4.2 The Difference between Forwards and Futures	601
19.4.3 Pricing of Commodity Forwards and Futures	602
19.4.4 Extracting Information from Forward Prices	606
19.4.5 Financial Forwards and Futures	607
19.4.6 Pricing of Financial Forwards and Futures	608
19.4.7 The Economic Functions of Futures and Forwards Markets	610
19.5 Swaps	611
19.5.1 Interest Rate Swaps	612
19.5.2 Total Return Swaps	613
19.5.3 Currency Swaps	615
19.5.4 Credit Default Swaps	616
19.5.5 Swap Contract Pricing	617
19.6 Fundamentals of Pricing Derivatives	617
19.6.1 Dynamic Replication and the BSM Options Pricing Model	618
19.6.2 The Binomial Model and Replication: Pricing Options	619
19.6.3 Dynamic Replication: Pricing Options	623
19.6.4 Pricing Any Derivative	626
Conclusion	627
Takeaways	627
Key Terms	628
Key Equations	628
Problems	629

Chapter 20 The Financial System and its Functions — 634

Chapter Overview	634
Learning Objectives	634
Introduction	635
20.1 The Financial System	636
20.2 Institutions and the Financial System	637
20.2.1 Market Costs and the Design of Institutions	638
20.2.2 Behavioral Biases and the Design of Institutions	638
Box 20.1 Simple for the Individual: A Learning-by-Doing User Interface That Never Changes	640
20.2.3 Sociological Effects and the Design of Institutions	641
20.3 The Functional Perspective and the Financial System	644
20.3.1 Functions of the Financial System	645
Box 20.2 The Return of the 30-Year Treasury	647
20.3.2 Levels of Analysis	650
20.4 Financial Innovation	653
20.4.1 Financial Innovation and Market Forces	653
20.4.2 The Financial Innovation Spiral	655
20.5 Trust and the Financial System	656
20.5.1 Trust and Financial Markets	656
20.5.2 Building Trust and Substitutes for Trust	657
Conclusion	657
Takeaways	658
Key Terms	658
Key Equations	659
Problems	659

Answers to Quick Check Questions	660
Glossary	705
Bibliography	722
Index	727

PREFACE

Why This Text?

Modern finance is both a scientific discipline and a practical necessity. As a scientific discipline, it is the study of the allocation of resources over time and under uncertainty. In practice, it is about budgeting, saving, investing, borrowing, lending, hedging, insuring, diversifying, cash management, and risk-taking. It is also about the markets and institutions that facilitate these activities: stocks, bonds, options, futures, swaps, banks, mutual funds, hedge funds, exchange-traded funds, rating agencies, insurance companies, and regulatory bodies.

Finance is of course relevant to those who work in the financial industry, but it is also relevant to those outside the field. Around the world, a basic knowledge of financial principles and practices is essential for success in almost every area of life—personal, business, and public affairs. Indeed, financial literacy is becoming a social and personal goal almost on par with literal literacy (knowing how to read and write). Governments everywhere list universal financial literacy—or financial capability—among their highest national priorities.

Since the 1950s, the field of finance has seen several fundamental advances in theory and in practice, and in the interplay between the two. Finance has become an applied science resting firmly on a set of common principles, widely accepted quantitative models, empirical research results, and best practices. However, oftentimes the breadth of content in finance, with a wide range of ever-changing institutional details, makes it challenging for students to understand the field. We believe that it is time for an introductory finance textbook to fully integrate foundational principles and fundamental advances in finance theory and practice in a coherent and systematic manner to help students learn about finance.

In this textbook, the foundation is a set of ten unifying principles that connect the concepts and topics covered throughout the book. This principle-based foundation is combined with coverage of important discoveries in the field of finance that have had a profound impact on practice. One prominent discovery is option pricing. Nobel Prizes have been awarded for discoveries related to option pricing, yet it is rarely covered in introductory courses. Option pricing has had a profound effect on both the theory and the practice of finance. As such, this book positions it on par with the time value of money and discounted value as a fundamental valuation tool, and presents it as the key to understanding risk and risk management.

Put and call options are important financial instruments and trade globally in large size. Their importance to the understanding of finance is even more consequential because their payoff structure and pricing can be used to analyze and value a wide array of assets and securities, including corporate stocks, bonds, mortgages, and capital investment projects. Option pricing is also the key to valuing the cost of flexibility in financial plans. Option pricing belongs in the core because it is a powerful tool of analysis applicable in every part of finance. Our book therefore introduces option pricing early (Chapter 7) and in an accessible way that emphasizes its structural application to decision making under uncertainty. Options are applied subsequently to both corporate finance (Chapter 14) in understanding corporate securities and project selection and asset pricing (Chapter 19), where the actual securities themselves are analyzed more technically.

The overall approach offers instructors and students a number of advantages. Instead of focusing on an excessive amount of often-confusing institutional details, this book focuses on a unifying set of core principles that apply to all subfields of finance, at all times, and in all places. This equips students with an understanding that will help them to comprehend many of the ever-changing developments in finance, as the principles and core topics covered in the textbook are applicable now and will continue to be applicable over time. Rather than focusing on topics that may be currently newsworthy but quickly outdated, the core concepts and techniques covered in the book will be applicable long into the future, and permit an understanding of changes in financial markets related to technology, innovations, and so forth. We further provide clear, accessible, step-by-step explanations of the foundational concepts, and emphasize how they connect to real-world practice.

Who Is This Book For?

Principles of Finance is written for MBA first courses in finance and is also appropriate and accessible for equivalent undergraduate or masters in finance courses. Most texts for these courses focus exclusively on corporate finance. We retain the emphasis on corporate finance, but our scope is much broader.

How We Approach the Teaching of Finance

Our book is divided into three parts. Part I covers core principles that apply across all subfields of finance, at all times, and in all countries. We treat the chapters in Part I as a base of common knowledge on which the instructor can build in several different directions. Part II covers corporate finance, and includes a chapter that applies option theory in a unified approach to valuation for the entire balance sheet of the firm. Part III covers asset pricing and capital markets, including the term structure of interest rates, portfolio theory, capital market equilibrium, and the pricing of corporate bonds, stocks, options, futures, and swaps. It ends with a chapter on the financial system that explains why financial institutions typically differ across geopolitical borders and change over time, and how changes in the financial system can be analyzed.

Flexibility

The book has a modular structure, so that it can be used in courses and course sequences that vary in length and topical emphasis. The text readily accommodates instructors teaching a traditional one-semester introductory course in corporate finance. An instructor who wishes to emphasize capital markets in the first course can cover the chapters in Part I and then select chapters from Parts II and III. The chapters employing option theory are coordinated with the other chapters so that instructors can omit them without disturbing the topical coverage of their existing course.

Pedagogical Features

Each chapter follows a consistent structure that uses pedagogical features designed to engage students and to impart and consolidate the important lessons of the chapter.

Learning Objectives
Each chapter starts with a list of learning objectives to alert students to the main ideas and concepts addressed in the chapter.

Equations You Know
Each chapter starts with a table of key equations introduced in previous chapters that will be utilized in the chapter, to ensure students learn these important models.

Finance Scenarios
A list of finance scenarios opens each chapter to present students with problems they will encounter in personal and corporate finance settings, which can be addressed with the information covered in the chapter. Students see early how their study will apply in real-world situations.

Ten Principles of Finance
Listed and explained in Chapter 1, the Ten Principles of Finance are signposted in the text whenever they are pertinent to the topics being discussed. This approach reminds students that all of the various topics they are learning about are built on a firm base of knowledge embodied in the ten principles.

Focus Boxes
- Through each chapter, focus boxes expand on topics covered in the chapter. Examples are Box 2.1 "Calculating Future Values" and Box 3.1 "Managing Your Personal Resources: Financial Literacy Is Trending around the World." These boxes help students engage in more depth on information of particular note or use to them in understanding and retaining information in the chapter.
- **World of Business** boxes present real-life, interesting, and accessible case studies about the use and effect of financial principles in business.
- **Excel in Practice** boxes show students how to follow the processes of common working in the field that they will need to apply as part of their finance practice.

Examples
Examples illustrate theory at work in making financial decisions. Hypothetical and real-world examples are included throughout to illustrate the concepts and tools of modern finance. Problem-solving examples are covered at an accessible level with clear step-by-step explanations of the math and underlying concepts. We also incorporate the use of Excel where appropriate in the examples and in the end-of-chapter problem sets. This includes detailed explanations of how to perform certain calculations in Excel and illustrative spreadsheets. The examples show students how to use Excel to solve problems and to explore the models introduced in the chapters in more depth.

Quick Check Questions
Quick Check questions throughout the chapters help students check their understanding of the material just presented. Answers to these questions can be found at the end of each chapter so students can check their work.

Homework Problems
End-of-chapter problems cover the full range of topics in each chapter. Complete step-by-step solutions for all problems are provided in the instructor's resources in a format that allows adopters of the text to distribute them to their students.

Takeaways
A list of main ideas and key takeaways end each chapter to consolidate student understanding. The takeaways consolidate the learning objectives that begin the chapter and ensure students have understood the key concepts of the chapter topic.

Key Terms
Key terms are highlighted in red throughout each chapter to ensure student engagement with the terminology of the field. Listed at the end of each chapter with convenient page number cross-referencing, they are a convenient revision tool for students.

Key Equations

The key equations introduced and used throughout the chapter are collated at the end of each chapter for ease of student reference and review. This consolidates the equations in the table at the beginning of the chapter as they have been recontextualized by the chapter content.

Online Resources

A full suite of online student and instructor resources accompany this text to assist in teaching and learning. This includes:

- solutions manual for end-of-chapter problems;
- key equations test bank: code generated adapted versions of select problems for revision of the key equations, 10 per problem;
- 800-question test bank written by finance academics and subject matter experts;
- instructor manual: includes model syllabi mapping the modular structure to any finance course, explanations of pedagogy, tips for teaching difficult concepts and formulas, and suggestions for revision and assessment using the available supplementary resources;
- concept videos demonstrating important theories, models and workings;
- chapter introduction videos. The authors introduce chapter topics and inspire students in their study of finance;
- lecture slides for each chapter;
- Excel apps with functionality that allows students to model and analyze finance problems; and
- LMS cartridges of the end-of-chapter problems.

ABOUT THE AUTHORS

Zvi Bodie is Professor Emeritus at Boston University. Robert C. Merton is Distinguished Professor of Finance at Massachusetts Institute of Technology (MIT), and recipient of the 1997 Nobel Memorial Prize in Economics. Richard T. Thakor is Associate Professor of Finance at the University of Minnesota.

The collaboration and friendship between Robert C. Merton and Zvi Bodie began in 1970 at MIT's Sloan School, when Bodie was a new PhD student in economics and Merton was a new assistant professor with a reputation as a brilliant original thinker. Both Merton and Bodie were inspired by their teacher, mentor, and friend Paul A. Samuelson. Samuelson, who had employed Merton as his research assistant and supervised Merton's thesis, later referred to Merton as "the Isaac Newton of finance."

In 2010, Richard T. Thakor entered the Sloan School to pursue his PhD in finance. While at MIT, Thakor served as Merton's teaching assistant and wrote his PhD dissertation under Merton's supervision. In recent years he has worked with Merton as collaborator and coauthor of several joint research papers.

Each member of this author team shares a passion for teaching, and a strong belief that the first course in finance should be structured around several basic principles. Their guiding motto is "current best practice is not good enough." They were not satisfied with the existing textbooks, and so decided to create their own. The combination of experience, thought, and areas of expertise has allowed Bodie, Merton, and Thakor to write a book that will benefit students from all over the world, now and in the future.

Zvi Bodie, Robert C. Merton, and Richard T. Thakor

ACKNOWLEDGMENTS

Contributors

We would especially like to acknowledge William E. Zieff (Bill) as a team member for very helpful discussions and for contributing valuable content for the book. We also especially thank Jane Tufts and Jane Adams for their extensive help in development editing for the book.

Special thanks to the subject matter experts who wrote the online resources that support this book: Bill Zieff for the instructor manual, Excel applications, and lecture slides; and Adrian Cecotto, William "Andy" Fletcher, Jiahao Gu, Fred Hoffman, and Ronald L. Moy for their contribution to the test bank and solutions manual.

Some portions of content in this book are based in part on *Financial Economics* by Bodie, Merton, and Cleeton, the rights of which are owned/held by the authors Zvi Bodie and Robert C. Merton. We thank all contributors to that book.

Reviewers

The authors and the Press would like to thank all the academics in business, finance, and economics who provided invaluable feedback during the writing stage.

Abhishek Ganguly, University of Oklahoma
Adam Harper, University of South Alabama
Adam Lei, Midwestern State University
Adrian Cecotto, Southwestern Adventist University
Alexander Núñez-Torres, CUNY, Lehman College
Amy Tan, University of Winchester
Andrea Xu, Farmingdale State College
Arjun Chatrath, University of Portland
Asad Dossani, Colorado State University
Atul K. Saxena, Georgia Gwinnett College
Barkat Ullah, Morgan State University
Bob Barghaus, Western Connecticut State University
Bobby Merriman, Texas Tech University
Brian Haughey, Marist College
Cagla Yildirim, New Mexico State University
Charlotte Meierdirk, University of Brighton
Chee Ng, Ithaca College
Christine Beaudin, Nichols College
Christopher Coles, University of Stirling
Danielle Xu, Gonzaga University
David Louton, Bryant University
Denada Ibrushi, St. Mary's University
Donghyup Woo, University of Pittsburgh at Greensburg
Duong Nguyen, University of Massachusetts Dartmouth
Emanuele Citera, St. Lawrence University
Emma Xu, University of New Mexico
Farid AitSahlia, University of Florida

Frank Howland, Wabash College
Frank Van Gansbeke, Middlebury College
Fred Hoffman, Rutgers Business School
Gökçe Soydemir, California State University, Stanislaus
Hao Zhang, Rochester Institute of Technology
Hari Adhikari, Enbry-Riddle Aeronautical University
Harry Turtle, Colorado State University
Heather Bono, University of West Georgia
Heng Wang, Elon University
Honggang Qiu, Framingham State University
Howard Finch, Samford University
Hui-Ju Tsai, Washington College
Imtiaz Mazumder, St. Ambrose University
James Forjan, York College of Pennsylvania
Jane (Qian) Xie, St. Edward's University
Janet D. Payne, Texas State University
Jason Lee, University of California, Merced
Jason Morrison, Alfred University
Jay Wright, Georgetown University
Jenny Gu, University of Dallas
Jiahao Gu, West Virginia University
Jianyu Ma, Robert Morris University, Pittsburgh
Jinghan Cai, University of Scranton
John Lynch, Hofstra University
Jungjun Park, St. Lawrence University
Kainan Wang, University of Toledo
Kandarp Srinivasan, Northeastern University
Kelly E. Carter, Morgan State University

Lynda S. Livingston, University of Puget Sound
Madhuparna Kolay, University of Portland
Marc F. LoGrasso, Canisius University
Mark D. Schild, Seton Hall University
Mark Hoven Stohs, California State University, Fullerton
Md Asif Ul Alam, University of Texas at El Paso
Mia L. Rivolta, Xavier University
Michael Densmore, University of New Brunswick
Michael Ice, University of Rhode Island
Michael J. Stewart, Essex County College
Nan Li, Penn West University
Nell Gullett, University of Tennessee at Martin
Nicholas Mangee, Georgia Southern University
Omid Sabbaghi, University of Detroit Mercy
Pedro Sottile, University of Wisconsin–Eau Claire
Pete Vatev, Virginia Commonwealth University
Peter Haslag, Vanderbilt University
Phillip Braun, Northwestern University
PJ Glandon, Kenyon College
Rachel Graefe-Anderson, University of Mary Washington
Raisa Velthuis, Villanova University
Ralph Lim, Sacred Heart University
Rama Malladi, California State University, Dominguez Hills
Richard Cloutier, Whitworth University
Rizeanu Sorin, University of Victoria
Robinson Reyes-Pena, Florida International University
Ronald L Moy, St. John's University
Rui Liu, Duquesne University
Scott Emge, Loyola University, Maryland
Sehoon Kim, University of Florida
Seongkyu (Gilbert) Park, Willamette University
Shuangshuang Ji, Middle Tennessee State University
Song Wang, Angelo State University
Steve Salopek, Ohio State University
Susan Ji, Christopher Newport University
Tammy Schlosky, University of Illinois Springfield
Ted Heling, DePaul University
Tim Kesssel, Dickinson State University
Tuan V. Le, University of Findlay
Uliana Filatova, Florida Atlantic University
Vivek Singh, University of Michigan, Dearborn
Wendy Ku, Santa Clara University
William "Andy" Fletcher, Bethany College
Yizhao (Andy) Wang, St. Lawrence University
Yuriy Zabolotnyuk, Carleton University
Zhiguang Wang, South Dakota State University
Zhuoming Peng, Pacific University Oregon

PART I
PRINCIPLES AND CORE CONCEPTS

Part I covers core concepts and principles that apply across all of finance, at all times, and in all places.

Chapter 1 introduces the Ten Principles that are the foundation for financial decision making. The principles apply to financial decisions and problems in all settings: corporate, small business, nonprofit, government, or personal, as well as across different countries with different sets of institutions.

Chapter 2 explains the principles and concepts related to the timing of when costs are paid and benefits are received, including compounding, discounting, and the concepts of present value, future value, and cost of capital.

Chapter 3 applies the tools from Chapter 2 to personal financial planning. It addresses the issues of how much to save for retirement and other personal goals, and how to take account of inflation.

Chapter 4 explores the process of valuing assets and liabilities and explains how one chooses a valuation approach that will accurately reflect what the market price would be if sold in a competitive market, an approach used in virtually all financial decisions.

Chapter 5 introduces the variety of financial instruments that exist in the global financial system, and shows how to calculate their rates of return. We introduce the term structure of interest rates as the foundation for planning for the future both in the short term and the long run. We also survey the history of risk-free rates of return as well as the returns on risky assets around the world.

Chapter 6 explains the principles of measuring and managing risk, and presents a systematic procedure that begins with identifying key risks faced by a firm or a household, quantifying them, and deciding what, if any, action to take to mitigate them. We dive into three methods for managing risk: diversifying, hedging, and insuring.

Chapter 7 covers options, financial contracts that allow holders a choice of whether to do a transaction with an asset in the future. Options are at the core of decision making under uncertainty, providing an important framework for understanding risk in finance. We discuss the mechanics of how options work and an overview of their role in financial decision making.

Chapter 8 is about the analysis of financial statements for companies. The chapter makes a clear distinction between accounting and finance. Financial statements provide valuable information that can be used in ascertaining a firm's true market value, and are used as templates for financial forecasting and planning.

1 THE TEN PRINCIPLES OF FINANCE

CHAPTER OVERVIEW

1.1	What Is Finance?	3
1.2	Overview of the Financial System	5
1.3	Ten Principles of Finance	6

> **LEARNING OBJECTIVES**
>
> After reading this chapter, you will be able to:
> - define finance and understand how it can help you think more systematically about different issues that arise in your life and your career;
> - identify the major players in the financial system and describe the roles they play;
> - list and describe the Ten Principles of Finance that are the conceptual basis of finance.

✚ You are the chief financial officer of a major pharmaceutical company, and you must decide whether to launch a new drug development project. This project is expected to cost $2 billion over the next few years, and has an unknown probability of success. If the project is successful, however, it will generate additional revenues of $1 billion per year until the patents expire in 10 years. What factors should you consider in deciding whether to invest in this new drug?

✚ You are considering launching a startup with three classmates and wonder whether you should pursue this idea or take a job at a large established company. How much money do you need to get started? What are the risks and rewards? How should you structure the startup to maximize the chances of success? How do these costs and benefits compare with those of taking the job with the established company? In thinking about this decision, how do you evaluate and compare the many possible outcomes?

✚ You are part of an international team at the World Bank, analyzing a small African country's application for a loan to finance a major hydroelectric power plant. This

plant will provide a steady supply of electricity to one million city inhabitants who currently live in brownout conditions that disrupt their lives daily. However, building the plant will flood much of a river valley, requiring the relocation of tens of thousands of farmers and ranchers. How do you decide what to recommend?

- You are renovating your home and thinking about installing a solar power system. Will this save you money? If you are adopting solar out of concern for the environment, is the question about saving money the correct one to ask?

- Scientific evidence of climate change is now well established, but the implications for public policy are much less clear because any intervention will inevitably involve trading off current expenditures for very distant future benefits. In some cases, the benefits are so far in the future that they will not benefit anyone in the current or next two generations. How can finance help us think about how to make these trade-offs?

Introduction

This chapter opens with a list of scenarios that are all examples of financial decisions. It introduces a scientific approach to analyzing and making such decisions. We first look at what finance is and at the various contributions a study of finance can make to individuals, firms, and societies. Next, we look at a general overview of the financial system and the roles that various actors play within it. We then explore ten unifying principles from which all the tools and techniques of modern finance can be derived.

Throughout this journey, keep in mind specific personal goals you might have for learning finance, so that you can bring the principles to life and make them more relevant to you. After completing your study, you will be able to think more systematically about and, in most cases, come up with rational answers to many different issues that arise in your business, your career, and your life.

1.1 What Is Finance?

Finance is the study of the allocation of resources over time. One of the most remarkable innovations of the human species—something that makes us unique among all the species that have ever existed on our planet—is the invention of money and credit and the global financial system that has developed from it. It is no exaggeration to say that much of modern civilization is attributable to the ability of firms and individuals to engage in various types of financial transactions such as loans, pooled investments, fractional ownership of large business ventures, and insurance. Although people have engaged in financial transactions since the beginning of recorded history, we have only relatively recently developed a formal theory of financial decision making.

Financial decisions differ from other types of resource management decisions in that the costs and benefits of financial decisions are spread out over time and the results are rarely known with certainty in advance, either by the decision makers or by anybody else. These two factors—time and risk—are what make the study and practice of finance challenging and interesting.

Finance is one of the most important subjects that you will learn as you pursue your career. Finance is not only the lifeblood and the common language of all of business and management, it is also the most common and systematic framework for evaluating *any* decisions about the future that involve money or credit. This is true for decision making in households, businesses, nonprofit organizations, or government agencies.

1.1.1 Why Study Finance?

There are four main reasons to study finance that underpin how a finance professional interacts with their study, life, and future professional career.

First is *dealing with the world of business*. Finance is critical for evaluating any decisions involving money in any type of organization anywhere in the world. For example, suppose you are considering launching a tech startup to create a mobile phone app that provides users with real-time alerts anytime they are within 100 feet of someone they deem "interesting." To do this, you will need to develop the software, attract users, create a business model to generate revenues, figure out how to pay all of the costs of setting up the business, and balance these costs against the uncertain benefits of future business that the app might bring in. Describing these issues requires the language of finance, and many of the key decisions involved—whether to fund the startup with your savings or with other people's money, how to compensate your first hires, and what kind of subscription model to propose for users—are mainly financial. To recognize the limits of what can be done in an organization, it is crucial to understand the terminology, concepts, and techniques employed in finance.

Second is *managing your personal resources*. Knowing some finance helps you to manage your own income and wealth. Can you get along without knowing anything about finance? Perhaps. But if you are completely ignorant about financial issues, then you are at the mercy of others. You may seek the help of experts and there are many professionals and firms that provide financial advice. But how do you evaluate the advice you are given if you know nothing about finance? The study of finance provides a conceptual framework to help you make better financial decisions and plans.

Third is *pursuing interesting and rewarding career opportunities*. There are varied and potentially rewarding career opportunities in the field of finance, and many possible paths you can follow as a finance professional. Most finance professionals work in the financial services sector of the economy, such as banking, insurance, or investment management. However, many others work in financial roles in nonfinancial firms or in government—for example, in Treasury departments of corporations or governments—overseeing how those organizations raise and spend money.

While there are many careers one can pursue specifically in the field of finance, even if you do not intend to specialize in finance as a career, a background in finance provides a good foundation for better understanding how organizations work, and for a career in general management. Many chief executives of major corporations around the world started in finance. More generally, the concepts in finance are fundamental to any role in any sector. Finance centers around decision making under uncertainty, which involves understanding risk and flexibility, something that is ever-present in any business (and personal) situation. Finance also provides a toolkit that allows one to analyze uncertainty and risk in a systematic way, which helps to better inform such decisions.

Fourth is *making informed public choices*. The financial system is an important part of the infrastructure of any society. Indeed, a sound set of financial institutions is believed by many to be an essential element in economic growth and development. As a voter, or maybe even a policy decision maker, you may have to make political choices that affect the functioning of the financial system. For example, do you want to vote for a political candidate who favors abolishing government insurance that protects depositors from losing all their money if their bank should go bankrupt, or one who would impose strict controls on stock-market trading, such as allowing traders to only make trades of fewer than 5,000 shares?

* * *

Finance has been, is, and will be, essential for dealing with society's greatest challenges. As a species, *Homo sapiens* have been remarkably successful in their short history on this planet, largely as a result of technological breakthroughs in agricultural, medical, industrial, computational, and financial technologies. These innovations have addressed many issues with food, clothing, and shelter, but as the world develops, new and difficult challenges continue to arise: climate change, pandemics, cancer, Alzheimer's disease, poverty, famine, the looming energy crisis once fossil fuels are exhausted, clean water, space exploration and colonization, and so on.

Although it is impossible to know today how we will solve these enormous problems in the future, one thing is certain: finance will figure prominently in the solutions because they will all require unprecedented levels of global cooperation and coordination, and lots of funding. This is what finance excels at. The more informed we are about how finance works, the more successful we will be at using it to achieve desirable goals while avoiding unintended and undesirable consequences. If used carelessly and irresponsibly, however, finance can do great harm, leading to failed companies and ruined lives.

1.2 Overview of the Financial System

The financial system is the set of markets and other institutions that establish and enforce financial contracts and facilitate the exchange of financial assets and risks (its functions).

1.2.1 The Institutions of the Financial System

The institutions that make up the financial system comprise a varying mixture of the following:

Capital markets, in which stocks (an equity security that represents an ownership share in a corporation), bonds (a debt security that represents a loan to a corporation), and other financial instruments are traded.

Financial intermediaries, such as banks and insurance companies, which act as go-betweens for parties engaged in financial transactions.

Financial service firms, such as tax preparers and financial advisors, which help people and firms understand the various parts and rules of the complex financial system and show them how they can take part in and benefit from it.

Regulators, such as the various governmental, economic, industrial, and business bodies that set and enforce the rules by which all participants in the financial system must operate. The financial system (and indeed all markets) requires rules to function at all, and requires additional rules to function well.

For a variety of reasons—including differences in size, complexity, and available technology, as well as differences in political, cultural, and historical backgrounds—financial institutions generally differ from country to country. They also change over time. Even when the names of institutions are the same, the functions they perform often differ dramatically. For example, banks in the United States today are very different from what they were in 1928 or in 1958, and banks in the United States today are very different from the institutions called banks in Germany or the United Kingdom today.

The second aspect of the financial system, its functions, provides a unifying conceptual framework for understanding how and why financial institutions differ from country to country and why they change over time.

1.2.2 The Functions of the Financial System

The functional perspective framework focuses (as you probably expect from its name!) on functions rather than institutions. The functional perspective rests on two basic premises:

- Financial functions are more stable than financial institutions; they change less over time and vary less from country to country.
- Institutional form follows function; innovation and competition among institutions ultimately result in greater efficiency in how well the financial system performs its functions.

The financial system achieves its overarching goal of allocating resources efficiently by performing six basic functions.

1. It provides ways to transfer economic resources through time, across borders, and among industries.
2. It provides ways to manage the risk inherent in a market economy.
3. It facilitates trade by clearing and settling payments to facilitate trade.
4. It enables people and businesses to pool resources for investment purposes and to subdivide ownership in various enterprises.
5. It provides price information to help coordinate decision making among market participants in various sectors of the economy.
6. It provides ways of dealing with the incentive problems created when one party to a transaction has information that the other party does not or when one party acts on behalf of another.

The breadth and depth of modern financial systems are unprecedented, thanks to the remarkable growth in financial innovation that has occurred over the past half-century. In the chapters that follow, we will build up your understanding of the structures and functions to enrich your understanding of the overall financial system.

1.3 Ten Principles of Finance

Now that we have a basic understanding of the key players and functions in the financial system, we are ready to introduce the Ten Principles of Finance, a foundation of core concepts that underlie all of finance and are applicable to the entire financial system, regardless of time and place.

Table 1.1 The Ten Principles of Finance

Principle 1.	A dollar today is not worth the same as a dollar tomorrow.
Principle 2.	Equivalent assets that can be freely bought and sold will have the same market price.
Principle 3.	There is no such thing as a free lunch in finance; everything has a cost.
Principle 4.	Every model is an incomplete, simplified description of a complex reality.
Principle 5.	The best estimate of an asset's value is usually its market price, which incorporates valuable information to guide the allocation of resources and risks.
Principle 6.	Risk is fundamental to financial analysis and must be explicitly considered in all financial decisions.
Principle 7.	There is a trade-off between risk and expected return.
Principle 8.	Flexibility in financial decisions has value, and the greater the uncertainty, the greater the value.
Principle 9.	Transparency, verification, and trust are all important to the proper functioning of the financial system.
Principle 10.	The basic functions of a financial system are essentially the same in all economies all over the world, past, present, and future, but the institutions used to perform these functions differ across geopolitical borders and over time.

Here, we provide a brief introduction to the Ten Principles of Finance. It's likely that you will not fully comprehend these principles right away, but don't worry—we expand on them greatly throughout the book. For now, they will give you a good idea of what finance is all about.

Principle 1. *A dollar today is not worth the same as a dollar tomorrow.*

This principle embodies a crucial concept in finance, the time value of money, which states that, at a positive interest rate, a sum of money will grow in value over time. For example, if you deposit $100 in a savings account and earn 2% interest per year, you will end up with $102 in one year. If you do not make any withdrawals, the amount in your account will grow exponentially at 2% per year. This principle focuses on the value of assets across time (e.g., in the future).

Principle 2. *(Law of one price) Equivalent assets that can be freely bought and sold will have the same market price.*

If you want to buy a share of General Motors (GM) stock, you can call a broker or look up on your computer how much it would cost you. You do not have to shop around for the cheapest price, because all shares of GM stock are equivalent and have the same price. The reason you and everyone else do not need to waste time and effort in shopping around is the law of one price, which states that in markets where assets can be freely bought and sold equivalent assets will sell for the same price. In contrast to Principle 1, which addresses asset value at different times, this principle focuses on an asset's value at one point in time: right now. The law of one price is a statement about the price of one asset relative to the price of another right now; it tells us that if the current price of GM stock on the New York Stock Exchange is $54 per share, we can be reasonably sure that its price in London is the same, £39 (= $54).

The law of one price is the most fundamental valuation principle in finance. If observed prices appear to violate the law, so that seemingly identical assets are selling at different prices, our first suspicion should not be that this is an exception to the law of one price, but that (1) something is interfering with the normal operation of the market or (2) there is some (perhaps undetected) economic difference between the two assets.

Principle 3. *There is no such thing as a free lunch in finance; everything has a cost.*

Finance deals with the allocation of scarce resources over time and under uncertainty, and this allocation *always* involves making trade-offs between costs and benefits. For example, when you borrow, you receive money in the present (a benefit) and pay it back with interest in the future (a cost). When you lend, you give money in the present (cost) and get it back with interest in the future (benefit).

Often, in finance, it *seems* that you can get a "free lunch" and receive a benefit without paying a cost. But be assured: Even when it seems like there is no cost, there is *always* a cost. Thus, if some financial transaction seems too good to be true, it is almost certain to not be true. Consider the following scenario: US Treasury (UST) bonds promise a 1% interest rate, which is risk-free: No matter what happens, you will earn 1% on the bond. Now suppose some company offers you a product or security that promises to pay a 5% interest rate, and, *from what you can determine*, there appears to be no risk involved. Like the UST, this product will pay its 5% interest no matter what happens. What should you do?

You might be tempted to grab the product with the greater return, but this is not the wisest choice. Instead, you should ask yourself why you (and probably others) are so lucky to get this high-interest product. "Why would others buy UST bonds at 1% when they could get 5%? Am I much smarter than those buying UST bonds?" The UST bond market is one of the largest in the world, and most of the direct investors in them are the largest and most sophisticated financial investment institutions in the world. If this 5% opportunity is truly risk-free, then why do these knowledgeable full-time investing professionals with enormous resources invest at 1% when they could purchase the same investment you are considering and earn 5% risk-free? Have you found a goldmine investment they do not know about despite their resources?

If you do not have a definitive answer to these questions, it is likely that this 5% security carries a risk (and likely a very large risk) that you will lose your money. And if you don't see what the risks are, it is wise to not buy it.

Principle 4. *Every model is an incomplete, simplified description of a complex reality.*

To determine the best model to analyze any given financial problem, situation, or decision, one must consider three criteria:

- What to include in the model: what factors to include, what factors to exclude.
- Who will be using the model: Does the model illuminate or explain what the user needs it to explain?
- What the model will be used for: Is the model to be used for making buy and sell decisions, making fundamental changes in how a company is organized, or for some other purpose?

For example, to run a small retail store the owner may require nothing more than a model that projects revenues, expenses, and profit or loss. The managers of a large multinational corporation, however, might require a highly detailed computer model to guide their decisions about how to allocate capital to each division in the firm. The lesson is that you need to carefully choose or develop a model so that it will lead you to a helpful solution or recommendation, and not lead you astray.

Principle 5. *The best estimate of an asset's value is usually its market price, which incorporates valuable information to guide the allocation of resources and risks.*

Many financial decisions boil down to figuring out how much assets are worth. For example, in deciding whether to invest in a security such as a stock or a bond or in a business opportunity, you have to determine whether the price being asked is high or low relative to other investment opportunities. In addition to investment decisions, there are many other situations in which you need to determine the value of an asset. For example, suppose the tax assessor in your town assesses your house at $500,000 for property tax purposes. Is this value too high or too low? Or suppose you and your siblings inherit some property, and you decide to sell it and share the proceeds equally among yourselves. How do you decide how much it is worth?

The key idea underlying all valuation procedures is that to estimate how much an asset is worth you must use information about one or more comparable assets whose market prices you know. For example, realtors arrive at the value of a house by looking at recently sold homes that are similar to the property they're trying to buy or sell in terms of location, size, condition, and features. These houses are then used to determine a home's fair market value.

Principle 6. *Risk is fundamental to financial analysis and must be explicitly considered in all financial decisions.*

Virtually *every* financial activity involves uncertainty and risk. And this risk must be measured and managed to successfully accomplish specific financial goals. For corporations, the goal is to maximize shareholder value; for individuals, the goal is to maximize their well-being.

Measuring risk starts with identifying something that has no risk attached to it. Once a risk-free asset or strategy has been identified, the risk of another asset can be measured in relation to what is risk-free.

Principle 7. *There is a trade-off between risk and expected return.*

The theory of finance assumes that people will avoid risk unless they are compensated for bearing it. The compensation takes the form of expected returns that are greater than the return that can be earned on a risk-free asset. Investors have to be compensated only for bearing risk that cannot be managed in any other way.

To illustrate, suppose you are considering whether to buy the stocks of two different companies. One company sells consumer electronics, and its sales depend heavily on how well the economy is doing; when the economy is doing well, consumers have money to spend on new gadgets. The other is a utility company, which provides electricity and gas to its customers. The demand for these goods changes very little over time because they are essential services. Compared to the utility company, the electronics company faces higher risk because how well it does changes more over time. For an investor to choose to invest in the electronics company over the utility company, they would demand the electronics company provide a higher expected return in exchange for the risk faced.

Principle 8. *Flexibility in financial decisions has value, and the greater the uncertainty, the greater the value.*

As Principle 6 notes, risk is an essential element of every financial decision. Risk stems from the fact that the future is inherently uncertain. With risk being an ever-present force in financial decisions, this means that having flexibility—the ability to decide what to do in the future after some uncertainty is resolved—is valuable because it can reduce the risk that is inherent in financial decisions. There are many everyday financial decisions that exemplify this. For example, consider the risk in buying a car—the ability to return it if it has previously undetected defects eliminates uncertainty. Flight insurance that allows you a refund if a flight is cancelled or significantly delayed eliminates a good deal of uncertainty with air travel.

There are a variety of financial contracts known as options, which allow the holder the ability to make decisions in the future once outcomes are known. For example, a type of option—a call option— allows the holder to make a decision about whether or not to purchase an asset (such as a share stock) for an agreed-upon amount in the future once the price is known. Since the holder can just walk away and decide not to purchase it once the price is known, the contract eliminates uncertainty about the price. In particular, purchasing an option now makes it possible for its owner to plan for making financial decisions about risky strategies in the future after uncertainty is resolved, whereas in general someone considering a financial decision must make their purchasing choice in advance of knowing how the risk will play out in the future.

By embedding flexibility into them, options allow an analysis of uncertainty and risk in financial decisions. A range of formal financial tools have been developed to analyze options, and thus uncertainty in many contexts. Indeed, underscoring this, the applications of options analysis in the real world are numerous, including financial markets, but also extending far beyond financial markets. Examples include financial contracts traded in markets, insurance contracts, product development decisions, research and development, and medical insurance.

Principle 9. *Transparency, verification, and trust are all important to the proper functioning of the financial system.*

Customers must pay to purchase financial products. With any such transaction, there is the danger that the other party may renege or otherwise not be able to deliver the product as agreed. For example, if you give your money to a financial advisor, you expect them to have the skills to make investments with the risk, return, and cost properties you've requested and to execute decisions in your best interests. Investors buying shares of a company's stock expect the managers running the company to make investments in its owners' interests. If you trust your financial advisor or investors trust a company's managers, then there is no impediment to these transactions taking place. But if there is a concern that the advisor or managers are either incompetent or have interests that conflict with yours, mutually beneficial financial transactions may not occur.

There are three ways to efficiently implement financial transactions: transparency, verification, and trust. Transparency means that all parties to a financial transaction have available to them all the relevant information they need to make an informed decision. Companies that sell their shares on established stock exchanges, for example, are required by law to disclose to investors information such as profit, loss, and risks. Companies that do not trade publicly can choose to voluntarily disclose such information. Transparency allows people to work with financial advisors to more confidently achieve their goals, and allows companies to more easily sell shares of stock to raise money.

Verification is the second process that encourages parties to enter into financial transactions. Verification means that information provided to the customer has been examined and certified by a third party to be true. For example, auditors perform the verification function of certifying that company financial statements are accurate and meet industry and legal standards.

Some financial products, such as financial advice, cannot be made transparent and are difficult to verify. In the absence of either sufficient transparency or verification, transactions involving such products can only succeed if the purchasers trust the provider. Trust is the belief that someone or something is reliable, truthful, and capable. In some cases, transparency or verification can be combined with trust; in other cases, trust is the only thing to rely on. Consider, for example, a self-directed retirement plan in which customers make contributions over many years and then draw the funds out after they retire. Today, most such plans offer no guaranteed outcome, so the risk is borne by the customer. But very few customers are capable of managing the fund on their own in a way that produces a secure, steady stream of income that will last a lifetime after retirement. To achieve their goal of a secure retirement, customers rely on the guidance of professional advisors and online tools. If the provider offers a credible guarantee (that the customer pays for) of a certain level of lifetime income, then the customer can trust that the provider will do a good job.

Principle 10. *The basic functions of a financial system are the same in all economies all over the world, past, present, and future, but the institutions used to perform these functions differ across geopolitical borders and change over time.*

Financial decisions are always made within the context of a financial system that both constrains and enables the decision maker. Effective financial decisions thus require an understanding of that system. Suppose, for example, that you want to further your education, buy a house, or start a new business. Where can you get the funds to do it? The answer to this question depends very much on where you are located. The roles played by families, governments, and private sector institutions (such as banks and securities markets) in financing economic activities vary considerably between countries. What's more, these roles change over time.

In this book, the functional and structural framework informs our discussions of financial systems. This approach allows us to understand the specific kinds of financial institutions, markets, instruments, contracts, and regulatory bodies that will or should evolve in response to underlying changes in a nation's technology, politics, demographics, and cultural norms.

As an illustration, in recent years advances in financial technology have provided new ways to make deposits to a bank account swiftly and reliably at low cost. As a result, the old system of walking into a bank, writing out a deposit form, and standing in line to wait for a human bank teller to be free to accept your deposit, is now an outmoded technology. Instead, a check can be deposited by accessing your bank's app and taking a picture of the check on your phone and submitting the photo to the bank. Even though the institutional form has changed, however, the function of clearing and settling deposits remains.

∗ ∗ ∗

It is a bold claim that these principles form the basis of *all* of modern financial analysis. But in short order it will become clear that at least one of these principles lies at the heart of every topic in this text. More importantly, a deep understanding of these principles will serve as a durable foundation for many rewarding career paths in business and will serve you well in making plans and decisions in many aspects of your life.

Conclusion

In this chapter we have provided a broad introduction of what finance is and why it is important to study, and given a general overview of the financial system. We also introduced the ten fundamental principles of finance that form the foundation of everything that we will talk about in this book, and from which all of the tools and techniques of modern finance come.

From this starting point, the subsequent chapters will delve into details and develop the necessary tools needed to understand the essential tenets of finance. In Part I we begin with the core toolkit and foundations needed to analyze financial decisions. Part II utilizes and expands this toolkit to examine financial decisions made by companies, while Part III does so for financial market investments. Throughout, we show how the core principles of finance are critical to understanding all decisions within the financial sector, whether for your own personal life or career path, or for the broad functioning of the economy.

Takeaways

- Finance is the study of how to allocate scarce resources over time. The two features that distinguish finance from other resource allocation decisions are that the costs and benefits of financial decisions are spread out over time and are usually not known with certainty in advance by either the decision maker or anybody else.
- There are at least four reasons to study finance: to deal with the world of business; to manage personal resources; to pursue interesting and rewarding career opportunities; and to make informed public choices as a citizen.
- The key institutions in the financial system are capital markets, financial intermediaries, financial service firms, and regulators. The functions carried out by these financial institutions are transferring economic resources, managing risk, facilitating trade, pooling resources, providing price information, and dealing with incentive problems.
- The Ten Principles of Finance underlie all of finance and are applicable to the entire financial system, regardless of time and place.

Key Terms

Capital markets   5
Financial intermediaries   5
Financial service firms   5
Financial system   5
Functions   5
Law of one price   7
Options   9

Regulators   5
Time value of money   7
Ten Principles of Finance   6
Transparency   10
Trust   10
Verification   10

2 BASICS OF VALUATION: THE TIME VALUE OF MONEY

CHAPTER OVERVIEW

2.1	Using Timelines to Analyze Cash Flows	14
2.2	Future Value and Compounding	15
2.3	Present Value and Discounting	26
2.4	Investment Decisions Using Net Present Value	34
2.5	Valuing Annuities	37
2.6	Valuing Perpetuities	41
2.7	Inflation and Discounted Cash Flow Analysis	44

> ### LEARNING OBJECTIVES
>
> After reading this chapter, you will be able to:
> - construct a timeline for analyzing cash flows;
> - describe the meaning and implications of compounding and future value, and discounting and present value;
> - calculate the current value of an asset by discounting future cash flows;
> - calculate net present value and use it to evaluate investment decisions;
> - calculate the value of annuities and perpetuities;
> - incorporate inflation and taxes into time value of money calculations.

✚ Your friend Kamal has just gotten a raise and is feeling generous. He offers to give you $100 and wants to know if you want it now or one year from now. What would you choose?

✚ You want to buy a new car in five years. You want to spend $30,000 on the car. To ensure that you can buy it in the future, you decide to invest money now in an account earning interest each year. How can you determine how much money you should put aside now?

- You are taking out a loan to fund the tuition for your MBA. The loan is for $80,000 and is paid off in monthly installments over ten years, and the loan provider quotes an interest rate of 10% APR. How much money you will actually have to pay each month and each year?

- You win a sweepstakes that your school is running with a cash prize, which allows you to receive a lump sum of money now or a regular payment each quarter for the next ten years. Which should you take?

- An insurance company representative offers you a savings product that will pay you, in exchange for some money now, a fixed amount of money each year for the next 30 years. The representative says that it's a great product for retirement. How can you assess whether this is the case?

- Your niece is 8 years old, and you are planning to open an account to provide for her first year of college education at age 18. Tuition for one year of college is now $15,000, but it has been rising with inflation each year. How can you determine how much you will need to put into the account each year?

Introduction

As we learned in Chapter 1, financial decisions involve calculating costs and benefits that are spread over time. Financial decision makers in households and firms all have to evaluate whether investing money today is justified by the benefits they expect to receive in the future. They must, therefore, compare the values of sums of money at different dates. However, sums of money at different dates cannot be valued in the same way. For example, if given the choice between $100 today and $100 one year from now, most people would likely choose to receive $100 today. As we will discuss, there are at least three reasons why this is true:

- Money can be invested or saved today and earn interest so that, after some period of time, you have more money in the future than you started with.
- The purchasing power of money can change over time because of inflation.
- The receipt of money expected in the future is, in general, uncertain, so it is better to receive money, for sure, today.

In this chapter, we examine more closely the reasoning and concepts behind **Principle 1:** *A dollar today is not worth the same as a dollar tomorrow.* We do so by presenting time value of money concepts and discounted cash flow techniques for valuing investment projects. For now, we assume that financial decision makers know with certainty exactly what future cash flows their investments will produce. In other words, we ignore the fact that investors usually do not know for certain that they will receive the returns they expect. We take up the effect of uncertainty on valuation in Chapters 4 and 5.

Understanding Principle 1 allows us to take a step toward one of the fundamental goals of finance: to understand value, how much something is worth, the amount of money someone is willing to pay for something. As we will see, almost anything has a value that can be placed on it: financial assets such as stocks, bonds, and contracts; tangible physical assets such as factories, houses, and cars; existing projects within companies; entire companies; and intangible assets such as a brand name, proposed projects, and knowledge. We often use the generic term asset as a catch-all term for any of these items. Valuation is the process of figuring out how much an asset is worth.

2.1 Using Timelines to Analyze Cash Flows

Before proceeding with our first steps in valuation, we need to introduce some tools and define some notation that will be used here and throughout the book when valuing assets.

At a fundamental level, the value of an asset comes from the cash flows that are associated with it—that is, from the amounts of money that the owner either receives or pays at various points in time. An essential tool in analyzing cash flows from any financial decision is a diagram known as a timeline, a linear representation of cash outflows and inflows over a period of time. A negative sign in front of a cash flow means that you are paying that amount of money (it's a cash *outflow* from you). No sign means that you are receiving an amount of money (it's a cash *inflow* to you).

When describing when cash inflows and outflows occur, we distinguish between discrete points in time and periods of time. We use t to indicate a point in time (usually a year), so that $t = 0$ refers to now, $t = 1$ refers to one year from now, $t = 2$ to two years from now, and so on. The end point of a particular series of cash flows is denoted with a capital T. A period of time is the time that elapses between two points in time. Thus, period 1 is the time between point 0 and point 1; period 2 is the time between point 1 and point 2; and period T is the last period between points $T - 1$ and T.

Consider the cash flows associated with borrowing and lending money for five years ($T = 5$) pictured in Figure 2.1 and 2.2. Figure 2.1 shows the cash flows faced by someone borrowing $1,000 for five years at an interest rate r of 10% per year. An interest rate is the percentage of an amount deposited, borrowed, or invested that will be paid each period. An interest rate is usually expressed in percent per year, and the amount paid is the interest. The amount deposited, borrowed, or invested is called the principal. Figure 2.2 shows the cash flows faced by the lender. Figure 2.1 shows that the borrower receives $1,000 (the principal) now, at time 0, pays the lender $100 in interest each year for four years, and at the end of year 5 pays the lender both the $100 interest and the $1,000 principal. Figure 2.2 shows that the lender faces the opposite cash flows: an outflow of $1,000 at time 0 and then inflows for years 1–5.

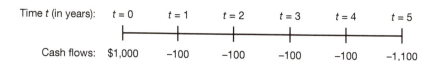

FIGURE 2.1 Borrower cash flow timeline (borrows $1,000 for five years at an interest rate of 10%). A depiction of cash flows to and from someone who borrows $1,000. Today ($t = 0$), the borrower receives a cash inflow of $1,000. Then at times $t = 1, 2, 3$, and 4 the borrower pays the lender an interest payment of $100. At the end of the five-year loan, period $t = 5$, the borrower pays the lender $100 interest and pays back the $1,000 principal.

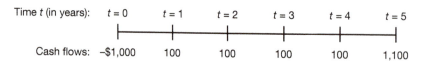

FIGURE 2.2 Lender cash flow timeline (lends $1,000 for five years at an interest rate r of 10%). A depiction of cash flows to and from someone who lends $1,000 to the borrower. Today ($t = 0$), the lender has a cash outflow of $1,000 when they lend to the borrower. The outflow shows a negative sign. At times $t = 1, 2, 3$, and 4 the lender receives a $100 cash inflow, the interest payment from the borrower. At the end of the five-year loan, period $t = 5$, the lender receives an inflow of $1,100 when the borrower pays $100 interest and pays back the $1,000 principal.

Cash flow timelines like the ones shown in Figures 2.1 and 2.2 help in analyzing cash flows over a period of time. As we will see throughout the book, timelines provide a very useful way to keep track of cash flows at different points in time, especially more complicated patterns of cash flows.

> **QUICK CHECK 2.1** Your friend asks to borrow $100 from you, which she will pay back in three years. In the meantime, she will pay you a 10% interest rate each year for the use of your money. Construct two timelines to illustrate this situation for you (the lender) and for your friend (the borrower).

2.2 Future Value and Compounding

You have just won $1,000 in a raffle and are given the following choice: You can receive $1,000 right now or you can receive $1,000 one year from now. Which of these two options would you choose? Most people would choose to receive the $1,000 right now, indicating that they perceive that $1 today is worth more than $1 in the future. As we noted earlier, there are a number of reasons for this. Embodied in these reasons, an important consideration is what other things you could do with the $1,000 if you received it today.

In particular, if you receive the $1,000 right now, you could invest it to produce more than $1,000 a year from now. For example, you could put it into an account or some other investment earning an interest rate r of 10% per year. In this case, the account will pay you 10% (0.10 as a decimal) of the $1,000 each year, or 10% × $1,000 = 0.1 × $1,000 = $100. At the end of period 1 (one year), you will have $1,000 + $100 = $1,100 in your account.

This $1,100 is the future value (FV) of today's present value (PV) of $1,000; it is what an investment made today is expected to be worth at some point in the future. Mathematically, we calculate this future value as:

$$\begin{aligned} FV &= PV \times (1+r) \\ &= \$1,000 \times (1+r) \\ &= \$1,000 \times (1+0.10) \\ &= \$1,100, \end{aligned}$$

where r is the interest rate of 10%, or 0.10.

2.2.1 Valuing Cash Flows over Multiple Periods

To illustrate how things change when we have cash payouts over multiple periods, suppose again that you put $1,000 (the present value) into an account earning an interest rate of 10% per year. How much will you have in five years, assuming you take nothing out of the account before then? In other words, what is the future value of $1,000 in five years at an interest rate of 10% per year? We can visualize the situation via a timeline (Figure 2.3).

> **QUICK CHECK 2.2** What is the future value of $1,000 one year from now at an interest rate of 20%?

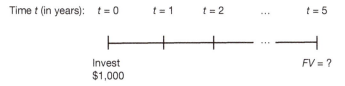

FIGURE 2.3 Timeline representing the future value of $1,000. This figure shows the future value of a $1,000 investment right now.

Let us calculate the future value in this example one step at a time. We already calculated that after the first year ($t = 1$) you will have your original $1,000 plus interest of $100, giving a future value at the end of year 1 of $FV_{t=1} = \$1,100$.

If you leave the $1,100 invested for another year, how much will you have at the end of year 2? During year 2 you will earn 10% interest on the entire $1,100. The interest earned is, thus, $0.1 \times \$1,100 = \$110$. You will therefore have $1,210 at the end of year 2. Mathematically we can write the future value in year 2 ($t = 2$) as:

$$FV_{t=2} = FV_{t=1} \times (1 + r)$$
$$= \$1,100 \times (1 + 0.10)$$
$$= \$1,210.$$

If we look at the above equation, we can recognize that this shows the original principal ($1,000) multiplied by 1.10 and then multiplied by 1.10 again:

$$FV_{t=2} = FV_{t=1} \times (1 + 0.10)$$
$$= \$1,000 \times (1 + 0.10) \times (1 + 0.10)$$
$$= \$1,000 \times (1 + 0.10)^2$$
$$= \$1,210.$$

Earning a return (i.e., interest) on an amount that has already earned interest is known as compounding.

2.2.2 Compound and Simple Interest

To gain a better understanding of the nature of compound interest, we can break this future value of $1,210 into its three components. First, there is the principal, the original invested amount of $1,000. Next there is the interest on this amount: $100 in the first year and another $100 in the second year. The interest on the original principal is called simple interest ($200 in our example). Finally, there is $10 of interest earned in the second year on the $100 of interest earned in the first year. Interest earned on interest already paid is called compound interest. The total interest earned ($210) is the sum of the simple interest ($200) plus the compound interest ($10).

Practically speaking, you do not care how much of your total interest of $210 is simple interest and how much is compound interest. All you really care about is how much you will have in your account in the future—that is, the future value of your $1,000. We can proceed in the same way as above to calculate the future value in three years (as of $t = 3$):

$$FV_{t=3} = FV_{t=2} \times (1 + 0.10)$$
$$= \$1,000 \times (1 + 0.10) \times (1 + 0.10) \times (1 + 0.10)$$
$$= \$1,000 \times (1 + 0.10)^3$$
$$= \$1,331.$$

Following this chain of reasoning, we can find future value after five years by repeated multiplication:

$$FV_{t=5} = \$1,000 \times (1 + 0.10) \times (1 + 0.10) \times (1 + 0.10) \times (1 + 0.10) \times (1 + 0.10)$$
$$= \$1,000 \times (1 + 0.10)^5$$
$$= \$1,610.51.$$

Thus, we have our answer to the original question. The future value of $1,000 at an interest rate of 10% per year for five years is $1,610.51. The total interest earned over the five years is $610.51, of which $500 is simple interest and $110.51 is compound interest.

2.2 FUTURE VALUE AND COMPOUNDING

Table 2.1 **Future value and compound interest.** This table shows the future value in five years of $1,000 at an interest rate of 10% per year.

Year, t	Beginning amount	Interest earned	Ending amount
1	$1,000.00	$100.00	$1,100.00
2	$1,100.00	$110.00	$1,210.00
3	$1,210.00	$121.00	$1,331.00
4	$1,331.00	$133.10	$1,464.10
5	$1,464.10	$146.41	$1,610.51
	Total interest earned	$610.51	

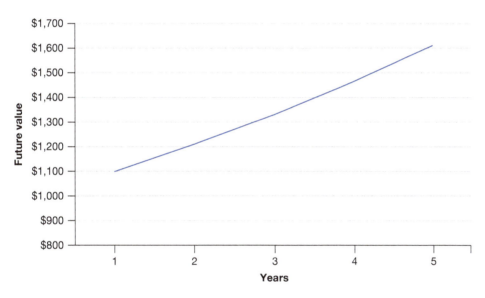

FIGURE 2.4 **Future value of $1,000 for different periods at a fixed interest rate.** This figure graphs the data from Table 2.1, showing the future value of a $1,000 investment at various points in the future at a 10% interest rate. The further out into the future, the higher the future value of the investment due to the interest earned.

To help in understanding the effect of compounding, Table 2.1 shows the growth of the amount in your account over the five-year period. Figure 2.4 graphs the data from Table 2.1.

2.2.3 The Future Value Equation

If r is the interest rate and T is the number of years, the future value of an initial deposit or investment PV as of year T is given by the formula:

$$FV_T = PV \times (1+r)^T, \tag{2.1}$$

where $(1+r)^T$ is known as the future value factor, and is what we multiply any current amount by to get its future value at the end of period T. The future value factor is greater the higher the interest rate and the longer the time the investment is held. Table 2.2 and Figure 2.5 illustrate this relationship for various interest rates and holding periods.

2 BASICS OF VALUATION

Table 2.2 Future value of $1 for different periods and interest rates. This table shows the future value of $1 for different holding periods at various interest rates. The higher the interest rate, the faster the future value grows.

Number of periods, T	Interest rate, r					
	2%	4%	6%	8%	10%	12%
1	$1.0200	$1.0400	$1.0600	$1.0800	$1.1000	$1.1200
2	1.0404	1.0816	1.1236	1.1664	1.2100	1.2544
3	1.0612	1.1249	1.1910	1.2597	1.3310	1.4049
4	1.0824	1.1699	1.2625	1.3605	1.4641	1.5735
5	1.1041	1.2167	1.3382	1.4693	1.6105	1.7623

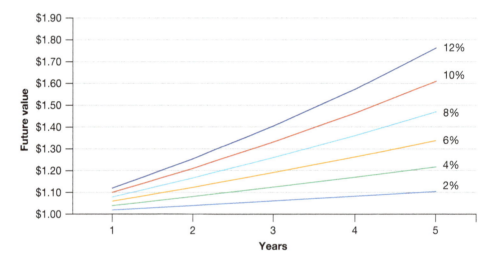

FIGURE 2.5 Future value of $1 for different periods and interest rates. This figure graphs the data from Table 2.2, showing the future value of a $1 investment at various points in the future at the indicated interest rates. Note that at higher interest rates the curves are steeper, indicating that the amount of money in the future gets progressively larger due to interest earned.

Box 2.1 Calculating Future Values

There are a number of ways to calculate future values in practice. Here are the most common tools and programs.

Financial Calculators

Special-purpose financial calculators are designed to make calculating future values easier than pen-and-paper calculations. By pressing the appropriately labeled keys, you enter the values for the number of periods (T), the interest rate (r), and the value of the investment (principal or present value PV). The calculator then computes the future value (FV) for you.

Spreadsheets

Spreadsheet programs such as Microsoft Excel or Google Sheets offer a simple and convenient way to compute future values. In an Excel spreadsheet, the future value is calculated using the built-in FV() function: =FV(r, T, 0, -PV). In Excel, cash outflows are represented by negative signs.

For this reason, the entry for the present value is negative: We are taking money out of our pocket (a cash outflow) and putting it into an account (a cash inflow).

Using the example shown in Table 2.1 and Figure 2.4 we would input the following numbers to the Excel formula. These values would be entered in column B:

$$= \text{FV}\left(10\%,\ 5,\ 0,\ -\$1{,}000\right).$$

The spreadsheet calculation gives us a future value of $1,610.51–the same future value we got from pen-and-paper calculations and the calculator. The resulting spreadsheet is shown in Figure 2.6. The companion Excel app to this chapter also shows how these formulas work and compares them to the manual calculations.

(a)

	A	B
1	*r*	10.00%
2	*T*	5
3	PV	-$1,000.00
4	FV	=FV(B1,B2,0,B3)

(b)

	A	B
1	*r*	10.00%
2	*T*	5
3	PV	-$1,000.00
4	FV	$1,610.51

FIGURE 2.6 **Excel spreadsheet inputs and outputs.** This figure shows the Excel inputs and outputs for calculating the future value of $1,000 in five years at an interest rate of 10%. (a) The formula used and the cells referred to; (b) the output.

The advantage of using a spreadsheet program is that it quickly recalculates the future value if any inputs change. For example, changing the interest rate in cell B1 from 10% (0.1) to 15% (0.15) would return a new future value in cell A4 equal to $2,011.36. Figure 2.7 illustrates this.

(a)

	A	B
1	*r*	15.00%
2	*T*	5
3	PV	-$1,000.00
4	FV	=FV(B1,B2,0,B3)

(b)

	A	B
1	*r*	15.00%
2	*T*	5
3	PV	-$1,000.00
4	FV	$2,011.36

FIGURE 2.7 **Excel spreadsheet inputs and outputs.** This figure shows the Excel inputs and outputs for calculating the future value of $1,000 in five years at an interest rate of 15%. (a) The formula used and the cells referred to; (b) the output.

The Rule of 72

There is a handy rule that can help you estimate future values when you do not have a calculator or computer available. The "Rule of 72" says that the number of years it takes for an amount of money to double in value (the "doubling time") is approximately equal to the number 72 divided by the interest rate r (expressed in percent per year):

$$\text{Doubling time} = \frac{72}{r}.$$

So, at an interest rate of 10% (0.10) per year, it should take approximately 72 / 0.10 = 7.2 years to double your money. If you start with $1,000, you will have $2,000 after 7.2 years, $4,000 after 14.4 years, $8,000 after 21.6 years, and so on.

2 BASICS OF VALUATION

Example 2.1 (Paying Back a Loan): One day, you get a letter from your local government notifying you that they have just discovered that you failed to pay a $100 tax bill 20 years ago. Because it was the government's oversight, it has decided to charge you an interest rate of only 6% per year. How much do you owe them?

Solution. The $100 bill (the present value, PV) has been accruing interest of 6% per year for 20 years. We therefore need to solve for the future value (FV) of $100 in 20 years at a 6% interest rate. We can visualize the situation with the following timeline:

Time t (in years): $t=0$ $t=1$ $t=2$ ... $t=20$

Present value $100

FV = ?

Using Equation 2.1, with PV = $100, T = 20, and r = 0.06, you owe the government $320.71:

$$FV_{T=20} = PV \times (1+r)^T$$
$$= \$100 \times 1.06^{20}$$
$$= \$320.71.$$

Example 2.2 (Saving): To save some money, each year you deposit $1,000 into an account paying an interest rate of 10% per year, starting immediately. How much will you have after two years if you do not withdraw any money before then?

Solution. We can visualize the problem using a timeline as follows:

Time t (in years): $t=0$ $t=1$ $t=2$

Deposit $1,000

FV = ?

At time 0 ($t=0$), we put $1,000 into the account, which after one year is:

$$FV_{T=1} = PV \times (1+r)^T$$
$$= \$1{,}000 \times 1.10$$
$$= \$1{,}100.00.$$

Now, at $t=1$ the end of year 1/beginning of year 2, we invest an additional $1,000 which gives us $2,100. This $2,100 then will gain in value at 10% interest for another year, giving us the future value at year 2:

$$FV_{T=2} = \$2{,}100 \times 1.10$$
$$= \$2{,}310.00.$$

Example 2.3 (Saving for Old Age): Suppose you are 20 years old, and considering putting $100 into a savings account that pays 8% interest per year for 45 years.

(a) How much will you have in the account in 45 years (at age 65)?
(b) How much of this total is simple interest and how much is compound interest?
(c) If you could find an account paying 9% per year, how much more would you have at age 65?

2.2 FUTURE VALUE AND COMPOUNDING

Solution.

(a) We want to find the future value of the $100 at $T = 45$:

Using Equation 2.1, you can find the future value (FV_T) of your $100 deposit ($PV$). Your $100 will earn (compound) interest over 45 years ($T = 45$) at an interest rate of $r = 8\% = 0.08$:

$$FV_T = PV \times (1+r)^T$$
$$FV_{T=45} = \$100 \times (1+r)^T$$
$$= \$100 \times (1+0.08)^{45}$$
$$= \$3{,}192.04.$$

(b) Because the original amount invested is $100, we take the future value of $3,192.04 from part (a) and subtract the original amount of $100 to calculate total interest earned of $3,092.04. The simple interest 8% is earned on the $100 each year for 45 years: $0.08 \times \$100 = \$8$. Because there are 45 years in the investment with simple interest of $8 per year, the total simple interest is $45 \times \$8 = \$360$. Compound interest makes up the rest of the total interest of $3,092.04, so the amount of compound interest is $\$3{,}092.04 - \$360 = \$2{,}732.04$.

(c) To find how much you would have after 45 years if the interest rate were 9%, use Equation 2.1 with the new interest rate of $r = 0.09$:

$$FV_{T=45} = \$100 \times (1+r)^T$$
$$= \$100 \times (1+0.09)^{45}$$
$$= \$4{,}832.73.$$

Thus, a seemingly small increase of 1% in the interest rate results in an extra $1,640.69 ($4,832.73 − $3,192.04) at age 65, when we compare our answer to part (a). This is more than a 50% increase from the amount we got in part (a): $1,640.69/$3,192.04 = 0.514. The general point of this example is that a small difference in interest rates can make a big difference in future values over long periods of time.

> **QUICK CHECK 2.3** Solve for the future value of $1,000 ten years from today at an interest rate of 5%.

2.2.4 The Frequency of Compounding

In the previous examples we calculated compounded interest each year. Interest rates on loans and savings accounts are usually stated in the form of an annual percentage rate (APR) (e.g., 6% per year), which makes comparisons and calculations of interest consistent if interest is earned annually. However, interest can be calculated at different frequencies, such as monthly or quarterly. Because the frequency of compounding can differ, it is important to have a way of making interest rates comparable to calculate the actual amount you will have in your account in the future.

To illustrate, suppose that you have $100 in your account, and it earns interest monthly at an APR of 6% per year. This means that you will have your interest added to your account every month, or 12 times per year. To calculate the interest rate per month, we divide the 6% APR by 12, giving 6%/12 = 0.5% per month (or 0.005 per month as a decimal). In general, if an amount of money earns interest m times per year, the interest rate per period is given by the APR divided by the number of periods:

$$\text{Interest rate per period} = \frac{APR}{m}. \quad (2.2)$$

In our illustration above, interest is paid monthly, so $m = 12$.

The APR is convenient in the sense that we can easily calculate what our interest rate each period is. It is also what is usually provided whenever you see an interest rate (e.g., when you take out a loan or put your money into a bank account). However, the APR does not paint the entire picture of how much money we will have at the end of the year, because it does not account for compounding that happens throughout the year. Consider our situation above, with an APR of 6% per year. You may be tempted to think that your $100 at the end of one year will be $100 × 1.06 = $106. However, this does not incorporate the fact that you earn interest every month that is compounded, so that any interest you earn in previous months earns additional interest. To incorporate this compounding correctly, we need to adjust our yearly APR into a rate that covers the number of compounding periods per year. An APR of 6% with monthly compounding is actually 0.5% per month (the annual rate of 6% divided by 12).

Generally, the future value of any amount PV in T years when it is compounded m times within the year is:

$$FV_{T,m} = PV \times \left(1 + \frac{APR}{m}\right)^{m \times T}. \quad (2.3)$$

Using Equation 2.3, the amount of money at the end of a year (FV) with $m = 12$ and $T = 1$ will be:

$$\begin{aligned} FV_{T=12, m=12} &= PV \times \left(1 + \frac{APR}{m}\right)^{m \times T} \\ &= \$100 \times \left(1 + \frac{0.06}{12}\right)^{12 \times 1} \\ &= \$100 \times (1 + .005)^{12} \\ &= \$106.16778. \end{aligned}$$

Compounding interest is earned every month over the year, which gives us slightly more than $106 at the end of year 1.

Another way of representing yearly interest rates is to use the effective annual rate (EAR), which is an annual rate that incorporates all of the compounding throughout the year. The formula to calculate the EAR when we are given the APR is:

$$EAR = \left(1 + \frac{APR}{m}\right)^m - 1. \quad (2.4)$$

The EAR based on our 12 months of compounding (m = 12) and 6% APR is:

$$EAR = \left(1 + \frac{APR}{m}\right)^m - 1$$
$$= \left(1 + \frac{0.06}{12}\right)^{12} - 1$$
$$= 0.0616778 \text{ or } 6.16778\%.$$

This rate tells us how much we would earn in a year, taking into account compounding within that year. We can verify that, with our monthly interest, we would earn $100 × (1 + EAR) = $100 × (1.0616778) = $106.16778 after one year, which is exactly what we calculated before.

The EAR is therefore useful in telling us what we will actually earn throughout the year if we have different compounding frequencies. These frequencies can vary a lot. Table 2.3 presents the EARs corresponding to an APR of 6% per year for different compounding frequencies.

If compounding is done once per year, then the EAR is the same as the annual percentage rate: APR = EAR. As the compounding frequency increases, the EAR gets larger and larger but approaches a limit. The extreme case is called continuous compounding, and represents the situation in which interest is compounded continuously—not just every hour, every minute, or every second, but at the smallest time intervals imaginable (even smaller than milliseconds!). You may think that this would make the amount grow to be infinite ... after all, we are compounding an infinite number of times. However, the amount of interest each period becomes divided up into minuscule amounts, leading to a finite rate in the end. With continuous compounding, the future value of $PV in T years with an APR of r becomes:

$$FV_{T,m=\infty} = PV \times e^{r \times T}, \qquad (2.5)$$

where e is the constant number 2.71828 (rounded to the fifth decimal place).

Table 2.3 Effective annual rates for an APR of 6%. This table shows the EAR for an APR of 6% for various compounding periods. The EAR gets larger than the APR when compounding is done more frequently than annually, reflecting the fact that the EAR reflects compound interest earned during the year.

Compounding period	m	EAR
Annually	1	6.00000%
Semi-annually	2	6.09000%
Quarterly	4	6.13636%
Monthly	12	6.16778%
Weekly	52	6.17998%
Daily	365	6.18313%
Continuously	∞	6.18365%

Box 2.2 Excel in Practice: Using Excel to Calculate the Effective Annual Rate

In Excel, the EAR can be calculated using the built-in function =EFFECT(APR, m). In an Excel cell, entering =EFFECT(10%, 4) would return 0.1038129, which says that a 10% APR with quarterly compounding corresponds to an EAR of 10.38129%.

The symmetric Excel built-in =NOMINAL() function calculates the APR corresponding to a given EAR and number of compounding periods per year. The syntax is =NOMINAL(EAR, m). Thus, entering =NOMINAL(12%, 12) in an Excel cell will return 0.1138655. This is interpreted to say that an EAR of 12% under monthly compounding corresponds to an APR of 11.38655%.

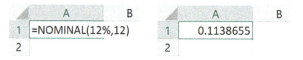

QUICK CHECK 2.4 If you take out a loan at an APR of 12% with monthly compounding, what is the EAR on your loan?

2.2.5 Future Value When Interest Rates Change over Time

In our previous examples, we have calculated future values assuming that the interest rate will stay the same in the future. However, this will not always be the case. The interest rate on an account may go up or down in the future. Or, you may decide to take your investment out of one account and put it into another account that pays a different rate.

To calculate future values when interest rates change in the future, we must take into account that any investment will earn interest compounded on any previous interest earned. In particular, if we invest $PV right now, the future value of it at year T is given by the following general formula:

$$FV_T = PV \times (1 + r_{0,1}) \times (1 + r_{1,2}) \times (1 + r_{2,3}) \times \cdots \times (1 + r_{T-1,T}). \quad (2.6)$$

The idea behind Equation 2.6 is as follows. You first invest your $PV in an account that will earn interest at a rate of $r_{0,1}$ from now (year 0) until year 1, leaving you with $PV \times (1 + r_{0,1})$ at the end of year 1. Assuming that the interest changes to $r_{1,2}$, this amount then will earn interest at a rate of $r_{1,2}$ from year 1 to year 2 (the previous interest is compounded), leaving you with $PV \times (1 + r_{0,1}) \times (1 + r_{1,2})$ in year 2. This process continues through year T. The amount you would have in each year is shown in Table 2.4.

As an illustration, suppose you invest $100 in an account that pays 1% from now until a year from now, and 2% for the next year: $r_{0,1}$ = 1% or 0.01 and $r_{1,2}$ = 2% or 0.02. We can calculate the future value at the end of the two-year period (T = 2) using Equation 2.6:

$$\begin{aligned} FV_{T=2} &= \$PV \times (1 + r_{0,1}) \times (1 + r_{1,2}) \\ &= \$100 \times (1 + 0.01) \times (1 + 0.02) \\ &= \$100 \times 1.01 \times 1.02 \\ &= \$103.02. \end{aligned}$$

2.2 FUTURE VALUE AND COMPOUNDING

Table 2.4 Future values when interest rates change over time. This table shows the future value (FV) of an amount PV at various future time points, when interest rates are not the same over time. $r_{t-1,t}$ represents the interest rate earned for investing money from time $t-1$ to time t.

Year	Amount (FV)
0	PV
1	$PV \times (1+r_{0,1})$
2	$PV \times (1+r_{0,1}) \times (1+r_{1,2})$
3	$PV \times (1+r_{0,1}) \times (1+r_{1,2}) \times (1+r_{2,3})$
4	$PV \times (1+r_{0,1}) \times (1+r_{1,2}) \times (1+r_{2,3}) \times (1+r_{3,4})$
5	$PV \times (1+r_{0,1}) \times (1+r_{1,2}) \times (1+r_{2,3}) \times (1+r_{3,4}) \times (1+r_{4,5})$
...	
T	$PV \times (1+r_{0,1}) \times (1+r_{1,2}) \times (1+r_{2,3}) \times (1+r_{3,4}) \times (1+r_{4,5}) \ldots \times (1+r_{T-1,T})$

Example 2.4 (Reinvesting at a Different Rate): You are faced with the following investment decision. You have $10,000 to invest for two years. You have decided to invest your money in bank certificates of deposit (CDs), which is a savings account into which you deposit your money and agree to not make withdrawals for a certain period of time. Two-year CDs are paying 7% per year and one-year CDs are paying 6%. What should you do?

Solution. You want to invest for two years, meaning that you can choose to either invest in the two-year CD, or invest in the one-year CD and then invest in a new one-year CD after the first year. You will want to invest in the choice that gives you the most money after two years.

Let us first consider how much money you would get from investing in the two-year CD. Because we have the same rate of 7% going forward ($r = 0.07$) for $T = 2$ years, we can use our future value Equation 2.1 with a PV of $10,000:

$$FV_{T=2} = PV \times (1+r)^T$$
$$= \$10,000 \times 1.07^2$$
$$= \$11,449.$$

Now let us consider investing in the one-year CDs. As we mentioned, this involves first investing now for one year at a rate of 6%, and then investing in a new one-year CD next year. However, note that the rate one year from now is not necessarily going to be 6%. To make your decision, you will need to decide what you think the interest rate on one-year CDs will be next year. Suppose that you are sure it will be 8% per year. This means that the rate from now until next year, r_1, is 6%, while the rate from next year to the year after, r_2, is 8%. Using these numbers in Equation 2.6 with a $T = 2$-year planning horizon, we get:

$$FV_{T=2} = PV \times (1+r_{0,1}) \times (1+r_{1,2})$$
$$= \$10,000 \times 1.06 \times 1.08$$
$$= \$11,448.$$

2 BASICS OF VALUATION

The difference is very small, but you are slightly better off with the two-year CD because it gives you $1 more after two years. Note that your answer may be different if you think that rates on CDs will be higher in one year, say $r_{1,2} = 9\%$. If that were the case, then we would have:

$$\begin{aligned} FV_{T=2} &= PV \times (1+r_{0,1}) \times (1+r_{1,2}) \\ &= \$10{,}000 \times 1.06 \times 1.09 \\ &= \$11{,}554. \end{aligned}$$

This outcome would lead us to choose to deposit the $10,000 into the two one-year CDs instead.

QUICK CHECK 2.5 Suppose that the one-year interest rate right now is 2%. The one-year interest rate one year from now (i.e., from year 1 to year 2) is expected to be 3%, and two years from now the one-year interest rate (i.e., from year 2 to year 3) is expected to be 3.5%. Assuming these expected interest rates hold, what is the value in three years of $1,000 invested at these rates?

2.3 Present Value and Discounting

In the previous section, we learned why it was more valuable to choose to receive $1,000 right now instead of in the future: If you invest it, it will turn into more than $1,000 in the future. We can also think about the choice in a different way: If you decide that you want to have $1,000 paid to you in one year (i.e., if you want to receive a cash inflow of $1,000 in one year), how much would you have to invest or save today so that you would have $1,000 available to you in one year? To determine *today's* value (called the present value, *PV*) of this future $1,000, we must convert money from the future into today's terms. We can visualize this in a timeline as follows:

```
Time t:        t = 0       t = 1
               |-----------|
Cash flow CFₜ: PV = ?      $1,000
```

To calculate the present value (*PV*) of the $1,000 you will receive one year from now, let us consider the setup from the previous section. In this case, however, we know the future value (*FV*) is $1,000. What we want to figure out is what amount of money we need today to have $1,000 at a future date if the interest rate is $(1 + r)$. If the interest rate is 10% ($r = 0.10$) we solve for the *PV* as follows:

$$\begin{aligned} FV &= PV \times (1+r) \\ \$1{,}000 &= PV \times (1+r) \\ \$1{,}000 &= PV \times (1+0.10) \\ PV &= \frac{\$1{,}000}{1.10} \\ &= \$909.09. \end{aligned}$$

This tells us that, given an interest rate of 10%, we need to invest $909.09 today in order to have $1,000 one year from now. Put differently, at a 10% interest rate, $1,000 in one year is worth $909.09 right now.

2.3 PRESENT VALUE AND DISCOUNTING

This example shows that calculating present value is the reverse of calculating future value. That is, it tells us the amount you have to invest today to have a certain amount in the future. The general formula for the present value of a future amount one period from today is:

$$PV = \frac{FV}{1+r}, \tag{2.7}$$

where r is the interest rate. The process of calculating present value by dividing a future amount by $1 + r$ is called discounting, because the present value of an amount is less than its future value. Because of this, in finance, the interest rate r is also called the discount rate, $1/1 + r$ is called the discount factor, and the calculation of present value is called discounted cash flow (DCF) analysis. An important thing to note in Equation 2.7 is that the higher the discount rate r, the lower the present value.

The concept of the time value of money summarized in **Principle 1** *(A dollar today is not worth the same as a dollar tomorrow)* gives us an important rule to follow when considering amounts of money that are paid out or "flow" at different times. Because the value of $1 today is not the same as the value of $1 one year from now, we cannot simply add together money from different periods of time—that would be like trying to add together £50 and ¥50. You cannot come up with a meaningful number because the amounts are in different currencies—you would have to convert pounds to yen or yen to pounds. Instead, we need to convert money that flows at different times into a common value, and we do this by discounting all future money flows to their present value.

> **QUICK CHECK 2.6** Solve for the present value of $1,000 one year from today at an interest rate of 5%. Is the present value higher or lower than when the interest rate is 10%? Why?

Now let us think about what the present value will be of a $1,000 cash flow that will occur in two years, at $t = 2$. To solve present value problems, it is a good first step to draw a timeline of the cash flows. There are no cash flows at $t = 0$ and $t = 1$, but at $t = 2$ you receive the $1,000 cash inflow:

Time t:	$t = 0$	$t = 1$	$t = 2$
Cash flow CF_t:	0	0	$1,000

Suppose the discount rate is 10%. To find the present value of this cash flow, we must discount the $1,000 at $t = 2$ back to now ($t = 0$) using Equation 2.7 to discount back one period at a time. First, consider what the value of the $1,000 would be at $t = 1$. Using Equation 2.7 to discount the $1,000 back one year:

$$\begin{aligned} PV_{t=1} &= \frac{CF_2}{1+r} \\ &= \frac{\$1{,}000}{1.10} \\ &= \$909.09. \end{aligned}$$

The present value of the $1,000 in year $t = 2$ as of year $t = 1$ ($PV_{t=1}$) is $909.09. To find the present value of the $1,000 as of now ($t = 0$), we need to discount back one more year from year 1 to year 0:

$$\begin{aligned} PV_{t=0} &= \frac{PV_{t=1}}{1+r} \\ &= \frac{\$909.091}{1.10} \\ &= \$826.45. \end{aligned}$$

The present value of $1,000 in two years, given a 10% interest rate, is $826.45. Note that we could have calculated this present value in one step, immediately discounting back two years:

$$PV_{t=0} = \frac{CF_2}{(1+r)^2}$$
$$= \frac{\$1,000}{1.10^2}$$
$$= \$826.45.$$

To double-check our calculation, let's use Equation 2.1. To arrive at a future value (*FV*) of $1,000 in two years at 10% interest, the present value (*PV*) must be

$$\$1,000 = PV \times (1+r)^t$$
$$\$1,000 = PV \times 1.10^2$$
$$PV = \frac{\$1,000}{1.10^2}$$
$$= \$826.45.$$

This illustrates the general formula for determining the present value of a cash flow that will occur at time *t*:

$$PV = \frac{CF_t}{(1+r)^t}. \tag{2.8}$$

In general, if the interest rate is the same each year, we calculate the present value of a stream of expected future cash flows by discounting each cash flow. In Equation 2.8, $1/(1+r)^t$ is called the discount factor for period *t*, and we multiply any cash flow that occurs in that period by the discount factor to get the present value of that cash flow. As we found before in our one-year case, the higher the discount rate *r*, the lower the present value, because a higher discount rate implies that we could make more money investing right now, and thus money promised to us in the future is relatively less valuable. Equation 2.8 also tells us that the further in the future the money is promised, the less valuable it is in the present (we divide by a larger and larger number as *t* increases). Figure 2.8 underscores this point by graphing the present value of $1 for different interest rates and different time horizons.

2.3.1 Present Value of Multiple Cash Flows in the Future

Although the above example involves a single cash flow that is expected to occur in the future, we can expand it to calculate the present value of multiple cash flows expected to occur at different points in time. The key is that once we have determined the present value of any cash flow as of right now (*t* = 0), we can add together any number of present values because they are in equivalent terms. This leads to the general equation for the present value of a series of future cash flows that end at time *T*:

$$PV = \frac{CF_1}{1+r} + \frac{CF_2}{(1+r)^2} + \frac{CF_3}{(1+r)^3} + \cdots + \frac{CF_T}{(1+r)^T}$$
$$= \sum_{t=1}^{T} \frac{CF_t}{(1+r)^t}. \tag{2.9}$$

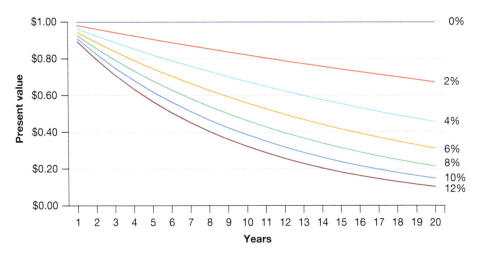

FIGURE 2.8 Present value of $1 for time horizons and interest rates. This figure depicts the present value (*PV*) of receiving $1 as of the indicated number of years in the future, given the interest rates shown on the right side of each line. The further out into the future the money will be received and the higher the interest rate, the lower the present value of that amount.

The summation sign in Equation 2.9 means that the individual elements for each date t from $t = 1$ to $t = T$ are added together. Equation 2.9 tells us that we first discount the year 1 ($t = 1$) cash flow, CF_1, back one year to year 0, by dividing by $1 + r$. We then add the year 2 ($t = 2$) cash flow, CF_2, discounted back two years by dividing by $(1 + r)^2$. We continue in this way for every cash flow through the end of the series at time T.

Example 2.5 (When a $100 Gift Is Not Really $100): It is your brother's tenth birthday, and he receives a $100 savings bond maturing in five years. This type of bond pays nothing until its maturity date. In adding up the value of his birthday "loot," he mistakenly writes down $100 for this bond. How much is it really worth if the discount rate is 8% per year and the bond does not mature for another five years? How can you explain your brother's mistake to him so that he will understand?

Solution. We are looking for the present value of $100 to be received in five years at a discount rate of 8% per year. The timeline of cash flows is as follows:

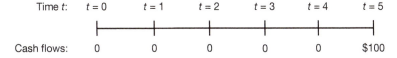

We can compute the present value of the $100 cash flow in year 5 using Equation 2.9:

$$PV = \frac{CF_t}{(1+r)^t}$$

$$= \frac{CF_5}{(1+r)^5}$$

$$= \frac{\$100}{1.08^5}$$

$$= \$68.06.$$

The future $100 bond payout is worth just over $68 right now. Explaining the answer to your brother is a tough assignment. Probably the best way to do it is to use the idea of future value rather than present value. You could explain to him that his $100 savings bond is worth only $68 because all he has to do to get $100 five years from now is put $68 into a savings account paying interest of 8% per year.

Example 2.6 (Investment with Multiple Cash Flows): Suppose we have an investment opportunity that lasts three years, with the following cash flows:

Time t:	$t = 0$	$t = 1$	$t = 2$	$t = 3$
Cash flows:	0	30	30	30

If the discount rate is 10%, what is the present value of this investment?

Solution. We have a series of cash flows in the future corresponding to each year t, to which we can apply Equation 2.9 using the discount rate of $r = 0.10$ to compute the present value:

$$PV = \frac{CF_1}{1+r} + \frac{CF_2}{(1+r)^2} + \frac{CF_3}{(1+r)^3}$$

$$= \frac{\$30}{1+0.10} + \frac{\$30}{(1+0.10)^2} + \frac{\$30}{(1+0.10)^3}$$

$$= \frac{\$30}{1.10} + \frac{\$30}{1.10^2} + \frac{\$30}{1.10^3}$$

$$= \$74.61.$$

The investment is thus worth about $74.61 today.

> **QUICK CHECK 2.7** What is the present value of $100 to be received each year over the next four years at an interest rate of 6% per year?

2.3.2 Discounting with Compounding More Frequently Than Annually

When interest is compounded more frequently than on an annual basis, we need to make the appropriate adjustments in the method for discounting. In particular, the formula for present value of a cash flow that occurs at year t would be modified to:

$$PV = \frac{CF_t}{\left(1 + \frac{APR}{m}\right)^{m \times t}}, \tag{2.10}$$

where APR is the annual percentage rate and m is the number of compounding periods within a year. In other words, we would need to change our discount rate from an annual discount rate to a discount rate that reflects the frequency of compounding (i.e., a monthly ($m = 12$), quarterly ($m = 4$), or semi-annual ($m = 2$) discount rate). As we saw before, we can do so by dividing the APR by the number of compounding periods m. The number of periods we discount by therefore changes from t (the number of years) to $m \times t$ (the number of periods overall).

2.3 PRESENT VALUE AND DISCOUNTING

To illustrate, suppose we want to determine the present value of $500 in five years with semi-annual compounding, at an annual rate (APR) of 10%. Using Equation 2.10, and noting that $m = 2$ with semi-annual compounding,

$$PV = \frac{CF_t}{\left(1 + \frac{APR}{m}\right)^{m \times t}}$$

$$= \frac{\$500}{\left(1 + \frac{0.10}{2}\right)^{2 \times 5}}$$

$$= \$306.96.$$

When interest is continually compounded (compounded an infinite number of times in a year), we need to adjust this equation. As we saw in Equation 2.5, the future value of a cash flow PV when we have continuous compounding ($m = \infty$) is $FV_{T,m=\infty} = \$PV \times e^{r \times T}$, where e is the constant number 2.71828. Thus, the present value of a cash flow occurring at year t with continuous compounding is:

$$\$PV = \$CF_t \times e^{-APR \times t}$$
$$= \frac{CF_t}{e^{APR \times t}}. \qquad (2.11)$$

Using the same numbers as before, with a future cash flow of $500 in year $t = 5$ at an interest rate of 10% compounded continuously, the present value of the $500 is $303.27. The intuition is that more frequent compounding results in a higher discount rate and therefore a lower present value for a given future value.

Box 2.3 Excel in Practice: Using Excel to Calculate Present Values

Excel is a convenient tool to use in calculating present values. Consider the problem of calculating the present value of $500 in five years at a 10% annual discount rate. We can use Excel directly to calculate this using our present value formula, $CF_5 / (1 + r)^5 = \$500 / 1.10^5$:

	A	B
1	r	10%
2	T	5
3	CF	$500
4	PV	=B3/(1+B1)^B2
5		$310.46

This will return $310.46.

Alternatively, we can use Excel's built-in present value formula, which takes the form =PV(rate, # periods, PMT, FV), where "rate" is the interest rate per time period, "# periods" is the number of periods, "PMT" represents any payments being made over time (in our example, we set it to 0), and "FV" is the amount you want to take the present value of (must be entered as a negative number). In this example, the command would be =PV(10%, 5, 0, -$500), and it will return $310.46.

If we want to incorporate compounding, we need to adjust the rate and # periods inputs. Suppose we have semi-annual compounding as in the previous illustration. Then we would have two half-years for five years, with a total of 2 × 5 = 10 periods. We would need to enter the interest rate per period, as in Equation 2.2, which would be APR / m = 10% / 2 = 5%. The formula would therefore become =PV(5%, 10, 0, -$500), which returns $306.96, a lower present value because the interest one earns—and thus the effective interest rate—is higher due to more frequent compounding.

	A	B
1	r	5%
2	T	10
3	CF	$500
4	PV	=PV(B1,B2,0,-B3)
5		$306.96

For continuous compounding, we cannot use the built-in =PV() function, and have to type out the formulas. To calculate $e^{-r \times t}$ in Equation 2.11, we can use Excel's =EXP() function, where anything in the parentheses in the function represents the exponent:

	A	B
1	10%	r
2	5	T
3	$500	CF
4	=A3*EXP(-A1*A2)	PV

This gives us $303.27, a present value that is lower still because compounding is done over even more periods, resulting in more interest and a still higher effective interest rate. These calculations can also be performed using the companion Excel app to this chapter.

Example 2.7 (Investments with Quarterly and Continuous Compounding): Consider a bond with a maturity of five years and a face value of $10,000. This means that the bond will pay you $10,000 in five years. The APR for equivalent investments is 10%. If interest on the bond is compounded every quarter, what should the price (i.e., present value) of the bond be? What if, instead, interest was continuously compounded?

Solution. The price of the bond is what it is worth right now, which is the same as the present value of the bond. First, consider if interest is compounded quarterly (four times per year). Because the bond pays $10,000 in year $t = 5$, we use Equation 2.10 with $m = 4$:

$$PV = \frac{CF_t}{\left(1 + \frac{APR}{m}\right)^{m \times t}}$$

$$= \frac{\$10,000}{\left(1 + \frac{0.10}{4}\right)^{4 \times 5}}$$

$$= \$6,102.71.$$

2.3 PRESENT VALUE AND DISCOUNTING

If interest were instead continuously compounded, we would use Equation 2.11:

$$PV = CF_t \times e^{-APR \times t}$$
$$= \frac{\$10{,}000}{e^{0.10 \times 5}}$$
$$= \$6{,}065.31.$$

If interest is compounded quarterly, the bond is worth more. This is because a higher frequency of compounding increases the discount rate, discounting the bond by a higher number and lowering its value.

2.3.3 Future Value with Negative Interest Rates

In all of our examples, the interest rates provided are positive. However, in some parts of the world interest rates on certain investments—such as bank accounts—can be negative. What this implies is that the future value of any money that you invest will be lower. For example, if an account has an interest rate of −1% (−0.01), then the future value in one year of $100 is (using Equation 2.1):

$$FV = \$PV \times (1 + r)$$
$$= \$100 \times (1 - 0.01)$$
$$= \$99.$$

Over time, you would have less and less money in your account. In this case, compounding makes the amount in your account go down at an increasing rate over time. Figure 2.9 shows the future value of $1.00 for various negative interest rates.

Why would someone ever invest at a negative interest rate? Sometimes the safety or convenience of putting money in an account is particularly valuable—for example, in places where it may be dangerous or just costly to keep your money "under a mattress." In other cases, inflation can reduce "actual" (i.e., real) interest rates over time enough to make them negative.

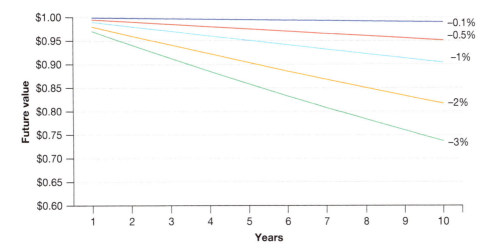

FIGURE 2.9 Future value of $1 for different periods and interest rates. This figure depicts the future value of a $1 investment at various points in the future at the indicated negative interest rates to the right of each line. Note that at interest rates that are more negative, money in the future gets progressively lower due to negative interest accrued over time.

2 BASICS OF VALUATION

For present values, negative interest rates imply that $1 in the future is actually worth more than $1 today, because if we invested $1 today it would turn into less than $1 in the future at a negative interest rate. For example, suppose the interest rate is −1% and you want to figure out the present value of a $100 cash flow that will occur in one year. Using Equation 2.7:

$$PV = \frac{FV}{1+r}$$
$$= \frac{\$100}{1-0.01}$$
$$= \$101.01.$$

The graph in Figure 2.10 shows the present value of $1 in the future, at various negative interest rates.

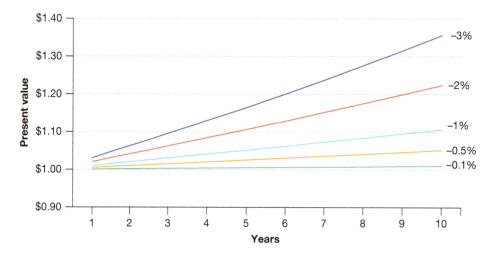

FIGURE 2.10 Present value of $1 in the future and negative interest rates. This figure depicts the present value of receiving $1 as of the indicated number of years in the future, given the negative interest rates shown to the right of each line. Negative interest rates imply that the present value of a future cash flow will be higher than the future value. The further out into the future the money will be received and the more negative the interest rate, the higher the present value of that amount.

> **QUICK CHECK 2.8** You are promised $10,000 in five years. The current interest rate is 10% APR with monthly compounding. What is this promised amount worth to you now?

2.4 Investment Decisions Using Net Present Value

The DCF concepts that we have studied so far in this chapter provide a powerful set of tools for determining the value of cash payments we expect to receive in the future, which can then be used in making investment decisions. The most common tool that comes from DCF analysis is the net present value (NPV) rule. Net present value is the difference between the present value of all current and future cash inflows (i.e., positive cash flows) minus the present value of all current and future cash outflows (i.e., negative cash flows):

$$NPV = -PV(\text{cash outflows}) + PV(\text{cash inflows}). \tag{2.12}$$

This rule is not only widely used and universally applicable (i.e., correctly used it never leads to the wrong decision), but it is also very intuitive. Simply put, the NPV rule is: Invest in any project for which the present value of the benefits (future cash inflows) exceeds the present value of the costs (the initial investment and future cash outflows). Make an investment if its NPV is positive; do not make an investment if its NPV is negative. When calculating an asset's NPV, you must be sure when you are comparing future cash flows (which happen some time from today) to present cash flows (which happen today) that you have made the cash flows comparable by first converting them to their present values.

For example, suppose that a $100 savings bond maturing in five years is selling for a price of $75 (this is the bond's present value at $t = 0$/today/now). Your next best alternative to investing in this bond is to put your $75 in a bank account paying 8%. Is the savings bond a good investment? We can use the NPV decision rule to evaluate this investment. The timeline for the cash flows of the savings bond is provided in Figure 2.11.

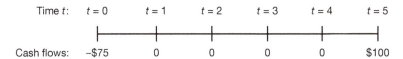

FIGURE 2.11 Savings bond example. This figure shows a timeline of the cash flows for the savings bond investment, where you pay $75 right now (time $t = 0$) in exchange for receiving $100 in five years.

The initial investment for the savings bond is $75, which is the cash outflow (this happens today, no discounting necessary). What is the present value of the cash inflows that the bond generates? It is the present value of $100 to be received five years from now. The relevant interest rate is 8%, the rate that the money could earn if it were deposited in a savings account and not invested in the bond. In this example, the opportunity cost of capital of investing in the savings bond is the 8% rate we could earn if we put our money in the bank account.

In general, the interest rate we use for the NPV calculation of any investment is known as the opportunity cost of capital (also called the *market capitalization rate*), the rate that the investment could earn somewhere else if we did not invest it in the project under evaluation. Using our knowledge of present value (Equation 2.8), we can compute the NPV of investing in this bond:

$$\begin{aligned} NPV &= -PV(\text{cash outflows}) + PV(\text{cash inflows}) \\ &= -\$75 + \frac{\$100}{1.08^5} \\ &= -\$75 + \$68.06 \\ &= -\$6.94. \end{aligned}$$

The $75 initial investment reflects the cash outflow (happening now), which is subtracted. We can see that the present value of the cash inflows ($100 in five years) is $68.06, which is less than the $75 we would have to pay for the bond. Because the NPV of the investment is negative, the investment in the bond is not worthwhile, and we should deposit our $75 in the savings account.

Another way to arrive at the same conclusion is to use a slightly different rule known as the future value rule, which says to invest in the project if its future value is greater than the future value of the next best alternative. Let us illustrate how the future value rule would work in the example we used to illustrate the NPV rule.

Investing in a savings bond (initial investment $75, future value of cash flows $100 in five years) leads to a future value of $100. Putting the money into a bank at 8% is the next best thing we can do with the money. Does the savings bond have a higher future value than we could get from depositing $75.00 in the bank?

Using our future value formula, the future value from the bank account is given by:

$$FV_{T=5} = \$PV \times (1+r)^T$$
$$= \$75 \times 1.08^5$$
$$= \$110.20.$$

So, $75 (the cost of the savings bond) invested in the bank account will give you $110.20 in five years. Alternatively, you could spend the $75 to buy the savings bond, which will give you $100 in five years. The bank account is clearly a better investment, which matches what we found using the NPV rule.

The future value rule is actually slightly more intuitive (and leads to the same decision as the NPV rule). The reason it is not used as often in practice is that in many circumstances (as we will see later in the book), the future value of an investment cannot be computed, whereas the NPV rule can always be computed.

Example 2.8 (Investing in Land): You have the opportunity to buy a piece of land for $10,000. You are sure that five years from now it will be worth $20,000. If you can earn 8% per year by putting your money in the bank, is this investment in the land worthwhile?

Solution. By the NPV rule, we know that the investment is worthwhile if it has positive NPV. We therefore want to calculate the NPV of this investment. We can draw out a timeline of the cash flows from the investment:

Time t:	$t=0$	$t=1$	$t=2$	$t=3$	$t=4$	$t=5$
Cash flows:	−$10,000	0	0	0	0	$20,000

Our cash inflow from the investment is $20,000 five years from now, the present value of which is:

$$PV(\text{cash inflow}) = \frac{\$20,000}{1.08^5}$$
$$= \$13,612.$$

Thus, the investment in the land has a present value of $13,612. Comparing this to the $10,000 cost of the land (the cash outflow today), it clearly seems like a bargain—its NPV is $13,612 − $10,000 = $3,612. The investment is therefore worthwhile.

We can also solve this problem using the future value rule. The future value (FV) of the land in five years is $20,000. In contrast, at an 8% interest rate, the future value in five years of investing $10,000 is:

$$FV(\text{cash inflow}) = \$10,000 \times (1.08)^5 = \$14,693.28.$$

The future value of the land in five years is higher, again leading us to the same conclusion: Invest in the land.

Example 2.9 (Other People's Money): Suppose that you need to borrow $5,000 to buy a car. You go to a bank and they offer you a loan at an interest rate of 12% per year. You then go to a friend who says he will lend you the $5,000 if you pay him $9,000 in four years. What should you do?

Solution. In the preceding example, we considered an investment in which you are required to lay out money in the present and receive cash at some future date. But often financial decisions involve the reverse, as in this case.

First, let's identify the investment that you need to evaluate. The cash flow that you want to evaluate is the $5,000 (today) you can borrow from your friend (a cash inflow). The investment you must make is the present value of the $9,000 repayment (a cash outflow) after four years. It is useful to draw a timeline to represent this:

Time t:	$t = 0$	$t = 1$	$t = 2$	$t = 3$	$t = 4$
Cash flow CF_t:	$5,000	0	0	0	−$9,000

The way to proceed is to calculate the NPV of the project. Because the opportunity cost of capital is 12% (the bank's rate, your next best alternative), the NPV is (Equation 2.12):

$$\begin{aligned} NPV &= -PV(\text{cash outflows}) + PV(\text{cash inflows}) \\ &= -\frac{\$9,000}{1.12^4} + \$5,000 \\ &= -\$5,719.66 + \$5,000 \\ &= -\$719.66. \end{aligned}$$

The NPV is negative, so you should not borrow from your friend. You are better off borrowing from the bank. We can also arrive at the same conclusion using the future value rule. The future value of the loan your friend offers is $9,000 in four years. In contrast, at a 12% interest rate, the future value of the $5,000 bank loan is:

$$FV(\text{cash inflow}) = \$5,000 \times (1.12)^4 = \$7,867.60.$$

The future value of the loan from your friend is higher, meaning that it is more expensive. You should borrow from the bank.

> **QUICK CHECK 2.9** Consider the previous savings bond example: You are looking at a $100 savings bond maturing in five years and selling for a price of $75. Instead of your opportunity cost of capital (next best alternative) being a savings account paying 8% interest per year, suppose the savings account is paying only 2%. What is the NPV of the savings bond? What is the NPV of the savings account? What investment should you make?

2.5 Valuing Annuities

Often the future cash flows from a financial product—a savings plan, an investment project, or a loan repayment schedule—follow a certain pattern. They might be the same each year, or grow each year in some pre-specified way. Sometimes the cash flows may last for a long period of time, say 30 years or more. In such a case, it may be difficult to discount each individual cash flow to get the present value of the stream of future cash flows. In this section, we explore this type of special cash flow, and learn how to easily find out its present value.

Often the future cash flows in a savings plan, an investment project, or a loan repayment schedule are the same each year. We call such a level stream of cash flows an annuity. Thus, the stream of payments on an installment loan, a lease, or a mortgage is considered an annuity.

If the cash flows start immediately, as in a savings plan or a lease, it is called an annuity due (sometimes also referred to as an immediate annuity). If the cash flows start at the end of the current period rather than immediately, it is called an ordinary annuity. A mortgage is an example of an ordinary

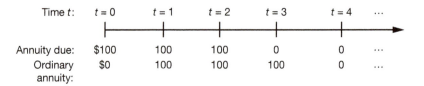

FIGURE 2.12 Cash flow timeline of a $100 annuity that lasts three years. This figure shows a timeline of the cash flows for an annuity due and an ordinary annuity which pay $100 each year for three years and then nothing after that. In an annuity due, the first cash flow occurs at $t = 0$, while in an ordinary annuity the first cash flow occurs at $t = 1$.

annuity. Figure 2.12 shows the timeline of the cash flows on immediate and ordinary annuities that last three years each, paying a cash flow of $100 each year. In finance, most annuities are ordinary annuities, and so henceforth when we talk about an annuity we will be referring to an ordinary annuity unless otherwise specified.

There are some convenient formulas, financial calculator functions, and spreadsheet programs for computing the future and present values of annuities, which come in handy when the stream of cash flows lasts for many periods. We will go over these now.

2.5.1 The Future and Present Values of an Annuity

To understand how to value an annuity, let's begin with the future value of an annuity that pays $100 each year for the next three years. We first consider how much money will have accumulated in three years at an interest rate of 10% per year. Note that we have three different cash flows. The first cash flow of $100 occurs at $t = 1$, and we use Equation 2.1 to determine that its future value at $t = 3$, given the 10% interest rate for two years (from $t = 1$ to $t = 3$) will be: $100 \times 1.10^2 = \$121$. The second cash flow of $100 occurs at $t = 2$, and its future value in one year at $t = 3$ will be: $100 \times 1.10 = \$110$. Finally, the third cash flow of $100 occurs at $t = 3$ and its future value at $t = 3$ is therefore $100. When we add up the future values of all of these cash flows at $t = 3$, we get: $121 + \$110 + \$100 = \$331$.

The general formula for the future value at time T of an annuity that gives you a cash flow CF of the same amount each year, given an interest of r, is:

$$FV_T = \$CF \times \frac{(1+r)^T - 1}{r}. \tag{2.13}$$

Our example would yield the following equation:

$$\begin{aligned} FV_3 &= \$CF \times \frac{(1+r)^T - 1}{r} \\ &= \$100 \times \frac{(1.10)^3 - 1}{0.10} \\ &= \$331. \end{aligned}$$

Often, we want to compute the present value rather than the future value of an annuity stream. The present value of this annuity is the sum of the present value of the three cash flows (Equation 2.9):

$$\begin{aligned} PV &= \frac{CF_1}{1+r} + \frac{CF_2}{(1+r)^2} + \frac{CF_3}{(1+r)^3} \\ &= \frac{\$100}{1.10} + \frac{\$100}{1.10^2} + \frac{\$100}{1.10^3} \\ &= \$248.69. \end{aligned}$$

2.5 VALUING ANNUITIES

Note that this present value is the same as the future value we calculated earlier using Equation 2.8, discounted back three years: $331 / 1.10^3 = \$248.69$.

While we can pretty easily calculate the present value as we always have for an annuity stream that will last for three years, sometimes an annuity stream will last for a much longer period. For example, a common length for a home mortgage is 30 years! Writing out 30 DCFs would take a lot of time. Luckily, there is a convenient formula for calculating the present value of an annuity for any length of time:

$$PV = \frac{\$CF}{r} \times \left[1 - \frac{1}{(1+r)^T}\right]. \qquad (2.14)$$

Example 2.10 (Buying an Annuity): You are 65 years old and are considering whether it pays to buy an annuity from an insurance company. For a cost of $10,000 the insurance company will pay you $1,000 per year for the rest of your life. Suppose you can earn 8% per year on your money in a bank account and expect to live until age 80. Is it worth buying the annuity?

Solution. The most direct way to make this investment decision is to compute the present value of the payments from the annuity and compare it to the annuity's $10,000 cost—in other words, compute the NPV of buying the annuity. The annuity is expected to make 15 payments of $1,000 each year starting at age 66 (next year) and ending at age 80. This time line shows the payment stream:

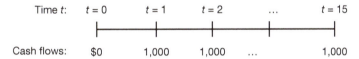

You could calculate the present value by discounting each of the $1,000 cash flows, but it is more convenient to use Equation 2.14. Given the interest rate of $r = 0.08$ and $T = 15$, the present value of this annuity is

$$PV = \frac{\$CF}{r} \times \left[1 - \frac{1}{(1+r)^T}\right]$$

$$= \frac{\$1,000}{0.08} \times \left[1 - \frac{1}{(1+0.08)^{15}}\right]$$

$$= \$8,559.48.$$

Note that we could also calculate the present value in Excel using the =PV() function. Recall that the syntax is =PV(rate, # periods, PMT, FV). In this case, we are getting a payment each period from the annuity ($1,000), so we want to enter −1000 as our PMT (given the negative sign convention in Excel). FV will be zero in this case because we do not receive a single amount at the end of the annuity; we just receive the same $1,000 each year. Therefore, we would enter =PV (8%, 15, −1000, 0), which returns the same number, $8,559.48, as shown below:

	A	B
1	r	8%
2	T	15
3	CF	$1,000
4	PV	=PV(B1,B2,-B3,0)
5		$8,559.48

This number indicates that to generate the same 15 annual payments of $1,000 each, you would need to invest $8,559.48 in a bank account paying 8% interest per year. The NPV of the investment in the annuity is, given that it costs $10,000:

2 BASICS OF VALUATION

$$\begin{aligned} NPV &= -PV\text{ (cash outflows)} + PV\text{ (cash inflows)} \\ &= -\$10{,}000 + \$8{,}559.48 \\ &= -\$1{,}440.52. \end{aligned}$$

The annuity is **not** worth buying, because it has a negative NPV.

Example 2.11 (Taking Out a Mortgage): You have just decided to buy a house and need to borrow $100,000. One bank offers you a mortgage loan to be repaid over 30 years in 360 monthly payments. If the interest rate is 12% per year (APR), what is the amount of the monthly payment (the monthly cash flow)?

Solution. First, note that the payments are monthly and the interest rate is quoted as an APR, so the monthly interest rate will be (based on Equation 2.4): 12%/12 = 1%. We want to calculate what the monthly payment will be, given that the present value of the mortgage is $100,000. We can set up the annuity equation with $r = 1\%$ and $T = 360$ months:

$$PV = \frac{\$CF}{r} \times \left[1 - \frac{1}{(1+r)^T}\right]$$

$$\$100{,}000 = \frac{\$CF}{0.01} \times \left[1 - \frac{1}{(1+0.01)^{360}}\right]$$

$$\$CF = \$1{,}028.61.$$

Your monthly mortgage payment will be $1,028.61.

> **QUICK CHECK 2.10** Calculate the present value of an annuity that pays $100 each year for ten years. The interest rate is 10%.

2.5.2 The Present Value of Growing Annuities

Not all annuities have the same cash flow in each period. A **growing annuity** is an annuity for which the cash flows increase by some rate with each period. This continues until the end of the annuity. Figure 2.13 shows what a growing annuity cash flow stream looks like, with a first cash flow of $100 followed by cash flows that grow at a rate g.

Equation 2.15 allows us to calculate a growing annuity's present value today ($t = 0$), given an initial cash flow of $\$CF_1$ that occurs in the next period (at $t = 1$), a discount rate of r, and a growth rate of g:

$$PV = \frac{\$CF_1}{r - g} \times \left[1 - \left(\frac{1+g}{1+r}\right)^T\right]. \quad (2.15)$$

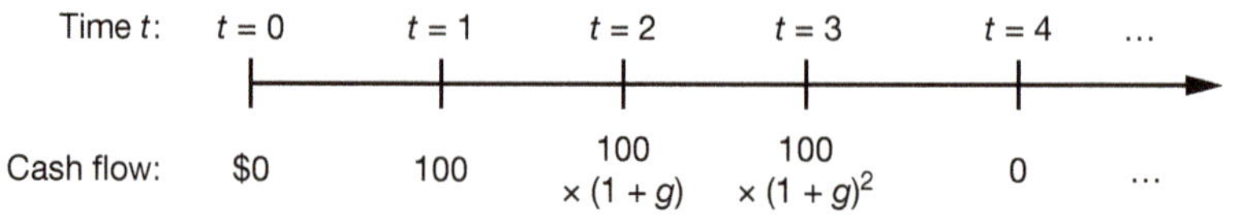

Time t:	$t = 0$	$t = 1$	$t = 2$	$t = 3$	$t = 4$	...
Cash flow:	$0	100	100 × (1 + g)	100 × (1 + g)²	0	...

FIGURE 2.13 Cash flow timeline of a $100 growing annuity that lasts three years.

The intuition behind this formula is that even though the cash flows are growing by g each period, when we discount them by r the present value of the future cash flows gets smaller.

It is important to note that this formula holds only when the growth rate g is not the same as the discount rate r. If they are the same ($r = g$), the equation must be modified to reflect this, so as to not divide by zero:

$$PV = \frac{\$CF_1 \times T}{1+r}. \tag{2.16}$$

Example 2.12 (Gift Exchange): It is your birthday today. You have a trust fund that promises to give you payments for your next 20 birthdays. The first payment will be $1 million dollars on your next birthday, exactly one year from now. After that, the yearly payments from the trust will grow at the rate of 5% every year, and the interest rate the trust fund earns is 10%. You are considering selling this stream of trust fund payments right now to buy a yacht. How much could you sell them for?

Solution. To determine the present value of these payments, we use Equation 2.15. The first payment next year is $\$CF = \$1$ million, $r = 10\%$, and the growth rate is $g = 5\%$. Putting these into the growing perpetuity formula (Equation 2.15), we have:

$$\begin{aligned} PV &= \frac{\$CF}{r-g} \times \left[1 - \left(\frac{1+g}{1+r}\right)^T\right] \\ &= \frac{\$1 \text{ million}}{0.10 - 0.05} \times \left[1 - \left(\frac{1+0.05}{1+0.10}\right)^{20}\right] \\ &= \$12.112 \text{ million.} \end{aligned}$$

You could therefore cash out and sell your stream of trust fund payments for $12.112 million today.

> **QUICK CHECK 2.11** Calculate the present value of an annuity that pays $100 each year (starting next year) for ten years, but grows at a rate of 2% per year after the first year. The interest rate is 10%.

2.6 Valuing Perpetuities

A *perpetual annuity* or *perpetuity* is a stream of cash flows that lasts *forever*. The classic example is the consol bond issued by the British government in the nineteenth century, which pays interest each year on the face value of the bond but has no maturity date. Perpetuities will feature prominently in our discussion of company valuation in Part II of this book, as we assume that there is no defined end to the cash flows that companies generate. Figure 2.14 shows what a perpetuity's cash flow stream looks like, with a cash flow of $100 each period.

A disturbing feature of any perpetual annuity is that you cannot compute the future value of its cash flows. Because the perpetuity never ends, its cash flows are infinite. Furthermore, calculating the present value of a perpetuity by discounting individual cash flows using Equation 2.9 is infeasible because the cash flows never end. Nevertheless, a perpetuity has a well-defined and determinable present value.

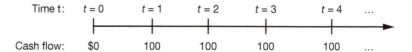

FIGURE 2.14 Cash flow timeline of a $100 perpetuity. This figure provides a timeline of a perpetuity that provides a cash flow of $100 each period and continues forever.

It might at first seem paradoxical that a series of cash flows that lasts forever can have a finite value today. To show the intuition behind this, consider a perpetual cash flow of $100 per year. If the interest rate is 10% per year, how much is this perpetuity worth today? You may think that it is worth an infinite amount of money. However, think about the present value of each of these cash flows. The present value of the year 1 cash flow is $100 / 1.1 = $90.91. The present value of the year 2 cash flow is $100 / 1.1^2 = $82.64. To go further forward, the present value of the year 40 cash flow is only $100 / 1.1^{40} = $2.21. The present values of cash flows that happen further in the future continue to decline, so that even though the perpetuity lasts forever, the present value of the cash flows that happen far in the future are minuscule. That is why the present value of the entire stream is finite.

As another way to see this, consider how much money you would have to put into a bank account offering interest of 10% per year in order to be able to take out $100 every year forever. If you put in $1,000, then at the end of the first year you would have $1,100 in the account. You would take out $100, leaving $1,000 for the second year. If the interest rate stayed at 10% per year, and you had a fountain of youth nearby, you could go on doing this forever. This illustrates that the present value of the perpetuity is $1,000.

More generally, the formula for the present value of a perpetuity with a cash flow $CF each period is:

$$PV = \frac{\$CF}{r}. \qquad (2.17)$$

In our previous example, the present value of a perpetuity that provides a cash flow of $100 each period (starting next period), with an interest rate of 10%, is:

$$\begin{aligned} PV &= \frac{\$CF}{r} \\ &= \frac{\$100}{0.10} \\ &= \$1,000. \end{aligned}$$

This matches the present value we solved for before.

Example 2.13 (Valuing a Gift): You are set to receive a gift that promises to pay you $1,000 each year forever, with the cash flows starting in year 3. You will receive the gift in two years. How much is it worth to you now, assuming an interest rate of 10%?

Solution. This is a perpetuity, but one that starts in year 3. A timeline clarifies the timing of the cash flows:

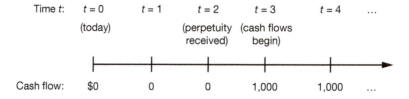

Let us first begin by considering the value of a perpetuity of $1,000 per year using the perpetuity formula (Equation. 2.17):

$$PV = \frac{\$CF}{r}$$
$$= \frac{\$1,000}{0.10}$$
$$= \$10,000.$$

It is critical to remember the timing of the perpetuity formula. The formula gives you the present value of a perpetuity of $1,000 per year that begins next year. Put differently, it tells you the present value of the perpetuity at $t = 2$ (i.e., what the present value would be if we were in year 2), because it is as of this date that the $1,000 payments begin in the next year. Another way of thinking about this is that whichever date's cash flow we put into the perpetuity (or any of the other) formulas, the formulas will give us the present value of the cash flow stream as of the date prior to that. Thus, putting the year $t = 3$ cash flow of $1,000 into the formula gives us the value of the subsequent perpetuity cash flows at $t = 2$. We can visualize this as follows:

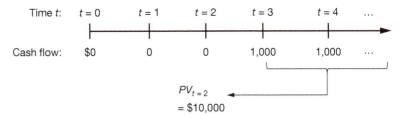

The last step notes that the $10,000 is the present value at $t = 2$. We want to determine the perpetuity's value as of now. To do so, we discount the value at $t = 2$ back two years to today:

$$PV = \frac{\$10,000}{1.10^2} = \$8,264.46.$$

A perpetuity that will start paying out in year 3 in the future is worth $8,264.46 today.

QUICK CHECK 2.12 What is the present value of a perpetuity that provides a cash flow of $1,000 each year (starting next year), with an interest rate of 5%?

2.6.1 Growing Perpetuities

Often the cash flows from an investment grow at a constant rate. A perpetuity with this characteristic is called a growth perpetuity or growing perpetuity. Figure 2.15 shows the timeline of a growing perpetuity that pays $100 in the first period, and then grows at rate g.

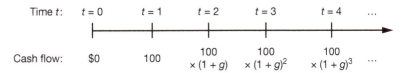

FIGURE 2.15 Cash flow timeline of a $100 growing perpetuity. This figure shows a timeline of a growing perpetuity, which pays $100 in $t = 1$, and continues to make payments each period that grow at rate g.

For example, suppose that you are considering investing in a property for which you expect the first year's cash flow to be $1,000, and you expect it to grow by 4% each year in perpetuity:

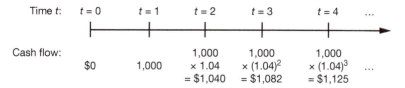

To evaluate such an investment, you need a formula for computing the present value of a growing perpetuity. To calculate the present value now ($t = 0$), given a first cash flow of $\$CF_1$ that occurs next period (at $t = 1$), a discount rate of r, and a growth rate of g, the formula is:

$$PV = \frac{\$CF_1}{r - g}. \tag{2.18}$$

Note that in Equation 2.18 it must be the case that the discount rate r is greater than the cash flow growth rate g ($r > g$). In Equation 2.18 the cash flows grow by g each period, but when we discount them by r, the present value of the future cash flows gets smaller. When the discount rate is greater than the growth rate ($r > g$), then the effect of the discounting overwhelms the effect of the growth, allowing us to have a finite present value. If this is the case, then, exactly as in the perpetuity formula, the present values of cash flows that happen far in the future will be extremely small: Even though the cash flows are growing, they are not growing faster than they are being discounted. If, however, the growth rate is larger than the discount rate ($g > r$), then the discounting cannot offset the growth in the cash flows. In that case, the cash flows will grow so fast that the present value of future cash flows will get larger and larger and the present value would be infinite.

To continue our example, suppose that the discount rate is 9%. The cash flow remains at $1,000 per year, and the growth rate of the cash flows is 4%. Then the present value of the property would be:

$$\begin{aligned} PV &= \frac{\$CF_1}{r - g} \\ &= \frac{\$1,000}{0.09 - 0.04} \\ &= \frac{\$1,000}{0.05} \\ &= \$20,000. \end{aligned}$$

> **QUICK CHECK 2.13** What is the present value of a growing perpetuity that gives $1,000 each year (starting next year), and grows at a rate of 2% per year after that, with an interest rate of 5%?

2.7 Inflation and Discounted Cash Flow Analysis

Throughout this chapter we have looked at how to determine the amount of money that an investment may provide at a future date, as well as the present value of a sum of money in the future. In our discussions we have assumed that the value of the money itself does not change. But the value of money does change over time—for example, groceries that cost $100 today may cost $200 ten years from now due to inflation, a general increase in the prices of everything over time. Not taking inflation into account in cash flow analysis can lead to distorted financial decisions. In some countries, the rate of inflation is high year to year, meaning that prices for the same goods over time increase substantially. In other countries, the rate of inflation is lower from year to year. Whether high or low, inflation has important implications for our valuation techniques.

For example, let us consider the issue of saving for retirement. At age 20 you save $100 and invest it at a dollar interest rate of 8% per year. The good news is that at age 65 your $100 investment will have grown to $3,192 ($100 × 1.08^{45}). The bad news is that if there is inflation it will cost you more to buy the same items you buy today. For example, if the prices of all the goods and services you want to buy also go up at 8% per year for the next 45 years, then your $3,192 will buy no more than your $100 will buy today. In a "real" sense, that is, in terms of the goods you can buy, you will not have earned any interest at all. Thus, to make truly meaningful long-run savings decisions, you must take account of inflation as well as interest.

To take account of both interest and inflation, we distinguish between nominal and real interest rates. The nominal interest rate is the rate denominated in dollars or some other currency, and the real interest rate is denominated in units of consumer goods. Put differently, the nominal interest rate does not take into account that money may have less purchasing power in the future; it does not account for inflation. The real interest rate, in contrast, adjusts for inflation because it reflects how much each dollar would actually be able to purchase.

The general formula relating the real rate of interest to the nominal rate of interest and the rate of inflation is:

$$1 + \text{real interest rate} = \frac{1 + \text{nominal interest rate}}{1 + \text{rate of inflation}}, \quad (2.19)$$

or, equivalently,

$$\text{Real interest rate} = \frac{\text{nominal interest rate} - \text{rate of inflation}}{1 + \text{rate of inflation}}. \quad (2.20)$$

To make our notation more compact, we will refer to the real interest rate as r_{real} and the nominal interest rate as $r_{nominal}$.

From this point forward in the book, when we talk about interest rates, we will be talking about nominal interest rates unless otherwise specified.

2.7.1 Inflation and Future Values

From a financial planning perspective for individuals and corporations, there is a great advantage to knowing the real interest rate. This is because ultimately it is what you can buy with your accumulated savings in the future that you care about.

Returning to our specific example of saving $100 at age 20, not to be taken out until age 65, let's now take into account that inflation is 5% per year. What we really want to know is how much you will have accumulated in the account when you reach age 65 in terms of real purchasing power. There are two alternative ways of calculating it—a short way and a long way. The short way is to compute the future value of the $100 using the real interest rate for 45 years. In this case, the real interest rate, using Equation 2.20, is:

$$\begin{aligned} r_{real} &= \frac{r_{nominal} - \text{rate of inflation}}{1 + \text{rate of inflation}} \\ &= \frac{0.08 - 0.05}{1.05} \\ &= 0.02857. \end{aligned}$$

The real rate of interest is therefore 2.857%. We can then calculate the future value using the rate of 2.857% per year for 45 years. We define this as the real future value:

$$\text{Real } FV_T = \$PV \times (1 + r_{real})^T$$
$$= \$100 \times (1 + 0.02857)^{45}$$
$$= \$355.$$

What this means is that instead of having $3,192 in the bank with which you can buy $3,192 worth of goods and services, you will have $3,192 in the bank with which you can buy only $355 worth of goods and services. So, in other words, your $100 will be worth $355 in real terms.

Alternatively, we can arrive at the same number in stages. First, we compute the nominal future value by using the nominal interest rate of 8% per year:

$$\text{Nominal } FV_T = \$PV \times (1 + r_{nominal})^T$$
$$= \$100 \times 1.08^{45}$$
$$= \$3,192.$$

Next, we figure out what the price level will be 45 years from now if the inflation rate is 5% per year (i.e., how many dollars 45 years from now would buy as much as $1 today):

$$\text{Price level in 45 years} = 1.05^{45}$$
$$= 8.985.$$

Thus, in 45 years, it will take about $8.99 to purchase as many goods and services as $1 would purchase today.

Finally, we divide the nominal future value by the future price level to find the real future value:

$$\text{Real } FV_T = \frac{\text{nominal } FV_T}{\text{price level in 45 years}}$$
$$= \frac{\$3,192}{8.985}$$
$$= \$355.$$

We find that by saving $100 today (age 20) and investing it for 45 years, we expect to have enough at age 65 to buy what would cost $355 at today's prices.

Thus, we see that there are two equivalent ways of computing the real future value of $355:

(a) Compute the future value using the real rate of interest.
(b) Compute the nominal future value using the nominal rate, and then adjust the nominal amount for the effects of inflation to find the real future value.

Which of the two equivalent approaches one adopts depends on the particular context.

One lesson from this is that future values are lower when we incorporate inflation. This has a number of practical implications that are important to take into account. For example, savings become less valuable over time when inflation rates are higher. On the other hand, when considering a plan for long-run savings, the amount of money you can afford to save each year is likely to rise with the general cost of living because your income will probably also be going up. One way to take account of this without having to make an explicit forecast of the rate of inflation is to make your plans in terms of constant real payments and a real rate of interest.

Borrowing money also becomes more attractive. Suppose you borrow $1,000 at an interest rate of 8% per year and have to pay back the principal and interest one year later (i.e., $1,080). If the rate of inflation turns out to be 8% during the year, the real interest rate on the loan is zero. Although you must pay back $1,080, its real value will be only $1,000. The $80 in interest just offsets the decline in the purchasing power of the $1,000 principal. Another way to state this is that you are paying back the loan with "cheaper" dollars than the ones you borrowed. No wonder that when the interest rate on a loan is fixed in advance, borrowers like unanticipated inflation and lenders do not.

> **QUICK CHECK 2.14** In this section we calculated the real future value of $100 assuming a nominal interest rate of 8% and an inflation rate of 5%. Now let's assume that the nominal interest rate is instead 6%. How does this affect the real future value calculations?

2.7.2 Inflation and Calculating Present Values

We now turn to how inflation affects present value calculations. For example, suppose you plan to buy a car four years from now and want to save enough money now to pay for it. The kind of car you have in mind now costs $10,000, and the interest rate you can earn on your money is 8% per year.

In attempting to figure out the amount to invest now, it is natural to compute the present value of $10,000 to be received in four years at 8%:

$$PV = \frac{\$10,000}{1.08^4} = \$7,350.$$

So, you might conclude that investing $7,350 now is adequate to pay for the car four years from now. But that would be a mistake! Almost surely, if the car you want costs $10,000 today, a similar car will cost more four years from now because of inflation. How much more? That depends on the rate of inflation. If inflation in car prices is 5% per year, then the car will cost $10,000 \times 1.05^4 = \$12,155$.

There are two equivalent ways to take account of inflation in problems such as this. The first is to compute the present value of the $10,000 real future amount using the real discount rate. From the previous section, we found that the real rate is 2.857%. Using this real rate to compute the present value of the $10,000, we use Equation 2.8:

$$PV = \frac{\$10,000}{1.02857^4} = \$8,934.$$

Thus, to have enough money in your account to purchase the car in four years (given how the price of the car will rise due to inflation), you would need to invest $8,934, not $7,350.

The second way to account for inflation is to compute the present value of the $12,155 nominal future cost of the car using the nominal discount rate of 8% per year:

$$PV = \frac{\$12,155}{1.08^4} = \$8,934.$$

Either way, we get the same result: You must invest $8,934 now to pay the car's inflated price in four years. The reason we at first mistakenly computed the amount we needed to invest as only $7,350 was that we discounted a real future amount of $10,000 at a nominal discount rate of 8% per year instead of the real discount rate of 2.857%.

The key lesson from these examples? **Always discount nominal cash flows by nominal interest rates, and real cash flows by real interest rates.** Never use a nominal interest rate when discounting real cash flows or a real interest rate when discounting nominal cash flows. By convention, interest rates are generally quoted as nominal rates unless specified otherwise. We return to this issue and the distinction between real and nominal rates throughout the book.

Example 2.14 (Saving for College): Your daughter is 10 years old, and you are planning to open an account to provide for her first year of college education at age 18. Tuition for a year of college is now $15,000.

If you put $8,000 into an account paying a nominal interest rate of 8% per year (assuming 0% inflation over the eight years), will you have enough to pay for her first year's tuition eight years from now? What if inflation is instead 5% per year?

Solution. If you compute the future value of the $8,000 at a nominal interest rate of 8% per year for eight years and 0% inflation, you find:

$$FV_{T=8} = \$8,000 \times 1.08^8$$
$$= \$14,807.$$

Because $14,807 is very close to $15,000, it might appear that saving $8,000 now is enough to provide for the first year's tuition. But the tuition level is a moving target because of inflation. For example, if inflation turns out to be 5% per year (instead of 0% per year), the cost of the first year's college tuition will be $15,000 × 1.05⁸ = $22,162. So, your $14,807 will be short by $7,355.

> **QUICK CHECK 2.15** In the example presented in this section, you planned to buy a car four years from now and wanted to save enough money now to pay for it. The kind of car you had in mind costs $10,000 now. Recalculate the amount you would need to invest now for the car in four years, assuming a nominal interest rate of 6% and an inflation rate of 5% per year.

2.7.3 Inflation and Investment Decisions

It is just as essential to take account of inflation in investment decisions as it is in saving decisions. When investing money in real assets such as real estate and plant and equipment, the future cash flows from the investment are likely to rise in nominal value because of inflation. If you fail to make the appropriate adjustments, you will tend to pass up worthwhile investment opportunities.

To see how important it is to take proper account of inflation, consider the following example. Suppose you currently heat your factory with oil and your annual heating bill is $20,000. By converting to gas heat, you estimate that this year you could cut your heating bill by $5,000 per year, and you think that the difference in cost between gas and oil is likely to remain the same for many years. The cost of installing a gas heating system is $100,000. If your alternative use of the money is to leave the $100,000 in a bank account earning an interest rate of 8% per year (this is your opportunity cost of capital), is the conversion worthwhile?

Note that there is no natural time horizon for this decision. We will, therefore, assume that the $5,000 cost differential between gas and oil heat will remain forever. We will also assume that the future cost of replacing the heating equipment ($100,000) will be the same under both the oil and gas alternatives, so that we can ignore them for the purposes of making this decision. Therefore, the investment is a perpetuity—you pay $100,000 now and get $5,000 per year forever.

Comparing this 5% per year rate of return to the 8% per year alternative, you might be inclined to reject the gas investment opportunity. *But* the 8% per year rate on the bank account is a nominal interest rate. Is the 5% per year rate of return on the investment in gas heat nominal or real?

If you think that the $5,000 cost differential between gas and oil will increase over time with the general rate of inflation, then the 5% rate of return on the investment is a real rate of return. You should, therefore, compare it to the expected real interest rate on the bank account. If you expect the rate of inflation to be 5% per year, then the expected real interest rate on the bank account is 2.857% (i.e., (0.08 − 0.05) / 1.05). The 5% per year real return on the investment in gas heat exceeds the real return on the bank account, so perhaps the investment is worthwhile after all.

This example leads us to the following rule: When comparing investment alternatives, never compare a real rate of return to a nominal rate of return when calculating discount rates (i.e., opportunity cost of capital).

Conclusion

In this chapter we have explored many aspects of **Principle 1:** *A dollar today is not worth the same as a dollar tomorrow.* This principle forms the basis of determining the value of any type of asset, be it a financial investment such as investing in a savings account, a project a company is thinking of undertaking, a financial instrument such as a stock, or an entire company.

We began the chapter by determining the future value of an investment—in other words, if you put your money into an investment that earns interest over time, how much money will you have in the future? We saw that the idea of compound interest allowed us to accurately answer this question, as it accounts for interest earned on previous interest. The ability to earn such interest on an investment is what underlies the time value of money summarized by Principle 1 and makes a dollar today not equal to a dollar in the future: The dollar invested today can earn interest at the interest rate, resulting in a different amount of money in the future.

The concept of future value then allowed us to examine a parallel question—if you face a financial transaction or investment that will pay you some amount of money in the future, what is that investment worth to you today? We answered this question by converting money to be received in the future into today's terms by calculating the present value of a future cash flow via a process known as discounting. We explored various examples of patterns of cash flows that reflect real-world financial decisions, and learned how to value them. This set the foundation for understanding many different types of financial decisions and transactions that we will explore throughout the book.

Takeaways

- **Principle** 1 states that a dollar today is not worth a dollar tomorrow. This chapter explores the concept of the time value of money, which means that $1 at different points in time is not worth the same amount.
- The future value of a sum of money is the amount after it has earned interest over time. Compounding reflects the fact that over time interest is continually earned on previous interest.
- Discounting is finding the present value of an amount you expect to receive in the future.
- By inverting the formula for the future value of a sum of money, we get the present value of an expected future amount.
- When compounding occurs at different frequencies within a year, discount rates must be adjusted to account for this through the appropriate use of annual percentage rates (APR) and effective annual rates (EAR).
- Investment decisions can be evaluated using the net present value rule, which states that an investment should be undertaken if the present value of the cash inflows exceeds the present value of the cash outflows.

- Annuities and perpetuities are special patterns of future expected cash flows. There are formulas that allow us to directly and easily calculate the present value of such cash flows.
- Real interest rates take inflation into account when calculating the value of cash flows. Never use a nominal interest rate when discounting real cash flows or a real interest rate when discounting nominal cash flows.

Key Terms

Annual percentage rate (APR)   21
Annuity   37
Annuity due, immediate annuity   37
Cash flows   14
Compound interest   16
Compounding   16
Continuous compounding   23
Discount factor   27
Discount rate   27
Discounted cash flow   27
Discounted cash flow analysis   27
Discounting   27
Effective annual rate (EAR)   22
Future value (FV)   15
Future value rule   35
Growing annuity   40
Growth or growing perpetuity   43

Inflation   44
Interest   14
Interest rate   14
Net present value (NPV)   34
Nominal interest rate   45
Opportunity cost of capital   35
Ordinary annuity   37
Perpetual annuity, perpetuity   41
Present value (PV)   15
Principal   14
Real interest rate   45
Simple interest   16
Timeline   14
Time value of money   13
Valuation   13
Value   13

Key Equations

Future value	$FV_T = \$PV \times (1+r)^T$	Eq. 2.1
Future value (changing interest rates)	$FV_T = \$PV \times (1+r_{0,1}) \times (1+r_{1,2}) \times (1+r_{2,3}) \times \ldots \times (1+r_{T-1,T})$	Eq. 2.6
Effective annual rate (EAR)	$EAR = \left(1 + \dfrac{APR}{m}\right)^m - 1$	Eq. 2.4
Present value	$PV = \dfrac{CF_1}{1+r} + \dfrac{CF_2}{(1+r)^2} + \dfrac{CF_3}{(1+r)^3} + \cdots + \dfrac{CF_T}{(1+r)^T}$	Eq. 2.9
Present value, annuity	$PV = \dfrac{\$CF}{r} \times \left[1 - \dfrac{1}{(1+r)^T}\right]$	Eq. 2.14
Present value, growing annuity ($r \neq g$)	$PV = \dfrac{\$CF_1}{r-g} \times \left[1 - \left(\dfrac{1+g}{1+r}\right)^T\right]$	Eq. 2.15
Present value, perpetuity	$PV = \dfrac{\$CF}{r}$	Eq. 2.17

Present value, growing perpetuity	$PV = \dfrac{\$CF_1}{r - g}$	Eq. 2.18
Real rate of interest	Real interest rate = $\dfrac{\text{nominal interest rate} - \text{rate of inflation}}{1 + \text{rate of inflation}}$	Eq. 2.19

Problems

1. (a) If you invest $1,000 today at an interest rate of 10% per year, how much will you have 20 years from now, assuming no withdrawals in the interim?
   (b) If you invest $100 every year for the next 20 years starting one year from today, how much will you have at the end of the 20 years?
   (c) How much must you invest each year if you want to have $50,000 at the end of the 20 years?
2. Suppose you want to make sure that you have $30,000 in five years so that you can purchase a new car. The annual interest rate is 6%. How much money should you invest at that interest rate in order to achieve your goal?
3. What is the present value of the following cash flows at an interest rate of 10% per year?
   (a) $100 received five years from now.
   (b) $100 received 60 years from now.
   (c) $100 received each year beginning one year from now and ending ten years from now.
   (d) $100 received each year for ten years, with the first payment occurring one year from today.
   (e) $100 received each year for ten years, with the first payment occurring today.
   (f) $100 each year beginning one year from now and continuing forever.
4. As winner of the Midas Touch Prime Lottery, you can choose one of the following prizes:
   (a) $60,000,000 now;
   (b) $80,000,000 at the end of six years;
   (c) $8,000,000 per year for ten consecutive years, with the first payment in one year;
   (d) $2,550,000 per year forever, with the first payment in one year;
   (e) $1,250,000 one year from now, which increases by 2% each year forever.
   If interest rates are 4% each year, which is the more valuable prize?
5. You take a one-year loan of $1,000 at an interest rate of 12% per year (1% per month) to be repaid in 12 equal monthly payments.
   (a) What is the monthly payment?
   (b) What is the total amount of interest paid over the 12-month term of the loan?
6. You are taking out a $100,000 mortgage loan to be repaid over 25 years in 300 monthly payments.
   (a) If the interest rate is 16% per year, what is the amount of the monthly payment?
   (b) If you can only afford to pay $1,000 per month, how large a loan could you take?
   (c) If you can pay $1,500 per month, need to borrow $100,000, and want a 25-year mortgage, what is the highest interest rate you can pay?
7. Suppose your ancestor purchased land in 1700, for $50.
   (a) If your ancestor had instead invested the cash in an account earning 6% per year compounded annually, how much money would be in the account as of 2020, 320 years later?
   (b) What if it were instead compounded semi-annually?
8. You win a $1 million lottery, which pays you $50,000 per year for 20 years. How much is your prize really worth, assuming an interest rate of 8% per year?
9. You borrow $100,000 from a bank for 30 years at an APR of 10.5%. What is the monthly payment?

10. Larry's bank account has a "floating" interest rate on certain deposits. Every year the interest rate is adjusted. Larry deposited $20,000 three years ago, when interest rates were 7% (annual compounding). Last year the rate was only 6%, and this year the rate fell again to 5%. How much will be in his account at the end of this year?

11. You have a choice between investing in a bank savings account that pays 8% compounded annually (BankAnnual), and one that pays 7.5% compounded daily (BankDaily). Based on effective annual rates, which bank would you prefer?

12. What are the EARs of the following:
    (a) 12% APR compounded monthly?
    (b) 10% APR compounded annually?
    (c) 6% APR compounded daily?

13. Your brother-in-law asks you to lend him $200,000 as a second mortgage on his vacation home. He promises to make level monthly payments for 15 years, 180 payments in all. Assume that a fair interest rate is 8% annually.
    (a) Calculate the appropriate monthly compounded interest rate.
    (b) What should the monthly payment be?

14. Charlie wants to borrow $80,000 to purchase a sailboat. He pledges to pay back the loan three years later (no payment will be made between now and three years). Consider the following three offers, quoted in APR:
    (a) 7.5% per year, daily compounding (based on 360 days per year);
    (b) 8.0% per year, monthly compounding;
    (c) 8.3% per year, quarterly compounding.
    For each offer, calculate the EAR. How much money will Charlie owe at the end of three years?

15. Suppose you know that you will need $2,500 two years from now in order to make a down payment on a car. BankOne is offering 4% interest (compounded annually) for two-year accounts and BankTwo is offering 4.5% (compounded annually) for two-year accounts.
    (a) If you know you need $2,500 two years from today, how much will you need to invest in BankOne to reach your goal?
    (b) How much will you need to invest in BankTwo?
    (c) Which bank account do you prefer?
    (d) Now suppose you do not need the money for three years, and the interest rates for the two banks apply for three-year accounts. How much will you need to deposit today in BankOne? BankTwo?

16. Lucky Lynn has a choice between receiving $1,000 from her great-uncle one year from today or $900 from her great-aunt today. She believes she could invest the $900 at a one-year return of 12%.
    (a) What is the future value of the gift from her great-uncle upon receipt one year from today?
    (b) Which gift should she choose?
    (c) How does your answer change if you believed she could invest the $900 from her great-aunt at only 10%? At what rate is she indifferent?

17. As manager of short-term projects, you are trying to decide whether or not to invest in a project that pays one cash flow of $1,000 one year from today. The total cost of the project is $950. Your alternative investment is to deposit the money in a one-year bank account, which will pay 4% per year.
    (a) Assuming the cash flow of $1,000 is guaranteed (there is no risk you will not receive it), what would be a logical discount rate to use to determine the present value of the cash flows of the project?

(b) What is the present value of the project if you discount the cash flow at 4% per year? What is the NPV of that investment? Should you invest in the project?

(c) What would you do if the bank increases its quoted rate on one-year accounts to 5.5%?

(d) At what one-year bank rate would you be indifferent between the two investments?

18. Calculate the NPV of the following cash flows: You invest $2,000 today and receive $200 one year from now, $800 two years from now, and $1,000 a year for ten years starting four years from now. Assume that the interest rate is 8%.

19. Suppose you have three personal loans outstanding to your friend Elizabeth. A payment of $1,000 is due today, a $500 payment is due one year from now, and a $250 payment is due two years from now. You would like to consolidate the three loans into one, with 36 equal monthly payments, beginning one month from today. Assume the agreed interest rate is 8% (EAR) per year.

(a) What is the APR you will be paying?

(b) How large will the new monthly payment be?

20. As CEO of ToysRFun, you are offered the chance to participate, without initial charge, in a project that produces cash flows of $5,000 at the end of the first period, $4,000 at the end of the next period, and a loss of $11,000 at the end of the third and final year.

(a) What is the NPV if the relevant discount rate (the company's cost of capital) is 10%?

(b) Would you accept the offer?

21. You must pay a creditor $6,000 one year from now, $5,000 two years from now, $4,000 three years from now, $2,000 four years from now, and a final $1,000 five years from now. You would like to restructure the loan into five equal annual payments due at the end of each year. If the agreed annual interest rate is 6%, what is the payment?

22. Find the future value of the following (ordinary) annuities (the payments begin one year from today and all interest rates compound annually):

(a) $100 per year for 10 years at 9%.

(b) $500 per year for 8 years at 15%.

(c) $800 per year for 20 years at 7%.

(d) $1,000 per year for 5 years at 0%.

(e) Now find the present values of the annuities in (a)–(d).

23. Suppose you will need $50,000 ten years from now. You plan to make seven equal annual deposits beginning three years from today in an account that yields 11% compounded annually. How large should the annual deposit be?

24. Suppose an investment offers $100 per year for five years at 5% beginning one year from today.

(a) What is the present value?

(b) How does the present value calculation change if one additional payment is added today?

(c) What is the future value of this ordinary annuity?

(d) How does the future value change if one additional payment is added today?

25. You are trying to decide whether to buy a car for 4.0% APR for the full $20,000 purchase price over three years or receive $1,500 cash back and finance the rest at a bank rate of 9.5%. Both loans have monthly payments over three years. Which should you choose?

26. You are looking to buy a sports car costing $23,000. One dealer is offering a special reduced financing rate of 2.9% APR on new car purchases for three-year loans, with monthly payments. A second dealer is offering a cash rebate. Any customer taking the cash rebate would be ineligible for the special loan rate and would have to borrow the balance of the purchase price from the local bank at the 9% annual rate. How large must the cash rebate be on this $23,000 car to entice a customer away from the dealer who is offering the special 2.9% financing?

27. As a pension manager, you are considering investing in a preferred stock, which pays $5,000,000 per year forever beginning one year from now. If your alternative investment choice is yielding 10% per year, what is the present value of this investment?
28. A new lottery game offers a choice for the grand prize winner. You can either receive a lump sum of $1,000,000 immediately or an annuity of $100,000 per year forever, with the first payment today. (If you die, your estate will still continue to receive payments.) If the relevant annual interest rate is 9.5%, what is the difference in value between the two prizes?
29. Find the future value of a $1,000 lump-sum investment under the following compounding periods. (Hint: Either figure out the EAR or change the number of periods and interest rate as the compounding period shortens.)
    (a) 7% compounded annually for 10 years.
    (b) 7% compounded semi-annually for 10 years.
    (c) 7% compounded monthly for 10 years.
    (d) 7% compounded daily for 10 years.
    (e) 7% compounded continuously for 10 years.
30. Sammy Jo charged $1,000 worth of merchandise one year ago to her MasterCard, which has a stated interest rate of 18% APR compounded monthly. She made 12 regular monthly payments of $50 at the end of each month, and refrained from using the card for the past year. How much does she still owe?
31. Suppose you are considering borrowing $120,000 to finance your dream house. The APR is 9% and payments are made monthly.
    (a) If the mortgage has a 30-year amortization schedule, what are the monthly payments?
    (b) What EAR would you be paying?
    (c) How do your answers to parts (a) and (b) change if the loan amortizes over 15 years rather than 30?
32. The interest rate on conventional ten-year Treasury bonds is a nominal rate of return of 7% per year, while the interest rate on ten-year TIPS (Treasury inflation-protected securities) is a real rate of return of 3.5% per year. You have $10,000 to invest in one of them.
    (a) If you expect the average inflation rate to be 4% per year, which bond offers the higher expected rate of return?
    (b) Which would you prefer to invest in?

3 PERSONAL FINANCE

CHAPTER OVERVIEW

3.1	Financial Decisions and Household Balance Sheets	57
3.2	A Discounted Cash Flow Model of Lifetime Labor and Consumption	59
3.3	Should You Defer Taxes through Voluntary Retirement Plans?	64
3.4	Should You Invest in a Professional Degree?	64
3.5	Should You Buy or Rent?	66

LEARNING OBJECTIVES

After reading this chapter, you will be able to:
- construct and interpret a household economic balance sheet;
- explain the concepts of human capital and consumption smoothing over time using a discounted cash flow model;
- analyze three major decisions using a discounted cash flow model: saving for retirement, investing in a professional degree, and choosing to rent or buy a home;
- describe what sensitivity analysis is and how it informs financial decisions.

EQUATIONS YOU KNOW

Present value	$PV = \dfrac{CF_1}{1+r} + \dfrac{CF_2}{(1+r)^2} + \dfrac{CF_3}{(1+r)^3} + \cdots + \dfrac{CF_T}{(1+r)^T}$	Eq. 2.9
Present value, annuity	$PV = \dfrac{\$CF}{r} \times \left[1 - \dfrac{1}{(1+r)^T}\right]$	Eq. 2.14
Real rate of interest	Real interest rate = $\dfrac{\text{nominal interest rate} - \text{rate of inflation}}{1 + \text{rate of inflation}}$	Eq. 2.20

- You're in college and are aiming for a high-paying job. But you heard that the job is very stressful, so you decide to only work in that job to save up enough money to live comfortably. How long will you have to work in your job, and how much money will you have to save up to achieve your goals?

- You are about to finish college, and are thinking about pursuing a master's degree. You know that getting the degree means that you will earn more when you get a job. But you will also need to pay tuition for two years for the program. How do you make this decision?

- You just graduated from college and you now have a job. You like the company you work for and are looking to stay for a long time. You are currently renting an apartment. You talk to your parents, and they encourage you to buy a house. Does their suggestion make sense financially?

- Your older sister is working, but saving a relatively low amount of money for retirement. She loves to travel and will want to keep up that lifestyle after she retires. What advice can you give her about how much to save?

Introduction

Most people do not become chief financial officers (CFO) of major corporations or corporate finance executives. But everybody will be their own CFO, and will have that job for their entire adult life. As your own CFO, you are responsible for earning a living, budgeting, borrowing, insuring, saving, and investing. Some of the financial decisions you may have to address include:

- whether to further your education and, if you do, how to pay for it;
- how much to save to pay off your debts, raise children, and retire some day; and
- whether to buy or rent your house or apartment.

These are all very practical decisions, and the methods of analyzing them make use of **Principle 1**: *A dollar today is not worth the same as a dollar tomorrow.* Economists have considered the management of personal financial resources over a lifetime to be a central issue worthy of serious study, and several Nobel Prizes in economics have been awarded for contributions in this area. And, as Box 3.1 shows, financial literacy for a nation's people is a goal being pursued by countries all over the world.

In this chapter we apply the basic insights and the models developed by those economists and make extensive use of the discounted cash flow (DCF) concepts covered in Chapter 2. Starting with the decision about how much to save for retirement, we develop a DCF model for lifetime financial planning. We then use DCF models to analyze various choices, such as whether to defer taxes or pay them immediately, whether to invest in a professional education, and whether to buy or rent a home.

> **Box 3.1** Managing Your Personal Resources: Financial Literacy is Trending around the World
>
> Financial literacy means knowing how to live within your means. It includes the ability to make a budget, distinguish between wants and needs, file a tax form, buy insurance, save for a rainy day, and borrow only as much as you can pay back. It is an essential part of being a responsible adult capable of leading an independent life in a market economy. Just as knowing how to read and write—literacy in the usual sense—is important for success in managing your work and leisure activities, financial literacy is important for avoiding poverty and financial distress.

Having a financially literate population is of great value to a country and a community. If everyone knows how to live within their means, a society can support a decent basic standard of living and its citizens can be relied upon to respect the property rights of others.

Governments around the world have taken an active interest in promoting financial literacy among their citizens because fraud and abuse of the financially uneducated have become a major political concern. A financially literate population is the best defense against most fraudulent schemes and bad financial advice.

Improving individuals' financial understanding and behaviors is a long-term policy priority in many countries. This trend has led to the development of a wide range of financial education initiatives by governments, regulators, and various other private and civil stakeholders, sometimes combined with financial consumer protection measures.

For example, in the United States, the Financial Literacy and Education Commission (FLEC) was established under the Fair and Accurate Credit Transactions Act of 2003. The Commission was tasked to develop a national financial education website (MyMoney.gov) and a national strategy on financial education. It is chaired by the Secretary of the Treasury and the vice chair is the Director of the Bureau of Consumer Financial Protection. The FLEC includes the following vision statement:

> The Commission's vision is of sustained financial well-being for all individuals and families in the U.S. In furtherance of this vision, the Commission sets strategic direction for policy, education, practice, research, and coordination so that all Americans make informed financial decisions.

In Europe, the Organization for Economic Cooperation and Development (OECD), a major institution headquartered in Paris that coordinates economic policies for 38 countries around the world, created the International Network on Financial Education (INFE) in 2008. The INFE is a network of more than 280 public institutions with the purpose of sharing the experience of developed and emerging economies on promoting and establishing programs to foster financial literacy. Similar initiatives have been launched in other countries across the globe. For example, in 2019 Malaysia launched a National Strategy for Financial Literacy, which included a multi-year plan to raise the country's low levels of financial literacy.

3.1 Financial Decisions and Household Balance Sheets

Households come in many forms and sizes. A household is typically defined as one or more people, related or not, who live together in a housing unit (house or apartment).

Households face four basic types of financial decisions:

- *Consumption and saving decisions:* How much of their current income should they spend on consumption? Because saving is defined as income minus consumption, this decision is the same as deciding how much of their current income they should save for the future.
- *Investment decisions:* How should they invest the money they have saved?
- *Financing decisions:* When and how should households use other people's money to implement their consumption and investment plans?
- *Risk-management decisions:* How and on what terms should households seek to reduce the financial uncertainties they face? (In this chapter we ignore the effects of uncertainty and risk on financial decisions, leaving them to Chapter 5 and the chapters on portfolio theory in Part III.)

3.1.1 Accounting and Economic Balance Sheets

As a result of saving part of their income for use in the future, people accumulate a pool of wealth, which can be held in any number of different forms. One form is bank accounts; another might be a piece of real estate or a share in a business venture. All of these are examples of an asset, which is anything that has economic value.

When people choose how to hold their pool of accumulated savings, it is called personal investing. In addition to investing in their own homes and businesses, people will often choose to invest in financial assets, such as stocks or bonds, or to invest in their own human capital by investing in their education.

When people borrow to purchase or invest in an asset, they incur a liability. A household's wealth or net worth is measured by the value of its assets minus its liabilities. For example, say you own a house worth $100,000 and have $20,000 in a bank account, but you also owe $80,000 to the bank on your home mortgage loan and have a $5,000 credit card debt outstanding. Your net worth is $35,000: your total assets ($120,000) minus your total liabilities ($85,000). These assets and liabilities can be displayed in a balance sheet such as the one shown in Table 3.1.

In finance, we distinguish between an accounting balance sheet (such as Table 3.1) and an economic balance sheet, which includes the expected future lifetime labor earnings as an asset. Economists define human capital as the present value of all expected future labor earnings. Let's assume this household's human capital is $1,200,000. Table 3.2 is the household's economic balance sheet. Because there are no offsetting liabilities, almost all the wealth in this example is in the form of human capital.

In our examination of household financial decisions, we will assume that when you start your adult life your only asset is your human capital. As you go through life, you will save part of your labor income and use it to accumulate assets by, for example, purchasing a car or a house or accumulating

Table 3.1 Household accounting balance sheet. This balance sheet shows what this household owns (its assets) and what it owes (its liabilities). The difference between the two is the household's net worth.

Assets		Liabilities	
Bank account	$20,000	Mortgage	$80,000
House	100,000	Credit card debt	5,000
TOTAL ASSETS	$120,000	TOTAL LIABILITIES	$85,000
		NET WORTH	**$35,000**

Table 3.2 Household economic balance sheet. Unlike the household accounting balance sheet, the economic balance sheet includes a household's human capital as one of its assets.

Assets		Liabilities	
Bank account	$20,000	Mortgage	$80,000
House	100,000	Credit card	5,000
Human capital	1,200,000		
TOTAL ASSETS	$1,320,000	TOTAL LIABILITIES	$85,000
		NET WORTH	**$1,235,000**

assets in a retirement account, so that you will be able to pay for consumption after you no longer have any labor income.

3.2 A Discounted Cash Flow Model of Lifetime Labor and Consumption

To understand how to undertake such lifetime financial planning, consider the following example. You are currently 35 years old and expect to retire in 30 years, at age 65. You plan on living for 15 more years until age 80.

After you retire you do not want your standard of living to decline; you want to be able to spend as much in each of the 15 years from age 65 to 80 as you spend in each of the 30 years from age 35 to 65. This approach to planning for your financial comfort over your lifetime is characterized by *consumption smoothing*, the shifting of one's earnings from periods of high income (such as the working years) to periods of lower income (such as the retirement years). This shift is accomplished by saving some current yearly income to finance yearly consumption in the future, when you are no longer earning any income.

Let's use some concrete numbers to see how this might work. Your current income is $60,000 per year, and you have not yet accumulated any assets other than your human capital. For now, we simplify the example by ignoring any taxes you pay on your income, so the amount of income you have available to spend is $60,000 per year. Also let us assume that your real labor income adjusted for inflation remains at $60,000 per year until age 65. In other words, we assume that your income will keep pace with inflation, but not beat it. We will assume that the nominal rate of interest is 3% per year, and inflation is 2% per year, so the real interest rate is 1%. Each year, you plan to spend part of the money you make on consumption C (i.e., purchases of food, housing, clothing, personal care items, etc.), and save the rest of the money S for retirement. Over the 30 years of your working life, how much should you spend on consumption C and how much should you save for retirement S?

Every dollar you save in years 1–30 will earn interest until you withdraw it to live on when you retire at 65. To execute your retirement saving plan, you must figure out how much consumption you can afford each year. We solve this problem in the next section by assuming that you smooth your consumption, so that C stays the same in real terms throughout your working life and retirement.

Before we begin, we need to clarify how economists use the terms "saving" and "savings." *Saving* (without an "s") is a flow variable, something that occurs over time, such as saving part of your income—say, $1,000—each year. *Savings* (with an "s") refers to the total amount of money saved from all saving deposits; it is a stock variable. If you deposit $1,000 of saving every year for three years, at the end of year 3 your savings will be $3,000 plus interest.

3.2.1 Saving to Maintain a Constant Standard of Living

We are now ready to build a *discounted cash flow (DCF) model* to find how much to consume and save over the next 45 years. We begin by acknowledging the constraint on your lifetime consumption—that is, the present value of lifetime consumption cannot exceed the present value of lifetime earnings. C can be less than or equal to, but you would never choose not to consume all that you could.

Over your lifetime you cannot spend more than you earn, so the present value of your lifetime labor income over the next 30 working years must equal the present value of your lifetime consumption spending over the next 45 years (30 working years plus 15 retirement years). As noted before, economists call the present value of one's future labor income *human capital*.

To decide how much to spend and how much to save in real terms, we can use the formulas we developed in Chapter 2. Because we have assumed that both salary income and consumption are constant in real terms, we can use the formula for the present value of an annuity (Equation 2.14) to determine what the level of consumption C should be:

$$PV = \frac{\$C}{r} \times \left[1 - \frac{1}{(1+r)^T}\right]. \tag{3.1}$$

Note that for Equation 3.1, the cash flow $\$CF$ that we previously used in Equation 2.14 is replaced by consumption C, thus indicating that the level of consumption each year is denoted as a dollar amount. We want to find the level of consumption C we can afford *each working year* that will enable us to save enough money to have the same level of consumption per year in our working and retirement years. To begin this journey we start with Equation 3.2, which states that the PV of lifetime earnings must equal the PV of lifetime consumption:

$$PV_{lifetime\ earnings} = PV_{lifetime\ consumption}. \tag{3.2}$$

Substituting Equation 3.1 into Equation 3.2, we can set up equations to determine the level of consumption that can be maintained. Remembering that earnings will occur over 30 years and that consumption will occur over 45 years, we can put in the numbers from our example to find:

$$PV_{lifetime\ earnings} = \frac{\$CF}{r} \times \left[1 - \frac{1}{(1+r)^T}\right] = \frac{\$60{,}000}{0.01} \times \left[1 - \frac{1}{(1+0.01)^{30}}\right] = \$1{,}548{,}462,$$

$$PV_{lifetime\ consumption} = \frac{\$C}{r} \times \left[1 - \frac{1}{(1+r)^T}\right] = \frac{\$C}{0.01} \times \left[1 - \frac{1}{(1+0.01)^{45}}\right] = \$1{,}548{,}462.$$

Notice that in the $PV_{lifetime\ consumption}$ equation there is one variable we don't know the value of: C, which is annual real consumption spending. To make our lifetime consumption plan work, we need to figure out how much we can spend each year of our 45 years of working and retirement. We find this number from the $PV_{lifetime\ consumption}$ equation.

The first step is to find the value of the bracketed term:

$$\left[1 - \frac{1}{(1+0.01)^{45}}\right] = 1 - 1/1.5648$$
$$= 1 - 0.6391$$
$$= 0.3609.$$

Now we have

$$\frac{\$C}{0.01} \times [0.3609] = \$1{,}548{,}462.$$
$$C \times 1/0.01 \times [0.3609] = \$1{,}548{,}462$$
$$C \times 36.09 = \$1{,}548{,}462.$$

The 36.09 is the present value factor of a $1.00 annuity for 45 years.

To find out how much of our $60,000 yearly earnings we can spend, we solve for C:

$$C = \$1{,}548{,}462.49 / 36.09 = \$42{,}900.22 = \$42{,}900 \text{ rounded to the nearest dollar.}$$

We have now arrived at the answer to our consumption-smoothing plan: In order to have consumption of $42,900 per year for 45 years, we will have to save $60,000 − $42,900 = $17,100 of our $60,000 yearly salary.

3.2.2 Using Excel to Plan for the Future

We can also make use of an electronic spreadsheet, such as Excel, to build our DCF planning model and explore its implications.

Figure 3.1 shows a lifetime financial plan generated from a DCF planning model using such a spreadsheet; this is included in the companion app to this chapter. It shows the inputs to and outputs from the model and graphs the outputs over the 45-year lifespan of the plan (from the current date until ending age). In this example, with real labor income of $60,000 per year for 30 years and a real

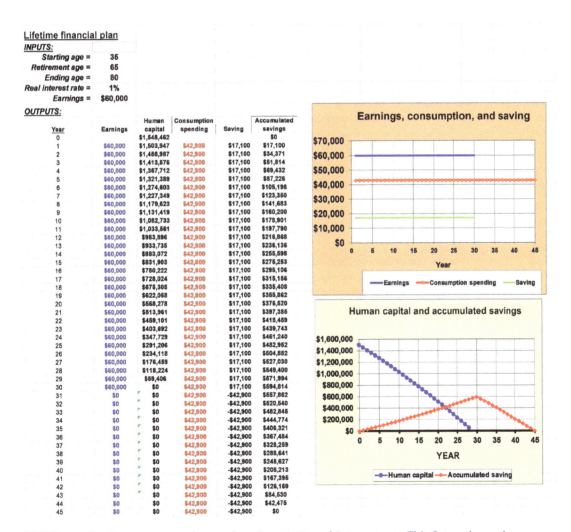

FIGURE 3.1 Earnings, consumption, and saving at 1% real interest rate. This figure shows the patterns of earnings, consumption, and saving over a person's working and retirement life. The top-left table shows the information (inputs) needed to determine how much to spend and how much to save to achieve a constant level of consumption in retirement. The bottom-left table lists the outputs from this information. The top-right graph shows lifetime earnings from working years 0 to 30. The bottom-right graph shows that human capital over time.

interest rate of 1%, your human capital is $1,548,462 at age 35, and your consumption is $42,900 per year. These parameters can be varied using the companion app.

The top left table shows the information (inputs) needed to determine how much to spend and how much to save to achieve a constant level of consumption in retirement. The bottom-left table lists the outputs from this information over the 45-year lifespan of the plan. The top-right graph shows lifetime earnings from working years 0–30; real earnings are constant at $60,000 per year. Consumption is constant at $42,900 per year during working years 0–30, *and* during retirement years 30–45. Saving is constant at $17,100 per year during working years 0–30.

The bottom-right graph shows that human capital declines every year during working years 0–29. When the working years end, human capital is at zero. At the start of the working years there is no accumulated saving, but every year from 1 to 30, $17,100 is saved and is added to the accumulated saving plus the 1% interest on the accumulated saving. At retirement (year 30), accumulated savings is at its peak ($600,000). While accumulated savings continues to earn interest, $42,900 per year is withdrawn to be spent on consumption during retirement.

We can also use our spreadsheet model to see what effect a higher interest rate has on consumption, saving, and human capital. We need only change the value of the real interest rate from 1% to 3%. As in the previous section, we assume that you are currently 35 years old, expect to retire in 30 years at age 65, and then live for 15 more years until age 80. Your real labor earnings are $60,000 per year, and you have not yet accumulated any assets.

Table 3.3 shows that at each higher interest rate, the initial value of human capital is lower. This occurs because of the inverse relationship between present value PV and the interest rate r. Even though the initial value of human capital is lower at higher interest rates, the higher interest rate paid on your accumulated savings allows you to consume more each year in your working and retirement years. As a result, you do not have to save as much during your working years. Figure 3.2 illustrates these effects.

Table 3.3 Human capital, consumption, and saving as functions of the real interest rate. This table shows that as the interest rate goes up, the initial value of human capital goes down, consumption spending per year goes up, and saving per working year goes down. With a higher real interest rate throughout your working and retirement years, you are better off because your consumption will be higher.

Real interest rate	Initial human capital	Consumption per year	Saving per year
0%	$1,800,000	$40,000	$20,000
1%	1,548,462	42,900	17,100
2%	1,343,787	45,567	14,433
3%	1,176,026	47,964	12,036
4%	1,037,522	50,073	9,927
5%	922,347	51,893	8,107
6%	825,890	53,435	6,565
7%	744,542	54,724	5,276
8%	675,467	55,785	4,215
9%	616,419	56,650	3,350
10%	565,615	57,348	2,652

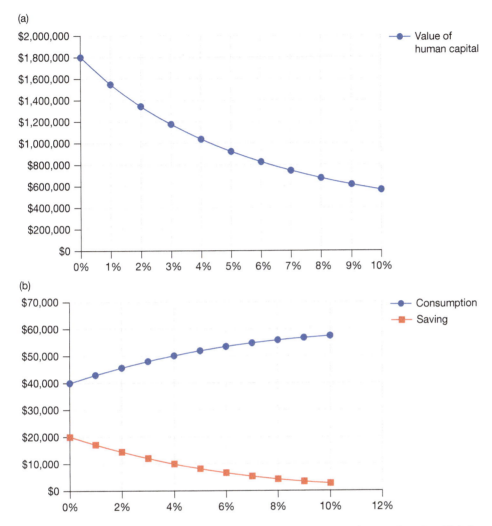

FIGURE 3.2 **Effect of the real interest rate on human capital, consumption, and saving.** This figure graphs the data from **Table 3.3.** (a) The effect of the interest rate on human capital. As the real interest rate increases, the value of human capital decreases. (b) The effects of the interest rate on consumption and saving. As the real interest rate rises, the level of consumption spending you can afford throughout life rises and the less you have to save.

QUICK CHECK 3.1 Georgette is currently 30 years old, plans to retire at age 65, and to live to age 85. Her labor income is $25,000 per year, and she intends to maintain a constant level of real consumption spending over the next 55 years. Assume no taxes, no growth in real salary, and a real interest rate of 3% per year.

- What is the value of Georgette's human capital?
- What is her sustainable consumption?

3.3 Should You Defer Taxes through Voluntary Retirement Plans?

In many countries, governments encourage voluntary saving for retirement through provisions in their tax codes. In the United States, people are permitted to establish tax-advantaged accounts, known as individual retirement accounts (IRAs). IRA contributions are deductible from current income for tax purposes, and interest earned on these contributions is not taxed until the money is withdrawn. These plans are called *tax deferred* rather than *tax exempt* because any amounts withdrawn from the plan are taxed at the time of withdrawal. How do we analyze the advantages of deferring paying taxes on retirement saving? Should you set up a retirement account that enables you to defer paying taxes on your income?

Consider the following example. Suppose you face a tax rate of 20% both before and after retirement. The nominal interest rate is 8% per year. In the 30 years before your retirement date, you contribute $1,000 each year to an IRA. Your total before-tax amount accumulated at retirement will be $1,000 \times 1.08^{30} = \$10,062.66$. If you choose to withdraw it all at once on the day of your retirement, you will have to pay taxes at the rate of 20% on the entire amount. Thus, your taxes will be $0.20 \times \$10,062.66 = \$2,012.53$, and you will be left with $8,050.12 after taxes.

If, instead, you choose not to contribute to an IRA but instead deposit your saving in an ordinary saving account, you have to pay 20% of the $1,000 or $200 immediately in additional taxes. The remaining $800 will go into the ordinary savings plan, and interest earnings on the $800 will be taxed each year. The after-tax interest rate earned is, therefore, $(1 - 0.20) \times 8\%$, or 6.4%. The amount accumulated at retirement from this ordinary savings plan is $\$800 \times 1.064^{30} = \$5,144.45$. Because you have paid the taxes on the original contribution and on the interest along the way, the amount accumulated is not subject to further tax.

The tax-deferred savings plan provides a larger after-tax benefit ($8,050.12 versus $5,144.45). Thus, even though you remain in the same 20% tax bracket both before and after retirement, the amount you have to spend in the future is almost twice as much under the tax-deferred savings plan.

When your tax rate remains unchanged, our example shows that with deferral you end up with an after-tax benefit of $8,050.12, whereas if you don't defer and you pay the tax immediately, you end up with an after-tax benefit of $5,144.45. Thus, the general rule is, if you can defer paying taxes on your income and the interest earnings by depositing money into a tax-deferred account, you should.

> QUICK CHECK 3.2 Suppose that the consumer tax rate is 30% instead of 20%. How large would be the advantage of tax deferral compared to our example with a 20% tax rate?

3.4 Should You Invest in a Professional Degree?

Education and training can be viewed as an investment in human capital. Although there may be many reasons for acquiring additional schooling, one purpose is to increase people's earning power—that is, to increase their human capital.

Let us consider the costs and benefits of additional education. The economic costs consist of explicit costs such as tuition, and the implicit costs are forgone earnings during the time spent in school. The economic benefits consist of the value of the increased stream of earnings attributable to the additional years of education. Like other investment decisions, the investment is worthwhile if the net present value (NPV) of the expected incremental benefits exceeds the NPV of the expected incremental costs.

For example, consider Jo Grad, who has just graduated from college and is deciding whether to go on for her master's degree. Jo figures that if she takes a job immediately, she can earn $30,000 per year in real terms for the remainder of her working years. If she goes on for two more years of graduate study, however, she can increase her earnings to $35,000 per year. The cost of tuition is $15,000 per year in real terms. Is this a worthwhile investment if the real interest rate is 1% per year?

Jo must give up $45,000 (tuition plus forgone earnings) in each of the next two years in order to increase her earnings by $5,000 per year over her remaining career.

Suppose Jo is 20 years old and expects to retire at age 65. The relevant cash flows for this investment are incremental outflows of $45,000 in each of the next two years and then incremental inflows of $5,000 in each of the succeeding 43 years.

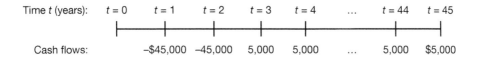

To compute the present value of the outflows, we use Equation 2.9:

$$PV = \frac{CF_1}{1+r} + \frac{CF_2}{(1+r)^2} + \frac{CF_3}{(1+r)^3} + \cdots + \frac{CF_T}{(1+r)^T}$$

$$= \frac{\$45,000}{1.01} + \frac{\$45,000}{1.01^2}$$

$$= \$88,668.$$

To compute the present value of the incremental cash inflows that start when Jo begins to work, we first find the present value two years from her graduate school graduation, and then discount that sum back to the present. We can use the equation for the present value of an annuity (Equation 2.14) to compute the present value of the cash inflows of $5,000 per year for 43 years that start two years after her graduation from college:

$$PV = \frac{\$CF}{r} \times \left[1 - \frac{1}{(1+r)^T}\right]$$

$$= \frac{\$5,000}{0.01} \times \left[1 - \frac{1}{(1.01)^{43}}\right]$$

$$= \$174,050.04.$$

But this value is as of two years from now, *after* Jo has finished her master's program. We therefore need to discount these $174,050 by two years, back to today:

$$PV = \frac{174,050}{1.01^2}$$

$$= \$170,621.$$

The present value of the outflows is $88,668; the present value of the inflows is $170,621. The net present value (NPV) is the difference between the two:

$$NPV = \$170{,}621 - \$88{,}668 = \$81{,}953.$$

The NPV of the investment in the degree is, therefore, $81,953, meaning it is worthwhile.

> QUICK CHECK 3.3 Suppose that Jo is 30 years old instead of 20. If all the other assumptions remain the same, does the investment in the graduate degree still have a positive NPV?

3.5 Should You Buy or Rent?

You are currently renting a house for $20,000 per year and have an option to buy it for $500,000. As an owner you would have to pay property taxes and maintenance costs of $6,000 each year. The real interest rate is 3% and you are going to own the house for ten years.

Let us assume that your objective is to provide yourself with housing at the lowest present value of cost. Should you buy or continue to rent?

The buy-or-rent decision is an investment decision. To save the $20,000 per year rental costs, you will incur the costs associated with buying the house: the $500,000 purchase price plus the annual costs of maintenance and property taxes of $6,000 per year. Offsetting the cost of purchasing the house will be a cash flow at time T when you sell the house. You decide to build a DCF model to analyze this decision, which involves calculating the present value of the cash flows from buying the house and comparing it to the present value of the cash flows from renting. You will choose the option that has the lower present value.

3.5.1 Present Values of Buying Costs

To clarify the cash flows of the costs of buying and owning the house, we construct a timeline. We assume that taxes and maintenance are paid at the end of the first year through the end of year 10. Because we are figuring the present value of the *costs* of buying, the amount received back from selling the house at time $T = 10$ is negative.

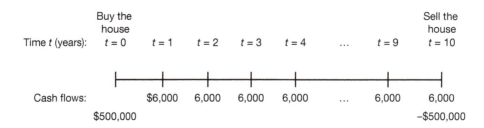

Our next step is to calculate the present value of the costs of buying, which is done in four steps.

Step 1: Present value of $500,000 at $t = 0$ is $500,000.
Step 2: Present value of $6,000 from $t = 1$ to $T = 10$ is:

$$PV = CF \times \frac{1}{r} \times \left[1 - \frac{1}{(1+r)^T}\right] \qquad (3.3)$$

$$= \$6,000 \times \frac{1}{0.03} \times \left[1 - \frac{1}{(1.03)^{10}}\right]$$

$$= \$6,000 \times 8.53 = \$51,181.$$

Step 3: Present value of −$500,000 at year 10 is:

$$PV = \frac{-\$500,000}{1.03^{10}} = -\$372,047.$$

Step 4: Add up the results of Steps 1–3 to get:

$$\begin{aligned} PV \text{ of costs of buying the house} &= \$500,000 + \$51,181 - \$372,047 \\ &= \$179,134. \end{aligned}$$

3.5.2 Present Value of Renting Costs

To clarify the cash flows of the costs of renting, we construct a timeline, assuming that the rent is paid at the end of the year for years 1–10.

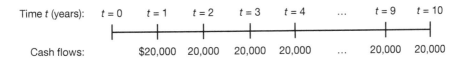

The present value of renting costs is found using Equation 3.3:

$$PV = \frac{\$CF}{r} \times \left[1 - \frac{1}{(1+r)^T}\right]$$

$$= \frac{\$20,000}{0.03} \times \left[1 - \frac{1}{(1+0.03)^{10}}\right]$$

$$= \$20,000 \times \left[\frac{1}{0.03} \times 1 - \frac{1}{(1+0.03)^{10}}\right]$$

$$= \$20,000 \times 8.53$$

$$= \$170,604.$$

The 8.53 in this equation is the present value of an annuity of $1 for 10 years at the interest rate of 3%.

3.5.3 The Decision
Because you choose the option with the lowest present value, you will choose to continue to rent.

3.5.4 Breakeven Rent
We are interested in knowing at what point we would choose to buy rather than rent. We know that to make buying more attractive the rent would have to be greater than $20,000 because we just saw that at $20,000 rent we would choose to continue to rent.

The rent at which you would be indifferent between buying and renting is called the breakeven rent. We find the breakeven rent X by setting the *PV* cost of buying equal to *PV* cost of renting and solving for X.

We know the *PV* cost of buying is $179,134. To find the breakeven rent, we must solve the equation

$$\begin{aligned} \text{Breakeven rent } X &= \text{annuity factor} \times \text{rent} = PV \text{ cost of buying} \\ &= 8.53 \times X = \$179{,}134 \\ &= \$21{,}000. \end{aligned}$$

Thus, if the rent is greater than $21,000 per year, you would choose to buy.

3.5.5 Sensitivity Analysis of the Buy versus Rent Decision
A natural question to ask is how dependent our decision is on the values we have assumed in our model for maintenance costs, property taxes, the length of time we plan to stay in the house, and the discount rate *r*. We can generate tables and graphs to aid us in this analysis. This type of analysis is called sensitivity analysis, and it is a stepping stone on the road to a full risk analysis (which we discuss in Chapter 6). In this final section of the chapter we will illustrate sensitivity analysis of the buy-or-rent decision in the preceding section. In particular, we will look at how sensitive the decision criterion is to our assumption about the time horizon *T* and the discount rate *r*.

The starting point in a sensitivity analysis is the breakeven point; that is, we start with values for the variables in the model that result in the breakeven point. In the previous section we found that the breakeven annual rental value was $21,000 per year when the other parameters and variables had the values shown in Table 3.4.

Table 3.4 **Values for the breakeven point.** This table summarizes all the data we currently know about the breakeven point.

Price of house	$500,000
Annual maintenance + property taxes	$6,000
Rent (breakeven)	$21,000
Time horizon	10 years
Interest rate	3%
Costs at breakeven point	
Present value of renting	$179,134.26
Present value of buying	$179,134.26

One of the most important variables in making the decision to rent or buy is the interest rate. To broaden our understanding of this choice, we can use sensitivity analysis to see how changes in the interest rate affect the present values of buying and renting, and thus, the rent-or-buy decision.

Sensitivity Analysis of Changes in the Interest Rate. Table 3.5 shows that buying is most advantageous (its present value is lowest) when the interest rate r is zero. As the interest rate r at which future cash flows are discounted increases, the present value of renting goes down while the present value of buying goes up. At 3%, the present values of buying and renting are equal and a person is indifferent between buying and selling. When r is less than 3%, buying is cheaper than renting, so you buy; when r is greater than 3%, buying is more expensive than renting, so you keep renting.

Use the Excel spreadsheet app for this chapter to perform this analysis using different assumptions for the variables.

Table 3.5 Interest rate effects on the costs of buying versus renting. Part (a) summarizes the information we know about some of the variables involved in the buy-or-rent decision. Part (b) shows how changes in the interest rate affect the present values of buying and renting costs. The breakeven interest rate is 3%, the point at which the present values of buying and renting are equal.

(a)

Price of house	$500,000
Annual maintenance + property taxes	$6,000
Rent	$21,000
Time horizon	10 years
Interest rate	?

(b)

Interest rate, r	PV rent	PV buy
0.0%	$630,000	$180,000
0.5%	$583,675	$236,249
1.0%	$541,962	$283,885
1.5%	$504,333	$324,214
2.0%	$470,326	$358,343
2.5%	$439,536	$387,210
3.0% (breakeven)	$411,609	$411,609
3.5%	$386,233	$432,213
4.0%	$363,133	$449,593
4.5%	$342,067	$464,233
5.0%	$322,821	$476,546
5.5%	$305,209	$486,880
6.0%	$289,061	$495,534

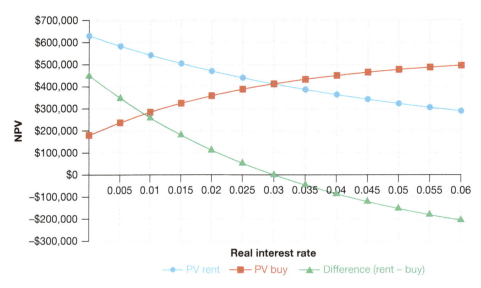

FIGURE 3.3 Effect of interest rate on present values of buying and renting. This graph plots the data from Table 3.5. It shows the effects that different interest rates have on the buy-or-rent decision. When the present value of buying curve is below the present value of renting curve, buying is the right choice. Three percent is the breakeven interest rate—the rate at which the present values of buying and renting are equal. Above 3%, renting is the right decision because the present value of renting is lower than the present value of buying.

Conclusion

This chapter has analyzed several of the basic financial decisions that people have to make at various stages of life, such as how to save for retirement and other life events and when to buy or rent. We have shown how the DCF concepts and formulas introduced in Chapter 2 can be employed in models that take account of the timing of cash flows involved in personal financial decisions. We have also seen how to take account of inflation in making these decisions. We return to the DCF model throughout the book, especially in Chapters 9 (company valuation) and 10 (capital budgeting decisions).

Takeaways

- A household balance sheet shows what a household owns (its assets) and what it owes (its liabilities). The difference between the two is the household's net worth.
- In making lifetime saving/consumption decisions: (1) Do the analysis in real terms to simplify the calculations and to avoid having to forecast inflation; and (2) start by computing the present value of your lifetime resources. The present value of your lifetime spending cannot exceed this amount.
- If you are in the same tax bracket before and after you retire, it is best to hold your retirement savings in a tax-deferred retirement account.
- Getting a professional degree or other training can be evaluated as an investment in human capital. As such, it should be undertaken if the net present value of the benefits (such as an increase in your earnings) exceeds the net present value of the costs (such as tuition and forgone salary).
- In deciding whether to buy or rent a house, choose the alternative with the lower present value of costs.

- Any financial decision depends on the particular values that are assumed for the variables that are relevant to the decision. Sensitivity analysis shows how a decision changes when the values of these variables change. The starting point of sensitivity analysis is the breakeven point at which a person is indifferent between two choices. From there, you can change the variables' values and see how it affects the decision.

Key Terms

Asset 58
Breakeven rent 68
Consumption smoothing 59
Household 57
Human capital 58
Liability 58
Net worth 58
Personal investing 58
Saving 59
Savings 59
Sensitivity analysis 68
Wealth 58

Key Equations

Present value, consumption annuity	$PV = \dfrac{\$C}{r} \times \left[1 - \dfrac{1}{(1+r)^T}\right]$	Eq. 3.1
Saving to maintain constant consumption	$PV_{lifetime\ earnings} = PV_{lifetime\ consumption}$	Eq. 3.2

Problems

1. Assume that you are 40 years old and wish to retire at age 65. You expect to be able to average a 6% annual rate of interest on your savings over your lifetime (both prior to retirement and after retirement). You would like to save enough money to provide $8,000 per year beginning at age 66 in retirement income to supplement other sources (social security, pension plans, etc.). Suppose you decide that the extra income needs to be provided for only 15 years (up to age 80). Assume that your first contribution to the savings plan will take place one year from now.
   (a) How much must you save each year between now and retirement to achieve your goal?
   (b) If the rate of inflation turns out to be 6% per year between now and retirement, how much will your first $8,000 withdrawal be worth in terms of today's purchasing power?

2. You are saving for retirement and you come across Table 3.6. It shows the percentage of your current salary that you should save for your retirement in order to retire with an annuity equal to 70% of your salary if you have not yet saved anything. It assumes that your annual salary will remain constant in real terms until retirement, and that you will live for 25 years after retiring. For instance, if you have 35 years left before you retire and earn 3.5% per year on your investments, then you should save 17.3% of your current salary. Fill in the missing numbers in Table 3.6.

Table 3.6 Savings rate needed to achieve 70% replacement rate.

Real interest rate	Years to retirement		
	15	25	35
3.5% per annum	?	?	17.30%
4.5% per annum	?	?	?

3. Continuing the previous problem, now fill in Table 3.7. Assume that instead of targeting a 70% replacement rate of preretirement income, your goal is to maintain the same level of consumption spending both before and after retirement.

Table 3.7 Saving to maintain lifetime consumption spending.

Real interest rate	Years to retirement		
	15	25	35
3.5% per annum	?	?	19.82%
4.5% per annum	?	?	?

4. Use the Lifetime Consumption and Earnings Excel app. Suppose you start working at age 25, aim to retire by age 65, and expect to live until age 85. You earn $50,000 per year. At an interest rate of 3%, what can you expect your constant consumption to be? How much will you have to save each year until retirement?

5. Again use the Lifetime Consumption and Earnings Excel app. In the same scenario as the previous question, suppose instead you earn $80,000 per year. How do your answers change? Explain why this makes sense.

6. Again use the Lifetime Consumption and Earnings Excel app. In the same scenario as from question 4, suppose instead that you begin working at age 18, skipping college, but expect to earn $30,000 per year as a result. How do your answers change? Explain why this makes sense.

7. Willie is 35 years old and plans to retire at 50, and to live to the ripe old age of 100. His labor income as a plumber is $150,000 per year, and he expects to maintain a constant level of real consumption spending for the remainder of his life. Assuming a steady real salary, the complete absence of taxes, and a real interest rate of 2% per annum:
   (a) What is the value of Willie's human capital?
   (b) What is the level of his sustainable consumption?

8. You are saving for retirement and you come across Table 3.8. It shows the increase in the annual benefit you can receive in retirement per dollar that you increase your annual retirement saving

Table 3.8 The increase in the annual benefit per dollar.

Interest rate	Years to retirement		
	20	25	30
0.0%	$1.00	$1.25	$1.50
0.5%	$1.10	$1.40	$1.70
1.0%	$1.22	$1.57	?
1.5%	$1.35	$1.75	$2.19
2.0%	$1.49	$1.96	$2.48
3.0%	$1.81	?	$3.20
3.5%	?	$2.74	$3.63
4.0%	$2.19	$3.06	$4.13
4.5%	$2.41	$3.43	$4.69
5.0%	$2.65	$3.83	?

in the years before retirement. It assumes that you will live for 20 years after retiring. For instance, if you have 30 years left before you retire and earn an interest rate of 3% per year, then you will obtain an increase of $3.20 in your annual retirement benefit for every $1 per year increase in annual saving. Fill in the missing table values.

9. George Thriftless is 45 years old, earns $50,000 per year, and expects that his future earnings will keep pace with inflation, but will not exceed inflation. He has not yet saved anything toward his retirement. His company does not offer a pension plan. George pays Social Security taxes equal to 7.5% of his salary, and he assumes that when he retires at age 65, he will receive $12,000 per year in inflation-adjusted Social Security benefits for the rest of his life. His life expectancy is age 85.

George buys a book on retirement planning that recommends saving enough so that when private savings and Social Security are combined, he can replace 80% of his preretirement salary. George buys a financial calculator and goes through the following calculations:

First, he computes the amount he will need to receive in each year of retirement to replace 80% of his salary: 0.8 × $50,000 = $40,000.

Since he expects to receive $12,000 per year in Social Security benefits, he calculates that he will have to provide the other $28,000 per year from his own retirement fund.

Using the 8% interest rate on long-term default-free bonds, George computes the amount he will need to have at age 65 as $274,908 (the present value of $28,000 for 20 years at 8% per year). Then he computes the amount he will have to save in each of the next 20 years to reach that future accumulation as $6,007 (the annual payment that will produce a future value of $274,908 at an interest rate of 8% per year). George feels pretty confident that he can save 12% of his salary (i.e., $6,007/$50,000) in order to ensure a comfortable retirement.

(a) If the expected long-term *real* interest rate is 3% per year, approximately what is the long-term expected rate of inflation?
(b) Has George correctly taken account of inflation in his calculations? If not, how would you correct him?
(c) How much should George save in each of the next 20 years (until age 65) if he wants to maintain a constant level of consumption over the remaining 40 years of his life (from age 45 to age 85)? Ignore income taxes.

10. You are 30 years old and are considering full-time study for an MBA degree. Tuition and other direct costs will be $15,000 per year for two years. In addition, you will have to give up a job with a salary of $30,000 per year. Assume tuition is paid and salary received at the *end* of the year. By how much does your salary have to increase (in real terms) as a result of getting your MBA degree to justify the investment? Assume a real interest rate of 3% per year and ignore taxes. Also assume that the salary increase is a constant real amount that starts after you complete your degree (at the end of the year following graduation) and lasts until retirement at age 65.

11. Suppose you currently rent an apartment and have an option to buy it for $200,000. Property taxes are $2,000 per year and are deductible for income tax purposes. Annual maintenance costs on the property are $1,500 per year and are *not* tax deductible. You expect property taxes and maintenance costs to increase at the rate of inflation. Your income tax rate is 40%, you can earn an *after-tax* real interest rate of 2% per year, and you plan to keep the apartment forever. What is the "breakeven" annual rent such that you would buy it if the rent exceeds this amount?

12. Use the Buy vs Rent Home Excel app. If the real interest rate changes to 5%, how does this affect your rent vs. buy decision? What if the interest rate was 2%? Explain.

13. You have decided to acquire a new car that costs $30,000. You are considering whether to lease it for three years or to purchase it and finance the purchase with a three-year installment loan. The lease requires no down payment and lasts for three years. Lease payments are $400 monthly

starting immediately, whereas the installment loan will require monthly payments starting one month from now at an annual percentage rate of 8%.
  (a) If you expect the resale value of the car to be $20,000 three years from now, should you buy or lease it?
  (b) What is the breakeven resale price of the car three years from now, such that you would be indifferent between buying and leasing it?
14. Using the finance concepts presented in this chapter, construct a personal balance sheet showing your assets, liabilities, and net worth.
  (a) Did you value your assets at cost or at current market value? Why?
  (b) Did you include your human capital as an asset? Why?
  (c) Did you include deferred taxes as a liability? Why?
15. Suppose you buy a house for $200,000 when you are 35 years old. You make a 20% down payment and borrow the other 80% from a mortgage lender. The mortgage loan is at a fixed interest rate of 8% per year for 30 years and requires level annual payments. At age 65 you plan to take out a "reverse mortgage" loan that will allow you to borrow a constant annual amount for the rest of your life to be paid off by the sale of your house when you die. Your life expectancy is age 85. The interest rate on both the original mortgage loan and the reverse mortgage will be 8% per year.
  (a) Suppose that you expect the inflation rate to be 3% per year and you can rent an equivalent house for $10,000 per year. Is it worth buying the house?
  (b) Show how buying the house will affect your assets, liabilities, and cash flow over the next 50 years.
  (c) Show how transaction costs associated with buying the house rather than renting it will affect the analysis.

4 PRINCIPLES OF VALUATION

CHAPTER OVERVIEW

4.1	The Crucial Role of Market Prices in Asset Valuation	77
4.2	Value Maximization and Financial Decisions	78
4.3	The Law of One Price and Arbitrage	79
4.4	How the Law of One Price Determines Financial Asset Prices	80
4.5	The Law of One Price and Valuation Models	82
4.6	Interest Rates and the Law of One Price	87
4.7	Market Prices and Information	89
4.8	The Law of One Price and Efficient Markets	97

LEARNING OBJECTIVES

After reading this chapter, you will be able to:
- define the law of one price and explain how it works in determining the value of a financial asset;
- describe how the process of arbitrage enforces the law of one price;
- explain how valuation models can be used to arrive at an estimate of the value of an asset;
- describe how markets incorporate information from market participants, and define the efficient markets hypothesis, which states that asset prices fully reflect all available information;
- explain how market efficiency implies that markets usually provide the best estimates of the value of an asset.

EQUATIONS YOU KNOW

Present value of a series of cash flows	$PV = \dfrac{CF_1}{1+r} + \dfrac{CF_2}{(1+r)^2} + \dfrac{CF_3}{(1+r)^3} + \cdots + \dfrac{CF_T}{(1+r)^T}$ $= \sum_{t=1}^{T} \dfrac{CF_t}{(1+r)^t}$	Eq. 2.9
Present value of a perpetuity	$PV = \dfrac{\$CF}{r}$	Eq. 2.17
Future value of a cash flow	$FV = PV \times (1+r)^T$	Eq. 2.1
Relationship between present value and future value one year from now	$PV = \dfrac{FV}{1+r}$	Eq. 2.7

- You are looking to invest your money by buying some shares of a company's stock, which is currently trading for $10 on the stock exchange. Your good friend says not to buy it because she thinks it is actually worth only $8. Who is likely correct?

- You work in the jewelry industry, and you notice that the price of gold bars that can be made into rings is substantially higher in New York than in Chicago. Can you make money based on this observation? How long should you expect this opportunity to last?

- You are a real estate agent, and you want to determine a fair market price to list a client's house for. What are some ways you could go about determining this price?

- You work as an equity analyst for an investment bank. You are looking at a stock, and you calculate based on a valuation model you know that the stock's price should be $100 per share. You see that the stock is actually trading on the market for $95. You think that makes it a good deal to buy. How confident should you be in your conclusion?

- You are thinking of whether to accept a job offer from a company. You are somewhat worried about taking the job because the company has struggled over the last year. However, you see on the news that the company's stock price suddenly went up substantially. Does this give you relevant information for your decision?

- The stock market suddenly plummeted 5% yesterday, and news pundits all offer wide-ranging explanations as to why. Your friend says this is evidence that markets are not rational. Is your friend correct?

Introduction

Most financial decisions boil down to figuring out how much an asset is worth. For example, in deciding whether to invest in a security such as a stock or a bond or in a business opportunity, you have to determine whether the price being asked is high or low relative to other investment opportunities in the years before retirement. It assumes that you will live for 20 years after retiring. For instance, if you have 30 years left before you retire and earn an interest rate of 3% per year, then you will obtain an increase of $3.20 in your annual retirement benefit for every $1 per year increase in annual saving. Fill in the missing table values.

9. George Thriftless is 45 years old, earns $50,000 per year, and expects that his future earnings will keep pace with inflation, but will not exceed inflation. He has not yet saved anything toward his retirement. His company does not offer a pension plan. George pays Social Security taxes equal to 7.5% of his salary, and he assumes that when he retires at age 65, he will receive $12,000 per year in inflation-adjusted Social Security benefits for the rest of his life. His life expectancy is age 85.

George buys a book on retirement planning that recommends saving enough so that when private savings and Social Security are combined, he can replace 80% of his preretirement salary. George buys a financial calculator and goes through the following calculations:

First, he computes the amount he will need to receive in each year of retirement to replace 80% of his salary: $0.8 \times \$50,000 = \$40,000$.

Since he expects to receive $12,000 per year in Social Security benefits, he calculates that he will have to provide the other $28,000 per year from his own retirement fund.

Using the 8% interest rate on long-term default-free bonds, George computes the amount he will need to have at age 65 as $274,908 (the present value of $28,000 for 20 years at 8% per year). Then he computes the amount he will have to save in each of the next 20 years to reach that future accumulation as $6,007 (the annual payment that will produce a future value of $274,908 at an interest rate of 8% per year). George feels pretty confident that he can save 12% of his salary (i.e., $6,007/$50,000) in order to ensure a comfortable retirement.

(a) If the expected long-term *real* interest rate is 3% per year, approximately what is the long-term expected rate of inflation?
(b) Has George correctly taken account of inflation in his calculations? If not, how would you correct him?
(c) How much should George save in each of the next 20 years (until age 65) if he wants to maintain a constant level of consumption over the remaining 40 years of his life (from age 45 to age 85)? Ignore income taxes.

10. You are 30 years old and are considering full-time study for an MBA degree. Tuition and other direct costs will be $15,000 per year for two years. In addition, you will have to give up a job with a salary of $30,000 per year. Assume tuition is paid and salary received at the *end* of the year. By how much does your salary have to increase (in real terms) as a result of getting your MBA degree to justify the investment? Assume a real interest rate of 3% per year and ignore taxes. Also assume that the salary increase is a constant real amount that starts after you complete your degree (at the end of the year following graduation) and lasts until retirement at age 65.

11. Suppose you currently rent an apartment and have an option to buy it for $200,000. Property taxes are $2,000 per year and are deductible for income tax purposes. Annual maintenance costs on the property are $1,500 per year and are *not* tax deductible. You expect property taxes and maintenance costs to increase at the rate of inflation. Your income tax rate is 40%, you can earn an *after-tax* real interest rate of 2% per year, and you plan to keep the apartment forever. What is the "breakeven" annual rent such that you would buy it if the rent exceeds this amount?

12. Use the Buy vs Rent Home Excel app. If the real interest rate changes to 5%, how does this affect your rent vs. buy decision? What if the interest rate was 2%? Explain.

13. You have decided to acquire a new car that costs $30,000. You are considering whether to lease it for three years or to purchase it and finance the purchase with a three-year installment loan. The lease requires no down payment and lasts for three years. Lease payments are $400 monthly

starting immediately, whereas the installment loan will require monthly payments starting one month from now at an annual percentage rate of 8%.
  (a) If you expect the resale value of the car to be $20,000 three years from now, should you buy or lease it?
  (b) What is the breakeven resale price of the car three years from now, such that you would be indifferent between buying and leasing it?

14. Using the finance concepts presented in this chapter, construct a personal balance sheet showing your assets, liabilities, and net worth.
  (a) Did you value your assets at cost or at current market value? Why?
  (b) Did you include your human capital as an asset? Why?
  (c) Did you include deferred taxes as a liability? Why?

15. Suppose you buy a house for $200,000 when you are 35 years old. You make a 20% down payment and borrow the other 80% from a mortgage lender. The mortgage loan is at a fixed interest rate of 8% per year for 30 years and requires level annual payments. At age 65 you plan to take out a "reverse mortgage" loan that will allow you to borrow a constant annual amount for the rest of your life to be paid off by the sale of your house when you die. Your life expectancy is age 85. The interest rate on both the original mortgage loan and the reverse mortgage will be 8% per year.
  (a) Suppose that you expect the inflation rate to be 3% per year and you can rent an equivalent house for $10,000 per year. Is it worth buying the house?
  (b) Show how buying the house will affect your assets, liabilities, and cash flow over the next 50 years.
  (c) Show how transaction costs associated with buying the house rather than renting it will affect the analysis.

available to you. In addition to investment decisions, there are many other situations in which one needs to determine the value of an asset. For example, suppose that the tax assessor in your town has assessed your house at $500,000 for property tax purposes. Is this value too high or too low? Or suppose you and your siblings inherit some property, and you decide to sell it and share the proceeds equally among yourselves. How do you decide how much it is worth?

In Chapter 2 we learned about one method for determining an asset's value: discounted cash flows. In this chapter, we explain other core methods of asset valuation, the process of estimating how much an asset is worth. Asset valuation is at the heart of much of financial decision making. For firms, value maximization (maximizing the wealth of shareholders) is assumed to be the main objective of management. For households, many financial decisions can be made by selecting the alternative that maximizes value.

Valuation models are mathematical tools used for estimating how much an asset is worth. The key idea underlying all valuation models is embodied in **Principle 2:** *Equivalent assets that can be freely bought and sold will have the same market price.* That two identical assets must have the same prices is known as the law of one price. If we need to determine the value of an asset, the law of one price states that if we find a comparable asset that is exactly the same, the price of the comparable asset will tell us the price of our asset. In reality, no two assets are *exactly* identical, but some assets may be similar or comparable in various ways to the one we wish to value. Valuation models help us adjust for differences between assets, and tell us which differences matter and which don't when it comes to determining an asset's price. There are many different models that one may use to value an asset, and the choice depends on the particular application at hand. In this chapter we explore how models are used in finance, and illustrate with two models: the discounted cash flow model covered in Chapter 2 and valuation using multiples.

4.1 The Crucial Role of Market Prices in Asset Valuation

The ultimate goal of all valuation models is to determine the price that an asset may trade at. Sometimes we do not know what this price is, and must use a valuation model to determine it. Other times we can observe prices of assets (e.g., shares of stock) traded in a market and compare the prices as determined by our valuation models to market prices. In general, market prices are the most accurate reflection of an asset's value because they incorporate the information that all market participants have when they decide to buy or sell the asset. Thus, market prices are an important source of information and should always be considered in any analysis of an asset's value.

In particular, market prices reflect the equilibrium price that results from the buying and selling activities of market participants. In real-world financial markets, traders make decisions based on the limited information directly available to them plus what they can glean from market prices. If there is a specific piece of significant information about a single stock (such as a merger or earnings announcement), known only by some market participants, this could affect the prices because it reflects information not available to everyone. However, in the markets for very widely traded stocks there is no single trading entity that knows anything close to all the information that can affect a stock's value. The stock's market price reflects and aggregates the combined information of all who are trading (or even choosing not to trade) at a point in time, which is more information than any one entity can possibly know. That is, an asset's market price contains information that no single market participant has. In that sense, a market price is itself a primary source of information for all to take into account in making financial decisions.

How does the market aggregate individual traders' information? Market prices are a weighted average of the information/actions taken in which the larger the trades, the greater the impact on the equilibrium market price. If those who control decisions for the largest pools of assets are in that position because they are better informed, then the market price weights the information from those sources more heavily than information from other sources. Participants that are more confident in their predictions about an asset's value will purchase more of the asset, an observable action that further weights the market price toward the better-informed view. Thus, market prices generally reflect more accurate information than the average trader's information in the market. In sum, the market is likely to be better informed than most individual traders, and all traders should use market prices as part of the information to analyze and arrive at their decisions.

4.2 Value Maximization and Financial Decisions

In many instances, personal financial decisions can be made by selecting the alternative that maximizes value to the individual. This is usually true even without considering details about the individual's spending habits or how much risk they are willing to take on. To give a simple example, consider the choice between two alternatives: (A) you get $100 today, or (B) you get $95 today.

Suppose you had to guess how a stranger, about whom you knew nothing at all, would choose. If the two alternatives are the same in every other respect and there is no chance that you will not get the money promised, then you would choose alternative A on the grounds that more wealth is better than less.

Few financial decisions are this simple and straightforward. Suppose, now, that the choice is between a share of a very risky stock (i.e., its price may change or drop substantially) and a completely safe bond (i.e., its price will not change), and that the stranger hates taking risks and thinks the stock's price will fall in the future. However, the current market price of the stock is $100, and the market price of the bond is $95.

Because the stranger hates taking risks and is pessimistic about the price of the stock in the future, you might predict that he would choose the bond. However, even if he ultimately wants to invest his money in safe bonds, the stranger should choose the stock.

Why? The answer is that the stranger can sell the stock for $100 and buy the bond for $95. As long as the costs of buying and selling the stock/bond (e.g., broker fees and other transaction costs) are less than the $5 difference in price, the stranger will come out ahead by choosing the stock. This simple example makes two important points:

1. Financial decisions can rationally be made purely on the basis of maximizing value, regardless of a person's risk preferences or expectations about the future.
2. The markets for financial assets provide the information needed to value the alternatives.

Just as households make many financial decisions based on the criterion of value maximization, so do firms. Managers of companies are faced with the question of how to raise money, make investment decisions, and manage resources. This leads to a general and simple rule for company decision making: Choose investments to maximize the value of the company. As we will see in later chapters, there are situations that may complicate this rule.

How can decision makers estimate the values of the assets and investment opportunities that are available to them? In some cases, they can look up the market price of the asset online. But some assets are not traded in any market and, therefore, we do not know their prices. To compare alternatives in such a case, we need to figure out what their market value would be *if* they were traded.

The essence of asset valuation in these cases is to estimate how much an asset is worth using information about one or more comparable assets whose current market prices we know. The method used to accomplish this estimation depends on the information available. If we know the prices of assets that are virtually identical to the asset whose value we want to estimate, then we can apply the law of one price.

> **QUICK CHECK 4.1** You win a contest, and the prize is a choice between a ticket to an opera and a ticket to a ball game. The opera ticket has a price of $100 and the ticket to the ball game has a price of $25. Assuming you prefer ball games to opera, which ticket should you choose?

4.3 The Law of One Price and Arbitrage

A core principle that underlies, in one way or another, the process of valuing *any* asset is the law of one price, which states that in a market where assets can be bought or sold freely, two equivalent assets should have the same market price. What do we mean by "equivalent"? The simplest case is when there are two assets that are identical in every significant way. If two assets differ in some dimensions (e.g., stock shares that have different serial numbers) but are perfect substitutes for one another in terms of the characteristics that affect why the assets are being bought or sold, then they can be considered to be equivalent.

The law of one price is enforced by a process called arbitrage, the purchase and immediate sale of equivalent assets in order to earn a sure (and potentially unlimited) profit from a difference in their prices. Let us demonstrate how arbitrage works using gold. For thousands of years, gold has been widely used as a store of value and as a means of payment. It is a well-defined commodity whose quality can be precisely determined. When we talk about the price of gold, we mean the price of an ounce of gold of standard quality.

Consider the following situation: Village A and Village B are a one-minute walk from each other. If the price of gold in Village A is $1,000 per ounce, what is its price in Village B?

Gold in the two places is equivalent. So, by the law of one price, the answer is that the price in Village B should also be $1,000 per ounce. To see why, let us consider what would happen if the price in Village B was different from $1,000 per ounce. Suppose, for example, that the price of gold in Village B is only $900. You could then buy gold in Village B for $900, walk to Village A, and sell it for $1,000. This would guarantee you a profit of $100. In this example of arbitrage your profit would be unlimited: If you can buy and sell as much gold as you want at these prices, you would never stop, and the amount of money you would make is infinite! Furthermore, if you could agree to not pay for buying the gold in Village B until after you sell in Village A, you wouldn't even need to spend any money upfront!

The main takeaway is that, when we look at prices when valuing an asset, we assume that *no* situation like the above exists and that there is no arbitrage. This relatively simple idea forms the basis for all valuation in finance; it tells us that when two assets are the same in all crucial characteristics, they should have the same price.

4.3.1 Limits to Arbitrage

The above illustration shows how the law of one price and arbitrage work *in theory*. In the real world, however, there are complications. In fact, you may have seen many situations in which the prices of two nearly identical items are different. The law of one price still holds in these types of situations, and provides a roadmap for why prices of similar assets may differ (and how different they may be).

To illustrate, consider the price of gold in Los Angeles compared to the price of gold in New York. Let's say that the price of gold in New York is $1,000 per ounce. What should the price in Los Angeles be? By the law of one price, we would expect the price of gold in Los Angeles to be *approximately* $1,000 per ounce. One reason why it is not *exactly* $1,000 is because New York and Los Angeles are far away from each other, not just one mile apart like Villages A and B. Consider how much it would cost to buy gold in Los Angeles and sell it in New York. There are the costs of shipping, handling, insuring, and fees for buying and selling. We call the totality of such costs transaction costs.

Say gold costs $950 in Los Angeles, and the transaction costs are $2 per ounce (it takes a day to ship the gold by air). If you buy gold in Los Angeles for $950 and sell it in New York for $1,000, then your profit would be $48 per ounce; you would buy gold where it is cheap and sell it where it is expensive.

If such a discrepancy in the price of gold between New York and Los Angeles ever developed, it is unlikely that you would be the first or only person to notice it. It is much more likely that gold dealers, who are in the business of buying and selling gold on a daily basis, would discover the discrepancy first. The first dealer to discover it would seek to buy as much as they could in Los Angeles at $950 an ounce. In addition to gold dealers, another group of market participants, called arbitrageurs, watch the price of many different assets—including gold—in different regions, searching for price discrepancies to exploit for profit.

Regardless of who or what group is doing the buying and selling, the acts of buying a lot of gold in Los Angeles and simultaneously selling it in New York would affect the forces of supply and demand, and quickly drive the price up in Los Angeles and down in New York. The arbitrage would stop only when the price in Los Angeles was within $2 per ounce of the price in New York. If the price in Los Angeles were *higher* than in New York (say the price of gold in New York is again $1,000 per ounce, but in Los Angeles it is $1,050), the force of arbitrage would work in the opposite direction. Gold dealers and arbitrageurs would buy gold in New York and ship it to Los Angeles until the price differential fell to $2 per ounce.

Thus, the force of arbitrage maintains a relatively narrow band around the price difference between the gold market in Los Angeles and the one in New York. The lower the transaction costs, the narrower the band. In addition to transaction costs, other factors can affect how different prices can be. For instance, there may be different tax rates in different locations or different laws restricting trade. These and other factors will determine how close prices of equivalent assets will be to each other.

> QUICK CHECK 4.2 If the price of silver is $20 per ounce in Chicago and the total transaction costs of shipping silver to New York are $1 per ounce, what can we say about the price of silver in New York?

4.4 How the Law of One Price Determines Financial Asset Prices

In the previous section, we saw how the law of one price and arbitrage work when the asset is a commodity. Now let us consider how it operates in the market for *financial* assets such as shares of stock. One feature of financial assets is that their transaction costs are much lower than those for gold—there is no need to physically transport them between locations, no need to store them, and so forth. To see how the law of one price operates with financial assets, let's look at shares of stock of a company called Financials Inc. These shares are traded on two different major stock exchanges: the New York Stock Exchange (NYSE) and the London Stock Exchange. If shares of Financials Inc. stock were selling for $90 each on the NYSE at the same time they were selling for $100 on the London Stock Exchange, what would happen?

If the transaction costs were negligible, investors would sell their shares in London and buy them in New York. Arbitrageurs could earn sure profits by buying 100,000 shares of Financials Inc. on the NYSE for a total of $9,000,000 (100,000 shares × $90 per share) and then immediately selling them on the London Stock Exchange for a total of $10,000,000 (100,000 shares × $100 per share). Because they pay only $9,000,000 for the shares bought in New York but receive $10,000,000 for the shares sold in London, they are left with $1,000,000 in profit.

Note that the arbitrageurs could do this without investing *any* of their own money. For example, they could borrow the money to initially buy the shares on the NYSE, sell the shares in London, and then immediately pay back whoever they borrowed from. Even though this set of transactions requires no cash outlays by the arbitrageurs at any time, they immediately increase their wealth by $1,000,000 as a result of these transactions. As long as the prices for Financials Inc. stock on the two exchanges are different, arbitrageurs can continue to increase their profits by making these transactions and can continue to get something for nothing.

This process would be like the mythical goose that laid golden eggs, except for an important fact: Such arbitrage opportunities do not persist for very long. The large profits earned by the arbitrageurs will attract attention to the price discrepancy. Other arbitrageurs will compete for the same arbitrage profits; as a result, this activity of buying and selling will drive down the price in London and drive up the price in New York. In the end, the stock prices in the two locations will converge.

As this simple example illustrates, the law of one price is a statement about the price of one asset *relative* to the price of another; it tells us that if we want to know the current price of Financials Inc. stock, it is enough to know its price on the NYSE. If that price is $90, we can be reasonably sure that its price in London is the same.

The law of one price is the most fundamental valuation principle in finance, and we will always assume that there can be no situations with arbitrage, an assumption we will refer to as the no-arbitrage condition. As long as there is no arbitrage, the law of one price holds. The no-arbitrage condition is the basis for **Principle 3:** *There is no such thing as a "free lunch" in finance; everything has a cost.* The possibility of engaging in arbitrage would imply that market participants are getting something valuable for free.

If observed prices appear to violate the law of price, so that seemingly identical assets are selling at different prices and there is an arbitrage opportunity, our first suspicion should not be that this is an exception to the law of one price and Principles 2 and 3. Instead, we should suspect that (1) something is interfering with the normal operation of the competitive market, or (2) there is some (perhaps undetected) economic difference between the two assets.

To see this point, consider the following example. Normally a US dollar bill is worth four quarters. We know that because we could take a dollar and exchange it costlessly for four quarters at a bank, a retail store, or with a person we meet on the street. Yet we can describe a situation in which a dollar bill will be worth *less* than four quarters. Suppose you are desperate to do your laundry right now. You need two quarters for the washer and one quarter for the dryer. You have no change, but you do have a dollar bill. If you are in a big hurry and the only other person at the laundromat has three quarters, you would likely agree to part with your dollar for three quarters.

When would a dollar be worth *more* than four quarters? Perhaps you are at a bus stop and are very thirsty. You find a beverage vending machine that will only accept dollar bills and not coins. Under those circumstances you may be willing to pay someone more than four quarters in exchange for a dollar.

These situations do not violate the law of one price because in each instance the dollar bill is not really equivalent to the four quarters in all respects that have a bearing on their value. At the laundromat, a dollar bill is useless because it will not start the washer or dryer. At the bus stop, quarters are useless because they will not operate the vending machine. And in both situations you do not have costless access to a party who will exchange the two in the normal ratio.

No two distinct assets are identical in *all* respects. For example, even two different shares of stock in the same company differ in their serial numbers. Nevertheless, we would expect the shares to have the same price because they are the same in all respects that have a bearing on their value to investors (e.g., expected return, risk, voting rights, marketability, and so on).

> QUICK CHECK 4.3 Under what circumstances might two 25-cent coins have different values?

4.4.1 When Arbitrage Is Not Possible, There Is Still Dominance

In our previous examples of arbitrage, a single agent unilaterally executed transactions in asset markets in order to make an instant amount of money. The arbitrageur could continue to do so with ever-larger trades until the arbitrage forces the prices to converge to the level at which the arbitrage opportunity disappears. This process creates a powerful force because it will happen even if just *one* person is able to do such trades. In reality, however, there may be limitations that prevent these types of trades from occurring. For example, it is common for stock trading platforms to impose limits on how many trades or how large a trade a person is able to execute. These limitations have the potential to prevent prices from converging in the way described above, since a single agent can no longer make the necessary arbitrage trades. However, even with restrictions on how much a single person may be able to trade, prices may still adjust to eliminate arbitrage opportunities if *many* people are able to find and trade on such opportunities.

To illustrate, suppose Financials Inc. stock is selling on the NYSE for $90 per share and on the London Stock Exchange for $100. If there were no barriers to arbitrage, a single individual could carry out one massive trade that would eliminate the price discrepancy. Now suppose that such a one-person arbitrage is not possible because there is a legal limit on the number of shares that can be purchased and sold by a single individual. Anyone wanting to buy Financials Inc. shares would be better off buying them in New York and anyone wanting to sell them would be better off selling them in London. If enough people act on this, the mechanism of price convergence is similar to the one for arbitrage—buy low and sell high. The difference is that it cannot be done by just one person, and requires others trading in those securities to observe or otherwise find out about the situation, and to act on it.

We refer to such a situation as market-force dominance. The idea behind market-force dominance is that if prices are such that an asset *dominates*—that is, the asset in one location trades at a lower price than an adjacent location, thus presenting a sure-profit opportunity—then prices can converge to eliminate the opportunity because multiple agents make the trade. This will occur even if there are limits to how much individuals can trade the asset.

Like no-arbitrage, no-dominance is a necessary condition for any mathematical model that helps us to determine financial prices. While no-dominance can produce the same result as actual arbitrage, it is less powerful because it requires enough agents to find and act on the dominance opportunity, whereas arbitrage can cause prices to converge with just one agent.

4.5 The Law of One Price and Valuation Models

The law of one price underlies *every* method of valuation used in finance. Generally speaking, the process of valuation requires that we find assets comparable to the one whose value we want to estimate and then make judgments about which differences have a bearing on their value to investors.

Valuation is fairly simple when we can apply the law of one price directly for two equivalent assets. However, because we almost never know the prices of assets that are exactly equivalent to the one we are evaluating, we cannot always apply the law of one price in such a direct and straightforward way. In these cases, we must employ some other method for estimating value from the known prices of other assets that are comparable but not quite the same. The quantitative method used to infer an asset's value from information about the prices of other comparable assets and market interest rates is called a valuation model. The intrinsic or fundamental value of an asset is an estimate of what an asset's price *should* be using some valuation model.

How we define "equivalent assets" is important when applying valuation models. For example, if the cash flows of two assets match in every possible outcome, that may be enough to consider them to be equivalent even if there are other differences. Later, as we develop models that incorporate uncertainty, we will define other notions of "equivalent" such as "two assets with the same/equivalent risk must have the same expected return." The reason the notion of equivalent assets is important is because of **Principle 2:** *Equivalent assets that can be freely bought and sold will have the same market price.* For any valuation model to work, there must be no arbitrage. This is because valuation models essentially try to compare an asset we're trying to value to other assets. If there is arbitrage, then the law of one price would fail and we could not perform this comparison because equivalent assets would have different prices.

4.5.1 Choosing Valuation Models

Chapter 2 introduced one type of valuation model—the discounted cash flow (DCF) model—and later in this section we review what the law of one price implies for DCF models. We cover many other types of valuation models throughout this book. The type of model to use depends on its specific purpose. If you want to estimate the value of an asset over which you have no control, you might use a different model than if you can influence the asset's value through your actions. Thus, if you are an individual estimating the value of a firm's stock as a personal investment, you should use a different model from the one used by a corporation contemplating taking over the firm and reorganizing it. In later chapters we explore in detail specific types of valuation models that are used in finance to value different kinds of assets for different purposes. Here, we provide some examples to illustrate some of the issues involved in selecting an appropriate valuation model.

For example, consider the valuation problem faced by the town assessor from the introduction to this chapter. She has to estimate the values of all houses in the town once each year. Because homeowners will have to pay taxes based on her assessments, the assessor must choose a valuation method that is perceived as fair and accurate. Valuation models used in real estate assessment vary significantly in their level of complexity and mathematical sophistication. Because the town's taxpayers will have to pay for the cost of the annual assessment, they will want the method chosen to be implementable at low cost.

Consider one simple model the assessor might use. She can collect all available data on prices of houses in the town that were sold since the last revaluation of houses one year ago, average them, and use that average as the assessed value for all houses. This model is certainly inexpensive to construct and implement, but it almost surely would not be perceived as fair by those homeowners with houses that are worth less than the average.

Another simple method would be to take the original purchase price of each house and adjust it by a factor reflecting the general change in house prices in the town from the date of purchase to the current date. Thus, suppose that house prices in the town have increased at an average rate of 4% per year for the past 50 years. A house bought 50 years ago for a price of $30,000 would then have a current assessed value of $30,000 \times 1.04^{50}$ or $213,200. But some homeowners are sure to object that this method ignores changes that have occurred over time in the house itself. Some houses will have undergone major improvements and others will have deteriorated. Moreover, the relative desirability of various locations in the town will have changed. The assessor faces a difficult problem in choosing among valuation methods and may wind up using more than one.

Models have great power and usefulness, but it is important to remember that all valuation models are *approximations* of reality. Reality is complex, with many different forces happening at the same time, and it is impossible to incorporate *everything* into one model. We will learn about many different valuation models over the course of this book. We will see that the choice between models depends on the given application and the user, and choosing the appropriate model that best reflects the financial decision process is critical. It is also important to understand the limitations of any financial decision model. This lesson is summarized in **Principle 4**: *Every model is an incomplete, simplified description of a complex reality.* We return to this principle again and again as we introduce new models throughout the book.

> QUICK CHECK 4.4 Can you offer the assessor a way to alter her valuation model so that it accounts for the specific neighborhood the house is located in?

4.5.2 Valuation Using Comparables

The most straightforward valuation model that directly uses the law of one price is valuation using comparables. The intuition behind this method is to find the value of another very similar—ideally *identical*—asset to the one you are trying to value. Because the law of one price states that two equivalent assets should have the same price, if we know the price of the very similar asset, we have zeroed in on the value of the asset we're trying to value.

For example, consider valuing a house using the observed prices of comparable houses. Suppose that you own a house and that each year you pay real estate taxes on it to the local town government that are computed as a proportion of the house's estimated market value. You have just received a notice from the town's real estate assessor notifying you that the estimated market value of your house this year is $500,000.

Suppose that your next-door neighbors just sold a house identical to yours for $300,000. You could justifiably appeal the town's $500,000 assessment for your house as being too high on the grounds that a house virtually identical to yours just sold for $200,000 less than your assessed value. If you do so, you are applying the law of one price in your valuation of your house. You are implying that if you were to put your house up for sale, your expectation is that it would fetch a price of $300,000, because a comparable house just sold for that amount.

Of course, the house next door is not *exactly* identical to yours because it is not located on your lot. And you probably cannot *prove* that if you actually put your house up for sale it would fetch only $300,000 rather than the $500,000 that the town's assessor says it is worth. Nonetheless, unless the town's assessor can point to some economically relevant feature of your house that would make it worth $200,000 more than your neighbor's house (such as more land or floor space or bathrooms), you would have a strong case for appealing the town's assessment.

We can also apply this same intuition to determining the value of a share of a company's stock. As before, if you can find a company identical in all respects, then you are done: By the law of one price, you can use that identical company's stock price as the price of the company you are valuing. Just as no houses are exactly the same, no two companies are exactly identical. However, there are companies that are *similar* in many respects—they operate in the same business areas, sell similar products, are roughly the same size, and so forth. We call companies that are similar comparable companies. A relatively simple model widely used in estimating the value of a share of a firm's stock is to take its most recent earnings per share and multiply it by a price/earnings multiple from comparable firms. A firm's price/earnings multiple is the ratio of its stock price to its earnings per share. The idea is that, because the comparable firms are very similar to the company we are trying to value, then for each share the market price should be a certain multiple of what the accounting earnings are. Thus, for the company we want to value, we take its accounting earnings per share and multiply by that number given by the comparable companies, and we will get an estimate of the stock price.

Suppose that you want to estimate the value of a share of XYZ stock, and XYZ's earnings per share are $2. Suppose further that comparable firms in the same line of business have an average price/earnings multiple of 10. Using this model, we would estimate the value of a share of XYZ stock to be:

$$\text{Value of a share of XYZ stock} = \text{XYZ earnings per share} \times \frac{\text{price}}{\text{earnings}} \text{ of comparables} \quad (4.1)$$

$$= \$2 \times 10 = \$20.$$

In applying the price/earnings multiple model, one must use great care to make sure that what is being measured is truly comparable. For example, shares of stock issued by two firms with identical assets but different debt–equity ratios are not really comparable. Moreover, firms classified as being in the same industry may have very different opportunities for profitable growth in the future and, therefore, differ in their price/earnings multiples. We go over this method of valuing using comparables to value stock shares as well as entire companies in detail in Chapter 8. The overall point is that even when the force of arbitrage cannot be relied on to enforce the law of one price, we still rely on its logic to value assets with various methods.

> QUICK CHECK 4.5 A firm's earnings per share are $5, and the industry average price/earnings multiple is 10. What would be an estimate of the value of a share of the firm's stock?

4.5.3 Valuation Using the Discounted Cash Flow Model

The discounted cash flow (DCF) model we covered in Chapter 2 is an example of a widely used valuation model, and the law of one price has direct implications for it and our concepts of present value. As we discussed in Chapter 2, we can figure out the present value (*PV*) of an asset or investment by discounting the future cash flows (*CF*) it provides by the appropriate discount rate. Assuming the discount rate does not change over time, this gives us (Equation 2.9):

$$PV = \frac{CF_1}{1+r} + \frac{CF_2}{(1+r)^2} + \frac{CF_3}{(1+r)^3} + \cdots + \frac{CF_T}{(1+r)^T}$$

$$= \sum_{t=1}^{T} \frac{CF_t}{(1+r)^t}. \quad (4.2)$$

To illustrate, consider the valuation problem for determining the value of a share of XYZ stock. If we do not have suitable comparable firms, as we did before, we could use the DCF valuation model. To do so, we would need to determine the cash flows that owning a share of XYZ stock yields. Cash payments that stocks provide their holders are known as *dividends*, and often companies announce that they will make such payments regularly. Suppose a company announces that it will pay stockholders a cash dividend payment of $5 per share of stock every year starting next year, and the discount rate is 5%. The cash flow stream would be a perpetuity, and thus the present value of the stock would be calculated using Equation 2.17, the perpetuity formula from Chapter 2:

4 PRINCIPLES OF VALUATION

$$PV = \frac{\$CF}{r} \quad (4.3)$$

$$PV = \frac{\text{Dividend}}{r}$$

$$= \frac{\$5}{0.05}$$

$$= \$100.$$

This gives us an estimated stock price of $100. In this case, using DCF analysis to discount future dividends is known as the **dividend discount model**. Given the assumptions we've made, this model is easy to work with. But such a model may be difficult to implement—if the dividends a company may pay are not known in advance, for example, we may be better off using another model. In later chapters we will go over the dividend discount model of valuing stock shares in more detail, and will learn about other valuation models that can be used to value stocks.

More generally, the law of one price tells us that equivalent assets should have the same price (ignoring factors such as transactions costs). In the context of determining present values through a DCF model, two assets will be **equivalent** if: (a) they are expected to give exactly the same cash flows; and (b) the appropriate discount rates for both are the same.[1] If these conditions hold, then the assets will have the same present value.

To illustrate, consider two identical investments, each of which promises you the following cash flows:

Time t:	$t = 0$	$t = 1$	$t = 2$	$t = 3$
Investment A cash flows:	0	$100	100	100
Investment B cash flows:	0	$100	100	100

Suppose each cash flow has a discount rate of 10% ($r = 0.10$). If we take the present value of these cash flows, we can see that each has an identical present value (applying Equation 4.2):

$$PV = \frac{CF_1}{1+r} + \frac{CF_2}{(1+r)^2} + \frac{CF_3}{(1+r)^3}$$

$$= \frac{\$100}{1.10} + \frac{\$100}{1.10^2} + \frac{\$100}{1.10^3}$$

$$= \$248.69.$$

This outcome is consistent with the law of one price: Because both investments are equivalent, they must have the same price (i.e., present value). If this were not the case, there would be an arbitrage opportunity. Suppose that Investment A had a discount rate of 10% and Investment B had a discount rate of 8%. In this case, Investment A would have a present value of $248.69. Investment B would have a present value of:

---

1 Two assets having the same discount rate implies that they have the same risk—that is, that their values are expected to move in the same way in the future. More generally, two assets that will give you the same cash flows *no matter what occurs in the future* would automatically imply that the two assets have the same discount rate, since they have the same risk. Note that two investments can have the same *expected* cash flows, but the risk of those cash flows (how widely the actual cash flows differ) can be different, which implies different discount rates.

$$PV = \frac{CF_1}{1+r} + \frac{CF_2}{(1+r)^2} + \frac{CF_3}{(1+r)^3}$$

$$= \frac{\$100}{1.08} + \frac{\$100}{1.08^2} + \frac{\$100}{1.08^3}$$

$$= \$257.71.$$

We could therefore buy Investment B (the higher-valued investment) and sell it, using the proceeds to buy Investment A and guaranteeing us a profit of $257.71 − 248.69 = $9.02.

This implies that if we are confident that our discount rate is the same across investments, and if we find an investment we want to value that has the same promised cash flows as another investment we know the price of, we don't even need to do any calculations—we know that the prices must be the same.

Another implication is that if we discover that the cash flows of an investment we want to value are the same as the *combination* of cash flows of two other assets for which we know the prices, then we automatically know the value of the investment: It is the sum of the two known assets' values. Along similar lines, if we know that the prices of Investments A and B are the same and the cash flows we expect to get from each are the same, then the discount rates for each must be the same.

Example 4.1 (Treasure Bond Prices and Arbitrage): You own a Treasury bond that currently sells for a price of $95.23, and guarantees to pay you $100 next year. You discover another Treasury bond trading in the marketplace that also promises to pay the holder $100 in one year. The appropriate discount rate for both bonds is 5%. (a) What should the price of the other Treasury bond be? (b) If the second bond were trading for a price of $90, what would be the arbitrage opportunity?

Solution. (a) It is stated that the two Treasury bonds have the same cash flows ($100 in one year) and the same discount rates (5%). By the law of one price, the bonds must have the same price: $95.23. (b) If, for some reason, the second bond is being sold for $90, then there would be an arbitrage opportunity. We would sell our higher-priced bond, use the money to buy the lower-priced one, and make a profit of $95.23 − $90 = $5.23. The bonds have the same cash flows and discount rates, so we would be making money without giving up anything.

QUICK CHECK 4.6 If two assets have the same expected cash flows but different discount rates, can their prices be the same according to the law of one price?

4.6 Interest Rates and the Law of One Price

Competition in financial markets ensures that not only the *prices* of equivalent assets are the same, but also that *interest rates* on equivalent assets are the same.

Suppose, for instance, that the US Treasury is currently selling one-year $1,000 bonds (called T-bills) that pay an interest rate of 5% per year. The World Bank is also offering one-year $1,000 bonds (denominated in dollars). Assume that both bonds are guaranteed to be free from default (i.e., risk-free), and will pay you what they promise. What interest rate would you expect a major institution such as the World Bank to pay on these bonds?

Your answer should be 5% per year. To see why, first consider what the future value of your $1,000 investment will be in one year for the US T-bills (using Equation 2.1):

$$\begin{aligned} FV &= PV \times (1+r) \\ &= \$1,000 \times (1+r) \\ &= \$1,000 \times (1+0.05) \\ &= \$1,050. \end{aligned}$$

You will therefore have $1,050 in one year.

We now want to find out what the interest rate on the World Bank bonds would have to be. Suppose that the World Bank offered significantly *less* than 5% per year. This would give investors a future value in a year of less than $1,050. Well-informed investors would not buy the bonds issued by the World Bank; instead, they would invest in one-year T-bills. Thus, if the World Bank expects to sell its bonds, it must offer at least as high a rate as the US Treasury.

Would the World Bank offer significantly more than 5% per year? If it did so, then investors would certainly all buy the World Bank's bonds instead of the US T-bills, since the World Bank's bonds would pay out more than $1,050. Assuming that it wants to minimize its borrowing costs (a higher interest rate being more expensive), the World Bank would offer no higher interest rate than is necessary to attract investors. Furthermore, because the United States wants to sell its bonds, it would likely respond by offering new bonds at a higher rate to attract investors.

Thus, interest rates on *any* risk-free bonds denominated in dollars with a maturity of one year will tend to be the same as the 5% per year interest rate on one-year US T-bills. More generally, if there are entities that have the ability to borrow and lend on the same terms at different interest rates, then they can carry out interest-rate arbitrage: borrowing at the lower rate and lending at the higher rate (a form of the old adage "buy low and sell high"). Their attempts to expand their activity will bring about an equalization of interest rates.[2]

Example 4.2 (Interest Rates and Arbitrage): Suppose that you are the manager of a bank. You are able to lend money to safe clients (meaning that they will always pay back the loans) at an interest rate of 6% per year. At the same time, you are able to borrow from the US Federal Reserve at an interest rate of 4% per year. Is there an arbitrage opportunity? How would you take advantage of it?

Solution. Because the interest rate you can borrow at is lower than the interest rate you can lend at, you can make essentially "free" money just by borrowing and lending. Consider the following. Suppose you decided to take a one-year loan for $100 from the Federal Reserve. You would then have to pay the $100 back with interest of $100 × 4% = $4 in one year. In terms of a cash flow timeline, you would get $100 today from the loan, and then have a negative cash flow in one year when you have to pay it back with interest:

```
t = 0              t = 1
├──────────────────┤
$100              −$104
```

Suppose you also decided to lend $100 to a client at an interest rate of 6%, to be paid back in one year. You would have a negative cash flow of $100 today given that you're lending money out, and then a positive cash flow of $100 plus interest of $100 × 6% = $6 in one year when the client pays back the loan:

---

2 Note that two bonds of otherwise identical promised terms may sell at significantly different promised interest rates if there is the possibility of default on payment—that is, the bonds are risky and may not pay what they promise. The valuation of risky credit bonds is covered in Part III.

4.7 MARKET PRICES AND INFORMATION

If we combine the two cash flows, we get:

Thus, for each transaction you would not need to spend any money today, and would get $2 in one year. You would therefore be making $2 for free, making this an arbitrage opportunity. If you are able to increase the amount that you borrow and lend in this way to millions of dollars, you could make an enormous (even unlimited) amount of money!

> **QUICK CHECK 4.7** Suppose you can borrow money at a yearly interest rate of 3%. At the same time, Treasury bonds sell in the marketplace for a price of $1,000 and promise to pay interest of 5% per year. What is the arbitrage opportunity that you face?

4.7 Market Prices and Information

The intrinsic value of an asset is produced by a valuation model. Another source of the value of an asset is the price that the asset trades at in the market. In an ideal world, the market price and intrinsic value of an asset will be the same. But they can and sometimes do differ. In this section we talk about why this may be the case, and how the market is a great tool for determining true value.

Market prices for assets are determined through the decisions of people who buy and sell assets. They must estimate what they think the assets are worth using a valuation model, and the equilibrium price is a weighted average of these estimates of intrinsic value.

This process can be exemplified through an auction, say for an antique desk. The person who owns the desk and is putting it up for auction may not know its value. All possible buyers will come to the auction (either in person or online) having used some valuation model to determine how much the desk is worth. For example, they may use what they know was the price of a similar desk at another shop (an example of using direct comparables as the valuation model) or in another auction. Participants will use their own valuation model, and the desk's selling price at the auction will incorporate the information of all the participants in the market for the antique desk.

Because the market price incorporates the information of all participants, it is good practice to assume that for assets that are bought and sold in well-functioning markets, price is an accurate reflection of value. If a valuation model produces an intrinsic value that differs significantly from the observed market price, then it may be a sign that the model should be adjusted. The important role of market information in determining an asset's value is summarized in **Principle 5:** *The best estimate of an asset's value is usually its market price, which incorporates valuable information to guide the allocation of resources and risks.*

As we will see, this assumption is generally warranted precisely because there are well-informed professionals who look for mispriced assets and profit by eliminating discrepancies between an asset's market price and its intrinsic value. We explain the intuition behind this process in the next section.

4.7.1 The Efficient Markets Hypothesis

Sometimes a corporation's stock price jumps in response to a public announcement about the company's future prospects. For example, suppose that QRS Pharmaceuticals Corporation announces that its research scientists have just discovered a drug that will cure the common cold. The stock price will probably rise dramatically on this news. On the other hand, if it is announced that a judge has just ruled against QRS Pharmaceuticals in a lawsuit involving the payment of millions of dollars in compensation to customers who bought one of its products, QRS's stock price will probably fall. Stock prices are also affected by announcements about various indicators of an economy's health. Box 4.1 discusses such responses during the COVID-19 pandemic of 2020.

Box 4.1 World of Business: Stock Market Reactions during the COVID-19 Pandemic of 2020

The global COVID-19 pandemic of 2020 led to an unprecedented public policy response and a near shutdown of the global economy in an attempt to contain the effects of the virus. The crisis led to a large decline in stock markets around the world in response to a continuous stream of negative economic news regarding unemployment, GDP, and other indicators. The US S&P 500, UK FTSE 100, and Japanese Nikkei stock markets each lost roughly one-third of their respective values between late February 2020 and late March 2020.

Even though negative news continued, however, stock markets rebounded. For example, by early August 2020 the S&P 500 had returned to the same level it was at before it dropped. The Nikkei similarly recovered to its pre-drop levels around the same time, with the FTSE index recovering to near its former level a few months later in the spring of 2021.

Many commentators, flabbergasted by how the market's reaction could differ so much from the bleak economic news, decried the irrationality of the stock market. However, others noted that the stock market reflects all participants' expectations about the *future*, while economic indicators are *backward* looking and measure what the situation was in the past. The interpretation is that the market's information about the future economic recovery was positive. This reaction—including the apparent disconnect from economic indicators—is consistent with previous crises, including the 2008 Financial Crisis, the Great Depression, and even the Spanish Influenza pandemic of 1917–1918. In all cases, the market recovered even in the midst of bad economic news, reflecting the information from all market participants regarding the future.

Sources: MarketWatch (2020). Market action a century ago suggests worst could be over for stocks, if not for the coronavirus pandemic. Baker, S. R., Bloom, N., Davis, S. J. et al. (2020). The unprecedented stock-market reaction to COVID-19. Kellogg Insight.

In such situations, people say that the stock market is reacting to the information contained in these announcements. Implicit in this statement is the view that at least some of the investors who buy or sell QRS stock (or the stock analysts advising them) are paying attention to the fundamental factors that determine the stock's value. Such factors include the company's expected future earnings, investments, and the risk of its operations. Chapter 9 presents details of stock valuation. When those fundamentals change, so does the stock price. Indeed, if the stock price does not move when an important news item is officially made public, many observers of the stock market would say that the news was already reflected in the stock price. It is this idea that is behind the efficient markets hypothesis. Box 4.2 on the *Challenger* space shuttle explosion provides a clear example of what can happen to a stock's price in response to an adverse event.

The efficient markets hypothesis (EMH) is the proposition that an asset's current price fully reflects all available information about future economic fundamentals affecting the asset's value. Thus, if you wanted to trade a stock after gathering information about a company, the EMH implies that all of the information you researched is already incorporated into the stock's price, making it impossible to profit off your information.

The reasoning behind the EMH can be explained by considering the following simplified description of the actions of typical analysts/investors in making decisions about a particular company's stock.

First, analysts collect the information or "facts" about the company and related matters that may affect the company. Such information would include the company's past sales, projections about future sales based on current market trends, the company's size and structure, and what its competitors are doing, among other things. Second, they analyze this information in such a way that helps them determine their best estimate (as of today, time $t = 0$) of the stock's price at a future date (time $t = 1$). This best estimate is the expected stock price at time $t = 1$, which we denote by $\bar{P}_1$. From looking at the current stock price, P_0, they can estimate an *expected* return on the stock, $\bar{r}$, which is what they anticipate the percentage change in the stock price to be:

$$\begin{aligned} \bar{r} &= \frac{\bar{P}_1 - P_0}{P_0} \\ &= \frac{\bar{P}_1}{P_0} - 1. \end{aligned} \tag{4.4}$$

However, the analysts' job is not finished. Because they recognize that their information is not perfect and is subject to error or unforeseen events that may occur, they must also consider a range of possible future prices. In particular, they must estimate how broad this range is around their best estimate, and how likely it is that a large or small deviation from this estimate will occur. This analysis then gives them an estimate of the deviations of the rate of return from the expected rate and the likelihood of such deviations. The more accurate their information, the smaller will be the dispersion around their estimated value and the less risky the investment.

Third, armed with their estimates of the expected rate of return and the dispersion that might occur around this expected rate, they make an investment decision about how much of the stock to buy or sell. How much they buy will depend on how high the expected return on this stock is compared to alternative investments available and on how much money they have to invest either personally or as an agent for others. The higher the expected return and the more money they have or control, the more of the stock they will want to buy or sell. The larger the dispersion (i.e., the less accurate their information), the smaller the amount of stock they will buy.

To see how the current market price of a stock is determined, we look at the aggregation of all analysts' estimates, and assume that the market is usually in equilibrium so that total demand equals total supply. Analysts' estimates may differ for two reasons:

1. They could have access to different amounts of information about the stock (although presumably public information is available to all).
2. They could analyze the information differently with regard to its impact on the stock's future price.

Nonetheless, each analyst comes to a decision as to how much to buy or sell at a given market price, P_0. The aggregation of these decisions gives us the total demand for shares of the company at the price, P_0.

If the price is too low, buyers will demand more shares than are available to buy. As buyers outbid each other to purchase the limited supply of shares, the price of the shares will rise. Similarly, if more shares are available at a given price than are demanded, suppliers will lower the share price until the amount buyers are willing and able to buy matches the amount sellers are willing and able to sell.

In asset markets, however, not all participants have an equal say in determining an asset's value; some participants' opinions are weighted more heavily than others. How are these weights determined? Because "votes" in the marketplace are cast with dollars, the analysts with the biggest impact will be the ones who control the larger amounts of money, and among these the ones who have the strongest opinions about the stock will have the most influence on the stock's price. Put differently, more weight is placed on the actions of those agents who decide on the larger transactions—that is, those with greater confidence in their beliefs and the most resources to put behind those beliefs.

Note that analysts with the strongest opinions have them because they believe that they have better information (resulting in a smaller dispersion around their best estimate). Furthermore, because analysts who consistently overestimate the accuracy of their estimates will eventually lose customers, one would expect that among the analysts who control large sums, the ones who believe that they have better information, on average, probably do.

From all these observations, we conclude that the market price of a stock will reflect the weighted average of analysts' opinions, with heavier weights on the opinions of those analysts who control more than the average amount of money and who have better than average information. Hence, the estimate of fair or intrinsic value provided by the market price will be more accurate than the estimate obtained from any individual average analyst.

Now, suppose that you are an analyst and you find a stock whose market price is low enough that you consider it a bargain (if you never find this situation, then there is no point to being in the analyst business). From the previous discussion, there are two possibilities:

1. You do have a bargain, and your estimate is more accurate than the market's—that is, you have either better than average information about future events that may affect stock price and/or you do a better than average job of analyzing information.
2. Others have better information than you do or process available information better, and your "bargain" is not a true bargain.

Your assessment of which possibility is true depends on how good the other analysts are relative to yourself. There are important reasons why you would expect the quality of other analysts to be high:

- Analysts who can consistently beat the average performance on predicting asset price movements will attract large numbers of intelligent and hardworking customers and will reap enormous rewards. The relative ease of entry into the analyst business implies that competition will force analysts to find better information and develop better techniques for processing this information just to survive.
- The stock market has been around long enough for these competitive forces to take effect.

Precisely because professional analysts compete with each other, the market price becomes a better and better estimate of fair value, and it becomes more difficult to find profit opportunities and beat the market.

> **Box 4.2** World of Business: The Space Shuttle *Challenger* Explosion and Market Efficiency
>
> An illustration of market efficiency at work comes from the market's reaction to the space shuttle *Challenger* disaster. On 28 Jan. 1986, the US space shuttle *Challenger* suddenly exploded at 11:39 a.m., soon after its launch. The cause was not immediately known, and it would be months before an investigative team created by the US government would come to a conclusion regarding the reason for the explosion.
>
> There were four major publicly traded companies involved in the construction of the shuttle: Morton Thiokol, Lockheed, Martin Marietta, and Rockwell International. All four companies experienced negative stock returns on the day of the disaster. However, even though the cause of the explosion was not known with certainty, the market quickly attributed blame to one company in particular—Morton Thiokol, which experienced returns of roughly −12%, compared to the other three companies whose returns fell in the range of −2% to −3%.
>
> After four months of study by a team of engineering experts and scientists, Morton Thiokol was definitively determined to be the culprit, because it had manufactured a critical part in the shuttle's booster rockets that lacked resiliency at different temperatures. The market thus came to the same conclusion within a day, demonstrating how markets can incorporate information from many different people.
>
> *Source:* Information based on Maloney, M. T. and Mulherin, J. H. (2003). The complexity of price discovery in an efficient market: the stock-market reaction to the Challenger crash. *Journal of Corporate Finance* 9(4): 453–479.

4.7.2 Valuation and the Efficient Markets Hypothesis

The notion of market efficiency is at the core of much of what we aim to do in finance, which involves understanding the *value* of assets. In some cases the market will directly inform us of asset values through market prices. In other cases we may not have an asset's market price, but we may use the prices of other comparable assets in the valuation process. At still other times we may have a direct market price, but still go through our valuation process and perhaps determine that the market price is incorrect and that the asset is either overvalued or undervalued.

In each of these cases we are implicitly taking a stand on market efficiency. Whenever we directly accept market prices as the true estimate of an asset's value, we are making the assumption that the market is efficient and therefore provides the best information possible in determining the asset's value. When we calculate values and then compare them to the market's price, we may decide that our calculations better reflect reality than the market. In these cases we are assuming that the market is not completely efficient. There may be various reasons for this. For example, we may believe that we have some sort of private information about the asset that is not fully reflected in the market price because no one else has that information. Indeed, it is because of these possibilities that Principle 5 is not an absolute statement—it states that the best estimate of an asset's value is *usually* the market price.

These different beliefs about market efficiency are categorized into three different degrees of efficiency.

Strong market efficiency refers to the notion that market prices reflect *all* available information in the economy, even information that is privately held by individuals. This form of market efficiency is what is hypothesized by the efficient markets hypothesis, and the ability of market prices to incorporate even privately held information is often referred to as "the wisdom of the crowds." Put differently, market prices often reflect information that no single decision maker (including entities such as governments and central banks) has. Box 4.3 discusses how information can be incorporated into prices almost instantaneously once it is known. Strong market efficiency carries with it the implication that, because market prices already incorporate everyone's information, it should be impossible to consistently outperform or beat the market. Put differently, it implies that the only way to get higher returns than the market is through taking on more *risk*, a finding we formalize in Chapter 17. In line with this, there are many empirical studies that have shown that even professional investors have significant difficulties in beating the market.

Box 4.3 World of Business: Instantaneous Trading on the News

One common critique of the efficient markets hypothesis (EMH) takes aim at its premise that new information can immediately be reflected in the market price of a stock. Humans, after all, take some time to read new information, process it, decide how to act, and then to execute any trades in response. But developments in the use of computers to automatically execute trades after interpreting news reports have undermined this critique of the EMH.

For some time now, investors have used computer programs that scan news reports and corporate announcements for specific terms that could have an impact on the investor's decision to buy, hold, or sell a stock. A spate of reports with the term "heat wave" could, for instance, suggest the purchase of shares of firms that manufacture cooling appliances. As impressive as this may be, computers have been able to move well beyond this level of interpretation.

Algorithms can be programmed to evaluate many years' worth of news issued by or about a given firm to determine how announcements of a certain kind have tended to affect its stock's share price. From this analysis, programs can, immediately upon receiving a new announcement, determine whether to buy or sell shares of the stock in question. In this framework it could potentially be the case that information, quite literally, travels instantaneously from machine to machine in a cycle beginning with computer-generated news and ending with computer-executed trading.

How might such a scenario bear on the EMH? First, we have to remember that the EMH supposes that the moment new information about a firm comes to light, that information is incorporated in the firm's stock price. When human investors must interpret news reports and analyze their content before executing trades, this hypothesis seems unrealistic. But in a world in which information travels, can be interpreted, and can lead to trades, all in less than a second, the EMH does not seem unreasonable. Indeed, the advent of this technology only serves to bolster the significance of the EMH.

Source: Van Duyn, A. (2007). Automatic news makes headlines and money. *Financial Times*, 15 Apr.

Semi-strong market efficiency posits that prices reflect all past price information and all public information (but not private information). Weak market efficiency posits that prices only reflect all past price information. Both semi-strong and weak market efficiency admit the possibility that market prices may be incomplete in the sense that they do not incorporate all relevant information.

In all examples of valuation we will view the market as providing important information, which sometimes yields inputs into our valuation calculations and sometimes directly yields the valuation itself. The notion that markets convey valuable information due to market efficiency also has other implications in practice. Box 4.4 provides an example of how the legal system uses market efficiency.

> QUICK CHECK 4.8 The DEF Corporation announces that over the next few years it will spend several billion dollars on developing a new product. The firm's stock price falls dramatically after the announcement. According to the EMH, what is the reason for the drop in price? If you were the president of DEF Corporation, what conclusions would you draw from the decline in your firm's stock price?

Box 4.4 Efficient Markets Hypothesis in the Law

The efficient markets hypothesis (EMH) has come to influence not only financial markets and economic theory, but also legal interpretation of market happenings. The EMH, as discussed in this chapter, essentially holds that the market price of a share of stock completely and correctly incorporates all public information pertinent to its worth. In this view, stock prices only ever rise or fall because new information becomes available. Such information, the EMH holds, is promptly reflected in the market price of a share.

The EMH has a special role in the legal world because it has been accepted by the US Supreme Court. In the 1988 case *Basic Inc. v. Levinson*, the Court accepted as a legal standard a concept known as "fraud on the market," which presupposes the validity of the EMH. "Fraud on the market" is concerned with deceptive news releases by firms. Such statements, the Court ruled, defraud traders who buy the firm's shares, whether their purchases were directly founded on the deceptive statements or not. After this ruling, civil cases invoking the "fraud on the market" standard multiplied rapidly. The EMH seems to have found its way into criminal prosecutions, too.

Consider the case of Mr. Jamie Olis, a tax accountant involved in a scandal at the energy company Dynegy. In 2004, Mr. Olis was sentenced to 24 years in prison for his role in "Project Alpha," a set of fraudulent accounting. The judge presiding over the case sentenced Mr. Olis to a prison term based on the calculated loss to Dynegy shareholders when the stock tanked upon news that Project Alpha was a scam. Though the sentence was reduced to 6 years on appeal, it is clear that the EMH has meant some serious time for at least one businessman.

The focus of Mr. Olis's appeal was the degree to which the stock's decline resulted specifically from news of Project Alpha's fraudulence. Economists working for both the prosecution and the defense were expected to estimate the loss due to the news of that scandal. The EMH was the foundation on which the case was built.

For years, however, the EMH—originally developed in the 1950s and 1960s—has come under fire by academics. A pair of scholars argued that even the world's most advanced financial markets are not, in practice, as efficient as the EMH would have us believe them to be. Certainly, these scholars claimed, such markets are not efficient enough to warrant the use of a stock price's decline to determine the magnitude of financial losses in a legal case.

Still, the standard in law has remained unchanged in the United States. In both civil and criminal cases, the EMH can play an important role. And so we see that the influence of this hypothesis expands well beyond the halls of the world's universities.

Source: Adapted from *The Economist* (2006). Dismal science, dismal sentence. *The Economist*, 7 Sept.

4.7.3 The Efficient Markets Hypothesis and Behavioral Finance

The EMH rests upon the assumption that individuals behave rationally—that is, that individuals trade assets based on all the relevant information they know, in a way that maximizes the profits that they make at any given time. If this is not the case, then information may not be effectively incorporated into market prices and market efficiency may not hold—in either strong, weak, or semi-strong forms. This, in turn, can cause market prices to move away from representing an asset's fundamental economic values. Behavioral finance is a subfield of finance that examines why individuals may not behave rationally, and explores the implications of this.

Behavioral finance was founded on the observation that we sometimes observe market prices behaving in a way that should not be the case if the EMH holds. These observations are known as market anomalies. For example, there have been a number of market crashes (such as the "dot com" bubble bursting in 2001 and the Financial Crisis of 2008–2009) in which market prices suddenly and unexpectedly experienced precipitous drops. In each case, certain conditions in the market were weak, but this reality was not incorporated into market prices, thus indicating that market prices were not properly aligned with true intrinsic values. Another example is the existence of very successful investors such as Warren Buffett, who seem to consistently "beat" the market over long periods of time, something that should not be possible according to the EMH.

Behavioral finance helps to explain these phenomena by appealing to psychology to understand the ways in which people may not behave rationally. For example, behavioral biases such as overconfidence (individuals excessively thinking they are correct), confirmation bias (individuals paying attention only to information that supports their already-formed opinions), and regret/loss aversion (people disliking losses more than gains) are well-documented psychological phenomena that also apply to investors or managers making decisions within companies.

As a simple illustration, investors that are subject to confirmation bias may ignore important information that contradicts their beliefs when investing, thus preventing that information from being incorporated into market prices. These behavioral biases can help explain why individuals may not behave rationally, thus leading to market anomalies that seemingly violate the EMH.

Some have argued that the body of evidence provided by behavioral finance effectively invalidates the EMH. Others point to examples of the EMH in action (see Box 4.2 on the *Challenger* explosion), and argue that efficient markets generally hold even if there are exceptions. There have also been attempts to reconcile these points of view. The adaptive market hypothesis, proposed by MIT financial economist Andrew Lo, posits that anomalies can exist within efficient markets. Markets change over time, and individuals adapt and evolve in response. This attempt to adapt to changing conditions can lead to apparent biases appearing, which are, in reality, rational responses to potentially unknown changes that individuals face.

The extent to which efficient markets holds is still a subject of academic debate. However, recall **Principle 5:** *The best estimate of an asset's value is usually its market price, which incorporates valuable information to guide the allocation of resources and risks*. This lesson, which runs throughout this book, emphasizes that markets will *always* provide important information that should never be ignored when making financial decisions, even if there are times when the information is not complete.

4.7.4 Extracting Information from Market Prices

A useful implication of Principle 5 is that, when armed with a valuation model, we can extract certain information from market prices. Put differently, we can observe some information from the market prices of certain assets when we view those prices through the lens of a valuation model, and then use the information in making financial decisions. As we will see in Chapter 16, one such application of this information is to use the information gained from the price of one asset to determine the value of *other* assets. More generally, we can glean information in this way that is important to various financial decisions.

To illustrate, suppose that a bank is offering you an interest rate of 4% to put your money in an account for one year. You are unsure whether this is a fair interest rate based on what is offered in the market. One way to find out this information is to ascertain what interest rate is implied by the market prices of other equivalent assets. One such asset may be a bond, trading at $95 right now and promising to pay the owner $100 one year from now. The discounted cash flow (DCF) model says that the price of the bond (its present value) must equal the cash flows it produces discounted by the interest rate (Equation 2.7):

$$PV = \frac{FV}{1+r}$$
$$\$95 = \frac{\$100}{1+r}$$
$$r = 5.3\%.$$

Using our DCF valuation model, we can therefore infer that, based on the market price of this bond, the interest rate for a one-year investment should be 5.3%. The 4% interest rate offered by the bank is lower than the interest you would earn from buying a bond, so the bank's offer is not a good one.

This shows how we can use market prices, in conjunction with a valuation model, to infer information about interest rates. In subsequent chapters we will use a variety of different models to illustrate various other types of information we can distill from market prices, including information about assets that would be difficult to directly measure.

4.8 The Law of One Price and Efficient Markets

Having discussed both the law of one price and the notion of efficient markets in detail, it is important to note that the law of one price and the efficient markets hypothesis are *different* concepts. The law of one price and no-arbitrage are fundamental forces that can drive markets toward informational efficiency, giving rise to the EMH. However, even if the EMH does not hold (and prices therefore do not reflect an asset's intrinsic economic values), the law of one price will still be valid and hold. Put differently, market efficiency may hold in its different forms—strong, semi-strong, or weak—or it may not hold at all, but the forces of arbitrage will still make it so that two equivalent assets have to sell for the same price.

The lesson: Principle 2 (the law of one price) and the notion of no-arbitrage is the most robust principle in finance and underlies the vast majority of financial analysis and decisions. Therefore, even if we encounter situations in which an asset's market price does not seem to reflect all information, it is important to understand that this does *not* imply that the law of one price is being violated and that there is an arbitrage situation.

Conclusion

In Chapter 2 we took a first step in learning how to value assets by discounting future cash flows. In this chapter, we discussed some more general principles involved in determining the values of assets, principles that underlie discounted cash flow (DCF) analysis, and all other valuation models.

The process of valuation rests upon **Principle 2**: *Equivalent assets that can be freely bought and sold will have the same market price.* This principle, known as the law of one price, holds because if equivalent assets had *different* prices, a market participant could earn unlimited profits through arbitrage (buying the lower-priced asset and selling it to another market participant for the higher price). Arbitrage ensures that any discrepancies in the prices of equivalent assets will quickly disappear.

In reality, because the majority of assets we encounter are not *exactly* the same, we cannot directly apply the law of one price when valuing an asset. Instead, we use valuation models that allow us to determine the value of assets by incorporating information on equivalent assets, and adjusting for any differences that may matter for the asset's value. In Chapter 2 we introduced a particular type of valuation model, the DCF model, which used information on future cash flows and interest rates (discount rates) to determine an asset's present value. There are many, many other models that can be used for valuation. In choosing a valuation model, it is crucial to keep in mind **Principle 4**: *Every model is an incomplete, simplified description of a complex reality.* For this reason, it is always important to understand the potential shortcomings of any model, and to be sure that the model takes into account variables that are pertinent to an asset's value.

Prices of comparable assets traded in the market provide another source of information about an asset's value. Market prices are formed through the buying and selling actions of many individuals, each of whom has some information about the asset. This collective information is reflected in the market price. The incorporation of information from thousands of buyers and sellers gives rise to **Principle 5**: *The best estimate of an asset's value is usually its market price, which incorporates valuable information to guide the allocation of resources and risks.* The efficient markets hypothesis (EMH) takes an even stronger stance and suggests that the buying and selling activity of market participants results in *all* available information being reflected in market prices, and thus it is not possible to "beat" the market. Although market anomalies have been observed that call the EMH into question, an important takeaway is that markets will always provide important information that should never be ignored when making financial decisions.

Takeaways

- The ability to value assets accurately is at the heart of the discipline of finance because many personal and corporate financial decisions can be made by selecting the alternative that maximizes value.
- The law of one price states that in a competitive market, if two assets are equivalent they will have the same price.
- The law of one price is enforced by a process called *arbitrage*, the purchase and immediate sale of equivalent assets in order to earn a sure profit from a difference in their prices.
- If arbitrage cannot be carried out in practice to enforce the law of one price, unknown asset values can still be inferred from the prices of comparable assets whose prices are known.
- The quantitative method used to infer an asset's value from information about the prices of comparable assets is called a *valuation model*. The best valuation model to employ varies with the information available and the intended use of the estimated value.
- In making most financial decisions, it is a good idea to start by assuming that for assets that are bought and sold in competitive markets, the market price accurately reflects the information available to market participants, and the value they assign to assets. This assumption is generally warranted precisely because there are well-informed professionals looking for mispriced assets who profit by eliminating discrepancies between the market prices and the fundamental values of assets.

- The proposition that an asset's current price fully reflects all publicly available (and some private) information about future economic fundamentals affecting the asset's value is known as the *efficient markets hypothesis*.
- The prices of traded assets reflect information about the fundamental economic determinants of their value. Analysts are constantly searching for assets whose prices are different from their fundamental value in order to buy or sell these bargains. In deciding the best strategy for the purchase or sale of a bargain, analysts have to evaluate the accuracy of their information.
- The market price of an asset reflects the weighted average of all analysts' opinions, with heavier weights on analysts who control large amounts of money and on those analysts who have better than average information.

Key Terms

Adaptive market hypothesis   96
Arbitrage   79
Arbitrageurs   80
Asset valuation   77
Behavioral biases   96
Behavioral finance   96
Comparable companies   84
Dividend discount model   86
Efficient markets hypothesis (EMH)   91
Fundamental value   83
Interest-rate arbitrage   88
Intrinsic value   83
Law of one price   77
Market anomalies   96
Market-force dominance   82
No-arbitrage condition   81
Price/earnings multiple   84
Semi-strong market efficiency   94
Strong market efficiency   93
Transaction costs   80
Valuation model   83
Valuation using comparables   84
Weak market efficiency   94

Key Equations

Price/earnings multiple model	Value of a share of XYZ stock $= $ XYZ earnings per share $\times \dfrac{\text{price}}{\text{earnings}}$ of comparables	Eq. 4.1
Present value of an asset with future cash flows	$PV = \dfrac{CF_1}{1+r} + \dfrac{CF_2}{(1+r)^2} + \dfrac{CF_3}{(1+r)^3} + \cdots + \dfrac{CF_T}{(1+r)^T}$ $= \sum_{t=1}^{T} \dfrac{CF_t}{(1+r)^t}$	Eq. 4.2
Present value of a perpetuity	$PV = \dfrac{\$CF}{r}$	Eq. 4.3
Expected percentage change in a stock price	$\bar{r} = \dfrac{\bar{P}_1 - P_0}{P_0}$ $= \dfrac{\bar{P}_1}{P_0} - 1$	Eq. 4.4

Problems

1. IBX stock is trading for $35 on the NYSE and $33 on the Tokyo Stock Exchange. Assume that the costs of buying and selling the stock are negligible.
   (a) How could you make an arbitrage profit?
   (b) Over time what would you expect to happen to the stock prices in New York and Tokyo?
   (c) Now assume that the cost of buying or selling shares of IBX is 1% per transaction. How does this affect your answer to part (a)?

2. Suppose you live in the state of Taxachusetts, which has a 16% sales tax on liquor. A neighboring state called Taxfree has no tax on liquor. The price of a case of beer is $25 in Taxfree and $29 in Taxachusetts.
   (a) Is this a violation of the law of one price?
   (b) Are liquor stores in Taxachusetts near the border with Taxfree going to prosper?

3. Suppose the price of white truffles is €400 per kilo in Paris and price of €1 is $1.453. With transportation and transactions costs, such as insurance, of 1% in moving truffles from Paris to New York, within what range do you expect to observe the price of white truffles in New York?

4. You own an annuity asset that promises to pay you $1,000 per year starting from next year and making its last payment 30 years from now. The interest rate on equivalent annuities is 5% per year. You discover another equivalent 30-year annuity being offered in the marketplace that is selling for a price of $10,000. Is there an arbitrage opportunity? If so, how would you take advantage of it?

5. You own a stock that currently sells for a price of $80, and you expect to pay dividends of $5 per share next year and in each subsequent year. The appropriate discount rate for the stock is 5%.
   (a) According to the dividend discount model, what should the price of the stock be?
   (b) Is there an arbitrage opportunity? If so, how would you take advantage of it?

6. You own a Treasury bond that currently sells for a price of $95, and promises to pay you $100 in two years. You discover another Treasury bond trading in the marketplace also promising to pay the holder $100 in two years. Both bonds do not pay any coupons. The appropriate discount rates (the one-year risk-free rate and two-year risk-free rate) for both bonds is 5%.
   (a) What should the price of the other Treasury bond be?
   (b) Is there an arbitrage opportunity? How would you take advantage of it?

7. You want to value a firm. The firm's earnings per share are $10, and the industry average price/earnings multiple is 5. What would be an estimate of the value of a share of the firm's stock?

8. You want to value a furniture firm, Huang's Discount Furniture. The furniture firm's earnings per share are $20; you find a competing furniture store and find that its price/earnings multiple is 10.
   (a) If you use the competing furniture store as a comparable, what would be an estimate of the value of a share of Huang's Discount Furniture?
   (b) Suppose that you find that Huang's Discount Furniture is trading at a price of $180 in the market. Does this mean that the market price is wrong, and there is an arbitrage opportunity? What is an alternative explanation?

9. There are two investments that your company is considering: Project A and Project B. Both projects are expected to produce cash flows of $1 million each year for the next four years.
   (a) If you calculate that the discount rates for the two projects are different, does this mean that there is an arbitrage opportunity?
   (b) Suppose you find that both projects are equivalent and have the same risk profiles, and that the appropriate discount rate for both is 8%. What is the present value of each investment?
   (c) If you find that you are able to sell Project B to another company in the marketplace for $4 million, is there an arbitrage opportunity? If so, how would you take advantage of it?

10. Suppose that you decide to lend money to trusted individuals (meaning that they will always pay back the loans) at an interest rate of 10% per year. At the same time, you are able to borrow from a bank at an interest rate of 5% per year. Is there an arbitrage opportunity? How would you take advantage of it?
11. Suppose the price/earnings ratio of ITT Corporation is 6 while the price/earnings ratio of the S&P 500 is 10. What might account for the difference?
12. Suppose the Federal Reserve is holding a meeting to address the question of whether to undertake actions to raise interest rates. If market participants are convinced that the Federal Reserve will raise interest rates, how will this be reflected in security prices?
13. The price of Singh Co. stock recently jumped when the sudden unexpected death of its CEO was announced. What might account for such a market reaction?
14. Suppose we study the returns earned by corporate officers trading on the basis of inside information—that is, information which is known to corporate insiders but not publicly available. If these types of trades produce above average returns, what does this tell us about market efficiency?
15. The current price of a share of Outel stock is $30, but your analysis leads you to believe that the price of Outel's stock should be $25 per share.
    (a) If you do not believe that you have access to special information about the company, what should you do?
    (b) If you believe that you have much better than average information, what should you do?
16. Suppose that Snoozer stock has earnings of $10 per share, and its industry price/earnings ratio is 10.
    (a) What would be an estimate of the value of a share of Snoozer stock?
    (b) Suppose that you determine that Snoozer will pay dividends of $10 per share each year going forward. The appropriate discount rate for it is 9%. Using the dividend discount model, what is an estimate of the value of Snoozer stock?
    (c) Suppose that Snoozer is trading for $90 in the market, and you believe that the dividend discount model is correct and gives its true value. Construct an arbitrage strategy to take advantage of this, assuming that you can borrow at a 2% interest rate.
    (d) Suppose instead that Snoozer is trading for $120 in the market, and you believe that the dividend discount model is correct and gives its true value. Construct an arbitrage strategy to take advantage of this, assuming that you can borrow at a 2% interest rate.
17. Consider again Snoozer stock from the previous question, with earnings of $10 per share and an industry price/earnings ratio of 10.
    (a) Suppose that Snoozer is trading for $120. If you believe that the price/earnings multiple approach gives the correct value and you can borrow at an interest rate of 0% each year, explain how you can make arbitrage profits.
    (b) If you do make a profit doing this strategy, explain what this implies about market efficiency.

5 FINANCIAL INSTRUMENTS AND RATES OF RETURN

CHAPTER OVERVIEW

5.1	Financial Markets and Instruments	103
5.2	Financial Market Rates: Interest Rates	107
5.3	Financial Market Rates: Stocks and Equity Funds	116
5.4	The Fundamental Determinants of Rates of Return	121
5.5	History of Stock and Bond Returns	123
5.6	Monte Carlo Simulation of Future Stock Market Performance	131

> **LEARNING OBJECTIVES**
>
> After reading this chapter, you will be able to:
> - identify the major types of financial instruments, and explain how they broadly work;
> - describe the meaning and determinants of market interest rates, and the term structure of interest rates;
> - calculate stock returns and explain how stocks differ from fixed-income instruments;
> - explain how individuals and firms can invest in many stocks at the same time;
> - describe how rates of return are determined at a fundamental level for all types of assets, and how rates of return relate to the principles of finance;
> - learn how to use past asset returns to simulate the possible future distribution of returns.

✚ You have inherited $1 million, and want to invest it to allow it to grow over time. What types of financial investments are available to you?

✚ You are looking to finance the purchase of a car, and notice that the dealership charges a different interest rate depending on whether you take out a two-year or five-year loan. What is the reason for this?

- Your company is considering raising money by issuing bonds to investors. How much money can your company expect to raise, and what sorts of payments can your company expect to make to investors?

- You want to invest your savings in an investment that pays out its returns regularly, and are considering investing in bonds. You want to minimize the risk that you will lose all or part of your investment. What type of bonds should you buy?

- You have heard on the news that inflation is picking up. How does this affect any investments you've made in bonds?

- You want to invest in the stock market, but don't feel you have the knowledge to choose individual stocks. What can you do?

- You are an investment advisor providing advice to clients on investing in stocks and investing in bonds. What kinds of returns have these investments had in the past?

Introduction

In the previous chapters we introduced some of the conceptual underpinnings of finance. To engage in any financial transaction, however, requires interacting with some part of the financial system. For example, if you want to deposit cash into a savings account, you will have to do so at a bank.

The financial system refers to the markets and institutions used to carry out the decisions that households, business firms, and governments make about managing their money and other financial assets. The financial system includes:

- financial markets in which stocks, bonds, and other financial instruments are traded;
- financial intermediaries, the institutions—such as banks and insurance companies—that act as go-betweens in financial transactions;
- financial service firms, such as tax preparers and financial advisors, that help people and firms understand the various parts of the financial system and how they can take part in and benefit from this complex system; and
- regulators, the various governmental, economic, industrial, and business groups that set and enforce the rules by which all participants in the financial system must operate. The financial system (and indeed all markets) require rules to function at all, and require additional rules to function well.

In this chapter we focus on financial markets, describe the major types of financial instruments, and explain how their rates of return are measured and determined. This will lay the groundwork for us to assess the performance and risk of a financial investment, and to understand whether an investment will serve the needs of the investor looking to put money into it. To better understand how to assess and measure financial performance, we look at what rates of returns on stocks and bonds have been in the past around the world. In the subsequent parts of this book, we delve more deeply into the other entities that make up the financial system.

5.1 Financial Markets and Instruments

Financial markets are organized marketplaces in which financial assets or instruments are bought and sold. A financial instrument is a contract between two parties that has some monetary value, and that involves an exchange of cash flows. A security is a tradable financial instrument. The company or other entity issuing (i.e., creating) the security to be traded is called the issuer.

A country's regulatory structure determines what instruments are considered securities. In some countries and languages, the term "security" is commonly used to mean any form of financial instrument, even though the underlying legal and regulatory regime may have a narrower definition. For example, in the United States a security is defined as any kind of tradable financial instrument.

Sometimes a market for a particular financial product has a specific geographic location, such as the New York Stock Exchange (NYSE) or the Osaka Options and Futures Exchange, which are institutions housed in buildings in New York City and in Osaka, Japan, respectively. Often, however, the market has no one specific location. Such is the case for the over-the-counter markets—or off-exchange markets—in stocks, bonds, and currencies, which are essentially global electronic networks linking those that buy and sell financial assets.

Financial assets can be issued (i.e., created and sold) by any sort of entity, typically in order to raise money. They are also used for the purposes of managing risk, as we will discuss in Chapter 6. The basic types of financial assets are *debt*, *equity*, and *derivatives*. We provide an overview of each of these in this section.

5.1.1 Debt

Debt securities are issued by anyone who *borrows* money—firms, governments, and households. By issuing and selling a debt security, the issuer (the borrower) is selling a loan to a buyer (the lender). The issuer receives money from the buyer, and the issuer promises to pay back that money (plus more) to the buyer over time.

A typical example of a debt security is a bond, a loan issued by a company or government. The issuer sells the bond in financial markets for whatever price a buyer is willing to pay. The cash the issuer gets from the buyer is the amount of money the issuer is borrowing. The issuer then must pay back to the holder (the buyer) of the bond a promised amount of money (called the par or principal or face value amount) at some date in the future (called the maturity of the bond). Often, an issuer also promises to pay to the buyer additional fixed amounts (some percentage of the principal) known as interest payments (also known as coupon payments in the case of bonds) at specified intervals. These payments are legal obligations and failure to pay either interest or principal payments (known as default) can cause the issuer of the bond to go into bankruptcy. Some bonds are *secured*, meaning that some pre-specified asset will be provided by the issuer to the owner of the bond in the event of default. Other bonds are unsecured, in which case the owner of the bond receives nothing if the issuer defaults.

For example, a company may issue a bond that is a promise to pay an amount (principal) of $1,000 in three years (the maturity) plus interest (coupon payments) of $100 each year (10% of the principal). The buyer of this bond is lending the company some amount of money now. If the amount that the buyer pays the company now is, say, $900, then the timeline of cash flows to the buyer is shown in Figure 5.1. It is important to remember that bonds typically also pay interest payments at maturity, in addition to the principal amount.

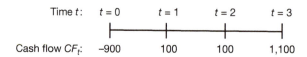

FIGURE 5.1 Example of a bond's cash flows. This figure illustrates a timeline of the cash flows to the buyer of a three-year $1,000 bond that costs $900 to purchase. This bond is a promise that the issuer will pay the holder the principal of $1,000 at maturity in three years and coupon payments of 10% of the principal each year.

The assets traded in debt markets include corporate bonds, government bonds, residential and commercial mortgages, and consumer loans. Debt instruments are also called fixed-income instruments because they promise to pay fixed sums of cash (interest) in the future. There are many terms for debt financial instruments, and those in finance often use these terms interchangeably. For clarity, throughout this text we will use "debt" when referring to the broad class of financial instruments related to borrowing, using more specific terms when it is necessary to distinguish between individual features of certain markets. The fact that debt instruments are traded means that the issuer must pay back the *owner* of the debt; this may be different from the person or entity that originally bought the debt (and thus lent money to the company), because the original purchaser can sell the debt to someone else.

Debt securities are classified by the maturity of the claims being traded. The market for short-term debt (which matures in less than one year) is called the money market, and the one for long-term debt (and equity securities) is called the capital market. Money market instruments are mostly interest-earning securities issued by governments (such as US Treasury bills) and reliable private sector borrowers (such as bonds issued by large corporations). Money markets are today globally integrated and liquid, where liquidity is defined by the relative ease, cost, and speed with which an asset can be converted into cash.

Some securities do not neatly fit into the classification of debt or equity. Hybrid securities, as the name suggests, combine some of the characteristics of debt and equity securities. Examples of hybrid securities include convertible bonds (bonds that can be converted into shares of common stock).

5.1.2 Equity

Equity is a financial instrument issued by a company that makes the purchaser of the instrument a partial owner of the firm. Equity securities issued by corporations are called common stocks or shares of stock (or just "stocks"). They are bought and sold in the stock market. By selling stock to investors, companies raise money that they can use for their operations. Investors typically buy shares of stock in the hope that the issuing firm will do well so that the share price (or value) will go up in the future, thus allowing them to make a profit when they sell the stock. Those who own shares of stock are known as shareholders.

Shares of stock may also give additional benefits to those that hold them. For example, the company may periodically give shareholders part of its profits through cash payments called dividends. Shareholders are also entitled to one vote on particular company matters. However, some corporations issue two classes of common stock, one with voting rights and the other without.

Common stock represents a residual claim on the assets of a corporation. The owners of common stock are entitled to any assets of the firm left over after it meets all of its other financial obligations. If, for example, the firm goes out of business and all of its assets are sold, common stockholders receive what, if anything, is left after all creditors (i.e., lenders to the company) are paid what they are owed.

Common stock also has the feature of limited liability. This means that if the firm is liquidated and the proceeds from the sale of its assets are not sufficient to pay off all the firm's debts, creditors cannot seek money from the common stockholders to meet this shortfall. The claims of the creditors of the corporation are limited to the assets of the firm. This characteristic also means that the price of a share of stock cannot go below zero, which would happen if a firm's creditors could demand money from shareholders that the firm could not pay.

In addition to common stock, a company can issue preferred stock, shares of stock that offer a fixed dividend that the issuing firm must pay before paying any dividend payments to common stock holders. Preferred stock is popular with income-seeking investors. However, as with common stock, failure to pay a preferred dividend on time does not precipitate bankruptcy.

5.1.3 Derivatives

Derivatives are financial instruments whose value is based on (derived from) the prices of one or more other assets such as equity securities, fixed-income securities, foreign currencies, or commodities such as gold and silver. Put differently, they are assets whose values are based on the behavior of the values of other assets. For example, a derivative might promise to pay you some amount of money if the price of another asset, such as a stock, goes above a certain level. The most common types of derivatives are options, forwards and futures, swap contracts, and asset-backed securities (ABS). Derivative instruments provide investors the ability to tailor investments to their specific needs—for example, by allowing them to earn a rate of return based on an asset without having to invest in the actual asset (such as gold), or to offset some sort of risk they have in their investment portfolios. Below, we provide a brief overview of what these types of contracts are; we provide the details of how they work and why investors may purchase them in Chapters 7 and 19.

Options. Options are financial contracts that allow the holder a choice in the future. A put option (or simply a put) is an option that gives its holder the right to sell or not sell an underlying asset at a specified price on or before some specified expiration date. When an owner of an asset buys a put option on that asset, she effectively is insuring it against a decline in its price below the price specified in the put-option contract. A call option (or simply a call) is an option that gives its holder the right to buy or not buy an underlying asset at a specified price on or before some specified expiration date. When an owner of an asset buys a call option on that asset, she is in a position to benefit if the asset's price rises above the price specified in the option contract.

Forwards and Futures. Forward contracts are instruments that *oblige* one party to the contract to buy, and the other party to sell, an asset at a specified price on a specified date. They permit buyers and sellers of the asset to eliminate the uncertainty about the future price—called the spot price—at which the asset will be exchanged. Futures contracts work in the same way as forward contracts, but offer standardized terms and are traded on financial exchanges.

Swaps. A swap is a financial contract that commits two parties to exchange the cash flows that come from two different financial assets. Swaps can be created based on almost any kind of financial instrument, such as ones based on interest rates, foreign currency exchange rates, or stock markets. This exchange of cash flows makes it possible for one investor to exchange cash flows they no longer want with another investor (for whom the cash flows may better meet their needs), and in turn gain cash flows that are more desirable. This cash flow swap allows investors to tailor their portfolio of investments to better suit their needs. For example, a party that owns assets whose cash flows might go up or down depending on how interest rates change can enter into a swap exchanging those possibly changing cash flows for cash flows based on a more stable or fixed interest rate.

Asset-backed securities. An asset-backed security (ABS) is a financial contract that provides cash flows to investors that are "backed" by some sort of underlying asset, such as mortgage loans or car loans. For example, an ABS could be created by a bank that has extended a number of mortgages to individuals to buy a house (this is known as a mortgage-backed security [MBS]). The mortgage payments that the individuals make to the bank are the cash flows that are paid to the ABS investors.

> QUICK CHECK 5.1 Provide an example of a debt security, an equity security, and a derivative security and explain the goals they allow buyers and sellers to achieve.

5.2 Financial Market Rates: Interest Rates

Through the news media and online, every day we are showered with reports of financial market indicators, which track how the various assets in financial markets described in the previous section are performing. In this section and the next, we explain the meaning of the various rates that are reported.

For debt securities, interest rates are an important indicator of the financial instrument's performance. An interest rate is a rate of return promised by a borrower to a lender in exchange for borrowing money. As we will describe in more detail shortly, interest rates incorporate both Principle 1, the time value of money, and Principle 7, the trade-off between risk and return, which we discuss in detail in Chapter 6. There are as many different interest rates as there are distinct kinds of borrowing and lending. For example, the interest rate that home buyers pay on the loans they take to finance their homes is called the mortgage rate, whereas the rate charged by banks on loans made to businesses is called the commercial loan rate.

The interest rate on any type of loan or debt instrument depends on a number of factors, but the most important are its time pattern of promised payments, its unit of account, and its default risk. Let us define each of these factors:

- The time pattern of promised payments varies with the type of debt instrument and its maturity—the length of the time period between when the instrument was issued until the last payment is made. The maturity of debt may be short (less than a year) or long (30 years), and some instruments promise to pay their holders some amount (in interest) every month until maturity, some pay every year until maturity, and some do not pay anything until maturity.
- The unit of account is the medium in which payments are denominated. The unit of account is usually a currency, such as dollars, pounds, euros, pesos, yen, and so on. Sometimes the unit of account is a commodity such as gold or silver or some standard "basket" of goods and services. The interest rate varies depending on the unit of account.
- Default risk is the possibility that some portion of the interest or the principal on a fixed-income instrument will not be repaid in full. The greater the instrument's default risk, the higher the interest rate the issuer must promise to investors to get them to buy it.

We begin by considering how each of these three factors affects interest rates in the real world. As we cover the various aspects that can cause differences in interest rates, it is important to keep in mind the core principle of the law of one price (Principle 2): Competition in financial markets ensures that interest rates on *equivalent* assets are the same.

5.2.1 How the Time Pattern of Promised Payments Affects Interest Rates

Different debt securities specify different time patterns of promised payments—that is, *when* the issuer is supposed to pay the holder of the security (both the maturity date and the dates of interest payments). As we introduced with Principle 1 in Chapter 2, interest rates reflect the time value of money, the fact that money in the future is worth less than money today. Interest rates differ depending on the maturity date: An interest rate for borrowing funds due to be repaid in three years is often different from an interest rate for borrowing funds due to be repaid in one year. This is because expectations for what will happen in three years are different from expectations for what will happen in the next year. Expectations about what will happen regarding economic growth, inflation, and government monetary policy all play a role in determining interest rates in the market.

To illustrate, consider a bond that matures in two years, and promises to make interest payments every year. The timeline of the cash flows if you own the bond is therefore:

Recall that the interest that bonds pay equals the interest rate times the promised principal amount. What interest rate should this bond pay? The answer depends on the prevailing interest rates in the economy. If an investor can earn higher interest rates by investing in, say, a one-year US Treasury bond or a two-year savings account, then the investor has no incentive to invest in this bond. The bond's issuer would therefore need to pay a higher interest rate, depending on what the interest rates are for both one-year and two-year horizons.

These differences in market interest rates over different time periods lead to differences in interest rates across debt with different maturities. Market interest rates for borrowing over different time periods is known as the term structure of interest rates. Figure 5.2 provides a visual description of the term structure of interest rates, where $r_{0,1}$ is the one-year spot interest rate, which is the interest rate charged right now for borrowing money for one year; and $r_{0,2}$ is the two-year spot interest rate, the interest rate charged right now for borrowing money over two years.

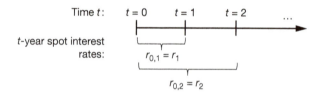

FIGURE 5.2 Term structure of interest rates. This figure provides a visualization of the term structure of interest rates, which represents interest rates charged right now for borrowing at different periods in the future. $r_{0,1}$ is the one-year spot interest rate; $r_{0,2}$ is the two-year spot interest rate, which is the interest rate charged right now for borrowing money over two years.

In understanding Figure 5.2, consider the two-year spot interest rate, denoted by $r_{0,2}$, or r_2 for short. This rate represents the interest rate for borrowing money now that will be paid back in two years. Interest rates are typically quoted in annual terms—in other words, the amount of money C you would have in two years is *not* $\$C \times (1 + r_2)$, but rather $\$C \times (1 + r_2)^2$.

These interest rates can be determined from the yields on zero-coupon bonds. Zero-coupon bonds are bonds that only pay at a single point in time. That is, they pay the principal at maturity but no interest in the interim.

The zero-coupon bonds issued by the US Treasury are called STRIPS (which stands for Separate Trading of Registered Interest and Principal of Securities). STRIPS are not issued or sold directly to investors, and are instead purchased through financial institutions and government securities brokers and dealers, which then sell them (or securities constructed from them) to investors. There are STRIPS of different maturities, which allow us to determine the interest rates they imply. For example, suppose you see the current price of a two-year STRIPS bond, which pays $100 in two years, is $95. The rate of return of this bond implied by this price is whatever rate the current price would need to grow by to eventually turn into the promised payment. Remember that these rates are all in annual terms (i.e., annualized), which is why we multiply by $(1 + \text{rate})^2$:

$$\text{Price} \times (1 + \text{rate})^2 = \text{Principal}$$
$$\$95 \times (1 + \text{rate})^2 = \$100$$
$$\text{Rate} = 5.26\%.$$

This rate of return is known as the bond's yield to maturity (YTM or yield). The YTM is formally defined as the internal rate of return of a bond, or the discount rate that sets the present value of the bond's payments equal to its price. It can also be calculated for coupon bonds, which pay cash payments over their lifetime. Thus, the YTM depends not only on its final maturity date, but also its pattern of payments. We go over YTM calculations in detail in Part III. Finding the yields for STRIPS of various maturities, which indicate the implied interest rates for each, allows us to construct a yield curve. The yield curve is a graphical description of the term structure of interest rates, and it shows how interest rates change given the particular time horizon considered.

Figure 5.3 shows the US Treasury zero-coupon yield curve on 10 July 2020. This yield curve depicts the relation between interest rates (yields) on fixed-income instruments issued by the US Treasury and the maturity of the instrument as of 10 July 2020 (the orange line). In Figure 5.3 we see that the annualized yield on one-year Treasury obligations was about 0.17% per year; on 30-year obligations, the YTM increased to about 1.53% per year.

The shape and the level of the yield curve change significantly over time. At times in the past, short-term rates have been higher than long-term rates, so that the yield curve has sloped downward from left to right. The blue line depicts what the same yield curve looked like one year prior, on 10 July 2019. Interest rates at that time were substantially higher.

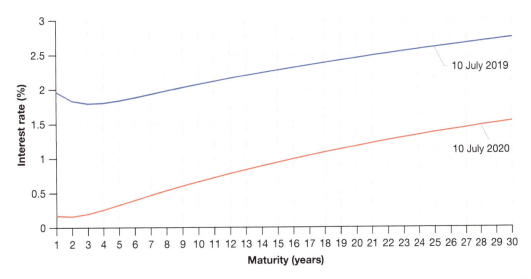

FIGURE 5.3 US Treasury zero-coupon yield curve. This figure depicts an example of the yield curve for zero-coupon US Treasury bonds on two dates, 10 July 2019 (blue line) and 10 July 2020 (orange line). The lines plot the YTM for zero-coupon Treasury bonds of the indicated maturities. Yields were higher in 2019, reflecting a drop in interest rates between 2019 and 2020.

The US Treasury reports information on par bonds, the prices of which can also be used to construct a yield curve. A par bond is a bond whose price equals its face value. To illustrate, consider a bond that matures in two years, with a face value of $100 that promises to make interest payments every year of 4% of its face value. If this bond trades at a price of $100, then it is a par bond. The promised interest payments (coupons) of par Treasury bonds provide information about interest rates in the economy over different time horizons. In many financial analyses we look at the yields of Treasury bonds because they allow us to examine the behavior of interest rates without having to consider the effects of default risk on a bond.

To illustrate the information we can get on yields from par bonds, consider how the interest rate on default-free par bonds varies with maturity. Figure 5.4 shows the yield curve for an example date of 30 Oct. 2020.

With a complete set of zero-coupon bonds for all different maturities into the future, it is possible to find the price of *any* fixed-income instrument that is free of default risk, because these zero-coupon interest rates represent the appropriate opportunity cost of capital for equivalent assets. This is because, as we noted in Chapter 4, if two assets both have no default risk and are otherwise equivalent (i.e., the same maturity), then by the law of one price (Principle 2) their implied interest rates would need to be the same.

Knowledge of the term structure of interest rates and the yield curve is the starting point for virtually any valuation model used in finance. This is because these rates give the basic rates of return for essentially any asset—that is, they give us a "base" for discount rates. This base can then be adjusted appropriately for various sources of risk (such as default risk). Because it gives us information on the base situation with *no* risk, the term structure of interest rates serves an important role in terms of Principles 4 (choosing the best valuation model) and 6 (dealing with uncertainty), which we discuss in detail in the next chapter.

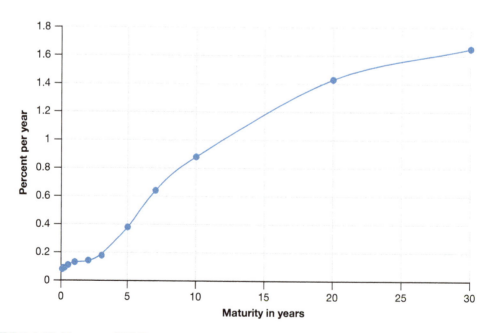

FIGURE 5.4 Yield curve of US Treasury par bonds, 30 Oct. 2020. This graph depicts the yield curve as of 30 Oct. 2020. Each point on the curve represents the YTM for US Treasury par bonds of the indicated maturity. The curve's upward slope indicates that the yields for bonds with longer maturities are higher.

Box 5.1 The History of STRIPS

Because of their use as riskless rates that can be used in discounting, the information on rates of return provided by STRIPS is a powerful tool for valuation. If we want to accurately value any cash flow, we would like to have the prices of zero-coupon bonds of all possible maturities. Until very recently, however, bond market price data rarely came in zero-coupon form. Even today, the US Treasury issues only two different security types: bills with maturities up to one year, which are issued in pure discount form, and notes and bonds with a semi-annual coupon, which are usually issued at or close to par. For many years "implied" interest rates on zero-coupon bonds with maturities longer than one year could only be inferred from the observed prices of coupon bonds.

More recently, investment banking firms have developed a secondary market for US Treasury STRIPS. These firms buy US Treasury bonds and sell off their component cash flows as if they were zero-coupon bonds. Observing the market prices of the resulting US Treasury STRIPS, investors can now have direct knowledge of the zero-coupon yield curve. This improvement in the information provided by financial markets was not the intention of the firms that created the US Treasury STRIPS, but rather was a byproduct of their profit-making activities. As the markets for fixed-income securities and their derivatives continue to evolve, more and more information useful in valuing other fixed-income instruments will become available.

> QUICK CHECK 5.2 Go to treasury.gov and discover what the level and shape of the US Treasury yield curve is.

5.2.2 How the Unit of Account Affects Interest Rates

The interest rate for a debt instrument also depends on the unit of account, which is the units in which the payments are denominated. A fixed-income instrument may be risk-free only in terms of its own unit of account, and interest rates vary depending on the unit of account. To see this, consider bonds denominated in different currencies.

Suppose the interest rate on UK government bonds is much higher than that on Japanese government bonds of comparable maturity. Because the bonds from both countries are free of default risk, shouldn't all investors prefer the UK bonds? The answer is no because the bonds are denominated in different currencies. The payments (and thus returns) on UK government bonds are denominated in pounds, and the payments and returns on Japanese government bonds are denominated in yen. Although the bonds offer a risk-free rate of return in their own currency, the rate of return in any other currency is uncertain because it depends on the exchange rate, the price of one currency in terms of the other, between the currencies when payments are received in the future.

For example, suppose you are investing for one year. The interest rate on a one-year Japanese government bond is 3%, and at the same time it is 9% on a one-year UK government bond. The exchange rate is currently 150 yen per pound. Suppose you are a Japanese investor who wants a safe investment in terms of yen. If you buy the Japanese bond, you will earn 3% for sure. If you buy the UK government bond, however, your rate of return *in yen* depends on the yen–pound exchange rate one year from now. If the value of the pound in terms of the yen falls by more than 6%, you will earn less than 3% in terms of yen on the UK bond.

Let's demonstrate this with numbers. Suppose you invest £100 in a UK bond. At an exchange rate of ¥150 to £1, this equates to 100 × 150 = 15,000 yen. To invest in the UK bond, you will have to convert ¥15,000 into pounds. Because the interest rate on the UK bond is 9%, you will receive £100 × 1.09 = £109 one year from now. The value of the £109 in yen is not known now because the future yen–pound exchange rate is unknown.

Your realized yen rate of return will be:

$$\text{Yen rate of return} = \frac{(\pounds 109 \times \text{future yen price of a pound }(\yen/\pounds)) - (\pounds 100 \times \text{current yen price of a pound }(\yen/\pounds))}{\yen 15{,}000}.$$

Suppose the yen price of the pound falls during the year, so that the yen–pound exchange rate is ¥140 to £1 one year from now. What will the realized yen rate of return on the UK bond be?

Substituting into the preceding expression, we get:

$$\begin{aligned}
\text{Yen rate of return} &= \frac{(\pounds 109 \times 140) - (\pounds 100 \times 150)}{\yen 15{,}000} \\
&= \frac{(\pounds 109 \times 140) - \yen 15{,}000}{\yen 15{,}000} \\
&= 0.0173.
\end{aligned}$$

Thus, your *realized* yen rate of return will be 1.73%, which is less than the 3% risk-free yen interest rate you could have earned on one-year Japanese bonds.

> **QUICK CHECK 5.3** From the discussion of the pound–yen exchange rate, recalculate the realized yen rate of return if the current yen–pound exchange rate were instead ¥140 to £1.

Example 5.1 (Rates of Return and Different Currencies): Suppose that the euro–dollar exchange rate is €1 to $1.3 now. It is expected to change to €1 to $1.4 in one year. If you invest $1,000 into an account denominated in euros that pays an interest rate of 5%, what is your rate of return for that account in dollars? If the US risk-free rate of return is 3%, is the euro account an attractive investment opportunity for you?

Solution. First, note that to invest in the euro account you must convert the $1,000 into euros. The exchange rate is $1.3 to €1, which means that $1 is equal to 1/1.3 = €0.77 today. Thus, $1,000 becomes $1,000 × 0.77 = €770. Now, at a 5% interest rate, this €770 will grow to 770 × 1.05 = 808.5 in one year. The €808.5 will then need to be converted back to dollars, and to do so we multiply by 1.4 (what we expect the exchange rate in a year will be). The rate of return in dollars, based on the initial investment of $1,000, will therefore be:

$$\text{Dollar rate of return} = \frac{(\text{\euro} 808.5 \times 1.4) - \$1{,}000}{\$1{,}000} = 13.2\%.$$

The key to calculating these rates of return is to make sure all components are expressed in the same currency—in this case, we want the rate of return in dollars.

Note that this rate of return is substantially higher than the US risk-free rate of 3%, making it an attractive investment if we are sure about what the exchange rate will be in one year.

Box 5.2   World of Business: Series I Saving Bonds

Series I Savings Bonds, or I bonds, are a savings bond issued by the US Treasury. The rate of an I bond adjusts to track inflation and it is guaranteed to never lose value.

First issued in 1998, Series I Savings Bonds (I bonds) are a type of savings bond sold by the US Treasury. I bonds are designed to guarantee a real rate of return, regardless of inflation, deflation, or what's happening in financial markets. To do this, I bonds adjust their rate every six months to track changes in the level of inflation as measured by the consumer price index for all urban consumers (CPI-U). Even in periods of deflation, I bonds protect your investment by never losing value because the US Treasury has set a floor on the rate at 0%.

Because I bonds cannot lose value and are backed by the US government, they are frequently chosen by investors over corporate or municipal bonds, which can default or lose value.

The US Treasury considers I bonds to be a long-term investment. As such, there are several limitations on I bonds that must be considered when analyzing your financial goals. I bonds have a one-year minimum hold time in which the bond cannot be redeemed. Additionally, bonds are subject to a three-month interest penalty if the bond is redeemed within five years of the issue date. Similar to other US Treasury bonds, I bonds continue to earn interest for 30 years. After that time, the matured bond is worth the face value plus the interest collected over that time.

Source: Treasury Direct (n.d.). I bonds.

5.2.3 How Default Risk Affects Interest Rates

All debt securities promise to pay back to their holders specific amounts of money in the future. However, the issuer of the debt security may sometimes default on the promised payments and not pay the full amount that they owe. A default can happen because the issuer—whether a company or a government—does poorly financially and does not have enough money to pay all of its obligations. The risk that an issuer will not make its promised debt payments is known as default risk. The higher the default risk on fixed-income instruments, the higher the interest rate, holding all other features constant. This is in line with Principle 6, that there is a trade-off between risk and expected return, with the interest rate determining the expected return for debt securities.

To illustrate why this is the case, consider two bonds issued by two different companies: A and B. For both, in exchange for you paying the company $100, the company promises to pay you back $100 in one year plus some interest on the $100 (denoted by r_A for the Company A bond and r_B for the Company B bond). From your perspective, the cash flows of each bond are as follows:

Time t:	$t = 0$	$t = 1$
Company A bond:	−100	$100 + (r_A \times 100)$
Company B bond:	−100	$100 + (r_B \times 100)$

Now suppose that you find out that Company B has a good chance of going out of business before next year, in which case you will receive *no* money at $t = 1$ from Company B. Would you purchase the bond from Company B? If the interest rates r_A and r_B are the same, then you would *never* buy the bond from Company B. For example, if the interest rates are both 10%, then for Company A you will receive $100 + (0.10 \times 100) = \$110$ for sure in one year in exchange for $100, while for Company B you *may* receive that $110 in exchange for your $100, but never more than $110 and you may receive less. For you to be persuaded to buy the bond from Company B, you would demand to be paid more in promised interest—that is, r_B would have to be greater than r_A. If the interest rate for Company B's bonds was not higher than that for Company A's bonds, Company A's bond would absolutely dominate Company B's bond. This situation would permit an arbitrage to be made by buying the bonds from Company A and selling the bonds from Company B. Competition in financial markets—enforced by the forces of arbitrage—ensures that interest rates on equivalent assets are the same; thus, interest rates on assets that are *not* equivalent must be different.

A risk-free asset is one without default risk, and the interest rate attached to that asset is a risk-free interest rate. There may be many different risk-free rates, based on the maturity being examined and currency (as we explain shortly). Table 5.1 shows the interest rates on US dollar-denominated bonds for issuers with different degrees of default risk. US Treasury bonds have the least default risk (and are the closest to risk-free), followed by high-quality corporate bonds (i.e., bonds issued by companies in good financial shape).

Table 5.1 Interest rates and yield spreads (relative to 20-year Treasury bonds) for corporate bonds. This table shows the interest rate (yield to maturity, YTM) and yield spread (the YTM minus the yield on Treasury bonds) for the indicated bonds. The yield for 20-year Treasury bonds is the lowest because it has the lowest possible default risk. Aaa-rated corporate bonds have higher yields than Treasury bonds because there is a small chance of default, and Baa-rated corporate bonds have the highest yields and yield spread because they have a higher default risk.

Bond	Interest rate (YTM)	Yield spread
20-year Treasury bonds	3.26%	–
Corporate bonds (Aaa-rated)	4.06%	0.80%
Corporate bonds (Baa-rated)	5.10%	1.84%

Note: Data are from the St. Louis Federal Reserve Bank's Economic Data. Rates are as of 25 June 2022. Corporate bonds yields are for 20-year and above maturity bonds. The 20-year Treasury bond is for a constant maturity.

The default risk of a corporate bond is summarized by its bond rating, a grade for individual bonds that is issued by financial companies called ratings agencies. Ratings agencies rate the bonds issued by corporations based on how likely the bonds are to default. A bond may be more likely to default because it is more "junior"—that is, the company is legally obligated to pay other financial claims before that bond—or because the company is not doing well financially. All of these factors are incorporated into a credit rating. For example, Moody's is a major credit rating agency in the United States that gives the highest-quality bonds—those least likely to default—a rating of Aaa. Bonds with a higher ("medium") likelihood of default are rated Baa. Bonds in the lowest rating, which are very likely to default (or have already defaulted), are rated C. Moody's also has ratings in between these different categories.

Consider the difference in yields—called the yield spread—between Treasury bonds with maturities of 20 years (3.26% per year) and corporate bonds of high quality with similar maturities (4.06% per year). The yield spread is 0.80% per year, which reflects the fact that corporate bonds are riskier than US Treasury bonds.

The risk-free interest rate and yield spread are important tools for measuring the risk of debt securities. The yield on a corporate bond is the *maximum* return that an investor can get. If there is a positive probability of default, then the *expected value* of the rate of return on the bond will be less than the quoted yield.

> QUICK CHECK 5.4 Go to the St. Louis Federal Reserve Economic Research website (https://fred.stlouisfed.org) and find information on Aaa corporate bond yields relative to ten-year Treasury bonds. What does this data series represent? Do you see any noticeable patterns?

5.2.4 How Inflation Affects Interest Rates

Inflation is the general rise in prices in the economy over time. People have long recognized that the prices of goods, services, and assets must be corrected for the effects of inflation in order to make meaningful economic comparisons over time. To correct for the effects of inflation, economists distinguish between what they call nominal prices, prices in terms of some currency, and real prices, prices that adjust for purchasing power in order to make meaningful comparisons across time.

Inflation affects interest rates because a high inflation rate implies that a given amount of money in the future will be less valuable (less able to purchase goods); this effect will be incorporated into the interest rates that investors demand. Because the rate of inflation can be different for different currencies, inflation is also an important force that interacts with the unit of account.

Just as we distinguish between nominal and real prices, so too we distinguish between *nominal* and *real* interest rates. The nominal interest rate on a bond is the promised amount of money you receive per unit you lend. The real interest rate is defined as the nominal interest rate you earn corrected for the change in the purchasing power of money. Because inflation usually erodes how much $1 can buy over time, real interest rates are generally lower than nominal interest rates. Real interest rates adjust for the fact that the amount you make in interest in the future can buy less because of inflation.

For example, if you earn a nominal interest rate of 8% per year and the rate of price inflation is also 8% per year, then the real rate of return is zero. The intuition is that you may have made $108 ($100 × 1.08) by investing/lending $100, but that $108 will only be able to buy as many goods as $100 today. You therefore will not have made any additional money if we consider what you can buy with it.

The unit of account for computing the real rate of return is some standardized basket of consumption goods. The real rate of return, therefore, depends on the composition of the basket of consumption goods. In discussions of real rates of return in different countries, the general practice is to take whatever basket is used to compute the national consumer price index (CPI). This basket includes items that people typically spend money on, such as housing costs, recreational expenses, groceries, and so forth. The CPI therefore tracks how much the price of that basket changes over time, which is used as a measure of inflation.

What is the real rate of return if the nominal interest rate is 8% per year, and the rate of inflation as measured by the proportional change in the CPI is 5% per year? Intuition suggests that it is the difference between the nominal interest rate and the rate of inflation, which is 8% − 5% = 3% per year in this case. That is approximately correct, but not exactly so.

To see why, let us compute the real rate of return precisely. For every $100 you invest now, you will receive $108 one year from now. But a basket of consumption goods, which now costs $100, will cost $105 one year from now. How much will your future value of $108 be worth in terms of consumption goods? To find the answer we must divide the $108 by the future price of a consumption basket: $108/$105 = 1.02857 baskets. Thus, for every basket you give up now, you will get the equivalent of 1.02857 baskets one year from now. The real rate of return (baskets in the future per basket invested today) is, therefore, 2.857% per year.

The general formula relating the real rate of return to the nominal rate of interest and the rate of inflation is:

$$1 + \text{real rate of return} = \frac{1 + \text{nominal interest rate}}{1 + \text{rate of inflation}}, \tag{5.1}$$

or equivalently,

$$\text{Real rate of return} = \frac{\text{nominal interest rate} - \text{rate of inflation}}{1 + \text{rate of inflation}}.$$

Substituting into this formula a nominal interest rate of 8% and a rate of inflation of 5%, the real rate of return becomes:

$$\text{Real rate of return} = \frac{0.08 - 0.05}{1.05} = 2.857\%.$$

If the expected rate of inflation is 5% per year, then the expected real rate of return is 2.857% per year. But if the rate of inflation turns out to be higher than 5%, the realized real rate will be less than 2.857%.

Note that a fixed-income instrument that is risk-free in nominal terms will not necessarily be risk-free in real terms. This is because rates of inflation are not known for certain in advance. This uncertainty introduces risk when we consider rates in real terms.

There are various ways to protect against inflation risk. Some bonds have their interest and principal denominated in terms of the basket of goods and services used to compute the cost of living in a particular country. For example, the government of the United Kingdom has been issuing such index-linked bonds since 1981. The US Treasury started issuing such bonds in January 1997. They are called Treasury Inflation Protected Securities (TIPS). The interest rate on these bonds is a risk-free real rate. In September 1998, the US Treasury added inflation-protected savings bonds.

To illustrate how TIPS work, consider one that matures in one year. Assume that it offers a risk-free real rate of interest of 3% per year. The rate of return in dollars is not known with certainty in advance because it depends on the rate of inflation. If the inflation rate turns out to be only 2%, then the realized dollar rate of return will be approximately 5%; if, however, the rate of inflation turns out to be 10%, then the realized dollar rate of return will be approximately 13%.

To summarize, an interest rate is a promised rate of return. Because most bonds offer an interest rate that is denominated in terms of some currency, their real rate of return in terms of consumption goods is uncertain. In the case of inflation-indexed bonds, the interest rate is denominated in terms of some basket of consumer goods and it is a risk-free real rate for that basket.

> QUICK CHECK 5.5 Suppose the risk-free nominal interest rate on a one-year US Treasury bill is 6% per year and the expected rate of inflation is 3% per year. What is the expected real rate of return on the Treasury bill? Why is the Treasury bill risky in real terms?

5.3 Financial Market Rates: Stocks and Equity Funds

As we discussed in the previous section, interest rates are *promised* rates of return on fixed-income instruments. As a result, they are a contractual obligation—the issuer *must* pay interest (or face the possibility of bankruptcy). However, many assets do not carry a promised rate of return. For example, if you invest in stocks, there is no promise of specified cash payments in the future. Because the cash flows (and therefore values) of such assets are not predictable, we say that they have an

5.3 FINANCIAL MARKET RATES: STOCKS AND EQUITY FUNDS

"inherent randomness" to them.[1] Let us now consider how to measure the rate of return on such risky assets.

5.3.1 Stocks

When you invest in common stocks, the *return* comes from two sources. The first source is cash payments called dividends that are paid to the stockholder by the firm that issued the stocks. These dividend payments are not contractually required, unlike interest payments. Dividends are paid to stockholders at the discretion of the firm's board of directors.

The second source of return to the stockholder is any gain (or loss) in the market price of the stock over the period it is held. This second type of return is called a capital gain or capital loss. The length of the holding period for measuring returns on stock can be as short as a day or as long as several decades.

To illustrate how returns are measured, suppose you buy shares of stock at a price of $100 per share. One day later the price is $101 per share and you sell. Your *rate of return R* for the day is 1%—a capital gain of $1 per share divided by the purchase price of $100:

$$R = \frac{\$101 - \$100}{\$100} = 1\%.$$

If stocks pay a dividend, however, calculating their return becomes slightly more complicated. When a stock pays a dividend, the share price goes *down* because the company must use up cash to pay its dividend—cash that the company no longer has, and thus no longer is incorporated into the stock price. Because investors receive the money from the dividend, we add the dividend back in to properly calculate the rate of return. The one-year rate of return R is therefore:

$$R = \frac{\text{ending price of a share} - \text{beginning price} + \text{cash dividend}}{\text{beginning price}}. \quad (5.2)$$

Suppose you hold the stock for a year. At the end of the year, the stock pays a cash dividend of $3 per share and the price of a share is $105 just after the dividend is paid. In this case, we have:

$$\begin{aligned} R &= \frac{\$105 - \$100 + \$3}{\$100} \\ &= 0.08 \text{ or } 8\%. \end{aligned}$$

If you decide *not* to sell your shares at the end of the year? The answer is that you measure the rate of return exactly the same way, whether or not you sell the stock. The price appreciation of $5 per share is as much a part of your return as is the $3 dividend. That you choose to keep the stock rather than sell it does not alter the fact that you could convert it into $105 of cash at the end of the year. Thus, whether you decide to realize your capital gain by selling the stock or to reinvest it (by not selling), your rate of return is 8%.

> **QUICK CHECK 5.6** You invest in a stock costing $50. It pays a cash dividend during the year of $1, and you expect its price to be $60 at year's end. What is your expected rate of return? If the stock's price is actually $40 at year's end, what is your realized rate of return?

---

[1] Bonds that have the possibility of default also have a randomness to them in the sense that they may not pay what they promised. In contrast, however, the lack of any sort of promised amounts for stocks adds a greater degree of randomness.

5.3.2 Market Indexes and Mutual Funds

It is useful for many purposes to have a measure of the overall level of stock prices. For example, people holding multiple stocks might want an indicator of the current value of their investment, or they might want a benchmark—a comparison group—against which to measure the performance of their own investment in stocks. A 5% increase in a stock's price may seem like good performance, but it's not if the overall stock market increased by 20% in the same period. A stock index represents the overall price level of a collection of stocks in a given industry (like the automotive industry or technology sector), country, or even globally. Table 5.2 lists the stock indexes generally reported in the financial press for the stocks traded on major national stock exchanges around the world.

Table 5.2 Major stock indexes around the world.

Country	Index
United States	Dow Jones Industrial Average, S&P 500, Russell 2000, NASDAQ
Japan	Nikkei, TOPIX
United Kingdom	FTSE
Germany	DAX
China	Shanghai Composite, Hang Seng
France	CAC 40
Europe, Australia, Asia	MSCI EAFE
India	Nifty, Sensex
Brazil	Bovespa
Global	MSCI World

Stock indexes provide common benchmarks for different stock investment strategies. Some investors purchase individual stocks and use stock indexes as a useful benchmark for performance—for instance, if you purchase a share of stock in Microsoft, an appropriate benchmark to compare performance may be an index representing the US technology sector. Other times, investors may put their money into an investment fund known as a mutual fund, which is run by a professional money manager who takes investors' money and invests it into a range of investments, sometimes including both stocks and bonds. Some mutual funds are actively managed, meaning that the money manager may buy and sell the fund's securities frequently according to some strategy. For other mutual funds, the goal is to match or beat the performance of an index such as the S&P 500 or an industry index.

An alternative goal of some mutual funds is indexing, an investment strategy that seeks to match the investment returns of a specified stock market index. When indexing, an investment manager attempts to replicate the investment results of the target index by holding all—or in the case of very large indexes, a representative sample—of the securities in the index. There is no attempt to use "active" money management (frequent buying and selling) or to make "bets" on individual stocks or narrow industry sectors in an attempt to outpace the index. There are two key advantages of indexing. First, holding many different stocks reduces risk through diversification, as we will discuss in the next chapter. Second, trading stocks infrequently reduces the trading fees and other transaction costs associated with buying and selling individual stocks.

To shed light on this second advantage—that indexing reduces transaction costs—consider the evidence on investing in an index compared to investing in individual stocks or mutual funds. Since

1926, the US stock market has provided investors with an average return of about 10% per year. That figure, however, does not take into account any costs associated with buying and selling stocks. These costs come in the form of an investment fund's expense ratio, which is how much a fund charges in fees as a percentage of money invested. The expense ratio covers the various expenses that the fund incurs, including advisory fees, distribution charges (the cost of sending money to investors), and other operating expenses. Portfolio transaction costs, which are costs for buying or selling individual securities, are also included.

Traditional mutual fund managers have high portfolio activity; the average fund's portfolio yearly turnover rate (the proportion of the assets that are sold and replaced) was 47% in 2005. This trading leads to a high expense ratio for these funds: In 2020, the average general-equity mutual fund had an annual expense ratio of 1.54% of investor assets. Thus, if you invested $100,000 in a fund, an expense ratio of 1.54% means that the fund will remove 1.54% × $100,000 = $1,540 from any profits you would normally make. In addition, these expenses take a significant bite out of the investment-return pie. Funds charging sales commissions swallow even more of the returns.

An index fund is a special type of mutual fund that aims to match the performance of a specific stock index. In contrast to other mutual funds, one of the key advantages of an index fund is its low cost. An index fund requires only minimal advisory fees, can keep operating expenses at the lowest level, and holds portfolio transaction costs to a minimum. Moreover, because index funds engage in much lower portfolio turnover than actively managed funds, there is a strong (but by no means assured) tendency for index funds to realize and distribute only modest—if any—capital gains to shareholders. Because these distributions are taxable for all shareholders, it is an advantage to defer their realization as long as possible. Over time, the broad stock market indexes have outperformed the average mutual fund that invests in stocks because of the higher transaction costs of the actively managed equity mutual funds.

Of course, there will always be actively managed funds that outperform index funds. It may just be luck—pure chance would say that some investment managers will provide exceptional returns and they may even have superior performance over lengthy winning streaks. Or, it may be skill: There may be some investment managers with truly outstanding abilities who can consistently earn superior returns over time. The problem in selecting actively managed funds is identifying in advance those that will be consistently superior over time.

5.3.3 Exchange-Traded Funds

A type of investment fund that is similar to a mutual fund is an exchange-traded fund (ETF). As the name implies, ETFs are investment funds that are traded on exchanges—just as stocks are—allowing any investor to buy a share of the fund. The fund invests in a variety of assets, as mutual funds do. When the value of the fund's investments goes up, the value of the shares that investors own go up in turn. Many ETFs seek to match the investment returns of indexes such as the S&P 500, thus giving investors an easy way to earn the returns of the broad market.

Exchange-traded funds give investors an alternative to giving their money to the money managers who run mutual funds. An investor can just go to an exchange like the NYSE and purchase a share in an ETF. Exchange-traded funds have two other advantages over mutual funds: greater liquidity and a tax advantage.

They offer relatively easy liquidity to investors, meaning that investors can more easily convert their ETF shares into cash by selling them through an exchange whenever the market is open. In contrast, because the cash invested in mutual funds is invested in various assets by money managers, an investor's request to withdraw money from the fund must go to the money manager and thus may not be immediate. Furthermore, the manager may charge fees or place other restrictions on withdrawals from the fund.

Exchange-traded funds also offer a tax advantage over mutual funds. Buying and selling securities is a necessary strategy for every fund, and any security that has appreciated in value results in a capital gain that is subject to a capital gains tax when it is sold. However, due to certain trading rules, ETFs are able to exchange securities "in kind," allowing them to avoid taxation on the capital gains that would be realized on many transactions. This, in turn, reduces the taxation hit that is passed along to investors.

> **Box 5.3** Different Stock Market Indexes
>
> In the United States, perhaps the stock index most often cited in the news is the Dow Jones Industrial Index (DJI), an index of the prices of 30 stocks of major industrial US corporations. While the DJI is a useful barometer of the performance of different sectors of the economy because it includes many of the leaders in those sectors, it has two major defects that limit its usefulness as a benchmark for measuring stock performance. One is that it is not diversified enough to accurately reflect the wide spectrum of stocks in the United States. The other is that it corresponds to a portfolio strategy that is unsuitable as a performance benchmark.
>
> Most investment professionals, therefore, prefer to use other indexes such as the Standard and Poor's 500 (S&P 500) as a performance benchmark. The S&P 500 index corresponds to a portfolio of 500 stocks selected from among the largest public corporations in the United States, with dollar amounts invested in each corporation in proportion to its share of the total market value.
>
> To illustrate the construction of these two types of indexes and to compare them, let us simplify matters by analyzing a hypothetical two-stock index. The two stocks in the index are IBM (International Business Machines) and HPQ (Hewlett-Packard Company). The DJI-type index is computed by taking the average current price of a share of each stock, dividing by the average price in the base year, and multiplying the result by 100.
>
> $$\text{DJI type index} = \frac{\text{average of current stock prices}}{\text{average of stock prices in base year}} \times 100.$$
>
> Let us say that in the base year the prices were $100 per share for IBM and $50 for HPQ. The average price per share, computed by adding the two prices and dividing by 2, is, therefore, $75. A year later, the prices are $50 per share for IBM and $110 per share for HPQ, and the average is $80. The DJI-type index would, therefore, show a value of 106.67, indicating an increase of 6.67%:
>
> $$\begin{aligned}\text{DJI type index value} &= \frac{\text{average of current stock prices}}{\text{average of stock prices in base year}} \times 100 \\ &= \frac{(50+110)/2}{(100+50)/2} \times 100 = 106.67.\end{aligned}$$
>
> The DJI-type index assumes that the benchmark portfolio consists of one share of each stock. Had investors bought one share of IBM stock and one share of HPQ in the base year, then their portfolio would have increased in value by 6.67%. Such a portfolio is not a natural benchmark for measuring performance. Suppose, for instance, that the total value of both stocks over this example period declined from $25 billion to $20 billion. This would be a 20% decline in the stocks' value, very different from the increase of 6.67% suggested by the index.

Investment professionals typically use a market-weighted index as a benchmark for measuring the performance of common stock mutual funds. Market-weighted stock indexes represent the price performance of a portfolio that holds each stock in proportion to its total market value. In the preceding example, suppose IBM accounted for 80% of the total value of the stock market and HPQ for 20%. A market-weighted index gives each stock these weights and reveals that the index has declined in value by 31.11% and not gained value of 6.67%:

$$\text{Market-weighted index value} = \frac{\text{weighted average of current stock prices}}{\text{weighted average of stock prices in base year}} \times 100$$

$$= \frac{0.8 \times \$50 + 0.2 \times \$110}{0.8 \times \$100 + 0.2 \times \$50} \times 100 = 68.89.$$

This implies a decline of 100 − 68.89 = 31.11%.

> **QUICK CHECK 5.7** What are the advantages of putting your money in a mutual fund, rather than investing individually in a few stocks?

5.4 The Fundamental Determinants of Rates of Return

As we will explain fully in Chapter 18, theory suggests that in equilibrium there are two fundamental rates of return: an expected rate of return on a market portfolio, a portfolio of all risky assets $E(R_m)$; and the risk-free interest rate on short-term (riskless) bonds R_f. The difference between $E(R_m)$ and R_f is called the risk premium on the market portfolio, and it represents how much more investors must be compensated for taking on risk.

There are four main factors that determine rates of return in a market economy:

1. productivity of capital goods, the expected rates of return on mines, dams, roads, bridges, factories, machinery, and inventories;
2. degree of uncertainty regarding the productivity of capital goods;
3. time preferences of people, the preference of people for consumption now versus consumption in the future; and
4. risk aversion, the amount of potential returns people are willing to give up to reduce their exposure to risk.

We now briefly discuss each of the four factors, and how they relate to the principles we have covered.

5.4.1 The Expected Productivity of Capital Goods

The first and maybe most important determinant of expected rates of return is the productivity of capital goods, the expected rates of return on mines, dams, roads, bridges, factories, machinery, and inventories.

Capital goods are goods produced in an economy that can be used to produce other goods. Typical examples of capital goods are mines, roads, canals, dams, power stations, factories, machinery, and inventories. In addition to such physical goods (tangible capital), capital also includes patents, contracts, formulas, brand-name recognition, and production and distribution system designs that contribute to output. Such nonphysical goods (intangible capital) are often the result of expenditures on research and development and advertising.

Capital's productivity can be expressed as a percentage per year, called the rate of return on capital. This return on capital is the source of the dividends and interest paid to the holders of the stocks, bonds, and other financial instruments issued by firms. These instruments represent claims on the return to a firm's capital. The expected rate of return on capital varies over time and place according to the state of technology, the availability of other factors of production such as natural resources and labor, and the demand for the goods and services the capital can produce. The higher the expected rate of return on capital, the higher the level of interest rates in the economy.

The fact that rates of return incorporate information on capital good productivity—as well as information on the other factors discussed below—reflects **Principle 5:** *Market prices contain valuable information for making financial decisions, and the market price of an asset is usually the best estimate of its true value.*

5.4.2 The Degree of Uncertainty about the Productivity of Capital Goods

The rate of return on capital is always uncertain for a host of reasons. The uncertainties of the weather affect agricultural output; mines and wells often turn out to be dry; machines break down from time to time; and the demand for a product may change unpredictably due to changing tastes or the development of substitutes. Above all, technological progress that comes from the development of new knowledge is by its nature unpredictable. Even the simple production process of storing goods in inventory for use at a future date is not risk-free because an unknown quantity could go bad or become obsolete.

Equity securities represent claims to the profits earned on capital goods. The greater the degree of uncertainty about the productivity of capital goods, the higher the return due to risk on equity securities. This is in line with **Principle 6:** *Risk is fundamental to financial analysis, and must be explicitly considered in all financial decisions.* When an individual is efficiently diversified, there is a trade-off between risk and expected return.

5.4.3 Time Preferences of People

Another factor determining the level of rates of return is the preference of people for consumption now versus consumption in the future. This observation is in line with **Principle 1:** *A dollar today is not worth the same as a dollar tomorrow.* Economists generally assume that the rate of interest would still be positive even if there were no capital goods to invest in and the only reason for borrowing and lending was that people wanted to alter their patterns of consumption over time. In general, the greater the preference of people for current consumption over future consumption, the higher the rate of interest in the economy.

One reason people may prefer greater consumption in the present than in the future is uncertainty about their time of death. They know they are alive now to enjoy their consumption spending, but there is some uncertainty about whether they will be around to enjoy it in the future. This manifestation of risk reinforces Principle 6.

5.4.4 Risk Aversion

As discussed, the rate of return on capital is always risky. How, then, is it possible for people to earn a risk-free rate of interest, and what determines the risk-free rate?

The answer is that the financial system provides contractual mechanisms for people who want to invest in risk-free assets to do so by giving up some of their expected return. People who are more tolerant of risk offer those who are more averse to risk the opportunity to earn a risk-free rate of interest in return for accepting a rate that is lower than the average expected rate of return on risky assets. The greater the degree of risk aversion of the population, the higher the return required in exchange for risk, and the lower will be the risk-free rate of interest. This is in line with Principles 6 and 7.

> QUICK CHECK 5.8 What are the fundamental determinants of rates of return? Which of the Ten Principles of Finance are these determinants an example of?

5.5 History of Stock and Bond Returns

How have the different types of securities actually performed over time? In this section we explore this question by looking at actual data. We study the history of rates of return on stocks and bonds in order to make forecasts about the future. The assumption is that the statistical distribution of historical rates of return will give us insight into the probability distribution of these rates in the future. To understand the data, we begin by explaining common return statistics and how to calculate them.

5.5.1 Calculating Historical Rates of Return and Volatility

Historical rates of return can be characterized by answering two questions:

1. If you invest $1 in an asset at the beginning of a period, do not withdraw any interest, reinvest any dividends paid, and never withdraw any money, how much will your $1 have turned into by the end of the period?
2. Over a time period, what might be or what have been the average returns on an asset?

5.5.1.1 Terminal Wealth

The answer to the first question ("How much will a $1 investment be worth at the end of a time period?") involves the concept of terminal wealth. An investment's terminal wealth at the end of a period is calculated using the terminal wealth ratio. Mathematically, if R_1 is the return (based on price appreciation and interest plus dividends) in the first period, R_2 is the return in the second period, and so forth until the last period T, then we calculate the terminal wealth ratio as follows:

$$\text{Terminal wealth ratio} = (1 + R_1) \times (1 + R_2) \times \cdots \times (1 + R_T). \tag{5.3}$$

We can calculate the return over this period, known as the cumulative return, by subtracting 1 from the terminal wealth ratio: $(1 + R_1) \times (1 + R_2) \times \cdots \times (1 + R_T) - 1$. Note that the terminal wealth ratio incorporates compounding, so the return in each subsequent period gets applied to all of the money made during the previous periods. To illustrate, suppose that you have a stock that gives you a return of 5% in period 1, 10% in period 2, and 8% in period 3. Your terminal wealth ratio would therefore be:

$$\begin{aligned}\text{Terminal wealth ratio} &= (1 + R_1) \times (1 + R_2) \times (1 + R_3) \\ &= 1.05 \times 1.10 \times 1.08 \\ &= 1.25.\end{aligned}$$

Thus, $1 invested would be worth $1.25 at the end of three years.

Note that if a company pays dividends, then those dividends must be factored back into the returns of the stock. Returns are often quoted as total returns, which means that the return is calculated assuming that any dividends paid out are automatically invested back into the investment in the stock.

5.5.1.2 Average Rates of Return

There are two ways to answer the second question ("Over a time period, what might be or what have been the average returns on an asset?").

The arithmetic average return (also called the arithmetic mean rate of return) is used to forecast the mean of the probability distribution for the future. That is, investors use the arithmetic average return to predict what the rate of return of an investment may be over a future period. It is calculated by taking a simple mean—that is, by adding together the returns R_t in each period t, and dividing by the total number of periods T:

$$\text{Arithmetic average return} = \frac{R_1 + R_2 + \cdots + R_T}{T}. \tag{5.4}$$

In our previous example, in which the stock had returns of 5%, 10%, and 8%, the arithmetic average return would be:

$$\frac{5\% + 10\% + 8\%}{3} = 7.7\%.$$

So, if an investor wanted to figure out what the stock's return will likely be in a future period, they would look at the arithmetic average return, which would tell them that they might expect, on average, a return on their investment of 7.7% in the future period.

The geometric average rate of return (also known as the **average compound rate of return**) is used to characterize *past* time series of returns, and explicitly incorporates the effects of compounding. The geometric average rate of return is defined as the constant annualized rate over a number of periods that would result in $1 growing to the terminal wealth ratio at the end of the periods. Put differently, the geometric average rate of return examines the terminal wealth at the end of a period (how much you actually made), and tells you on average what return you would have had to have each period to get that terminal wealth. The geometric average is the answer to the question: "What compound rate of return has this asset earned over a period?" To calculate the geometric average return, we use the following formula:

$$\text{Geometric average return} = \left((1 + R_1) \times (1 + R_2) \times \cdots \times (1 + R_T)\right)^{1/T} - 1. \tag{5.5}$$

With our previous example, the geometric average return becomes:

$$= \left((1 + R_1) \times (1 + R_2) \times (1 + R_3)\right)^{\frac{1}{3}} - 1$$

$$= \left((1 + .05) \times (1 + .10) \times (1 + .08)\right)^{\frac{1}{3}} - 1$$

$$= 0.076 \text{ or } 7.6\%.$$

This means that an investment growing at a constant annualized rate of 7.6% over the three periods would result in $1 growing to the terminal wealth ratio of 1.25.

In this case, the arithmetic and geometric means are very similar to each other. Over longer time horizons and in different circumstances, they can differ substantially, as we will see. The geometric average is always less than the arithmetic average.

5.5.1.3 Volatility

Finally, it is informative to understand how much the rates of return have *varied* in the past. The standard deviation of annual rates of return measures the volatility of the annual rates. The standard deviation σ of a series of returns is given by the formula:

$$\sigma = \sqrt{\frac{1}{N} \times \sum_{i=1}^{n} \left(R_i - \mathbb{E}[R]\right)^2}, \tag{5.6}$$

where N is the total number of observations, i is a period, R_i is the rate of return in period i, $\mathbb{E}[R]$ is the expected return, and $\sum_{i=1}^{n}$ · indicates a summation for each i from 1 to N (that is, all of the $(R_i - \mathbb{E}[R])^2$ terms for each i are added together).

The standard deviation measures how much the individual historical returns, R_i, differ from their expected return, $\mathbb{E}[R]$. A larger standard deviation indicates greater volatility. In calculations, $\mathbb{E}[R]$ is measured by the arithmetic average return (Equation 5.4). Thus, using our previous average return of 7.7%, the standard deviation would be

$$\begin{aligned}
\sigma &= \sqrt{\frac{1}{N} \times \sum_{i=1}^{n}(R_i - \mathbb{E}[R])^2} \\
&= \sqrt{\frac{1}{N} \times \left[(R_1 - \mathbb{E}[R])^2 + (R_2 - \mathbb{E}[R])^2 + (R_3 - \mathbb{E}[R])^2\right]} \\
&= \sqrt{\frac{1}{3} \times \left[(0.05 - 0.077)^2 + (0.10 - 0.077)^2 + (0.08 - 0.077)^2\right]} \\
&= 0.021 \text{ or } 2.1\%.
\end{aligned}$$

That is, future returns are likely to fall within bands of 2.1% of the arithmetic average return, depending on how frequently each return occurs. For example, the returns may form a *normal* distribution, meaning that returns near the arithmetic average occur more frequently than returns that are very different from the average. A graph of such a distribution of returns would form a bell-shaped curve.

If our historical returns reflect a normal distribution, then, based on the existing data, there is a roughly 2/3 chance that future returns will be within one standard deviation band of the arithmetic average return—that is, 7.7% ± 2.1% or between 9.8% and 5.6%. Future returns, based on the existing data, have a very high chance (99.7%) of being within three standard deviations of the arithmetic average return: 7.7% ± (3 × 2.1%) = 1.4% or 14%. This is illustrated in Figure 5.5. These estimates,

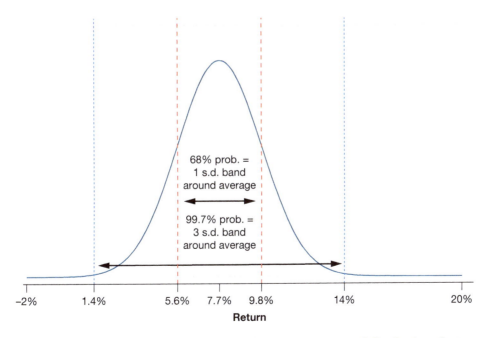

FIGURE 5.5 Probability distribution of returns. This figure shows a normal distribution of returns, with a mean return of 7.7% and the probability that the return will fall within the indicated bands.

however, are dependent on how representative the data points we observe are of the actual distribution of possible data points. In our example, we use only three datapoints; statistical confidence in our ability to ascertain the possible bounds for future returns increases with more data points.

Let's illustrate further with a simple example where we have five years of data on stocks in Example 5.2.

Example 5.2 (Calculating the Wealth Ratio, Returns, and Volatility): Consider the following yearly stock returns shown in **Table 5.3**.

Table 5.3 Yearly stock returns for Example 5.2.

Year	Return
2017	5%
2018	−10%
2019	3%
2020	15%
2021	20%

What is the terminal wealth ratio? What are the arithmetic average and geometric average rates of return for this stock? What is the standard deviation of the returns?

Solution. For the terminal wealth ratio, we use Equation 5.3:

$$\begin{aligned}\text{Terminal wealth ratio} &= (1+R_1)\times(1+R_2)\times(1+R_3)\times(1+R_4)\times(1+R_5)\\ &= (1+0.05)\times(1-0.10)\times(1+0.03)\times(1+0.15)\times(1+0.20)\\ &= 1.343.\end{aligned}$$

Using Equation 5.4, the arithmetic average return is the simple average of these returns:

$$\begin{aligned}\text{Arithmetic average return} &= \frac{R_1+R_2+R_3+R_4+R_5}{5}\\ &= \frac{0.05-0.10+0.03+0.15+0.20}{5}\\ &= 0.07 \text{ or } 7.0\%.\end{aligned}$$

This represents a forecast of the mean of the probability distribution of the rate of return over the next year—that is, of all the possible returns, it is likely that the return on this stock will be around 7.0%. The geometric average rate of return is calculated using Equation 5.5:

$$\begin{aligned}\text{Geometric average return} &= \left((1+R_1)\times(1+R_2)\times(1+R_3)\times(1+R_4)\times(1+R_5)\right)^{\frac{1}{5}}-1\\ &= \left((1+0.05)\times(1-0.10)\times(1+0.03)\times(1+0.15)\times(1+0.20)\right)^{\frac{1}{5}}-1\\ &= 0.061 \text{ or } 6.1\%.\end{aligned}$$

Note that the arithmetic average of 6.6% exceeds the geometric average of 6.1% by 0.5%. The arithmetic average rate of return is always either greater than or equal to the geometric average. The difference between the two depends on the volatility of the series of returns. If there is zero volatility, the arithmetic and geometric averages are equal.

Finally, the standard deviation of the returns is given by Equation 5.6:

$$\sigma = \sqrt{\frac{1}{N} \times \sum_{i=1}^{n}(R_i - E[R])^2}$$

$$= \sqrt{\frac{1}{N} \times \left[(R_1 - E[R])^2 + (R_2 - E[R])^2 + (R_3 - E[R])^2 + (R_4 - E[R])^2 + (R_5 - E[R])^2\right]}$$

$$= \sqrt{\frac{1}{5} \times \left[(0.05 - 0.07)^2 + (-0.10 - 0.07)^2 + (0.03 - 0.07)^2 + (0.15 - 0.07)^2 + (0.20 - 0.07)^2\right]}$$

$$= 0.104 \text{ or } 10.4\%.$$

Thus (assuming a normal distribution), the majority of returns fall within 7.0% ± 10.4%.

Excel can make these calculations simpler. To compute the arithmetic returns in Excel, we can use the =AVERAGE() function, which takes a simple average of all the numbers in the indicated cells:

	A	B	C	D	E
1	Year	Return	1+Return		
2	2010	0.05	1.05	=AVERAGE(B2:B6)	
3	2011	-0.10	0.90		
4	2012	0.03	1.03		
5	2013	0.15	1.15		
6	2014	0.20	1.20		
7					

To compute the terminal wealth ratio and geometric average, we first create two columns: column B with the annual rates of return in decimal form, and column C with one plus the returns. The terminal wealth ratio is calculated by multiplying 1 + R in each period. To do so, we can use the =PRODUCT() function, which multiplies together all of the numbers in the indicated cells:

	A	B	C	D	E
1	Year	Return	1+Return		
2	2010	0.05	1.05	=PRODUCT(C2:C6)	
3	2011	-0.10	0.90		
4	2012	0.03	1.03		
5	2013	0.15	1.15		
6	2014	0.20	1.20		

To calculate the geometric mean, we can proceed in two different ways. The first way is to use the =PRODUCT() function, and apply our formula:

	A	B	C	D	E	F
1	Year	Return	1+Return			
2	2010	0.05	1.05	=(PRODUCT(C2:C6))^(1/5)-1		
3	2011	-0.10	0.90			
4	2012	0.03	1.03			
5	2013	0.15	1.15			
6	2014	0.20	1.20			
7						

The second and simpler way is to use the =GEOMEAN() function, which takes the product of 1 + R and automatically raises it to the power of 1/T.

	A	B	C	D	E
1	Year	Return	1+Return		
2	2010	0.05	1.05	=GEOMEAN(C2:C6)-1	
3	2011	-0.10	0.90		
4	2012	0.03	1.03		
5	2013	0.15	1.15		
6	2014	0.20	1.20		
7					

Finally, we can compute the standard deviation using the =STDEV.P() function:

	A	B	C	D	E
1	Year	Return	1+Return		
2	2010	0.05	1.05	=STDEV.P(B2:B6)	
3	2011	-0.10	0.90		
4	2012	0.03	1.03		
5	2013	0.15	1.15		
6	2014	0.20	1.20		

You can verify that we get the same answers in each of these cases.

> **QUICK CHECK 5.9** What are the arithmetic and geometric average returns for a stock that posted returns of 5%, 20%, and −5% in three consecutive years?

5.5.2 Historical Equity and Bond Returns across the World

Every year, partnering with LSE, UBS Research, the research analysis wing of the Union Bank of Switzerland, publishes the *Global Investment Returns Yearbook* (previously published by Credit Suisse). This comprehensive historical cross-country database starts with data from 1900 and includes data on the returns to various investments from ~23 countries (this number can change from one edition to the next) (Figure 5.6). These data were initially gathered and analyzed by financial historians Elroy Dimson, Paul Marsh, and Mike Staunton, who published them in their 2002 book *Triumph of the Optimists*. Since then Dimson, Marsh, and Staunton have updated the database annually.

From Figure 5.6 one might draw the conclusion that investing in stocks is a "no-brainer." An investment of $1 in 1900, assuming no withdrawals from the portfolio, grew to $1,937 after adjusting for inflation. An investment of a dollar in bonds, on the other hand, grew to only $10.90 after adjusting for inflation. And a strategy of rolling over and reinvesting in bills grew to only $2.60. We turn to a discussion of this potential conclusion in detail in the next section, and point out the dangers of such a conclusion.

Table 5.4 contains country data giving average returns (both arithmetic and geometric) and risk measures (standard deviation) for Europe, Japan, Switzerland, the United Kingdom, the United States, and the world as a whole. In line with the previous points, the geometric average return is always less than the arithmetic average, and the volatility (standard deviation) of bond returns for each country is lower than the volatility of stock returns for that country, indicating that bond returns are less risky than stock returns.

5.5 HISTORY OF STOCK AND BOND RETURNS

Table 5.4 Real equity and bond returns in selected markets, 1900–2023. This table provides return characteristics for equity and bond returns for individual countries and for the world.

Country	Geometric average (%)	Arithmetic average (%)	Standard deviation (%)	Minimum return (%)	Maximum return (%)
Real equity returns					
Europe	4.1	5.9	19.7	−48.0	75.2
Japan	4.2	8.6	28.9	−85.5	121.1
Switzerland	4.5	6.3	19.3	−37.8	59.4
United Kingdom	5.3	7.1	19.5	−56.6	99.3
United States	6.4	8.3	19.9	−38.6	55.8
World	5.0	6.5	17.4	−42.9	67.6
Real bond returns					
Europe	1.3	2.5	15.8	−52.6	72.2
Japan	−0.8	1.7	19.4	−77.5	69.8
Switzerland	2.4	2.7	9.3	−21.4	56.1
United Kingdom	1.9	2.7	13.5	−29.9	59.4
United States	2.0	2.5	10.3	−18.1	35.2
World	2.0	2.5	10.9	−31.6	16.0

Note: Europe and World indexes are in a common currency (USD).

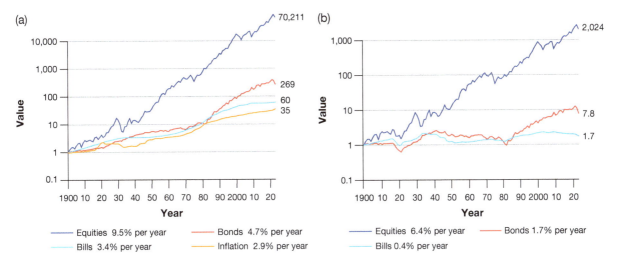

FIGURE 5.6 The value of $1 invested in stocks, bonds, and bills, 1900 to 2023. This figure shows the (a) nominal and (b) real value of a dollar invested in a world portfolio of each of three different asset classes: stocks, bonds, and bills (i.e., the terminal wealth ratio over time).
Source: © 2023 Elroy Dimson, Paul Marsh and Mike Staunton.

Summarizing the results for the world portfolio, we see that the geometric average real annualized rate of return on stocks was 5.0% compared with 2.0% for bonds. The arithmetic average for the future real annual rate of return on stocks is 6.5% compared to 2.5% for bonds. The volatility (standard deviation) of the real rate of return on stocks is 17.4% compared to 10.9% for bonds. The higher average rate of return but higher volatility for stocks underscores the trade-off between risk and expected return emphasized in Principle 6.

The numbers also show that, while on average the investments shown have done well, they do not necessarily *always* do well—there is risk in the investments, which is illustrated by the standard deviations and the fact that each of the investments has experienced minimum and maximum returns that are large in magnitude. Box 5.4 illustrates this fact by exploring the performance of professional investment managers. We explore the implications of this further in the next section.

Box 5.4 World of Business: Even Successful Investment Managers Are Not Always Successful

We often hear stories of successful investment managers, who have earned spectacular rates of return on their clients' money. For example, Warren Buffett, who runs the holding company Berkshire Hathaway, has a net worth of over $70 billion as a result of successful investments. Warren Buffett's success is often attributed to the focused and careful research he undertakes to get to know the details of the assets he's looking to invest in. For example, Buffett researches how competent and trustworthy a company's management team is.

Other successful investors have taken different approaches. For instance, James Simons, the founder and CEO of Renaissance Technologies, a hedge fund with $22 billion under management, formerly worked as a code breaker for the NSA before turning to academia. He used computer-based models to drive his investment strategy and to attempt to predict price changes, resulting in average returns of 35% annually.

However, even these well-known managers do not *always* produce such stellar returns, and there can be substantial variability in performance from year to year. The co-founder and CEO of Viking Global Investors, a fund managing around $30 billion, returned 41% in 2008 and 13.4% in 2021. Furthermore, even the best investment managers who deliver stellar historical performance have periods of underperformance. A recent study found that approximately 97% of the top mutual fund managers had at least one three-year period where they underperformed their target benchmark. Furthermore, there is a substantial amount of evidence that the *majority* of fund managers who actively manage their funds end up underperforming their targets. One report showed that the performance of more than three-quarters of active mutual fund managers fell behind the S&P 500 in 2021.

Sources: The Big 4 Accounting Firms (2024). The best hedge fund managers of all time. Williams, S. (2020). 6 reasons Warren Buffett is such a successful investor. Baird (2014). The truth about top-performing money managers. Meyers, J. (2022). New report finds almost 80% of active fund managers are falling behind the major indexes. CNBC.

5.6 Monte Carlo Simulation of Future Stock Market Performance

What can we say about the possible outcomes of wealth in the long run from investing in stocks? The previous section illustrated how much an investor could earn when investing in stocks over a long time horizon. When looking at Figure 5.6, it is tempting to think that, even though there are some drops within the period of time, in the *long run* they are *sure* to outperform investments like government bonds and bills. In other words, if you just invest in stocks and hold on to your investment for long enough, you will always achieve higher returns by investing in stocks. However, this view ignores the fact that stock investments have *risk*–they may fall in value. In fact, for any given investment we only observe *one* observation over the long run. That is, if we look at only one outcome, there is bias when examining successes, and one is tempted to use the successful experiences as a predictor of the future. In reality, the outcomes may have turned out very differently, and they may turn out differently in the future.

We illustrate this point using a technique called Monte Carlo simulation, which is an analytical technique that uses existing data to demonstrate possible outcomes that could occur in the future. In a Monte Carlo simulation we pretend to invest $1 in a representative stock portfolio and then use a computer model to generate many alternative, possible future 20-year periods of performance. We assume that any dividends received along the way are reinvested in the portfolio.

For our historical data set we use the annual real rates of return on a value-weighted portfolio of all stocks traded on the New York Stock Exchange (NYSE) over the 96 years from 1926 to 2024 (Figure 5.7). The chart includes the geometric and arithmetic averages as well as the standard deviation for the annual real rates of return over the full period. The curve on panel (b) represents how a hypothetical portfolio would grow at the geometric average rate of 6.78% every individual year over the entire period. Panel (c) includes a logarithmic scale on the vertical axis, which causes the hypothetical curve with constant growth rate to become a perfectly straight line whose slope reflects the growth rate.

Figure 5.8 shows the annual real returns over the period 1926–2024, which shows the frequency with which we see smaller or larger annual returns. The distribution of annual real returns may be approximated by a normal distribution with a mean of 8.59% and standard deviation of 19.14%.

The Monte Carlo simulation can be run in the companion workbook in two different ways:

1. Generate yearly returns by sampling from a normal distribution with mean and standard deviation specified as inputs, such as mean of 8.59% and standard deviation of 19.14%. Put differently, one can create a new data set of random returns that matches how the distribution of the original data looks statistically.
2. Generate yearly returns by bootstrap sampling from the historical data set of annual real returns from 1926 to 2021.

Bootstrap sampling (or simply "bootstrapping") was applied in the Monte Carlo simulation discussed here and is depicted in Figures 5.9 and 5.10. Bootstrap sampling is a method of simulating returns that generates a return for each year by randomly selecting *actual* past returns. The idea is that any of the observed returns over the sample could, in principle, occur at any time. Thus, for any given year, we randomly select from the observed returns. More specifically, the bootstrap sampling procedure is as follows: for each 20-year period, the method randomly selects a year from 1926 to 2024, and then assigns that year's return to be the return for year 1 in the simulation run return sequence being created. It then does the same thing for year 2, and so on, up to year 20. Together, the 20 sampled returns establish one possible trajectory for the wealth ratio. This is repeated many times to provide many possible trajectories or "sample paths." The distribution of wealth ratios is assumed to represent the possibilities for the future.

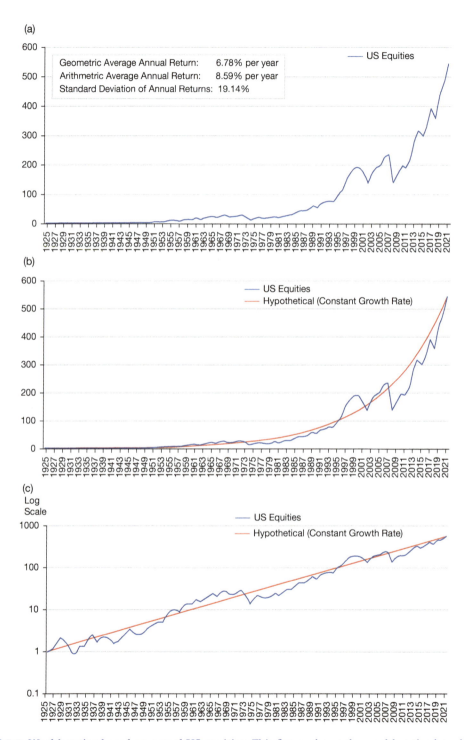

FIGURE 5.7 **Wealth ratios based on actual US equities.** This figure shows the wealth ratios based on annual real rates of return on a value-weighted portfolio of all stocks traded on the NYSE from 1926 to 2021. (a) The real value of the portfolio (blue line). (b) The value growth of a hypothetical portfolio at the geometric average rate of 6.78% every year over the entire period (red line). (c) The same data using a logarithmic scale on the vertical axis (red line).
Source: Data from the Center for Research in Security Prices (CRSP).

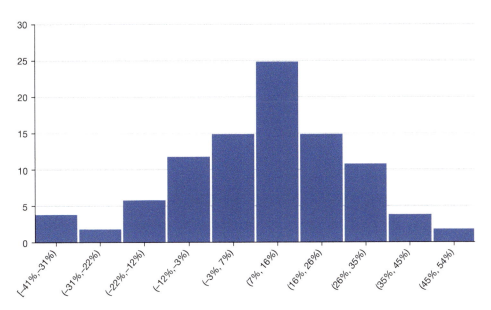

FIGURE 5.8 **Histogram of annual real returns from 1926 to 2021.** This figure shows the distribution of annual real rates of return on a value-weighted portfolio of all stocks traded on the NYSE over the 96 years from 1926 to 2021.
Source: Data from the Center for Research in Security Prices (CRSP).

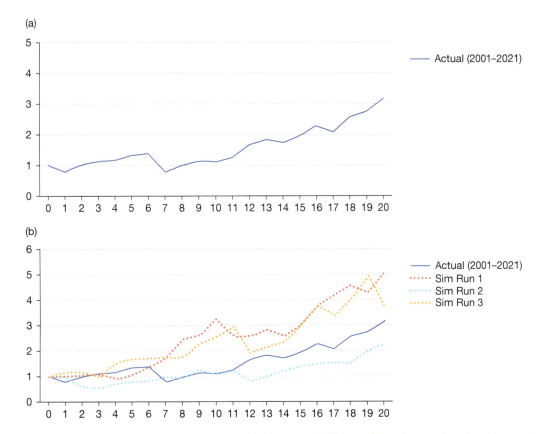

FIGURE 5.9 **Actual data and simulated Monte Carlo runs.** (a) The wealth ratio over time for the actual data. (b) The wealth ratio for three different simulated runs.
Source: Data from the Center for Research in Security Prices (CRSP).

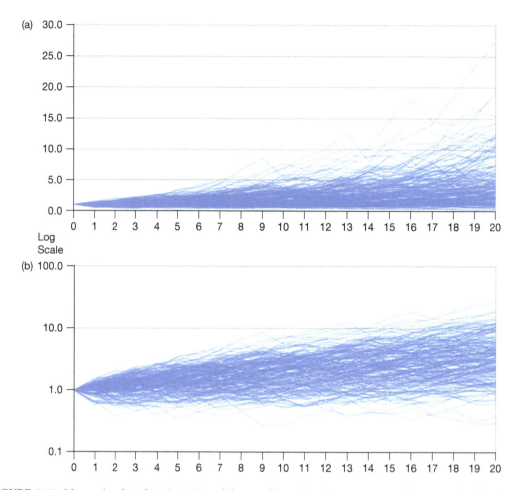

FIGURE 5.10 Many simulated trajectories of the wealth ratios. Bootstrap sampling: 200 simulated runs. The wealth ratios for 200 simulated runs, illustrating potential performance based on the characteristics of the underlying data. (a) The wealth ratio over time for each simulated run. (b) The wealth ratio on a logarithmic scale for each simulated run.

Figure 5.9(a) shows the actual historical path of the wealth ratio for the 20 years ending 2021. Figure 5.9(b) adds three simulated trajectories. Figure 5.10 shows the result of 200 simulation runs.

The simulation results show just how differently things may turn out based on the actual risk of the investment. While there are some trajectories that do well, there are many trajectories where the terminal wealth ratio is less than 1.[2] In other words, in many cases even after 20 years investors can experience a loss in the real value of their portfolio. The Monte Carlo simulation shows just how differently things may turn out when we consider this investment. This illustrates the dangers of using just one historical observation as a predictor of the future—when accounting for the randomness of an investment, there are potentially many outcomes that can occur.

---

2 The distribution of terminal wealth ratios is lognormal. This result follows from the Central Limit Theorem. You are encouraged to experiment using the companion workbook to conduct additional Monte Carlo simulations.

Conclusion

In this chapter we learned about the major financial markets and the basic types of financial instruments that are traded in those markets. We also demonstrated how rates of return of common financial instruments—such as bonds and stocks—are calculated, as well as what these returns have actually been historically. Calculating rates of return and looking at past patterns allowed us to explore how some of the conceptual underpinnings of finance—such as the trade-off between risk and return—inform the investment decisions that people are able to make in financial markets.

In subsequent chapters we will explore how the financial markets and instruments we discussed in this chapter can be used to achieve specific financial goals, such as managing risk. We will also show how the return calculations we introduced will be essential elements in measuring the performance and risk of financial investments. In later parts of the book we explore in more detail other entities that make up the financial system.

Takeaways

Financial markets are where financial contracts are traded. The basic types of financial assets traded in markets are *debt*, *equity*, and *derivatives*:

- Debt instruments are issued by anyone who borrows money—firms, governments, and households.
- Equity is the claim of the owners of a firm. Equity securities issued by corporations are called stocks.
- Derivatives are instruments such as options, swaps, and futures contracts that derive their value from the prices of one or more other assets.
- An interest rate is a promised rate of return, and there are as many different interest rates as there are distinct kinds of borrowing and lending.
- Interest rates vary depending on the unit of account, the maturity, and the default risk of the credit instrument.
- A *nominal* interest rate is denominated in units of some currency; a *real* interest rate is denominated in units of some basket of goods and services. Bonds that offer a fixed nominal interest rate have an uncertain real rate of return. Inflation-indexed bonds offering a fixed real interest rate have an uncertain nominal rate of return.
- From 1900 to 2023, historical returns of stocks and bonds have followed the pattern of the risk–return trade-off in Principle 6, with stocks posting the highest returns but exhibiting the highest risk, and government bonds posting the lowest returns but the least risk.

Key Terms

Actively managed	118	Common stocks or shares	105
Arithmetic average return	124	Debt securities	104
Asset-backed security (ABS)	106	Default	104
Benchmark	118	Default risk	107
Bond	104	Derivatives	106
Bond rating	114	Dividends	117
Bootstrap sampling	131	Equity	105
Call option (or call)	106	Exchange rate	111
Capital gain or capital loss	117	Exchange-traded fund	119
Capital market	105	Expense ratio	119

Face value   104
Financial instruments   103
Financial intermediaries   103
Financial markets   103
Financial service firms   103
Financial system   103
Fixed-income instruments   105
Forward contracts   106
Futures contracts   106
Geometric average rate of return   124
Hybrid securities   105
Index fund   119
Indexing   118
Inflation   115
Interest payments (coupon payments)   104
Interest rate   107
Issuer   103
Limited liability   105
Liquidity   105
Maturity   104
Money market   105
Monte Carlo Simulation   131
Mutual fund   118
Nominal interest rate   115
Nominal prices   115
Options   106
Over-the-counter markets or off-exchange markets   104
Par bonds   110

Par or principal or face value amount   104
Preferred stock   105
Productivity of capital goods   121
Put option (or put)   106
Rate of return on capital   122
Real interest rate   115
Real prices   115
Regulators   103
Residual claim   105
Risk-free asset   114
Risk-free interest rate   114
Security   103
Shareholders   105
Spot interest rate   108
Spot price   106
Standard deviation   124
Stock index   118
Stock market   105
STRIPS   108
Swap   106
Term structure of interest rates   108
Terminal wealth   123
Terminal wealth ratio   123
Time pattern of promised payments   107
Unit of account   107
Yield curve   109
Yield spread   114
Yield to maturity (YTM or yield)   109
Zero-coupon bonds   108

Key Equations

Relation between real and nominal rates	$1 + \text{real rate of return} = \dfrac{1 + \text{nominal interest rate}}{1 + \text{rate of inflation}}$	Eq. 5.1
Stock rate of return	$R = \dfrac{\text{ending price of a share} - \text{beginning price} + \text{cash dividend}}{\text{beginning price}}$	Eq. 5.2
Terminal wealth ratio	$\text{Terminal wealth ratio} = (1 + R_1) \times (1 + R_2) \times \cdots \times (1 + R_T)$	Eq. 5.3
Arithmetic average return	$\text{Arithmetic average return} = \dfrac{R_1 + R_2 + \cdots + R_T}{T}$	Eq. 5.4
Geometric average return	$\text{Geometric average return} = ((1 + R_1) \times (1 + R_2) \times \cdots \times (1 + R_T))^{1/T} - 1$	Eq. 5.5
Standard deviation of returns	$\sigma = \sqrt{\dfrac{1}{N} \times \sum_{i=1}^{n} (R_i - \mathbb{E}[R])^2}$	Eq. 5.6

Problems

1. Name one financial function that each of the three basic types of financial assets—debt, equity, and derivatives—can perform.
2. If you observe that the yield spread of a corporate bond has increased, for what reasons might it have increased?
3. Draw a timeline of cash flows for a five-year $1,000 bond that costs $950 to purchase. This bond is a promise that the issuer will pay the holder the principal of $1,000 at maturity in five years and coupon payments of 5% of the principal each year.
4. If a one-year STRIPS bond with a principal amount of $100 trades at a price of $96, what is the bond's yield to maturity (YTM)?
5. Suppose you see the current price of a two-year STRIPS bond, which pays $1,000 in two years, is $970. What is the bond's yield to maturity?
6. Go to the US Treasury's website and graph the current yield curve for US zero-coupon bonds.
7. Suppose that the pound–euro exchange rate is £1 to €1.4 now, but is expected to change to £1 to €1.2 in one year.
    (a) If you invest €1,000 into an account denominated in pounds that pays an interest rate of 3%, what is your rate of return for that account in euros?
    (b) If the euro risk-free rate of return is 5%, is the pound account an attractive investment opportunity for you?
8. If there is inflation, should real interest rates be higher or lower than nominal interest rates? Explain why.
9. Suppose you have an investment opportunity that provides a nominal interest rate of 5%, but the current rate of inflation is 6%. What is your expected real rate of return? What might be a better alternative investment choice for you?
10. Suppose you see a zero-coupon bond issued by the US Treasury with a maturity of two years and a par amount of $1,000. You also see a zero-coupon bond issued by a risky company with a maturity of two years and the same par amount of $1,000. Can the yields of the two bonds be different? If so, which should be higher? Explain why.
11. You track a stock, and notice that its price went from $50 last year to $48 this year.
    (a) What is the rate of return on the stock based on these prices?
    (b) Suppose you discover that the stock paid a dividend of $3 per share over the course of this period. Does this affect your return calculations? If so, explain why and recalculate the return of the stock given this new information.
12. What are the benefits of investing in index funds as opposed to actively managed funds?
13. What are the arithmetic and geometric average returns for a stock that posted returns of 10% and 30% in two consecutive years?
14. What are the terminal wealth ratio, arithmetic average return, and geometric average return for the set of yearly stock returns shown in Table 5.5? What is the standard deviation?

Table 5.5

Year	Return
1	2%
2	5%
3	−3%
4	18%
5	23%
6	−16%

15. What are the terminal wealth ratio, arithmetic average return, and geometric average return for the set of yearly stock returns shown in Table 5.6? What is the standard deviation?

Table 5.6

Year	Return
1	1%
2	−3%
3	−8%

16. Why are stock returns typically higher than bond returns?
17. Use the companion Excel app for this chapter. Run 10 simulations over 20 years. What is the highest ending value that you get? What is the lowest? Why can they be so different?

6 PRINCIPLES OF RISK MANAGEMENT

CHAPTER OVERVIEW

6.1	What Is Risk?	140
6.2	Risk and Financial Decisions	142
6.3	Risk Management	149
6.4	The Three Dimensions of Risk Transfer: Diversifying, Hedging, and Insuring	153
6.5	Risk Transfer and Economic Efficiency	162
6.6	Risk Management in Practice	164

LEARNING OBJECTIVES

After reading this chapter, you will be able to:
- define what risk is and describe how it is incorporated into financial decisions;
- calculate the expected return of assets, and understand the trade-off between risk and return;
- explain how risk is incorporated into valuation calculations;
- perform calculations to measure the financial risk of assets;
- describe what risk management is, and identify the three dimensions of risk transfer: diversifying, hedging, and insuring.

EQUATIONS YOU KNOW

Future value	$FV_T = PV \times (1+r)^T$	Eq. 2.1

- You like to avoid risks in life. How does this affect your choice of financial investments?

- As part of your retirement plan investment choices, you can invest in assets with more or less risk. On which investments can you expect to earn a higher return?

- You are investing in a company that describes its current project investment pipeline. The company's performance will depend on how likely its projects are to succeed. How can you measure the company's expected risk and return?

- Your wealth consists of your current yearly income, your savings, and investments in stocks and bonds. What are your sources of financial risk? How can you manage these risks?

- You are a manager of a grain distribution company. You identify that the company is exposed to risks related to the weather and to whether farmers have large or small crop yields. What can you do to manage the company's risks?

Introduction

In the previous chapters we introduced the concept of valuation, which involved converting cash flows that are expected to happen in the future into today's terms, and we learned about the returns on various assets and how to analyze the past performance of financial instruments to inform investment decisions. However, the future is not known for sure. The cash flows that occur may be different from what we initially expect, and the value (and rates of return) of financial instruments change over time. In this chapter, we introduce a fundamental concept in finance: Uncertainty about the future can affect valuation and decision making.

We begin by defining what risk is in finance, and how it affects financial decisions. We then dive into how risk can be managed, which includes identifying relevant risks, assessing how they can affect one's financial situation, and then determining appropriate techniques that can be used to reduce these risks. We go into detail analyzing the risk management technique that plays the greatest role in financial markets—transferring specific risks to others that would prefer to bear them—and provide examples of how this can be done. We conclude by briefly describing how risk management is performed in practice, and some difficulties in doing so.

6.1 What Is Risk?

When we make a decision to invest in something (real estate, a business, a bond, a stock, a work of art), we are concerned about what money or value it will provide us in the future. Most of the time, however, we do not know what the future will bring and the outcome of some decision, action, or event is uncertain. After you make an investment, for example, you may not know for sure what cash flows it will give you in the future. Risk is uncertainty that matters to someone because it affects their welfare. The flip of a coin has an uncertain outcome, but it is risky only if there is something at stake on its outcome. If you make a bet that if the coin lands heads up you win some money and if it lands tails up you lose some money, you now have a risky situation. Because you can now win or lose money, the outcome of the coin flip matters to you.

Finance is the study of allocating resources over time under conditions of uncertainty. Virtually *every* financial activity—saving, investing, borrowing, lending—involves risk. As a result, much of finance has to do with measuring and managing risk, as summarized in **Principle 6:** *Risk is fundamental to financial analysis and must be explicitly considered in all financial decisions.*

In many risky situations, the possible outcomes can be classified either as losses or gains in a simple and direct way. For example, if you invest in the stock market and the value of your stock portfolio goes down, it is a loss; if it goes up, it is a gain. People normally consider the downside possibility of losses to be the risk, not the upside potential for a gain. However, in typical measures of risk in finance, we consider both upside *and* downside potential—for example, a stock that jumps up in price could very well fall by the same amount in the future.

This general preference of individuals—that all else being equal, we prefer to *not* take risks—is called risk aversion. Put differently, if provided with two alternatives that cost the same, a risk-averse individual will select the one with lower risk.

To illustrate, consider the following two investment opportunities. For Opportunity A, you invest $100 now and receive $105 for sure tomorrow. The probability of this outcome occurring is 100%: You will definitely receive $105 tomorrow.

OPPORTUNITY A

For Opportunity B, you invest $100 now and then flip a coin tomorrow: If the coin comes up heads, you receive $110, but if it comes up tails, you receive $100. The probability of the heads outcome is 50% and the probability of the tails outcome is 50%. Thus, there is a 50% probability that you will receive $110 and a 50% probability that you will receive $100.

OPPORTUNITY B

With Opportunity A, there is *no* risk: You will make $5 no matter what happens. With Opportunity B, however, there *is* risk: You may make money ($10) or you may not make any money. Because there are two possibilities, we can calculate the *expected* value of Opportunity B's payoff: Payoff 1 multiplied by its probability of occurring plus Payoff 2 multiplied by its probability of occurring: $110 × 0.50 + $100 × 0.50 = $105. Thus, the expected value of Opportunity B is the same as the risk-free payoff of Opportunity A. Because both options have the same expected payoff ($105) but a different level of risk, a risk-averse person would select the first option, the one with no risk. We will return to this example in more detail shortly. Risk aversion is a deeply ingrained human behavior, and we will therefore assume that typical investors are risk-averse. As we will see, this assumption leads to a number of deep insights about optimal financial decision making.

If you face a particular type of risk because of your job, the nature of your business, or your pattern of consumption, you are said to have a risk exposure. For example, if you are a temporary office worker, your exposure to the risk of a layoff is relatively high. If you are a tenured professor at a major university, your exposure to the risk of a layoff is relatively low. If you are a farmer, you are exposed both to the risk of a crop failure and to the risk of a decline in the price at which you can sell your crops. If your business significantly involves imports or exports of goods, you are exposed to the risk of an adverse change in currency exchange rates. If you own a house, you are exposed to the risks of fire, theft, storm damage, and earthquake damage, as well as the risk of a decline in its market value.

While the previous examples may seem clear in terms of risk, the riskiness of an asset or a transaction cannot be assessed in isolation. In one context, the purchase or sale of a particular asset may add to your risk exposure; in another, the same transaction may be risk-reducing. Thus, if you buy an insurance policy on your life, it is risk-reducing to your family because the benefit offsets their loss in income in the event that you die. If people unrelated to you buy the policy on your life, they are not reducing risk; they are betting that you will die during the year. Similarly, if a farmer with wheat ready to be harvested enters a contract to sell their wheat at a fixed price in the future, the contract is risk-reducing for the farmer: They know for certain what they will sell their wheat for in the future. But if someone with no wheat to sell enters into that same contract, they are expecting that wheat prices will fall because they profit only if the market price at the contract delivery date is below the contractually fixed price. In this case, the contract increases the person's risk because, while they hope wheat prices will fall, the prices might actually rise, and they will lose out on the possibility of making more money.

Speculators are people who hope to increase their wealth by investing in assets that increase their exposure to certain risks. In contrast, hedgers are people who hope to preserve their wealth by investing in assets that decrease their exposure to certain risks. The same person can be a speculator in some circumstances and a hedger in others.

> **Box 6.1** Knight's Approach to Risk and Uncertainty
>
> The precise relationship of risk to uncertainty is something that has long been a subject of debate. The definition of risk that we provide in this book is uncertainty that "matters" because it affects welfare. University of Chicago economist Frank Knight introduced a different distinction between risk and uncertainty in 1921.
>
> According to Knight, risk is *measurable* or quantifiable, whereas uncertainty is not. Using our previous example of Opportunity B, Knight would identify this as risky because the value of the investment opportunity may become $110 or $100 because we know that each outcome has a 50–50 chance of occurring. Knight's approach would identify Opportunity B as uncertain (but not risky) if we knew that the value may become $110 or $100, but did not know the probabilities of these potential outcomes.
>
> Knight's version of uncertainty is sometimes referred to as *ambiguity*. Studies of human behavior have indicated that humans treat ambiguity differently from normal risk; in particular, humans tend to avoid situations that contain ambiguity. This is referred to as *ambiguity aversion*, and can affect decision making by individuals.
>
> Researchers have attempted to incorporate Knight's concept of uncertainty and ambiguity into models in finance and economics, and this remains an area of active research. For example, it has been shown that, in the presence of ambiguity, demand for uncertain assets is reduced, and prices can be increasingly based on randomness, leading to increased volatility.

6.2 Risk and Financial Decisions

To fully understand why risk must be considered in all financial decisions, we need to incorporate the concept of risk into the toolkit that we have been developing for determining the time value of money, asset values, and market returns. We continually return to the issue of risk as we expand our toolkit throughout the book.

6.2.1 Risk and Returns in Financial Investments

When making decisions about investing, households, firms, and even the government must take into account the fact that things might not work out as expected. In investment decisions, a basic concept that serves as an important benchmark for evaluating the risk of any asset is that of a risk-free asset.

A risk-free asset is an asset that will pay its promised amount no matter what happens in the future. An example of a risk-free asset would be an investment where you invest $100 today (at $t = 0$) and receive $105 *for sure* in one year (at $t = 1$):

Today $t = 0$ **Next year $t = 1$**

Invest $100 ⟶ $105

The return of the risk-free asset is therefore $105/$100 − 1 = 0.05 or 5%. We call the return of a risk-free asset the risk-free rate of return or risk-free rate. This is also sometimes referred to as a riskless interest rate. We denote it r_f.

Finance practitioners often use some form of a US Treasury bond as a risk-free asset when performing financial analysis. These bonds are backed by the guarantee of the US government, and thus are widely accepted as being nearly risk-free because it is unlikely that the US government will default on its obligations. For every currency there will be a different risk-free rate. An investment that offers a US dollar risk-free interest rate is risky in terms of Japanese yen, because currency exchange rates can change over time.

Risk-free assets are important because they are well-defined, and because they allow us to define risky assets, which is any asset that is not risk-free. As a result, risk-free assets are crucial to measuring risk. In reality, no asset is completely risk-free; after all, even for US Treasury bonds it is possible—although unlikely—that some decision by the government leads to it intentionally not paying its bonds back. In modeling how financial decisions are made, however, the risk-free asset is an extremely useful simplification, in line with **Principle 4:** *Every model is an incomplete description of a more complex reality.*

To see the effects of risk or to analyze how risk is incorporated into valuation, let us consider a risky asset, an asset in which we invest $100, but do not know for certain what its value in the future will be. Let's say that we think there is a 50–50 chance of the value being $130 or $90 a year from now. We do not know for sure which of these outcomes will happen. But we can calculate what we mathematically *expect* the rate of return to be. In particular, in the best-case scenario, the rate of return will be ($130 − $100) / $100 = 0.30, and in the worst-case scenario the return will be $90 − $100 / $100 = −0.10:

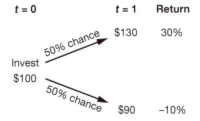

The expected rate of return $\mathbb{E}[R]$ of an asset is the sum over all possible outcomes of each possible rate of return multiplied by the respective probability of an outcome happening. Put differently, it is a probability-weighted mean of the future returns:

$$\begin{aligned}\mathbb{E}[R] &= p_1 \times R_1 + p_2 \times R_2 + \cdots + p_n \times R_n \\ &= \sum_{i=1}^{n} p_i \times R_i,\end{aligned} \qquad (6.1)$$

where there are n possible outcomes in the future, and p_i represents the probability that a return R_i will be realized. Finance practitioners usually look at a stock's past performance (about which there is a lot of information) to assess what the possible values of an asset may be in the future.

The expected rate of return for our risky asset, given that the probability of each outcome is 50% (or 0.50), is given by the following (note that since the probabilities have to add up to 100% (or 1), it must be the case that $p_2 = 1 - p_1$):

$$\begin{aligned} \mathbb{E}[R] &= p_1 \times R_1 + p_2 \times R_2 \\ &= 0.50 \times 30\% + 0.50 \times -10\% \\ &= 10\%. \end{aligned}$$

The expected rate of return of the risky asset is therefore 10%.

Note that the expected rate of return of the risky asset is higher than the rate of return of the risk-free asset (which was 5%). This illustrates a general but important point: To be compensated for more risk, investors will generally expect a *higher* rate of return. In other words, receiving a higher expected rate of return from an investment is not "free," but comes at the "cost" of higher risk. It is because this insight has such important implications in finance that it serves as Principle 7.

This insight is also consistent with the notion of risk aversion that we discussed earlier: A risk-averse investor is generally willing to accept a lower expected rate of return on an investment because it is more predictable (i.e., less risky). When choosing among investment alternatives with the *same* expected rate of return, a risk-averse individual will choose the alternative with the *lowest* risk. As a result, if a riskier investment does not offer a higher expected return to compensate an individual for taking on the greater risk, a risk-averse individual would likely not choose that investment.

This insight also connects with the discounted cash flow (DCF) analysis introduced in Chapter 2. As we noted in that chapter, the discount rate for an investment is also known as the opportunity cost of capital because it reflects the rate that we could earn somewhere else if we did not invest in the opportunity/project under consideration. In the case of DCF analysis, the opportunity cost of capital represents the rate of return we could earn elsewhere *for an investment with equivalent risk*. Thus, the higher the risk of a project, the higher the return we would require in order to invest in the project, and therefore the higher the discount rate should be. We analyze this outcome in more detail in the next section.

> **QUICK CHECK 6.1** Suppose there are two investments: (1) a riskless bond that sells for a price of $100 and promises to pay you $105 in a year; and (2) a stock that sells for a price of $100 and has a 50–50 chance of either going up in value to $110 or staying at $100. What is the expected return of each investment? Which would a risk-averse investor choose?

6.2.2 Valuation and Risk

The concept of risk also alters the valuation toolkit introduced in Chapter 2 in important ways. In that chapter, we examined what happens if we invest $100 in an account that pays 5% in interest per year. We saw that after one year, the future value is (Equation. 2.1):

$$\begin{aligned} FV &= \$100 \times (1 + r) \\ &= \$100 \times (1 + 0.05) \\ &= \$105. \end{aligned}$$

This calculation tells us that, if we make an initial outlay of $100, the account will give us $105 in one year. However, there is no notion of risk in this calculation. We are in a case of certainty and are essentially assuming we are guaranteed to have $105 in our account in one year.

What if this were not the case? Suppose that you find another investment opportunity that also promises to pay you interest, but there is some possibility that the company offering you this opportunity will run out of money, and you will lose money. In other words, instead of having $100 \times (1 + r)$ for sure in one year, you have the following possible future values: There is a 50% chance you have $100 \times (1 + r)$ and, say, a 50% chance that you have only $90. With this risk, would you put your money into this account if it gave you a 5% interest rate? Your answer would certainly be *no*—you are better off putting your money into the first investment account, which leaves you with $105 for sure, instead of $105 or $90 (depending on how the company fares).[1]

Now, suppose the new investment promises you a higher interest rate, say 25%? In this case, if the account pays you, you would receive $100 \times (1 + 0.25) = \$125$. You therefore have the following possible outcomes in one year:

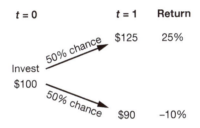

In this case, you may choose to go with the new investment because you have a chance to make more money given the higher interest rate, and earn a higher return. In particular, your *expected* return is higher: $0.5 \times 25\% + 0.5 \times -10\% = 7.5\%$. If it is likely that you will lose even more money in the case of the bad outcome, then you may require an even higher interest rate to convince you to make the investment. This example illustrates a general point: To be compensated for more risk, investors will generally demand a higher rate of return (Principle 7).

The rate of return that investors demand given the amount of risk they face is called the required rate of return. This required rate of return is the discount rate we use when we calculate present values in DCF analysis.

This example illustrates two important points about dealing with risk or uncertainty when valuing an asset or investment opportunity. First, instead of using certain future cash flows, we use *expected* future cash flows. Second, we adjust for cash flows being riskier by using a *higher* discount rate. Higher risk therefore generally means that money promised in the future becomes *less* valuable today because we are less certain that we will receive the expected money.

The present value of expected future cash flows is known as the intrinsic value of an asset. One of the main ways of expressing the criterion for making the investment decision when incorporating risk is to compute the present value of expected future cash flows (intrinsic value) of the investment and compare it to the initial outlay (price) for the investment. If the intrinsic value is greater than price, then the investment should be made.

6.2.3 Measuring Financial Risk

The previous examples showed an asset that is more risky than a risk-free asset. However, as we note in Principle 6, it is essential to be able to measure *how* risky an asset is. One way to do so is by measuring how wide the range of possible rates of return on the asset might be. This range is called an asset's

---

[1] In fact, such a situation would constitute an arbitrage, since the opportunity without risk is better in every regard.

volatility. The larger an asset's volatility, the wider the range of possible outcomes, the more likely it is to have returns at the extremes of the range, and the riskier the asset is.

To illustrate, consider two different stocks: Risco and Genco. The returns over the next year on each stock depend on how well the economy does (Table 6.1). These possible outcomes can be illustrated with a timeline.

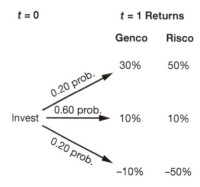

Table 6.1 Possible rates of return on Risco and Genco.

State of the economy	Rate of return on Risco	Rate of return on Genco	Probability
Strong	50%	30%	0.20
Normal	10%	10%	0.60
Weak	−30%	−10%	0.20

We can calculate the expected returns of both Genco and Risco using Equation 6.1. For Genco we have:

$$\mathbb{E}[R_{Genco}] = p_1 \times R_1 + p_2 \times R_2 + p_3 \times R_3$$
$$= 0.20 \times 30\% + 0.60 \times 10\% + 0.20 \times -10\%$$
$$= 10\%.$$

For Risco, we have:

$$\mathbb{E}[R_{Risco}] = p_1 \times R_1 + p_2 \times R_2 + p_3 \times R_3$$
$$= 0.20 \times 50\% + 0.60 \times 10\% + 0.20 \times -30\%$$
$$= 10\%.$$

As we can see, Genco and Risco have the *same* expected return, but the range of these returns differs. Risco's range of returns varies from 50% to −50%; Genco's is 30% to −10%. Intuitively, Risco is riskier because it is less certain how big the gain or loss will be.

Another way of visualizing volatility is by graphing the probability distribution of returns, which charts how likely it is for each return to be realized. Figure 6.1 shows that the probability distribution of Risco's returns is wider than that of Genco, and therefore Risco's returns are more volatile.

We can quantify how volatile a stock's return is. The statistic that is used most widely in finance to quantify and measure the volatility of a stock's probability distribution of returns is the standard deviation σ (sigma). Standard deviation measures how widely a stock's possible future returns may vary. The standard deviation is computed as follows:

$$\sigma = \sqrt{\sum_{i=1}^{n} p_i \times (R_i - \mathbb{E}[R])^2}. \tag{6.2}$$

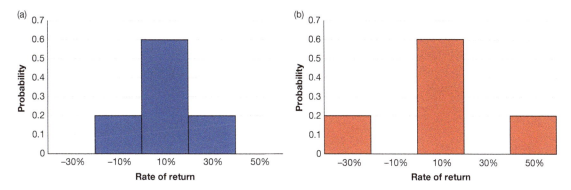

FIGURE 6.1 Probability distribution of returns for Genco (a) and Risco (b). The bars show the probability that each stock will achieve the indicated rate of return. Risco has a chance of lower or higher returns than Genco, indicating that Risco is riskier.

In Equation 6.2, σ calculates how far away each possible realized return, R_i, is from the expected return, $\mathbb{E}[R]$, and weights each of these possibilities by the probability that they will occur, p_i. Thus, if there are realizations where the returns are very different from the expected return, $R_i - \mathbb{E}[R]$, and there are high probabilities p_i of these realizations occurring, this will contribute to a higher standard deviation—the possible future returns are far away from the expected return.

A higher standard deviation indicates higher volatility, and a standard deviation of zero (the lowest possible number) indicates no risk. The standard deviation for a risk-free investment with a certain 5% return is zero:

$$\begin{aligned} \sigma &= \sqrt{\sum_{i=1}^{n} p_i \times (R_i - \mathbb{E}[R])^2} \\ &= \sqrt{1.0 \times (5\% - 5\%)^2} \\ &= 0. \end{aligned}$$

For this risk-free investment, there is only one possible outcome (which occurs with a probability of 1), and that one outcome is therefore the same as the expected return.

Coming back to Genco and Risco, the standard deviation for Genco stock is:

$$\begin{aligned} \sigma_{Genco} &= \sqrt{\sum_{i=1}^{n} p_i \times (R_i - \mathbb{E}[R])^2} \\ &= \sqrt{p_1 \times (R_1 - \mathbb{E}[R])^2 + p_2 \times (R_2 - \mathbb{E}[R])^2 + p_3 \times (R_3 - \mathbb{E}[R])^2} \\ &= \sqrt{0.2 \times (30\% - 10\%)^2 + 0.6 \times (10\% - 10\%)^2 + 0.2 \times (-10\% - 10\%)^2} \\ &= 12.65\%. \end{aligned}$$

The standard deviation for Risco stock is:

$$\begin{aligned} \sigma_{Risco} &= \sqrt{\sum_{i=1}^{n} p_i \times (R_i - \mathbb{E}[R])^2} \\ &= \sqrt{p_1 \times (R_1 - \mathbb{E}[R])^2 + p_2 \times (R_2 - \mathbb{E}[R])^2 + p_3 \times (R_3 - \mathbb{E}[R])^2} \\ &= \sqrt{0.2 \times (50\% - 10\%)^2 + 0.6 \times (10\% - 10\%)^2 + 0.2 \times (-30\% - 10\%)^2} \\ &= 25.30\%. \end{aligned}$$

6 PRINCIPLES OF RISK MANAGEMENT

For each of these stocks, the expected return ($\mathbb{E}[R]$) is 10%, as we previously calculated. Risco's standard deviation is twice that of Genco. Therefore, Risco's risk is higher because the possible deviations from its expected value are twice those of Genco.

Standard deviation is just one way to measure the risk associated with an asset. In Part III we will examine more closely the implications of the standard deviation and learn about other ways to measure risk.

> **QUICK CHECK 6.2** Suppose that XYZ stock's rate of return can take three possible values: −50%, 50%, and 100%, each with equal probability. What is XYZ's expected rate of return and its standard deviation?

Example 6.1 (Calculating Expected Return and Standard Deviation): Suppose two stocks have the possible outcomes shown in **Table 6.2**.

Table 6.2 Possible outcomes for Example 6.1.

Scenario	Stock A	Stock B	Probability
1	30%	40%	0.25
2	20%	15%	0.25
3	10%	5%	0.25
4	−20%	−15%	0.25

Which stock has the higher expected return? Which is riskier?

Solution. First, using Equation 6.1, calculate each stock's expected return. Stock A's expected return is:

$$\mathbb{E}[R_A] = p_1 \times R_1 + p_2 \times R_2 + p_3 \times R_3 + p_4 \times R_4$$
$$= 0.25 \times 30\% + 0.25 \times 20\% + 0.25 \times 10\% + 0.25 \times -20\%$$
$$= 10\%.$$

Stock B's expected return is:

$$\mathbb{E}[R_B] = p_1 \times R_1 + p_2 \times R_2 + p_3 \times R_3 + p_4 \times R_4$$
$$= 0.25 \times 40\% + 0.25 \times 15\% + 0.25 \times 5\% + 0.25 \times -15\%$$
$$= 11\%.$$

Stock B has the higher expected return.

To determine which stock is riskier, use Equation 6.2 to find the standard deviation of each stock's expected return.

Stock A's standard deviation is:

$$\sigma_A = \sqrt{\sum_{i=1}^{n} p_i \times (R_i - \mathbb{E}[R])^2}$$
$$= \sqrt{p_1 \times (R_1 - \mathbb{E}[R])^2 + p_2 \times (R_2 - \mathbb{E}[R])^2 + p_3 \times (R_3 - \mathbb{E}[R])^2 + p_4 \times (R_4 - \mathbb{E}[R])^2}$$
$$= \sqrt{0.25 \times (30\% - 10\%)^2 + 0.25 \times (20\% - 10\%)^2 + 0.25 \times (10\% - 10\%)^2 + 0.25 \times (-20\% - 10\%)^2}$$
$$= 18.708\%.$$

Stock B's standard deviation is:

$$\begin{aligned}\sigma_B &= \sqrt{\sum_{i=1}^{n} p_i \times (R_i - \mathbb{E}[R])^2} \\ &= \sqrt{p_1 \times (R_1 - \mathbb{E}[R])^2 + p_2 \times (R_2 - \mathbb{E}[R])^2 + p_3 \times (R_3 - \mathbb{E}[R])^2 + p_4 \times (R_4 - \mathbb{E}[R])^2} \\ &= \sqrt{\begin{array}{l}0.25 \times (40\% - 10\%)^2 + 0.25 \times (15\% - 10\%)^2 \\ + 0.25 \times (5\% - 10\%)^2 + 0.25 \times (-15\% - 10\%)^2\end{array}} \\ &= 19.843\%.\end{aligned}$$

Stock B has a higher standard deviation than Stock A, and thus Stock B is riskier—the higher expected return of Stock B comes with a higher risk.

6.3 Risk Management

The systematic attempt to analyze and deal with risk is known as the risk management process. The process can be broken down into five steps:

1. risk identification;
2. risk assessment;
3. selection of risk management techniques;
4. implementation of risk management techniques; and
5. review of the outcomes of the risk management plan.

As noted in Principle 6, managing risk is an essential element to every financial decision, which underscores the importance of the risk management process.

6.3.1 Risk Identification

The first step in the risk management process is risk identification: figuring out what the most important risk exposures are for the decision maker (individual, household, firm, or some other entity). Sometimes risks are explicitly financial. In previous sections, for example, the risks of Risco and Genco stocks were based on how high or how low the potential stock returns in the future may be. Other times, the risks may not be explicitly financial (i.e., may not involve low financial returns as in the Risco–Genco example), but most risks will, one way or the other, affect the financial position of the decision maker. Households or firms are sometimes not aware of all of the risks to which they are exposed. For example, a person who has never missed a day of work because of illness or injury may give little thought to the risk of disability. Buying insurance against disability risk might make sense, but may not even be considered. Box 6.2 describes how the Securities Exchange Commission (SEC) defines several types of risks faced by investors.

For effective risk identification, it is a good idea to have a checklist that covers all of the risks to which the decision maker might be exposed and how, if at all, the risks are related to each other. For example, you may have an investment account that you are using to pay for your homeowner's insurance. If your investment account faces a large loss so that you can no longer afford to pay for your homeowner's insurance, the risk of owning your house will be directly related to the risk of your investment account. The risks a household might face include:

- *Sickness, disability, and death*: The risk of loss arising from unexpected sickness, accidental injuries, or death imposes large costs because of the need for treatment and care and because of the loss of income caused by the inability to work.
- *Unemployment risk*: This is the risk of losing one's job.
- *Consumer durable-asset risk*: This is the risk of loss arising from ownership of a house, car, or other consumer durable asset. Losses can occur due to hazards such as fire or theft, or due to obsolescence arising from technological change or changes in consumer tastes.
- *Liability risk*: This is the risk that others will have a financial claim against you because they suffer a loss for which you can be held responsible. For example, if you cause a car accident through reckless driving, you would be required to cover the cost to others of personal injury and property damage.
- *Financial asset risk*: This is the risk arising from holding different kinds of financial assets such as equities or fixed-income securities denominated in one or more currencies. The underlying sources of financial asset risk are the uncertainties faced by the firms, governments, or other economic organizations that have issued these securities.

These and other risks faced by households influence virtually all of their economic decisions.

Firms must also identify the risks they face. Firms are organizations whose primary economic function is to produce goods and services. A firm is exposed to risk in virtually every one of its activities: purchasing, manufacturing, financing, distribution, investing, and so on.

Detailing the risks that a firm is exposed to requires detailed knowledge about the economics of the industry in which the firm competes, the technology the firm uses, and its sources of supply. A firm that produces baked goods, for example, faces a number of risks, such as:

- *Production risk*: This is the risk that machines (e.g., ovens, delivery trucks) will break down, that deliveries of raw materials (e.g., flour, eggs) will not arrive on time, that workers will not show up for work, or that a new technology will make the firm's existing equipment obsolete.
- *Price risk of outputs*: This is the risk that the demand for the baked goods produced by the bakery will change unpredictably. For example, an unanticipated shift in consumer preferences (e.g., celery becomes a popular substitute for bread at restaurants) might cause the market price of baked goods to fall. Or if competition intensifies, the bakery might be forced to lower its prices.
- *Price risk of inputs*: This is the risk that the prices of some of the bakery's inputs will change unpredictably. Flour can become more expensive, or wage rates can rise. If the bakery borrows money to finance its operations at a floating interest rate, it is exposed to the risk that the interest rate might rise.

The size and organizational form of the firm itself can also be affected by risk. Bakeries come in many different types and sizes. At one extreme are small production and retail operations owned and operated by a single individual or family. At the other extreme are large corporations such as Hostess Brands, with a workforce of thousands of people and an even larger number of shareholder owners. One purpose (and usually not the only one) of organizing as a large corporation is to better manage the production, demand, or price risks of the business.

The business risks faced by a firm are borne by its stakeholders: shareholders, creditors, customers, suppliers, employees, and government. If profitability is low or if the production technology changes, for instance, employees may be forced to take a pay cut or even lose their jobs altogether. The financial system can be used to transfer risks faced by firms to other parties. Specialized financial firms, such as insurance companies, perform the service of pooling and transferring risks. Ultimately, however, all risks faced by firms are borne by people.

Expertise in managing risks is essential to a firm's success. A bakery's management team can manage some of its risks in the following ways: It can keep extra flour in inventory to protect itself against delays in delivery; it can maintain spare parts for its machinery; and it can subscribe to services that forecast trends in the demand for its products. It can also buy insurance against some risks, such as accidental injury to its employees or theft of its equipment. Making trade-offs between the costs and benefits of risk-reducing measures is an essential part of managing a firm. We discuss risk management techniques in the next few sections.

> QUICK CHECK 6.3 Think of a fast-food restaurant. What risks is such a business exposed to, and who bears them?

Box 6.2 Investment Risk Defined by the SEC

The US Securities and Exchange Commission (SEC) defines investment risk as "the degree of uncertainty and/or potential financial loss inherent in an investment decision." There are many different financial assets one can invest in, and thus many different sources of the investment risks faced by firms and households. According to the SEC, these sources of investment risk include:

- *Business risk*: The returns on investments in stocks depend on how well the companies do.
- *Volatility risk*: Every company's stock price moves up or down, even when there is not a particular danger of the company failing. Investors are thus exposed to the risk of these up and down movements.
- *Inflation risk*: Inflation refers to a general upward trend in prices that, over time, reduces a currency's purchasing power. Inflation reduces the real returns on an investment.
- *Interest rate risk*: Interest rates can go up and down over time. As we saw in Chapter 2, such movements affect a financial asset's value. For example, an increase in interest rates makes the present value of an asset go down because the future cash flows must be discounted by a higher rate.
- *Liquidity risk*: This refers to the risk that investors will not be willing to buy or sell a certain financial product when they want to. Because many financial strategies rely on precise timing for trading, liquidity risk can change the nature of investment decisions.

Source: Investor.gov (n.d.). What is risk?

6.3.2 Risk Assessment

The next step in the risk management process is risk assessment. Risk assessment is the quantification of the costs associated with the risks identified in the first step of the risk management process. For example, a crop farmer may identify bad weather—such as flooding—as a major risk exposure. To assess the farmer's exposure to the risk of flooding, they need information. Based on past weather data, how likely is flooding in the farmer's location? If flooding occurs, what will be the cost to the farmer in terms of damage to crops and lost revenue?

In some cases, such information may be costly to gather. One of the main functions of insurance companies is to provide this kind of information. They employ actuaries, who are professionals specially trained in mathematics and statistics, to gather and analyze data and estimate the probabilities of natural disasters (such as flooding or forest fires), illness, accidents, and other such risks.

The costs associated with financial asset risks revolve around how much money one may lose in an investment. To illustrate, let's return to our previous example, where investing $100 led to a value next year of either $130 (a return of 30%) or $90 (a return of −10%). The risk comes from not knowing what the value will be in one year, particularly the possibility of a −10% return, and thus a loss from the investment. Calculating the volatility of this investment in the way we did in the previous section would be one way to quantify this investment's risks.

Households and firms often need expert advice in assessing their exposures and in quantifying the trade-offs between the risks and rewards of investing in various categories of assets, such as stocks and bonds. They typically turn to professional investment advisors, mutual funds, or other financial intermediaries and service firms to help them make those assessments.

6.3.3 Selection of Risk Management Techniques

After risk assessment, the next step is to choose how to *reduce* risk by choosing among risk management techniques. In all forms, risk involves possible changes in some outcome in the future; risk exists because no one can perfectly predict the future. However, employing suitable risk management techniques, financial decision makers may be able to reduce some—or even all—of the uncertainty, no matter what occurs in the future. There are four basic techniques available for reducing risk:

- *Risk avoidance*: A conscious decision not to be exposed to a particular risk. People may decide to avoid the risks of going into certain professions and firms may avoid certain lines of business because they are considered too risky. But it is not always feasible to avoid risks. For example, all people are inevitably exposed to the risk of illness by virtue of being human—they cannot avoid it.
- *Loss prevention and control*: Actions taken to reduce the likelihood or the severity of losses. Such actions can be taken prior to, concurrent with, or after a loss occurs. For example, you can reduce your exposure to the risk of illness by eating well, getting plenty of sleep, not smoking, and keeping your distance from people known to have contagious illnesses. If you catch a cold, you can stay in bed and reduce the possibility of having it turn into pneumonia. Similarly, a restaurant can reduce its risk of a kitchen fire by regularly cleaning cooking oil build-up around appliances.
- *Risk retention*: Absorbing the risk and covering losses out of one's own resources. This sometimes happens by default, as for example when one is unaware that there was any risk or one chooses to ignore it. But one may make a conscious decision to absorb certain risks. For example, a farmer may decide to not buy crop insurance against bad weather if the farmer does not want to pay the cost of the insurance. In that case, the farmer knows that crop losses due to bad weather will come out of their own savings.
- *Risk transfer*: Transferring the risk to others. Selling a risky asset to someone else and buying insurance are examples of this technique of risk management. Taking no action to reduce risk and relying on others to cover your losses is another example. There are three basic methods of accomplishing the transfer of risk: diversifying, hedging, and insuring. We explain these in detail later in this chapter.

6.3.4 Implementation of Risk Management Techniques

Following a decision about how to handle identified risks, one must implement the techniques selected. The underlying principle in this step of the risk management process is to minimize the *costs* of implementation. Thus, if you decide to buy automobile insurance of a certain kind, you should shop around for the lowest-cost provider. If you have decided to invest in the stock market, you should compare the costs of doing so through mutual funds or buying stocks through an online trading platform.

6.3.5 Review of Outcomes

The final step in risk management is a dynamic feedback process in which decisions are periodically reviewed and revised. As time passes and circumstances change, new risk exposures may arise, information about the likelihood and severity of risks may become more readily available, and techniques for managing them may become less costly. Thus, you will probably decide not to purchase life insurance if you are single, but reverse that decision if you get married and have children. A shipping company that has operated in the midwestern United States but expands to Florida may suddenly need to worry about the risk of hurricanes to its inventory, a risk that was not salient before.

> **QUICK CHECK 6.4** Identify a major risk in your life and describe the steps you take to manage it.

6.4 The Three Dimensions of Risk Transfer: Diversifying, Hedging, and Insuring

Among the four techniques of risk management listed in the previous section, transferring some or all of the risk to others is where the financial system plays the greatest role. The most basic method of transferring risk is to simply sell the asset that is the source of the risk. For example, an owner of a house is subject to at least three risk exposures: fire, storm damage, and the risk that the market value of the house will decline. By selling the house, the owner gets rid of all three of those exposures.

If one either cannot or does not choose to sell the asset that is the source of the risk, it is possible to manage some of the risks of ownership in other ways. For example, one can buy insurance against fire and storm damage, and thereby retain only the market value risk of the house. In some cases, it may be possible through risk transfer to completely eliminate a risk (but at a cost!).

There are three methods for transferring risks, called the three dimensions of risk transfer: diversifying, hedging, and insuring.

6.4.1 Risk Transfer by Diversifying

The first dimension of risk transfer is diversifying, which means spreading an investment among many small risks that are not perfectly correlated instead of investing in one big risk. Put differently, diversification limits the exposure to risk that comes from investing in just one asset.

Consider the diversification of business risks. Suppose that you are thinking about investing $100,000 in the biotechnology business because you believe that the discovery of new genetically engineered drugs offers great profit potential over the next several years. You could invest all $100,000 in a single firm that is developing a single new drug. In that case, your biotech investment would be concentrated, not diversified.

Diversification can be implemented by an individual or firm by investing directly in a market or by investing through a financial intermediary. Thus, you can diversify your investment in the biotechnology business by:

- investing in several firms, each of which is developing a new drug;
- investing in a single firm that is developing many drugs; and
- investing in a mutual fund that holds shares in many firms that are developing new drugs.

To illustrate how diversification reduces the exposure to risk, suppose that you have two investment opportunities. With the first, Opportunity A, you can invest $100,000 in the development of a single new drug. Success means that you will quadruple your investment and receive $400,000 in one year, but failure means you lose your $100,000 investment. There is a 50–50 chance of success or failure. Thus, your investment opportunity looks like this:

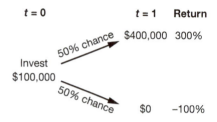

INVESTMENT OPPORTUNITY A

Now suppose that you have an alternative, Opportunity B, where instead of investing in a single drug, you can diversify and invest $50,000 in the development of each of two different drugs. Each drug again has a 50-50 chance of failure or success, and will quadruple your investment and pay you $200,000 if it succeeds. Importantly, suppose that the outcomes of each of the two drugs are not correlated—that is, they do not depend on each other. If one succeeds, it does not mean the other necessarily succeeds. The payoffs of each investment are:

INVESTMENT OPPORTUNITY B

Now let us compare the two investment opportunities. In Opportunity A, which is all or nothing, the expected return (Equation 6.1) is

$$\begin{aligned} \mathbb{E}[R] &= p_1 \times R_1 + p_2 \times R_2 \\ &= 0.5 \times 300\% + 0.5 \times -100\% \\ &= 100\%, \end{aligned}$$

and the standard deviation (Equation 6.2) is

$$\begin{aligned} \sigma &= \sqrt{\sum_{i=1}^{n} p_i \times (R_i - \mathbb{E}[R])^2} \\ &= \sqrt{p_1 \times (R_1 - \mathbb{E}[R])^2 + p_2 \times (R_2 - \mathbb{E}[R])^2} \\ &= \sqrt{0.5 \times (300\% - 100\%)^2 + 0.5 \times (-100\% - 100\%)^2} \\ &= 200\%. \end{aligned}$$

These numbers indicate that the expected return is 100% and the standard deviation is 200%.

In Opportunity B, as we noted, the success of one drug does not affect the success of the other drug. Therefore, there is still a chance of winding up with either $400,000 (if both drugs succeed) or nothing (if both drugs fail). However, there is also the intermediate possibility that one drug succeeds and the other fails. In that event, you will wind up with $200,000 (four times your investment of $50,000 in the drug that succeeds and zero from the drug that fails). Thus, there are four possible outcomes with Opportunity B, each with a 25% chance of occurring:

1. both drugs succeed, and you receive $400,000;
2. Drug 1 succeeds and Drug 2 doesn't, so you receive $200,000;
3. Drug 2 succeeds and Drug 1 doesn't, so you receive $200,000; and
4. both drugs fail, and you receive nothing.

Therefore, the possible outcomes of the *combined* investment are the following:

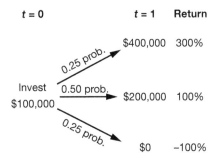

We can calculate the expected return (Equation 6.1) and standard deviation (Equation 6.2) of the diversified investment:

$$\mathbb{E}[R] = p_1 \times R_1 + p_2 \times R_2 + p_3 \times R_3$$
$$= 0.25 \times 300\% + 0.5 \times 100\% + 0.25 \times -100\%$$
$$= 100\%,$$

$$\sigma = \sqrt{\sum_{i=1}^{n} p_i \times (R_i - \mathbb{E}[R])^2}$$
$$= \sqrt{p_1 \times (R_1 - \mathbb{E}[R])^2 + p_2 \times (R_2 - \mathbb{E}[R])^2 + p_3 \times (R_3 - \mathbb{E}[R])^2}$$
$$= \sqrt{0.25 \times (300\% - 100\%)^2 + 0.5 \times (100\% - 100\%)^2 + 0.25 \times (-100\% - 100\%)^2}$$
$$= 141\%.$$

Note that with the diversified investment, the expected return is the same as investing in a single drug. But the risk as measured by the standard deviation of the returns is lower! By diversifying and holding a portfolio of two drugs, you reduce the probability of losing your entire investment to 25%, just one-half of what it would be without diversification. On the other hand, the probability of winding up with $400,000 has fallen from 50% to 25%. The other two possible outcomes result in your receiving $200,000.

This example shows how spreading your money across different investments (rather than "putting all your eggs in one basket," as the saying goes) can reduce risk. It is transferring your risk exposure across a number of different assets/investments. In the next subsection we expand upon this example by showing the effect with many different drugs.

Note that diversification does not reduce your risk exposure if the individual drugs you invest in always either succeed or fail together. That is, in the two-drug example, if there is no chance that one drug succeeds and the other fails, it would make no difference to your risk whether you invested all $100,000 in a single drug or split your investment between the two. Either way, there are only two possible outcomes—either you wind up with $400,000 (from success on both drugs) or you lose your entire investment (from the failure of both drugs). In such a case, the risks of commercial success for each separate drug are said to be *perfectly correlated* with each other—they move exactly in line with each other. In order for diversification to reduce your risk exposure, the risks must be less

> **QUICK CHECK 6.5** How might farmers reduce their exposure to risks of crop failure through diversification?

than perfectly correlated with each other. Furthermore, there are some types of risk that cannot be reduced through diversification—for example, risks that affect *many* assets (such as broad economic events like recessions) are examples of nondiversifiable risk. By contrast, risk that can be diversified (such as the random risk attributable to a particular drug) is known as diversifiable risk. We explore these types of risk in detail in Part III.

Diversification is a broad principle that can reduce risks in many financial situations for households, companies, or investors. But it is worth noting that, when looking at the performance of an investor that diversifies, it may not look as "magical" as the performance of an investor that does not—the more spectacular winners are most likely to come from among undiversified investors. But this is also the group that produces the more spectacular losers. By diversifying your portfolio, you reduce your chances of ending up at either extreme.

To underscore this point, let us return to the previous example of investing in the development of new drugs. For each drug that succeeds, you quadruple your investment; but for each that fails, you lose your entire investment. Thus, if you concentrate your $100,000 investment in a single drug, you wind up with $400,000 or nothing. You may find yourself labeled an investment "genius" for quadrupling your money, or a "dunce" for the colossal failure of losing your entire investment. There is a 50–50 chance of either outcome happening. If you diversify, however, you are most likely to make "only" $200,000, and thus be labeled an "average" performer. Of course, one always prefers to be a big winner and called a genius. But if that can only be accomplished by a decision now that results in either being a big winner or a big loser after the fact, then perhaps it is preferable to choose an alternative that leaves you in the middle.

As obvious as this point may seem, people often lose sight of it. Good luck is often interpreted as skill. Thus, it is not uncommon to find press reports about the spectacular successes of particular stock market investors who do not diversify their portfolios but concentrate instead in a single stock. Although such investors may indeed be investment geniuses, it is more likely that they are simply lucky. It is also not uncommon to find stories about big losers who are portrayed as foolhardy for not choosing the stocks that had big payoffs. A more valid criticism might be that they were undiversified.

> **QUICK CHECK 6.6** In the example of drug investment, suppose instead that Drug 2 pays off $100,000 if it is successful. What is the expected return and standard deviation of Drug 2 now? Recalculate the expected return and standard deviation of the combined investment.

6.4.1.1 The Power of Diversification

In the previous example, we showed how investing in two drugs resulted in a diversification effect that reduced risk relative to investing in only one drug. To expand upon the previous example and further illustrate the risk-reducing effect of diversification, consider what happens to the mean and standard deviation of the portfolio when we invest in *many* different drugs.

To illustrate this, consider Opportunity A from the previous section.

6.4 THE THREE DIMENSIONS OF RISK TRANSFER

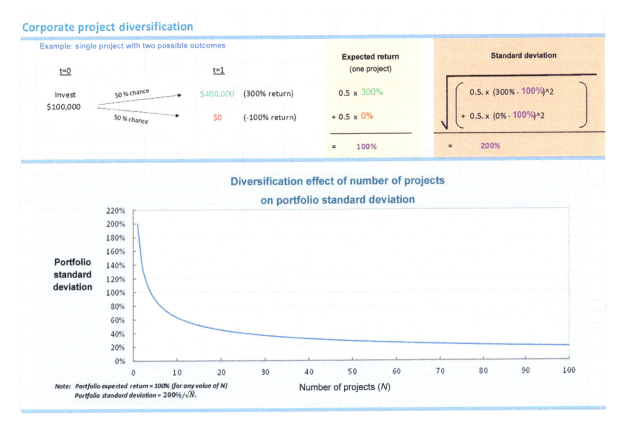

FIGURE 6.2 Diversification effect. This figure illustrates diversification by showing the effect of increasing the number of projects on the portfolio standard deviation. The top of the figure shows the payoffs of an individual project, which consists of investing $100,000, and in return having a 50% chance of making $400,000 and a 50% chance of making $0. The expected return and standard deviation of this project is calculated. The bottom of the figure shows how the total standard deviation of a portfolio of these projects decreases when the number of projects goes up.

Figure 6.2 shows the portfolio expected return and standard deviation as a function of the number of projects, N. The portfolio expected return stays the same for all N, but the portfolio standard deviation goes down as N increases. This outcome is due to the diversification effect. The standard deviation is equal to $200\% / \sqrt{N}$. The companion app to this chapter allows you to perform this exercise with different assumptions.

In this example it is important to add an additional assumption to realize the risk-reducing effects of diversification. As we add more and more projects, the scale of the drug company grows, so we need to add more and more investors to keep the scale of the investment at $100,000. In other words, the process of diversification consists of *pooling* risks and *subdividing* the required investment. This can be accomplished by creating a corporation or a mutual fund and issuing shares to the investors. See Box 6.3 for a real-world example that shows that diversification is a tool with wide-ranging possibilities in drug development not only for those who invest, but also for those who benefit from the fruits of those investments.

> **Box 6.3** World of Business: Diversification and Expanding Drug Development
>
> The concept of diversification is broad and powerful, and has the potential for a wide variety of applications. One such example is through the proposed concept of a drug "megafund," introduced by MIT economist Andrew Lo and colleagues.
>
> A challenge in the race to develop life-saving drugs for critical disease groups, such as cancer, is that development in many areas is very expensive (it can take upward of $2 billion to bring a drug to market) and risky (only about 1–2 out of 10 drugs make it to market). For example, it is estimated that it cost nearly $3 billion to bring the drug Nuplazid, for the treatment of Parkinson's disease and related disorders, to the market. The combination of great expense and great risk results in unattractive returns for investors looking to invest in these companies and provide them with money. With increasing development costs for drugs, many have raised the concern that treatments for critical diseases may go unfunded, at the cost of lives.
>
> A proposed solution for this conundrum—the drug "megafund"—comes directly from the concept of diversification. The idea is to financially pool together the development of many different types of drugs into one portfolio, and issue securities to investors based on the financial prospects of that portfolio. The drugs included would be for many different diseases, so the success of these drugs would be naturally uncorrelated, thus providing the ideal benefits of diversification. The reduction in risk provided by diversification improves the risk–reward trade-off of the portfolio of drugs, thus providing a more enticing investment opportunity for investors to purchase securities issued by the portfolio. The increased attractiveness for investors therefore enables additional money to be raised for the development of the drugs.
>
> *Sources:* Fernandez, J.-M., Stein, R. M., and Lo, A. W. (2012). Commercializing biomedical research through securitization techniques. *Nature Biotechnology* 30(10): 964–975. Lo, A. W., and Thakor, R. T. (2022). Financing medical innovation. *Annual Review of Financial Economics* 14: 231–270. Wouters, O. J., McKee, M., and Luyten, J. (2020). Estimated research and development investment needed to bring a new medicine to market, 2009–2018. *JAMA* 323(9): 844–853.

6.4.2 Risk Transfer by Hedging

The second dimension of risk transfer is hedging. The dictionary defines hedging as "protecting oneself against loss on (a bet or investment) by making balancing or compensating transactions." In finance, hedging refers to an action that reduces an investor's exposure to a loss while simultaneously eliminating the investor's exposure to a gain. For example, farmers who enter into a contract before the harvest to sell their future crops at a fixed price eliminate the risk of a low price at harvest time but give up the possibility of profiting from high prices at harvest time. They are hedging their exposure to the price risk of their crops. If you subscribe to a magazine for three years instead of subscribing one year at a time, you are hedging against the risk of a rise in the price of the magazine. You eliminate the potential loss due to an increase in the price of a subscription, but you give up the gain from a potential drop in subscription prices.

In practice, hedging often involves investing in an asset whose value moves in the *opposite* direction of the value of a risky asset.

To illustrate, consider a potential investment by an airline company. The company can invest $5 million now to purchase an airplane that will subsequently generate revenue of $5.5 million. However, the company expects that operating costs will change depending on the price of oil. Suppose that the company expects the price of oil in one year will be either $20 per barrel or $70 per barrel with a 50–50 chance, and that the company will need the equivalent of 10,000 barrels of oil to fuel its new plane. Thus, the company expects to incur oil costs of either $200,000 or $700,000: The revenue after fuel costs will be either $5.3 million or $4.8 million. We can represent the return on the $5 million investment as follows:

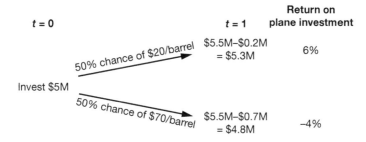

To hedge against the possibility of having a –4% return, the airline could invest in another asset where the returns are expected to move in the opposite direction. Such an asset would have a relatively higher return in the case where the risky asset goes down in value (if oil ends up being $70 per barrel), but a relatively lower return in the case where the risky asset goes up in value (if oil ends up being $20 per barrel). Because the airline's costs go up (and therefore returns go down) when the price of oil goes up, it should invest in oil at the same time. This action allows the company to hedge its investment in the plane:

(a) If the price of oil goes up, the airline makes money on its oil investment and loses money on its plane investment. The higher return on oil offsets the lower return on the plane.
(b) If the price of oil goes down, the airline loses money on its oil investment and makes money on its plane investment. The higher return on the plane offsets the lower return on oil.

Here's how this hedge would work: Suppose that the airline purchased 10,000 barrels of oil today for $40 per barrel, with the expectation that the price of oil will be either $20 or $70 per barrel in one year. The payoffs from this investment in oil would be:

We can see from these timelines that the airline makes money when oil prices are higher, which is when it would incur the highest fuel costs and lose money on its plane investment. Conversely, the airline loses money when oil prices are lower, and it would make money on its plane investment. If the airline made the initial plane investment and simultaneously invested in oil as a hedge, its situation would be as follows:

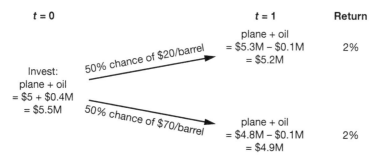

Note that we have not only reduced our overall risk—we have eliminated it, illustrating what is known as a "perfect hedge." But on the upside of the plane investment, our return has gone down: Instead of the original 6%, we have 2%. We therefore have removed the downside, but have given up some of the upside. The amount of the lost return can be viewed as part of the price the airline pays in the end for eliminating the risk of a big loss.

One can choose the degree to which one hedges risks—how "fully" one chooses to hedge depends on how much of the downside loss one wants to reduce (at the expense of reducing upside gain). Many times, a loss can put an individual or company in such a bad position that it makes sense to give up potential gains, making hedging a valuable tool to reduce risk. Financial markets offer a variety of mechanisms for hedging against risks such as those associated with changes in commodity prices, stock prices, interest rates, and exchange rates. Derivative contracts often offer a convenient way to hedge. For instance, in the previous example, the airline invested directly in oil to hedge against the fuel price risk it faced on its airplane investment. The airline could actually buy barrels of oil at $20 per barrel, but issues such as storing it would make this approach complicated. In practice, however, investors use financial contracts that allow them to agree to purchase an asset (such as oil) in the future, and earn returns based on that commodity's value in the future, without having to actually buy or sell the commodity itself. Such an arrangement is an example of a derivatives contract known as a forward contract. We describe how these contracts and other derivative contracts work in detail in Chapter 19.

> **QUICK CHECK 6.7** A restaurant that serves dishes made out of corn is exposed to the risk of corn prices going up. If the restaurant wants to hedge against this risk, what could it do?

6.4.2.1 Hedging Shortfall Risk by Matching Assets to Liabilities
Insurance companies and other financial intermediaries that sell insured savings plans and other insurance contracts need to assure their customers that the product they are buying is free of default risk. One way to assure customers is for insurance companies to hedge their liabilities in the financial markets by investing in assets that match the characteristics of their liabilities.

For example, suppose that an insurance company sells a customer a guaranteed investment contract that promises to pay $1,000 five years from now for a one-time premium today of $783.53. (This implies that the customer is earning an interest rate of 5% per year.) The insurance company can hedge this customer liability by buying a default-free zero-coupon bond with a face value of $1,000 issued by the government.

The insurance company is matching its assets (the $1,000 bond) to its liabilities (the contract that promises to pay $1,000). In order to earn a profit on this set of transactions, the insurance company has to be able to buy the five-year government bond for less than $783.53. (In other words, the interest rate on the five-year government bond must be greater than 5% per year.) If, instead of hedging its liability by buying a bond, the insurance company invests the customer's $783.53 premium in a portfolio of stocks, then there will be a risk of a shortfall—the value of the stocks in five years may turn out to be less than the $1,000 promised to the customer.

Many financial intermediaries pursue hedging strategies that involve matching their assets to their liabilities. In each case, the objective is to reduce the risk of a shortfall. The nature of the hedging instrument varies with the type of customer liability.

Thus, if a savings bank has customer liabilities that are short-term deposits earning an interest rate that floats, the appropriate hedging strategy would be to purchase a floating-rate bond, or to buy short-term bonds and use the proceeds when they mature to buy new short-term bonds at new interest rates that offset the risk of the short-term deposits.

6.4.3 Risk Transfer by Insuring

The final dimension of risk transfer is *insuring*, which is when a person or entity enters into a contract that provides protection against risks by giving payments in specific cases of loss. Those who buy insurance pay the insurance company in advance a payment called a *premium*, which keeps the insurance contract/policy in force. By buying insurance, you pay some cost now (the premium you pay for the policy) in exchange for compensation when you suffer a loss. Insuring is a type of risk transfer because the entity selling you the insurance—usually an insurance company or some other financial institution—takes on your risk (promising to pay you when you would take a loss).

For example, if you buy a car, you usually must buy some insurance against the risks of damage, theft, and injury to yourself and others. The premium may be $1,000 today to insure your car for the next year against the potential losses stemming from these contingencies. The cost now—a sure loss of $1,000—is substituted for the risk of losses that could be tens of thousands of dollars.

We can illustrate using our financial asset example from earlier, where a $100 investment has a 50% chance of going up to $130 and a 50% chance of going down to $90. Insuring would be paying a premium now to ensure a payoff when you would normally lose money (i.e., when your investment would go down in value to $90 and the return would be negative). Fully insuring this loss would involve paying a premium (let's say $2) to purchase an insurance policy that pays $10 only when your asset goes down in value, thus offsetting the loss:

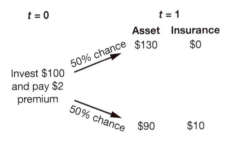

In this case, the overall risk is reduced specifically by eliminating the possible downside loss that you might incur from the asset. You may be able to insure a financial asset in this way through a policy bought from an insurance company. Compared to hedging, insuring is more precise—you do not give up the upside, but only eliminate the downside. Why hedge instead of insure? The answer is that the costs and benefits differ—hedging may be less expensive to undertake because you may lose money in the future by doing it, but insuring will provide more of a payoff for what is paid. Thus, one method may be preferred for an individual, depending on the circumstances. We show this in more detail in Part III.

6.4.3.1 Basic Features of Insurance Contracts

In discussing insurance contracts and understanding how to use them to manage risk, it is important to understand some basic terms and features. Four of the most important features of insurance contracts are exclusions, caps, deductibles, and copayments.

Exclusions and Caps: Exclusions are losses that might *seem* to meet the conditions for coverage under the insurance contract but are specifically excluded. For example, life insurance policies pay benefits if the insured party dies, but such policies typically exclude payment of death benefits if the insured person takes their own life within the first two years of coverage. Health insurance policies may exclude from coverage pre-existing conditions—that is, certain illnesses the insured party had *before* the policy was purchased. Some common pre-existing conditions are diabetes, cancer, and epilepsy.

Caps are limits placed on compensation for particular losses covered under an insurance contract. Thus, if a health insurance policy is capped at $1 million, it means the insurance company will pay no more than this amount for the treatment of an illness.

Deductibles: A deductible is an amount of money that the insured party must pay out of their own resources before receiving any compensation from the insurer. Thus, if your automobile insurance policy has a $1,000 deductible for damage due to accidents, you must pay the first $1,000 in repair costs and the insurer will pay for the amount in excess of $1,000. Deductibles create incentives for insured parties to control their losses. Research has shown that people with automobile insurance who have to pay more of the repair costs out of their own pockets tend to drive more carefully than drivers with no deductibles.

Copayments: A copayment feature in an insurance policy means that the insured party must cover a fraction of the loss. For example, an insurance policy might stipulate that the insured must pay 20% of any loss, and the insurance company pays the other 80%.

Copayments are similar to deductibles in that the insured party winds up paying part of the losses. The difference is in the way the partial payment is computed and in the incentives created for the insured party to control losses. For example, consider the case of a health insurance policy that covers visits to the physician. With a copayment feature, the patient must pay part of the fee for each visit. If the policy had a $1,000 deductible instead of a copayment feature, the patient would pay the entire cost of all visits until the $1,000 deductible was met, and then nothing for additional visits. Thus, the deductible feature does not create any incentive for patients to forgo additional visits once the $1,000 deductible is met; a copayment feature does create an incentive for patients to limit their visits to the doctor. Insurance policies can contain both deductibles and copayments.

6.4.3.2 Financial Guarantees

Any financial agreement is subject to credit risk, the risk that the other party to a contract into which you have entered will default. To manage this risk, there is a special type of insurance contract called a financial guarantee, in which an entity known as the guarantor promises to step in and pay what is owed if one party in a financial agreement is not able to. A *loan guarantee*, for example, is a contract that obliges the guarantor (which could be another financial intermediary or the government) to make the promised payment on a loan if the borrower fails to do so. Loan guarantees are pervasive in the economy and play a critical role in facilitating trade.

For example, consider credit cards, which in today's world have become a principal means of payment used by consumers. Banks and other issuers of credit cards guarantee to merchants that they will stand behind all customer purchases made with their credit cards. Credit card issuers thus provide merchants with insurance against credit risk.

Banks, insurance companies, and, on occasion, governments offer guarantees on a broad spectrum of financial instruments ranging from credit cards to interest rate and currency swaps. Parent corporations routinely guarantee the debt obligations of their subsidiaries. Governments guarantee residential mortgages, farm and student loans, loans to small and large business firms, and loans to other governments. Governments sometimes serve as the guarantor of last resort, guaranteeing the promises made by guarantors in the private sector such as banks and pension funds.

6.5 Risk Transfer and Economic Efficiency

As stated in Principle 6, risk management is an important objective in finance, given that any financial situation exposes people and firms to some type of risk. If there were no ways to limit or eliminate these risks, then businesses and individuals could experience massive losses, leading them to become financially insolvent, thus reducing economic efficiency, and potentially leading to a recession in the economy.

The transfer of risk, which is made possible by the financial system, contributes to economic efficiency in two distinct ways:

1 Even with no change in total output or total risk, redistributing the way the risk is borne can improve the welfare of the individuals involved.
2 Risk transfer can allow investments to be made that otherwise would not.

6.5.1 Improving Welfare through Redistributing Risks

Consider the hypothetical case of two investors in very different economic circumstances. The first is a retired widow who has an accumulated nest egg of $100,000, which is her sole source of income. The second is a college student who has $100,000 and who anticipates a good stream of earnings in the future after graduating from college.

Typically, the widow is assumed to be a more conservative investor and the student more aggressive. That is, we would expect the widow to be concerned primarily with the safety of her stream of investment income, whereas we might expect the student to be willing to bear more risk in exchange for a higher expected return.

Suppose the widow currently holds all of her wealth in the form of a portfolio of stocks left to her by her recently deceased husband, and suppose the college student has all of her wealth in a bank savings account that her parents started for her years before. Both would be better off if they could somehow swap their assets so that the widow ends up holding the savings account and the student the stock portfolio.

One of the most important functions of the financial system is to facilitate such transfers of risk. One way for this transfer of risk to take place is for the widow to simply sell her stocks and for the student to buy them. The widow could then invest the proceeds of the sale in a bank savings account. The student, on the other hand, could withdraw the money out of her savings account and use the money to buy stocks.

In this set of transactions, no immediate change occurs in the wealth of either party (except that each must pay the cost of carrying out the transactions, such as trading fees and bank charges). The student and the widow each had $100,000 of assets before, and immediately afterwards they each have $100,000 (less fees). The sole purpose and result of the transactions is to allow each party to hold the portfolio of assets that offers them the combination of risk and expected return most attractive for their circumstances.

6.5.2 Allowing More Investments through Risk Transfer

The ability to reallocate risks can facilitate the undertaking of valuable projects that might not otherwise be undertaken because they are too risky. The ability to pool and share risks can lead to an increase in inventive activity and the development of new products.

Let's look again at the case of creating new pharmaceuticals. The research and development effort that goes into the discovery, testing, and production of new drugs requires enormous amounts of investment extended over a considerable period of time. The return on that investment is highly uncertain. Even if an individual investor had the wealth necessary to finance the development of a new drug, risk aversion might deter them from doing so on their own.

To be more specific, suppose that a scientist discovers a new drug designed to treat the common cold. She requires $1 million to develop, test, and produce it. At this stage, the drug has a small probability of commercial success. Even if the scientist has $1 million in her bank account, she might not be willing to risk it all on the drug. She might instead set up a firm to develop the drug, and bring in other investors to share both the risks and the potential rewards of her discovery.

In addition to risk pooling and sharing, specialization in the bearing of risks can also facilitate undertaking risky investments. Potential investors may be willing to accept some of the risk exposure associated with a business enterprise, but not other risks. For example, suppose a real estate developer is planning to construct a new shopping mall in a downtown location. A consortium of banks and other lending institutions agrees to finance the project, but only on the condition that it is insured against fire. That is, the lenders accept the risk that the mall might not be a commercial success, but they do not accept the exposure of their investment to the risk of a fire. The existence of specialized insurance companies that accept the risk of fire makes possible the financing of the new shopping mall.

6.6 Risk Management in Practice

Given the benefits of risk transfer, over the centuries various economic organizations and contractual arrangements have evolved to facilitate a more efficient allocation of risk bearing both by expanding the scope of diversification and by permitting greater specialization in the management of risk.

In the last few decades, the rate of introduction of innovations that facilitate risk management has greatly accelerated because of changes on both the supply side and the demand side of the markets for risk bearing. Derivative financial contracts and marketplaces for trading them, such as exchanges, are examples of institutions whose primary economic function is to facilitate risk management. New discoveries in telecommunications, information processing, and finance theory have significantly lowered the costs of achieving greater global diversification and specialization in the bearing of risks. At the same time, increased volatility of exchange rates, interest rates, and commodity prices has increased the demand for ways to manage risk. Thus, the rapid and widespread development of futures, options, and swap contracts starting in the 1970s and 1980s can largely be explained as market responses to these cost and demand factors.

In an ideal world, all risks will be perfectly allocated to those that are ideally suited to bear them. But the theoretical ideal of complete markets for allocating risks is challenging to achieve because in the real world there are a number of limiting factors that can never be overcome entirely. Two factors that limit the efficient allocation of risks are transaction costs and incentive problems.

Transaction costs include the costs of establishing and running institutions such as insurance companies or securities exchanges, and the costs of writing and enforcing contracts. These institutions will not come into existence unless the benefits from their creation exceed the costs.

The primary incentive problems standing in the way of the development of institutions for efficient risk sharing are moral hazard and adverse selection. The moral hazard problem exists when having insurance against some risk causes the insured party to take greater risk or to take less care in preventing the event that gives rise to the loss. Consider the example of insurance companies. Moral hazard can lead to unwillingness on the part of insurance companies to insure against certain types of risk. For example, if a warehouse owner buys fire insurance, the existence of the insurance reduces his incentive to spend money to prevent a fire. Failure to take the same precautions makes a warehouse fire a more likely occurrence. In an extreme case, the owner may be tempted to actually start a fire in order to collect the insurance money if the coverage exceeds the market value of the warehouse. Because of this potential moral hazard, insurance companies may limit the amount they will insure or simply refuse to sell fire insurance under certain circumstances.

Another class of incentive problems is adverse selection—those who purchase insurance against risk are more likely than the general population to be at risk. For example, a life insurance policy pays the policyholder's beneficiary (usually a family member) in the case of the death of a policyholder. An insurance company may not be able to perfectly see if the person purchasing the policy is healthy. If the insurance company is not able to charge a price for the policies appropriately based on the policyholder's life expectancy, a disproportionately large number of the policies sold may be bought by unhealthy people who expect to live only a short time. The insurance company would then lose a significant amount of money, and in the extreme case, induce insurance companies to not want to sell *any* policies.

Conclusion

In this chapter we learned about the concept of risk, which is a component of every financial decision that one can make. We introduced ways to measure the financial risk of an investment, and then discussed the concept of risk management—ways to identify risks and reduce them. An important way to reduce risk in financial transactions is through transferring the risk to another party, and is made possible through financial contracts via hedging, insuring, and diversifying.

In subsequent chapters we will show how risk affects financial decisions in the context of investments (such as through stocks and bonds) and corporate decisions (the choice of project and financial instruments). We will also provide details of specific financial contracts that can be used to manage risk, starting in the next chapter, which introduces options.

Takeaways

- Risk is defined as uncertainty that matters to people. Principle 6 states that risk is fundamental in all financial decisions, and must be measured and considered explicitly in financial analysis. When an individual is efficiently diversified, there is a trade-off between risk and expected return. Financial risk can be measured using the standard deviation of returns of investments, which tells us how far away returns may be from what we expect.
- The process of risk management is the systematic attempt to analyze and deal with risk.
- All risks are ultimately borne by people in their capacity as consumers, stakeholders of firms and other economic organizations, or taxpayers. The riskiness of an asset or a transaction cannot be assessed in isolation; it depends on the specific frame of reference. In one context, the purchase or sale of a particular asset may add to one's risk exposure; in another, the same transaction may reduce risk. Many resource allocation decisions, such as saving, investment, and financing decisions, are significantly influenced by the presence of risk and, therefore, are partly risk management decisions.
- There are five major categories of risk exposures for households: sickness, disability, and death; job loss; consumer durable-asset risk; liability risk; and financial asset risk. Firms face several categories of risks: production risk, price risk of outputs, and price risk of inputs.
- There are five steps in the risk management process:
    1. risk identification;
    2. risk assessment;
    3. selection of risk management techniques;
    4. implementation; and
    5. review.
- There are four techniques of risk management:
    1. risk avoidance;
    2. loss prevention and control;
    3. risk retention; and
    4. risk transfer.
- There are three dimensions of risk transfer: diversification, hedging, and insuring. Diversification involves spreading an investment among many small risks that are not perfectly correlated instead of investing in one large risk. Hedging involves reducing the downside loss of a risk by giving up some upside. Insuring involves paying a premium to avoid a much larger loss.
- From society's perspective, risk management institutions contribute to economic efficiency by shifting risk away from those who are least willing or able to bear it to those who are most willing

to bear it. By allowing people to reduce their exposure to the risk of undertaking certain business ventures, they may encourage entrepreneurial behavior that can benefit society.
- Over the centuries, various economic organizations and contractual arrangements have evolved to facilitate a more efficient allocation of risk bearing by expanding the scope of diversification and the types of risk that are shifted.
- Among the factors limiting the efficient allocation of risks are transaction costs and problems of adverse selection and moral hazard.

Key Terms

Adverse selection   164
Caps   162
Copayment   162
Credit risk   162
Deductible   162
Diversifiable risk   156
Diversifying   153
Exclusions   161
Expected rate of return   143
Financial guarantee   162
Hedgers   142
Hedging   158
Incentive problems   164
Insuring   161
Intrinsic value   145
Moral hazard problem   164
Nondiversifiable risk   156
Opportunity cost of capital   144

Premium   161
Probability distribution   146
Required rate of return   145
Risk   140
Risk assessment   151
Risk aversion   141
Risk exposure   141
Risk identification   149
Risk-free asset   143
Risk-free rate of return or risk-free rate   143
Risk management process   149
Risk management techniques   152
Risky assets   143
Speculators   142
Standard deviation   146
Three dimensions of risk transfer   153
Transaction costs   164
Volatility   146

Key Equations

Expected rate of return	$$\mathbb{E}[R] = p_1 \times R_1 + p_2 \times R_2 + \cdots + p_n \times R_n = \sum_{i=1}^{n} p_i \times R_i$$	Eq. 6.1
Standard deviation σ	$$\sigma = \sqrt{\sum_{i=1}^{n} p_i \times (R_i - \mathbb{E}[R])^2}$$	Eq. 6.2

Problems

1. Suppose you are aware of the following investment opportunity: You could open a coffee shop around the corner from your home for $25,000. If business is strong, you could net $15,000 in after-tax cash flows each year over the next five years.
   (a) If you knew for certain the business would be a success, would this be a risky investment?
   (b) Now assume this is a risky venture and that there is a 50% chance it is a success and a 50% chance you go bankrupt within two years. You decide to go ahead and invest. If the business

subsequently goes bankrupt, did you make the wrong decision based on the information you had at the time? Why or why not?

2. Suppose your new business venture will last only one year. For $110,000 you plan to purchase 20 acres of farmland next to a site that may be developed into a retail shopping mall. You will sell the land in one year and, based on the outcome of the zoning hearing, there is an equal chance that it will be worth either $100,000, or $125,000, or $145,000 next year. The bank is willing to make you a riskless loan to finance the purchase of the property at an interest rate of 10%. The loan balance in total will be paid in one year when you sell the property. What is the most the bank will be willing to lend?

3. Which risk management technique has been chosen in each of the following situations?
    (a) Installing a smoke detector in your home.
    (b) Investing in many different stocks rather than just one stock.
    (c) Deciding to purchase collision insurance on your car.
    (d) Purchasing a life insurance policy for yourself, to be paid to your immediate family.

4. Suppose you are a fanatical follower of a particular Major League Baseball team (e.g., the Cubs) about to start playing in the World Series. You know that if your team loses again this time you will need serious psychological help and expect you will probably have to spend thousands of dollars on counseling services. Is there a way to insure against this risk? Would you be considered a speculator if you gambled on the World Series?

5. What dimension of risk transfer are you engaged in if you make a restaurant reservation for your party of six? Why do some restaurants refuse to take reservations?

6. Suppose you are interested in financing your new home purchase. You have your choice of many financing options. You could enter into any one of the following agreements: 8% fixed rate for 7 years, 8.5% fixed rate for 15 years, or 9% fixed rate for 30 years. In addition, you could finance with a 30-year variable rate that begins at 5% and increases and decreases with the rates in the economy.
    (a) Suppose you believe that interest rates are on the rise. If you want to completely eliminate your risk of rising interest rates for the longest period of time, which option should you choose?
    (b) Would you consider that hedging or insuring? Why?
    (c) Suppose you believe interest rates are going to fall; which option should you choose?
    (d) What risk do you face in that transaction?

7. Suppose you are thinking of investing in real estate. How might you achieve a diversified real estate investment?

8. Many insurance policies ranging from automobile, to homeowner's, to health insurance contain deductible provisions. A deductible is a fixed amount per claim, or over a given period of time, which is not reimbursed under the policy. What efficiency role do deductibles play in insurance markets?

9. Suppose you have an investment opportunity with a 50% probability of providing a 5% return, and a 50% probability of providing a 3% return. Calculate the expected return and standard deviation of this investment. If this riskless interest rate is 5%, would you put your money into the investment opportunity or into the riskless asset? Explain.

10. Suppose you have an investment with a 20% probability of providing a 60% return, and an 80% probability of providing a 10% return. Calculate the expected return and standard deviation of this investment.

11. Use the companion app for this chapter. Put the investment of the above project into the app (a 20% probability of providing a 60% return, and an 80% probability of providing a 10% return). Run the Monte Carlo simulation assuming that you have a portfolio of these investments consisting of: 1, 5, 10, 50, 100, and 1,000 projects. What is the overall expected return and standard deviation in each of these scenarios? Comment on how they change as you increase the number of projects and why.

12. Use the companion app for this chapter. Now suppose the investment project is as follows: a 100% probability of providing a 60% return, and a 0% probability of providing a −10% return. Run the Monte Carlo simulation assuming that you have a portfolio of 100 and 1,000 projects. What is the overall expected return and standard deviation in both cases? Comment on why things changed or did not change.
13. Consider the two stocks shown in Table 6.3.

Table 6.3

Rate of return on Stock A	Rate of return on Stock B	Probability
20%	80%	0.30
5%	20%	0.60
−10%	−90%	0.10

Calculate the expected rate of return and standard deviation for both stocks. Which stock is riskier?

14. Consider the two stocks shown in Table 6.4.

Table 6.4

Rate of return on Stock X	Rate of return on Stock Y	Probability
80%	120%	0.1
50%	20%	0.2
−50%	−20%	0.4
−80%	−95%	0.3

Calculate the expected rate of return and standard deviation for both stocks. Which stock is riskier?

15. Suppose we have the information shown in Table 6.5 on prices for a share of Taltavull Transfer Corporation (TTC) stock.

Table 6.5

Year	1 Jan. price	31 Dec. price
2020		$65.00
2021	$65.00	$72.00
2022	$72.00	$77.00
2023	$77.00	$80.00
2024	$80.00	$79.00
2025	$79.00	$85.00

Calculate the annual total rates of return on an investment in TTC. Using each year as an observation, what is the expected annual total rate of return?

16. Find the expected return and variability of the returns measured as the standard deviation from the return distribution shown in Table 6.6.

Table 6.6

Probability	Return
15%	50%
25%	40%
25%	25%
25%	10%
10%	−30%

17. Suppose Table 6.7 represents the historical returns for Microsoft and Apple.

Table 6.7

Year	MSFT	Apple
1	10%	9%
2	15%	12%
3	−12%	−7%
4	20%	18%
5	7%	5%

(a) What is the expected return for Microsoft? For Apple?
(b) What is the standard deviation of returns for Microsoft? For Apple?

7 ANALYZING UNCERTAINTY: OPTIONS

CHAPTER OVERVIEW

7.1	How Options Work	174
7.2	The Put–Call Parity Relation	180
7.3	Option Trading in Markets	187
7.4	Investment Strategies with Options	189
7.5	Valuing Options: The Black–Scholes–Merton Model	195

> **LEARNING OBJECTIVES**
>
> After reading this chapter, you will be able to:
> - identify options and their uses in financial and nonfinancial applications;
> - explain the mechanics of financial option contracts, the decisions they allow a holder to make, and how they are traded;
> - construct investment strategies using options to modify exposure to particular investment risks, such as the possibility that a stock will drop in value;
> - construct diagrams that illustrate payoffs for different option positions;
> - explain the pricing relationships that exist among calls, puts, stocks, and bonds;
> - determine the price of an option;
> - identify the factors that affect option values as shown by the Black–Scholes–Merton model;
> - demonstrate how implied volatility can be inferred from the Black–Scholes–Merton model.

✚ You work for a large publicly traded company, which pays you a bonus in the form of stock options. What is the value of these options?

✚ You believe that a stock will go up in value and want to invest in it, but the stock costs $1,000 per share and you do not want to invest too much money. Your friend Mosab suggests that you buy call options on the stock. How do the options work, and what is their relationship to the stock?

+ You are the CEO of a company, and want to pay employees so that they benefit when the company does well. However, you do not want to issue additional shares of stock at the moment. Is there a financial contract you can use?

+ You own a large number of shares of stock in a friend's company, and want to hold on to them to show your support. However, you are concerned that the stock price will drop and cause a large decline in your wealth. How can you invest to protect against this scenario?

+ The CFO of your company decides to raise funding with a new type of security that starts out as debt but can turn into equity if the company does well enough. You are asked to determine what price investors would be willing to pay for the security, and thus how much the company could raise by issuing it. How can you do so?

+ You want to construct an investment strategy that will pay you money whether the market goes up or down in the future. How can you do so, and how much would such a strategy cost?

Introduction

In the previous chapter we discussed what risk is and how managing risk is an essential element of every financial decision. Risk stems from uncertainty about the future. In this chapter, we introduce and explain financial contracts—options—that help resolve uncertainty by allowing an asset to be traded at a fixed price in the future after observing outcomes. More specifically, *put* options allow the choice to sell or not sell an underlying asset in the future, while *call* options allow the choice to buy or not buy an underlying asset in the future. The owner does not *have* to sell (in the case of a put) or buy (in the case of a call) in the future if it is not beneficial to them. Thus, the value of option contracts is that they embed flexibility—the owner makes the decision after the market price of the underlying asset is observed. However, because there is no such thing as a free lunch (Principle 3), this flexibility comes at a price.

Options are at the core of decision making under uncertainty. Refer to **Principle 6:** *Risk is fundamental to financial analysis and must be explicitly considered in all financial decisions.* In particular, purchasing an option now makes it possible for its owner to plan for making financial decisions in the future after uncertainty is resolved, whereas in general someone considering a risky financial purchase must make their purchasing choice in advance of knowing how the risk will play out in the future. For example, consider the risk in buying a house—the ability to walk away from it if it has previously undetected defects eliminates this uncertainty. Flight insurance that allows you a refund if a flight is cancelled or delayed eliminates a big uncertainty with air travel. If you purchase a stock and a put option on that stock that pays you if the stock drops in value, you have eliminated your financial risk.

The ability to choose to buy or sell an asset after its future price becomes known is as valuable as the ability to make a perfect forecast of the asset's price. Consider the following example (presented in Merton 1981). Suppose you pursue one of two strategies:

1. you invest $1,000 every month in stocks; or
2. you invest $1,000 each month in months when stocks outperform bonds, and invest the $1,000 in bonds when bonds outperform stocks.

Without the ability to perfectly forecast the future prices of stocks and bonds, pursuing Strategy 1 would have resulted in an ending value of $67,527 after 50 years. But a strategy of investing in stocks only in months where they outperform bonds and in bonds in the other months would have resulted after 50 years in $5,362,212,000! This strategy is equivalent to having a free option every month, as it allows one to costlessly buy assets when uncertainty is resolved (price changes are known), and is very profitable. Since there is no free lunch, that means the options will have a price that reflects their value.

Option pricing is foundational to decision making under uncertainty. One of our Ten Principles is **Principle 8:** *Flexibility in financial decisions has value, and the greater the uncertainty, the greater the value.* Just as timelines and discounted cash flow (DCF) analysis are fundamental tools in dealing with the time dimension of financial decisions (i.e., **Principle 1:** *A dollar today is not worth the same as a dollar tomorrow*), options analysis is fundamental for dealing with uncertainty.

Although the option pricing model was originally derived in order to evaluate stock options, its uses are far broader and more consequential. As we will see in this chapter and the rest of the book, the range of applications of option analysis in finance is extensive and includes asset management, capital markets, corporate finance, public finance, household decisions, and government policy. We describe some of these applications in more detail later in the chapter. Thus, the topic of options is important to finance, no matter what part of finance you work in and whether or not you are a "quantitative" finance practitioner.

There are as many kinds of option contracts as there are items to buy or sell. Stock options, interest-rate options, foreign-exchange options, and commodity options are traded both on and off organized exchanges all around the world.

The foundational model for the pricing of options is the Black–Scholes–Merton (BSM) model developed in the early 1970s entirely in theory, as there were no traded options exchanges to provide price data for empirical testing at that time. The discovery of the option pricing formula by Black and Scholes (1973), and Merton's (1973b) dynamic replication methodology, ushered in a revolution in the theory and practice of finance in a fashion similar to the revolution in molecular biology that followed the discovery of the double-helix structure of DNA in 1953. The double-helix model gave birth to the field of genetic engineering; the option pricing model gave birth to financial engineering.

The Chicago Board Options Exchange (CBOE), the first public options exchange, began its operations in April 1973, coinciding with the publication of the BSM model. By 1975, the BSM model was the dominant model of choice used by traders to value and hedge the risk of their option positions.

Such a rapid transition from theory to practice on such a large scale was unprecedented in the history of finance. As we will see, option pricing expertise has since been applied to the pricing of a wide array of other financial contracts, and it has played a fundamental role in supporting the creation of new financial products and markets around the globe.

Although the option pricing model was originally derived to evaluate stock options, its uses are far broader and more consequential. As we will see in this chapter and the rest of the book, the range of applications of option analysis in finance is extensive and includes asset management, capital markets, corporate finance, public finance, household decisions, and government policy. Box 7.1 provides an overview of some of these applications.

Box 7.1 Options Are Everywhere

The implications of options are broader than just financial options traded in marketplaces. Indeed, options are *everywhere*—both in financial contracts and real-economy decisions.

Financial contracts that embed options in them include:

- Deposit insurance: Many bank accounts are explicitly insured by governments if banks fail. This type of insurance is a put option because it pays the holder of the bank account when the value of the bank declines below its ability to pay the accountholder.

- Loan guarantees: Companies and governments often guarantee that they will pay off loans if a borrower fails to make payments (default), an example of a put option because the guarantee pays off when the loan's value becomes low.
- The ability to analyze corporate debt and equity, as well as many other types of financial claims issued by companies, as combinations of options. We cover this in detail in Chapter 14.
- Employee stock options: Employees and executives within companies are frequently paid in call options on the company's stock.
- Consumer product-obsolescence insurance: With technological change, consumer items such as smartphones and computers can quickly become obsolete. Many manufacturers and retailers offer plans that permit the consumer to exchange their product for a new one for a fee.

Beyond financial contracts, options also appear in nonfinancial decisions. These are known as *real options* and refer to decisions that can be analyzed (and valued) using an options framework. The common element for using option pricing here is the same as in the preceding examples: The future is uncertain and in an uncertain environment having the flexibility to decide what to do after some of that uncertainty is resolved is an option. Examples of such real options include:

- Concert or game tickets: Once purchased, the ticket holder has the right (but not the obligation) to attend the concert, or let the option expire by skipping the concert.
- Power-generating plants: The ability to increase or decrease power generation based on current conditions.
- Drug discovery: Breaking a drug's development into phases and at the end of each phase making a decision based on new information whether to continue financing its development or stop the clinical trials, which creates an option to abandon the trials and save further expenditures.
- Expanded manufacturing capacity: The decision to increase/decrease manufacturing of products can be made after market information is learned. Similarly, decisions about research and development into new products can be made once market information about existing products is known.
- Medical insurance: Healthcare insurance contains varying degrees of flexibility, a major one being whether the consumer agrees in advance to use only a pre-specified set of doctors and hospitals (HMO plan) or retain the right to choose an out-of-plan doctor or hospital. In making the decision on which to take, the consumer solves an option pricing problem as to the value of that flexibility.

Source: Merton, R. C. (2022a). Emergence of financial engineering from financial science: an MIT story. Killian Lecture, MIT, 28 Mar.

We begin this chapter by explaining how options work and how they can be used to create a variety of payoff patterns contingent on the price of the underlying asset. We then apply the law of one price (**Principle 2:** *Equivalent assets that can be freely bought and sold will have the same market price*) to derive a relation between the price of a call and the corresponding put. The BSM option pricing formula is introduced and applied.

7.1 How Options Work

As explained in the introduction to this chapter, an option is a contract that allows the owner to trade an asset in the future at a fixed price. However, there are two types of options, ones that allow the owner to sell if they choose and ones that allow the owner to buy. A put option is a contract that gives its owner the right, but not the obligation, to sell a specified asset in the future at a pre-specified price. A call option is a contract that gives its owner the right, but not the obligation, to buy a specified asset in the future at a pre-specified price. The owner of an option can thus choose to sell (in the case of a put) or buy (in the case of a call) the asset at the fixed price in the future, or the owner can simply choose to take no action and let the option expire. An example of a put option is a contract that allows you to sell a share of Microsoft Corporation stock in one year for a price of $100. In one year's time, if, based on the market stock price, it is a good deal for you to sell the share of stock for $100 (e.g., if the price of Microsoft stock falls below $100), you can do so; otherwise, if the market price is above $100, you can simply let the contract expire. Thus, option contracts permit you to wait until after you know whether there will be a gain before deciding whether to take an action or not.

Knowing the cost of acquiring such flexibility is fundamental to making financial decisions of all kinds. If having the flexibility to not make a decision until the future is revealed were free, choosing to acquire that flexibility is easy: take it. But no one in the financial sector is going to give away flexibility for free, and so the core of decision making under uncertainty involves assessing the benefits of flexibility and the cost of acquiring it. Option pricing models provide estimates of that cost.

In order to understand how options work, it is useful to think about what you would do if you owned the different types of option contracts. We begin by illustrating with an example of a put option on a share of stock.

7.1.1 Put Options

As stated above, a put option is one that gives you the right to sell a stock in the future. Here we will look at an example of potential opportunities of owning a put option on a share of stock.

Consider our example of a put option contract that allows you to sell a share of Microsoft Corporation stock one year from now for $100. This is a European option, as the trade decision can only be done on a fixed date in the future, as opposed to an American option, where it can be made at any time during the contract's life. The underlying asset, the item that can be bought or sold, is a share of Microsoft stock. The initial expiration or maturity date, the date the option can be exercised (bought or sold), is one year from now, and we will denote this date as T. The strike price, or exercise price, the fixed price the underlying asset on the option contract can be traded at, is $100, and we will denote this price as K.

The put option allows you to sell Microsoft stock one year from now for a price of $100. At the decision time (i.e., expiration) one year from now, would you do so? The answer depends on the price of Microsoft's stock in the market at that time.

If Microsoft's stock price one year from now is $50, would it be a good deal for you to sell it for $100? The answer is yes. You would be selling an asset worth $50 for $100 and your payoff—the value of the option at expiration—is positive. Note that we are only considering the payoff and not the profit, since we are ignoring the price initially paid for the put option; in Section 7.3 we will show how to derive this option price. More specifically, you would buy a share of Microsoft stock in the market for $50, and turn around and sell via the put option for $100 (i.e., exercise the put option). Your payoff from this transaction would be $100 − $50 = $50. However, suppose that rather than declining to $50, Microsoft's stock price increases to $120. Would it be a good deal for you to sell it for $100? The answer is no—you would have to buy the stock for $120 in the market, and then sell it by exercising the option for $100, resulting in a negative payoff (i.e., loss) of $100 − $120 = −$20. In this case, you are better off not exercising the option and letting the contract expire, resulting in a payoff of zero, which, while not positive, is also not a loss.

In each case, we can also represent the payoff of the put option at expiration, which we will denote by P_T, mathematically as:

$$P_T = \max(K - S_T, 0). \tag{7.1}$$

Equation 7.1 thus states that, at expiration, you will choose whichever is larger—the payoff from buying the stock for S_T and selling it for K, or the payoff from leaving the option unexercised and getting zero. In the case where Microsoft's stock became worth $50, the payoff of the put option if you were to exercise it would be $K − S_T$ = $100 − $50 = $50; this is greater than 0, and therefore you would choose to exercise the option and receive this payoff. In contrast, in the case where Microsoft's stock became worth $120, the payoff of the option if you were to exercise is $K − S_T$ = $100 − $120 = −$20; this is less than zero, and you would choose to let the option expire unexercised and get a payoff of $0.

Table 7.1 provides the decision you would make, given various possible values of Microsoft's stock.

The different payoffs from Table 7.1 are shown as a payoff diagram in Figure 7.1. The payoff diagram shows that put options pay off on the downside of the underlying asset—the owner gains a greater payoff as the stock price goes lower, below the strike price. In other words, once the stock price goes below the strike price, the payoff of the put increases one-for-one as the stock price decreases.

Subtracting the price of the put from the payoff shows the net payoff, often called the profit. It is shown as the dashed line below the payoff. In this example, we assume the price of the put is $10. In one year (at the expiration date of the option), if Microsoft's stock price ends up at 80, then the owner would exercise the $100 strike price option, the payoff will be $K − S_T$ = $100 − $80 = $20, and the profit will be $20 − $10 = $10. If the stock price is $120, then the payoff is zero and there is a loss of $10.

Put options provide insurance against the loss in value of the underlying asset below the strike price. As we saw in Chapter 6, insuring is one of the three core tools of risk management. There is an important difference between the value of insurance provided by puts and other forms of insurance, like homeowner's insurance: The put provides insurance regardless of what causes the loss in asset value. A homeowner's policy will pay for a loss in value from specified covered events, like a fire, weather damage, or a flood, but not for a loss from events that are not covered, like an increase in property taxes. In contrast, the put covers the loss in value whatever the cause.

Table 7.1 **Long put option payoffs at expiration.** Possible payoffs at expiration date T from holding a put option with a strike price of K = $100 based on various future values of Microsoft stock with a price of S_T at expiration. The table shows exercise decision best practice in each case.

Stock price, S_T	Exercise decision	Put option payoff, P_T
$0	Exercise	$100
50	Exercise	50
80	Exercise	20
100	Indifferent	0
120	Do not exercise	0
150	Do not exercise	0

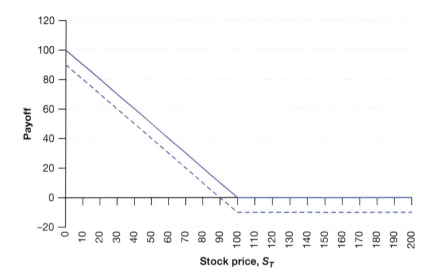

FIGURE 7.1 **Payoff diagram of a long put option: buying value insurance.** This figure shows the payoff diagram of a long position in a put option with a strike price of $100. The solid line shows the payoff, and the dashed line shows the net payoff assuming an initial option price of $10.

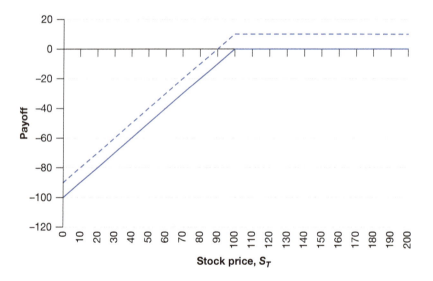

FIGURE 7.2 **Payoff diagram of a short position in a put option: writing value insurance.** This figure shows the payoff diagram of a short position in a put option with a strike price of $100. The solid line is the payoff, while the dashed line shows the net payoff assuming an initial price of $10.

Buying and owning an option is called a long position, and it enables the holder to make the exercise decision. Selling or writing the option is called a short position, and an obligation to buy from the put option holder or sell to the call option holder should the option be exercised. The payoff of the short position of a put option is shown in Figure 7.2; it is effectively the negative, or mirror image along the horizontal axis, of the payoff of the long position since it represents the opposite side of the transaction.

Consider our example of a put option on Microsoft stock with a strike price of $K = \$100$. If Microsoft's stock price ends up greater than $100, the long position would not exercise the option, resulting in a payoff of zero and a profit of $10 for the short position. But suppose Microsoft's stock price ends up $80, so S_T = $80. The owner of the option—the long position—would exercise the option (sell Microsoft stock for $100), resulting in a payoff of $100 − $80 = $20 and a profit of $10. What about the payoff and the profit of the short position? The short position would have to give the long position $100 in exchange for the stock whose market price is only $80. This results in a payoff of $80 − $100 = −$20 to the short position (the solid line in Figure 7.2). Since the short position received a premium of $10 when it sold the put, the net payoff would be a loss of $10 (the dashed line in Figure 7.2).

As the value of the underlying asset decreases, the holder of a long put option receives a greater payoff while the short put position incurs a greater loss. The short put position benefits when the underlying asset's value goes up: In our example above, if the stock price ends up above $100, the strike price, both the long and short put options have a payoff of zero, since the option expires unexercised, but the short position makes a net profit from selling the put option in the first place, while the long position is out by the price of the put.

> **QUICK CHECK 7.1** Create a payoff diagram for a long position in a put option on a share of stock with a strike price of $200. What is the maximum payoff from the long position, and at what stock price does that happen? Create payoff and profit diagrams for the long and short positions, assuming that the option is bought at a price of $40.

7.1.2 Call Options

A call option is a contract that allows the holder to buy an asset for a pre-specified price in the future. To understand a call, we will work through the actions you would take if you owned one. The option in our example allows you to buy Microsoft stock one year from now (but does not require you to do so) for a price of $100. At the decision time, one year from now (T = 1), would you do so? Again, the answer depends on the price of Microsoft's stock at that time.

If Microsoft's stock price one year from now is $50, would it be a good deal for you to buy it for $100? The answer is no—you would not want to buy an asset worth $50 for $100 (you could just go to the stock market and buy it for $50 if you wanted to). In this case, you would not exercise the call option (i.e., leave it unexercised, or let it expire). Your payoff—the value of the option at expiration—is zero in this case.

If Microsoft's stock price one year from now is $120, would it be a good deal for you to buy it for $100? The answer is yes! By exercising the option to buy Microsoft, you would be buying an asset worth $120 for $100, providing a payoff of $120 − $100 = $20. Note again that we are only considering the payoff and ignoring the price paid for the call option.

We can also represent the payoff of the call option at expiration, which we will denote by C_T, mathematically as:

$$C_T = \max(S_T - K, 0), \tag{7.2}$$

where S_T is the price of the underlying asset (i.e., the stock price in our example) when the option expires at time T, and K is the pre-specified strike price ($100 in our example). Equation 7.2 thus states that, at expiration, you will choose whichever is larger—the payoff from exercising the option or from leaving the option unexercised for a payoff of zero. For example, in the case where Microsoft's stock ended up being worth $50, the payoff of the option if you were to exercise it would have been $S_T - K$ = $50 − $100 = −$50; this is less than 0 (you would lose money), and therefore you would choose to let the option expire unexercised and get a payoff of $0. Put differently, the call option is worthless at expiration in this scenario. In contrast, in the case where Microsoft's stock ended up being worth $120, the payoff of the option if you were to exercise is $S_T - K = \$120 - \$100 = \$20$, and since this is greater than 0 you would thus choose to exercise the option and receive this payoff. Table 7.2 provides the decision you would make given various possible values of Microsoft's stock.

We depict the different payoffs from Table 7.2 in Figure 7.3. The payoff diagram of the call option has the shape of a hockey stick. It captures the upside potential of the underlying asset—the owner gains a greater payoff the higher the stock price or the value of the underlying asset rises. Once the stock price is greater than the strike price, the option payoff increases one-for-one with the stock price. This feature of call options also makes them well-suited to compensation, and it is common for companies to pay their employees with call options. The idea is that when a company performs well, employees can expect a higher payoff from the options, thus aligning their incentives to take actions to improve the company's value. We discuss this in detail in Chapter 11.

Call options also limit the downside loss—the most the owner of a call can lose is the premium paid for it. The dashed line in Figure 7.3 shows the net payoff. To break even on purchasing the call, the

Table 7.2 **Long call option payoffs at expiration.** Possible payoffs at expiration date T from holding a call option with a strike price of $K = \$100$ based on different future values of Microsoft stock with a price of S_T at expiration. The table shows exercise decision best practice in each case.

Stock price, S_T	Exercise decision	Call option payoff, C_T
$0	Do not exercise	$0
50	Do not exercise	0
80	Do not exercise	0
100	Indifferent	0
120	Exercise	20
150	Exercise	50

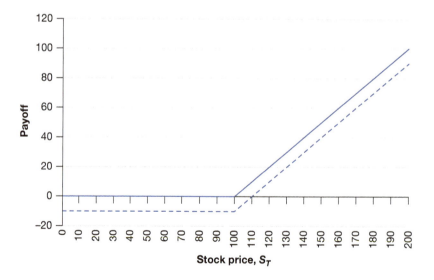

FIGURE 7.3 **Payoff diagram of a long call option.** This payoff diagram shows a long position in a call option with a strike price of $K = \$100$. The solid line shows the payoff diagram, while the dashed line shows the net payoff diagram, assuming an initial price of $10 and an expiration date of one year.

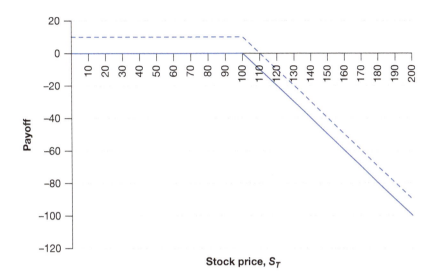

FIGURE 7.4 Payoff diagram of a short call option. This payoff diagram shows a short position in a call option with a strike price of $K = \$100$. The solid line shows the payoff diagram, while the dashed line shows the net payoff diagram, assuming an initial price of $10.

stock price at expiration of the option has to be $110, providing a payoff of $10 to cover the $10 cost of the option.

Figure 7.4 shows the payoff for the short position, the one who wrote the call. As before, the payoff of the short position is the opposite of the payoff of the long position.

To illustrate, consider our example of a call option based on Microsoft stock with a strike price of $K = \$100$. Suppose Microsoft stock ends up worth $120, so $S_T = \$120$. We saw that the holder of the option—the long position—would exercise the option (buy Microsoft stock for $100), resulting in a payoff of $120 − $100 = $20. What about the payoff of the short position? The short position has to comply with whatever the long position decides. Thus, the long position would decide to exercise the option and buy Microsoft stock for $100, paying the short position $100. However, the short position must give a share of Microsoft to the long position and will have to buy it in the market for $120. This results in a payoff of $100 − $120 = −$20 to the short position, the negative of the long position. Alternatively, if Microsoft stock ends up being worth $50, as noted above, the long position would choose to not exercise the option, resulting in a payoff of zero. As the short position would not have to buy the shares at market price, the payoff of the short position would also be zero.

The loss to the short position is potentially limitless given that there is no ceiling to how high stock prices can go. It is for this reason that financial marketplaces that allow trading in options limit the size of such positions. What benefit therefore is there to holding the short position in options trading? The holder of a short position benefits from the initial option sale and can potentially make a profit when the stock goes down in value. For instance, when the stock price goes lower than the strike price, the payoff of the call option becomes zero. In that case, the short position makes a net profit ($10) from selling the option in the first place. We can see this from the net payoff diagram in Figure 7.4 (the dashed line); the short position makes a positive profit when the option expires unexercised, since it retains the future value of the initial $10 price paid, and does not lose any money from the option payoff. The short call position will lose money if the stock price is above the strike price, but net of (the future value of) the initial option price (here $10) received when the contract was created.

> **QUICK CHECK 7.2** Create a payoff diagram at expiration for a long position in a call option on a share of stock, with a strike price of $200. Create a payoff diagram for the long and short positions. Also create net payoff diagrams for the long and short positions, assuming that the option was bought at a price of $40.

7.2 The Put–Call Parity Relation

In this section we show that there is a relationship between the prices of European puts and calls, that follows from **Principle 2**: *Equivalent assets that can be freely bought and sold will have the same market price.* This will be useful for a few reasons. First, it provides us with a deeper understanding of the relationships between different types of options, and how one can combine options to achieve specific investment goals. Second, it gives us insight into the price one would pay for an option. As we discussed, the flexibility embedded in options is valuable, as stated in **Principle 8**. *Flexibility in financial decisions has value, and the greater the uncertainty, the greater the value.* This value does not come for free, and this is reflected in the price of the option.

7.2.1 Payoff Diagrams for Stocks and Riskless Bonds

A key insight in understanding the price of options is that there is an equivalence relationship between options and stocks and bonds—the payoffs of a put (call) option are the same as a specific combination of stocks, bonds, and call (put) options. Since the payoffs are the same, this means the prices of the combinations must be the same by the law of one price, thus giving us a way to infer option prices. In order to illustrate further, it is useful to first consider what the payoff diagrams of two familiar assets look like: stocks and risk-free bonds.

First, consider a position in a zero-coupon risk-free bond that matures one year from today, and promises to pay its owner $100 at maturity. The payoffs of the risk-free bond will be a constant $100, as shown in the second column of Table 7.3 and Figure 7.5a.

Now consider a position in a stock. One year from today, given that you already own the share of stock, the payoff (i.e., value or amount of money you would get if you sold it) is simply the stock price itself. Thus, if the stock ends up being worth $S_T = \$50$ one year from now, your payoff from the stock is $50; if the stock ends up worth $100 a year from now, your payoff is $100. These payoffs are provided in the third column of Table 7.3 and in Figure 7.5b.

Table 7.3 **Stock and risk-free bond payoffs.** This table provides various possible payoffs of a zero-coupon risk-free bond with a principal amount of $100 and a share of stock as the underlying asset.

Stock price, S_T	Risk-free bond payoff	Stock payoff
$0	$100	$0
50	100	50
100	100	100
150	100	150
200	100	200
250	100	250

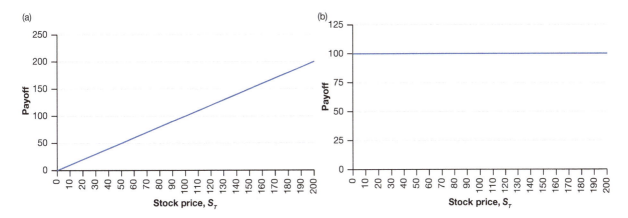

FIGURE 7.5 **Payoff diagram of (a) a stock and (b) a risk-free bond.** This figure shows the payoff diagram of a share of stock (a) and a zero-coupon risk-free bond (b) with a principal amount of $100, as of the maturity date of the bond, and with respect to the stock as the underlying asset.

With the payoff diagrams for stocks and bonds defined, we can now examine how they can be combined and the relationship between these payoffs and options.

7.2.2 The Relationship between the Payoffs of Options, Stocks, and Bonds

Now consider the payoffs of two different strategies that have the exact same payoff structures:

(1) Long a stock + long a put option with a strike price of $100 and expiration of one year.
(2) Long a zero-coupon risk-free bond with a principal amount of $100 + long a call option with a strike price of $100 and expiration of one year.

Begin with Strategy 1. As we previously noted in Section 7.1.1, a put option provides its owner downside protection (insurance). Thus, Strategy 1, by combining a stock with a put option, results in an insured investment in the stock. This combination is commonly known as a protective put (also shown in Table 7.4).

For example, if the stock price is $50 at expiration, the investor will exercise the put option and it will pay off (Equation 7.1): $P_T = \max(K - S_T, 0) = \max(100 - 50, 0) = \$50$. The payoff of the stock will simply be the stock price, $50. The combined payoff of the positions will be $50 + $50 = $100. Thus, the put option provides a payoff to compensate for the loss in value of the stock below $100. If, in contrast, the stock price is $S_T = \$150$ at expiration, the put option will be unexercised and pay off (Equation 7.1): $P_T = \max(K - S_T, 0) = \max(100 - 150, 0) = \$0$. The payoff of the stock will again be the stock price, $150. The combined payoff of the positions will be $0 + $150 = $150. In this case, the investor will still enjoy the upside of the stock. Figures 7.6 and 7.7 provide the payoff diagrams for the individual and combined positions from Table 7.4. As the diagram shows, the combination ensures an investor a minimum payoff if the stock price falls.

Strategy 1 allows an investor who owns a stock to insure against downside risk by purchasing a put option. Another way of creating that same pattern of payoffs is shown in Strategy 2: buy a zero-coupon riskless bond and a call option. Consider the payoffs of Strategy 2 (long a risk-free bond and long a call option), shown in Table 7.4. For example, if the stock price ends up being $50, the investor will not exercise the call option (i.e., via Equation 7.2: $C_T = \max(S_T - K, 0) = \max(50 - 100, 0) = \$0$) and the risk-free bond will pay off $100, resulting in a combined payoff of $0 + $100 = $100. If the stock price ends up being $120, the investor will exercise the call option ($C_T = \max(S_T - K, 0) = \max(120 - 100, 0) = \$20$) and the risk-free bond will pay off $100, resulting in a combined payoff of $20 + $100 = $120. The payoffs for each strategy and the combined payoffs are provided in Table 7.4, with the payoff diagram shown in Figure 7.7.

Table 7.4 **Payoffs of the two strategies.** Possible payoffs, based on the eventual stock price, of two strategies: (1) Long a stock + long a put option with strike price $100 and expiration of one year; and (2) long a zero-coupon risk-free bond with principal amount $100 + long a call option with strike price $100 and expiration of one year.

Stock price, S_T	"Protective put" Strategy 1: stock + put			Strategy 2: bond + call		
	Long put	Long stock	Combined	Long risk-free	Long call	Combined
$0	$100	$0	**$100**	$100	$0	**$100**
50	50	50	**100**	100	0	**100**
100	0	100	**100**	100	0	**100**
150	0	150	**150**	100	50	**150**
200	0	200	**200**	100	100	**200**
$S_T < 100$	$100 - S_T$	S_T	**100**	100	0	**100**
$S_T > 100$	0	S_T	S_T	100	$S_T - 100$	S_T

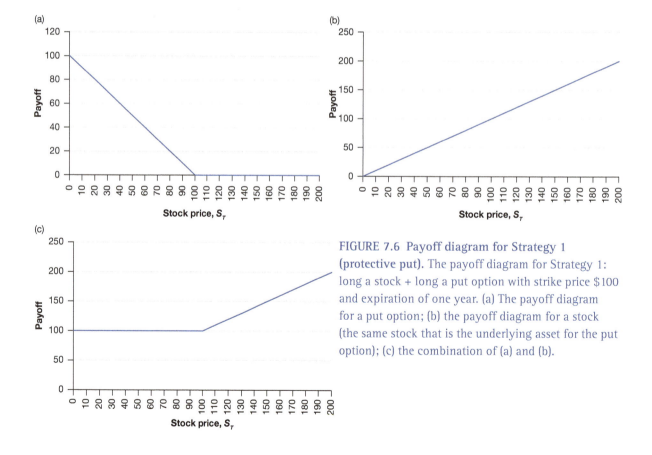

FIGURE 7.6 **Payoff diagram for Strategy 1 (protective put).** The payoff diagram for Strategy 1: long a stock + long a put option with strike price $100 and expiration of one year. (a) The payoff diagram for a put option; (b) the payoff diagram for a stock (the same stock that is the underlying asset for the put option); (c) the combination of (a) and (b).

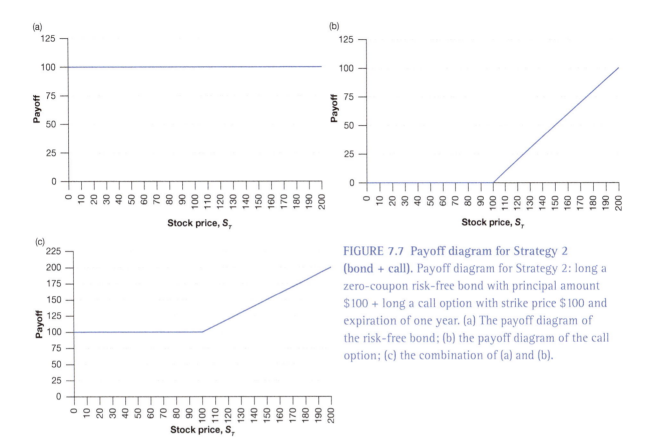

FIGURE 7.7 Payoff diagram for Strategy 2 (bond + call). Payoff diagram for Strategy 2: long a zero-coupon risk-free bond with principal amount $100 + long a call option with strike price $100 and expiration of one year. (a) The payoff diagram of the risk-free bond; (b) the payoff diagram of the call option; (c) the combination of (a) and (b).

By examining both the tables and the combined payoff diagrams in Figures 7.6 and 7.7, we can see that the payoffs of the two strategies at expiration are identical. Thus, we can achieve a protective-put strategy of stock plus put by an insured-equity strategy of purchasing a risk-free bond and a call option. We can express this relationship more generally. Suppose we have the following positions and payoffs:

1. A risk-free (zero-coupon) bond that matures at time T and pays a principal amount of K. The payoff at maturity will be K.
2. A call option on a stock with a strike price K that expires at time T. The payoff at expiration will be (Equation 7.1): $C_T = \max(S_T - K, 0)$.
3. A put option on a stock with a strike price K that expires at time T. The payoff at expiration will be (Equation 7.2): $P_T = \max(K - S_T, 0)$.
4. A share of stock. The payoff at expiration will be S_T.

As our example in Table 7.4 and Figures 7.6 and 7.7 show, the payoffs of the four positions above satisfy the following relationship at the expiration date T:

$$S_T + P_T = C_T + K. \tag{7.3}$$

This provides us with two key insights. First, buying options, whether puts or calls, is buying insurance and writing (selling) options is always selling insurance. This comes directly from the equivalence between calls and puts, and the fact that puts are direct insurance against a fall in the value of the underlying asset. Second, the prices of call options and put options are linked, and so if you know one, you can infer the other. We focus on this second insight next.

7.2.3 Option Prices and the Put–Call Parity

The put–call parity relationship derived above states that the payoffs at expiration of a put option and a call option, when combined, must be the same as the combined payoffs of the underlying stock and a bond (when the options are based on the same stock, and the options/bond have the same expiration/maturity and strike price/principal). This carries an important implication for the prices of options: Because the end payoffs (at maturity) of the two strategies are the same, the prices of the two strategies must be the same (**Principle 2:** *Equivalent assets that can be freely bought and sold will have the same market price*). Since the payoffs of the two strategies are the same, they are equivalent assets.[1]

If we take the present value of the payoffs in Equation 7.3, we will get the following pricing relationship based on the put–call parity:

$$S_0 + P_0 = C_0 + \frac{K}{(1+r_f)^T}, \qquad (7.4)$$

where S_0 is the current stock price (at time $t = 0$), P_0 is the current price of the put option, C_0 is the current price of the call option, and the term $K / (1 + r_f)^T$ represents the price of the risk-free bond (i.e., the principal amount K discounted by the risk-free interest rate r_f). Equation 7.3 is known as the put–call parity relation. Importantly, as in our example in Table 7.4 and Figures 7.6 and 7.7, for the relationship to hold, the options and risk-free bond must have the same maturity T and same strike price/principal amount K. Note that the put–call parity only holds strictly for European options.

The put–call parity provides us with a useful insight into understanding the prices of options. As can be seen from Equation 7.4, the price of any one of the four securities can be determined from the values of the other three. In addition, Equation 7.4 can be used as a recipe for synthesizing any one of the four from the other three and in the following sections we will use it to examine these securities.

For example, by rearranging Equation 7.4 we find that a call (C_0) is equivalent to holding a share of the stock, borrowing the present value of the exercise price (i.e., selling short a risk-free zero-coupon bond with face value K), and buying a put:

$$C_0 = S_0 + P_0 - \frac{K}{(1+r_f)^T}. \qquad (7.5)$$

An important feature of the put–call parity formula is that it is not model-dependent: It holds regardless of what we assume the underlying stock price dynamics are. Equation 7.5 is the version that

---

[1] Institutional features may cause the payoffs of the two strategies to differ to a certain extent. For example, the tax treatment of the two strategies may be different depending on the type of investor (i.e., taxable or nontaxable investor).

considers the nature of a call option. In effect, it says that the characteristics of a call option can be broken into three components:

1. buying the stock (S_0);
2. borrowing part of the money to do so (leverage, $-K / (1 + r_f)^T$); and
3. buying insurance against downside risk (the put, P_0).

Equation 7.5 can be used to convert a put into a call, and vice versa. For example, suppose that the values on the right side of Equation 7.5 are: $S_0 = \$100$, $K = \$100$, $T = 1$, $r_f = 0.08$, and $P_0 = \$10$. Then the price of the call option, C_0, would have to be:

$$C_0 = S_0 + P_0 - \frac{K}{(1+r_f)^T}$$

$$= 100 + 10 - \frac{100}{1.08}$$

$$= 17.41.$$

Principle 2: *Equivalent assets that can be freely bought and sold will have the same market price*, and **Principle 3:** *There is no such thing as a free lunch in finance; everything has a cost* are the two principles that ultimately enforce the put–call parity in the market. Put differently, if the put–call parity relationship does *not* hold, then it would be possible to make unlimited profits in the marketplace; this can be illustrated via a strategy of put–call arbitrage. Suppose that the price of the call in the marketplace is $19 instead of $17.41, and that there are no barriers to arbitrage. Then the call's price in the market is too high relative to what it should be according to put–call parity. An arbitrageur can therefore profit by buying (going long) "synthetic" calls—that is, the combination of stocks, puts, and bonds that are equivalent to call options via the put–call parity—using a replicating strategy at a cost of $17.41, and simultaneously selling calls in the market for a price of $19. The arbitrageur would buy a "synthetic" call by buying a stock (a cash outflow), selling a bond with a face value of $100 for $100/1.08 = $92.59 (a cash inflow), and buying a put for $10 (a cash outflow). The result will be a total cash outflow of $17.41. At the same time, the arbitrageur would sell a call in the marketplace for $19 (a cash inflow), resulting in a net profit right now of $19 − $17.41 = $1.59. At expiration, the arbitrageur would neither owe nor make any money—there would be no net payoff—since the cash flows of the positions cancel each other out.

Thus, the arbitrageur gained the initial profit "for free," and could repeat this as many times as necessary to make unlimited amounts of money! As we have seen with **Principle 3:** *There is no such thing as a free lunch in finance; everything has a cost*, such a situation cannot exist for long, and the price of the call option therefore must be $17.41—the put–call parity relationship must hold. This arbitrage strategy is presented in Table 7.5.

Equation 7.4 can be rearranged to show the relation among puts, calls, stocks, and bonds to create a "synthetic" stock or a risk-free bond as follows:

$$S_0 = C_0 - P_0 + \frac{K}{(1+r_f)^T},$$

$$\frac{K}{(1+r_f)^T} = S_0 - C_0 + P_0.$$

(7.6)

Table 7.5 Put–call arbitrage. This table shows how an arbitrage strategy can be constructed if a call option were trading for $19 instead of $17.41. By selling the call option, and buying a synthetic call (a combination of a stock, bond, and put option that produces the same payoffs as the call option), riskless profits can be achieved regardless of what the cash flows end up being at the option expiration date.

Position	Immediate cash flow	Cash flow at expiration date	
		If $S_T < \$100$	If $S_T < \$100$
Sell a call	$19	$0	$-\$(S_T - 100)$
Buy replicating portfolio (synthetic call):			
Buy a stock	−100	S_T	S_T
Sell a bond with face value $100	92.59	−100	−100
Buy a put	−10	$(100 - S_T)$	0
	$111.59 − $110	$S_T - 100 + (100 - S_T)$	$-\$(S_T - 100) + S_T - 100$
Net cash flows	$1.59	0	0

In these forms:

- A stock can be replicated with a long call option, a short put option, and a long risk-free bond.[2]
- A risk-free bond can be replicated with a long stock, a short call option, and a long put option.

Thus, in the same way that we can view options, stocks, and bonds as building blocks that comprise options, so too can we view options and stocks as the building blocks comprising bonds and options and bonds as the building blocks comprising stocks. This will provide many insights into the pricing of shares of stock and bonds, as well as corporate financial decision making, which we will discuss in detail in Chapter 14.

> QUICK CHECK 7.3 If the price of the call option with a strike price of 80 and a maturity of two years is 30.328, the price of the put option is 8.752, and the risk-free interest rate is 1% per year, what must be the price of the underlying stock?

With a conceptual understanding of how options work, we next turn to details of how they are traded in practice in marketplaces around the world.

---

[2] In the case of the "synthetic" stock, one practical difference between purchasing a stock directly and replicating the stock using options is that a position with a stock is indefinite, while a position using options has an explicit expiration date. One can view the synthetic stock replicated using options and bonds as therefore consisting of long-dated bonds/options; alternatively, the contracts can be rolled forward if there are defined holding periods, but this may introduce roll-over risk.

7.3 Option Trading in Markets

Now that you understand the nature of options, in this section we are going to discuss how investors actually buy and sell them in practice. Options are widely traded in financial markets around the globe. Exchange-traded options have standard contract terms defined by the options exchange. The exchange matches buyers and sellers and guarantees payment in the event of default by either party. Figure 7.8 shows that billions of option contracts are traded each year, representing trillions of dollars of transactions. Options not traded on an exchange are called over-the-counter (OTC) options, which means that they are contracts that are arranged directly between two parties. This allows greater customization of terms to fit specific investment needs, but since they are not on exchanges, one cannot trade such contracts as freely.

The largest options exchange in the world is the Chicago Board Options Exchange (CBOE); other significant exchanges that allow trading in options include the Eurex Exchange in Frankfurt, Germany and the Tokyo Stock Exchange. On the CBOE, a typical single call option contract gives its owner the right to buy 100 shares of the underlying stock and is of the American type. Original maturities of CBOE options vary from three months to three years, and they all expire on the third Friday of the month in which they mature. CBOE options with maturities of one year and longer are called long-term equity anticipation securities (LEAPS).

An option is identified by its type (call or put), the name of the underlying security, its strike price, and its expiration date. For exchange-traded options, the characteristics of options offered on the exchange are determined by the rules of the exchange.

Table 7.6 shows an example of how options are listed and traded on exchanges using option prices for Home Depot (HD) stock as of Monday, 26 June 2025, with HD stock trading at $36.64 per share.

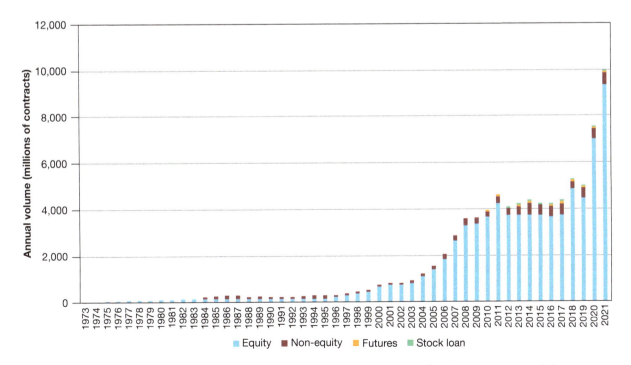

FIGURE 7.8 Options trading in marketplaces. This figure shows the number of options contracts traded in the United States each year from 1973 to 2021, in millions of contracts.
Source: Merton, R. C. (2022b). Data from the Options Clearing Corporation.

Table 7.6 **Home Depot option prices.** This table provides option prices based on Home Depot (HD) stock. Closing prices are as of Monday, 26 June 2025. Quotes are based on an underlying stock price of 36.64.

	Calls				Puts		
Strike	**Expiration**	**Last sale**	**Open interest**	**Strike**	**Expiration**	**Last sale**	**Open interest**
32.50	July	4.30	313	32.50	July	0.15	722
35.00		2.40	4,635	35.00		0.25	4,278
37.50		0.45	8,953	37.50		1.45	7,136
40.00		0.05	6,727	40.00		3.40	842
32.50	Aug.	4.60	310	32.50	Aug.	0.25	761
35.00		2.65	8,476	35.00		0.65	8,462
37.50		1.40	16,612	37.50		1.65	17,212
40.00		0.30	16,364	40.00		3.60	30,992

Source: CBOE: www.cboe.com/DelayedQuote.

In the table, the first row lists a strike price of 32.50 and the expiration month of July. On 26 June, the July HD call options had just a bit less than one month left to go before expiration. The entry in the column labeled "Last sale" gives the price at which the July HD call traded was 4.30, which means $430 per contract. The next column, "Open interest," is the total number of CBOE contracts of that type in existence on 26 June. The final two columns give the closing price and open interest for the July 32.50 put option.

The hypothetical value of an option if it were expiring immediately (i.e., for a call option, the current stock price minus the strike price or zero, whichever is larger) is called its intrinsic value (or tangible value). This gives an investor a sense of payoffs based on where the stock price currently is relative to the strike price, and thus what the potential future payoffs at expiration might be. Because the price of HD stock was 36.64 per share and the option's exercise price is 32.50, the value of the call if exercised immediately would be 36.64 − 32.50 = 4.14 per share of stock. The option's price of 4.30, therefore, exceeds its intrinsic value by 0.16. This difference between an option's price and its intrinsic value is called the option's time value.

An option's time value is greater the longer it has to go before expiration. For example, in Table 7.6, look at the prices of HD 35 calls that were expiring in July and August. Both had the same intrinsic value of 1.64 (36.64 − 35.00 = 1.64), but the prices of the call options were 2.40 and 2.65, respectively. Similar patterns hold for HD 35.00 put options.

The table also demonstrates some patterns regarding the prices of options. There is an inverse relation between the price of a call and its strike price. Put differently, consider two call options on the same stock with the same expirations, except that one has a strike price of $50 and the other has a strike price of $100. The call option with the higher strike price—$100 in this example—will trade for a lower price. For put options, this relationship is reversed. This can be seen in Table 7.6 for the options that expire in July. As the strike price goes from 32.50 to 40.00, the prices of the calls go from 4.30 to 0.05, and the prices of the puts go from 0.15 to 3.40.

In addition to options on individual securities such as HD stock, there are also many other types of options that are traded. One example is index options, which are options where the underlying asset is a financial index such as a stock market index. For example, the CBOE offers trading in calls and puts

Table 7.7 **Listing of S&P 500 index options.** Option prices based on the S&P 500 Index. Quotes based on an underlying index value of 1244.56.

		Calls					Puts		
Strike	Expiration	Last sale	Vol.	Open interest	Strike	Expiration	Last sale	Vol.	Open interest
1,245	June	7.00	429	205	1,245	June	8.10	127	558
1,260		1.90	765	369	1,260		16.00	56	7
1,275		0.60	2,068	840	1,275		29.90	0	16
1,245	July	19.00	530	3,745	1,245	July	17.00	153	14,001
1,260		10.80	1,535	20,206	1,260		24.00	117	19,838
1,275		5.40	1,322	76,551	1,275		33.60	52	63,534
1,245	Aug.	29.00	3	33	1,245	Aug.	24.10	50	59
1,260		20.00	30	1,613	1,260		30.00	1	2,025
1,275		13.00	411	22,403	1,275		37.00	1	5,178

Source: www.cboe.com/DelayedQuote.

on the S&P 500 stock index under the symbol SPX. SPX options are calls or puts on a hypothetical index fund that invests in a portfolio composed of the stocks that make up the S&P 500 index, each of the 500 companies in proportion to the total value of its shares outstanding. Index options do not require actual exchange of the underlying stock, as in the previous examples of call and put options, a process known as cash settlement.

Table 7.7 shows a listing of the prices and trading activity for SPX options on Tuesday, 26 June 2025. SPX options are of the European type and can, therefore, only be exercised at expiration. In addition to the "Open interest" column, the table shows the trading volume during the day. The SPX contract specifies that if the call option is exercised, the owner of the option will receive a cash payment of $100 times the difference between the index value and the strike price.

For example, assume that when the July 1,260 call option listed in Table 7.7 expired on July 24, 2025, the value of the index was 1,275. Upon expiration its owner would have received $1,500, which is: $100 \times (1,275 - 1,260) = 1,500$.

This section provided some details of how individual options are actually traded in marketplaces. We next turn to goals that investors can achieve through this trade: the ability to trade different options enables investors to achieve a payoff structure that they desire. We dive into this notion in detail in the next section.

> QUICK CHECK 7.4 Using Table 7.6, compute the intrinsic value and the time value of the August HD 37.50 call. Do the same for the put.

7.4 Investment Strategies with Options

In this section, we demonstrate how options can be combined with other positions to achieve desired patterns of payoffs.

7.4.1 Using Options to Modify Payoff Patterns from Stock Exposure

First, as we previously noted, buying or selling options provides an alternative way for a person who does not own the underlying asset (i.e., the stock) to take a position. The price of a call option is only a fraction of the price of the underlying stock (you can see this by examining payoff diagrams—the payoff of holding a stock is always higher than the payoff of holding an option, which implies that the price of the stock must be higher). As a result, investing the same amount of money in calls as in the stock provides a leveraged position—a position equivalent to investing your own money and borrowing additional money to invest.

To illustrate, suppose that you are bullish on stocks and have $100,000 to invest. Assume that the price of a share of stock is $100 and the stock pays no dividends, and the price of a call option on that stock is $10, one-tenth of the stock price. Consider three different investment strategies:

(1) Invest all $100,000 in the stock (i.e., buy 1,000 shares of the stock).
(2) Invest all $100,000 in call options on the stock, with a strike price of $100 and an expiration of one year. Thus you would buy calls on 10,000 shares of stock.
(3) Invest $90,000 in the risk-free asset, and $10,000 in call options on the stock, with a strike price of $100 and an expiration of one year. Thus, you would buy calls on 1,000 shares of stock.

Also assume that the riskless interest rate is 5% per year. Now consider what your rate of return from investing in each strategy would be after a year. This will depend on what the stock price ends up being.

First, suppose that the stock price ends up being $120 in one year. Under Strategy 1, your investment will be worth (given 1,000 shares) $120 × 1,000 = $120,000. Thus, your return will be $120,000/100,000 − 1 = 20%.

Under Strategy 2, use Equation 7.2 to calculate the payoff of each call option at:

$$\max(S_T - K, 0) = \max(\$120 - \$100, 0) = \$20.$$

With 10,000 call options, the investment will be worth $20 × 10,000 = $200,000. What will be the rate of return for Strategy 2? Given the $100,000 investment, it will be $200,000/100,000 − 1 = 100%. This is five times greater than the return on investing the same amount in the stocks.

Under Strategy 3, since the risk-free asset has an interest rate of 5%, the $90,000 investment will become: $90,000 × 1.05 = $94,500. The option investment, given that the payoff of each option is $20, will be (given 1,000 call options): $20 × 1,000 = $20,000. The total investment's value in one year will therefore be $94,500 + $20,000 = $114,500, giving a return on the $100,000 investment of $114,500/100,000 − 1 = 14.5%. Strategy 3 therefore provides a return that is in between that of Strategies 1 and 2.

Now suppose that the stock price ends up *lower*, at $90 in one year. Under Strategy 1, your investment will be worth (given 1,000 shares) $90 × 1,000 = $90,000. Thus, your return will be $90,000/100,000 − 1 = −10%. Under Strategy 2, the payoff of each call option at expiration will be (Equation 7.1) $\max(S_T - K, 0) = \max(\$90 - \$100, 0) = \$0$; you would not exercise the call options, and thus the investment will be worth $0. In other words, your rate of return will be, $0/100,000 − 1 = −100%! The return on investing in the options is therefore much lower than the return on just investing in the stock when the stock goes down. Finally, consider Strategy 3. Since the risk-free asset has an interest rate of 5% no matter what happens to the stock, the $90,000 investment will again become: $90,000 × 1.05 = $94,500. The option investment value will be $0. The total investment's value in one year will therefore be $94,500 + $0 = $94,500, giving a return on the $100,000 investment of: $94,500/100,000 − 1 = −5.5%. Strategy 3 therefore provides a less-negative return than Strategies 1 and 2.

The scenarios above underscore the point that investing in call options is a leveraged investment, providing amplified exposure to the underlying stock—the returns move in the same direction as the stock, but are higher than the stock when the stock goes up, and more negative than the stock when the stock goes down. Strategy 3 illustrates that mixing a risk-free asset with options allows an investor to reduce the amount of return amplification provided by options. Table 7.8 illustrates this by providing the returns of each strategy for a wide range of potential scenarios; Figure 7.9 shows these returns in a graph.

Figure 7.9 shows that none of the three strategies dominates the other two. All three are bullish: You would only choose them if you believe that the stock price is likely to rise. But to determine which of the three is best for you, you must define more precisely your expectations about the stock price and your tolerance for risk. For example, suppose you anticipate that the economy will be in a boom, and the stock price will increase to $150. Under Strategy 1 (100% stocks), your rate of return would be 50%. Under Strategy 2 (100% call options), your options will be worth $500,000 at expiration, and your rate of return will be 400%. Under Strategy 3 (10% call options), your options would be worth $50,000 and your bonds $94,500, so your rate of return would be 44.5%. Strategy 2 would thus provide the highest return in this scenario.

However, none of the strategies always outperforms the others. Strategy 2 (100% invested in call options) performs best when stock prices rise significantly and worst when stock prices fall. Strategy 3 performs best when stock prices fall, but worst when they rise significantly. Strategy 1 performs best when stock prices either remain the same or rise slightly (to $110), but comes in second in all other scenarios.

The fact that none of the strategies dominates the others is consistent with **Principle 7**: *There is a trade-off between risk and expected return.* Depending on their preference, the investor might choose any one of them. Indeed, a very risk-averse investor might rationally prefer the strategy of investing all $100,000 in the risk-free asset to earn 5% for sure.

Table 7.8 Payoffs and returns of strategies. Payoffs and returns of Strategies 1, 2, and 3 for various possible values of the stock price in one year. Strategy 1 consists of investing $100,000 in a stock. Strategy 2 consists of investing $100,000 in call options on the stock, with a strike price of $100 and an expiration of one year. Strategy 3 consists of investing $90,000 in the risk-free asset, and $10,000 in call options on the stock, with a strike price of $100 and an expiration of one year.

Stock price in one year	Payoffs			Returns		
	Strategy 1	Strategy 2	Strategy 3	Strategy 1	Strategy 2	Strategy 3
50	$50,000	$0	$94,500	−50%	−100%	−5.5%
60	$60,000	$0	$94,500	−40%	−100%	−5.5%
70	$70,000	$0	$94,500	−30%	−100%	−5.5%
80	$80,000	$0	$94,500	−20%	−100%	−5.5%
90	$90,000	$0	$94,500	−10%	−100%	−5.5%
100	$100,000	$0	$94,500	0%	−100%	−5.5%
110	$110,000	$100,000	$104,500	10%	0%	4.5%
120	$120,000	$200,000	$114,500	20%	100%	14.5%
130	$130,000	$300,000	$124,500	30%	200%	24.5%
140	$140,000	$400,000	$134,500	40%	300%	34.5%
150	$150,000	$500,000	$144,500	50%	400%	44.5%

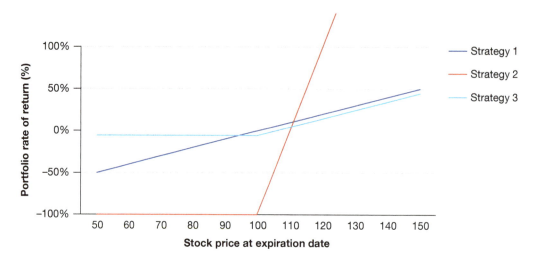

FIGURE 7.9 **Returns of strategies.** Returns of Strategies 1, 2, and 3 for various possible values of the stock price in one year. Strategy 1 consists of investing $100,000 in a stock. Strategy 2 consists of investing $100,000 in call options on the stock, with a strike price of $100 and an expiration of one year. Strategy 3 consists of investing $90,000 in the risk-free asset, and $10,000 in call options on the stock, with a strike price of $100 and an expiration of one year.

> **QUICK CHECK 7.5** Suppose there is another strategy to invest $96,000 in the riskless asset and $4,000 in call options. What is the minimum guaranteed rate of return? Draw the graph (payoff diagram) of this strategy's return depending on what the stock's price is in one year.

7.4.2 Options as Building Blocks to Create Tailored Investment Strategies

Basic investment strategies with call options can provide different exposures to an underlying stock and payoff diagrams can be used to illustrate how options can be used to tailor investment strategies according to a wider range of specific goals. Therefore, options-based investment strategies can be used to achieve a very wide range of payoffs. For example, you may be unsure if a stock's price will go up or go down. Or you may strongly believe that a stock's price will remain about the same in the future. Options strategies can be constructed so that you benefit in each of these situations.

Suppose you believe that a stock is likely to experience large price changes—greater price volatility—in the next few months than is generally anticipated, but you are unsure whether those changes will be up or down. You could implement an investment strategy reflecting that combined view by purchasing both a call option and a put option on the stock. Suppose the stock price is currently $75, and you think the price movement will occur within three months. With a maturity date set to three months, if you hold (i.e., go long) a call option with a strike price of $75 and go long a put option with a strike price of $75, the payoff profile based on possible values of the stock is shown in Table 7.9. Such a combined position is called a straddle. A straddle is also a way to protect or insure against the risk of greater volatility with large moves in future stock prices.

If the stock price is $S_T = \$50$ at expiration, the exercised put option will pay off (Equation 7.1): $P_T = \max(K - S_T, 0) = \max(75 - 50, 0) = \$25$. The call option will expire unexercised, thus paying off (Equation 7.2): $C_T = \max(S_T - K, 0) = \max(50 - 75, 0) = \$0$. Thus, the combined payoff of the positions will be $25 + $0 = $25. If the stock price is $S_T = \$100$ at expiration, the put option will expire unexercised and pay off (Equation 7.1): $P_T = \max(K - S_T, 0) = \max(75 - 100, 0) = \$0$. However, the investor will exercise the call option, and it will pay off $C_T = \max(S_T - K, 0) = \max(100 - 75, 0) = \$25$. The combined position will pay off $0 + $25 = $25. Thus, the combination pays off both if the stock price ends up rising or falling. Figure 7.10 provides the payoff diagrams for the individual and combined positions from Table 7.9.

Table 7.9 **Call and put option combined payoffs.** Possible payoffs of a long call option and a long put option on a stock, each with a strike price of $75.

Stock price, S_T	Long put option payoff	Long call option payoff	Combined payoff
$0	$75	$0	$75
25	50	0	50
50	25	0	25
75	0	0	0
100	0	25	25
125	0	50	50
150	0	75	75

Note: To construct a table like this it is important to include at a minimum a value of 0, any strike prices of any options, and at least one possible value above the highest strike price.

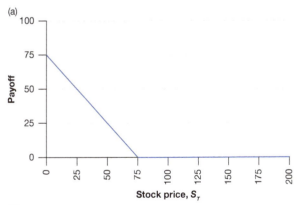

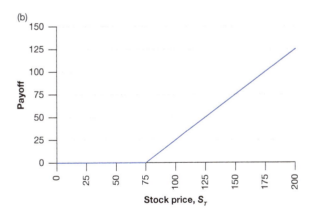

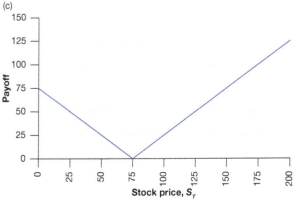

FIGURE 7.10 **Call and put option (straddle) payoff diagram.** Possible payoffs of (a) a long call option, (b) a long put option, and (c) the straddle (combined) on a stock, each with a strike price of $75.

Of course, being able to customize portfolios to pay off in any eventuality does not come for free—the investors in the above examples would need to purchase the options.

You can use the companion Excel app for this chapter to construct combined payoff diagrams with up to four different component positions.

> **QUICK CHECK 7.6** Choosing to deploy a straddle investment strategy, suppose that the put option had a strike price of $50 and the call option had a strike price of $80. This is also called a "strangle." Draw the payoff and profit diagram of the straddle.

Example 7.1 (Butterfly Spread): A trader believes that a significant price move in the next six months is unlikely on a stock currently worth $61. They want a strategy that produces its largest payoffs if the future stock price is close to the current one. The trader buys (goes long) one call with a $55 strike price, (goes long) one call with a $65 strike price, and sells (goes short) two calls with a $60 strike price. Draw the payoff diagram of this strategy.

Solution. First, create a table with the payoffs of the individual positions based on what the stock price may be, and then calculate the combined payoffs as shown in **Table 7.10**:

Table 7.10 Combined payoffs for Example 7.1.

Stock price, S_T	Long call, $K = 55$	Long call, $K = 65$	Short two calls, $K = 60$	Combined payoff
$0	$0	$0	$0	$0
50	0	0	0	0
55	0	0	0	0
60	5	0	0	5
65	10	0	−10	0
70	15	5	−20	0

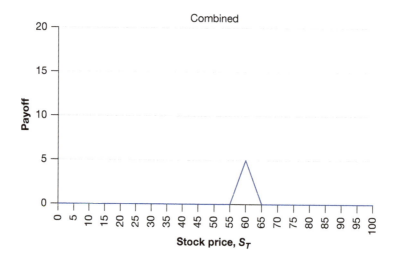

Figure 7.11 Payoff diagram providing the payoffs at expiration of a combination of a long call option with a strike price of $55, a long call option with a strike price of $65, and two short call options with strike prices of $60.

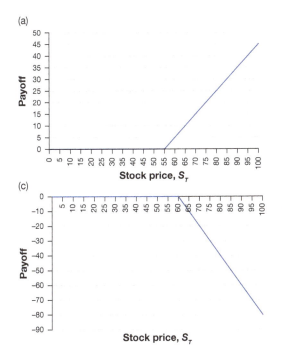

Figure 7.12 Payoff diagrams of the individual positions at expiration: (a) a long call with a strike price of $55, (b) a long call with a strike price of $65, and (c) short two calls with strike prices of $60. **Figure 7.11** is (a) + (b) + (c).

For the short position, calculate the payoffs as follows. If the stock price is $70, the long position would choose to exercise the option and gain a payoff of $10 per option. The short position therefore has a negative payoff of −$10 per option. Since the position is short two calls, the payoff is 2 × −10 = −20. The payoff patterns indicate that, after the stock price goes beyond 60, the short calls begin to reverse the positive payoffs of the long call with strike price of 55. But then after a stock price of 65, the long call with $K = 65$ becomes active, leveling out the payoff at zero. The payoff diagram of the combined position is shown in **Figure 7.11**. We can also view this as the combination of the individual positions, as shown in **Figure 7.12**.

In this section and the previous sections we have shown how options can reduce future uncertainty, and furthermore how option positions can be used or combined in order to create investment strategies that are tailored to an individual's needs. However, as we noted, this valuable flexibility does not come for free. In the next section we provide a methodology for determining the value of an option.

7.5 Valuing Options: The Black–Scholes–Merton Model

In Section 7.3 we covered the put–call parity relation, which allows us to express the price of a call in terms of the price of the underlying asset, the riskless rate of interest, and the price of the corresponding put. However, this relies on us knowing the price of a call or the price of the corresponding put to drive the equation.

In the early 1970s, Fischer Black and Myron Scholes as co-authors and Robert C. Merton separately achieved a major breakthrough in determining the price of an option. Merton and Scholes received the 1997 Nobel Prize in Economics Sciences for this work (Fischer would have shared in it, but passed away before the awarding). Known as the Black–Scholes–Merton (BSM) model, the formula they derived is based on a model of stock price dynamics that requires estimating the volatility of the underlying asset's future price.

7.5.1 The Black-Scholes-Merton Formula

The BSM formula gives us a way to calculate our goal of determining the price of a call option right now (at time $t = 0$), C_0, given a set of five characteristics of the stock and the option. These inputs are:

- the current price of the stock (i.e., at time $t = 0$), S_0;
- the strike price of the option, K;
- the time to maturity (expiration date) of the option in years, T;
- a measure of the risk of the stock: the standard deviation of the rate of return of the stock, σ; and
- the riskless interest rate, r_f.[3]

With these inputs, the price of a call option can be computed as follows:

$$C_0 = S_0 \times N(d_1) - \frac{K}{e^{r_f \times T}} \times N(d_2), \tag{7.7}$$

where

$$d_1 = \frac{\ln\left(\frac{S_0}{K}\right) + \left(r_f + \frac{\sigma^2}{2}\right) \times T}{\sigma \times \sqrt{T}}.$$

$$d_2 = d_1 - \sigma \times \sqrt{T}$$

In Equation 7.7, ln is the natural logarithm, e is the base of the natural log function (approximately 2.718282) to reflect the fact that interest is continuously compounded, and $N(d)$ is the probability that a random draw from a standard normal distribution will be less than d.

In deriving their formula, Black and Scholes assumed that no dividends are paid during the life of the option. The model was generalized by Merton to allow for a constant continuous dividend yield. Whenever a stock pays a dividend, the stock price goes down (since it is paying cash), and this version of the formula incorporates this effect.

The intuition behind the BSM model (Equation 7.7) is that the payoffs of an option can be replicated using stocks and riskless borrowing. Put differently, a synthetic call can be constructed using only stocks and riskless borrowing. Thus, by **Principle 2**: *Equivalent assets that can be freely bought and sold will have the same market price*, we know that the price of the call must equal the cost of the synthetic call that we have constructed.

The BSM formula in Equation 7.7 derives the price of a call option. We can derive the formula for the value of a put option by using the put-call parity formula (Equation 7.4) and replacing C_0 with Equation 7.7 (we also replace the normal discounting with continuously compounded discounting to be consistent with Equation 7.7):

$$\begin{aligned} P_0 &= C_0 - S_0 + \frac{K}{e^{r_f \times T}} \\ &= \left(N(d_1) - 1\right) \times S_0 + \left(1 - N(d_2)\right) \times \frac{K}{e^{r_f \times T}}. \end{aligned} \tag{7.8}$$

---

[3] Note that σ is the standard deviation of the annualized continuously compounded rate of return of the stock. By the same token, the riskless rate r_f is the annualized continuously compounded rate on a safe asset with the same maturity as the option.

7.5 VALUING OPTIONS: THE BLACK–SCHOLES–MERTON MODEL

Using the BSM formula requires five inputs: the stock price, the strike price K, expiration date T, the volatility of the stock's returns σ, and the riskless interest rate r_f. Each will be known from market data or the terms of the option contract, with the exception of volatility, σ. In the real world, the volatility σ of a stock is not known with certainty, and may change over time. In practice, the volatility is typically estimated using the standard deviation of the stock's past returns. The Excel app for this chapter can be used to calculate the price of an option, given the underlying characteristics.

Consider an option on a stock with a strike price of $100 and an expiration of six months. The underlying stock's returns have an annualized volatility of 20%. The riskless interest rate is 8%. We therefore have the following inputs into the BSM formula:

- $S_0 = 100$
- $K = 100$
- $T = 0.5$
- $\sigma = 0.2$
- $r_f = 0.08$.

With these inputs, using Excel app 7.1, we get a call option price of $7.71 and a put option price of $3.79. Example 7.2 shows how to perform these calculations in a more manual way.

Example 7.2 (Price of a Call Option): Suppose that there is a stock with a current price of $41 and an annual volatility of 30%. What is the price of a call option with a strike price of $40 and an expiration of three months? What is the price of a put option with the same characteristics? The riskless rate is 8%.

Solution. In this case, we have that $S_0 = 41$, $K = 40$, $T = 0.25$, $\sigma = 0.3$, $r_f = 0.08$. Let us use Equation 7.7 to calculate the price of the call option. First, we need to calculate d_1 and d_2. This gives us:

$$d_1 = \frac{\ln\left(\frac{S_0}{K}\right) + \left(r_f + \frac{\sigma^2}{2}\right) \times T}{\sigma \times \sqrt{T}}$$

$$= \frac{\ln\left(\frac{41}{40}\right) + \left(0.08 + \frac{0.3^2}{2}\right) \times 0.25}{0.3 \times \sqrt{0.25}}$$

$$= 0.373,$$

$$d_2 = d_1 - \sigma \times \sqrt{T}$$

$$= 0.373 - 0.3 \times \sqrt{0.25}$$

$$= 0.223.$$

This will allow us to find $N(d_1)$ and $N(d_2)$. This can be done by looking up a normal CDF (cumulative density function) table, or using the Excel function =NORMSDIST(). The syntax would be =NORMSDIST(0.373), to reflect that this is a distribution that is standard normal (mean = 0 and standard deviation = 1) and is a cumulative function. This gives:

$$N(d_1) = N(0.373) = 0.645,$$
$$N(d_2) = N(0.223) = 0.588.$$

Plugging these numbers for the price of the call option into the BSM formula gives us (Equation 7.7):

$$C_0 = S_0 \times N(d_1) - \frac{K}{e^{r_f \times T}} \times N(d_2)$$

$$= 41 \times 0.645 - \frac{40}{e^{0.08 \times 0.25}} \times 0.588$$

$$= 3.391.$$

This gives the price of the call option. The price of the put option can be calculated via Equation 7.8, either using the put–call parity formula or the formula with the price of the call option already substituted in. Using the put–call parity formula, we get:

$$P_0 = C_0 - S_0 + \frac{K}{e^{r_f \times T}}$$

$$= 3.391 - 41 + \frac{40}{e^{0.08 \times 0.25}}$$

$$= 1.599.$$

Equivalently:

$$P_0 = (N(d_1) - 1) \times S_0 + (1 - N(d_2)) \times \frac{K}{e^{r_f \times T}}$$

$$= (0.645 - 1) \times 41 + (1 - 0.588) \times \frac{40}{e^{0.08 \times 0.25}}$$

$$= 1.599.$$

These numbers can be verified using the BSM calculator included in the Excel app to this chapter.

The BSM model allows a convenient calculation of any call or put option, but requires a calculator or app to utilize. In some special cases, we can use "shortcuts" to provide a quick calculation when such a calculator may not be easily accessible. For the special case in which the price of the underlying stock equals the present value of the strike price (i.e., $S = K / e^{r_f \times T}$), there is a convenient approximation to calculate option prices:

$$\frac{C_0}{S_0} \approx 0.4 \times \sigma \times \sqrt{T}. \tag{7.9}$$

This approximation is also valid for the price of the put. Thus, if the stock price is $100, the strike price is $108.33, the maturity is one year, the riskless interest rate is 8%, and volatility 0.20, then the approximate price of the call and of the put is 0.08 of the stock price, or $8. If we instead use Equations 7.7 and 7.8 to calculate these option prices, we find that the approximation is not bad: The prices of the call and put options are both $7.97. The approximation will be most accurate for small values of T.

The BSM model also indicates what does and does not matter in terms of defining option prices. For example, an important takeaway of the BSM formula is that the expected return on the stock, which can be difficult to measure, does not explicitly appear in the option pricing formula. What does matter is the stock price: Any change in expectations about the future stock price or in the expected return required on the stock will cause the stock price to change and thereby change the price of the call. But at any given stock price, the option price can be derived without knowing the expected return on the stock. Analysts who disagree about the expected return on the stock will nevertheless agree about the right price for the option, given the current observed price of the stock.

7.5 VALUING OPTIONS: THE BLACK–SCHOLES–MERTON MODEL

The variables in the BSM formula can also tell us how the price of an option will change when the characteristics of the underlying stock or the option change (holding all other variables constant). These relationships are known as the Greeks, and are denoted by Greek letters.

Delta (Δ): How an option's price changes when the stock price changes. In other words, it is the sensitivity of the option's price to a change in the stock price. Delta can also refer to the change in an option's price if the option strike price changes. This helps to gauge how likely an option is to expire "in the money" (i.e., with a positive payoff): The more likely that is, the higher the option price. We find the following specific relationships:

- An increase in the price of the underlying stock results in an increase in the price of the call and a decrease in the price of the put.
- An increase in the strike price results in a decrease in the price of the call and an increase in the price of the put.

Gamma (Γ): How much an option's delta changes when the stock price changes. Gamma is important because it tells us how fast the delta is changing. For example, if a stock price is at $1,000 and the strike price of a call option is $100, an increase of $1 in the stock price will not affect the option's price much, as measured by delta. In contrast, if the stock price is at $99, a $1 increase in the stock price will affect the option price proportionately more. Gamma will be at its highest when an option is "at the money."[4]

Vega (v): How an option's price changes when the stock's volatility changes. An increase in volatility results in an increase in the prices of both the call and the put.

Theta (θ): How an option's price changes when the time to expiration of the option increases. For American-type options, an increase in the time to expiration results in an increase in the price of the call and an increase in the price of the put. For European-type options, an increase in the time to expiration may either increase or decrease option prices.

Rho (ρ): How an option's price changes when the riskless interest rate changes. An increase in the interest rate results in an increase in the price of the call and a decrease in the price of the put.

Psi (Ψ): How an option's price changes when the dividend yield of the stock increases. Since a company's stock price drops when it pays a dividend, an increase in the dividend yield results in a decrease in the price of the call and an increase in the price of the put.

This is summarized in Table 7.11.

Table 7.11 **Determinants of option prices.** How call and put option prices change when the variable (in the second column) increases, holding all other variables the same.

Greek measure	Increase in	Change in call price	Change in put price
Delta (Δ)	Stock price, S	Increase	Decrease
Delta (Δ)	Strike price, K	Decrease	Increase
Gamma (Γ)	Delta (Δ)	–	–
Vega	Volatility, σ	Increase	Increase
Theta (Θ)	Time to expiration, T	Increase for American, ambiguous for European	Increase for American, ambiguous for European
Rho (ρ)	Interest rate, r	Increase	Decrease
Psi (Ψ)	Dividend yield, div	Decrease	Increase

---

[4] In Chapter 19 we discuss the relationship of gamma to replicating the payoffs of an option using stocks and bonds, which is the intuition underlying the BSM formula.

An increase in volatility results in an increase in the prices of an option; this is an important insight with a variety of implications, as we discuss in the next section.

> **QUICK CHECK 7.7** Suppose that the volatility of the underlying stock is 0.3. With a stock price of $100 (equal to the present value of the strike price), a strike price of $108.33, a maturity of one year, the riskless interest rate is 8%. What is the approximate and exact price of the call and put option?

7.5.2 Volatility and Option Prices

One of the insights of the BSM model is that the higher the volatility of a stock's price, the higher the prices of both puts and calls on that stock. Figure 7.13 helps to explain why. The top row of the figure compares the probability distribution of outcomes for a security with high volatility or low volatility. The tick marks in each rug plot, which shows the frequency with which observations in the distribution occur, are most concentrated in the center where there is the highest likelihood of outcomes. As the likelihood of observations is diminished in both tails, the tick marks become more sparse. Figure 7.13(c) shows the probability distributions and the rug plots together for both high volatility and low volatility. When superimposed together like this, it provides a perspective on differences in the relative frequency of observations for both high and low volatility. The middle row of Figure 7.13 shows the payoff diagrams for a put option with a strike price equal to $20 at low volatility, high volatility, and both. Finally, the bottom row combines and superimposes the rug plots from the top row onto the payoff diagram from the middle row. These payoff-probability (or payoff-density) charts show the payoff diagram but at the same time provide an indication of the likelihood that various payoffs may be achieved. Figure 7.13(i) superimposes the payoff-probability when there is high volatility with the payoff-probability plot when there is low volatility. The takeaway is that the payoff diagrams are identical, but the probabilities associated with each, and therefore the rug plots that lay on top of them, are different, with a greater probability of higher payoffs with higher volatility.

The reasoning behind greater volatility resulting in higher options prices is as follows. The payoff from an option at expiration cannot be negative. At worst, the option will be worthless and not be exercised. With greater volatility, the oscillations of the stock price are greater in both directions: Greater volatility implies that the probability of small price changes declines and the probability of large price changes increases, thus raising the potential for a higher option payoff for both a put and a call at expiration. This can be seen in the rightmost columns of Figures 7.13 and 7.14.

To illustrate, consider a put option on a stock. Greater volatility means that the possible severity of a loss on the stock is greater, which makes the put more valuable. Puts are insurance, and if the loss is going to be potentially twice as big, the buyer is going to be willing to pay more (think of the example of hurricane insurance with a bigger storm). While the buyer of the put would desire the option even more if the possible loss-protection is larger, the seller/writer of the option will need more compensation to cover the greater potential loss, leading to a higher price. Given the relationship between puts and calls through the put–call parity relationship, the same logic also applies to call options: The more volatile the underlying asset, the larger the potential upside for the call option payoffs is.

So, an increase in a stock's volatility, holding constant the current price, will cause the prices of puts and calls on that stock to rise. Moreover, the put–call parity relation implies that an increase in stock price volatility will result in the exact same increase in the price of both the call and the corresponding put (i.e., the put with the same maturity and exercise price as the call).

7.5 VALUING OPTIONS: THE BLACK–SCHOLES–MERTON MODEL

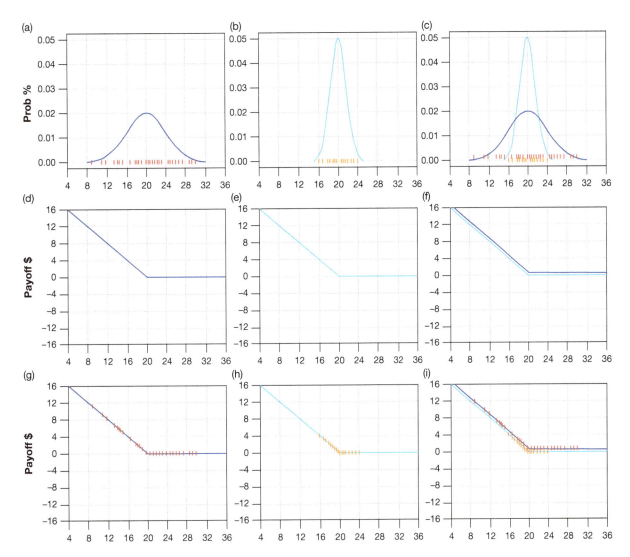

FIGURE 7.13 **Payoff diagram distributions for low and high volatility put option.** The top three graphs compare probability distribution of outcomes for a security when it has high volatility and low volatility. (a) The security at high volatility; (b) the security at low volatility; (c) low and high volatility together. Each chart includes a rug plot of the frequency with which observations from the distribution would occur at the base of each curve. In (c), the probability distributions and the rug plots are shown together for both high volatility and low volatility. The middle three graphs show the payoff diagrams for an option with strike price equal to $20 at low volatility (yellow), high volatility (blue), and both. The bottom three graphs combine and superimpose the rug plots from the top row onto the payoff diagram from the middle row. Note that in (i), the plots have been shifted slightly to make the differences stand out.

This result implies that an increase in risk (i.e., greater uncertainty) for the option's underlying asset will increase the option's value. This underlies **Principle 8:** *Flexibility in financial decisions has value, and the greater the uncertainty, the greater the value.* As we will see throughout the book, this insight has a number of important implications. For example, in Chapter 14 we will show that corporate equity can be viewed as a type of call option. Principle 8 immediately leads to the insight that corporate stock prices will rise when the risk of the underlying company increases, which in turn leads to important implications for the incentives that managers who run companies face (discussed in Chapter 11).

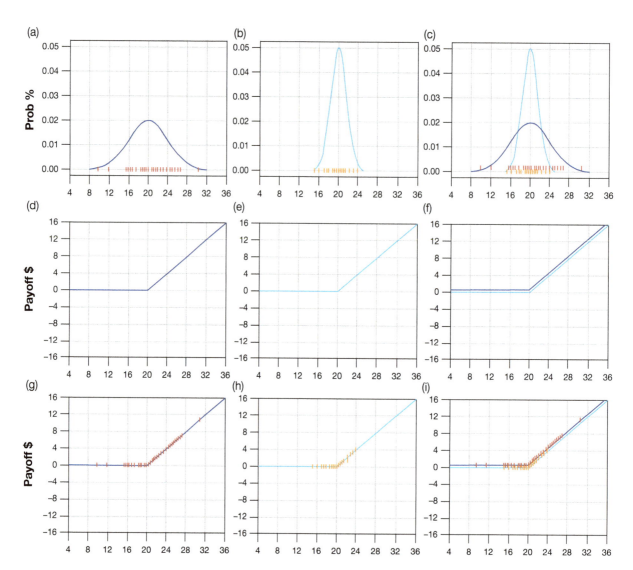

FIGURE 7.14 Payoff diagram distributions for low and high volatility call option. The top three graphs compare probability distribution of outcomes for a security when it has high volatility and low volatility. (a) The security at high volatility; (b) the security at low volatility; (c) low and high volatility together. Each chart includes a rug plot of the frequency at the base of each curve. In (c), the probability distributions and the rug plots are shown together for both high volatility and low volatility. The middle three graphs show the payoff diagrams for an option with strike price equal to $20 at low volatility (yellow), high volatility (blue), and both. The bottom three graphs combine and superimpose the rug plots from the top row onto the payoff diagram from the middle row. Note that in (i), the plots have been shifted slightly to make the differences stand out.

> **QUICK CHECK 7.8** Suppose that there is a stock with a current price of $100 and an annual volatility of 20%. What is the price of a call option with a strike price of $100 and a maturity of one year if the riskless rate is 2%? Compare this to the price of the call when the stock's volatility is instead 30%.

7.5.3 Implied Volatility

A key input into the BSM model is the underlying asset's volatility, σ—that is, how much the value of the asset moves around. As important as volatility is, it is often difficult to measure. For example,

7.5 VALUING OPTIONS: THE BLACK–SCHOLES–MERTON MODEL

consider a company's stock. If we want to measure the true volatility (i.e., overall risk) of the stock, a common way is to take the standard deviation of the stock's return over a past period, say the last 90 days. However, this type of measure suffers from the fact that it is backward looking, and may not necessarily reflect the risk of the company now.

Option prices indicate what the market views as the current volatility of the stock, giving a potentially more accurate estimate of it, in line with **Principle 5**: *The best estimate of an asset's value is usually its market price, which incorporates valuable information to guide the allocation of resources and risks*. We refer to this as implied volatility, and it is defined as the value of σ that makes the observed market price of the option equal to the value computed using the option pricing formula. Put differently, if we observe an option price in the market, implied volatility is the value of σ that will set that price equal to the price given by the BSM formula (Equation 7.7), given the other variables.

To illustrate, suppose we observe a call option that is trading for $7.97, and the call option has a maturity of one year and a strike price of $108.33. The current stock price is $100, and the riskless interest rate is 8%:

- $C_0 = 7.97$
- $S_0 = 100$
- $K = 108.33$
- $T = 1$
- $r_f = 0.08$
- $\sigma = ?$

The implied volatility is found by substituting the variables' information into Equation 7.7 and solving for σ. If we do so, we get the volatility implied by this option's price, which is $\sigma = 0.2$.

For any given stock, the availability of prices for multiple options with different maturities infers the term structure of implied volatility, which is the implied volatility of options with various maturities. Just as we can use the DCF formula to convert bond prices to yield to maturity, we can use the BSM formula to convert option prices to implied volatility. Just as we use bonds of different maturities to derive a term structure of yields, so we use options of different expiration times to derive an implied volatility term structure. In exchange-traded options markets, there are different maturities for every strike price of an option. There are also traded options on stock market indexes such as the S&P 500 Index, which allows one to infer the implied volatility of the entire market. Figure 7.15 shows the term structure of implied volatility based on S&P 500 options. The implied volatility term structure is generally not flat. Figure 7.15 shows the term structure of volatility on 6 Oct. 2021. It

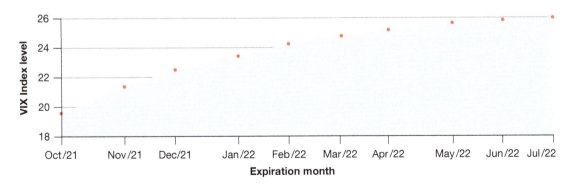

FIGURE 7.15 **Implied volatility term structure for S&P 500 options.** This figure shows the term structure of implied volatility based on options on the S&P 500 Index. This is referred to as the VIX Index. Implied volatility is plotted for options at various future expiration dates.
Source: CBOE.

rises from left to right, from a value of 19.56 for the option expiring on 15 Oct. 2021 to a value of 25.99 for the option expiring on 15 July 2022.

Conclusion

In this chapter we introduced options, which are financial contracts that embed flexibility: The owner can make a decision after the market price of an underlying asset is observed. Call options allow the owner to buy an asset in the future for a predetermined price, while put options allow the owner to sell an asset in the future for a predetermined price. We explained the mechanics of call options and put options, and how they are traded in financial marketplaces. We further showed how options can be used to construct specific investment strategies, and explored how the price of an option can be determined.

Options are important because they are at the core of decision making under uncertainty, which is a key aspect of finance (**Principle 6:** *Risk is fundamental to financial analysis and must be explicitly considered in all financial decisions*). This insight is so fundamental that it formed one of our principles (**Principle 8:** *Flexibility in financial decisions has value, and the greater the uncertainty, the greater the value*). Indeed, underscoring this, the applications of options analysis in the real world are numerous and extend far beyond financial markets. In future chapters throughout the book, we will explore many of these in more detail.

Takeaways

- A call option is the right but not the obligation to buy a specified asset for a predetermined price (known as the strike price) at some point in the future. A put option is the right but not the obligation to sell a specified asset for a predetermined price at some point in the future.
- Options can be used to modify an investor's exposure to investment risk. By combining the risk-free asset and stock index call options, an investor can achieve a guaranteed minimum rate of return plus substantial upside participation in the stock market.
- Options can be combined in order to achieve particular desired payoff profiles in the future.
- A portfolio consisting of a stock plus a European put option is equivalent to a riskless bond with a face value equal to the option's exercise price plus a European call option. Therefore, by the law of one price, there is a relationship between their prices called put–call parity. This relationship does not depend on the model of underlying price dynamics.
- The Black–Scholes–Merton (BSM) formula determines the price of an option given five inputs: the underlying asset's price, the volatility of the underlying asset's price, the riskless interest rate, the maturity of the option, and the strike price of the option.
- The BSM formula provides a way of converting prices of options into implied volatilities of the underlying assets.

Key Terms

American option	174	Exercise price	174
Black–Scholes–Merton (BSM) formula	195	Expiration/maturity date	174
Call option	174	Greeks	199
Cash settlement	189	Implied volatility	203
European option	174	Index options	188
Exchange-traded options	187	Intrinsic value/tangible value	188

Leveraged position 190
Long position 176
Net payoff 175
Options 171
Over-the-counter (OTC) options 187
Payoff 174
Payoff-probability/payoff-density charts 200
Profit 175
Protective put 181
Put option 174
Put–call parity relation 184
Short position 176
Straddle 192
Strike price 174
Term structure of implied volatility 203
Time value 188
Underlying asset 174
Writing 176

Key Equations

Payoff of a put option	$P_T = \max(K - S_T, 0)$	Eq. 7.1
Payoff of a call option	$C_T = \max(S_T - K, 0)$	Eq. 7.2
Put–call parity payoffs	$S_T + P_T = C_T + K$	Eq. 7.3
Put–call parity	$S_0 + P_0 = C_0 + \dfrac{K}{(1+r_f)^T}$	Eq. 7.4
Value of a call option from the put–call parity	$C_0 = S_0 + P_0 - \dfrac{K}{(1+r_f)^T}$	Eq. 7.5
Value of a stock and a risk-free bond from the put–call parity	$S_0 = C_0 - P_0 + \dfrac{K}{(1+r_f)^T}$ $\dfrac{K}{(1+r_f)^T} = S_0 - C_0 + P_0$	Eq. 7.6
Value of a call option, BSM formula	$C_0 = S_0 \times N(d_1) - \dfrac{K}{e^{r_f \times T}} \times N(d_2)$ $d_1 = \dfrac{\ln\left(\dfrac{S_0}{K}\right) + \left(r_f + \dfrac{\sigma^2}{2}\right) \times T}{\sigma \times \sqrt{T}}$ $d_2 = d_1 - \sigma \times \sqrt{T}$	Eq. 7.7
Value of a put option	$P_0 = C_0 - S_0 + \dfrac{K}{e^{r_f \times T}}$ $= (N(d_1) - 1) \times S_0 + (1 - N(d_2)) \times \dfrac{K}{e^{r_f \times T}}$	Eq. 7.8
Approximation to calculate option prices	$\dfrac{C_0}{S_0} \approx 0.4 \times \sigma \times \sqrt{T}$	Eq. 7.9

Problems

1. Which has unlimited downside risk, a long or short position in a call option? A long or short position in a put option? Explain your answers.
2. Describe the key defining characteristics of a put or call option on any asset.
3. Graph the payoff for a European put option selling for a premium of $5 with exercise price ($K$) of $50, written on a stock with value S, when:
   (a) you hold a long position (i.e., you buy the put);
   (b) you hold a short position (i.e., you sell the put).
4. Graph the payoff to a portfolio of one European call option and one European put option, each with the same expiration date and each with exercise price (E) of $25, when both options are on a stock with value S. What is the portfolio payoff if the stock price is $40 at expiration? What if the price is $20?
5. Draw the payoff diagrams (at maturity) for the following combinations of ABC stock and its options. Assume all put and call options on ABC have the same strike price $K = \$100$ and maturity T, and any risk-free bonds have a par amount of $100 and a maturity T.
   (a) Purchased (long) one share of ABC stock, sold (short) one call option.
   (b) Short two shares of ABC stock, long three put options.
   (c) Long one risk-free bond, short one call option.
   (d) Long one share of ABC stock, short two call options, long one put option.
6. Draw payoff diagrams for the following combination of securities at maturity:
   (a) Short one share of stock, long one call option with a strike price of $100.
   (b) Long one risk-free bond with a par value of $100, long one call option with a strike price of $100.
   (c) Long one put option with a strike price of $100, long one call option with a strike price of $50.
   (d) Short one put option with a strike price of $50, long one put option with a strike price of $100.
   (e) Long two call options with a strike price of $100, short two call options with a strike price of $150.
   (f) Short one put option with a strike price of $50, long one call option with a strike price of $100.
7. Suppose that Superior Industries is currently trading at $20 per share. You believe that the current market valuation is fair, but believe that the market consensus expectation of the volatility of Superior over the next year is too high. As such, you plan to use European calls and puts to build a so-called "butterfly spread," which pays off if Superior's stock price does not move outside of a given range within the next year. The desired payoff for your butterfly spread is given in Figure P7.1.
   Using the Excel app, recreate this payoff diagram in two different ways. List the details of the instruments that you use to do so.
8. Merck is currently trading at $30. You have just purchased two options (one put with a strike of $15 and one call with a strike of $45) on Merck (MRK). The options have a maturity of one year.
   (a) Draw the payoff diagram of your portfolio of the two options.
   (b) If the price of Merck were to drop to $10, which of your options would be in the range in which you would exercise the option if it were at maturity (also called "in-the-money")?
   (c) Why would you take on both a put and a call option? Explain briefly.
9. Glad Triton Industries (GTI) is currently trading at $100. Kwong, a Singapore-based relative value hedge fund manager, buys 1,000 put options with a strike of 100, buys 1,000 shares of the stock, and sells 1,000 call options with a strike of 100. Both options are European and have a maturity of one year. The puts are priced at $18 and the calls are selling for $30. What does this strategy cost Kwong? Draw the payoff diagram of this strategy at the maturity of the options. Be sure to label all relevant prices and axes.

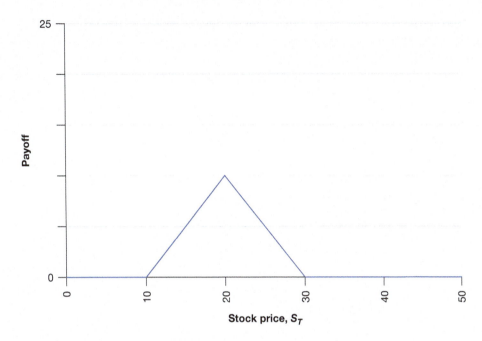

Figure P7.1 Desired payoff for butterfly spread.

10. If an investor paid a $4.75 premium to obtain a long position in a put option with an exercise price of $47, the underlying asset breakeven point corresponds to what price? Diagram the position.
11. The risk-free one-year rate of interest is 4%, and the Globalex stock index is at 100. The price of one-year European call options on the Globalex stock index with an exercise price of 104 is 8% of the current price of the index. Assume that the expected dividend yield on the stocks in the Globalex index is zero. You have $1 million to invest for the next year. You plan to invest enough of your money in one-year Treasury bills to ensure that you will at least get back your original $1 million, and you will use the rest of your money to buy Globalex call options. If you think that there is some chance that the Globalex index one year from now will be up 12%, some chance that it will be up 40%, and some chance that it will be down 20%, what are your possible portfolio rates of return?
12. Given the following variables: $S = \$55$, $K = \$75$, $T = 1$ year, $r = 5\%$, and $P = \$20$; if the call option is selling for $10 ($C = \$10$), what arbitrage opportunity exists? Outline the strategy and the profit to be realized.
13. Using the put–call parity relation:
    (a) Show how one can replicate a one-year pure discount bond (zero-coupon bond) with a face value of $100 using a share of stock, a put, and a call.
    (b) Suppose that $K = \$100$, $S = \$100$, $P = \$10$, and $C = \$15$. What must be the one-year interest rate?
    (c) Show that if the one-year risk-free interest rate is lower than in your answer to part (b), there would be an arbitrage opportunity.
14. A 90-day European call option on a share of the stock of Wimendo is currently trading at €20, whereas the current price of the share itself is €24. Ninety-day zero-coupon securities issued by the government of France are selling for €98.55 per €100 of face value. Infer the price of a 90-day European put option on this stock if both the call and put have a common exercise price of €20.

15. Gordon Gekko has assembled a portfolio consisting of ten 90-day US Treasury bills, each having a face value of $1,000 and a current price of $990.10, and 200 90-day European call options, each written on a share of Paramount stock and having an exercise price of $50. Gekko is offering to trade you this portfolio for 300 shares of Paramount stock, which is currently valued at $215 per share. If 90-day European put options on Paramount stock with a $50 exercise price are currently valued at $25,
    (a) infer the value of the calls in Gekko's portfolio; and
    (b) determine whether you should accept Gekko's offer.

16. The stock of Kakkonen, Ltd., a hot tuna distributor, currently lists for $50 per share, whereas one-year European call options on this stock, with an exercise price of $20, sell for $40 and European put options with a similar expiration date and exercise price sell for $8.457.
    (a) Infer the yield on a one-year, zero-coupon US government bond sold today.
    (b) If this yield is actually at 9%, construct a profitable trade to exploit the potential for arbitrage.

17. Which has more value, (a) a portfolio composed of call options on ten different stocks or (b) a single call option on a portfolio composed of the same ten stocks? Assume the exercise price of (b) is equal to the sum of the exercise prices of the call options in (a) and all option expiration dates are identical. Explain your answer.

18. The share value of Drummond, Griffin, and McNabb (DGM), a New Orleans publishing house, is currently trading at $100 but is expected, 90 days from today, to rise to $150 or to decline to $50, depending on critical reviews of its new biography of Ezra Pound. Assuming the risk-free interest rate over the coming 90-day period is 1%, can you value a European call option written on a share of DGM stock if the option carries an exercise price of $85?

19. Using the Black–Scholes–Merton (BSM) model, find the price of a call option with an exercise price of $35 on a share currently priced at $40. Assume the riskless rate of 10% per annum and the option has six months to expiration. The risk of the stock is measured by a value of 0.25. Decompose the premium into intrinsic value and time value.

20. Use the BSM formula to find the price of a three-month European call option on a nondividend-paying stock with a current price of $50. Assume the exercise price is $51, the continuously compounded risk-free interest rate is 8% per year, and the volatility is 0.4.

21. Use the put–call parity relation to find the BSM formula for the price of the corresponding put option in the previous problem.

22. Suppose XYZ is a nondividend-paying stock. The current stock price is $S = \$100$, the volatility is $\sigma = 40\%$, and the risk-free interest rate is $r = 2\%$.
    (a) Using the BSM formula or a BSM calculator, find the price of a two-year European call option on XYZ with a strike price of $80.
    (b) Using put–call parity, find the price of a two-year European put option on XYZ with the same strike price.

23. As a financial analyst at Yew and Associates, a Singaporean investment house, you are asked by a client if she should purchase European call options on Rattan, Ltd. stock, which are currently selling in US dollars for $30. These options have an exercise price of $50. Rattan stock currently exhibits a share price of $55, and the estimated rate of return variance of the stock is 0.04. If these options expire in 25 days and the risk-free interest rate over that period is 5% per year, what do you advise your client to do?

24. Use the BSM model to infer the volatility of the returns on the underlying share of stock paying no cash dividend. Assume the following parameters: $S = 90$, $K = 100$, $r = 10\%$, $T = 0.5$. What is σ? If the call option premium is $3.05? What if the premium is $5.52?

8 FINANCIAL STATEMENTS: ANALYZING AND FORECASTING

CHAPTER OVERVIEW

8.1	Financial Statements	210
8.2	Balance Sheet	211
8.3	Income Statement	214
8.4	Statement of Cash Flows	217
8.5	Notes to Financial Statements	220
8.6	The Difference between Market Values and Accounting Book Values	221
8.7	Financial Ratio Analysis	225
8.8	Using the Financial Ratios: Information about Performance	235
8.9	Using the Financial Ratios: Market Valuation	237
8.10	Limitations of Financial Ratios	240
8.11	Future Financial Planning and Projections	241

LEARNING OBJECTIVES

After reading this chapter, you will be able to:
- explain how basic financial statements are constructed, and interpret the information they provide;
- describe the difference between market values and book values;
- calculate and interpret key financial ratios;
- use financial statements to plan out a company's future.

EQUATIONS YOU KNOW

Rate of return from investing in a stock	$r = \dfrac{\text{ending share price} - \text{beginning share price} + \text{dividends}}{\text{beginning share price}}$	Eq. 5.2

- You are looking to invest in the stock of a company, but want to understand its current and recent financial positions; where can you find this information?

- You are a financial analyst, and a company you are following just released its latest financial information. How do you interpret this information?

- A company you have invested in releases its accounting statements, but the company's valuation on those statements is very different from how the market values the company based on its stock price. Why are they different, and which reflects the company's true value?

- Your company wishes to provide its existing and potential investors with forward-looking statements based on what it anticipates will happen to the company in the future. How are these statements constructed?

Introduction

In this chapter we review an important source of information about companies: financial statements. Financial statements are reports published by businesses and other organizations that provide investors and other stakeholders with information about a firm's assets, liabilities, existing and potential cash flows, and so on. The core financial statements, which are usually published quarterly and annually, are the balance sheet, the income statement, and the statement of cash flows. Financial statements provide information about a firm's current and past financial state, information that is key in figuring out a firm's current economic value and the outlook on how the firm may perform in the future.

The material in this chapter advances our understanding of the topics we have covered so far in a number of ways. The financial investments introduced in previous chapters—stocks, bonds, options, and so on—are usually available from actual companies. Thus, to better understand the potential performance of those investments, it is important to have a more complete picture of the companies that issue those financial instruments. Financial statements can provide such information. Furthermore, subsequent chapters will present models for estimating what the current intrinsic, or economic, value of a company *should* be. As we will see, in order to do so, we need to model what we expect the future financial state of the company will be, based on its past information. The information presented in financial statements is essential to developing and applying such models.

We begin with a discussion of the three basic types of financial statements. We then discuss the difference between a firm's market value (determined by trading in financial markets) and its accounting book values as reflected in its balance sheet information. Finally, we show how a company uses financial statements as templates for planning its financial future. Throughout this chapter, to help explain the contents of the financial statements and what they tell us, we will consider a hypothetical manufacturing company called Generic Consumer Products (GCP) and how it creates and uses financial statements.

8.1 Financial Statements

Financial statements serve three important functions:

- *Function 1*: Financial statements provide information to a firm's stakeholders about the company's current status and past financial performance. Knowing the details of a firm's income, expenses, debt, equity, assets, and liabilities is crucial to understanding its present and future values. And understanding these values enables financial decision makers inside and outside the firm to make informed financial decisions—for example, whether purchasing the firm's stock is a good decision—and to undertake strategies that enhance the functioning of the firm, as we discuss in detail in Part II.

- *Function 2*: Financial statements provide information that allows us to estimate a firm's intrinsic economic value. As we will see throughout this book, we can use the information provided by financial statements to estimate the true or intrinsic economic value of a firm. Financial statements provide measures of the value of a firm, but these *accounting* values do not necessarily reflect a firm's true *economic* value. The information about a firm's current or past state can help us construct informed estimates of the likely future cash flows that a firm will generate, which we can use to value the firm (a process we cover in subsequent chapters).
- *Function 3*: Financial statements provide a convenient way for a firm's owners and managers to plan for its future. Financial statements provide different stakeholders with information that allows them to plan for the future. A firm's managers and owners use current and past financial statements to prepare future projections of income statements, balance sheets, and statements of cash flow. These projections allow managers and owners to calculate performance targets, and allow decision makers to engage in financial planning for the future and to estimate the firm's future profits and financing requirements. A firm's creditors use financial statement information to determine what, if any, borrowing restrictions should be set on the firm going forward.

There are three standard financial statements that perform these functions: the balance sheet, the income statement, and the statement of cash flows. Although other templates can be used to summarize a firm's status and performance, these three are the most commonly used by a firm's managers, investors, and regulators.

8.2 Balance Sheet

A firm's balance sheet shows its assets (what it owns) and its liabilities (what it owes) at a given point in time, called the balance sheet date. The difference between assets and liabilities (assets − liabilities) is the firm's net worth, also called shareholders' equity for a corporation. A firm's balance sheet answers the question "What are a firm's resources and what does it owe at a particular point in time?" This information provides valuable insights into a firm's financial strength.

Because the balance sheet is a snapshot of a firm's finances at one point, its numbers are accounting *stock* values, not *flows*. An accounting stock value (note that this is different from shares of a company's stock) represents an amount that exists at a particular point in time (e.g., how much cash you had at the end of last year). In contrast, an accounting flow variable measures how much something increased or decreased over a period of time (e.g., how much cash you spent over the past year).

The values of assets and liabilities on a company's balance sheet are measured at their *historical* acquisition costs in accordance with Generally Accepted Accounting Principles (GAAP). That is, these values do not necessarily reflect the current values of assets and liabilities, but instead reflect the values of the assets and liabilities when the company first acquired them. (We discuss the implications of this difference in Section 8.6.) The GAAP rules are determined and modified periodically by the Financial Accounting Standards Board, an independent organization that sets accounting reporting standards in the United States. Any corporation from any country that wants to list its shares on an exchange in the United States must conform to the GAAP accounting standards and report regularly (often quarterly, always annually) on its activities. It does so by filing financial statements with the Securities and Exchange Commission (SEC), the US government agency whose goals are to protect investors; maintain fair, orderly, and efficient markets; and facilitate capital formation. Firms in other countries often follow other standards—for example, the International Financial Reporting Standards (IFRS) (an international not-for-profit agency responsible for developing global accounting standards) has been adopted by numerous firms across the globe.

We will now start looking at our hypothetical company, Generic Consumer Products, and its financial statements. GCP's balance sheet as of 31 Dec. 2025 and, for comparison, as of 31 Dec. 2024 is shown in Table 8.1. It is not required that all balance sheets show the previous year's numbers, but it's usually good practice and most companies do so.

Table 8.1 Balance sheet for GCP. This balance sheet shows values (in millions of US dollars) of GCP's assets and liabilities as of 31 Dec. for the years 2025 and 2024.

Assets	2024	2025
Current assets		
Cash and marketable securities	$100.0	$120.0
Accounts receivable	50.0	60.0
Inventories	150.0	180.0
Total current assets	*300.0*	*360.0*
Noncurrent assets		
Property, plant, and Equipment (PP&E)	400.0	490.0
less accumulated depreciation	(100.0)	(130.0)
Net PP&E	300.0	360.0
Intangible assets	100.0	100.0
Total noncurrent assets	*400.0*	*460.0*
Total assets	**700.0**	**820.0**
Liabilities and stockholders' equity		
Current liabilities		
Accounts payable	60.0	72.0
Short-term debt	90.0	184.6
Total current liabilities	*150.0*	*256.6*
Noncurrent liabilities		
Long-term debt	150.0	150.0
Total liabilities	*300.0*	*406.6*
Stockholders' equity		
Stockholders' equity (1 million shares outstanding)	400.0	413.4
Paid-in capital	200.0	200.0
Retained earnings	200.0	213.4
Total liabilities and equity	**700.0**	**820.0**

Note: All figures are in millions of US dollars. Values are as of 31 Dec.

8.2 BALANCE SHEET

8.2.1 Assets

The first section of a balance sheet lists a firm's assets—what it owns. These are typically split between current assets and noncurrent assets.

Current assets are short-term assets a company owns that are either currently cash or will be converted into cash within one year. As Table 8.1 shows, GCP's current assets include: cash and marketable securities (such as Treasury bills which can easily be sold for cash), accounts receivable (the amount owed to GCP by customers), and inventories (raw materials, goods in the process of production, and finished goods that will likely be sold shortly). When combined, these three items make up GCP's total current assets, $360 million.

The next asset account is noncurrent assets, also called long-term assets, or fixed assets. These are assets that a company owns that are either not expected to be sold or cannot be easily sold in the short term. GCP's noncurrent assets consist of property, plant, and equipment (PP&E)—items the firm owns such as buildings, land, manufacturing machines, and so on. The reported value of these assets is $490 million in 2025. However, as noted earlier, assets on the balance sheet are reported at their historical values (when they were acquired). Because the value of such assets goes down over time (depreciates), we subtract $130 million in depreciation so that net PP&E in 2025 is $360 million.

Another asset account that frequently appears as a noncurrent asset on a balance sheet is intangible assets, items related to brand recognition and intellectual property that have value but are not physical assets. An example of this is goodwill, which results when one firm acquires another firm at a price greater than its book value. GCP's intangible assets are $100 million. To get total assets, we add current assets and noncurrent assets to get $820 million.

8.2.2 Liabilities

The next section of a balance sheet lists a firm's liabilities: what it owes to others. Similar to assets, liabilities are usually split between current liabilities and noncurrent liabilities.

Current liabilities are items a company owes that must be paid off within a year. For GCP, these include accounts payable (the amount the company owes to its suppliers) of $72 million, and short-term debt (loans the company has taken that are due within a year) of $184.6 million. These two items combine to make up total current liabilities of $256.6 million in 2025.

The difference between a firm's current assets and its current liabilities (current assets − current liabilities) is called net working capital (NWC). Net working capital provides a measure to gauge the short-term financial health of a company. A positive number indicates that a company has greater resources than it owes in the short run, while a negative number indicates that a company owes more than it currently has in the short run. It does not explicitly appear as an item on the balance sheet, but it is important in figuring out the anticipated cash flows of a company in Part II of the text, which covers valuation of companies. GCP's NWC at the end of 2025 is $103.4 million: current assets of $360 million minus current liabilities of $256.6 million.

The next item on the liabilities part of the balance sheet is noncurrent liabilities, the long-term debt that a company is obligated to pay in more than one year. The largest part of a company's noncurrent liabilities is usually the bonds it has issued to borrow money and that are due to mature in more than one year. GCP has bonds outstanding that obligate it to pay a face value of $150 million when the bonds mature in 2031.

The final category is shareholders' equity, the residual value of a firm's assets that may be paid to the firm's owners (i.e., its shareholders) once its liabilities have been paid. Put differently, it represents the value that remains from the firm's assets once its liabilities (debt and other money it owes) have been paid off. This item is also called the *book value of equity*, and it usually differs from the *market* value of the firm's shares. We explain the reasons for this difference in Section 8.4. For GCP's shareholders, equity consists of paid-in capital (the amount raised in the past by issuing common stock) and retained earnings, the cumulative amount of past earnings that have been kept as cash in the business. These items are valued at $200 million and $213.4 million, respectively, thus summing to $413.4 million.

As its name states, a balance sheet must be in balance—that is, the firm's assets must equal its liabilities and stockholders' equity. We can see that this is indeed the case for GCP: Its total assets are $820 million, and its liabilities plus stockholders' equity is $820 million.

> **QUICK CHECK 8.1** What difference would it have made to the end-of-year balance sheet if GCP had issued an additional $50 million in long-term debt during 2025 and added that amount to its holdings in cash and marketable securities?

8.3 Income Statement

An income statement provides information about a company's profitability—its revenues minus its expenses—over a period of time. The income statement is also referred to as the statement of earnings or the statement of profit and loss (P&L). Unlike the balance sheet, which is a snapshot of what a company owns and owes at a particular point in time, the income statement provides information on accounting *flows* related to money earned and paid over a period of time. It answers the question "How profitable have a company's operations been over a period of time?" Table 8.2 shows the income statement for GCP in 2025. In the table, numbers for each line item *not* in parentheses represent positive numbers (revenues), while numbers within parentheses represent negative numbers (expenses).

8.3.1 Revenues

The first item listed in the income statement is sales revenue, the total amount of money a firm receives for sales. While GCP's revenue for 2025 comes entirely from sales of its products, other companies may earn revenue from royalties, renting out property, providing services, and other activities.

Table 8.2 Income statement for GCP as of 31 Dec. 2025 (in millions of US dollars).
This income statement shows GCP's revenues, expenses, taxes, and net income for the year ending 31 Dec. 2025. Numbers in parentheses represent negative numbers (expenses).

Sales revenue	$200.0
Cost of goods sold	(80.0)
Gross margin	120.0
Sales, general, and administrative expenses	(30.0)
Depreciation expense	(30.0)
Operating income/earnings before interest and taxes (EBIT)	60.0
Interest expense	(21.0)
Taxable income	39.0
Income taxes	(15.6)
Net income	23.4
Note: All figures are in millions of US dollars.	

8.3.2 Expenses

After revenues are listed, the income statement then lists a firm's various expenses: all the money it pays out. These expenses are broken down into five major categories: cost of goods sold, sales, general, and administrative expenses, depreciation expense, interest expense, and income taxes.

The first category is cost of goods sold (COGS), which is the expense GCP incurred in manufacturing the products it sold during the year, including materials and labor used in the manufacturing process. Compensation of employees and executives is typically included in this item as well. Compensation can include not only wages, but other forms of compensation such as options (see Box 8.1). In 2025, GCP's total COGS was $80 million.

The line item below the COGS, the gross margin, is the difference between revenues and COGS (revenue minus COGS). Gross margin focuses on the profits generated directly from the goods the firm produces—that is, revenues from sales of goods minus how much it costs to produce those goods. GPC's gross margin in 2025 was $200 million – $80 million = $120 million.

The second expense category is sales, general, and administrative (SG&A) expenses. This broad category includes the expenses incurred in managing the firm, such as salaries, advertising and distributing costs for the products produced during the year, rent, and other general overhead costs. GCP's SG&A expenses were $30 million.

The third expense category is depreciation expense, which tallies the amount that assets such as equipment depreciated in value during the year. The idea behind depreciation is that it allows a firm to allocate large expenditures over time, rather than all at once. Even though this is an "expense," the actual cash paid for the asset—that is, the cash outlay—occurred at the time it was initially purchased. For example, suppose you purchase machinery for $100 million in cash that will be worth nothing after five years, and decide to depreciate it over five years. Even though you technically paid $100 million in cash at the beginning, each year you can reduce your accounting income by $20 million due to the depreciation, thus reducing your tax bill each year.

Note that depreciation is *not* the same as an actual decline in value. For example, suppose a company purchases a building for $500,000. It can tally the building as going down in value over time and depreciate it on an accounting basis (saving taxes as a result). But if the real estate market is booming, then the property can actually go *up* in market value even as its depreciation is accounted for as an expense. Amortization is also often included as a separate expense line item. Amortization is the same thing as depreciation but applied to intangible assets such as trademarks or brand goodwill. GCP had $30 million in depreciation expense in 2025.

The next expense line item is operating income, gross margin less SG&A and depreciation expenses. Operating income is a measure of a firm's overall profits that are generated from its operational activities. It takes into account its revenues generated from sales and all its operational expenses, including direct expenses from production (COGS), more general business expenses (SG&A), and noncash expenses (depreciation and amortization). GCP's gross margin was $90 million and its SG&A and depreciation were $30 million. Its operating income was therefore $120 million – $60 million = $60 million. Operating income is also known as earnings before interest and taxes (EBIT), since we have not yet subtracted interest expense or tax payments.

The fourth expense category is interest expense, the amount of interest a company has paid on its debt. As noted in the balance sheet above, GCP has a total of $184.6 million in short-term debt and $150 million of long-term debt, and this borrowed money requires interest payments to be paid each year. GCP's interest payments totaled $21 million in 2024.

The next line item is taxable income, gross margin minus interest expense—the income the company reports that can be taxed by the government. We subtract interest expense from gross margin because the amount a company pays in interest can be deducted from its income to reduce the company's tax bill, an important point that we will revisit in later chapters. GCP's taxable income was $60 million – $21 million = $39 million.

The fifth and final expense category is income taxes, the amount of taxes the company pays to the government. In 2025, GCP faced an average tax rate of 40% on its taxable income of $39 million, so its tax bill was $39 million × 40% = $15.6 million.

> **QUICK CHECK 8.2** What difference would it have made to the income statement if GCP instead had SG&A expenses of $50 million?

The last line item on the income statement is net income, the final profits of the company (revenues minus expenses). One can think of net income as the "bottom line" of the firm over a period of time: It represents the profits that are left after all expenses have been paid out. To get net income, we take GCP's taxable income and subtract income taxes, which gives us a net income of $39 million − $15.6 million = $23.4 million.

Box 8.1 World of Business: Accounting for Employee Stock Options

Call options (the option to buy shares of a company's stock) are frequently used by companies to pay their employees and executives. Because the payoff of a call option increases when the price of the underlying stock increases, the option holder has an incentive to strive to improve the company's performance.

Even though options are widely used in compensation packages, the accounting rules governing options have long been a source of controversy. Because options have value (**Principle 8:** *Flexibility in financial decisions has value, and the greater the uncertainty, the greater the value*), options granted by the company to employees should be viewed as a compensation *expense* at the time they are granted to the employee, and should be entered on the income statement in the sales, general, and administrative expenses (SG&A) category. However, historically this is not how companies have taken account of stock option grants.

To make SG&A more accurately and fully reflect the use of call options in compensation, in 1972 the Financial Accounting Standards Board (FASB) issued a rule specifying that the cost of options should be measured by their intrinsic value—the difference between the current fair market value of the stock and the exercise price of the option. As a result, if an option's exercise price was set to the current market value, the accounting value of an option was set to *zero*; in other words, companies did not have to report it as an expense and it looked like they had more profit (the same revenues, but lower expenses) than they actually had.

The accounting rules governing options became much more consequential after 1973, when stock option grants experienced a boom, the Black–Scholes–Merton option pricing model was introduced, and options trading made it clear that options with no intrinsic value nevertheless had value. Those in favor of *not* expensing stock options had argued that they do not represent real costs to a company or that such costs cannot be estimated.

By not reporting option grants as a compensation expense, companies provide a distorted picture of their true economic performance. For example, had AOL Time Warner—a large communications and media conglomerate that formed following a merger in 2000—reported employee stock options as an expense in 2001, it would have shown an operating loss of $1.7 billion as opposed to the $700 million profit it actually reported.

After much heated controversy, in 1995 the FASB compromised and created a new standard that *recommended* (but did not require) companies to report the cost of options granted and their fair market value using option pricing models. This cost was to be reported as an expense (typically in SG&A) on their income statements. In 2004, there was a further revision that *required* companies to report stock options as a business expense at their fair market value (using an option pricing model) as of the award date of the option. The FASB does not specify which model to use, but the Black–Scholes–Merton model is commonly used and may be the best to ensure that a company's accounting expenses over time and expenses among different companies are directly comparable.

Source: Bodie, Z., Kaplan, R. S., and Merton, R. C. (2003). For the last time: stock options are an expense. *Harvard Business Review* 81(3): 62–71.

8.4 Statement of Cash Flows

The last of the three major financial statements is the statement of cash flows, which tracks the actual cash that has flowed in and out of the firm during a period of time. Understanding a firm's cash flows reveals exactly how a company runs its operations by examining where its money comes from and where it goes. Cash flow statements answer the question "How much money came into and went out of the company over a period of time, and where did that money come from and go to?"

A company's statement of cash flows often provides a better picture of what is going on with its operations than do its balance sheet and income statement. In particular, the statement of cash flows focuses attention on what is happening to the firm's actual cash position over time. Profitable firms can easily run short of cash and have difficulty meeting their financial obligations. Such problems can be difficult to see when just looking at the income statement, because income is affected by accounting conventions and subjective judgments on the part of management about issues such as how to value inventory and how quickly to depreciate assets. For example, on its income statement a firm can recognize income or expenses in a period based on transactions that occur, but the firm may not actually see the money come in or go out until the next period. The statement of cash flows is not influenced by such accounting decisions.

To get at the total change in cash for a firm, we start with the accounting earnings of the firm (net income), and then adjust them to reflect the sources of actual cash paid out or received (as opposed to noncash accounting expenses such as depreciation) over a time period. Many of these adjustments come from changes in the accounts on the balance sheet in Table 8.1. Table 8.3 presents GCP's statement of cash flows for 2025. It organizes cash flows into three categories, depending on where the cash is coming from: operating activities, investing activities, and financing activities.

Table 8.3 Statement of cash flows for GCP for 2025 (in millions of US dollars). The statement of cash flows for the cash that has flowed into and out of a firm during a period of time. The flows are categorized according to where the cash comes from.

Cash flow from operating activities	
Net income	$23.4
+ Depreciation	+30.0
− Increase in accounts receivable	−10.0
− Increase in inventories	−30.0
+ Increase in accounts payable	+12.0
Total cash flow from operations	*+25.4*
Cash flow from investing activities	
− Investment in plant and equipment	−90.0
Total cash flow from investing activities	*−90.0*
Cash flow from financing activities	
− Dividends paid	−10.0
+ Increase in short-term debt	+94.6
Total cash flow from financing activities	*+84.6*
Total change in cash and equivalents	**$20.0**
Note: All figures are in millions of US dollars.	

8.4.1 Cash Flow from Operating Activities

The cash flow from operating activities (or cash flow from operations) is the cash received from the regular business of a firm (i.e., selling the firm's products), minus the cash paid for expenses (such as materials and labor to produce the products).

To calculate this cash flow, we begin with the company's accounting net income of $23.4 million from its income statement. (GCP's income statement is in Table 8.2.) When calculating net income for the income statement, we subtract depreciation from revenues, which reduces the company's reported earnings and reduces its tax bill. However, depreciation is designed to spread out the cost of a previously purchased physical asset over a period of time; depreciation does *not* involve any actual cash leaving the company in the periods over which the asset is depreciated. In calculating cash flows, then, we need to add depreciation back to net income. GCP's depreciation charges for 2025 were $30 million, which we add to net income.

The second cash flow from operating activities item is an *increase in accounts receivable*. Accounting income is recorded on the balance sheet (Table 8.1) and it represents the amount of product a firm has sold for cash and credit in the current time period. Accounts receivable represent the amounts that customers or other parties are expected to pay the firm in the future. An increase in accounts receivable (i.e., more promises of payment in the future) is included as a part of net income, but because the firm has not actually received cash from these sources, it does not yet represent cash going into the firm. To accurately reflect the cash the firm is receiving, we must reduce net income by subtracting the increase in accounts receivable. The cash flow from accounts receivable is the difference between the revenue recognized during the year (net income) and the actual cash collected from customers. GCP's balance sheet (Table 8.1) shows that its accounts receivable were $60 million in 2025, but $50 million in 2024. This $10 million increase in accounts receivable is subtracted from net income on GCP's cash flow statement.

The third item is an *increase in inventories*, the increase in the value of a firm's inventories—the stock of goods ready to be sold that the firm is holding—at the end of the year. As shown on its balance sheet, GCP's inventories had increased by $30 million between the end of 2024 and the end of 2025. For the value of inventories to increase, GCP would have to spend cash to purchase or produce goods to increase its inventory. Thus, GCP spent $30 million in cash to increase its inventories which was not accounted for when figuring its net income on its income statement. To accurately reflect cash flowing out of the firm, we have to subtract the $30 million increase in inventories from GCP's net income.

The fourth item that makes up cash flow from operations is an *increase in accounts payable*. Accounts payable (found on a firm's balance sheet) represent business expenses that a firm has promised to pay others (such as suppliers and employees) in the future. Net income includes expenses such as a bill to pay a supplier, but these bills are due in the future and are not paid in cash right away. Because these are not yet actual cash outflows, they need to be added back to net income (otherwise the cash paid out would seem higher than it actually is). GCP's balance sheet (Table 8.1) shows that its accounts payable increased from 2024 to 2025 from $60 million to $72 million. Thus, we add the increase in accounts payable of $12 million.

These steps give us a *total cashflow from operations* of $25.4 million.[1] Note that because of the various accounting adjustments that do not reflect the actual movement of cash, the total cash flow from operations differs from the net income reported on the income statement ($23.4 million). This difference underscores that by stripping away accounting adjustments, cash flow statements can be particularly important to understanding the actual picture of a company's financial situation. Because it makes these accounting adjustments, the total cash flow from operations is useful for making comparisons of companies in different countries that report their net income using different accounting standards.

---

[1] Some firms use cash basis accounting, which recognizes revenues and expenses when cash is actually received or paid out. In such cases, the cash flow from operations will be directly given by net income, without the need to add depreciation or add/subtract changes in accounts payable/receivable and inventory.

8.4.2 Cash Flow from Investing Activities

The second portion of the statement of cash flows is cash flows from investing activities, which represent the cash used to make investments in the company, such as buying machinery, equipment, buildings, and so on. For GCP, this consists of just one item, which is $90 million spent on *investment in plant and equipment*. This gives us a total cash flow from investing activities of –$90 million.

8.4.3 Cash Flow from Financing Activities

The third section of the statement of cash flows is cash flows from financing activities, which track the cash that the company either receives from or pays out to its investors. GCP has gotten funding from selling stock and bonds to investors. After selling stock to investors, a company may elect to pay cash to stockholders in the form of dividends. The amount that a company pays in dividends goes into the statement of cash flows as dividends paid. GCP paid its investors $10 million in dividends and subtracts this amount as a cash outflow.

The next line item in the cash flow statement is an *increase in short-term debt*, which indicates the amount of funds a company has borrowed that must be paid back during the year. GCP's balance sheet shows that it took on $94.6 million in short-term debt. This money may have come from GCP issuing and selling new short-term bonds during the year, or from GCP taking out a loan from a bank or some other financial institution. Because GCP actually received this amount in cash during the year, we add $94.6 million to the cash flow from financing activities.

Together, dividends paid and the increase in short-term debt give us a total cash flow from GCP's financing activities of –$10 + $94.6 = $84.6 million.

8.4.4 Total Change in Cash and Equivalents

The final number on the cash flow statement is the total change in cash and equivalents, which sums the cash flows from operating, investing, and financing activities to show how a company's cash flow has changed over the year. ("Equivalents" are items such as US Treasury bills that have a predictable value and are very liquid—that is, easy to sell and thus readily converted into cash.) In 2025, GCP had a net cash inflow of $25.4 – $90.0 + $84.6 = $20 million.

We've now examined all aspects of a firm's three most important financial statements. It's been quite a slog, but rest assured that your understanding of what these numbers mean and what they can tell you are crucial to just about every topic covered in the remaining chapters of the book. Table 8.4 provides a summary of the three main financial statements.

Table 8.4 Summary of financial statements.

	What it is	What it tells us
Balance sheet assets = liabilities + stockholders' equity	• A snapshot of the value of a firm's assets and liabilities at a given point. • Asset values are given at historic cost and depreciated over time.	What a firm's resources are at a particular point in time, and what it owes.
Income statement net income = revenues – expenses	• Records revenues and expenses over a period. • Use of accrual accounting principles implies that net income usually does not equal net cash flow.	How profitable a company's operations were over a period of time.
Statement of cash flows total cash flow = cash from operating activities + cash from financing activities + cash from investing activities	• Shows how much cash has flowed into and out of a firm over a period. • Cash flows are categorized by where the cash is flowing from or flowing to.	How much money flowed into and out of a company over a period of time, and where that money came from or went to.

> **QUICK CHECK 8.3** What difference would it have made to the cash flow statement if GCP had retained all of its net income instead of paying out cash dividends of $10 million?

8.5 Notes to Financial Statements

Many times, the information provided in the three main financial statements does not provide all of the relevant details about a company's financial condition. As a result, companies also include notes to financial statements, which are addendums or footnotes to a given financial statement that provide additional, often important, details.

Unlike the three main financial statements, there is no standard, specific format for notes to financial statements. However, certain information is expected to be provided by companies in the notes. Some of the information included in the notes to financial statements include:

- *An explanation of accounting methods used.* Because firms are allowed some discretion in how they report certain costs (e.g., the method of depreciation or inventory-costing methods), the notes must explain which specific methods the company has used. In addition, when accounting standards change, companies may restate prior year results in the notes using the new standards.
- *Greater detail regarding certain assets or liabilities.* The notes provide details regarding certain assets or liabilities. For example, the debt that appears on the balance sheet may be short term (expiring within a year) or long term (expiring in more than a year). The notes to financial statements often provide the expiration dates of the debt—that is, when the company will need to pay it off. The notes also provide information on special conditions of the debt. For example, when companies borrow money, they often must agree to certain terms imposed by the lender, such as limits on additional borrowing.
- *Information regarding the equity structure of the firm.* The notes provide details about shares of the firm's stock, such as what types of shares there are (some shares may have different voting rights, be entitled to priority dividend payments, etc.).
- *Documentation of changes in operations.* Two activities that can have a great impact on financial statements are acquisitions of assets or other companies, and sales of (divestitures of) assets or companies. The notes explain whether these events occurred and what impact they had on a company's finances.
- *Off-balance-sheet items.* Off-balance-sheet items are common financial contracts entered into by a firm that do not appear on its balance sheet because they are not required to be entered as line items on this financial statement. For example, a firm may enter into derivative contracts such as swaps or options that can profoundly affect its financial condition. Other off-balance-sheet items include contingent liabilities, such as lawsuits or regulatory actions the firm is currently facing. These liabilities can sometimes be very large. For example, in 2016 the car manufacturer Volkswagen agreed to a $14.7 billion settlement after the company was taken to court over allegations that it had falsified emissions results for its cars. Because there are no accounting standards that require such an expenditure to be reported on a balance sheet, such expenditures are often disclosed in the notes to financial statements.

> **QUICK CHECK 8.4** What potentially important information about a firm can be found in the footnotes to its financial statements?

8.6 The Difference between Market Values and Accounting Book Values

The financial statements reviewed above contain useful information about a company's financial position, including a number for the total value of its assets as well as its shareholders' equity. One of our main goals throughout the book will be to arrive at this number and figure out what a firm is worth. Indeed, Function 2 of financial statements is to provide information that can allow us to estimate a firm's economic value. As you will learn in the upcoming chapters, however, determining a firm's economic value is not as straightforward as the financial statements suggest.

8.6.1 Why Market and Book Values Differ

The numbers provided in the financial statements, as useful as they are, are not sufficient to enable financial analysts to determine a company's value for the purpose of investment decisions. The official accounting values in financial statements are called book values. Book values represent economic values calculated based on accounting conventions, which typically describe how the company was in the *past*. In contrast, finance is mainly interested in a firm's market value (sometimes called fair value), which is what the economic value is *now*.

Market and book values can sometimes be very different. This is especially apparent when looking at the difference between the book and market values of a share of stock. The market price of a share is how much it sells for in the stock market, while the book value per share is found from the balance sheet (stockholders' equity divided by the number of shares). Table 8.5 illustrates how the market and book values per share differ for a number of well-known corporations.

Accounting conventions are why book values are not the same as market values. First, the book value provided in accounting statements like the balance sheet does not include all of a firm's assets and liabilities. For example, if a firm builds up a good reputation for the quality and reliability of its products, this will not appear as an asset on the balance sheet. Similarly, if a firm builds up a

Table 8.5 Market and book values for large companies (as of 31 Mar. 2024).

Company	Book value per share	Market value per share
Apple Inc. (AAPL)	$ 4.84	$ 171.48
Microsoft Corporation (MSFT)	$ 34.06	$ 420.72
Alphabet Inc. (GOOG)	$ 23.65	$ 152.26
Best Buy Co., Inc. (BBY)	$ 14.17	$ 82.03
Amazon.com, Inc. (AMZN)	$ 20.83	$ 180.38
Delta Air Lines, Inc. (DAL)	$ 17.39	$ 47.87
The Walt Disney Company (DIS)	$ 54.35	$ 122.36
General Motors Company (GM)	$ 60.54	$ 45.35
Anheuser-Busch Inbev SA/NV (BUD)	$ 41.26	$ 60.78
Sumitomo Pharma Co., Ltd. (4506.T)	¥392.82	¥404.00
Alibaba Group Holding Limited (BABA)	$ 405.38	$ 72.36
Roche Holding AG (ROG.SW)	36.77 CHF	229.70 CHF

Source: Yahoo! Finance

knowledge base as the result of past research and development spending or as the result of training its workforce, these too will not appear as assets. These kinds of assets, called intangible assets, add to a firm's economic value and are relevant when making investment decisions about a company. As we saw earlier, one common type of intangible asset, goodwill, *is* an intangible asset that is recorded on a firm's balance sheet if it acquires another firm for a price that exceeds the target's book value. Although this particular intangible asset is recorded on the firm's accounting balance sheet because accounting convention states that it must be included, many other intangible asset values are not recorded on any accounting financial statements.

The accounting balance sheet also omits some significant liabilities. For example, if the firm has lawsuits pending against it that would involve a payout to consumers or other firms, these possible payouts will not appear as liabilities on the balance sheet. However, a lawsuit or regulatory action against a firm could greatly affect its value. A market value will incorporate these possible damages, but a book value will not. The existence and amount of such liabilities should be disclosed in the footnotes to the financial statements.

A second reason why accounting conventions lead to a difference between book and market values is that most, but not all, firms value the assets and liabilities included on their balance sheets at their *original* acquisition costs, and then depreciate them over time. Many firms, however, do not update their assets and liabilities to their current market values. As an example, suppose a company buys a building for $100,000. A year later, suppose real estate prices increase substantially, so that the market value of the building increases to $150,000. On an accounting basis, the value of the building would remain at $100,000 (or perhaps lower if it is depreciated). However, the increase in value would make the company more valuable in market terms. Such changes in the market values of a company's assets or liabilities can substantially change the view of how financially healthy the company is. Box 8.2 provides an example of this with high-profile bank failures that occurred in 2023.

The distinctions made about market values and book values carry over to our notions of income discussed in Chapter 3. For example, suppose your wages over the year were $50,000, but you have assets in the form of stock that declined in value by $20,000 because the market went down. In general, accountants would ignore this decline of $20,000 in the market value of your assets because it is "unrealized," that is, because you have not sold the stocks. An economist, on the other hand, would say that the decline in value must be counted in the income calculation because it affects your ability to spend money, which is currently $20,000 less than at the beginning of the year. Thus, the "market value" of your income would only be $30,000.

In recent years, there has been a move toward more fair-value, market-value-based accounting. For example, assets held by corporations in their pension funds are now reported at current market values rather than acquisition cost. Revaluing and reporting a firm's assets and liabilities at their current market prices is called marking to market. Some companies report what is called a market value balance sheet, which reports assets and liabilities at estimated market values rather than accounting values.

It should be noted that the choice of different accounting conventions or different types of balance sheets, such as the accounting balance sheet and market value balance sheet, depend on the goal of the user, and it is important to use the "right" tool for the task to be performed (**Principle 4:** *Every model is an incomplete, simplified description of a complex reality*). For some financial analyses, consistency or comparability across different companies may be important, in which case accounting conventions help to provide that consistency.

> QUICK CHECK 8.5 Why does the market price of a firm's stock usually differ from its book value?

> **Box 8.2** World of Business: The Rapid Failure of Silicon Valley Bank
>
> In 2023, two of the largest bank failures in US history occurred: Silicon Valley Bank (SVB) and Signature Bank. The failures occurred very quickly, with many depositors withdrawing their funds from the banks at the same time, a classic example of a bank run.
>
> One of the reasons this occurred was due to market conditions. Since March 2022, the US Federal Reserve had been aggressively raising interest rates to fight rapidly rising inflation. Yields on one-year US government Treasury notes rose from under 0.5% at the beginning of 2022 to 5.25% as of March 2023. As interest rates in the economy go up, cash flows are discounted by the higher rates, and the prices of bonds go down. For example, just a 2 percentage point increase in the yield on a 30-year US Treasury bond can cause its market value to drop by 32%!
>
> Banks, like all other types of companies, have assets and liabilities on their balance sheets. In the case of SVB, a large share of its assets was invested in US government bonds with a long maturity, as well as other types of bonds. The increase in interest rates meant that the market value of these assets went down substantially. However, SVB also had deposit accounts as short-term liabilities; depositors are free to withdraw their money whenever they want, and the bank must honor this liability. As depositors withdrew their funds and SVB's liabilities came due, SVB had a lack of cash reserves to meet its depositors' demands for their funds, forcing it to start selling its assets. To meet its obligations, it sold $21 billion of its asset portfolio at a loss of $1.8 billion due to the drop in the value of the bonds. This shed light on the poor financial state of SVB to its investors and customers, inducing more depositors to pull their money out, and sealing its demise.
>
> The failure of SVB led to concerns about the financial strength of other banks. Shortly after the failure of SVB, Signature Bank also experienced a large number of depositors withdrawing their money, putting it in a similar situation to SVB. This caused the third-largest bank failure in US history.
>
> *Source:* PBS News Hour (2023). Analysis: why Silicon Valley Bank and Signature Bank failed so fast.

8.6.2 Calculating Returns with Market and Book Values

The difference between market and book values extends to how company performance is calculated. When shareholders of a company ask how well their company performed in a particular period (a quarter, a year, or several years), they want to know how much their wealth increased as a result of their investment in the company. Recall from Chapter 5 (Equation 5.2, repeated here as Equation 8.1) that the total rate of return from investing in a stock is

$$r = \frac{\text{ending share price} - \text{beginning share price} + \text{dividends}}{\text{beginning share price}}. \tag{8.1}$$

In other words, the rate of return from a stock comes from any increase in the share price while you hold the stock, plus any cash dividends the company pays you. By dividing by the beginning share price, we get a rate of return. This is also called the total shareholder return; it is based on the stock's market price or value.

However, there are also a number of accounting measures of performance that look similar to this, and also measure "returns" in various ways. One such measure that is commonly used is return on equity (ROE), which is defined as net income (i.e., profit) this year divided by the book value of shareholders' equity from the previous year (some analysts divide by an average of the end-of-year and beginning-of-year equity values). Net income is taken from the income statement, while shareholders' equity is taken from the balance sheet.

$$\text{Return on equity (ROE)} = \frac{\text{net income from current year}}{\text{shareholders' equity from previous year}}. \qquad (8.2)$$

Note that this ratio is similar in spirit to the return calculated in Equation 8.1 because it takes the company's increase/decrease in profit, and examines how much of that increase/decrease is based on the equity that shareholders put into the firm the previous year.

However, even though the two returns are similar in logic, there may be no correspondence at all between them. Let us go through an example using GCP's numbers to illustrate.

Example 8.1 (Calculating Total Shareholder Return and ROE): Suppose GCP's stock price at the end of 2024 was $200.00, and the stock price at the end of 2025 was $187.20. GCP paid shareholders $10 in cash dividends per share over this time. Calculate GCP's total shareholder return and GCP's ROE.

Solution. First, let us look at GCP's total shareholder return. Using the information on GCP's stock provided, we can directly calculate this return using **Equation 8.1**:

$$\begin{aligned} r &= \frac{\text{ending share price} - \text{beginning share price} + \text{dividends}}{\text{beginning share price}} \\ &= \frac{\$187.20 - \$200 + \$10}{\$200} \\ &= -0.014 \text{ or } -1.4\%. \end{aligned}$$

So, GCP provided shareholders a negative total return of −1.4%.

Now let us calculate GCP's ROE. We can use **Equation 8.2** and the information for GCP provided in the balance sheet (**Table 8.1**) and income statement (**Table 8.2**). Specifically, GCP's net income in 2025 was $23.4 million. GCP's shareholders' equity in the previous year, 2024, was $300 million. Putting these values into the ROE equation gives us:

$$\begin{aligned} \text{ROE} &= \frac{\text{net income from current year}}{\text{shareholders' equity from previous year}} \\ &= \frac{\$23.4 \text{ million}}{\$300 \text{ million}} \\ &= 0.078 \text{ or } 7.8\%. \end{aligned}$$

Note that the two numbers are completely different! The actual share price return was negative, while the ROE based on accounting numbers was positive.

This example underscores how there may be no relation between market value returns and accounting returns. While analysts, regulators, and investors may look at accounting returns because they are informative about the operations of the company in the past, finance focuses on market returns and valuations to determine whether something is a worthwhile investment. For example, a young electric car startup could have lost a lot of money last year (a negative ROE) because it is not yet selling cars. Its shareholder return could have been positive, however, because the company generated really good news about future sales in the coming years, and that news was incorporated in the stock price.

With this point in mind, in the next section we discuss how we can use some of the accounting information and measures to estimate market values and returns.

> **QUICK CHECK 8.6** In 2025, X7 VGI corporation reported earnings per share of $5 and paid a cash dividend to shareholders of $3.00 per share. Its beginning-of-year book value per share was $30, and its market price was $40. At the end of the year, the book value per share was $32 and the market price was $35. Compare VGI's total shareholders' returns and ROE.

8.7 Financial Ratio Analysis

The accounting information from a firm's financial statements helps us to construct financial ratios, numbers that conveniently summarize key aspects of a firm's performance and financial condition. These ratios can also be used to compare how the firm is doing relative to other firms.

Financial ratios can help us use the information in financial statements to achieve two of their main functions: Function 1 (providing information about a firm's current and past performance) and Function 2 (providing information that allows us to estimate a firm's intrinsic economic value). In terms of Function 1, financial ratios directly provide us with convenient statistics about a company's performance. In terms of Function 2, financial ratios can be used to provide estimates of what the market values a firm at, as well as what the market believes the future value of the firm might be. The future, of course, is uncertain and thus subject to risk, and we discuss in later chapters how taking risk into account might affect our conclusions about how well or poorly a firm is performing or how we expect it to perform. When analyzing a firm's financial ratios, we need first to establish two things:

- Whose perspective to adopt—shareholders, creditors, or some other group of stakeholders. As we will see in more detail later in the book, some indicators can benefit one group more than another.
- What benchmark to use—that is, are we interested in comparing the company to how it has done in the past, to other companies in the industry, or to broader information about financial markets?

As we will see in many examples throughout the book, changing either the perspective or benchmark can lead to very different conclusions about how we view company performance.

We first introduce some common financial ratios, and what they measure. We then discuss how to use these ratios to get to the market's assessment of a firm's current value and future growth potential. Finally, we talk about the limitations of using financial ratios: As convenient as they may be, the picture they paint is often incomplete.

While many different financial ratios are used in practice, they can broadly be classified into five different categories: profitability, asset turnover, financial leverage, liquidity, and market value. For each of these categories, we will go over a handful of commonly used ratios, and use the numbers from GCP's financial statements to illustrate how to calculate and interpret them. The Excel app for this chapter also provides these calculations, and allows you to change the financial statements for GCP and see how the calculations of the ratios are affected.

8.7.1 Profitability Ratios

Profitability ratios are various measures that indicate how well a firm is performing. These ratios typically examine a company's income or profit compared to some baseline, such as the company's sales or asset value, with higher numbers indicating higher profitability. A profitability ratio for a given company measured right now can be compared to the same ratio measured in the past to see whether a company has improved over time, or it can be compared to other companies.

The first profitability ratio is return on sales (ROS), a firm's profits as measured by EBIT compared to its sales revenue in period t. Both of these numbers are found on a firm's income statement, and the ROS ratio tells us how much each dollar of sales generates in profit (EBIT) for the firms. Put differently, ROS helps analysts to answer the question: How effectively is a company turning its sales revenue into actual profit?

$$\text{Return on sales (ROS)} = \frac{\text{EBIT}_t}{\text{sales}_t}. \tag{8.3}$$

As in previous chapters, the subscript t refers to a number in a particular time period, while subscript $t-1$ refers to the number in the previous period. A ratio equal to 1 means that each dollar of sales is transformed into $1 of profits; a ratio greater than 1 indicates that each dollar of sales is transformed into more than $1 of profits and that a company is more effective at making profits from its sales. For most companies, the ROS ratio is less than 1.

GCP's ROS for 2025 is its EBIT in 2025 ($60 million from the income statement, Table 8.2) divided by its sales in 2025 ($200 million also from the income statement), thus yielding a return on sales of $60 / $200 = 30%. This means that every dollar of sales generated $0.30 in profit.

The second profitability ratio is return on assets (ROA), which compares profits (EBIT, from the income statement) to the accounting value of a company's average total assets (from the firm's balance sheet, Table 8.1). A firm's ROA tells us how much profit each dollar of assets generates:

$$\begin{aligned}\text{Return on assets (ROA)} &= \frac{\text{EBIT}}{\text{average total assets}} \\ &= \frac{\text{EBIT}_t}{\left(\text{total assets}_t + \text{total assets}_{t-1}\right)/2}.\end{aligned} \tag{8.4}$$

A higher number indicates that the firm is more efficient at utilizing its assets to generate profits. Note in the Equation 8.4 that EBIT comes from the income statement, which covers flows over a period of time (a flow variable), while total assets comes from the balance sheet, which is a stock variable, a fixed amount at a point in time. To adjust for this mismatch in timing, whenever a financial ratio contains one item from the income statement and another from the balance sheet, the practice is to take the average of the previous period ($t-1$) and current period (t) balance sheet numbers, and use this average as the denominator.

GCP's EBIT in 2025 is $60 million from the income statement, while average total assets from the balance sheet (using the 2024 and 2025 numbers) is ($700 + $820) / 2 = $760 million, yielding an ROA of 7.9%. That is, every dollar in assets generated $0.079 in profit in 2025.

The third profitability ratio is return on equity (ROE), which compares a firm's income to its shareholders' equity:

$$\begin{aligned}\text{Return on equity (ROE)} &= \frac{\text{net income}}{\text{average shareholders' equity}} \\ &= \frac{\text{net income}_t}{\left(\text{shareholders' equity}_t + \text{shareholders' equity}_{t-1}\right)/2}.\end{aligned} \tag{8.5}$$

When calculating ROE, the convention is to use net income from the income statement rather than EBIT from the balance sheet. As we noted in our earlier discussion of the income statement, net income is calculated by subtracting interest and tax expenses from the base profits as measured by EBIT. The reason we want to use net income is because our base for calculating performance is the shareholders' equity of the firm, and stockholders get paid only after interest and taxes are paid out. We take the average of shareholders' equity because this number comes from the balance sheet. ROE tells us how much profit is generated based on the value that shareholders have.

For GCP, net income is $23.4 million in 2025. Shareholders' equity is $400 million in 2024 and $413.4 million in 2025, yielding an average of ($400 + $413.4) / 2 = $406.7 million. The ROE is therefore $23.4 / $406.7 = 5.8%. That is, each dollar of value in shareholders' equity produced $0.058 in profits (net income) this year.

Note that the three profitability measures are different because they each measure a firm's profit performance related to different benchmarks (i.e., sales, assets, or equity). These benchmarks help to tell us how well a company is generating profits, and thus can provide different views on the question of how profitable a company is. For example, a company with a relatively higher return on sales can indicate that each sale the company makes produces a good amount of profit (e.g., because sales costs are low), but if that company also has a relatively low ROA, that may suggest that it has a lot of assets that are not being deployed productively to produce profits.

8.7.2 Turnover Ratios

The set of ratios known as asset turnover ratios captures a firm's ability to use its assets productively to create revenue.

The first of these ratios is the inventory turnover ratio, which examines how fast a company is able to sell its inventory, which in turn gives an indication of how efficiently a company is using its inventory and turning it into sales. The inventory turnover ratio examines cost of goods sold (COGS) (from the income statement) divided by average inventory (from the balance sheet):[2]

$$\text{Inventory turnover} = \frac{\text{cost of goods sold (COGS)}}{\text{average inventory}} \\ = \frac{\text{COGS}_t}{(\text{inventory}_t + \text{inventory}_{t-1})/2}. \tag{8.6}$$

A higher inventory turnover ratio is generally viewed as good for a company because it indicates that the company is effectively turning its inventory into sales. In contrast, a lower number may indicate that the inventory is just sitting in a warehouse and not being sold, and therefore not generating revenue to pay for the costs of acquiring or producing the goods to be sold. These interpretations depend on the exact measure of inventory turnover and the units, however. In Equation 8.5 the unit of measure would be "times," meaning that inventory turned over a certain number of times during the year. In this case, a higher number indicates more efficiency, and is better. Alternatively, inventory turnover can be calculated in "days," meaning the amount of time it takes the inventory to turn over during a period; a lower number in this case indicates more efficiency, and is better. Note that we divide by average inventory because merchandise sales can fluctuate significantly from year to year.

GCP's cost of goods sold (COGS) in 2025 was $110 million from the income statement, and its average inventory was ($180 + $150) / 2 = $165 based on balance sheet inventory of $180 million in 2025 and $150 million in 2024. Its inventory turnover is therefore $110 / $165 = 0.7, and we would say that its inventory "turned over" 0.7 times over the year. Put differently, this means that for each dollar's worth of inventory GCP held, it sold $0.70 of it.

---

[2] An alternative way to calculate this ratio is to take sales revenue from the income statement and divide by average inventory.

The second turnover ratio is the asset turnover ratio, which examines how effectively a company uses its existing assets to make sales. The asset turnover ratio takes sales (from the income statement) and divides by the average total assets (from the balance sheet):

$$\begin{aligned} \text{Asset turnover} &= \frac{\text{sales}}{\text{average total assets}} \\ &= \frac{\text{sales}_t}{\left(\text{total assets}_t + \text{total assets}_{t-1}\right)/2}. \end{aligned} \qquad (8.7)$$

A higher turnover ratio indicates that a company is more efficiently using its assets to sell goods; put differently, it shows that a company was able to generate more sales for each dollar of assets it held. Whether an asset turnover ratio is high or low for a given company depends on both the company's asset turnover ratio in the past (a drop in this number may indicate reduced efficiency) and other factors such as the industry the company is in (an online retail company may naturally sell far more products compared to a biotechnology company primarily working on research and development).

According to its income statement, GCP's sales in 2025 were $200 million, while its average total assets from the balance sheet (using the 2024 and 2025 numbers) were ($700 + $820) / 2 = $760 million. GCP's asset turnover ratio is therefore $200 / $760 = 0.3. This turnover ratio indicates that GCP's assets turned over into sales 0.3 times over the year, and that each dollar of GCP's assets was able to generate $0.30 in sales.

8.7.3 Financial Leverage Ratios

Financial leverage ratios highlight how much a firm has borrowed through debt, and how much of a burden that debt is to the firm. This information is a key factor in understanding a firm's financial health: A firm is legally obligated to pay back its debt over time, and failure to do so (defaulting on its debt) will cause the firm to go bankrupt. The two most commonly examined financial leverage ratios are the debt ratio and the times interest earned ratio.

The debt ratio, often called the leverage ratio, relates a company's debt to its assets at a given time.

$$\text{Debt ratio} = \frac{\text{debt}_t}{\text{total assets}_t}. \qquad (8.8)$$

Because both debt and total assets are stock values (values as of a specific point in time) that come from the balance sheet, there is no need to take an average of total assets as we did with previous ratios. Debt in this case is total debt: the sum of long-term debt and short-term debt. (Note that we do not include other liabilities in this ratio; we are only concerned with loans that the company has taken out.)

A higher debt ratio means the firm has greater leverage—that is, it has a bigger obligation to pay back the people or firms that lent it money. Put differently, it means that what a firm owes in debt is relatively high compared to what it owns in assets that can be used to pay back the debt. A debt ratio of less than 1 means that the firm must pay back less in debt in the future than it currently owns in assets; a debt ratio equal to 1 means that the firm owes so much debt in the future that the current accounting value of all of its assets is just enough to cover the amount owed. It is possible for the debt ratio to be above 1, which implies that the firm owes *more* in the future than it currently holds in assets.

In 2025, GCP's total debt was $334.6 million ($184.6 million of short-term debt plus $150 million of long-term debt). Its total assets in 2025 were $820 million, giving us a debt ratio of $334.6 / $820 = 41%. This ratio means that in accounting ("book") terms, 41% of GCP's assets was funded by debt (and 59%

was funded by equity); it also means that for every dollar of assets that GCP owns, it owes $0.41 debt in the future.

There are two important things to note about debt ratios. First, while a higher ratio can potentially indicate that a firm is in trouble—that is, it would have to use/sell a substantial portion of the assets it owns to pay off its debt and thus put it in a tenuous position—a higher ratio is not *necessarily* bad for the firm. As we will see when we cover capital structure in Part II, having more debt can have its benefits. Second, this debt ratio is in accounting (book) values, which are based on past information about the firm. This perspective can be informative, but in finance we want to get a more accurate picture of the current (and future) state of the firm, so we are generally more interested in seeing debt ratios in *market value* terms, which can sometimes be very different! For example, suppose GCP's stock price at the end of 2025 was $187.20. GCP has one million shares outstanding, which means that the total market value of its equity (combined value of all of its stock) is $187.20 × 1 million = $187.20 million. The market value of GCP's total assets would be the sum of this market equity value ($187.20) and its debt ($334.6 million), which is $334.6 + $187.20 = $521.8 million. The market debt ratio would be total debt over this number, or $334.6 / $521.8 = 64%, which is higher than GCP's debt ratio in accounting terms of 41%. This indicates that GCP's debt may be more burdensome than suggested by the book debt ratio because the market is valuing GCP's equity (and thus its assets) lower than the values in the balance sheet. (Part II delves into the topic of how firms may choose their debt ratios and what this implies for the value of the firm.)

The second of the financial ratios is the times interest earned ratio, which estimates how easily a company can make the interest payments on its debt (interest expense) given how much it earns (EBIT). Both of these numbers come from a firm's income statement.

$$\text{Times interest earned} = \frac{\text{EBIT}_t}{\text{interest expense}_t}. \tag{8.9}$$

A higher times interest earned is generally considered to indicate stronger financial health for a company, because it means that the company has relatively more income than it needs to pay interest on its debt (which it must do, or go bankrupt). A ratio of greater than 1 indicates that the profits a company has earned from its operations were more than sufficient to meet the interest obligations on its debt over the past period. A ratio of less than 1 indicates that the profits a company has earned was not enough to pay what it owed in interest payments, and thus the company would have needed to use money from other sources (such as its cash reserves).

In 2025, GCP's EBIT was $60 million and its interest expense was $21 million, so its times interest earned is $60 / $21 = 2.9. This means that GCP earned 2.9 times as much as it owed in interest payments, which in turn means that it generated more than enough profit in 2025 to pay back the interest it owed.

8.7.4 Liquidity Ratios

Liquidity ratios measure the ability of a firm to meet its short-term obligations, such as paying its bills and revealing the resources the firm has available to meet its current liabilities.

The first liquidity ratio, the current ratio, tells us how much of its current, near-term liabilities a company could pay using the short-term assets it has access to, money due from customers in the near term, or money raised by selling off its inventory. The current ratio can be an important indication of a company's immediate financial health. and it is defined as current assets divided by current liabilities (both of which are on a company's balance sheet):

$$\text{Current ratio} = \frac{\text{current assets}_t}{\text{current liabilities}_t}. \tag{8.10}$$

A ratio of greater than 1 indicates that a company has more than enough assets to meet its obligations in the near future, which can be an indication of strong current financial health. In contrast, a ratio of less than 1 indicates that the short-term assets a company has access to are not enough to pay off what it owes in the near future, which might indicate that the company needs to tap into additional financing sources (e.g., by selling off inventory to raise money) immediately to survive.

GCP's 2025 current assets are $360 million, and its current liabilities are $256.6 million. Its current ratio is therefore $360 / $256.6 = 1.4, meaning that it has 1.4 times its liabilities in current assets and thus has sufficient resources to cover what it owes in the near future.

The second liquidity ratio is the quick ratio, sometimes referred to as the acid test, which tells us how much of a firm's current, near-term liabilities it could pay using only its most liquid short-term assets. The quick ratio is similar to the current ratio, but is more stringent because it considers only a firm's most liquid current assets—cash, marketable securities (securities such as Treasury bonds that can be easily sold for cash), and accounts receivable (amounts that others have pledged to pay the firm in the short run). The quick ratio does not include inventory (as does the current ratio) because it may be difficult for a firm to quickly sell off its inventory in a pinch. The quick ratio gives us a sense of how much money a company has access to in case it needs to quickly pay off its liabilities. The cash, marketable securities, and accounts receivable numbers and the current liabilities appear on a firm's balance sheet.

The quick ratio is:

$$\text{Quick ratio} = \frac{\text{cash and marketable securities}_t + \text{accounts receivable}_t}{\text{current liabilities}_t}. \tag{8.11}$$

The interpretation of the quick ratio is the same as that of the current ratio. A higher quick ratio indicates a company can more easily meet its upcoming obligations and is thus in stronger financial health. A ratio greater than 1 indicates that a company has more than enough liquid assets to meet its near-term obligations. A ratio of less than 1 indicates that the company holds insufficient assets that can be turned very quickly into cash in order to meet its upcoming obligations.

For GCP, cash and marketable securities in 2025 was $120 million, accounts receivable was $60 million, and current liabilities was $256.6 million. GCP's quick ratio was therefore ($120 + $60) / $256.6 = 0.7. It therefore has 0.7 times its current liabilities in items it could quickly turn into cash. Note that this paints a different picture compared to the current ratio. While the current ratio was above 1, the quick ratio is below 1; thus, while GCP has enough short-term assets to cover its upcoming liabilities, it may not be feasible to quickly turn all those short-term assets into cash to make its payments. This suggests that GCP may want to raise additional money or have another contingency plan to meet its short-term obligations and survive.

8.7.5 Market Value Ratios

The final set of financial ratios is the market value ratios. These ratios compare a firm's accounting values to its market values and help us understand the market's view of the company's future growth prospects. As we will see in the next section, we can use market value ratios to arrive at an estimate of what we think a firm's market value is or should be.

The first commonly used market value ratio is the price to earnings (P/E) ratio. This ratio takes the stock price per share (from the market) and divides it by the accounting earnings per share (typically estimated as net income from the income statement divided by the number of shares outstanding from the balance sheet):

$$\text{Price to earnings } (P/E) \text{ ratio} = \frac{\text{price per share}_t}{\text{earnings per share}_t}. \tag{8.12}$$

The P/E ratio tells us a company's stock price relative to its profits per share. The specific value of a P/E ratio is difficult to interpret in isolation, but offers valuable insights when compared to a company's past P/E ratios or a different company's P/E ratio. A higher P/E ratio indicates that, per share of stock, the market assesses the company's stock value relatively higher compared to the earnings it currently generates. As we discuss in more detail when we examine stock valuation in Part II, the market valuation of a company's stock incorporates market participants' assessment of the stock's future prospects. This means that a higher P/E ratio can be interpreted as the market assessing that a stock's *future* (measured by the price) is relatively promising compared to its *current* profits (EBIT).

For GCP, we supposed that its stock price at the end of 2025 was $187.20 per share. GCP's net income was $23.4 million and there are one million shares outstanding, so earnings per share were $23.40. Thus, the P/E ratio for GCP is $187.20 / $23.4 = 8.0, meaning that GCP's stock price is eight times what it currently earns per share. If this number is higher than GCP's past P/E ratios, then this can indicate that the market is now more positive about GCP's growth prospects. Similarly, this number can be used to compare GCP to other companies to gain insights into how the market views GCP's growth prospects compared to others.

There are, however, challenges in using the P/E ratio. While a relatively higher P/E ratio can be interpreted as positive future growth opportunities, a common rule of thumb is that if a company's P/E ratio is "too high" (e.g., if its stock price is more than 50 times what it earns, then the market price is valuing the stock too highly, and the price is likely to drop in the future). Put differently, a P/E ratio that is too high indicates that a company's stock price cannot be justified based on its current earnings. Similarly, some companies (such as startup companies that are growing) may have *negative* earnings, making the interpretation of the ratio very difficult. As we discussed earlier, it is important to note that there is no absolute standard with which to judge whether ratios are too high or too low, and sometimes a very high ratio can be justified because the company has very good growth prospects.

The second commonly used market value ratio is the market to book (M/B) ratio. This is calculated by taking the stock price per share from the market and dividing it by the accounting book value of equity per share derived from the balance sheet:

$$\text{Market to book (M/B) ratio} = \frac{\text{price per share}_t}{\text{book value of equity per share}_t}. \quad (8.13)$$

The market to book ratio helps us understand how the market's assessment of a stock's value differs from the accounting value of the stock; put differently, it compares the stock's market value to the benchmark value provided by the balance sheet. A ratio equal to 1 means that the market's value of a company's stock matches that of the accounting statements. A ratio greater than 1 indicates that the market views a stock's current value as being *higher* than its accounting book value, while a ratio that is less than 1 indicates that the market views the stock's value as being *lower* than its accounting book value.

Analysts and investors use the M/B ratio in a variety of ways. For example, an M/B ratio of less than 1 (often called "undervalued") can potentially mean that the market should value a company higher given the baseline value from its accounting statements. Such an undervalued stock might be a good investment. Along similar lines, an M/B ratio of greater than 1 (often called "overvalued") may indicate that the market's valuation of a company is higher than justified by the accounting statements, and thus one may want to sell the stock. However, M/B ratios must be interpreted with caution. As we discussed in Section 8.6, market values may differ from accounting values for a variety of reasons, such as accounting conventions and the fact that book values are often historical (backward-looking) numbers. This opens up the M/B ratio to other interpretations.

For instance, in a similar way to the P/E ratio, the M/B ratio can also be interpreted as a relative measure of future growth prospects, with a higher value suggesting that market participants view the future (measured by the market value) as bright compared to the historical value, and thus the company may be a good investment.

For GCP, the price per share in the stock market is $187.20. The book value of equity is shareholders' equity from the balance sheet, which was $413.4 million. Because there are one million shares, the book value of equity per share is $413.4. The market to book ratio is therefore $187.20 / $413.4 = 0.5.

The final common market valuation ratio is the enterprise value to EBITDA (EV/EBITDA) ratio. Enterprise value (also called total value) is the market value of a company's total assets (combined debt and equity). The enterprise value incorporates market participants' assessment of the future prospects of the company as a whole.

EBITDA (earnings before interest, taxes, depreciation, and amortization) is found on the income statement:

$$\text{Enterprise value to EBITDA (EV/EBITDA) ratio} = \frac{\text{enterprise value}_t}{\text{EBITDA}_t}. \tag{8.14}$$

The EV/EBITDA ratio tells us how much value the market places on a company's assets relative to its current profits. It is similar to the P/E ratio, except instead of focusing on just the equity (stock) value of a company as does the P/E ratio, it examines the value of the entire company (the total assets). Just as with the P/E ratio, a higher EV/EBITDA ratio indicates that the company's total market value is high relative to its current earnings. Like the P/E ratio, the EV/EBITDA ratio is difficult to interpret in isolation, but it can provide valuable insights when compared to a company's past ratios or a competitor's current ratio. Analysts and investors can use the EV/EBITDA ratio as an indication of the market's assessment of the future of the company relative to how it is now. A higher EV/EBITDA ratio can be interpreted as the market assessing that a company's future is relatively promising compared to the cash generated by its current activities.

We calculate GCP's EV/EBITDA ratio as follows: To determine enterprise value, recall that this is not the same as the book value of GCP's assets found on the balance sheet; we are interested in the *market* value of its assets. We can calculate this market value by adding together the market value of GCP stock (equity) and the value of its debt. The total value of GCP's stock, given a stock price of $187.20 in 2025 and one million shares outstanding, is $187.20 million.

The value of GCP's total debt is $334.6 million. Note that here we are taking the *book* value of the debt from the balance sheet, since we are not given information about the market value of this debt. This is often done in practice, because the book value of debt is often similar to the market value. Furthermore, it can be difficult to get proper information about debt market values; in Chapter 14 we present valuation models that can be used to estimate debt market values. In contrast, as we learned earlier, the market value of equity is often far different from the book value of equity.

Adding together the values of GCP's equity and debt, we find that GCP's enterprise value is $187.20 million + $334.6 million = $521.8 million.

We calculate GCP's EBITDA from its income statement by adding its $30 million depreciation back to its EBIT of $60 million. GCP's EBITDA is $90 million. Putting these numbers together, GCP's EV/EBITDA = $521.8 / $90 = 5.8, meaning that GCP has an enterprise value that is 5.8 times its current earnings.

Table 8.6 shows the various financial ratios reviewed above, and the calculations we did, and Table 8.7 provides the specific calculations for GCP.

Table 8.6 Summary of financial ratios.

Ratio	Formula	Source	What it means
Profitability			
Return on sales (ROS)	$\dfrac{\text{EBIT}}{\text{sales}}$	Income statement	How well a company turns sales into profits: the amount of profit generated for each $1 of sales
Return on assets (ROA)	$\dfrac{\text{EBIT}}{\text{average total assets}}$	Income statement and balance sheet	How much money the firm's assets generated: the amount of profit generated for each $1 in assets the company has
Return on equity (ROE)	$\dfrac{\text{net income}}{\text{average shareholder's equity}}$	Income statement and balance sheet	How much profit is made from the value that shareholders have: the amount of profit generated for each $1 in shareholder's equity
Asset turnover			
Inventory turnover ratio	$\dfrac{\text{cost of goods sold}}{\text{average inventory}}$	Income statement and balance sheet	How efficiently a company is utilizing its inventory and turning the inventory into sales: the amount sold for each $1 in inventory
Asset turnover ratio	$\dfrac{\text{sales}}{\text{average total assets}}$	Income statement and balance sheet	How effectively a company uses its existing assets to make sales: the amount sold for each $1 in assets the company has
Financial leverage			
Debt ratio	$\dfrac{\text{total debt}}{\text{total assets}}$	Balance sheet	The amount of debt compared to the assets held: how much is owed in the future for each $1 in assets the company has
Times interest earned	$\dfrac{\text{EBIT}}{\text{interest expense}}$	Income statement	How easily a company is able to make interest payments on its debt given how much it earns: the amount of profit a firm had in order to pay each $1 in interest it owed

Table 8.6 (cont.)

Ratio	Formula	Source	What it means
Liquidity			
Current ratio	$\dfrac{\text{current assets}}{\text{current liabilities}}$	Balance sheet	The amount of current assets a company has that it could use to meet its current liabilities: the amount of short-term assets a company owns that could be used to pay off $1 in short-term obligations
Quick ratio	$\dfrac{\text{cash and marketable securities} + \text{receivables}}{\text{current liabilities}}$	Balance sheet	The amount of easily sellable current assets a company has that it could use to meet its current liabilities: the amount of "liquid" short-term assets a company owns that could be used to pay off $1 in short-term obligations
Market value			
Price to earnings (P/E) ratio	$\dfrac{\text{price per share}}{\text{earnings per share}}$	Market prices and income statement	A company's stock price relative to its profits per share
Market to book (M/B) ratio	$\dfrac{\text{price per share}}{\text{book value per share}}$	Market prices and balance sheet	How the market's assessment of a stock's value differs from the accounting value of the stock
Enterprise value to EBITDA (EV/EBITDA) ratio	$\dfrac{\text{enterprise value}}{\text{EBITDA}}$	Market prices, balance sheet, and income statement	How much value the market places on a company's assets relative to its current profits

Table 8.7 Financial ratios for GCP.

Ratio	Formula	Calculation
Profitability		
Return on sales (ROS)	$\dfrac{\text{EBIT}}{\text{sales}}$	$\dfrac{\$60}{\$200} = 30\%$
Return on assets (ROA)	$\dfrac{\text{EBIT}}{\text{average total assets}}$	$\dfrac{\$60}{(\$700 + \$820)/2} = 7.9\%$
Return on equity (ROE)	$\dfrac{\text{net income}}{\text{average shareholder's equity}}$	$\dfrac{\$23.4}{(\$400 + \$413.4)/2} = 5.8\%$

(Continued)

Table 8.7 (cont.)

Ratio	Formula	Calculation
Asset turnover		
Inventory turnover ratio	$\dfrac{\text{cost of goods sold}}{\text{average inventory}}$	$\dfrac{\$110}{(\$180+\$150)/2} = 0.7$ times
Asset turnover ratio	$\dfrac{\text{sales}}{\text{average total assets}}$	$\dfrac{\$200}{(\$700+\$820)/2} = 0.3$ times
Financial leverage		
Debt ratio	$\dfrac{\text{total debt}}{\text{total assets}}$	$\dfrac{\$334.6}{\$820} = 41\%$
Times interest earned	$\dfrac{\text{EBIT}}{\text{interest expense}}$	$\dfrac{\$60}{\$21} = 2.9$ times
Liquidity		
Current ratio	$\dfrac{\text{current assets}}{\text{current liabilities}}$	$\dfrac{\$360}{\$256.6} = 1.4$ times
Quick ratio	$\dfrac{\text{cash and marketable securities + receivables}}{\text{current liabilities}}$	$\dfrac{\$180}{\$256.6} = 0.7$ times
Market value		
Price to earnings (P/E) ratio	$\dfrac{\text{price per share}}{\text{earnings per share}}$	$\dfrac{\$187.20}{\$23.4} = 8.0$
Market to book (M/B) ratio	$\dfrac{\text{price per share}}{\text{book value per share}}$	$\dfrac{\$187.20}{\$413.4} = 0.5$
Enterprise value to EBITDA (EV/EBITDA) ratio	$\dfrac{\text{enterprise value}}{\text{EBITDA}}$	$\dfrac{\$521.8}{\$90} = 5.8$

> **QUICK CHECK 8.7** What are the five types of financial ratios used to analyze a company's performance?

8.8 Using the Financial Ratios: Information about Performance

As we discussed above, financial ratios can directly provide us with convenient statistics about a company's performance. However, as we also noted with many of the ratios, the interpretation of a specific number may not be entirely clear and can depend on the benchmark used. For example, a "low" return on sales (ROS) or asset turnover ratio (ATO) may or may not be a sign of a troubled firm. Each of these ratios must be interpreted relative to some industry or firm norms and benchmarks. For example, a Rolls Royce dealership will almost certainly have a higher ROS and lower turnover than a Chevrolet dealership.

8 FINANCIAL STATEMENTS: ANALYZING AND FORECASTING

Table 8.8 **Hypothetical financial ratios for growth industries.** This table provides financial ratios for the past three years (with t being the current year) for a hypothetical company called Growth Industries. The ratios provided are ROE, ROA, ROS, debt ratio, and asset turnover.

	Return on equity, ROE	Return on assets, ROA	Return on sales, ROS	Debt ratio	Asset turnover, ATO
$t-1$	25%	5%	10%	80%	0.3
$t-2$	13%	5%	10%	70%	0.3
$t-3$	10%	5%	10%	60%	0.3

To illustrate these points further, consider an example of a hypothetical company called Growth Industries. Growth Industries has been rapidly growing in terms of ROE over the last three years. However, it has been earning a lower (and flat) ROS. Table 8.8 shows various ratios for Growth Industries.

For simplicity, let us assume that net income = EBIT for Growth Industries each year. Note that, at first glance, Growth Industries appears to have grown tremendously over the past three years, with a return on equity (ROE) that has gotten larger each year. However, the return on assets (ROA), return on sales (ROS), and asset turnover (ATO) have stayed flat over time. The company therefore appears to be growing according to one metric, but stagnant according to other metrics. What is going on here?

The answer can be seen through what is known as *ratio decomposition*, which allows us to see the relationships between the different ratios. First note that we can express ROA as the following:

$$\begin{aligned} \text{ROA} &= \frac{\text{EBIT}}{\text{average total assets}} \\ &= \frac{\text{EBIT}}{\text{sales}} \times \frac{\text{sales}}{\text{average total assets}} \\ &= \text{ROS} \times \text{ATO}. \end{aligned} \quad (8.15)$$

This shows us that the ROA of Growth Industries depends on both the ROS and the ATO ratio. Because both ROS and ATO are not growing, ROA also is not growing.

We can do the same analysis for ROE using what is known as the *Du Pont Identity*, which decomposes ROE and allows us to relate it to other ratios (such as ROA and the debt ratio) in order to analyze the possible reasons for a change to ROE:

$$\begin{aligned} \text{ROE} &= \frac{\text{net income}}{\text{average shareholder's equity}} \\ &= \frac{\text{net income}}{\text{EBIT}} \times \frac{\text{EBIT}}{\text{sales}} \times \frac{\text{sales}}{\text{average total assets}} \times \frac{\text{average total assets}}{\text{average shareholder's equity}} \\ &= \frac{\text{net income}}{\text{EBIT}} \times \text{ROA} \times \left(\frac{1}{1 - \text{average debt ratio}}\right). \end{aligned} \quad (8.16)$$

In Equation 8.16, note that the total assets of a company equal its debt plus shareholders' equity, and therefore 1 − debt ratio = equity / total assets. Also recall that we assumed that net income for Growth Industries equals its EBIT, and therefore, net income / EBIT = 1 in the above. We can then see from Equation 8.16 that a company's ROE depends on its ROA and on the amount of debt it has.

In other words, for Growth Industries, the ROE is increasing each year solely because it is taking on more debt. The reason for this is that an increased proportion of debt makes the amount of equity relatively smaller, which implies that any dollar of earnings generates a higher return (because of a smaller equity base).

Put differently, the "growth" that we see in Growth Industries based on its ROE is not because the company is actually expanding and growing, but rather because it is increasing its debt ratio. This illustrates how examining ratios in isolation may give a distorted picture of a company's performance, and how the perspective (i.e., whether examining the return of the company's overall assets or the company's equity) matters.

8.9 Using the Financial Ratios: Market Valuation

Financial ratios, especially the ones related to market value, can be used to directly estimate the current economic (market) value of a company. Market values incorporate the market's assessment of the firm's current economic value, which takes into account what the market thinks the firm is likely to do in the future. Because financial ratios directly relate the market's valuation of a company to the accounting information reported by the company, they allow us to use the accounting information provided by the company to estimate its market valuation and to see what the market thinks about the firm's future.

We first examine how to use financial ratios for valuation, and then explore the information they provide about a firm's growth prospects. The valuation techniques we introduce here are a crucial first step in the toolkit that we will use for estimating the value of a company; we discuss other valuation techniques in much more detail in future chapters.

8.9.1 Valuation Using Comparables

The method of using financial ratios to arrive at an estimate for the market value of a company is called valuation using comparables. There are two steps to this valuation method.

1. Find one or more comparable firms—that is, firms similar to the one being valued in terms of type of industry, size, products produced/sold, risk, customer market, and so on.
2. Use the financial ratios of the comparables and the accounting information of the firm we want to value, and combine them to get an estimate of the market value of the firm we are trying to value.

Suppose we are trying to estimate the stock price of a sofa manufacturing company. You first find a comparable, which could be another very similar sofa manufacturer, or an average of a number of such manufacturers. You find that a comparable company has a price to earnings ratio of 12—that is, it has a stock price that is 12 times its earnings per share. If we believe that the other firms are truly similar to the sofa firm we are trying to value, then the sofa firm should *also* have a stock price that is 12 times its earnings per share. If we know that our firm has earnings per share of $1.50, then this implies that its stock price should be $1.50 × 12 = $18.

More generally, if we want to figure out the stock price of a firm using the price to earnings ratio, we use the following formula:

$$\text{Stock price} = EPS \times \left(\frac{P}{E}\right)_{comparable}, \qquad (8.17)$$

where EPS is the earnings per share of the company we are trying to figure out the stock price of, and $(P/E)_{comparable}$ is the comparable's price to earnings ratio. Another way of loosely viewing how this formula works is that if we assume that our firm and the comparable are very similar, the EPS and the earnings per share E of the competitor in Equation 8.17 are essentially canceling each other out, leaving the stock price P that we want. This valuation model allows us to estimate the price of a stock, but does not require complex calculations.

Often we can compare our estimate of the stock price to the actual stock price in the stock market. If our estimate is higher than the actual stock price, this may indicate that the stock is undervalued by the market and thus a good investment. In contrast, if our estimate is lower than the actual stock price, this may indicate that the stock is overvalued by the market and it may be best to avoid the stock (or sell it). However, it is important to remember two finance principles when making such assessments. First, as we discuss in more detail below, valuation by comparables is a valuation model and may provide inaccurate estimates if its assumptions are not met, in line with **Principle 4:** *Every model is an incomplete, simplified description of a complex reality.* Second, market value estimates can sometimes be incorrect, but are usually the best estimate of an asset's value, in line with **Principle 5:** *The best estimate of an asset's value is usually its market price.*

Suppose we instead want to figure out a firm's enterprise value (the market value of a firm's assets). To do so, we can use the EV/EBITDA ratio (Equation 8.14), and proceed in the same way, using the following formula:

$$\text{Enterprise value} = \text{EBITDA} \times \left(\frac{\text{EV}}{\text{EBITDA}}\right)_{comparable}, \qquad (8.18)$$

where EBITDA is the earnings before interest, taxes, depreciation, and amortization of the company whose enterprise value we are trying to determine, and $(\text{EV}/\text{EBITDA})_{comparable}$ is the enterprise value to EBITDA ratio of the comparables.

Because we are using a financial ratio and multiplying accounting earnings by it to get an estimate of value, the ratio is sometimes called a multiple, and this method is often referred to as valuation by multiples.

To illustrate valuation by multiples, consider a real-world example: Microsoft Corporation and Apple Inc. both produce consumer electronics and software, and are close competitors. Suppose we try to arrive at an estimate of Apple's enterprise value, using Microsoft as its comparable. Apple's EBITDA as of March 2023 was $125.29 billion. Microsoft's EV/EBITDA ratio at the same time was 20.75. Therefore, our estimate of Apple's enterprise value using Microsoft as a comparable would be $125.29 billion × 20.75 = $2.60 trillion. It turns out that this estimate matches Apple's actual enterprise value as provided by the market: $2.60 trillion.

As discussed earlier, however, valuation by comparables can also have limitations. To illustrate, consider another real-world example: The Coca-Cola Company and PepsiCo Inc. make competing soft drinks, and most people would consider them close competitors. Suppose we try to arrive at an estimate of Coca-Cola's enterprise value, using PepsiCo as its comparable. Coca-Cola's EBITDA as of March 2023 was $13.51 billion. PepsiCo's EV/EBITDA ratio at the same time was 18.82. Therefore, our estimate of Coca-Cola's enterprise value using PepsiCo as a comparable would be $13.51 billion × 18.82 = $254.26 billion. Coca-Cola's actual enterprise value, however, was $290.99 billion—we are thus off by about $36.73 billion! One reason why these numbers are off is that Coca-Cola and PepsiCo are not actually as similar as we thought. In contrast to Coca-Cola, for example, PepsiCo has many snack food divisions that make up a significant portion of its revenue.

This example underscores that selecting proper comparables is critical to correctly using this valuation methodology. Valuation by multiples will give the most accurate answer when the comparables are very similar to the company we are looking at. If they are not, then our answer may be very inaccurate. As the example with Coca-Cola and PepsiCo illustrates, the comparison firms may in fact be different in important ways that at first glance may not be obvious.

In practice, valuation using multiples typically gives a reasonable first pass at valuation that is easy to calculate, and gives us a place to start when examining a company.

Example 8.2 estimates the share price and enterprise value of GCP using these methods.

Example 8.2 (Valuation Using Comparables): We are interested in valuing GCP using comparables, and choose two firms of similar size that are also in manufacturing. These firms have the following financial ratios:

Comparable:	P/E ratio	EV/EBITDA ratio
Consumer Products Inc.	8.5	6.5
Manufacturing Products Inc.	7.0	5.0

Using the appropriate numbers from GCP's financial statements, estimate what GCP's stock price and enterprise value should be.

Solution. To calculate GCP's stock price, we will look at the P/E ratios of GCP's comparables. Note that we could choose just one comparable, but it is common practice to take an average of their P/E ratios. The average P/E ratio for the two is 7.75. From its income statement and based on one million shares outstanding from the balance sheet, we know GCP has earnings per share (EPS) of $23.40. Using Equation 8.17, GCP's estimated stock price is:

$$\begin{aligned}\text{Stock price} &= EPS \times \left(\frac{P}{E}\right)_{comparable} \\ &= \$23.4 \times 7.75 \\ &= \$181.35.\end{aligned}$$

To calculate GCP's enterprise value, we use the comparables' EV/EBITDA ratios, the average of which is 5.75. From GCP's income statement, we know that its EBITDA is $90 million, and so its estimated enterprise value is (Equation 8.18):

$$\begin{aligned}\text{Enterprise value} &= EBITDA \times \left(\frac{EV}{EBITDA}\right)_{comparable} \\ &= \$90 \text{ million} \times 5.75 \\ &= \$517.50 \text{ million}.\end{aligned}$$

You may note that we already had GCP's actual stock price ($187.20), and enterprise value ($521.8 million) based on the stock price and amount of debt on the balance sheet. Many times this will not be the case, and we will go through these calculations to arrive at these numbers. Other times, we may go through these calculations to understand whether the market's assessment of a company's value is correct or not.

Using the comparables method, we estimated GCP's stock price as $181.35 (vs. its actual price of $187.50), while its enterprise value estimate was $517.50 million (vs. its actual enterprise value of $521.8 million). These estimates are very close, likely reflecting that the comparables used were good choices.

8.9.2 Using Ratios to Assess Firm Growth Prospects

In addition to helping us estimate how the market values a company in the present, financial ratios can also tell us the market's view of a company's future growth potential.

Both the price to earnings (P/E) and enterprise value to EBITDA (EV/EBITDA) ratios look at the market's assessment of either stock price or overall firm value (in the numerator), compared to the firm's current earnings or firm value (in the denominator). As we will emphasize throughout the book, market values distill the market's assessment of the current economic value of the firm, considering what the firm is likely to do in the future. A higher value of either of these ratios therefore means that the market views the value of the firm to be relatively high compared to its current accounting earnings.

Similarly, the market to book ratio (M/B) takes the current price per share and compares it to the book value per share (derived from the balance sheet). A higher ratio indicates that the market's valuation of the company is higher than the accounting valuation of the company, and this can be viewed as a sign of the company's potential growth opportunities. Consider GCP's market to book ratio, which we calculated as $187.20 / $413.4 = 0.5 earlier. The fact that the market values GCP's stock as substantially lower than its book value (i.e., the market to book ratio is much lower than 1) indicates that the market views GCP as having poor future growth opportunities.

Versions of these ratios (P/E, EV/EBITDA, and M/B) have been created to assess the overall stock market. One example is the Shiller P/E ratio or CAPE ratio (cyclically adjusted price earnings ratio), created by Nobel Prize-winning financial economist Robert Shiller, which calculates a price to earnings ratio for the S&P 500 market index using average earnings over the past ten years (adjusted for inflation).

> QUICK CHECK 8.8 Suppose you see two companies in the same industry with the same EBITDA. If Company A has a higher EV/EBITDA ratio than Company B, what does that tell you about the growth prospects of the two companies? Which company would you expect to have a higher enterprise value?

8.10 Limitations of Financial Ratios

Financial ratios can provide useful information to us about a company's current state and future prospects. A financial ratio is a convenient shortcut or *heuristic* that summarizes various details about a company in a single number that we can interpret and use in making finance and investment decisions. It is important, however, to be aware of the limitations of financial ratios; the most important to keep in mind are:

Financial ratios rely on accounting conventions: All of the ratios we discussed rely on accounting numbers, which are often calculated in arbitrary ways. For example, accounting earnings are adjusted for things such as depreciation, which may help to lower tax bills, but provide a distorted view of the company's actual earnings. Furthermore, accounting numbers are based on past information, which may not accurately reflect the current state of the company.

Comparable companies are difficult to define: As we have seen, one use of financial ratios is to determine the value of a company based on the value of comparable companies. However, it is often difficult to identify a set of comparable firms because firms can differ in important ways that are not always easy to see.

There is no set standard for judging financial ratios: Sometimes we look to see if ratios are "too low" or "too high," but there is no absolute standard to allow us to judge if this is the case. For example, a very high market value ratio might indicate that a company's market valuation is unrealistic compared to its current accounting earnings. If a firm is going to grow tremendously in the future, however, the high ratio is warranted. Other times, financial ratios can be high or low because of factors other than what is explicitly included in the numerator or denominator of the ratio. For example, a high return on equity (ROE) may indicate that the company is producing a lot of profit for each dollar of value that the shareholders have, but it may also indicate that a company has a high amount of debt. As we saw with the Du Pont Identity (Equation 8.16), ROE can be written as a function of debt ratio, since a higher amount of debt will crowd out shareholders' equity.

Financial ratios do not give us a complete picture about risk: The future of any firm is uncertain; it is exposed to risk, and things may not end up as we expect them to. While the ratios provide us with convenient snapshots of a company's performance or value, they do not tell us about how that value may or may not change in the future, and what sorts of events might affect it in the future.

Although financial ratios are useful, as a rough guide to a company's health and prospects, they should not be relied upon exclusively when making financial decisions. In making such decisions, it is essential to use other methods that give a more nuanced and detailed understanding of a company's current and future values. In later chapters, we learn about other valuation methods, and learn how to evaluate how the risks a company faces affect its value.

8.11 Future Financial Planning and Projections

Much of our discussion of financial statements thus far has focused on Function 1 (information to a firm's stakeholders about the company's current status and past financial performance). Beyond examining a company's current and past performance, financial statements can also be used to plan for a company's *future* development. Thus, financial statements fulfill Function 3—providing a convenient way to plan for the future—through their use in financial planning. As we will see in Part II, future financial projections will also be an important step for other methods of estimating a firm's economic value (Function 2).

Financial planning is the continual process of making plans for a company's profitability and growth, implementing them, and revising them as actual results are known. The starting point of a firm's financial plan is the strategic plan which guides the financial planning process by establishing overall business development guidelines and growth targets. These growth targets, and the specifics about what planning might be possible given the current state of the company, are guided by the information provided in the firm's financial statements.

When making a financial plan for a company, a manager needs to specify the plan's horizon—that is, how far out in the future the plan covers. In general, the longer the horizon, the less detailed the financial plan. This is because we do not know what the future will be, and we will be less certain about the far-off future. Many companies choose to create a five-year financial plan. Longer-horizon financial plans will typically consist of what are called pro forma financial statements, a set of forecasted income statements and balance sheets that show only general categories with few details. Multiyear plans are usually revised every year, and annual plans are often revised every quarter. Firms also have monthly plans, which feature detailed forecasts of revenues and expenses for specific product lines and detailed projections of cash inflows and outflows.

The financial planning cycle can be broken down into several steps:

1. *Determine future external demand and market conditions.* Managers forecast the key external factors that determine the demand for the firm's products and the costs of production. These factors include details about the markets in which the firm operates, economic activity in broader markets (e.g., exchange rates, interest rates, the overall market), and what competitors are doing.

2. *Develop a production and investment plan.* Based on these external factors, managers must plan how much product to produce, how much it will cost to produce that quantity, and how much to spend on investment in equipment, research, and marketing.
3. *Forecast the firm's revenues and expenses.* With the information on demand, markets, production, and investment in hand, managers then forecast the firm's revenues, expenses, and cash flows over the financial planning horizon.
4. *Estimate the need for financing.* To implement its plan, the firm may need to obtain additional funds through external financing. Managers must therefore include obtaining such financing in their plan, and account for any difficulties involved in doing so.
5. *Establish performance targets.* Based on the plan, senior managers establish specific performance targets for themselves and their subordinates.
6. *Measure actual performance.* Actual performance is then measured at regular intervals (either monthly or quarterly), and is regularly compared to the targets set in the plan. If the actual numbers for the company deviate from the targets, corrective actions are taken as needed, and management may adjust the targets.

At the end of each year, rewards (e.g., bonuses or raises) are distributed and the planning cycle starts again. It is important throughout the planning cycle for managers to check that the firm's likely future financial results are consistent with their strategic plan for creating value for shareholders, and that financing is available to implement the plan. If there are any inconsistencies, then managers revise their decisions until they come up with a workable plan, which becomes a blueprint for the firm's operating decisions during the year.

An important thing to keep in mind is that the financial planning process involves *estimates* of the future, and these estimates involve the *risk* that the future may end up being substantially different from managers' predictions. It is always good practice to make contingency plans in case some of the forecasts turn out to be wrong. For example, if sales for a company end up being much lower than expected, the company may have to borrow money to cover its expenses. By borrowing money, the company then has to pay more in interest payments in the future. These increased interest payments may make it harder for the company to spend money according to its original plan, but if the company does not pay the interest payments, it will go bankrupt. In its financial planning process, a company should attempt to anticipate and develop a plan for various contingencies.

In the next section we provide an example of financial planning through constructing future financial statements.

8.11.1 Constructing Pro Forma Financial Statements

To illustrate what a financial plan looks like and how it can be created, let's construct hypothetical *pro forma*, or future projected, financial statements for GCP. To construct these pro forma statements, we use the accounting information in GCP's past financial statements, and assume that this is the only information we have available. Table 8.9 provides balance sheet and income statement information from the past three years (2023–2025). Our goal is to construct GCP's financial statements for one year in the future, 2026.

To estimate GCP's 2026 accounting values, we proceed in three steps:

1. Determine which items on the balance sheet and income we can estimate based on projected sales data.
2. Estimate what we think sales are likely to be next year.
3. Calculate estimated numbers for the remaining items by looking at patterns in the data.

8.11 FUTURE FINANCIAL PLANNING AND PROJECTIONS

Table 8.9 Financial statements for GCP for 2023–2025. Pro forma financial statements are based on accounting information from a few years of a firm's past financial statements. All figures are in millions of US dollars.

Income statement	2023	2024	2025
Sales revenue	$138.9	$167.7	$200.0
Cost of goods sold	(55.6)	(66.7)	(80.0)
Sales, general, and administrative expenses	(20.8)	(25.2)	(30.0)
Depreciation expense	(30.0)	(30.0)	(30.0)
Earnings before interest and taxes (EBIT)	*32.5*	*45.8*	*60.0*
Interest expense	(15.0)	(17.0)	(21.0)
Income taxes	(7.0)	(11.5)	(15.6)
Net Income	*10.5*	*17.3*	*23.4*

Balance sheet	2022	2023	2024	2025
Assets				
Cash and marketable securities	69.5	83.3	100.0	120.0
Accounts receivable	34.7	41.7	50.0	60.0
Inventories	104.2	125.0	150.0	180.0
Property, plant, and equipment (PP&E)	264.4	325.2	400.0	490.0
Intangible assets	100.0	100.0	100.0	100.0
Liabilities				
Accounts payable	41.7	50.0	60.0	72.0
Short-term debt	21.4	43.9	90.0	184.6
Long-term debt	150.0	150.0	150.0	150.0

The first step involves using the percent-of-sales method, a method that identifies which items in the financial statement tend to be a certain ratio of sales. For example, a company's COGS (expenses for selling goods) is usually close to a fixed percentage of its sales revenue. If we know these two numbers and have a sense of what sales might be in the future, then we will have an estimate for these items in the future.

As a first step in the percent-of-sales method, we examine the past financial data to determine *which* items on the income statement and balance sheet have maintained a fixed ratio to sales (i.e., they are the same proportion of sales each year). This enables us to decide which items can be forecast strictly on the basis of our projected sales, and which items require another method.

One way to determine each item's ratio to sales is to rewrite the income statement and balance sheet, and represent all numbers as percentages of the sales number in that year; that is, divide all of the numbers by sales in that year. Table 8.10 provides these calculations. The items in blue show a constant ratio to sales.

As we can see in Table 8.10, the following items are always a fixed percentage of yearly sales: cost of goods sold; SG&A expenses; cash and marketable securities; accounts receivable; inventories; and accounts payable. Thus, for these items, once we've projected what sales will be in 2026, we will have their estimated values by multiplying estimated sales in 2026 by the percentages in the table.

Table 8.10 GCP financial statements as a percentage of yearly sales for 2023–2025. This table shows financial statement categories as a percentage of yearly sales. The ratio to sales is constant for the items in blue. All figures are in millions of US dollars.

Income Statement	2023	2024	2025
Sales revenue	100%	100%	100%
Cost of goods sold	40%	40%	40%
Sales, general, and administrative expenses	15%	15%	15%
Depreciation expense	22%	18%	15%
Earnings before interest and taxes (EBIT)	23%	27%	30%
Interest expense	11%	10%	11%
Income taxes	5%	7%	8%
Net Income	8%	10%	12%

Balance sheet	2023	2024	2025
Assets			
Cash and marketable securities	60%	60%	60%
Accounts receivable	30%	30%	30%
Inventories	90%	90%	90%
Property, plant, and equipment (PP&E)	234%	239%	245%
Intangible assets	72%	60%	50%
Liabilities			
Accounts payable	36%	36%	36%
Short-term debt	32%	54%	92%
Long-term debt	108%	89%	75%

The next step is to estimate what we believe sales in 2026 are likely to be. We can estimate sales for 2026 by looking for patterns in the sales data that we have for the three years prior. One such pattern is that sales increased by roughly 20% every year between 2023 and 2025. Given this pattern, we can assume that sales will also increase by 20% between 2025 and 2026, and thus will rise from $200 million in 2025 to $240 million in 2026.

With this estimated sales number of $240 million, we will get the estimated numbers for the items in blue in Table 8.10 by multiplying by the respective percentages. For example, COGS has been 40% of sales, so our estimated COGS for 2026 is 40% × $240 million = $96 million.

The final step is to estimate the remaining items that are not in blue in Table 8.10: depreciation expense, interest expense, income taxes, PP&E, intangible assets, and short-term and long-term debt. One simple way to do so is to proceed as we did for sales in step (b), and check to see if there are any patterns in the ways these items have been increasing. Table 8.11 shows by what percent these items grew compared to the previous year for 2024 and 2025.

In Table 8.11, the following items have a constant percentage increase over time: depreciation, PP&E, intangible assets, short-term debt, and long-term debt. Thus, for the 2026 numbers, we will assume that we can use the same percentage increases. For example, intangible assets for 2026 would be the same as for 2025 (since we assume a 0% increase), or $100 million, while estimated 2026 PP&E would be the 2025 numbers increased by 23%, or $490 million × 1.23 = $602.7 million.

8.11 FUTURE FINANCIAL PLANNING AND PROJECTIONS

Table 8.11 **Growth of remaining GCP financial items compared to previous year.** This table shows the percentage increase in other items from GCP's financial statements compared to the previous year. Items with a constant percentage increase are in orange.

Income statement	2024	2025
Depreciation expense	−20%	−20%
Earnings before interest and taxes (EBIT)	41%	31%
Interest expense	13%	24%
Income taxes	64%	36%
Net income	65%	35%

Balance sheet	2024	2025
Assets		
Property, plant, and equipment (PP&E)	23%	23%
Intangible assets	0%	0%
Liabilities and stockholders' equity		
Short-term debt	105%	105%
Long-term debt	0%	0%

There are just a few items that remain to be filled in on GCP's pro forma financial statements.

EBIT and net income are both calculated as sums of other numbers we've estimated. EBIT is sales revenue minus cost of goods sold (COGS), sales, general, and administrative expenses (SG&A), and depreciation, and net income is EBIT minus interest expense and taxes.

Interest expense can be estimated in most cases by taking the interest rate for each type of debt, and multiplying it by the previous year's amount of debt. There are two types of debt: short-term and long-term. In this case, let us assume that the interest rate on both is 8% (the interest rates on debt is information that is often provided by the firm). The interest expense for 2026 would be the amount of total debt in 2025 ($184.6 million + $150 million = $334.6 million) multiplied by the interest rate of 8%, so $334.6 million × 8% = $26.8 million.

Finally, for income taxes, we should have an idea of the company's tax rate. Here, GCP's tax rate is 40%. If we apply this tax rate to GCP's 2025 taxable income of $39 million (its EBIT of $60 million minus interest expense of $21 million), we arrive at an estimate for GCP's income taxes of $15.6 million.

Table 8.12 presents the calculated pro forma numbers for all of the items on GCP's income statement and balance sheet, showing the previous years' numbers for comparison. To calculate total assets, we subtract accumulated depreciation from the other items on the balance sheet, which was $100 million in 2024 and $130 million in 2025, and therefore projected to be $160 million in 2026.

The Excel app included with this chapter allows you to construct pro forma statements for GCP based on different assumptions. In particular, the app allows you to reconstruct Tables 8.10–8.12 assuming different percent-of-sales and growth numbers for the balance sheet and income statement, thus providing different forecasts for the 2026 numbers.

Note from these figures that we are estimating an increase in net income from $23.4 million in 2025 to $30.7 million in 2026, due to increased sales. This increase in net income comes at a cost, and we see that expenses also go up from $110 million ($80 million COGS and $30 million SG&A) to

Table 8.12 Actual and pro forma financial statements for GCP for 2023–2026. Using the numbers from Tables 8.9–8.11, we have developed a pro forma statement for 2026 (in the blue column). We show the previous years' numbers for comparison. All figures are in millions of US dollars.

Income statement	2023	2024	2025	Estimated 2026
Sales revenue	$138.9	$167.7	$200.0	$240.0
Cost of goods sold	(55.6)	(66.7)	(80.0)	(96.0)
Sales, general, and administrative expenses	(20.8)	(25.2)	(30.0)	(36.0)
Depreciation expense	(30.0)	(30.0)	(30.0)	(30.0)
Earnings before interest and taxes (EBIT)	*32.5*	*45.8*	*60.0*	*92.6*
Interest expense	(15.0)	(17.0)	(21.0)	(26.8)
Income taxes (40% rate)	(7.0)	(11.5)	(15.6)	(17.0)
Net income	*10.5*	*17.3*	*23.4*	*30.7*

Balance sheet	2022	2023	2024	2025	Estimated 2026
Assets					
Cash and marketable securities	69.5	83.3	100.0	120.0	144.0
Accounts receivable	34.7	41.7	50.0	60.0	72.0
Inventories	104.2	125.0	150.0	180.0	216.0
Property, plant, and equipment (PP&E)	264.4	325.2	400.0	490.0	602.7
Intangible assets	100.0	100.0	100.0	100.0	100.0
Less accumulated depreciation	40.0	70.0	100.0	130.0	160.0
Total assets	*532.8*	*605.2*	*700*	*820*	*974.7*
Liabilities and stockholders' equity					
Accounts payable	41.7	50.0	60.0	72.0	86.4
Short-term debt	21.4	43.9	90.0	184.6	193.8
Long-term debt	150.0	150.0	150.0	150.0	150.0
Total liabilities	*213.1*	*243.9*	*300*	*406.6*	*430.2*
Stockholder's equity	*319.7*	*361.3*	*400*	*413.4*	*544.5*

$132 million ($96 million COGS and $36 million SG&A). These increased expenses need to be paid for somehow. In the example above, we assume that GCP pays for this increase by borrowing more: Their short-term debt increases from $184.6 million to $193.8 million. However, a company may plan to finance such an increase in other ways, as we discuss in the next section.

8.11.2 Working Capital and Liquidity Management

In most businesses, cash must be paid out to cover expenses before any cash is collected from the sale of the firm's products. As a result, a typical firm's investment in assets such as inventories and accounts receivable exceeds its liabilities such as accrued expenses and accounts payable. The difference between current assets and current liabilities is called working capital. If a firm's need for working capital is permanent rather than seasonal, it usually seeks long-term financing for it by issuing more stock or bonds (or a combination). Seasonal financing needs are usually met through short-term financing arrangements, such as a loan from a bank.

Given the importance of working capital to meeting a company's short-term funding needs, companies must pay attention to how these needs might change in the future. That is, the company must engage in working capital management. The main principle behind the efficient management of a firm's working capital is to minimize the amount of the firm's investment in nonearning assets (such as receivables and inventories) and maximize the use of "cheap" credit such as prepayments by customers, accrued wages, and accounts payable. These three sources of funds are cheap to the firm in the sense that they usually bear no explicit interest charge.[3]

Policies and procedures that shorten the lag between the time that the firm sells a product and the time that it collects cash from its customers reduce the need for working capital. (Ideally, the firm would like its customers to pay in advance.) The firm can also reduce its need for working capital by extending the time between when it purchases its inputs and when it pays for them.

Figure 8.1 shows the relation between these time lags and a firm's investment in working capital and illustrates a firm's working capital and cash flow cycle.

The cash cycle time is the number of days between the date the firm must start to pay cash to its suppliers and the date it begins to receive cash from its customers. The cash cycle time is the difference between the sum of the inventory and receivables periods on the one hand, and the payables period on the other:

$$\text{Cash cycle time} = \text{inventory period} + \text{receivables period} - \text{payables period}. \quad (8.19)$$

The firm's required investment in working capital is directly related to the length of its cash cycle time. If the payables period (the amount of time between when a company receives an invoice from suppliers and it actually pays suppliers) is long enough to cover the sum of the inventory and receivables periods (the time between when a good first arrives in inventory and the firm gets cash for selling it), then the firm does not need any working capital at all.

A firm can take a variety of actions to reduce its need for working capital:

- *Reduce the amount of time that goods are held in inventory.* This can be accomplished by improving the inventory control process or by having suppliers deliver raw materials exactly when they are needed in the production process, rather than having them sit a long time in inventory.

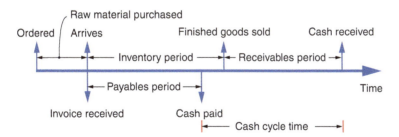

FIGURE 8.1 **The working capital and cash flow cycle.** This figure depicts the typical steps and time between when a product is ordered by consumers and when the cash is received for the product by the firm. A product is ordered (on the left), it goes into inventory and becomes a payable for the company until cash is paid by the company, and the finished product is then sold to the customer and becomes a receivable until cash is received from the customer.

---

[3] If, however, the firm gives price discounts on its products to customers who pay in advance, then the size of this discount represents an implicit interest charge. Similarly, if the firm forgoes a discount from its suppliers by delaying payment to them, this forgone discount represents an implicit interest charge. It is important to note that this should not be interpreted as these sources of funds being without risk. For example, if something unexpected happens and the firm is unable to pay back these funds, then this would negatively affect its value.

- *Collect accounts receivable more quickly.* Among the methods available to speed up how fast money is collected from customers are improving the efficiency of the collection process, offering discounts to customers who pay faster or in advance, and charging interest on accounts that are overdue.
- *Pay its own bills more slowly.* When possible, if a company can pay its bills more slowly, it will reduce the payables period.

Another important consideration related to working capital management is liquidity. Liquidity refers to how able a company is to make immediate payments, either for a purchase or to pay off debt. Illiquidity is a situation in which a company does not have the means to make an immediate payment. Note that a firm may have enough *assets* to make a payment, but if those assets cannot be converted quickly and easily into cash, then the firm still has an illiquidity problem. Assets such as cash and marketable securities (such as US Treasury bonds) would be considered liquid, while assets such as vast tracts of land or specialized factories that may be hard to sell would be considered illiquid.

> QUICK CHECK 8.9 How can a firm reduce its need for working capital?

Firms should always forecast their cash outflows and inflows carefully so that they will not be affected by the difficulties caused by illiquidity. A plan that shows these forecasts is called a cash budget.

Conclusion

In this chapter we learned about financial statements, reports produced by companies that summarize their current and past financial condition. Financial statements allow analysts and investors to understand the assets that a company owns, the revenues that those assets produce, and the various expenses that the firm has to pay. As we explored, this information is valuable in understanding the company's health and its economic value. This information can also aid a company in planning for its future.

Later chapters will show how the information produced in financial statements is a key ingredient in models used to estimate a company's economic value. In particular, financial statements can be used to estimate the future cash flows that a company may produce, which can then be used in financial models to estimate what the company's market value should be. Investors can use these crucial estimates to decide whether or not to invest in a company, and managers running companies can use them to determine whether a particular financial decision can improve or harm their company's value.

Takeaways

- Financial statements are standardized reports that serve three important functions:
  Function 1: They provide information to a firm's stakeholders about the company's current status and past financial performance.
  Function 2: They provide information that allows us to estimate a firm's intrinsic economic value.
  Function 3: They provide a convenient way for a firm's owners and managers to plan for its future.
- The three most common financial statements are
  - the *balance sheet*, which shows a firm's assets and the claims against them at a particular point in time;
  - the *income statement*, which reports the results of a firm's operations over a period of time (such as a year), and shows its revenues and costs over that period; and
  - the *statement of cash flows,* which summarizes a firm's cash flows from different types of activities over a period of time.

- Additional relevant financial information is provided in the *notes to financial statements*. The information provided by the three basic financial statements and the notes to them allow financial statements to serve Function 1 by providing information about the company's current status and past financial performance.
- Financial ratios are numbers that are derived from the numbers reported on financial statements and from other information. They are convenient heuristics that can tell us a company's strengths and weaknesses and what its prospects are. They can also provide estimates of the company's current enterprise value.
- A firm's financial ratios are often compared with those of a comparable set of companies and to the ratios of the firm's recent past periods. There are five types of ratios: *profitability, turnover, financial leverage, liquidity,* and *market value* ratios. Financial ratios serve financial statement Functions 1 and 2 (provide information about the firm's current status and past financial performance, and provide information that allows us to estimate a firm's intrinsic value).
- Although financial statements and the financial ratios derived from them provide useful information about the state of a company in convenient terms, they have important limitations. For example, balance sheets do not include all economically important assets and liabilities, and they report assets and liabilities at their book values, rather than their current market values. Financial ratios also rely on accounting conventions and various assumptions that affect their accuracy.
- Financial statements and ratios omit one crucial characteristic: They do not give us a complete picture of a company's risk—how its value and condition may change in the future. Different accounting conventions and types of financial statements may provide information such as market values or risk metrics. However, the choice between these different financial statements and metrics depends on the goal of the user and the task to be performed. For example, as we will go over in detail in Part II, certain models that aim to estimate the value of a company may use information from the balance sheet (such as the amount of debt) and income statement (such as EBIT).
- Financial statements can be used to construct pro forma (projected future) financial statements that a firm can use to plan its future over various time horizons. The tangible outcome of the financial planning process is a set of blueprints in the form of projected financial statements and budgets. The longer the time horizon, the less detailed the financial plan will be.
- In the short run, financial planning is concerned primarily with the management of working capital. The need for working capital arises because many firms have a need for cash to conduct production and sales activities before cash flows in. The longer this time lag (which is called the length of the cash flow cycle), the more working capital a firm needs. Working capital management is important to a firm's financial health because even a profitable firm can get into financial distress or even go bankrupt if it does not have the cash to meet its financial obligations.

Key Terms

Acid test 230
Asset turnover ratio (ATO) 227
Assets 211
Balance sheet 211
Book values 221
CAPE ratio 240
Cash budget 248
Cash cycle time 247
Cash flow from operating activities 219
Cash flows from financing activities 219
Cash flows from investing activities 219
Comparable firms 237
Cost of goods sold (COGS) 215
Current assets 213
Current liabilities 213
Current ratio 229
Debt ratio 228
Depreciation expense 215
Dividends paid 219
Du Pont Identity 236

Earnings before interest and taxes (EBIT)   215
Enterprise value to EBITDA (EV/EBITDA) ratio   232
Fair value   221
Financial leverage ratios   228
Financial planning   241
Financial ratios   225
Financial statements   210
Fixed assets   213
Generally Accepted Accounting Principles (GAAP)   211
Goodwill   213
Gross margin   215
Illiquidity   248
Income statement   214
Intangible assets   222
Interest expense   215
Inventory turnover ratio   227
Leverage ratio   228
Liabilities   211
Liquidity   248
Liquidity ratios   229
Long-term assets   213
Market to book (M/B) ratio   231
Market value   221
Market value balance sheet   222
Market value ratios   230
Marking to market   222
Multiple   238
Net income   216
Net working capital   213
Net worth   211

Noncurrent assets   213
Noncurrent liabilities   213
Notes to financial statements   220
Operating income   215
Paid-in capital   214
Percent-of-sales method   243
Price to earnings (P/E) ratio   230
Pro forma   241
Profitability ratios   225
Quick ratio   230
Ratio decomposition   236
Retained earnings   214
Return on assets (ROA)   226
Return on equity (ROE)   226
Return on sales (ROS)   235
Sales revenue   214
Sales, general, and administrative (SG&A) expenses   215
Shareholders' equity   211
Shiller P/E ratio   240
Statement of cash flows   217
Statement of earnings   214
Statement of profit and loss (P&L)   214
Taxable income   215
Times interest earned ratio   229
Total change in cash and equivalents   219
Total shareholder return   223
Valuation by multiples   238
Valuation using comparables   237
Working capital   246
Working capital management   247

Key Equations

Rate of return from investing in a stock	$r = \dfrac{\text{ending share price} - \text{beginning share price} + \text{dividends}}{\text{beginning share price}}$	Eq. 8.1
Return on equity, ROE	$ROE = \dfrac{\text{net income from current year}}{\text{shareholders' equity from previous year}}$	Eq. 8.2
Return on sales, ROS	$ROS = \dfrac{EBIT_t}{Sales_t}$	Eq. 8.3

KEY EQUATIONS

Return on assets, ROA	$\text{ROA} = \dfrac{\text{EBIT}}{\text{average total assets}}$ $= \dfrac{\text{EBIT}_t}{\left(\text{total assets}_t + \text{total assets}_{t-1}\right)/2}$	Eq. 8.4
Return on equity, ROE	$\text{ROE} = \dfrac{\text{net income}}{\text{average shareholders' equity}}$ $= \dfrac{\text{net income}_t}{\left(\text{shareholders' equity}_t + \text{shareholders' equity}_{t-1}\right)/2}$	Eq. 8.5
Inventory turnover	$\text{Inventory turnover} = \dfrac{\text{cost of goods sold (COGS)}}{\text{average inventory}}$ $= \dfrac{\text{COGS}_t}{\left(\text{inventory}_t + \text{inventory}_{t-1}\right)/2}$	Eq. 8.6
Asset turnover	$\text{Asset turnover} = \dfrac{\text{sales}}{\text{average total assets}}$ $= \dfrac{\text{sales}_t}{\left(\text{total assets}_t + \text{total assets}_{t-1}\right)/2}$	Eq. 8.7
Debt ratio	$\text{Debt ratio} = \dfrac{\text{debt}_t}{\text{total assets}_t}$	Eq. 8.8
Times interest earned	$\text{Times interest earned} = \dfrac{\text{EBIT}_t}{\text{interest expense}_t}$	Eq. 8.9
Current ratio	$\text{Current ratio} = \dfrac{\text{current assets}_t}{\text{current liabilities}_t}$	Eq. 8.10
Quick ratio	$\text{Quick ratio} = \dfrac{\text{cash and marketable securities}_t + \text{accounts receivable}_t}{\text{current liabilities}_t}$	Eq. 8.11
Price to earnings ratio	$\text{Price to earnings (P/E) ratio} = \dfrac{\text{price per share}_t}{\text{earnings per share}_t}$	Eq. 8.12
Market to book (M/B) ratio	$\text{Market to book ratio} = \dfrac{\text{price per share}_t}{\text{book value of equity per share}_t}$	Eq. 8.13
EV/EBITDA ratio	$\text{Enterprise value to EBITDA ratio} = \dfrac{\text{enterprise value}_t}{\text{EBITDA}_t}$	Eq. 8.14

ROA ratio decomposition	$$\text{ROA} = \frac{\text{EBIT}}{\text{average total assets}}$$ $$= \frac{\text{EBIT}}{\text{sales}} \times \frac{\text{sales}}{\text{average total assets}}$$ $$= \text{ROS} \times \text{ATO}$$	Eq. 8.15
Du Pont Identity	$$\text{ROE} = \frac{\text{net income}}{\text{average shareholder's equity}}$$ $$= \frac{\text{net income}}{\text{EBIT}} \times \frac{\text{EBIT}}{\text{sales}} \times \frac{\text{sales}}{\text{average total assets}} \times \frac{\text{average total assets}}{\text{average shareholder's equity}}$$ $$= \frac{\text{net income}}{\text{EBIT}} \times \text{ROA} \times \left(\frac{1}{1 - \text{average debt ratio}}\right)$$	Eq. 8.16
Stock price valuation using comparables	$$\text{Stock price} = \text{EPS} \times \left(\frac{P}{E}\right)_{comparable}$$	Eq. 8.17
Enterprise value valuation using comparables	$$\text{Enterprise value} = \text{EBITDA} \times \left(\frac{\text{EV}}{\text{EBITDA}}\right)_{comparable}$$	Eq. 8.18
Cash cycle time	Cash cycle time = inventory period + receivables period − payables period	Eq. 8.19

Problems

1. Suggest if and how the following assets and liabilities would be recorded on their owners' balance sheets:
   (a) a lottery ticket
   (b) a successful song
   (c) an unsuccessful movie
   (d) a warehouse
   (e) a customer that owes money for a past order
   (f) a loan taken out to expand a company's office space.
2. Show how the following events and transactions should appear on your personal income statement, balance sheet, and cash flow statement.
   (a) On 1 July 2025, you receive $20,000 in gifts upon graduation from school and pay off a $10,000 student loan.
   (b) On 1 Aug. 2025, you get a job as a finance intern at General Financial Services Inc. You are promised a salary of $4,000 per month, payable on the last day of each month.
   (c) On 31 Aug. 2025, you receive your first statement of GFS salary and benefits showing the following items:

Gross salary	$4,000
Income tax withholding	1,400
Social Security and Medicare tax	500
Healthcare premium	150
Contribution to pension plan	200
Employer Social Security tax	300
Employer contribution to pension plan	200
Employer contribution to healthcare	150
Amount credited to employee checking account at GFS Bank	1,750
Total employer benefit	650

(d) On 1 Sept. 2025, you purchase a new car for $20,000. You make a down payment of $5,000 and borrow the remaining $15,000 from GFS bank at a monthly interest rate of 1%. Your monthly payment is $498.21 for 36 months.

3. As an individual or a household, why might you want to maintain a balance sheet? How often would you update it? Should you mark-to-market or leave your assets and liabilities at their historical values?

4. The Ruffy Stuffed Toy Company's balance sheet at the end of 2022 is given in Table 8.13.

Table 8.13 Balance sheet for Ruffy Stuffed Toy Company, end of year 2022.

Assets		Liabilities and shareholders' equity	
Cash	$27,300	Payables	
Accounts receivable	35,000	Accounts payable	$65,000
Inventory	57,000	Salary payable	3,000
Total current assets	119,300	Utilities payable	1,500
Property, plant, and equipment		Loans (long-term debt)	25,000
Equipment	25,000	Total liabilities	94,500
Less accumulated depreciation	(2,500)	Common stock	45,000
Net equipment	22,500	Retained earnings	16,300
Furniture	16,000	Total shareholders' equity	61,300
Less accumulated depreciation	(2,000)	**Total liabilities and equity**	**155,800**
Net furniture	14,000		
Total prop, plant, and equipment	36,500		
Total assets	**155,800**		

During 2023, the Ruffy Stuffed Toy Company recorded the following transactions:

- Early in the year, purchased a new toy stuffing machine for $21,000. It paid $9,000 in cash and signed a three-year note for the balance of $12,000.
- Had cash sales of $115,000 and sales on credit of $316,000.
- Purchased raw materials from suppliers for $207,000.
- Made payments of $225,000 to its raw materials suppliers.
- Paid rent expenses totaling $43,000.
- Paid insurance expenses totaling $23,000.

- Paid utility bills totaling $7,500; $1,500 of this amount reversed the existing payable from 2022.
- Paid wages and salaries totaling $79,000; $3,000 of this amount reversed the payable from 2022.
- Paid other miscellaneous operating expenses totaling $4,000.
- Collected $270,000 from its customers who had made purchases on credit.
- The interest rate on the loan payable is 10% per year. Interest was paid on 31 Dec. 2023.

Other information:
- The existing equipment has been estimated to have a useful life of 20 years, with no salvage value. Two years have been depreciated through 2022.
- The existing furniture has been estimated to have a useful life of eight years (no salvage value), of which one year has been depreciated through 2022.
- The new stuffing machine has been estimated to have a useful life of seven years, and will have no salvage value.
- The corporate income tax rate is 35% and taxes are paid on 31 Dec. 2023.
- Dividend payout, if possible, will be 10% of net income.
- Cost of goods sold for the year's sales were $250,000.
- Accounts receivable ending balance = beginning balance − cash received from credit customers + sales on credit.
- Accounts payable ending balance = beginning balance + purchases − cash payments to suppliers.
- Inventory ending balance = beginning balance + purchases of raw material − cost of goods sold.
- The company's stock price at market close on 31 Dec. 2023 was $4.625. It has 20,000 shares outstanding.

(a) Construct the income statement for operations during the year 2023.
(b) Construct the balance sheet for the Ruffy Stuffed Toy Company as of 31 Dec. 2023.
(c) Construct a cash flow statement for the year 2023.
(d) Calculate the following profitability ratios: return on sales, return on assets, return on equity.
(e) Calculate the following asset turnover ratios: receivables turnover, inventory turnover, asset turnover.
(f) Calculate the following financial leverage and liquidity ratios: debt, times interest earned, current ratio, and quick (acid) test.
(g) What is Ruffy's book value per share at the end of 2023?
(h) (Excel app) Using the Excel App, calculate the financial ratios from Table 8.14 for Ruffy.
(i) Calculate the firm's price to earnings ratio and the ratio of its market share price to its book value per share.

5. You have the information shown in Table 8.14, taken from the 2001 financial statements of Computronix Corporation and Digitek Corporation. Compare and contrast the financial performance of the two companies using the following financial ratios: ROS, ROA, ROE, market to book, and price to earnings.

Table 8.14 Financial information on Computronix and Digitek Corporations. All figures are in millions of US dollars, except for the second and final three rows.

	Computronix	Digitek
Net income	$153.7	$239.0
Dividend payout ratio	40%	20%
EBIT	$317.6	$403.1
Interest expense	54.7	4.8
Average assets	2,457.9	3,459.7
Sales	3,379.3	4,537.0
Average shareholders' equity	1,113.3	2,347.3
Market price of the common stock:		
beginning of year	$15	$38
end of year	$12	$40
Shares of common stock outstanding	200 million	100 million

6. You are thinking of taking a trip to Florida for your spring vacation, which begins two months from now. You use a free online travel service to find the cheapest round-trip fare from Boston to Fort Lauderdale. It tells you that the cheapest airline is AirCheapo. You have never heard of this airline before and are concerned that it may go out of business before you can use your ticket two months from now. How could you use available online financial data to investigate the risk to you of buying an AirCheapo ticket? Which firms are in the relevant comparables group for your purposes?

7. Your company currently has earnings per share of $90 and an EBITDA of $50 million. Your financial analyst says that she found comparable companies, and lists the following data for them.

Comparable	P/E ratio	EV/EBITDA ratio
A	9.5	20.3
B	7.0	16.1
C	6.0	13.2

Using each comparable company, provide an estimate of what you think the stock price and enterprise value of your company should be. Then provide an estimate using the averages of the ratios across all comparables. What sorts of things might you be concerned about in performing this exercise?

8. Go to a site like Yahoo! Finance. Choose a company that you want to value. Now try to value it using the following steps: (a) Find a comparable company; (b) look up that comparable company's P/E and EV/EBITDA ratios; (c) use that information and the accounting information provided for the company you chose to calculate estimates of the company's stock price and enterprise value. Comment on how close you were to the actual stock price and enterprise value, and possible reasons why.

9. Consider the financial statements shown in Table 8.15 for the Give Me Debt company.

Table 8.15 Give Me Debt Company financial statements.

Income statement	2024	2025	2026
Sales	$1,200,000	$1,500,000	
Cost of goods sold	750,000	937,500	
Gross margin	450,000	562,500	
Operating expenses			
Advertising expense	50,000	62,500	
Rent expense	72,000	90,000	
Salesperson commission expense	48,000	60,000	
Utilities expense	15,000	18,750	
EBIT	265,000	331,250	
Interest expense	106,000	113,000	
Taxable income	159,000	218,250	
Taxes (35%)	55,650	76,388	
Net income	103,350	141,863	
Dividends (40% payout)	41,340	56,745	
Change in retained earnings	62,010	85,118	

Balance sheet	2024	2025	2026
Assets			
Cash	$300,000	$375,000	
Receivables	200,000	250,000	
Inventory	700,000	875,000	
Property, plant, equipment	1,800,000	2,250,000	
Total assets	3,000,000	3,750,000	
Liabilities and shareholders' equity			
Liabilities	300,000	375,000	
Payables			
Short-term debt (10% interest)	500,000	989,882	
Long-term debt (7% interest)	800,000	900,000	
Shareholders' equity	1,100,000	1,100,000	
Common stock			
Retained earnings	300,000	385,118	
Total liabilities and equity	3,000,000	3,750,000	

(a) Using the income statements and balance sheets, determine which items varied in constant proportion to sales between 2024 and 2025.
(b) Determine the rate of growth in sales that was achieved from 2024 to 2025.
(c) What was the firm's return on equity for 2025? For 2024?
(d) What was the firm's external (additional) funding requirement determined to be for 2025?

(e) Prepare the income statement for 2026 with the following assumptions:
- Rate of growth in sales = 15%.
- The firm intends to keep its debt levels the same as 2025.
- The firm's dividend payout in 2026 will be reduced to 30%.
- The firm anticipates an increase in the corporate tax rate to 38%.

(f) Complete the balance sheet for 2026.

(g) What would be the firm's forecasted return on equity for 2026? How much additional funding will the firm need for 2026?

(h) Take the financial statements developed in the previous parts, and revise them assuming a growth rate in sales from 2025 to 2026 of 10%.

(i) Develop financial statements for 2027 assuming a growth rate in sales of 20% from 2026 to 2027.

(j) Suppose that after analyzing the results of 2026 and forecasting the financial statements for 2027, the Give Me Debt Company anticipates an increase in total assets of $50, an increase in retained earnings of $25, and an increase in payables of $40. Assume that other than the payables, the firm's liabilities include short-term and long-term debt, and that its equity includes common stock and retained earnings. The chief financial officer of the company asks you to determine the required amount of additional funding in 2027. What do you tell the CFO?

(k) What actions can the Give Me Debt Company undertake to address the situation you have found?

10. Place the following planning events in their likely order of occurrence within the planning cycle:
- Funding needs for implementation of tactical plans are estimated.
- The final firm-wide plan and budgets are completed.
- The CEO and top management team establish strategic objectives for the firm (e.g., increase market share from 10% to 12%).
- Line managers devise action plans to support strategic objectives.
- Revisions are made to the strategic plan and divisional budgets based on feedback from divisional managers with regard to resource (money, people) requirements.
- Decisions are made as to which sources of external financing to tap.
- Integration of divisional budgets into a preliminary firm-wide budget by the CEO and top management team.
- The firm determines the amount of required external financing.
- Tactical plans and budgets are reviewed with division management; priorities are assigned to planned activities.
- Division managers review the strategic objectives with their line (or tactical) management.

11. Suppose it is 13 Mar. 2022, and you just received your monthly credit card statement with a new balance of $2,000. The payment is due on 5 Apr. 22, but your spouse panics at the sight (and size) of the balance and wants to pay it immediately. If you practice the principles of cash cycle time management in your personal finances, when would you make the payment? Why? What danger exists in adopting this strategy?

12. Suppose you own a firm that manufactures pool tables. Thirty days ago, you hired a consultant to examine your business and suggest improvements. The consultant's proposal, if implemented, would allow your firm to shorten the time between each sale and the subsequent cash collection by 20 days, slightly lengthen the time between inventory purchase and sale by only 5 days, but shorten the time between inventory purchase and your firm's payment of the bill by 15 days. Would you implement the consultant's proposal? Why?

13. In general, the principles of cash cycle time management call for a firm to shorten the time it takes to collect receivables, and lengthen the time it takes to pay amounts it owes to suppliers. Explain what trade-offs need to be managed if the firm offers discounts to customers who pay early, and the firm also forgoes discounts offered by its suppliers by extending the time until it pays invoices.
14. Some furniture companies conduct highly advertised annual sale events in which customers can either take an up-front discount for a cash or credit card purchase, or defer finance charges for up to one year on their purchases by charging it to the company's credit account. Assume that the two options do not present a time value of money advantage for the company. In terms of cash cycle management:
    (a) Why does the company offer the discount?
    (b) Why might the company be willing to forgo cash collection for one year if a customer chooses to defer? What risk does the company assume in the deferment case that it does not assume in the discount case?
15. (Excel app) Construct pro forma financial statements using the percent-of-sales method for GCP assuming that 2025 sales will be $300 million, a 30% tax rate on income, and that cost of goods sold will be 20% of sales in 2025.

PART II

CORPORATE FINANCE

Part II of this book is about corporate finance, which examines decision making *within companies* and also how investors and other stakeholders may react to those decisions.

Chapter 9 explores how to use the financial information introduced in Chapter 8 to determine the total value of a company, applying the principles and valuation techniques introduced in Part I. It provides a framework for understanding how a company's financial decisions may affect the company, which we explore in the subsequent chapters.

Chapter 10 applies valuation techniques to examine investment decisions within companies. Managers within companies will ideally want to invest in projects that increase the value of the firm.

Chapter 11 explores forms of business organization for companies, and explains how separation of ownership and control may be conducive to the functioning of companies. However, this may result in conflicts between the various company stakeholders. We examine corporate governance mechanisms that companies may use to resolve these conflicts.

Chapter 12 focuses on when companies have excess cash, and whether it is optimal for them to either keep that cash or return it to shareholders in the form of payout: dividends or repurchases. We examine how this may impact a company's value.

Chapter 13 focuses on the capital structure decision—how companies may choose to finance themselves. We examine the consequences of this choice, and how it may affect the value of the company, utilizing the valuation framework introduced in Chapter 9. We also show how capital structure interacts and may either exacerbate or ameliorate the conflicts discussed in Chapter 11.

In Chapter 14, we introduce a framework to understand corporate decision making based on options, covered in Chapter 7. We cover how this framework based on option pricing can be used to value a wide variety of claims that a company may issue, including equity, debt, and securities that have features of both, such as convertible bonds. We also show how it can be used to examine project decisions within companies in a different way from Chapter 10.

In Chapter 15 we pull together the various topics discussed in the previous chapters to explore financing decisions over the life of a firm, from startup to windup. Included are examinations of venture capital, bank loans, private equity, initial public offerings (IPOs), and mergers and acquisitions (M&A). It draws on all of the previous chapters in Part II.

9 COMPANY VALUATION

CHAPTER OVERVIEW

9.1	Company Value	261
9.2	Calculating Company Value: Valuation Using Comparables	263
9.3	Calculating Company Value: Discounted Cash Flow Analysis	265
9.4	Calculating Equity Value	278

LEARNING OBJECTIVES

After reading this chapter, you will be able to:
- define a company's total value, and distinguish it from the value of the company's debt and equity;
- explain how valuation models can be used to estimate a company's value;
- identify different models that are widely used to value companies;
- perform calculations using these models to estimate the value of a company;
- calculate the equity value of a company using different models.

EQUATIONS YOU KNOW

Stock price valuation using comparables	Stock price = $EPS \times \left(\dfrac{P}{E}\right)_{comparable}$	Eq. 8.17
Total company value valuation using comparables	Total company value = $EBITDA \times \left(\dfrac{EV}{EBITDA}\right)_{comparable}$	Eq. 8.18
Present value, perpetuity	$PV = \dfrac{\$CF}{r}$	Eq. 2.17
Present value, growing perpetuity	$PV = \dfrac{\$CF_1}{r - g}$	Eq. 2.18

- You want to acquire a company, and need to determine the price to pay for it. How do you do this?

- You are looking to invest in a company and want to determine whether the price of its stock or bonds is "fair."

- You want to determine how management decisions will impact a company's value (or perhaps *your* company faces a decision and you want to understand how that will affect the company's value).

- You are an equity analyst and must determine whether the value of a stock you are reviewing should be greater or less than its current market price.

- A company you are looking to invest in claims that its new plan will increase its cash flows over the long run by 1% and you want to know how this will affect its value.

- An investment company analyst says that their model indicates that a certain company is much more valuable than the market consensus and you wish to evaluate this claim.

Introduction

In previous chapters, we introduced the fundamental principles behind understanding the value of financial investments, such as stocks, bonds, and options. However, many of these investments (such as shares of stock or bonds issued by a company or call options that allow the holder to purchase shares of a company's stock) are based on specific companies. To fully understand such investments, it is necessary to better understand the companies that they are based on. In Chapter 8 we examined company financial statements as a first step toward analyzing companies in more detail. We now expand upon this and explore how the information from financial statements can be used to estimate the economic *value* of a company.

In this chapter we focus on further developing and applying our valuation tools to better understand company value. We begin by taking the perspective of an observer examining a company from the "outside," that is, someone who cannot influence the way a company is run. In other words, given how a company is being managed by its current managers, what should its value be? Starting in the next chapter, we will consider the perspective of a manager from *within* a company, and determine how the actions of those running a company can affect its value.

9.1 Company Value

There are various definitions of company value. We will focus on the total value of a company's assets. Total value is also referred to as total company value or the enterprise value of a company. Conceptually, a company's decision makers and stakeholders should optimally make decisions that maximize the total value of the company. If managers maximize total value, then they can make all stakeholders better off economically.

The total value of a company is the *combined* value of the company's stock (equity) and bonds or loans (debt). This is because the investors that provide money to the company are entitled to receive some part of its cash flows, which are generated by the assets financed by the stock, bonds, or loans, and therefore are part of the company's value. In particular, a company's debtholders are promised

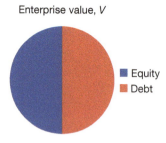

FIGURE 9.1 Total value, debt, and equity. A company's total value is the sum of its equity (blue) and debt (red).

cash payments in the future (in the form of interest and principal), which are paid out from the company's cash flows. The remaining cash flows go to the stockholders, who may receive cash payments in the form of dividends, and/or see the cash flows reinvested in the company and reflected in the value of their shares. We can represent this relationship between a company's total value V and the value of its debt D and equity E through Equation 9.1:

$$V = D + E. \tag{9.1}$$

Figure 9.1 shows one possible allocation of a company's value between debt and equity. The split may be even, as shown in the figure, or a company could choose to finance itself with relatively more debt or equity. The proportion of debt and equity that a company chooses is known as the company's capital structure. As we will discuss in more detail in Chapter 13, the capital structure a company chooses can affect its total value.

Oftentimes when the media refer to a company's value they are referring only to the value of the company's *equity*. As we will see, in some circumstances we may be specifically interested in determining the value of a company's equity, while in other circumstances we may be focused on a company's total value. However, it is important to keep in mind that the two values are distinct. Let's illustrate the difference between total value and equity value using Microsoft, a large publicly traded corporation. Table 9.1 provides the total, equity, and debt values for Microsoft. As the table shows, the total value is $3,236 billion, the sum of the equity and debt values.

Recall from Chapter 8 that there is distinction between a firm's book value and its market value. Book values represent values calculated based on accounting conventions, which are typically acquisition or historical costs less cumulative depreciation. In this chapter we focus on *market values* because we are interested in determining a company's economic value now.

Determining the value of a company requires a valuation model, as discussed in Chapter 4. In choosing an appropriate valuation model, we put to work two of our principles:

Principle 2: *Equivalent assets that can be freely bought and sold will have the same market price.* Because the law of one price is the driving force that determines values/prices, it is at the core of every valuation model.

Principle 4: *Every model is an incomplete, simplified description of a complex reality.* Because no model is perfect, we must determine which valuation model is most appropriate to use, given the specific situation at hand.

We will cover the two most commonly used valuation models for calculating a company's total value: valuation using comparables and valuation using discounted cash flow (DCF) analysis. As we will discuss, the use of either of these valuation models involves understanding a company and identifying the numbers that are relevant to helping us achieve that understanding.

Table 9.1 Firm values of Microsoft (as of 31 Mar. 2024).

Equity value	$3,130 billion
Debt value	+ 106 billion
Total value	$3,236 billion
Source: Yahoo! Finance.	

9.2 Calculating Company Value: Valuation Using Comparables

Valuation by comparables is a method of valuation that uses relevant information about comparable—ideally *identical*—companies. This method is based on the intuition that because the law of one price (Principle 2) states that two equivalent assets should have the same price, if we know the value of an identical company, we can use it to estimate the value of the company that we're trying to value. In reality, no two companies are completely identical. However, companies that are comparable to each other—for example, close competitors in the same industry—can provide useful information for calculating company value.

A widely used model based on this concept is to calculate the total value of a company using *multiples* or *ratios* that come from comparable companies and can be used to estimate the value of the company of interest. To illustrate, we will calculate the total value of Generic Consumer Products (GCP), the manufacturing firm we examined in Chapter 8. Suppose we know that the current earnings of GCP (as measured by EBITDA, earnings before interest, taxes, depreciation, and amortization) are $10 million, but do not have any other information. However, we are able to identify a comparable company, ProductWorld, which is a manufacturing firm that produces consumer products similar to those made by GCP. We note that ProductWorld's enterprise value to EBITDA (EV/EBITDA) ratio is 20.00, meaning that ProductWorld has an enterprise value that is 20 times its current earnings (EBITDA). If GCP and ProductWorld are truly comparable companies, then GCP should also have an enterprise value that is 20 times its current earnings. By this method, an estimate of GCP's enterprise value would be:

$$V = \$10 \text{ million} \times 20.00 = \$200 \text{ million}.$$

More generally, we can write out the methodology to calculate a firm's enterprise value using the EV/EBITDA ratio as (as we also saw in Equation 8.18):

$$V = \text{EBITDA} \times \left(\frac{\text{EV}}{\text{EBITDA}}\right)_{comparable}. \tag{9.2}$$

In Equation 9.2, EBITDA comes from the company you are trying to value, and $(\text{EV/EBITDA})_{comparable}$ comes from a comparable company (or an average across a set of comparable companies).

In this example, our goal is to determine the overall company value of GCP. As we noted, sometimes we are interested in specifically estimating the price of a company's equity or stock. To do so, we can use the same methodology, but apply different ratios. In particular, we can use the price-to-earnings (P/E) ratio of a company or set of companies (the stock price divided by earnings per share), and multiply by the earnings per share of the company whose stock we wish to value (as we also saw in Equation 8.17):

$$\text{Stock price} = EPS \times \left(\frac{P}{E}\right)_{comparable}. \tag{9.3}$$

Using multiples or ratios from comparables is a useful valuation method in many circumstances. First, it does not require the same amount of detailed data (or future projections) about a company as other valuation methods. This makes it particularly useful when valuing companies such as private companies, which may not have a lot of readily accessible data. Second, it is quick and straightforward, and therefore can give a first pass at valuation before using more detailed methods.

However, when using this model, it is important to note its limitations. This method is the most accurate when we can identify truly comparable companies—ones that are similar in terms of their characteristics and the nature of their business. If we use a company that is not a good comparable, our estimates may be substantially off. This is why understanding the company we are trying to value—its operations, industry, and competitors—is critically important. Knowing these characteristics gives us a basis for correctly identifying comparable companies. Because it is practically impossible to find one company that is a perfect comparable, analysts usually find a number of comparable companies within the same industry, and take an average of their ratios when using comparables to estimate a company's total value.

To see how the comparables model of valuation works, suppose we want to estimate the total value of the Coca-Cola Company. Using comparables requires an understanding of Coca-Cola's business in order to identify appropriate comparable companies. Coca-Cola is primarily in the business of manufacturing and distributing beverages, and a primary competitor that comes to mind for its brand-name drink is Pepsi. Let's therefore use PepsiCo Inc. as our comparable company. To estimate Coca-Cola's total value using Equation 9.2, we first need its earnings (EBITDA), which were estimated to be $14.65 billion over the past year as of March 2024. We next need to find out PepsiCo's EV/EBITDA ratio, which is 18.11. Our model's estimate of Coca-Cola's total value is therefore:

$$V = \text{EBITDA} \times \left(\frac{\text{EV}}{\text{EBITDA}}\right)_{comparable}$$
$$= \$14.65 \times 18.11$$
$$= \$265.31 \text{ billion}.$$

How does our estimate compare to Coca-Cola's actual enterprise value in March 2024? Coca-Cola had an actual enterprise value of $297.16 billion, a difference in value from our estimate of about $31.8 billion!

Why is our estimate off? There are two possibilities. First, it may be that the market's assessment of enterprise value is wrong, and Coca-Cola is truly worth less—in other words, it is overvalued. While there may be cases when we believe the market's appraisal of value is incorrect (as discussed in Chapter 4), Principle 5 generally holds, and the best estimate of an asset's value is usually its market price, which incorporates valuable information to guide the allocation of resources and risks.

Second, the amount by which our estimate differs from the market's suggests that our model is wrong in some way. An important way in which it may be wrong is the comparable firm we used. While Coca-Cola and PepsiCo's namesake drink products are close competitors, the companies differ in other important ways. For example, a large part of PepsiCo's business consists of food product brands such as Lay's, Doritos, and Tostitos snacks and Quaker Oats, which serve different markets than Coca-Cola. A better approach would have been to select another comparable company, or to use an average across several carefully selected comparable companies. Alternatively, one can decompose the company into its major divisions and use a comparable EV/EBITDA ratio for each component business. This underscores the importance of selecting appropriate comparable companies, which involves understanding the story of and operational details about the company we are trying to value.

QUICK CHECK 9.1 Suppose you want to value a furniture company, and you see that a typical one has a stock price that is 12 times its earnings per share. If the company you aim to value has earnings per share of $1.50, what is an estimate of its stock price?

9.3 Calculating Company Value: Discounted Cash Flow Analysis

A widely used valuation model is the discounted cash flows (DCF) model, which we introduced in Chapters 2 and 4. The logic behind the DCF model is that the value of a company, like the value of any asset, will be given by the present value of the company's cash flows. We focus on *present* value, in accordance with **Principle 1:** *A dollar today is not worth the same as a dollar tomorrow.* To value a company using the DCF model, we proceed in three steps:

(1) Estimate the company's projected future cash flows, known as the company's free cash flows (FCFs).
(2) Determine the correct discount rate for the cash flows, which is the company's overall cost of capital.
(3) Discount the free cash flow from Step 1 using the cost of capital in Step 2 as the discount rate.

Let's work through an example. Suppose that a company's future expected FCFs are summarized in the following cash flow timeline:

Time t:	$t=0$	$t=1$	$t=2$	$t=3$	$t=4$	$t=5$	...
Free cash flow FCF_t:		FCF_1	FCF_2	FCF_3	FCF_4	FCF_5	...

We can therefore represent our DCF approach to calculating company value through the following equation:

$$V = \frac{FCF_1}{1+r_A} + \frac{FCF_2}{(1+r_A)^2} + \frac{FCF_3}{(1+r_A)^3} + \frac{FCF_4}{(1+r_A)^4} + \frac{FCF_5}{(1+r_A)^5}\cdots, \quad (9.4)$$

where FCF_t represents the free cash flow that is projected to occur at time t in the future, and r_A represents the company's overall discount rate (cost of capital). We refer to the discount rate as r_A because it represents the rate of return that investors expect from the company's total *assets* which generate the FCFs.

9.3.1 Projecting a Company's Cash Flows

The first step in using the DCF model to calculate company value is to estimate the free cash flows that the company will generate in the future. We do not know exactly what the future will bring for a given company. We therefore need to paint a picture about the future of the company—develop a story about the likely development of the firm's revenues and expenses—and translate that likely future into numbers. We can create our best estimates of the future based on past information we have about the company's operations, combined with our current understanding of the company and our judgment regarding how its operations are likely to change.

A company's accounting information typically forms the basis for determining a company's future expected cash flows. As we learned in Chapter 8, companies provide what are known as pro forma accounting statements, which are management estimates of the company's accounting numbers over the next few years. These include both balance sheet and income statement projections.

However, it is important to note that reported accounting quantities, such as earnings, include a number of adjustments that help companies estimate their accounting earnings but potentially obscure the true amount of cash they are expecting to generate. For example, suppose a company spends $1 million on factory equipment. That $1 million cost may not be expensed for this year, but may be depreciated over, say, the next five years at $200,000 per year. The $200,000 each year for the next five years reduces the net income of the company for those years, but does not reflect the reality that all the cash for the investment was spent this year. As a result, once we have the accounting projections, it is necessary to strip out various adjustments to arrive at an estimate of a company's actual cash flow.

More specifically, we can use the following formula to arrive at an estimate of a company's free cash flow in any given year:

$$\text{FCF} = \text{EBIT} \times (1-\tau) + \text{depreciation} - \text{CapEx} - \Delta\text{NWC}. \tag{9.5}$$

In this equation, we start with the accounting measure of the firm's profits, earnings before interest and taxes (EBIT). Since this is measured before the company pays taxes to the government, we need to adjust for this by multiplying by $(1-\tau)$, where τ represents the tax rate (equivalently, we can view this as taking EBIT and subtracting taxes, EBIT $\times \tau$). This adjustment reflects the government's claim on the value of the company. Depreciation is the depreciation that was applied to the accounting earnings. We add this in because depreciation is used in accordance with accrual accounting to reduce a company's earnings (and thus its tax bill), but this does not reflect an actual cash outflow. We then subtract capital expenditures, CapEx, to account for cash that a company plans to spend for future investments. Finally, ΔNWC represents the change in net working capital (NWC) from the previous period to the current period. Net working capital is the difference between the amount of current assets (items such as inventory and accounts receivable) and the amount of current liabilities (items such as accounts payable). It is generally interpreted as the funds that the company needs to use for short-run operations. Net working capital is, therefore, a use of the company's cash that is deducted from the FCF to account for any funding that is expected to flow in or out of the company in the short run. For example, an increase in inventories would imply that NWC would go up. We subtract this change because the company would have to pay for the increase in inventories, which would be a cash outflow.

As noted above, it is typical for a company to provide pro forma estimates for a few years in the future that can be used to calculate FCF. We can therefore use those estimates as the basis for our FCF calculations. In Chapter 8 we went over the details of how companies can construct pro forma statements. To illustrate how those pro forma figures can be used to estimate FCF, consider the following pro forma projections for GCP for the next year. (These values are taken from the GCP financial statements in Chapter 8.)

Suppose that GCP faces a tax rate of 30%. We can plug the numbers from Table 9.2 into the free cash flow formula (Equation 9.5) to arrive at an estimate of GCP's FCF for next year. Before we do,

Table 9.2 GCP pro forma projections. GCP's pro forma projections are based on the GCP financial statements presented in Chapter 8. All numbers are in millions of US dollars.

	Current year ($t = 0$)	Next year ($t = 1$)
EBIT		$1,000
Capital expenditures		100
Depreciation		50
Current assets	$100	50
Current liabilities	50	100

note that we need to figure out the net working capital (NWC) for GCP in $t = 0$ and $t = 1$. Since NWC equals current assets − current liabilities, at $t = 0$, NWC = \$100 − \$50 = \$50, and at $t = 1$, NWC = \$50 − \$100 = −\$50. The change is therefore: ΔNWC = −\$50 − \$50 = −\$100. We can now use our FCF formula (Equation 9.5) directly:

$$\begin{aligned} \text{FCF} &= \text{EBIT} \times (1 - \tau) + \text{depreciation} - \text{CapEx} - \Delta\text{NWC} \\ &= \$1{,}000 \times (1 - 0.30) + \$50 - \$100 - (-\$100) \\ &= \$750. \end{aligned}$$

Our estimated free cash flow for GCP for next year is therefore \$750 million.

In practice, how does a company come up with its pro forma projections, as in the above example? At a broad level, companies can draw from their recent experiences or planned strategy to paint a picture of the future:

- **EBIT**: Companies can use projected sales, based on previous years, as well as cost growth rates to project future earnings.
- **Depreciation**: When a company makes a large purchase, say for equipment, it chooses a depreciation schedule to depreciate the value over time. An example of such a method is straight-line depreciation, where the value is depreciated by the same amount each year. The company can then estimate future annual depreciation expense.
- **CapEx**: Companies typically have plans for large capital investments in the short run, and thus some sense of how much they will spend to make those investments.
- **ΔNWC**: Projections regarding sales and expenses will translate into expected changes in accounts payable and accounts receivable, which are important components of net working capital. Beyond this, companies typically engage in working capital management, which includes how they can maintain or change their level of inventory.

Example 9.1 (Calculating Free Cash Flows): At the end of 2025, you are looking to value a company. You need to determine its free cash flows as a first step in your valuation. It has the current (2025) and pro forma (2026 onward) financing information (in millions of US dollars) shown in Table 9.3.

Table 9.3 Finance information for Example 9.1.

	2025	2026	2027	2028
Sales	6,000.0	6,600.0	7,200.0	7,416.0
EBIT	2,100.0	2,310.0	2,520.0	2,595.6
CapEx − depreciation	10.0	30.0	30.0	10.8
Accounts receivable	390.0	400.0	468.0	500.0
Inventory	200.0	275.0	300.0	309.0
Accounts payable	640.0	704.0	800.0	791.0

What are the company's projected free cash flows for years 2026, 2027, and 2028? Assume that the tax rate is 35%.

9 COMPANY VALUATION

Solution. The calculations are summarized in Table 9.4.

Table 9.4 Summary of calculations for Example 9.1.

	2025	2026	2027	2028
EBIT		$2,310.00	$2,520.00	$2,595.60
Taxes (at 35%)		808.50	882.00	908.46
EBIT $\times (1-\tau)$		1,501.50	1,638.00	1,687.14
$-$(CapEx $-$ depreciation)		30.00	30.00	10.80
$-\Delta$NWC		21.00	$-$3.00	50.00
$=$ Free cash flow		$1,450.50	$1,611.00	$1,626.34
Accounts receivable	$390.00	400.00	468.00	500.00
Inventory	200.00	275.00	300.00	309.00
Accounts payable	640.00	704.00	800.00	791.00
Net working capital, NWC	$-$50.00	$-$29.00	$-$32.00	18.00
Change in NWC, ΔNWC		21.00	$-$3.00	50.00

We can calculate the FCFs for each of the years using Equation 9.5, which we can rewrite to reflect CapEx and depreciation as given:

$$\text{FCF} = \text{EBIT} \times (1-\tau) - (\text{CapEx} - \text{depreciation}) - \Delta\text{NWC}.$$

EBIT and the tax rate τ are given, so EBIT $\times (1-\tau)$ can be computed using the information in the question. For example, in 2026, EBIT is $2,310, the tax rate is 35%, taxes are $808.5, and EBIT $\times (1-\tau)$ is $1,501.5.

To obtain the change in net working capital (ΔNWC), we first compute the level of NWC, and then compute the difference relative to the preceding year. Remember that NWC equals current assets $-$ current liabilities. Current assets in this case include accounts receivable and inventory (because these are what the company has or expects to receive), while current liabilities include accounts payable (what the company expects to pay out). In this case, NWC is:

$$\text{NWC} = \text{accounts receivable} + \text{inventory} - \text{accounts payable}.$$

For example, for 2025 this is:

$$\text{NWC} = 390 + 200 - 640 = -50.$$

For 2026 this is:

$$\text{NWC} = 400 + 275 - 704 = -29.$$

Hence, ΔNWC for 2026 is $-29 - (-50) = 21$ (NWC increased by 21).

Putting everything together, the FCF in 2026 is: $1,501.5 - 30 - 21 = \$1,450.5$ million. We obtain the FCFs for the other years by repeating this process.

> **QUICK CHECK 9.2** What are the different components of free cash flow? How would a typical company estimate the level of each of these components in the future?

9.3.2 Terminal Values and Long-Run Growth Rates

To calculate a company's estimated total value, we must discount the company's projected future free cash flows (FCFs) by the company's discount rate. In Chapter 8 we discussed how to project out these future FCFs over subsequent years using pro forma financial statements. Companies typically provide these pro forma statements for a few years into the future. However, we assume that companies will continue to operate *indefinitely*, and thus the future FCFs will not stop. In other words, our standard assumption is that a given company will continue to operate (and thus generate FCFs) for the foreseeable future. This is also why, while a company's bonds may mature, equity does not have an expiration date and in theory a company has an infinite timeline.

To calculate the total value of a company and estimate Equation 9.4, analysts typically project cash flows up to a certain date in the future, and then calculate the expected value of the firm at that future date. This value, called the terminal value, represents the present value of all future cash flows as of that future date (the end of the projected cash flows).

One can conceptually calculate a terminal value as of *any* future date. In practice, these dates are commonly $t = 5$ (five years in the future) or $t = 10$ (ten years in the future). The future date at which you calculate a terminal value depends on the particular situation. The terminal value assumes that the cash flows follow a particular pattern (e.g., they stay the same or grow at some rate after a certain point or time). Thus, you typically want to calculate a terminal value as of the date that you are reasonably sure the cash flows will follow such a pattern. If you expect the cash flows to move up and down based on fluctuating sales over the next few years, you would likely be best off projecting individual cash flows further out into the future before calculating a terminal value. For example, consider a new clothing store. Its sales over the next few years (and thus cash flows) may initially grow rapidly, with customers being excited to try out its products, but then is likely to settle into a more stable amount of sales each year. The point in time at which the sales stabilize would represent a reasonable choice for calculating the terminal value of the company.

To illustrate, suppose that we have estimated the expected free cash flows for GCP for the next three years into the future (i.e., up to $t = 3$). To keep our calculations simple, let us say we determine that after year $t = 3$ it is reasonable to assume that the FCFs are likely to follow a pattern and not fluctuate randomly. To calculate GCP's terminal value as of year 3, we would incorporate the estimated present value as of year $t = 3$ of all cash flows from year $t = 4$ and onwards:

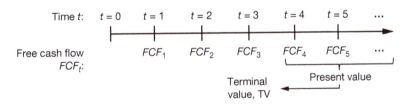

Mathematically, incorporating this year 3 terminal value into Equation 9.4 allows us to rewrite it as:

$$V = \frac{FCF_1}{1+r_A} + \frac{FCF_2}{(1+r_A)^2} + \frac{FCF_3}{(1+r_A)^3} + \frac{FCF_4}{(1+r_A)^4} + \frac{FCF_5}{(1+r_A)^5} \cdots$$

$$= \frac{FCF_1}{1+r_A} + \frac{FCF_2}{(1+r_A)^2} + \frac{FCF_3}{(1+r_A)^3} + \frac{TV_3}{(1+r_A)^3}.$$

(9.6)

In Equation 9.6, by discounting future FCFs for years 4, 5, 6, and beyond back to year $t = 3$, we can determine GCP's terminal value in year 3, TV_3, which now makes it feasible to discount the endless stream of FCFs and calculate the company value. More generally, if we calculate a terminal value as of year T in the future, Equation 9.6 would be expressed as:

$$V = \frac{FCF_1}{1+r_A} + \frac{FCF_2}{(1+r_A)^2} + \frac{FCF_3}{(1+r_A)^3} + \frac{FCF_4}{(1+r_A)^4} + \frac{FCF_5}{(1+r_A)^5} \cdots$$
$$= \frac{FCF_1}{1+r_A} + \frac{FCF_2}{(1+r_A)^2} + \frac{FCF_3}{(1+r_A)^3} + \cdots + \frac{FCF_T}{(1+r_A)^T} + \frac{TV_T}{(1+r_A)^T}. \quad (9.7)$$

Calculating a terminal value first requires assuming how the free cash flows will act after a certain point in time (in our example above, after $t = 3$). A common assumption is that the FCFs will either stay at a certain level or continue to grow at some steady-state growth rate after that point in time. Suppose that we assume the FCFs will stay at the year $t = 3$ level indefinitely, that is, the cash flows will not grow. We can therefore represent GCP's cash flows as:

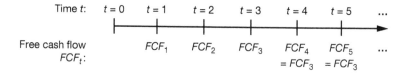

Note that the cash flows after $t = 3$ stay at the $t = 3$ level, and therefore are a perpetuity (discussed in Chapter 2). This allows us to use the perpetuity formula (Equation 2.17), which states that the present value of a stream of cash flows C that start next period and last forever will be C / r, given a discount rate of r. Thus, as of $t = 3$, the present value of all the cash flows that occur after that point in time ($t = 4$ and onwards) will be given by:

$$TV_3 = \frac{FCF_4}{r_A} = \frac{FCF_3}{r_A}.$$

Note that in this equation, the cash flow in year 3 is the same as the cash flow in year 4, so we can assume a perpetuity. It is important to remember the timing of the perpetuity formulas: The formula C / r provides the present value of a cash flow stream assuming that the cash flows start in the *next* period. Therefore, by inserting the year $t = 4$ cash flow into the perpetuity formula, we arrive at the present value of the cash flow stream as of year $t = 3$.

With this terminal value calculated, we can then calculate the value of the firm by plugging it into Equation 9.6. More generally, if we want to calculate the terminal value at some date T in the future, and the cash flows after that date are those of a perpetuity, we would use the following formula:

$$TV_T = \frac{FCF_{T+1}}{r_A}. \quad (9.8)$$

This terminal value would then be substituted into Equation 9.7.

Alternatively, suppose we assume that the FCFs will grow forever at some rate g each year after year $t = 3$. This would correspond to a company that has achieved a long-run "steady" growth rate. We refer to such a growth rate as the terminal growth rate or long-run growth rate. We can then represent the cash flows of GCP as:

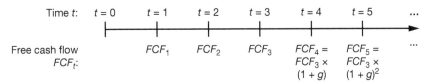

Notice that the cash flows after $t = 3$ are a *growing perpetuity*. To calculate the terminal value, then, we can use the growing perpetuity formula introduced in Chapter 2. Equation 2.18 states that the present value of a stream of cash flows C that start next period and grow forever at a rate g will be $C/(r-g)$, given a discount rate of r. Thus, as of $t = 3$, the present value of all the cash flows that occur after that point in time ($t = 4$ and onwards) will be given by:

$$TV_3 = \frac{FCF_4}{r_A - g} = \frac{FCF_3 \times (1+g)}{r_A - g}.$$

We can then calculate the value of the firm by plugging this terminal value into Equation 9.6. More generally, if we want to calculate the terminal value at some date T in the future, and the cash flows after that date are a growing perpetuity, we would use the following formula:

$$TV_T = \frac{FCF_{T+1}}{r_A - g}. \quad (9.9)$$

We would then plug this into Equation 9.7.

To illustrate, suppose that GCP expects free cash flows (FCFs) of $10 million next year ($t = 1$), $20 million two years from now ($t = 2$), and $30 million three years from now ($t = 3$). You are informed that its cash flows are expected to stay constant at $30 million each year from $t = 4$ onward. We can represent its cash flows with the following timeline:

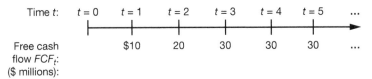

Suppose further that GCP's overall cost of capital is 10%. To solve for GCP's total value, let us first calculate the terminal value as of $t = 3$. Examining the timeline of cash flows, $t = 3$ is a logical point of time to calculate the terminal value because the cash flows exhibit a pattern after this point in time: they stay constant at $30. Using the perpetuity formula (Equation 9.8):

$$TV_3 = \frac{FCF_4}{r_A} = \frac{30}{0.10} = 300.$$

Then, using the terminal value of 300 and discounting the other cash flows, we can arrive at the company's total value using Equation 9.6:

$$\begin{aligned}
V &= \frac{FCF_1}{1+r_A} + \frac{FCF_2}{(1+r_A)^2} + \frac{FCF_3}{(1+r_A)^3} + \frac{FCF_4}{(1+r_A)^4} + \frac{FCF_5}{(1+r_A)^5} \cdots \\
&= \frac{FCF_1}{1+r_A} + \frac{FCF_2}{(1+r_A)^2} + \frac{FCF_3}{(1+r_A)^3} + \frac{TV_3}{(1+r_A)^3} \\
&= \frac{\$10}{1+0.10} + \frac{\$20}{(1+0.10)^2} + \frac{\$30}{(1+0.10)^3} + \frac{\$300}{(1+0.10)^3} \\
&= \$273.554.
\end{aligned}$$

GCP's total value at time 0 is therefore $273.554 million.

If GCP anticipates its cash flows will grow after year $t = 3$ at a rate of $g = 1\%$ each year, the cash flow timeline would change to:

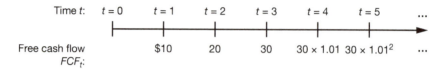

Then our calculation of the terminal value changes to (using Equation 9.9):

$$TV_3 = \frac{FCF_4}{r_A - g} = \frac{FCF_3 \times (1+g)}{r_A - g} = \frac{\$30 \times 1.01}{0.10 - 0.01} = \$336.667.$$

Using this new (larger due to growth) terminal value and discounting the other cash flows, we arrive at the following company value:

$$\begin{aligned} V &= \frac{FCF_1}{1+r_A} + \frac{FCF_2}{(1+r_A)^2} + \frac{FCF_3}{(1+r_A)^3} + \frac{FCF_4}{(1+r_A)^4} + \frac{FCF_5}{(1+r_A)^5}\cdots \\ &= \frac{FCF_1}{1+r_A} + \frac{FCF_2}{(1+r_A)^2} + \frac{FCF_3}{(1+r_A)^3} + \frac{TV_3}{(1+r_A)^3} \\ &= \frac{\$10}{1+0.10} + \frac{\$20}{(1+0.10)^2} + \frac{\$30}{(1+0.10)^3} + \frac{336.667}{(1+0.10)^3} \\ &= \$301.102. \end{aligned}$$

The company value is now greater because there is long-term growth.

For a given company, how is the terminal growth rate g estimated for the terminal value calculation? Long-term cash flow growth rates for similar companies or other firms in the same industry—adjusting for firm size and GDP growth rates across time periods—can often provide reasonable estimates for g. It is important to keep in mind that g represents a long-run, "steady-state" growth rate we expect a given company to maintain indefinitely. As a result, while a company may have achieved a growth rate over the past few years of, say, 20% per year, setting $g = 20\%$ will almost certainly give you an unrealistically large number for your company's total value! Box 9.1 discusses some practical issues related to choosing these growth rates when implementing DCF models.

Box 9.1 Calculating Cash Flow Growth Rates in Practice

Discounted cash flow, or DCF, models are widely used to value companies. When projecting free cash flows, it is typical to think of what stage the company is in and how long it can sustain the growth rate of its cash flows given that stage. For example, a company in its early stage of expansion may achieve a high rate of growth and generate cash flows that grow over 10% each year for the next few years. This rapid growth stage is often followed by a flatter growth phase, where a company is unable to maintain a high growth rate due to increased competition. It may grow, but not by as much; as a company evolves closer to maturity, we often assume a growth rate of about 5–8%. It is through this stage that we will explicitly project out free cash flows, and then assume that a company will reach maturity and grow at the terminal growth rate, which corresponds to g in the terminal value calculations we discussed previously.

At this "mature" stage, we assume that a company's growth is minimal as more of the company's focus is on using its resources to defend its existing market share from competitors. A positive terminal growth implies that a company will grow in perpetuity, while a negative terminal growth rate implies that a company's operations will eventually not continue. In practice, typical terminal growth rates range between the historical inflation rate and the average GDP growth rate. If we assume that a terminal growth rate is higher than the average GDP growth rate, we are in effect assuming that the company expects to outperform the economy on average forever.

A significant amount of judgment is needed to implement this model, and to determine if and when a company is likely to progress into the next stage of its growth and reach maturity. In addition, care must be taken in selecting the terminal growth rate. A choice of a terminal growth rate that is too high may give you a company value that is larger than the GDP of the economy, which is clearly unrealistic!

Source: Vipond, T., (n.d.). Terminal growth rate. Corporate Finance Institute, https://corporatefinanceinstitute.com

Finally, note that there are other ways to estimate the terminal value. Because a terminal value is an estimated future total company value, any valuation model that can be used to estimate total value can also be used to estimate a terminal value. For example, in Section 9.2 we used EV/EBITDA multiples to calculate total value by multiplying the EV/EBITDA of comparable companies by the EBITDA of the target company to arrive at the estimate of the total value. For terminal value calculations, this means that we can get an estimate of the terminal value by multiplying the *expected* EBITDA of the target company for the future date by the comparable's EV/EBITDA ratio.

> **QUICK CHECK 9.3** Recalculate the total value in the example given in Section 9.3.2, with a growth rate g of 4%.

Example 9.2 (Calculating Total Company Value): Suppose that Expander Inc. has the following free cash flows projected for the next few years (currently it is $t = 0$):

Year	1	2	3	4
Free cash flows	$100	$200	$400	$500

The company's cost of capital is 10%.
(a) If the terminal value of Expander Inc. in year 4 is $4,000, what is the total value of the company?
(b) Suppose instead that you are told that Expander Inc. projects that its free cash flows will grow at a rate of 1% each year forever after year 4. What is its terminal value of year 4? What is its total value?
(c) Instead of the information in parts (a) and (b), you are only told that similar companies that have sold have had an enterprise value multiple, EV/EBITDA, of 18.00. Expander Inc.'s EBITDA in year 4 is $200. Using this multiple, estimate Expander Inc.'s terminal value in year 4. What is its total value now?

Solution. (a) Using Equation 9.7 we can discount the future free cash flows (FCFs) and the terminal value back to today:

$$V = \frac{FCF_1}{1+r} + \frac{FCF_2}{(1+r)^2} + \frac{FCF_3}{(1+r)^3} + \frac{FCF_4}{(1+r)^4} + \frac{\text{terminal value}}{(1+r)^4}$$

$$= \frac{100}{1.10} + \frac{200}{1.10^2} + \frac{400}{1.10^3} + \frac{500}{1.10^4} + \frac{4{,}000}{1.10^4}$$

$$= \$3{,}630.285.$$

(b) The terminal value is a growing perpetuity. The growth starts after year 4, so the growing perpetuity will have an initial cash flow of $\$500 \times (1+g)$ in year 5 and a growth rate $g = 0.01$, which as of year 4 is worth (Equation 9.9):

$$TV = \frac{FCF_5}{r_A - g} = \frac{FCF_4 \times (1+g)}{r_A - g} = \frac{\$500 \times 1.01}{0.10 - 0.01} = \$5{,}611.111.$$

The total company value repeats the calculation from part (a), but substitutes the terminal value we just calculated:

$$V = \frac{FCF_1}{1+r} + \frac{FCF_2}{(1+r)^2} + \frac{FCF_3}{(1+r)^3} + \frac{FCF_4}{(1+r)^4} + \frac{\text{terminal value}}{(1+r)^4}$$

$$= \frac{100}{1.10} + \frac{200}{1.10^2} + \frac{400}{1.10^3} + \frac{500}{1.10^4} + \frac{5{,}611.111}{1.10^4}$$

$$= \$4{,}730.695.$$

(c) To estimate the terminal value in this case, we can use the enterprise value multiple provided, multiplied by the company's estimated EBITDA in year 4 (Equation 9.2 using the future estimated EBITDA):

$$\text{terminal value} = \text{EBITDA} \times \frac{EV}{\text{EBITDA}} = \$200 \times 18.00 = \$3{,}600.$$

Using this terminal value, we can calculate the total company value:

$$EV = \frac{FCF_1}{1+r} + \frac{FCF_2}{(1+r)^2} + \frac{FCF_3}{(1+r)^3} + \frac{FCF_4}{(1+r)^4} + \frac{\text{terminal value}}{(1+r)^4}$$

$$= \frac{100}{1.10} + \frac{200}{1.10^2} + \frac{400}{1.10^3} + \frac{500}{1.10^4} + \frac{3{,}600}{1.10^4}$$

$$= \$3{,}357.08.$$

9.3.3 Calculating Company Discount Rates

When using the DCF model to calculate a company's total value, the discount rate r_A that we use should be the discount rate that represents the cost of capital for the entire company's assets. That is, the cost of capital should reflect the rates of return that a company's equity and debt investors demand. As noted in Section 9.1, a company's total value is the sum of the values of the company's debt and equity, because that is how a company is financed. As a result, the discount rate r_A used in the DCF valuation model should reflect the company's mix of financing: If a company is funded entirely through equity (stock), then the discount rate should be its equity's cost of capital, the rate of return that shareholders expect to earn. If the company is also financed by debt, then the discount rate should reflect its debt's cost of capital (the rate of return that debt holders expect) and its equity's cost of capital.

This understanding leads us to one method of calculating a company's overall cost of capital: the **weighted-average cost of capital (WACC)**. The WACC is the discount rate for the overall company, and it incorporates an average of the rates of return that the company's equity and debt investors demand, which we denote by r_E and r_D, respectively. We can write the WACC as follows:

$$r_A = \text{WACC} = \left[\frac{E}{V} \times r_E\right] + \left[\frac{D}{V} \times r_D\right]. \tag{9.10}$$

Note that the r_A in this equation is calculated assuming that the company does not pay taxes. For this reason, Equation 9.10 is called the pre-tax WACC. If a company pays taxes, then it also saves money on its taxes whenever it makes debt interest payments. We discuss below how this affects Equation 9.10.

The WACC takes the required rates of return for equity (r_E) and debt (r_D), and weights each by the proportion of the company's value made up of equity E/V and debt D/V.

Calculating the required rates of return for equity (r_E) and debt (r_D) for a company requires data on the company (from its financial statements and financial markets) and a *valuation model*. As we discussed in Chapter 4, choosing the appropriate valuation model—and understanding the limitations of that model—is a key part of the financial valuation process. We go into detail about valuation models that can be used to calculate the cost of capital in Chapters 13 and 18.

It is important to note that one should always use market values when calculating E/V and D/V in Equation 9.10, rather than book values. This is because our valuation calculations seek to determine the company's value via its future cash flows. As noted in Chapter 8, book values are typically based on historical or past information about a company. In contrast, the market value is based on the market's appraisal of the company's current equity and debt values, which incorporates the market's best estimate of the company's prospects.

Another version of the WACC is the **after-tax WACC** $r_A^{\text{after-tax}}$, which incorporates the fact that debt requires interest payments that are tax-deductible for a company. We refer to these tax savings as the **debt tax shield**. The debt tax shield is incorporated into the WACC formula by *lowering* the cost of debt $(D/V) \times r_D$ by multiplying it by $1 - \tau$, where τ is the company's tax rate:

$$\text{After-tax WACC } r_A^{\text{after-tax}} = \left[\frac{E}{V} \times r_E\right] + \left[\frac{D}{V} \times r_D \times (1 - \tau)\right]. \tag{9.11}$$

Thus, the more debt a company holds, the more tax savings it receives (reflected by a lower WACC), and the higher its value is (since we discount the company's free cash flow by a lower discount rate). We cover the tax savings associated with holding debt in Chapter 13, along with other issues related to a company's choice of how much debt and equity to hold.

We can see how to use the WACC to determine a company's cost of capital and then to value the company using the DCF valuation model by extending our previous example to include an explicit calculation for the cost of capital. Suppose again that GCP expects free cash flows (FCFs) of $10 million next year ($t = 1$), $20 million two years from now ($t = 2$), and $30 million three years from now ($t = 3$). After year $t = 3$, GCP expects its cash flows to grow at a rate of $g = 1\%$ each year. GCP expects to maintain a capital structure where debt makes up half of its firm value (so $D/V = E/V = 50\%$). Its equity cost of capital is 15%, its debt cost of capital is 6%, and its tax rate is 30%. To calculate GCP's total value in this case, we again want to use Equation 9.6, but we first need to calculate GCP's cost of capital. Using Equation 9.11 with $r_E = 0.15$, $r_D = 0.06$, $\tau = 0.30$, and $D/V = 0.50$, we get:

$$\begin{aligned} r_A^{after-tax} &= \text{after-tax WACC} = \left[\frac{E}{V} \times r_E\right] + \left[\frac{D}{V} \times r_D \times (1-\tau)\right] \\ &= [0.50 \times 0.15] + [0.50 \times 0.06 \times (1-0.30)] \\ &= 0.096. \end{aligned}$$

With this new cost of capital, we then need to calculate the terminal value as of year 3 using Equation 9.9:

$$TV_3 = \frac{FCF_4}{r_A - g} = \frac{FCF_3 \times (1+g)}{r_A - g} = \frac{\$30 \times 1.01}{0.096 - 0.01} = \$352.326.$$

Finally, using this terminal value and the cost of capital, we can discount GCP's cash flows as we did before with Equation 9.6:

$$\begin{aligned} V &= \frac{FCF_1}{1+r_A} + \frac{FCF_2}{(1+r_A)^2} + \frac{FCF_3}{(1+r_A)^3} + \frac{FCF_4}{(1+r_A)^4} + \frac{FCF_5}{(1+r_A)^5} \cdots \\ &= \frac{FCF_1}{1+r_A} + \frac{FCF_2}{(1+r_A)^2} + \frac{FCF_3}{(1+r_A)^3} + \frac{TV_3}{(1+r_A)^3} \\ &= \frac{\$10}{1+0.096} + \frac{\$20}{(1+0.096)^2} + \frac{\$30}{(1+0.096)^3} + \frac{352.326}{(1+0.096)^3} \\ &= \$316.177. \end{aligned}$$

At the given discount and tax rates, GCP's total value is $316.18 million.

A final note on the cost of capital over time. In the above examples, we use the same cost of capital to discount all future cash flows. However, a company's cost of capital may *change* over time—for example, if its capital structure (amount of debt and amount of equity) is expected to change. If that is the case, then the WACC will typically also change over time, and we would need to incorporate this into our calculations. We tackle this issue in detail in Chapter 13.

> QUICK CHECK 9.4 Recalculate the total company value in the example using $r_E = 0.20$ and $r_D = 0.07$.

Example 9.3 (Calculating WACC and Total Company Value): Trek Technologies is a company you are considering acquiring. It has 100,000 shares of stock outstanding, and its current stock price is $50. It also has debt in the amount of $10 million (market value). You do some research, and find that its equity cost of capital is 20% and its debt cost of capital is 8%. The company currently projects free cash flows of $1.65 million next year, and expects them to grow at a rate of 1% thereafter. Assume that there are no corporate taxes. What is the value of Trek Technologies?

Solution. We are given Trek Tech's free cash flows, to value the company we need to discount them. To begin, we need to calculate the company's cost of capital. Since there are no taxes, we can use WACC Equation 9.10 (or Equation 9.11 with $\tau = 0$).

To do so, first note that we need to calculate E/V and D/V. The value of equity is the number of shares outstanding multiplied by the price per share: $E = 100{,}000 \times \$50 = \$5$ million. The value of debt is given as $D = \$10$ million. Because $V = D + E$:

$$\begin{aligned} r_A &= \text{WACC} = \left[\frac{E}{V} \times r_E\right] + \left[\frac{D}{V} \times r_D\right] \\ &= \left[\frac{5}{5+10} \times 0.20\right] + \left[\frac{10}{5+10} \times 0.08\right] \\ &= 0.12. \end{aligned}$$

The company projects FCFs of $1.65 million starting next year, expected to grow 1% thereafter. We can therefore apply the growing perpetuity formula (Equation 9.9) to value the company with $FCF_1 = 1.65$ and $g = 0.01$:

$$V = \frac{FCF_1}{r_A - g} = \frac{1.65}{0.12 - 0.01} = 15.$$

Trek Technologies is therefore worth $15 million.

9.3.4 Sensitivity Analysis and Valuation Adjustments

As the previous sections illustrated, the various inputs into our calculations can have a large impact on our final numbers. Many of the inputs—such as the terminal growth rate and estimates of future cash flows over the next few years—require assumptions regarding the company's future state. To derive other inputs—such as the cost of capital—the analyst must choose an appropriate valuation model. In many cases there may be multiple choices for each of these inputs that are reasonable, so it is important to consider how our answers may differ when we alter our input choices. This process is known as sensitivity analysis (also known as scenario analysis). If our final calculated answers (and the decisions based on them) result in changes that are critical or sizable when we change our inputs, then we should take a step back and carefully consider which input choices are correct. In contrast, if we arrive at the same decision despite changing inputs, then we can have more confidence in our decisions about what model to use and what inputs to put into the model.

Spreadsheets are often a handy way of undertaking sensitivity analyses, because they allow for easily changing or holding constant certain inputs to examine how answers change and how these changes affect decision making. Box 9.1 describes using the companion Excel app to do sensitivity analyses.

Box 9.2 Excel in Practice: Sensitivity Analysis

The Excel app for this chapter provides a calculator that allows you to calculate a company's value given different inputs for the cash flows, cost of capital, and terminal growth rate.

In the app, you can input the free cash flows (FCFs) for years 1–5 for a company, the company's cost of capital, and the terminal growth rate. To illustrate, suppose that we have the following FCFs:

Year	1	2	3	4	5
Free cash flows	1,000	1,100	1,200	1,300	1,400

> Suppose we set the company's cost of capital to 10%. Starting with a terminal growth rate of 1%, we can see how much the company's value changes when we increase the growth rate by increments of 0.5%:
>
> | Terminal growth rate g | Company value |
> | --- | --- |
> | 1.0% | $14,232 |
> | 1.5% | $14,857 |
> | 2.0% | $15,560 |
> | 2.5% | $16,357 |
> | 3.0% | $17,268 |
>
> Now suppose we keep the company's terminal growth rate at 2.0%, and vary the company's cost of capital:
>
> | Cost of capital | Company value |
> | --- | --- |
> | 9.0% | $17,859 |
> | 9.5% | $16,633 |
> | 10.0% | $15,560 |
> | 10.5% | $14,615 |
> | 11.0% | $13,774 |
>
> We can see in this case that changes in both the terminal growth rate and the cost of capital affect company value in similar ways. You can choose different numbers for each of these (as well as different projected FCFs for the first five years) to see how these change company value. In some cases, either the terminal growth rate or the cost of capital may matter relatively more in terms of how they affect company value.

Finally, it should be noted that there may be additional adjustments to the DCF methodology described above when applied in practice. For example, a firm may have existing assets (such as buildings) or cash reserves that are not factored into future free cash flows that the company will generate. In such cases, these assets may need to be added to the DCF total value when calculated as described. Furthermore, there are other special circumstances that can change the valuation of a firm, such as control premiums when valuing a company that is an acquisition target (i.e., the firm is more valuable when run by one person compared to another). Similarly, if a firm cannot easily be sold to another party, there may be a discount based on lack of marketability. We discuss some of these issues in further detail in Chapter 15.

9.4 Calculating Equity Value

The previous section discussed how to use DCF analysis to estimate a company's total value. In some cases, we are specifically interested in calculating the *equity* value of the company. For example, you may be interested in investing in the stock of a company that is going public for the first time (i.e., selling its stock to investors for the first time), and want to see if the price being offered by the underwriter is reasonable. There are a variety of different approaches based on the DCF valuation method that allow us to estimate equity value.

9.4.1 Equity Value Using the Dividend Discount Model

A first way to calculate equity value is through the dividend discount model that we introduced in Chapter 4. This model rests on the idea that equity holders receive cash flows, in the form of dividend payments, from holding shares of stock. Often, companies announce that they will make such payments regularly. The dividend discount model uses DCF analysis to discount these payments to arrive at the value of a stock based on the premise that the value of a share of stock P equal the discounted present value of all future dividends the stock provides:

$$P = \frac{Div_1}{1+r_E} + \frac{Div_2}{(1+r_E)^2} + \frac{Div_3}{(1+r_E)^3} + \cdots. \tag{9.12}$$

In Equation 9.12, Div_t is the expected dividend payment the stock will provide at date t. The appropriate discount rate to use is the cost of equity capital r_E. Note that Equation 9.12 provides an estimate of the value P of *one* share of stock. To arrive at an estimate of the total equity value of a company, we multiply P by the total number of shares of stock outstanding.

To illustrate, suppose a company announces that it will pay stockholders a cash dividend payment of $5 per share of stock every year starting next year, and the discount rate r_E is 5%. The company has 50,000 total shares outstanding. The cash flow stream would be a perpetuity, and thus the present value of the stock would be calculated using Equation 2.17, the perpetuity formula from Chapter 2:

$$PV = \frac{CF}{r} \tag{9.13}$$

$$PV = \frac{dividend}{r}$$

$$= \frac{\$5}{0.05}$$

$$= \$100.$$

This gives us an estimated stock price of $100. Because there are 50,000 total shares outstanding, the total equity value of the company is $100 × 50,000 = $5 million.

A difficulty with the dividend discount model is that it may be difficult to implement because the dividends a company may pay are not known with certainty in advance. In this case, we may be better off using another model to estimate a company's equity value. This again reinforces **Principle 4:** *Every model is an incomplete, simplified description of a complex reality.*

In the next sections, we look at a few of the most common models used to determine a company's equity value.

9.4.2 Equity Value Using the DCF Method

Another method for calculating equity value is to calculate total company value as described in Section 9.3, and subtract the value of the company's debt. Put differently, once an estimate of V has been arrived at using the DCF method, we can rearrange Equation 9.1 to estimate equity value:

$$E = V - D. \tag{9.14}$$

The logic behind this equation is that total value is the combined value of debt and equity. If we subtract the portion of the company's value that is promised to debt holders, then the remainder is the value that accrues to equity holders.

To illustrate, suppose that GCP has debt valued at $100 million. At a cost of capital of 9.6%, we previously estimated GCP's total value to be $316.177 million. Using Equation 9.14, the value of GCP's equity is therefore:

$$\begin{aligned} E &= V - D \\ &= \$316.177 - \$100 \\ &= \$216.177 \text{ million.} \end{aligned}$$

9.4.3 Equity Value Using the Flows to Equity Model

A second model for calculating equity value that is based on the DCF method is the flows to equity (FTE) or free cash flow to equity (FCFE) model. This model involves discounting the portion of a company's cash flows that flow to equity holders, keeping in mind that equity holders are the residual claimants after the company has paid off its other obligations. This contrasts with the DCF method, where we calculated the total cash flows that the company produced (which go to either the debt holders or the equity holders).

To calculate the equity value using the FTE method, we proceed in two steps. First, we estimate the company's projected future free cash flows to equity (FCFE), which are the cash flows that accrue specifically to equity holders. To estimate these, we can take the overall free cash flows (FCFs) of the company, and adjust them to determine what goes to equity holders. The formula for FCFE at date t is:

$$\begin{aligned} FCFE_t &= FCF_t - \text{interest}_t + \text{tax shield}_t + \Delta \text{debt}_t \\ &= FCF_t - \left[\text{Interest}_t \times (1 - \tau) \right] + (D_t - D_{t-1}). \end{aligned} \quad (9.15)$$

In Equation 9.15, FCF_t is the free cash flow of the company at date t, which can be calculated from Equation 9.4. We then subtract interest payments that the company must make to the debt holders. As previously noted, interest payments the company makes are tax-deductible, which we refer to as the debt tax shield. We add the value of the tax shield because these tax savings create value for equity holders. Finally, we add in proceeds that a firm gets from issuing debt, proceeds from which equity holders gain value.

Once we have estimated the future FCFE for the company, we take the present value of those future cash flows by discounting them. Because we are valuing equity, the appropriate discount rate is the cost of equity capital, r_E, which reflects the risk of equity.

We calculate equity value with the FTE model using the perpetuity formulas to calculate a continuation value (also known as an *equity terminal value* or *exit price*) at future period as we did when we used the DCF model to calculate a company's total value.

$$\begin{aligned} E &= \frac{FCFE_1}{1 + r_E} + \frac{FCFE_2}{(1 + r_E)^2} + \frac{FCFE_3}{(1 + r_E)^3} + \frac{FCFE_4}{(1 + r_E)^4} + \frac{FCFE_5}{(1 + r_E)^5} + \ldots \\ &= \frac{FCFE_1}{1 + r_E} + \frac{FCFE_2}{(1 + r_E)^2} + \frac{FCFE_3}{(1 + r_E)^3} + \ldots + \ldots + \frac{FCFE_T}{(1 + r_E)^T} + \frac{\text{continuation value}_T}{(1 + r_E)^T}. \end{aligned} \quad (9.16)$$

Example 9.4 (Setting Up a Subsidiary): Suppose that your company is considering setting up a subsidiary firm. The firm will generate the free cash flows and plans to hold the debt indicated in the schedule below. The company will also pay interest on the previous year's debt amount at a rate of 6%.

9.4 CALCULATING EQUITY VALUE

	Year 0	Year 1	Year 2	Year 3
Free cash flows	–	$200	$300	$300
Debt	$100	50	0	0
Interest (at 6% rate)	0	6	3	0

The tax rate is 30% and the equity cost of capital is 15% in each year. After year 3, the FCFs of the company will stay constant at $300 each year while debt (and thus interest payments) stay at 0. Using the flows to equity (FTE) model (Equation 9.16), calculate the equity value of the company.

Solution. Our first step is to calculate the free cash flows to equity holders (FCFE) in each year using Equation 9.15. Starting with year 3:

$$\begin{aligned} FCFE_{t=3} &= FCF_3 - \text{interest}_3 \times (1-\tau) + (D_3 - D_2) \\ &= \$300 - \$0 \times (1-0.30) + \$0 \\ &= \$300. \end{aligned}$$

Note that we need to calculate the FCFE for year 3 because the amount of debt in the previous year changes versus the year before that. Year 3's FCF is the same as year 2's ($300) and it remains at that level from year 3 into the future.

To arrive at our estimate for the equity value, we must calculate the free cash flows to equity for years 1 and 2:

$$\begin{aligned} FCFE_{t=2} &= FCF_2 - \text{interest}_2 \times (1-\tau) + (D_2 - D_1) \\ &= \$300 - [\$3 \times (1-0.30)] + (\$0 - \$50) \\ &= \$247.90, \end{aligned}$$

$$\begin{aligned} FCFE_{t=1} &= FCF_1 - \text{interest}_1 \times (1-\tau) + (D_1 - D_0) \\ &= \$200 - [\$6 \times (1-0.30)] + (\$50 - \$100) \\ &= \$145.80. \end{aligned}$$

Setting up our final valuation Equation 9.16 (with the cash flows after year 2 making up a perpetuity) using a discount rate of $r_E = 0.15$ gives us:

$$\begin{aligned} E &= \frac{FCFE_1}{1+r_E} + \frac{FCFE_2}{(1+r_E)^2} + \frac{FCFE_3}{(1+r_E)^3} + \frac{FCFE_4}{(1+r_E)^4} + \frac{FCFE_5}{(1+r_E)^5} \cdots \\ &= \frac{FCFE_1}{1+r_E} + \frac{FCFE_2}{(1+r_E)^2} + \left(\frac{FCFE_3}{r_E}\right) \times \frac{1}{(1+r_E)^2} \\ &= \frac{\$145.80}{1.15} + \frac{\$247.90}{1.15^2} + \left(\frac{\$300}{0.15}\right) \times \frac{1}{1.15^2} \\ &= \$1,826.518. \end{aligned}$$

Using the flows to equity (FTE) model, we find that the company's equity value E is $1,826.518.

Conclusion

In this chapter, we have covered ways to estimate the overall economic value of a company, known as its total company value (also total value or enterprise value). Estimating the total value of a company requires the use of a valuation model, and the appropriateness of a specific valuation model depends on the situation at hand. We examined the details of calculating total company value via valuation using comparables, which involved using information from similar companies to form estimates, and also discounted cash flow (DCF) analysis, which involved calculating estimated future free cash flows that a company may generate and discounting them back to the present. We also explored methods of determining specifically the equity value of a company.

The methods in this chapter use the concepts we have explored previously to further analyze companies, and this in turn forms the basis for models that help us determine total company value. In subsequent chapters, we will expand upon these models to explore how choices made by a company's managers—such as choosing to finance the company using either debt or equity—can increase or decrease company value. The methods we covered in this chapter will allow us to be able to evaluate these choices and whether they are beneficial for a company.

Takeaways

- A company's total value is the total value of its assets. This is the same as the combined value of the company's debt and the company's equity.
- A valuation model is required to estimate company value. Valuation models include using comparables and discounting the firm's cash flows (discounted cash flow [DCF] model).
- The DCF model involves projecting a company's free cash flows and discounting them by the company's overall cost of capital, known as the weighted-average cost of capital (WACC), which incorporates the required rates of return of the company's equity and the company's debt.
- A company's equity value can be estimated using the dividend discount model, DCF model, or flows to equity (FTE) model.

Key Terms

After-tax WACC   275
Capital structure   262
Continuation value   280
Cost of capital   265
Debt tax shield   275
Dividend discount model   279
Enterprise value to EBITDA ratio (EV/EBITDA)   263
Flows to equity (FTE) model   281
Free cash flows (FCF)   265

Free cash flows to equity (FCFE) model   280
Long-run growth rate   270
Price-to-earnings (P/E) ratio   263
Terminal growth rate   270
Terminal value   269
Total company value   261
Total value   261
Valuation by comparables   263
Weighted-average cost of capital (WACC)   275

Key Equations

Total company value, debt and equity	$V = D + E$	Eq. 9.1
Total value, valuation by comparables	$V = \text{EBITDA} \times \left(\dfrac{\text{EV}}{\text{EBITDA}}\right)_{comparable}$	Eq. 9.2
Stock price, valuation by comparables	$\text{Stock price} = EPS \times \left(\dfrac{P}{E}\right)_{comparable}$	Eq. 9.3
Free cash flow	$\text{FCF} = \text{EBIT} \times (1-\tau) + \text{depreciation} - \text{CapEx} - \Delta \text{NWC}$	Eq. 9.5
Total company value using DCF	$\begin{aligned} V &= \dfrac{FCF_1}{1+r_A} + \dfrac{FCF_2}{(1+r_A)^2} + \dfrac{FCF_3}{(1+r_A)^3} + \dfrac{FCF_4}{(1+r_A)^4} + \dfrac{FCF_5}{(1+r_A)^5} \cdots \\ &= \dfrac{FCF_1}{1+r_A} + \dfrac{FCF_2}{(1+r_A)^2} + \dfrac{FCF_3}{(1+r_A)^3} + \cdots + \dfrac{FCF_T}{(1+r_A)^T} + \dfrac{TV_T}{(1+r_A)^T} \end{aligned}$	Eq. 9.7
Terminal value (no growth)	$TV_T = \dfrac{FCF_{T+1}}{r_A}$	Eq. 9.8
Terminal value (growth)	$TV_T = \dfrac{FCF_{T+1}}{r_A - g}$	Eq. 9.9
Weighted-average cost of capital (WACC)	$r_A = \text{WACC} = \left[\dfrac{E}{V} \times r_E\right] + \left[\dfrac{D}{V} \times r_D\right]$	Eq. 9.10
After-tax weighted-average cost of capital	$\text{After-tax WACC } r_A^{\text{after-tax}} = \left[\dfrac{E}{V} \times r_E\right] + \left[\dfrac{D}{V} \times r_D \times (1-\tau)\right]$	Eq. 9.11
Stock price, dividend discount model	$P = \dfrac{Div_1}{1+r_E} + \dfrac{Div_2}{(1+r_E)^2} + \dfrac{Div_3}{(1+r_E)^3} + \cdots$	Eq. 9.12
Equity value	$E = V - D$	Eq. 9.14
Free cash flows to equity	$\begin{aligned} FCFE_t &= FCF_t - \text{interest}_t + \text{tax shield}_t + \Delta \text{debt}_t \\ &= FCF_t - \left[\text{interest}_t \times (1-\tau)\right] + (D_t - D_{t-1}) \end{aligned}$	Eq. 9.15
Equity value, flows to equity/free cash flow to equity	$\begin{aligned} E &= \dfrac{FCFE_1}{1+r_E} + \dfrac{FCFE_2}{(1+r_E)^2} + \dfrac{FCFE_3}{(1+r_E)^3} + \dfrac{FCFE_4}{(1+r_E)^4} + \dfrac{FCFE_5}{(1+r_E)^5} + \cdots \\ &= \dfrac{FCFE_1}{1+r_E} + \dfrac{FCFE_2}{(1+r_E)^2} + \dfrac{FCFE_3}{(1+r_E)^3} + \cdots + \dfrac{FCFE_T}{(1+r_E)^T} + \dfrac{\text{continuation value}_T}{(1+r_E)^T} \end{aligned}$	Eq. 9.16

Problems

1. Suppose you want to value the Stop Thief Alarm Company (STAC), which sells security systems. You see that the stock price of a comparable firm is 15 times its earnings per share. If STAC has earnings per share of $3.00, what is an estimate of its stock price? If STAC's actual stock price is very different from that forecast, why might that be the case?

2. Using a finance website such as Yahoo! Finance, estimate the total company value of a target publicly traded company using comparables by: (a) identifying a comparable company, (b) finding that comparable company's EV/EBITDA ratio, and (c) multiplying the target company's EBITDA by the comparable company's ratio. Find the actual total value of the target company. How close was your estimate? How similar was the comparable company to your target company, and how did that affect your estimate?

3. Suppose you want to value Nice Ice, a company that makes cake decorating supplies. You see that similar manufacturers have an enterprise value to EBITDA multiple of 30.00. Nice Ice's current EBITDA is $3 million. What is an estimate of its total value?

4. Consider a company with the following free cash flows (FCFs) for each year:

Year	1	2	3
Free cash flows	$500	$900	$1,200

    In year 4, the company expects its FCF to stay at its year 3 level. The company's overall cost of capital is 8%.
    (a) Calculate the company's terminal value as of year 3.
    (b) What is the total value of the company now (year 0)?

5. Consider a company with the following free cash flows for each year:

Year	1	2	3
Free cash flows	$100	$200	$300

    In year 4, the company expects its free cash flow to stay at $300. However, after that it expects the free cash flows to grow by 1% per year. The company's overall cost of capital is 8%.
    (a) Calculate the company's terminal value as of year 3.
    (b) What is the total value of the company now (year 0)?

6. Consider a firm with zero net working capital (NWC) right now ($t = 0$). The firm has the following projected accounting information for next year ($t = 1$):
    - The firm's EBIT is expected to be $10 million.
    - Depreciation and capital expenditures are each expected to be $1 million.
    - The firm expects zero NWC.

    The firm expects its free cash flows after $t = 1$ to stay the same as its $t = 1$ free cash flow. The firm has a 0% tax rate, an equity cost of capital of 15%, and a debt cost of capital of 3%. It has a leverage ratio (D/V) of 50%. What is the firm's total value?

7. Suppose that a company has the following free cash flows projected for the next few years (right now it is $t = 0$):

Year	1	2	3	4
Free cash flows	$100	$200	$400	$500

The company's cost of capital is 10%.
(a) If the terminal value of the company in year 4 is $4,000, what is its total value?
(b) Suppose instead that you are told the company projects free cash flows of $500 in year 5, which grows at a rate of 1% forever thereafter. What is the terminal value of the company as of year 4? What is its total value?
(c) Instead of the information in parts (a) and (b), you are only told that similar companies that have sold have had an enterprise value multiple, EV/EBITDA, of 18.00. The company's EBITDA in year 4 is $200. Using this multiple, estimate the company's terminal value in year 4. What is its total value now?

8. The Voilà Tile Company (VTC) has the accounting information projected for the next 3 years in Table 9.5.

Table 9.5

	Year 0	Year 1	Year 2	Year 3
EBITDA	–	100.0	800.0	400.0
CapEx	–	20.0	20.0	20.0
Net working capital	10.0	15.0	10.0	5.0

VTC expects its free cash flows to stay at their year 3 level after year 3. It has a cost of capital of 4.3%. What is VTC worth (i.e., what is its total value)?

9. You are the CEO of a major conglomerate in 2023, and are thinking of acquiring Reboot Tech Inc. (RTI). You are wondering what price would be appropriate to offer. You look at RTI's financial statements, and see that it expects the accounting numbers for the next four years (in thousands of dollars) as shown in Table 9.6.

Table 9.6

	2024	2025	2026	2027
EBIT	5,000	7,000	8,000	9,000
Capital expenditures	3,000	3,500	4,000	5,000
Depreciation	100	300	400	600
Accounts receivable	600	800	1,000	1,000
Accounts payable	400	900	1,000	1,000

(a) The current corporate tax rate is 35%. RTI's overall cost of capital is 9.4%. RTI says that it will be able to sustain its cash flows at the 2027 level indefinitely after 2027. Net working capital in 2023 is 0.
(b) What are RTI's free cash flows from 2024 to 2027?
(c) What is RTI's terminal value as of 2027? What is the present value of this terminal value?
(d) What is RTI's total company value in 2023?

10. Suppose company ABC's equity cost of capital is 13.4%, the firm's pre-tax cost of debt is 7%, and the tax rate is 40%. ABC's leverage ratio is 0.5. What is ABC's total value if its EBIT is $100 per year perpetually, its investment in PP&E (property, plant, and equipment) is equal to its annual depreciation every year, and its NWC (net working capital) is constant through time?

11. Suppose instead that ABC's equity cost of capital is 9.6%. Its pre-tax cost of debt is 5%, and the tax rate is 40%. ABC's leverage ratio in market value terms at present is 0.6. What is the market value of ABC's equity if its EBIT next year is $1,000 and it is expected to grow perpetually after that at 2% per year? Assume that NWC remains constant over time, and that capital expenditures and depreciation are zero each year.

12. Spray-On Grass Company (SOG) has the free cash flows for each year shown in Table 9.7.

    Table 9.7

	Year 1	Year 2	Year 3
EBIT	100	200	300
Depreciation	10	10	10
Capital expenditures	30	40	50
Net working capital	−10	10	0

    Assume that net working capital (NWC) in year 0 equals 0. After year 3, SOG will grow its free cash flows by 1% per year. Its overall cost of capital is 7%. Assume a tax rate of 30%.
    (a) Calculate SOG's free cash flows in years 1, 2, and 3.
    (b) Calculate its terminal value as of year 3.
    (c) What is SOG's total company value now (year 0)?

13. Suppose that we are now in year 0. You are interested in valuing Gilgen, a biotech company. Gilgen currently has the accounting quantities for year 0 and for the next 2 years (in millions of dollars) shown in Table 9.8.

    Table 9.8

	Year 0	Year 1	Year 2
EBIT	0	0	5,000
Depreciation	0	300	200
Capital expenditures	0	100	0
Net working capital	0	−100	0

    Year 2 is when Gilgen expects to launch its blockbuster drug, Icuritall. After year 2, Gilgen projects that the drug will be able to generate free cash flows that will increase at a rate of 2% per year from its year 2 numbers. Gilgen faces a corporate tax rate of 20%. Gilgen has stated that it will maintain a constant percentage of debt in its capital structure equal to 20%. In other words, its $D/V = 0.20$ in each year. Gilgen has an equity cost of capital of 20% and a debt cost of capital of 6%.
    (a) What are Gilgen's free cash flows in years 1 and 2?
    (b) What is Gilgen's weighted-average cost of capital (WACC)?
    (c) Determine Gilgen's total company value.

14. Consider the company Terminal Inc., which has the following free cash flows projected for the next few years (right now it is $t = 0$):

Year	1	2	3	4
Free cash flows	100	200	400	500

    After year 4, the FCFs remain constant at 500. The company's cost of capital is 10%.
    (a) Calculate Terminal Inc.'s terminal value as of year 5.
    (b) Calculate Terminal Inc.'s terminal value as of year 4.
    (c) Calculate Terminal Inc.'s terminal value as of year 3.
    (d) Compare your answers to parts (a) through (c), and explain why they are the same or different.
    (e) Calculate Terminal Inc.'s total company value.

15. Consider company Planes R Us (PRU), which has the following free cash flows projected for the next few years (right now it is $t = 0$):

Year	1	2	3	4
Free cash flows	200	300	400	500

    After year 4, the FCFs will increase at a rate of 1%. The company's cost of capital is 10%.
    (a) Calculate PRU's terminal value as of year 4.
    (b) Calculate PRU's terminal value as of year 3.
    (c) Calculate PRU's terminal value as of year 5.
    (d) Calculate the total company value of PRU.

10 CAPITAL BUDGETING

CHAPTER OVERVIEW

10.1 Choosing between Investment Projects: Capital Budgeting — 289
10.2 The Net Present Value Investment Rule — 292
10.3 Other Project Decision Criteria: IRR and Payback — 298
10.4 Inflation and Capital Budgeting — 305

> ### LEARNING OBJECTIVES
>
> After reading this chapter, you will be able to:
> - evaluate a company's investment project, and determine its financial value;
> - identify the advantages and disadvantages of commonly used decision rules for choosing between investment projects;
> - explain the net present value method for evaluating investment projects and compare it to alternative methods;
> - describe how to compare projects and choose the project that will maximize company value.

EQUATIONS YOU KNOW

Net present value	$NPV = PV(\text{cash inflows}) - PV(\text{cash outflows})$	Eq. 2.12
Present value of a perpetuity	$PV = \dfrac{\$CF}{r}$	Eq. 2.17
Free cash flow	$FCF = EBIT \times (1-\tau) + \text{depreciation} - CapEx - \Delta NWC$	Eq. 9.5

✚ You are a manager in a company, and members of your team propose three different new products that the company could develop. You can only develop one new product. How do you choose which one to pursue?

✚ You are tasked with coming up with a new app for the software company you work for, and you need to convince your bosses that spending money and time on it is a good investment for the company. How can you make and present your case?

- You are thinking of investing some money in the stock of a company, and the company's CEO enthusiastically announces a new product line that will significantly increase the company's value. How can you evaluate the validity of this claim?
- You work at a consumer electronics company, and have come up with the plans for a revolutionary new touchscreen tablet. However, it will be about five years before the project is profitable. Your boss is not enthusiastic about the idea, saying that it will take too long to make money. How can you show that the project does have value?

Introduction

In the previous chapter we examined how to value entire companies. To do so, we took the perspective of someone—such as an investor—looking at the company from the outside and determining its value based on how it currently operates.

In this chapter, we shift to the perspective of someone *within* the company, and shift our unit of analysis from the firm as a whole to the investment projects within a firm. Company value and project choice are tightly connected because managers try to choose projects that will *increase* the company's value. In this chapter, we examine how to evaluate a firm's investment projects and look at how managers can choose projects that increase company value the most.

10.1 Choosing between Investment Projects: Capital Budgeting

Companies need to use their resources—such as materials, labor, and capital—to survive, compete, and grow. These resources are used to accomplish two basic goals: the funding of the company's daily operations (operating expenses such as salaries, rent, and utilities), and the funding of long-term capital investments that will increase the company's value. An operating budget typically refers to expenditures for the short-term day-to-day regular operations of the company. In contrast, a capital budget typically refers to expenditures for new investments with a focus on the longer-term growth of a company. Examples of capital investments include launching a new product, building or purchasing new research laboratories, factories, warehouses, showrooms, or machinery, launching a marketing campaign, and training to improve employee skills or knowledge. Capital budgeting is the process of analyzing capital investment decisions. Although the details vary from firm to firm, any capital budgeting process consists of four steps:

(1) coming up with proposals for investment projects;
(2) evaluating the projects;
(3) deciding which projects to accept; and
(4) choosing how to finance the project(s).

In this chapter we focus on the first three steps. We touch on Step 4, but because the decision about how to finance a project is a part of a firm's capital structure decision, we discuss Step 4 in detail in Chapter 11.

The basic unit of analysis in the capital budgeting process is an individual investment project. Investment projects start with an idea for increasing company value by producing a new product, improving the way an existing product is produced, or adding to the scale of production. Investment projects are analyzed as a sequence of decisions and possible events over time. After a potential investment project is proposed, a company assesses the costs and benefits of implementing it, and devises an optimal strategy for implementing the project over time.

In general, we will analyze investment projects by looking at the financial value they add to the firm; a value we determine by projecting the cash flows they will create, and determining the value of those cash flows using different evaluation methods.

10.1.1 Where Do Investment Ideas Come From?

Most investment projects requiring capital expenditures fall into three categories: new products, cost reduction, and replacement of existing assets. Here are some examples:

- Should the firm start a new product line that requires investment in plant, equipment, and inventories?
- Should the firm invest in automated equipment that will allow it to reduce its labor costs?
- Should the firm replace an existing plant to expand capacity or lower operating costs?

Ideas for investment projects can come from external sources, such as customers or competitors, or from internal sources, such as current employees. For example, surveys of customers, both formal and informal, can suggest new demands that can be met by producing new products and services or by improving existing ones: A computer manufacturer may discover that providing a repair service for its computers is a profitable new line of business.

Market competitors are another source of project ideas. For example, if a company knows that a competitor is working on a new upgrade to its competing product, the company may want to upgrade its own product. Or it may want to consider acquiring the competitor—and the upgraded product. Acquisitions can be a way to expand capacity and/or add a new product line, and thus are capital budgeting projects. Box 10.1 discusses some prominent examples of this.

Internally, many firms establish a research and development (R&D) department to identify potential new products that are technologically feasible to produce and that seem to satisfy a perceived customer demand. In the pharmaceutical industry, for example, R&D activity is the source of virtually all new product ideas.

Ideas for product improvement or cost reduction often come from the production divisions of corporations. For example, engineers, production managers, or other employees who are in close contact with the production process may spot ways to cut costs by reorganizing an assembly line or by replacing labor-intensive operations with automated equipment requiring a capital outlay.

In corporations with incentive systems that encourage managers and other employees to think about opportunities for profitable growth and operating improvements, there is generally a regular flow of proposals for investment projects. The rest of this chapter discusses techniques for evaluating projects and deciding which ones are likely to enhance shareholder value.

Box 10.1 World of Business: Microsoft's Expanding Empire Using Acquisitions

Tech giant Microsoft has used acquisitions to expand its footprint in various arenas in the technology space over the past decades, and to compete against companies such as Google. Microsoft now owns names in many fields, ranging from social media to gaming. Among its major acquisitions, in 2022 Microsoft announced its intent to acquire Activision Blizzard, a major video game publisher, which it completed in 2023 for $69 billion. This followed on the heels of its acquisition of Mojang (the developer of hit game Minecraft) in 2014 for $2.5 billion, on top of acquisitions of other game developers such as Bungie. In 2016, Microsoft bought the business networking social media platform LinkedIn for $26.2 billion. In 2011, Microsoft purchased video-chat company Skype for $8.5 billion. Microsoft purchased online storage and developer platform company GitHub in

2018 for $7.5 billion, giving it another entry point into software development.

Microsoft has used acquisitions to expand investments in key areas, in addition to its internal capital investments in software. In many cases, Microsoft has used acquisitions to catch up to rivals. For example, it purchased advertising firm aQuantive in 2007 for $6.3 billion only one month after Google had purchased DoubleClick, another major advertising technology firm. Microsoft has continued to push forward in the area, purchasing advertising technology firm Xandr in 2022.

Firms can also acquire individual project ideas from other firms. For example, in the drug development sector, Krieger et al.'s (2022) research has shown that pharmaceutical firms often purchase drug projects (which can include patents, property rights, and/or research teams) from other companies when the need arises to work on a new project, as opposed to developing new projects in-house.

Sources: De Vynck, G. (2022). LinkedIn, Candy Crush and Minecraft: Microsoft's empire goes far beyond Windows and Word. *The Washington Post*, 18 Jan. Krieger, J. L., Li, X., and Thakor, R. T. (2022). Find and replace: R&D investment following the erosion of existing products. *Management Science* 68(9): 6552–6571.

QUICK CHECK 10.1 Where do you think new project ideas come from in the movie business?

10.1.2 Evaluating Projects

We analyze investment projects by determining the financial value they will add to the firm. We determine this potential added value by projecting the cash flows they create, and determining the value of those cash flows. To illustrate the process of investment project analysis, suppose you are a film industry executive whose job is to come up with proposals for new movies and to analyze their potential value to your company's shareholders. Typically, producing a movie for the mass market involves major outlays of cash over several years before there are any cash inflows from customers who pay to see it. Roughly speaking, the movie will increase company value only if the present value of the expected future cash inflows exceeds the present value of the outlays.

Forecasting the likely cash outlays and inflows from a movie is a complicated task. The cash flows will depend on a sequence of decisions and actions that are under your control and on a sequence of events that are not under your control. At each stage in the project's life, from conceiving the idea for the movie to the distribution of the final product to movie theaters and streaming services, unpredictable events will occur that affect the cash flows. At each stage, you will have to decide whether to continue the project, discontinue it, delay it, or accelerate it. You will also have to decide whether to reduce the level of spending (e.g., by eliminating some costly scenes) or to increase it (e.g., by launching a television advertising campaign).

Forecasting a project's cash flows and evaluating its likely effect on the company's value are complex and difficult processes because forecasts are, by definition, uncertain. To simplify our discussion of project analysis, we proceed in stages. First, we analyze projects as if the future cash flows can be estimated and their uncertainty accounted for. We can then use a discounted cash flow valuation to find the present value of those cash flows, based on **Principle 1**: *A dollar today is not worth the same as a dollar tomorrow*, as discussed in Chapters 2 and 4. In Chapter 14 we will consider alternative ways to take account of uncertainty and of the value of managerial options.

Finally, we will discuss three common decision criteria that are used to measure value and evaluate projects: net present value (NPV), internal rate of return (IRR), and payback.

10.2 The Net Present Value Investment Rule

In this section we cover the NPV rule, which is an investment rule that utilizes the same concept of present value introduced in Chapter 2, and which is also the most correct way to evaluate projects. We first introduce the idea behind the rule and the calculations, and then discuss details about how to determine the cash flows and discount rate for an investment project.

10.2.1 Calculating Net Present Value

One of the most widely used decision rules is net present value, or NPV (discussed briefly in Chapter 2 and shown in Equation 2.12), which is the difference between the present value of a project's cash inflows (revenues) and the present value of the project's cash outflows (initial investment and costs):

$$NPV = PV(\text{cash inflows}) - PV(\text{cash outflows}). \tag{10.1}$$

Net present value therefore makes use of our familiar discounted cash flow model (as in Equation 2.9) to evaluate investment projects, but also includes any initial cash flows CF_0 that may be immediately needed to launch the project after the investment decision is made, such as any initial investments or costs.

A project that has an NPV greater than zero (the NPV of doing nothing) will result in value being added to the firm. This provides us with the NPV rule, which states that projects with the highest total NPV should be undertaken. Projects with positive NPV add value to the company (and should be advanced); projects with negative NPV take away value (and should be rejected).

While *all* available projects with a positive NPV should be undertaken by a firm, that is not always feasible. In practice, firms face resource constraints and may not have enough available capital to undertake all positive-NPV projects. In such cases, the NPV rule would mean that the company must choose the set of projects that provides the highest NPV that falls within the firm's budget constraints. And some projects may be mutually exclusive—that is, the firm must choose one or the other, but not both (e.g., a utility company can choose to run electricity wires either above or below ground).[1]

The amount and timing of the project's cash flows are estimates and thus present some uncertainty or risk. According to **Principle 6: *Risk is fundamental to financial analysis and must be explicitly considered in all financial decisions.*** In NPV analysis, project risk is accounted for in the project's cost of capital, which is used as the discount rate. As we emphasize throughout this chapter, when information about a project's cash flows and its cost of capital are available, NPV is the *only* correct method for evaluating projects.

To illustrate how to calculate a project's NPV, we present the following example. Generic Jeans Company, a manufacturer of casual clothing, is considering whether to produce a new line of jeans called Protojeans. It requires an initial outlay of $100,000 for new specialized equipment, and the firm's marketing department forecasts that given the nature of consumer preferences for jeans, the product will have an economic life of three years. The cash flow forecasts for the Protojeans project are:

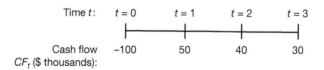

---

[1] A directly related capital budgeting criteria to the NPV rule is the profitability index, which is defined as the present value of a project's future cash inflows divided by the initial investment cost. By providing a ratio, projects can be ranked, which can be helpful in choosing the projects that provide the highest total NPV when one cannot invest in all feasible projects.

A negative sign in front of a cash flow forecast indicates a cash outflow: a cost or an investment of capital. In the case of the Protojeans project, there is only one negative cash flow, and that is at the start of the project (time zero). Subsequent cash flows are all positive: $50,000 at the end of the first year, $40,000 at the end of year 2, and $30,000 at the end of year 3. If the appropriate discount rate for the project is 8%, we can calculate the NPV of the project using Equation 10.1, including the initial investment:

$$NPV = -100 + \frac{50}{1.08} + \frac{40}{1.08^2} + \frac{30}{1.08^3}$$
$$= \$4,404.82.$$

To the nearest penny, the NPV of the Protojeans project is $4,404.82. This means that by going forward with the Protojeans project, management expects to increase the value of the Generic Jeans Company by $4,404.82.

Applying the NPV rule requires discounting cash flows, and thus: (1) forecasting the amount and timing of the project's cash flows, and (2) estimating the appropriate discount rate for the project.

> **QUICK CHECK 10.2** Suppose that the Protojeans project is expected to have a year 3 cash flow of only $10,000 instead of $30,000. If all other cash flows are the same and the discount rate is still 8% per year, what would be its NPV?

10.2.2 Estimating a Project's Cash Flows

Forecasts of the amount and timing of project cash flows can be created from estimates of the incremental revenues and costs associated with the project—that is, from estimates of a project's sales volume, selling price, and costs.

Suppose you are a manager in the personal computer division of AirCleaners Corporation, a firm that manufactures air filtration systems for commercial buildings. You come up with an idea for a new type of air purifier system that uses ultraviolet light to eliminate bacteria and viruses, which you call the UV1000. You must prepare a capital appropriation request that details the amount of capital required and the projected benefits to the corporation from undertaking the project.

Your estimates assume that sales will be 4,000 units per year at a price of $5,000 per unit, yielding sales revenue of $4,000 \times \$5,000 = \$20$ million. Production equipment will have to be purchased at a cost of $2.8 million. The equipment will be depreciated over seven years using the straight-line method. In addition, you estimate a need for $2.2 million for additional working capital—primarily to finance parts inventories—thus bringing the total initial cash outlay required to $2.8 + $2.2 = $5 million. This investment in the project is a negative cash flow that occurs immediately (at year $t = 0$).

Now consider the project's expected cash flows *in the future*. We can use the following formula, derived from the formula for free cash flow introduced in Chapter 9 (Equation 9.5), to calculate the net cash inflows from the project:

$$\text{Cash flow} = \text{revenue} - \text{total expenses} - \text{taxes} + \text{noncash expenses}. \quad (10.2)$$

The intuition behind this formula is as follows. We first calculate the project's profits (revenue minus expenses) and subtract taxes paid to the government from these profits. We then add back noncash expenses—depreciation is a typical example—because these are originally included in total expenses to reduce a company's tax bill, but are not actual cash outflows. It is also important to note that prior costs associated with a project that have already occurred, which are sunk costs, should not be included in the cash flows when evaluating a project.

To apply this to the UV1000 project, we first need to determine how long the project will generate cash flows. The natural planning horizon to use is seven years, the equipment's lifespan. At the end of seven years, the firm would have to decide whether to renew the investment, since the equipment's useful life will be "used up." Suppose that total expenses in each of the next seven years will be $18.5 million, and taxes will be $600,000 per year. The only noncash expense is depreciation. Because the purchase cost of $2.8 million is depreciated using the straight-line method over the seven years, the depreciation will be $2.8 / 7 = $0.4 million or $400,000 each year. Using Equation 10.2, we therefore estimate the cash inflows for each of the next seven years as:

$$
\begin{aligned}
\text{Cash flow} &= \text{revenue} - \text{total expenses} - \text{taxes} + \text{noncash expenses} \\
&= \$20 - \$18.5 - \$0.6 + \$0.4 \\
&= \$1.3 \text{ million.}
\end{aligned}
$$

To complete the cash flow forecast, we need to estimate another cash flow in the final year (year 7) of the planning horizon. The natural assumption to make in this case is that the equipment will have no residual or market value at the end of the seven years, but that the working capital (such as inventories) will still be intact. If the project ends, that $2.2 million of working capital can be reabsorbed back into the company as a positive cash flow. Note that the project will not *necessarily* end, but that another capital budgeting decision (i.e., to refinance it or not) would have to be made at the end of the seven-year horizon. We can summarize these cash flows using the following timeline:

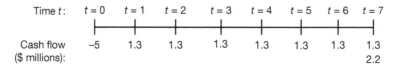

If the discount rate for the project is 15%, the NPV is:

$$
\begin{aligned}
NPV &= -5 + \frac{1.3}{1.15} + \frac{1.3}{1.15^2} + \frac{1.3}{1.15^3} + \frac{1.3}{1.15^4} + \frac{1.3}{1.15^5} + \frac{1.3}{1.15^6} + \frac{1.3 + 2.2}{1.15^7} \\
&= \$1.236 \text{ million.}
\end{aligned}
$$

The project has a positive NPV and will therefore add value to AirCleaners Inc., and so it should undertake the investment.

> **QUICK CHECK 10.3** What would be the NPV of the UV1000 project if the production equipment cost $3 million instead of $2.8 million?

Example 10:1 (NPV of a Project, No Noncash Expenses): The firm you work for is considering a project with expected revenues of $40 million each year for the next three years, expenses of $20 million each year for the next three years, and will incur taxes of $10 million each year for the next three years. There are no noncash expenses. The project requires a $40 million investment right now and the appropriate discount rate for the project is 15%. Is the project worth pursuing?

10.2 THE NET PRESENT VALUE INVESTMENT RULE

Solution. For each year for the next three years ($t = 1$ to $t = 3$), the project will produce the following cash flows (using Equation 10.2):

$$\begin{aligned} \text{Cash flow} &= \text{revenue} - \text{total expenses} - \text{taxes} + \text{noncash expenses} \\ &= \$40 - \$20 - \$10 \\ &= \$10 \text{ million.} \end{aligned}$$

The timeline of cash flows, including the initial investment, is:

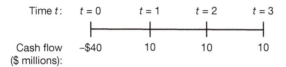

Given that the appropriate discount rate for the project is 15%, we can calculate the NPV of the project using Equation 10.1:

$$\begin{aligned} NPV &= -40 + \frac{10}{1.15} + \frac{10}{1.15^2} + \frac{10}{1.15^3} \\ &= -\$17.168 \text{ million.} \end{aligned}$$

With a negative NPV, the project is therefore *not* worth pursuing. You can also see this from the timeline of cash flows, as the undiscounted value of the future cash flows do not equal the initial investment cost.

Example 10.2 (NPV of a Project with Noncash Expenses): ElecWorld is launching its own in-house tablet line. Given the rapidly changing trends in this industry, the new line is predicted to have a five-year lifespan. Projected sales are forecasted as shown in Table 10.1.

Table 10.1 Project sales for Example 10.2.

Year	Sales ($ thousands)	Total expenses ($ thousands)	Taxes ($ thousands)
1	0	100	0
2	2,000	1,125	800
3	4,000	2,245	1,600
4	6,000	3,290	2,400
5	2,000	1,125	800

The equipment that produces these tablets costs $500,000. It will be purchased immediately, depreciated on a straight-line basis over the next five years, and have no value at the end of its life. The appropriate cost of capital for this project is 18%. What is the NPV of the new tablets?

Solution. We will need to determine the cash flows from the project for each of the years. Sales represent the revenues the project generates. Given that the equipment is depreciated on a straight-line basis and has no salvage value, depreciation is $500,000 / 5 = $100,000. This represents noncash expenses. Therefore, using Equation 10.2, the project's cash flows in each year will be as shown in Table 10.2.

Table 10.2 Project cash flows for Example 10.2 ($ thousands).

	1	2	3	4	5
Revenue	0	2,000	4,000	6,000	2,000
Total expenses	100	1,125	2,245	3,290	1,125
Taxes	0	800	1,600	2,400	800
Depreciation	100	100	100	100	100
Cash flows	0	175	255	410	175

Including the initial investment cost, the timeline of cash flows will be:

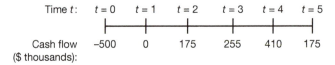

To calculate the NPV, we discount these cash flows at the cost of capital of 18%:

$$NPV = -500 + \frac{0}{1.18} + \frac{175}{1.18^2} + \frac{255}{1.18^3} + \frac{410}{1.18^4} + \frac{175}{1.18^5}$$
$$= \$68,850.70.$$

The project has a positive NPV, and therefore will add value to ElecWorld.

10.2.3 Analyzing Cost-Reducing Projects

Our analysis of the UV1000 project was an example of a decision about whether to launch a new product. Another major category of capital budgeting projects is cost saving.

For example, suppose a firm is considering an investment proposal to automate its production process to save on labor costs. It can invest $2 million now in equipment and thereby save $700,000 per year in pretax labor costs. If the equipment has an expected life of five years and if the firm pays income tax at the rate of 33⅓% and its cost of capital is 10%, is this a worthwhile investment?

To answer, we must compute the incremental cash flows (i.e., the net effect on the company's cash flows) generated by this investment. Table 10.3 shows the cash inflows and outflows associated

Table 10.3 Cash flows with and without investment in labor-saving equipment.

	Without investment (1)	With investment (2)	Difference in cash flow due to investment (3)
Revenue	$5,000,000	$5,000,000	0
Labor costs	1,000,000	300,000	−$700,000
Other cash expenses	2,000,000	2,000,000	0
Depreciation	1,000,000	1,400,000	400,000
Pretax profit	1,000,000	1,300,000	300,000
Income taxes (at 33⅓%)	333,333	433,333	100,000
After-tax profit	666,667	866,667	200,000
Add back depreciation	1,000,000	1,400,000	400,000
Net cash flow (after-tax profit + depreciation)	$1,666,667	$2,266,667	$600,000

10.2 THE NET PRESENT VALUE INVESTMENT RULE

with this project. Column 1 shows the firm's revenues, costs, and cash flow without the investment; column 2 shows them with the investment. Column 3, the difference between columns 1 and 2, is the incremental change in cash flows due to the investment.

There is an initial cash outflow of $2 million to purchase the equipment. Then, as Table 10.3 shows, in each of the five subsequent years there is a cash inflow of $600,000, which is the increased net profit of $200,000 plus the $400,000 in annual depreciation charges (depreciation, although an accounting expense, is not a cash outflow). The cash flow diagram for this project is:

```
Time t:           t = 0   t = 1   t = 2   t = 3   t = 4   t = 5
                    ├───────┼───────┼───────┼───────┼───────┤
Cash flow          -2     0.6     0.6     0.6     0.6     0.6
($ millions):
```

Now consider the impact of the project on the firm's value. The firm must give up $2 million now, but in return it will receive an incremental after-tax cash flow of $600,000 at the end of each of the next five years. If the project's cost of capital is 10%, then the NPV is:

$$NPV = -2 + \frac{0.6}{1.10} + \frac{0.6}{1.10^2} + \frac{0.6}{1.10^3} + \frac{0.6}{1.10^4} + \frac{0.6}{1.10^5}$$
$$= \$274,472.$$

Thus, the labor cost savings are worth $274,472 more than the $2 million cost of acquiring them, and this is the expected increase to the firm's value if the project is undertaken. Given the positive NPV, the project should be accepted.

> **QUICK CHECK 10.4** Suppose that investing in the equipment would reduce labor costs by $650,000 per year instead of $700,000. Would the investment still be worthwhile?

10.2.4 A Project's Cost of Capital

The risk-adjusted discount rate to use in computing a project's NPV is the project's cost of capital, which takes into account the project's expected risk and thus investors' required rate of return. The standard way of dealing with uncertainty about future cash flows is to use a larger discount rate. We develop the ways for making this adjustment and calculating appropriate discount rates to use in Chapters 13 and 18. There are, however, three important points to keep in mind when figuring out a project's cost of capital so that the NPV calculation is accurate:

1. The risk of a particular project may be different from the risk of the firm's existing assets.
2. The cost of capital must be estimated using a model.
3. The risk that is relevant in computing a project's cost of capital is the risk of the project's cash flows and not the risk of the financing instruments (stocks, bonds, etc.) the firm issues to finance the project.

The first point to keep in mind is that the discount rate relevant to a particular project may be different from the rate that is relevant to the value of a firm and its existing assets. For a project typical for the company, that is, similar to its existing operations, and funded by its existing mix of equity and debt, it may be appropriate to use the company's overall discount rate. But if the project is different from what the company usually does or is funded in a very different way, then a different discount rate would be appropriate. Consider a railway company whose average cost of capital for its existing assets is 16% per year. In evaluating a project, should the firm use a 16% discount rate? If the project is to lay a new set of railroad tracks identical to those it already operates and is financed by the firm's mix of capital, then the answer is yes. However, if the tracks or the financing is different in any significant way, then the answer is no. Thus, in general, using the firm's existing average cost of capital to evaluate specific new projects will not be correct.

Sometimes it may be necessary to use a cost of capital that is totally unrelated to the cost of capital of the firm's current operations. For example, if the railway company decided to suddenly undertake a project to develop an airplane, then using a cost of capital faced by firms in the aerospace industry would be more appropriate. We discuss techniques for finding appropriate rates in Chapter 13.

The second point to make about a project's cost of capital is that it must be estimated. The cost of capital represents the rate of return that investors should expect in order to provide money for the project, given its risk, and not for other opportunities. As we will see in Chapter 18, estimating this and assessing the expected risk of the project's cash flows that is relevant for the cost of capital is not always straightforward. In particular, it often requires a model to estimate the returns investors should expect from a project, and different models make assumptions on what types of risk may matter in such a calculation. Because of this, sensitivity analysis (also called scenario analysis), as we discussed in Chapter 9, is important in capital budgeting. Sensitivity analysis involves how robust project decision conclusions are to different assumptions about expected cash flows and discount rates. For example, if assuming a discount rate that is a few percentage points higher or lower does not change a company's decision to invest/not invest in a project, the company can be more confident in its decision.

The final point to keep in mind is that the risk that is relevant in computing a project's cost of capital is the risk of the project's cash flows and not necessarily the risk associated with the financing instruments used to fund the project. For example, suppose that AirCleaners Corporation is planning to finance the $5 million outlay required to undertake the UV1000 project by issuing bonds. Because AirCleaners has almost no debt outstanding, it has a high credit rating and, therefore, can issue $5 million worth of bonds at an interest rate of 6% per year. It would be a mistake to use 6% per year as the cost of capital in computing the NPV of the UV1000 project. As we will see in Chapter 13, the way a project is financed can have an effect on its NPV, but that effect is not measured correctly by discounting the project's expected future cash flows using the cost of the project's financing (in this case, the interest rate on the bonds).

> **QUICK CHECK 10.5** Suppose that the average cost of capital for AirCleaners' existing mix of businesses is 12% per year. Explain why this might not be the right discount rate to use in computing the NPV of the UV1000 project.

10.3 Other Project Decision Criteria: IRR and Payback

In addition to the NPV rule, there are other criteria that companies commonly use to evaluate investment projects. In this section, we describe two such criteria: the internal rate of return and the payback period. Even though companies often use these criteria to evaluate possible projects, the NPV method is the *only* correct project decision method; using other decision criteria can lead to potentially incorrect project decisions.

10.3.1 Internal Rate of Return

The internal rate of return (IRR) of a project is the average rate of return that the project is expected to provide. It can be defined mathematically as the discount rate that results in a project's NPV being zero. Let I_0 be the initial cost of a project and let CF_t be the cash flow of the project in year t. Then the IRR is defined as the discount rate *IRR* that makes the following equation hold:

$$NPV = 0 = -I_0 + \frac{CF_1}{1+IRR} + \frac{CF_2}{(1+IRR)^2} + \cdots + \frac{CF_T}{(1+IRR)^T},$$

$$I_0 = \frac{CF_1}{1+IRR} + \frac{CF_2}{(1+IRR)^2} + \cdots + \frac{CF_T}{(1+IRR)^T}. \tag{10.3}$$

As Equation 10.3 shows, solving for the IRR is usually infeasible to do by hand, and thus a financial calculator or computer program (such as Excel) is needed.

Companies often use the IRR of a project as a decision rule by choosing a project if the IRR is "high enough." In other words, a company may accept a project if its IRR is above some threshold, which is known as the hurdle rate. For multiple projects above that threshold, a company will typically pick the project with the highest IRR. Oftentimes the threshold is greater than or equal to the project's or company's cost of capital.

Companies may use both the IRR and NPV together when making a decision about a project. The IRR can be a useful statistic in making capital budgeting decisions because it summarizes the project's rate of return. However, the IRR has three main disadvantages compared to using the NPV rule.

First, there may be multiple or nonexistent IRRs. The first disadvantage comes from the math needed to calculate the IRR. Mathematically, depending on the pattern of the cash flows of a project, there may be more than one IRR that satisfies Equation 10.3. If that is the case, then these different rates of return are all technically mathematically "correct," but we do not have a way of telling what the "true" IRR of the project is. Furthermore, it may be the case that there is *no* IRR that satisfies Equation 10.3, and thus the IRR cannot be calculated. Such situations commonly occur when there are negative future cash flows forecast for a project.

Second, IRR makes an implicit assumption that cash flows received can be reinvested at the IRR rate, which may lead to incorrect decisions. The second disadvantage is that IRR calculations make a key implicit assumption that any cash flows received over time can be reinvested at the IRR rate. Because it may not be possible for a firm to reinvest payments at a rate as high as the IRR, this assumption can lead to the amount of money at the end of the project being smaller than the IRR would imply. While this is not a problem for projects where there is one cash inflow at the end of the project's life, it is a problem for the many projects that expect multiple cash flows over the project's life.

As an example, consider a project that costs a $100 investment today and promises to pay $100 next year ($t = 1$) and $75 in two years ($t = 2$). The IRR of the project will therefore be (Equation 10.3, and using Excel or the chapter app to calculate):

$$I_0 = \frac{CF_1}{1+IRR} + \frac{CF_2}{(1+IRR)^2} + \frac{CF_3}{(1+IRR)^3} + \cdots$$

$$\$100 = \frac{\$100}{1+IRR} + \frac{\$75}{(1+IRR)^2}$$

$$IRR = 0.50 \text{ or } 50\%.$$

This earns a rate of return of 50% each year. At this rate of return, the future value of the cash inflows as of $t = 2$ (i.e., the amount of money you will have in two years) is $\$100 \times (1 + 50\%) + 75 = 225$. But note that this assumes that the $100 received at $t = 1$ can also be invested at the 50% rate of return. Suppose instead that at time $t = 1$, the product market changes and the firm can only achieve a 10%

rate of return. The future value of the investment will therefore be $100 \times (1 + 20\%) + 75 = 185$. The actual amount of money that the project generates ends up being lower than what the IRR would suggest because the $100 cannot be reinvested at as high a rate.

The third disadvantage of using the IRR to determine a project's desirability is that the IRR provides a project's rate of return, but does not take into account the size or scale of projects. This can cause a company to rank projects incorrectly. For example, if project choices are mutually exclusive, such that the firm can only invest in one of them, the firm should choose the project with the highest NPV because that project will add the most value to the firm, and management should always try to maximize firm value. However, if the firm ranks projects according to their IRR, management may choose the project with a higher IRR but a smaller NPV than other projects, and as a result the firm does not maximize shareholder value.

For example, suppose that you own a parcel of land and have two alternatives for developing it. You can construct an office building on it, requiring an initial outlay of $20 million, or you can make a parking lot out of it, requiring an initial outlay of $10,000. If you build an office building, you estimate that you will be able to sell it in one year for $24 million and your IRR is, therefore (Equation 10.3):

$$I_0 = \frac{CF_1}{1 + IRR} + \frac{CF_2}{(1 + IRR)^2} + \frac{CF_3}{(1 + IRR)^3} + \cdots$$

$$\$20 \text{ million} = \frac{\$24 \text{ million}}{1 + IRR}$$

$$IRR = 0.20 \text{ or } 20\%.$$

If you make it into a parking lot, you estimate that you will have a cash inflow of $10,000 per year forever. This cash flow pattern is a perpetuity, so you would use the perpetuity formula (Equation 2.17) to determine the parking lot's IRR:

$$I_0 = \frac{CF_1}{1 + IRR} + \frac{CF_2}{(1 + IRR)^2} + \frac{CF_3}{(1 + IRR)^3} + \cdots$$

$$\$10,000 = \frac{\$10,000}{1 + IRR} + \frac{\$10,000}{(1 + IRR)^2} + \frac{\$10,000}{(1 + IRR)^3} + \cdots$$

$$\$10,000 = \frac{\$10,000}{IRR}$$

$$IRR = 1 \text{ or } 100\%,$$

Based on IRRs, which project should you choose? The parking lot has the higher IRR, but you would not necessarily want to choose it because at any cost of capital below 20% per year, the NPV of the office building is greater. For example, if the cost of capital is 15%, the NPV of the office building is ($24 million / 1.15) − $20 million = $869,565, whereas the NPV of the parking lot is ($10,000 / 0.15) − $10,000 = $56,667. Therefore, at that cost of capital, the office building project adds more value than the parking lot project.

Figure 10.1 shows the NPV profiles of both projects plotted as a function of the cost of capital. The discount rate used to compute the project's NPV (the project's cost of capital) is measured along the horizontal axis and the NPV is measured along the vertical axis. The figure shows that a discount

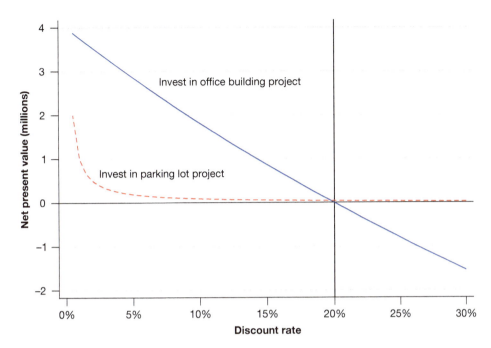

FIGURE 10.1 NPV as a function of the discount rate. This graph provides the NPV of the parking lot and office building projects as a function of the discount rate. At discount rates above 0.2 (20%) per year the parking lot has a positive NPV and should be invested in, while the office building project has a negative NPV and should not be invested in. At rates below 0.2 (20%), both projects have a positive NPV, but the NPV of the office building is higher and should be chosen over the parking lot project.

rate of 20% per year is the critical "switch-over point" for the two mutually exclusive projects. At any discount rate above 20% per year the parking lot has a higher NPV, and at rates below 20% the office building has a higher NPV.

The fact that a project's IRR is independent of its scale makes IRR a poor measure for ranking mutually exclusive projects. In our example, the parking lot has a very high IRR, but its scale is small compared to the office building. If the parking lot were on a larger scale, it might offer a higher NPV than the office building. To illustrate, suppose that the parking lot project requires an initial outlay of $200,000 to build a multistory facility and that the annual net cash flow will then be $200,000 per year forever. The NPV of the parking lot project would then be 20 times greater than before. And if its annual cash flows were large enough, the parking project would have an NPV greater than the building's NPV.

> **QUICK CHECK 10.6** Assuming its initial outlay is equal to its annual cash flow, what would the scale of the parking project have to be to make its NPV equal to the office building's NPV? The cost of capital remains at 15%.

Box 10.2 Excel in Practice: Calculating NPV and IRR

A project has the following cash flows for each year. (The negative cash flow is the initial investment.)

	Year 0	Year 1	Year 2	Year 3
CF	−70	30	30	30

What is the project's NPV, assuming a discount rate of 10%? What is its IRR? If the company decides to accept only projects with an IRR greater than 15% (the hurdle rate), will it accept this project?

Solution. Starting first with NPV, using Equation 10.1, we have:

$$NPV = -70 + \frac{30}{1.10} + \frac{30}{1.10^2} + \frac{30}{1.10^3}$$
$$= 4.606.$$

We can use Excel to calculate this using the =NPV() function. The =NPV(rate, cash flows) function requires you to first specify a discount rate, and then the future cash flows starting in year 1 onwards. Note that the initial cost has to be separately accounted for:

	A	B	C	D	E
1	Year	0	1	2	3
2	Cash-flow	-70	30	30	30
3					
4	=NPV(0.10,C2:E2)+B2				

Now let us solve for the IRR. Using Equation 10.3, IRR solves the following equation:

$$I_0 = \frac{CF_1}{1+IRR} + \frac{CF_2}{(1+IRR)^2} + \frac{CF_3}{(1+IRR)^3},$$

$$70 = \frac{30}{1+IRR} + \frac{30}{(1+IRR)^2} + \frac{30}{(1+IRR)^3}.$$

Let us use Excel to solve this. The simplest way is to use the IRR() function. Type the cash flows in the table into separate cells, and use the function "=IRR()" and refer to those cells:

	A	B	C	D	E
1	Year	0	1	2	3
2	Cash-flow	-70	30	30	30
3					
4	=IRR(B2:E2)				
5					

Excel will give you **IRR = 13.7%**. With a hurdle rate of 15%, the company would not undertake the project.

Note that if the particular project you are looking at has more than one IRR, then Excel will only return one of the IRRs. If you have a situation with multiple IRRs, one way to solve for them is to "guess and check" within Excel—pick different possible IRRs, and see which ones give you a project NPV equal to zero.

10.3.2 Payback Period

Another common decision rule uses a project's payback period to determine whether it should be undertaken. The payback period is the length of time it takes for the future cash flows to earn back the initial investment. The payback decision rule states that a company should choose projects whose payback periods are less than some predefined length of time. Some companies may impose a payback constraint, first filtering out projects that have payback periods that are too long, and then applying decision rules (such as the NPV rule or IRR hurdles) on the remaining projects.

To illustrate how to calculate a payback period, consider again the UV1000 project with the following cash flows:

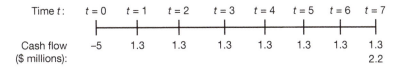

The initial cash outlay is $5 million. For this project, it takes four years with annual cash flows of $1.3 million each, totaling $5.2 million to make back the initial investment of $5 million.

The payback period provides a simple and easy-to-calculate metric for determining how long a project takes to turn a profit based on its initial investment. Companies may feel the need to avoid projects that take too long to do so—for example, a company anticipating funding shortfalls in the future.

However, the payback decision rule has two main disadvantages which can cause a company to reject positive NPV investments that would otherwise add value to the company.

The first disadvantage is that the basic version of the payback period does *not* consider the time value of money—as shown above, we simply add cash flows from different time periods together, treating cash flows at different times as the same. This of course is not correct, and violates **Principle 1:** *A dollar today is not worth the same as a dollar tomorrow.* Indeed, with a high discount rate, cash flows that occur in the far future may be much less valuable, given their present values. Furthermore, the discount rate incorporates the risk of the project in an NPV calculation, including situations such as the potential for funds not being available in the future for the firm. As noted before, this potential lack of future funding is sometimes cited to justify the use of the payback period, but properly adjusting the discount rate in NPV calculations will account for such situations (we cover these calculations in Chapter 13). Because of the disadvantage of not discounting, the discounted payback period is sometimes used instead, which applies the same methodology but discounts the cash flows.

The second disadvantage is that the payback period is primarily concerned with the time it takes to make up the initial investment. A project may provide a large cash flow in the more distant future—making it a positive-NPV investment—but the project may be disregarded if its payback period is longer than the company is willing to consider. To illustrate, suppose that a project initially costs $7 million, and provides cash flows of $1 million for the next six years, and then $20 million in year 7. The timeline of cash flows would be:

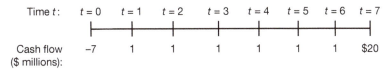

The payback period here is seven years. If we assume a discount rate of 10%, the project also has a positive NPV (of $9.62 million) due to the $20 million cash flow in year 7. However, if the company has a payback constraint of six years, the project would be thrown out despite it having a positive NPV and therefore the potential to add value to the company.

In a similar fashion, the payback period also disregards *costs* that occur after the payback period. For example, it is possible for a project to have a relatively short payback period but still be negative NPV—and thus value-destroying for a firm—because the project requires large costs to maintain far out in the future. Budgeting processes in firms and especially governments sometimes make this mistake, leading to negative-NPV decisions. Processes sometimes only take account of costs or cash flows out to some specified period (e.g., ten years), and so instead of buying equipment, a firm or government leases the equipment and as a result gets a positive payback in the ten years, even if the lease rate is greater than the cost of borrowing and investing in the equipment up front.

> **QUICK CHECK 10.7** What are the disadvantages of the payback criterion?

Box 10.3 sheds light on how managers make use of these various capital budgeting decision rules in the real world. In practice, managers make decisions based on the NPV rule, but also may use other factors to determine how to invest in projects.

Box 10.3 World of Business: Capital Budgeting Decisions in Practice

A key takeaway to keep in mind for the various capital budgeting decision criteria is that the NPV rule is the most correct criteria versus other rules. This is because the NPV rule properly quantifies value added, while other decision criteria often do not.

It is worth considering how companies actually use these decision rules in practice. Surveys done by economists Graham and Harvey (2001) and Graham (2022) revealed the following practices by companies:

- roughly 3/4 of CFOs always or almost always use NPV;
- roughly 3/4 of CFOs always or almost always use IRR; and
- about 60% of CFOs always or almost always use payback criterion.

That these numbers add up to more than 100% indicates that CFOs use more than one decision criterion at the same time.

One reason to compute IRR and payback is that they play a role in sensitivity analysis (also called scenario analysis), which examines how robust conclusions are to different assumptions about the cost of capital or projected cash flows. The IRR can tell you how high the cost of capital can be and still have a positive NPV. The discounted payback period tells you how long the cash flow must continue to still have a positive NPV.

While IRR and payback can provide useful statistics about a project, we have emphasized that the main decision about whether to invest should rest upon the NPV. Thus, it's acceptable to examine what the other criteria are saying as long as companies are relying on the NPV rule. However, a study of companies in the United Kingdom showed that over a 20-year period from 1975 to 1992, up to 14% of companies used payback as their *only* capital budgeting rule, indicating that companies are likely using both IRR and payback as key factors in deciding between projects.

Companies that rely on criteria other than NPV run the risk of making incorrect project decisions. However, there may be special circumstances in which the use of criteria such as a payback constraint can be valuable, such as to prevent actions by some managers who may be deliberately making bad decisions (e.g., Thakor 2021). For example, in practice companies have implemented a payback constraint because they have observed managers proposing long-term projects to get a higher wage, but then the project ends up being a bad project—and by the time the company realizes that, the manager has moved on to a new job. While such situations are not the norm, firms may still need to take actions to defend against such possibilities.

Sources: Graham, J. R., and Harvey, C. R. (2001). The theory and practice of corporate finance: evidence from the field. *Journal of Financial Economics* 60(2–3): 187–243. Graham, J. R. (2022). Presidential address: corporate finance and reality. *The Journal of Finance* 77(4): 1975–2049. Lefley, F. (1996). The payback method of investment appraisal: a review and synthesis. *International Journal of Production Economics* 44(3): 207–224. Thakor, R. T. (2021). Short-termism, managerial talent, and firm value. *The Review of Corporate Finance Studies* 10(3): 473–512.

10.4 Inflation and Capital Budgeting

An important consideration in analyzing investment projects is how to account for inflation. Consider an investment that requires an initial outlay of $2 million. In the absence of inflation, it is expected to produce an annual after-tax cash flow of $600,000 for five years, and the cost of capital is 10% per year. Under these assumptions, the project has an NPV of:

$$NPV = -2,000,000 + \frac{600,000}{1.10} + \frac{600,000}{1.10^2} + \frac{600,000}{1.10^3} + \frac{600,000}{1.10^4} + \frac{600,000}{1.10^5}$$
$$= \$274,472.$$

Now let us assume an inflation rate of 6% per year. The nominal cash flow projections are inflated at the rate of 6% per year to reflect our expectations in terms of "then-year dollars." The real cash flow projections are in terms of "today's dollars." In terms of a cash flow timeline, the real and nominal cash inflows of the project would be:

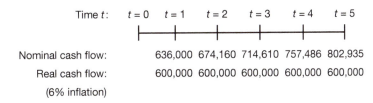

Just as we distinguish between real and nominal cash flow projections, so too we distinguish between the real and nominal cost of capital. The real rate is the rate that would prevail in a zero-inflation scenario. The nominal rate is the rate that we actually observe. Even if a firm does not explicitly set its cost of capital in real terms, setting it in nominal terms implies a certain real rate. For example, if the nominal cost of capital is 14% per year, and the expected rate of inflation is 6% per year, then the implied real cost of capital is approximately 8% per year.

There are two correct ways to account for inflation when computing NPV:

1. use the nominal cost of capital to discount nominal cash flows; and
2. use the real cost of capital to discount real cash flows.

We have already computed the NPV and IRR using the second approach that uses real cash flow estimates and a real cost of capital of 10% per year: NPV = $274,472. Because the NPV is positive, this project is worthwhile.

Now let us take the nominal approach. Before doing so, we must make a slight modification to the way we calculate the nominal rate. For most purposes it is perfectly adequate to approximate the nominal rate as 16%: the real rate of 10% plus the 6% expected rate of inflation. But in this case, we want to be exact in order to demonstrate the exact equivalence of using the real and nominal approaches to capital budgeting, so we must present the exact relation between nominal and real rates.

The exact relation between the nominal and real rates is:

$$\text{Nominal rate} = (1 + \text{real rate}) \times (1 + \text{expected inflation}) - 1. \tag{10.4}$$

Therefore, in our example the nominal rate would be:

$$\text{Nominal rate} = 1.1 \times 1.06 - 1 = 0.166 \text{ or } 16.6\%.$$

So, the nominal rate would be 16.6% rather than 16% per year. Using this 16.6% rate to compute the NPV of the nominal cash flow estimates above will produce an NPV of:

$$NPV = -2{,}000{,}000 + \frac{636{,}000}{1.166} + \frac{674{,}160}{1.166^2} + \frac{714{,}610}{1.166^3} + \frac{757{,}486}{1.166^4} + \frac{802{,}935}{1.166^5}$$
$$= \$274{,}472.$$

This is the same result as we obtain using the real approach (slight differences are due to rounding). This is logical because the increase in the current value gain from undertaking the project should not be affected by the unit of account—that is, whether we use inflated dollars or dollars of constant purchasing power.

These same conclusions also apply to other decision criteria beyond the NPV of a project. For example, when calculating an IRR, one may use nominal or real cash flows, and decisions are made comparing the IRR to a hurdle rate or the company's cost of capital. For a correct apples-to-apples comparison, one must never compare the IRR computed using real cash flow estimates to a nominal cost of capital; the proper approach is to compare the IRR from real cash flows to a real cost of capital, or to compare the IRR from nominal cash flows to a nominal cost of capital.

> **QUICK CHECK 10.8** Consider the same project as before, which requires an initial outlay of $2 million, and, in the absence of inflation, is expected to produce an annual after-tax cash flow of $600,000 for five years with a cost of capital of 10% per year. Analyze the same project assuming an expected rate of inflation of 8% per year instead of 6%.

Conclusion

In this chapter we have examined capital budgeting, the process by which companies decide which investment projects to undertake. Managers running companies should choose projects which add to the overall value of the company. To determine which add value, we explored different types of investment rules for evaluating projects. The most widely used criterion is net present value (NPV), the difference between the present values of a project's cash inflows and its outflows. A project that has a positive NPV adds value to a company.

Calculating the NPV of a project follows the same approach we introduced in Chapter 2 and utilized with company valuation in Chapter 9, and is an application of Principles 1 (a dollar today is not worth the same as a dollar tomorrow) and 6 (risk is fundamental to financial analysis and must be explicitly considered in all financial decisions). In subsequent chapters we explore additional considerations that are important to capital budgeting, such as when managers may be tempted to make project choices that benefit themselves but not the firm (Chapter 11), the effect of financing choices on NPV calculations and project decisions (Chapter 13), how flexibility can affect project decisions (Chapter 14), and methods of calculating discount rates in NPV calculations (Chapter 18).

Takeaways

- Capital budgeting is the process firms use to evaluate and select investment projects that require capital allocation and create a series of cash flows over time.
- The objective of capital budgeting procedures is to assure that only projects that increase company value (or at least do not reduce it) are undertaken.

- Most investment projects requiring capital expenditures fall into three categories: new products, cost reduction, and replacement. Ideas for investment projects can come from external sources, such as a firm's customers and competitors, or from internal sources, such as a firm's own R&D or production departments.
- Projects should be evaluated using a discounted cash flow analysis: estimate the incremental cash flows associated with the project and calculate its net present value (NPV). The discount rate should be risk-adjusted, reflecting the risk of the project, of its financing, or of the firm itself.
- The internal rate of return (IRR) is the average rate of return that creates an NPV = 0. Companies may use the IRR as a decision rule by selecting projects that have an IRR above a certain rate, known as a hurdle rate.
- A project's payback period is the amount of time it takes the cumulative cash generated by the project to exceed the initial investment. Companies may use the payback period to eliminate projects that have payback periods that are longer than some threshold.
- When a project's cost of capital and future cash flows are available, the NPV rule is the *only* correct decision criterion. Other decision rules like IRR and payback have disadvantages that can lead firms to reject value-creating projects and accept value-losing projects.
- It is always important to check whether cash flow forecasts have been properly adjusted to account for inflation over a project's life. There are two correct ways to make the adjustment: (a) use the nominal cost of capital to discount nominal cash flows; or (b) use the real cost of capital to discount real cash flows. Either approach results in the same NPV.

Key Terms

Capital budgeting 289
Discounted payback period 303
Hurdle rate 299
Internal rate of return (IRR) 298
Net present value (NPV) 292
NPV rule 292
Payback constraint 303
Payback decision rule 303
Payback period 303
Sensitivity analysis 298

Key Equations

Net present value	$NPV = PV(\text{cash inflows}) - PV(\text{cash outflows})$	Eq. 10.1
Project net cash flows	Cash flow = revenue − total expenses − taxes + noncash expenses	Eq. 10.2
Internal rate of return (IRR)	$NPV = 0 = -I_0 + \dfrac{CF_1}{1+IRR} + \dfrac{CF_2}{(1+IRR)^2} + \cdots + \dfrac{CF_T}{(1+IRR)^T}$ $I_0 = \dfrac{CF_1}{1+IRR} + \dfrac{CF_2}{(1+IRR)^2} + \cdots + \dfrac{CF_T}{(1+IRR)^T}$	Eq. 10.3
Nominal rate of return	Nominal rate = $(1 + \text{real rate}) \times (1 + \text{expected inflation}) - 1$	Eq. 10.4

Problems

1. New Futuristics Company is thinking about marketing a new software product. Upfront costs to market and develop the product are $10 million. Starting in year 1, the product is expected to generate cash flows of $1.5 million per year for 15 years. The company will have to provide product

support expected to cost $200,000 per year in perpetuity, a cost that has not been included in the cash flows just mentioned. Assume all cash flows (except for the upfront costs) occur at the end of each year.
   (a) What is the net present value (NPV) of this investment if the cost of capital is 5%? Should the firm undertake the project?
   (b) Repeat the analysis for discount rates of 1% and 15%. Should the company undertake the project in these two cases?
   (c) What is the payback period of the project? (Note: You only need to consider the upfront costs in this calculation.)
   (d) How many IRRs does this investment opportunity have? (Hint: Plot the project NPV as a function of the discount rate—that is, creating a graph that shows what the NPV is for a broad range of discount rates.)
   (e) Can the IRR rule be used to evaluate this investment? Explain your answer.
2. Your firm is considering two investment projects with the patterns of expected future net after-tax cash flows (in millions) shown in Table 10.4.

Table 10.4

Year	Project A	Project B
1	$1	$5
2	2	4
3	3	3
4	4	2
5	5	1

The cost of capital for both projects is 10%. If both projects require an initial outlay of $10 million, which is the better project?

3. Consider the previous problem. Given the patterns of the two cash flow series, does the ranking of the projects depend on the cost of capital? Explain your answer.
4. A firm is considering investing $10 million in equipment that is expected to have a useful life of four years and is expected to provide cash flows of $4 million per year. Assume the firm pays a 40% tax rate on accounting profits and uses the straight-line depreciation method. What is the after-tax cash flow from the investment in years 1 through 4? If the firm's discount rate for this investment is 15% per year, what are the investment's IRR and NPV? Should the firm make this investment? Explain your answer.
5. Leather Goods Inc. wants to expand its product line into wallets. It is considering producing 50,000 wallets per year. The price will be $15 per wallet in the first year, and the price will increase 3% per year thereafter. The cost is expected to be $10 per wallet and will increase by 5% per year. The machine will cost $400,000, and will have an economic life of five years. It will be fully depreciated using the straight-line method. The discount rate is 15% and the corporate tax is 34%. What is the NPV of the investment?
6. Suppose that you are choosing to invest in one of two mutually exclusive projects, each with the following projected cash flows:
   - Project A has cash flows of $1 million for five years, starting next year. It costs $3 million today to invest in.
   - Project B has cash flows of $100,000 forever, starting next year, which will grow at a rate of 0.5% each year thereafter. It costs $1.1 million today to invest in.

Your company's cost of capital is 15%.
(a) What is the NPV of each project? Which project should you choose?
(b) If your company implements a payback restriction so that it will not approve any project with a payback period greater than five years, which project gets eliminated?
(c) Suppose that your business partner calculates that Project A has an IRR of 15.1%. What is the IRR of Project B? Based on IRRs, which project is better?

7. Pepe's Ski Shop is contemplating replacing its ski boot foam injection equipment with a new machine. The old machine has been completely depreciated but has a current market value of $2,000. The new machine will cost $25,000 and will have a life of ten years and no value after this time. The new machine will be depreciated on a straight-line basis assuming no salvage value. The new machine will increase annual revenues by $10,000 and increase annual nondepreciation expenses by $3,000. Assume a 50% tax rate for all income—that is, the capital gains tax rate on the sale of the old machine is also 50%.
(a) Draw a timeline of the expected cash flows of the project. What is the additional after-tax net cash flow realized by replacing the old machine with the new machine?
(b) What is the IRR of this project?
(c) At a cost of capital of 12%, what is the NPV of this cash flow stream?
(d) At a cost of capital of 12%, is this project worthwhile?

8. Healthy Hopes Hospital Supply Corporation is considering an investment of $500,000 in a new plant for producing disposable diapers. The plant has an expected life of four years. Sales are expected to be 600,000 diapers per year at a price of $2 per diaper. Costs excluding depreciation of the plant are $200,000 per year, in addition to costs of $1.20 per unit. The plant will be depreciated over four years using the straight-line method with zero salvage value. The discount rate for the project is 15% per year, and the corporation pays income tax at the rate of 34%. Find the IRR, NPV, and payback period.

9. Kitchen Supplies, Inc. must replace a machine in its manufacturing plant that has no salvage value. It has a choice between two models. The first machine will last five years and will cost $300,000. It will generate annual revenues of $50,000. Annual maintenance costs will be $20,000. The machine will be fully depreciated using the straight-line depreciation method and will have no salvage value. The second machine will last seven years and will cost $600,000. It will generate annual revenues of $70,000. This machine will also be fully depreciated using the straight-line depreciation method, but is expected to have a salvage value of $60,000 at the end of the seventh year. The annual maintenance cost is $15,000. The annual tax rate is 35% and the cost of capital is 10%. Which machine should the company purchase?

10. Assume the three mutually exclusive projects shown in Table 10.5, each of which requires an initial outlay of $10,000 and has the shown after-tax cash flow streams.

Table 10.5

Year	Project 1	Project 2	Project 3
1	$0	$2,000	$4,000
2	$2,500	$2,000	$4,000
3	$10,000	$8,000	$4,000

Which project should be undertaken if the cost of capital is 8%? What if the cost of capital is 10%?

11. *Challenge question*: Your firm is considering two investment projects with the following patterns of expected future net after-tax cash flows:

Year	Project A	Project B
1	$0	$2,000
2	$2,500	$200

Suppose both projects require an initial outlay of $2,000 and have identical costs of capital. Determine a complete decision rule conditional on the cost of capital for undertaking the projects if it is possible to invest in one or both projects. Repeat the decision rule if they are mutually exclusive. (Hint: Calculate the project IRRs and NPVs of the two projects at alternative costs of capital equal to 0%, 5%, 10%, and 15%.)

12. The Big Bear Brew Pub is considering buying more machinery that will allow the pub to increase its portfolio of beers on tap. The new machinery will cost $65,000 and will be depreciated on a ten-year basis. It is expected to have no value after ten years. The improved selection is anticipated to increase sales by $30,000 for the first year and increase at the rate of inflation of 3% for each year after that. Production costs are expected to be $15,000 for the first year and are also expected to increase at the rate of inflation. The real discount rate is 12% and the nominal risk-free interest rate is 6%. The corporate tax rate is 34%. Should Big Bear's owner buy the machinery?

13. You are a financial analyst at a company and you are considering two mutually exclusive projects, shown in Table 10.6. Unfortunately, the figures for Project 1 are in nominal terms and the figures for Project 2 are in real terms. The nominal discount rate for both projects is 17%, and inflation is projected to be 3%.
    (a) Calculate the NPV of each project in real and nominal terms. Also calculate the IRR of each project.
    (b) Determine which project to choose. Comment on the difference between the two in real and nominal terms.

Table 10.6

	Project 1	Project 2
0	−$100,000	−$90,000
1	30,000	25,000
2	60,000	55,000
3	75,000	80,000

14. Patriots Foundry (PF) is considering getting into a new line of business: producing souvenir statues of Paul Revere, the famous eighteenth-century American silversmith. This will require purchasing a machine for $40,000. The new machine will have a depreciable life of two years and no salvage value. PF will depreciate the machine on a straight-line basis. The firm thinks it will sell 3,000 statues per year at a price of $10 each, and costs will be $1 per statue with expenses (not including depreciation) of $2,000 per year. PF's cost of capital is 10%. Assume that there will be no inflation. The tax rate is 40%.
    (a) What is the series of expected future cash flows?
    (b) What is the expected NPV of this project? Is the project worth undertaking?

Now assume instead that there will be inflation of 6% per year during each of the next two years and that both revenues and expenses, except depreciation, increase at that rate. Assume that the real cost of capital remains at 10%.

(c) What is the series of expected nominal cash flows?
(d) What is the NPV of this project, and is this project worth undertaking now?
(e) Why does the NPV of the investment project go down when the inflation rate goes up?

15. Mr. Salles is considering a business venture in which he would lead guided tours of the romantic Greek isles and the Italian countryside. After four years, Mr. Salles intends to retire. The initial investment would be $50,000 in a computer and phone system. This investment would be depreciated on the straight-line method, and is expected to have no salvage value. The corporate tax rate is 35%. The price of each tour paid to Mr. Salles will be $5,000 per customer and the price will remain constant in real terms. Mr. Salles will pay himself $50 per hour and anticipates an annual increase in salary of 5% in real terms. The cost to Mr. Salles for each customer is $3,500 per tour, and this cost is expected to increase annually by 3% in real terms. Assume that all revenues and costs occur at year end. The inflation rate is 3.5%. The risk-free nominal rate is 6% and the real discount rate for costs and revenues is 9%. Using the additional following data, calculate the NPV of the project.

	Year 1	Year 2	Year 3	Year 4
Number of customers	100	115	130	140
Hours worked	2,080	2,080	2,080	2,080

16. Camille, the owner of the Germanos Tree farm has contracted with the government of his native land to provide cedar tree saplings to aid in that government's efforts to reforest part of the country and return the cedar tree to its past glory. The project is expected to continue in perpetuity. At the end of the first year, the following nominal and incremental cash flows are expected:

Revenues	$125,000
Labor costs	$65,000
Other costs	$45,000

Camille has contracted with an air freight shipping company to transport the saplings. The contract is for a fixed payment of $35,000 in nominal terms per year. The first payment is due at the end of the first year. Revenues are expected to grow at 4% in real terms. Labor costs are expected to grow at 3% per year. Other costs are expected to decrease at 0.5% per year. The real discount rate for revenues and costs is 8% and inflation is expected to be 3.5%. There are no taxes and all cash flows occur at year end. What is the NPV of the contract?

11 AGENCY COSTS AND GOVERNANCE

CHAPTER OVERVIEW

11.1	Organizational Structure of Companies	314
11.2	Agency Problems	319
11.3	Corporate Governance and Strategies: Internal Governance	322
11.4	Regulation and Market Discipline: External Governance	324
11.5	The Challenge of Multiple Objectives	329

LEARNING OBJECTIVES

After reading this chapter, you will be able to:
- describe the different kinds of organizational structures companies use in order to operate efficiently to achieve their objectives;
- explain how forms of business organization and the separation of ownership and control can help companies to be run efficiently;
- describe how agency problems may cause suboptimal decisions to be made within companies;
- explain how corporate governance can help to prevent these problems from occurring, and improve company operations;
- identify the challenges of firm multiple objectives to efficiently running a company and making optimal decisions.

✚ You are looking to start a new company using your own money. How should you organize the company, and who should control it?

✚ You are looking to invest in the stock of a company. The company has an ownership structure involving many different debtholders and shareholders. How can this affect the operations of the company?

- You are currently a shareholder of a well-known company, and you and other shareholders are unhappy with the way the CEO has been running the company. What can you and the other shareholders do to replace the CEO?

- The company you work for is targeted by a well-known financial investor, who is trying to gain control over the operations of the company. Is this good or bad for the company?

- You are running a startup which is expanding its operations. Other companies in this field have had problems where certain managers and employees have made project decisions that were good for them personally but were not good for the company. How can you avoid this in your company?

Introduction

In the previous chapter we focused on decisions within companies, and discussed decision rules that managers can follow to choose investment projects. A key takeaway is that managers should make project decisions that increase the value of the company. In this chapter, we explore how organization structure can support decision making that increases value. We also consider how in some circumstances it can cause poor decisions to be made that disadvantage the firm.

Many firms separate ownership and control—the people who run companies and make decisions (referred to as agents) are not always the same people who own the companies (known as principals). This separation offers many benefits, helping to guide companies toward optimal investment and operating decisions. However, it can also result in bad decisions being made. For example, managers and other stakeholders may have their own interests and take actions that benefit themselves but not the company. We refer to situations that result from such conflicts of interest as agency problems (sometimes referred to as incentive problems). When agency problems cause decisions to be made that reduce a company's value, we refer to this as an agency cost.

As we will describe in more detail, the fact that such agency problems may arise within companies can interfere with the proper functioning of the company. For example, if you are looking to invest your money in a company's stock and you trust the company's managers, then there is no impediment to you buying the stock. However, if there is a concern that the managers have interests that conflict with yours, then you and others may not invest in the company, which can prevent the company from securing funding that it needs to make investments. Thus, systems that are put in place to reduce agency costs are important for companies to function. Examples include organizational structures that enhance trust by ensuring that managers cannot take certain actions, disclosures by the company to increase transparency to investors, and examinations by regulators which provide verification of the company's actions. These issues are so important that they are summarized in **Principle 9:** *Transparency, verification, and trust are all important to the proper functioning of the financial system.*

To better understand these issues, this chapter discusses the various types of organizational forms that firms may take. It then describes the structure of ownership and control in companies, and how agency problems may come about. Given the potential for agency problems, the chapter then discusses what actions companies can take to prevent or resolve these types of problems. In addition to actions that companies themselves can take, financial markets can also impose discipline on companies which can help to resolve agency problems. The chapter concludes with a short discussion of challenges that firms can face in resolving agency problems if they have multiple objectives beyond simply maximizing their value.

11.1 Organizational Structure of Companies

In this section, we describe the typical organizational structures that companies use and why they use them. While there are many advantages to different structures, this also allows us to understand how agency problems may arise within organizations, which we devote much of the rest of the chapter to discussing.

11.1.1 Forms of Business Organization

There are three basic types of company organization: sole proprietorships, partnerships, and corporations. A sole proprietorship is a firm owned by an individual; the assets and liabilities of the firm are the personal assets and liabilities of the proprietor. A sole proprietor has unlimited liability for the debts and other liabilities of the firm. This means that if the firm cannot pay its debts, the proprietor's personal assets can be seized to satisfy the demands of the firm's creditors.

Frequently a business such as a restaurant, a real estate agency, or a small workshop will remain a sole proprietorship throughout its existence. Many firms start out as sole proprietorships and then change their organizational form as they become established and expand, for example.

A partnership is a firm with two or more owners, called the partners, who share the equity in the business. A partnership agreement usually stipulates how decisions are to be made and how profits and losses are to be shared. Unless otherwise specified, all partners have unlimited liability. There can, however, be limited partners, who have limited liability but do not have the power to make day-to-day business decisions of the partnership. In this form, what is known as the general partner has unlimited liability for the debts of the firm and makes the day-to-day business decisions.

A corporation is a firm that is a legal entity distinct from its owners, unlike a sole proprietorship or a partnership, in which the firm is not separated from its owners. Corporations can own property, borrow, and enter into contracts, and have liability for the corporation's actions. They can sue and be sued. They are usually taxed according to rules that differ from the rules that apply to the other forms of business organization.

Individuals who buy shares of the corporation become the shareholders or owners of the corporation. Their personal liability is limited, and they are entitled to a share of any distributions from the corporation (e.g., cash dividends) in proportion to the number of shares they own. Usually there is one vote per share, but sometimes there are different classes of stocks with different voting rights. The shareholders elect a board of directors, which in turn selects managers to run the business. A corporation has a charter that sets down the rules that govern it, written by the founders of the corporation. We discuss the role of the shareholders and board of directors in more detail later in this chapter.

The different forms of business organizations each offer certain advantages. Sole proprietorships and partnerships typically have simple structures which may be ideal for small businesses run by only one or a handful of people. These types of businesses also have fewer filing and legal reporting requirements compared to corporations. However, corporations also offer advantages. One advantage of the corporate form is that ownership shares can usually be transferred without disrupting the business. Another advantage is shareholders' limited liability, which means that if the corporation fails to pay its debts, the creditors can seize the assets of the corporation but have no recourse to the personal assets of the shareholders. In that sense, a corporation serves the same function as a general partner in a partnership, and its shareholders are like limited partners.

Around the world, large firms are almost always organized as corporations, although ownership of the corporation may be restricted to a single person or family. Corporations with broadly dispersed ownership and with shares that trade in public stock markets are called publicly traded corporations (also known in the United States as public corporations); those with concentrated ownership held privately are called private corporations. Laws governing the corporate form of organization differ in their details from country to country, and even within a country. In the United States, for example, laws governing corporations are created and administered at the state level, with certain regulatory oversight imposed nationally. In the European Union (EU), EU directives govern the formation of companies across member countries and allow cross-country activities, but individual countries are able to enforce and implement their own laws so long as they are in compliance with EU directives.

An important aspect of organizational form, beyond the advantages and considerations noted above, is whether the people who own the company are the same people who make decisions within the company. As we will see throughout the rest of the chapter, this distinction can create a number of advantages as well as challenges.

> QUICK CHECK 11.1 A corporation owned by a single person is not a sole proprietorship. Why?

11.1.2 Separation of Ownership and Control

In private company sole proprietorships and many partnerships, often the owners and the managers of the business are the same people. However, in many firms, especially large ones, the owners do not manage the business: They delegate that responsibility to professional managers who do not own any part of it. This is known as a separated structure. There are four major reasons for the owners of a firm to turn over the running of the business to others to manage in this structure.

First, professional managers may have a superior ability to run the business. They may have better technological knowledge, more experience, a more suitable personality to run the business, or a greater ability to gather important information. For example, managers can gather the most accurate information available about the firm's production technology, the costs of its inputs, and the demand for its products. The owners of the firm need to know relatively little about the technology of the firm, the intensity at which it is being operated, and the demand for the firm's products. Consider the entertainment industry: The information needed to successfully manage the production and distribution of a movie is substantial. Although information about top actors and directors who might be hired to star in a movie is readily available at low cost, this is not so with respect to other resource inputs to movie production and distribution. Establishing information networks of agents and jobbers is costly and is most efficiently handled by having movie executives specialize in doing it. In a structure in which the owner is also the manager, the owner must have both the talents of a manager and the financial resources necessary to own a company. In the separated structure, no such happenstance is required.

The people most qualified to manage a film studio or a television network may not have the financial resources to own the business, and the people with the wealth to own such a business may have no ability to manage it. Therefore, it makes sense for the managerially competent people to deal with creatives and the media landscape and for the wealthy people to simply provide the capital.

Second, to achieve efficient scale, a business may require more capital than any one owner can provide and multiple owners cannot efficiently manage, whereas a single manager can. For example, the cost of producing a single movie is in the tens of millions for a low-budget film, and for the average feature-length movie it is around $100 million. To achieve an efficient scale of production and raise these millions of dollars calls for a structure with many owners, not all of whom can be actively involved in managing the business.

Third, owners may want to diversify their risks by investing across many firms. If they have to also manage the firms they invest in, there may be no way they can diversify across as many firms as they want. As we noted in Chapter 6, to diversify optimally requires the investor to hold a portfolio of assets, in which each security is but a small part. Such efficient diversification is difficult to achieve without separation of ownership and management. For example, suppose an investor-owner thinks that firms in the entertainment industry will do well over the next few years and would like to buy a diversified stake in that industry. They would not be physically capable of then also managing those firms. Along similar lines, an investor that wants to diversify across firms within the service industry could invest in multiple restaurants in different locations, but it would be impossible for the investor to cook the food and serve customers in each restaurant. The corporate form is especially well suited to facilitating diversification by investor-owners because it allows them to own a relatively small share of each firm.

Fourth, there is the learning curve or going-concern effect, which ensures that management knowledge stays with the company, not the owners. Suppose an owner-manager wants to sell all or part of their shares either now or at a later date and give up both roles (i.e., owner and manager) at the company. The new owners will have to replace a manager. However, if the owner is not a manager, then when the business is sold there can be continuity of management under the new owners. Using the entertainment industry as an example, a studio producing a series for a streaming platform could be sold to a new owner while retaining the series' director, writers, and actors, thus ensuring no disruption in the production of new episodes.

The corporate form is especially well suited to the separation of owners and managers because it allows relatively frequent changes in owners by share transfer to have no effect on the firm's operations. Millions of shares in corporations around the world change hands and rarely is there any effect on the management or operations of the business. Furthermore, companies can change from being a sole proprietorship or partnership to a corporation without a disruption in operations—when a company issues shares to the public for the first time, the original owner-managers often continue to manage the business, even if they own fewer or no shares in the business.

> QUICK CHECK 11.2 What are the main reasons for having a separation of ownership and management of firms?

Overall, separating ownership and control can confer a number of advantages for companies. We next describe specifics of how firms structure themselves to implement this separation.

11.1.3 Structure of Ownership and Control in Companies

Across the globe, in order to separate ownership and control, companies structure themselves as corporations. There is a structure of four groups that is common across most corporations: shareholders, debtholders, managers, and the board of directors.

Shareholders own stock in a company, which entitles them to an ownership share (equity) of the company. For a private company, there may be just one shareholder who is also the owner and manager, and who maintains complete control of the company. For a public company, there are usually many shareholders (based on potentially thousands or even millions of shares outstanding), and the shares of stock that they own are freely traded in a stock exchange. In practice, shareholders' equity claim entitles them to some portion of ownership of the assets of the company and thus the profits the company's assets generate, paid in the form of dividends. Shareholders can also exercise their ownership and control rights by *voting* on important decisions during shareholder meetings. Examples of such decisions may include electing members of the board of directors, approving mergers or acquisitions, dividend policy, or holding a vote of confidence in the company's CEO.

Shares of stock in a company are typically divided into two types: common stock, regular shares of a company, and preferred stock, shares that carry a specified dividend that must be paid before the dividends of the common stock. Common stock is also often just called shares, so when we refer to the corporation's shareholders, we mean the holders of its common stock. Common stock confers on its holder the residual claim to the corporation's assets. In other words, after all other parties with a claim on the corporation have been paid, whatever is left goes to the holders of the common stock in the form of share value and dividends. Often there is more than one class of common stock, which can differ in terms of voting rights imparted and the rights of the holder to sell them to other parties. For example, some corporations issue Class A common stock that has voting rights and Class B common stock that does not (or has fewer voting rights). Restricted stock cannot be sold for a certain number of years.

Preferred stock differs from common stock in that it carries a specified dividend that must be paid before the firm can pay any dividends to the holders of the common stock. It is in this sense that it is preferred over common stock. Failure to pay preferred dividends does not trigger a default in the way that failure to pay interest on debt would. However, preferred stockholders typically receive only their promised dividends and do not receive any voting rights, in contrast to common stockholders. Most of the time, shareholders have an incentive to act in a way that maximizes company value—they own stock, and actions that improve company value will result in their shares of stock increasing in value.

Debtholders (creditors) have provided debt financing—have lent money—to the company. Corporate debt is a contractual obligation on the part of the company to make promised future payments in return for the resources provided to it. Debt financing in its broadest sense includes loans and debt securities, such as bonds and mortgages, as well as other promises of future payment by the corporation, such as accounts payable, leases, and pensions. For many corporations, long-term lease and pension liabilities may be much larger than the amount of debt in the form of loans, bonds, and mortgages. Debt also typically includes terms, known as covenants, which restricts what a company can do in an effort to ensure that the company does not take actions that will put it in a position where it cannot pay back debt. An example of a covenant is a contractual clause that prevents a company from paying dividends unless it is in a position where it can comfortably pay back its debt first.

Debtholders have an ownership and control claim over a company because making payments on debt is a contractual obligation. If a company defaults on its debt—it does not pay what debtholders are owed or violates a covenant—then debtholders are able to exercise this claim. Importantly, in this case debtholders have priority over the claims of shareholders and other stakeholders.

Debtholders want to get paid back what they are owed (both interest and principal) and this is most likely to occur when the company does well. Thus, debtholders will seek to make control decisions that improve company value and give them the best chance of getting paid. For example, when a company defaults, the debtholders may choose to forgive the default or renegotiate the terms in the debt, allowing the company to continue operations as normal in the hopes that it will be able to repay the full amount. However, if a debtholder feels the company's prospects are poor and it is unlikely to be able to improve and repay the loan, then the debtholders may choose to take the company into bankruptcy and potentially liquidate (sell off) parts of the company in order to receive what is owed.

Managers, from divisional managers to the chief executive officer (CEO), are the people making operational and investment decisions. The managers of a public corporation owe their primary allegiance to the shareholders, and in many legal jurisdictions managers can be held liable for failure to fulfill their fiduciary responsibilities to the shareholders. Managers typically have a lot of discretion about how to utilize a firm's resources, but their incentives are usually aligned with the firm's incentives. For example, if a company does poorly and ceases to exist, a manager will not get paid their salary. Compensation arrangements can offer explicit incentives. For example, it is common to pay managers by giving them stock or options of the company, so that making good decisions that improve company value and increase the value of the stock or options will benefit the managers.

The board of directors is a group of individuals (often about a dozen) that oversees the proper functioning of a company. After being nominated through sub-committees of the existing board, members are elected (and can subsequently be fired) by the shareholders through a shareholder vote. The CEO is often a member of the board of directors, and sometimes can serve as the chair of the board, and thus may play a dual role as a manager and director. Boards usually meet a set number of times each year to decide on a range of important policy issues for the company, including:

- hiring and firing the CEO and other top managers, such as the chief financial officer (CFO);
- approving the compensation of the CEO and other top managers;
- determining dividend and payout policy for the company;
- approving mergers and acquisitions; and
- deciding company charter issues that include the structure and organization of the company, incorporation details, and voting rights.

Figure 11.1 summarizes the structure of ownership and control in a corporation, and the relationships between the four different groups we described above. The separation of ownership and management within companies has a number of advantages, such as allowing those with expertise to run the firm (managers) while owners focus on providing capital (stockholders). The various stakeholders that own and control a company will typically have an incentive to act in the best interests of the company because their interests are aligned—they benefit when the company benefits. Furthermore, the relationships between the groups that we described above can help to further align incentives—shareholders elect members of the board of directors, and the board elects/fires the CEO, thus providing checks and balances between the groups. However, there is also the potential for problems, which we will cover in the next section.

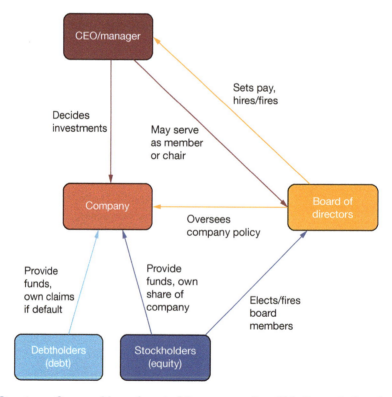

FIGURE 11.1 **Structure of ownership and control in a corporation.** This figure depicts the ownership and control structure of a typical corporation, and the relationship between the shareholders, bondholders, CEO/manager, and board of directors.

> **QUICK CHECK 11.3** Briefly describe the four main groups of stakeholders that own and control corporations. Why would each group usually take actions that are good for the company?

11.2 Agency Problems

The separated structure of ownership, control, and management can create what is known as agency problems. Agency problems are when there is a conflict of interest between the different stakeholders of a company, which arises when one stakeholder is expected to work in the best interest of the other stakeholders (making that stakeholder an *agent* of the others), but may take different actions that are in the stakeholder's own interests. This can result in actions being taken that are detrimental to the firm, such as bad investments. In this section we describe common agency problems that may occur within companies.

11.2.1 Conflicts with Shareholders and Debtholders

There are times when shareholders may make decisions that are not in the best interest of the company. These can arise because even if an action is beneficial to a company—that is, a good (positive-NPV) investment—the benefits do not necessarily accrue equally to all of the owners of the company. Thus, when a shareholder sees that an action may not benefit them (i.e., their share price is reduced), they will make decisions to prevent that action.

11.2.1.1 Conflicts between Shareholders

Conflicts between shareholders occur when a group of shareholders act to prioritize the value of their holdings at the expense of other shareholders and the company. For example, a company may need to sell additional shares of stock to raise money to fund an investment, but this will dilute the original shares, which means they are less valuable to the shareholders and their voting share becomes less influential. The investment may have a positive NPV and be good for the firm, and new investors may be eager to buy new shares of the firm because of this, but the value added by the investment may not be enough to offset the dilution caused to the original shareholders.

To illustrate, suppose that a company has 100 shares of stock outstanding and each share is worth $10, making the total equity value $100 \times \$10 = \$1,000$. Now suppose that the company wants to issue 50 new shares of stock to undertake an investment. The net present value (NPV) of the investment is $100, so the company's total equity value will be $1,100. The company will have 150 shares of stock with an equity value of $1,100, so each share will then be worth $1,100 / 150 = \$7.33$. Furthermore, before the share issuance each share of stock provided one vote out of 100; after the share issuance it provides only one vote out of 150, making each vote relatively less important. Shareholders can prevent the company from issuing additional stock through using their voting rights, pressuring management, or pressuring the board, whom they elect, which in turn pressures management. Managers who are paid in stock or options will also face this conflict of interest. Thus stockholders prevent the company they own shares in from investing in projects that have a positive NPV.

11.2.1.2 Conflicts between Shareholders and Debtholders

Misalignment of shareholders (and managers acting in the interest of shareholders) and debtholders incentives can also create a conflict of interest. This can arise because shareholders have limited liability, meaning that the value of their shares cannot fall below $0, which creates little incentive for shareholders to limit the firm's losses in the event of a bankruptcy. Shareholders (or managers paid in stock or acting in the best interests of shareholders) may undertake riskier investments that could increase the wealth of shareholders at the expense of ensuring the debtholders are paid back their debt. This problem becomes more severe if the firm has a significant amount of debt.

For example, suppose a firm's assets are worth $100 million. The firm has debt with a face value of $104 million maturing one year from now. Stockholders have the choice: invest all $100 million in riskless Treasury bills (T-bills) maturing in one year that pay an interest rate of 4%, or invest $100 million in a venture that will either be worth $200 million or nothing one year from now. Even if the probability of the new venture succeeding is quite small, the firm (in line with shareholders' best interests) will choose to undertake the risky venture. If shareholders invest in T-bills, the value of the firm's assets in one year would be exactly what it owes to the debtholders, and there is no residual value left to shareholders. However, if the firm has some chance, no matter how small, of being worth more than $104 million one year from now, then the shares will have some value now. From the shareholders' perspective, the risky venture will either fail and leave them with no value—exactly the same situation as if the firm invested in T-bills—or will pay off and leave a residual value to them of $200 million − $104 million = $96 million. The debtholders in this example bear all the downside risk of the risky venture—if the firm invested in the T-bills, the debtholders would get paid what they are owed, but if the firm invests in the risky venture they will likely get nothing. In contrast, the shareholders get all of the incremental upside potential for gain.

In firms with large amounts of debt, stockholders might have an incentive to redeploy the firm's assets in a way that actually reduces the firm's total value (the size of the whole pie) in order to increase share price (the size of the equity piece). This can result in negative consequences for the firm, such as excessively risky (and potentially negative-NPV) investments being made that have the potential to boost share prices in the short term, but reduce firm value (or pull the company into bankruptcy) when they fail. Because creditors are aware that under certain adverse circumstances managers might be tempted to take actions at their expense, they will limit their lending in the first place or charge a higher interest rate. Debt covenants that restrict certain firm investments or actions are also often put in place in order to try to mitigate this problem. However, these may not always be effective at preventing such a situation from occurring—it can be difficult to identify such projects in advance.

11.2.2 Managerial Conflicts of Interest

Managers ideally should make investment and other decisions to maximize company value. However, managers may neglect their obligations to the company in deference to their personal interests and, in extreme cases, may even act contrary to the interests of their shareholders. Adam Smith, the founder of classical economics, summed it up in *The Wealth of Nations* as follows:

> The directors of such [joint-stock] companies, however, being the managers rather of other people's money than of their own, it cannot well be expected, that they should watch over it with the same anxious vigilance with which the partners in a private copartnery frequently watch over their own.... Negligence and profusion, therefore, must always prevail, more or less, in the management of the affairs of such a company.

There are a number of ways in which managers may do this. When managers have a lot of discretion about how to allocate a firm's cash flows, there can be a temptation to use the cash to invest in projects that benefit them but do not increase the value of the company, also known as the free cash flow problem (Jensen 1986). Examples include investments with negative NPV that increase the power, prestige, or perks of the managers. To illustrate, consider a CEO of a major hotel chain that has the choice of two investment projects:

1. building a new hotel in the same city as the company's headquarters; or
2. building a new resort hotel in the Bahamas, with the ability to use the company's private jet to "check" on the progress of the hotel at any time.

Because of the extra perks that come with the hotel in the Bahamas (warm weather, beaches, and use of a private jet), a CEO may be tempted to invest in the second option even if it has a lower NPV than the first. If the company has a lot of cash, then it becomes substantially easier for the CEO to make this decision with little oversight because it is harder for others to notice, given how much cash there is. In contrast, an investment made by a company with very little cash would likely be very noticeable; that company likely would need to raise funds from outside investors, who would also put additional scrutiny on what the money is being used for.

Managers may also make investments (such as acquisitions) that expand the size of the company, because they enjoy the prestige and often higher compensation of a larger company (often referred to as "empire building"). These additional benefits, which are often difficult to quantify, are referred to as private benefits.

The threat of being fired can provide a powerful incentive for managers to make decisions for the good of the company. However, managers can make this difficult through entrenchment: making investments or implementing policies that make it harder to fire them. Examples include "manager-specific" investments, where a manager intentionally invests in projects that require the manager's expertise. Another example is when a CEO intentionally blocks an efficient merger deal because of the possibility that they will be fired from the new joint company.

11.2.3 Conflicts of Interest and the Board of Directors

The board of directors may also not act in the company's best interest. This can occur for a number of reasons.

There can be a captured board: The CEO has the board "in their pocket," and the board "rubber stamps" the CEO's proposals, or at least is unlikely to stand in the way of the CEO's agenda. With a captured board, CEOs can also *de facto* nominate members to the board (such as friends and allies) to further consolidate their power. One reason why a captured board may come about and persist is because the CEO is often also the board chair, and thus sets the board's agenda. Another reason why a captured board may persist is the way that board members are hired and fired: through a shareholder vote. While requiring a shareholder vote provides shareholder oversight, the majority of shareholders, especially individual shareholders who are passively invested in the company through mutual funds or exchange-traded funds, may have little knowledge or even understanding of board activities. This can make it easy to approve board members friendly to the CEO and challenging for shareholders to hold a successful campaign to oust a director if they are not doing a good job.

Another challenge with the board of directors is that members may not invest enough time or effort to provide diligent oversight for the company, creating board inattention. Board members that have been successful in the industry are often sought out for a board, as they can potentially provide good guidance to the company based on their experience. At the same time, that person may be pressed for time or not be paid enough to expend a lot of effort for the company. For example, the annual salary for a board member of a large publicly traded company can be around $250,000. While that is a large sum of money to most people, it may not be enough money to motivate someone who previously made a great deal of money as a successful CEO!

Overall, various agency problems can stem from conflicts of interest between shareholders, debtholders, managers, and members of the board of directors. These agency problems can cause a reduction in company value and present a challenge for the proper functioning of any company. In the next section we detail ways in which these types of agency problems can be reduced or avoided.

> **QUICK CHECK 11.4** Briefly describe how there may be agency problems associated with the different stakeholders that own and control corporations.

11.3 Corporate Governance and Strategies: Internal Governance

In order to prevent these problems from occurring, companies pay particular attention to corporate governance: systems put into place to prevent or correct such agency problems. These systems include internal mechanisms—such as compensation contracts offered by firms to managers, corporate structure, and company actions such as financial policy and disclosure—and external forces such as regulation and market discipline. In this section we describe internal governance mechanisms, and in Section 11.4 we cover external governance.

11.3.1 Pay and Contracts

Setting pay and compensation contracts is one way to try to solve some of these agency problems. One common practice is to pay managers with stock (or call options on the firm's stock). The CEO's or manager's actions should directly affect how well the company does, and thus its stock price. An increase in the stock price will make the shares of stock more valuable; as discussed in Chapter 7, it will also increase the value of call options based on that stock since a call option enables the owner to buy the stock at a predetermined price and thus benefit from an increase in price. If managers get a large portion of compensation from stock or options, then they have an increased incentive to make decisions that add value to the firm. If a manager owns, or could own through options, stock in the company, an increase in stock price will increase their personal wealth. Similarly, paying members of the board of directors in stock and options may incentivize them to put more effort into overseeing the company.

Managers' compensation contracts often also come with additional features to further ensure that incentives are aligned. One common feature is including vesting periods for stock or options. If a manager is paid in stock with a vesting period, the manager cannot sell the stock until the vesting period ends. Similarly, a vesting period for options prevents the holder from exercising the option (i.e., buying the stock for the exercise price) until the vesting period has ended. Vesting periods help to ensure that CEOs and other managers focus on the long-term value of the company. Otherwise, a manager may be able to take some action that raises the price of the stock in the short run—thus enabling the manager to sell the stock for a profit—but is revealed to not be a good decision in the long run. For example, the manager could announce earnings targets that are unrealistically high, which misleads investors and can cause the value of the firm to plummet when the firm doesn't reach the target, or investing in a negative-NPV project that has the appearance of being a good project.

Another feature frequently included in the compensation contracts of CEOs or top managers is a golden parachute, which is a large payment made to a CEO if they are forced to leave that position—for example, when there is a change of control in the company, such as a merger or acquisition. As discussed, managers have an incentive to entrench themselves to protect their jobs, and one way of doing so is to intentionally prevent an efficient merger from happening. A golden parachute provides an incentive for a manager to not stand in the way of such a deal, because management will be compensated.

Contracts related to compensation help to solve some conflicts of interest. The particular contract used depends on the "right tool for the job," namely, the contract or instrument should match the incentive needed. For example, paying stocks or options to employees whose job performance will have a nonmeasurable impact on the stock price may be a poor incentive as it exposes them to risk that they have no influence on (e.g., the stock price).

However, some problems are difficult to solve even with a properly designed compensation structure. For example, if a manager highly values the private benefits that a particular project provides, then paying the manager in stock or offering different types of compensation may not be enough to incentivize the manager to choose the better project. Thus, other mechanisms of corporate governance are needed, such as ensuring oversight between stakeholders and policies the company can implement.

11.3.2 Shareholder Voting and Board Composition

An important aspect of corporate governance is the shareholder vote, which provides oversight on the company's operations. For example, shareholders can place a vote of no confidence in a company's CEO if the CEO is performing poorly, which puts pressure on the board of directors to fire the CEO. Furthermore, shareholders can vote to include particular people on the board of directors who are likely to enhance the company's corporate governance.

It is considered a good corporate governance practice to include outside directors—that is directors who are unaffiliated with the company itself—as members of the board. Thus, outside directors are not previous employees of the company and do not have a previous connection with the company (such as a previous business relationship with the company's CEO). The idea behind outside directors on the board is that they are more likely to be objective compared to "insiders," and can provide a different perspective on company matters.

Another practice is to include blockholders on the board. A blockholder is the owner of a large number (or block) of the company's shares—commonly at least 5% of the outstanding shares of the company. That they own a large number of shares means that this is likely valuable and significant to the blockholder's wealth, which gives the blockholder an incentive to be an attentive board member. Furthermore, the large number of shares allows the blockholder to exert substantial influence through voting rights.

11.3.3 Financial Policy

The firm's financial policy can also be a powerful force in mitigating some of the agency problems discussed above. These policies include paying out earnings to investors and capital structure choices.

The free cash flow problem—where a manager can use cash to easily invest in suboptimal projects—results when the company is holding a substantial amount of cash. A straightforward solution is therefore to find ways to reduce the amount of excess cash that the company is holding through the company's financial policies. Payout policy, which determines cash distributions to stockholders by paying dividends or repurchasing stock, is one way that companies can drain excess cash by "giving money back" to investors (discussed in detail in Chapter 12). Using debt is another way that companies can mitigate the free cash flow problem. Debt forces management to distribute cash to the firm's debtholders in the form of prescheduled payments of interest and principal, thereby reducing the amount of free cash flow available to managers.

Issuing debt can also help to improve corporate governance in other ways. Paying interest and principal to debtholders is mandated by law, and if a company reneges on its obligation, the debtholders can pull the company into bankruptcy. Such a situation has a good chance of resulting in the management of the firm being fired. To avoid this, the management may be more careful about selecting good investments and making decisions that benefit the company. Covenants that restrict the company from making ad hoc investments can also reinforce this incentive. This is the disciplining effect of debt. Finally, debtholders also have an incentive to monitor the operations of the company to detect violations of covenants (thus providing verification to other stakeholders and investors), and can at times directly intervene to block inefficient investments or company actions.

11.3.4 Voluntary Disclosure

Transparency is an important part of corporate governance that prevents agency problems. Transparency entails providing details about a company to investors and regulators, assuring them that the company is being run efficiently and is not engaging in fraudulent activities. Companies may disclose (or communicate) information to investors voluntarily through announcements of new products, large investments, announcing earnings targets, and so on.

The idea behind increased voluntary disclosure is that the more information that investors and regulators have regarding a company's operations, the more likely they are to be able to prevent agency problems from occurring. However, there can be disadvantages for a company too. Any information that is disclosed publicly will be seen by a company's competitors. For example, a smartphone company may want to provide investors with information about an upcoming phone that is likely to be successful, to improve investor confidence in the prospects of the company. However, these details will also be seen by competing manufacturers, who can then start to design their own products in response. This will hurt the sales of the smartphone company's upcoming phone.

Overall, the above actions that firms can directly take—compensation, corporate structure, financial policy, and transparency—all help to solve agency problems and ensure the efficient functioning of the firm. These actions are in line with **Principle 9:** *Transparency, verification, and trust are all important to the proper functioning of the financial system.* Beyond what the company itself can do, there are also forces *outside* the company that help to ensure its proper functioning. We discuss these next.

> **QUICK CHECK 11.5** What is corporate governance, and how can it help to solve agency problems?

11.4 Regulation and Market Discipline: External Governance

In addition to internal choices made within a company, external governance is applied by regulators or from markets. External governance refers broadly to forces outside the company that align the incentives of managers with those of the firm. These forces can be as effective or ineffective as internal governance systems, and produce similar results. These forces and systems include regulation by government authorities that companies must abide by, and incentives imposed on managers by the market.

11.4.1 Regulation

Laws and regulations require companies to disclose certain information to the government and to investors. In countries across the world, publicly traded companies are required to file audited accounting statements (such as balance sheets and income statements) with regulators on a regular basis. In certain jurisdictions, such as the EU, some private companies are also required to disclose such accounting information. Additional regulations require some companies to file additional information, such as statements describing the mechanisms the company has in place to prevent fraud, and attestations by independent auditors of the company's financials (one example of such a law is the Sarbanes–Oxley Act–see Box 11.1).

Laws and regulations can also more directly prevent problems by making certain actions illegal. One example is laws that prevent insider trading, where a manager or some other individual working with a company trades on the company's stock, knowing details about the company's future actions that other (outside) investors do not. At a minimum, beyond being unfair to investors, insider trading can remove incentives for managers to work hard and improve the value of the firm. Other laws require the company's managers and directors to be accountable to the shareholders. These types of laws collectively can increase the confidence that investors have in how the company is run, and thus can increase trust in the firm and therefore enhance its operations (Principle 9).

However, there are costs: Complying with accounting regulation (preparing forms in a certain way, creating account systems, hiring auditors) can be expensive for companies and can even influence decisions based on their effects on the financials.

> **Box 11.1 World of Business: The Sarbanes–Oxley Act**
>
> The Sarbanes–Oxley (SOX) Act was legislation passed in the United States in July 2002, and was aimed at improving accounting standards and oversight with the goal of protecting investors from fraudulent financial reporting. The law was passed in response to a series of high-profile scandals involving publicly traded companies, such as Enron Corporation and WorldCom. Enron, a large US energy and commodities company that operated in multiple countries, filed for bankruptcy in 2001 after it became known that it engaged in massive accounting fraud over many years. The bankruptcy also caused the downfall of Enron's auditor, the large accounting firm Arthur Andersen, due to its questionable accounting practices that permitted Enron to operate fraudulently. WorldCom, the second-largest US telecommunications company, filed for bankruptcy in 2002 due to an accounting scandal led by the CEO and top executives. At the time, the bankruptcies were two of the largest in US history (and the largest at the time due to scandal). These scandals led to reduced trust in financial reporting in general.
>
> There were many provisions of SOX that strengthened oversight. For example, criminal penalties were codified, including prison terms, for executives who knowingly signed off on inaccurate financial statements or did not retain accurate records for long enough. Other provisions required firms to file specific reports. Section 404 of SOX required that all firms of a certain size (with publicly traded stock not held by insiders greater than $75 million in value) file a "Management Report," in which the manager has to opine on the quality of the firm's "Internal Control over Financial Reporting"—potential risks in the financial reporting that may lead to misrepresentation or fraud. Examples of such risks include inaccurate recordings of sales revenues. An independent auditor's report attesting to these controls must also be included.
>
> The passing of the law had a positive impact on corporate governance, with an increased focus on ethics and corporate responsibility, and a change in the structure and oversight of corporations. For example, there has been more of a shift in corporate control from the CEO to the board of directors since SOX was passed. Many have considered SOX to be a success, contributing to a limited number of financial accounting scandals. Furthermore, similar legislation has been passed in other countries based on SOX. For example, EU rules set in 2014 and expanded in subsequent years established requirements for audits and a framework for imposing sanctions to protect investors.
>
> *Source:* Peregrine, M. W. (2021). The lasting, positive impact of Sarbanes-Oxley. Harvard Law School Forum on Corporate Governance, corpgov.law.harvard.edu.

11.4.2 Market Discipline: Hostile Takeovers

A hostile takeover happens when a company (the target) is acquired by another company or individual (the acquirer) against the wishes of the target firm's management, as opposed to a friendly merger with amicable and negotiated terms. The threat of a takeover can play an important role in resource allocation and in disciplining managers and boards, compelling them to act in the best interests of the company.

A hostile takeover begins when an acquirer identifies a target company and purchases a large number of shares of the company. The targets of such a takeover are usually significantly mismanaged firms—ones whose management has chosen an investment plan that leads the firm to be significantly undervalued, given the firm's resources. However, takeovers can differ depending on the intention of the acquiring firm. In some cases, once the takeover is complete, the acquirer will use its control rights to replace the existing managers (and/or board) of the company (with ones that can better operate it). This will result in an increase in value of the target, and the acquirer can then sell shares of the firm at the new market price for a profit.

In other cases, once the takeover is complete and the acquiring firm obtains control, it may have no interest in continuing to run the firm. Instead, it may choose to liquidate the target firm, selling the individual assets (e.g., factories, equipment, buildings) to the highest bidder. Why might such a strategy be profitable to an acquirer? For a well-run firm, the strategy and decisions made by management usually adds value (i.e., synergy) to the individual assets of the company, making them more valuable together than as standalone assets. In this case, the value of the whole company will be greater than the sum of the value of its individual parts. However, a company that is poorly run by its management can substantially take away value from the assets, implying that the assets would be more valuable separately than together under the control of the management. In this case, an acquirer can purchase the entire company for a relatively low price, and sell off the assets individually to make a profit.

Once an acquirer has made an initial investment in a target company, it will increase its control by purchasing more shares. The acquirer may be able to purchase enough shares on its own to gain complete control. In other cases, it may not be able to obtain more than 50% ownership (and therefore control) of the company because there are not enough shares of stock being sold on the open market. In that case, the acquirer may be able to organize a shareholder meeting to convince other shareholders to either vote to approve the acquirer's plan, or the acquirer may offer to buy the other shares at a premium.

The threat of a takeover and the subsequent replacement of management provides a strong incentive for current managers (acting in their self-interest) to act in the interests of the firm by maximizing market value. Indeed, even in the absence of any explicit instructions from the shareholders or knowledge of management theory, one might expect managers to move in the direction of value maximization as a matter of self-preservation. Moreover, it should be noted that it does not matter whether the source of the mismanagement is incompetence or the pursuit of different objectives, the takeover mechanism serves equally well to correct either one.

Hostile takeovers were widespread in the 1980s, and still occur today. However, they are less common today for a few reasons. First, the effectiveness of the takeover mechanism has been reduced by government policies that have been put in place since the 1980s. For example, in an attempt to prevent the formation of monopolies, regulators such as the US Department of Justice and EU antitrust regulators will take legal action under antitrust laws to prevent mergers or acquisitions that might reduce competition. Because it is more likely that a supplier, customer, or competitor will be the takeover bidder who identifies the mismanaged firm, this public policy will tend to reduce the threat of takeover. Other laws, such as regulations that require shareholders to disclose their intent once they accumulate a large enough ownership stake in a company (currently 7.5% in the United States) partly remove the potential advantage of "surprise" that an acquirer may have had.

Second, many companies incorporate explicit defenses against hostile takeovers. These are sometimes referred to as shark repellent policies. A common example is a poison pill, where in the likely event of a takeover attempt (e.g., if a single shareholder obtains a certain proportion of company ownership), a company's outstanding shares experience an automatic dilution or other shareholders are enabled to purchase shares at a discount. Such a contingency can be built into a company's charter. Another example is a provision that a higher proportion of shareholders (e.g., over 80%) approve mergers, rather than a simple majority. Another type of shark repellent policy is that some firms may even intentionally engage in mergers or take on high levels of debt as a tactic to complicate an acquiring firm's strategy (Disney engaged in this strategy to fend off a takeover attempt, as described in Box 11.2).

The efforts by regulators to make hostile takeovers more difficult are motivated by negative outcomes, such as economic inefficiency from viable companies in a temporary downturn being liquidated, flowing on to the human costs that come from the loss of jobs. In addition, acquirers have engaged in games to enrich themselves through takeover attempts. One example is known as greenmail, which is when an acquirer purchases a large portion of the target company's shares, and threatens to purchase additional shares unless the company agrees to buy out the acquirer's shares at a premium (leaving the acquirer with a large profit). While it may be tempting for a company to make such an agreement to eliminate the immediate threat, it then signals to others that they can successfully do the same thing!

Managers or boards may have divergent interests or incorrect knowledge, and thus the takeover mechanism can provide a powerful incentive for managers and boards to run their companies more efficiently. This is especially important with publicly traded firms with dispersed ownership of the shares. Thus, while these efforts to reduce hostile takeovers can mitigate some of the downsides of takeovers, they can also reduce their positive incentive effects.

> **QUICK CHECK 11.6** How does the threat of a takeover serve as a mechanism to deal with the conflict of interest between owners and managers of a corporation?

Box 11.2 World of Business: The Hostile Takeover Attempt on Disney

In June 1984, Walt Disney Productions Inc. was the subject of a takeover attempt by Saul Steinberg, a well-known corporate raider. Steinberg announced a purchase of 6.3% of outstanding Disney stock and his intention to increase his holdings to 25%. When the CEO of Disney, Ron Miller, responded by engaging in acquisitions of other companies to complicate Steinberg's strategy, Steinberg made a public offer for 49% control of Disney. Disney was trading for $54.25 per share at the time, and Steinberg's offer involved a premium of about $13–18 per share.

The takeover attempt came at a time when Disney had experienced lackluster financial performance, struggling with attendance at its theme parks and cost overruns from theme park construction. Steinberg's goal, if he were to acquire Disney, was to sell off the company in pieces (particularly making a profit on the land that Disney's theme parks—Disneyland and Disney World—were sitting on).

With the prospect of Disney facing liquidation, and the understanding that many shareholders would find Steinberg's offer appealing, given Disney's financial struggles, the company paid Steinberg approximately $77.50 per share to buy out his holdings of Disney, thus ending the takeover attempt.

However, after this, Disney's stock price fell because this induced other corporate raiders to make their own raids, seeing that greenmail strategies were effective. Disney's board of directors, perturbed by the course of events, bought out all of the raiders and recognized that the company was not being run effectively, thus allowing such a situation to occur. The board fired Ron Miller as CEO, and hired Michael Eisner as the new CEO, with a new corporate strategy based on creating films to bolster the intellectual property of the company, which its merchandise and theme parks were based on. Disney's current corporate strategy continues to leverage its content creation, and thus remains rooted in the strategy that Eisner put into place.

Source: Bruner, R. F. (2017). Walt Disney Productions, June 1984. *Darden Business Publishing Cases.* https://doi.org/10.1108/case.darden.2016.000346.

11.4.3 Market Discipline: Activist Shareholders

Another form of external governance comes from shareholders known as activist shareholders. Activist shareholders are individuals who own large numbers of shares of a company—and thus wield substantial influence—and are also outspoken to other shareholders and the media regarding their views on company policy. This can exert pressure on the company's management to undertake specific actions that are beneficial to the shareholders, such as paying out excess cash in the form of dividends or repurchases (which can help to solve the free cash flow problem) or not engaging in suboptimal acquisitions.

The influence of activist shareholders is closely related to the mechanism of takeovers, since activists may engage in a takeover attempt or rally a vote to oust the management team. Often activist shareholders use their influence to vote and convince other shareholders to vote on specific changes in a company, such as ousting the company's existing management. This strategy may be beneficial to an activist investor as it allows them to change corporate strategy to increase value via organized persuasion of other large shareholders, without having to pay a premium to acquire actual control of a company. Activist investors may also try to secure seats for themselves on the company's board of directors. Box 11.3 describes a real-world example of how activist shareholders can influence well-known large companies in the United States and abroad.

In sum, external forces such as regulation and investors in the marketplace can serve as forms of corporate governance and potentially improve company value. However, in practice, companies may have further objectives beyond improving company value, which can present additional challenges.

Box 11.3 World of Business: Activist Investors, Netflix, and Japan

In November 2012, streaming video company Netflix was engaged in a fight with Carl Icahn, a well-known activist investor. From July 2011 to November 2012, shares of Netflix had fallen from $300 to $80, a decline of 73%. Carl Icahn, upon seeing this decline, increased his stake in Netflix to just under 10%. Netflix's stock price increased in response to this, due to the possibility that Icahn's activism would improve Netflix's strategy and performance, or that Icahn would position Netflix to be acquired by another company at a premium over its current stock price. Indeed, Icahn publicly commented on the need for change by management, including the possibility of Netflix being acquired by a larger technology or media company.

In response to Icahn's purchase, Netflix undertook a poison pill defense, which would allow shareholders the right to buy more shares of stock if any individual shareholder owned more than 10% of the stock, thus making control more difficult for Icahn. Icahn blasted the move as an example of "poor corporate governance."

In the end, the poison pill did not deter Icahn, and he raised his stake to about 12%. However, Netflix's stock price took off afterwards, as the CEO was determined to show that his strategy for the company was viable, validating the effects of Icahn's activism. Carl Icahn sold his shares in 2015, providing him a profit from his investment of roughly $1.6 billion.

The role and effect of activist investors is similar in countries across the globe. In Japan, for example, the structure of companies has been criticized by international investors as generally holding too much cash and not focusing enough on profitability. Reforms implemented by the Japanese government in 2014 were aimed to make companies engage more with shareholders through increased corporate governance, such as encouraging the use of restricted stock in paying senior management. As a result, there has been an increase in activity by activist investors in Japan, and nearly 70% of Japanese firms expect more activist investor activity. This has affected many of the largest and most well-known Japanese firms. After years of clashing with activist investors, Toshiba's shareholders voted to add two activist investors to board seats in 2022. In 2023, Toyota Motor's longtime CEO has found himself the target of activist investors who are seeking to unseat him over the company's climate disclosure policies.

Sources: Gustin, S. (2012). Raiders of the lost stream: Netflix fight with Carl Icahn escalates over "poison pill." *Time*, 6 Nov. Yamazaki, M. (2022). Toshiba board gains two directors from activist funds in historic shift. *Reuters*. Long, K. (2022). The rise of activist investors in Japan. *The Banker*.

11.5 The Challenge of Multiple Objectives

The primary objective of a firm is to maximize value; however, firms increasingly have additional objectives that managers need to consider in addition to value maximization. These objectives involve stakeholders—people with an interest in the company's operations—other than investors or those running the company. For example, firms often have environmental, social, and governance (ESG) objectives, where a firm invests in projects that advance environmental goals (such as emissions reduction) or social goals (such as programs to help youth in the local community). Other such stakeholders may be the employees of the company itself, and an additional objective for the company may be to increase benefits or perks for employees. These goals may even be pursued by activist investors; Box 11.4 explains how an activist investor successfully pushed Exxon-Mobil, one of the world's largest oil companies, to pursue investments in renewable energy.

There are benefits and challenges to a firm having multiple objectives. A number of academic research papers have suggested that firms pursuing these additional objectives may increase their value (see Gillan et al. 2021). For example, investment in the local community (an ESG objective) has a social benefit, but also has a positive impact on existing employees who live there, which improves their productivity. It also may attract good new employees. In this way, such goals may be aligned with value maximization.

However, implementing multiple objectives for the management of a firm introduces challenges, as the pursuit of some objectives may be at the expense of others. First, it becomes difficult and perhaps almost impossible to prove that management is doing a poor job of running the company if they have the excuse of serving one or more of the company's stakeholders (including, at the extreme, the good of society at large). Second, it may not be feasible for managers to deviate much from value maximization without the risk of takeover and change in control (and thus getting fired). Put differently, a firm that is sacrificing value maximization in favor of other objectives may be easily taken over, which creates a disincentive for managers to pursue such goals.

> **Box 11.4** World of Business: An Activist Investor Gains Three Seats on Exxon-Mobil's Board
>
> As of June 2021, Christopher James' hedge fund Engine No. 1 had won three seats on the board of directors of Exxon-Mobil Corp., one of the world's largest oil companies. His victory came as he had called on Exxon to slash expenses on projects that might lose money when oil and gas prices are low, realign management incentives, and develop a plan to invest in renewable energy. James' arguments won him the support of shareholders, including some of Wall Street's biggest money managers, who voted to award board seats to three of his handpicked candidates.
>
> He benefited from good timing. Exxon had been weakened by a $22 billion loss in 2020, making it more vulnerable to investors' fears about shrinking profits and concerns about the company's future.
>
> James' victory was a watershed moment in the efforts to seek more ESG modifications at the nation's biggest companies. His argument was that the giants of the oil industry would drop in value unless they embraced a transition to renewable energy.
>
> *Sources:* Baer, J., and Lim, D. (2021). The hedge-fund manager who did battle with Exxon—and won. *Wall Street Journal.* Matthews, C. M. (2021). Activist likely to gain third seat on Exxon board. *Wall Street Journal.*

Finally, just as in the classic challenge of managerial perks described earlier in the chapter, there are potential agency conflicts from other individual stakeholders with small economic interests in the firm that may press for value-destroying actions that benefit their causes or compensation. For example, a local politician may put pressure on a company to halt construction of a new building, citing environmental concerns, when in fact the politician is trying to curry favor with certain groups.

Overall, it is important to keep in mind that the benefits of pursuing multiple objectives may not be as simple as they might appear.

Conclusion

In this chapter we have examined the organizational structure of companies, and how ownership and control can be divided within companies. The separation of ownership and control, which is a feature of the corporate form, permits a number of advantages, such as allowing managers to specialize in running the firm while owners focus on providing capital. However, a separated structure also introduces the potential for agency conflicts, where different stakeholders pursue their own interests at the expense of other stakeholders or the firm. Corporate governance includes both internal policies and external forces such as markets and regulations which aim to reduce agency problems and ensure the proper functioning of a company. Many firms also pursue multiple objectives in addition to maximizing firm value, which can complicate things.

This chapter continues our examination of decision making within firms, and explores the reasons why, even though firms *should* make decisions that improve company value—such as investing in positive-NPV projects as we discussed in the previous chapter—they may not. The considerations discussed in this chapter are central to the investment decisions of firms, but also the sources of financing that firms may decide to tap into. In subsequent chapters we will explore more of these implications, how they can confer certain advantages or disadvantages to particular places that firms can turn to for funding, and how we can formally analyze some of these considerations within models.

Takeaways

- Agency problems happen when different stakeholders of companies take actions that benefit themselves at the expense of the company. Agency problems arise because there is a separation of ownership, control, and management within companies—the people running companies are not always those who own the companies and/or who control the decision making.
- In a typical corporation there are four key groups of stakeholders: shareholders, debtholders, managers, and the board of directors.
- Corporate governance refers to systems put into place to prevent or reduce agency problems. Mechanisms of corporate governance include pay and contracts, shareholder voting, financial policy (all internal governance mechanisms), and laws and regulations.
- The market can act as a form of external governance, imposing discipline on managers. Hostile takeovers and activist shareholders are two examples of how the market can induce companies to take actions that maximize value.
- Firms may sometimes try to pursue multiple objectives in addition to value maximization. Such objectives may not be as simple to implement without unintended negative consequences.

Key Terms

Activist shareholders 327
Agency costs 313
Agency problems 313
Agents 313
Blockholders 323
Board inattention 321
Board of directors 317
Captured board 321
Common stock 316
Corporate governance 322
Corporation 314
Covenants 317
Debtholders 317
Default 317
Dilute 319
Disciplining effect of debt 323
Disclose 324
Entrenchment 321
Environmental, social, and governance (ESG) 329
External governance 324
Free cash flow problem 320
General partner 314
Golden parachute 322
Greenmail 326
Hostile takeover 325
Incentive problems 313
Limited liability 314
Limited partners 314
Managers 317
Monitor 323
Outside directors 323
Partnership 314
Payout policy 323
Poison pill 326
Preferred stock 316
Principals 313
Private corporations 315
Public corporations 314
Publicly traded corporations 314
Restricted stock 317
Separated structure 315
Shareholder meetings 316
Shareholders 316
Shark repellent policies 326
Sole proprietorship 314
Transparency 323
Unlimited liability 314
Vesting period 322

Problems

1. You are thinking of starting your own business, but have no money.
   (a) Think of a business that you could start without having to borrow any money.
   (b) Now think of a business that you would want to start if you could borrow any amount of money at the going market interest rate.
   (c) What are the risks you would face in this business?
   (d) Where can you get financing for your new business?
2. While there are clear advantages to the separation of management from ownership of business enterprises, there is also a fundamental disadvantage in that it may be costly to align the goals of management with those of the owners. Suggest at least two methods, other than the takeover market, by which the conflict can be reduced, albeit at some cost.
3. Consider a poorly run local coffee shop with its prime location featuring a steady stream of potential clients passing by on their way to and from campus. How might an active takeover market help to improve the coffee shop's operations?
4. Recently, legislation has been proposed that would limit the deductibility of interest paid on so-called junk bonds when the bonds were issued to pay for the takeover of a corporation by another group (such bonds generally have relatively high coupon rates, reflecting the relatively high risks). What do you think is the reasoning behind the proposal? Which corporate stakeholders would gain and/or lose from such legislation?

5. The Griffey-Lang Food Company faces a difficult problem. In management's effort to grow the business, it has accrued a debt of $150 million while the value of the company is only $125 million. Management must come up with a plan to alleviate the situation in one year or face certain bankruptcy. Also upcoming are labor relations meetings with the union to discuss employee benefits and pension funds. Griffey-Lang at this time has three choices: (1) launch a new, relatively untested product that, if successful (probability of 0.12), will allow Griffey-Lang to increase the value of the company to $200 million; (2) sell off two food production plants in an effort to reduce some of the debt and the value of the company, thus making it even less likely to avoid bankruptcy (0.45 probability of success); or (3) do nothing (probability of failure = 1.0).
   (a) As a creditor, what would you like Griffey-Lang to do, and why?
   (b) As an investor?
   (c) As an employee?
6. Explain the tools that shareholders can use to replace a CEO that is performing badly.
7. Explain why the owner of a small, family-run business with no plans to significantly expand may prefer to operate as a sole proprietorship or partnership.
8. A member of the board of directors of a company is not properly fulfilling his duties. An activist investor calls attention to this, and wants a shareholder meeting to replace the member. However, the activist finds it difficult to rally enough shareholders to hold an effective meeting. What might be the cause of this?
9. Are there circumstances in which shareholders may make decisions that are bad for firm value? Explain.
10. Why might a company's shareholders not like the company holding a large amount of cash?
11. Explain how compensation contracts can be designed to solve agency problems.
12. What are the costs and benefits of regulation in ensuring the efficient operation of companies?
13. You observe a company that is the target of an activist shareholder, who has signaled that they want to acquire the company because it is underperforming. The company responds by introducing a poison pill. Is this action good or bad for company value? Explain.
14. Explain how the existence of hostile takeovers can enhance firm value.
15. You see a local manufacturing company installing state-of-the-art emissions-reduction equipment, with a commitment to update that equipment to the latest technology each year, no matter the cost. What are the benefits and challenges with this strategy?

12 PAYOUT POLICY

CHAPTER OVERVIEW

12.1	Forms of Payout	334
12.2	Does Payout Policy Matter? Payout in a Frictionless Environment	336
12.3	How Payout Policy Can Add Value: Payout with Frictions	340
12.4	Stock Dividends and Splits	346

LEARNING OBJECTIVES

After reading this chapter, you will be able to:
- describe how dividends and share repurchases work, and how they can be used by companies to distribute funds back to investors;
- explain why investors do not gain any value from payout policy when there are no frictions in the market;
- understand and explain the reasons why, when there are frictions in the market, payout policy can create value for companies and investors;
- explain why companies may choose to pay investors dividends rather than do share repurchases, or vice versa;
- rationalize the use of stock splits and stock dividends.

EQUATIONS YOU KNOW

Total company value	$V = D + E$	Eq. 9.1

✚ You are deciding between some company stocks to invest in, and notice that one company pays dividends regularly. How might this affect your choice of what to invest in?

✚ You are the CFO of a company, and decide to give some of the cash your company holds back to investors. What are your options?

- A company you own stock in announces a plan to buy back a large number of shares from investors. As a shareholder, what do you think of this?

- You are the manager of a company that has been successful over the past year and has generated a lot of cash. You decide that you should hold onto the cash just in case, but some of your investors question this decision. Who is correct?

- You work in the consumer retail division of a tablet manufacturing company. The company has regularly been paying a cash dividend to investors for a long time. This year, consumer demand has been down and the company is getting short on cash. Your boss comes to you and explains that the company has decided to suspend some project investments so that it can keep paying its dividend to investors. You are surprised by this decision—what might rationalize it?

Introduction

In the last few chapters we have considered financial and strategic decisions made within companies, and whether they improve the value of the company. In this chapter we continue examining company decisions, and focus on a particular financial decision—the payout decision, which considers whether a company keeps the cash it holds or gives it back to investors. As we will show, this decision is important because firms can potentially increase their value—and benefit their investors—through their choice of whether to pay out cash to investors. Furthermore, as we discussed in the previous chapter, agency problems may arise when companies hold onto large amounts of cash due to managerial conflicts of interest. Thus, payout can serve an important role in corporate governance.

Payout policy refers to the various ways a company can choose to distribute funds back to stockholders. Companies generate cash internally through their operations, and externally through financing (e.g., borrowing funds or issuing shares). Companies may keep a reserve of cash on the balance sheet in order to fund future investments or operations. However, they also distribute excess cash back to shareholders via a variety of payout methods. We will examine the reasons they may do so in this chapter.

We will introduce the different ways to implement payout policy. This consists of direct cash payments to shareholders (dividends), and purchases of shares of stock from investors by the company (share repurchases). We then examine why a company may engage in different policies, and whether they affect shareholder wealth and/or the value of the firm. The first half of the chapter considers payout policy in a frictionless financial environment, where there are no taxes, no market imperfections, and no other inefficiencies, to consider how shareholder wealth is unaffected by the firm's payout policy. This provides the basic foundation for understanding why payout policy may matter to both companies and investors in practice: in the real world, there are frictions which can cause payout policy to have an effect on the wealth of shareholders. These include taxes, regulations, reducing agency costs, and the informational or "signaling" content of dividends, which we will cover in detail.

12.1 Forms of Payout

There are two ways a corporation can distribute funds, or payout, to its shareholders: a cash dividend, which is a cash payment delivered directly to holders of a company's stock, or a stock repurchase (or stock buyback), which is when the company buys shares of its stock back from shareholders.

When a company pays a cash dividend, all shareholders receive cash payments in amounts proportional to the number of shares they own. For example, if you own 100 shares of stock in a company and the company announces a cash dividend of $2 per share, you will receive a payment of $2 × 100 = $200. Cash dividends are referred to by different names, depending on their frequency and the type of share the dividend is paid on.

Regular dividends are scheduled cash dividend payments that happen at a regular frequency, often quarterly. A company declares to investors that it intends to pay regular dividends according to the schedule it announces. Regular dividends typically refer to dividends on common stock. Special dividends are one-time cash payments made to shareholders, which a company might not repeat in the future. Preferred dividends are dividends paid regularly on preferred stock, and a company must prioritize these payments over payments to common stockholders. Companies differ widely in terms of their dividend policy. For example, Berkshire Hathaway (run by Warren Buffett) has never paid dividends to investors, and Alphabet Inc. (the parent company of Google) never paid a dividend until 2024. In contrast, Stanley Black & Decker, a manufacturer of industrial tools, has paid a regular dividend for over 140 years.

Share repurchases are another way that companies can distribute money back to shareholders, while also reducing the number of shares outstanding. In a share repurchase, a company pays cash to buy shares of its stock in the stock market. The company keeps the shares that it has repurchased as treasury stock (i.e., stock that had been issued but is no longer outstanding and can be reissued to raise cash in the future) or retires them (once retired, the shares no longer exist). The shareholders who choose to sell shares to the company will receive a payment in cash. The shareholders who choose to keep their shares may receive value in the form of an increased stock price (a capital gain; these shareholders may also gain more of a voting share, given there are fewer other shareholders). We will discuss in the following sections why the stock price would increase following a share repurchase. The fact that the number of shares outstanding decreases due to a repurchase is another reason companies may use the mechanism—it can offset dilution caused by issuing new shares.

There are two main types of share repurchases. In an open-market repurchase, a company instructs a broker to purchase its stock on a stock exchange, such as the New York Stock Exchange (NYSE) or London Stock Exchange. The company buys its own stock for the current market price, in the same way as any investor would buy the company's stock. In a tender-offer repurchase, a company goes to the shareholders directly and offers to buy back a predetermined number of shares at a certain price. For example, suppose that a company currently has 100,000 shares of stock outstanding that are trading at a price of $50. In a tender-offer repurchase, the company may offer to buy back, say, up to 10,000 shares of stock from interested investors at a price of $55. The company thus offers a price above the current market price in order to incentivize shareholders to sell. Any interested shareholders can take part in the repurchase until all of the offered shares are bought.

Another aspect of payout policy is actions corporations can take which provide additional shares of stock to investors. A stock split transforms each outstanding share into more than one share. For example, a two-for-one stock split means that each old share will now be counted as two shares. Thus, a firm with 500,000 shares outstanding will have one million shares outstanding. This serves to increase the number of shares outstanding, which may be beneficial because it can help enhance trading (liquidity) of a company's stock—a company with a small number of shares outstanding may trade at a very high price (some companies have had shares that trade for hundreds of thousands of dollars apiece), making it difficult for many investors to invest in the company. In the case of a stock dividend, the corporation distributes additional shares of stock to each stockholder. A stock dividend is intended to provide investors compensation in the form of shares of stock; as opposed to cash dividends or repurchases, the company does not spend any cash to pay out to shareholders. Companies may choose to do stock dividends because they do not want to spend cash to do cash dividends or repurchases.

> **QUICK CHECK 12.1** What do stockholders receive from dividends and repurchases?

Having introduced the different forms of payouts, we now turn to understanding how payout policy may matter—that is, whether it affects a company's value—and therefore why firms may choose to engage in payout. The following section will introduce a framework—a frictionless environment—that will allow us to start to analyze the question of why certain payout policies are adopted.

12.2 Does Payout Policy Matter? Payout in a Frictionless Environment

As the previous section showed, there are a number of different forms of payout policy and many different potential real-world considerations in understanding their impact on firms and investors. For example, paying dividends or doing repurchases requires cash, which may affect the investments that companies can make (as we discussed in Chapter 11). Dividends provide direct income to investors, while repurchases may confer capital gains (stock price appreciation), which carries tax implications as income and capital gains tax rates may differ. There are many other considerations beyond this, which we will discuss.

Given the number of possible considerations that may matter, in order to systematically understand why payout policy may matter to investors and guide the decisions of managers, we will begin with a more basic framework to guide our thinking. In particular, we will start with a simplified setting that abstracts away from complications and has no frictions, which are imperfections that prevent markets from functioning perfectly and affect decision making. Frictions include government taxes, costs of doing business in markets (transaction costs), differences in information between market participants (asymmetric information), agency costs (arising from conflicts of interest, as discussed in Chapter 11), and so on. By doing so, we can understand any fundamental value that payout policy may generate, and also understand in a systematic way how payout policy may have value given each individual friction. This will help guide us and tell us what matters—and what does not—in terms of payout policy decisions.

In a "frictionless" financial environment, according to the Miller–Modigliani (M-M) Dividend Proposition (Miller and Modigliani 1961), a firm's payout policy has no effect on the wealth of its current shareholders. The essence of the M-M argument is that shareholders can achieve the effect of any corporate dividend policy by reinvesting dividends or selling shares of stock on their own. Thus, at a very basic level, payout policy should not "matter" to firms and investors if there are no frictions. This tells us that frictions are the key to understanding the value of payout policy, as we will discuss in later sections.

We will begin by illustrating the M-M argument in the context of dividends, and then show that the same logic extends to repurchases.

12.2.1 Dividends in a Frictionless Environment

The M-M argument is that shareholders can achieve the effect of any corporate dividend policy by costlessly reinvesting dividends or selling shares of stock on their own.

To illustrate how this works, consider the case of Generic Consumer Products (GCP), a typical manufacturer of consumer goods. GCP has 500,000 shares of stock outstanding that trade at a market price of $20 per share, so GCP's market value of equity is $E = \$20 \times 500{,}000 = \$10$ million. GCP has debt valued at $D = \$2$ million, making its total value $V = D + E = \$2 + \$10 = \$12$ million. GCP has cash of $2 million and other assets of $10 million.

First, consider the effects when GCP decides to pay a dividend of $2 per share using its cash reserves. In this case, GCP will spend a total of $\$2 \times 500{,}000 = \$1$ million of cash for dividend payments, which will reduce its cash reserves and therefore equity value by $1 million. As a result, GCP's stock price will go down after the dividend payment. Specifically, with 500,000 shares and a new total equity value of $9 million, the new price per share will be $9 million/500,000 = $18. We refer to the share price immediately after a dividend has been paid as the ex-dividend price. However, shareholders are indifferent to GCP paying or not paying a dividend, since that does not affect their wealth. If GCP pays the dividend, shareholders have, per share, $18 of stock and $2 of cash, for a total wealth of $20. If GCP does not pay, they have shares of stock worth $20 each. In any case, shareholder wealth is equal to $20 per share.

What if GCP had issued additional debt of $1 million, rather than using its existing cash, and used the debt proceeds to pay for the dividend? The total company value V of GCP will be unchanged after the debt issue and dividend payment. The total debt value D will increase to $3 million, and the total equity value E will decrease to $9 million, so that $V = D + E = \$3 + \$9 = \$12$ million. As the $1 million in cash raised by the debt issue is immediately paid out as a dividend, the company will still have $2 million in cash and $10 million in other assets. Therefore, we will be in the same situation as when GCP used its cash reserves to pay a dividend: Shareholders are left with shares worth $18 each and $2 of cash per share.

Thus, in either case, GCP's investors retain the same total value irrespective of whether the firm pays dividends: If it does, some shareholder value is now in the form of cash, but total shareholder value remains unchanged. Table 12.1 summarizes each of these situations. It should

Table 12.1 **The effect of cash dividends for GCP. Market value balance sheets under various scenarios.** There are 500,000 shares outstanding. The top of the table represents the original scenario before the firm pays a dividend. The middle of the table shows assets, debt, and equity after the firm has paid a dividend of $1 million; stockholders have the same value as before when considering the share price plus the cash received. The bottom of the table shows outcomes after the firm has raised $1 million in debt to pay a dividend; stockholders have the same value.

Original situation			
Assets		**Debt and equity**	
Cash	$2 million	Debt, D	$2 million
Other assets	$10 million	Equity, E	$10 million
Total	$12 million	Total, V	$12 million
	Price per share: $20		
After cash dividend paid using cash reserves			
Assets		**Debt and equity**	
Cash	$1 million	Debt, D	$2 million
Other assets	$10 million	Equity, E	$9 million
Total	$11 million	Total, V	$11 million
	Price per share: $18		
	Cash per share: $2		
After cash dividend paid by raising debt			
Assets		**Debt and equity**	
Cash	$2 million	Debt, D	$3 million
Other assets	$10 million	Equity, E	$9 million
Total	$12 million	Total, V	$12 million
	Price per share: $18		
	Cash per share: $2		

> **QUICK CHECK 12.2** Recreate Table 12.1, assuming that GCP paid a dividend of $4 per share.

be noted that the same arguments hold no matter where GCP decides to get the cash from—GCP could have issued additional shares of stock or decided to cut investments and use that money to pay dividends—the total value to shareholders would not increase.

Under the assumptions of M-M, investors could sell shares of stock for cash or buy stock using the cash from the dividends, and thus are indifferent between the firm paying or not paying a dividend. Put differently, they could create the same outcome themselves. To see this, suppose that GCP's managers decide not to pay out the $1 million in cash as dividends. Suppose a shareholder who owns 100 shares of GCP stock would have liked to have a cash dividend of $2 per share, which would give a total cash payment of 100 × $2 = $200. The shareholder can simply sell 10 shares of stock (= $200 / $2) at the current market price of $20. The shareholder winds up with GCP stock worth $1,800 (90 shares at $20 per share) and the desired cash amount of $200. Note that this is exactly the same result as if the company had paid a dividend of $2 per share—in that case, the shareholder would have cash from dividends of $200 and GCP stock worth $1,800 (100 shares at $18 per share). Now suppose GCP pays out a cash dividend of $2 per share, and a shareholder who owns 100 shares of GCP stock does not want the cash. After the dividend payment, the shareholder has $200 in cash and $1,800 in stock. They can easily re-establish their original position by using the $200 in cash to buy more shares of the stock at the new price of $18 per share.

Overall, the key intuition of the M-M dividend proposition is that any increase in shareholder wealth relative to the base case does *not* come from dividend policy, since any dividend can be reproduced by investors. This provides us with a number of useful insights. First, in contrast to what someone might intuitively think, paying shareholders cash via dividends is not necessarily valuable to them. In the M-M framework, the only way for a company to add to its value is through making positive-NPV (net present value) investments. Second, because of this, any value that a firm or its shareholders derive from dividends must be due to reasons other than just the distribution of cash. Put differently, the M-M framework assumes that there are no frictions; this tells us that the frictions that we have not considered may be what makes dividends valuable. We consider this shortly. Before we do, we show that the M-M argument also applies to repurchases, and thus more broadly to payout policy in general.

12.2.2 Share Repurchases in a Frictionless Environment

The intuition behind the M-M dividend result also applies to share repurchases. To see this, consider again the example of GCP, which has an equity value of $10 million. Suppose that instead of paying a dividend, GCP decides to repurchase $1 million of shares in an open-market operation.

At a share price of $20, this equates to purchasing $1 million / $20 = 50,000 shares, leaving 450,000 shares outstanding (here we assume the firm retires the shares). Let us consider the effects, ignoring, for the moment, where the money to purchase the shares comes from. The shareholders that choose to sell to GCP have the same wealth both before and after—previously, they held stock worth $20 each, but now they hold $20 in cash. The remaining shareholders hold the fewer remaining shares: There are now 450,000 outstanding shares with an equity value of $10 million, which implies a new share price of $10 million / 450,000 = $22.22. This is a commonly cited reasoning for why companies do repurchases—it results in a capital gain for shareholders. However, it is important to note that this does not account for *how* GCP purchased the shares.

First, suppose that GCP spends $1 million cash to purchase the shares. In that case, GCP's cash reserves will fall by $1 million (from $2 million to $1 million), as will the total value of its equity (from $10 million to $9 million, because the repurchased shares are retired). With 450,000 shares remaining, the new price per share after the repurchase will be $9 million / 450,000 = $20. Thus, the share price remains exactly the same: The capital gain caused by there being fewer shares is offset by the fact that GCP must spend its cash to purchase the shares.

The same situation occurs if GCP funded the repurchase in another way. Suppose that GCP instead decides to raise an additional $1 million of debt in order to purchase the shares. Keep in mind that we are still in a frictionless environment—the total value V of GCP will be unchanged after the debt issue and repurchase. When the debt is issued, total debt D will increase to $3 million and cash will increase to $3 million. The share repurchase will then decrease cash by $1 million and decrease equity by $1 million (as explained above). So, after the share repurchase, debt will be $3 (= 2 + 1) million, cash will be $2 (= 2 + 1 − 1) million, equity will be $9 (= 10 − 1) million, and $V = D + E = \$3 + \$9 = \$12$ million. With 450,000 shares, the new price per share after the repurchase will again be $9 million / 450,000 = $20. Both scenarios are summarized in Table 12.2.

Table 12.2 The effect of share repurchases for GCP. Market value balance sheets under various scenarios. The top of the table represents the original scenario before the firm makes a repurchase. The middle of the table shows assets, debt, and equity after the firm has repurchased 50,000 shares; stockholders have the same share price as before. The bottom of the table shows outcomes after the firm has raised $1 million in debt to fund the repurchase of shares; stockholders have the same value.

Original situation			
Assets		**Debt and equity**	
Cash	$2 million	Debt, D	$2 million
Other assets	$10 million	Equity, E	$10 million
Total	$12 million	Total, V	$12 million
	Price per share: $20		
	Shares outstanding: 500,000		
After repurchase funded using cash reserves			
Assets		**Debt and equity**	
Cash	$1 million	Debt, D	$2 million
Other assets	$10 million	Equity, E	$9 million
Total	$11 million	Total, V	$11 million
	Price per share: $20		
	Shares outstanding: 450,000		
After repurchase funded by raising debt			
Assets		**Debt and equity**	
Cash	$2 million	Debt, D	$3 million
Other assets	$10 million	Equity, E	$9 million
Total	$12 million	Total, V	$12 million
	Price per share: $20		
	Shares outstanding: 450,000		

> **QUICK CHECK 12.3** Suppose GCP instead decided to repurchase 100,000 shares. Recreate Table 12.2 for this scenario.

Thus, in both scenarios shareholder wealth is unchanged, as asserted by M-M. Those shareholders who chose to sell shares receive cash, but their wealth is the same as before they sold the shares. The others experience no change in the market value of their shares. Note also that shareholder wealth is exactly the same as if GCP paid a dividend. Thus, neither dividends nor repurchases affect shareholder wealth under the assumptions of frictionless markets.

To sum up, we saw from the previous section that M-M tells us that, in the absence of frictions, paying a dividend does not add value for shareholders. In this section we saw that this insight also applies to repurchases: Repurchasing shares of stock does not increase shareholder value. This provides us with a valuable base case with which to assess why repurchases may be used. In particular, one common argument for why repurchases are used is that they provide a capital gain for shareholders due to the number of shares outstanding being reduced. The argument above shows that this is *not* the reason for why the share price goes up following a repurchase. As with dividends, the M-M framework thus helps to clarify what matters and what does not in assessing repurchases—it is the frictions that we have not considered in our analysis that may add value from payout policy. In the next section we consider these frictions explicitly in our analysis and how they rationalize the use of payout.

12.3 How Payout Policy Can Add Value: Payout with Frictions

We have seen that in a hypothetical, frictionless financial environment, dividend policy does not impact shareholder wealth. This is a valuable starting point for understanding the rationale behind a firm paying dividends or undertaking repurchases, as it explains that any value that is created from doing so is not because of the money the company is distributing to shareholders, since that money is offset by changes in the share price itself. Rather, any value created from payout must be due to frictions, market imperfections that affect decision making, which include taxes, transaction costs, asymmetric information, agency costs, and many others. In this section we consider some of the most important ones that firms face, and how—once these frictions are considered—payout policy can be valuable to shareholders because it can help to resolve some of the inefficiencies that arise from frictions.

12.3.1 Asymmetric Information and Signaling

Firms engage in dividends and repurchases due to the friction of asymmetric information—that the managers and other insiders running a company know more about the company's operations and future prospects than investors and other outsiders. Given this, firms can use payout to demonstrate to investors that the firm is doing well, and thus increase value.

With asymmetric information, the announcement that a firm intends to pay regular dividends (or increase its previously announced dividend amount) can serve as information content. In particular, it can be a positive signal—an action that conveys good news about the company—to the market. The intuition behind this effect is that when a company announces that it will pay regular dividends, it is telling shareholders that it will pay a dividend of a certain amount regularly (say, every quarter). In order for the company to sustain these regular dividend payments, it will have to successfully generate strong cash flows. Managers that are beginning to pay dividends or increasing the amount that the company is paying are therefore implicitly telling investors that they are confident that they will have the cash flows to sustain the dividend payments.

Dividend announcements can thus cause a company's stock price to increase because the market is incorporating this new information.

On the other hand, dividend cuts—when a company either does not pay a scheduled dividend payment or pays a lower payment—are perceived as a very negative signal—an action that conveys bad news about the company—by the market. Although dividend payments are not legally required (in the same way as interest payments), a firm cutting a dividend payment tells investors that the firm, or at least its ability to generate cash flows, may have poor future prospects. This can cause a firm's stock price to decrease significantly.

These effects are borne out empirically. Research has shown that dividend initiations (when a firm announces it will pay dividends for the first time) and increases have positive stock price announcement effects, on the order of +3.4% to +3.7% for initiations and +0.4% for increases (Asquith and Mullins 1983). In contrast, dividend omissions (not paying a dividend) or cuts have even larger negative stock price effects: −7.0% for omissions and −1.3% for cuts.

This positive response by the market to dividend initiations or increases and the negative response to dividend omissions or cuts has a number of implications. First, companies can view dividends as inflexible once they start paying them, and avoid eliminating or cutting them. Firms may even cut their investments instead of cutting their dividend payments. Box 12.1 provides examples of these market incentives.

Second, it makes it feasible for firms with good prospects to signal their quality to investors. If firms with poor prospects (such as those that are badly run) were able to freely use dividends to "mimic" high-quality firms and take advantage of the stock price gain, then dividends would not be an effective signal to investors. However, the fact that low-quality firms are punished by the market when they fail to pay a dividend—which is likely since they are low-quality—makes low-quality firms hesitant to use dividends as a signal.

Share repurchases can also signal to investors, but in a different way from dividends. Share repurchases are viewed as more flexible than dividends, since investors have no expectation of future repurchases. In fact, there are laws that prevent a regular schedule of share repurchases the way regular dividend payments are set up.

To understand the signaling benefit of repurchases, consider a company undertaking an open-market repurchase. The company purchases shares at the current market price. The implication of this to the market is that if the company thinks that its shares are undervalued by the market (trading for less than their true value), or it knows that good news will come in the future that will increase value, then there is an incentive for the company to repurchase shares (and reissue shares when the price is higher—that is, buying low and selling high). Knowing this, investors may view the repurchase as a positive signal of a firm's future prospects, causing an increase in the stock price due to this information getting incorporated when the repurchase is announced.

The signaling effect is different for tender-offer repurchases. Tender-offer repurchases typically have stronger signaling value than open-market repurchases, and may even have stronger signaling value than dividends. In a tender-offer repurchase, the firm typically offers a price to investors that is above the current market price. Furthermore, managers typically abstain from selling their own shares of stock to boost the credibility of the repurchase. This tells investors that the company is very confident, based on its internal information, that its stock price will go up substantially in the future and can cause the firm's stock price to increase when the repurchase is announced. Figure 12.1 depicts the situation with repurchases and signaling.

> **QUICK CHECK 12.4** Explain how a firm's stock price might increase when it begins paying dividends or does a repurchase.

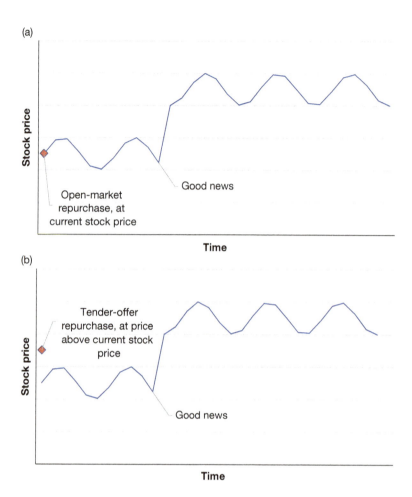

FIGURE 12.1 Signaling with repurchases. (a) This graph shows how open-market repurchases can serve as a signal. The firm repurchases stock at the current price and knows that the price will increase after good news is released. (b) This graph shows how tender-offer repurchases can serve as a signal. The firm repurchases stock at a price higher than the current market price, forecasting that the price is likely to rise even higher after good news is released.

Box 12.1 World of Business: Signaling with Dividends

There has been a long-held argument that the payment of regular dividends is seen as a good sign to the market about a company's prospects, and companies often take actions that are consistent with this notion. If companies are struggling and are in a position where paying dividends is difficult, they will still try hard to avoid cutting dividend payments. For example, in early 2023 Intel Corp.—a major global computer chip manufacturer—struggled with a large and rapid drop in earnings due to supply chain issues and weak global economic conditions inducing depressed demand for its products. Intel looked to preserve cash for the company's turnaround efforts. However, Intel announced at the time that it "remained committed to paying a competitive dividend." Instead of reducing its payout to preserve cash, Intel took other actions, including reducing its executives' pay—the leadership team had its pay reduced by 15% on average, with CEO Pat Gensler taking a 25% salary cut.

In some cases, however, companies cannot avoid cutting dividends. For instance, in 2020 during the COVID-19 pandemic, many companies across the globe suspended or reduced their dividend payments. However, in line with the strong incentives companies face to continue their dividend payouts, once firm balance sheets and profits strengthened in 2021, dividends bounced back strongly globally: 90% of companies across the world increased their dividends or maintained them steadily in 2021, with the greatest rebounds coming from countries that experienced the greatest cuts in dividends during the pandemic, such as the UK and Australia. The UK, for example, had total dividend payouts of roughly £60 billion in 2020, and in 2021 this rose about 45% to over £93 billion. The strong rebound can be viewed as a credible signal of returning to strength of earnings and cash flow among companies, and their respective countries' economies.

Sources: King, I. (2023). Intel slashing CEO, managers' pay in a bid to preserve cash. *Bloomberg News*. Kilincarslan, E. (2022). Demystifying the "dividend puzzle" and making sense of government regulations in times of pandemics. *LSE Business Review*. Blog entry

12.3.2 Agency Frictions

Dividends and repurchases can add value to a company by helping to resolve agency problems, which are when stakeholders of a company act in their own interests at the expense of other stakeholders or the company itself (see Chapter 11).

Payout can be helpful in resolving the free cash flow problem, when managers have a lot of discretion about how to allocate a firm's cash flows and use the cash to invest in projects that do not increase the value of the company. Examples of the free cash flow problem include investments that may not have high NPV or even positive NPV, but which increase management's monetary or non-monetary (i.e., private) benefits: the power, prestige, or perks of the managers. A straightforward way of solving the free cash flow problem is to ensure that the firm is not holding excess amounts of cash. Thus, both dividends and repurchases reduce cash reserves. Box 12.2 provides examples of the use of payout policy by Apple and Microsoft to reduce their cash holdings, a strategy that investors have liked.

Another agency problem that can be solved via repurchase is that of lack of effort by a manager. When a firm repurchases shares, the firm's managers typically do not participate in the buyback, and if they have an ownership share it will increase as the number of outstanding shares decreases. For example, suppose that a manager owns 100 shares of stock and there are 900 other shares outstanding. If the firm buys back 400 shares from other shareholders, the manager continues to have 100 shares but there are only 500 other shares outstanding. The manager's proportional ownership stake therefore increases (from 100 / 1,000 = 10% of all shares to 100 / 600 = 16.7% of all shares). This can better align the incentives of the manager and the company, since the manager now has a proportionally larger share of it, driving them to make better decisions for the company.

Given asymmetric information and signaling effects, when a firm starts paying a dividend, the firm views the payments as inflexible, as we described above. This inflexibility can further help to ameliorate agency problems. The pressure to keep paying dividends—in order to avoid the punishment the market imposes on firms that cut dividends—means that firms keep spending cash in order to pay them. This can help to discipline managers—provide a penalty if they don't make good decisions for the firm—who must now be more hesitant to spend cash on things that do not generate positive cash flows.

> **Box 12.2** World of Business: Global Tech Companies Reduce Cash Using Payout
>
> Global tech giants Apple Inc. and Microsoft Corporation have authorized large share repurchase and dividend programs, reflecting a desire by investors to reduce their large cash reserves. Apple has been a leader in terms of payout policy, conducting roughly $550 billion in repurchases over a ten-year period. In 2021 alone, Apple spent $85.5 billion on repurchases and $14.5 billion on dividends. In 2021, Microsoft announced a $60 billion share repurchase plan, on top of previous plans such as a $40 billion repurchase program and a dividend increase in 2016. These plans have continued in 2023.
>
> In general, investors have liked these moves, as reflected in stock price reactions, indicating that investors do not see better uses by the companies for the large amount of excess cash. In 2021 Microsoft held over $130 billion in cash (or equivalents) on its balance sheet. These large cash holdings had enabled Microsoft to acquire a number of different companies, a strategy that investors were critical of due to the poor performance of many of them. Investors have therefore taken Microsoft's commitment to payout as a sign that it will be more disciplined going forward.
>
> *Source:* Bass, D. (2016). Microsoft plans another $40 billion buyback, boosts dividend. *Bloomberg*, 20 Sept.

> **QUICK CHECK 12.5** Explain how dividends and repurchases can help to reduce agency problems.

12.3.3 Capital Structure Effects

Payout policy decisions can be closely connected to capital structure decisions, since firms can pay for dividends or repurchases using internal or external funds (i.e., debt and equity). A firm can use repurchases as a mechanism for changing its capital structure—for example, by issuing debt and then using the proceeds from the issuance to buy back its stock. As a result, the firm will have taken on more debt but without carrying additional cash, which may expose the firm to the free cash flow problem.

Using external financing to fund dividends and repurchases can also help to amplify some of the positive effects of these forms of payout. A firm that uses debt to finance dividends will use up more excess cash via both dividend and interest payments, and this will exert more discipline on managers. Debt can be used as a positive signal of future prospects when there is asymmetric information, since management is signaling that the firm is likely to have strong cash flows in order to support its promised interest and principal payments. (We will go into more detail on this in Chapter 13.) Since dividends (and repurchases) can also be used as a signal, it follows that funding payout with debt will serve as an even stronger signal.

> **QUICK CHECK 12.6** What are some potential disadvantages of funding dividends or repurchases with debt?

Repurchases can also be used to correct some of the potential distortions of external financing. For example, shareholders experience dilution when a firm issues stock as there are more shares outstanding, resulting in a potentially lower share price (all else being equal) and a smaller ownership stake in the company, which can be offset by a repurchase that reduces shares outstanding and subsequentially increases ownership stake.

12.3.4 Transaction Costs, Taxes, and Regulations

Frictions related to transaction costs, taxes, and regulations can affect the relative attractiveness of dividends and repurchases to companies.

Firms that do not use their internal cash reserves to pay dividends can raise funds externally. However, raising funds externally entails transaction costs—which are costs, both in terms of money and time/effort, associated with financial transactions. For example, the investment bankers who intermediate the sale of new shares to outside investors have to be paid, and it is the firm's current shareholders who bear that cost.

In some countries, such as Singapore, dividends are mostly tax-free. In most countries, however, including the United States, the tax authorities require shareholders to pay personal income taxes on cash dividends. Put differently, a shareholder that receives a dividend is receiving a cash payment; this payment is taxed as income for the shareholder. Thus, if a corporation distributes cash by paying dividends, it forces all of its shareholders to pay taxes, often at the ordinary income tax rate.[1] If, instead, the firm distributes the cash by repurchasing shares, any tax costs borne by the shareholders come in the form of capital gains taxes when the investors sell their shares. From a shareholder tax perspective, the relative advantage of dividends compared to repurchases depends on whether the tax rate for dividends (often the ordinary income rate) is higher or lower than the tax rate for capital gains. For example, in the United States the capital gains tax rate has historically been lower than the average ordinary income tax rate, creating a shareholder tax advantage for repurchases. This may be a consideration for management in making payout decisions, since shareholders may have more demand for the stocks of companies that do repurchases as opposed to dividends. However, keep in mind that tax codes vary substantially across countries and also over time within the same country, complicating this factor.

Regulations can also affect whether firms are more inclined to use dividends or repurchases. As we previously mentioned, there are laws that prevent corporations from using share repurchase as an alternative to dividends as a regular mechanism for paying cash to shareholders. The authorities take the view that taxes ought to be paid on these distributions of cash, and that repurches can be used as a way to either avoid the payment of personal taxes on dividends or to avoid a higher tax rate. Laws in different countries have also restricted or outright banned the use of certain types of payout; Box 12.3 goes into the details of regulations on repurchases across the globe.

Box 12.3 The Legal Landscape of Share Repurchases across the Globe

Share repurchases, or buybacks, are used by companies in countries around the world. In 2018, nearly 80% of US companies and roughly 40% of companies in other countries used share repurchases. Shareholders of companies in different countries broadly have similar reactions to repurchases: They generate significant and positive excess returns in both the short run and the long run, consistent with repurchases having a beneficial effect and shareholders viewing them as adding value. Past estimates have pegged the short-run positive announcement returns of repurchases globally at around 1.3–3%, and the long-run positive abnormal returns over 3–4 years at around 25–30%. This is in line with repurchases being used for value-adding reasons by companies, such as reducing free cash flow problems and signaling positive prospects to the market.

However, it has also been argued that repurchases can be used for nonvalue-maximizing reasons, such as distorting earnings per share and other metrics (buybacks reduce the number of shares outstanding, thus mechanically affecting metrics that use the number of shares), enriching managers and increasing their ownership stake in companies, and potentially favoring some investors over others when companies make repurchase transactions. These potential reasons have often

---

[1] There are exceptions in the tax law. For example, in the United States "qualified" dividends refer to dividends received when a stock has been held for a sufficient amount of time around the dividend payment date. The tax rate is lower for qualified dividends than for ordinary dividends.

spurred countries to regulate and restrict the ability of companies to undertake repurchases, and regulations are constantly shifting. For example, Japan, France, and Hong Kong have restrictions on when companies can use repurchases, such as close to earnings announcements. Other countries have price restrictions, such as Canada and Japan, where the repurchase price can be no higher than the previous day's price. Finally, some countries have outright banned or severely restricted repurchases. Companies in China were previously banned from share repurchases in most cases, but in 2018 regulators allowed them to do buybacks for certain purposes. In 2023, India's market regulator announced that it will phase out open-market repurchases and trim the time period under which tender-offer repurchases can be done, due to allegations that certain shareholders can disproportionately benefit from the actions compared to others.

Sources: Small, R. C. (2014). Buybacks around the world. *Harvard Law School Forum on Corporate Governance.* Shen. M., (2018). China eases restrictions on company share buy-backs: Xinhua. *Reuters.* Vishnoi, A. (2022). India overhauls stock buyback mechanism to aid small investors. *Bloomberg.* Williamson, S. K., Babcock, A. F., and He, A. (2020). The dangers of buybacks: mitigating common pitfalls. *Harvard Law School Forum on Corporate Governance.*

12.3.5 Flexibility and Firm Life Cycles

We noted that, because repurchases cannot be used regularly in the same way as dividends, investors have no expectation of future repurchases once started, and thus share repurchases are viewed as more flexible than dividends. This difference in flexibility means that, in terms of payout policy, different types of firms in different segments of the economy may choose either dividends or repurchases. Large, mature firms tend to use dividend payouts, as they have relatively more stable cash flows and future prospects, and can be more confident in their ability to keep paying dividends. In contrast, small, growing firms have more uncertain cash flows, and thus added flexibility is important to such firms. These types of firms are more likely to rely on share repurchases.

These insights can also help to explain long-term trends in the use of dividends and repurchases. Academic research has shown that the proportion of firms paying dividends dropped substantially over the latter half of the twentieth century, from roughly 90% of firms in 1950 to roughly 20% of firms in 2000 (Fama and French 2001). Although this proportion has rebounded somewhat between 2000 and 2020, in contrast the proportion of firms doing repurchases has exhibited a continuous upward trend (Michaely and Moin 2022). These trends can be partially explained by changes in the relative tax rates on ordinary income and capital gains. However, changes in the composition of the economy have also contributed. Since the 1990s, younger firms in industries that were nascent at the time, such as tech companies, became a larger segment of the global economy. Many of these firms have uncertain future cash flows, thus making the use of repurchases—and the flexibility that comes with them—more beneficial than dividends. As these types of firms matured, they used dividends, which may help to explain the rebound in the proportion of firms using dividends over the past two decades.

> **QUICK CHECK 12.7** Why may tax considerations and regulations favor the use of repurchases over dividends?

12.4 Stock Dividends and Splits

Apart from dividends and repurchases, there are other corporate actions—stock splits and stock dividends—that are commonly used by companies and are closely related to payout policy. A **stock split** is when a company decides to split each of its existing shares outstanding into multiple shares.

For example, a 3-for-1 stock split means that each share that an investor owns is turned into three shares. A stock split is used by a company as a tool for increasing the number of its shares in circulation. A stock dividend is when a company pays dividends to its shareholders, but instead of paying cash the company provides additional shares of its own stock. Stock dividends are used by companies that are looking to pay shareholders a dividend, but prefer to not use cash.

Both types of corporate actions are related to payout policy because they both result in increases in the number of shares outstanding, the opposite of what happens with a share repurchase. To fully understand why a company may engage in these actions—and how they may provide value to shareholders—we will proceed to analyze stock splits and stock dividends in the same way as we did repurchases: We start with a frictionless environment to understand the basic mechanisms and establish if they add any value to the firm, and then consider real-world frictions and the uses of these mechanisms given those.

Assume again that we are in a frictionless environment, and consider our previous example of GCP, which has 500,000 shares outstanding, a current share price of $20, and total equity value of $10 million. Suppose that GCP's management declares a 2-for-1 stock split. This means that each old share will now be counted as two shares. The total number of GCP shares outstanding will increase from 500,000 to one million. Note that this action does not involve GCP spending any cash or making any investments, so in a frictionless environment it will not affect total shareholder wealth. With its total equity value of $10 million remaining unchanged and one million shares outstanding after the split, the price per share will change from $20 to $10 million / 1 million = $10. However, each shareholder now holds more shares and so shareholders' wealth remains unchanged: A shareholder that held 100 shares before the split had a position worth 100 × $20 = $2,000, while that shareholder's position after the split (with 200 shares) will be worth 200 × $10 = $2,000. Thus, when there are no frictions, a stock split does not add any shareholder value, as with dividends and repurchases; any value from stock splits must be due to frictions.

Now consider stock dividends and suppose that GCP instead decides to pay a 10% stock dividend. This means that shareholders will receive one new share for every ten old shares they own, and the company keeps any cash that would have been paid in cash dividends. Again, this action does not involve GCP spending any cash or making any investments, and so in a frictionless environment it will not affect total shareholder wealth. Instead, there will be 10% more shares outstanding, so GCP's number of shares will go from 500,000 to 550,000. With its total equity value of $10 million remaining unchanged and 550,000 shares outstanding after the stock dividend, the price per share will change from $20 to $10 million / 550,000 = $18.18. The value of each shareholder's position will also remain unchanged. A shareholder that held 100 shares before the stock dividend had a position worth 100 × $20 = $2,000, while that shareholder's position after the stock dividend (with the number of shares going from 100 to 110) will be worth 110 × $18.18 = $2,000. As with stock splits and other forms of payout, with no frictions a stock dividend does not increase shareholder value. Table 12.3 summarizes each of these situations.

This analysis shows that, for stock splits and stock dividends to be valuable to shareholders, there must be frictions. One such friction is encouraging market liquidity. The above scenarios showed that stock splits and stock dividends lower the prices of individual shares of stock (although the total value of equity remains unchanged). If the stock price of a company is high enough, this can introduce frictions where individual shareholders may not be able to invest in the company at all because a single share is unaffordable. For example, in March 2022 Amazon Inc. announced a 20-for-1 stock split, with its shares trading at $2,785 apiece at the time of the announcement. Other companies, such as Berkshire Hathaway class A shares, traded in 2023 for over $500,000 per share! Stock splits are especially effective at increasing the number of shares outstanding and therefore lowering the price per share, and therefore may benefit investors that want to purchase the stock (and potentially increase the funding the company receives when issuing new shares of stock).

Table 12.3 The effect of stock splits and stock dividends for GCP. Market value balance sheets under various scenarios with no frictions. The top of the table shows the original situation. The middle of the table shows the firm's situation after engaging in a 2-for-1 stock split. The bottom of the table shows the firm's situation after paying a 10% stock dividend. In all situations, shareholder value is unchanged.

Original situation			
Assets		**Debt and equity**	
Cash	$2 million	Debt, D	$2 million
Other assets	$10 million	Equity, E	$10 million
Total	$12 million	Total, V	$12 million
	Price per share: $20		
	Shares outstanding: 500,000		
After 2-for-1 stock split			
Assets		**Debt and equity**	
Cash	$2 million	Debt, D	$2 million
Other assets	$10 million	Equity, E	$10 million
Total	$12 million	Total, V	$12 million
	Price per share: $10		
	Shares outstanding: 1,000,000		
After stock dividend			
Assets		**Debt and equity**	
Cash	$2 million	Debt, D	$2 million
Other assets	$10 million	Equity, E	$10 million
Total	$12 million	Total, V	$12 million
	Price per share: $18.18		
	Shares outstanding: 550,000		

Another benefit of improving market liquidity via increasing the number of shares and lowering the share price is to enhance market efficiency. As we stressed with **Principle 5:** *The best estimate of an asset's value is usually its market price, which incorporates valuable information to guide the allocation of resources and risks.* Every trade in a market is itself a signal, reflecting information that helps guide the allocation of resources and risks. However, there can be cases where there are so few shares of a stock being traded (i.e., the stock has low liquidity) that prices are not able to accurately reflect all valuable information because too many agents are priced out of the stock. A stock split or a stock dividend that increases the number of outstanding shares and decreases the price of each can help to add liquidity and improve market efficiency.

As we noted previously, stock splits are primarily aimed at increasing the number of shares outstanding, and thus can play a key role in improving the liquidity of the company's stock. While stock dividends functionally also increase the number of shares, they do so to a lesser extent, and thus the primary use of stock dividends by companies is different. A possible source of value from stock dividends derives from taxes—investors receiving a cash dividend typically have to pay personal taxes on the income, whereas if they receive a share of stock as a dividend it will not be taxed until the investor sells the share of stock.

> **QUICK CHECK 12.8** What would be the effect of GCP paying a 20% stock dividend?

Conclusion

In this chapter we continued our examination of financial decisions within companies, and focused on the payout decision—when companies choose to give excess cash that it doesn't need for its operations back to investors. We examined how two primary forms of payout policy work. Companies could make direct cash payments to investors via cash dividends, or they could use share repurchases (buybacks) to purchase outstanding shares from investors. In order to analyze the consequences of these decisions, we first considered a framework with no frictions—no market imperfections such as taxes, differences in information, agency costs, etc. We saw that payout policy in such a framework does not affect overall shareholder value, and thus does not "matter" to shareholders. This gave us the conclusion that payout policy can have value due to frictions, and we discussed a number of important frictions in practice that can drive companies to undertake repurchases or pay dividends. Payout can play an important role in mitigating free cash flow problems by reducing the amount of cash a company holds. Dividends and repurchases can signal to investors that the company is likely to have good prospects going forward. And regulations and tax advantages for dividends or repurchases can lead a company to prefer one or another. Companies can also engage in other related corporate actions which functionally increase the number of shares outstanding—stock splits and stock dividends—which can have value due to frictions involving liquidity and taxes.

This chapter focuses on how companies can take financial actions related to their cash reserves. This introduces tools that can help to correct agency problems, and thus connects directly with issues we discussed in Chapter 11. Since firms can also take on additional cash by raising money from capital markets, payout policy also directly connects with issues related to capital structure, which we discuss in the next chapter.

Takeaways

- Payout policy is how a corporation can distribute funds to its shareholders. Payout policy takes two main forms: A firm can pay a cash dividend, or it can repurchase stock (also referred to as a stock buyback).
- Regular dividends are scheduled cash dividend payments that happen at a regular frequency. Preferred dividends are dividends to preferred shareholders, which take priority over payments to common stockholders. Special dividends are one-time payments made to shareholders, which a company may not repeat in the future.
- An open-market repurchase is when a company goes to a stock exchange and places an order to purchase its own stock. A tender-offer repurchase is when a company goes to shareholders directly and offers to buy back a predetermined number of shares at a certain price.
- The Modigliani–Miller (M-M) Dividend Proposition states that in a "frictionless" financial environment, a firm's dividend policy has no effect on the wealth of its current shareholders. The same intuition applies to the effect of share repurchases. Thus, any value from payout policy is due to frictions.

- With asymmetric information, announcing dividends can serve as a positive signal of a firm's prospects, since the firm is telling investors that it can sustain dividends going forward. Firms that announce that they will pay regular dividend payments receive an increase in their share price as a result of the market incorporating this information. Firms that cut or don't pay scheduled dividend payments are punished by the capital markets.
- Repurchases can also serve to signal a firm's future prospects. Tender-offer repurchases have stronger signaling value than open-market repurchases, and may even have stronger signaling value than dividends.
- Payout policy can help to solve agency problems by using up excess cash and disciplining managers.
- Firms can use payout as a mechanism to change their capital structure, or can fund payout with debt or equity, thus connecting the payout policy decision to the capital structure decision.
- Transaction costs, taxes, and regulations can change the relative attractiveness of dividends and repurchases to investors and firms.
- In a frictionless environment, other corporate actions such as stock dividends and splits only increase the number of shares outstanding, and do not change shareholder value. With frictions, such actions may have some value.

Key Terms

Agency problems 343
Asymmetric information 340
Cash dividend 334
Ex-dividend price 337
Free cash flow problem 343
Frictionless 334
Miller–Modigliani (M-M) Dividend Proposition 336
Negative signal 341
Open-market repurchase 335
Payout 334

Payout policy 334
Positive signal 340
Preferred dividends 335
Regular dividends 335
Special dividends 335
Stock dividend 335
Stock repurchase/stock buyback 334
Stock split 335
Tender-offer repurchase 335
Transaction costs 345
Treasury stock 335

Problems

1. Suppose that a company has had an extraordinarily profitable year, and it announces that it will use most of its net cash inflow to buy back shares of its stock in the market. Would you expect the price of its stock to rise or fall when the announcement is made? Explain.
2. Consider the company Payer Inc., shown in Table 12.4.

Table 12.4

Assets		Debt and equity	
Cash	$5 million	Debt, D	$10 million
Other assets	$15 million	Equity, E	$10 million
Total	$20 million	Total, V	$20 million

Suppose that Payer Inc. has 100,000 shares outstanding. Assume there are no frictions.
   (a) What is Payer Inc.'s price per share?
   (b) Suppose Payer Inc. pays a cash dividend of $10 per share. Rewrite Table 12.4 after it pays the dividend. What would be the new price per share?
   (c) Suppose instead that Payer Inc. uses cash to repurchase 10,000 shares of stock. Rewrite Table 12.4 after the repurchase. What would be the new price per share?

3. Consider the current balance sheet of the Ostende Oar Company, which has 2,000,000 shares outstanding at a price per share of €20 (Table 12.5). Derive the new balance sheet after the payment of a 25% stock dividend and compute the new share price.

Table 12.5

Assets		Liabilities and equity	
Cash	€10,000,000	Debt	€20,000,000
Other assets	€50,000,000	Equity	€40,000,000
Total	€60,000,000	Total	€60,000,000

4. Divido Corporation is an all-equity financed firm with a total market value of $100 million. The company holds $10 million in cash equivalents and has $90 million in other assets. There are 1,000,000 shares of Divido common stock outstanding, each with a market price of $100. What would be the impact on Divido's stock price and on the wealth of its shareholders of the payment of a cash dividend of $10 per share? What if the company instead repurchased 100,000 shares?

5. Continuing the previous problem, analyze the impact on Divido's stock price and on the wealth of its shareholders of the company:
   (a) paying a 10% stock dividend;
   (b) making a 2-for-1 stock split; and
   (c) investing $10 million in an expansion that has an expected rate of return on investment equal to the firm's cost of capital.

6. Explain two reasons why companies may want to initiate (start paying) regular dividend payments.

7. Explain two advantages of using repurchases compared to dividends.

8. Explain the reasons why a company may choose to engage in a tender-offer repurchase instead of starting to pay regular dividends.

9. Suppose that a company had been paying dividends regularly, but suddenly missed a dividend payment to investors. What would you expect to happen, and why?

10. Company CashCo has $50 million in equity and no debt. It holds $20 million in cash and $30 million in other assets. It has 100,000 shares outstanding. Analyze the effect on CashCo's total equity value and price per share of the following situations:
    (a) CashCo spends cash to do an open-market repurchase of 20,000 shares.
    (b) CashCo pays a dividend of $10 per share.
    (c) CashCo does a 6-for-1 stock split.
    (d) Suppose CashCo does each of these actions sequentially, starting with part (a) and ending with part (c). What will be its total equity value and share price after these actions?

11. If the government announces that personal income taxes will increase but capital gains taxes will remain the same, what would you predict regarding companies' use of dividends compared to repurchases? Explain.

12. Consider a young tech startup firm that is looking to distribute extra cash to shareholders. Would you predict that it is more likely to use dividends or repurchases? Why?

13. "A firm's stock price will rise after a share repurchase because the number of remaining shares outstanding decreases." Critique this statement.

14. Explain why regular dividends may be more effective at solving the free cash flow problem than repurchases.

15. Shady Inc. is an electronics manufacturer that specializes in overpriced electronics that frequently break down. It has mounting concerns of declining customer satisfaction, but its CEO refuses to

address quality concerns within the company. It observes that its competitor, Quality Electronics Corporation, has decided to start paying dividends. Quality Electronics Corporation's stock price rises significantly as a result.
(a) What does the increase in Quality Electronics Corporation's stock price tell you about the prospects of the company?
(b) Shady Inc.'s CEO wants to start paying dividends to also gain the benefits that Quality Electronics gained. Shady Inc.'s CFO advises against it. What is the logic behind the CFO's advice?

16. Buyback Inc. is a company that is well-known for having a management team that deeply cares about the company's success, and it won an award for its high-quality corporate governance. It recently did an open-market repurchase, yet its stock price remained essentially unchanged. How might you rationalize this?

17. Microhardware Inc. has been recently acquiring a variety of companies using its cash reserves. Many shareholders criticized this string of acquisitions. Microhardware recently announced a large share repurchase, and that it would begin to pay regular dividends. Based on this information, would you expect the company's stock price to go up or down after the announcement? Why?

18. You are the CFO of a smartphone manufacturer. The development of the product has been very positive, and you expect consumers to receive the product well. You have been telling your investors that development is going well, but this seems to not have had much of an impact on your share price. How can you use payout policy to convey your optimism to investors? Why might that work?

13 CAPITAL STRUCTURE

CHAPTER OVERVIEW

13.1	Internal and External Financing	356
13.2	Capital Structure and the Modigliani–Miller Propositions (No Frictions)	357
13.3	Capital Structure with Default/Bankruptcy Risk	368
13.4	Capital Structure with Frictions: Taxes	373
13.5	Capital Structure with Other Frictions	388
13.6	Optimal Capital Structure	396

LEARNING OBJECTIVES

After reading this chapter, you will be able to:
- identify the factors that underlie a firm's choice between debt and equity in its capital structure;
- discuss how the choice of capital structure affects company value;
- understand what the Modigliani–Miller framework predicts about the effects of a capital structure change on the costs of equity, debt, and WACC, and be able to calculate these costs and the firm's value given the company's choice of capital structure;
- explain the effects of taxes on capital structure decisions;
- describe the costs of bankruptcy and their effects on capital structure decisions;
- explain the "frictions" that affect capital market decisions and how to minimize their effects.

EQUATIONS YOU KNOW

Company value	$V = D + E$	Eq. 9.1
Calculating company value, DCF method	$V = \dfrac{FCF_1}{1+r_A} + \dfrac{FCF_2}{(1+r_A)^2} + \dfrac{FCF_3}{(1+r_A)^3} + \dfrac{FCF_4}{(1+r_A)^4} + \dfrac{FCF_5}{(1+r_A)^5}\cdots,$	Eq. 9.4
Present value of a perpetuity	$PV = \dfrac{\$CF}{r}$	Eq. 2.17

Present value of a growing perpetuity	$PV = \dfrac{\$CF_1}{r - g}$	Eq. 2.18
Pre-tax weighted-average cost of capital (WACC)	$r_A = \text{WACC} = \left[\dfrac{E}{V} \times r_E\right] + \left[\dfrac{D}{V} \times r_D\right]$	Eq. 9.10

+ Your business currently uses no debt, but a friend of yours that works in the financial industry tells you that there are many advantages to using debt to finance the business. However, you have read many stories of businesses that have gone under because of using debt. How do you reconcile these views and reach a decision?

+ You are a financial analyst, and a firm you are covering pays no corporate income tax because it has been losing money. You need to write a report evaluating whether its choice of financing is optimal compared to other firms that do have to pay taxes. What can you say about the situation?

+ You are the CEO of Orr Oil Company. It needs $10 million to finance the test drilling of some land it owns in New Guinea. If the tests are favorable, the company will need an additional $10 million to develop the site. Orr Oil common stock is currently selling at $10 per share, and earnings are $2 per share. Other firms in the oil industry are selling at 10–12 times earnings. Orr Oil's debt ratio is 25%, compared to an industry average of 40%. Total assets on the most current balance sheet were $105 million. Should you finance the drilling using debt or equity?

+ Your family company, Gormeh Inc., operates a chain of gourmet food stores in the southeastern United States. It is owned by you and your four sisters, each of whom holds one-fifth of the outstanding stock. The company is profitable, but rapid growth has put it under severe financial strain. The real estate is all heavily mortgaged, the inventory is being used to secure a bank line of credit, and the accounts receivable are being factored. With total assets of $15 million, the company now needs an additional $2 million to purchase equipment for the shipping department. What are the potential benefits and costs of borrowing to raise the additional money?

+ Mumbai Textile Company manufactures cotton cloth in India and exports about half of it to small clothing companies operating in Singapore. The company's plant and equipment have been financed in part by a loan from the government, and this is its only long-term debt. It pays cash for its inputs, and offers 60 days' credit to its customers in Singapore. Recent growth in its export sales to $5 million per year has created the need for an additional $500,000 in financing. As the manager of the company, how should you raise the additional financing?

+ Jarvis Holey has been driving a cab in Philadelphia for five years, and has saved up $50,000 toward the purchase of a Burger Queen franchise. Burger Queen Corporation (BQC) requires that each of its franchisees invest at least $100,000 of equity capital, and then BQC arranges debt financing for the remainder. Holey has just learned that the owner of an existing Burger Queen franchise in his neighborhood wants to sell out for $250,000, and Holey wants to buy the business from him. How should Holey raise the money to do so?

+ Lee Productions is a small independent movie production company that has recently attracted attention because of the unexpected success of its film, *Red Tide Rising*. There are currently ten owners, and they want to double the number of new movies the company produces. The company recently incorporated and now wants to raise $10 million from outside investors through selling shares of stock. Is this the best way to raise the money?

Introduction

In previous chapters we explored how to calculate the value of a company, given decisions that it had already made. In subsequent chapters we then focused on decisions that a manager within a company could make, and how they affect company value, such as project investment decisions. In this chapter we continue to examine decisions made by companies, and focus on a particularly important decision—the *financing decision*. Capital structure is the mix of financing sources that a firm uses to fund its operations, growth, and investment projects. A firm may choose to use internal funding from operations, or use external funding from issuing debt (bonds) or equity (stock), or other financing instruments.

Firms can choose a wide range of potential capital structures consisting of any split between debt and equity. For example, a company could choose to rely entirely on equity, obtaining all of its funding from stock issuances. Alternatively, a company could choose to finance itself almost entirely through debt. Any combination of the two is also possible: 10% debt and 90% equity, 50% debt and 50% equity, and so forth. The central question that underlies the firm's choice of the optimal capital structure is how that choice affects the value of the firm. The managers and owners of the firm ideally want to make capital structure decisions that maximize the value of the firm.

As we will cover in this chapter, in the real world things such as contract law, regulations, transaction costs, taxes, differences in information, and moral hazard can affect the relative advantages or disadvantages of using debt or equity—and therefore will cause capital structure to affect the value of the firm. For example, debt interest payments are tax deductible by law, which can lower a company's tax bill if it holds debt. However, companies that hold substantial amounts of debt may have trouble paying it off and thus struggle financially, with a negative impact on operations. The sheer number of different factors can make it difficult to even begin to understand the capital structure decision. As a starting point to develop a framework to understand this decision, we abstract away from as many of these factors as possible, and analyze corporate capital structure in a frictionless financial environment, defined as one in which there are no market imperfections, such as taxes, transaction costs, differences in information between participants, agency costs, etc. The key insight is that, in this environment, the overall value of the firm is not affected by its financing mix. Therefore, at a basic level abstracting away from many real-world considerations, policies that change only the firm's capital structure, such as borrowing to repurchase stock or issuing new stock to retire debt, will not affect the firm's value. This tells us that any value that comes from changing financial capital structure must therefore be related to these frictions, such as the potential to reduce the costs introduced by them.

Because contract law, taxes, and regulations differ from place to place and change over time, we find that there is no single optimal financing mix that applies to all firms. Rather, finding the optimal capital structure for a corporation involves making trade-offs that depend on the corporation's particular legal and tax environment.

We will begin the chapter by giving an overview of the financing choice that companies face, in particular whether to fund internally (through cash holdings) or externally (raising debt or equity). In order to then understand the external financing decision and the choice between raising debt or equity, we introduce a foundational framework: the Modigliani–Miller (M-M) Proposition. The framework allows us to analyze, at a basic and fundamental level abstracting away from frictions, whether and how the capital structure choice matters in terms of firm value and risk. This will also allow us to expand upon our toolkit introduced in Chapter 9 for determining firm value, and understand how the choice of capital structure affects the toolkit. With this as our foundation, we then begin to analyze how complications in the real world affect our analysis. We first add the possibility of bankruptcy and how that can change the cost of debt and potentially complicate the analysis. We then introduce individual frictions that are commonplace in practice, and analyze how changing a firm's capital structure may affect value. These frictions include taxes, costs of financial distress, agency problems, asymmetric information, and the structure of debt. We conclude the chapter by putting everything together and thinking about what the different considerations discussed entail for the optimal choice of capital structure by companies.

13.1 Internal and External Financing

In analyzing capital structure decisions, it is important to distinguish between internal and external sources of funds. Internal financing is funding generated from the operations of the firm and reinvested in the company. It can be generated by managing elements of net working capital—for example, accrued wages or accounts payable—and/or by earning a profit. For example, if a firm earns profits and reinvests them in new plant and equipment for their own operations, this is internal financing. External financing is generated from outside the firm from lenders or investors. If a corporation issues bonds or stocks to generate funds to finance the purchase of new plant and equipment, it is using external financing.

The decision processes are usually different for internal and external financing. In both cases, managers will analyze how the capital could fund investments that add value to the firm, as discussed in Chapter 10. For project and other expenses that would require extraordinarily large amounts of funds, internal financing decisions are often routine and almost automatic. For example, purchasing disposable safety equipment on a monthly basis for workers in a company's factory may be done in each case using the company's cash reserves. The amount of managerial time and effort required to make internal financing decisions and the degree of scrutiny of planned expenditures are usually less than for external financing. For internal financing, the process typically involves approval within the firm of the uses of the cash by managers. Smaller expenditures like the example above could simply be done by a divisional manager, perhaps with the approval of higher-level management. Larger expenditures may be directly decided by top managers like the CFO or CEO. In most cases the spending of cash can be done directly by companies, although large expenses by firms may draw scrutiny by shareholders or the board of directors. If a corporation raises funds from external sources, the process can be more complicated and time-consuming. In general, outside providers of funds are likely to want to see detailed plans for the use of the funds and will want to be convinced that the investment project will produce sufficient future cash flows to justify the expenditure and support their return on investment. They will scrutinize the plans and are likely to be more skeptical about the prospects for success than the corporation's own managers. External financing, therefore, subjects the corporation's plans more directly to the discipline of the capital market than internal financing does. We will discuss exactly how this may be the case later in this chapter.

> **QUICK CHECK 13.1** How does the need for external financing impose market discipline on a corporation?

13.2 Capital Structure and the Modigliani–Miller Propositions (No Frictions)

We noted that there are a large number of potential factors, due to frictions, that may affect the capital structure decision and may make firms prefer either debt or equity. Given the number of possible considerations that may matter, in order to systematically understand why capital structure may matter to investors and guide decisions of managers, we will begin with a more basic framework to guide our thinking. In particular, we will start with a simplified setting that abstracts away from complications and has *no* frictions. This will allow us to understand at a more basic level how capital structure may affect a company to clarify what matters and what does not matter in the decision, and also allow us to isolate the effects of particular frictions that can help guide managerial actions.

In this section we will begin our analysis, assuming that we are operating in a frictionless environment. A frictionless environment (or market) is one where there are:

- no income taxes;
- no transaction costs of issuing debt or equity securities;
- no information asymmetries—investors, firms, and everyone else in the economy can see the same information; and
- no agency costs in the form of conflicts of interest between the various stakeholders of the firm.

In our development in this section, we make a further simplifying assumption: The corporation's debt is risk-free—that is, the amount of debt the company has is sufficiently small that there is no default risk and no bankruptcy, and the company will surely pay its debt obligations. We will discuss the implications of relaxing this assumption in Section 13.3.

13.2.1 Modigliani–Miller and the Irrelevance of Capital Structure to Firm Value

In the 1950s, economists Franco Modigliani and Merton Miller examined the question, "Does the choice of capital structure affect the value of a firm?" By considering the question in a frictionless market (a market without taxes or transaction costs) to isolate capital structure from all other costs, they showed that the choice of capital structure has no impact on firm value (Modigliani and Miller 1958). As a result, when there are no frictions, there is no particular "optimal" capital structure that maximizes value for a given firm. We refer to this insight as Modigliani–Miller (M-M) Proposition 1: Capital structure is irrelevant to overall firm value (the combined value of debt and equity), but does affect the individual components of firm value. Modigliani and Miller discovered that the total market value of the firm is determined by the cash flows the firm's assets provide, which in turn are created by the firm's investments, and not by the way the firm chooses to fund those investments. Thus, the firm cannot add value to the company by choosing more debt or more equity.

Miller explained the M-M capital structure proposition in terms of a pie. Think of the firm as a gigantic pizza, divided into quarters: If you cut each quarter in half into eighths, the M-M Proposition says that you will have more pieces, but not more pizza. That is, regardless of how much you change the firm through capital structure and financing choices and how each part functions, the fundamental size/shape (or value) of the firm will stay the same.

This is visually represented in Figure 13.1. On the left side of the figure, consider a firm whose total market value (represented by the size of the circle) is composed of 25% debt (red) and 75% equity (blue). This split represents the identity we introduced in Chapter 9, that a company's total value (also

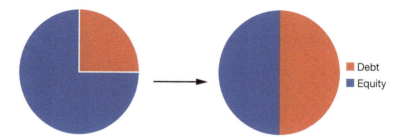

FIGURE 13.1 Representation of Modigliani–Miller Proposition 1. Capital structure is irrelevant to the overall firm value (the combined value of debt and equity), but does affect the individual components of firm value. This figure depicts a change in capital structure that increases the proportion of debt (red) relative to equity (blue). The size of the circle represents the total value of the firm.

called enterprise value, denoted V) is made up of the combined market value of its debt (denoted D) and equity (denoted E):

$$V = D + E. \tag{13.1}$$

Now suppose this same firm decides to increase its leverage (i.e., increase the amount of debt it has), and change its capital structure to be 50% debt and 50% equity (and therefore $D/V = 50\%$ and $E/V = 50\%$). It may do so by issuing bonds or taking out additional loans, and then using the proceeds to buy back its own stock in the market. It is important to note that the firm is not making any investment or changing its operations in any way, it is only changing its capital structure. The right side of Figure 13.1 illustrates what M-M Proposition 1 says: The size of the "pizza" (i.e., the total value of the firm) does not change; only the split between debt and equity (the relative proportion of red and blue) will change. The total company value remains unchanged because the addition of new debt (increasing the red area) causes the value of the equity (the blue area) to go down by the amount of equity repurchased with the proceeds of the debt.

For example, let's consider our example firm from previous chapters: Generic Consumer Products (GCP), a typical US manufacturing firm, and a similar firm, Levered Generic Consumer Products (LGCP), which have two different capital structures. Suppose that GCP's management decides that it will hold no debt, and thus its capital structure is 100% equity (composed of shares of common stock). Since GCP has no debt, it is unlevered. Assume that GCP has total earnings (earnings before interest and taxes [EBIT]), and thus free cash flows, of $10 million each year and a cost of capital r_A of 10%. The timeline of GCP's cash flows is therefore:

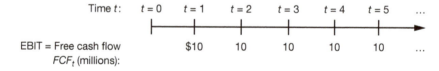

Since these earnings are in perpetuity, GCP's total firm value V will be given by applying the perpetuity formula (based on Equation 2.17, where $EBIT = CF$):

$$\begin{aligned} V^{GCP} &= \frac{EBIT}{r_A} \\ &= \frac{10}{0.10} \\ &= \$100 \text{ million.} \end{aligned}$$

13.2 CAPITAL STRUCTURE AND THE M-M PROPOSITIONS

For GCP, since it is only composed of equity, $V^{GCP} = E^{GCP}$.

Now consider LGCP. As it is identical to GCP, LGCP's earnings stream (EBIT) is expected to also be $10 million each year, and it has the same risk characteristics as GCP's earnings. However, LGCP differs from GCP in that it has some debt financing: It is levered. LGCP has issued bonds that have a face value of $40 million at an interest rate of 8% per year, meaning that the bonds promise to pay a coupon of $3.2 million per year (0.08 × $40 million). Assume that the bonds are issued in perpetuity—that is, with no maturity.

Assume that LGCP's bonds are default-risk-free and that the riskless rate of interest is 8% per year. The interest payments will be the same $3.2 million per year regardless of the realized value of EBIT. First, consider the earnings available to LGCP's shareholders each year after the payment of the $3.2 million of interest on the bonds:

$$\begin{aligned} \text{LGCP's earnings to shareholders} &= EBIT - \$3.2 \\ &= \$10 - \$3.2 \\ &= \$6.8 \text{ million}. \end{aligned}$$

The total cash flows to LGCP's bondholders and stockholders combined (i.e., the free cash flows) are:

$$\begin{aligned} \text{LGCP's total cash flows} &= \text{LGCP's earnings to shareholders} + \text{interest payments} \\ &= \$6.8 + \$3.2 \\ &= \$10 \text{ million}. \end{aligned}$$

LGCP's combined cash flows to its stakeholders each year are the same as GCP's payments to its stakeholders: $10 million. The only difference is that the cash flows of GCP go to only one stakeholder (its stockholders), while the cash flows of LGCP go to both its bondholders and its stockholders. Since the cash flows are the same for GCP and LGCP, and the risk of the earnings is the same for both, it follows that both companies will have the same total firm value. Put differently, $V^{GCP} = V^{LGCP}$, and LGCP's capital structure does not cause its firm value to be different from GCP's.

It is important to note that, although LGCP's leverage does not influence its total firm value, the components of firm value are different between GCP and LGCP. The value of GCP's equity, since it is 100% equity financed, is the same as its total firm value: $V^{GCP} = E^{GCP} = \$100$ million. For LGCP, the value of its debt is the present value of its bond cash payments discounted by the riskless rate (since it is default-risk-free) using the perpetuity formula:

$$\begin{aligned} D^{LGCP} &= \frac{3.2}{0.08} \\ &= \$40 \text{ million}. \end{aligned}$$

Since the total value of the firm is $100 million and $V = D + E$ by Equation 13.1, it follows that the value of LGCP's equity is:

$$\begin{aligned} E^{LGCP} &= V^{LGCP} - D^{LGCP} \\ &= \$100 - \$40 \\ &= \$60 \text{ million}. \end{aligned}$$

This compares to GCP's equity value of $100 million, which was the same as the total company value. The effect of LGCP's leverage is therefore to lower the value of equity, while maintaining the same overall firm value. Thus, as anticipated by M-M Proposition 1: Capital structure is irrelevant to overall firm value (the combined value of debt and equity), but does affect the individual components of firm value. We discuss this point in more detail shortly.

Table 13.1 Arbitrage with GCP and LGCP.

Position	Cash flows now (t = 0)	Cash flows each subsequent year (t ≥ 1)
Short-sell GCP stock	$110 million	−$10 million
Buy LGCP equity	−$60 million	$6.8 million
Buy LGCP debt	−$40 million	$3.2 million
Total cash flows	$10 million	$0

We can also prove the fact that LGCP must have the same value as GCP using **Principle 2**: *Equivalent assets that can be freely bought and sold will have the same market price.* Suppose that GCP was instead worth $110 million. If LGCP was still worth $100 million, we would have an arbitrage. To see this, suppose that you make a short-selling arrangement where you sell all of GCP's stock right now in exchange for paying back the $10 million EBIT stream in the future. This brings you $110 million now. Now suppose that you buy LGCP's debt and equity for a total of $100 million. Your net profit right now is $10 million. But note that the total cash flows each year that you get from LGCP (3.2 + 6.8 = $10 million) are exactly equal to the cash flows you owe for GCP ($10 million) each year (and as we previously noted, they have the exact same risk). This therefore allows you to make $10 million now, and have a net zero cash flow each year going into the future. This situation is illustrated in Table 13.1. As we have emphasized, such an arbitrage cannot persist, and by the law of one price GCP and LGCP must be worth the same.

> **QUICK CHECK 13.2** If GCP were to announce an issue of $50 million of debt to be used to repurchase and retire common stock, what would be the effect on its total company value and equity value?

13.2.2 Modigliani–Miller and the Effect of Capital Structure on the Firm's Risk and Cost of Capital

M-M Proposition 1 has a host of important implications for our previous calculations of firm value that we introduced in Chapter 9, where we used the discounted cash flow (DCF) approach to valuing a company. In particular, as we will show below, M-M Proposition 1 implies that in a frictionless environment the overall risk of a firm—and thus the firm's overall discount rate or cost of capital—will not change when a firm changes its capital structure. However, the risk of the firm's equity will change.

Recall our DCF approach to calculating firm value. In it, we first determined a company's expected future free cash flows (FCF), which can be represented via the following cash flow timeline:

Time t: $t = 0$, $t = 1$, $t = 2$, $t = 3$, $t = 4$, $t = 5$, ...

Free cash flow FCF_t: FCF_1, FCF_2, FCF_3, FCF_4, FCF_5, ...

We then discounted these FCFs by the company's overall cost of capital r_A (see Equation 9.4):

$$V = \frac{FCF_1}{1+r_A} + \frac{FCF_2}{(1+r_A)^2} + \frac{FCF_3}{(1+r_A)^3} + \frac{FCF_4}{(1+r_A)^4} + \frac{FCF_5}{(1+r_A)^5} \cdots. \qquad (13.2)$$

Now consider the implication of a company changing its capital structure (i.e., its mix of equity and debt). Since the company is not changing its investments or obtaining additional earnings and thus cash, the FCFs will not change in Equation 13.2. What about the discount rate r_A? The answer is that the discount rate also cannot change, since otherwise the value of the company V would change, and we have established that V will not change according to M-M Proposition 1.

This insight has a number of deep implications. First, since the firm's overall discount rate r_A reflects the risk of the firm as a whole, this implies that capital structure also does not affect a company's risk. Second, it upends long-held beliefs prior to the introduction of M-M Proposition 1 about the effect of a firm's capital structure by demonstrating how risk shifts between debt and equity.

To explain this point, recall from Chapter 9 (Equation 9.10) the formula for calculating the discount rate (i.e., cost of capital) for a company when there are no taxes. This was called the pre-tax weighted-average cost of capital (WACC):

$$r_A = \text{WACC} = \left[\frac{E}{V} \times r_E\right] + \left[\frac{D}{V} \times r_D\right]. \tag{13.3}$$

In Equation 13.3 the WACC takes the required rates of return for equity (r_E) and debt (r_D), and weights each by the proportion of the company's value made up of equity and debt (E/V and D/V). As we noted, we are assuming that the company's debt is risk-free, and thus the expected/required rate of return of the debt (r_D) will be the same as the promised return (yield), which is also the same as the risk-free interest rate.

Note that, as a general point, the cost of debt (expected rate of return on debt) r_D will always be less than the cost of equity (expected rate of return on equity) r_E, $r_D < r_E$. This is not because we are assuming that the company's debt is risk-free and the equity is not, but rather because the interest and principal payments made to debtholders have legal priority over any payments to shareholders. Shareholders get the residual cash flows that the company generates after debtholders are paid. Thus, the cash flows to shareholders are riskier—less likely to occur—than the cash flows to debtholders, and so shareholders require a higher rate of return than debtholders. Because $r_D < r_E$, debt is often referred to as being "cheaper" than equity for the firm, and the long-held belief was that the firm can lower its overall cost of capital by using more debt (i.e., increasing D/V in Equation 13.3 and thus putting more weight on r_D).[1]

Modigliani and Miller demonstrated that this way of thinking is incorrect, since the overall risk of the firm does not change because the value does not change. Changing a firm's capital structure will cause the firm's cost of equity r_E and cost of debt r_D to also change, and these changes will keep the overall risk of the company the same.

First, imagine that a firm increases the proportion of debt in its capital structure, and thus that D/V goes up. In Equation 13.3 more weight is placed on the cost of debt r_D, which is lower than the cost of equity r_E. However, at the same time, the increase in debt will cause the cost of equity r_E to increase. Why? Because with more debt, more of the cash flows go to debtholders and less to shareholders. As a result, the equity becomes riskier: Shareholders are already last in line to be paid after the debtholders, and adding additional debt to the capital structure makes it even less likely that they will be paid. A company's cash flows are risky, and the more debt that it has to pay, the higher the likelihood that

---

[1] Although the term "cost" is widely used to refer to the expected returns on debt and equity, it should be clarified that the higher "cost" of equity comes from the fact that the expected return is higher for equity due to the greater risk being borne by equity. The term "cost" has the intuitive interpretation that substituting debt for equity may appear to reduce the cost for the firm, which aligns with the long-held belief prior to M-M. As we will describe, M-M showed that this line of thinking is incorrect.

the company will fall short, leaving the possibility that shareholders receive nothing. As a result of this increased risk, shareholders will require a higher rate of return.

Here, since we are still assuming that the company's debt has no default risk, the cost of debt r_D stays the same after the change in capital structure.

The net effect of an increase in the leverage ratio on the company's overall cost of capital is summarized as:

$$r_A = \left[\frac{E}{V} \times r_E\right] + \left[\frac{D}{V} \times r_D\right].$$
$\quad\leftrightarrow\quad\quad\;\downarrow\;\uparrow\uparrow\quad\quad\;\;\uparrow\;\leftrightarrow$

As the firm increases its leverage ratio D/V, r_E increases; however, more weight is shifted toward r_D, which is lower than the cost of equity. The end result is that the effects cancel each other out, leaving the overall cost of capital unchanged. The effect of a decrease in leverage is symmetrical, with the overall cost of capital again remaining unchanged:

$$r_A = \left[\frac{E}{V} \times r_E\right] + \left[\frac{D}{V} \times r_D\right].$$
$\quad\leftrightarrow\quad\quad\;\uparrow\;\downarrow\downarrow\quad\quad\;\;\downarrow\;\leftrightarrow$

The main takeaway is that, so long as the assumptions of M-M hold (i.e., there are no frictions), any changes a firm makes to its capital structure will not affect either its cost of capital or firm value. This provides us with guidance for undertaking DCF calculations to determine firm value when a firm changes its capital structure—as we demonstrate in Example 13.1—but also provides guidance for calculating a firm's cost of capital, as we discuss next.

Example 13.1 (Capital Structure and Company Value When There Are No Frictions): Suppose a railroad company is undertaking a new investment to lay train tracks, similar to many of the tracks it has already constructed. You need to calculate the appropriate discount rate to value this project. Suppose the company's cost of debt is 7% and the return that equity holders demand is 10%. The company is financed with 30% debt and 70% equity. Assume that the company operates in a frictionless environment.

(a) What is the company's weighted-average cost of capital (WACC)?
(b) If the company expects free cash flows of $1 million each year forever, beginning next year, what is its total value?
(c) Now suppose that the company increases its leverage, and changes its capital structure to 40% debt and 60% equity. What are the company's overall cost of capital and total company value now?

Solution.

(a) We can use Equation 13.3, plugging in the information given ($r_E = 0.10$, $r_D = 0.07$, $D/V = 0.30$, and $E/V = 0.70$):

$$\begin{aligned} r_A = \text{WACC} &= \left[\frac{E}{V} \times r_E\right] + \left[\frac{D}{V} \times r_D\right] \\ &= \left[0.70 \times 0.10\right] + \left[0.30 \times 0.07\right] \\ &= 0.091 \text{ or } 9.1\%. \end{aligned}$$

(b) The company's total value is found, via the DCF method, by discounting its future free cash flows by the WACC. The FCFs make up a perpetuity, so we can calculate the total company value by applying the perpetuity formula with the WACC calculated in part (a):

$$V = \frac{FCF}{r_A}$$
$$= \frac{1}{0.091}$$
$$= \$10.989 \text{ million}.$$

(c) Since M-M holds in this situation, we know that the overall cost of capital will remain at 9.1%, and furthermore the total company value will also be unchanged. It may be tempting to take the WACC formula from Equation 13.3 and simply plug in the new leverage ratios ($D/V = 0.40$ and $E/V = 0.60$), resulting in a new WACC. However, this is incorrect because when the firm changes its capital structure, the cost of equity r_E would also change. Therefore, using the same numbers as before for these rates will lead to a wrong answer.

QUICK CHECK 13.3 Consider a company that decides to go from a leverage ratio (D/V) of 70% of firm value to 50% of firm value. If the assumptions of M-M hold (i.e., there are no frictions), explain how you expect this to affect the firm's overall cost of capital, its cost of equity, and its cost of debt.

In the previous two sections we showed the implications of M-M Proposition 1 on firm value and firm risk. In particular, with no market frictions, the choice of debt or equity does not change the overall value of a company, or its risk (and thus its cost of capital). In the next section we show how these insights can provide useful guidance for performing firm valuation calculations.

13.2.3 Calculating the Cost of Capital

The key insights of Modigliani and Miller are the effect of a change in a firm's capital structure on the value of a company, as well as the risk of the company's debt and equity. In Chapter 9 we introduced the DCF methodology for calculating company value, which involved discounting a company's expected future free cash flows by the company's cost of capital. Thus, the insights of Modigliani and Miller provide a helpful methodology for determining the cost of capital of a company, and in particular how the cost of equity and cost of debt for a company may change if the company changes its capital structure.

Modigliani and Miller state that an increase in the leverage ratio of a company leads to the cost of equity r_E increasing, since shareholders are exposed to more risk. By exactly how much the cost of equity changes is formalized by Modigliani–Miller (M-M) Proposition 2:

$$r_E = r_U + \frac{D}{E} \times (r_U - r_D). \tag{13.4}$$

In Equation 13.4, r_U represents the unlevered cost of capital, the cost of capital for the firm if it had no debt, and D/E is the debt-to-equity ratio (note that we are dividing by equity, not total firm value V as in previous formulas). If $D/E = 0$, the cost of equity is equal to the unlevered cost of capital—that is, the cost of equity is the same as the entire firm's cost of capital because there is no debt. If the amount of debt the company has increases, then D/E will go up and cause r_E to go up.

In addition to a firm's debt-to-equity ratio, Equation 13.4 requires knowing the firm's cost of debt r_D and unlevered cost of capital r_U. The cost of debt can be inferred from information about a company's issued bonds as well as different valuation models; we will go over these details in Part III. We can calculate the unlevered cost of capital r_U by combining two different insights. First, if there are no frictions (i.e., if M-M Proposition 1 holds), then r_U will be the same as a company's pre-tax WACC (Equation 9.9):

$$r_U = \left[\frac{E}{V} \times r_E\right] + \left[\frac{D}{V} \times r_D\right]. \tag{13.5}$$

Because capital structure does not change the WACC, according to M-M Proposition 1 the firm's cost of capital with no debt will be the same as the cost of capital with debt, and both are equal to the firm's WACC. Of course, if we want to calculate the WACC, we need r_E in the first place!

The second insight is based on the idea of comparables: Two comparable companies should have the same fundamental operating risk, and thus the same unlevered cost of capital. Note that these comparable companies should be similar, ideally identical, in terms of their business and operations, but they may have different financial capital structures. The unlevered cost of capital allows us to conveniently compare costs of capital without having to worry about the effects of leverage. Thus, if we have appropriate information about a comparable company, we can calculate the unlevered cost of capital for the comparable using Equation 13.5, and this will give us an estimate of r_U for the company we are trying to value.

When combined, these insights provide the following steps for calculating a company's equity cost of capital, which can then be used to calculate the WACC or calculate how the company's equity cost of capital changes if capital structure changes:

1. Find a comparable company.
2. Calculate the unlevered cost of capital r_U for the comparable company using Equation 13.5 and data from the comparable company.
3. Using this unlevered cost of capital from step (b), calculate the equity cost of capital r_E (also called re-levering the cost of capital—that is, adding back the effect of leverage) using the target company's capital structure information (D/E).

To illustrate, consider the example of GCP and LGCP, which are comparable companies since they are identical except for their capital structures. GCP has a total company value of $100 million and is 100% equity financed, and LGCP also has a total value of $100 million composed of 40% debt and 60% equity (so D^{LGCP} = $40 million and E^{LGCP} = $60 million). LGCP's cost of debt r_D is 8% and GCP's WACC r_A is 10%. What is LGCP's cost of equity and WACC?

First, GCP is a comparable, unlevered company to LGCP. Second, GCP has no debt, and so its unlevered cost of capital will be the same as its overall cost of capital (WACC): 10%. We use this unlevered cost of capital to plug into Equation 13.4 and then subsequently into the WACC calculation (Equation 13.3), using the data from LGCP:

$$\begin{aligned} r_E^{LGCP} &= r_U + \frac{D^{LGCP}}{E^{LGCP}} \times \left(r_U - r_D^{LGCP}\right) \\ &= 0.10 + \frac{40}{60} \times (0.10 - 0.08) \\ &= 0.1133, \end{aligned}$$

13.2 CAPITAL STRUCTURE AND THE M-M PROPOSITIONS

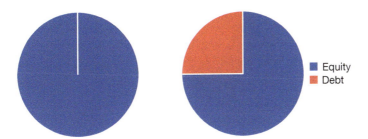

FIGURE 13.2. **The difference between unlevered cost of capital and cost of equity.** This figure depicts the difference between the unlevered cost of capital and the cost of equity. The left figure depicts a firm with no debt, only equity (blue). The right figure depicts the same firm with debt (red). The cost of capital corresponds to the risk of different parts of each circle. The unlevered cost of capital r_U is the cost of capital of the entire firm if the firm had no debt, and corresponds to the risk of the entire blue circle (left). The cost of equity r_E is the expected rate of return of equity given the amount of debt the firm has, and corresponds to the blue portion of the firm's value on the right.

$$\begin{aligned} r_A = WACC &= \left[\frac{E^{LGCP}}{V^{LGCP}} \times r_E^{LGCP}\right] + \left[\frac{D^{LGCP}}{V^{LGCP}} \times r_D^{LGCP}\right] \\ &= \left[\frac{60}{100} \times 0.1133\right] + \left[\frac{40}{100} \times 0.08\right] \\ &= 0.10. \end{aligned}$$

LGCP's cost of equity is greater than GCP's cost of equity (which is equal to GCP's WACC), since LGCP has debt. However, consistent with Modigliani and Miller, the WACC of LGCP is the same as the WACC of GCP, since they are the same except for their capital structure.

Finally, it is important to note that the unlevered cost of capital is different from the cost of equity. The cost of equity is the required rate of return for a company's equity given the amount of debt it already has. The unlevered cost of capital is the required rate of return for the entire company if we imagined that it had no debt. In general, the cost of equity will always be at least as large as the unlevered cost of capital. The two will be equal if a company actually holds no debt. This is illustrated in Figure 13.2.

Example 13.2 (Calculating WACC Using a Comparable Company When There Are No Frictions): Your company currently has 50% debt and 50% equity in its capital structure. It only recently went public, so you do not have reliable data about its cost of equity. You were able to calculate that its required return on debt is 6%, however. You find that a similar competitor has a cost of equity of 12%, a cost of debt of 5%, and has 20% debt and 80% equity in its capital structure. Assume no taxes or other frictions.

(a) What is your company's equity cost of capital?
(b) What is your company's WACC? If you expect your company to generate free cash flows of $1 million each year forever, starting next year, what is the total value of your company?
(c) Suppose that your company now changes its capital structure to 25% debt and 75% equity. Assume that the cost of debt is unchanged. What is your company's equity cost of capital now? What is its WACC now? Will the total company value change?

Solution.

(a) Since we have a comparable company, we can follow the previous steps to compute the unlevered cost of capital using Equation 13.5. Note that we use the appropriate numbers for the *competitor*:

$$r_U = \left[\frac{E}{V} \times r_E\right] + \left[\frac{D}{V} \times r_D\right]$$
$$= [0.80 \times 0.12] + [0.20 \times 0.05]$$
$$= 0.106.$$

Next, we calculate the cost of equity using Equation 13.4 with our just-calculated value for r_U, and the numbers for *your* company:[1]

$$r_E = r_U + \frac{D}{E} \times (r_U - r_D)$$
$$= 0.106 + \frac{0.50}{0.50} \times (0.106 - 0.06)$$
$$= 0.152.$$

Your company's cost of equity capital is therefore 15.2%.

(b) We can use the estimate for the cost of equity from part (a) of $r_E = 0.152$ along with the cost of debt provided of $r_D = 0.06$ to plug into Equation 13.3:

$$r_A = \left[\frac{E}{V} \times r_E\right] + \left[\frac{D}{V} \times r_D\right]$$
$$= [0.50 \times 0.152] + [0.50 \times 0.06]$$
$$= 0.106.$$

Note that no calculation is necessary, however, because we know that, according to the M-M framework, in the frictionless world r_U = WACC and the WACC for both firms is equal, since capital structure does not affect firm value or WACC.

The cash flows are $1 million each year, which is a perpetuity. Applying the perpetuity formula and the estimate of the WACC to discount these cash flows gives us the total company value:

$$V = \frac{FCF}{r_A}$$
$$= \frac{\$1}{0.106}$$
$$= \$9.434 \text{ million.}$$

(c) We can apply Equation 13.4 with the new capital structure for your company. When a firm changes its capital structure, note that the unlevered cost of capital will remain unchanged, since the unlevered cost of capital reflects the situation when a company has no debt. We therefore have:

$$r_E = r_U + \frac{D}{E} \times (r_U - r_D)$$
$$= 0.106 + \frac{0.25}{0.75} \times (0.106 - 0.06)$$
$$= 0.121.$$

Your company's new equity cost of capital is 12.1%, which is lower than in part (a) because your company has less debt.

By the M-M framework, we know that the WACC of the firm will be unchanged. As a result, since the FCFs do not change, the total company value will also not change. We can recalculate it using the new cost of equity (and unchanged cost of debt) to confirm:

$$\begin{aligned} r_A &= \left[\frac{E}{V} \times r_E\right] + \left[\frac{D}{V} \times r_D\right] \\ &= [0.75 \times 0.121] + [0.25 \times 0.06] \\ &= 0.106. \end{aligned}$$

---

[1] In the subsequent calculations, note that we can calculate D/E by using the leverage ratios D/V and E/V. In particular, mathematically it will be the case that $(D/V) / (E/V) = D/E$. Therefore, we can rewrite Equation 11.4 as: $r_E = r_U + ((D/V) / (E/V)) \times (r_U - r_D)$. It should be noted that the previous unlevered cost of capital formula (Equation 13.5) can be applied here because the competitor does not have any debt and thus there is no effect of the tax shield. However, when there are taxes, to calculate the unlevered cost of capital the effect of the tax shield must be removed and Equation 13.5 will not generally apply. One formula for calculating the unlevered cost of capital is:

$$r_U = \frac{r_D \times (1-\tau) \times \frac{D}{E} + r_E}{1 + (1-\tau) \times \frac{D}{E}}.$$

QUICK CHECK 13.4 Suppose LGCP were instead composed of $50 million of debt and $50 million of equity. Would its equity cost of capital be higher or lower than what we calculated? Recalculate its equity cost of capital (assume that the cost of debt remains unchanged).

13.2.4 Summary of the Implications of the M-M Framework

According to Modigliani and Miller, if a firm operates in a frictionless environment and increases its leverage ratio:

1 firm value will be unchanged;
2 the firm's equity value will decrease (increasing debt will push out equity value, since firm value remains constant);
3 the firm's overall cost of capital (WACC or r_A) will be unchanged; and
4 the firm's equity cost of capital (r_E) will increase.

These relationships are summarized in Figures 13.3 and 13.4, again assuming that there is no possibility of debt default and/or bankruptcy.

In this section we have explored a basic framework–that of Modigliani and Miller–to begin to understand the implications of financing a company using either debt or equity. We saw that, when abstracting away from many complications in the real world in order to focus on the core intuition, the choice of capital structure does not fundamentally affect the value or risk of the entire firm. However, it does affect the risk of the equity or debt of the firm, and thus may be relevant to the financiers of a company. This framework tells us that value gained from capital structure choices

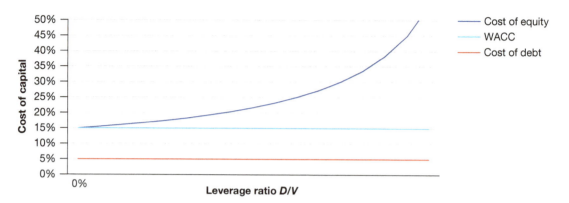

FIGURE 13.3 The costs of capital for equity, debt, and the firm based on the leverage ratio. This figure depicts the cost of equity (dark blue line), debt (red line), and overall firm cost of capital (light blue line) as a function of the leverage ratio, D/V. The figure assumes a WACC of 15% and that the assumptions of the M-M framework hold, with no bankruptcy.

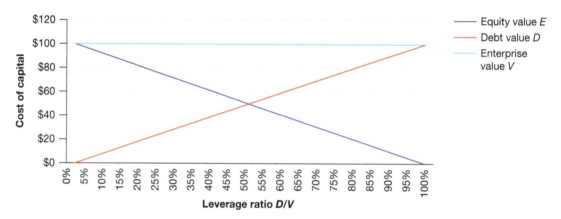

FIGURE 13.4 The values of equity, debt, and the entire firm based on the leverage ratio. Numbers are in millions of dollars, and assumes perpetual free cash flows of $15 million per year and a WACC of 15%. The dark blue line represents equity value, the red line represents debt value, and the light blue line represents the total value of the firm.

must therefore come from the considerations that we left aside from the M-M framework—the real-world frictions and other considerations. In the next section we relax one of the simplifying assumptions we made—that the firm's debt is default-risk-free—to understand how this affects the analysis. We then turn to the effects of individual real-world frictions on the capital structure choice.

13.3 Capital Structure with Default/Bankruptcy Risk

In the previous sections we made a simplifying assumption that a firm's debt is risk-free, which means that the firm will not default on its debt and there is no bankruptcy. This also implied that any change in the firm's capital structure did not change the cost of debt. This is a reasonable assumption in some cases, especially when the firm being examined is highly rated or does not have a substantial amount of debt (and thus the amount of debt does not affect the analysis). However, in other cases it may be an inappropriate assumption. In this section we discuss how the possibility of bankruptcy may affect the previous analysis, in particular the conclusions of how the risk of debt and equity change when the company's capital structure changes. Throughout this section, we will continue to assume that there are no taxes or other frictions, and thus the original assumptions of the M-M framework hold, so that we can focus on the effects without worrying about these other considerations.

13.3.1 Bankruptcy Risk and the Cost of Debt

When debt is risk-free, the promised yield on a company's bonds will be the same as the cost of debt r_D. To illustrate, consider a one-year zero-coupon bond issued by a company with a par amount of $1,000 and trading for a current price of $950. If there is no possibility that the firm will default, then the timeline of cash flows for the bond can be represented as:

```
Time t:            t = 0          t = 1
                   ├──────────────┤
Company bond:      Price          $1,000
                   = $950
```

In this case, there is no uncertainty about the cash flows. As we saw in Chapter 5, the yield of the bond is defined as the rate that the price would grow at to turn into the promised payment. In the above example, this is given by:

$$\text{Price} \times (1 + y) = \text{par},$$
$$\$950 \times (1 + y) = \$1{,}000$$
$$y = 5.26\%.$$

With no possibility of bankruptcy, the expected return on debt will be the same as the promised yield, since there is no uncertainty. Thus, $y = r_D$.

What if, instead, there is a possibility that the firm defaults on its debt and doesn't pay what it promised? For example, suppose there is some probability that the bond defaults and does not pay what is promised, but otherwise the bond keeps its promised payment. In the event of default, bonds will often pay the bondholder some amount of money less than what it has promised (whatever the company can afford to pay). The difference between the actual amount bondholders receive in default compared to what they were promised is known as the loss given default.

To illustrate, suppose there is a one-year coupon bond with a par value of $1,000 that is trading at a price of $920. The promised yield on this bond is therefore:

$$\$920 \times (1 + y) = \$1{,}000,$$
$$y = 8.70\%.$$

However, let us assume instead that there is a 50% chance that the bond will default and only pay $950 to the bondholder at maturity, while there is a 50% chance that the bond will pay what is promised. The situation is then:

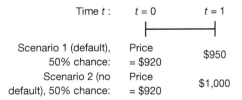

In scenario 1, the realized return of the bond is $y = (\$950 / \$920) - 1 = 3.333\%$, while in scenario 2 the realized return of the bond is the same as the promised yield of 8.7%. The expected return of the bond is the weighted average of these scenarios:

$$r_D = 0.5 \times 3.33\% + 0.5 \times 8.7\%$$
$$= 6.02\%.$$

The cost of debt when there is the possibility of default is therefore *less* than the promised yield, since investors expect their return to be lower, given that the firm may default.

More generally, suppose that a company's bonds have a promised yield of y, but may default with probability p, in which case bondholders experience a loss rate of L (i.e., they expect to lose L per \$1 they are promised). Then the return that bondholders can expect can be represented as:

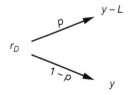

Mathematically, we can calculate the expected return on debt r_D as:

$$r_D = \left[(1-p) \times y\right] + \left[p \times (y - L)\right]$$
$$= y - p \times L. \tag{13.6}$$

In practice, information for each of these variables can be readily obtained for any given company's bonds. For example, credit rating agencies publish estimates of the probability of default p and projected loss rates for bonds of publicly traded companies they examine. Box 13.1 describes how these estimates work.

Box 13.1 World of Business: Bond Ratings

Bond ratings are published by financial intermediaries known as rating agencies. The three largest rating agencies in the world are Moody's, Fitch, and Standard & Poor's (S&P). A rating agency examines corporate bonds issued by companies, and issues them a "grade" based on their analysis of the financial strength of the company. Agencies also provide ratings on other types of debt, such as bonds issued by countries. The higher the rating, the "safer" the bond—it is expected to have a lower probability of default and a lower loss rate if the company defaults. A downgrade can represent a significant event for a company or a country, reflecting that investors can expect a higher risk of default and thus investors will likely demand a higher rate of return in exchange for buying the bond. This makes financing more expensive for the entity.

Table 13.2 shows examples of ratings by Moody's. The highest rating is "AAA," while the lowest rating is "CC-C." As the table shows, on average, the highest-rated bonds have a negligible chance of defaulting, while the lowest-rated bonds have an average default rate of 12.9%. These estimates are published along with estimated loss rates for each bond in the event that they default.

Table 13.2 **Credit ratings and default probabilities.** This table provides the average default probabilities of a bond with the indicated rating, as provided by Moody's, a credit rating agency using data from 1920 to 2008. The top row shows default rates on average, while the bottom row shows default rates during recessions.

	Rating							
	AAA	AA	A	BBB	BB	B	CCC	CC-C
Default rate								
Average	0.0%	0.0%	0.2%	0.4%	2.1%	5.2%	9.9%	12.9%
In recessions	0.0%	1.0%	3.0%	3.0%	8.0%	16.0%	43.0%	79.0%

However, as Table 13.2 shows, default rates can be very different during recessions. For instance, the probability of default of a CC-C bond in recessions is 79%, nearly 68 percentage points higher than on average! Varying estimates can greatly affect the estimates of the prices of bonds, the cost of debt of a company, and the appraisal of risk. The complexities of accurately estimating expected default rates again highlights **Principle 4:** *Every model is an incomplete, simplified description of a complex reality.*

Source: Moody's (2009). Corporate defaults and recovery rates, 1920–2008.

Example 13.3 (Calculating Cost of Debt Using Bond Data): A prominent pet food company has AA-rated, ten-year bonds outstanding with a promised yield to maturity of 2.05%. Based on their AA rating, you believe that the company's bonds have a 1% chance of default, and their expected loss rate in the event of default is 10%. What is your estimate of the expected return for these bonds?

Solution. For the pet food company's bonds, $y = 0.0205$, $p = 0.01$, and $L = 0.10$. Applying Equation 13.6, we have:

$$\begin{aligned} r_D &= y - p \times L \\ &= 0.0205 - 0.01 \times 0.10 \\ &= 0.0195. \end{aligned}$$

The company's expected cost of debt is therefore close to the yield on its bonds, given the low chance of default and relatively small loss rate in the event of default.

QUICK CHECK 13.5 Recalculate the expected rate of return on debt in Example 13.3 assuming that there is a 10% chance the company's bonds will default.

13.3.2 Changes in Capital Structure with Default Risk

In Section 13.2 we assumed that corporate debt was risk-free, and discussed the implications of changing a company's capital structure according to the M-M framework. However, in cases where the credit risk is substantial, the DCF method of firm valuation we previously developed to value firms may not be the right tool/model to use. In the case where there are no frictions but there is default risk, then the conclusions and intuition of Modigliani and Miller—which are that a change in capital structure does not affect firm value but does affect the risk of the firm's equity—still obtain. However, in addition to these effects, an added complication is that the risk of the firm's debt will also change (Merton 1977, 1992a).

To illustrate, suppose that a firm increases the proportion of debt in its capital structure, and thus that D/V goes up. Suppose now that the company's debt is also risky, and thus it may default. As previously concluded in Section 13.2, the company's overall risk and cost of capital remain the same and the cost of equity will still increase, but this will be offset by a lower weight placed on equity in the WACC calculation.

However, in this case the increase in debt will also cause the cost of debt r_D to increase, since by similar logic the firm's cash flows will be split across more debtholders, making each individual claim riskier. However, since debtholders as a group are first in line to get paid, the increase in the required rate of return of debt will be much lower than that of equity. In many cases one can reasonably assume that an increase in a company's leverage ratio will have a negligible effect on its cost of debt (especially if the increase in debt is small and the company starts with little leverage). As a result, we will often assume that the cost of debt remains the same when capital structure changes.

The net effect of an increase in the leverage ratio on the company's overall cost of capital is summarized as:

$$r_A = \left[\frac{E}{V} \times r_E\right] + \left[\frac{D}{V} \times r_D\right].$$
$$\leftrightarrow \quad\quad\quad \downarrow \uparrow\uparrow \quad\quad\quad \downarrow \quad \uparrow$$

As the firm increases its leverage ratio D/V, more weight is shifted toward r_D, which is lower than the cost of equity. While r_D increases slightly, r_E increases substantially, which offsets the higher weight being put on debt. The end result is that the effects cancel each other out, leaving the overall cost of capital unchanged. The effect of a decrease in leverage is symmetrical, with the overall cost of capital again remaining unchanged:

$$r_A = \left[\frac{E}{V} \times r_E\right] + \left[\frac{D}{V} \times r_D\right].$$
$$\leftrightarrow \quad\quad\quad \uparrow \downarrow\downarrow \quad\quad\quad \downarrow \quad \downarrow$$

Figure 13.5 shows how the cost of capital evolves with respect to the leverage ratio (represented by debt divided by equity, D/E) in this setting.

Properly reflecting the changing cost of debt due to credit risk presents challenges in a DCF model. Thus, overall, in cases where the credit risk of a firm is not substantial, a DCF model to value a firm or its financial claims can provide a reasonable answer or approximation. However, in cases where the amount of debt is substantial enough to have first-order effects on the analysis, then DCF analysis may be the wrong tool for the situation, since it relies on proper estimation of the rates of return of debt and equity (which are changing). This reflects **Principle 4:** *Every model is an incomplete, simplified description of a complex reality.* In Chapter 14 we will present a different approach to valuing company claims, including risky debt, which addresses this challenge and can serve as a better tool in such situations.

To sum up, in this section we relaxed one of the previous simplifying assumptions we made—that a company's debt is default-risk-free—and saw how this real-world effect can add important considerations in the capital structure choice. In the next sections we add additional real-world considerations to the capital structure choice by considering frictions that companies face. Modigliani and Miller showed that, absent these frictions, the capital structure choice does not affect overall company value and risk. As we will see, this implies that the existence of frictions can potentially change company value and the overall risk of the company.

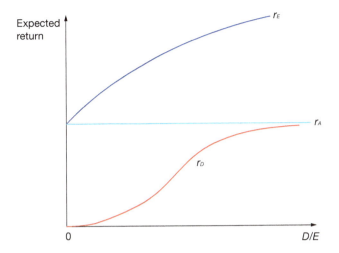

FIGURE 13.5 The costs of capital for equity, debt, and the firm with the possibility of default. The respective expected rates of return are plotted with respect to the debt-to-equity ratio, D/E. The top curve represents the cost of equity capital r_E, the bottom curve represents the cost of debt capital r_D, and the straight line between them is the overall firm cost of capital r_A.
Source: Merton, R. C. (1974). On the pricing of corporate debt: the risk structure of interest rates. *Journal of Finance*, 29(2): 449–470.

13.4 Capital Structure with Frictions: Taxes

The previous sections examined the capital structure decision through a foundational framework—the M-M framework—which excluded the many frictions that firms face in the real world. We saw that in the absence of frictions, the capital structure decision does not affect overall firm value or the risk of the firm. But it does affect the risk of the debt and the equity of the firm. This also provides us with a key takeaway: Any value added from the choice of capital structure must be related to the frictions that we assumed away. Put differently, capital structure may create value by helping to overcome the frictions that companies face. In this section we explore this point and begin to introduce these various frictions, and examine how they may affect the capital structure decision. There are a long list of frictions that companies are exposed to, and so to proceed in a systematic way and understand the core economics behind each one, we will analyze the most important of them one by one and see how each may affect our basic takeaways from the M-M framework. After considering each friction individually, we will then wrap up the chapter by thinking of how to combine them.

In this section we will look at one important friction: taxes. In addition to shareholders and creditors, taxes introduce an additional claimant to the earnings generated by a firm: the government tax authority. Some taxes are paid at the corporate level, such as corporate income tax, where a company must pay some portion of its profits to the government. Other taxes are at the level of the individual shareholder, such as personal income taxes on dividends, bond interest, and realized capital gains. We will first consider the effect of taxes at the corporate level, including touching upon the effect of taxes at the individual level (see Box 13.2). As we will discuss, a primary way that taxes will change things versus our original M-M framework is because of the ability of companies to deduct interest payments from their tax bills, which then generates value from having additional debt. We start by discussing conceptually how this works, and then incorporate these effects in the context of our previous calculations and using different valuation models.

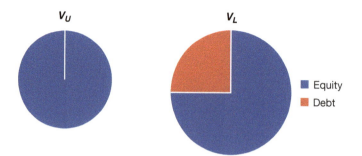

FIGURE 13.6 **Unlevered and levered firm value with taxes.** This figure depicts a change in capital structure that increases the proportion of debt (red) relative to equity (blue). The size of the circle represents the total value of the firm. The left circle shows the value of a firm with no debt, referred to as the unlevered firm. The right circle shows the value of the same firm with some debt, referred to as the levered firm. The size of the right circle is larger than the left circle, reflecting that firm value increases due to the tax shield that comes from having debt.

13.4.1 Corporate Taxes

A key consideration with corporate taxes is that in most countries, interest paid by the firm is tax deductible—in other words, the firm can reduce its taxable income by the amount of interest it pays. Therefore, debt financing can reduce the amount of cash flow that must be paid to the government tax authority by reducing the firm's tax burden.

This interest tax deduction changes things in a few ways from our M-M capital structure foundation. In particular, suppose that we are still operating in a frictionless environment *except* firms pay taxes, so we can isolate the effect that taxes have on our analysis. Then the overall value of the firm will *increase* when the firm has more debt, because the firm's taxes are reduced. Put differently, with taxes as a friction, capital structure does matter because it affects the size of the claim that the government tax authority has on the firm. We refer to the tax savings created by the interest deductibility of debt as the interest tax shield or debt tax shield.

Figure 13.6 shows the effect of taxes and the interest tax shield on firm value. The left circle represents the value of a firm if it had no debt—that is, the unlevered firm value V_U. The right circle represents the value of the firm with debt—that is, the levered firm value V_L. Without taxes and other frictions, $V_U = V_L$. However, after introducing taxes, $V_U < V_L$ due to the tax shield reducing tax expenditures. This is reflected by the fact that the right circle is larger than the left circle, and thus the firm value is higher.

To find out how much firm value the debt adds due to these tax savings, we need to calculate the present value of this tax shield. This requires a valuation model. Two common models are the after-tax WACC method and the adjusted present value (APV) method. Each model has various trade-offs to keep in mind, in line with **Principle 4:** *Every model is an incomplete, simplified description of a complex reality.*

QUICK CHECK 13.6 With taxes, why is firm value changed when a firm changes its capital structure?

13.4.2 The After-Tax WACC Method

The after-tax WACC method is commonly used in practice and was introduced in Chapter 9. This method calculates the total value of the firm by discounting the free cash flows by the firm's overall cost of capital, and incorporating the effect of the tax shield directly into the cost of capital. Consider general cash flows as follows:

13.4 CAPITAL STRUCTURE WITH FRICTIONS: TAXES

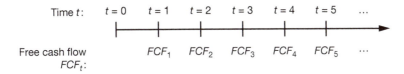

We can represent the DCF valuation method as:

$$V = \frac{FCF_1}{1+r_A} + \frac{FCF_2}{(1+r_A)^2} + \frac{FCF_3}{(1+r_A)^3} + \frac{FCF_4}{(1+r_A)^4} + \frac{FCF_5}{(1+r_A)^5}\cdots. \quad (13.7)$$

The after-tax WACC method involves using the after-tax weighted average cost of capital (after-tax WACC) as the discount rate in Equation 13.7:

$$r_A^{after-tax} = \text{after-tax WACC} = \left[\frac{E}{V} \times r_E\right] + \left[\frac{D}{V} \times r_D \times (1-\tau)\right]. \quad (13.8)$$

In Equation 13.8 we take the proportion of the company's value made up of equity multiplied by the equity cost of capital, and add that to the proportion of the company's value made up of debt multiplied by the debt cost of capital adjusted for taxes. The debt tax shield is thus incorporated into the WACC formula by lowering the cost of debt (through multiplying by $1 - \tau$, where τ is the company's tax rate). The term $r_D \times (1 - \tau)$ is sometimes referred to as the after-tax debt cost of capital. Thus, the more debt a company holds, the more tax savings it receives, which lowers the WACC, and the higher its value is, since we discount the company's free cash flows by a lower discount rate.

It is important to note that in Equation 13.8 and the subsequent equations in this chapter, the ratios E/V and D/V should be calculated using market values, and not book values. This is because the cost of capital should reflect the state of the company going forward, and as we stressed in **Principle 5:** *The best estimate of an asset's value is usually its market price, which incorporates valuable information to guide the allocation of resources and risks.* Book values, as we discussed in Chapter 8, are backward-looking and reflect the past state of the company.

Taxes also lead to a revised version of M-M Proposition 2, which incorporates the tax rate:

$$r_E = r_U + \frac{D}{E} \times (r_U - r_D) \times (1-\tau). \quad (13.9)$$

Taxes therefore also reduce the equity cost of capital, all else being equal, because the savings from the tax shield will benefit the shareholders (equity holders). In Equation 13.9, it is important to note that the unlevered cost of capital r_U will remain unchanged even when a firm changes its capital structure, because this refers to the risk of the company if it had no debt.

We can see these effects visually in Figure 13.7, which shows how the relationship between a firm's leverage ratio and its costs of capital changes when taxes are introduced. For simplicity, let us again assume no debt default risk or bankruptcy. As before, the cost of equity goes up when a firm's leverage ratio goes up. The unlevered cost of capital remains the same, since it refers to the hypothetical situation in which the firm has no debt, and is unaffected by the firm's actual capital structure. However, in contrast to the situation with no taxes, the firm's after-tax WACC goes down when the firm's leverage ratio increases. Figure 13.8 shows the analogous effects for firm value—as the leverage ratio increases, total firm value increases.

To illustrate these effects, let us reconsider our previous example of GCP and LGCP. As before, GCP has no debt, while LGCP has debt. Let's assume that the expected EBIT of both are again $10 million each year, starting next year, but that both companies face a tax rate of $\tau = 40\%$.

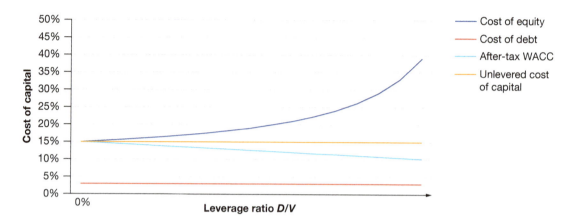

FIGURE 13.7 **The costs of capital for equity, debt, and the firm with corporate taxes based on the leverage ratio.** This figure depicts the cost of equity (dark blue line), debt (red line), the unlevered cost of capital (orange line), and overall firm cost of capital (light blue line) as a function of the leverage ratio D/V. Figure assumes WACC = 15% and that the assumptions of M-M hold with no bankruptcy.

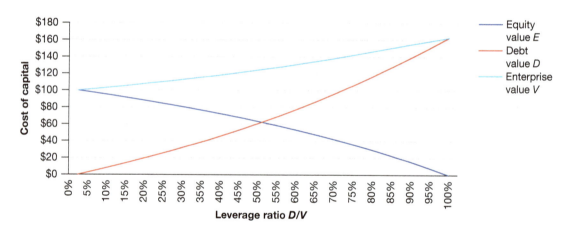

FIGURE 13.8 **The values of equity, debt, and the entire firm based on the leverage ratio.** Amounts are in millions of dollars, and assume FCFs of $15 million per year and the after-tax WACC numbers from Figure 13.7. The dark blue line represents equity value, the red line represents debt value, and the light blue line represents the total value of the firm.

As before, we assume no depreciation, capital expenditures, or change in net working capital. The free cash flows will be less since we are introducing taxes; specifically, they will be: $FCF = EBIT \times (1 - \tau) = \$10 \times (1 - 0.40) = \$6$ million. This reduction in free cash flows represents the fact that the government now has a claim on the company's cash flows that has priority over the claims of debtholders and shareholders. We can view the cash flows in the following timeline:

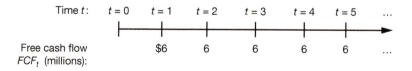

13.4 CAPITAL STRUCTURE WITH FRICTIONS: TAXES

As before, suppose that GCP has an unlevered cost of capital (which is the same as its WACC since it has no debt) r_A of 10%, and that LGCP has a cost of debt r_D of 8%. What are the total company values of GCP and LGCP?

First, let us consider GCP. We are given its WACC, and thus its value via the perpetuity formula is:

$$V^{GCP} = \frac{FCF}{r_A^{GCP}}$$
$$= \frac{6}{0.10}$$
$$= \$60 \text{ million.}$$

GCP's value is lower than before because we now have taxes.

Now, consider LGCP's firm value. Since LGCP has leverage and there are now taxes, its WACC will be different from GCP's. In examining the after-tax WACC (Equation 13.6), we can note that we have the cost of debt capital, $r_D = 0.08$. We do not have the equity cost of capital, but we can calculate it via Equation 13.7; the D/V ratio is still 40%. What about the firm's capital structure D/V and E/V? Note that the previous leverage ratio of D/V = 40% no longer applies because the value of the firm (V, the denominator in the leverage ratio) is lower due to tax payments to the government, but the firm also gains a tax shield to partly offset this. Let us assume that the new leverage ratio is D/V = 49% when incorporating these effects. This presents a challenge when considering the proper leverage ratio to use since we are trying to calculate V (with the effect of the tax shield incorporated) in the first place. We discuss this issue later in the section.

We will proceed by calculating the equity cost of capital r_E. To do so, we can utilize Equation 13.9, using an unlevered cost of capital of $r_U = 0.10$, which we get from GCP, and D/V = 0.49 (E/V = 0.51), $r_U = 0.08$, and $\tau = 0.40$:

$$r_E^{LGCP} = r_U + \frac{D}{E} \times (r_U - r_D) \times (1 - \tau)$$
$$= 0.10 + \frac{0.49}{0.51} \times (0.10 - 0.08) \times (1 - 0.40)$$
$$= 0.112.$$

We now can plug this into Equation 13.8 to calculate LGCP's after-tax WACC:

$$r_A^{LGCP} = \left[\frac{E}{V} \times r_E\right] + \left[\frac{D}{V} \times r_D \times (1 - \tau)\right]$$
$$= [0.51 \times 0.112] + [0.49 \times 0.08 \times (1 - 0.40)]$$
$$= 0.081.$$

LGCP's after-tax WACC is thus lower than GCP's overall cost of capital (10%), which was also the case without taxes. Thus, LGCP's firm value will be higher than that of GCP, given that they have the same cash flows. We can confirm that this is the case:

$$V^{LGCP} = \frac{FCF}{r_A^{LGCP}}$$
$$= \frac{6}{0.081}$$
$$= \$74.1 \text{ million.}$$

The difference in the values of GCP and LGCP when we consider taxes is entirely due to the tax shield that LGCP gets from holding debt. In particular, our calculations show that this tax shield is equal to: $V^{LGCP} - V^{GCP} = \$74.1 - \$60 = \$14.1$ million.

Example 13.4 (Calculating Company Value Using the After-Tax WACC): Company Leverager has free cash flows of $4.25 million next year, $5 million in year 2, and $6 million in year 3. After that, it expects its cash flows to continue growing at a rate of 1% each year. It currently has a capital structure of 50% debt and 50% equity (as a percentage of firm value), and it will keep that capital structure indefinitely. Its cost of debt is 6%. The tax rate it faces is 35%.

As additional information, you see that Leverager has a close competitor that is 100% equity financed, and has an equity cost of capital of 8%.

What is the value of Leverager?

Solution. Our goal is to value the company, and therefore discount its free cash flows by the appropriate after-tax WACC. First, we can draw a timeline of Leverager's cash flows:

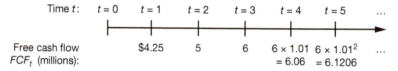

Note that since the cash flows are composed of a growing perpetuity after year 3, we discount year 1–3 cash flows separately and can calculate a terminal value as of year 3 using the growing perpetuity formula:

$$V = \frac{4.25}{1+r_A} + \frac{5}{(1+r_A)^2} + \frac{6}{(1+r_A)^3} + \frac{1}{(1+r_A)^3} \times \frac{6 \times 1.01}{r_A - g}.$$

We thus need to calculate the after-tax WACC. From Equation 13.8, we have all of the needed information except for the equity cost of capital. We can use Equation 13.9 to calculate the equity cost of capital, but further note that we are not provided with the unlevered cost of capital r_U and must solve for it using the "close competitor" as a comparable.[1] Doing so as our first step, we can use Equation 13.5:

$$\begin{aligned} r_U &= \left[\frac{E}{V} \times r_E\right] + \left[\frac{D}{V} \times r_D\right] \\ &= 1 \times 0.08 \\ &= 0.08. \end{aligned}$$

Next we calculate the equity cost of capital:

$$\begin{aligned} r_E &= r_U + \frac{D}{E} \times (r_U - r_D) \times (1 - \tau) \\ &= 0.08 + \frac{0.50}{0.50} \times (0.08 - 0.06) \times (1 - 0.35) \\ &= 0.093. \end{aligned}$$

We can now plug all of the needed numbers into the after-tax WACC formula:

$$\begin{aligned} r_A &= \left[\frac{E}{V} \times r_E\right] + \left[\frac{D}{V} \times r_D \times (1 - \tau)\right] \\ &= [0.50 \times 0.093] + [0.50 \times 0.06 \times (1 - 0.35)] \\ &= 0.066. \end{aligned}$$

In the final step, we turn back to the first equation we set up for the value of the firm, and plug this after-tax WACC into it:

$$V = \frac{4.25}{1+r_A} + \frac{5}{(1+r_A)^2} + \frac{6}{(1+r_A)^3} + \frac{1}{(1+r_A)^3} \times \frac{6 \times 1.01}{r_A - g}$$

$$= \frac{4.25}{1.066} + \frac{5}{1.066^2} + \frac{6}{1.066^3} + \frac{1}{1.066^3} \times \frac{6 \times 1.01}{0.066 - 0.01}$$

$$= 102.673.$$

The total value of Leverager is therefore $102.673 million.

[1] It should be noted that the previous unlevered cost of capital formula (Equation 13.5) can be applied here because the competitor does not have any debt and thus there is no effect of the tax shield. However, when there are taxes, to calculate the unlevered cost of capital the effect of the tax shield must be removed and Equation 13.5 will not generally apply. One formula for calculating the unlevered cost of capital is:

$$r_U = \frac{r_D \times (1-\tau) \times \frac{D}{E} + r_E}{1 + (1-\tau) \times \frac{D}{E}}.$$

QUICK CHECK 13.7 Recalculate the value of LGCP if it instead held 30% debt and 70% equity. Assume that the cost of debt remains at 8%. Compare your value to that calculated in the chapter.

13.4.3 The After-Tax WACC Method with a Changing Capital Structure

In the previous examples we used the after-tax WACC as our discount rate in the perpetuity formula (Equation 2.17). This effectively uses the same after-tax WACC to discount all of the company's future expected free cash flows. It is important to note that this will only be correct to do if the firm's capital structure does not change over time. While this was the case in our previous examples, in practice the capital structure of companies frequently changes over time.

The key insight is that if a company's capital structure does change, then the company's after-tax WACC will also change. This means that the company's discount rate will change over time, something that we must account for in our calculations.

To illustrate, let's return to our example of LGCP. Suppose it has the same after-tax FCFs of $6 million each year, and right now it has the same capital structure of 40% debt and 60% equity. But now suppose that it will change its capital structure in year 1 to be 50% debt and 50% equity. We can write out its cash flows and capital structure as follows:

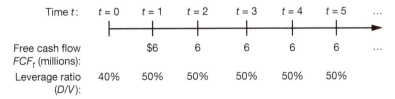

Note that, with taxes, the after-tax WACC for discounting the cash flows in years 2 and onward will change compared to the discount rate in year 1. To see this, first note that the after-tax WACC when the leverage ratio (D/V) is 40% is 8.2%, as we calculated in Section 13.4.2. Next, consider the after-tax WACC when the leverage ratio is 50%. The equity cost of capital in this case (using our previous numbers of $r_U = 0.10$ and $r_D = 0.08$) is:

$$r_E = r_U + \frac{D}{E} \times (r_U - r_D) \times (1 - \tau)$$

$$= 0.08 + \frac{0.50}{0.50} \times (0.10 - 0.08) \times (1 - 0.40)$$

$$= 0.092.$$

The after-tax WACC in this situation is:

$$r_A = \left[\frac{E}{V} \times r_E\right] + \left[\frac{D}{V} \times r_D \times (1 - \tau)\right]$$

$$= [0.50 \times 0.092] + [0.50 \times 0.08 \times (1 - 0.40)]$$

$$= 0.07.$$

The after-tax WACC for LGCP for a leverage ratio of 40% is, therefore, 7%.

To account for the changing discount rates, we can calculate the value of LGCP in two steps. The first step is to calculate the value of LGCP as of time $t = 1$ by discounting all of the cash flows that occur after $t = 1$ (i.e., $t = 2$ and onwards) back to $t = 1$. Note that this calculation is the same as the calculation of a terminal value as of this date. The WACC of 7% (at a leverage ratio of 50%) will be the appropriate discount rate for these cash flows. These cash flows are a perpetuity, and thus we can apply the perpetuity formula:

$$V_{t=1}^{LGCP} = \frac{\$6}{r_{A,t=1}^{LGCP}}$$

$$= \frac{6}{0.07}$$

$$= \$85.714 \text{ million.}$$

The next step is to discount this value and the $t = 1$ cash flow back to today ($t = 0$). The rate that applies for discounting from $t = 1$ back to today is the 8.2% WACC using the leverage ratio of 40%. We therefore discount $V_{t=1}^{LGCP}$ and the $6 million cash flow occurring at $t = 1$ back one year at this rate:

$$V_{t=0}^{LGCP} = \frac{\$6}{1 + r_{A,t=0}^{LGCP}} + \frac{V_{t=1}^{LGCP}}{1 + r_{A,t=0}^{LGCP}}$$

$$= \frac{6}{1.082} + \frac{85.714}{1.082}$$

$$= \$84.763 \text{ million.}$$

This results in a firm value of $84.763 million.

Example 13.5 (Calculating Company Value with a Changing Capital Structure Using the After-Tax WACC): Tablet Company manufactures tablet computers, and has announced that it anticipates the following free cash flows (FCFs) (in millions of dollars) and leverage ratios going forward:

Year	t = 0	t = 1	t = 2
FCF	–	150	200
D/V	50%	55%	60%

13.4 CAPITAL STRUCTURE WITH FRICTIONS: TAXES

It announces that it intends to keep its leverage ratio at 60% after year 2. Assume that after year 2 the free cash flows stay constant at $200 million each year. The unlevered cost of capital is 17%, the debt cost of capital is constant at 8%, and the tax rate is 40%. What is the value of the firm as of each year?

Solution. Note that Tablet's leverage ratio changes each year. Thus, we will first calculate the after-tax WACC in each year, and in the final step discount the free cash flows by the appropriate WACC.

In order to calculate the WACC, note that we are not provided with the equity cost of capital, so we will need to calculate it with the given information. Using Equation 13.9, we have for each of the years:

$$r_{E,t=2} = r_U + \frac{D}{E}\bigg|_{t=2} \times (r_U - r_D) \times (1-\tau)$$
$$= 0.17 + \frac{0.60}{0.40} \times (0.17 - 0.08) \times (1 - 0.40)$$
$$= 0.251,$$

$$r_{E,t=1} = r_U + \frac{D}{E}\bigg|_{t=1} \times (r_U - r_D) \times (1-\tau)$$
$$= 0.17 + \frac{0.55}{0.45} \times (0.17 - 0.08) \times (1 - 0.40)$$
$$= 0.236,$$

$$r_{E,t=0} = r_U + \frac{D}{E}\bigg|_{t=0} \times (r_U - r_D) \times (1-\tau)$$
$$= 0.17 + \frac{0.5}{0.5} \times (0.17 - 0.08) \times (1 - 0.40)$$
$$= 0.224.$$

Next, we can calculate the after-tax WACC for each year (Equation 13.8):

$$r_{A,t=2} = \left[\frac{E}{V}\bigg|_{t=2} \times r_{E,t=2}\right] + \left[\frac{D}{V}\bigg|_{t=2} \times r_D \times (1-\tau)\right]$$
$$= [0.4 \times 0.251] + [0.6 \times 0.08 \times (1-0.40)]$$
$$= 0.129,$$

$$r_{A,t=1} = \left[\frac{E}{V}\bigg|_{t=1} \times r_{E,t=1}\right] + \left[\frac{D}{V}\bigg|_{t=1} \times r_D \times (1-\tau)\right]$$
$$= [0.45 \times 0.236] + [0.55 \times 0.08 \times (1-0.40)]$$
$$= 0.133,$$

$$r_{A,t=0} = \left[\frac{E}{V}\bigg|_{t=0} \times r_{E,t=0}\right] + \left[\frac{D}{V}\bigg|_{t=0} \times r_D \times (1-\tau)\right]$$
$$= [0.5 \times 0.224] + [0.5 \times 0.08 \times (1-0.40)]$$
$$= 0.136.$$

In the final step, we calculate the firm value in each year. Let us start at the last period given ($t = 2$), and work backward. It is useful to draw out the timeline to begin:

13 CAPITAL STRUCTURE

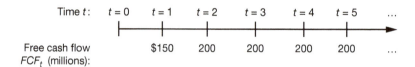

As of time $t = 2$, the subsequent cash flows are a perpetuity. Thus, we can calculate the value of the firm as of $t = 2$ (i.e., the terminal value) using the perpetuity formula:

$$V_{t=2} = \frac{FCF_{t=3}}{r_{A,t=2}}$$

$$= \frac{200}{0.129}$$

$$= \$1{,}550.39 \text{ million.}$$

Now, for time $t = 1$, we discount this and the year-2 free cash flow back one year by the $t = 1$ WACC:

$$V_{t=1} = \frac{FCF_{t=2} + V_{t=2}}{1 + r_{A,t=1}}$$

$$= \frac{1{,}550.39 + 200}{1.133}$$

$$= \$1{,}544.91 \text{ million.}$$

Finally, for time $t = 0$, we proceed in the same way, discounting this value at the free cash flow for year 1 back a year:

$$V_{t=0} = \frac{FCF_{t=1} + V_{t=1}}{1 + r_{A,t=0}}$$

$$= \frac{1{,}544.92 + 150}{1.136}$$

$$= \$1{,}492.01 \text{ million.}$$

QUICK CHECK 13.8 Suppose instead that LGCP chose to change its leverage ratio to 50% starting in year 2. Recalculate LGCP's firm value.

13.4.4 The Adjusted Present Value Method

The adjusted present value (APV) method is another valuation model for incorporating the tax shield, which takes a different approach from the after-tax WACC method. In the after-tax WACC method, we account for the value of the tax shield by adjusting the discount rate. The APV method incorporates the tax shield by considering the tax savings as cash flows and discounting them to arrive at the present value of the tax shield.

The APV method works by separately calculating the value of a company if it had no debt (i.e., the unlevered value of the company), and then adding the present value of the debt tax shield:

13.4 CAPITAL STRUCTURE WITH FRICTIONS: TAXES

Value of firm = value if all equity financed + present value of tax shield,

$$V_L = V_U + PV(\text{debt tax shield}), \quad (13.10)$$

where V_L represents the levered firm value (i.e., value of the firm with debt) and V_U is unlevered firm value (the value of the firm if it had no debt). This implies that the only difference between the value of a levered and unlevered firm comes from the tax shield.

To use the APV method:

1. Calculate unlevered firm value V_U.
2. Calculate the present value of the debt tax shield.
3. Sum to find the firm value.

In the first step, we must calculate the unlevered value of the firm V_U. To do so, we discount the firm's future expected free cash flows by the unlevered cost of capital r_U.

In the second step, we must calculate the amount of the tax savings that make up the tax shield, and then find its present value. Note that in any given year, the amount of money that a firm saves due to the tax shield is:

$$\text{Tax shield}_t = D_{t-1} \times r_D \times \tau, \quad (13.11)$$

where D_{t-1} is the amount of debt the firm has in the previous year, r_D is the debt cost of capital, and τ is the tax rate. The equation says that the firm will enjoy tax saving in a given year equal to the expected interest payments (calculated by multiplying the previous year's debt by the cost of debt) multiplied by the tax rate. Once we calculate the tax savings for each year we can discount them as cash flows. We use a discount rate that appropriately reflects the risk of the tax shield. Since the tax shield is due to the debt the firm carries, an appropriate discount rate is the cost of debt capital r_D.

To illustrate, we will consider LGCP. LGCP has $40 million in debt at an interest rate of 8% per year, and it will keep this amount of debt on its balance sheet every year. Assume taxes are 40% and after-tax free cash flows are $6 million each year.

Applying the APV method, first calculate the unlevered firm value V_U. To do so, discount LGCP's cash flows by the unlevered cost of capital, which we previously calculated as $r_U = 0.10$. Therefore, applying the perpetuity formula:

$$V_U^{LGCP} = \frac{FCF}{r_U}$$
$$= \frac{6}{0.1}$$
$$= \$60 \text{ million}.$$

The unlevered value of LGCP, the value if it had no debt, is $60 million.

Then calculate the present value of LGCP's tax shield. Note that in this case, since LGCP will always have $40 million in debt, LGCP's actual tax savings in each year from year 1 onward will be (applying Equation 13.10):

$$\text{Tax shield}_t = D_{t-1} \times r_D \times \tau$$
$$= \$40 \times 0.08 \times 0.40$$
$$= \$1.28 \text{ million}.$$

By holding debt, LGCP thus saves $1.28 million in tax payments. Since these tax savings occur every year, they are a perpetuity, and we can calculate the present value using the perpetuity formula and discounting by the debt cost of capital r_D:

$$PV(\text{tax shield}) = \frac{1.28}{r_D}$$
$$= \frac{1.28}{0.08}$$
$$= \$16 \text{ million}.$$

Finally, add the unlevered firm value and the present value of the tax shield (Equation 13.8):

$$V_L^{LGCP} = V_U^{LGCP} + PV(\text{debt tax shield})$$
$$= \$60 + \$16$$
$$= \$76 \text{ million}.$$

Thus, according to the APV method, LGCP is worth $76 million when accounting for the tax shield. We can visualize LGCP's cash flows, amount of debt, and tax shield in each year in a timeline:

Time t:	$t=0$	$t=1$	$t=2$	$t=3$	$t=4$	$t=5$	...
Free cash flow FCF_t (millions):		$6	6	6	6	6	...
Amount of debt (millions):	$40	40	40	40	40	40	
Tax shield (millions):		$1.28	1.28	1.28	1.28	1.28	

The example of LGCP illustrates the special case of fixed and perpetual debt, where a company chooses to keep the same amount of debt on its balance sheet indefinitely. Since the amount of debt is the same in each year, the tax shield will also be the same in each year ($D \times r_D \times \tau$), and can be discounted using the perpetuity formula. In this case, things simplify to:

$$V_L = V_U + PV(\text{debt tax shield})$$
$$= V_U + \frac{D \times r_D \times \tau}{r_D} \quad (13.12)$$
$$= V_U + D \times \tau.$$

There are a few potential complications to bear in mind when applying the APV method in practice. First, when calculating the unlevered cost of capital, a different formula for calculating from Equation 13.5 may need to be used, depending on the firm's leverage policy. These alternative formulas involve methods of undoing the effect of the tax shield on the cost of capital when calculating the unlevered cost of capital. Second, as with the unlevered cost of capital, a firm's capital structure policy can affect the calculation of the debt tax shield. In particular, if a firm has a particular leverage policy, such as periodically adjusting its levered ratio or keeping an amount of debt that ensures that its earnings can cover the interest payments, then this has implications for the risk of the tax shield and may require a different discount rate to calculate its present value of the tax shield.

We now have two models for calculating firm value while accounting for capital structure when there are taxes. However, you may have noticed that, in our example of LGCP above, the value we derived using the APV method was different from the value calculated using the after-tax WACC method in Section 13.4.2. This is because each respective method requires different modeling assumptions and approaches the calculations differently. A natural question to ask is whether one model is better than the other. The answer, as we stressed with **Principle 4**: *Every model is an incomplete, simplified description of a complex reality*, is that the after-tax WACC and APV models use different assumptions, and so their best use depends on the situation.

The after-tax WACC method offers a relatively straightforward way of incorporating the tax shield, since it confines the calculations to the discount rate. However, it requires information about a firm's expected capital structure (D/V and E/V), and the firm's equity and debt costs of capital. Uncertainty about a firm's future equity value (which will vary depending on the market) can sometimes create challenges regarding which numbers to use for the capital structure ratios.

This was the case in the calculations for LGCP. With the after-tax WACC method, we needed a leverage ratio for LGCP—while we continued to assume that $D = \$40$ million, the V to use in D/V required incorporating taxes and the tax shield, which we needed to calculate in the first place. A changing capital structure also complicates the calculations for the after-tax WACC, especially when calculating a terminal value, because the perpetuity formulas utilize one discount rate, which will be incorrect unless a firm's leverage ratio is expected to stay constant from the terminal value data onward. Furthermore, calculating the firm's equity cost of capital requires a model (in this chapter we used M-M Proposition 2—that is, Equation 13.9); as we will explore in Part III, there are numerous models to choose from.

In contrast, the APV method does not require information about a firm's leverage ratio, only information about the amount of debt the firm expects to have. In our example with LGCP, this will lead to the more accurate value. However, the APV method requires calculating the unlevered cost of capital, which requires the use of a model (i.e., Equation 13.5) and comparable companies.

The analysis above has only considered corporate income taxes. However, there are also other sources of taxes that investors face that can alter the capital structure decision, and that can also be incorporated into our analysis. Box 13.2 goes over these taxes.

Example 13.6 (Calculating Firm Value Using the APV Method): Slab Company manufactures tablet computers. The amount of debt the firm will maintain is predetermined and shown below for years 0, 1, and 2. After year 2, the firm will maintain a fixed level of debt equal to $700 million. The free cash flow (FCFs) of the firm for years 0–2 (in millions of dollars) are:

Year	$t = 0$	$t = 1$	$t = 2$
FCF	–	150	200
Debt	900	800	700

Assume that after year 2 the FCF has a constant growth rate of 2% per year. The unlevered cost of capital is 17%, the cost of debt is 8%, and the tax rate is 40%. Calculate the value of the firm.

Solution. First, calculate the unlevered value of the firm by discounting the FCFs by the unlevered cost of capital $r_U = 0.17$ (and using the perpetuity's constant growth rate to account for the cash flows after $t = 2$):

$$V_U = \frac{FCF_1}{1+r_U} + \frac{FCF_2}{(1+r_U)^2} + \frac{1}{(1+r_U)^2} \times \frac{FCF_3}{r_U - g}$$

$$= \frac{150}{1.17} + \frac{200}{1.17^2} + \frac{1}{1.17^2} \times \frac{200 \times 1.02}{0.17 - 0.02}$$

$$= 1,267.81.$$

Second, calculate the tax shield and find its present value. We will use Equation 13.9 to calculate the tax savings for each year. This is represented by the following timeline:

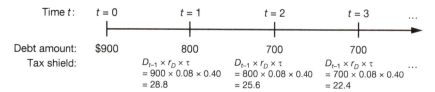

Note that since the amount of debt stays constant at $700 million after $t = 2$, the tax shield will also stay constant and we can thus apply the perpetuity formula. Using a discount rate of $r_D = 0.08$, the present value of the tax shield is thus:

$$PV(\text{tax shield}) = \frac{\text{tax shield}_{t=1}}{1+r_D} + \frac{\text{tax shield}_{t=2}}{(1+r_D)^2} + \frac{1}{(1+r_D)^2} \times \frac{\text{tax shield}_{t=3}}{r_D}$$

$$= \frac{28.8}{1.08} + \frac{25.6}{1.08^2} + \frac{1}{1.08^2} \times \frac{22.4}{0.08}$$

$$= 288.67.$$

In the final step, add the unlevered value of the firm and the present value of the tax shield (Equation 13.11):

$$V_L = V_U + PV(\text{debt tax shield})$$

$$= 1{,}267.81 + 288.67 = \$1{,}556.48 \text{ million.}$$

> **QUICK CHECK 13.9** What are the steps involved in calculating the value of a firm using the APV method?

Box 13.2 Debt and Other Taxes

So far, we have focused on the effect of corporate income taxes, but there are also other taxes, such as personal taxes. This is important because investors—stockholders and bondholders—must pay these taxes. This can affect how attractive stocks and bonds are to them, and therefore how much they are willing to pay for them (and thus the value of debt and equity).

An investor that owns the bonds of a company receives interest payments from the company. This interest income is taxed as regular income in most countries. An investor that owns shares of stock may receive dividends and/or realize a capital gain when the stock is sold. Both are taxable, but the tax rate on capital gains has usually been lower than the tax rate on qualified dividends, which in turn is lower than the rate on ordinary income, such as interest, in the United States. This higher tax rate on bond interest reduces the attractiveness of investing in bonds compared to stocks. This diminishes the value of debt, and thus the debt tax shield (Miller 1977). This effect may be stronger or weaker in different countries, depending on the specific tax code. For example, in Singapore dividends are mostly tax-free. Thus, based on taxes, investors would find stocks to be even more attractive, which would further diminish the value of the debt tax shield. Furthermore, many countries, such as France and other countries in the European Union, limit the amount of interest tax deduction that investors can take advantage of.

To show how this affects our calculations, consider the special case of fixed and permanent debt, where a company continually keeps an amount of debt D on its balance sheet. With corporate taxes of τ, the present value of the tax shield (shown in Equation 13.12) in such a situation is:

$$PV(\text{debt tax shield}) = D \times \tau. \tag{13.13}$$

Now suppose that investors also face personal taxes (that they also pay on interest income) of τ_p and capital gains taxes of τ_g. In such a case, the present value of the tax shield will instead be given by:

$$PV(\text{debt tax shield}) = D \times \left(1 - \frac{(1-\tau) \times (1-\tau_g)}{1-\tau_p}\right). \tag{13.14}$$

The value of the debt tax shield is therefore lower due to the taxes that investors must pay.

To illustrate, consider again the case of LGCP, which has perpetual debt of $40 million and faces a corporate tax rate of $\tau = 40\%$. As we saw in Section 13.4.4, the present value of LGCP's tax shield is:

$$\begin{aligned} PV(\text{tax shield}) &= D \times \tau \\ &= \$40 \times 0.40 \\ &= \$16 \text{ million.} \end{aligned}$$

Now suppose that investors face personal taxes on ordinary income of $\tau_p = 30\%$, and capital gains taxes of $\tau_g = 15\%$. The present value of the debt tax shield then becomes (using Equation 13.14):

$$\begin{aligned} PV(\text{debt tax shield}) &= D \times \left(1 - \frac{(1-\tau) \times (1-\tau_g)}{1-\tau_p}\right) \\ &= 40 \times \left(1 - \frac{(1-0.40) \times (1-0.15)}{1-0.30}\right) \\ &= \$10.857 \text{ million.} \end{aligned}$$

13.4.5 Calculating the Cost of Capital for Projects

To this point, we have discussed capital structure decisions of firms in the abstract without considering motive. However, as we pointed out in Chapter 10, financing decisions are directly connected to project investment decisions since the firm must decide how to pay for them. For example, a company that manufactures aircraft and decides to develop and construct a new aircraft model may change its capital structure (e.g., issue additional debt or equity) in order to raise funds to do so.

A firm's capital structure decision can change the appropriate discount rate used to discount the firm's cash flows. In the same vein, the decision of how to finance a project can affect the appropriate discount rate used in the net present value (NPV) calculation for the project. A key consideration in determining this discount rate is whether the risk of a particular project's cash flows is different from the risk of the firm's existing assets—that is, from the overall risk of the firm.

If the risk of a project's cash flows is the same as the risk of the firm's existing assets (e.g., an aircraft manufacturer investing to expand construction of its existing airplane models), then it may be appropriate to use the firm's overall cost of capital to discount the project's cash flows. In particular, this is because the project's unlevered cost of capital should be the same as the overall firm's unlevered cost of capital: The unlevered cost of capital captures the fundamental operational risk of a company absent of debt, and a project exactly in line with the company's operations should have this same risk. r_U can therefore be calculated for the firm, and then be used as a base to calculate the project's cost of capital, which should reflect the firm's capital structure (after the project financing decision has been made). For example, if a firm takes on additional debt for the project, this will in turn affect the firm's capital structure and cost of capital due to the tax shield, which can be calculated via the after-tax WACC or APV methods discussed previously.

In contrast, if the risk of a project's cash flows is different from the overall risk of the firm's cash flows, then the project's unlevered cost of capital will be different from the firm's unlevered cost of capital. For example, if the aircraft manufacturer decides to start a project in a completely different industry, such as manufacturing electric cars, an appropriate unlevered cost of capital, r_U, can be found by taking the unlevered cost of capital from comparable companies or projects (e.g., electric car companies). This unlevered cost of capital would then be adjusted based on the capital structure of the aircraft company.

Beyond this, the financing decision can also materially change the project investment decision in other ways due to frictions such as agency conflicts between financiers. We discuss such situations in detail in Section 13.5.

> **QUICK CHECK 13.10** As in the discussion above, suppose that your aircraft manufacturing company is considering building a new electric car. The electric car project costs $10 million now, and will generate $5 million in cash flows each year for the next three years. Your company currently has 50% debt and 50% equity in its capital structure, and it will continue to have this capital structure after issuing financing for the project. The unlevered cost of capital for electric car manufacturers is 15%. Your company's cost of debt is 5%, and the tax rate is 35%. What is the appropriate discount rate and NPV of the project?

13.5 Capital Structure with Other Frictions

Frictions are imperfections that prevent markets from functioning perfectly, and they affect decision making. Frictions include government taxes, costs to doing business in markets (transaction costs), differences in information between market participants (asymmetric information), agency costs (arising from conflicts of interest, as we discussed in Chapter 11), and so on. In the previous sections we went over the Modigliani–Miller theory for understanding capital structure decisions, which states that in the case with no taxes or frictions, capital structure does not affect overall firm value. We then introduced one friction—taxes—and showed that additional debt caused firm value to increase. With taxes as our only friction, the optimal capital structure to maximize firm value is 100% debt! Of course, in the real world we do not observe many firms that finance themselves exclusively with debt. What is missing from our framework is the effect of other frictions in addition to taxes. In this section we will explore how each of these frictions affect the capital structure decision and company value.

We will begin by considering frictions that add disadvantages to holding debt, which include the financial distress that comes with holding substantial amounts of debt and agency costs. We then discuss frictions that add advantages to holding debt. We conclude the section with additional considerations that can create a preference for debt or equity, such as asymmetric information and the structure of debt.

13.5.1 Costs of Financial Distress

As the proportion of debt in a firm's capital structure increases, so too does the likelihood that the firm might default on that debt should future cash flow be less than expected. Firms that are in imminent danger of defaulting on their debt obligations are said to be in financial distress. In such circumstances, firms usually incur significant costs that reduce the firm's total value. This is an additional friction associated with debt financing.

There are two types of costs of financial distress: direct costs and indirect costs. Direct costs of financial distress are the costs that firms incur if they enter into bankruptcy proceedings. If a firm defaults on its debt, it may liquidate and cease operations; however, viable firms may enter into bankruptcy proceedings in court, with the aim of renegotiating the firm's standing agreements and contracts so that the firm can continue operations after the proceedings (this is known as chapter 11 bankruptcy in the United States, and as restructuring plans in the UK and many other countries). Such proceedings are costly, as the firm must pay administrative and legal fees to lawyers, as well as fees to accountants, consultants, and others involved in the proceedings. Box 13.3 provides a real-world example of these costs.

Indirect costs of financial distress are costs to a firm that are not part of bankruptcy proceedings, but are imposed on firms that are close to defaulting. This includes things like the cost of the time and effort the firm's managers spend avoiding bankruptcy, and business that is lost because customers, suppliers, and employees become greatly concerned by the threat of bankruptcy followed

---

Box 13.3 World of Business: Toys "R" Us and Direct Costs of Financial Distress

Long-time international toy retailer Toys "R" Us filed for chapter 11 bankruptcy in late September 2017, with over $5 billion in debt resulting in $400 million of interest payments each year, and declining sales in the face of online retailers such as Amazon. However, the mood in the courtroom was hopeful when the firm initiated its proceedings, as the company had built up a solid brand image among American families, and was confident in its ability to turn around the company. Toys "R" Us hoped to shed some of its debt and reorganize its business through the proceedings.

However, in March 2018 reality sunk in and Toys "R" Us announced that it would close down all of its stores, thus effectively liquidating. Throughout the bankruptcy proceedings the company had been steadily losing money, spending nearly $50 million on legal, banking, and consulting fees in the four months since entering into chapter 11 proceedings. Alongside weaker-than-expected sales during the holiday season, the firm's lenders had determined that they had had enough of the company burning through cash, and thus chose to sell off the company's inventory and real estate, rather than continue to lose money through the proceedings.

In 2021, a few years after the shuttering of all Toys "R" Us stores, a management company known as WHP Global acquired the rights and revived Toys "R" Us as a "store-within-a-store" concept, selling toys within Macy's department stores.

Source: Corkery, M. (2018). Toys 'R' Us case is test of private equity in age of Amazon. *New York Times.*

by the possibility of a liquidation of the firm. This can put the firm in a weakened position versus its competitors.

How large are these indirect costs? The answer is that it depends on the operations of each specific firm and the kind of "product" it sells. For example, consider the following question: Would a consumer purchase a car from a manufacturer that is in danger of going bankrupt? While some consumers might if the company reduces its prices substantially, many consumers may worry that the firm will not be able to provide proper maintenance and parts, so instead shop at a competitor. The manufacturer may experience large costs of financial distress through lost sales. In contrast, many airlines have gone through bankruptcy proceedings with little effect on their sales, as consumers understand that taking a trip on an airplane is a service that is independent of future trips—once you take the trip, you are not necessarily expecting anything further from the airline. Put differently, the airline being in financial distress is less likely to turn customers away than a car manufacturer.

Economists have attempted to quantify the costs of financial distress, and estimates indicate that they can range, on average, between 4.5% and 20% of firm value, with the higher end of the estimates being for firms in bankruptcy (Andrade and Kaplan 1998; Almeida and Philippon 2007). These financial distress costs represent a disadvantage of holding debt. However, as we saw in Section 13.4, the advantage of holding debt comes from the tax shield. Indeed, empirically it has been estimated that the tax benefits of debt are roughly 4.3–9.7% of firm value, roughly in line with the empirical magnitude of average costs of financial distress (Graham 2000). This is the essence of the trade-off theory of capital structure, which predicts that firms will choose an optimal level of debt, trading off the tax benefits of debt with the financial distress costs of debt.

In the trade-off theory, a firm will continue to borrow—thereby increasing its firm value through the tax shield—until the amount of debt gets large enough to begin to decrease firm value through the higher financial distress costs that come with it. Companies that face higher financial distress costs, such as our previous example of an automobile manufacturer, will optimally hold less debt, as their costs of financial distress will inhibit firms from taking on more debt to take advantage of the tax shield. In contrast, companies with low financial distress costs, such as our previous example of airlines, will optimally hold more debt, as they can take more advantage of the cash savings from the tax shield without having to worry about the costs of financial distress. This is illustrated in Figure 13.9.

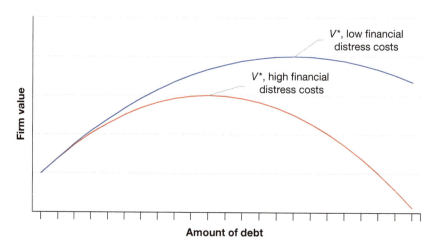

FIGURE 13.9 **Firm value with taxes and financial distress costs.** The red curve represents firm value if the firm has high financial distress costs, while the blue curve represents firm value if the firm has low financial distress costs. The optimal amount of debt is denoted by V^*.

The trade-off theory of capital structure is useful in understanding how firms choose their optimal capital structure. How well does it explain capital structure in practice? According to empirical work, even companies that seem to be far away from financial distress or face low costs of financial distress do not hold as much debt as they could in order to maximize their value. Put differently, firms hold less debt than the trade-off predicts they should; in particular, a typical firm could add roughly 17% to its firm value by adding more debt and gaining more benefit from the tax shield (Graham 2000).

This suggests that the trade-off theory of capital structure is incomplete and does not fully explain firms' choices of capital structures. We now explore frictions such as moral hazard and asymmetric information that can help us complete the picture.

> QUICK CHECK 13.11 How would a decrease in the costs of financial distress affect corporate capital structure?

13.5.2 Conflicts between Shareholders and Debtholders

We have discussed the costs of financial distress and showed how they limit the optimal amount of debt in a firm's capital structure. An additional friction comes from moral hazard, which can happen if a stakeholder of the firm takes an action at the expense of others, and potentially at the expense of the firm itself.

A moral hazard problem can stem from a misalignment of incentives between shareholders (and managers acting in the interest of shareholders) and creditors. This incentive problem friction arises because shareholders have little incentive to limit the firm's losses in the event of a bankruptcy, since they stand to receive nothing in that case. Managers acting in the interests of shareholders may choose to undertake volatile investments that have the potential to increase the wealth of shareholders at the expense of debtholders. This is referred to as risk shifting. In some cases, this can even result in negative-NPV investments being undertaken.

For example, suppose the firm's current assets are worth $100 million. The firm has debt with a face value of $104 million maturing one year from now. Management has two choices: (1) investing all $100 million in riskless Treasury bills (T-bills) maturing in one year that pay an interest rate of 4%; or (2) investing $100 million in a venture that will either be worth $200 million one year from now with probability 30%, or nothing with probability 70%:

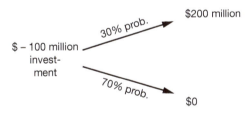

With a riskless interest rate of 4%, the net present value (NPV) of this investment can be calculated as:

$$NPV = \frac{1}{1.04} \times (0.70 \times \$200 + 0.30 \times \$0) - \$100$$
$$= -\$34.615 \text{ million.}$$

In theory, since option 2 has a negative NPV, management should not choose this investment. However, management (acting solely in the interest of shareholders) will choose to undertake the risky venture because if management invests in T-bills, the value of the firm's shares will fall to zero: The investment will be worth $104 million in one year, but all of the money will go to pay off bondholders, leaving shareholders with nothing. However, with the risky venture the firm has some chance, no matter how small, of being worth more than $104 million one year from now, and then the shares will have some value. More specifically, if the investment succeeds and is worth $200 million, then the shareholders will gain value of $200 − $104 = $96 million after creditors are paid.

The creditors in this example bear all the downside risk of the risky venture, and the shareholders get all of the incremental upside potential for gain: If the risky venture fails, shareholders receive nothing (what they would have received anyway with the riskless investment) and creditors will also receive nothing (in contrast to what they would have received with the riskless investment).

Creditors have to consider the potential moral hazard problem when they lend to certain firms with large amounts of debt; managers might have an incentive to redeploy the firm's assets in a way that reduces the firm's total value (the size of the whole pie) in order to increase share price (the size of the equity piece). Because creditors are aware that under certain adverse circumstances managers might take actions that might be at creditors' expense, they will limit their lending in the first place.

Risk shifting typically involves risky (and sometimes even negative-NPV) projects being undertaken due to conflicts between shareholders and creditors. Another problem that stems from moral hazard involves debt preventing good (positive-NPV) projects from being undertaken, because they may increase the value of debt more than the value of equity. This is referred to as the debt overhang problem, when a firm has debt that is so large it cannot take on additional financing for investment.

To illustrate, consider the following investment opportunity. A firm with no internal funds is considering issuing stock to raise $110 million from new shareholders. The investment will generate $140 million in revenue one year from now with 80% probability, or $100 million one year from now with 20% probability:

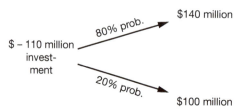

Suppose that the appropriate discount rate is 5%, and the firm already owes $100 million in debt that it must pay back in one year. The project's NPV is:

$$\begin{aligned} NPV &= \frac{1}{1.05} \times \left(0.80 \times \$140 + 0.20 \times \$100\right) - \$110 \\ &= \$15.714 \text{ million.} \end{aligned}$$

This project thus has a positive NPV, and the firm should invest in it to increase firm value. However, it is unlikely that the firm will gain new shareholders to provide the $110 million to undertake the investment because the generated profit will not result in any shareholder payout—shareholders are paid less money than they gave to the firm due to what the firm has to pay the debtholders. To see this, note that shareholders will either receive nothing after creditors are paid $100 million (in the case when the investment generates $100 million), or will receive $40 million (in the case when the investment generates $140 million). Either case results in shareholders losing value by providing $110 million upfront, so they will not provide the funding. The firm will therefore not be able to invest in the project, despite it having a positive NPV, since all of the upside of the project is going to pay off the debtholders. More generally, managers may internalize these incentives in their project choices if they are acting on behalf of the shareholders. Box 13.4 shows that debt overhang can also cause difficulties in raising additional financing from new debtholders.

> **Box 13.4** World of Business: Petrobras' Capital Structure and Debt Overhang
>
> In 2016, an oil glut caused by excess supply and declining demand had wrecked the expansion plans of many oil and gas companies, and deteriorated their profitability severely. This caused the cash flows of these companies to dry up, forcing them to raise additional debt. Petroleo Brasileiro Petrobras, a Brazilian oil company, experienced a reduced ability to generate cash flows, while its leverage ratio had gone up considerably over the last few quarters.
>
> However, in contrast to its peers, Petrobras had not raised a large amount of debt to meet its capital spending needs in the last two years. This is primarily because the company's balance sheet already had a large amount of debt, and the company had not been in a position to raise additional debt at attractive rates.
>
> This illustrates that debt overhang can also affect a company's ability to raise capital through debt financing. A company with a large amount of existing debt that wishes to raise new debt must approach new creditors, who recognize that the firm will likely need to prioritize its existing creditors. This will lead to new creditors demanding higher interest rates or other terms in exchange for funds, which may be prohibitive to the company seeking funding, resulting in missed investments.
>
> *Source*: Trefis (2016). A look at Petrobras' capital structure. *Forbes*.

> **QUICK CHECK 13.12** How might conflicts between shareholders and creditors affect a company's investments?

13.5.3 Advantages of Debt

In Chapter 11 we discussed the problem of conflicts of interest between the managers and shareholders of corporations. When managers have discretion about how to allocate a firm's cash flows, there is a temptation to use the cash to invest in projects that do not increase the wealth of shareholders, but their own: the free cash flow problem. Examples include investments with negative NPV that increase the power, prestige, or perks of the managers. In order to mitigate this incentive problem created by free cash flow, a certain amount of debt may be a good thing.

Debt forces management to distribute cash to the firm's debtholders in the form of prescheduled payments of interest and principal. Issuing debt to repurchase shares can create value for the shareholders by reducing the amount of free cash flow available to managers. The required interest payments can impose discipline on managers in terms of their investment and financing decisions, as poor decisions that result in the firm generating insufficient cash to meet its interest and principal obligations can lead to the firm going bankrupt, and the manager therefore being out of a job.

Debt can also signal to investors that the firm has good future prospects. Since managers understand they should only use debt if the company can maintain the debt through enough cash flow, their choice of using debt can demonstrate managers' confidence in the firm's prospects to outside investors.

> **QUICK CHECK 13.13** What are the advantages to a firm of having debt?

13.5.4 Asymmetric Information

Another important friction is asymmetric information—that is, a firm's managers know more about the operations and future prospects of a firm than outside investors do. Asymmetric information can cause a firm to have a preference for using cash, debt, or equity. In particular, managers may strategically make certain financing choices based on the information only they know; investors may infer this information upon seeing the financing choice, thus potentially creating advantages and disadvantages from certain financing choices.

To illustrate, imagine that a company is developing a new consumer product, which management knows the details/prospects of, but investors do not. The firm is deciding whether or not to raise funding through issuing equity. First, suppose that management finds out information that proves the product has good prospects—for example, internal testing reveals that consumers love the product. Will the managers of the firm choose to issue equity now? The answer is no. The reason is that right now the stock is undervalued compared to what managers know to be the true value. Management could simply wait until the product launch, when the market information becomes public and shows the value to raise more money. Managers, acting in the interest of the existing shareholders (and probably owning shares of stock themselves), will be diluting their shares of stock if they issue equity before the expected stock price increase when the product launches. Managers therefore have an incentive to not issue stock when they know good news is likely to come.

Now suppose that management finds out bad news about the product that no one else has—for example, internal testing reveals that consumers have a negative reaction to the product. Will the managers of the firm choose to issue equity now? The answer is yes. The managers, acting in the interest of the existing shareholders and acting on the information they have that the market doesn't, will want to sell shares of stock and raise money for the company at a high price now, since they know the price will fall in the future. When the share price falls once the product launches, the company can repurchase stock at a lower price. These two situations are summarized in Figure 13.10.

When there is asymmetric information, firms have an incentive to issue equity before bad news about their product arrives, but not to issue equity until good news arrives. Investors, knowing these incentives, may view equity issuance before a product launch as a bad signal and therefore penalize the firm when assigning a price to the equity.

The asymmetric information friction has less or no impact when not related to issuing equity; payoffs of debt are less dependent on the future state of the firm than equity, and are thus less affected. If a firm has internal funds (i.e., cash) on hand, then the problem is avoided entirely since no new equity is issued. This is known as the pecking order theory of capital structure: In the presence of asymmetric information, firms seeking to finance their operations should do so in the following order:

> QUICK CHECK 13.14 Suppose a firm expects good news to happen in the future. Why might the firm's management decide to not issue stock?

1. internal funds (cash)
2. debt
3. equity.

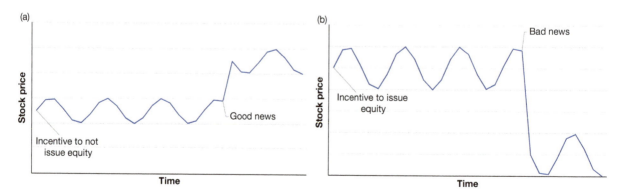

FIGURE 13.10 Issuing equity under asymmetric information. (a) The situation where the firm knows there will be good news in the future. (b) The situation where the firm knows there will be bad news in the future.

13.5.5 The Structure of Debt: Maturity and Seniority

The structure of a company's debt can also be important in understanding a company's capital structure decisions. Debt can be acquired in multiple instances, from multiple sources under multiple conditions that require the firm to approach it in different ways. The approach a firm can take to its debt can differ depending on the debt's seniority. Debt that is more senior takes priority in terms of repayment compared to debt that is less senior (i.e., more junior, also referred to as subordinated debt). Senior debt refers to debt at the top of the repayment list, mezzanine debt refers to debt in the middle of the repayment list, and junior debt refers to debt at the bottom of the repayment list. A company may have many different tiers or tranches of debt, which refer to the order of their seniority. More senior debt also typically has legal priority over more junior debt in terms of claims in bankruptcy proceedings. For these reasons, the more senior the debt, the less risk the debtholder is exposed to, and the lower the rate of the return investors demand of the company.

The calculations we've worked through in this chapter assumed that a company had one type of debt, with a single required rate of return, r_D. However, when a firm has a debt structure, each seniority of debt has a different risk profile and thus a different cost. This should be incorporated into the calculations and is straightforward, as we can simply split the debt terms into the type of debt. For example, a company with senior debt of D_{Senior} and junior debt of D_{Junior} would have a pre-tax WACC given by:

$$\text{WACC} = r_A = \left[\frac{E}{V} \times r_E\right] + \left[\frac{D_{Senior}}{V} \times r_{D,Senior}\right] + \left[\frac{D_{Junior}}{V} \times r_{D,Junior}\right], \tag{13.15}$$

where $V = E + D_{Senior} + D_{Junior}$. Thus, the WACC formula remains similar, except we separately consider the proportion of the firm's value made up of senior debt multiplied by the cost of the senior debt, and the proportion of the firm's value made up of junior debt multiplied by the cost of the junior debt. A company can also have hybrid securities, which have aspects of both debt and equity. We go into detail about such securities in Chapter 14. Estimating the rates of returns on such securities, as well as debt of different seniorities, can be challenging. In Chapter 14 we discuss methodologies of valuing debt that do not rely on DCF calculations.

Another way in which debt can differ is in terms of maturity—when the principal amount owed is due. Debt can be short term (typically due in one year or less) or long term, where long-term debt can vary substantially (e.g., 5 years or 30 years). Debt of different maturities will typically have different interest rates, since interest rates in the economy at different horizons differ. We will examine this issue in more detail in Part III.

The structure of debt can introduce important considerations for a company's capital structure decisions. For example, consider a firm that has short-term junior debt due in one year and long-term senior debt due in five years:

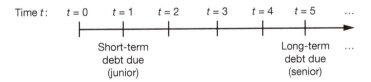

The long-term debt has priority over the short-term debt as it is senior. However, imagine a company that is doing well enough through year $t = 1$ to pay off the short-term debt, but then runs into financial trouble in year $t = 3$ and is unable to pay off the long-term debt. Even though the long-term debt is "senior," in reality the more junior debt ended up carrying less risk and being paid off since it was

> **QUICK CHECK 13.15** What is debt seniority and maturity?

short-term debt. The potential for such situations can affect the pricing of the debt that a company wishes to issue, can affect negotiations among creditors and the covenants placed on debt, and a company's investment decisions along the lines of the effects discussed in the previous sections.

13.6 Optimal Capital Structure

We have established that in a frictionless economic environment, capital structure does not affect the value of the firm, but in the real world there are frictions of many sorts that must be accounted for by capital structure. Finding the optimal capital structure for a corporation involves determining trade-offs that depend on the company's particular environment.

For some firms, agency conflicts may be very important, but for other firms they may be less relevant—for example, due to good corporate governance (as we discussed in Chapter 10). Some firms may be younger and thus less well known to investors, in which case there is a more substantial amount of asymmetric information between managers and investors regarding the firm's operations and prospects; some firms may be exposed to more financial distress costs than others. All of these possibilities and the subsequent effects may be more or less relevant depending on the firm under consideration. Conceptually, the optimal capital structure is a firm choosing the level of debt that maximizes the benefits of debt while minimizing the costs—taking on too much debt can cause the costs to outweigh the benefits, and thus the value of the firm to decline. This is illustrated in Figure 13.11, and we can also represent this as:

$$\text{Value of firm} = V_U + PV(\text{debt tax shield}) + PV(\text{agency benefits of debt}) \\ - PV(\text{agency costs of debt}) - PV(\text{financial distress costs of debt}). \tag{13.16}$$

The agency benefits of debt include reducing free cash flow problems and disciplining managers, while the agency costs of debt include risk shifting and the debt overhang problem. We can calculate

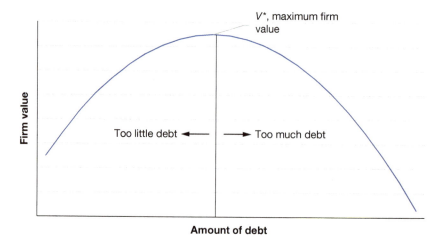

FIGURE 13.11 Optimal capital structure. The optimal amount of debt is represented by V^*, which maximizes firm value. A firm that holds too little debt will not take enough advantage of the benefits of debt, and can increase its firm value V by holding more debt. A firm that holds too much debt is affected by the costs of debt, and can increase firm value V by reducing its amount of debt. The optimal amount of debt trades off the costs and benefits, and maximizes firm value V^*.

an amount for some of these effects, which require a valuation model. For example, in Section 13.4 we saw methods of calculating the value of a firm's tax shield given its debt. Assessing the impact on valuation of some effects, such as risk shifting and debt overhang, will require different valuation models, which we will introduce in Part III.

Other effects, such as conflicts between shareholders and debtholders and the effect of the free cash flow problem, are difficult to place a value on even with a model. It is important to note that there is no single valuation model that explains all of these different effects. As we stressed with **Principle 4:** *Every model is an incomplete, simplified description of a complex reality.* Ultimately, properly understanding the structure of the firm you are examining, and the incentives of all of the stakeholders, is critical to understanding how important a given friction may be.

Conclusion

In this chapter we continued our examination of decision making within companies, and focused on an important financial decision that companies face: the capital structure decision, the choice of what mix of financing a firm uses to fund its operations, growth, and investment projects. Companies may use internal funds to finance themselves, or they may raise financing externally from investors through debt (borrowing) or equity (e.g., issuing stock). In order to focus on the core economic intuition behind the decision and ground our analysis, we explored a framework—that of Modigliani and Miller—which examines this choice while abstracting away from many of the complications such as market imperfections (frictions) that companies face in the real world. We saw that in a world without frictions, the choice of capital structure does not affect overall firm value or the risk of the firm. But it does affect the risk of the debt and equity of the firm. An implication of this is that any value added from the choice of capital structure must be due to frictions.

With the M-M framework as our foundation, we then examined individual frictions that companies face in the real world, and analyzed how they may affect the capital structure choice. With taxes, we saw that having additional debt can add value to a firm due to the tax deductibility of interest payments, and we could explicitly measure this effect in our calculations. Frictions such as the potential of financial distress and conflicts between investors while holding large amounts of debt added disadvantages to holding debt. On the other hand, we explored other advantages of debt, such as the potential of agency costs. Finally, we explored additional considerations that may be important in understanding the choice between debt and equity, such as differences in information between firms and investors, and how debt is structured.

Overall, there is a long list of considerations that companies have to bear in mind when making a decision about how to finance themselves. Certain frictions may be more important to some firms than to others. For example, a large and financially secure firm likely does not need to worry much about financial distress costs, whereas these costs may be important for a young firm without stable profits. As a result, there is no "one size fits all" policy that every firm can follow when it comes to capital structure: Each firm must individually weigh the different costs and benefits when making their choice.

We were able to expand upon our previous analytical framework for firm value in this chapter and incorporate the choice of capital structure. Subsequent chapters will further develop this in a variety of ways. In Chapter 14 we will introduce a different analytical framework that will delve further into issues pertaining to the capital structure choice, such as incorporating the possibility of default risk and including the choice of financing tools that are a blend of debt and equity. In Chapter 15 we will explore specific *sources* of debt and equity financing—for example, venture capital, private equity, and bank financing—and understand how the details of these sources combined with the insights from this chapter can help us to better understand companies' choices of financing.

Takeaways

- To fund its operations, a firm may choose internal financing, such as cash generated from its operations, or external financing, such as debt or equity.
- A firm's capital structure is its choice of the mix of debt and equity it uses to finance itself.
- The starting point of analyzing capital structure decisions is M-M Proposition 1, which states that in a world with no frictions, capital structure does not affect firm value. This also implies that capital structure does not affect a firm's cost of capital.
- An increase in the proportion of debt in a firm's capital structure increases the risk of a firm's equity, although the overall cost of capital is unchanged. M-M Proposition 2 provides a formula to calculate how the cost of equity changes depending on a firm's capital structure.
- When there are taxes, a friction, firm value increases when a firm takes on more debt because of the debt tax shield: Interest payments are tax deductible.
- The value of the tax shield can be incorporated into calculations to determine firm value in two ways. The after-tax WACC method incorporates the tax shield into the firm's discount rate by lowering the WACC. The APV method separately calculates the value of the unlevered firm and the tax shield savings; the two discounted cash flow streams are then added together.
- Costs of financial distress are costs that a firm incurs related to being in or close to bankruptcy, and can reduce firm value. This represents a disadvantage of debt.
- The trade-off theory of capital structure predicts that firms will choose an optimal amount of debt that trades off the tax benefits of debt with its costs of financial distress.
- Conflicts between shareholders and creditors are a cost of holding substantial amounts of debt, and can lead to suboptimal investment. Risk shifting happens when a firm has an incentive to invest in excessively risky projects, because debtholders bear the brunt of the risk. Debt overhang happens when a firm does not undertake good projects because the benefits flow primarily to the debtholders.
- Debt can be used to help solve the free cash flow problem by limiting the amount of cash a firm has on hand because of interest and principal payments. Debt can also impose discipline on managers, inducing them to make good decisions.
- The pecking order theory predicts that, if there is asymmetric information, firms should first turn to internal funds, then debt, and finally equity as a last resort when funding themselves.
- Maturity and seniority are aspects of debt that can be important considerations when analyzing a firm's capital structure.
- A given firm's optimal capital structure trades off the costs and benefits of debt in order to maximize firm value. Estimating the exact impact on the value of the firm requires a valuation model, and it is important to keep in mind that all valuation models are simplifications of a complex reality.

Key Terms

Adjusted present value (APV) method   374
After-tax WACC method   374
After-tax weighted average cost of capital (after-tax WACC)   375
Asymmetric information   393
Debt overhang problem   392
Debt-to-equity ratio   363
Direct costs of financial distress   389

Discipline   393
External financing   356
Financial distress   389
Fixed and perpetual debt   384
Free cash flow problem   393
Frictionless environment   357
Indirect costs of financial distress   389
Interest tax shield   374

Internal financing 356
Junior debt 395
Leverage 358
Levered 359
Long-term 395
Maturity 395
Mezzanine debt 395
Modigliani–Miller (M-M) Proposition 1 357
Modigliani–Miller (M-M) Proposition 2 363
Moral hazard 391
Optimal capital structure 388
Pecking order theory 394
Pre-tax weighted-average cost of capital (WACC) 361
Re-levering 364
Risk shifting 391
Senior debt 395
Seniority 395
Short-term 395
Signal 393
Subordinated debt 395
Trade-off theory of capital structure 390
Unlevered 358
Unlevered cost of capital 363

Key Equations

Total company value	$V = D + E$	Eq. 13.1
Firm value (DCF)	$V = \dfrac{FCF_1}{1+r_A} + \dfrac{FCF_2}{(1+r_A)^2} + \dfrac{FCF_3}{(1+r_A)^3} + \dfrac{FCF_4}{(1+r_A)^4} + \dfrac{FCF_5}{(1+r_A)^5} \cdots$	Eq. 13.2
Pre-tax weighted-average cost of capital (WACC)	$r_A = \text{WACC} = \left[\dfrac{E}{V} \times r_E\right] + \left[\dfrac{D}{V} \times r_D\right]$	Eq. 13.3
Modigliani–Miller Proposition 2 (cost of equity)	$r_E = r_U + \dfrac{D}{E} \times (r_U - r_D)$	Eq. 13.4
Unlevered cost of capital (no taxes)	$r_U = \left[\dfrac{E}{V} \times r_E\right] + \left[\dfrac{D}{V} \times r_D\right]$	Eq. 13.5
Cost of debt	$r_D = y - p \times L$	Eq. 13.6
Firm value, DCF valuation with after-tax WACC	$V = \dfrac{FCF_1}{1+r_A} + \dfrac{FCF_2}{(1+r_A)^2} + \dfrac{FCF_3}{(1+r_A)^3} + \dfrac{FCF_4}{(1+r_A)^4} + \dfrac{FCF_5}{(1+r_A)^5} \cdots$	Eq. 13.7
After-tax WACC	$r_A^{after\text{-}tax} = \text{after-tax WACC} = \left[\dfrac{E}{V} \times r_E\right] + \left[\dfrac{D}{V} \times r_D \times (1-\tau)\right]$	Eq. 13.8
Modigliani–Miller Proposition 2 with taxes (cost of equity)	$r_E = r_U + \dfrac{D}{E} \times (r_U - r_D) \times (1-\tau)$	Eq. 13.9
Value of firm, APV method	$V_L = V_U + PV(\text{debt tax shield})$	Eq. 13.10
Yearly tax shield	$\text{Tax shield}_t = D_{t-1} \times r_D \times \tau$	Eq. 13.11
Value of firm, APV method with fixed and perpetual debt	$V_L = V_U + D \times \tau$	Eq. 13.12

Value of tax shield, fixed and perpetual debt	$PV(\text{debt tax shield}) = D \times \tau$	Eq. 13.13
Value of tax shield including personal and capital gains taxes	$PV(\text{debt tax shield}) = D \times \left(1 - \dfrac{(1-\tau) \times (1-\tau_g)}{1-\tau_p}\right)$	Eq. 13.14
WACC with senior and junior debt	$WACC = r_A = \left[\dfrac{E}{V} \times r_E\right] + \left[\dfrac{D_{Senior}}{V} \times r_{D,Senior}\right] + \left[\dfrac{D_{Junior}}{V} \times r_{D,Junior}\right]$	Eq. 13.15
Value of firm with costs and benefits of debt	Value of firm $= V_U + PV(\text{debt tax shield}) + PV(\text{agency benefits of debt})$ $- PV(\text{agency costs of debt}) - PV(\text{financial distress costs of debt})$	Eq. 13.16

Problems

1. What are examples of both internal and external financing options available to pay for your school tuition?

2. Divido Corporation is an all-equity financed firm with a total market value of $100 million. There are 1,000,000 shares of Divido common stock outstanding, each with a market price of $100. Divido Corporation has decided to issue $20 million of bonds and to repurchase $20 million worth of its stock. What will be the impact on the price of its shares and on the wealth of its shareholders? Why? Assume that there are no frictions.

3. According to M-M Proposition 1, the capital structure of a firm doesn't matter. From the perspective of an equity holder, does this imply that leverage also shouldn't matter? Explain briefly.

4. The Tiberius Company expects an EBIT of $100,000 every year forever. Tiberius can borrow at 10%. Tiberius currently has no debt, and its cost of equity is 14%. If the corporate tax rate is 34%, what is the value of the firm? What will the value be if Tiberius borrows $200,000 and uses the proceeds to buy up stock? Explain your answers and state concisely any assumption you make.

5. Comfort Shoe Company of England has decided to spin off its Tango Dance Shoe Division as a separate corporation in the United States. The assets of the Tango Dance Shoe Division have the same operating risk characteristics as those of Comfort. The capital structure of Comfort has been 40% debt and 60% equity in terms of marketing values, and is considered by management to be optimal. The required return on Comfort's assets (if unlevered) is 16% per year, and the interest rate that the firm (and the division) must currently pay on their debt is 10% per year. Sales revenue for the Tango Dance Shoe Division is expected to remain indefinitely at last year's level of $10 million. Variable costs are 55% of sales. Annual depreciation is $1 million, which is exactly matched each year by new investments. The corporate tax rate is 40%.
    (a) How much is the Tango Dance Shoe Division worth in unlevered form?
    (b) If the Tango Dance Shoe Division is spun off with $5 million in debt, how much would it be worth?
    (c) What rate of return will the shareholders of the Tango Dance Shoe Division require?

6. Based on Problem 5, suppose that Foxtrot Dance Shoes makes custom-designed dance shoes and is a competitor of Tango Dance Shoes. Foxtrot has similar risks and characteristics as Tango, except that it is completely unlevered. Fearful that Tango Dance Shoes may try to take over Foxtrot in order to control their niche in the market, Foxtrot decides to lever the firm to buy back stock. If there are currently 500,000 shares outstanding, what is the value of Foxtrot's stock?

7. Suppose that a TV manufacturing company is currently financed with 20% debt and 80% equity (at market values). The required return on equity is 12%, and the required return on debt is 4%. For all parts of this question, assume that the Modigliani–Miller theorem holds (i.e., there are no frictions such as taxes, costs of financial distress, asymmetric information, etc.).
   (a) What is the company's WACC?
   (b) The company decides to raise additional funds by issuing some more debt. After doing so, its capital structure changes to 40% debt and 60% equity. Assume, for now, that the issue is sufficiently small to not change the cost of debt (which therefore continues to be 4%). What is the company's WACC after the debt issuance?
   (c) What is the required return on the company's equity?
   (d) Assume now that the capital structure change described did raise the cost of debt after all, from 4% to 5%. What is the company's WACC after the debt issuance, given that the cost of debt has risen to 5%? What is the required return on the company's equity?

8. You are in the midst of valuing a large, risky investment in an offshore wind farm. You are faced with two options: using generic turbines or using new-technology turbines. Building the wind farm with generic technology is cheaper: A generic wind farm costs $20 million while a new-technology wind farm has a price tag of $30 million. Either option will create $3 million in free cash flows next year that will grow at a rate of 3.2% in perpetuity.

   To evaluate your project, you find two comparable companies. Your generic technology comparable has an expected equity return of 15% and an expected cost of debt of 11%. Your new-technology comparable has an expected equity return of 17% and an expected cost of debt of 12%.

   You are extremely averse to taking on any debt and so, regardless of your choice of technology, you plan on financing your wind farm with no debt whatsoever. Answer the following questions:
   (a) What is the unlevered cost of capital for the generic technology comparable?
   (b) What is the unlevered cost of capital for the new-technology comparable?
   (c) Which technology would you choose for your wind farm?

9. Company LVG has free cash flows of $4.25 million in the next year and continuing forever. Its cost of equity is 8.67%. It currently has no debt in its capital structure. LVG is considering issuing $18.29 million in market value of debt, which would carry an interest rate of 6%. With the debt, its capital structure would be 33% debt and 67% equity. With the debt, the cost of equity would also increase to 9.52%. Assume that the tax rate LVG faces is 35%, and that the cost of debt stays constant.
   (a) What is the WACC of the firm before the debt is issued, and after the debt is issued?
   (b) Using the WACCs from part (a), calculate the value of the firm before and after the debt is issued.
   (c) Now calculate the annual tax shield each year. What is the present value of this tax shield? What is the value of the firm with the tax shield?

10. Suppose that your company is considering setting up a subsidiary firm. The firm has a single project, which generates the following free cash flows:

Year	0	1	2
FCF	–	200	300

    The unlevered cost of capital is 15%, the return on debt is flat at 6%, the tax rate is 30%, and the company has stated that it will maintain a constant leverage ratio of 50% of firm value. After year 2, the FCFs of the company will stay constant at 300 each year. Using the after-tax WACC method, what is the value of the firm right now?

11. Suppose that your company is considering setting up a subsidiary firm. The firm has a single project, which generates the following free cash flows and debt schedule:

Year	0	1	2
FCF	–	200	300
Debt	100	50	0

The unlevered cost of capital is 15%, the return on debt is flat at 6%, and the tax rate is 30%. After year 2, the FCFs of the company will stay constant at 300 each year while debt stays at 0. Using the APV method, what is the value of the levered firm right now?

12. The Griffey-Lang Food Company faces a difficult problem. In management's effort to grow the business, they accrued a debt of $150 million while the value of the company is only $125 million. Management must come up with a plan to alleviate the situation in one year or face certain bankruptcy. Also upcoming are labor relations meetings with the union to discuss employee benefits and pension funds. Griffey-Lang at this time has three choices they can pursue: (1) launch a new, relatively untested product that, if successful (probability of 0.12), will allow Griffey-Lang to increase the value of the company to $200 million; (2) sell off two food production plants in an effort to reduce some of the debt and the value of the company, thus making it even less likely to avoid bankruptcy (0.45 probability of success); or (3) do nothing (probability of failure = 1.0).
    (a) As a creditor, what would you like Griffey-Lang to do, and why?
    (b) As an investor?
    (c) As an employee?

13. Tablet Company is looking to set up a wholly owned subsidiary firm, which will sell cheap, rugged computers in developing countries. Suppose Tablet announced that it will aim to have a certain leverage ratio. Thus, its free cash flows and leverage ratio are:

Year	0	1	2
FCF	–	150	200
D/V	50%	55%	60%

It announces that it intends to keep its leverage ratio at 60% after year 2. Assume that after year 2 the FCFs grow at a rate of 1% each year. The unlevered cost of capital is 17%, the return on debt is constant at 6%, and the tax rate is 40%.
    (a) Calculate the cost of equity for years 0, 1, and 2.
    (b) Using your answers from part (a), calculate the after-tax WACC for years 0, 1, and 2.
    (c) Calculate the total value of the firm using the after-tax WACC method for years 0, 1, and 2. (Hint: Work backward starting at year 2, using your after-tax WACCs from part (b).)

14. Consider Tablet Company again, with the following free cash flows:

Year	0	1	2
FCF	–	150	200

Tablet announces that it will aim to have a constant leverage ratio of 60% (D/V). Assume that after year 2 the FCFs grow at a rate of 1% each year. The unlevered cost of capital is 15%, the expected return on debt is 5%, and the tax rate is 40%.
    (a) Calculate the cost of equity.
    (b) Calculate the after-tax WACC.
    (c) Calculate the total value of the firm using the after-tax WACC method right now (year 0).

15. Tablet Company continues to sell cheap, rugged computers in developing countries. The debt schedule for the firm is predetermined and shown below for years 0, 1, and 2. After year 2, the firm will maintain a fixed level of debt equal to 700. The free cash flows of the firm for years 0–2 are:

Year	0	1	2
FCF	–	150	200
Debt	900	800	700

Assume that after year 2 the FCFs grow at a rate of 1% each year. The expected return on debt is 5%, and the tax rate is 40%.
  (a) Suppose you find a competitor to the firm Tablet is considering setting up, which holds 50% debt and 50% equity in its capital structure. The competitor has a cost of debt of 4% and a cost of equity of 26%. What is the competitor's unlevered cost of capital? Use that number for your estimate of r_U for the rest of the problem.
  (b) Calculate the value of the firm as of year 2 using the APV method. Be sure to include the value of the tax shield in your calculations.
  (c) Use the APV method to calculate the levered value (total value) of the firm as of year 0 and year 1.

16. Suppose you estimate that your firm has an equity cost of capital of 13.4% and cost of debt is 7%, and the tax rate is 40%. The leverage ratio of the firm is 0.5. What is the total value of the firm if its EBIT is $100 per year perpetually, its investment in PP&E (property, plant, and equipment) is equal to its annual depreciation every year, and its net working capital (NWC) is constant through time?

17. Suppose your firm has an equity cost of capital of 9.6%. The firm's cost of debt is 5%, and the tax rate is 40%. The leverage ratio of the firm in market value terms at present is 0.6, and will remain the same. What is the total value of the equity of this firm if its EBIT next year is $1,000 and expected to grow perpetually after that at 2% per year? Assume that NWC remains constant over time, and that capital expenditures and depreciation are zero each year.

18. IKEA has made a booming business out of selling low-cost yet stylish furniture. Now it is looking to launch a new hotel chain, Moxy Inc., designed to serve the traveling needs of the budget-minded traveler.

    To launch Moxy Inc., IKEA is expected to invest $490 million today (year 0). The hotel chain is expected to generate free cash flows of $24 million per year, starting at the end of the first year (year 1). Thereafter, these free cash flows are expected to grow at 3% in perpetuity.

    You are asked to assess the potential value of the new hotel chain. Since you are pressed for time, you ask Göran Lööf, your assistant, to help you gather financial data. Göran reports recent financial data for a couple of publicly traded firms:

Company	MV of equity	MV of debt	Equity cost of capital
La-Z-Boy Furniture Inc.	1,000	50	13.5%
Intercontinental Hotels Group	7,500	2,500	10%

He also reports that the risk-free interest rate is 2%. Both companies in the table above had constant leverage ratios in the past, and their debt is very highly rated for both (i.e., risk-free). Based on guarantees pledged by IKEA, Moxy's debt is also expected to be very highly rated (i.e., risk-free). Assume that the corporate tax rate of 30%.
  (a) If Moxy Inc. is 100% equity financed, what is a reasonable estimate of the required rate of return on Moxy's equity? What is Moxy's WACC?

(b) What is the value of launching Moxy Inc.? Is it worth pursuing, when considering the initial investment today of $490 million?

(c) Suppose instead that Moxy Inc. is financed by 50% debt and 50% equity. Would this make it more attractive? Explain your answers without calculations.

(d) Recalculate the value of launching Moxy Inc., given the capital structure in part (c). Is it worth pursuing?

19. Suppose that you are looking to value your company. You anticipate free cash flows of $2 million each year starting next year and continuing until five years from now (so from years 1 through 5), after which you believe that the free cash flows will grow at a rate of 1% forever. You anticipate maintaining a flat leverage ratio (D/V) of 30% going forward, and your company has a cost of debt of 8%. The tax rate is 30%. There is a very similar company to your company which has 50% leverage (D/V), and has a cost of debt of 8% and a cost of equity of 15%.

(a) What is an estimate of the market value of your company?

(b) Now suppose that you are given advice that you should use more debt. You therefore intend to increase the company's leverage ratio to D/V = 70%. What is the total value of the company now? Assume that the company's r_D will remain the same, even with the new leverage ratio.

14 A UNIFIED APPROACH TO THE VALUATION OF CORPORATE ASSETS AND CAPITAL STRUCTURE

CHAPTER OVERVIEW

14.1	Analyzing Corporate Equity and Debt	407
14.2	Corporate Debt Structure	416
14.3	Guarantees and Other Securities	422
14.4	Project Valuation Using Real Options	426
14.5	Applications of Real Options outside Firms	432
14.6	The Options-Based Approach versus DCF	433

LEARNING OBJECTIVES

After reading this chapter, you will be able to:
- explain how the options framework can be used to analyze a variety of corporate decisions—including financing and project investment decisions—and gain new insights to better understand these decisions;
- calculate the value of a company's equity and debt, including debt of different seniority, and analyze their risk using an options framework;
- identify incentives that companies have in making capital structure decisions;
- describe a unifying theory for valuing the capital structure of the firm;
- explain how alternative securities that firms use to finance themselves—such as hybrid securities—work, how they can be valued, and why they are used;
- identify flexibility in capital budgeting decisions, and how this flexibility in project decisions has value that can be analyzed and realized;
- compare the options framework and the DCF model for valuing the firm and its component capital.

14 VALUATION OF ASSETS AND CAPITAL STRUCTURE

EQUATIONS YOU KNOW

| Total company value | $V = D + E$ | Eq. 9.1 |

+ You work as a financial analyst for a large corporation, and have been tasked with determining the value of the equity of a potential acquisition target. You know the current market value of the target, but do not have enough confidence in cash flow forecasts or discount rate calculations to do a DCF analysis. What is an alternative method you can use to value the target?

+ Palmart Corporation has announced that it is offering two types of bonds to investors, each with a different seniority. You are examining these bonds as a potential investment. What is the difference between them, and how can you determine what their values should be?

+ You invest in a company's bonds, and then find out that the US government has decided to guarantee the company's credit. How can you analyze this guarantee and its value?

+ You work for an office construction company, and are deciding whether to spend some money up-front to clear some land of debris. If you do, it gives you the ability to decide later on whether it will be profitable to construct an office building on the land, or sell off the land to a residential developer. How can you value this project, given the flexibility you have in making the decision in the future?

Introduction

Throughout Part II we have focused on determining and understanding the value within firms on both sides of the balance sheet. Chapters 9 and 10 focus on valuing the assets of the firm—understanding how to value the entire firm (its total assets) as well as individual projects undertaken within the firm. Chapter 13 focuses on understanding the value of the liabilities and equity of the firm, and how this side of the balance sheet can be structured through a firm's capital structure. Our workhorse tool set for analyzing these issues was discounted cash flow (DCF) analysis. In this chapter, we introduce a different valuation tool, option pricing analysis, as an improved valuation framework that allows us to explore these topics.

In Chapter 7 we introduced options, financial contracts which provide their holder with the flexibility to either buy (call) or sell (put) at a preset price, after the value of the underlying asset is known. The holder is not obligated to buy or sell the asset in the future if it is not beneficial. Thus, option contracts embed flexibility, which can reduce or eliminate uncertainty. The ability to do so has value, as reflected in one of our principles: **Principle 8:** *Flexibility in financial decisions has value, and the greater the uncertainty, the greater the value.* This embedded flexibility makes option theory a fundamental tool for modeling the impact of uncertainty (i.e., risk) on financial decisions, as embedded in **Principle 6:** *Risk is fundamental to financial analysis and must be explicitly considered in all financial decisions* and **Principle 7:** *There is a trade-off between risk and expected return.*

In this chapter, we explore how option theory can be applied to vastly enhance core corporate finance decisions. We begin by showing how the choice between equity (stock) and debt (bonds) can be analyzed and valued using option pricing models. For example, common stock is analogous to a call option on the assets of the firm and so can be valued as such. The basic insight stems from **Principle 2**: *Equivalent assets that can be freely bought and sold will have the same market price.* We will show that the payoffs of equity and debt are equivalent to options or combinations of options and other assets, and thus their values can be derived using options models. This provides a unified general valuation framework for a firm's capital structure, which means it offers a single framework that can be applied to analyze and value any type of capital structure that a company may have. This includes typical debt and equity structures that we have analyzed previously with DCF models, but as we will see, the options-based framework will allow us to glean additional insights and permit more accurate valuation compared to other models. In addition, we will use this framework to analyze more complex capital components including (but not limited to) debt securities of different seniority, other types of tranched securities, hybrid securities that have aspects of both debt and equity, and performance guarantees provided by companies as well as governments. We will look at how option pricing also provides a tool for valuing corporate claims that cannot be valued using DCF models, such as situations where there is risk of debt default.

Beyond capital structure, the unified options valuation framework can be used to analyze project valuation and capital budgeting decisions, offering an alternative to typical DCF analyses. Many projects—such as building a power plant, producing a movie, investing in the development of a new phone, or developing a new drug—require decisions to be made that depend on how uncertainty in the future resolves, and are more effectively analyzed using an options framework. For example, a company can delay decisions until after some uncertainty has been resolved, and option pricing theory provides a way to assess that value. The company can decide to abandon or expand a project depending on how circumstances change. This application of option theory to physical/nonfinancial projects is known as real options. Real options analysis provide a powerful framework to supplement DCF analysis, as standard net present value (NPV) calculations are not able to capture the value of these types of choices. Incorporating the flexibility value of such choices explicitly can sometimes lead to the conclusion that projects evaluated using DCF that have negative NPV—and which would be discarded if based solely on that analysis—should actually be pursued! Section 14.5 provides a summary discussion of "the best tool for the job," comparing the DCF and option pricing approaches to valuation to help identify which is the more effective tool in various circumstances, including using both for different aspects of the capital budgeting and capital structure decisions.

We begin by applying option theory analysis to the capital structure of a company, analyzing equity and risky corporate debt. We then delve into more complex types of capital structures involving various financial securities, such as different types of debt, guarantees, and hybrid. This is followed by a discussion of option pricing analysis for project decisions. We conclude with a discussion comparing the options-based approach to the standard DCF approach to valuation.

14.1 Analyzing Corporate Equity and Debt

In this section we will show how to use option pricing theory to value the debt and equity of a firm, and then discuss the insights into corporate financing decisions. We will begin by showing that the payoffs of equity correspond to those of a call option, and thus equity can be analyzed as a call option. We then show how corporate debt—which has the possibility of default—can be analyzed in a similar way via an options lens. We show how these insights allow us to use options valuation techniques to value a company's equity and debt.

14.1.1 Equity

To begin, consider a hypothetical firm, Landco, that is in the real estate business. It has issued two types of securities: stock (one million shares) and zero-coupon bonds with a total face value of $80 million (80,000 bonds, each with a face value of $1,000). Landco's bonds mature one year from now. Note that $80 million is not the market value of the debt, but rather the promised future payment; the market value will be the present value of the $80 million, accounting for the fact that the debt is risky—it may default (not pay the entire $80 million). Let us assume that we know that the total market value (i.e., enterprise value) V of Landco's assets is $100 million.

Suppose that we want to determine the separate market values of Landco's debt and equity. Recall from Chapter 9 (Equation 9.1) that the total value of a company is made up of the combined market value of the company's debt (D) and equity (E): $V = D + E$. Therefore, we want to determine what portion of the $100 million total company value is composed of debt and what portion is composed of equity.

To determine the value of the equity, consider the possible payoffs of the company's equity in the future, specifically when the debt matures one year from now. These payoffs will depend on how much the company's overall assets are worth one year from now, which is uncertain and can depend on many things (e.g., land prices, the mortgage market, etc.). First, suppose that the value of Landco's assets in one year is zero: The company has gone bankrupt and owns nothing of value. Then both equity and debt will get no payoff, and their values will be zero. Now suppose that the value of Landco's assets in a year is $40 million. Then the debtholders do not get what they are owed—$80 million—and instead receive whatever Landco has, which is $40 million. Landco defaults on its debt in this situation, and goes bankrupt; since debtholders have a priority claim on the company's assets in the event of default, they then receive whatever the assets are worth. The debtholders may decide to liquidate the firm—terminating the assets and selling them individually at market value—or keep the firm as a going-concern by reorganizing it through the bankruptcy process. This distinction can be important, as the assets of a firm when liquidated may be worth more or less than the firm as an intact entity. In the subsequent analysis, we assume the case where there is a costless transfer of operations of the firm to the debtholders.[1]

Equity holders, being the residual claimants after the debt has been paid off, receive a payoff of zero—there is no value left in the company after the debtholders have been paid.

Now suppose that Landco's assets end up being worth more than what they owe to the debtholders: $V = $100 million. In this case, the company has enough value to pay off everything that it owes to the debtholders, and it has value leftover for the equity holders as the residual claimants. Thus, the debtholders will be paid $80 million, and after that the equity holders get the $20 million that remains. If Landco's assets are worth $120 million, the company has enough value to pay off everything that it owes to the debtholders ($80 million), and has additional value leftover, $40 million, that goes to the equity holders. A summary of these payoffs for both equity and debt is provided in Table 14.1.

For the equity payoffs in one year, if the firm's value is less than the promised amount to the debtholders, then the equity holders get nothing. However, if the firm's value is greater than the

---

[1] In practice, the managers of a firm may choose to liquidate the firm's assets even if there is no debt and it is not bankrupt, because it is worth more disassembled. As we noted in Chapter 11, one way this can occur is due to the firm being poorly managed. Alternatively, a firm may go through the bankruptcy process in order to reorganize and continue as a going-concern—potentially under new owners—because the firm as an intact entity is worth more than its individual assets. The bankruptcy process can entail costs through a disruption of company operations; for that reason, mechanisms which allow a costless transfer of operations between owners have been proposed.

Table 14.1 **Landco's equity and debt payoffs.** Possible payoffs (in millions of dollars) of Landco's debt and equity at maturity date $T = 1$ based on Landco's possible total company value at that time, and a total principal amount of debt of $80 million.

Total company value in one year, V_1	Debt payoff in one year	Equity payoff in one year
$0	$0	$0
20	20	0
40	40	0
60	60	0
80	80	0
100	80	20
120	80	40

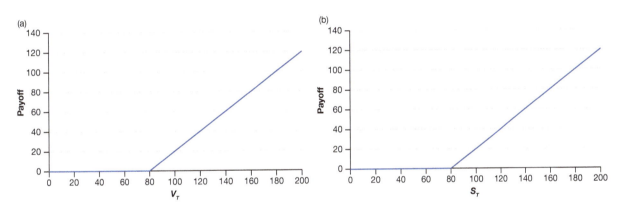

FIGURE 14.1 **Equity payoffs at maturity.** (a) The various possible payoffs of Landco's equity at maturity date $T = 1$ based on Landco's possible total company value at that time, and a total principal amount of debt of $80 million. All payoffs are in millions of dollars. For comparison, panel (b) provides the payoff diagram for a call option on a stock with a strike price of $80.

promised amount to the debtholders, then the equity holders get whatever value remains after the debtholders are paid what they are owed (if anything remains). We can draw a diagram that depicts these payoffs depending on what the firm's value is when the debt comes due; this is shown in Figure 14.1(a).

Note that the payoff diagram is identical to that of a call option, which you can see in Figure 14.1(b), which depicts the payoff diagram of a call option with a strike price of $80 based on a stock. A call option allows the owner of the option to buy the underlying asset at a fixed exercise price at the expiration of the option. In Chapter 7, the underlying asset in most of the examples was a share of stock; thus, a call option allowed you to buy stock in the future at a fixed exercise price K, providing a payoff at expiration of $C_T = \max(S_T - K, 0)$. As can be seen in Figure 14.1(b), the payoff diagram for a call option on a stock with an exercise price of $80 looks identical to that of Landco's equity in Figure 14.1(a). In the case of equity payoffs, however, the underlying asset is the entire firm itself, and the exercise price of the option is the amount of outstanding debt (face value of the debt). Mathematically, we can express the payoffs of equity when the debt matures (denoted as time T) as follows:

$$E_T = \max(V_T - B, 0), \qquad (14.1)$$

where V_T is the total value of the firm at time T, and B is the promised payment of the firm's debt. Note that Equation 14.1 is exactly analogous to Equation 7.1 in Chapter 7, the payoff of a call option at maturity.

This provides us with a key insight: A firm's equity can be analyzed as a call option on the firm's assets, with an exercise price equal to the face value of the firm's debt (plus accrued interest). In other words, the shareholders are long a call on the firm's assets. The underlying logic is that the payoffs of the two are the same, and thus they are equivalent assets (and must also have the same value, as noted in **Principle 2:** *Equivalent assets that can be freely bought and sold will have the same market price*). As we will describe in the sections to follow, this provides us with a wide range of important insights into the value of a firm's equity, and how that value may change depending on the firm's actions.

> **QUICK CHECK 14.1** Recreate Table 14.1 and Figure 14.1 for equity assuming that the firm's debt matures in two years and the total face value of the debt is $120 million.

14.1.2 Debt

Our analysis of Landco's equity also allows us to examine its debt in a similar way using options. A key to this, as our equity analysis showed, is that Landco's debt is risky and may default, not paying all it promised. We will show that debt can be analyzed as a combination of a (put) option and a riskless bond. If the firm's value is less than the promised amount to the debtholders, then the debtholders get whatever the firm's assets are worth—that is, there is a change of ownership through bankruptcy and debtholders take possession of the firm's assets/the entire firm. However, if the firm's value is greater than the promised amount to the debtholders, then the debtholders get exactly what they are owed—$80 million in Landco's case. In effect, it is as if the debtholders own the assets of the firm and the equity holders have an option to buy those assets by paying the debtholders the amount they were promised. We can mathematically express the payoffs of debt at the maturity of debt at time T as:

$$D_T = \min(V_T, B). \qquad (14.2)$$

In Equation 14.2, at the maturity date of the debt T, debtholders get the minimum of the value of the assets of the firm V_T and what they were promised B. Thus, if the firm's assets are greater than what the debtholders promised, the firm is able to pay the promised amount and the debtholders get B. However, if the firm's assets end up being worth less than B, then the firm defaults and the debtholders receive the remaining value V_T. We can also graph the payoffs of Landco's debt from Table 14.1, provided in Figure 14.2.

Unlike equity, the payoff diagram for the firm's debt is not the same as any of the single option diagrams we covered in Chapter 7. However, debt payoff can be shown as analogous to a *combination* of two positions:

- a riskless bond; and
- a short put option.

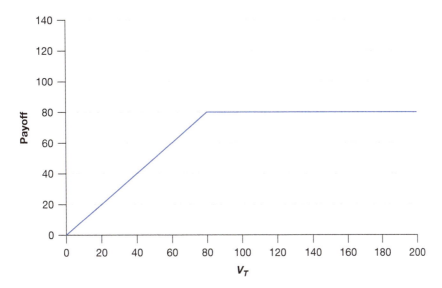

FIGURE 14.2 Debt payoffs at maturity. Various possible payoffs of Landco's debt at maturity date $T = 1$ based on Landco's possible total company value at that time, and a total principal amount of debt of $80 million. All payoffs are in millions of dollars.

To see this, consider a riskless bond with a maturity of one year and a principal amount of $80 million. Now consider writing a put option with a strike price of $80 million, where the underlying asset is the entire firm itself.[2] Recall that a put option allows the holder to sell an asset in the future at the strike price K, resulting in a payoff at expiration date T (if the underlying asset is a stock) of $P_T = \max(K - S_T, 0)$; writing a put option—which results in a short put position—provides the negative of these payoffs to its issuer, since it is the opposite side of the transaction. Table 14.2 shows the combined payoffs of the riskless bond and the short put option—as you can see, when compared to Figure 14.2, the payoff is identical to the firm's debt.

Figure 14.3 shows this graphically. Figure 14.3(a) shows the payoff of riskless debt with a promised amount of $80 million, while Figure 14.3(b) shows a short put option with a strike price of $80 million. Combining these two parts of Figure 14.3 provides us with Figure 14.3(c), which is identical to the payoff diagram of Landco's debt in Figure 14.2. Because the payoffs of Landco's debt in Figure 14.2 and the combination in Figure 14.3 are identical, they can be viewed as equivalent assets. Thus, the firm's risky debt can be seen as the payoff on riskless debt net of the payoff of a put option. This provides a useful and intuitive relationship between risky corporate debt (which may default) and riskless debt. In particular, if we compare riskless debt (Figure 14.2(a)) and risky debt (Figure 14.2(c)), we see that for the same principal amounts, the payoff of riskless debt will always be

---

[2] Note that there are other ways to replicate the firm's debt payoffs as well. Going long the firm itself (the assets of the firm) and writing a call option with a strike price equal to the outstanding amount of debt will also produce the same payoffs, and is equivalent to this combination of the riskless bond and writing a put option. Under the law in most countries, the management is a fiduciary for the equity holders and therefore required to operate in their best interests. Thus, there will be an inherent conflict between equity holders (and management who represents them) and debtholders. The presence of moral hazard can exacerbate this and lead to deleterious outcomes for the firm. When a firm is in financial distress even before it goes through the legal bankruptcy process, the fiduciary duty of management changes from one to the current equity holders to the debtholders. In that situation, management is bound to consider the debtholders' best interests, which would not be the extreme risk-shifting behavior illustrated above.

Table 14.2 **Replicating Landco's debt payoffs.** Payoffs of a combination of riskless debt with a principal amount of $80 million and writing a put option with a strike price of $80 on Landco's assets at maturity date $T = 1$, based on Landco's possible total company value at that time.

Total company value in one year, V_1	Riskless bond, par = $80 million	Write a put option, K = $80 million	Combined	Landco debt payoffs
$0	$80	−$80	$0	$0
20	80	−60	20	20
40	80	−40	40	40
60	80	−20	60	60
80	80	0	80	80
100	80	0	80	80
120	80	0	80	80

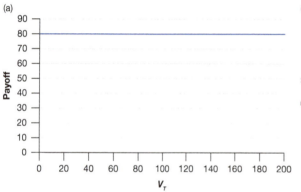

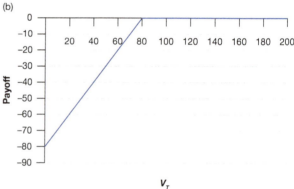

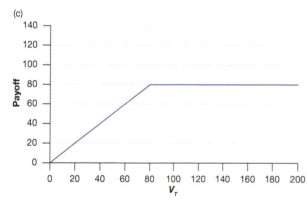

FIGURE 14.3 **Replicating Landco's debt payoffs.** This figure provides the payoffs of a combination of (a) riskless debt with a principal amount of $80 million and (b) writing (short) a put option with a strike price of $80 on Landco's assets at maturity date $T = 1$, based on Landco's possible total company value at that time. (c) The combination of (a) and (b).

14.1 ANALYZING CORPORATE EQUITY AND DEBT

at least as high as that of risky debt—the risky debt will pay less than the riskless debt when the value of the firm gets low enough. This is due to the default risk of corporate debt, and it is the put option (Figure 14.2(b)) that incorporates this default risk. As a result, as we will see, the price of risky debt will be less than that of equivalent riskless debt due to default risk.

> **QUICK CHECK 14.2** Recreate Table 14.2 and Figure 14.2 for debt, assuming that the firm's debt matures in two years and the total face value of the debt is $120 million.

The fact that the payoffs of both the equity and debt are identical to option payoffs allows us to analyze equity and debt directly using the valuation and risk insights we learned about options in Chapter 7. The insight that the combinations of options and bonds above exactly replicate the payoffs of Landco's debt and equity means that if we know how to value the options that replicate the structure of debt and equity, we can determine the value of the debt and equity. This is due to the law of one price (**Principle 2**: *Equivalent assets that can be freely bought and sold will have the same market price*). Since the payoffs are identical, the prices must also be the same, otherwise there is an arbitrage. This provides us with an alternative method to the DCF approach to value a company's debt and equity.

14.1.3 Determining the Values of Equity and Debt

In this section we continue our analysis of examining debt and equity using option pricing theory. In the previous section we saw that equity was equivalent to a call option, and debt is equivalent to a riskless bond combined with a short put option. By **Principle 2**: *Equivalent assets that can be freely bought and sold will have the same market price*, this means that the values also must be the same. As we covered in Chapter 7, we have methodologies for determining option prices. This allows us to use those techniques in order to value equity and debt.

Let us begin with equity. As shown, equity can be viewed as a call option on the firm's assets. This means that if we know how to value this call option, we can value the firm's equity. From Chapter 7, the Black–Scholes–Merton (BSM) model used to determine option value can be applied in this situation. Note that the underlying asset in this case is the entire firm (the assets of the firm), and not just its stock, which is a specific claim on these assets. The BSM formula requires the following inputs:

1. The current price of the underlying asset. Since the underlying asset is the firm itself, this will be the current total value (i.e., enterprise value) of the firm, V_0. Continuing our example, we assume that Landco's total value is $V_0 = \$100$ million.
2. The strike price of the option. This is the promised payment on the firm's outstanding debt at maturity, which we will denote as B, which is $80 million. Note that this is different from the current market value of the debt, which is the present value of this promised $80 million payment.
3. The expiration date of the option in years T, which is the maturity of the firm's debt. In this case, $T = 1$ year.
4. The volatility of the underlying asset σ. This will be the volatility (standard deviation) of the total value of the firm. Let us assume that $\sigma = 0.3$.
5. The riskless interest rate r_f. Let us assume that $r_f = 0.08$.

Putting these numbers into the BSM formula yields a value for the call option of $28.24 million; this is the value of the firm's equity. Box 14.1 highlights the process of obtaining these numbers in practice and provides a real-world example.

Now, let us consider debt. We can use the identity that the value of total assets of the firm equals the value of all the claims on those assets, $V = D + E$, and thus $D = V - E = 100 - 28.24 = \$71.76$ million. Thus, Landco's debt, which promises to pay $80 million in one year, is currently worth $71.76 million. The fact that the current market value is lower than $80 million reflects both the time value of money (**Principle 1**: *A dollar today is not worth the same as a dollar tomorrow*) and the fact that the debt is risky and may not in fact pay the full $80 million (**Principle 7**: *There is a trade-off between risk and expected return*).

Deriving the value of the debt using the fact that the debt is a combination of a riskless bond and a short put option on the assets allows us to determine the values of more complicated debt structures, which is discussed in Section 14.2. Landco's debt can be viewed as a combination of a riskless bond with a maturity of one year and a principal amount of $80 million, and a short put option with a strike price of $80 million. Since the riskless bond promises $80 million in one year, its value can be found by discounting this principal amount by the riskless interest rate (we discount using the continuously compounded discount rate to be consistent with the BSM formula values, which assume continuous compounding):

$$PV \text{ riskless bond} = \frac{80}{e^{0.08}}$$
$$= 73.85.$$

For the value of the put option, we use the BSM formula for put options. We can also use the put–call parity formula (Equation 7.4) to determine the value of the put option given the call option value:

$$\text{Put option value} = \text{call value} - V_0 + \frac{B}{e^{r \times T}}$$
$$= 28.24 - 100 + \frac{80}{e^{0.08}}$$
$$= 2.09.$$

The value of the put option is 2.09. The value of Landco's debt is therefore the value of the riskless debt we calculated above, minus the value of the put option:

$$D = \text{riskless debt} - \text{put option}$$
$$= 73.85 - 2.09$$
$$= 71.76.$$

This gives us the same answer: The risky debt which promises to pay $80 million in one year has a current market value of $71.76 million. And, because of the possibility of default that is reflected in the short put option, the value of risky corporate debt is less than the value of riskless debt with the same principal amount: An investor would be willing to pay more for $80 million face value in riskless debt than $80 million face value in risky debt.

This provides an alternative to the standard DCF model for determining the value of a company's equity and debt. In the next section we highlight these differences and the circumstances in which one or the other may be more beneficial to use.

> **QUICK CHECK 14.3** Calculate the value of Landco's debt and equity assuming instead that the firm's debt matures in two years and the total face value of the debt is $120 million. Assume that the other characteristics of the firm remain the same as above.

Box 14.1 Applying the BSM Formula to Value Equity in Practice

Applying the Black–Scholes–Merton (BSM) formula to determine the values of debt or equity requires knowing the following:

1. the current value of the firm's assets, since that value is pledged as collateral for debt (i.e., the total value of the firm V);
2. the firm's promised debt payments: the amount and maturity of the promised payments;
3. the volatility (standard deviation) of the value of the firm's assets; and
4. the riskless interest rate r_f.

In practice, some research or calculations may be needed to determine these inputs. The first is the value of a firm's assets V. If the debt and the equity of the firm are traded, we can take the sum of the market prices of both in order to get $V = D + E$. Otherwise, a DCF model can determine V (as in Chapter 9) through forecasting expected future cash flows and discounting them at the estimated cost of capital of the firm.

The second input is information on the firm's promised debt payments, in particular the amount and maturity of the debt. The principal payment at maturity becomes the options' strike price, and the debt's maturity date becomes the options' expiration date.

The third input needed is the standard deviation of the company's value V, which can be estimated using historical data on the firm's value. Note that this conceptually is the volatility of the asset value V of the firm; however, in practice a firm's stock return volatility is often used as a proxy. We explained how to calculate the volatility of a firm's stock returns in Chapter 5. The final input, the riskless interest rate, can be derived using information on the yields of US Treasury bonds, as we also discussed in Chapter 5.

To provide an example, consider how we can estimate what the equity value of IBM should be. If we go to a resource such as Yahoo! Finance, we can obtain information we can use as the relevant inputs. IBM's enterprise value (V) on 30 June 2023 was $121.90 billion according to market data (this consists of its stock capitalization plus the outstanding amount of debt); absent a readily available source like this, one could do a DCF calculation to determine the company's total value, as in Chapter 9. The total outstanding amount of debt was $60.3 billion according to its balance sheet, but incorporating this into our calculation can be challenging because we also need a maturity date for the debt, and IBM likely has multiple types of debt with different maturities. We cover the details of how to deal with more complicated debt structures in Section 14.2, but for now we can make an assumption that the debt matures in ten years. The volatility of IBM can be inferred from the standard deviation of its stock returns. Taking the annualized standard deviation of IBM's daily stock returns over the previous year through 30 June 2023 yields a volatility of 20.2%. Finally, the riskless rate can be found from market sources. On 30 June 2023, the ten-year US Treasury rate was 3.81%. Putting these inputs into the BSM calculator in the Excel app provides an equity value of $125.24 billion. For reference, IBM's actual market capitalization on 30 June 2023 was $121.90 billion.

14.2 Corporate Debt Structure

The options-based valuation methodology in the previous section also provides us with an additional framework to gain a better understanding of the capital structure and project choices that we discussed in Chapters 10 and 13. In this section we will begin by looking at how the choice of capital structure can create incentives that prevent good project investment choices from being made. Our options-based framework will provide calculations to illustrate this effect. We will then use our framework to examine more detailed capital structure choices related to different types of debt that firms can use.

14.2.1 Capital Structure and Investment Decisions

Our framework can help us understand the capital structure and project investment decisions managers and firms make by showing us the impact of such choices on the value of a firm's equity. The framework can show us how and why some firms will fall prey to certain agency problems as a result of debt and capital structure. To illustrate, we will continue to use our example firm, Landco, with the following assumptions:

- total company value is $V_0 = \$100$ million;
- face value of the firm's outstanding debt is $B = \$80$ million;
- maturity of the firm's debt is $T = 1$ year;
- volatility of total value of the firm is $\sigma = 0.3$; and
- the riskless interest rate is $r_f = 0.08$.

As we saw, the BSM formula yielded a value of $28.24 million for Landco's equity (see Section 14.1.3).

Recall from Chapter 7 one key insight from the pricing of options is that an increase in the volatility of the underlying asset results in an increase in the value of a call or put option. This insight has important implications for understanding a firm's choice between debt and equity. To illustrate, suppose that the CEO of Landco has a choice to invest in a project—building a shopping mall in an area prone to earthquakes—that has an NPV of zero (and thus does not affect Landco's total company value). However, the project is very risky and will cause the volatility of Landco to increase from $\sigma = 0.3$ to 0.5.

Note that investing in this project will result in a change in the value of Landco's equity. Recalculating the value of the call option via the BSM formula with the new volatility of $\sigma = 0.5$ (and the previous parameters) gives a value of $33.21 million for the value of Landco's equity. Thus, if Landco were to invest in the risky project, the value of Landco's equity will increase by $4.97 million, or an increase of 18% from $28.24 to $33.21 million.

From a capital budgeting perspective, the project itself does not increase the value of the firm since the NPV is zero. Thus, a manager would be indifferent between doing it or not in the best interests of the total value of the firm. However, it can be shown to increase the volatility of the firm, which can be an incentive to shareholders. So, the manager may have a moral hazard incentive to choose to do this investment. As we discussed in Chapter 11, moral hazard is an agency problem when a stakeholder of the firm takes an action that benefits them at the expense of other stakeholders and the firm. In this case, the moral hazard problem—due to the increase in the value of the equity—originates from the fact that the shareholders have little incentive to limit the firm's losses in the event of a bankruptcy—the creditors bear all the downside risk of the risky project, and the shareholders get all of the incremental upside potential for gain. Managers acting solely for shareholders (or themselves paid with shares or options on the stock) may undertake more volatile investments that increase the wealth of shareholders at the expense of the debtholders. This is known as risk shifting, and can even result in negative-NPV investments being undertaken. Risk shifting occurs due to a moral hazard problem and large amounts of debt in a firm. The incentive for managers to increase risk gets stronger when there is more debt. For example, suppose that Landco had $100 million in debt outstanding. In this case, a project increasing the volatility of Landco from $\sigma = 0.3$ to 0.5 will result (using the BSM formula) in an increase in equity value from $15.71 million to $23.06 million, an increase of 47%!

The increase reflects the fact that, with $100 million in debt outstanding, the equity holders see an even greater upside potential for gain from increased risk (volatility). With an even larger amount of outstanding debt (holding everything else fixed), the value of the equity will be even smaller to begin with, magnifying the effect—shareholders will likely be left with very little value if they don't increase the risk since it will accrue to the bondholders.[3]

The options-based framework also illustrates a number of other effects related to investment decisions. For example, another problem that stems from moral hazard involves debt preventing good (i.e., positive-NPV) projects from being undertaken, because they may increase the value of debt more than the value of equity—which benefits debtholders, not shareholders and invested managers. This is referred to as the debt overhang problem. We illustrate this effect in Example 14.1.

> **QUICK CHECK 14.4** In the Landco example in this section, suppose instead that the project reduces the volatility of Landco to $\sigma = 0.1$. Recalculate Landco's equity value assuming the project is undertaken. Explain why the equity value changes in the way it does.

Example 14.1 (Analyzing Equity Using Options): Suppose a company's total value is currently $100 million, the volatility of its assets is 20%, and the company has debt outstanding with a principal amount of $130 million that is due in one year. The current risk-free interest rate is 2%.

(a) What is the value of the company's equity? Interpret this number.
(b) Suppose that the company has a project investment opportunity with an NPV of $10 million, which thus would increase the total value of the company by $10 million. How much would the value of the company's equity increase if it made this investment?
(c) Suppose the project cost $2 million to invest in. If the company needed to sell new shares of equity to raise this money, would new potential shareholders buy the stock?
(d) Suppose that the company was able to reach a deal to retire some of its debt so that it has debt outstanding of $90 million instead. Would new potential shareholders buy the stock for $2 million in this case?

Solution.

(a) We can use the BSM calculator to determine the value of the equity. The inputs are as follows: $V_0 = \$100$ million (current value of the underlying asset), $B = \$130$ million (strike price of the option), $T = 1$ year (expiration date), $\sigma = 0.1$ (volatility of the underlying asset), and $r_f = 0.02$. With these numbers, we get

---

[3] Under the law in most countries, the management is a fiduciary for the equity holders and therefore required to operate in their best interests. Thus, there will be an inherent conflict between equity holders (and management who represents them) and debtholders. The presence of moral hazard can exacerbate this and lead to deleterious outcomes for the firm. When a firm is in financial distress even before it goes through the legal bankruptcy process, the fiduciary duty of management changes from one to the current equity holders to one to the debtholders. In that situation, management is bound to consider the debtholders' best interests, which would not be the extreme risk shifting behavior illustrated above.

a call option value (value of equity) of $1.232 million. The reason that this number is low relative to the total value of the firm is because the firm must pay $130 million in one year, given that it is currently worth $100 million. With a volatility of only 20% per year, there is little chance that the value of the company will climb high enough to exceed $130 million, and thus right now the equity is worth little. This is an example of a company in what would typically be called financial distress.

(b) If the company invests in the new project, the new total company value will be V_0 = $100 million. Putting this number into the BSM calculator with the other numbers, we get a new equity value of $3.177 million. The increase in equity value will therefore be $1.945 million in total.

(c) The project has positive NPV ($10 million) and thus increases the value of the company. Thus, it *should* be invested in. However, note that from the perspective of new equity holders looking to give the company money in exchange for stock, the *total* increase in equity value is less than $10 million, since much of the gain goes to debtholders. Equity holders only gain $1.945 million in value. Thus, new equity holders would likely conclude that it is not a good deal to part with $2 million in exchange for sharing in a gain of $1.945 million.

(d) If the company instead had $90 million in outstanding debt, the BSM calculator inputs to determine the company's equity value are as follows: V_0 = $100 million (current value of the underlying asset), B = $90 million (strike price of the option), T = 1 year (expiration date), σ = 0.2 (volatility of the underlying asset), and r_f = 0.02. With these numbers, we get a call option value (value of equity) of $14.807 million. Now consider investment in the project. The new total company value will be V_0 = $100 million. Putting this number into the BSM calculator with the other numbers, we get a new equity value of $23.121 million. The increase in equity value will therefore be $8.314 million in total, above the $2 million the equity holders would need to purchase the stock, since now most of the gains accrue to the equity given the lower amount of debt.

14.2.2 Multiple Debt Issues: Debt Seniority

Seniority, or the order within which debt must be repaid, is one of the ways debt may differ within a firm. Typically, not all debt obligations of the company have the same repayment priority: A company may prioritize the repayment of a particular bond issue over another bond issue. In fact, a company may have many different tiers or tranches of debt, ranked in order of their seniority. Senior debt has the highest priority in terms of the order of repayment. Junior or subordinated debt refers to debt below that on the repayment list. For example, in their 2022 Annual Report, IBM notes that they have senior long-term debt and commercial paper (which is unsecured short-term debt). More-senior debt also typically has legal priority over more-junior debt in terms of their claims in bankruptcy proceedings. For these reasons, the more senior the debt, the less risk the debtholder is exposed to—the firm will use its cash flows to make payments on that debt before other types of debt—and the lower the expected rate of the return demanded by the debtholders, all else being equal. Figure 14.4 illustrates this ranking: Senior debt receives the highest priority, followed by junior debt; equity receives the residual after these claims are paid.

The options valuation framework can be used to determine the value of each type of debt in this corporate debt structure, thus allowing us to value a corporate capital structure that is closer to what we often observe in the real world in a way that is more straightforward than other methodologies, such as DCF, that may require estimation of multiple discount rates and other factors. A similar intuition with this structure applies as when valuing equity and debt—cash flows to debt first go to the more-senior debt and then the less-senior debt. To illustrate, consider again our example of Landco, but now assume that Landco's $80 million of debt outstanding is split between senior and junior debt: Senior debt comprises $60 million and junior debt comprises $20 million. Apart from this, Landco has the same characteristics as before:

- total company value is $V_0 = \$100$ million;
- maturity of the firm's debt is $T = 1$ year;
- volatility of the total value of the firm is $\sigma = 0.3$; and
- riskless interest rate is $r_f = 0.08$.

What are the values of Landco's senior and junior debt? To answer this question, we apply **Principle 2**: *Equivalent assets that can be freely bought and sold will have the same market price*, and determine the combinations of options (and other assets whose values we know) that perfectly replicate the payoffs of the senior and junior debt; adding the values of these option combinations will yield the values of the senior and junior debt.

Suppose that the value of Landco's assets in one year is zero. Then, as before, neither type of debt nor equity gets any payoffs, and their values will be zero. However, suppose that the value of Landco's assets in a year is $40 million. The senior debtholders, who are first in priority, do not get what they are owed—$60 million—but instead receive whatever Landco has, which is $40 million. Note that there is no value left to pay off either junior debtholders or equity holders, and so both receive zero as their payoff. If Landco's assets are worth $60 million, the senior debtholders get exactly what they are owed, $60 million, but there is no value left in the company after that to accrue to junior debtholders or equity, so their payoffs are again zero. Now suppose that Landco's assets are worth $80 million. In this case, the company has enough value to pay off everything that it owes to the senior debtholders, and it has value leftover that then goes to the junior debtholders ($20 million, enough to pay what they are owed). There is no value left over for equity holders in this case. If the value of Landco's assets is greater than $80 million, then equity holders will receive a positive residual value. These payoffs are summarized in Table 14.3.

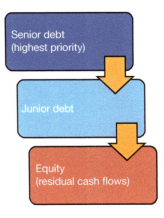

FIGURE 14.4 Hierarchy of priority with debt seniority. The hierarchy of repayment priority when a firm has senior and junior debt. Senior debt receives the highest priority and assets are used to pay it off first, followed by junior debt. Equity receives residual assets after these claims are paid.

If we draw the payoff diagram for the debt payoffs, we get Figure 14.5. We can see that the figure for senior debt is familiar—it looks like the payoff diagram for the single type of corporate debt from

Table 14.3 **Landco's senior and junior debt payoffs.** This table shows various possible payoffs of Landco's senior debt, junior debt, and equity at maturity date $T = 1$ based on Landco's possible total company value at that time, and a principal amount of debt of $60 million for senior debt and $20 million for junior debt.

Total company value in one year, V_1	Senior debt payoff in one year	Junior debt payoff in one year	Equity payoff in one year
$0	$0	$0	$0
20	20	0	0
40	40	0	0
60	60	0	0
80	60	20	0
100	60	20	20
120	60	20	40

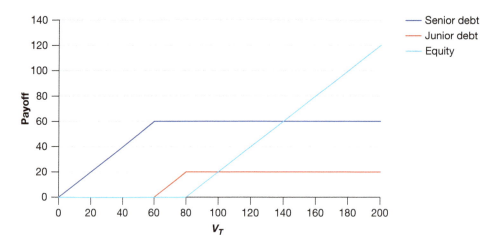

FIGURE 14.5 Senior and junior debt payoffs at maturity. This figure depicts the various possible payoffs of Landco's senior debt (dark blue line), junior debt (red line), and equity (light blue line) at maturity date $T = 1$ based on Landco's possible total company value at that time, and a principal amount of debt of $60 million for senior debt and $20 million for junior debt.

the previous examples (see Figure 14.2). We covered in Section 14.1.3 that such a payoff can be viewed as a combination of a riskless bond and a short put option. In this case, it would be a riskless bond with a maturity of one year and a principal amount of $60 million and a short put option with a strike price of $60 million (corresponding to the minimum total company value for the senior debt to be fully paid, where the payoffs in the graph flatten). The value of the riskless bond in this case is PV (riskless bond) $= 60 / e^{0.08} = 55.39$. The put option in this case can be calculated using the BSM formula for put options or the put–call parity formula (Equation 7.4), using a strike price of $60 (and the same for other inputs). Doing so yields a put price of $0.20 million. The value of the senior debt can therefore be calculated as:

$$D_{Senior} = 55.39 - 0.20$$
$$= 55.19.$$

The value of Landco's senior debt is therefore very similar to the value of riskless debt. This reflects the fact that Landco's current total value is $100 million, and Landco owes $60 million on its senior debt, payable in one year. With a volatility of 30%, it is relatively unlikely that Landco's total company value will fall to the level that it will be unable to pay off the $60 million in senior debt.

The value of the junior debt can be derived in a similar manner. Note that we can replicate the graph for the junior debt using a combination of a long call option (on the underlying assets of Landco) with a strike price of $60 million, and a short call option with a strike price of $80 million.[4] Using the BSM model to gauge the price of both options (with the same underlying asset characteristics as before) yields a value for the junior debt of: $D_{Junior} = \$44.82 - \$28.24 = \$16.58$ million. Note that the combined value of the senior and junior debt is the same (rounded) as when there was only one type of debt: $16.58 + 55.19 = 71.77$; the value is thus just split between the two types. The equity value is also the same in this case, $28.24 million, since the different types of debt do not affect equity's payoffs (it is still paid off after all debt).

---

[4] An alternative, but entirely equivalent, combination would be a long riskless bond with a principal amount of $20 million, a short put option with a strike price of $80 million, and a long put option with a strike price of $60 million.

14.2 CORPORATE DEBT STRUCTURE

This option model for valuing a company's debt has advantages over the standard DCF model, since it avoids the need to estimate different discount rates for each type of debt. Furthermore, the method can be generalized for multiple levels (tranches) of debt as well, as Example 14.2 illustrates.

Example 14.2 (Analyzing Corporate Debt): Your company, Choices Inc., currently has a total company value of $150 million, and has three different tranches of debt: senior, mezzanine, and junior. The senior debt always gets paid first, followed by the mezzanine debt and then the junior debt. Each type of debt matures in two years and has a principal amount of $30 million. The volatility of Choices' assets is 40%, and the riskless interest rate is 2%. What is the value of each type of debt?

Solution. To answer this question, we will again determine which combinations of options and other positions perfectly replicate the payoffs of each type of debt; adding the values of these combinations will yield the values of the respective types. To do so, it is useful to start by constructing a payoff diagram for each type at maturity.

Figure 14.6 helps us to determine what combinations of positions replicate each of the types of debt. One such combination is:

- senior debt = riskless bond with principal $30 million − put option with K = $30 million;
- mezzanine debt = long call with K = $30 million − call with K = $60 million; and
- junior debt = long call with K = $60 million − call with K = $90 million.

The riskless bond price is calculated by discounting (back two years) the principal amount of $30 million by the riskless rate: PV (riskless bond) = $30 / e^{2 \times 0.02}$ = 28.82. We can determine the option prices using the BSM model (calculator) as follows:

Position	Value
Put with K = $30 million	$0.02 million
Call with K = $30 million	$121.19 million
Call with K = $60 million	$93.31 million
Call with K = $90 million	$69.03 million

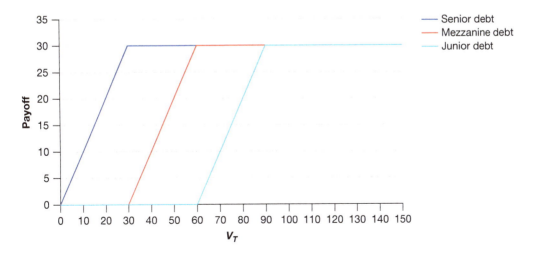

Figure 14.6 This figure depicts the various possible payoffs of Choices Inc.'s senior debt (dark blue line), mezzanine debt (red line), and junior debt (light blue line) at maturity date T = 2 based on Choices' possible total value at that time, and a principal amount of debt of $30 million for each type of debt.

Using these numbers, the valuations for each debt are:

- senior debt = 28.82 − 0.02 = $28.80 million;
- mezzanine debt = 121.19 − 93.31 = $27.88 million; and
- junior debt = 93.31 − 69.03 = $24.28 million.

> **QUICK CHECK 14.5** Considering Landco with senior and junior debt, suppose instead that the principal amounts for the senior and junior debt were $40 million each. What would be the values of the senior and junior debts in this case?

14.3 Guarantees and Other Securities

The division of a firm's capital structure into different debt seniorities is common across the corporate world. However, in addition to equity and types of debt, some companies also have other types of financial securities that are part of their capital structure. The options-based framework can be applied to a variety of corporate claims and securities other than debt or equity, such as credit guarantees and hybrid securities that have features of both debt and equity.

14.3.1 Credit Guarantees

Guarantees against credit risk pervade the financial system and play an important role in corporate and public finance. A guarantee is a security that states that a debt will be repaid to a debtholder by another party if the borrower defaults. Parent corporations routinely guarantee the debt obligations of their subsidiaries. Commercial banks and insurance companies offer guarantees in return for fees on a broad spectrum of financial instruments, ranging from traditional letters of credit to interest rate and currency swaps. The largest providers of financial guarantees are governments and governmental agencies. Across the world, governments provide a wide range of financial guarantees. One that is of prime importance, both economically and politically, is deposit insurance, where the federal government or a central banking authority will explicitly cover a shortfall (up to a limit) that depositors experience if a bank goes under.

However, government guarantees are also used extensively elsewhere. In the corporate sector, the government has guaranteed the debt of small businesses and on occasion it has done so for very large businesses. The Pension Benefit Guarantee Corporation (PBGC) provides limited insurance of corporate pension plan benefits. Residential mortgages and farm and student loans are examples of noncorporate obligations that the government has guaranteed. Box 14.2 gives an overview of the types of government guarantees that are commonly found.

> **Box 14.2** Government Guarantees
>
> Guarantees are provided by the government for a variety of different financial institutions worldwide. Oftentimes these guarantees are provided by the government in order to extend credit to populations that are viewed as facing barriers to accessing traditional financial services. Examples of such guarantees include:
>
> - Small business loans: Governments often directly provide loans or guarantee loans for small and early-stage companies in order to promote entrepreneurship. For example, in the United

> States, the Small Business Administration (SBA) guarantees loans that are provided by banks to such companies. In Europe, individual countries have agencies that provide loans or guarantees to companies operating in different sectors—for example, the KfW bank in Germany, run by the German government, provides loans to support small businesses that are guaranteed by the government.
> - Mortgages: In the United States, the Federal Housing Administration (FHA) supports residential mortgages by offering insurance on such loans to banks, so that banks are more willing to provide mortgages to individuals and families to allow them to purchase houses.
> - Agriculture: Farms are critical to food production, but are often small family-run businesses that can struggle financially. Loan programs in many countries aim to support the agricultural sector. In the United States, the US Department of Agriculture (USDA) supports loan guarantees for banks lending to farmers, and the government also offers direct loans to farmers in addition to programs such as crop insurance. In Canada, the Canadian Agricultural Loans Act is a loan guarantee program designed to increase loan availability for farms and agricultural cooperatives. Similar support programs include the European Agricultural Guarantee Fund (EAGF) in Europe and agricultural loans by the Japan Finance Corporation (owned by the government) in Japan.
>
> *Source:* Peterdy, K. (n.d.). Government guarantee. Corporate Finance Institute, corporatefinanceinstitute.com.

Guarantees are also implicit every time a loan is made. To see this, we will consider the following formulas to show where the guarantee is in both risky and default-free loans:

$$\text{risky loan} + \text{loan guarantee} = \text{default-free loan}, \quad (14.3)$$

$$\text{risky loan} = \text{default-free loan} - \text{loan guarantee}. \quad (14.4)$$

To see more clearly, think of the lending activity as taking place in two steps: (1) the purchase of a guarantee; and (2) the taking of a loan. Suppose that the guarantor and the lender are two distinct entities. In the first step, the borrower buys a guarantee from the guarantor for $10. In the second step, the borrower takes this guarantee to the lender and borrows $100 in default-free debt with an interest rate of 10% per year. The borrower winds up receiving a net amount of $100 − $10 = $90 in return for a promise to pay back $110 in one year.

Of course, often the lender and the guarantor are the same entity—for example, a commercial bank—and the borrower simply receives the net $90 from the bank in return for a promise to repay $110 in one year. The promised interest rate on the loan is then stated as 22.22%—that is, ($110 − $90)/$90. This promised rate reflects both the riskless interest rate and the charge for the guarantee. The purchase of any real-world loan is, thus, functionally equivalent to the purchase of a pure default-free loan and the simultaneous issue of a guarantee of that loan. In effect, the creditor simultaneously pays for the default-free loan and receives a "rebate" for the guarantee of that loan. The magnitude of the value of the guarantee relative to the value of the default-free loan component varies considerably. A high-grade bond rating such as AAA denotes a nearly default-free loan with a very small guarantee component. A below-investment-grade or "junk" rating, on the other hand, typically indicates a bond with a large guarantee component.

Options theory can be used to analyze the efficient management and value of guarantees. Guarantees are, functionally, put options. The guarantor must make the promised payment on a financial contract if the borrower fails to do so. The loss to the guarantor is equal to the difference between the promised payment on the guaranteed contract and the price received from the sale of the assets that are available from the issuer as collateral—all assets, even unpledged, that a loan issuer can seize, for this obligation. This difference is called the shortfall. It is generally assumed that the issuer will only default if the shortfall is nonnegative. We can see this in our previous Landco risky debt example in Section 14.2. With corporate debt of Landco—which is risky—debtholders were paid the full amount owed when Landco's assets had sufficient value, and then it was assumed that the debtholders received whatever the assets were worth if there was a positive shortfall. We also saw that Landco's debt had equivalent payoffs to a riskless bond and a short put option. This is in line with Equation 14.4—the put option represents the guarantee on the debt, which is subtracted from the default-free or riskless component of it.

Example 14.3 illustrates how option pricing can be used to value guarantees on debt.

Example 14.3 (Valuing a Guarantee): Consider a company, Debtco, which has a total company value of $100 million and a total principal amount of debt of $80 million that matures in one year. The debt is valued at $71.759 million. The volatility of Debtco's asset value is 30%, and the riskless interest rate is 8%. Suppose that a bank, insurance company, or the government undertakes to guarantee the debt of Debtco against default. What is the fair market value of this guarantee?

Solution. One way to compute this value is to take the difference between the present value of riskless bonds promising the same cash flows as Debtco bonds and the value of Debtco bonds without the guarantee. With the guarantee in place, Debtco's debt becomes risk-free.

Because the riskless interest rate is 0.08 per year continuously compounded, and the debt promises $80 million at maturity one year from now, its value as risk-free debt is

$$PV \text{ (riskless debt)} = \frac{80}{e^{0.08}} = \$73.849 \text{ million}.$$

The value of the guarantee must, therefore, be the difference between the value of Debtco's debt if it was riskless (i.e., the value with the guarantee included) and the value of the debt without the guarantee:

$$\begin{aligned} \text{Value of guarantee} &= \text{value with guarantee} - \text{value without guarantee} \\ &= \$73.849 - 71.759 \\ &= \$2.09 \text{ million.} \end{aligned}$$

But there is another way to compute the value of the guarantee. The credit guarantee is equivalent to writing a put option on Debtco's assets with a strike price equal to the face value of the debt. The guarantee's value can, therefore, be computed using the BSM formula applied to put options, with the following inputs: underlying asset value of $100 million, strike price of $80 million, time to expiration of one year, volatility of 30%, and a riskless interest rate of 8%. Doing so again results in a value of $2.09 million.

14.3.2 Hybrid Securities

Hybrid securities are financial instruments that have features of both debt and equity, while not being strictly like them.

One such hybrid instrument is a convertible bond, which is a bond that has the same functions as a regular bond, but can also be converted at a later point in time to equity. A convertible bond is thus a corporate bond with a warrant (a call option on a company's stock that is issued by the company) attached to it with a face value equal to the exercise price of the warrant so that the convertible bond can be exchanged for shares of stock when exercised.

A company that issues a convertible bond raises money from the investors that purchase it, and the security initially functions as a bond—it issues coupon payments and will default if the company reneges on the payments. However, the holder of the bond may pay a conversion fee to convert the bond into a predetermined number of shares of stock (equity). Once converted to equity, the holder of the convertible bond does not have the ability to reverse the conversion. Specific features of convertible bonds can vary—for example, in some cases the company itself may have the ability to force conversion.

Conversion bonds lend naturally to options analysis since they provide the holder of the bond an option: The holder can pay the conversion fee and convert to equity (i.e., exercise the option to convert) if the company is doing well (and thus the equity is sufficiently valuable), but can choose not to convert (let the option expire) and leave the instrument as a bond if the company is not doing as well. Thus, the conversion feature gives the holder of a convertible bond both unlimited upside potential if the bond is converted (as with holding equity but unlike holding a bond) and downside coupon payments (as with a bond but unlike holding equity).

This can functionally be viewed as a bond with an option attached to it, and the value can be analyzed using options analysis. Since the conversion option is valuable to the holder of a bond, investors would be willing to pay a premium for such a bond relative to a regular bond with similar terms (i.e., the same maturity and promised coupons). This provides one reason why companies sometimes opt to issue such bonds: They can expect to raise more capital per bond relative to a typical issue.

There are also hybrid securities with other types of features. For example, "callable" bonds allow a company to buy back bonds that are sold to investors. "Putable equity" allows investors that hold shares of stock to sell their equity back to the company at a set price. There are many other types of hybrid securities; in all cases, the options-based analysis provides a general framework to analyze and value them.

In the previous sections we covered how the option pricing framework can be used to value and analyze specific corporate financial claims: equity, types of debt, and guarantees. However, options analysis can be applied to an even wider range of other securities that companies can issue. These include convertible bonds, multiple tranches of debt beyond just senior and junior debts, warrants (options on the shares of a firm's stock issued by the firm itself), and so forth. Indeed, the framework can be used to look at *any* financial claim on the firm, including a variety of alternative financing designs. This is why the options-based framework is frequently used by financial practitioners to price and assess new issues of securities meant to raise funds. In this sense, the options-based approach is unified because it allows analyses of more complex and realistic capital structures that often exist in practice. Other methodologies, such as DCF, face challenges when examining more complicated capital structures—for example, the DCF methodology requires estimation of a different discount rate for each financial instrument considered.

This approach is also powerful because it allows an analysis of new financial innovations—that is, new types of securities that are introduced and may not yet be known or used in practice.

As we have seen in the previous sections, options give us a powerful and versatile framework with which we can analyze the company's financial claims that comprise the liabilities and equity of the company. However, the applications of options don't end with the capital structure decisions, but can also be used to value the other side of the balance sheet—the assets of the company. In the remainder of this chapter, we now turn to how the options-based framework can be used as a tool to analyze and value the assets companies hold and the projects that they can invest in.

14.4 Project Valuation Using Real Options

The previous sections focused on using option pricing to value the capital structure of the firm and analyze financing instruments that companies can issue. However, option pricing applications can also be used when considering physical projects. The family of such applications is called real options. In a seminal paper, Stewart C. Myers was the first to coin and develop the analysis of real options (Myers 1977). The most developed area for real-options application is investment decisions by firms. However, real-options analysis has also been applied to real-estate investment and development decisions.

The common element for using option pricing here is the same as in the preceding examples: The future is uncertain (if it were not, there would be no need to create options because we would know now what we will do later), and in an uncertain environment having the flexibility to decide what to do after some of that uncertainty is resolved definitely has value (**Principle 8:** *Flexibility in financial decisions has value, and the greater the uncertainty, the greater the value*). Option pricing theory provides the means for assessing that value where other project evaluation techniques (such as DCF analysis) may have more challenges. In particular, for many types of generic projects it may be reasonable to assume certainty and use an approach such as DCF with a constant discount rate. However, for projects with optionality, DCF will not be the proper tool for analysis because of uncertain and changing risks in the future: The ability to stop, expand, or change things can be first-order effects for certain types of projects, and not properly incorporating them into the analysis may cause misjudgment (**Principle 6:** *Risk is fundamental to financial analysis and must be explicitly considered in all financial decisions*).

The major categories of options within project investment valuations are the option to:

- initiate or expand;
- abandon or contract; and
- pause, slow down, or speed up development.

There are growth options—creating excess capacity as an option to expand, or researching and development of new products and even new businesses—but with no obligation to do so if not economically viable. An example of an application of the real-options technology is in the generation of electric power. A power plant can be constructed to draw on oil/natural gas, wind, or solar power, or it can be built to operate on all of these. The value of that option is the ability to use the least-cost fuel available at each point in time and the cost of that option is manifest in both the higher cost of construction and less efficient energy conversion than with the corresponding specialized equipment. This is in addition to any cost to the environment.

The movie industry provides a good example of the importance of real-option values in evaluating investment projects. Often a movie studio will buy the rights to a movie script and then wait to decide if and when to actually produce it. Thus, the studio has the option to wait. Once production starts, and at every subsequent step in the process, the studio has the option to discontinue the project in response to information about cost overruns or changing tastes of the moviegoing public. Another important real option in the movie business is the option of the film studio to make sequels. If the original movie turns out to be a success, then the studio has the exclusive right to make additional movies with the same title and characters. The option to make sequels can be a significant part of a movie project's total value.

There is a fundamental similarity between the options in investment projects and call options on stocks: In both cases the decision maker has the right, but not the obligation, to buy something of value at a future date. Put differently, the flexibility to make a decision in the future—and to not have to make it now—is valuable and can be assessed using option pricing. Recognizing the similarity between call options and real options is important for three reasons:

- It helps in structuring the analysis of the investment project as a sequence of managerial decisions over time.
- It clarifies the role of uncertainty in evaluating projects.
- It gives us a method for estimating the option value of projects by applying the quantitative models developed for valuing call options on stocks.

14.4.1 Types of Real Options

Real options are categorized by the type of flexibility they offer to the terms of a real investment opportunity, and each can be valued like a type of financial option.

The option to postpone the beginning of an investment project is a deferral option and can be mapped nicely into an American call option. Here the option exercise price is the project's required initial investment and its maturity date corresponds to the final decision point. An option to abandon a project corresponds to an American put option. The exercise price for the option is the amount that must be paid to terminate the project. This could be a contracted amount or simply the market value of the project if it is liquidated. On both sides of a deferral option and an option to abandon may lie possibilities to exercise an option to rescale the project, where the project can be expanded or contracted for some fixed price.

More complex real options include switching options, which require the payment of a fixed amount to change operating or production modes. The option to close down and restart a production line, or exit and then reenter a market, are also examples of switching options that can be modeled as portfolios of American put and call options.

Complex investment projects, which are typically organized into a set of alternative stages with critical decisions at the end of each stage, can be analyzed as compound options in which options on options exist. For example, a major drug company's product cycles consist of a research stage in which alternative compounds are tested, a product development stage in which clinical trials are conducted, and a marketing stage in which the final product is brought to market. Each stage involves new investments that are conditional on exercise of an option to proceed from the previous stage.

Real options can help in analyzing investment projects that have optionality. We will look at this application to consider how some real options are analogous to call options. To illustrate, we will consider a film studio's decision on purchasing the movie rights to a book currently being written by a best-selling author that is due to publish one year from now.

Assume the author charges $1 million for the exclusive right to make a movie out of her novel. If the book is a success on publication, then the film studio will make a movie out of it, but if the book is a commercial failure the studio will not exercise its right to make it into a movie. Figure 14.7 shows this investment project as a decision tree.

The studio's current decision is whether to pay the $1 million price the author demands. This is represented by a decision box at the left of the tree. The right branch coming out of the first decision box corresponds to a decision to pay the $1 million for the movie rights and the lower branch corresponds to a decision not to pay the $1 million.

The circle represents an event not under the control of management: whether the book is a commercial success. The upward branch coming from the circle directs to the possibility that the

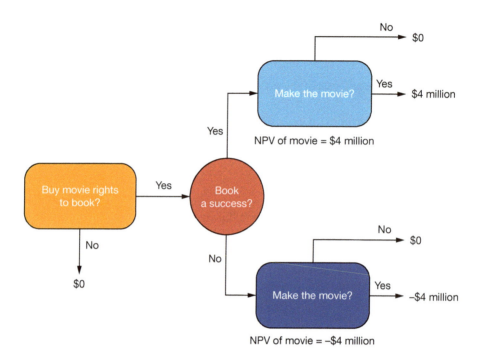

FIGURE 14.7 Decision tree for a movie project. The initial decision to buy movie rights or not is shown in the rectangle on the left. If movie rights are not bought, there is no money spent, reflected by the down arrow. If movie rights are bought, then whether the book was a success is examined (center). If not, then the rectangle on the bottom is reached to decide whether to make the movie. Deciding to make it gives an NPV of −$4 million, deciding not to gives an NPV of zero. If the book was a success, the rectangle at the top is reached to decide whether to make the movie. Deciding to make it gives an NPV of $4 million, deciding not to gives an NPV of zero. The tree includes outcomes that have negative payouts, which are technically not well defined because their value depends on their owner's willingness and capability to pay. A more rigorous approach would attach a riskless bond to the project, with the same maturity and face value as the pay-in (in this case $4 million) to eliminate any need for future pay-in. This is collateral that assures that the promised pay-in will be made, which then releases the valuation from depending on its owner (Merton 1977).

novel is a success, and the downward branch to the possibility that the novel is a failure. Each has a probability of 0.5. Analysts at the studio estimate that if the book is a success, then the NPV of the movie will be $4 million. If, however, the book is a failure then the NPV of the movie one year from now will be −$4 million.

Note that each branch extending from the event circle ends in another decision box representing the decision that management must make about whether to actually produce the movie. If the project were analyzed without taking account of management's ability to abandon it one year from now, then the project would be rejected, because the project's expected present value today would be zero at any cost of capital, no matter how low, since $0.5 \times 4 + 0.5 \times -4 = 0$. Management would surely not spend $1 million to buy the rights to make a movie that has an expected present value of zero. However, this is a mis-specification of the investment opportunity; because management would purchase the right and not the obligation to make the movie, management does not have to make the movie in one year at an NPV of −$4 million. Put differently, management has a choice to say no once reaching the rectangles on the right, and would say no to making the movie if the book ends up not being a success. This will change the present value calculation and make it positive instead of zero. The option to abandon the movie will increase the value of buying the movie rights. Thus, we see that it is extremely important in structuring the analysis of the project to take account of management's ability to change course in the future. Options analysis thus accounts for the hidden value that comes from flexibility in the face of uncertainty, which a typical NPV analysis would not allow us to see.

How important is the value of managerial options as a component of an investment project's total value? The answer depends on the type of project, but it is difficult to think of any investment project where management has no discretion to alter its plans once the project has begun. It is especially important to take option value into account when considering investments in research and development. The use of the financial theory of options in capital budgeting has been adopted by large pharmaceutical companies. In general, the greater the uncertainty about future outcomes of the project, the greater the need to account explicitly for any options. Box 14.3 provides examples of real options for movie rights and drug development in practice.

Box 14.3   World of Business: Real Options in Practice

Real options can be seen in many different industries. One is with movie rights—studios will often pay for the rights to *possibly* make a movie in the future based on a book; sometimes a book that hasn't even been written yet. In 1993, Universal Pictures made a $3.75 million deal for the rights to make a movie based on the next book from John Grisham, a best-selling author of legal thrillers. The deal, at the time, represented the most ever paid for an unfinished book, and highlights the value movie companies place on books they believe will turn into big dollars at the box office, value that can be seen as real options. Similar examples abound. Paramount purchased the film rights to *The Godfather* from Mario Puzo when he had only 100 pages of the book written.

Real options are at the heart of decision making in other industries, such as drug development. In a *Harvard Business Review* interview with Merck CFO Judy Lewent, she details how the real-options framework is critical for what they do as a company:

> Merck invests approximately $1 billion per year in research, which has given us extraordinary insight into the risky nature and high cost of pharmaceutical research ... Think about drug research for a minute. We may know at the beginning of a project that there is a market for a specific treatment that includes many thousands of people, and once we reach a certain point in the process, we may know that a certain compound may be effective. But we still aren't 100% certain that the compound will prove so safe and effective that it can be turned into a drug. So we have to ask ourselves, "Do we continue to invest?" Those are the kinds of decisions we face every day. And they aren't investments that easily lend themselves to traditional financial analysis. Remember that we need to make huge investments now and may not see a profit for 10 to 15 years. In that kind of situation, a traditional analysis that factors in the time value of money may not fully capture the strategic value of an investment in research, because the positive cash flows are severely discounted when they are analyzed over a very long time frame. As a result, the volatility or risk isn't properly valued ... Option analysis, like the kind used to value stock options, provides a more flexible approach to valuing our research investments than traditional financial analysis because it allows us to evaluate those investments at successive stages of a project.

When you make an initial investment in a research project, you are paying an entry fee for a right, but you are not obligated to continue that research at a later stage. Merck's experience with R&D has given us a database of information that allows us to value the risk or the volatility of our research projects, a key piece of information in option analysis. Therefore, if I use option theory to analyze that investment, I have a tool to examine uncertainty and to value it.

Sources: Eller, C. (1993). Movie deal on unwritten Grisham book sets record: film: Universal will pay $3.75 million for rights to next legal thriller by best-selling author of "The Firm." *Los Angeles Times*, 17 July. Schall, E. (2021). "The Godfather": how Paramount got the Mario Puzo bestseller for $12,500. Showbiz CheatSheet, 14 May. Nichols, N. A. (1994). Scientific management at Merck: an interview with CFO Judy Lewent. *Harvard Business Review*.

14.4.2 Determining the Value of a Real Option

Now that we have recognized the importance of taking account of the option value in investment opportunities, how do we quantify that value? In this section we will apply the Black-Scholes-Merton (BSM) formula to determine this value of real options using an acquisition and an investment opportunity as examples.

14.4.2.1 Acquisition of a Firm

Suppose that a firm, Rader Inc., is considering acquiring another firm, Bullseye Inc. They are both 100% equity financed—that is, neither firm has any debt outstanding. Each firm has one million shares of common stock outstanding that can be freely bought and sold in a competitive market. The current market value of Bullseye's assets is $100 million and the standard deviation of the proportional change in its value is 0.20. Suppose that Bullseye's management offers Rader an option to acquire 100% of Bullseye's shares one year from now for $106 million. The riskless interest rate is 6% per year.

If the option costs $6 million, is the investment worthwhile? From Rader's perspective this is a capital budgeting decision. The initial outlay is the $6 million cost of the option to acquire Bullseye's assets one year from now. To determine the value of this option we can use the BSM valuation model developed in Chapter 7 to price a European call option on a stock, since in this case the offer is explicitly a call option (the option to buy) shares of Bullseye's stock. The relevant inputs to the BSM formula would therefore be:

- the current price of the stock (i.e., at time $t = 0$), $S_0 = \$100$ million;
- the strike price of the option, $K = \$106$ million;
- the time to maturity (expiration date) of the option in years, $T = 1$ year;
- a measure of the risk of the stock: the standard deviation of the rate of return of the stock, $\sigma = 20\%$; and
- the riskless interest rate, $r_f = 6\%$.

Applying the BSM formula yields an option value of approximately $8 million. The NPV of the investment opportunity is $2 million, the option's value to Rader less its cost $8 million – $6 million, so the project should be undertaken.

> **QUICK CHECK 14.6** In the example in this section, if Bullseye's stock volatility increases to 30%, what happens to the value of the option to Rader? Explain why this is the case.

14.4.2.2 Project Decisions

Option theory can help to evaluate an investment opportunity that does not involve the explicit purchase of an option but does contain a managerial option. For example, an electricity firm, Electro Utility, has the opportunity to invest in a project to build a power-generating plant. In the first phase, an initial outlay of $6 million is required to build the facility to house the equipment. In the second phase, one year from now, equipment costing $106 million must be purchased. Viewed from today's perspective, suppose that the value of the completed plant one year from now is a random variable with a mean of $112 million and a standard deviation of 0.2. The riskless interest rate is 6% per year.

Suppose we do a conventional DCF analysis of this investment opportunity. At a discount rate of r, the present value of the completed plant is $12 million / (1 + r). Because the $106 million investment outlay for power-generating equipment is known for certain, its present value is computed by discounting at the riskless rate, giving a present value of the outlay of $106 million / 1.06 = $100 million. So, the total present value of the initial investment in the plant ($6 million) and the investment in equipment (PV = $100 million) is $106 million. Suppose that the company's discount rate r = 12%, we have a project NPV of:

$$NPV = \frac{\$112 \text{ million}}{1+r} - \$100 \text{ million} - \$6 \text{ million}$$
$$= \frac{\$112 \text{ million}}{1.12} - \$106 \text{ million}$$
$$= -\$6.0 \text{ million.}$$

Thus, the project has negative NPV and should be discarded. In fact, note that the NPV will be negative for any discount rate r greater than 5.66%.

But to do this is to ignore the important fact that management has the right to abandon the project one year from now. In other words, management will invest an additional $106 million in the second stage of the project *only* if the value of the plant turns out to be more than $106 million. (We assume for simplicity that the $6 million initial outlay is lost completely if the plant is not completed; that is, the salvage value is zero.) How can we evaluate this investment taking management's flexibility into account? The answer is that we can apply the same method we just applied in evaluating Rader Inc.'s option to buy Bullseye Inc. Although the circumstances are somewhat different, the two situations have the same structure and even the same payoffs.

To see this, note that by undertaking the first phase of the project, Electro Utility would in effect be paying $6 million to "buy an option" that will mature in one year. The option is to undertake phase two of the project, and its "exercise price" is $106 million. The present value of the completed project, which is the present value of the cash inflows (excluding the investment cost) is $112 million / 1.12 = $100 million. The inputs that are needed for the BSM formula—and their analogies to the inputs into the formula when the option is based on a stock—are shown in Table 14.4.

The BSM formula says that this option is worth approximately $8 million. The project, therefore, has positive NPV of $2 million instead of the negative NPV computed when we ignored management's option to discontinue the project after the first year. In other words, it is worth investing the $6 million right now in order to unlock the option to purchase the equipment one year from now. Our conclusion is that taking management's flexibility explicitly into account increases a project's NPV. In particular, we see in this case that a project that has negative NPV according to standard DCF calculations—and thus would be discarded based on that analysis—is actually worth pursuing when incorporating the real option into the analysis.

Table 14.4 Black–Scholes–Merton formula input correspondence for the Electro Utility real option. This table provides the inputs to the BSM formula for the real option that Electro Utility can consider, and the analogous inputs when the underlying asset is a stock. One year from now, equipment costing $106 million must be purchased. The value of the completed plant one year from now is a random variable with a mean of $112 million and a standard deviation of 0.2. The company's discount rate is 12%. The riskless interest rate is 6% per year.

BSM input (based on a stock)	Variable	Real option input	Value
Current stock price	S	PV of project cash flows	$\dfrac{\$112 \text{ million}}{1.12} = \$100$ million
Exercise price	K	Future investment cost	$106 million
Stock return volatility	σ	Volatility of project value	20%
Time to expiration	T	Time to investment	1 year
Risk-free rate	r_f	Risk-free rate	6%

Moreover, from the theory of option pricing, we know that the value of flexibility increases with the volatility of the project. Again, consider the example of Electro Utility. Suppose that the value of the power-generating plant is actually more volatile than was at first thought. Instead of the standard deviation being 0.20, suppose it is 0.40. This makes the investment project more attractive. Applying the BSM formula, we find that the option value is now $16 million. The project's NPV is, therefore, $10 million, rather than the $2 million computed earlier.

Virtually all future investment opportunities can be viewed as call options because firms can almost always wait before making their initial outlay and can decide not to proceed with it. The amount of time the firm can wait is analogous to the option's time to expiration; the initial outlay is analogous to the exercise price; and the present value of the project's expected future cash flows is analogous to the price of the underlying stock. The project's conventionally computed NPV is, thus, analogous to the option's intrinsic value—that is, what it would be worth if it were expiring immediately. Conventional NPV understates the value of the project because it ignores the option's time value.

> **QUICK CHECK 14.7** What is the option value of the Electro Utility investment project if the volatility of the power-generating plant is 0.3 instead of 0.2?

14.5 Applications of Real Options outside Firms

Beyond project decisions within firms, there are a wider array of decisions—such as household or government policy decisions—that can be formulated as real option problems. Formulating such decisions as options affects not just value pertaining to those decisions, but also the risk that is inherent in those decisions.

Deciding how much vocational education you should acquire can be formulated as an option valuation problem in which the optimal exercise conditions reflect when to stop training and start working. In the classic labor–leisure trade-off, the job that provides the flexibility to increase or decrease the number of hours worked and, hence, total compensation, on relatively short notice has a valuable option relative to jobs with fixed available work hours. Wage, welfare, and pension plan floors that provide for minimum compensation have an optionlike structure.

Healthcare insurance contains varying degrees of flexibility, a major one being whether the consumer agrees in advance to use only a prespecified set of doctors and hospitals (HMO plan) or retain the right to choose an out-of-plan doctor or hospital. In making the decision the consumer solves an option pricing problem as to the value of that flexibility. Much the same structure of valuation occurs in choosing between pay-per-view and flat-fee payment for cable television services.

Option value can be a significant proportion of the total value of government-granted offshore drilling rights and pollution rights. Option pricing analysis quantifies the government's economic decision to build roads in less populated areas depending on whether it has the policy option to abandon rural roads if they are not used enough. Various legal and tax issues involving policy and behavior can be addressed using the option model. For example, the valuation of plaintiffs' litigation options, bankruptcy laws including limited-liability provisions, tax delinquency on real estate and other property as an option to abandon or recover the property by paying the arrears, tax evasion, and valuing the tax timing option for the capital-gains tax in a circumstance when only realization of losses and gains on investments triggers a taxable event.

Option theory is also a fruitful framework for the analysis of strategic decisions for governments. Early strategic applications are in energy- and power-generation industries that need long-term planning horizons and have major fixed-cost components on a large scale with considerable uncertainty. Because energy and power generation are fundamental in every economy, this use for derivatives offers mainline applications in both developed and developing countries. Option models can thus be important and insightful tools for implementing strategic objectives.

14.6 The Options-Based Approach versus DCF

In the previous sections we examined the options-based approach to valuing the equity and debt of a company, as well as valuing projects within a firm. However, in Chapters 9–13, we used the discounted cash flow (DCF) model to value debt and equity and projects. Each approach is a tool for analysis and each will be the "right" tool depending on the situation being analyzed. In this section we will look at different situations and discuss which valuation tool is most appropriate.

For valuing an entire firm (i.e., determining V as in Chapter 9), the DCF approach—estimating a company's expected future cash flows and discounting by the overall cost of capital—can be considered the most reasonable methodology to use. However, the DCF approach is a poor tool for valuing the components of capital structure (i.e., debt D and equity E) because the input required to use it is too complex. It requires a detailed knowledge of cash flows of each capital structure component over time, their fluctuations, and the impact of those fluctuations on the cost of capital of each component. In sharp contrast, the options valuation approach does not require estimates of either the cost of capital or the future expected cash flows.

For project valuation the most appropriate valuation method depends on the nature of the project. For projects whose characteristics are "fixed" in the future and not expected to change, the DCF model is a reasonable approach to valuation. However, for projects where the future is uncertain—such as our book/movie example above, where the risk of the project can change and decisions must be made based on how the project changes—then analyzing projects as real options using the BSM model is a more accurate approach.

Overall, it is important to keep in mind that there are multiple tools that can be used for any situation, and no one tool that uniformly works in every case, as stated in **Principle 4**: *Every model is an incomplete, simplified description of a complex reality.*

Conclusion

In this chapter we have examined a unified theory of valuation based on options that can be used to analyze financial securities that a company may use to fund itself as well as the projects that a company may invest in. We introduced how equity can be viewed as a call option on the assets of a company, and debt can be viewed as the combination of a riskless bond and a short put option. This insight allowed us to use option valuation tools as an alternative methodology for determining the value of a company's equity and risky debt. The insights of these option valuation tools also allowed us to better understand more about the debt structure of a company, such as why having a substantial amount of debt may introduce moral hazard, and how to analyze complicated debt structures involving multiple seniorities. The framework also allowed us to understand and analyze guarantees and other types of financial securities such as "hybrid securities."

The option-based framework also permitted us to value and analyze the assets of a company, including project decisions. These are known as real options, and involve decisions that companies may make in the future. We saw that the ability to make a project decision in the future can be viewed as an option, and this flexibility has value that is not properly incorporated into DCF analysis. The options framework allowed us to ascertain what that value is.

This chapter connected to the topics in Chapters 10, 11, and 13 by introducing a powerful new alternative framework that allowed us to explore the project and capital structure decisions introduced in those chapters in more depth. We will explore additional situations that incorporate options when examining company choices in Chapter 15, and further examine details of the options methodology—introducing another way to value options—in Chapter 19.

Takeaways

- Corporate financial structure can be analyzed using an options framework. Equity can be viewed as a call option on a company's assets, with a strike price equal to the principal amount of outstanding debt. Debt can be viewed as a combination of a riskless bond and a put option.
- Option pricing analysis provides an alternative means of determining the values of equity and debt, which is often more practical given DCF's complexity.
- More complicated financial structures, such as debt of different seniority, convertible bonds, and other financial claims, lend themselves to being analyzed with an options framework.
- An extremely important feature of investment projects to take into account is the ability of managers to delay the start of a project, or once started, to expand it or to abandon it. Failure to take account of these management options will cause an analyst evaluating the project to systematically and often materially underestimate its NPV.
- Recognizing the similarity between financial options and real managerial options is important for three reasons: (1) It helps in structuring the analysis of the investment project as a sequence of managerial decisions over time; (2) it clarifies the role of uncertainty in evaluating projects; and (3) it gives us a method for estimating the option value of projects by applying the quantitative models developed for valuing call options on stocks.

Key Terms

Collateral 424
Compound options 427
Conversion fee 425
Convertible bond 424
Debt overhang problem 417
Deferral option 427
Hybrid securities 407
Junior/subordinated debt 418
Moral hazard 416
Option to abandon 427
Option to rescale 427
Optionality 426
Options 406
Real options 407
Residual claimants 408
Risk shifting 416
Seniority 407
Shortfall 424
Switching options 427
Tranched securities 407

Key Equations

Equity value at debt maturity	$E_T = \max(V_T - B, 0)$	Eq. 14.1
Debt value at debt maturity	$D_T = \min(V_T, B)$	Eq. 14.2

Problems

1. Suppose Notaboek Tablets Company has a current market value balance sheet with $250 million. Suppose the highly leveraged company has its entire debt financed with a single issue of zero-coupon bonds with aggregate face value of $240 million. These bonds mature in one year. Use the Black–Scholes–Merton (BSM) model to calculate the aggregate market value of the firm's equity if the riskless interest rate is 8% and the standard deviation of the rate of return on the firm's assets is 10%.

2. Referring to Problem 1, suppose the company is stunned to learn that the government has just canceled a major supply contract. This immediately decreases the market value of Notaboek's assets while also increasing the standard deviation of the rate of return on the firm's assets. How do you expect this to impact on the equity value of the firm?

3. Consider a firm that has $50 million of debt outstanding due in one year. The firm's current total company value is $45 million, and its assets have a volatility of 20%. The current risk-free interest rate is 1%.
   (a) Draw a payoff diagram of the firm's debt and equity as a function of its total company value at the maturity of its debt.
   (b) What is the value of the firm's debt and equity?

4. Suppose a company's total value is currently $70 million, the volatility of its assets is 20%, and the company has senior debt outstanding with a principal amount of $50 million as well as junior debt outstanding with a principal amount of $100 million. All of the debt is due in one year. The current risk-free interest rate is 2%.
   (a) Draw a payoff diagram for the company's equity, junior debt, and senior debt as a function of the company's asset value at the maturity of the debt.
   (b) Using the BSM formula, what is the value of the company's equity?
   (c) Using any combination of put/call options, risk-free bonds, and the underlying assets of the company, recreate the payoffs from the junior and senior debt. Be sure to give the details of the individual positions.
   (d) What is the current market value of the senior debt?
   (e) What is the current market value of the junior debt?

5. Suppose that you are examining a company as a potential acquisition target. Your analyst did a DCF analysis, and you know that the company has a total value of $150 million. Your analyst looked at the numbers over time, and estimated that the volatility of its assets is 30%. You want to put in an offer to purchase all of the equity of the company, because that would give you control. The company has (zero-coupon) risky debt outstanding with a principal amount of $70 million. All of the debt is due in two years, and it all has the same seniority. The current risk-free interest rate is 4%.

   (a) Draw a payoff diagram of the company's equity and debt as a function of the company's asset value in two years (i.e., the maturity of the debt). Draw them on the same graph.

   (b) What is the value of the company's equity, given the amount of debt it has outstanding? You may use a BSM calculator.

   (c) Before you are able to make your offer to purchase the company's equity, the company announces that it is splitting its debt into two different seniorities. It will now have senior debt with an outstanding principal amount of $30 million, and junior debt with an outstanding principal amount of $40 million. Draw a payoff diagram of the company's senior debt and junior debt as a function of the company's asset value in two years. Draw them on the same graph.

   (d) You wonder whether the company's decision should affect your offer. What is the market value of the company's equity after the company splits its debt? Compare your answer to part (b), and explain.

   (e) What is the market value of the company's junior debt?

   (f) What is the market value of the company's senior debt?

6. Your company, Options Inc., is currently worth (has a total company value of) $100 million, and it currently has $100 million (par value) of total debt outstanding which is due in one year and is split between senior and junior debt—the senior debt has a par amount of $50 million and the junior debt also has a par amount of $50 million. The current risk-free interest rate is 2%. Suppose that you know the following put option prices (each has a maturity of one year and is based on an asset with the same current underlying value and volatility as Options Inc.):

Strike price K	Price of put option ($ millions)
$50 million	0.421
$100 million	14.743

   (a) Draw a payoff diagram of the company's equity as a function of the company's asset value in one year (i.e., the maturity of the debt).

   (b) Using the put–call parity, provide the prices of the equivalent call options in the above table (i.e., call options with strike prices of $K = \$50$ million and $K = \$100$ million, each with a maturity of one year and based on an asset with the same current underlying value and volatility as Options Inc.).

   (c) What is the value of the company's equity?

   (d) Draw a payoff diagram of the company's junior debt and senior debt as a function of the company's asset value in one year (i.e., the maturity of the debt). You may draw them on either the same graph or different graphs.

   (e) Using any combination of the underlying assets of the company, call options, put options, and risk-free bonds, replicate (i.e., copy) the payoffs of the junior debt and the senior debt. Be sure to specify the par amounts (for bonds) and strike prices (for options) that you use.

   (f) What is the value of the company's junior debt and senior debt?

7. Suppose that a biotech company has decided to raise money by only issuing convertible bonds with a total face value of $50 million. The terms of the bond are that in one year holders can choose to either be paid the face value or to convert the bonds into equity (for a conversion price equal to the face value of the bonds). The total assets of the company are currently worth $50 million and the risk-free interest rate is 5%.
   (a) Draw the payoff diagram of the convertible bonds as a function of the value of the company's assets in one year. (Assume that the company has no existing outstanding equity, so ignore any dilution effects with existing equity.)
   (b) How would you replicate (i.e., copy) the payoffs of the convertible bonds using risk-free bonds, put options, and call options? Be sure to mention the number of contracts, type of position (i.e., short or long), and the strike price of each contract that you would use.
   (c) If a call option on the company's assets with a strike price of $50 million is currently worth $10.896 million, and a call option on the company's assets with a strike price of $100 million is currently worth $1.582 million, what is the amount of money that the biotech company can raise with the convertible bonds (i.e., what is the value of the convertible bonds)?
   (d) Suppose instead that the company issued regular debt with a face value of $50 million. What would the value of this debt be? Which instrument allows the company to raise more money—regular debt or convertible debt? Why?

8. Suppose a company's total value is currently $100 million, the volatility of its assets is 10%, and the company has debt outstanding with a principal amount of $120 million that is due in one year. The current risk-free interest rate is 1%.
   (a) What is the value of the company's equity? Interpret this number.
   (b) Suppose that the company has a project investment opportunity with an NPV of $10 million, which thus would increase the total value of the company by $10 million. By how much would the value of the company's equity increase if it made this investment?
   (c) Suppose the project costs $2 million to invest in. The company decides to issue additional debt, which will be junior debt while the existing debt becomes senior debt. At what principal amount of junior debt would the company be able to raise enough money through junior debt to pay for the project?

9. Suppose that the current value of a company's operating assets is $100 million. The company has ten-year zero-coupon debt outstanding (the only debt it has) with a principal amount at maturity of $155 million. Its debt has a yield to maturity of 10%.
   (a) Draw a payoff diagram of the company's debt at maturity as a function of the value of its assets then. Be sure to label all relevant payoffs and axes.
   (b) Suppose that the government announces that the company is "too big to fail," so it will fully and unconditionally guarantee the debt of the subsidiary, meaning that the government will ensure that its bonds always pay off the full amount that they owe. Draw the payoff diagram of the company's debt with the guarantee included.
   (c) What is the value of the guarantee? You can assume a risk-free rate of 5%. (Hint: Calculate the value of the debt in part (a), and the value of the combined debt and guarantee in part (b). You can then infer the value of the guarantee based on those.)

10. Tony knows that, at any point in time over the next five years, he can close down half of his production facilities and liquidate the property, building, and equipment for a sum of $10 million. However, the value of the remaining operations would be adversely impacted and the decline in value would be 40%. Describe the option involved in terms of the underlying risky asset, the exercise price, the time to maturity, and the volatility.

11. Refer to the Electro Utility example in Section 14.4.2.2. What is the breakeven riskless interest rate for the project? What is the breakeven risk level for the plant?
12. Commercial banks make a significant share of their fee-based income from establishing precommitted lines of credit. In exchange for a fee assessed against the limit on the borrowing line, they guarantee to lend at a predetermined fixed or floating rate. From the borrower's point of view, what option position do they have, what is the underlying uncertainty, and what is the exercise price?
13. Suppose that company XYZ is a manufacturing company that builds microprocessors for mobile devices. Suppose that the company has the opportunity to invest in project A, which generates free cash flows of $1 million each year starting next year. The company's cost of capital is 10%. The project costs $11 million to undertake. Undertaking the project allows a follow-on investment in two years of $20 million, which then would likely generate a cash flow of $25 million in year 5. The nature of the investment is highly uncertain though, and it is estimated that its value fluctuates with a standard deviation of 40% per year. The risk-free interest rate is 2%.
    (a) What is the NPV of the two projects?
    (b) Calculate the value of the follow-on project as a real option, using the BSM formula. Based on this, is it optimal to invest in project A?
14. Your biotech company has the opportunity to invest in a new drug project. The project costs $10 million up-front to invest in. It is projected to generate free cash flows of $2 million per year (starting next year) for ten years, after which the patent expires and the cash flows will go to zero. The company's cost of capital is 20%.
    (a) What is the NPV of the project? Based on this NPV, should you undertake the drug project?
    (b) You discover that, if you invest in the project, you will have the opportunity to test the compound involved across new indications. Doing so will require a cost of $20 million in year 5. However, it is expected to yield a valuable patent which the company could sell for $25 million in year 6. What is the NPV of this follow-on project? Based on the combined NPV of the new drug project and the follow-on project, is it optimal to invest in these?
    (c) What is the value of the follow-on project as a real option? Suppose that the value of the follow-on investment fluctuates with a standard deviation of 50% per year, and the risk-free interest rate is 1%. Based on this, would you invest in the new drug project?
    (d) Suppose that you were mistaken about the volatility of the value of the follow-on project, and that it instead fluctuates only with a standard deviation of 30%. What is the value of the follow-on project as a real option now? Based on this, would you invest in the new drug project? If your answer to whether you would invest has changed, explain why.
15. Suppose Microstuff Corporation has the opportunity to invest in a new computer technology that would use television sets to connect to the internet. In the first phase an initial outlay of $100 million is required for a pilot project to determine the feasibility of the technology. In the second phase, one year from now, an additional investment of $1 billion would be required. Suppose that viewed from today's perspective the value of the project one year from now is a random variable with a mean of $1.1 billion. The required rate of return on the project is 10% per year. The standard deviation of the continuously compounded rate of return on this project is 0.2. The continuously compounded riskless interest rate is 5%. Use the BSM options pricing model to help determine whether this is a worthwhile investment.
16. Referring to Problem 15, what is the breakeven value for the riskless interest rate? What is the breakeven value for the risk of the project?

15 FINANCING OVER A FIRM'S LIFE

CHAPTER OVERVIEW

15.1	Life of a Firm and Financing Sources	441
15.2	Sources of External Private Firm Financing	443
15.3	Going Public or Staying Private	450
15.4	Mergers and Acquisitions	456
15.5	Bankruptcy and Liquidation	461

LEARNING OBJECTIVES

After reading this chapter, you will be able to:
- identify the sources that a company may use to obtain financing at different stages of its life;
- describe the institutional features of specific financing sources available to private firms, including venture capital and bank loans;
- discuss the main considerations a company faces in its decision to be privately or publicly owned;
- describe the reasons why companies merge, and the factors that contribute to the added value of mergers or acquisitions;
- explain the bankruptcy and liquidation process.

EQUATIONS YOU KNOW

Total company value (terminal value calculated as of $t = 4$)	$$V = \frac{FCF_1}{1+r_A} + \frac{FCF_2}{(1+r_A)^2} + \frac{FCF_3}{(1+r_A)^3} + \frac{FCF_4}{(1+r_A)^4} + \frac{FCF_5}{(1+r_A)^5} \cdots$$ $$= \frac{FCF_1}{1+r_A} + \frac{FCF_2}{(1+r_A)^2} + \frac{FCF_3}{(1+r_A)^3} + \frac{FCF_4}{(1+r_A)^4} + \frac{TV_4}{(1+r_A)^4}$$	Eqs. 9.4 and 9.6

Total company value using comparables (EV/EBITDA)	$V = EBITDA \times \left(\dfrac{EV}{EBITDA}\right)_{comparable}$	Eq. 9.2
Free cash flow	$FCF = EBIT \times (1-\tau) + \text{depreciation} - CapEx - \Delta NWC$	Eq. 9.5
After-tax WACC	$r_A^{after-tax} = \left[\dfrac{E}{V} \times r_E\right] + \left[\dfrac{D}{V} \times r_D \times (1-\tau)\right]$	Eqs. 9.11 and 13.8

✢ You have an innovative idea for a new type of pillow for pets. You need funds in order to finish the development, testing, and manufacturing of the pillow, and you do not have enough money in your personal savings. Where can you get the necessary capital?

✢ Your startup company has had a successful year in sales, and is looking to expand further. A venture capital firm approaches you and offers to provide $2 million in exchange for 60% ownership of the company. What are the considerations in deciding whether to accept this offer?

✢ You are the CEO of a large private company that manufactures shoes, and your CFO approaches you and advises you to take the company public in order to raise large amounts of capital, expand further, and highlight the brand's image more broadly. What are the costs and benefits of doing so?

✢ You run an electronics manufacturing company that makes tablets for consumers. You identify a firm that produces chips which could be adapted to your tablets and potentially streamline your manufacturing process. Should you acquire the firm, and what price should you pay for it?

✢ Your company has been struggling to make payments on its debt, and you predict that it will run out of cash by the end of the year. However, you think that the core business idea is viable if you can rearrange some operations and renegotiate debt payments. What can you do?

Introduction

In Chapter 13 we saw that the general choice of financing—debt or equity—affected overall firm value only due to frictions such as agency problems or asymmetric information. Debt and equity financing can come from many different sources in the financial system, and the institutional details of these sources can introduce important considerations for the firms seeking financing. In this chapter we explore the different sources of financing that may be available and/or feasible for firms to use at various stages of their lives: from new startup firms to mature and stable publicly traded corporations. Broadly speaking, the global financial system successfully meets the financial needs of the many different types of firms that operate in the economy. However, firms are constantly in flux, and as a result so are their financial needs. While the financial sources we discuss in this chapter continue to be important to the financial system, in response to the evolving nature of firms, new financial innovations and different ways of financing are always being introduced.

We open by giving an overview of the life of a company from when it is a new startup to when it matures into a larger firm, and how the ownership structure (private versus publicly traded) and financing sources may differ from one extreme to the other. We then begin our discussion by exploring the sources of financing that startup companies and other private firms have access to, including banks, venture capital, and alternative financing sources. After this, we describe the factors that may drive a private company to become a publicly traded company (and vice versa), the process by which they do so, and how the financing sources of publicly traded companies can differ from privately held ones. We then discuss mergers and acquisitions, which represent a potential key event in a firm's life, where it combines with another firm. We conclude the chapter by discussing the end of a firm's life—when it shuts down via bankruptcy.

15.1 Life of a Firm and Financing Sources

All firms originate as ideas by entrepreneurs. An entrepreneur may think of a new product, for example, and begin to make that product to sell to customers. The entrepreneur can form a startup firm to support the sales of the product, potentially allowing production and sales to increase. If the product is successful, the firm can continue to expand in size. Each year entrepreneurs across the world start millions of new businesses, as shown in Figure 15.1.

It is common for entrepreneurs to contribute their own personal wealth to finance a startup. However, this exposes the entrepreneur to substantial risk, and will likely not be sufficient when the firm grows. The profits a firm generates from sales may sometimes be sufficient to fund a company, but early-stage companies may not have any profits, and the investment costs of growing a company often outstrip the firm's profits.

This need for capital means that firms must often tap external sources of funding, and as they mature—grow larger and more established—their funding needs expand. However, as firms become larger and more mature, additional potential financing sources become available to them (Figure 15.2).

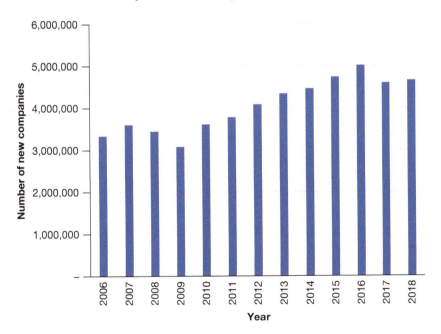

FIGURE 15.1 Number of new companies, 2006–2018. Each bar represents the total number of new registered limited-liability (or equivalent) firms in each year across all countries in the World Bank's database combined with new business formations in the United States. Each year, millions of new companies are formed worldwide.
Sources: United States Census and World Bank Entrepreneurship Database.

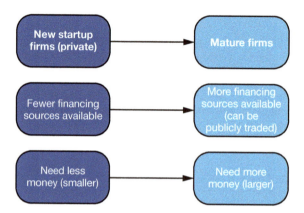

FIGURE 15.2 **Financing over a firm's life.** This figure shows financing sources and needs for firms at two different stages of their lives. The left side shows new startup firms, which are smaller and have fewer financing sources available. The right shows a mature firm at a later stage, which is larger and can be publicly traded, with more financing sources available.

In various life stages, firms may be *young*, at founding or the beginning of their existence, or *mature* and old or established, small or large, and privately owned or publicly traded. While all firms start as privately owned, as firms mature they may become publicly owned, which can be a key milestone in the life of a company. Private companies are usually owned by a small number of individuals or investors, and do not have access to public capital markets—stock and bond markets—to raise money; public companies are owned by many different shareholders, and may raise additional funds in the public financial markets.

Firms across the life spectrum, from small startup firms to large, mature corporations, can be private or public. For example, while many publicly traded firms have been in existence for decades—such as Microsoft, Toyota Motor Corporation, and Samsung Electronics—there are relatively young firms that are able to become public. There are also well-known and established large firms that choose to remain privately owned, such as Cargill (a US food and drink company) and Lush Retail Ltd. (a UK cosmetics retailer). As we cover in the sections to come, these traits influence the types of financing firms can obtain.

There tends to be a typical order to the type of financing from the beginning of a company's life to its end. At the start of their lives, firms tend to use the personal financial resources of their founders. When they grow and need external financing due to the founders' resources no longer being sufficient, firms often will turn to bank loans, which are available to private and public firms alike. In developing countries, where the financial system may not be as well established, "microfinance" organizations such as the World Bank provide loans to businesses for startup capital or investment. Once a private firm's business model has become more established and these sources alone may not be enough, firms may tap into sources of financing such as venture capital. Finally, firms that have grown to the extent that they need additional risk capital often become publicly traded, thus raising funds through financial markets. We discuss each of these throughout the rest of the chapter, highlighting the functional role that each source plays in providing funding to firms.

In the following section we begin by examining the various sources of external financing available to private firms. In Section 15.3, we will discuss the various considerations related to the choice between being private or public.

15.2 Sources of External Private Firm Financing

As discussed above, all new startup firms begin as privately held. Private firms are companies that are owned by a small number of individuals or investors, and do not have access to public capital markets. Both new startups run by entrepreneurs and larger, mature firms can be private. In this section we describe the sources of financing that are typically available to private firms, including bank loans, venture capital funding, and other smaller sources of financing.

15.2.1 Bank Loans

Private companies can access funding through borrowing, typically from banks, financial institutions that hold and lend money to individuals and businesses. Bank loans function in the same way as other types of borrowing, and are a common source of financing for both private and publicly traded companies across the world. A bank lends a firm money, and requires interest and principal to be paid back over time. A sample timeline of a typical loan is provided in Figure 15.3. Bank loans may be structured in a variety of different ways, with differing details regarding the maturity or term of the loan, the collateral required to secure the loan, and the form of the loan—for example, an amortized loan (money for specific needs in exchange for scheduled payments including principal and interest) or a line of credit (where businesses can flexibly draw upon a portion of a loan when needed).

Bank loans represent an important source of financing for firms, both public and private, as well as individuals. As of June 2023, the total amount of commercial bank loans in the United States totaled $17.3 trillion (values from Statista.com, 2023). In addition to financing, banks also provide valuable services such as check writing, safekeeping (through depository services), and providing financial advice. Financing through bank loans has a further advantage as it allows relationship lending. Relationship lending is when a bank knows a borrower through a previous loan and there is less asymmetric information about the borrower; as a result the bank lends more and charges a relatively lower interest rate. Trust can also be built through that relationship over time, thereby further facilitating credit, in line with **Principle 9:** *Transparency, verification, and trust are all important to the proper functioning of the financial system.* Banks collect "hard" information about a borrower's characteristics at the time of a credit application, such as credit scores, income, and assets. Relationship lending allows a lender to collect what is known as "soft" information, such as the borrower's preferences and perceived trustworthiness. This can be particularly beneficial for smaller private firms

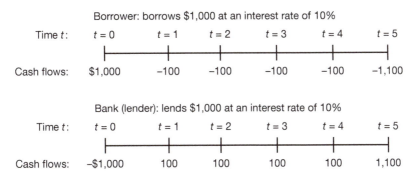

FIGURE 15.3 Sample timeline of a bank loan. This figure provides a sample timeline of a bank loan. The top timeline shows the cash flows from the perspective of a borrower that has borrowed $1,000 to be repaid in five years at an annual interest rate of 10%. The bottom timeline shows the cash flows from the perspective of the bank (lender) that has provided the funds to the borrower.

where outside investors know relatively little about the firm and would therefore offer more expensive financing terms to cover the risk. Bank loans allow flexibility compared to other forms of financing—for example, renegotiating the terms of a bond requires contract changes with (potentially many) investors that hold the bonds, while negotiations can be done with a bank directly. Banks can also monitor borrowers' operations—examining what the borrowers are doing to verify that the funds are being used properly—to the extent that they have information about the borrower.

One unique feature of bank loans is how banks can generate funds via qualitative asset transformation: Banks take money from bank deposits made by their account holders and turn it into loans. Banks can finance themselves through traditional debt and equity, like other firms; however, they also have access to the money (deposits) that individuals and firms (depositors) put into the bank via checking and savings accounts. Banks do not keep all deposits on hand as they typically do not need to meet all possible withdrawals at once, but rather they keep a portion of the money on hand and lend out the rest. Because of the relatively low interest rates that banks pay to their depositors, deposits represent a less-expensive source of financing than other forms of debt or equity (see, e.g., Merton and Thakor 2019). This resulting lower cost of funding means that banks have an increased willingness to provide credit or charge lower interest rates to firms or individuals seeking loans. Figure 15.5 shows the basic structure of qualitative asset transformation and the bank loan process.

In practice the institutional details of banks are complicated, and risks from the banking sector can affect the ability of firms to borrow money. We discuss this in further detail in Chapter 20. An extreme example is the global financial crisis of 2007–2009, which emanated from the financial system and caused sharp declines in both commercial and business credit, leading to reductions in investment and employment by firms. Such events are rare but represent important circumstances, and thus it is of importance to address the possibility of such events through means such as government policy to ensure the proper functioning of the financial system. Even outside such rare events as the financial crisis, there is evidence that reductions in loan supply by banks can have negative effects on

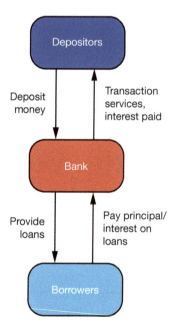

FIGURE 15.4 **The basic structure of banks.** This figure shows how banks work. A bank (center) receives money from depositors (top), and in exchange provides interest payments and transaction services. The bank uses those funds to provide loans to borrowers (bottom), who in exchange pay principal and interest on loans.

borrowing firms. Box 15.1 provides more details about the size and importance of the banking sector. However, the system typically functions well and successfully deploys great amounts of capital to the economy.

> QUICK CHECK 15.1 What are the features of banks that enhance their ability to lend to firms?

Box 15.1 World of Business: The Banking System

Banks held nearly $183 trillion dollars globally in assets as of 2021. The United States has the largest financial system in the world, which enables large amounts of capital to flow to businesses. As of the end of 2021, there were roughly 4,800 FDIC-insured commercial banks and savings institutions operating in the United States, with a total asset value of $23.7 trillion dollars. US banks collected a vast amount of money in deposits from both businesses and individuals—the total amount of domestic deposits as of the end of 2021 was around $18.2 trillion. The volume of deposits highlights the critical safekeeping function of banks for individuals and businesses. Banks had also extended $11.2 trillion in loans to businesses and individuals as of the end of 2021.

The amount of assets in the banking sector, as well as the amounts of loans, have been steadily increasing over time, as shown in Figure 15.5. From 2010 to 2022, total assets in the banking sector increased by $10 trillion, the amount of loans increased by almost $5 trillion, and the amount of deposits more than doubled from $7.8 trillion to $17.7 trillion. The magnitudes of these amounts highlight the functional role of banks in providing a large amount of funding to firms and individuals.

Academic research has also provided a wide range of evidence showing the importance of bank funding for the operations of all types of firms. As one example, Aghamolla et al. (2021) have shown that even important institutions such as hospitals rely on bank loans for financing, and a reduction in the availability of those loans can cause worse healthcare provision and even lead to increased mortality.

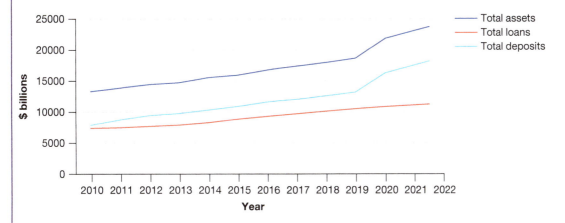

FIGURE 15.5 Assets in the banking sector, 2010–2022. This graph shows the amount of assets in the banking sector as well as the amounts of loans over time and how they have been steadily increasing.

Sources: Federal Deposit Insurance Corporation (FDIC) (various years). Statistics at a glance, historical trends. Statista (2024). Total assets of banks worldwide from 2002 to 2022. Aghamolla, C., Karaca-Mandic, P., Li, X., & Thakor, R. T. (2024). Merchants of death: The effect of credit supply shocks on hospital outcomes. American Economic Review, 114(11), 3623-3668.

15.2.2 Venture Capital

Venture capital (VC) is money provided by financial firms directly (i.e., not through a public market transaction) to entrepreneurs and companies. Venture capital firms, often referred to as VC funds, pool together investor money and use that money to invest, in exchange for ownership (equity) stakes and control rights. Venture capital represents a unique source of funding in that it brings not only money, but also often the management expertise of the venture capitalist to the entrepreneur.

Venture capital is a valuable funding source for private firms. The average (median) size of a VC funding round is $11 million, which can be a sizable amount for a small firm (Gompers et al. 2020). Also, the funds come in exchange for equity, avoiding the obligations of debt, such as regular repayments of interest and/or principal that can burden the firm's operations or even create costs of financial distress, as we discussed in Chapter 13.

In 2022 there were approximately 40,000 VC deals with a total value of $493.5 billion globally. The United States is the largest VC market, with a total deal value of $238.3 billion in 2022 over 16,000 deals. While the majority of new businesses do not receive VC funding, there is evidence that VC funding is an important source for many successful companies: VC-backed companies account for about 15% of industrial innovations, and 5–7% of US employment is generated by VC-backed companies. Furthermore, roughly 43% of public companies are VC-backed when they go public. This has included very successful companies such as Microsoft, Apple, Google, Amazon, Starbucks, and many others (see Gornall and Strebulaev 2015).

VC funds get money from general partners (GPs) and limited partners (LPs), as investors. General partners are sometimes referred to broadly as venture capitalists, and are the managers of the VC fund. They decide which companies to invest in, earning a fee for managing the pool of funding from LPs, and also put some of their own money into the fund (which helps to align incentives). Limited partners are outside investors that put their money into the fund, such as public/corporate pension funds, insurance companies, wealthy individuals, foundations, family offices, sovereign wealth funds, and so forth. Limited partners are paid a certain percentage of profits from the fund, and commit to investing in the fund for a specified period of time. Figure 15.6 depicts the structure of VC investments.

As any investors do, VC funds invest in firms in order to maximize their returns. They screen and select deals based on characteristics of the target firm and the market, such as the quality of

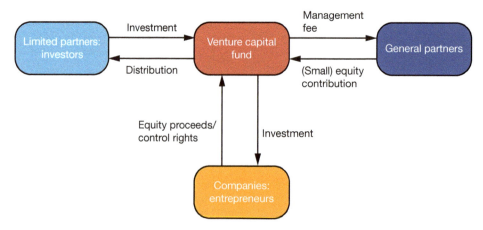

FIGURE 15.6 Venture capital investment structure. This figure shows the typical structure of a venture capital firm. The VC fund receives money from limited partners (left), and pays them with distributions. General partners (right) manage the fund in exchange for a fee and also provide some funds. Companies are run by entrepreneurs (bottom), and receive money from the VC fund in exchange for an equity stake.

management and the product, the size of the market, competition in the industry, and similar factors. They typically have an exit strategy, as they do not intend to hold their ownership stake indefinitely, but plan to sell their ownership shares in the future after the invested company has grown, often after an initial public offering (IPO).

Venture capital investments are typically done via staged financing, where not all the money is provided at once but portioned in stages over time. This protects the VC fund from some downside risk (and structures the VC investment as a real option, which we will introduce in Part III). The money is provided in exchange for both ownership stakes and control rights, which means that in specific circumstances (for example, not meeting profit targets), the VC fund may deny further funding or even take full control of the invested company (i.e., fire the entrepreneur). This introduces the potential for holdup problems, where agency issues create conflict between the VC fund and the entrepreneurs, causing investments to not be made. For example, the venture capitalist may disagree with viable business ideas and prevent them from going forward, and the entrepreneur may disagree with the VC and do the same. Entrepreneurs may also put in less effort if they see that the profits are mostly going to the VC firm.

Despite the potential for holdup problems, both the entrepreneur (or firm) and the venture capitalist benefit from VC investment. The entrepreneur can typically expect to receive not only funds from the venture capitalist, but also valuable expertise, experience, skill, advice (e.g., accounting, legal, etc.), and industry connections that can help the firm to grow and increase returns on investment. For example, a biotechnology startup that has a VC investor with experience in the biotech industry will receive added value as the VC firm can connect the startup to scientists, guide the firm in issues related to property rights, and help secure additional funding at terms that are appropriate for the industry. A venture capitalist can also serve as a disciplinarian, monitoring the entrepreneur and advising on changes in direction of the firm. As the venture capitalist performs these roles, it provides a natural synergy between the venture capitalist and the entrepreneur, which can also enhance the VC fund's decision about continuing or exiting at each stage of financing. Furthermore, with their equity stake, VC funds have skin in the game, but with staged financing they are not locked in. Staged financing provides option value via this flexibility (**Principle 8:** *Flexibility in financial decisions has value, and the greater the uncertainty, the greater the value*) to the venture capitalist, and enables many of the benefits that VC is able to provide.

The two main aspects of arranging VC deals is how the VC fund values the company that is asking for money and how the VC contracts are structured. That is, if a company asks a VC fund for $2 million, how much equity (ownership percentage) the VC fund will demand will be relative to their understanding of the firm's value, and subsequently, what sort of control rights will be included in the contract. The first step is the VC fund doing due diligence and assessing the value of the target company. A venture capitalist will determine the appropriate ownership stake to demand based on their calculation of the firm's value. If the venture capitalist determines that the firm's value is $10 million and the entrepreneur is asking for $2 million, then a 20% ownership stake may be appropriate in exchange for the $2 million, since $10 million $\times$ 20% = $2 million. Similarly, if the venture capitalist calculated a firm value of $6 million, then a 33% ownership stake in exchange for the $2 million may be appropriate. Thus, the venture capitalist's valuation of the firm is relevant for the entrepreneur asking for money—for example, if $2 million is needed to grow the business but the VC firm only values the company at $4 million, that would imply that the entrepreneur would need to give up half of the ownership of their company; this is not an appealing prospect! The discounted cash flow (DCF) valuation method (Chapter 9) and the options-based valuation method (Chapter 14) provide tools that a VC fund can employ to value a target.

Consider the DCF valuation method, where the target firm's value is determined by first projecting its future free cash flows (FCFs) up to a certain point in time (say, four years into the future), calculating a terminal value (*TV*), and discounting the FCFs by the appropriate cost of capital:

$$\begin{aligned} V &= \frac{FCF_1}{1+r_A} + \frac{FCF_2}{(1+r_A)^2} + \frac{FCF_3}{(1+r_A)^3} + \frac{FCF_4}{(1+r_A)^4} + \frac{FCF_5}{(1+r_A)^5} \cdots \\ &= \frac{FCF_1}{1+r_A} + \frac{FCF_2}{(1+r_A)^2} + \frac{FCF_3}{(1+r_A)^3} + \frac{FCF_4}{(1+r_A)^4} + \frac{TV_4}{(1+r_A)^4}. \end{aligned} \quad (15.1)$$

However, there are numerous challenges with implementing such a DCF model. First, the future cash flows may be particularly hard to predict, since the target firm is likely young and growing. Furthermore, the cash flows and growth estimates should reflect the VC fund's contributions not only of capital but also of intangibles such as advice and connections. The terminal value calculation should reflect the VC fund's exit strategy, but also may be difficult to calculate for the same reasons. Finally, models to calculate discount rates for private firms can be difficult to estimate, and as we know from **Principle 4**: *Every model is an incomplete, simplified description of a complex reality.*

Valuation by comparables (Chapter 9) uses data from similar/comparable companies along with information from the target firm in order to arrive at an estimate of value. One such piece of information, the enterprise value to EBITDA multiple (EV/EBITDA), provides an estimate of total company value:

$$V = \text{EBITDA} \times \left(\frac{\text{EV}}{\text{EBITDA}}\right)_{comparable}. \quad (15.2)$$

A VC fund may have knowledge of similar companies (perhaps in its own investment portfolio) from which it can pull a multiple. This method, however, presents its own set of challenges. For example, the target company may be a unique investment (which may be why the VC company is investing in the first place) that does not have good comparable companies. Furthermore, it is possible that the target company is not profitable yet, in which case using its EBITDA would produce a negative total value. The challenges with choosing and implementing an appropriate model further reflects **Principle 4**: *Every model is an incomplete, simplified description of a complex reality.* The choice of the appropriate model will therefore depend on the information available and the specifics of the investment. Box 15.2 provides a depiction of this valuation process in popular culture.

The second step in assessing a VC deal is to determine the details of the contract: the control rights afforded the VC fund, how many stages of investment to offer, etc. Tighter control rights can increase the potential for holdup problems, but can also protect the VC fund from downside risk, which includes not only the potential for failure, but also incentive and agency problems (such as entrepreneurs investing in bad projects), as discussed in Chapter 11. If a VC fund feels that there is a strong potential for such problems, then a restrictive contract may be beneficial. The inclusion of these terms may further motivate a venture capitalist to provide the funds that a young startup company needs to grow.

> **QUICK CHECK 15.2** What are the reasons why entrepreneurs would want to seek venture capital funding? Why would venture capitalists want to provide money to entrepreneurs?

> **Box 15.2** World of Business: *Shark Tank* and Venture Capital
>
> The business reality television show *Shark Tank*, which has run from 2009 until the present, has helped to popularize VC in the United States and across the globe. *Shark Tank* is the American franchise of the international format *Dragons' Den*, which has run in the UK since 2005 and is based on a format started in Japan. There are now franchises of *Shark Tank* or *Dragons' Den* in over 40 countries. In the show, a panel of four or five respected venture investors, known as the "sharks," listen to the pitches of entrepreneurs who are requesting a certain amount of money to grow their businesses. If any of the sharks think the idea is worth investing in, they then compete and provide deals to the entrepreneur: the money being asked in exchange for an ownership stake in the company. The basic structure of the show thus mirrors the basic structure of VC investments.
>
> As of 2013, the average statistics in these deals were: $182,000 raised (versus $210,000 requested by entrepreneurs), $466,000 valuation (versus $1 million requested by entrepreneurs), and a 39% equity stake (versus 20% requested by entrepreneurs). The deal amounts have increased over time while equity stakes have decreased over time: as of 2019, the average deal amount was $286,000 and average equity was 27%. The median valuation multiples were 4.2 times revenues and 10.0 times profits. How does this compare to traditional early-stage venture investment terms? An investment seed survey suggests that the monies raised outside *Shark Tank* were almost five times larger (giving the startups more resources to work with) at a valuation that was almost 13 times higher. So, instead of giving up 39% of their company, they would only be giving up to 15–30%. Granted there are differences in the types of deals, but there is still a large gap between *Shark Tank* and VC reality.
>
> Thus, *Shark Tank* is designed to make for good television, but it is not necessarily an accurate guide to what the normal VC fund-raising process looks like or where typical valuations end up. Contributing to this is the fact that contestants must make rushed decisions with a "now or never" mentality. However, *Shark Tank* is very good at helping the contestants get a national springboard for their brands and increasing awareness of their products.
>
> *Sources:* Deeb, G. (2013). Comparing "Shark Tank" to venture capital reality. *Forbes*. Crockett, Z. (2020). Shark Tank deep dive: a data analysis of all 10 seasons. *The Hustle*.

15.2.3 Alternative Sources of Financing

There are various other external financing sources available to private firms. Angel investors are typically high-net-worth individuals who invest an equity stake in a company. Angels are typically local investors, and entrepreneurs can encounter them through business or social networks (Prowse 1998). Angel investors are similar in concept to venture capitalists. A common difference is that angel investments are not structured as formally as VC investments: There tend to be fewer control rights issues, and financing is usually not staged. Furthermore, angel investors tend to provide less funding, in terms of absolute amounts, than VC funds.

Crowdfunding is very early-stage financing, where many different contributors provide small amounts of money. Entrepreneurs list their idea and funding goal on an online platform, and anyone on the platform can contribute money toward the goal. These investors typically do not get an equity stake in the company, but may gain some other type of nonpecuniary benefit from investing in the product or firm (such as early access to the product). A potential advantage of crowdfunding to entrepreneurs is that it can allow a "test" of the demand for the product: Not meeting stated funding goals typically does not allow the entrepreneur to raise enough money, which can signal that there is likely to be weak demand for the eventual product. Overall, crowdfunding can be an attractive source of equity-type financing for entrepreneurs, but it raises a much smaller amount of funding, which limits the usefulness of this type of funding for firms.

Credit from financial technology lenders (fintech lenders) is another alternative form of lending. Fintech lenders are financial companies that lend money but do not fund themselves with deposits (unlike banks). Such loans are typically initiated and extended via online platforms—for example, LendingClub and Prosper Marketplace. From a functional perspective, this form of lending is the same as bank financing—firms are borrowing money from lenders—but since they do not accept deposits these types of firms are not subject to the same regulations as banks. We discuss these issues in Chapter 20.

Finally, other types of financial innovations have emerged to provide financing to businesses and individuals who may not have access to the financing sources described above. In developing countries, microfinance has emerged as an innovation in the financial system that has expanded access to financial services by underserved populations. Microfinance refers broadly to financial services such as loans, insurance, savings, or fund transfers to small businesses or individuals that do not have access to traditional banking services. Such transactions can be similar to traditional loans, or can take the form of other repayment arrangements. Institutions providing microfinance services range from global financial institutions (such as the World Bank) to nonprofits and government agencies. While the amounts funded are smaller than other forms of financing (e.g., loans of less than $100 may be offered in developing countries), as of 2022, 173 million individuals and small businesses had used microfinance (Convergences 2023).

In this section we have provided an overview of the sources of financing that startups and other privately owned firms have access to. While these can be important sources of funding for firms, a firm may also be at the point in its life when these sources are insufficient to meet all of its financing needs. If that is the case, then a firm may decide to tap into external financial markets and become publicly traded. We discuss this in the next section.

15.3 Going Public or Staying Private

A critical juncture in the life of a firm is the choice of whether to stay privately owned or to "go public"—that is, to sell stock (and thus ownership shares) to outside investors.

Private ownership confers a number of advantages. First, there is less separation of ownership and control, and thus less reason to worry about agency costs, as described in Chapter 11. Second, public ownership requires reporting specific information, such as periodic financial reports filed with government agencies (e.g., the US Securities and Exchange Commission [SEC] or the European Securities and Markets Authority [ESMA]). This information is then public and available to competitors as well as investors and regulators, which can potentially be damaging to firms (e.g., Aghamolla and Thakor 2022a). Finally, public firms often have stringent governance rules and regulations—sometimes expected by investors and other times mandated by governments—that require them to file reports, conduct audits, and maintain internal controls in order to ensure investors that the firm's management is not engaging in fraudulent activities.

These disadvantages must be weighed against the advantages of access to public capital markets—stock markets as well as bond markets—which enable companies to raise large amounts of funds. In this section we describe this choice and the process of going public.

15.3.1 Initial Public Offerings

A private company issues stock to public shareholders for the first time in an initial public offering (IPO). The primary reason a firm does an IPO is that it increases the ability to obtain capital at a lower cost—firms gain access to equity markets, which allows the firm to raise larger amounts of capital at a fair price. This includes the initial proceeds from the IPO itself, which can be sizable, as well as setting up the opportunity to raise additional money in the future. After a firm has done an IPO and become publicly traded, at any point in the future it can sell additional new shares of stock to investors—called a seasoned equity offering (SEO)—in order to raise funds.

Other advantages of doing an IPO include the continuous confirmation of the firm's valuation through the ongoing trading of the company's stock, generating prices from willing buyers and sellers. This demonstrates **Principle 5**: *The best estimate of an asset's value is usually its market price, which incorporates valuable information to guide the allocation of resources and risks.* As well as value confirmation, being a publicly traded company can discipline management to focus on maximum value creation due to stock market corporate governance pressures, as we discussed in Chapter 11, and management "best practices," such as building positive employee compensation incentives and enhancing credibility with all stakeholders. Doing an IPO and receiving large amounts of capital can also help firms more effectively compete against competitors (see Aghamolla and Thakor 2022b). Finally, being publicly traded can help a firm receive better terms for debt financing, as more information is available to debtholders about the firm, both from required disclosures through financial reports and information generated through trading in the company's stock.

In an IPO, a firm offers a specific number of shares to investors at an offering price. The number of shares offered is based on the ownership portion it chooses to offer to outside investors. The offering price is determined with the help of a financial intermediary such as an investment bank, known as the underwriter, which also markets the shares to investors. The proceeds from the sale of those shares (net of any fees paid to the underwriter, which may be 6–7% of the proceeds) go to the issuing firm. Table 15.1 provides the typical anatomy of an IPO in the United States, which can be a

Table 15.1 The typical anatomy of an IPO. This table shows the usual process through which a firm does an initial public offering. The approximate timeline and events are based upon the process in the United States. The left column provides the date of each event relative to the start of the process. The right column shows the major events in the IPO process from beginning to end.

Event time (days)	Activity
<0	*"Bake off"*: Underwriter selection meeting. Multiple investment banks make presentations, and one is chosen.
0	*Organization "all hands" meeting:* Issuing firm underwriters, accountants, and lawyers meet to agree on terms of equity offering. "Quiet period" begins (management refrains from sharing information).
15–44	*Due diligence:* Underwriter interviews management, customers, suppliers, etc. Financials are reviewed.
45	*Registration (announcement) date:* Firm files registration statement with regulators (the SEC in the US case) announcing its intention to "go public."
45–75	*Regulatory review period:* Underwriter assembles a syndicate of investors and prepares the "road show."
50	Preliminary prospectus ("red herring") distributed.
60–75	*"Road show":* Underwriter and issuing firm management present offering to interested institutional and other investors.
99	Underwriter prices offering. Regulator gives final approval of registration statement.
100	Stock issued (IPO) and begins trading.
108	*Settlement date:* Underwriter distributes net proceeds to issuing firm.
After market	Underwriter may support new equity by acting as a market maker, providing "price stabilization."

time-consuming and resource-intensive process for a firm. The specific regulatory requirements for the IPO process vary between countries.

The price offered in the IPO determines the amount of money the offering firm stands to collect, but setting the appropriate price offers a challenge. A price that is too low "leaves money on the table": the firm may have been able to raise even more money for its investments and operations. In contrast, setting a price that is too high will not attract investors, and may also result in smaller proceeds than desired. Conceptually, underwriters set an offering price by implementing the types of valuation methods that we have described throughout the book; however, as discussed in Section 15.2, challenges exist for valuing IPOs. For example, determining proper comparable companies and estimating growth rates may be difficult if the company is a startup with a new market and no comparable companies or competitors. The high-profile IPO of eBay, discussed in Box 15.3, highlights some of these issues.

Initial public offerings represent a significant cash inflow for firms. For example, in the United States the median IPO size in 2021 was roughly $180 million (values from Statista 2023); in 2021 total proceeds of IPOs was roughly $119 billion in the United States (Figure 15.7). This latter figure reached $184.3 billion globally. Figure 15.7 depicts the number of US IPOs and total proceeds since 2009. The magnitude of these numbers underscores how effectively the IPO process deploys large amounts of capital to firms.

As Figure 15.7 shows, the number of IPOs and proceeds increased sharply in 2020 and 2021. This spike is reflective of the recent trend of using Special Purpose Acquisition Companies (SPACs). SPACs, also called "blank-check" companies, are shell companies set up by (typically experienced) investors (private equity firms, hedge funds) which do not contain any assets. SPACs go public through an IPO, with the explicit intention of finding a private company to acquire. Investors that purchase the stock of SPACs at their IPO are therefore placing their money in the hands of the investors operating the SPAC, and betting that the SPAC management team acquires a good target. After acquiring the company, the SPAC itself dissolves and the acquired company therefore becomes a public company. In

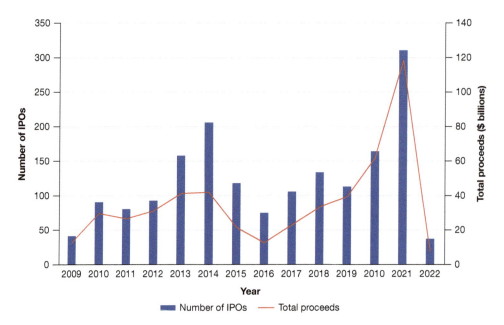

FIGURE 15.7 Annual IPO transactions and proceeds. This figure provides the number and total proceeds of US IPOs each year from 2009 to 2022.
Source: Ritter, J. R. (various years). IPO data. Warrington College of Business.

2020 and 2021, SPACs accounted for the majority of IPO funding. One reason that has been proposed for the popularity of SPACs is that they allow companies to go public and also bypass many of the expensive and burdensome regulations involved in the IPO process, including the need to disclose information during the IPO process. In response, regulators have placed additional scrutiny on SPACs and there has been a reduction in their popularity. The drop in IPOs in 2022, as shown in Figure 15.7, is reflective of the smaller number of SPACs, combined with an uncertain economic outlook and high inflation.

> QUICK CHECK 15.3 What are the reasons why a firm may do an initial public offering?

Box 15.3 World of Business: eBay's IPO

In the 1990s, online companies were in their infancy. By the late 1990s, there was a proliferation of new online companies, and many of them carried high stock market valuations reflecting investors' expectations of future growth. However, the majority of these companies had not yet generated profits. For example, Amazon was founded in 1995, but did not deliver positive profits until 2002. In 1998, eBay was one of the few profitable online companies. In 1999 it made the decision to go public through an IPO. Filings indicated that, as of 30 June 1998, it had an operating profit of $2.7 million and revenue of $14.9 million. A challenge to the pricing of the IPO was the lack of suitable comparable firms (i.e., profitable online companies) and the uncertainty about eBay's future growth prospects.

Goldman Sachs, the lead underwriter, priced the IPO at $18 per share in September 1998, which seemed high at the time in light of comparables analysis. However, the stock opened trading at $53.50 and closed the first day at $47.38. This represents a 160% price gain for those who bought the IPO at the offer price, and despite a 1.87% drop in the Dow Jones Industrial Index on the same day. John Fitzgibbon, the editor of the *IPO Reporter*, remarked that "You really don't justify the market cap. Investors are really caught up in the sizzle of eBay's steak without any of the meat."

The total proceeds for the IPO for eBay were $67 million. In the short term, eBay continued to do well, with its stock price rising roughly 700% to $323 per share in the six months following the IPO.

Source: Burnett, J., and Schill, M. J. (1998). Ebay Inc.

15.3.2 Going Private and Private Equity

While there are many advantages to being a public company, a firm may decide that the costs of remaining public outweigh the benefits, and thus may decide to go private—that is, no longer having its equity being freely sold to investors and traded in stock markets. This may be because the company no longer needs the funds that can come from public capital markets, or because the company finds the regulatory requirements of being a publicly traded corporation to be too costly. For example, in 2002 the United States passed the Sarbanes–Oxley Act (SOX) as an effort to reduce accounting fraud, which required compliance with new auditing and reporting requirements. The costs of these requirements are significant, and academic research has shown that these costs induced some public firms—particularly smaller public firms—to consider going private (Kamar et al. 2009; Leuz et al. 2008).

Going-private transactions involve a company delisting from public stock exchanges and the government regulator (such as the SEC) that supervises publicly listed companies, and retiring its publicly traded stock. If a company is able to organize a shareholder vote to agree to the action, the company can then retire its publicly traded stock by paying current stockholders an amount per share (sometimes referred to as a liquidating dividend). If the company does not immediately have enough votes to convert to private ownership, it may opt to buy back shares of stock via a tender offer in order to meet the necessary vote threshold.

While companies themselves are often the ones to decide whether to do an IPO or revert to being private, the decision is sometimes also caused by financial firms—private equity firms—that invest in companies and make operational decisions. A private equity (PE) firm is a financial fund that raises money from investors, and invests that money in companies through equity stakes with an exit strategy in mind, with the goal of maximizing profits from the investment. They tend to invest in more mature companies as opposed to early-stage companies, which are often the investment targets of VC firms and tend to take more (and often complete) control of their target companies. Figure 15.8 depicts trends in the total number and value of PE deals worldwide—in 2021, the total value of PE deals reached $1 trillion, with an average deal size of $1.2 billion; this reflects how significant the actions of PE firms are in financial markets.

Broadly speaking, PE firms undertake two main types of strategies: (1) They invest in private firms, take over operations, and sell later on; or (2) they invest in public firms with the purpose of taking them private and following the same process as strategy 1. First, they invest in the equity of developed small and mid-sized private firms, often taking complete ownership and aiming to improve management and operations. Thus, PE firms are a potential source of financing for private firms, but often at the owners' expense of losing control of the company. After a PE firm invests in the target company and makes operational improvements (thus generating profits), the PE firm realizes a return by selling its stake to another firm or taking the target firm public through an IPO. The profits are distributed to the PE firm's investors net of fees.

A second PE strategy is to invest in the equity of publicly traded firms, take operational control of the firms, and then take them private. With direct control the PE firm can then improve the target

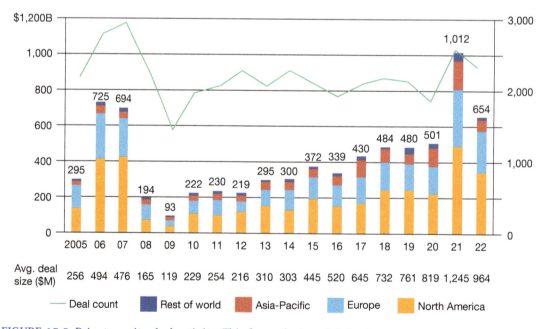

FIGURE 15.8 **Private equity deal activity.** This figure depicts global private equity deals from 2005 to 2022. The bars show the number of deals, split by region: Asia-Pacific, Europe, North America, and the rest of the world. The green line shows the number of deals in each year.
Source: Bain & Company (2023). Global private equity report 2023.

company's performance and does not have to deal with various issues related to public companies, such as governance or agency problems, or reporting and regulatory burdens. After improving the company's operations, the PE firm then exits its investment by selling its stake, often through taking the company public again.

Private equity serves a number of functional roles. For example, as we discussed in Chapter 11, one aspect of being public is agency problems between managers and other stakeholders, especially shareholders. Since PE firms often buy the entirety of target firms in order to gain control, this eliminates the agency problems related to being public. Also, there can be times when the economic function of a firm no longer works; that is, management is mismanaging the firm. Private equity can potentially improve operations as a type of activist shareholder (see discussion in Chapter 11). Sometimes it is also optimal to downsize or simply shut down firms, and PE firms can perform that economic function.

A common way for PE firms to purchase companies is through a leveraged buyout (LBO). An LBO occurs when a PE firm funds the purchase of a company using significant amounts of debt. The debt is collateralized by the assets of the target firm, and the interest and principal payments of the debt are paid using the cash flows from the target firm's operations. It is common for LBOs to result in leverage ratios (i.e., D/V) of 90% or higher as a percentage of total assets. There are a number of reasons why PE firms utilize LBOs. First, an LBO allows the PE firm to take advantage of the benefits of debt, such as the debt tax shield. Second, an LBO allows for risk shifting, discussed in Chapter 13. By taking on significant amounts of debt, the equity stake of the target company (which the PE firm owns) gets riskier, and the required rate of return increases. However, the PE firm is exposed to little of the downside risk: Since the debt is secured by the assets of the target firm and paid through the target firm's cash flows, the PE firm itself does not bear the brunt of the risk.

The institutional features, as well as the profit maximization goal, of PE raises an important question: Do PE firms add value to the companies they acquire and control? On the one hand, the goal of profit maximization can lead PE firms to make operational improvements to firms. For example, academic research has demonstrated that PE-owned restaurants are cleaner, safer, and better maintained compared to equivalent non-PE-owned restaurants (Bernstein and Sheen 2016). There is also research that has suggested that PE-owned hospitals experienced increased income and some improvements in care quality. On the other hand, other research has suggested that the profit maximization objective can cause PE ownership to lead to worse outcomes. For example, PE-owned universities have been shown to charge higher tuition, have lower graduation rates, and deliver worse education quality (Eaton et al. 2020). Recent evidence has suggested that PE-owned nursing homes take a greater advantage of government subsidies, but have higher mortality rates, suggesting worse care quality (Gupta et al. 2024). Furthermore, there may be negative spillover effects from PE investments; recent research has provided evidence that acquisitions of hospitals by PE firms lead to higher healthcare costs. Thus, the effect of PE ownership on the quality of firm products and services is an open question, and may depend in part on the details of the particular firm.

In this section we examined the decision of a privately held company to become publicly traded and able to tap into capital markets. We also discussed how sometimes publicly traded firms may revert back to being privately owned. Private equity firms can play a role in both decisions through their strategy to invest and take operational control of companies. We will now look more broadly at the decision to acquire another company (as was the case with private equity) or combine with another company, which often represents an important milestone in a company's life.

> QUICK CHECK 15.4 What is a leveraged buyout? Why is it common for PE firms to acquire companies in this manner?

15.4 Mergers and Acquisitions

At various points in a firm's life, a firm may merge with another firm by acquiring or being acquired. For the firm doing the acquisition, acquiring another firm can offer a way to supplement its assets—for example, an acquisition may allow a firm to procure project infrastructure belonging to an acquired firm that supplements its operations. For a target firm, being acquired may enable it to expand further and/or faster. For example, as we discussed in the previous section, acquisitions by PE firms constitute a potential source of financing for target firms. Also, the operations of a private firm can potentially expand after being acquired by a publicly traded firm, as the public firm's capital market financing can be deployed to expand the operations of the private firm.

A merger and acquisition (M&A) transaction is when two companies combine. The combination can be one that results in a new company that combines aspects of the operations of both companies, which is considered a merger, or when one company purchases another and absorbs the target's operations, which is known as an acquisition. Companies typically initiate M&A transactions after they have reached the middle (flat growth) phase of their life. In other words, a company seeking to acquire another company will typically not be an early startup, but a middle- or mature-stage company seeking future growth potential. M&A is often viewed as a tool to fill strategic holes (e.g., pursuing growth, diversifying an asset profile, or expanding the geographic footprint).

In an M&A, an acquiring company must purchase enough equity in the target company to gain operational control. For privately held targets, acquiring firms must present an offer to the controlling parties in exchange for their equity stakes. For publicly traded targets, an acquiring company will typically be unable to purchase a significant enough equity stake through an open-market stock purchase—that is, by buying stock from those that were already trying to sell—to gain control because shares of stock are numerous and spread across many different shareholders, not all of which are looking to sell. As a result, acquiring firms must usually convince shareholders to sell their stakes by presenting a tender-offer purchase, where the target company shareholders are given the opportunity to sell their shares for a price above the current market price of the target. The amount by which the offer price exceeds the current market price is called the acquisition premium; the average premium is between 20% and 30% of the current market price. Why would an acquiring firm be willing to pay an above-market price for a target? Typically, because the acquiring company believes that the operations and/or assets of the target will increase the firm's value when combined with the acquiring company, which is known as synergy. Synergy is the value derived from benefits produced by combining two companies.

The price offered by the acquiring firm relative to the other measures of value for a firm is shown in Figure 15.9. The market value of a target firm is the current price assessed by the market, and is typically higher than the book value of the firm (which is the historical cost of the firm's assets) due to firm growth. For firms that are run properly by management, the market value of a firm is also higher than the liquidation value of a firm, which is the value of the firm's assets when sold separately (i.e., the value obtained by selling off its component parts). This is because the firm's assets when put together and run by management's strategy generates value over the stand-alone value of those assets. However, if a company is run poorly, it is possible that the value of the assets when put together becomes negative and the liquidation value of a company is higher than the market value. In that case, as we described in Chapter 11, it is possible for an acquirer to profit by purchasing the firm at the market price, dissolving the firm, and then selling off the assets individually.

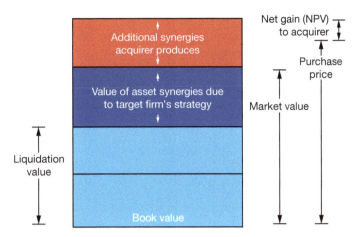

FIGURE 15.9 M&A acquisition price. This figure depicts the price for acquiring a company. Each portion of the rectangle represents a factor that contributes to the value of a company. The bottom light blue rectangle is the book value, the historical cost of the firm's assets. The bottom two light blue rectangles combined represent the liquidation value of the company, which is the market value of the assets sold individually. The dark blue rectangle represents the added value from combining the firm's assets together under the firm's management, which when added to the other rectangles gives the market value of the company. The red rectangle represents the synergy value the acquisition target gives to the acquirer. The purchase price must be above the market value. For the acquisition to be value-added, the purchase price must be below the combined value of the rectangles.

The red portion of Figure 15.9 represents the additional value that the acquisition would produce due to synergies. Since an acquirer must pay a price above the current market price, the key to an acquisition that adds value to an acquiring firm (i.e., a positive-NPV acquisition) is to set the purchase price above the market value of the target but also below the market value plus the synergies that the acquisition generates. If the purchase price is set too high—that is, above the red portion of the figure—the acquisition will have a negative NPV and decrease firm value. Determining the appropriate acquisition price is easier when the M&A transaction is between two companies that are publicly traded, since there is market information about the value of the companies (reflecting **Principle 5:** *The best estimate of an asset's value is usually its market price, which incorporates valuable information to guide the allocation of resources and risks*); determining the appropriate price is more difficult with private companies.

A merger may decrease firm value if the acquiring firm overestimates the synergies that come from the merger, and thus overpays (sets too high a purchase price). In some cases, the synergy value between firms in an M&A can even be negative—for example, M&A transactions between firms with disparate operations or a mismatch between the firms' cultures, as discussed in Box 15.4. Thus, the correct valuation and the correct choice of valuation model (as we emphasized with **Principle 4:** *Every model is an incomplete, simplified description of a complex reality*) is critical for successful acquisitions. Conceptually, an appropriate valuation model will allow an acquirer to:

1. determine the correct market value of the target firm as a stand-alone entity, if we cannot observe or affirm the market price;
2. determine the value of the target firm given any post-acquisition improvements or synergies; and
3. set an offer price in between these two values.

Applying the valuation model for (b)—determining the value of a firm post-acquisition—is often the step that acquiring firms get wrong because it requires the application of a valuation model with different assumptions and furthermore an estimation of what value may be added in the future.

To illustrate the correct valuation procedure of an M&A deal, consider the DCF valuation model we introduced in Chapter 9, where we would first determine the FCFs and WACC of a target firm:

$$\text{FCF} = \text{EBIT} \times (1 - \tau) + \text{depreciation} - CapEx - \Delta NWC, \tag{15.3}$$

$$r_A = \text{WACC} = \left[\frac{E}{V} \times r_E\right] + \left[\frac{D}{V} \times r_D \times (1 - \tau)\right]. \tag{15.4}$$

We would then discount the free cash flows by the WACC, incorporating a terminal value calculation with a long-term growth rate g (let us assume that we are projecting out cash flows five years into the future, and then calculating the terminal value):

$$\begin{aligned} V &= \frac{FCF_1}{1+r_A} + \frac{FCF_2}{(1+r_A)^2} + \ldots + \frac{FCF_5}{(1+r_A)^5} + \frac{FCF_6}{(1+r_A)^6} + \ldots \\ &= \frac{FCF_1}{1+r_A} + \frac{FCF_2}{(1+r_A)^2} + \ldots + \frac{FCF_5}{(1+r_A)^5} + \underbrace{\frac{1}{(1+r_A)^5} \times FCF_5 \times \left(\frac{1+g}{r_A - g}\right)}_{\text{terminal value}}. \end{aligned} \tag{15.5}$$

Since the value of a firm's equity is the focus in M&A transactions, a final step would be to determine the value of equity by subtracting the value of debt from V (e.g., $E = V - D$), and then the price per share by subsequently dividing E by the number of shares outstanding.

How does an acquiring firm incorporate improvements and synergies into the valuation calculation, in order to determine an appropriate upper limit on the offer premium? Projected improvements in sales could factor into Equation 15.4, resulting in increased free cash flows through a higher EBIT. The acquiring firm could also anticipate that synergies will increase the long-run growth rate of free cash flows, g, which factors into the terminal value calculation. Alternatively, the acquiring firm may choose to change the capital structure applied to the target firm—for example, increasing leverage and thus taking advantage of the debt tax shield, and lowering the WACC in Equation 15.4. An acquiring firm that overestimates these effects is more likely to end up with an M&A transaction that decreases firm value, while a firm that correctly incorporates these effects is more likely to create an M&A transaction that increases firm value.

> QUICK CHECK 15.5 Consider the DCF valuation model in Equation 15.5. How might overestimating synergies affect the inputs into calculating the model?

15.4 MERGERS AND ACQUISITIONS

Example 15.1 (Assessing an Offer Price): Your company is a beverage distributor, and is examining a bottle manufacturing firm to acquire. The firm anticipates the following free cash flows (in millions of dollars) over the next three years:

Year (t)	1	2	3
Free cash flow	20	30	40

After year 3, it anticipates that its free cash flows will grow at a rate of 1% per year. You determine that the appropriate discount rate for the target firm is 10%. You further expect that, due to synergies between the two companies, the long-run growth rate is likely to increase to 2%.

The target bottle manufacturing firm has $100 million in debt (market value), and has ten million shares outstanding. What would be an appropriate range for an offer price to acquire the bottle manufacturing firm?

Solution. We must first calculate the share price of the target company as-is, and then the share price incorporating synergies. The appropriate target price will lie in between the two prices.

To calculate the share price of the target company now, discount the free cash flows, calculating the terminal value, to determine the total company value:

$$V = \frac{FCF_1}{1+r_A} + \frac{FCF_2}{(1+r_A)^2} + \frac{FCF_3}{(1+r_A)^3} + \frac{1}{(1+r_A)^3} \times FCF_3 \times \left(\frac{1+g}{r_A - g}\right)$$

$$= \frac{20}{1.10} + \frac{30}{1.10^2} + \frac{40}{1.10^3} + \frac{1}{1.10^3} \times 40 \times \left(\frac{1.01}{0.10 - 0.01}\right)$$

$$= \$410.285 \text{ million.}$$

The equity value of the firm is found by subtracting the amount of debt:

$$E = V - D = 410.285 - 100 = \$310.285 \text{ million.}$$

Since there are ten million shares outstanding, the price per share is given by $310.285 million/10 million shares = $31.03 per share. This is the lower bound of the offer price that your company can set to acquire the bottle manufacturer.

Now, when incorporating synergies, the growth rate g increases to 2%. Redoing our calculations with this number gives:

$$V = \frac{FCF_1}{1+r_A} + \frac{FCF_2}{(1+r_A)^2} + \frac{FCF_3}{(1+r_A)^3} + \frac{1}{(1+r_A)^3} \times FCF_3 \times \left(\frac{1+g}{r_A - g}\right)$$

$$= \frac{20}{1.10} + \frac{30}{1.10^2} + \frac{40}{1.10^3} + \frac{1}{1.10^3} \times 40 \times \left(\frac{1.02}{0.10 - 0.02}\right)$$

$$= 456.198 \text{ million.}$$

The equity value of the target company in this case is $E = V - D = 456.198 - 100 = \$356.198$ million. With ten million shares outstanding, the price per share incorporating synergies is $356.198 million/10 million shares = $35.62 per share.

Your company can therefore set a target offer price between $31.03 and $35.62 per share, and the transaction will have a positive NPV.

> **Box 15.4** World of Business: Culture and M&As

Culture is an important consideration related to potential synergies between two companies merging. Culture is often defined as the "unwritten rules" and "norms" of behavior that determine how people behave even outside the explicit incentives produced by contracts (e.g., whether employees are collaborative, creative on their own, strictly regimented/disciplined, etc.). Why is culture important in M&A deals? One reason is because many target company employees will leave if they do not fit into the acquirer's culture, resulting in a loss of institutional memory and human capital. Furthermore, cultural mismatch can result in lower productivity in the combined company if, for example, employees do not communicate or work together effectively. Culture can also affect financial returns in other ways, such as the amount of risk a company is willing to take and its target capital structure.

The majority of mergers "fail" in the sense that they produce negative subsequent returns, and many of these failures have been attributed to cultural mismatch. Underscoring this, an analysis (Cameron and Mora 2003) has been conducted of 106 company mergers over a ten-year period. The Capital Asset Pricing Model (CAPM) (which we discuss in Chapter 18) was used to measure the success of the merger. Successfully merged companies were defined as achieving over 20% above expected financial returns (relative to what the CAPM predicted), and unsuccessfully merged companies as achieving worse than −20% below expected financial returns. Using only a measure of organizational culture, it was possible to predict the successful and the unsuccessful mergers 96 percent of the time. The study concluded that corporate culture is important to keep in mind in M&A deals, because it can directly affect the financial returns (through enhancing or reducing synergies) that are possible. Other research has reinforced the role of culture in M&A performance. For example, Bereskin et al. (2018) find that companies with similar cultures that merge experience greater synergies and better long-run operating performance.

There are many individual examples of culture-based M&A failures and successes. In 1999, America Online (AOL), an internet service, search engine, and email provider, and Time Warner, an American cable television company, merged to form a combined company. However, the merged company never integrated the cultures of the two companies, and the quality of their product suffered in the market. The merger was widely considered one of the most high-profile M&A failures of all time.

Another example of a culture-based failure was the combination of two large automobile brands in 1998—Daimler-Benz (the makers of Mercedes-Benz cars) and Chrysler (the makers of Chrysler, Dodge, Jeep, and Ram brands). Daimler effectively paid $36 billion (a 33% premium) for Chrysler in a "merger of equals," forming a combined company called Daimler-Chrysler. Chrysler was sold a few years later to Cerberus Capital Management, a PE firm, for $500 million. To put the value dissipation in a different perspective, Daimler's equity was worth $51 billion in market value and Chrysler's equity was worth $27 billion at the time of the merger. Just 15 months later, the combined company Daimler-Chrysler was worth only $48 billion. Despite the potential operation synergies between two car manufacturers, the cultures of the two companies were a bad fit—Chrysler had a more open and free-wheeling culture, while Daimler had a more traditional top-down culture. This filtered through to the products that customers saw, resulting in lower customer satisfaction for the cars produced by the combined company.

However, there are also examples of successful culture-based mergers. One example is the oil companies British Petroleum (BP) and Amoco. The merger was a success, with the companies taking what was best in each company's cultures (even though they were a bit different) and blending them together. For example, the BP performance management process and Amoco capital allocation and budgeting process were adopted. Beyond this, the merged company encouraged employees of both companies to socialize and work together.

Sources: Bradt, G. (2015). The root cause of every merger's success or failure: culture. *Forbes*. Cameron, K. S., and Mora, C. M. (2003). Corporate culture and financial success of mergers and acquisitions. University of Michigan Business School. Bereskin, F., Byun, S. K., Officer, M. S., and Oh, J.-M. (2018). The effect of cultural similarity on mergers and acquisitions: evidence from corporate social responsibility. *Journal of Financial and Quantitative Analysis*, 53(5): 1995–2039.

15.5 Bankruptcy and Liquidation

One possible outcome in a firm's life is to cease operations. This may occur voluntarily, for example, when the sole owner of a privately owned firm decides to retire and shut down operations rather than attempting to transfer them to a new owner. It can also occur involuntarily, when a firm cannot generate revenues that meet or exceed their expenses. For example, a firm's product market strategy may not generate the sales that were anticipated, and the firm cannot afford to pay the required interest payments on its debt. When a firm cannot meet its financial obligations, it is usually pulled into bankruptcy proceedings, a legal process to resolve the state of the company's operations.

In such situations, a firm may liquidate, which involves ceasing all operations and selling off any remaining assets via the legal court proceedings involved with liquidation. These are referred to generally as liquidation proceedings in countries around the world; in the United States they are referred to as chapter 7 bankruptcy. Through the court's guidance, the firm's assets are sold off and the proceeds used to pay off any debtors of the firm. Liquidation bankruptcy is often used when the firm does not have a viable way to change its operations in order to be successful. For example, many small businesses are created solely around the sales of a single product. If such a product is a commercial failure, then there may not be avenues to save those businesses. Debtholders can often expect to be paid less than they are owed in such proceedings. Oftentimes, the firm does not have enough cash on hand to pay off debtors (since that is why the firm is in bankruptcy in the first place), and the sales of assets may also not generate sufficient funds. In some cases, assets may be specialized for the particular firm, with few outside users being willing or able to pay for them, leading to the assets being sold at a discount. Furthermore, court and legal fees can be substantial, and must be paid before debtholders are paid.

An alternative option is for a firm to attempt to reorganize itself through the bankruptcy process, in which case the firm enters into court proceedings with the aim of reorganizing its operations and debt obligations. This is generally known as restructuring, and laws (and terms) vary across countries; the process is known in France as the rescue procedure, administration in the UK, and chapter 11 bankruptcy in the United States. In a chapter 11 bankruptcy and similar procedures in other countries, a firm must also submit a plan of reorganization, detailing the changes it will make in order to turn itself around and become successful. These changes may include selling off some assets, downsizing, shifting operational focus, etc. Debtholders may work with the firm and accept a reorganization plan because it increases the likelihood that they will be paid what they are owed; if a firm successfully turns itself around, debtholders may be repaid in full. However, debtholders must work with the firm and the court to agree upon a restructuring plan, and renegotiation of debt repayment terms or other contracts. If a firm has many debtors, this can present a challenge, as debtors may object to certain plans or disagree with each other or the firm. This can also cause proceedings to be lengthy, increasing the direct costs of bankruptcy (i.e., continued interest payments, court fees, etc.). Indeed, in the event that chapter 11 or administration bankruptcy proceedings are not successful, a firm's debtors may push the case into converting to liquidation or chapter 7 bankruptcy and liquidate the firm.

Filing for bankruptcy offers protection for firms in the sense that required payments and other contractual obligations are "paused" during the bankruptcy proceedings. Each year, a substantial number of new businesses file for bankruptcy; at the same time, hundreds of thousands of new businesses start up each year.

> **QUICK CHECK 15.6** What is the difference between chapter 7 and chapter 11 bankruptcy for a business?

Conclusion

In this chapter we have explored sources of financing over the life of a firm, from when it is a new startup to a larger mature firm. We first went over sources that are available to privately owned firms, which include startup companies. These include bank loans, VC financing, and others. We then discussed the choice of a firm in deciding to become publicly traded through an IPO—and being able to tap into broader capital markets—or being privately owned. An important possible event in the life of a firm includes when two firms are combined through an M&A, and we discussed the conceptual framework behind that decision. Finally, many firms end their lives by becoming bankrupt, and formal legal proceedings are in place in countries around the world to deal with this.

In previous chapters in Part II we discussed at a general level how firms make financing choices, such as the choice between debt and equity, and how that influences firm value. This chapter directly connects to those considerations, but examines at a more detailed level specific *sources* of debt and equity financing, institutional details about them, and important considerations firms need to take into account when choosing these sources.

Takeaways

- Startup firms may be able to use sources of funds such as the entrepreneur's own wealth, but when a firm grows to a certain size this will generally not be enough. Firms must therefore turn to external sources of funding.
- Private companies are owned by a small number of individuals, and do not have access to public capital markets in order to raise money. For public companies, the ownership of the company is spread across many different shareholders, and companies may raise additional larger amounts of funds than it otherwise would be able to if private.
- Venture capital firms are financial funds that typically invest in small private companies, in exchange for ownership stakes and control rights. In addition to access to funding, VC firms bring many advantages to entrepreneurs, such as advice, connections, and discipline.
- Both private and public firms are able to use debt financing through bank loans. Institutional features of banks help them to provide credit to firms on relatively attractive terms.
- When a firm gets to the point that public financing is beneficial, it can do an initial public offering (IPO) and sell its stock to investors in capital markets for the first time. Firms may also benefit from other aspects of being a publicly traded company, such as the better external governance.
- Public firms may decide that they want to go private, if, for example, they no longer gain much benefit from public stock markets or feel that the regulatory and reporting guidelines are too expensive. Private equity firms are financial firms that often purchase public companies, take them private, and then make improvements to their operations with the intention of gaining a profit.
- A firm may merge together with another firm by acquiring or being acquired. For the firm doing the acquisition, acquiring another firm can offer a way to supplement the assets of the acquiring firm. For a target firm, being acquired by another firm may enable the target firm to expand further. An acquiring firm must purchase the equity of a target firm in order to gain control of it. Choosing an appropriate valuation model is a key aspect of assessing M&A deals.
- One possible conclusion to a firm's life is to cease operations. Chapter 7 bankruptcy protection seeks to sell off the assets of a company in order to pay back its obligations; the company then ceases to operate. Chapter 11 bankruptcy seeks to reorganize a company and its obligations in order for the company to continue to operate.

Key Terms

Acquired company 452
Acquiring company 456
Angel investors 450
Bank loans 443
Bankruptcy 461
Banks 443
Chapter 7 bankruptcy 461
Chapter 11 bankruptcy 461
Crowdfunding 450
Deposits 444
Early-stage 441
Exit strategy 446
Fintech lenders 450
General partners (GPs) 446
Going private 444
Holdup problems 447
Initial public offering (IPO) 451
Leveraged buyout (LBO) 455
Limited partners (LPs) 446
Liquidate 461
Liquidation value 456
Merger and acquisition (M&A) 456
Microfinance 450
Premium 456
Private companies 442
Private equity (PE) 454
Public companies 442
Qualitative asset transformation 444
Relationship lending 443
Seasoned equity offering (SEO) 451
Services 443
Staged financing 446
Synergy 456
Target company 456
Underwriter 451
VC funds 446
Venture capital 446

Key Equations

DCF valuation	$V = \dfrac{FCF_1}{1+r_A} + \dfrac{FCF_2}{(1+r_A)^2} + \dfrac{FCF_3}{(1+r_A)^3} + \dfrac{FCF_4}{(1+r_A)^4} + \dfrac{FCF_5}{(1+r_A)^5} \cdots$ $= \dfrac{FCF_1}{1+r_A} + \dfrac{FCF_2}{(1+r_A)^2} + \dfrac{FCF_3}{(1+r_A)^3} + \dfrac{FCF_4}{(1+r_A)^4} + \dfrac{TV_4}{(1+r_A)^4}$	Eq. 15.1
Valuation by comparables	$V = \text{EBITDA} \times \left(\dfrac{EV}{\text{EBITDA}}\right)_{comparable}$	Eq. 15.2
Free cash flow formula	$FCF = \text{EBIT} \times (1-\tau) + \text{depreciation} - CapEx - \Delta NWC$	Eq. 15.3
After-tax WACC	$r_A = \text{WACC} = \left[\dfrac{E}{V} \times r_E\right] + \left[\dfrac{D}{V} \times r_D \times (1-\tau)\right]$	Eq. 15.4
Total company value	$V = \dfrac{FCF_1}{1+r_A} + \dfrac{FCF_2}{(1+r_A)^2} + \cdots + \dfrac{FCF_5}{(1+r_A)^5} + \dfrac{FCF_6}{(1+r_A)^6} + \cdots$ $= \dfrac{FCF_1}{1+r_A} + \dfrac{FCF_2}{(1+r_A)^2} + \cdots + \dfrac{FCF_5}{(1+r_A)^5} + \dfrac{1}{(1+r_A)^5} \times FCF_5 \times \underbrace{\left(\dfrac{1+g}{r_A - g}\right)}_{\text{terminal value}}$	Eq. 15.5

Problems

1. What are the advantages of a firm getting a loan from a bank?
2. Why is staged financing a good idea from the perspective of a VC firm? What is a potential disadvantage of staged financing?
3. Describe how a holdup problem might occur in a VC deal?
4. Explain some of the difficulties that a VC firm may have in valuing a startup firm in the context of the DCF model.
5. Explain some of the difficulties that a VC firm may have in valuing a startup firm in the context of the valuation by comparables model.
6. Why do most mergers fail (i.e., destroy value)?
7. If the equity liquidation value of a firm is higher than the equity market value of that firm, what would be a profitable strategy for an acquirer to undertake after acquiring the target firm?
8. Describe the different steps in the IPO process.
9. Explain why a publicly traded firm may decide to go private.
10. What is the difference between a general partner (GP) and a limited partner (LP) in a VC fund?
11. What are the strategies of PE firms? Why might they want to take a firm they own public or private?
12. In an M&A transaction, does an acquirer typically offer a purchase price above or below the current market value of the target firm's stock? Why?
13. You observe a publicly traded company announce that it intends to acquire another company, and the stock price of the acquirer immediately drops. What does this tell you about how the market views the acquisition? Why might this be the case?
14. Suppose that you are looking to acquire a company. The target company anticipates free cash flows of $2 million each year starting next year and continuing until five years from now (so from years 1 through 5), after which it believes that the free cash flows will grow at a rate of 1% forever. The target company has stated that it will maintain a flat leverage ratio (D/V) of 30% going forward, and has a cost of debt of 8%. The tax rate is 30%. There is a very similar company to your target company which has 50% leverage (D/V), and has a cost of debt of 8% and a cost of equity of 15%.
    (a) What is an estimate of the market value of the target company? If it has 10,000 shares outstanding, what would its price per share be?
    (b) Now suppose that, when you acquire the company, you plan to operate it as a stand-alone entity, but you intend to increase its leverage ratio to $D/V = 70\%$. There are no other synergies with the acquisition. What is the total value of the company to you once it is acquired? Assume that the company's cost of debt capital will remain the same, even with the new leverage ratio.
15. Suppose that we are given the following information about a target company:
    - target firm's equity cost of capital is 15.5%;
    - current (date 0) debt = $525 million;
    - the firm's current leverage ratio in market value terms $D/V = 0.4635$ (and we plan to keep this capital structure the same after the acquisition);
    - ten million shares are outstanding and current stock price of target is $66.67;
    - assume existing (year 0) NWC = $200 million;
    - the tax rate is 40% and cost of debt for the firm is 8%; and
    - total company value assuming $TV = PV$ of FCF in year 5 growing perpetually at 1%.

You are also given the following forecasted (pro forma) financial information:

Year	0	1	2	3	4	5
EBIT × (1 − τ)		$120	$120	$180	$240	$240
Depreciation − CapEx		−$10	−$50	$0	−$100	−$50
NWC	$200	$225	$220	$270	$230	$180

How much would you be willing to pay for this target?

16. Under what circumstances might a firm file for chapter 7 bankruptcy? When would chapter 11 bankruptcy be more appropriate?

PART III

ASSET PRICING AND FINANCIAL MARKETS

Part III covers asset valuation and financial markets, focusing on the management of wealth, and the trade-off between risk and expected return. Whereas Part II analyzed corporate balance sheets (assets, liabilities, and equity) from the perspective of an insider, a manager of a corporation, Part III looks at them from the perspective of an outsider, a security analyst or an investor.

We begin our coverage of security valuation and wealth management in Chapter 16, with an analysis of the term structure of interest rates on default-free financial instruments such as government bonds (a topic first introduced in Chapter 5). We start with zero-coupon bonds and their use in hedging by matching assets to liabilities. We then explain how information from such bonds can be used to derive spot and forward interest rates. We then define and explain how this information can be used to price bonds.

Interest rates are directly observable, whereas expected returns on risky assets have to be inferred using theory. Development of that theory is the subject of Chapters 17 and 18. Chapter 17 develops the theory of portfolio selection, starting with a single safe asset and a single risky asset. The theory is then expanded to look at many risky assets and different time horizons. Chapter 18 deals with the equilibrium implications of the models presented in Chapter 17, to understand how the returns investors expect can be estimated.

Chapter 19 describes and analyzes derivatives, including forward contracts, futures, and swaps, and covers options. We show how these derivatives are used to modify the payoffs from investor portfolios, allowing investors to achieve various financial goals, and we derive what their prices must be.

In Chapter 20, the final chapter of the book, we cover the financial system as a whole. The chapter provides a broad overview of the current structure of financial markets and institutions around the world, and it shows that the way the basic financial functions are performed changes over time and differs across borders. We introduce a functional perspective in which the basic economic functions of the system are the same everywhere, but the institutional structure can vary across geopolitical borders. This perspective provides students with the tools they need to understand and analyze financial systems as they exist now in different countries, and how they may evolve in an ever-changing world.

16 THE TERM STRUCTURE OF INTEREST RATES

CHAPTER OVERVIEW

16.1	Interest Rates for Different Borrowing Horizons	470
16.2	Determining Interest Rates from Pure Discount Bonds	474
16.3	Coupon Bonds	481
16.4	Uncertainty in Interest Rates	492
16.5	Measuring Interest Rate Risk	496
16.6	Real versus Nominal Interest Rates	506

LEARNING OBJECTIVES

After reading this chapter, you will be able to:
- describe how interest rates at various horizons can meet investor needs, and how they can be derived;
- calculate interest rates from the prices of current default-free bonds, and use the information to price claims with certain cash flows;
- identify what zero-coupon and coupon bonds are, and calculate their prices and yields;
- explain the relationship between the term structure of default-free interest rates and bond prices;
- describe what interest rate risk is, and perform calculations to measure interest rate risk through duration and convexity;
- understand how interest rates can be adjusted for inflation, and how to use them in analysis.

EQUATIONS YOU KNOW

Future value	$FV_T = PV \times (1+r)^T$	Eq. 2.1
Present value of an amount one period from today	$PV = \dfrac{FV}{1+r}$	Eq. 2.7
Present value of a future cash flow	$PV = \dfrac{CF_t}{(1+r)^t}$	Eq. 2.8
Real interest rate	real interest rate = $\dfrac{\text{nominal interest rate} - \text{rate of inflation}}{1 + \text{rate of inflation}}$	Eq. 2.20

+ You anticipate needing $1,000 three years from now. How can you invest today to ensure that you will have this money available in the future?

+ You find an investment opportunity that offers a certain stream of cash flows for the next five years, with no possibility of default. What is the fair price for such an opportunity?

+ You are seeking to put your savings in a safe investment, and choose US Treasury bonds. However, there are a wide variety of bonds, each with different promised payment rates, maturities, and prices. What are the cash flows that these bonds will pay you over time, and what will be your rate of return for each?

+ You have your retirement savings invested in a portfolio of bonds. How much will the value of your investment change when interest rates change?

+ You are working for the finance division of your company, and are considering issuing a bond to raise money. You also notice that interest rates have been changing recently. How can you structure the bond, and how does the interest rate environment affect the price of the bond?

+ You are a portfolio manager at an investment management company. Your clients want to invest in fixed-income investments, yet are concerned about how market conditions and interest rates in the economy may affect the value of their investments. How can you measure this and give them advice on the types of investments that might be suitable?

Introduction

In Chapter 5 we defined interest rates, promised rates of exchange for borrowing money, and the term structure of interest rates, which is how interest rates for borrowing money over different time horizons vary. As we saw, these interest rates are essential for determining the prices of bonds. However, interest rates are also used to determine discount rates for valuing projects and companies, which we covered in Part II. Thus, this concept is critically important in all areas of finance because interest rates provide the foundation to allow investors to meet their investment needs, and to value assets as well as to manage risk. In other words, interest rates are not just about determining the cost of borrowing. In this chapter we go deeper into how interest rates can be determined, the features of bonds, and how to measure and understand uncertainty in future interest rates.

Throughout this chapter, we will assume that any cash flows we examine are fixed and certain; this allows us to focus on how valuation is affected when interest rates change without the added complications of cash flows also changing. Financial investments that approximate this well are US Treasury bonds, because their promised cash flows are fixed and will be paid with near-certainty. We will begin with the case where all interest rates in the future are known and are the same in order to fix ideas in the most basic case. We then go through the case where interest rates change in the future, but there is no uncertainty, so we know exactly how the rates will change; this will allow us to move closer to reality and to understand how and why future interest rates usually differ depending on the borrowing period. In the real world, future interest rates are not predictable, so we look at how our analysis changes in a world with uncertainty about future interest rates. We conclude by providing methodologies for measuring the risk that comes from changing interest rates, and also how one can incorporate inflation into interest rate calculations.

16.1 Interest Rates for Different Borrowing Horizons

When individuals or companies borrow money, the time period at which they need to pay it back is not always the same. For example, you could take out a loan that matures in one year, or one that matures in five years. As we noted in Chapter 5, the interest rates for loans of these different borrowing horizons often differ because expectations of what will happen at different points in time in the future—such as about economic growth, government monetary policy, etc.— differ.

In this section we take a first step in understanding how to derive these interest rates for different horizons. The term structure of interest rates is how interest rates for borrowing money over different time horizons vary. To do so, we will first consider the most basic environment—when future interest rates at different horizons are all the same and do not change over time—in order to provide the intuition of the methodology we will use. We will then discuss how things change when interest rates in the future may change over time. This will lay the foundation for deriving interest rates in practice, when environments are even more complicated.

16.1.1 Certain and Constant Interest Rates

The most basic environment of interest rates is when all interest rates in the future are known for certain and are also exactly the same or constant. Where all interest rates in the future are the same is a flat term structure of interest rates. In our analysis in this section, interest rates are risk-free (or riskless): There is no chance of default in borrowing, and interest rates will not change in the future.[1]

To illustrate, suppose that r represents the economy's yearly interest rate for borrowing money in the future. This means that if you borrow $100 now (at time $t = 0$) that must be paid back in one year (time $t = 1$), you will owe $100 \times (1 + r)$ in one year. Now suppose instead that you borrow $100 now ($t = 0$) that must be paid back in two years. Then the amount that must be paid back represents interest accrued at the interest rate r for two years: in one year this amount is $100 \times (1 + r)$, and then after another year (at $t = 2$) this amount is $100 \times (1 + r) \times (1 + r) = \$100 \times (1 + r)^2$.

Consider an example. Investors can invest in bills, bonds with maturities of a year or less, or bonds with longer maturities. Suppose an investor has a choice of purchasing bills which mature in one year or in bonds which mature in two years. Each pays off $1,000 at maturity (the par/face value/principal amount), and the two-year bonds are assumed to not have any payout at the end of the first year. Figure 16.1 provides a timeline of the cash flows of the bill and the bond.

---

[1] The notion of a "risk-free" interest rate depends on the horizon at which one is planning to use money, and default-free need not necessarily mean risk-free. For example, a 25-year US Treasury bond is default-free in that it will surely provide its promised payment, but may be risky to hold for a one-year horizon when interest rates change. We show this explicitly later on in this chapter.

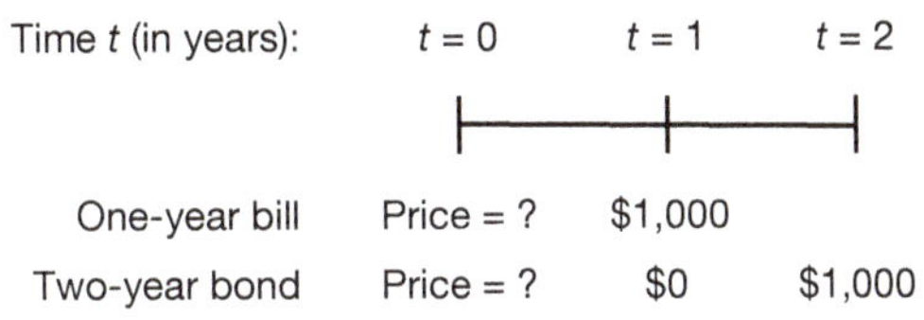

16.1 INTEREST RATES FOR DIFFERENT BORROWING HORIZONS

Time t (in years):	$t = 0$	$t = 1$	$t = 2$
One-year bill	Price = ?	$1,000	
Two-year bond	Price = ?	$0	$1,000

FIGURE 16.1 Timeline of cash flows for a one-year bill and a two-year bond. This figure depicts the timeline of cash flows for a bill that matures in one year and pays $1,000, and a bond that matures in two years and pays $1,000.

Suppose that the interest rate is 1% per year. Then the price that the one-year bill sells for will be determined by the $1,000 promised payment in year 1 discounted by the interest rate:

$$\text{Price of bill} = \frac{\$1,000}{1+r} = \frac{\$1,000}{1.01} = \$990.10.$$

Similarly, the price of the two-year bond will be determined by the $1,000 promised payment in year 2 discounted by the interest rate:

$$\text{Price of bond} = \frac{\$1,000}{(1+r)^2} = \frac{\$1,000}{1.01^2} = \$980.30.$$

Note that, since interest rates are fixed and certain, we can also determine how much the two-year bond will be worth one period from now (at $t = 1$). At $t = 1$, the bond will pay out $1,000 in one year (at $t = 2$). The interest rate at $t = 1$ will still be 1%. Thus, the price of the bond at $t = 1$ will be:

$$\text{Price of bond at } t = 1 : \frac{\$1,000}{1+r} = \frac{\$1,000}{1.01} = \$990.10.$$

We can see that the price of the bond will increase between $t = 0$ and $t = 1$, and in particular the percentage increase will be equal to the interest rate: $980.30 × (1.01) = $990.10. At $t = 2$, the bond's value will again increase by the interest rate, and it will be worth exactly what it has promised to pay off: $980.30 × (1.01)^2 = $1,000. Put differently, the annual rate of return from holding this bond, given a flat and certain term structure of interest rates, is the same as the interest rate. This highlights a more general point: Because there is no uncertainty, bonds of different maturities must all earn the same return over any specified holding period, according to the law of one price, **Principle 2**: *Equivalent assets that can be freely bought and sold will have the same market price.* Thus, a two-year bond held for one year must earn the identical return as a one-year bond held for that same year. As will be shown in Section 16.4, this equating of returns on bonds of different maturities over a specified holding period will not hold if future interest rates are uncertain.

What if interest rates were higher instead, say, 2%? Then the prices of the bonds will decrease, as they are discounted by a larger rate:

$$\text{Price of bill} : \frac{\$1,000}{1+r} = \frac{\$1,000}{1.02} = \$980.39,$$

$$\text{Price of bond} : \frac{\$1,000}{(1+r)^2} = \frac{\$1,000}{1.02^2} = \$961.17.$$

As discussed in Chapter 5, the annualized rate of return to investors who buy and hold a bond until it matures is known as the yield to maturity (YTM). Thus, with flat and certain interest rates, we can see that the yields of bonds of different maturities are the same and are equal to the fixed interest rate.

Since, as demonstrated, we can determine the yields of bonds from bond prices, the yield is simply a transformation of the price. We will return to this insight in more detail later.

> **QUICK CHECK 16.1** Suppose that interest rates in the economy are 0.5% instead. Recalculate the prices of the one-year bill and the two-year bond.

16.1.2 When Interest Rates Differ by Maturity

In most cases, interest rates for future horizons vary by maturity, which denotes when a borrowed amount is paid back. For example, a person considering investing money in a Treasury security will observe that the interest rate depends on its maturity—a Treasury bond maturing in two years will have a different promised interest rate than a Treasury bond maturing in five years.

In general, for any given future date for which a borrowed amount would be due, there is a different risk-free interest rate, and these different rates comprise the term structure of interest rates. Figure 16.2 visually depicts the idea of interest rates for different horizons. Interest rates charged right now for borrowing for a certain length of time are known as spot interest rates. In Figure 16.2, $r_{0,1}$ represents the one-year spot interest rate, the interest rate for borrowing money now (at time $t = 0$) that must be paid back in one year (time $t = 1$). The two-year (spot) interest rate, denoted by $r_{0,2}$, or r_2, represents the interest rate per year for borrowing money now due in two years ($t = 2$). It is important to note that these rates are per-year interest rates (i.e., stated in annual terms), so if you borrow $100 today for two years, you would need to pay back $100 \times (1 + r_2)^2$.

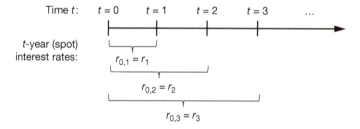

FIGURE 16.2 Interest rates over different horizons. $r_{0,1}$ (r_1) is the interest rate for borrowing money now (at time $t = 0$) that must be paid back in one year (time $t = 1$). $r_{0,2}$ (r_2) is the yearly interest rate for borrowing money now (at time $t = 0$) that must be paid back in two years (time $t = 2$). $r_{0,3}$ (r_3) is the yearly interest rate for borrowing money now (at time $t = 0$) that must be paid back in three years (time $t = 3$).

For now, we continue to assume that there is no uncertainty in interest rates, so we know exactly how the rates will change. The interest rate for borrowing money now for one year is $r_{0,1}$, and the interest rate for borrowing money now for two years is, $r_{0,2}$. Given these interest rates, we know for certain what the interest rate will be at $t = 1$ for borrowing money in one year (i.e., due at $t = 2$): $r_{1,2}$.

Interest rates serve many crucial functions in finance, such as allowing individuals to meet their saving and investment needs more precisely. To illustrate, consider the same two-period example. Investors can invest in bills, which mature in one year, or in bonds, which mature in two years. Each pays off $1,000 at maturity, and the two-year bonds are assumed to not have any payout at the end of the first year. It is possible to buy new one-year bills in one year. The timeline of the cash flows of the bill and the bond is, as before:

16.1 INTEREST RATES FOR DIFFERENT BORROWING HORIZONS

Time t (in years):	$t = 0$	$t = 1$	$t = 2$
One-year bill	Price = ?	$1,000	
Two-year bond	Price = ?	$0	1,000

Suppose now that the one-year interest rate r_1 (i.e., the interest rate for one-year bills) is 1%, and the two-year interest rate r_2 (i.e., the interest rate for two-year bills) is 2% per year. Then the price that the one-year bill sells for will be determined by the $1,000 promised payment in year 1, discounted by the one-year interest rate:

$$\text{Price of bill} = \frac{\$1,000}{1 + r_1} = \frac{\$1,000}{1.01} = \$990.10.$$

Similarly, the price of the two-year bond will be determined by the $1,000 promised payment in year 2 discounted by the two-year interest rate:

$$\text{Price of bond} = \frac{\$1,000}{(1 + r_2)^2} = \frac{\$1,000}{1.02^2} = \$961.17.$$

The interest rates also give us the yield to maturity (YTM): the rate of return earned by the bond and bill if held until maturity. The bill provides $1,000 in one year, thus providing a yearly return of ($1,000 / $990.10) − 1 = 1%. The bond provides $1,000 in two years, thus providing a return of ($1,000 / $961.17) − 1 = 4% over two years or an average return of 2% per year; 2% is therefore the YTM.

In this situation, where interest rates are changing, consider how much the two-year bond's price will change from now to one period from now (at $t = 1$). As of $t = 1$, the bond will pay out $1,000 in one year (at $t = 2$). The interest rate at $t = 1$ for borrowing for a year, however, will not be the same. Note that we know that the interest rate from now until $t = 1$, $r_{0,1} = r_1 = 1\%$. This means that the value of the bond increases by 1% in one year: $961.17 × 1.01 = $970.78; as we previously noted, this return must be the same as that earned by the one-year bill over the same horizon, according to **Principle 2:** *Equivalent assets that can be freely bought and sold will have the same market price.* However, note that this 1% return earned by the bond in one year is different from the 2% YTM. Thus, if you sell the bond before maturity, it can potentially provide a very different rate of return from what would be earned by holding the bond to maturity (i.e., the two-year interest rate of 2%). In contrast, if you hold the bond to maturity, you will surely earn the two-year interest rate of 2%.

This example highlights two takeaways. First, if a bond is held until maturity, then you will earn the YTM on the bond. However, if you do not hold the bond until maturity—that is, you sell it before the maturity date—then the actual earned rate of return may be substantially different.

Example 16.1 (Calculating Bond Prices When Interest Rates Vary): Consider the following spot interest rates for borrowing now, with the indicated maturity:

Horizon T	Spot interest rate	
1	r_1	2%
2	r_2	3%
3	r_3	5%

Consider three different bonds, each with a maturity corresponding to the horizons above. What is the price of each bond if it pays off $1,000 at each indicated horizon (and nothing else)?

Solution. First, we can draw a timeline of the cash flows for the bond of each horizon:

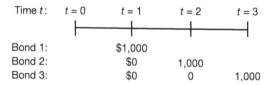

We can use the indicated interest rates to discount each bond's cash flows to determine the prices:

$$\text{Price of bond } 1 = \frac{\$1{,}000}{1+r_1} = \frac{\$1{,}000}{1.02} = \$980.392,$$

$$\text{Price of bond } 2 = \frac{\$1{,}000}{(1+r_2)^2} = \frac{\$1{,}000}{1.03^2} = \$942.596,$$

$$\text{Price of bond } 3 = \frac{\$1{,}000}{(1+r_3)^3} = \frac{\$1{,}000}{1.05^3} = \$863.838.$$

> **QUICK CHECK 16.2** Suppose that $r_1 = 2\%$ and $r_2 = 1\%$. Recalculate the prices of the bill and the bond. What would be your rate of return if you sold the bond at $t = 1$?

In this section we have introduced the foundations for understanding what interest rates represent, and how they can differ depending on the borrowing period. In the next section we show how these interest rates can actually be calculated using data from the market.

16.2 Determining Interest Rates from Pure Discount Bonds

Interest rates can be used to formulate the discount rates that investors can use to determine the present value of financial contracts securities promising a stream of known cash flows. The basic idea is that the cash flows produced by any fixed-income financial security can be replicated (copied) using a combination of simple bonds that reflect borrowing over different horizons. By the law of one price, since the cash flows are the same between the security and combination of simple bonds, that means the prices must be the same. Because the simple bonds incorporate the interest rates of various horizons, this means that these interest rates can be calculated and can also be used to determine the price of the financial security. In this section we will discuss the logic behind this process and how these calculations can be performed.

Pure discount bonds, also called zero-coupon bonds, are bonds that promise a single payment of cash at the maturity date. They are called this because the prices of the bonds will be less than (i.e., at a discount to) the promised amount in the future due to the time value of money (**Principle 1:** *A dollar today is not worth the same as a dollar tomorrow*) when interest rates are positive. The bonds also do not provide any payments (coupons) over time, and so as we will also see, providing a simple cash flow pattern allows straightforward discounting to infer prices. Such bonds issued by the US Treasury are known as STRIPS (Separate Trading of Registered Interest and Principal of Securities). The one-year bill and two-year bond from the previous section are examples of pure discount bonds. The promised cash payment at maturity is its face value, par value, or principal amount. The interest earned by investors on pure discount bonds is the difference between the price paid for the bond and the face value received at the maturity date. Thus, for a pure discount bond with a face value of $1,000 maturing in one year and a purchase price of $990, the interest earned is the $10 difference between the $1,000 face value and the $990 purchase price.

Pure discount bonds are the basic building blocks for valuing all contracts promising streams of known cash flows. This is because we can always deconstruct any contract—no matter how complicated its pattern of certain future cash flows—into its component cash flows, discount each one separately, and then add them up.

To illustrate the idea behind this, consider a contract that has a maturity of three years and pays a certain amount (i.e., there is no risk of it paying less) of $5,000 at $t = 1$, $7,000 at $t = 2$, and $9,000 at $t = 3$. We are unsure of what the price of this contract should be. However, suppose we know the prices of three pure discount bonds: A one-year bond with face value $1,000 sells for $990.10, a two-year bond with face value $1,000 sells for $961.17, and a three-year bond with face value $1,000 sells for $915.14. Figure 16.3 provides a timeline of the cash flows for the contracts.

As Figure 16.3 demonstrates, if we combine five one-year bonds, we will receive the same cash flows as the $t = 1$ cash flows of the contract. Similarly, if we combine seven two-year bonds, we will receive the same cash flows as the $t = 2$ cash flows of the contract. Finally, combining nine three-year bonds will replicate the $t = 3$ cash flows of the contract. Ascribing to **Principle 2:** *Equivalent assets that can be freely bought and sold will have the same market price*, since the cash flows of the contract are exactly the same as the cash flows of the combined pure discount bonds, the combined price of the pure discount bonds must be the same as the price of the contract (otherwise there will be an arbitrage). Thus, the price of the contract is:

$$\begin{aligned} \text{Price} &= 5 \times (\text{1-year bond price}) + 7 \times (\text{2-year bond price}) + 9 \times (\text{3-year bond price}) \\ &= 5 \times \$990.10 + 7 \times \$961.17 + 9 \times \$915.14 = \$19{,}914.95. \end{aligned}$$

The prices of pure discount bonds can also be used to determine interest rates for different maturities, which can in turn be used as discount rates in valuing contracts promising a stream of known cash flows. To see this, consider the price of a pure discount bond that matures in year T and pays par. Let us denote y_T as the bond's yield to maturity (YTM, or yield), which is the annualized rate of return to investors who buy it and hold it until it matures. For such a bond, an investor paying a price of P_T and receiving a sure payoff of par will therefore receive a yield defined by $P_T \times (1 + y_T)^T = \text{par}$. Rearranging this expression, we can express the price of the bond as:

$$P_T = \frac{\text{par}}{(1 + y_T)^T}. \tag{16.1}$$

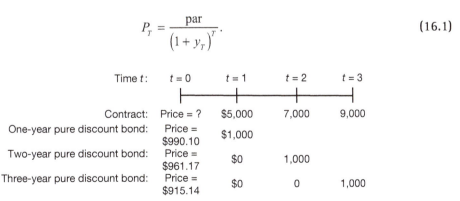

FIGURE 16.3 Timeline of contract and pure discount bonds. This figure shows the timeline of cash flows for a contract with a maturity of three years and which pays a certain amount of $5,000 at $t = 1$, $7,000 at $t = 2$, and $9,000 at $t = 3$. Below are the cash flows for three pure discount bonds with face values of $1,000 with one-, two-, and three-year maturities.

The prices of bonds and yields thus go in opposite directions—if yields go up, bond prices fall, and vice versa. Equation 16.1 also demonstrates that you can determine the price of such a bond by discounting the par amount by the appropriate interest rate (i.e., the T-year interest rate):

$$P_T = \frac{\text{par}}{(1+r_T)^T}. \tag{16.2}$$

In comparing Equations 16.1 and 16.2, we can see that the yield y_T for this pure discount bond will be the *same* as the T-year spot interest rate. Therefore, we can utilize the prices of pure discount bonds to determine spot interest rates. In particular, we can calculate the yield for T-year bonds (and therefore the T-year interest rate) as:

$$\begin{aligned} y_T &= \left(\frac{\text{par}}{P_T}\right)^{\frac{1}{T}} - 1 \\ &= r_T. \end{aligned} \tag{16.3}$$

This provides us with another way to utilize pure discount bonds in order to value streams of known cash flows: Determine the spot interest rates from pure discount bonds, and then use those rates to discount the cash flows. We can therefore generally express the present value of a stream of known cash flows CF_t that occur at each date t until date T as:

$$\begin{aligned} PV &= \frac{CF_1}{1+r_1} + \frac{CF_2}{(1+r_2)^2} + \cdots + \frac{CF_T}{(1+r_T)^T} \\ &= \sum_{t=1}^{T} \frac{CF_t}{(1+r_t)^t}. \end{aligned} \tag{16.4}$$

To see this, consider again the contract and pure discount bonds from Figure 16.3. We can value the contract by first calculating the yield of each pure discount bond, and then use those rates to discount the contract's cash flows. The one-year pure discount bond's yield is (using Equation 16.1):

$$\$990.10 = \frac{\$1,000}{1+y_1},$$

$$\begin{aligned} y_1 &= \frac{\$1,000}{\$990.10} - 1 \\ &= 0.01 = r_1. \end{aligned}$$

The yield of the one-year pure discount bond—and thus the one-year spot interest rate r_1—is therefore 1%. The two-year pure discount bond's yield is given by (directly using Equation 16.3):

$$\begin{aligned} y_2 &= \left(\frac{\$1,000}{\$961.17}\right)^{\frac{1}{2}} - 1 \\ &= 0.02 = r_2. \end{aligned}$$

Finally, the yield of the three-year pure discount bond—and thus the three-year spot interest rate r_3—is given by:

$$\begin{aligned} y_3 &= \left(\frac{\$1,000}{\$915.14}\right)^{\frac{1}{3}} - 1 \\ &= 0.03 = r_3. \end{aligned}$$

With these interest rates in hand, we can then use them to discount the cash flows of the contract to arrive at its price (Equation 16.4):

$$\begin{aligned} \text{Price} &= \frac{\$5{,}000}{1+r_1} + \frac{\$7{,}000}{(1+r_2)^2} + \frac{\$9{,}000}{(1+r_3)^3} \\ &= \frac{\$5{,}000}{1.01} + \frac{\$7{,}000}{(1.02)^2} + \frac{\$9{,}000}{(1.03)^3} \\ &= \$19{,}914.95. \end{aligned}$$

This is exactly the same price as before.

To conclude, when observed yields of pure discount/zero-coupon bonds are not the same for all maturities, value a contract or a security promising a stream of known cash payments by discounting each of the payments at the rate corresponding to a pure discount bond of its maturity. Then, sum the individual payment present values.

With a complete set of pure discount bonds for all relevant maturities, it is possible to derive the relevant information that investors need to discount any financial contract that pays a certain amount in the future. In Table 16.1 we show how this information would look for a hypothetical set of pure discount bonds with maturities ranging from 1 to 30 years. Figure 16.4 provides a plot of the information in the table. Note that it is standard practice to express the prices of pure discount bonds per unit of currency (i.e., per dollar of face value). Thus, in our previous example, the one-year bond with face value of $1,000 selling for $990.12 would be expressed as having a price of 0.99012 or selling for 99.012% of par. Figure 16.4 visually depicts the prices (per $1 of par) of pure discount

Table 16.1 Discount function, yield curve, and forward rates. Hypothetical data for the price per $1 of par and YTM (yield), derived for pure discount bonds of varying maturities. The price per $1 and yields can be used to determine the present value of a certain cash flow that occurs the indicated number of years in the future.

Years to maturity	Price per $1	YTM	Years to maturity	Price per $1	YTM
1	0.99	1.00%	16	0.67	2.50%
2	0.98	1.10%	17	0.65	2.60%
3	0.96	1.20%	18	0.62	2.70%
4	0.95	1.30%	19	0.59	2.80%
5	0.93	1.40%	20	0.56	2.90%
6	0.91	1.50%	21	0.54	3.00%
7	0.89	1.60%	22	0.51	3.10%
8	0.87	1.70%	23	0.48	3.20%
9	0.85	1.80%	24	0.46	3.30%
10	0.83	1.90%	25	0.43	3.40%
11	0.80	2.00%	26	0.41	3.50%
12	0.78	2.10%	27	0.38	3.60%
13	0.75	2.20%	28	0.36	3.70%
14	0.73	2.30%	29	0.34	3.80%
15	0.70	2.40%	30	0.32	3.90%

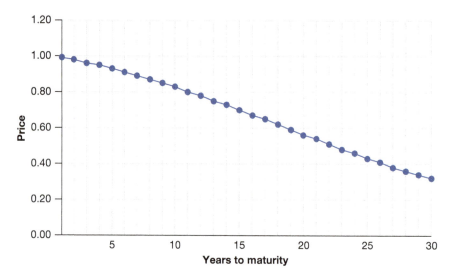

FIGURE 16.4 Discount function. This figure plots the discount function derived from zero-coupon bonds at the indicated maturities, based on the data in **Table 16.1**. Each point of the curve represents the price per $1 of purchasing a pure discount bond of the indicated maturity. These prices can be used to determine the present value of certain cash flows occurring at the indicated maturity dates.

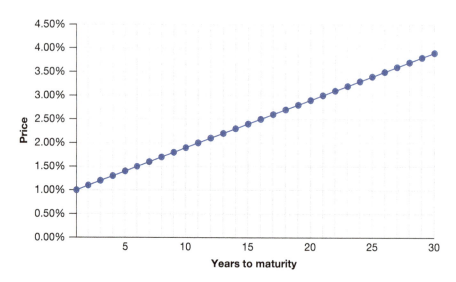

FIGURE 16.5 Yield curve. This figure plots the YTM for zero-coupon bonds at the indicated maturities, based on the data in **Table 16.1**. Yields increase for higher maturities, indicating an upward-sloping yield curve. These yields can be used as discount rates to derive the present value of certain cash flows occurring at the indicated maturity dates.

bonds for various maturities, known as the discount function, since these prices can be used as discount rates for future cash flows, as we saw above. Figure 16.5 plots the yields of these bonds for the different maturities, a plot known as the yield curve, which shows how interest rates change depending on the maturity of borrowing. In this particular example, yields are higher for longer maturities, which results in an upward-sloping yield curve. A flat yield curve is when yields for shorter and longer maturities are the same. Box 16.1 discusses how the slope of the yield curve—whether upward-sloping or downward-sloping (when yields are lower for longer maturities)—can be interpreted by practitioners.

In this chapter the cash flows have been certain (i.e., risk-free). As we noted in Part I, if a cash flow is risk-free, then a risk-free interest rate is an appropriate discount rate to use to value that cash flow. However, if a cash flow is uncertain or risky, then the expected cash flow must be discounted by a different rate adjusted to reflect this risk, in line with **Principle 7:** *There is a trade-off between risk and expected return.* In the subsequent chapters we will introduce models that take this into account. However, these models all use risk-free interest rates, as we have derived, as their starting points.

Box 16.1 The Shape of the Yield Curve and Recessions

The shape of the yield curve is sometimes used as a barometer to gauge whether there is an impending economic recession. The yield curve in periods of economic growth is typically upward-sloping: yields (i.e., interest rates) for longer-maturity Treasury bonds are usually higher than those for short-maturity Treasury bonds. However, the yield curve can sometimes be downward-sloping, where yields on longer-maturity Treasury bonds are lower than those for shorter-maturity Treasury bonds. In other words, the yield curve is downward-sloping. This is often referred to as an "inverted" yield curve.

An inverted yield curve is often viewed as a signal of an impending economic downturn. One reason inverted yield curves happen is because investors are selling stocks and shifting their money to long-term bonds because they've lost confidence in the economy, and are wary of the downside risk of stocks. This increases the demand for bonds, causing their prices to go up and their yields to fall.

Historically, inverted yield curves have preceded every recession since 1956. Indeed, before the tech bubble burst in 2001 there was an inversion of the yield curve. And in December 2005 the yield curve inverted, in advance of the Great Recession due to the financial crisis of 2007–2009. Recessions have tended to follow inverted yield curves an average of 22 months after the inversion. Figure 16.6 illustrates this by graphing the difference in the yields of a ten-year and

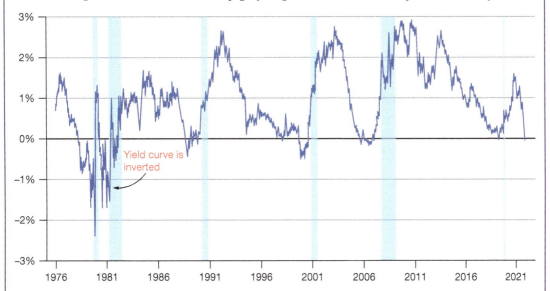

FIGURE 16.6 This graph shows the slope of the yield curve in the US economy. The blue vertical bars show the dates of recession. Generally an inverted yield curve can provide an indicator of an impending recession. Note the inverted yield curve falls before these dates.
Source: US Federal Reserve.

a two-year Treasury bond. Negative difference indicates that the two-year bond has a higher yield, and thus the yield curve is downward-sloping. The shaded bars indicate historical recession dates.

However, an inversion of the yield curve is not a perfect indicator of impending recessions. A brief inversion may simply be an anomaly—there are a number of inversions that have not preceded recessions. Furthermore, inversions may happen due to factors outside the regular movement of markets. For example, to the extent central banks such as the Federal Reserve can control short-term interest rates, it may be the case that the rates set are higher than what the market would dictate they should be.

Sources: Lewis, A. (2019). The inverted yield curve explained and what it means for your money. CNBC. Wessel, D., and Kovalski, M. A. (2018). The Hutchings Center explains: the yield curve—what it is, and why it matters. Brookings Institution.

Example 16.2 (Valuing an Annuity Based on the Yield Curve): An insurance company offers default-free annuity contracts to its retail customers. Using the discount function in **Table 16.1**, what should the price be of a 30-year default-free annuity of $1,000 per year?

Solution. We can begin by drawing a timeline of the cash flows of the annuity:

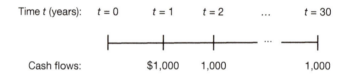

To discount these cash flows using the discount function, we must add all the prices in column 2 of **Table 16.1**—which give us the present value of $1 as of each maturity date—and multiply by 1,000 to reflect the fact that the annuity gives cash flows of $1,000 each year. The sum of the 30 prices is $20.28, so the cost of the annuity should be $20,280.

Example 16.3 (Valuing a Financial Contract Based on the Yield Curve): Suppose instead that the insurance company offers a default-free five-year contract to its retail customers, promising to pay $1,000 in the first two years (starting next year), and $2,000 for the remaining three years. Using the yields in **Table 16.1**, what should the price of this contract be?

Solution. It is useful to begin by drawing a timeline of the cash flows of the contract:

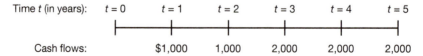

To value the contract, we can take each of these cash flows and discount them by the yields in the first five rows of **Table 16.1**, with the maturities corresponding to the time t that the cash flows occur. From **Table 16.1**, we get the following discount rates: $r_1 = 0.010$, $r_2 = 0.011$, $r_3 = 0.012$, $r_4 = 0.013$, and $r_5 = 0.014$. This allows us to calculate the price (Equation 14.6):

16.3 COUPON BONDS

$$\begin{aligned}\text{Price} &= \frac{\$1{,}000}{1+r_1} + \frac{\$1{,}000}{(1+r_2)^2} + \frac{\$2{,}000}{(1+r_3)^3} + \frac{\$2{,}000}{(1+r_4)^4} + \frac{\$2{,}000}{(1+r_5)^5} \\ &= \frac{\$1{,}000}{1.010} + \frac{\$1{,}000}{(1.011)^2} + \frac{\$2{,}000}{(1.012)^3} + \frac{\$2{,}000}{(1.013)^4} + \frac{\$2{,}000}{(1.014)^5} \\ &= \$7{,}663.14.\end{aligned}$$

The fair price of the contract is thus $7,663.14.

QUICK CHECK 16.3 Using the yields from Table 16.1, recalculate the value of the contract from the section that has a maturity of three years and pays a sure amount of $5,000 at $t = 1$, $7,000 at $t = 2$, and $9,000 at $t = 3$.

In this section we show how market interest rates can be calculated by using the prices of bonds known as pure discount bonds, which reflect borrowing at different horizons. We also saw how these interest rates form the basis of discount rates used to calculate the present value of future cash flows. In the next section we apply these insights to analyzing bonds that are commonly seen in financial markets.

16.3 Coupon Bonds

Pure discount or zero-coupon bonds are bonds that pay a promised amount only at maturity and nothing in the interim. However, many actively traded types of bond pay the holder before maturity. In this section we discuss the pricing and characteristics of such bonds, known as coupon bonds. A coupon bond obligates the issuer to make periodic payments of interest—called coupons or coupon payments—to the bondholder for the life of the bond, and then to pay the face value (i.e., par or principal amount) on maturity. The periodic interest payments are called coupons because at one time the actual bond contract (printed on paper) was given to the bondholder with paper coupons attached; when a coupon came due, the bondholder would tear off the coupon and present it to the bond issuer for payment. If the bond were sold, the coupons passed to the new bondholder.

In this section we will cover the details of how coupon bonds work and the cash flows they provide an owner. We will then cover how to calculate the price of a coupon bond using the insights we discussed in the previous section. As we will see, the pricing of bonds which offer cash flows over multiple periods is directly connected to the prices of pure discount bonds—the interest rates derived from such pure discount bonds are directly used to value the cash flows of coupon bonds. By this logic, as we discussed in the previous section, the cash flows of coupon bonds can be viewed as a series of pure discount bonds paying at different dates in the future. We will then go over how to calculate rates of return for coupon bonds, which provide additional insights into the structures of these bonds, before concluding the section with a discussion of additional features sometimes found in these bonds.

16.3.1 Coupon Payments

Coupon payments (denoted here by C) are the periodic payments of interest to bondholders between the issuing of the bond and maturity. The coupon rate of the bond is the interest rate applied to the face value to compute the coupon payment. The coupon rate denotes what percentage of the face value of the bond is paid out as a coupon payment each period. Thus, a bond with a face value of

$1,000 that has a coupon rate of 10% obligates the issuer to pay $C = 0.10 \times \$1,000 = \$100$ every year. For a typical bond contract this $100 annual coupon payment is fixed at the time the bond is issued and remains constant until the bond's maturity date. It is because these payments are fixed in this way that bond investments are often referred to as fixed-income investments. It is important to note that the coupon payment is also made on the maturity date itself, along with the principal payment. Thus, if the bond's maturity is six years, then at the end of six years the issuer pays the last coupon of $100 and the face value of $1,000. Figure 16.7(a) shows a timeline of the cash flows to the holder of a bond, while Figure 16.7(b) shows a timeline of the cash flows for a holder of a general coupon bond. We can see that the stream of promised cash flows has an annuity component (a fixed per-year amount) of $100 per year, and a lump sum balloon or bullet payment of $1,000 at maturity.

> **QUICK CHECK 16.4** Create a timeline of cash flows for a five-year bond with a face value of $1,000 and a coupon rate of 8%.

16.3.2 Prices of Coupon Bonds

At a fundamental level, we can derive the price of a coupon bond by discounting each payment (as shown in Figure 16.7) by the appropriate discount rate for that period, as in Equation 16.4:

$$P = \frac{C}{1+r_1} + \frac{C}{(1+r_2)^2} + \cdots + \frac{C + \text{par}}{(1+r_T)^T}. \tag{16.5}$$

To illustrate, consider two different two-year coupon bonds: one with a coupon rate of 5% and the other with a coupon rate of 10%. Assuming a face value of $1,000 for each, we can draw out the timeline of cash flows for both as follows:

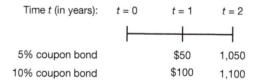

To determine the prices of these bonds, we need to discount the above cash flows at the appropriate interest rates corresponding to the dates they occur. As we noted above, we can get these

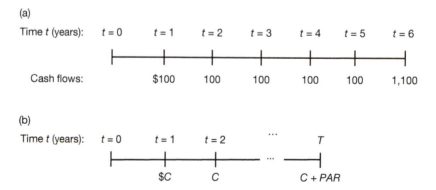

FIGURE 16.7 Timeline of cash flows of a coupon bond. (a) The timeline for a six-year coupon bond with a face value of $1,000 and a coupon rate of 10%. (b) The timeline for a general coupon bond with a maturity of T, that pays a face value of par and coupon payments of C.

interest rates from pure discount bonds. Suppose the yield on one-year pure discount bonds (i.e., r_1) is 4%, while the yield on two-year pure discount bonds (i.e., r_2) is 6%. Then, we can solve for the price of the 5% coupon bond by discounting its cash flows by the appropriate discount rates (i.e., Equation 16.5):

$$P_{5\% \text{ bond}} = \frac{\$50}{1+r_1} + \frac{1{,}050}{(1+r_2)^2}$$

$$= \frac{\$50}{1.04} + \frac{1{,}050}{(1.06)^2}$$

$$= \$982.57.$$

Similarly, for the 10% coupon bond:

$$P_{10\% \text{ bond}} = \frac{\$100}{1+r_1} + \frac{1{,}100}{(1+r_2)^2}$$

$$= \frac{100}{1.04} + \frac{1{,}100}{(1.06)^2}$$

$$= \$1{,}075.15.$$

As noted in Section 16.2, the yields on pure discount bonds are equivalent to the prices of these bonds. Thus, we can also determine the prices of these bonds by multiplying the year 1 cash flows by the price (i.e., discount factor) of a one-year pure discount bond, and adding that to the year 2 cash flows multiplied by the price (i.e., discount factor) of a two-year pure discount bond.

The 5% coupon bond has a price that is lower than its face value of $1,000. We refer to such a bond as a discount bond (differentiated from a pure discount bond because it pays a coupon). In contrast, the 10% coupon bond has a price that is higher than its face value of $1,000. Such a bond is known as a premium bond. When a bond has a price equal to its face value, it is known as a par bond. On the date a bond is issued, the coupon is usually set by the issuer so that it is a par bond.

After issuance, the price of a coupon bond and its face value can change and they become premium or discount bonds. This situation can occur if the interest rates in the economy change after the bond is issued. For example, suppose that a one-year 10% coupon bond with a face value of $1,000 was originally issued as a 20-year-maturity bond 19 years ago. At that time, the yield curve was flat at 10% per year, so the price of the bond at issuance was (Equation 16.5):

$$P = \frac{\$100}{1.10} + \frac{100}{(1.10)^2} + \cdots + \frac{1{,}100}{(1.10)^{20}}$$

$$= \$1{,}000.$$

The bond was therefore issued as a par bond. Now the bond has one year remaining before it matures, and the interest rate on one-year bonds is 5% per year. The price of the bond now is:

$$P = \frac{\$1{,}100}{1.05}$$

$$= \$1{,}047.62.$$

The bond is therefore now a premium bond, since the price is above its face value.

Over time the prices of discount bonds and premium bonds move toward their face value as they approach maturity. This is because their price must equal their face value (plus one coupon payment

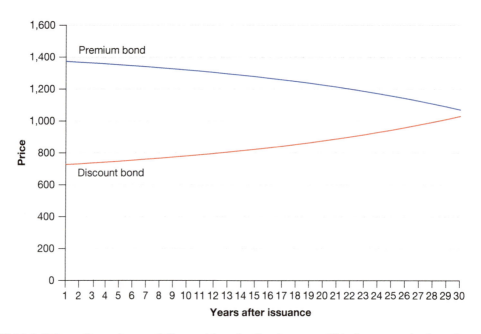

FIGURE 16.8 Prices of premium and discount bonds after issuance. This figure graphs the prices of a 30-year premium bond (blue line) and a 30-year discount bond (red line) after issuance. The term structure of interest rates is assumed to be flat at 5% over time. The discount bond has a coupon rate of 3%, while the premium bond has a coupon rate of 7%, and the face value of both bonds is $1,000. The prices of both bonds converge toward their face values plus a coupon payment.

for coupon bonds) at maturity. This implied price pattern is illustrated for the case of 30-year coupon bonds in Figure 16.8. The figure plots the prices of a 30-year discount bond and a 30-year premium bond over time after issuance. Assuming interest rates do not change over time, the figure shows that the prices of these bonds move toward their face value in the years after issuance. Later in this chapter we will go over how bond prices change when interest rates change over time.

QUICK CHECK 16.5 In the example of the 20-year maturity bond, suppose when the bond has one year remaining before it matures the interest rate on one-year bonds is instead 11% per year. What is the price of the bond now? Is it a discount, premium, or par bond?

Example 16.4 (Calculating Coupon Bond Prices and Determining Coupon Rates): Suppose there are three US Treasury bonds traded in the marketplace, each with a face value of $1,000 and paying annual coupons as follows:

Bond	Maturity (years)	Coupon rate
A	1	3.5%
B	2	5.0%
C	3	4.5%

Assume that the one-year interest rate is 3%, the two-year interest rate is 4%, and the three-year interest rate is 5%. What is each bond's price? If the Treasury issued a new three-year bond that it wanted initially traded as a par bond, what coupon rate would it need to set?

Solution. We can start by creating a timeline of the cash flows for each bond:

```
Time t:    t = 0      t = 1      t = 2      t = 3
           ├──────────┼──────────┼──────────┤
Bond A:              $1,035
Bond B:               $50       1,050
Bond C:               $45         45        1,045
```

We are told that $r_1 = 0.03$, $r_2 = 0.04$, and $r_3 = 0.05$. We can use these to calculate the prices of each bond (Equation 16.5):

$$P_A = \frac{\$1,035}{1+r_1}$$
$$= \frac{1,035}{1.03}$$
$$= \$1,004.85,$$

$$P_B = \frac{\$50}{1+r_1} + \frac{1,050}{(1+r_2)^2}$$
$$= \frac{\$50}{1.03} + \frac{1,050}{1.04^2}$$
$$= \$1,019.33,$$

$$P_C = \frac{\$45}{1+r_1} + \frac{45}{(1+r_2)^2} + \frac{1,045}{(1+r_3)^3}$$
$$= \frac{\$45}{1.03} + \frac{45}{1.04^2} + \frac{1,045}{1.05^3}$$
$$= \$988.00.$$

Finally, consider the potential new bond. For it to be a par bond, the price would have to equal the face value. Therefore, coupon C would have to satisfy the following (Equation 16.7):

$$1,000 = \frac{C}{1.03} + \frac{C}{(1.04)^2} + \frac{C+1,000}{(1.05)^3}$$

$$136.162 = \frac{C}{1.03} + \frac{C}{1.04^2} + \frac{C}{1.05^3}$$

$$136.162 = C \times \left[\frac{1}{1.03} + \frac{1}{1.04^2} + \frac{1}{1.05^3}\right]$$

$$C = 49.347.$$

This is the coupon payment each year. As a percentage of the face value, this is 49.347 / 1,000 = 0.049, so the coupon rate would have to be 4.9% for the bond to be issued as a par bond.

16.3.3 Yields of Coupon Bonds

The yields of coupon bonds provide useful information related to the prices of coupon bonds, such as whether a bond's current price is relatively high or low compared to the promised par amount, as well as help us understand the relationship between bond prices and interest rates. There are two different measures of yield that we can compute for coupon bonds, the current yield and the yield to maturity (YTM), which have different applications.

The current yield is the annual coupon as a percentage of the bond's price:

$$\text{Current yield} = \frac{C}{P}. \tag{16.6}$$

The current yield provides a measure of the return the bondholder can expect each year based on the coupon payment the bond will pay. To illustrate, again consider a two-year bond with a face value of $1,000 and a coupon rate of 10%, which trades for a price of $1,075.15. The one-year interest rate (r_1) is 4%, while the two-year interest rate (r_2) is 6%. The current yield of this bond would therefore be (using Equation 16.6):

$$\begin{aligned}\text{Current yield} &= \frac{C}{P} \\ &= \frac{\$100}{\$1,075.15} \\ &= 0.093 \text{ or } 9.3\%.\end{aligned}$$

Although this can be an informative measure to estimate an investor's return, the current yield will mis-state the true return on a coupon bond because it does not incorporate the face value the investor receives at maturity as well as coupon payments along the way. To account for this, we compute a different yield measure for coupon bonds: the yield to maturity (YTM). Mathematically, the YTM for a coupon bond is defined as the discount rate y that makes the present value of the bond's stream of promised cash payments equal to its price:

$$P = \frac{C}{1+y} + \frac{C}{(1+y)^2} + \cdots + \frac{C + par}{(1+y)^T}. \tag{16.7}$$

Conceptually, the interpretation of the YTM for a coupon bond is the same as that for a zero-coupon bond: It provides the annualized rate of return to investors who buy the bond and hold it until it matures. Each bond will have its own YTM, which incorporates information about the bond's current price, future payments, and the term structure of interest rates. Because it incorporates this information, the YTM is an often-quoted metric for bonds when they are traded in the marketplace, and has a direct relationship to a bond's price.

Consider again the same bond. Equation 16.7 will give us the YTM of the bond (we discuss the details of these calculations below):

$$\$1,075.15 = \frac{\$100}{1+y} + \frac{\$1,100}{(1+y)^2}$$

$$y = 0.0591 \text{ or } 5.91\%.$$

Comparing the YTM to the current yield of the bond, we see that the YTM is much smaller. Thus, if you used the current yield of 9.3% as a guide to what you would be earning if you bought the bond, you would be seriously misled.

Calculating the YTM of a bond with a maturity of greater than one year, as in the example above, can be substantially more complicated than calculating the YTM of a one-year bond (as we did in Section 16.2). For bonds of higher greater maturities, calculating y in Equation 16.7 involves solving equations with higher-order exponents, which can be more efficiently processed with financial calculators or Excel. Box 16.2 provides details of how to use Excel to calculate the YTM for a bond.

Box 16.2 Excel in Practice: Calculating YTM

Excel has a number of convenient ways of calculating the YTM of a bond, including YIELD, IRR, and Goal Seek functions.

Yield Function: Formulas > Financial > YIELD. YIELD(settlement, maturity, coupon rate, price, redemption, frequency). To use this function, you must first indicate the date that you are trading a bond (settlement), the maturity date of the bond (maturity), the coupon rate (coupon rate), the current price of the bond per $100 face value (price), the redemption price per $100 (redemption), and the compounding frequency (frequency). Note that the dates must be in Excel date format. For example, consider the two-year bond with a face value of $1,000 and a coupon rate of 10%, which traded for a price of $1,075.15. To set dates, suppose the date we traded the bond is 1/1/2024 and we type this date into cell A1, and therefore the maturity date two years later is 1/1/2026 and we type this into cell A2. The =YIELD function inputs would be: =YIELD(A1, A2, 10%, 107.515, 100, 1), which returns 0.059. Note that the format of the numbers matters. The settlement and maturity dates must either refer to cells with dates in them, or be in serial number format referencing dates. Note that the current price and redemption amounts are as of $100 face value.

IRR Function: Formulas > Financial > IRR. To use this function, the cash flows of the bond must be placed in order in consecutive cells, beginning with a cash outflow (i.e., negative cash flow) equal to the price of the bond. To illustrate, we can calculate the YTM of the two-year bond with face value of $1,000, a coupon rate of 10%, and price of $1,075.15 as:

	A	B	C	D	E
1		t=0	t=1	t=2	
2	Cash Flows:	-$1,075.15	$ 100	$ 1,100	=IRR(B2:D2)

	A	B	C	D	E
1		t=0	t=1	t=2	
2	Cash Flows:	-$1,075.15	$ 100	$ 1,100	5.91%

Goal Seek. The YTM is defined as the discount rate which sets the present value of a bond's cash flows equal to its price. Excel can be used to "guess" what this rate must be. For example, suppose we set up a spreadsheet where we take the same two-year bond's cash flows, and discount by some rate to produce a price. We can begin by guessing a YTM of 20%:

	A	B	C	D
1		t=0	t=1	t=2
2	Cash Flows:		$ 100	$ 1,100
3	Price:	=C2/(1+B4)+D2/(1+B4)^2		
4	YTM	20%		

This produces a price of $847.22, lower than the price of $1,075.15 for the bond. Thus, the YTM cannot be 20%. We can then check a lower YTM (say, 19%), and proceed until we find the rate that sets the price equal to $1,075.15.

Excel has a way to automate this process, known as Goal Seek. To use this, we can go to the "Data" tab, select "What-If Analysis" and then "Goal Seek ... ".

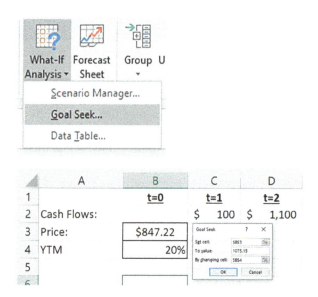

Doing so brings up a menu where we can specify to Excel that we want it to choose a value for the cell containing the YTM ("By changing cell") so that the price ("Set cell") is equal to $1,075.15 ("To value"). Doing so returns the YTM of the bond:

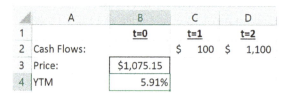

As Equation 16.7 shows, the YTM has a direct connection to the price of a bond. This provides us with three simple relationships for bonds:

- *Bond pricing relationship 1, par bonds:* If a bond's price equals its face value, then its yield equals its coupon rate.
- *Bond pricing relationship 2, premium bonds:* If a coupon bond has a price higher than its face value, its YTM is less than its current yield, which is in turn less than its coupon rate: YTM < current yield < coupon rate.
- *Bond pricing relationship 3, discount bonds:* If a coupon bond has a price lower than its face value, its YTM is greater than its current yield, which is in turn greater than its coupon rate: YTM > current yield > coupon rate.

To illustrate these relationships, consider the bonds from the previous section:

- a two-year bond with a face value of $1,000 and a coupon rate of 5%; and
- a two-year bond with a face value of $1,000 and a coupon rate of 10%.

We calculated that the price of the 5% coupon bond was $982.57 (a discount bond), and the price of the 10% coupon bond was $1,075.15 (a premium bond). Now also assume that there is a two-year bond with a face value of $1,000 selling for a price of $1,000 (a par bond), with a coupon rate of 5.94%. The timeline of cash flows for each bond is:

16.3 COUPON BONDS

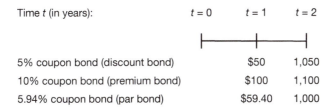

	Time t (in years):	$t = 0$	$t = 1$	$t = 2$
	5% coupon bond (discount bond)		$50	1,050
	10% coupon bond (premium bond)		$100	1,100
	5.94% coupon bond (par bond)		$59.40	1,000

Table 16.2 **Prices and yields of discount, premium, and par bonds.** The prices, current yields, and yields to maturity for three two-year bonds with face value of $1,000 each: a 5% coupon bond, a 10% coupon bond, and a par bond (with a 5.94% coupon). Prices and rates are calculated assuming that the one-year interest rate (r_1) is 4%, and the two-year interest rate (r_2) is 6%.

Bond	Price	Current yield	YTM
5% coupon bond (discount bond)	$982.57	5.09%	5.95%
10% coupon bond (premium bond)	$1,075.15	9.30%	5.91%
5.94% coupon bond (par bond)	$1,000.00	5.94%	5.94%

Table 16.2 provides the prices and yields of each bond. As the table shows, for the par bond, the YTM is the same as the coupon rate, in line with bond pricing relationship 1. For the premium bond, the coupon rate (10%) is greater than the current yield (9.30%), which is greater than the YTM (5.91%), in line with bond pricing relationship 2. Finally, for the discount bond, the coupon rate (5%) is less than the current yield (5.09%), which is less than the YTM (5.95%), in line with bond pricing relationship 3.

The examples above show how prices and yields for coupon bonds are related. They also help to clarify some misconceptions about yields. As you can observe in the recent examples and Table 16.2, bonds with the same maturity can have different yields to maturity. This was the case with the 5% coupon bond and 10% coupon bond above. Since yields and prices are tightly linked, is this a violation of **Principle 2:** *Equivalent assets that can be freely bought and sold will have the same market price*? The answer is no. In fact, for bonds with different coupon rates, when the yield curve is not flat, the law of one price implies that bonds of the same maturity will have different yields to maturity because their cash flows are different—in other words, they are not equivalent assets.

Example 16.5 (Calculating a Bond's Yield to Maturity): Consider again three US Treasury bonds traded in the marketplace, each with a face value of $1,000, paying annual coupons, and having prices as follows:

Bond	Maturity (years)	Coupon rate	Price
A	1	3.5%	$1,004.85
B	2	5.0%	$1,019.33
C	3	4.5%	$988.00

What is each bond's yield to maturity (YTM)?

Solution. We can set up Equation 16.7 for each bond (using the same timeline of cash flows as in Example 16.4). The equations will be:

$$\$1,004 = \frac{\$1,035}{1 + y_A},$$

$$y_A = \frac{1,035}{1,004} - 1$$

$$= 0.0309,$$

$$\$1{,}019.33 = \frac{\$50}{1+y_B} + \frac{1{,}050}{(1+y_B)^2},$$

$$\$988.00 = \frac{\$45}{1+y_C} + \frac{45}{(1+y_C)^2} + \frac{1{,}045}{(1+y_C)^3}.$$

We can calculate the YTM for Bond A by hand, since it has a maturity of one year. For Bonds B and C, we can use Excel to calculate the YTM. We do so with the =IRR function:

	A	B	C	D	E	F
1		t=0	t=1	t=2	t=3	YTM
2	Bond B:	-$1,019.33	$50.00	$1,050.00		=IRR(B2:D2)
3	Bond C:	-$988.00	$45.00	$45.00	$1,045.00	=IRR(B3:E3)

	A	B	C	D	E	F
1		t=0	t=1	t=2	t=3	YTM
2	Bond B:	-$1,019.33	$50.00	$1,050.00		3.98%
3	Bond C:	-$988.00	$45.00	$45.00	$1,045.00	4.94%

This provides a YTM of 3.98% for Bond B, and a YTM of 4.94% for Bond C.

However, in the past, some investment companies that invest exclusively in US Treasury bonds have advertised yields that appear much higher than the interest rates on other known investments of the same maturity. The yields that they are advertising are current yields, and the bonds that they are investing in are premium bonds that have relatively high coupon rates. Thus, according to bond pricing relationship 2, the actual return you will earn is expected to be considerably less than the advertised current yield.

To illustrate, suppose that you have $10,000 to invest for one year. You are deciding between putting your money in a one-year, government-insured, bank certificate of deposit (CD) offering an interest rate of 5% and investing in the shares of a US Treasury bond fund that holds one-year bonds with a coupon rate of 8%. The bonds held by the fund are selling at a premium over their face value: For every $10,000 of face value that you will receive at maturity one year from now, you must pay $10,285.71 now. The current yield on the fund is $800 / $10,285.71 or 7.78%, and this is the yield that the fund is advertising. If the fund charges a 1% annual fee for its services, what rate of return will you actually earn?

If there were no fees at all for investing in the fund, your rate of return for the year would be 5%, precisely the same rate of return as on the bank CD. This is because investing your $10,000 in the fund will achieve the same return as buying an 8% coupon bond with a face value of $10,000 for a price of $10,285.71:

$$\text{Rate of return} = \frac{\$10{,}800 - \$10{,}285.71}{\$10{,}285.71} = 5\%.$$

However, because you have to pay the fund a fee equal to 1% of your $10,000, your rate of return will be 4% instead of 5%.

QUICK CHECK 16.6 Suppose that the one-year interest rate (r_1) is 4%, the two-year interest rate (r_2) is 5%, and the three-year interest rate (r_3) is 6%. What would be the price and YTM of a three-year coupon bond with a face value of $1,000 and a coupon rate of 4% per year?

16.3.4 Other Effects on Bond Yields

There are many other features that can differentiate bonds, which can cause their prices and yields to differ; for example:

- Callability. This feature gives the issuer of the bond the right to redeem it at a prespecified price (i.e., "call it back" from the owner) before the final maturity date. A bond that has this feature is a callable bond.
- Convertibility. This feature gives the holder of a bond issued by a corporation the right to convert the bond into a prespecified number of shares of common stock. A bond that has this feature is a convertible bond.

These additional features can increase or decrease the price of an otherwise identical bond (i.e., one which offers the same stream of promised cash flows and the same maturity) compared to one that does not have the feature. Any feature that makes the bond more favorable to the issuer and thus less favorable to the bondholder may lower its price, since bond buyers will want to pay less for it. In contrast, any feature that makes it more favorable to the bond buyers will increase its price, since they will be willing to pay more for the feature. Thus, callability will cause a bond to have a lower price (and a higher yield to maturity). Convertibility will cause a bond to have a higher price and a lower yield to maturity (see Section 14.3.2).

16.4 Uncertainty in Interest Rates

In the real world, unlike the predictable interest rate framework we have used so far in this chapter, interest rates are not predictable and change in uncertain ways. For example, upon the unexpected start of the global financial crisis in late 2007, central banks around the world dropped interest rates substantially in order to help boost the economy.

However, the basics of valuation in such a situation are the same: When considering cash flows of a certain horizon even in situations of uncertainty in interest rates, the risk-free asset for that horizon is the zero-coupon bond (i.e., pure discount bond) for that horizon. For example, if your horizon is that you need money for sure in ten years, then a ten-year zero-coupon bond is the risk-free asset for that. When there are multiple payments in a world of uncertainty about interest rates, then we proceed by determining the cash flows for each horizon, and then multiplying these cash flows by the price of the zero-coupon bond (i.e., the discount factor) maturing in that horizon. The logic is due to the law of one price, as per Principle 2—if two series of cash payments are identical, the prices of the cash flows must also be the same.

Thus, we can determine the current value of known future payments in a situation with uncertain interest rates by using the same tools that we have covered thus far. However, investment values change over time when interest rates change, and with uncertain interest rates, investment values will also change in uncertain ways over time. Thus, knowing how interest rates may change in the future will help us estimate the value of the investments those interest rates effect.

In this section we describe conceptually how uncertainty in interest rates can affect investments, and how potential changes in interest rates can be inferred. We then provide details of these calculations in practice.

16.4.1 Uncertainty in Interest Rates and Investments

To illustrate how we can incorporate interest rate uncertainty into our framework, consider the example from Section 16.1: Investors can invest in bills, which mature in one year, or in bonds, which mature in two years. Each pays $1,000 at maturity, and the two-year bonds are assumed to not have any payout at the end of the first year. Suppose that the interest rate is 1% per year.

The price that the one-year bill sells for is determined by the $1,000 promised payment in year 1 discounted by the interest rate:

$$\frac{\$1,000}{1+r} = \frac{\$1,000}{1.01} = \$990.10.$$

Similarly, the price of the two-year bond is determined by the $1,000 promised payment in year 2 discounted by the interest rate:

$$\frac{\$1,000}{(1+r)^2} = \frac{\$1,000}{1.01^2} = \$980.30.$$

We knew in Section 16.1 exactly what the price of the two-year bond will be in one year at $t = 1$ since interest rates were fixed and certain. However, how can we find out what the price is if there is uncertainty about interest rates?

Assume there are two investors, Green and Purple. Green needs $1,000 one year from now, and Purple needs $1,000 two years from now. To eliminate all risk, Green could invest $990.10 exclusively in one-year bills, and Purple could invest $980.30 exclusively in two-year bonds. Thus, each investor has matched the investment to the horizon, a concept we refer to as maturity matching. It is also worth noting, in line with our discussions in Chapter 6, that each investor has an own risk-free asset depending on their investment needs. For Green, the risk-free asset is bills, and for Purple the risk-free asset is bonds. Broadly speaking, this example illustrates how interest rates of different horizons can meet the needs of different investors.

In practice, when a firm or an individual pursues a matching strategy, it has to match the unit of account as well as the maturity of its liabilities. Consider, for example, an insurance company selling life annuities around the world. Customers can choose the currency and can even link the payments to the cost of living. With a full menu of fixed-income securities of different maturities, investors are able to choose the risk-free asset that meets their individual needs.

Note that there is also another strategy that Purple could undertake. Instead of matching the maturity of her investment to her two-year horizon, Purple could invest in a one-year bill, and when it matures she can reinvest in another one-year bill, which is known as rolling over. Why might Purple be tempted to do that? She might think that bill interest rates are going to rise by a lot over the coming year, and if she invests $990.10 in a strategy of rolling over one-year bills, she will wind up with more than $1,000. The timeline of this possible investment strategy is given by:

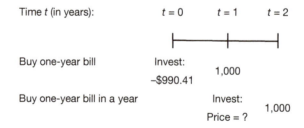

However, this strategy involves taking a risk, because no one knows what the one-year spot interest rate will be a year from now.

16.4.2 Forward Rates of Interest

The interest rate one year from now (i.e., what the one-year spot interest rate will be a year from now) is known as the one-year forward rate of interest. A forward rate is the rate at which you could borrow or lend with certainty over a specified future period (in our example, one year in the future). In a world of interest rate uncertainty, forward rates may or may not be the same as expected future spot rates. One reason why forward rates can be different from future spot rates is due to the risk premium, the additional return an asset is expected to provide beyond the risk-free rate of return, stemming from uncertainty in interest rates.

Forward rates of interest can be quoted for different horizons—for example, what the two-year interest rate will be one year from now—as well as for different time points in the future—for example, what the one-year interest rate will be two years from now. We will denote forward rates of interest by $f_{t,T}$, where t is the future date when the interest rate occurs, and T is the maturity of the borrowing. Thus, the one-year interest rate two years from now will be denoted to as $f_{2,3}$, since it reflects borrowing that occurs in year $t = 2$ for one year (until year $t = 3$). Figure 16.9 represents this for one-year forward interest rates.

We can calculate forward rates of interest by inference through observed market spot interest rates (i.e., actual transactions). In particular, based on current market spot interest rates, and in keeping with **Principle 2:** *Equivalent assets that can be freely bought and sold will have the same market price*, Purple's strategy should not give her any guaranteed profits (i.e., an arbitrage) versus buying and selling the one-year bill and two-year bond. Put differently, as of right now, the new one-year rate would have to be set so that Purple's strategy does not make any profit. Note that for each dollar invested, Purple's strategy of buying the one-year bill and then another one-year bill will yield at $t = 2$: $(1 + r_1) \times (1 + f_{1,2})$. In contrast, her strategy of buying the two-year bond will yield $(1 + r_2)^2$ at $t = 2$ for each dollar invested. The forward rate will set these two amounts equal to each other:

$$(1 + r_1) \times (1 + f_{1,2}) = (1 + r_2)^2$$

$$(1 + f_{1,2}) = \frac{(1 + r_2)^2}{(1 + r_1)}$$

$$f_{1,2} = \frac{(1.02)^2}{1.01} - 1$$

$$= 0.0301 \text{ or } 3.01\%.$$

Thus, the one-year forward rate of interest in this setting is 3.01%.

16.4.3 Estimating Forward Rates of Interest

Forward rates of interest are a tool for investors to meet their investment needs, so it is useful to know how to estimate them. For example, forward rates are often assumed to be forecasts of what investors expect future interest rates to be, an idea known as the expectations theory of the term structure of interest rates. Under this assumption, they can be used in models which use information about future interest rates (see Chapter 19). We can calculate forward rates of interest as of any date and over any time horizon by incorporating information on spot interest rates:

$$f_{t,T} = \frac{(1 + r_T)^T}{(1 + r_t)^t} - 1, \qquad (16.8)$$

where $T > t$.

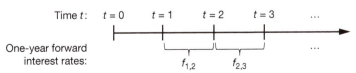

FIGURE 16.9 Forward rates of interest. This figure depicts one-year forward interest rates. $f_{1,2}$ represents the interest rate for borrowing at $t = 1$, with repayment at $t = 2$. $f_{2,3}$ represents the interest rate for borrowing at $t = 2$, with repayment at $t = 3$.

The prices of pure discount bonds can also be used to determine forward interest rates by the same logic. In particular, we can take Equation 16.8 and rearrange it to discover that forward interest rates can be determined by taking the ratio of prices of pure discount bonds of different maturities:

$$f_{t,T} = \frac{(1+r_T)^T}{(1+r_t)^t} - 1 = \frac{\frac{\text{par}}{(1+r_t)^t}}{\frac{\text{par}}{(1+r_T)^T}} = \frac{P_t}{P_T} - 1. \qquad (16.9)$$

With a complete set of pure discount bonds for all relevant maturities, it is possible to extract forward rates for different horizons in the future. Table 16.3 shows the same pure discount bonds with maturities ranging from 1 year to 30 years as was used in Table 16.1.

Table 16.3 Discount function, yield curve, and forward rates. Hypothetical data for the price per $1 of par value, YTM (yield), and one-year forward interest rates derived for pure discount bonds of varying maturities. The price per $1 and yields can be used to determine the present value of a certain cash flow that occurs the indicated number of years in the future.

Years to maturity	Price per $1	Yield to maturity	One-year forward rate
1	0.99	1.00%	1.20%
2	0.98	1.10%	1.40%
3	0.96	1.20%	1.60%
4	0.95	1.30%	1.80%
5	0.93	1.40%	2.00%
6	0.91	1.50%	2.20%
7	0.89	1.60%	2.40%
8	0.87	1.70%	2.60%
9	0.85	1.80%	2.80%
10	0.83	1.90%	3.01%
11	0.80	2.00%	3.21%
12	0.78	2.10%	3.41%
13	0.75	2.20%	3.61%
14	0.73	2.30%	3.81%
15	0.70	2.40%	4.01%
16	0.67	2.50%	4.21%
17	0.65	2.60%	4.41%
18	0.62	2.70%	4.62%
19	0.59	2.80%	4.82%
20	0.56	2.90%	5.02%
21	0.54	3.00%	5.22%
22	0.51	3.10%	5.42%
23	0.48	3.20%	5.63%
24	0.46	3.30%	5.83%

Table 16.3 (cont.)

Years to maturity	Price per $1	Yield to maturity	One-year forward rate
25	0.43	3.40%	6.03%
26	0.41	3.50%	6.23%
27	0.38	3.60%	6.44%
28	0.36	3.70%	6.64%
29	0.34	3.80%	6.84%
30	0.32	3.90%	

Example 16.6 (Calculating Forward Rates of Interest): Consider the following spot interest rates for borrowing now until the indicated time horizon:

Horizon T	Spot interest rate	
1	r_1	2%
2	r_2	3%
3	r_3	5%

What are the one-year forward rates of interest as of $t = 1$ and $t = 2$?

Solution. First, we can draw a timeline of the cash flows for the bond of each horizon:

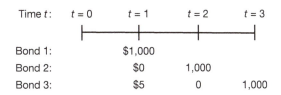

We can then calculate the one-year forward rates using Equation 16.9:

$$f_{1,2} = \frac{(1+r_2)^2}{1+r_1} - 1 = \frac{(1.03)^2}{1.02} - 1 = 0.0401,$$

$$f_{2,3} = \frac{(1+r_3)^3}{(1+r_2)^2} - 1 = \frac{(1.05)^3}{(1.03)^2} - 1 = 0.0912.$$

> **QUICK CHECK 16.7** Suppose that the two-year interest rate was the same as the one-year interest rate: 1%. What would the one-year forward interest rate be for $t = 1$?

In this section we discussed the concept of uncertainty in interest rates, when interest rates may change in the future. We went over ways to estimate future interest rates using current market data. Changes in interest rates stemming from this uncertainty can significantly impact the value of investments. In the next section we show how this may be the case, and ways to measure how susceptible investments may be to this interest rate risk.

16.5 Measuring Interest Rate Risk

As we have discussed, uncertainty about interest rates can change the value of investments substantially over time. Normally, we think of buying government bonds as a conservative investment policy because there is no risk of default involved. However, an economic environment of unpredictably changing interest rates can produce big gains or losses for investors in bonds. For example, consider a zero-coupon bond that pays $1,000 in ten years:

Time t (years): $t = 0$ $t = 1$ $t = 2$ ...   10
                       0   0 $1,000

If the term structure of interest rates is flat at 5%, then the value (price) of this bond is, using (Equation 16.2):

$$P = \frac{\$1,000}{(1+0.05)^{10}} = \$613.91.$$

Now let's say that right after you buy the bond, interest rates suddenly increase to 10%. Then the price of the bond will change to:

$$P = \frac{\$1,000}{(1+0.10)^{10}} = \$385.54.$$

Thus, the value of your investment goes down substantially. While the value of this bond will be the face value at maturity (as we discussed previously), a change in interest rates may pose significant issues for investors who are looking to sell the bond in the interim. Put differently, all bonds—even US Treasury bonds with no default risk—are exposed to interest rate risk, changes in value due to movements in interest rates. This is another example of **Principle 6:** *Risk is fundamental to financial analysis and must be explicitly considered in all financial decisions.*

In this section we discuss how bond values may change when interest rates change, and ways to measure how sensitive bond prices are to changes in interest rates.

16.5.1 Duration

A widely used measure of the interest rate sensitivity of a bond's value—how much a bond's value changes when interest rates change—is duration. Duration is related to a bond's time to maturity, and the higher a bond's duration, the more sensitive its value is to changes in interest rates. This is because the present value of cash flows further out into the future are more affected by changes in discount rates due to the time value of money (**Principle 1:** *A dollar today is not worth the same as a dollar tomorrow*).

To illustrate, consider the example of a ten-year zero-coupon bond. Given a flat term structure of interest rates, when rates increased from 5% to 10% the price of the bond decreased from $613.91 to $385.54, a drop in value of 37.2%:

$$P = \frac{\$1,000}{(1+0.05)^{10}} = \$613.91,$$

$$P = \frac{\$1,000}{(1+0.10)^{10}} = \$385.54.$$

Now consider if the bond were a one-year bond instead. Then the prices at 5% and 10% interest rates would be:

$$P = \frac{\$1,000}{1 + 0.05} = \$952.38,$$

$$P = \frac{\$1,000}{1 + 0.10} = \$909.09.$$

In this case, an increase in interest rates leads to a drop in value from $952.38 to $909.09, a decrease of 4.5%. Thus, the value of the longer-maturity bond is more sensitive to changes in interest rates. Figure 16.10 demonstrates this by showing how the prices of zero-coupon bonds of different maturities each respond to changes in interest rates, assuming a flat term structure of interest rates. As the graph shows, the prices of the longer-maturity bonds change by more when interest rates change, in line with them having a greater duration.

There are two common measures of duration that we can calculate: Macaulay duration and modified duration. First is Macaulay duration:

$$\begin{aligned}
\text{Macaulay duration} &= \frac{1}{P} \times \sum_{t=1}^{T} PV(CF_t) \times t \\
&= \frac{1}{P} \times \left(\frac{CF_1}{1+r_1} \times 1 + \frac{CF_2}{(1+r_2)^2} \times 2 + \cdots + \frac{CF_T}{(1+r_T)^T} \times T \right),
\end{aligned} \quad (16.10)$$

where T is the maturity of the bond, $PV(CF_t)$ is the present value of the cash flow of the bond at date t, and P is the price of the bond. Note that one could alternatively use the bond's YTM (y) to derive the present values of the cash flows instead of spot interest rates.

Macaulay duration attempts to assess how long-term an investment the bond is (and thus how sensitive it is to interest rate changes), accounting for both the maturity and when the cash flows occur during the life of the bond. It does so by taking a weighted average of the maturity of the bond, placing more weight on the dates that deliver more of the bond's value (i.e., the dates where there are cash

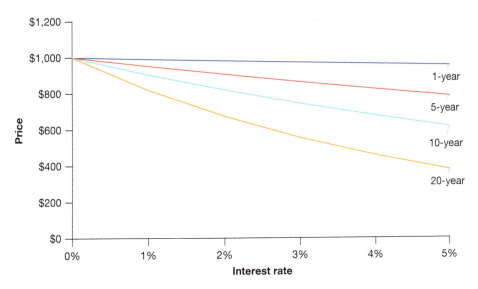

FIGURE 16.10 Interest rate changes and bond prices of different maturities. This figure graphs the prices of zero-coupon bonds of different maturities—1 year, 5 years, 10 years, and 20 years—for different interest rates, assuming that the term structure of interest rates is flat at the indicated rate over all maturities. The prices of longer-maturity bonds change by more than the prices of shorter-maturity bonds when interest rates change.

flows that contribute relatively more to the price of the bond). These differences, based on when payments are made during a bond's life, are why duration is needed as a measure, in addition to simply the time to maturity, which is just the time until the last payment of a bond. Because of **Principle 1: A dollar today is not worth the same as a dollar tomorrow**, we know that an instrument with $100 of its payments in year 3 and $1 in year 10 is very different from a (zero-coupon) bond that makes a $101 payment in year 10.

To illustrate, consider two different three-year bonds: the first is a zero-coupon bond with a face value of $1,000, and the second is a coupon bond with a face value of $1,000 and a coupon rate of 10%:

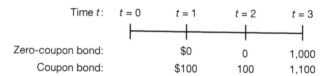

Assume that the term structure of interest rates is flat at 5%. The price of the zero-coupon bond is thus:

$$P = \frac{\$1,000}{(1+0.05)^3} = \$863.84,$$

while the price of the coupon bond is:

$$P = \frac{\$100}{1+0.05} + \frac{\$100}{(1+0.05)^2} + \frac{\$1,100}{(1+0.05)^3} = \$1,136.16.$$

Note that the bonds have the same maturity; however, their durations are different because some of the value of the coupon bond comes from the cash flows at $t = 1$ and $t = 2$, while all of the value of the zero-coupon bond is from the cash flow at $t = 3$; each of these time periods imply different interest rate sensitivities. The Macaulay duration of the zero-coupon bond is, using (Equation 16.10):

$$\text{Macaulay duration} = \frac{1}{P} \times \left(\frac{CF_3}{(1+r_3)^3} \times 3 \right)$$

$$= \frac{1}{\$863.84} \times \left(\frac{\$1,000}{(1+0.05)^3} \times 3 \right)$$

$$= 3 \text{ years.}$$

The Macaulay duration for the zero-coupon bond is thus three years, the same as its maturity. In fact, in general, for a zero-coupon bond the Macaulay duration is equal to its maturity. This is because all of the cash flows for a zero-coupon bond occur at maturity.

For the coupon bond, the Macaulay duration is:

$$\text{Macaulay duration} = \frac{1}{P} \times \left(\frac{CF_1}{1+r_1} \times 1 + \frac{CF_2}{(1+r_2)^2} \times 2 + \frac{CF_3}{(1+r_3)^3} \times 3 \right)$$

$$= \frac{1}{\$1,136.16} \times \left(\frac{\$100}{1+0.05} \times 1 + \frac{\$100}{(1+0.05)^2} \times 2 + \frac{\$1,100}{(1+0.05)^3} \times 3 \right)$$

$$= 2.75 \text{ years.}$$

The coupon bond thus has a duration of 2.75 years, *less* than the maturity of three years. The reason is that some of the cash flows occur before the maturity date of $t = 3$, and those create weight at the earlier dates. However, the largest payment occurs at the maturity date, so the duration is still close to three years.

Macaulay duration is useful for understanding the relative sensitivities of different bonds to interest rates: the prices of bonds with higher Macaulay durations will move more when interest rates move.

The second measure of duration tells us how much prices will change when interest rates change. This measure is known as modified duration, and is useful for understanding exactly how much a bond investment's value will rise or fall when interest rates change. This is in contrast to Macaulay duration, which informs about relative sensitivities between bonds (i.e., that one bond is more sensitive to interest rate changes than another). Modified duration can be calculated through the following formula:

$$\text{Modified duration} = \frac{\text{Macaulay duration}}{\left(1 + \frac{y}{T}\right)}, \quad (16.11)$$

where y is the YTM of the bond. The modified duration tells us by what percent a bond's price will fall when interest rates increase by 1 percentage point or 100 basis points (bps), given what interest rates are now. Basis points, known as bps or "bips," are used to describe percentage change in value. One basis point is equivalent to 0.01% (1/100th of a percent) or 0.0001 in decimal form.

For the three-year coupon bond, note that since the term structure of interest rates is flat at 5%, its YTM must also be 5%, so $y = 0.05$ (you can also see this by looking at Equation 16.9 and comparing it to the equation we set up for the price). Thus, the modified duration of this bond will be:

$$\begin{aligned}\text{Modified duration} &= \frac{\text{Macaulay duration}}{\left(1 + \frac{y}{T}\right)} \\ &= \frac{2.75}{\left(1 + \frac{0.05}{3}\right)} \\ &= 2.70.\end{aligned}$$

This tells us that this bond's price will decrease by 2.7% if interest rates increase by 1 percentage point.

Box 16.3 Excel in Practice: Calculating Duration

Calculating the duration of a bond by hand can become cumbersome for bonds with longer maturities. Fortunately, spreadsheet programs like Excel can make these calculations much quicker and easier.

The built-in Excel function =MDURATION calculates the Macaulay duration of a bond. The syntax is =MDURATION(settlement, maturity, coupon rate, y, frequency). Similar to the =YIELD function, the settlement date is the date the bond is traded, and the maturity date is when it matures. Frequency refers to the compounding frequency; we would select 1 for yearly bond payments. Consider the example of a two-year bond with a face value of $100 and a coupon rate of 10%, which traded for a price of $107.515. The =YIELD function inputs, as we saw in Box 16.2, were: =YIELD(A1, A2, 10%, 107.515, 100, 1), where cell A1 contained the trading date 1/1/2024 and cell A2 contained the maturity date 1/1/2026, which returns 0.059 as the YTM y. As previously noted, the format of the numbers matters—the settlement and maturity dates must either refer to cells with dates in them, or be in serial number format referencing dates. For our duration formula, we would have: =DURATION(A1, A2, 10%, 5.9%, 1), which returns 1.91 years:

	A	B	C	D
1	1/1/2024	=DURATION(A1,A2,10%,5.9%,1)		
2	1/1/2026			

	A	B	C
1	1/1/2024	1.912182	
2	1/1/2026		

The companion Excel app to this chapter also shows these calculations, given inputs for the cash flows of a bond.

QUICK CHECK 16.8 Calculate the modified duration of the three-year zero-coupon bond which had a face value of $1,000 and a price of $863.84.

(Excel) Example 16.7 (Calculating Bond Duration): Consider a three-year bond with a coupon rate of 5% and a face value of $1,000. The one-year interest rate (r_1) is 4%, the two-year interest rate (r_2) is 5%, and the three-year interest rate (r_3) is 6%. What is the Macaulay duration and modified duration of this bond? If interest rates were to increase by 1.5 percentage points (150 bps), how much would you expect the price of the bond to change? If the bond instead paid no coupons, would you predict that its price would be more or less sensitive to interest rates than the coupon bond?

Solution. First note the timeline of cash flows for this bond:

Time t: $t=0$ $t=1$ $t=2$ $t=3$

Cash flows: $50   50   1,050

To use the duration formulas, we first need to calculate the bond's price. With information on the term structure of interest rates, we can use Equation 16.7:

$$P = \frac{C}{1+r_1} + \frac{C}{(1+r_2)^2} + \cdots + \frac{C+PAR}{(1+r_T)^T}$$

$$= \frac{\$50}{1+0.04} + \frac{\$50}{(1+0.05)^2} + \frac{\$1,050}{(1+0.06)^3}$$

$$= \$975.03.$$

The YTM (y) will be used in the duration formulas, so our next step is to calculate that. It is convenient to use Excel to do so:

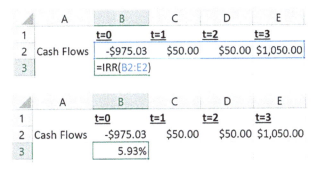

Now let us use the Macaulay duration formula (Equation 16.10). We could discount by the spot interest rates to take present values, but for practice we will use the newly calculated YTM y instead:

$$\text{Macaulay duration} = \frac{1}{P} \times \left(\frac{CF_1}{1+y} \times 1 + \frac{CF_2}{(1+y)^2} \times 2 + \frac{CF_3}{(1+y)^3} \times 3 \right)$$

$$= \frac{1}{\$975.03} \times \left(\frac{\$50}{1.0593} \times 1 + \frac{\$50}{(1.0593)^2} \times 2 + \frac{\$1,050}{(1.0593)^3} \times 3 \right)$$

$$= 2.86 \text{ years.}$$

Now, for the modified duration (Equation 16.11):

$$\text{Modified duration} = \frac{\text{Macaulay duration}}{\left(1 + \frac{y}{T}\right)}$$

$$= \frac{2.86}{\left(1 + \frac{0.0593}{3}\right)}$$

$$= 2.80.$$

We can expect this bond's price to decrease by 2.8% if interest rates were to increase by 1 percentage point. This allows us to answer the question of how much the bond's price will change if interest rates increased by 150 bps: In this case, the bond's price will decrease by 2.8% × 1.5 = 4.2%.

Finally, we are asked about how much prices would change if the bond were instead a zero-coupon bond. Note that the Macaulay duration of a zero-coupon bond is simply equal to its maturity, so the Macaulay duration would be three years if the bond paid no coupons. This is higher than the Macaulay duration of the coupon bond, so the bond's price would be *more* sensitive to interest rate changes if it paid no coupon.

16.5.2 Convexity

Duration is a useful measure of how sensitive bonds are to changes in interest rates. However, the full picture of how much a bond's value may change when interest rates change depends on the current level of interest rates.

The amount by which a bond's price sensitivity to interest rates changes as interest rates change is known as convexity. A bond's convexity measures how much the bond's duration changes when interest rates change. Why does bond price sensitivity change when interest rates change? The reason is that a 1 percentage point (100 bps) change in interest rates can have a different effect depending on the current interest rate. For example, at a 1% interest rate, a 1 percentage point (100 bps) increase is a doubling of the interest rate to 2% (or in other words, an increase of 100%). In contrast, at a 10% interest rate, a 1 percentage point (100 bps) increase is an increase of 10%. This magnitude of interest rate change is reflected in the prices of bonds. Not accounting for convexity when examining interest rate risk can result in an inaccurate appraisal of the true interest rate risk that an investor faces.

To illustrate how a bond price changes at different interest rates, consider three different bonds each with a face value of $1,000: a 30-year 8% coupon bond, a 10-year 8% coupon bond, and a 30-year zero-coupon bond. Figure 16.11(a) shows what their prices would be at different interest rates, assuming that interest rates do not vary by maturity (i.e., the term structure of interest rates is flat).

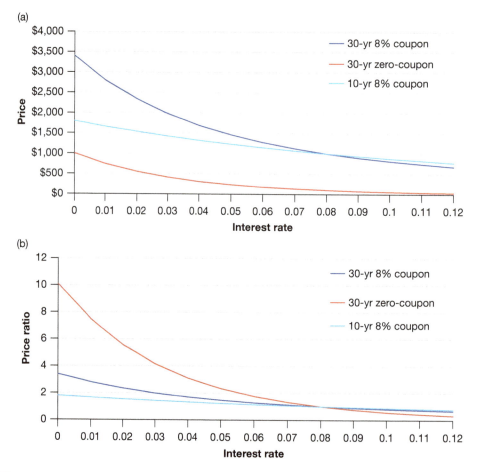

FIGURE 16.11 Interest rate changes and bond prices of different maturities. This figure graphs the prices of three bonds—a 30-year 8% coupon bond, a 10-year 8% coupon bond, and a 30-year zero-coupon bond—at various interest rates, assuming a flat term structure of interest rates. (a) The prices of each bond at the indicated interest rates; (b) the price ratio, defined as prices scaled by each bond's price, given an interest rate of 8%. How much prices change given a 1% change in interest rates depends on what the current interest rate is.

For example, at interest rates of all maturities (or a YTM) of 8%, the 30-year 8% coupon bond would be priced at the par value of $1,000. If instead interest rates at all maturities were 6%, the same bond would sell for a premium at $1,275.30, while at rates of 10% the bond would become a discount bond and sell for $811.46. Examining the curves, we can see that the changes in price to a 1% change in interest rates are different depending on what the interest rate is. Consider the 30-year 8% coupon bond. Going from an interest rate of 1% to 2% causes the price of the bond to drop by 16% (from a price of $2,807 to $2,344). However, going from an interest rate of 10% to 11% causes the price of the bond to drop by only 9%. This shows us that a 1% change in interest rates can cause either smaller or larger bond price reactions, depending on the level of interest rates.

Figure 16.11(b) shows the prices of the bonds relative to what their prices are at a reference interest rate of 8%. For example, at the 8% interest rate, the price of a 30-year 8% coupon bond with a face value of $1,000 would be $1,000. At a 1% interest rate, the price is $2,806.54, whereas at a 10% interest rate its price is $811.46. The ratio of its price at a 1% interest rate to its price at the reference 8% interest rate is, therefore, $2,806.54 / $1,000 = 2.8065. In contrast, the ratio of its price at the 10% interest rate to its price at the reference 8% interest rate is $811.46 / $1,000 = 0.8115. We can see that the relative price movements when interest rates change are sharper when interest rates are lower, reflected by the steeper curve at lower interest rates. Note also that the zero-coupon bond has an even steeper curve, reflecting the fact that the convexity of such a bond is greater: Interest rate changes at lower interest rates have an even more dramatic influence on the price of the zero-coupon bond, because all of its value comes from the more distant future. Finally, the 10-year bond has the flattest curve, which shows that convexity is lower for bonds with shorter maturities.

We can calculate convexity using the following formula:

$$\text{Convexity} = \frac{1}{P \times (1+y)^2} \times \sum_{t=1}^{T} \left[PV(CF_t) \times (t^2 + t) \right]$$

$$= \frac{1}{P \times (1+y)^2} \times \sum_{t=1}^{T} \left[\frac{CF_t}{(1+y)^t} \times (t^2 + t) \right]. \qquad (16.12)$$

With the convexity measure in hand, we can estimate how much a bond's price will change when yields/interest rates change by Δy:

$$\%\Delta P = -(\text{modified duration}) \times \Delta y + \frac{1}{2} \times \text{convexity} \times (\Delta y)^2. \qquad (16.13)$$

To illustrate the more accurate view of a bond's sensitivity to interest rates by accounting for convexity, we will calculate the convexity of the 30-year zero-coupon bond, and use it to gauge how much the bond's price will change if interest rates fall by 3 percentage points. Assume that the yield curve is currently flat at 8%. To begin, note that the Macaulay duration of the bond will be 30 years, since it is a zero-coupon bond. The modified duration of the bond (Equation 16.11) will be:

$$\text{Modified duration} = \frac{\text{Macaulay duration}}{\left(1 + \frac{y}{T}\right)}$$

$$= \frac{30}{\left(1 + \frac{0.08}{30}\right)}$$

$$= 29.920.$$

This tells us that the bond's price will go up by 29.92% if interest rates fall by 1 percentage point. This would imply that the bond's price will go up by 29.92 × 3 = 89.76%. Note that the bond's price given a yield of 8% is (Equation 16.3):

$$P = \frac{\$1,000}{1.08^{30}}$$
$$= \$99.38.$$

This implies that the bond's price will rise to $99.38 × 1.8976 = $188.58 when interest rates fall by 3%. However, let us now calculate the bond's convexity and account for it when examining how the bond's price will change. First, we calculate the bond's convexity using Equation 16.12:

$$\text{Convexity} = \frac{1}{P \times (1+y)^2} \times \sum_{t=1}^{T} \left[\frac{CF_t}{(1+y)^t} \times (t^2 + t) \right]$$

$$= \frac{1}{99.38 \times (1+0.08)^2} \times \left[\frac{1,000}{(1+0.08)^{30}} \times (30^2 + 30) \right]$$

$$= 797.304.$$

Now, using Equation 16.13 we can see what the price change should be for a 3 percentage point decrease in yields ($\Delta y = -0.03$) when accounting for convexity:

$$\%\Delta P = -(\text{modified duration}) \times \Delta y + \frac{1}{2} \times \text{convexity} \times (\Delta y)^2$$

$$= -29.920 \times -0.03 + \frac{1}{2} \times 797.304 \times (-0.03)^2$$

$$= 1.256.$$

Thus, we would predict that the bond's price would instead increase by 125.6% if interest rates fell by 3 percentage points.

Both convexity and duration are important tools for accurately assessing the interest rate risk of any fixed-income investment, especially ones of longer maturities where interest rate changes affect value the most.

> **QUICK CHECK 16.9** Between a five-year zero-coupon bond and a ten-year zero-coupon bond, which would you anticipate convexity would matter more for when ascertaining interest rate sensitivity?

Example 16.8 (Calculating Bond Price Changes Using Convexity): Consider the same bond we used in Example 16.7, a three-year bond with a coupon rate of 5% and a face value of $1,000. Accounting for convexity, if interest rates were to increase by 1.5 percentage points (150 bps), by how much would you predict the price of the bond would change?

Solution. From Example 16.7 we saw that the price of the bond was $975.03, the YTM was 5.93%, and the modified duration was 2.80. Based on the modified duration, we calculated a 4.2% decrease in the price of the bond. Now, calculating the convexity, we have (Equation 16.12):

$$\text{Convexity} = \frac{1}{P \times (1+y)^2} \times \sum_{t=1}^{T} \left[\frac{CF_t}{(1+y)^t} \times (t^2 + t) \right]$$

$$= \frac{1}{975.03 \times (1+0.0593)^2} \times \left[\frac{50}{(1+0.0593)} \times (1^2+1) + \frac{50}{(1+0.0593)^2} \times (2^2+2) + \frac{1{,}050}{(1+0.0593)^3} \times (3^2+3) \right]$$

$$= 9.976.$$

Using Equation 16.13, we can determine the price change given $\Delta y = 0.015$:

$$\%\Delta P = -(\text{modified duration}) \times \Delta y + \frac{1}{2} \times \text{convexity} \times (\Delta y)^2$$

$$= -2.80 \times 0.015 + \frac{1}{2} \times 9.976 \times (0.015)^2$$

$$= -0.041.$$

Incorporating convexity, we would predict that the price of the bond would fall by 4.1%, which is close to the fall predicted using duration alone. This reinforces the point that convexity has less bite for bonds with shorter maturities.

16.6 Real versus Nominal Interest Rates

Most interest rates are quoted as nominal interest rates, which are interest rates in terms of some currency (e.g., US dollars). However, people often care about real interest rates, which are denominated in units of consumer goods. Real interest rates adjust for inflation, the general increase in the prices of those goods over time. The nominal interest rate does not take into account that money may have less purchasing power in the future; it does not account for inflation. The real interest rate, in contrast, adjusts for inflation because it reflects how much each dollar would actually be able to purchase.

In some countries the rate of inflation is high year to year, meaning that prices for the same goods over time increase substantially. In other countries, the rate of inflation is lower from year to year. Real rates can be very different from nominal rates due to inflation. Furthermore, central banks in countries may increase nominal rates in order to combat inflation.

The general formula relating the real rate of interest to the nominal rate of interest and the rate of inflation is:

$$1 + \text{real interest rate} = \frac{1 + \text{nominal interest rate}}{1 + \text{rate of inflation}}, \quad (16.14)$$

or equivalently,

$$\text{Real interest rate} = \frac{\text{nominal interest rate} - \text{rate of inflation}}{1 + \text{rate of inflation}}. \quad (16.15)$$

When examining interest rates and performing the analyses we discussed in this chapter, it is important to keep the rate of inflation in mind as it can affect the actual rate of return on an investment, by considering how many goods can be purchased using that return. While the majority of bonds are quoted using nominal interest rates, there are some that explicitly use real interest rates. For example, in the UK, index-linked gilts are bonds that have been traded since 1981 and which adjust their payments based on the prevailing rate of inflation. Other countries also offer similar products; for example, the United States offers Treasury Inflation Protected Securities (TIPS). Savers may be interested in purchasing such bonds if they fear that the purchasing power of their saved money becomes eroded over time due to inflation. For instance, suppose that nominal interest rates are 5% per year and the inflation rate is 10% per year. Then a $100 investment will become $100 × 1.05 = $105 in a year, but would not be able to purchase the same amount of goods as the investment initially could (those goods would cost $100 × 1.10 = $110 in one year).

Conclusion

In this chapter we have gone through the details of what interest rates are, and characteristics of interest rates such as how they can vary depending on the length of borrowing and how they can change in uncertain ways in the future. We went over methodologies of calculating interest rates based on market data, and how interest rates directly relate to the prices of bonds and other fixed-income securities which promise specified cash flows in the future. We also discussed ways to measure the potential impact of changes in interest rates on investments.

This chapter relates to previous chapters in Parts I and II as it provides a methodology for determining discount rates in order to take the present value of certain cash flows in the future; in other words, riskless cash flows. In subsequent chapters we use the interest rates derived in this chapter as a foundation for taking the present value when cash flows are uncertain, which allows us to value a wide array of financial securities and also to determine appropriate discount rates to value companies, as we introduced in Part II.

Takeaways

- The term structure of interest rates reflects the interest rates for borrowing at different horizons in the future. Different interest rates for different horizons allow investors to engage in maturity matching—matching investments to needs that occur at certain horizons—thus granting investors the ability to better manage investment goals.
- Spot interest rates are annual rates for default-risk-free borrowing now until some point in the future. Forward interest rates are estimates of what interest rates for new borrowing will be at different points in the future. Forward interest rates can be inferred from current spot interest rates.
- Market interest rates can be calculated from the prices of pure discount bonds, also called zero-coupon bonds, which are risk-free bonds that pay a single amount at maturity. The prices of pure discount bonds form the building blocks for valuing any stream of certain cash flows in the future. The YTM (yield) of pure discount bonds, defined as the annualized rate of return to investors who buy and hold the bonds until maturity, are the appropriate interest rates that correspond to the maturity of the bond. The complete set of such rates at all maturities in the future is called the yield curve.
- Coupon bonds are bonds that pay periodic payments before maturity in addition to a final principal amount. Coupon bonds can be priced using interest rates derived from pure discount bonds. A change in market interest rates causes a change in the opposite direction in the market values of all existing contracts promising fixed payments in the future.
- Differences in the prices of default-free fixed-income securities of a given maturity arise from differences in coupon rates, maturity, and other features such as callability and convertibility.

- Over time the prices of bonds converge toward their face value. Before maturity, however, bond prices can fluctuate a great deal as a result of changes in market interest rates, even though there is no default risk associated with US Treasury bonds. Duration is a measure of how sensitive a bond's price is to a change in interest rates.
- When interest rates change, the sensitivity of a bond's price to further interest rate changes can also change—that is, a bond's duration will vary depending on the current level of interest rates. This is known as convexity, and accounting for it as well as duration provides a more accurate appraisal of a bond's price sensitivity to interest rate changes.

Key Terms

Basis points 499
Bills 470
Callable bond 491
Convertible bond 491
Convexity 502
Coupon bonds 481
Coupon rate 481
Coupons/coupon payments 481
Current yield 486
Discount bond 483
Discount function 478
Discount rates 469
Downward-sloping yield curve 479
Duration 496
Expectations theory 493
Face value/par value 474
Fixed income 482
Flat term structure of interest rates 470

Forward rate of interest 492
Interest rate risk 496
Interest rate sensitivity 496
Interest rates 469
Macaulay duration 497
Maturity 472
Maturity matching 492
Modified duration 499
Par bond 483
Premium bond 483
Pure discount bonds/zero-coupon bonds 474
Risk premium 493
Risk-free/riskless 470
Rolling over 492
Term structure of interest rates 469
Upward-sloping yield curve 478
Yield curve 478
Yield to maturity (YTM) 486

Key Equations

Price of a zero-coupon bond	$P_T = \dfrac{\text{par}}{(1+y_T)^T}$	Eq. 16.1
Price of a zero-coupon bond	$P_T = \dfrac{\text{par}}{(1+r_T)^T}$	Eq. 16.2
Yield for a T-year bond	$y_T = \left(\dfrac{\text{par}}{P_T}\right)^{\frac{1}{T}} - 1$ $= r_T$	Eq. 16.3

Price of a known stream of cash flows	$$PV = \frac{CF_1}{1+r_1} + \frac{CF_2}{(1+r_2)^2} + \cdots + \frac{CF_T}{(1+r_T)^T}$$ $$= \sum_{t=1}^{T} \frac{CF_t}{(1+r_t)^t}$$	Eq. 16.4
Price of a coupon bond	$$P = \frac{C}{1+r_1} + \frac{C}{(1+r_2)^2} + \cdots + \frac{C+\text{par}}{(1+r_T)^T}$$	Eq. 16.5
Current yield	$$\text{Current yield} = \frac{C}{P}$$	Eq. 16.6
Yield to maturity equation	$$P = \frac{C}{1+y} + \frac{C}{(1+y)^2} + \cdots + \frac{C+\text{par}}{(1+y)^T}$$	Eq. 16.7
Forward rate of interest	$$f_{t,T} = \frac{(1+r_T)^T}{(1+r_t)^t} - 1 = \frac{\frac{\text{par}}{(1+r_t)^t}}{\frac{\text{par}}{(1+r_T)^T}} = \frac{P_t}{P_T} - 1$$	Eq. 16.9
Macaulay duration	$$\text{Macaulay duration} = \frac{1}{P} \times \sum_{t=1}^{T} PV(CF_t) \times t$$ $$= \frac{1}{P} \times \left(\frac{CF_1}{1+r_1} \times 1 + \frac{CF_2}{(1+r_2)^2} \times 2 + \cdots + \frac{CF_T}{(1+r_T)^T} \times T \right)$$	Eq. 16.10
Modified duration	$$\text{Modified duration} = \frac{\text{Macaulay duration}}{\left(1 + \frac{y}{T}\right)}$$	Eq. 16.11
Convexity	$$\text{Convexity} = \frac{1}{P \times (1+y)^2} \times \sum_{t=1}^{T} \left[PV(CF_t) \times (t^2 + t) \right]$$ $$= \frac{1}{P \times (1+y)^2} \times \sum_{t=1}^{T} \left[\frac{CF_t}{(1+y)^t} \times (t^2 + t) \right]$$	Eq. 16.12
Change in bond price when interest rates change	$$\%\Delta P = -(\text{modified duration}) \times \Delta y + \frac{1}{2} \times \text{convexity} \times (\Delta y)^2$$	Eq. 16.13

Problems

1. Suppose you purchase a Treasury bill that matures in three years. The bill is a pure discount instrument paying its face value of $100,000 at maturity. If the bill is priced to yield 1% over the three years, what is its current selling price?
2. Suppose you decide to sell the Treasury bill from Problem 1 one year after you purchased it. At the time of the sale, suppose the bill's yield is 0.75% over the remaining two years. What is the price of the bond at that time?
3. Consider the following spot interest rates for borrowing now until the indicated time horizon:

Horizon T	Spot interest rate	
1	r_1	5%
2	r_2	6.5%
3	r_3	7%
4	r_4	8%

    What is the price of a bond that pays off $1,000 at each indicated horizon (and nothing else)? What are the one-year forward rates of interest as of $t = 1$, $t = 2$, and $t = 3$?
4. Using the spot interest rates in Problem 3, provide the price of a default-free security that promises to pay the following amounts in the future:

Horizon T	
1	$3,000
2	$10,000
3	$4,000
4	$2,000

5. Suppose you observe the following prices for zero-coupon bonds (pure discount bonds) that have no risk of default:

Maturity	Price per $1 of face value	YTM
1 year	0.97	3.093%
2 years	0.90	?

    (a) Find the missing entry in the table.
    (b) What should be the price of a two-year coupon bond that pays a 6% coupon rate and a principal amount of $1,000, assuming coupon payments are made once a year starting one year from now?
    (c) What should be the YTM of the two-year coupon bond in part (a)?
    (d) Why are your answers to parts (b) and (c) of this question different?
6. Consider a pure discount bond with ten years remaining to maturity selling for $61.39133 per $100 of face value. If the bond's yield remains constant over the next three years, what price will the bond be selling for with nine, eight, and seven years remaining to maturity? How high would the yield have to rise in order that, with six years remaining to maturity, the bond's price would be the same as two years prior, when it had eight years remaining to maturity?
7. Comment on the following statement: Ruling out negative interest rates, an upward-sloping term structure for zero-coupon Treasury notes and bonds implies the relationship between prices and time remaining to maturity is inverse for such pure discount instruments.

8. Assume a 50-year zero-coupon bond with $1,000 face value is priced to yield 10%. If the yield were to instantly drop to 5%, what would be the new price for the bond? How does the change in yield compare in a relative manner to the change in the price?

9. What is the current yield on a five-year 5% coupon bond priced to yield 7%? Assume annual compounding.

10. State the relationships among the current yield, the coupon rate, and the YTM based on the bond's price relative to its par, or face value.

11. A coupon bond's price can be broken down into two components. The bond's price is the sum of the present value of the coupon interest payments and the present value of the repayment of the face value. Under a flat term structure that remains constant over time, how do these two components change as time progresses?

12. Suppose there are three US Treasury bonds traded in the marketplace, each with a face value of $1,000 and paying annual coupons as follows:

Bond	Maturity (years)	Coupon rate
A	1	5.0%
B	2	6.5%
C	3	5.5%

Assume that the one-year interest rate is 2%, the two-year interest rate is 3%, and the three-year interest rate is 4%. What is each bond's price?

13. Suppose the Treasury issued a new ten-year bond that it wanted initially traded as a par bond. If the term structure of interest rates is flat at 5%, what coupon rate would it need to set?

14. Suppose the Treasury issued a new two-year bond that it wanted initially traded as a par bond. If the one-year interest rate is 2% and the two-year interest rate if 4%, what coupon rate would it need to set?

15. Suppose you want to know the price of a ten-year 7% coupon Treasury bond that pays interest annually.
    (a) You have been told that the YTM is 8%. What is the price (per $100 of face value)?
    (b) What is the price if coupons are paid semi-annually, and the YTM is 8% per year?
    (c) Now you have been told that the YTM is 7% per year. What is the price? Could you have guessed the answer without calculating it? What if coupons are paid semi-annually?

16. Assume a year ago the US Treasury yield curve was flat at a rate of 4% per year (with annual compounding) and you bought a 30-year US Treasury bond. Today it is flat at a rate of 5% per year (with annual compounding). What rate of return did you earn on your initial investment:
    (a) If the bond was a 4% coupon bond?
    (b) If the bond was a zero-coupon bond?

17. Repeat Problem 16 with semi-annual compounding. Now the yields and rates of return will be given as APRs with semi-annual compounding. The initial flat term structure was at 4% per year with annual compounding. What rate per year with semi-annual compounding produces the same effective annual rate? Make a similar adjustment for the current rate.

18. Assume that all of the bonds listed in the following table are the same except for their pattern of promised cash flows over time. Prices are quoted per $1 of face value. Use the information in the table and the law of one price to infer the values of the missing entries. Assume that coupon payments are annual.

Coupon rate	Maturity	Price	YTM
6%	2 years		5.5%
0	2 years		
7%	2 years		
0	1 year	$0.95	

19. You would like to create a two-year synthetic zero-coupon bond. Assume you are aware of the following information: one-year zero-coupon bonds are trading for $0.93 per dollar of face value and two-year 7% coupon bonds (annual payments) are selling at $985.30 (face value = $1,000).
    (a) What are the two cash flows from the two-year coupon bond?
    (b) Assume you can purchase the two-year coupon bond and unbundle the two cash flows and sell them. How much will you receive from the sale of the first payment? How much do you need to receive from the sale of the two-year Treasury STRIP to break even?

20. Suppose you have the following information from the market for zero-coupon bonds:

Maturity	Price per $100 face value	Yield (APR with semi-annual compounding)
1 year	$95.181	5.0%
2 years	$95.624	4.5%

   (a) What would be the price of a two-year 5% coupon bond paying interest annually? What would be its YTM?
   (b) What would be the price of a two-year 4.5% coupon bond paying interest annually? What would be its YTM? Why is this bond a discount bond?

21. What effect would adding the following features have on the market price of a similar bond which does not have this feature? Answer qualitatively (i.e., would the price to a buyer be higher or lower if the feature were added?).
    (a) Ten-year bond is callable by the company after five years (compare to a ten-year noncallable bond);
    (b) bond is convertible into ten shares of common stock at any time (compare to a nonconvertible bond);
    (c) ten-year bond can be "put back" to the company after three years at par (puttable bond) (compare to a ten-year nonputtable bond).

22. All else being equal, if interest rates rise along the entire yield curve, you should expect that:
    (i) Bond prices will fall.
    (ii) Bond prices will rise.
    (iii) Prices on long-term bonds will fall more than prices on short-term bonds.
    (iv) Prices on long-term bonds will rise more than prices on short-term bonds.
    Choose one of the following (and explain your answer):
    (a) (ii) and (iv) are correct.
    (b) We can't be certain that prices will change.
    (c) Only (i) is correct.
    (d) Only (ii) is correct.
    (e) (i) and (iii) are correct.

23. Consider two ten-year bonds: one with a 5% coupon rate and the other with a 10% coupon rate, both paying annual interest. Assuming the term structure remains flat, price these bonds

at three alternative yields: 5%, 10%, and 15%. Draw a diagram showing how the prices vary with the YTM.

24. Consider two 10% coupon bonds, one with five years to maturity and the other with ten years to maturity, both paying annual interest. Assuming the term structure remains flat, price these bonds at three alternative yields: 5%, 10%, and 15% (APRs compounded annually). Draw a diagram showing how the prices vary with the YTM. If the yield is currently 10% for both bonds, which bond's price will be more sensitive to a given change in the yield?

25. Calculate the duration of each bond in the previous example using Excel.

26. Consider a three-year 10% coupon bond with a face value of $1,000, paying annual coupons. Assume that the term structure of interest rates is flat at 5%.
    (a) Calculate the bond's price.
    (b) Calculate the bond's Macaulay duration and modified duration.
    (c) Calculate the bond's convexity.
    (d) If interest rates were to fall by 2 percentage points to 3%, based on your calculations from the previous parts, by what percent would you predict the bond's price would change?

27. The price of a coupon bond has two parts: the present value of the coupon interest stream and the present value of the face value repayment. Consider a five-year, 8% coupon bond paying semi-annual interest. What would be the pattern of the bond's price and the breakdown into the two component parts over time if the term structure is flat at 10% (APR with semi-annual compounding) and remains so over the next five years? Make these calculations for the bond today and each subsequent year until it matures. Draw a diagram showing the bond prices and components as a function of years remaining to maturity.

17 PORTFOLIO THEORY

CHAPTER OVERVIEW

17.1 The Process of Portfolio Selection by Individuals — 515
17.2 Forming Portfolios: The Trade-Off between Expected Return and Risk — 518
17.3 Portfolios of Multiple Risky Assets — 527
17.4 Mean-Variance Analysis and Asset Management — 546

LEARNING OBJECTIVES

After reading this chapter, you will be able to:
- identify what causes investors to make different portfolio choices, such as personal circumstances and risk tolerance;
- describe the theory and practice of selecting assets to form a portfolio in order to manage financial wealth;
- understand how to evaluate possible portfolios, and whether they may be suitable for an individual to invest in, by calculating their risk and return characteristics given by expected return, standard deviation, and the Sharpe ratio;
- explain and calculate how the characteristics of assets that comprise a portfolio affect the portfolio's overall characteristics, which provides guidance for how to construct or change the makeup of portfolios based on individual preferences;
- construct a portfolio of assets which provides an optimal trade-off between risk and reward;
- describe how investment management professionals can work with individual investors in order to provide them with an optimal portfolio that meets their needs and preferences.

EQUATIONS YOU KNOW

Expected return of an asset	$\mathbb{E}[R] = p_1 \times R_1 + p_2 \times R_2 + \cdots + p_n \times R_n$ $= \sum_{i=1}^{n} p_i \times R_i$	Eq. 6.1

Volatility of an asset	$\sigma = \sqrt{\sum_{i=1}^{n} p_i \times (R_i - \mathbb{E}[R])^2}$	Eq. 6.2

- After years of paying off student loans, at age 40 you finally have some money to invest from an unexpected bequest of about $1,000,000. Although you have taken a course in personal finance as an undergraduate, you know almost nothing about investing. How should you invest your bequest?

- You have been earning money from your job and want to invest it. There are many different stocks you could invest in, and you are unsure how many different stocks to invest in and how much money to put into each. How do you go about making this decision?

- Your wealth is invested in a portfolio made up of a large number of stocks. You decide that the return hasn't been large enough for your tastes. You don't mind taking on additional risk. How could you change your portfolio accordingly?

- You currently have your money invested in a portfolio of stocks that you decided to pick. Your financial advisor proposes that you invest your money instead in a completely different portfolio. How can you evaluate which one is "better" from a financial perspective?

- You have got your first job out of college as an investment advisor. You are supposed to provide clients with different investment portfolio possibilities that fit their preferences, but there are an overwhelming number of possibilities. How can you systematically come up with potential portfolios for your clients?

Introduction

In the previous chapter we explored how to determine the interest rates (rates of return) for risk-fee assets (i.e., investments with no default risk); however, individuals and investment professionals invest their wealth in not only risk-free assets, but also *risky* assets. There are a great number of risky assets, such as individual stocks, that individuals can potentially invest in, and thus individuals can form a portfolio of different assets. In addition to choosing which assets to invest in, individuals must also choose how much to invest in each asset. The process through which people choose assets to invest their wealth in is called portfolio selection.

This chapter explores the concepts and techniques you need to know to manage your portfolio efficiently. Two main principles guide the process of portfolio selection for all risk-averse people: **Principle 6:** *Risk is fundamental to financial analysis and must be explicitly considered in all financial decisions* and **Principle 7:** *There is a trade-off between risk and expected return.* People choose assets in portfolio selection to meet their specific financial goals which will have varying degrees of risk. To that end, this risk must be measured and managed. Measuring risk starts with identifying something that has no risk attached to it—a risk-free asset, which was the focus of Chapter 16. The risk of another asset can be measured in relation to what is risk-free—that is, relative to the rates of return we derived in the previous chapter. The basics of risk management were covered in Chapter 6. This chapter looks at risk management and measurement for investing in multiple assets, extending what we learned in Chapter

6. On top of this, individuals desiring a higher expected return for their investments must take on more risk. In this chapter, we will analyze the quantitative trade-off between risk and expected return, which will be key to selecting portfolios that meet an individual investor's needs.

We begin by examining the role of portfolio selection in the context of a person's lifetime financial planning process and show why there is no single strategy that is best for all people. We will examine how the investor's preferences (time horizon and risk tolerance) affect portfolio selection. We then explore ways to create an appropriate portfolio that can maximize return for the investor's risk tolerance, based on diversification. We begin with the simplest risky portfolio, with one risky asset and one riskless asset, and finish by examining optimal portfolio selection with many risky assets. We then discuss how these portfolio construction techniques can be implemented in practice by investment management professionals.

17.1 The Process of Portfolio Selection by Individuals

A portfolio is a combination of financial assets. Portfolio selection involves trading off risk and expected return to find the best portfolio of assets and liabilities. A narrow definition of portfolio selection includes only decisions about how much to invest in stocks, bonds, and other securities. A broader definition includes decisions about all of the financial investments in an individual's life, such as whether to buy or rent a home, what types and amounts of insurance to purchase, and how to manage liabilities. An even broader definition includes decisions about investing in your human capital—that is, yourself, such as by furthering your professional education. The common element in all of these decisions is the trade-off between risk and expected return (**Principle 7**). In this section we will cover how individuals make portfolio selection decisions based on their individual circumstances—age and planning horizon—and also their preferences for risk.

17.1.1 Personal Circumstances and Portfolio Selection

Portfolio selection strategy depends on an individual's personal circumstances (age, family status, occupation, income, wealth, etc.). For some people, holding a particular asset may add to their total risk exposure, but for others the same asset may be risk-reducing. An asset that is risk-reducing at an early stage of life may not be at a later stage. For example, for a young person at the start of their career it may be optimal to complete an MBA and take out a student loan to pay for it, because the risk of the loan is offset by the potential return of a higher wage over a longer career. For an older person who is about to retire, upskilling is not a valuable investment as the risk from the student loan will not be offset, as potential wage increase is lower if they are already senior in their field and their life stage leaves them less time to pay off the loan, which may burden them into retirement.

An example of two individuals at the same stage, but with different personal circumstances affecting asset choice, can be shown via life insurance. The optimal insurance policy for Miriam, a parent with dependent children, will differ from the policy appropriate for Veena, a single person with no dependents, even if the two people are the same in all other respects (age, income, occupation, wealth, etc.). Miriam would be concerned about protecting her family in the event of her death and would, therefore, want a policy that provides cash benefits payable to her children upon her death. Veena, on the other hand, would not be concerned about benefits payable if she dies; therefore, the purchase of life insurance would not be risk-reducing for her. At a later stage in her life, Miriam too may find that her children can provide for themselves and no longer need the protection afforded by life insurance. People of the same age, with the same income and wealth, may have different perspectives on buying a house or buying life insurance and the same is true of investing in stocks, bonds, and other securities. For example, Min is 30 years old and works as a security analyst on Wall Street. Her current and future earnings are very sensitive to the performance of the stock market—if stocks go down significantly,

Wall Street will likely struggle financially and may lay off large numbers of people. Ibrahim is also 30 years old and is a schoolteacher. His current and future earnings are not very sensitive to the stock market. For Min, investing a significant proportion of her investment portfolio in stocks would be riskier than it would be for Ibrahim, since Min's income is already *de facto* exposed to that risk.

The broad takeaway is that there is no single portfolio that is best for all people.

> **QUICK CHECK 17.1** How would the investment portfolio that is best for a young person with a secure job differ from the one that is best for a retired person whose only source of income is an investment portfolio?

17.1.2 Time Horizons

Formulating a plan for a portfolio begins with goals and time horizons—that is, lengths of time into the future that are considered in an analysis. This includes a planning horizon, a decision horizon, and a trading horizon. The planning horizon is the total length of time planned for. The longest time horizon would typically correspond to the retirement goal and would be the balance of one's lifetime. Thus, for a 25-year-old who expects to live to age 85, the planning horizon would be 60 years. As a person ages, the planning horizon typically shrinks (Box 17.1 discusses ways to determine an individual's planning horizon). Some people plan not only for their own lifetimes but also for those of future generations. For them the planning horizon might be very long, perhaps infinite. There are also shorter planning horizons that correspond to specific financial goals, such as paying for a child's education. For example, if you have a child who is three years old and plan to pay for her college education when she reaches age 18, the planning horizon for this goal is 15 years.

The decision horizon is the length of time between the points in time when a portfolio owner deciding to revise the portfolio. The length of the decision horizon is controlled by the individual. Some people review their portfolios at regular intervals—for example, once a month (when they pay their bills) or once a year (when they file income tax forms). People of modest means with most of their wealth invested in bank accounts might review their portfolios very infrequently and at irregular intervals determined by some triggering event, such as getting married or divorced, having a child, or receiving a bequest. A sudden rise or fall in the price of an asset might also trigger a review of the portfolio.

People with substantial investments in stocks and bonds might review their portfolios every day or even more frequently. The shortest possible decision horizon is the trading horizon, defined as the minimum time interval over which investors can revise their portfolios. The length of the trading horizon is not within an individual's control. Whether the trading horizon is a week, a day, an hour, or a minute is determined by the structure of the markets in the economy (e.g., when the securities exchanges are open or whether organized off-exchange markets exist). In the global financial environment, trading in many securities is carried out somewhere on the globe around the clock. For these kinds of securities the trading horizon is very short.

Portfolio decisions you make today are influenced by what you think might happen in the future over your planning horizon. A plan that takes account of future decisions in making current decisions is called a strategy. How frequently investors can revise their portfolios by buying or selling securities—which is influenced by the decision and trading horizons—is an important consideration in formulating investment strategies. If you know that you can adjust the composition of your portfolio frequently, you may invest differently than if you cannot adjust it. For example, a person may adopt a strategy of investing "extra" wealth in stocks—that is, wealth in excess of the amount needed to insure a certain threshold standard of living. If the stock market goes up over time, a person may increase the proportion of the portfolio invested in stocks. However, if the stock market goes down, a person may reduce the proportion invested in stocks. If the stock market falls to the point at which the person's threshold standard of living is threatened, the investor may get out of stocks altogether. An investor pursuing this particular strategy is more likely to have a higher threshold if stocks can only be traded infrequently.

> **Box 17.1** Computing Life Expectancy
>
> Your life expectancy is the number of years that you are expected to live, and is the basis for one's planning horizon. It is computed using statistics on mortality (i.e., death) rates collected and analyzed by actuaries, who are professionals that specialize in the mathematical techniques relevant to computing insurance premiums. To estimate the probability of death at a given age, actuaries use mortality tables such as Table 17.1, which is for US residents. For each age from 60 to 95 the table states the mortality rate in terms of deaths per 1,000 people and the expectation of life (expected value of the number of years remaining before death). There are separate statistics given for males and females.
>
> Table 17.1 A mortality table.
>
> | Age | Males Deaths per 1,000 | Life expectancy (years) | Females Deaths per 1,000 | Life expectancy (years) |
> |---|---|---|---|---|
> | 60 | 13.5 | 20.5 | 7.9 | 23.7 |
> | 61 | 14.6 | 19.7 | 8.5 | 22.9 |
> | 65 | 18.9 | 16.9 | 11.3 | 19.7 |
> | 70 | 26.1 | 13.6 | 16.6 | 15.8 |
> | 75 | 40.6 | 10.5 | 27.7 | 12.3 |
> | 80 | 65.6 | 7.7 | 47.1 | 9.1 |
> | 85 | 109.1 | 5.5 | 83.4 | 6.4 |
> | 90 | 182.6 | 3.7 | 147.0 | 4.4 |
> | 95 | 288.6 | 2.6 | 239.5 | 3.1 |
>
> The life expectancy numbers given here form the basis of the planning horizon, as individuals may make financial decisions based upon this. For example, if you target a certain amount of money to leave as a bequest for your children, you may see that you can achieve that amount by investing in riskless Treasury bonds for the remainder of your life expectancy. Your life expectancy will also determine your financial goals in retirement—the amount that you should have will vary depending on whether that income must support you for 5 years compared to 20 years. This, in turn, will affect how much money you decide to save versus spend on a day-to-day basis before you reach retirement, or if you should invest in a financial product like a lifetime annuity. While life expectancy numbers can be computed as above, people often underestimate their life expectancy. For example, research from Canada shows that on average people 50 years and older think they will live to be around 80 years old; in actuality, men aged 50 will live on average to age 84 and women to age 87. This potentially leaves a gap in financial planning and can affect investment strategies, as it implies an additional 4–7 years of income is needed and potentially not accounted for.
>
> *Source:* US Social Security 2020 period life table. Canada Life (2023). New retirement gap looms as people underestimate life expectancy. www.canadalife.co.uk.

> **QUICK CHECK 17.2** What is your current planning horizon? How might your planning horizon change in the future?

17.1.3 Risk Tolerance

A person's risk tolerance, the amount of risk they are willing to bear, is a major determinant of portfolio choices. Risk tolerance is influenced by characteristics such as age, family status, job status, wealth, and other attributes that affect and are affected by your ability to maintain your standard of living in the face of drops in the market value of your investment portfolio. Your personal attitude toward risk also plays a role in determining your tolerance for bearing risk. People with the same apparent personal, family, and job characteristics may have a greater willingness to take risk than others.

When we refer to a person's risk tolerance in our analysis of portfolio selection, we do not distinguish between capacity to bear risk and attitude toward risk. Thus, whether a person has a relatively high tolerance for risk because they are young or rich, because they handle stress well, or because they were brought up to believe that taking chances is the morally right path, all that matters is that they are more willing than the average person to take on additional risk to achieve a higher expected return.

> **QUICK CHECK 17.3** Do you think that risk tolerance increases with a person's wealth? Why?

The previous sections introduced how individuals may formulate a strategy to form portfolios, and how this varies between individuals based on their circumstances. In the next section we go over the details of the types of assets that investors can include in their portfolios, and how to measure the risk and return characteristics of the portfolios that investors may form.

17.2 Forming Portfolios: The Trade-Off between Expected Return and Risk

In this section we look at the analytical framework that can be used by professional portfolio managers to examine the quantitative trade-off between risk and expected return. The objective is to find the portfolio that offers the highest expected rate of return for any degree of risk we are willing to tolerate.

Portfolio optimization is often done as a three-step process:

1. define the appropriate riskless asset;
2. find the optimal combination of risky assets; and
3. mix this optimal risky-asset portfolio with the riskless asset.

In this section we will begin by defining a riskless asset. Then, we go over how to perform portfolio calculations by combining assets. In order to introduce some of the calculations needed to construct and analyze portfolios consisting of the optimal combination of risky assets in the second step, we move to the third step: mixing a single risky asset and a riskless asset. The general insights of combining assets will then be applied to combining risky assets—forming a risky-asset portfolio—in Section 17.3 in the second step. And since a portfolio of many risky assets chosen in an optimal way is itself a risky asset, the combined analysis will provide a guide for forming a portfolio consisting of a riskless asset and multiple risky assets.

17.2.1 What Is a Riskless Asset?

As we noted in the introduction to the chapter, the foundation of portfolio analysis is **Principle 6:** *Risk is fundamental to financial analysis and must be explicitly considered in all financial decisions* and **Principle 7**: *There is a trade-off between risk and expected return.* Thus, portfolio analysis fundamentally consists of choosing assets with varying degrees of risk. As a starting point, then, we will consider the case where a portfolio contains an asset with *no* risk. This is important for two reasons. First, it gives us a reference point so that we can assess the characteristics of risky assets *relative* to an asset with no risk. Second, for investors that want little or no risk, it permits them to invest their money in an asset that achieves this goal.

In the theory of portfolio selection, a riskless asset is defined as a security that offers a perfectly predictable rate of return in terms of the unit of account selected for the analysis and the length of the investor's decision horizon. When not related to a specific investor, a riskless asset is an asset that offers a predictable rate of return over the trading horizon (i.e., the shortest possible decision horizon). Thus, if the US dollar is taken as the unit of account and the trading horizon is one year, the riskless rate—the rate of return provided by a riskless asset—is the interest rate on US Treasury bills maturing next year. In Chapters 5 and 16 we discussed interest rates and showed that there is a different riskless asset (and thus riskless rate) that corresponds to each possible unit of account (dollars, yen, etc.) and to each possible maturity. Thus, a ten-year, dollar-denominated, zero-coupon bond that offers a default-free yield-to-maturity of 6% per year is riskless only in terms of dollars and only if held to maturity. The dollar rate of return on that same bond is uncertain if it is sold before maturity because the price to be received is uncertain, since interest rates and bond prices may change over time. And even if held to maturity, the bond's rate of return denominated in yen or in terms of consumer purchasing power is uncertain because future exchange rates and consumer prices are uncertain.

An example would be a US Treasury bill trading for $100 and promising $105 in the next year (thus, a $100 principal amount and $5 coupon):

Today $t = 0$	Next year $t = 1$
Invest $100	→ $105

The return of this risk-free asset, the riskless rate denoted by r_f, is therefore $105 / $100 − 1 = 0.05 or 5%.

> **QUICK CHECK 17.4** What is the riskless asset if the unit of account is the euro and the length of the decision horizon is one week?

17.2.2 What Are Risky Assets?

Risky assets are assets that do not offer a certain return. A risky asset may be a financial asset such as a share of stock or a physical asset such as a house. We can calculate measures of the expected return and risk of a risky asset in order to assess *how* risky it is and what sort of return is provided in exchange for that risk. Throughout the analysis we will often refer to risky assets generally or use stocks as an example, but a risky asset can refer to a wide variety of financial assets, including stocks, options, insurance policies, and so on. As explained in the preceding sections of this chapter, the riskiness of a particular asset depends critically on the specific circumstances of the investor.

To illustrate, suppose that an asset has some probability p of providing a return of R_1 next year, and some probability $1 - p$ of providing a return of R_2 next year:

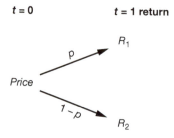

As we went over in Chapter 6, the expected return of this risky asset will be given by:

$$\mathbb{E}[R] = p \times R_1 + (1 - p) \times R_2. \tag{17.1}$$

We also saw in Chapter 6 that we could calculate a measure of risk, the volatility (measured by standard deviation) of the risky asset, via:

$$\sigma = \sqrt{p \times (R_1 - \mathbb{E}[R])^2 + (1 - p) \times (R_2 - \mathbb{E}[R])^2}. \tag{17.2}$$

In reality, it may be infeasible to perform these calculations. For example, we may not have the appropriate information to be able to calculate the probability p, and we may not know the possible returns associated with each of these probabilities. As a result, in practice we typically look at the *past* performance of a given risky asset in order to inform us about what to expect in the future. In particular, in order to estimate the expected return of a risky asset $\mathbb{E}[R]$, we typically will use the average return that the asset has historically provided. For example, if a risky asset provided returns of 5%, 6%, and 8% each respective year over the past three years, then an estimate of its expected annual return would be the average of these returns:

$$\mathbb{E}[R] = \frac{5\% + 6\% + 8\%}{3} = 6.33\%.$$

Similarly, we can estimate the asset's volatility by taking the standard deviation of these returns:

$$\sigma = \sqrt{\frac{1}{3} \times (5\% - 6.33\%)^2 + \frac{1}{3} \times (6\% - 6.33\%)^2 + \frac{1}{3} \times (8\% - 6.33\%)^2} = 1.53\%.$$

In portfolio calculations it is common to use a long window of past returns in order to estimate an asset's expected return and volatility. However, some assets have return histories that go too far back in time, even many decades, which makes the amount of data difficult to manage. In that case, it can sometimes be uncertain what the correct window of time is to perform these calculations. We return to this issue in Chapter 18.

Having introduced what riskless and risky assets are, and how one can calculate risk and return for individual assets, we now turn to how to calculate and analyze the risk and return of a portfolio consisting of a riskless and a risky asset.

17.2.3 Combining a Riskless Asset and a Single Risky Asset

Suppose that you have $100,000 to invest. You are choosing between a riskless asset with an interest rate of 0.02 (2%) per year and a risky asset with an expected rate of return of 0.14 (14%) per year and standard deviation of 0.20 (20%). How much of your $100,000 should you invest in the risky asset? The answer will depend on your goal in terms of the desired amount of risk you wish to bear, and therefore the return you can expect given that risk. To see this, we will explore possible combinations of the riskless asset and the risky asset, and determine the expected return and risk of the resulting portfolios.

First, note that the expected return on your portfolio will depend on what percentage of your $100,000 you invest in the risky asset and what percentage you invest in the riskless asset. If w is the fraction of your money you invest in the risky asset, then $1 - w$ is the fraction of your money invested in the riskless asset. The portion of the money in your portfolio that is invested in a particular asset is known as a portfolio weight. The expected return of your portfolio, $\mathbb{E}[R_P]$, will be a weighted average of the expected return of the risky asset (denoted by $\mathbb{E}[R_S]$) and the return of the riskless asset (denoted by r_f):

$$\mathbb{E}[R_P] = w \times \mathbb{E}[R_S] + (1-w) \times r_f. \qquad (17.3)$$

Next, note that the volatility of your portfolio, which we will denote by σ_P, will also depend on the fraction of money w you invest in the risky asset, as well as the volatility (standard deviation) of the risky asset, which we will denote by σ_S. In particular, the portfolio's volatility will be given by:

$$\sigma_P = w \times \sigma_S. \qquad (17.4)$$

Note that the volatility of the riskless asset is, by definition, zero, and thus does not enter into Equation 17.4.

Now consider combinations of the riskless and risky assets. Start with the base case of investing nothing in the risky asset and all of your money in the risk-free asset. As a result, $w = 0$. With $r_f = 0.02$, we get that the portfolio expected return and volatility are (Equations 17.3 and 17.4):

$$\begin{aligned}
\mathbb{E}[R_P] &= w \times \mathbb{E}[R_S] + (1-w) \times r_f \\
&= 0 + 1 \times r_f \\
&= 0.02, \\
\sigma_P &= w \times \sigma_S \\
&= 0.
\end{aligned}$$

Investing all of your money in the riskless asset will, unsurprisingly, construct a portfolio with the same exact risk–return characteristics as the riskless asset.

Next, consider investing 50% in the risky asset and 50% in the riskless asset, so $w = 0.50$. With $r_f = 0.02$, $\mathbb{E}[R_S] = 0.14$, and $\sigma_S = 0.20$, we have (Equations 17.1 and 17.2):

$$\begin{aligned}
\mathbb{E}[R_P] &= w \times \mathbb{E}[R_S] + (1-w) \times r_f \\
&= 0.5 \times 0.14 + 0.5 \times 0.02 \\
&= 0.08, \\
\sigma_P &= w \times \sigma_S \\
&= 0.5 \times 0.20 \\
&= 0.10.
\end{aligned}$$

Investing your wealth evenly between the risky and the riskless assets produces a portfolio with an expected return of 0.08 or 8% and risk (standard deviation) of 0.10 or 10%, exactly halfway between the risky and riskless assets.

Table 17.2 provides the expected return and volatility for portfolios of these and various other combinations of the risky and riskless assets. The case in which you invest all of your money in the riskless asset corresponds to portfolio F in the first row of Table 17.2. Column 2 in Table 17.2 gives the proportion of the portfolio invested in the risky asset (0%) and column 3 gives the proportion invested in the riskless asset (100%). The proportions always add to 100%. Columns 4 and 5 of Table 17.2 give the expected return and standard deviation that correspond to portfolio F: $\mathbb{E}[R_P]$ of 0.02 per year and σ_P of 0.00. The other extreme case, in which you invest all of your money in the risky asset, corresponds to Portfolio S in Table 17.2. In between, the table provides results for portfolios with 25%, 50%, and 75% invested in the risky asset. In each of these cases, the expected return and standard deviation of the portfolio are in between those of either the risky or riskless asset.

Figure 17.1 shows the portfolio expected return and volatility of each of the portfolios provided in Table 17.2. In Figure 17.1 the portfolio expected rate of return $\mathbb{E}[R_P]$ is measured along the vertical axis, and the standard deviation (volatility) σ_P along the horizontal axis. The portfolio proportions are not explicitly shown in Figure 17.1; however, we know what they are from Table 17.2. The line

Table 17.2 **Portfolio expected rate of return and standard deviation as a function of the proportion invested in the risky asset.** This table provides the portfolio expected rate of return and standard deviation (volatility) for portfolios formed from different combinations of the risky and riskless asset. Each portfolio is constructed assuming the given proportion of money invested in the risky asset, w, and proportion of money invested in the riskless asset, $1 - w$.

Portfolio	Proportion invested in risky asset, w	Proportion invested in riskless asset, $1 - w$	Expected rate of return, $\mathbb{E}[R_P]$	Standard deviation (volatility), σ_P
(1)	(2)	(3)	(4)	(5)
F	0%	100%	0.02	0.00
G	25%	75%	0.05	0.05
H	50%	50%	0.08	0.10
J	75%	25%	0.11	0.15
S	100%	0%	0.14	0.20

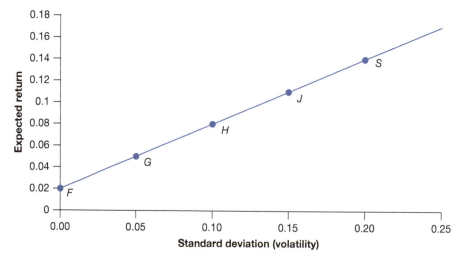

FIGURE 17.1 **The risk-reward trade-off line.** This figure shows the expected return and standard deviation for each of the portfolios provided in Table 17.2. At point F, the portfolio is 100% invested in riskless securities offering a rate of 0.02 per year. At point S, it is 100% invested in the risky asset, with an expected rate of return of 0.14 per year and a standard deviation of 0.20. At point H, the portfolio is half in the risky asset and half in the riskless asset.

connecting points F, G, H, J, and S in Figure 17.1 represents the set of alternatives open to you by choosing different combinations (portfolios) of the risky asset and riskless asset. Each point on the line corresponds to the mix of these two assets given in columns 2 and 3 of Table 17.2.

Figure 17.1 also illustrates the trade-off between risk and reward, in line with **Principle 7**: *There is a trade-off between risk and expected return*. As a result, the line depicting the expected return and standard deviation for various combinations of a risky asset and a riskless asset is known as the risk–reward trade-off line. At point F on the vertical axis in Figure 17.1, with $\mathbb{E}[R_P]$ of 0.02 per year and σ_P of zero, all of your money is invested in the riskless asset. You face no risk, and your expected return is 0.02 per year. As you shift money out of the riskless asset and into the risky asset, you move to the right along the trade-off line and face both a higher expected rate of return and a greater risk.

We can also see this trade-off mathematically by rearranging the expression for the portfolio expected return in Equation 17.3:

$$\begin{aligned} \mathbb{E}[R_P] &= w \times \mathbb{E}[R_S] + (1-w) \times r_f \\ &= r_f + w \times [\mathbb{E}[R_S] - r_f]. \end{aligned} \tag{17.5}$$

Equation 17.5 can be interpreted as follows. The base rate of return for any portfolio is the riskless rate (0.02 in our example above). The portfolio is expected to earn an additional return over the riskless rate based on how much of the portfolio is invested in the risky asset. This additional return depends on: (1) the risk premium on the risky asset, which is defined as the amount by which the expected return on the risky asset exceeds the riskless rate, $\mathbb{E}[R_S] - r_f$ (0.14 − 0.02 = 0.12 in our example); and (2) the proportion of the portfolio invested in the risky asset, denoted by w.

As another way of seeing the relationship between risk and return, we can derive the equation for the trade-off line in Figure 17.1. To do so, we can rearrange Equation 17.4 to find that $w = \sigma_P / \sigma_S$. Substituting this for w in Equation 17.5 gives us the equation for the trade-off line, which relates a portfolio's expected return and standard deviation:

$$\begin{aligned} \mathbb{E}[R_P] &= r_f + w \times [\mathbb{E}[R_S] - r_f] \\ &= r_f + \frac{\sigma_P}{\sigma_S} \times [\mathbb{E}[R_S] - r_f] \\ &= r_f + \frac{\mathbb{E}[R_S] - r_f}{\sigma_S} \times \sigma_P. \end{aligned} \tag{17.6}$$

Equation 17.6 shows that the portfolio's expected rate of return expressed as a function of its standard deviation is a straight line, with a slope equal to the extra expected return the market offers for each unit of extra risk an investor is willing to bear. In our example, this slope is:

$$\begin{aligned} \frac{\mathbb{E}[R_S] - r_f}{\sigma_S} &= \frac{0.14 - 0.02}{0.2} \\ &= 0.60. \end{aligned}$$

This means that each additional unit of risk a portfolio is exposed to (i.e., an increase in standard deviation of 1.0) provides an additional expected return over the riskless rate of 0.60. Put differently, suppose that the volatility of the portfolio increases by 0.10. This would correspond to moving from portfolio G to J. This would imply that the portfolio expected return should increase by 0.60 × 0.10 = 0.06, which is exactly the increase in expected return achieved by moving from portfolio G to J. This again reinforces the insights of **Principle 7**: *There is a trade-off between risk and expected return*.

> **QUICK CHECK 17.5** Locate the point corresponding to portfolio J in Figure 17.1. Consult Table 17.2 for the portfolio's composition, its expected rate of return, and standard deviation. How much of your $100,000 would be invested in the risky asset if you chose portfolio J?

17.2.4 Achieving a Target Expected Return or Risk

From Figure 17.1, we can see that it is possible to construct a portfolio using the risky and riskless assets in the previous example to achieve a wide range of risk–expected return combinations (anything on the line in Figure 17.1). Investors often have specific goals in mind for their investments. For example, an investor may want to construct a portfolio that offers a certain expected return, known as a target expected return, or a portfolio that contains a certain amount of risk, known as a target risk. In deciding what is needed for the desired return or risk, an investor can find the portfolio combination for *any* point on the trade-off line (see Figure 17.1), which we will now discuss.

First, let us examine how to work out the investment needed to achieve a target expected return. Suppose that we desire an expected return of 0.09, between the expected returns of portfolios H and J (which are 0.08 and 0.11, respectively, according to Table 17.2). We want to know what portion of our wealth we should invest in the risky asset, w, and therefore what portion we should invest in the riskless asset, $1 - w$. To do this, we can use Equation 17.5 using a target $\mathbb{E}[R_P] = 0.09$, and solve for what value of w will provide us with that target:

$$\mathbb{E}[R_P] = r_f + w \times [\mathbb{E}[R_s] - r_f],$$
$$0.09 = 0.02 + w \times [0.14 - 0.02]$$
$$w = \frac{0.09 - 0.02}{0.14 - 0.02}$$
$$w = 0.583.$$

To achieve an expected portfolio return of 0.09 or 9%, we would therefore need to invest 58.3% of our money in the risky asset, and $1 - w = 1 - 0.583 = 0.625$ or 41.7% of our money in the riskless asset. Doing so will produce a portfolio with a standard deviation (volatility) of (Equation 17.4):

$$\sigma_P = w \times \sigma_S$$
$$= 0.583 \times 0.2$$
$$= 0.117.$$

The portfolio standard deviation is thus 0.117.

Next, work out the investment needed to achieve a target risk, as measured by standard deviation or volatility; for example, a target standard deviation of 0.14. To do so, we can use Equation 17.4 and solve for w:

$$\sigma_P = w \times \sigma_S$$
$$0.14 = w \times 0.2$$
$$w = 0.7.$$

Therefore, investing $w = 0.7$ or 70% of your wealth in the risky asset and $1 - w = 0.3$ or 30% of your wealth in the riskless asset will produce a portfolio with a desired standard deviation of 0.14. The expected return of such a portfolio would be (Equation 17.5):

$$\mathbb{E}[R_P] = r_f + w \times [\mathbb{E}[R_s] - r_f]$$
$$= 0.02 + 0.7 \times [0.14 - 0.02]$$
$$= 0.104.$$

Your portfolio's expected return would therefore be 10.4%.

> **QUICK CHECK 17.6** Suppose that the risk-free rate was instead 0.03 per year and the expected rate of return on the risky asset was 0.10 per year. Recreate Table 17.2 with these new numbers. If you wanted to create a portfolio with a target expected return of 0.05 per year, what portion of your money would need to be invested in the risky asset?

17.2.5 Investing More Than Your Entire Wealth

In Table 17.2 it was possible to invest up to 100% of your wealth into the risky asset by choosing $w = 1.0$. However, by glancing at Figure 17.1, you may notice that the line extends to the right past portfolio S, which represents the portfolio corresponding to a 100% investment in the risky asset. This is because it is possible to invest more than 100% of your wealth in the risky asset by borrowing money. Doing so allows an investor the possibility of taking on even more risk to achieve an even greater expected return.

To illustrate, consider our original situation where you have $100,000 to invest. One possible strategy is to invest all $100,000 in the risky asset, borrow an additional $20,000 at the riskless rate, and invest that $20,000 in the risky asset. Your total investment in the risky asset would be $120,000, and therefore your portfolio weight in the risky asset would be $w = 120{,}000 / 100{,}000 = 1.2$. Note that even in this case, the weights must add up to 1.0. So the weight in the riskless asset will be *negative*: $1 - w = 1 - 1.2 = -0.2$. The negative weight reflects the fact that you must pay back interest on the amount that you borrowed, thus facing a negative return on the riskless asset. We also refer to this as a short position in the riskless asset (as opposed to a long position, where the weight is positive).

What is the expected return and risk of this portfolio? We can again use Equations 17.4 and 17.5:

$$\begin{aligned}
\mathbb{E}[R_P] &= r_f + w \times \left[\mathbb{E}[R_S] - r_f\right] \\
&= 0.02 + 1.2 \times [0.14 - 0.02] \\
&= 0.164, \\
\sigma_P &= w \times \sigma_S \\
&= 1.2 \times 0.2 \\
&= 0.24.
\end{aligned}$$

Thus, you can achieve an even higher expected return, 0.164, than the risky asset (which has a return of 0.14). However, this is at the expense of higher risk, a standard deviation of 0.24 compared to the risk asset's standard deviation of 0.2.

Theoretically, it is possible to achieve an unboundedly high expected return if an investor is willing to borrow an increasingly greater portion of money. This, of course, means that the investor is exposed to potentially unbounded risk. Because of the potential dangers of such a strategy, in practice there are restrictions on how much borrowing an investor can do in this way (i.e., how large a short position an investor can take).

> **QUICK CHECK 17.7** If an investor wanted to achieve a target expected return of 0.20, what position would the investor need to take?

17 PORTFOLIO THEORY

Example 17.1 (Risky Assets): Suppose that the riskless asset provides a return of 0.02, and the risky asset provides a return of 0.08 with a standard deviation of 0.15.

(a) What is the expected return and volatility of your portfolio if you invested half of your wealth in the risky asset and half of your wealth in the riskless asset?
(b) What is the expected return and volatility of your portfolio if you invested 150% of your wealth in the risky asset by borrowing at the riskless rate?
(c) Find the portfolio corresponding to an expected rate of return of 0.06 per year. What is its standard deviation?
(d) Find the portfolio corresponding to a standard deviation of 0.20 per year. What is its expected return?

Solution.

(a) To determine the expected return, we can use Equation 17.5, given that $r_f = 0.02$, $\mathbb{E}[R_s] = 0.08$, and $w = 0.5$ (since half of your wealth is invested in the risky asset):

$$\begin{aligned}
\mathbb{E}[R_P] &= r_f + w \times \left[\mathbb{E}[R_s] - r_f\right] \\
&= 0.02 + 0.5 \times \left[0.08 - 0.02\right] \\
&= 0.05.
\end{aligned}$$

To arrive at the volatility, we can make use of Equation 17.4, given that $\sigma_s = 0.15$:

$$\begin{aligned}
\sigma_P &= w \times \sigma_s \\
&= 0.5 \times 0.15 \\
&= 0.075.
\end{aligned}$$

(b) Now, $w = 1.5$ since 150% of your wealth is invested in the risky asset. Using Equations 17.4 and 17.5, we have:

$$\begin{aligned}
\mathbb{E}[R_P] &= r_f + w \times \left[\mathbb{E}[R_s] - r_f\right] \\
&= 0.02 + 1.5 \times \left[0.08 - 0.02\right] \\
&= 0.11, \\
\sigma_P &= w \times \sigma_s \\
&= 1.5 \times 0.15 \\
&= 0.225.
\end{aligned}$$

The portfolio's expected return is therefore 0.11, and its standard deviation is 0.225.

(c) With a target $\mathbb{E}[R_P] = 0.06$, we can solve for w using Equation 17.5:

$$\begin{aligned}
\mathbb{E}[R_P] &= r_f + w \times \left[\mathbb{E}[R_s] - r_f\right], \\
0.06 &= 0.02 + w \times \left[0.08 - 0.02\right], \\
w &= \frac{0.06 - 0.02}{0.08 - 0.02} \\
w &= 0.667.
\end{aligned}$$

Thus, investing 66.7% of your wealth in the risky asset and $1 - w = 1 - 0.667 = 33.3\%$ of your wealth in the riskless asset will give a portfolio with an expected return of 0.06. The standard deviation of this portfolio will be (Equation 17.4):

$$\begin{aligned} \sigma_P &= w \times \sigma_S \\ &= 0.667 \times 0.15 \\ &= 0.10. \end{aligned}$$

(d) With a target $\sigma_P = 0.20$, we can use Equation 17.4 to determine w:

$$\begin{aligned} \sigma_P &= w \times \sigma_S, \\ 0.20 &= w \times 0.15, \\ w &= 1.333. \end{aligned}$$

Investing 133.3% of your wealth in the risky asset and $1 - w = 1 - 1.333 = -0.333$ or -33.3% of your wealth in the riskless asset (i.e., borrowing the equivalent of 33.3% of your wealth at the riskless rate) will produce a portfolio with a standard deviation of 0.20. The expected return corresponding to this is (Equation 17.5):

$$\begin{aligned} \mathbb{E}[R_P] &= r_f + w \times \left[\mathbb{E}[R_S] - r_f \right] \\ &= 0.02 + 1.333 \times \left[0.08 - 0.02 \right] \\ &= 0.10. \end{aligned}$$

17.3 Portfolios of Multiple Risky Assets

We have discussed possible portfolio combinations involving the combination of one risky asset and a riskless asset. However, there are many potential risky assets and resulting combinations of those assets and the riskless asset that investors could put together to form a portfolio. How do we evaluate such portfolios, and determine what the best combinations are for investor needs?

In this section, we first go over the concept of portfolio efficiency, which helps us to evaluate different portfolio combinations and filter out the ones that are suboptimal or strictly inferior to others from a risk and return perspective. We then detail the calculations involved in forming and assessing portfolios composed of two risky assets. After that, we discuss how one can apply the concept of portfolio efficiency and calculate which of the possible portfolios is optimal. We then add a riskless asset to the mix, and show how this enables an investor to select a wider choice of optimal portfolios based on their preferences. Finally, we discuss how the calculations change when we go into the more realistic situation with more than two risky assets.

17.3.1 Portfolio Efficiency

Investors face a very large number of possible portfolios that they could form. Not only are there many different financial assets—thousands of different stocks, options, bonds, etc.—investors can also choose how much of their money to put into each asset. However, there are some portfolios that investors would not select, which offer a lower expected return for a given level of risk, and thus are not efficient. An efficient portfolio is defined as the portfolio that offers the investor the highest possible expected rate of return at a specified level of risk. Investors would only want to consider efficient portfolios, which helps to reduce the number of choices they need to make.

To illustrate how to evaluate the many potential portfolio combinations investors could put together, we will use the portfolios shown in Table 17.2, but add a second risky asset.

Suppose that Risky Asset 2 has an expected return of 0.08 per year and a standard deviation of 0.15. In Figure 17.2, we plot Risky Asset 2 with the previously constructed portfolios. From the

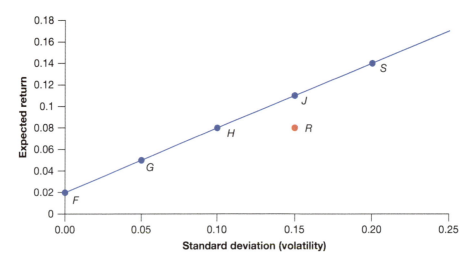

FIGURE 17.2 Risk–return of previous portfolios and Risky Asset 2. This figure shows the expected return and standard deviation for each of the portfolios provided in **Table 17.2**, and Risky Asset 2, denoted by point *R*. At point *R*, the portfolio is 100% invested in Risky Asset 2, offering an expected return of 0.08 and a standard deviation of 0.15. The investor can have both a higher expected rate of return and a lower standard deviation at any point on the line connecting points *H* and *J*.

figure, we can see that an investor requiring an expected rate of return of 0.08 per year could achieve this by investing all of their money in Risky Asset 2 and, thus, would be at point *R*. However, an investor would likely not choose point *R* because they can achieve at least as high a return for the same or lower risk from other portfolios. For example, from Table 17.2 we know that at point *H* the standard deviation is only 0.10 and that this is achieved by holding 50% of the portfolio in Risky Asset 1 and 50% in the riskless asset. Indeed, we can see that a risk-averse investor would be better off at *any* point along the trade-off line connecting points *G* and *S* than at point *R*. All of these points can be achieved by mixing Risky Asset 1 with the riskless asset. As another example, portfolio *J* has a standard deviation equal to that of Risky Asset 2 (0.15), but its expected return is 0.11 per year rather than 0.08. From Table 17.2, we know that its composition is 75% Risky Asset 1 and 25% riskless asset. More generally, we can use Equations 17.3 and 17.4 to find the composition of other efficient portfolios that lie between points *H* and *J* and, therefore, have both a higher expected rate of return and a lower standard deviation than Risky Asset 2.

We would refer to point *R* as *inefficient* because the investor can get a higher expected return for the same amount of risk.

Holding Risky Asset 2 by itself is inefficient, but what about holding portfolios that mix the two risky assets? Or portfolios that mix the two risky assets with the riskless asset? Will this make the portfolio efficient? In the next section we will look at how combining Risky Asset 2 with other assets can improve the risk and return of what is attainable through the benefits of diversification—spreading an investment across multiple assets which reduces overall risk, as we introduced in Chapter 6. We will explore the ways to efficiently combine three assets in two steps: consider the risk and return combinations attainable by mixing only Risky Assets 1 and 2, and then add the riskless asset.

17.3.2 Portfolios of Two Risky Assets

Combining two risky assets in a portfolio is similar to combining a risky asset with a riskless asset, as discussed in Section 17.2. When one of the two assets is riskless, the standard deviation of its rate of return and its correlation with the other asset are zero. When both assets are risky, the analysis of the risk and return trade-off is somewhat more involved.

The expected return of a portfolio with two risky assets is still the weighted average of the returns of the two assets, where the weights are the proportions invested in the assets. Let $\mathbb{E}[R_1]$ be the expected return of Risky Asset 1 and $\mathbb{E}[R_2]$ the expected return of Risky Asset 2. If an investor puts a proportion w in Risky Asset 1 and a proportion $(1 - w)$ in Risky Asset 2, the portfolio expected return is given by:

$$\mathbb{E}[R_P] = w \times \mathbb{E}[R_1] + (1 - w) \times \mathbb{E}[R_2]. \tag{17.7}$$

Equation 17.7 is essentially the same as Equation 17.3, except that the expected return on Risky Asset 2, $\mathbb{E}[R_2]$, is substituted for the interest rate on the riskless asset, r_f. Thus, Equation 17.7 is a more general form of Equation 17.3.

Calculating the risk of a portfolio with two risky assets is more complicated as it depends on the standard deviation of Risky Assets 1 and 2 (σ_1 and σ_2, respectively), the proportion of wealth invested in Risky Asset 1, w, as well as the *correlation* between the returns of the risky assets—whether and how much the returns of the two assets move together—denoted by $\rho_{1,2}$.

ρ represents the correlation coefficient between the returns of the two assets, and takes a value between -1 and 1. A positive value of ρ indicates that the two returns tend to move together—that is, an increase in the return of one asset tends to be followed by an increase in the return of the other asset. $\rho = 1$ indicates that the two returns move entirely in sync, an increase in the return of one asset is always followed by a proportional increase in the return of the other. In contrast, a negative value of ρ indicates the two returns move in opposite directions—an increase in the return of one asset tends to lead to a *decrease* in the return of the other assets. $\rho = -1$ indicates that the two returns move in sync in opposite directions, an increase in the return of one asset is always followed by a proportional decrease in the return of the other.

The formula for the variance of a portfolio, which is the standard deviation squared, is:

$$\sigma_P^2 = w^2 \times \sigma_1^2 + (1 - w)^2 \times \sigma_2^2 + 2 \times w \times (1 - w) \times \rho_{1,2} \times \sigma_1 \times \sigma_2. \tag{17.8}$$

To calculate the portfolio's standard deviation, we would take the square root of Equation 17.8, which is a more general form of Equation 17.4: When Asset 2 is riskless, then $\sigma_2 = 0$ and Equation 17.8 simplifies to Equation 17.4. As we will see, the reason why the portfolio's risk depends on whether and how much the two assets move together—the correlation between the risky assets—is because movements by each of the assets have the potential to offset each other, thus reducing the overall risk of the portfolio. This reduction in risk is known as diversification—spreading an investment among different assets with risks not perfectly correlated, reduces overall risk. We discussed the concept of diversification in Chapter 6. It is important to note that diversification refers to the fact that the returns of different assets that do not perfectly move together can cancel each other out, resulting in reduced risk. There are misconceptions in practice about diversification; Box 17.2 discuss some of these issues.

To illustrate, suppose that Risky Assets 1 and 2 have expected returns of 0.14 and 0.08, respectively, and standard deviations of 0.20 and 0.15, respectively (see Table 17.3). We will examine the overall portfolio expected return and risk given different assumptions about the correlation of their returns.

Table 17.3 Expected return and risk of Risky Assets 1 and 2.
This table provides the expected return $\mathbb{E}[R]$ and standard deviation σ of Risky Assets 1 and 2.

	Risky Asset 1	Risky Asset 2
Expected return, $\mathbb{E}[R]$	0.14	0.08
Standard deviation, σ	0.20	0.15

First, assume that the two assets have a correlation of 0.50; they tend to move in the same direction, but not always. Suppose we invested 0% of our wealth in Risky Asset 1 and 100% in Risky Asset 2, so $w = 0$; in effect, the portfolio is fully invested in Risky Asset 2. The expected return of the portfolio would be (Equation 17.7):

$$\begin{aligned} \mathbb{E}[R_P] &= w \times \mathbb{E}[R_1] + (1-w) \times \mathbb{E}[R_2] \\ &= 0 \times 0.14 + 1.0 \times 0.08 \\ &= 0.08. \end{aligned}$$

The standard deviation would be (Equation 17.8, then taking the square root):

$$\begin{aligned} \sigma_P^2 &= w^2 \times \sigma_1^2 + (1-w)^2 \times \sigma_2^2 + 2 \times w \times (1-w) \times \rho_{1,2} \times \sigma_1 \times \sigma_2 \\ &= 0 \times 0.20^2 + 1 \times 0.15^2 + 2 \times 0 \times 1 \times 0.50 \times 0.20 \times 0.15 \\ &= 0.0225, \\ \sigma_P &= \sqrt{0.0225} = 0.15. \end{aligned}$$

This produces a portfolio with an expected return of 0.08 and a standard deviation of 0.15, which is the return and risk of Risky Asset 2. Now suppose that instead we formed a portfolio with 25% invested in Risky Asset 1 and 75% invested in Risky Asset 2, so $w = 0.25$. Then our calculations would be:

$$\begin{aligned} \mathbb{E}[R_P] &= w \times \mathbb{E}[R_1] + (1-w) \times \mathbb{E}[R_2] \\ &= 0.25 \times 0.14 + 0.75 \times 0.08 \\ &= 0.095, \\ \sigma_P^2 &= w^2 \times \sigma_1^2 + (1-w)^2 \times \sigma_2^2 + 2 \times w \times (1-w) \times \rho_{1,2} \times \sigma_1 \times \sigma_2 \\ &= 0.25^2 \times 0.20^2 + (1-0.25)^2 \times 0.15^2 + 2 \times 0.25 \times (1-0.25) \times 0.50 \times 0.20 \times 0.15 \\ &= 0.0208, \\ \sigma_P &= \sqrt{0.0208} = 0.1442. \end{aligned}$$

This produces a portfolio with a higher expected return than our previous portfolio, but higher standard deviation—that is, more return and more risk.

We can continue in this way by going through *all* possible combinations of the risky assets (values of *w*). Table 17.4 provides the expected return and standard deviation for a wide range of possible portfolios. Given an assumed correlation of 0.5 between the returns of the two assets, we can see the above two portfolio combinations listed in the table. The table further provides the calculated values given different possible assumptions about the correlation between the two risky assets, ρ.

Table 17.4 shows a few notable results. First, for a given set of portfolio weights, the expected returns of the portfolio are independent of the correlation coefficient. As we can see from Equation 17.7, the expected return on any portfolio of risky assets is a simple weighted average of the expected returns of the assets in the portfolio, where the weights are the proportions invested in the assets. For example, a 50–50 mix between the two risky assets produces a portfolio with an expected return of 11% = 50% × 14% + 50% × 8%. This result is independent of the correlation between the returns of the pair of assets.

Second, the risk of a given portfolio, as measured by standard deviation, is dependent on the correlation coefficient. When the risky assets have a perfect positive correlation ($\rho_{1,2} = +1.0$) the portfolio risk–return relationship is linear and there is always a trade-off between higher variability and higher return. Put differently, the more money invested in Risky Asset 1, which has a higher expected return and higher risk, the higher the expected return and risk of the portfolio. However, in the case of less

17.3 PORTFOLIOS OF MULTIPLE RISKY ASSETS

Table 17.4 **The risk–reward trade-off for portfolios of two risky assets.** The expected return and standard deviation of portfolios constructed from the given combinations of Risky Assets 1 and 2, denoted by w, as well as different assumptions of the correlation between the returns of the assets, ρ. Risky Asset 1 has an expected return of 0.14 and a standard deviation of 0.20. Risky Asset 2 has an expected return of 0.08 and a standard deviation of 0.15.

Correlation, ρ	Proportion invested (%) in Risky Asset 1, w	Proportion invested (%) in Risky Asset 2, $1-w$	Expected rate of return (%), $\mathbb{E}[R_P]$	Standard deviation (%), σ_P
1.0	0	100	8.0	15.0
1.0	25	75	9.5	16.3
1.0	50	50	11.0	17.5
1.0	75	25	12.5	18.8
1.0	100	0	14.0	20.0
0.5	0	100	8.0	15.0
0.5	25	75	9.5	14.4
0.5	50	50	11.0	15.2
0.5	75	25	12.5	17.2
0.5	100	0	14.0	20.0
0.0	0	100	8.0	15.0
0.0	25	75	9.5	12.3
0.0	50	50	11.0	12.5
0.0	75	25	12.5	15.5
0.0	100	0	14.0	20.0
−0.50	0	100	8.0	15.0
−0.50	25	75	9.5	9.8
−0.50	50	50	11.0	9.0
−0.50	75	25	12.5	13.5
−0.50	100	0	14.0	20.0
−1.0	0	100	8.0	15.0
−1.0	25	75	9.5	6.3
−1.0	50	50	11.0	2.5
−1.0	75	25	12.5	11.3
−1.0	100	0	14.0	20.0

than perfect positive correlation, the risk–return trade-off becomes nonlinear, and in fact an investor may experience an increase in expected return but a decrease in risk. This is illustrated in Table 17.4 when the correlation coefficient is zero ($\rho_{1,2} = 0.0$). Starting with a portfolio fully invested in Risky Asset 2, as money is initially shifted toward Risky Asset 1 the expected return of the portfolio increases while the standard deviation decreases. With all the funds invested in Risky Asset 2, the expected return is 8% and the standard deviation is 15%, but with 25% in Risky Asset 1 and 75% in Risky Asset 2, the expected return rises to 9.5% and the standard deviation declines to 12.31%. However, note that investing more in Risky Asset 1 (so that w = 50%) starts to *increase* the portfolio standard deviation.

This suggests that, for a given correlation, there is a particular portfolio combination (value of *w*) that maximizes the diversification effect and produces a portfolio with the *least* amount of risk. Such a portfolio is called the minimum variance portfolio, which is discussed in the Appendix to this chapter. However, as explained in the next section, rather than simply finding the portfolio with the least risk, investors are concerned with finding the portfolio that produces the best risk–reward trade-off.

> **Box 17.2** The Fallacy of Time Diversification
>
> There is a widespread—but mistaken—belief that stocks are less risky in the long run than in the short run. The thinking behind this belief is that holding a risky asset over many periods allows one to diversify risk over *time*. Put differently, the same way that diversification reduces risk as an investor holds many assets over a given period, proponents of *time diversification* argue that risk can be reduced by holding a given risky asset over many periods.
>
> Based on this belief, an investor should invest more of their money in stocks the longer their planned holding period.
>
> Two propositions are used to prove that the time diversification effect is valid:
>
> - The longer the investor's holding period, the smaller the standard deviation of the annualized rate of return on stocks.
> - The longer the investor's holding period, the lower the probability that stocks will earn a rate of return less than the corresponding risk-free interest rate on bonds (provided that the expected log return is greater than the risk-free rate).
>
> Although they are true, these propositions do not support the validity of the idea that stocks are less risky in the long run than in the short run or that you should invest more in stocks because you have a longer planned holding period.
>
> The first proposition, that the standard deviation of the annualized rate of return declines as the holding period increases, is merely an expression of investment performance in terms of the annualized rate of return. There is no genuine diversification in this situation; you care about the amount of wealth you will have at the end of the holding period, and there is no decline in its standard deviation. For example, compare the results of investing all of your money in stocks versus risk-free bonds for one year and for 25 years. Even though the standard deviation of your annualized rate of return for the 25-year period is approximately one-fifth of the one-year result, the standard deviation of your ending wealth for the 25-year holding period is five times greater than the one-year standard deviation.
>
> As for the second proposition, it is true that the longer the holding period, the lower the probability of a *shortfall*, defined as the stock portfolio's earning less than the risk-free interest rate over that same period. However, the risk the loss incurred due to a shortfall depends on its severity when it happens as well as its probability of happening. If we consider measures of risk that take account of both the severity and the probability of a shortfall, there is no decline in risk as the holding period lengthens. For example, consider as a measure of risk the price of insuring a stock portfolio against a shortfall. It actually increases with the length of the holding period.
>
> In contrast to the notion of time diversification, diversifying one's portfolio through combining multiple risky assets is a robust and mathematically well-founded technique for reducing investment risk.
>
> A related strategy to time diversification is known as "dollar cost averaging," and refers to the strategy of investing a constant amount at fixed intervals over a period of time. While one

17.3 PORTFOLIOS OF MULTIPLE RISKY ASSETS

purported benefit of dollar cost averaging is the notion of time diversification, dollar cost averaging need not imply a very long holding period and also confers other advantages. The main idea behind dollar cost averaging is to avoid attempts to "time" the market—that is, trying to predict whether to buy (sell) assets because prices are relatively low (high)—and also to avoid "regret" at making a poor investment due to bad luck with timing. The disadvantage of dollar cost averaging versus a strategy of purchasing a desired position at one time is the potential of lower returns (due to holding onto money as cash for longer) and higher transaction costs in the form of fees.

QUICK CHECK 17.8 What are the mean and standard deviation of a portfolio that is 60% Risky Asset 1 and 40% Risky Asset 2, if the correlation coefficient is 0.1?

17.3.3 The Optimal Combination of Risky Assets

In the previous section we saw that the process of diversification between risky assets allowed a reduction in risk. However, investors may instead want to take on additional risk in order to gain a higher expected return (**Principle 7**). There are many different portfolio combinations that an investor may be able to choose in order to do so. Furthermore, there are some combinations that clearly dominate other combinations. For example, consider the case in Figure 17.3, where the correlation between the assets is equal to −0.5. There could be a portfolio with a standard deviation of 0.1 and an expected return of roughly 0.95, or a portfolio with the same standard deviation of 0.1 but a *higher* expected return of roughly 0.115. In this case, the latter option is clearly better, but other potential

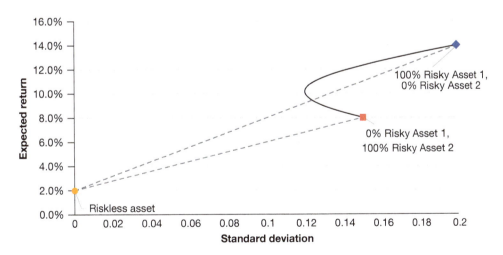

FIGURE 17.3 Risk–reward trade-off for different portfolios. This figure depicts the risk–reward trade-off for a portfolio consisting of 100% in Risky Asset 1 and 0% in Risky Asset 2 (represented by the blue diamond), and a portfolio consisting of 0% in Risky Asset 1 and 100% in Risky Asset 2 (represented by the red square). The orange circle represents the riskless asset, and the dashed line the risk–reward trade-off line corresponding to each portfolio. A steeper risk–reward trade-off line represents a greater return for each unit of risk. Risky Asset 1 has an expected return of 0.14 and a standard deviation of 0.20. Risky Asset 2 has an expected return of 0.08 and a standard deviation of 0.15. The riskless rate of return is 2%.

portfolios may offer better or worse risk–reward trade-offs. In this section we consider how we can choose an optimal portfolio, one that provides the best risk–reward combination.

In order to assess whether a portfolio is optimal, we need to quantify the risk–reward trade-off of a particular portfolio. Doing so requires knowing the rate of return provided by the riskless asset, which provides a point of reference for understanding how much additional return an investor will receive for taking on risk. In particular, recall the risk–reward trade-off line from Figure 17.1. We can quantify the risk–reward trade-off of investing in a particular risky asset by examining the slope between that asset and the riskless asset, which shows the extra expected return the market offers (beyond the riskless rate of return) for each unit of extra risk an investor is willing to bear. This slope is referred to as a Sharpe ratio, and for any risky asset or portfolio of assets P is given by:

$$\text{Sharpe ratio} = \frac{\mathbb{E}[R_P] - r_f}{\sigma_P}. \tag{17.9}$$

A higher value of the Sharpe ratio indicates a greater expected return per unit of risk, and thus a better portfolio in terms of its risk–reward trade-off.

Suppose, as before, that the riskless rate of return is 0.02. For simplicity, assume that the correlation between the risky assets is 0, so $\rho = 0$. We can calculate the Sharpe ratio of different portfolio combinations. First, consider the portfolio where we invest 0% in Risky Asset 1 and 100% in Risky Asset 2. From Table 17.4, the portfolio expected return is 0.08 and the standard deviation is 0.15. The Sharpe ratio is therefore (Equation 17.9):

$$\begin{aligned} \text{Sharpe ratio} &= \frac{\mathbb{E}[R_P] - r_f}{\sigma_P} \\ &= \frac{0.08 - 0.02}{0.15} \\ &= 0.4. \end{aligned}$$

Now consider the portfolio where we invest 100% in Risky Asset 1 and 0% in Risky Asset 2. From Table 17.4, the portfolio expected return is 0.14 and the portfolio standard deviation is 0.20. The Sharpe ratio for this portfolio is:

$$\begin{aligned} \text{Sharpe ratio} &= \frac{\mathbb{E}[R_P] - r_f}{\sigma_P} \\ &= \frac{0.14 - 0.02}{0.20} \\ &= 0.6. \end{aligned}$$

With a higher Sharpe ratio, this portfolio presents a better risk–reward trade-off. Figure 17.3 shows both portfolios as points on either end of the curve representing all possible portfolio combinations, along with risk–reward trade-off lines connecting the riskless asset and the respective portfolios. In line with the higher Sharpe ratio, the risk–reward trade-off line for the second portfolio has a steeper slope.

However, by looking at Figure 17.3, you may notice that it is possible to construct a steeper line than either of these portfolios by connecting the riskless asset to certain combinations of Risky Asset 1 and Risky Asset 2 (represented by the curve). To explore this, we can examine the risk–reward trade-off in this way for all possible portfolios consisting of combinations of Risky Asset 1 and Risky Asset 2. Table 17.5 provides the Sharpe ratio for the combinations provided in Table 17.4, given a correlation of 0. As the table shows, the risk–reward trade-off can be very different across the portfolios. Out of the possible combinations shown in the table, investing 50% in Risky Asset 1 and 50% in Risky Asset 2 provides the highest Sharpe ratio of 0.72.

Table 17.5 **The risk–reward trade-off for portfolios of two risky assets.** This table provides the expected return, standard deviation, and Sharpe ratios of portfolios constructed from the given combinations of Risky Assets 1 and 2, denoted by w. It is assumed that the correlation between the returns of the assets, ρ, is zero. Risky Asset 1 has an expected return of 0.14 and a standard deviation of 0.20. Risky Asset 2 has an expected return of 0.08 and a standard deviation of 0.15.

Proportion invested in Risky Asset 1, w	Proportion invested in Risky Asset 2, $1-w$	Expected rate of return, $\mathbb{E}[R_P]$	Standard deviation, σ_P	Sharpe ratio, $\dfrac{\mathbb{E}[R_P]-r_f}{\sigma_P}$
0%	100%	8.0%	15.0%	0.40
25%	75%	9.5%	12.3%	0.61
50%	50%	11.0%	12.5%	0.72
75%	25%	12.5%	15.5%	0.68
100%	0%	14.0%	20.0%	0.60

The portfolio combination that provides the *best* risk–reward trade-off is the optimal combination of risky assets (OCRA). One approach to finding the OCRA is to calculate the Sharpe ratio for every possible portfolio weight of Risky Asset 1, w, in addition to the ones listed in Table 17.5. However, it turns out that there is a formula that provides this optimal portfolio weight:

$$w = \frac{\left[\mathbb{E}[R_1]-r_f\right]\times \sigma_2^2 - \left[\mathbb{E}[R_2]-r_f\right]\times \rho_{1,2}\times \sigma_1 \times \sigma_2}{\left[\mathbb{E}[R_1]-r_f\right]\times \sigma_2^2 + \left[\mathbb{E}[R_2]-r_f\right]\times \sigma_1^2 - \left[\mathbb{E}[R_1]-r_f + \mathbb{E}[R_2]-r_f\right]\times \rho_{1,2}\times \sigma_1 \times \sigma_2}. \quad (17.10)$$

Thus, in our case, we can calculate the OCRA as (Equation 17.10):

$$\begin{aligned}
w &= \frac{\left[\mathbb{E}[R_1]-r_f\right]\times \sigma_2^2 - \left[\mathbb{E}[R_2]-r_f\right]\times \rho_{1,2}\times \sigma_1 \times \sigma_2}{\left[\mathbb{E}[R_1]-r_f\right]\times \sigma_2^2 + \left[\mathbb{E}[R_2]-r_f\right]\times \sigma_1^2 - \left[\mathbb{E}[R_1]-r_f + \mathbb{E}[R_2]-r_f\right]\times \rho_{1,2}\times \sigma_1 \times \sigma_2} \\
&= \frac{[0.14-0.02]\times 0.15^2 - [0.08-0.02]\times 0 \times 0.20 \times 0.15}{[0.14-0.02]\times 0.15^2 + [0.08-0.02]\times 0.20^2 - [0.14-0.02+0.08-0.02]\times 0 \times 0.20 \times 0.15} \\
&= 0.529.
\end{aligned}$$

Thus, the OCRA consists of investing 52.9% in Risky Asset 1 and 47.1% (= $1-w = 1-0.529 = 0.471$) in Risky Asset 2. Doing so produces a portfolio with an expected return and standard deviation of (Equations 17.7 and 17.8):

$$\begin{aligned}
\mathbb{E}[R_P] &= w\times \mathbb{E}[R_1] + (1-w)\times \mathbb{E}[R_2] \\
&= 0.529 \times 0.14 + 0.471 \times 0.08 \\
&= 0.112, \\
\sigma_P^2 &= w^2 \times \sigma_1^2 + (1-w)^2 \times \sigma_2^2 + 2\times w \times (1-w)\times \rho_{1,2}\times \sigma_1 \times \sigma_2 \\
&= 0.529^2 \times 0.20^2 + (1-0.529)^2 \times 0.15^2 + 2\times 0.529 \times (1-0.529)\times 0 \times 0.20 \times 0.15 \\
&= 0.016, \\
\sigma_P &= \sqrt{0.016} = 0.127.
\end{aligned}$$

The Sharpe ratio is thus (Equation 17.9):

$$\text{Sharpe ratio} = \frac{\mathbb{E}[R_P] - r_f}{\sigma_P}$$

$$= \frac{0.112 - 0.02}{0.127}$$

$$= 0.7244.$$

This portfolio produces the best risk–reward trade-off possible by combining Risky Assets 1 and 2, and thus the highest Sharpe ratio possible.

Figure 17.4 graphically shows the risk–reward trade-off line corresponding to this portfolio. As this portfolio gives the best possible risk–reward trade-off, the line has a steeper slope than the lines for other portfolios. Also note that the portfolio represents the point of tangency where the curve representing all possible portfolio combinations meets the risk–reward trade-off line. For this reason, the portfolio consisting of the optimal combination of risky assets is known as the tangency portfolio. Box 17.3 shows how Excel can be used to calculate a tangency portfolio; the companion Excel app to this chapter allows you to perform these calculations given different assumptions on the underlying assets.

This risk–reward trade-off is superior to the risk–reward trade-off (found in Section 17.2.3), 0.60, when we combined the riskless asset with just Risky Asset 1. Put differently, investors are better off here because they can achieve a higher expected rate of return for any level of risk they are willing to tolerate, due to the diversification benefit of the combination of two risky assets.

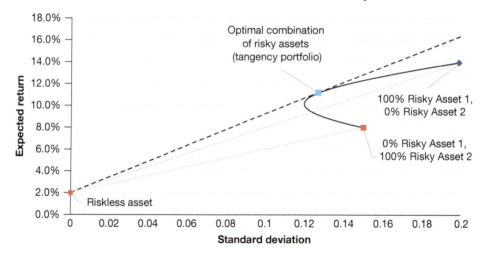

FIGURE 17.4 **Risk–reward trade-off for optimal combination of risky assets.** This figure depicts the risk–reward trade-offs for a portfolio consisting of the optimal portfolio of risky assets (the light blue square). The red circle represents the riskless asset, and the dashed line the risk–reward trade-off line corresponding to the portfolio consisting of the optimal combination of risky assets. Risky Asset 1 has an expected return of 0.14 and a standard deviation of 0.20. Risky Asset 2 has an expected return of 0.08 and a standard deviation of 0.15. It is assumed that the correlation between the returns of the assets, ρ, is zero.

> **QUICK CHECK 17.9** Recalculate the optimal combination of Risky Asset 1 and Risky Asset 2 assuming a correlation between the two of 0.50. What is the Sharpe ratio of this optimal combination?

17.3 PORTFOLIOS OF MULTIPLE RISKY ASSETS

Example 17.2 (Expected Return, Standard Deviation, and Sharpe Ratio on Risky Assets): Suppose that there are two risky assets with the following characteristics:

	Risky Asset 1	Risky Asset 2
Expected return, $\mathbb{E}[R]$	0.20	0.15
Standard deviation, σ	0.40	0.30

Assume a correlation coefficient of −0.75 between the risky assets, and a riskless interest rate of 2%. What is the optimal combination of risky assets? For this portfolio, calculate the expected return, standard deviation, and Sharpe ratio.

Solution. The portfolio weight corresponding to the investment in Risky Asset 1, w, for the OCRA is given by Equation 17.10:

$$w = \frac{\left[\mathbb{E}[R_1]-r_f\right]\times \sigma_2^2 - \left[\mathbb{E}[R_2]-r_f\right]\times \rho_{1,2}\times \sigma_1 \times \sigma_2}{\left[\mathbb{E}[R_1]-r_f\right]\times \sigma_2^2 + \left[\mathbb{E}[R_2]-r_f\right]\times \sigma_1^2 - \left[\mathbb{E}[R_1]-r_f + \mathbb{E}[R_2]-r_f\right]\times \rho_{1,2}\times \sigma_1 \times \sigma_2}$$

$$= \frac{[0.20-0.02]\times 0.30^2 - [0.15-0.02]\times -0.75 \times 0.40 \times 0.30}{[0.20-0.02]\times 0.30^2 + [0.15-0.02]\times 0.40^2 - [0.20-0.02+0.15-0.02]\times -0.75 \times 0.40 \times 0.30}$$

$$= 0.43.$$

The optimal investment in Risky Asset 2 is therefore:

$$1-w = 1-0.43$$
$$= 0.57.$$

Now, given these weights, the expected return of this portfolio is provided by Equations 17.7 and 17.8

$$\mathbb{E}[R_P] = w \times \mathbb{E}[R_1] + (1-w)\times \mathbb{E}[R_2]$$
$$= 0.43 \times 0.20 + 0.57 \times 0.15$$
$$= 0.172,$$

$$\sigma_P^2 = w^2 \times \sigma_1^2 + (1-w)^2 \times \sigma_2^2 + 2\times w \times (1-w)\times \rho_{1,2}\times \sigma_1 \times \sigma_2$$
$$= 0.43^2 \times 0.40^2 + (1-0.43)^2 \times 0.30^2 + 2 \times 0.43 \times (1-0.43)\times -0.75 \times 0.40 \times 0.30$$
$$= 0.015,$$

$$\sigma_P = \sqrt{0.015} = 0.121.$$

Finally, the Sharpe ratio can be calculated using these numbers and Equation 17.9:

$$\text{Sharpe ratio} = \frac{\mathbb{E}[R_P]-r_f}{\sigma_P}$$
$$= \frac{0.172-0.02}{0.121}$$
$$= 1.26.$$

Box 17.3 Excel in Practice: Portfolio Calculations

Spreadsheet programs such as Excel offer convenient ways to perform the portfolio calculations that we have discussed. As mentioned in Section 17.2, the expected return and standard deviation of a risky asset can be estimated using previous stock return data, and then used in the portfolio calculations. To illustrate, suppose that there are two stocks with data on five years' worth of returns each. We can estimate the expected return $\mathbb{E}[R]$ using the =AVERAGE Excel function, and the standard deviation can be calculated using the =STDEV.S function:

	A	B	C
1	Year	Stock 1 Returns	Stock 2 Returns
2	1	0.05	0.2
3	2	-0.02	0.25
4	3	0.06	0.02
5	4	0.1	-0.15
6	5	-0.01	0.01
7			
8	Expected Return:	=AVERAGE(B2:B6)	=AVERAGE(C2:C6)
9	Standard Deviation:	=STDEV.S(B2:B6)	=STDEV.S(C2:C6)

The correlation between the returns can be estimated using the =CORREL function in Excel:

	A	B	C
1	Year	Stock 1 Returns	Stock 2 Returns
2	1	0.05	0.2
3	2	-0.02	0.25
4	3	0.06	0.02
5	4	0.1	-0.15
6	5	-0.01	0.01
7			
8	Expected Return:	=AVERAGE(B2:B6)	=AVERAGE(C2:C6)
9	Standard Deviation:	=STDEV.S(B2:B6)	=STDEV.S(C2:C6)
10	Correlation:	=CORREL(B2:B6,C2:C6)	

This provides the following numbers:

	A	B	C
1	Year	Stock 1 Returns	Stock 2 Returns
2	1	0.05	0.2
3	2	-0.02	0.25
4	3	0.06	0.02
5	4	0.1	-0.15
6	5	-0.01	0.01
7			
8	Expected Return:	0.04	0.07
9	Standard Deviation:	0.05	0.16
10	Correlation:	-0.64	

Excel also offers a time-saving way to perform calculations such as solving for the tangency portfolio. Through Excel formulas, it is possible to choose many different possible portfolio combinations (investment weights for the risky assets, w and $1 - w$), and to calculate the weight that yields the lowest risk or highest Sharpe ratio. Alternatively, Excel can be asked to solve for the weights directly. To do so, let us assume a riskless rate of 0.01. Using Equations 17.7–17.9, we can first set up formulas to calculate the portfolio expected return, standard deviation, and Sharpe ratio given some weight (let's put $w = 0.5$ for now):

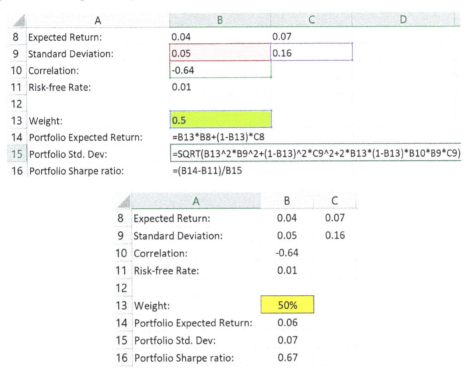

Now we can ask Excel to find the desired portfolios using Solver. To do so, we go to the *Data* tab and click on *Solver* (this may need to be enabled under *Add-ins* in Excel's options). To solve for the OCRA in a similar way, note that the optimal combination produces the highest Sharpe ratio. Thus, using Solver, we ask Excel to instead *Set Objective* to maximizing the Sharpe ratio (cell B16) by changing the portfolio weight (cell B13):

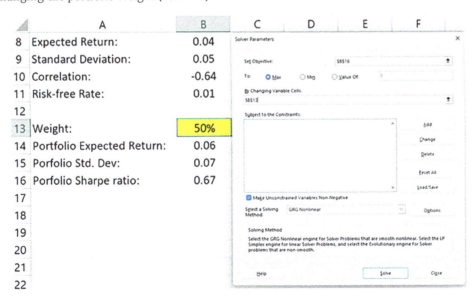

After clicking *Solve*, Excel will produce the tangency portfolio by replacing the value in the weight cell. Here, the tangency portfolio is produced by setting the weight to 78%:

	A	B	C
8	Expected Return:	0.04	0.07
9	Standard Deviation:	0.05	0.16
10	Correlation:	-0.64	
11	Risk-free Rate:	0.01	
12			
13	Weight:	78%	
14	Portfolio Expected Return:	0.05	
15	Portfolio Std. Dev:	0.03	
16	Portfolio Sharpe ratio:	1.16	

17.3.4 Selecting a Preferred Portfolio with Risky and Riskless Assets

We have now gone through how an investor may form a portfolio composed entirely of a combination of risky assets, and how to assess such a portfolio. However, an investor may also add the *riskless* asset to their portfolio, as we saw in Section 17.2.3. An investor can therefore choose to invest part of their money in the optimal combination of risky assets, and part in the riskless asset. Would an investor want to invest any part of their money in the riskless asset, and if so, what combination of riskless asset and optimal risky portfolio would an investor prefer?

To answer this question, assume that the correlation between the risky assets is zero and the riskless rate of return is 0.02. In the previous section we saw that the OCRA (i.e., tangency portfolio) consisted of investing 52.9% in Risky Asset 1 and 47.1% in Risky Asset 2, with an expected return of 0.112 and a standard deviation of 0.127. If we view the tangency portfolio as a single risky asset, then we can combine it with the riskless asset using the methodology of Section 17.2.3.

Let us use T to denote the tangency (risky asset) portfolio, so w_T is the proportion of money invested in the tangency portfolio, and thus $1 - w_T$ is the proportion invested in the riskless asset. Suppose first that an investor chooses to invest nothing in the tangency portfolio, so $w_T = 0$. Then the resulting portfolio will be composed entirely of the riskless asset and will provide an expected return $\mathbb{E}[R_P] = 0.02$ and a standard deviation of $\sigma_P = 0$. At the other end of the spectrum, suppose that an investor chooses to invest everything in the tangency portfolio and nothing in the riskless asset, so $w_T = 1$. This simply produces the tangency portfolio, which has an expected return $\mathbb{E}[R_T] = 0.112$ and a standard deviation of $\sigma_T = 0.127$, resulting in a Sharpe ratio of 0.72.

Suppose that an investor decides to invest half in the tangency portfolio and half in the riskless asset, so $w_T = 0.5$ and $1 - w_T = 0.5$. Since the correlation coefficient between a risky and riskless asset is 0, we can determine the expected return and standard deviation of the resulting portfolio using the methodology of Section 17.2.3 (Equations 17.3 and 17.4):

$$\begin{aligned}
\mathbb{E}[R_P] &= w_T \times \mathbb{E}[R_T] + (1 - w_T) \times r_f \\
&= 0.5 \times 0.112 + 0.5 \times 0.02 \\
&= 0.066, \\
\sigma_P &= w_T \times \sigma_T \\
&= 0.5 \times 0.127 \\
&= 0.0635.
\end{aligned}$$

Note that the tangency portfolio itself is composed of 52.9% in Risky Asset 1 and 47.1% in Risky Asset 2, so the composition of this portfolio is: 50% riskless asset, 0.5 × 52.9% = 26.45% Risky Asset 1, and 0.5 × 47.1% = 23.55% Risky Asset 2. Thus, if you were investing $100,000 in this portfolio, you would invest $50,000 in the riskless asset, $26,450 in Risky Asset 1, and $23,550 in Risky Asset 2.

We can calculate the Sharpe ratio of this portfolio as (Equation 17.9):

$$\text{Sharpe ratio} = \frac{\mathbb{E}[R_P] - r_f}{\sigma_P}$$

$$= \frac{0.066 - 0.02}{0.0635}$$

$$= 0.7244.$$

Note that this results in the *same* Sharpe ratio as investing everything in the tangency portfolio itself. Table 17.6 provides the calculations for various portfolios consisting of the tangency portfolio and the riskless asset. Included in the calculations is investing more than 100% of wealth in the tangency portfolio (i.e., investing everything in the tangency portfolio and borrowing more at the riskless rate to invest further in the tangency portfolio). Note that every possible combination of the riskless asset and the tangency portfolio provide the exact same Sharpe ratio, indicating that the combinations are equivalent from a risk–return standpoint. Put differently, the optimal portfolio is any combination of the riskless asset and the tangency portfolio. This is also shown visually in Figure 17.5; each portfolio lies on the same risk–reward trade-off line between the riskless asset and the tangency portfolio.

If all combinations result in an equivalent risk–reward ratio, how would an investor choose between the portfolios? The answer is that it depends on the person's preferences, which in turn depend on such things as the person's stage in life, planning horizon, and risk tolerance. For example, an investor that does not have a high risk tolerance (i.e., is more risk-averse) may choose portfolio (2) in Table 17.6 and Figure 17.5, choosing a relatively lower amount of risk. In contrast, an investor that is more risk-tolerant may choose portfolio (5) (investing everything in the tangency portfolio) or even portfolio (6), taking on even more risk for a higher expected return.

It is important to note that in finding the optimal combination of risky assets (the tangency portfolio), we do not need to know anything about investor wealth or preferences. The composition of this

Table 17.6 **Portfolios consisting of the tangency portfolio and riskless asset.** This table provides the expected return, standard deviation, and Sharpe ratios of portfolios constructed from the given combinations of the tangency portfolio and the riskless asset. The tangency portfolio itself is composed of 69.2% in Risky Asset 1 and 30.8% in Risky Asset 2, with expected return and standard deviation given in Table 17.3, assuming zero correlation between the risky assets.

Portfolio	Proportion invested in tangency portfolio, w_T	Proportion invested in riskless asset, $1 - w_T$	Expected rate of return, $\mathbb{E}[R_P]$	Standard deviation, σ_P	Sharpe ratio, $\frac{\mathbb{E}[R_P] - r_f}{\sigma_P}$
(1)	0%	100%	0.020	0.000	—
(2)	25%	75%	0.043	0.032	0.72
(3)	50%	50%	0.066	0.064	0.72
(4)	75%	25%	0.089	0.095	0.72
(5)	100%	0%	0.112	0.127	0.72
(6)	125%	−25%	0.135	0.159	0.72

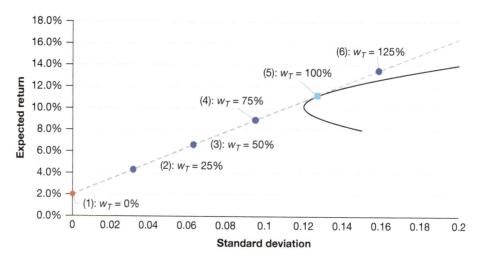

FIGURE 17.5 Risk–reward trade-off for portfolios consisting of the tangency portfolio and riskless asset. This figure depicts the risk–reward trade-offs for the portfolios shown in Table 17.6, consisting of the tangency portfolio and the riskless asset. Each portfolio lies on the same risk–reward trade-off line as the tangency portfolio.

portfolio depends only on the expected rates of return and standard deviations of Risky Asset 1 and Risky Asset 2, on the correlation between them, and on the risk-free rate. This implies that all investors who agree on the probability distributions for rates of return will want to hold this same tangency portfolio in combination with the riskless asset. Investors could then create their own portfolio, a combination of the risk-free asset and the tangency portfolio, to suit their individual risk tolerance by adjusting the weight invested in the risk-free asset.

This is a general result that provides insights into how portfolio managers can provide a menu of choices to investors. In particular, a manager can mix the OCRA in advance without having to know any detail about which choice the customer might make. Once that choice is made, the manager can quickly provide the portfolio mix the customer wants—a mix of just the riskless asset and the OCRA—based on the customer's preferences. This insight carries over to the case in which there are many risky assets in addition to Risky Asset 1 and Risky Asset 2: There is always a particular optimal portfolio of risky assets that all risk-averse investors who share the same forecasts of rates of return will combine with the riskless asset to reach their most preferred portfolio. We discuss this in detail in Section 17.4.

> **QUICK CHECK 17.10** Suppose an investor chooses to invest 75% of their wealth in the tangency portfolio and 25% in the riskless asset. What is the expected rate of return and standard deviation of this portfolio? If the investor has $100,000, how much will they invest in each of the three assets?

Example 17.3 (Achieving a Target Expected Return): Suppose you have $100,000 to invest and want an expected rate of return of 0.10 per year. Given the same information on the risky assets and riskless asset provided in Section 17.3.4, what is the composition of the portfolio you would need to form to achieve this expected return?

17.3 PORTFOLIOS OF MULTIPLE RISKY ASSETS

Solution. We need to solve for the weight (investment in the tangency portfolio) w_T that provides an expected return of $\mathbb{E}[R_P] = 0.10$. To do so, we can utilize Equation 17.3, given $r_f = 0.06$ and $\mathbb{E}[R_T] = 0.122$:

$$\mathbb{E}[R_P] = r_f + w_T \times \left[\mathbb{E}[R_T] - r_f\right],$$
$$0.10 = 0.06 + w_T \times \left[0.122 - 0.06\right],$$
$$w_T = 0.645.$$

Thus, 64.5% of the $100,000 must be invested in the OCRA and 35.5% in the riskless asset. The standard deviation of this portfolio is given by Equation 17.4:

$$\sigma_P = w_T \times \sigma_T$$
$$= 0.645 \times 0.146$$
$$= 0.094.$$

Because the OCRA is itself composed of 69.2% Risky Asset 1 and 30.8% Risky Asset 2, the composition of the final desired portfolio with expected return of 0.10 per year is found as follows:

Weight in riskless asset:	35.5%
Weight in Risky Asset 1:	$0.645 \times 69.2\% = 44.6\%$
Weight in Risky Asset 2:	$0.645 \times 30.8\% = 19.9\%$
Total:	100%

Example 17.4 (Forming a Portfolio with the OCRA): Suppose that there are two risky assets with the following characteristics:

	Risky Asset 1	Risky Asset 2
Expected return, $\mathbb{E}[R]$	0.40	0.10
Standard deviation, σ	0.60	0.15

The correlation between the two risky assets is 0.50. There is also a riskless asset with a rate of return of 0.05.

(a) What is the optimal combination of Risky Asset 1 and 2? What is the resulting expected return and standard deviation? What is the Sharpe ratio?
(b) If you wanted to achieve an expected return of 0.35, what combination of the tangency portfolio and the riskless asset would you need? What is the resulting Sharpe ratio?

Solution.

(a) The portfolio weight corresponding to the investment in Risky Asset 1, w, for the OCRA (denoted by T, since it represents the tangency portfolio) is given by Equation 17.8:

$$w_T = \frac{\left[\mathbb{E}[R_1] - r_f\right] \times \sigma_2^2 - \left[\mathbb{E}[R_2] - r_f\right] \times \rho_{1,2} \times \sigma_1 \times \sigma_2}{\left[\mathbb{E}[R_1] - r_f\right] \times \sigma_2^2 + \left[\mathbb{E}[R_2] - r_f\right] \times \sigma_1^2 - \left[\mathbb{E}[R_1] - r_f + \mathbb{E}[R_2] - r_f\right] \times \rho_{1,2} \times \sigma_1 \times \sigma_2}$$

$$= \frac{\left[0.40 - 0.05\right] \times 0.15^2 - \left[0.10 - 0.05\right] \times 0.50 \times 0.60 \times 0.15}{\left[0.40 - 0.05\right] \times 0.15^2 + \left[0.10 - 0.05\right] \times 0.60^2 - \left[0.40 - 0.05 + 0.10 - 0.05\right] \times 0.50 \times 0.60 \times 0.15}$$

$$= 0.714.$$

The optimal investment in Risky Asset 2 is therefore:

$$1 - w_T = 1 - 0.714$$
$$= 0.286.$$

Now, given these weights, the expected return of this portfolio is provided by Equations 17.7 and 17.8:

$$\mathbb{E}[R_T] = w_T \times \mathbb{E}[R_1] + (1 - w_T) \times \mathbb{E}[R_2]$$
$$= 0.714 \times 0.40 + 0.286 \times 0.10$$
$$= 0.314,$$
$$\sigma_T^2 = w_T^2 \times \sigma_1^2 + (1 - w_T)^2 \times \sigma_2^2 + 2 \times w_T \times (1 - w_T) \times \rho_{1,2} \times \sigma_1 \times \sigma_2$$
$$= 0.714^2 \times 0.60^2 + (1 - 0.714)^2 \times 0.15^2 + 2 \times 0.714 \times (1 - 0.714) \times 0.50 \times 0.60 \times 0.15$$
$$= 0.204,$$
$$\sigma_T = \sqrt{0.204} = 0.452.$$

Finally, the Sharpe ratio can be calculated using these numbers and Equation 17.9:

$$\text{Sharpe ratio} = \frac{\mathbb{E}[R_T] - r_f}{\sigma_T}$$
$$= \frac{0.314 - 0.05}{0.452}$$
$$= 0.584.$$

(b) We need to solve for the weight (investment in the tangency portfolio) w_T that provides an expected return of $\mathbb{E}[R_P] = 0.35$. To do so, we can utilize Equation 17.5, given $r_f = 0.05$ and $\mathbb{E}[R_T] = 0.314$ from part (a):

$$\mathbb{E}[R_P] = r_f + w_T \times [\mathbb{E}[R_T] - r_f],$$
$$0.35 = 0.05 + w_T \times [0.314 - 0.05],$$
$$w_T = 1.136.$$

Thus, 113.6% of wealth must be invested in the OCRA and 1 − 1.136 = −0.136 or −13.6% in the riskless asset. Put differently, to achieve the desired expected return, an investor would need to invest all of their money in the tangency portfolio, and then borrow at the riskless interest rate and invest that money in the tangency portfolio. So if the investor had $100,000, the investor would need to invest the $100,000 in the tangency portfolio, borrow $13,600 at the riskless interest rate, and then invest that in the tangency portfolio for a total investment of $113,600 in the tangency portfolio. The standard deviation of this portfolio is given by Equation 17.4:

$$\sigma_P = w_T \times \sigma_T$$
$$= 1.136 \times 0.452$$
$$= 0.5134.$$

Finally, the Sharpe ratio is (Equation 17.9):

$$\text{Sharpe ratio} = \frac{\mathbb{E}[R_P] - r_f}{\sigma_P}$$
$$= \frac{0.35 - 0.05}{0.5134}$$
$$= 0.584.$$

The Sharpe ratio is the exact same with this portfolio, reinforcing the conclusions from this section.

17.3.5 Portfolios with Many Risky Assets

Investors can, of course, invest in many more than two risky assets. When there are many risky assets we use the two-step method of portfolio construction used in the previous section, where we construct portfolios from the risky assets only, and then find the tangency portfolio of risky assets combined with the riskless asset. In particular, conceptually we form portfolios consisting of different possible combinations of risky assets, and determine the expected return and volatility of each portfolio. This then allows us to determine the portfolio that is the optimal combination of risky assets (OCRA), which can then be invested in along with the riskless asset. Figure 17.6 illustrates this. Each individual dot represents the expected return and risk of each individual risky asset as well as possible portfolios made up of combinations of the assets. The blue curve outlining the top of the cluster of dots represents the portfolio combinations of the risky assets which offer the highest possible expected rate of return for any given standard deviation, called the efficient frontier. The number of dots underscores the fact that there is an uncountable number of possible portfolios, but the vast majority of these dots do not need to be considered because they would never be selected over the ones on the efficient frontier (the curve) which provide a higher expected return for any given volatility. Out of the portfolios on the efficient frontier, the OCRA is the point of tangency between a straight line from the point representing the riskless asset (on the vertical axis) and the efficient frontier of risky assets. The straight line connecting the riskless asset and the tangency point representing the OCRA is the best risk–reward trade-off line achievable.

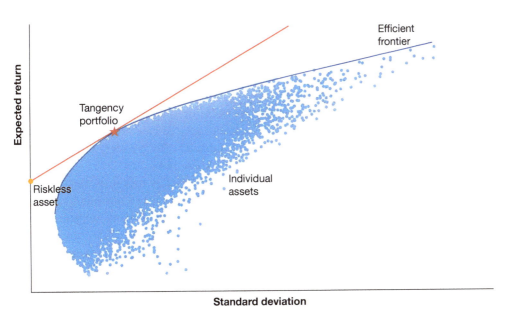

FIGURE 17.6 **Efficient portfolio frontier.** The efficient portfolio frontier is the blue curve outlining the top portion of the cluster of dots. It is made of the portfolio combinations that provide the highest expected return for a given amount of risk. The blue dots are individual risky assets and portfolios formed of combinations of the assets. The OCRA is the tangency portfolio (the red star), found by the line that runs from the riskless asset and is tangent to the efficient frontier.

Because the computations involve complex calculations, in practice it is usually best to use computers to determine the tangency portfolio when there are many risky assets. To illustrate, if there are N risky assets, then the equations for the portfolio expected return and variance are given by:

$$\mathbb{E}[R_P] = \sum_{i=1}^{N} w_i \times \mathbb{E}[R_i], \tag{17.11}$$

$$\sigma_P^2 = \sum_{i=1}^{N} w_i^2 \times \sigma_i^2 + \sum_{i=1}^{N}\sum_{i \neq j} w_i \times w_j \times \sigma_i \times \sigma_j \times \rho_{i,j}. \tag{17.12}$$

Equation 17.7 and 17.8 are specific versions of these equations, with $N = 2$ (Merton 1972). These equations quickly become very tedious to calculate by hand as the number of assets increases. The tangency portfolio is found by determining the values w_i for each risky asset i that produces a portfolio expected return and standard deviation (using Equations 17.11 and 17.12) with the best risk–reward trade-off (i.e., highest Sharpe ratio) among all possible portfolio combinations. Computer optimization programs are best to solve for the appropriate combination.

In the previous sections we explored how investors can form portfolios and perform calculations in order to determine the risk and return characteristics of portfolios, and select one that offers the best risk–return trade-off and also matches one's preferences. However, the calculations involved can sometimes be onerous. In the next section we describe how this process can be accomplished in practice.

17.4 Mean-Variance Analysis and Asset Management

The optimal decision for individuals is to invest in some combination of the tangency portfolio—consisting of a specific combination of risky assets and the riskless asset. In theory, individuals can purchase these assets on their own and determine the relative proportion of their money they want to invest in the riskless asset.

Most people have neither the knowledge nor the time to carry out the analyses required to select an optimal portfolio. Therefore, they hire an investment advisor to do it for them or they buy a "finished product" from a financial intermediary. Intermediaries such as banks, asset management firms, securities firms, investment companies, and insurance companies offer a variety of products for individuals (or their advisors who help select the products) to choose from.

When financial intermediaries decide what asset choices to offer to households, they are in a position analogous to a restaurant deciding on its menu. There are many ingredients available (the basic stocks, bonds, and other securities issued by firms and governments) and an infinite number of possible ways to combine them, but only a limited number of items will be offered to customers. The portfolio theory developed in this chapter shows how to find the least number of items that cover the full array a portfolio owner needs.

Frictions such as large transaction costs from purchasing individual assets in the marketplace, fees, and time spent purchasing assets are some of the reasons individuals delegate to asset managers. Individuals also often lack the financial and statistical knowledge and the data necessary to perform portfolio calculations. Such calculations are also not easy to do—as we saw in the previous sections, calculating the optimal portfolio even for just two risky assets is not a trivial exercise, much less with hundreds or thousands of assets! Thus, the division of such labor—delegating these tasks to intermediaries—can be optimal for individuals. However, since individuals need to rely on institutions for asset management, the features of these institutions matter, and can either help or hinder the end goal for the consumer. We discuss the importance of institutional design for a well-functioning financial system in more detail in Chapter 20.

How can a financial intermediary, such as a firm offering mutual funds to the investing public, decide on the "menu" of asset choices to offer to its customers? We just showed that the composition of the OCRA depends only on the expected returns, standard deviations, and correlation coefficients of the basic risky assets, and therefore the OCRA portfolio can be created independent of investor preferences. This general approach is known as mean-variance optimization.

Indeed, all that the buyers of the offered portfolios (i.e., individual investors) need to see in order to make a decision is the menu of risk and expected return combinations available, as displayed on the lines in Figures 17.5 and 17.6. Because customers do not need to know the individual component securities, their allocated weights, or their estimated means, variances, and correlation coefficients in order to select portfolios, the asset portfolio provider can offer its array of portfolios and still keep valuable proprietary information from its competitors as "trade secrets."

This is analogous to a restaurant offering a menu of dishes to customers. There are an uncountable number of different offerings based on combinations of ingredients that a chef could show customers, but customers need only be shown a subset of them—those that might be chosen—since the restaurant does not want to offer dishes that no one will eat. By doing so, the restaurant also preserves its proprietary recipes as trade secrets from competitors because it does not need to show the exact ingredients. By offering a menu of choices, the restaurant does not need to know the preferences of the customers. As a result, providing such a menu becomes a true decentralization of information.

This powerful insight, known as mutual fund separation, allows portfolio managers to offer choices to customers—and customers to be able to choose what is best for themselves—in a way that is very efficient for both the consumer and the provider: forming a menu of all optimal portfolios that any investor might select (Merton 1972). As noted above, a manager can mix the OCRA in advance without having to know any details about which choice the customer might make, by using only information on the expected returns, variances, and correlation coefficients of the individual securities.

After the OCRA is mixed, customers can then make a choice of the appropriate OCRA, and of the appropriate combination of that OCRA, w_T, and the riskless asset based on their individual preferences. Once this choice is made, the manager can quickly mix the portfolio the customer wants.

Thus, the manager need only provide the customer with information on the expected returns and standard deviations associated with possible mixes of the OCRA and the riskless asset, and the customer can choose their desired proportion to invest in the OCRA, which then determines their portfolio expected return and standard deviation. This is illustrated in Figure 17.7. When given the OCRA, a particular customer need only choose the proportion w_{opt} to invest in the OCRA (and thus $1 - w_{opt}$ in the riskless asset), thus achieving an expected return of $\bar{R}_{opt}$ and a standard deviation of σ_{opt}. A different customer, with different preferences, may choose a different proportion, say 100% invested in the OCRA, corresponding to an expected return and standard deviation of $\bar{R}^*$ and σ^*, respectively.

Overall, this means that the only meaningful information the customer needs is portfolios on the efficient frontier, instead of all the uncountable possible combinations of all the (possibly tens of thousands of) underlying assets. So although in principle individual investors have thousands of assets to choose from, in practice they make their choices from a menu of relatively few products that package together a large variety of individual assets offered by financial intermediaries. Examples include stock and bond mutual funds, and real estate. This makes investing accessible to less-knowledgeable individual investors.

The static mean-variance model thus leads to a basic theory of mutual fund financial intermediation, allowing a very complicated, data-intensive, custom product to be made into a very customer-friendly and relatively easy product for the provider to deliver at scale. Customers can delegate the task of forecasting expected asset returns, standard deviations, and correlations, of determining the optimal proportions to invest in individual assets, and of assembling the portfolio. Then, the only choice the customers need to make is the proportion w to invest in the OCRA portfolio.

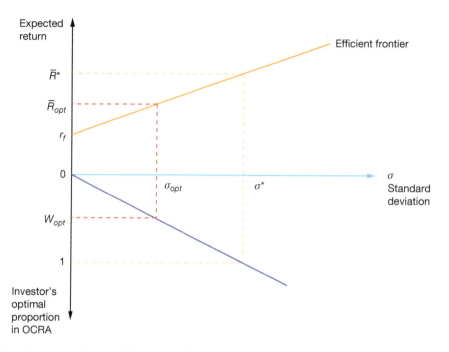

FIGURE 17.7 A customer's portfolio choice. The top line shows the efficient frontier (sometimes referred to as the "capital allocation line"), with the expected return (top portion of the vertical axis) and standard deviation (horizontal axis) of different mixes of the riskless asset and the OCRA. The bottom line illustrates the proportional investment in the OCRA (bottom portion of the vertical axis), and corresponding standard deviation. $\bar{R}_{opt}$, σ_{opt}, and w_{opt} are the expected return, standard deviation, and optimal proportion invested in the OCRA, respectively, for one investor's optimal portfolio choice. R^* and σ^* are the expected return and standard deviation, respectively, for a different investor's optimal portfolio choice corresponding to $w = 1$.

The basic mean-variance approach to quantitative investment management is still the dominant one used in the practice of asset management. However, the complexity of the individual investment objectives has led to modifications of the basic approach. As we discussed in Section 17.1.2, the time horizons considered in making portfolio decisions can differ across people and also over time for a given person. For example, the basic mean-variance approach may work well as long as you are making decisions over the trading horizon, but the planning horizon may reflect what you care about going forward. Thus, running a mean-variance approach over just one time period may not be sufficient. Optimal portfolio selection has expanded to include dynamic versions that integrate intertemporal optimization of the lifetime consumption-saving decisions with the allocation of those savings among alternative investments (see Merton 1969 for foundational work on incorporating these aspects into such models). In these models the demands for individual assets depend on more than just the optimal diversification presented here; they also come from the desire to hedge various risks not included in the original model, such as mortality risk and stochastic changes in interest rates, in the trade-off between expected return and risk, in returns to human capital, and in relative consumption goods prices. These models provide a richer theory for the role of securities and financial intermediation than the static mean-variance model.

These models of portfolio selection provide design guidance for investment firms to offer a wider "family" of mutual funds beyond just the optimal combination of risky assets and the riskless asset. Those additional funds represent optimal portfolios more tailored to the needs of different clienteles.

For example, individuals may face specific risks—such as exposure to one's human capital or other non-traded assets—which would benefit from more customized risk management. The investment firm can create integrated products from its funds by putting various combinations of its member funds together in proportions that reflect the right mix for customers in various stages of their lives.

Conclusion

In this chapter we have gone over the theory behind how investors can form portfolios of assets. We began by noting that portfolio selection depends on an investor's own circumstances, such as their appetite for risk, the time horizon that they are looking at, their stage of life, etc. As a result, there is no single portfolio that is universally optimal for everyone. We then went over the process by which investors form portfolios. We saw that investors can choose between risky (such as stocks) and riskless assets (such as US Treasury bonds). We went over empirical methods for calculating the expected return, risk, and risk-reward trade-off of portfolios, and found how to compute the combination of assets that provides the optimal portfolio. A key insight is that, given a selection of risky assets, there will be an optimal combination of them that maximizes the risk-reward trade-off. An investor would then construct a portfolio by placing some money in that combination and some money in the riskless asset. The exact proportion in each depends on the preferences of the investor. Finally, the insights of portfolio theory also permit investors to delegate many of the specific steps and calculations to investment managers.

In previous chapters we learned about types of individual assets investors can purchase and how to calculate risk and return characteristics for those assets (Chapter 5), and general principles of risk management with investments (Chapter 6). We also learned about riskless assets and the rates of return that they provide (Chapter 16). This chapter synthesizes these insights and applies them to analyze portfolios that investors may construct, and to provide guidance on optimal decisions investors can make. The next chapter expands upon these insights by specifying exactly what the tangency portfolio (OCRA) should be in practice, which carries a number of implications that touch upon many of the topics covered in the book.

Takeaways

- There is no single portfolio selection strategy that is best for all people.
- Stage in life is an important determinant of the composition of a person's optimal portfolio of assets and liabilities.
- Time horizons are important in portfolio selection. We distinguish among three time horizons: the planning horizon, the decision horizon, and the trading horizon.
- In making portfolio selection decisions, people can, in general, achieve a higher expected rate of return only by exposing themselves to greater risk.
- Risk may be reduced without reducing expected return by diversifying more completely either within a given asset class or across asset classes.
- The power of diversification to reduce the riskiness of an investor's portfolio depends on the correlations among the assets that make up the portfolio. In practice, the vast majority of assets are positively correlated with each other because they are all affected by common economic factors. Consequently, one's ability to reduce risk through diversification among risky assets without lowering expected return is limited.
- Although in principle people have thousands of assets to choose from, in practice they make their choices from a menu of relatively few products that package together a large variety of individual assets offered by financial intermediaries. Examples include bank accounts, stock and bond mutual funds, and real estate.

Key Terms

Decision horizon 516
Diversification 515
Efficient frontier 545
Efficient portfolio 527
Expected return 520
Human capital 515
Lifetime financial planning process 515
Long position 525
Mean-variance optimization 547
Minimum variance portfolio 532
Mutual fund separation 547
Optimal combination of risky assets (OCRA) 535
Optimal portfolio 534
Planning horizon 516
Point of tangency 536
Portfolio selection 514
Risk premium 523
Risk tolerance 515
Riskless asset 519
Riskless rate 519
Risk–reward trade-off line 523
Risky assets 519
Sharpe ratio 534
Short position 525
Strategy 516
Tangency portfolio 536
Target expected return 524
Target risk 524
Time horizon 515
Trading horizon 516
Variance 529
Volatility 520

Key Equations

Expected return of an asset with two possible values	$\mathbb{E}[R] = p \times R_1 + (1-p) \times R_2$	Eq. 17.1
Standard deviation of an asset with two possible values	$\sigma = \sqrt{p \times (R_1 - \mathbb{E}[R])^2 + (1-p) \times (R_2 - \mathbb{E}[R])^2}$	Eq. 17.2
Expected return, portfolio with one risky asset and a riskless asset	$\mathbb{E}[R_P] = w \times \mathbb{E}[R_S] + (1-w) \times r_f$	Eq. 17.3
Volatility, portfolio with one risky asset and a riskless asset	$\sigma_P = w \times \sigma_S$	Eq. 17.4

Expected return, portfolio with one risky asset and a riskless asset	$\mathbb{E}[R_P] = r_f + \dfrac{\mathbb{E}[R_S] - r_f}{\sigma_S} \times \sigma_P$	Eq. 17.6
Expected return, portfolio with two risky assets	$\mathbb{E}[R_P] = w \times \mathbb{E}[R_1] + (1-w) \times \mathbb{E}[R_2]$	Eq. 17.7
Volatility, portfolio with two risky assets	$\sigma_P^2 = w^2 \times \sigma_1^2 + (1-w)^2 \times \sigma_2^2 + 2 \times w \times (1-w) \times \rho_{1,2} \times \sigma_1 \times \sigma_2$	Eq. 17.8
Sharpe ratio	Sharpe ratio $= \dfrac{\mathbb{E}[R_P] - r_f}{\sigma_P}$	Eq. 17.9
Weight of asset 1, OCRA	$w = \dfrac{[\mathbb{E}[R_1] - r_f] \times \sigma_2^2 - [\mathbb{E}[R_2] - r_f] \times \rho_{1,2} \times \sigma_1 \times \sigma_2}{[\mathbb{E}[R_1] - r_f] \times \sigma_2^2 + [\mathbb{E}[R_2] - r_f] \times \sigma_1^2 - [\mathbb{E}[R_1] - r_f + \mathbb{E}[R_2] - r_f] \times \rho_{1,2} \times \sigma_1 \times \sigma_2}$	Eq. 17.10
Expected return, portfolio with N assets	$\mathbb{E}[R_P] = \sum_{i=1}^{N} w_i \times \mathbb{E}[R_i]$	Eq. 17.11
Variance, portfolio with N assets	$\sigma_P^2 = \sum_{i=1}^{N} w_i^2 \times \sigma_i^2 + \sum_{i=1}^{N}\sum_{i \neq j} w_i \times w_j \times \sigma_i \times \sigma_j \times \rho_{i,j}$	Eq. 17.12

Problems

1. Suppose that your 58-year-old father works for the Ruffy Stuffed Toy Company and has contributed regularly to his company-matched savings plan for the past 15 years. Ruffy contributes $0.50 for every $1.00 your father puts into the savings plan, up to the first 6% of his salary. Participants in the savings plan can allocate their contributions among four different investment choices: a fixed-income bond fund; a "blend" option that invests in stocks of large companies and small companies, and in the fixed-income bond fund; a growth-income mutual fund whose investments do not include other toy companies; and a fund whose sole investment is stock in the Ruffy Stuffed Toy Company. Over Thanksgiving vacation, your dad realizes that you have been majoring in

finance and decides to reap some early returns on that tuition money he's been investing in your education. He shows you the most recent quarterly statement for his savings plan, and you see that 98% of its current value is in the fourth investment option, that of the Ruffy company stock.

(a) Assume that your dad is a typical risk-averse person who is considering retirement in five years. When you ask him why he has made the allocation in this way, he responds that the company stock has continually performed quite well, except for a few declines that were caused by problems in a division that the company has long since sold off. In addition, he says, many of his friends at work have done the same. What advice would you give your dad about adjustments to his plan allocations? Why?

(b) If you consider the fact that your dad works for Ruffy in addition to his 98% allocation to the Ruffy stock fund, does this make his situation more risky, less risky, or does it make no difference? Why?

2. Determine the expected rate of return and standard deviation for Stock A and Stock B.

State of the economy	Probability	Stock A: rate of return	Stock B: rate of return
Moderate recession	0.05	−0.02	−0.20
Slight recession	0.15	−0.01	−0.10
2% growth	0.60	0.15	0.15
3% growth	0.20	0.15	0.30

3. Suppose that there is a risky asset with an expected rate of return of 10% and a standard deviation of 15%. If the riskless rate of return is 2%, what is the expected rate of return and standard deviation of a portfolio consisting of the following:
   (a) A 0% investment in the risky asset and 100% investment in the riskless asset?
   (b) A 10% investment in the risky asset and 90% investment in the riskless asset?
   (c) A 50% investment in the risky asset and 50% investment in the riskless asset?
   (d) A 75% investment in the risky asset and 25% investment in the riskless asset?
   (e) A 150% investment in the risky asset and −50% investment in the riskless asset?

4. Given the information below about the risks and returns of five alternative portfolios, plot the risks and returns. Which portfolio is not an efficient portfolio?

Portfolio	Expected return	Risk
I	0.050	0.00
II	0.075	0.12
III	0.075	0.05
IV	0.075	0.04
V	0.050	0.05

5. If the risk–reward trade-off line for a riskless asset and a risky asset results in a negative slope, what does that imply about the risky asset vis-à-vis the riskless asset?

6. Consider two assets with expected returns and risk given in the table below.

	Blau	Zwartz
Expected return	0.15	0.12
Standard deviation	0.10	0.08

If these asset returns have a correlation coefficient of +0.5, what is the risk and return of a portfolio equally divided between the two securities? What mix of the two securities produces the portfolio having the lowest risk? What level of risk is this?

7. Repeat the previous problem assuming that the two assets are uncorrelated.

8. An investor has two risky assets with uncorrelated returns ($\rho = 0$). The first asset has levels of expected return and risk equal to twice the level of the expected return and risk of the second asset, or in other words it offers twice the level of expected return for bearing twice the level of risk ($\mathbb{E}[R_1] = 2 \times \mathbb{E}[R_2]$ and $\sigma_1 = 2 \times \sigma_2$). In particular, assume $\mathbb{E}[R_2] = 0.06$ and $\sigma_2 = 0.02$. Suppose you wish to bear the same level of risk as that offered by the second asset. Can you construct a portfolio composed of both assets with the same risk as the second asset but a higher expected rate of return? What is the composition of this portfolio? How much of an expected return premium does this portfolio offer over that of the second asset?

9. Consider two uncorrelated assets with expected returns and risk given in the table below.

	Blanc	Rouge
Expected return	0.075	0.125
Standard deviation	0.050	0.075

Assume a riskless rate of 0.02.
   (a) What is the portfolio expected return and standard deviation, given a 50–50 investment between the two assets? What is the Sharpe ratio of this portfolio?
   (b) What is the optimal combination of the assets? What is the Sharpe ratio of this combination?

10. When the riskless rate is 0.04, assume the optimal combination of risky assets produces a portfolio with an expected rate of return equal to 0.13 and a standard deviation of 0.10. Along the efficient trade-off line, what is the reward-to-risk ratio (Sharpe ratio)? Suppose you wish to tolerate only three-quarters of the risk present in the optimal risky portfolio. How must you divide your investment between the risk-free asset and the optimal risky portfolio? What expected rate of return do you achieve?

11. Referring to the previous question, suppose your mother prefers to tolerate a good deal of risk. In fact, she wishes to bear twice the risk as offered by the optimal risky portfolio. How can she build a portfolio from the risk-free asset and the optimal risky portfolio with the risk level she desires? When she satisfies her appetite for risk what will be the level of expected return on her portfolio?

12. Refer to Table 17.2 in the text.
   (a) Perform the calculations to verify that the expected returns of each of the portfolios (F, G, H, J, S) in the table (column 4) are correct.
   (b) Do the same for the standard deviations in column 5 of the table.

13. Referring to Problem 12, assume that you have $1 million to invest. Allocate the money as indicated in Table 17.2 for each of the five portfolios and calculate the expected dollar return of each of the portfolios. Which of the portfolios would someone who is extremely risk-tolerant be most likely to select?

Use the following information to answer Problems 14–18. Suppose that you have the opportunity to buy stock in AT&T and Microsoft.

	AT&T	Microsoft
Expected return	0.10	0.21
Standard deviation	0.15	0.25

14. What is the minimum variance portfolio of AT&T and Microsoft in the following cases?
    (a) The correlation between the two stocks is 0.
    (b) The correlation between the two stocks is 0.5.
    (c) The correlation between the two stocks is 1.
    (d) The correlation between the two stocks is −1.
    (e) What do you notice about the change in the allocations between AT&T and Microsoft as the correlation coefficient moves from −1 to 0? From 0.5? To +1? Why might this be?
    (f) What is the standard deviation of each of these minimum-risk portfolios?
15. What is the optimal combination of these two securities in a portfolio for each of the four given values of the correlation coefficient in the previous problem, assuming the existence of a money market fund that currently pays a risk-free rate of 0.045? Do you notice any relation between these weights and the weights for the minimum variance portfolios? What is the standard deviation of each of the optimal portfolios? What is the expected return of each of the optimal portfolios?
16. Derive the risk–reward trade-off line for the optimal portfolio when the correlation is 0.5. How much extra expected return can you anticipate if you take on an extra unit of risk?
17. Using the optimal portfolio of AT&T and Microsoft stock when the correlation of their price movements is 0.5, along with the results of problem 16, determine the following.
    (a) The expected return and standard deviation of a portfolio that invests 100% in a money market fund returning a current rate of 0.045. Where is this point on the risk–reward trade-off line?
    (b) The expected return and standard deviation of a portfolio that invests 90% in the money market fund and 10% in the portfolio of AT&T and Microsoft stock.
    (c) The expected return and standard deviation of a portfolio that invests 25% in the money market fund and 75% in the portfolio of AT&T and Microsoft stock.
    (d) The expected return and standard deviation of a portfolio that invests 0% in the money market fund and 100% in the portfolio of AT&T and Microsoft stock. What point is this?
18. Again using the optimal portfolio of AT&T and Microsoft stock when the correlation of their price movements is 0.5, take $10,000 and determine the allocations among the riskless asset, AT&T stock, and Microsoft stock for the following:
    (a) A portfolio that invests 75% in a money market fund and 25% in the portfolio of AT&T and Microsoft stock. What is this portfolio's expected return?
    (b) A portfolio that invests 25% in a money market fund and 75% in the portfolio of AT&T and Microsoft stock. What is this portfolio's expected return?
    (c) A portfolio that invests nothing in a money market fund and 100% in the portfolio of AT&T and Microsoft stock. What is this portfolio's expected return?
19. A mutual fund company offers a safe money market fund whose current rate is 0.05. The same company also offers an equity fund with an aggressive growth objective that historically has exhibited an expected return of 0.20 and a standard deviation of 0.25.
    (a) Derive the equation for the risk–reward trade-off line.
    (b) How much extra expected return would be available to an investor for each unit of extra risk that she bears?
    (c) What allocation should be placed in the money market fund if an investor desires an expected return of 0.15? What risk will the investor bear with this investment?
20. In a portfolio composed of two risky assets (A and B) it is possible to obtain a riskless portfolio if the assets have a correlation coefficient of −1.0. If w is the proportion invested in Asset A, how should w be set so as to obtain a riskless portfolio?

21. What strategy is implied by moving further out to the right on a risk–reward trade-off line beyond the tangency point between the line and the risky asset risk–reward curve? What type of investor would be most likely to embark on this strategy? Why?
22. Suppose the most efficient risky portfolio to combine with a risk-free asset paying 0.05 is a portfolio with an expected return of 0.12 and a standard deviation of 0.10. What is the expected return and risk of a leveraged investment where for each $100 of your own funds you borrow $50 at the risk-free rate and invest the entire $150 in the optimal risky portfolio? What is the Sharpe ratio of this investment?
23. Suppose the mix of risky assets and risky portfolios is unchanged, but the risk-free rate increases. Explain what will happen to the reward-to-risk ratio and the optimal risky portfolio in terms of its expected return and risk characteristics.
24. Suppose there are three risky assets, with the following expected return and standard deviation:

	Expected return	Standard deviation
Asset 1	0.50	0.80
Asset 2	0.15	0.20
Asset 3	0.20	0.25

Assume that the correlation between the returns of each respective asset is 0.25. Consider a portfolio that invests an equal amount in each asset. What is the portfolio's expected return and standard deviation?

APPENDIX

17.A.1 The Minimum Variance Portfolio

In Section 17.3.2 we found that mixing two risky assets together could reduce a portfolio's standard deviation through the diversification effect. This implies that, given a correlation between the returns of the assets, there is a particular portfolio combination (value of w) that maximizes the diversification effect and produces a portfolio with the *least* amount of risk. This portfolio is called the minimum variance portfolio.

To illustrate, Figure 17.A.1 plots the expected returns and standard deviations for all possible portfolios of Risky Assets 1 and 2 (including portfolio combinations not shown in Table 17.4, given the indicated correlations. Thus, the top and bottom rows of Table 17.A.1 correspond to the end points of the curves in Figure 17.3: portfolios composed of investing either only in Risky Asset 1 (bottom row of Table 17.4 or upper-right end point in Figure 17.A.1) or only in Risky Asset 2 (top row of Table 17.4 or lower-left end point in Figure 17.A.1). Risky Asset 1 has an expected return of 14% with a standard deviation of 20% and Risky Asset 2 has an expected return of 8% with a standard deviation

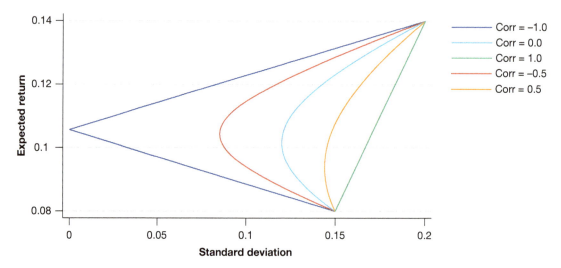

FIGURE 17.A.1 Risk and expected return of portfolios of Risky Assets 1 and 2. This figure provides the risk and expected return for different portfolios consisting of combinations of Risky Assets 1 and 2. Each curve represents a different assumed correlation between the returns of the two assets.

17.A.1 THE MINIMUM VARIANCE PORTFOLIO

Table 17.A.1 Minimum variance portfolios composed of Risky Assets 1 and 2. This table provides the combinations of Risky Assets 1 and 2 that form the minimum variance portfolio, given the indicated correlation between the assets.

Correlation, ρ	Proportion invested in Risky Asset 1, w	Proportion invested in Risky Asset 2, $1 - w$	Expected rate of return, $\mathbb{E}[R_p]$	Standard deviation, σ_p
1.0	0%	100%	8.0%	15.0%
0.5	23%	77%	9.4%	14.4%
0.0	36%	64%	10.2%	12.0%
−0.5	41%	60%	10.4%	8.5%
−1.0	43%	57%	10.6%	0.0%

of 15%. For each curve (which represents an assumed correlation between the two risky assets), the minimum variance portfolio is the left-most point of the curve.

The minimum variance portfolio can be found by experimenting with different weights to see which weights produce the portfolio with the smallest standard deviation out of all possible portfolios. Table 17.A.1 provides the portfolio weights that produce the minimum variance portfolio for each assumed correlation—in other words, the portfolios that correspond to the points on the curves furthest to the left in Figure 17.A.1. In line with the numbers shown in Table 17.2, the diversification benefit can be substantial, and the lower the correlation between the assets, the greater the potential risk reduction. In fact, if the assets are perfectly negatively correlated (a correlation of −1.0), the risk of the portfolio can be almost eliminated! Box 17.A.1 explains how to use spreadsheet programs such as Excel to find the portfolio weights corresponding to the minimum variance portfolio.

Box 17.A.1 Excel in Practice: Calculating the Minimum Variance Portfolio

Spreadsheet programs such as Excel also offer convenient ways to determine the minimum variance portfolio. Consider the previous stock returns from Box 17.3:

	A	B	C
1	Year	Stock 1 Returns	Stock 2 Returns
2	1	0.05	0.2
3	2	-0.02	0.25
4	3	0.06	0.02
5	4	0.1	-0.15
6	5	-0.01	0.01
7			
8	Expected Return:	0.04	0.07
9	Standard Deviation:	0.05	0.16
10	Correlation:	-0.64	

Through Excel formulas it is possible to choose many different possible portfolio combinations (investment weights for the risky assets, w and $1 - w$), and calculate the weight that yields the lowest risk. Alternatively, Excel can be asked to solve for the weights directly. To do so, let us assume a riskless rate of 0.01. Using Equations 17.5–17.7, we can first set up formulas to calculate the portfolio expected return, standard deviation, and Sharpe ratio given some weight (let's use $w = 0.5$ for now):

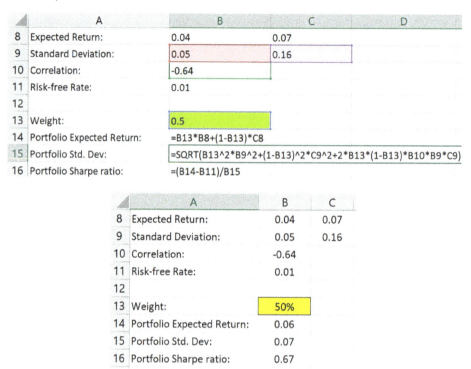

Now we can ask Excel to find the desired portfolio using Solver. To do so, we go to the *Data* tab and click on *Solver*. To solve for the minimum variance portfolio, we ask Excel to *Set Objective* to be setting the portfolio standard deviation (cell B15) to its minimum value, by changing the portfolio weight (cell B13):

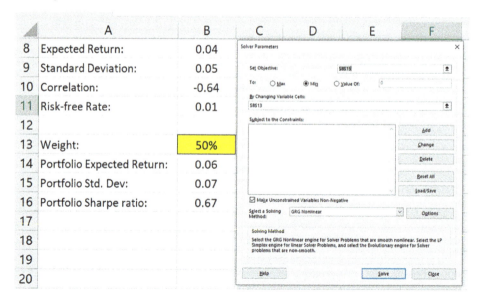

After clicking *Solve*, Excel will produce the minimum variance portfolio by replacing the value in the weight cell. Here, the minimum variance portfolio is produced by setting the weight to 80%:

	A	B	C
8	Expected Return:	0.04	0.07
9	Standard Deviation:	0.05	0.16
10	Correlation:	-0.64	
11	Risk-free Rate:	0.01	
12			
13	Weight:	80%	
14	Portfolio Expected Return:	0.05	
15	Portfolio Std. Dev:	0.03	
16	Portfolio Sharpe ratio:	1.15	

18 CAPITAL MARKET EQUILIBRIUM

CHAPTER OVERVIEW

18.1	The Capital Asset Pricing Model	562
18.2	Applying the CAPM in Practice	571
18.3	Calculating Discount Rates Using the CAPM	579
18.4	Alternatives to the CAPM	585

LEARNING OBJECTIVES

After reading this chapter, you will be able to:
- explain the theory behind the Capital Asset Pricing Model (CAPM);
- demonstrate how to use the CAPM to establish benchmarks for measuring the performance of investment portfolios;
- perform calculations using the CAPM to understand the correct risk-adjusted discount rate to use in discounted cash flow valuation models;
- explain how the CAPM has been modified and supplemented by other theories to add greater realism.

EQUATIONS YOU KNOW

Sharpe ratio	Sharpe ratio $= \dfrac{\mathbb{E}[R_P] - r_f}{\sigma_P}$	Eq. 17.9
Total company value, combination of debt and equity	$V = D + E$	Eq. 9.1
Total company value, DCF	$V = \dfrac{FCF_1}{1+r_A} + \dfrac{FCF_2}{(1+r_A)^2} + \dfrac{FCF_3}{(1+r_A)^3} + \dfrac{FCF_4}{(1+r_A)^4} + \dfrac{FCF_5}{(1+r_A)^5} + \cdots$	Eq. 9.4
(Pre-tax) weighted-average cost of capital (WACC)	$r_A = \text{WACC} = \left[\dfrac{E}{V} \times r_E\right] + \left[\dfrac{D}{V} \times r_D\right]$	Eq. 9.10

Present value of a perpetuity	$PV = \dfrac{\$CF}{r}$	Eq. 2.17
Present value of a growing perpetuity	$PV = \dfrac{\$CF}{r - g}$	Eq. 2.18

- You are at a party at which you meet a lot of strangers. You are introduced as a student majoring in finance. A small crowd gathers around you and one of them asks you what stock they should invest in. How might you answer?

- You are a portfolio manager, and decide to add a stock to your portfolio. What rate of return should you expect to be "fair," given the risk of the stock?

- You are the manager of a division of a company, and are contemplating a project to invest in. You know the discount rate to calculate the value of the project depends on the rate of return that investors would expect from the project, given its risk. How can you estimate this?

- You have the choice between investing in many individual stocks or funds that offer an investment in the overall market. Which offers a better investment from a risk–reward standpoint?

- You are examining the stocks of two different companies, and are thinking about investing in one of them. When you measure the volatility of the stock returns of the companies to measure the risk, you notice that one has a much higher risk than the other. Does that necessarily mean that you can expect a higher return from that stock?

- You are a financial advisor, and you recommend that your client invests in a mutual fund that tracks the broad stock market. However, your client is averse to taking on much risk. How can you adjust your recommendation?

- You are valuing a company to acquire, and want to perform a discounted cash flow analysis. How can you calculate the appropriate discount rate for the company?

Introduction

In the previous chapter we went over the process by which investors form portfolios, how to measure the risk and return of a given portfolio, and how an optimal portfolio can be chosen from a riskless asset and a set of risky assets. We saw that the optimal portfolio consists of holding some portion of one's money in the riskless asset and some portion in the tangency portfolio consisting of the optimal combination of risky assets (OCRA). In this chapter we introduce the capital asset pricing model (CAPM), which specifies exactly what the OCRA should be. The CAPM predicts, under a set of assumptions, that the OCRA consists of holding *all* assets in the market in proportion to their value. Thus, all investors should hold some combination of the market portfolio and the riskless asset because it is most efficient.

This insight provides a host of implications that connect to many previous topics that we have covered. First, it prescribes a specific optimal strategy for investors to maximize their risk–reward trade-off, as we covered in Chapter 17. Second, the CAPM specifies what is meant by risk, and that types of risk should be compensated for in the market. By theorizing that all investors should optimally hold the same assets—the riskless asset and the market portfolio—the CAPM implies that it is only risk related to the market that investors should hold. A fundamental insight of the CAPM is that not every type of risk will result in a higher expected return. For example, a small single-molecule biotechnology company's stock may have a far higher volatility than a cruise ship company, but could also have a much smaller expected return. This is because other nonmarket-related risk can be diversified away, and thus investors need not hold it or be compensated for it. The realization adds depth to **Principle 7**: *There is a trade-off between risk and expected return.*

By explaining the source of risk that matters to investors, the CAPM provides a way of estimating the rate of return that investors should expect for any given asset. This has uses for a variety of different financial applications. As we covered in Parts I and II, the discount rate used to determine the present value of an investment depends on the rate of return that investors would expect from investing in an alternative with the same risk. For example, the discounted cash flow (DCF) models used in Part II to evaluate company projects and calculate company values make use of risk-adjusted expected rates of return as discount rates. Since the CAPM specifies how we can measure this risk, the CAPM can be used to estimate such discount rates. At its core, the CAPM helps us to better understand risk and incorporate it into financial analysis, and thus its importance stems from **Principle 6**: *Risk is fundamental to financial analysis and must be explicitly considered in all financial decisions.*

We begin this chapter by explaining the CAPM and the assumptions that underlie it. We show how risk and expected returns can be calculated using the CAPM, and how it relates to the measures we introduced in Chapter 17 and earlier chapters. We then discuss how the CAPM can be used in practice, and how one can use real-world financial data and apply the CAPM. After this, we go into detail about how the CAPM can be used in corporate finance applications, to calculate discount rates to value projects within companies or to value companies, as well as how it can help in the analysis of capital structure decisions. We conclude the chapter by discussing proposed alternative models to the CAPM.

18.1 The Capital Asset Pricing Model

In the early 1960s, William F. Sharpe was a graduate student in economics at UCLA, studying under Harry Markowitz, who pioneered the model of portfolio selection that we covered in Chapter 17. Sharpe developed the CAPM, for which he subsequently received the 1990 Nobel Prize in economics. Since its inception, the CAPM has been one of the most widely used models by finance practitioners around the world.

The CAPM helps an investor develop an optimal investment strategy from a risk–reward perspective, and provides a theoretical justification for indexing. Indexing is a widespread form of passive indexing where an investor holds a diversified portfolio of securities in the same relative proportions of value as in a broad market index such as the S&P 500 or the Morgan Stanley index of international stocks. Trillions of dollars invested worldwide by pension funds, mutual funds, and other institutions are managed passively by indexing. Indexing provides a simple feasible benchmark that active investment strategies are measured against. The CAPM also provides a way of estimating expected rates of return for use in a variety of financial applications.

In this section we will look at the intuition and assumptions that underlie the CAPM, and how the CAPM figures into the portfolio selection framework. We then introduce how risk can be measured using the CAPM, and how to estimate an asset's expected return using the model.

18.1.1 The Capital Asset Pricing Model in Brief

The capital asset pricing model (CAPM) is a mathematical model that provides the expected rate of return for an asset, given the amount of risk the asset has. It predicts that the expected rate of return on an asset depends on the amount of risk related to the market that an asset has, as well as the riskless rate of return and the rate of return investors can get from investing in the market. Part of the power of the CAPM is that it can theoretically be applied to *any* asset, be it a stock, bond, investment project, or entire company.

At its heart, the CAPM rests upon two principles: **Principle 6**: *Risk is fundamental to financial analysis and must be explicitly considered in all financial decisions* and **Principle 7**: *There is a trade-off between risk and expected return*. The fundamental idea behind the CAPM is that in equilibrium the market rewards people for bearing risk. Because people generally exhibit risk-averse behavior, there must be a positive risk premium—that is, an expected return above the riskless rate—to get investors to willingly hold any risky asset. However, the CAPM makes a distinction between different *types* of risk. The CAPM notes that the market does not reward people for holding inefficient portfolios—that is, for exposing themselves to risks that could be eliminated by optimal diversification behavior. The risk premium on any individual security is, therefore, not related to the security's "stand-alone" risk, but rather to its contribution to the risk of an efficiently diversified portfolio as a participant in that portfolio. Measurement of this type of risk, which the CAPM predicts investors should be rewarded for, is thus a critical component of the CAPM, underscoring Principle 6.

We learned in Chapter 17 that every efficient portfolio can be constructed by mixing two particular assets: the riskless asset and the optimal combination of risky assets (OCRA—that is, the tangency portfolio, which is the portfolio with the highest Sharpe ratio and thus gives the best trade-off in terms of expected return and total risk/volatility). Put differently, anything other than the combination of the tangency portfolio and the riskless asset is inefficient. Based on this, to derive the CAPM we need two additional assumptions:

- *Assumption 1*: Investors agree in their forecasts of expected rates of return, standard deviations, and correlations of the risky securities, and they, therefore, optimally hold risky assets in the same relative proportions.
- *Assumption 2*: Investors behave optimally. In equilibrium, the prices of securities adjust so that when investors are holding their optimal portfolios, the aggregate demand for each security is equal to its supply.

Given these two assumptions, and because every investor's proportional holdings of risky assets are the same, the only way the asset market can achieve equilibrium is if those optimal relative proportions are how they are valued in the marketplace. A portfolio that holds all assets in proportion to their market values is called the market portfolio. The CAPM specifies that the tangency portfolio (e.g., optimal combination of risky assets, OCRA) will specifically be the market portfolio—a portfolio consisting of all risky assets, with weights equal to how much of the total market's value each asset comprises. While in the examples we present we use shares of stock, conceptually the market portfolio consists of *all* assets, whether traded or untraded. This includes (among many other things) corporate bonds and corporate equity that are frequently traded on exchanges, other types of financial assets such as derivative contracts, personal assets such as owner-occupied houses and cars, and assets that are not traded and potentially hard to measure, such as human capital or knowledge.

This provides three key insights. First, since holding the market portfolio (in combination with the riskless asset) is efficient, this is what every investor should do. Investors will hold more of the riskless asset and less of the market portfolio if they are more risk-averse, and less of the riskless asset and more of the market portfolio if they are more risk-tolerant. Each investor holds the same market portfolio—made up of identical proportions of its component risky assets—but varies the relative amount invested in the market versus the riskless asset.

Second, the more money an investor puts into the market portfolio, the more the investor will be compensated for that risk with a higher expected return. Third, since the market represents the only source of efficient risk—that is, risk that is compensated for by sufficient return—investors will not be compensated for other types of risk—that is, risk unrelated, or uncorrelated, to the market. This implies that assets with risk that are more closely related to the market will earn higher expected returns.

The definition of the market portfolio is central to the CAPM.

In the market portfolio, the fraction (weight) w_i allocated to security i equals the ratio of the market value of that security (MV_i) to the outstanding market value of all assets outstanding:

$$w_i = \frac{MV_i}{MV_1 + MV_2 + \cdots + MV_N} = \frac{MV_i}{\sum_{i=1}^{N} MV_i}, \tag{18.1}$$

where in Equation 18.1 we assume that there are N assets in the market. For example, suppose that there are only three assets: GM stock, Toyota stock, and the risk-free asset. The total market values of each at current prices are $66 billion for GM, $22 billion for Toyota, and $12 billion for the risk-free asset. The total market value of all assets is $100 billion. The composition of the market portfolio is, therefore, the total value of each divided by the total market value of $100 billion: 66% GM stock ($66 billion / $100 billion), 22% Toyota stock ($22 billion / $100 billion), and 12% risk-free asset ($12 billion / $100 billion).

As we saw in Chapter 17, investors may optimally hold any combination of the tangency portfolio and the riskless asset—each combination represents the same risk-reward trade-off and is thus equally optimal—and the specific choice depends on the investor's individual preferences (i.e., risk aversion). This insight carries through to the CAPM. Thus, depending on their risk aversion, investors hold different mixes of risk-free and risky assets, but the relative holdings of risky assets (the market portfolio) are the same for all investors.[1] Thus, in our simple example, all investors will hold GM and Toyota stock in the proportions of 3 to 1 (i.e., 66 / 22)—in other words, for any money that an investor decides to put into risky assets, the investor should put 75% (66 / (66 + 22)) of it into GM stock and 25% (22 / (66 + 22)) of it into Toyota stock.

For example, consider two investors, each with $100,000 to invest. Investor 1 has risk aversion equal to the average for all investors and, therefore, holds each asset in the same proportions as the market portfolio: $66,000 in GM, $22,000 in Toyota, and $12,000 in the risk-free asset. Investor 2 is more risk-averse than average and, therefore, chooses to invest $24,000 (twice as much as Investor 1) in the risk-free asset and $76,000 in risky assets. Investor 2's investment in GM stock will be $0.75 \times \$76,000 = \$57,000$, and the investment in Toyota stock will be $0.25 \times \$76,000 = \$19,000$. Thus, both investors will hold three times as much in GM stock as in Toyota stock: The amount of each stock they own is different, but the proportion of each stock they own in their risky portfolio is the same.

> **QUICK CHECK 18.1** Investor 3 has a $100,000 portfolio with nothing invested in the risk-free asset. How much is invested in GM and how much in Toyota?

18.1.2 The Capital Market Line

The CAPM tells us that holding some combination of the market portfolio and the riskless asset will be efficient, and thus investors will be compensated for risk related to the market. A mathematical model can be constructed to quantify this.

To see this, recall the risk-reward trade-off line we developed in Chapter 17, which plots the expected return and standard deviation of a selected portfolio. Figure 18.1 shows the risk-reward trade-off line facing each investor according to the CAPM, called the capital market line (CML).

---

[1] This implies that the market risk premium is a linear function of the aggregate average degree of risk aversion. If using returns that are not at an annual frequency, at this step it is typical to annualize the returns.

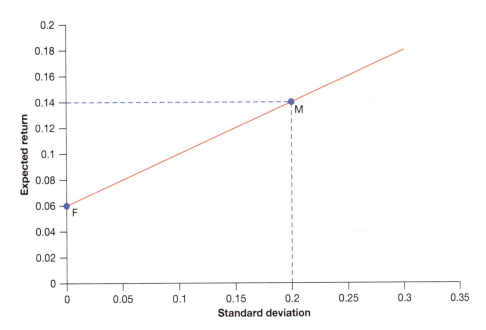

FIGURE 18.1 The capital market line. This figure illustrates a CML assuming a riskless rate of $r_f = 0.06$ and a Sharpe ratio of $\mathbb{E}[R_M] - r_f / \sigma_M = 0.40$. Each point on the line represents an investment in the risk-free asset and the market portfolio. Point F represents an investment entirely in the risk-free asset, and point M represents an investment entirely in the market portfolio. The slope of the line is the same as the Sharpe ratio of investing in the market portfolio.

Because the tangency portfolio or OCRA is the same as the market portfolio, the market portfolio is located somewhere on the risk–return trade-off line. Point M represents the market portfolio, point F is the risk-free asset, and the CML is the straight line connecting these two points. The CAPM says that in equilibrium, the CML represents the *best* risk–reward combinations available to all investors. Put differently, any point on the CML provides the highest Sharpe ratio possible, and that Sharpe ratio is given by (Equation 18.2):

$$\text{Sharpe ratio} = \frac{\mathbb{E}[R_M] - r_f}{\sigma_M}, \qquad (18.2)$$

where $\mathbb{E}[R_M]$ is the expected rate of return of the market portfolio, r_f is the risk-free rate of return, and σ_M is the standard deviation of the market portfolio. Although everyone will strive to achieve points that are above the CML (thus providing a higher Sharpe ratio), the forces of competition will move asset prices so that everyone expects to achieve points that are on the line.

Since the Sharpe ratio in Equation 18.2 gives the incremental expected return (over the riskless rate) given an additional unit of risk on the CML, it is the slope of the CML. Thus, we can represent the CML mathematically as:

$$\mathbb{E}[R] = r_f + \frac{\mathbb{E}[R_M] - r_f}{\sigma_M} \times \sigma. \qquad (18.3)$$

As we emphasized in Chapter 17 with the general risk–reward trade-off line, any point along the CML is equally efficient because the line itself represents portfolios with the same Sharpe ratio. The point an investor would choose on the CML depends on the risk preferences of the individual investor. A more risk-averse investor may choose a point in between F and M, perhaps closer to F, opting for a lower expected return but lower risk. A more risk-tolerant investor may choose point M (investing all money in the market portfolio), or even a point to the right of M along the line (investing all money in the market portfolio and borrowing additional money to invest in the market).

This leads to a few important implications. First, the CAPM implies that most investors can achieve their objectives by combining the risk-free asset with an index fund holding risky assets in the same proportions as in the market portfolio. By focusing on this choice of investing in just these two assets, rather than making investors consider individual positions in the thousands of potential risky assets in the market, investors don't need to conduct their own data gathering, analysis, and trading of individual stocks. Instead, investors can benefit from delegating those tasks to investment professionals—those with the skills, resources, and specialization to do so full-time and at scale. This is the same intuition as the "mutual fund separation" insight we discussed in Chapter 17, which provided a basic model of asset management: All the buyers of the offered portfolios do not need to know the expected returns and covariances of (potentially thousands of) individual assets to make an investment decision—they only need to hold the market portfolio and/or the riskless asset. And investment professionals do not need to know an investor's individual preferences or wealth to offer a menu of options to investors—different combinations of the market portfolio and riskless asset—which investors can choose from.

Second, since only points along the CML are efficient, the CAPM implies that the risk premium on any individual security, $\mathbb{E}[R] - r_f$, depends only on its contribution to the risk of the market portfolio. Put differently, since only combinations of the riskless asset and the market portfolio are efficient, the risk of the overall market portfolio is the only thing that matters to the ultimate investor. As a result, it is an individual asset's marginal contribution to the risk of the overall market portfolio that matters (i.e., how much of the overall market risk is provided by the asset), and not the stand-alone volatility of an individual asset. This implies that the way for an investor to get a higher expected return is to take on more exposure to the market portfolio, and thus that the risk of an asset will be compensated with a higher rate of return only if it contributes more to or is more closely related to the risk of the market portfolio. Thus, according to the CAPM, in equilibrium, investors get rewarded with a higher expected return *only* for bearing market risk.

We also refer to market risk as systematic risk, since it is an irreducible or necessary risk that investors must take to get their desired expected return. In contrast, we refer to a security's stand-alone risk as idiosyncratic risk (or unsystematic risk). Investors are rewarded for systematic risk, but *not* for idiosyncratic risk. The logic here is that because all efficient risk–reward combinations can be achieved simply by mixing the market portfolio and the risk-free asset, the only risk an investor needs to bear to achieve an efficient portfolio is market risk. Therefore, the market does not reward investors for bearing any nonmarket risk.

The market does not reward investors for choosing inefficient portfolios. Such portfolios contain risk that investors do not need to hold (idiosyncratic risk), since such risk can be diversified away by holding the market portfolio. Sometimes this implication of the CAPM is emphasized by saying that only the market-related risk of a security "matters."

18.1.3 Betas and Expected Returns

One of the key conclusions of the CAPM is that investors are only compensated for market-related, or systematic, risk. Thus, for an asset to provide a higher expected rate of return according to the CAPM, it will need to have more systematic risk. Until this point, we have measured the risk of an asset via the standard deviation of its returns, σ, and we have made the point that the higher the risk, the higher the expected return (Principle 7). The CAPM again reinforces this point—as inspection of the CML in Figure 18.1 illustrates—but makes the important distinction that it only applies to *efficient* portfolios. Specifically, it is an increase in the risk of an efficient portfolio (i.e., the market portfolio) that leads to a larger equilibrium expected return. Thus, on the CML, since it is combinations of the market portfolio and risk-free asset, σ does not just reflect any type of risk but specifically *systematic* or market risk. According to the CAPM, any other type of risk (i.e., idiosyncratic risk) does not provide a higher expected return. In a more general setting in which we consider assets or portfolio that may not be efficient, however, the standard deviation of an asset's returns does not measure just the systematic risk of securities, it will include both idiosyncratic *and* systematic risk. To numerically calculate exactly how much of a higher expected rate of return an asset should have, we specifically measure this systematic risk (again underscoring Principle 6) by calculating its beta β.

Technically, beta describes the marginal contribution of that security's return to the standard deviation of the market portfolio's return. The formula for the beta of a security i is given by:

$$\beta_i = \rho_{i,M} \times \frac{\sigma_i}{\sigma_M}. \tag{18.4}$$

In Equation 18.4, $\rho_{i,M}$ is the correlation between the returns of the market portfolio and asset i, σ_i is the standard deviation of the returns of asset i, and σ_M is the standard deviation of the returns of the market portfolio. Beta thus provides a number, unique to each asset i, of how closely related the asset's returns are to the market portfolio. Assets with a higher beta have greater systematic risk, and thus the CAPM states that they should have a higher expected return. In contrast, assets with a lower beta have less systematic risk, and the CAPM states that they should have a lower expected return.

This relationship between an asset's beta and its expected return is made explicit in the core equation of the CAPM:

$$\mathbb{E}[R_i] - r_f = \beta_i \times [\mathbb{E}[R_M] - r_f]. \tag{18.5}$$

According to the CAPM, in equilibrium the risk premium on any asset ($\mathbb{E}[R_i] - r_f$) is equal to its beta times the risk premium on the expected return of the market portfolio $\mathbb{E}[R_M] - r_f$. The term $\mathbb{E}[R_M] - r_f$ in Equation 18.5 is known as the market risk premium, and it represents how much more of a return investors can expect from investing in the market compared to the riskless rate. Note that the insights of the CAPM and Equation 18.5 apply to *any* asset, be it a stock, bond, investment project, or entire company. This underscores the appeal and theoretical versatility of the CAPM, as it can apply in a variety of contexts, which we will describe in the coming sections.

The relationship between the risk premium of an asset and its beta, known as the security market line (SML), is depicted in Figure 18.2, where we plot the security's beta on the horizontal axis and its expected excess return on the vertical axis, assuming a market risk premium of $\mathbb{E}[R_M] - r_f = 0.08$. This is known as the SML relation, and its slope is the risk premium on the market portfolio. Thus, in this example, because the market risk premium is 0.08, the SML is given by the equation $\mathbb{E}[R_i] - r_f = 0.08 \times \beta_i$. The fact that the line is upward-sloping demonstrates that a higher beta leads to a higher expected return (and higher risk premium).

If any security had an expected return and beta combination that was not on the SML, it would be a contradiction of the CAPM. For example, point J in Figure 18.2 lies below the SML because its expected return is "too low" to support equilibrium. The existence of such a situation contradicts the CAPM because it implies either that the market is not in equilibrium, that investors do not agree on the distribution of returns, or that investors are not behaving as mean-variance optimizers. Under the assumptions of the CAPM, investors could improve their portfolios by investing less in security J and more in the other securities.

The estimate of an asset's beta carries a number of different interpretations. First, a higher beta implies a higher expected return since it implies that the asset carries more systematic risk. Second, beta provides a proportional measure of the sensitivity of an asset's returns to the returns on the

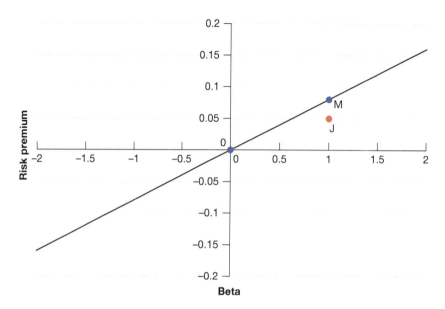

FIGURE 18.2 The security market line. This figure illustrates an SML assuming a market risk premium of 0.08. Each point on the line represents some investment in the risk-free asset and the market portfolio. Point M represents an investment entirely in the market portfolio. Point J represents an expected return–beta combination that is inconsistent with the CAPM.

market portfolio. Thus, if the return on the market portfolio is expected to go up by N%, then the return on asset i is expected to change by $\beta_i \times N\%$. Thus, an asset with a beta of 1 implies that its return moves on a one-to-one basis with the market. Assets with high betas (greater than 1) are called "aggressive" because their returns tend to accentuate or amplify those of the overall market portfolio, going up by more than the market when the market increases, and going down by more than the market when the market decreases. In contrast, securities with low betas (less than 1 but greater than zero) have returns that, when the market moves, have muted responses. It is also possible for an asset's beta to be negative, which implies that the asset's returns move in the opposite direction to the market.

To illustrate, suppose you examine a stock with a beta of 0.5. If the market risk premium is 0.08, then we would expect the stock's risk premium to be (Equation 18.5):

$$\begin{aligned} \mathbb{E}[R_i] - r_f &= \beta_i \times [\mathbb{E}[R_M] - r_f] \\ &= 0.5 \times 0.08 \\ &= 0.04. \end{aligned}$$

This means that the stock is expected to have a return that is 0.04, or 4%, above that of the risk-free rate, given the amount of market risk the stock has (i.e., the stock's beta). This risk premium is lower than that of the market risk premium of 0.08, since the beta is less than 1. Furthermore, a beta of less than 1 means that, given a movement in the market, the asset's expected return will move by less than the market. If the market's expected return (and thus market risk premium) were to increase by 1%, then we would expect the risk premium of the stock to increase by $0.5 \times 0.01 = 0.005$ or 0.5%. Suppose instead that the stock has a beta of 1.5. Then the risk premium on the stock will be (Equation 18.5):

$$\begin{aligned} \mathbb{E}[R_i] - r_f &= \beta_i \times [\mathbb{E}[R_M] - r_f] \\ &= 1.5 \times 0.08 \\ &= 0.12. \end{aligned}$$

The risk premium on the stock is thus higher, at 0.12 or 12%, and is even higher than the market risk premium. This is because the stock, with a beta of 1.5, has amplified systematic risk compared to the market. In line with this, the asset's return will amplify any movement in the market. If the market's expected return (and thus market risk premium) were to increase by 1%, then we would expect the risk premium of the stock to increase by 1.5 × 0.01 = 0.015, or 1.5%.

The beta of a particular asset, such as a stock, is determined by how much it co-moves (i.e., moves in lockstep) with the market portfolio, as indicated in Equation 18.4. The relative size of an asset's beta often mirrors how much that asset should move with the market, given the asset's characteristics. For example, utility company stocks typically have betas that are well below 1 (and close to 0). Thus, the expected returns of such stocks do not co-move substantially with the market. This aligns with the fact that the demand such companies face is not very dependent on the state of the market—utilities are heavily regulated, and consumer demand for electricity will not change based on whether the market is up or down. In contrast, retail company stocks (such as clothing companies) tend to have betas close to or higher than 1, indicating that they co-move substantially with the market. This aligns with the fact that such spending is more discretionary for consumers, and thus more responsive to economic prospects—if the market is down substantially, a person's wealth is likely lower and thus the person will probably spend less on new clothes.

Finally, note that betas can be calculated for any combination of assets by taking a weighted average of the individual betas, weighted by the values of the respective assets. Thus, the beta of a portfolio, β_P, is given by the sum of the betas of the individual assets i multiplied by the proportion of the portfolio's value composed of each asset, w_i:

$$\begin{aligned} \beta_P &= w_1 \times \beta_1 + w_2 \times \beta_2 + \cdots + w_N \times \beta_N \\ &= \sum_{i=1}^{N} w_i \times \beta_i. \end{aligned} \tag{18.6}$$

For example, any portfolio that lies on the CML (i.e., any portfolio formed by mixing the market portfolio and the riskless asset) has a beta equal to the fraction of the portfolio invested in the market portfolio. Consider the beta of a portfolio that is formed by investing 75% of your wealth in the market portfolio and 25% of your wealth in the risk-free asset. The beta of the market portfolio is, by definition, 1. The beta invested in the risk-free asset is, by definition, 0 (it is completely unrelated to the market's expected return). With a weight of 0.75 in the market and 0.25 in the risk-free asset, the portfolio beta is (Equation 18.6):

$$\begin{aligned} \beta_P &= 0.75 \times 1 + 0.25 \times 0 \\ &= 0.75. \end{aligned}$$

> **QUICK CHECK 18.2** Suppose you are examining a stock that has a beta of 0.8. According to the CAPM, what should be its risk premium, given a market risk premium of 0.08?

Example 18.1 (Calculating Expected Returns and Betas Using the CAPM): Suppose the expected return on the market portfolio is 0.11, and the riskless rate is 0.01. You see two assets being traded in the marketplace, the first with a beta of 0.1 and the other with a beta of 1.7.

(a) What is the risk premium for each asset, according to the CAPM?
(b) You have $1,000 to invest. If you decide to invest half of your money in the first asset and half in the second asset, what is the beta, risk premium, and expected return for the resulting portfolio? If the

market expected return were to increase by 1%, by how much would the portfolio's expected return increase?

(c) A new asset has a standard deviation of 0.2 and a correlation with the market's return of 0.3. If the standard deviation of the market's return is 0.3, what is the beta of this new asset? What is its expected return?

Solution.

(a) We can calculate the risk premium for each asset as follows (Equation 18.5):

$$\mathbb{E}[R_1] - r_f = \beta_1 \times \left[\mathbb{E}[R_M] - r_f\right]$$
$$= 0.1 \times [0.11 - 0.01]$$
$$= 0.01,$$
$$\mathbb{E}[R_2] - r_f = \beta_2 \times \left[\mathbb{E}[R_M] - r_f\right]$$
$$= 1.7 \times [0.11 - 0.01]$$
$$= 0.17.$$

Asset 2 has a higher expected return, given the higher beta.

(b) With a 50% investment in each asset, we can first use Equation 18.6 to calculate the portfolio beta, using a weight of 0.5 for each asset:

$$\beta_P = 0.5 \times 0.1 + 0.5 \times 1.7$$
$$= 0.9.$$

With this portfolio beta, we can calculate the risk premium for the portfolio using the CAPM Equation 18.5:

$$\mathbb{E}[R_P] - r_f = \beta_P \times \left[\mathbb{E}[R_M] - r_f\right]$$
$$= 0.9 \times [0.11 - 0.01]$$
$$= 0.09.$$

The expected return for the portfolio can be found by adding the risk-free rate to the risk premium: $\mathbb{E}[R_P] = 0.09 + 0.01 = 0.10$. If market expected returns were to increase by 1%, with a beta of 0.9, the portfolio's expected return would increase by $0.9 \times 1\% = 0.9\%$.

(c) We are given that $\rho_{i,M} = 0.3$, $\sigma_i = 0.2$, and $\sigma_M = 0.3$. Using Equation 18.4, we can calculate the beta of this new asset:

$$\beta_i = \rho_{i,M} \times \frac{\sigma_i}{\sigma_M} = 0.3 \times \frac{0.2}{0.1} = 0.6.$$

Using Equation 18.5 (and adding the risk-free rate to both sides), we can calculate the new asset's expected return according to the CAPM:

$$\mathbb{E}[R_P] = r_f + \beta_P \times \left[\mathbb{E}[R_M] - r_f\right]$$
$$= 0.01 + 0.6 \times [0.11 - 0.01]$$
$$= 0.07.$$

18.1.4 The Security Market Line or the Capital Market Line?

In the previous sections we introduced and used two representations of the CAPM: the security market line (SML) and the capital market line (CML). These representations are often confused since they both examine the relationship between risk and return, but the specific trade-offs differ. The SML predicts what risk premium (expected return above the riskless rate of return) we can expect from any asset given its beta (i.e., how much systematic risk it has). The CML represents the relationship between an asset's expected returns and its volatility (i.e., the risk–reward trade-off based on *total* risk). This leads to a natural question: When is each line the more appropriate and more useful model?

The use of one versus the other depends on the specific purpose of the user. For example, for an individual concerned about total wealth, the total amount of risk—and seeing how diversification may reduce that risk—may be most important, and thus examining the CML, with its basis in total volatility as measured by standard deviation, would be most appropriate. If an analyst is evaluating whether an asset is over- or under-valued based on the CAPM (i.e., generates alpha), then the SML—where the measure of risk is beta—will be most appropriate to use. From a firm's point of view, understanding the type of risk that investors will price is the most salient concern. In firm valuation or capital budgeting, as discussed in Chapters 9 and 10, the appropriate discount rate for a firm or a project will depend on the amount of priced risk—that is, risk that affects the project or firm's required returns—and thus the SML may be appropriate in determining this.

In this section we have gone over how the CAPM can be applied by investors and financial professionals in practice to analyze and guide investment decisions. The uses of the CAPM, however, go beyond this. The CAPM can also be used in the process of evaluating corporate investment decisions, including valuing and choosing projects and determining the value of companies. In the next section we go over these applications.

18.2 Applying the CAPM in Practice

The CAPM has a wide variety of applications to financial practice. In this section we explore how the CAPM is used by investment professionals in portfolio selection, and then discuss various issues related to applying the CAPM to real-world data.

18.2.1 Using the CAPM in Portfolio Selection

As we saw in Section 18.1, the CAPM implies that the market portfolio of risky assets is an efficient portfolio. This means that an investor will do at least as well by simply following a passive portfolio selection strategy of combining a market index fund and the risk-free asset than by following an active strategy of picking stocks and other assets to try to beat the market. This has deep implications for the process of investing and portfolio selection. In particular, the CAPM suggests a simple passive portfolio strategy:

- diversify your holdings of risky assets to match the proportions of the market portfolio; and
- mix this portfolio with the risk-free asset to achieve a desired risk–reward combination.

To illustrate, suppose that you have $1 million to invest. You are deciding how to allocate it between two risky asset classes—stocks and bonds—and the risk-free asset. You know that, in the economy, the net relative supplies of these three asset classes are 60% in stocks, 40% in bonds, and 0% in the risk-free asset. This, therefore, is the composition of the market portfolio. If you have an average degree of risk aversion, then you will invest $600,000 in stocks, $400,000 in bonds, and nothing in the risk-free asset. If you are more risk-averse than average, you will invest some of your $1 million in the risk-free asset and the rest in stocks and bonds. Whatever amount you invest in stocks and bonds will be allocated in the proportions 60% in stocks and 40% in bonds.

The CAPM predicting that the passive strategy of investing in the market portfolio will provide the best risk–reward trade-off also provides a useful benchmark, or comparison, for measuring the performance of active portfolio selection strategies. In assessing the performance of portfolio managers on a risk-adjusted basis, the CAPM provides a simple benchmark based on the CML: comparing the rate of return earned on the managed portfolio to the rate of return attainable by simply mixing the market portfolio and risk-free asset in proportions that would have produced the same volatility. This is equivalent to comparing the managed portfolio's Sharpe ratio to that of portfolios on the CML, which includes the market portfolio; we saw that every portfolio on the CML—that is, any combination of the market portfolio and the riskless asset—has the same Sharpe ratio. Figure 18.3 shows a portfolio which lies above the CML (portfolio A), and thus has a better risk–reward trade-off than what the CAPM would predict, and a portfolio that lies below the CML (portfolio B); the CAPM predicts managed portfolios should be either below or, at best, on the CML.

This method of calculating performance requires an estimate of the expected return of the managed portfolio as well as the volatility of the returns. In practice, the average returns over a relevant period—for instance, the last ten years—are used as the estimate of expected returns. Similarly, the standard deviation of the managed portfolio's returns over the same time period is used as the estimate of volatility. The risk-free rate can be obtained from data on US Treasury bond yields, as we discussed in Chapter 17. With these numbers in hand, Equation 17.9 can be used to calculate the Sharpe ratio for the managed portfolio:

$$\text{Sharpe ratio} = \frac{\mathbb{E}[R_P] - r_f}{\sigma_P} \qquad (18.7)$$

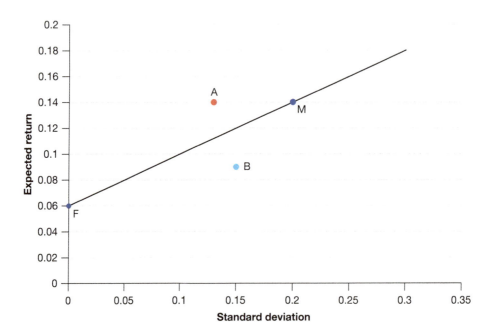

FIGURE 18.3 The capital market line and managed portfolios. This figure illustrates a CML assuming a riskless rate of $r_f = 0.06$ and a Sharpe ratio of $\mathbb{E}[R_M] - r_f / \sigma_M = 0.40$. Each point on the line represents some investment in the risk-free asset and the market portfolio. Point F represents an investment entirely in the risk-free asset, and point M represents an investment entirely in the market portfolio. Point A represents a portfolio that has a better risk–reward trade-off (Sharpe ratio) than the market, while point B represents a portfolio that has a worse risk–reward trade-off than the market.

The managed portfolio's Sharpe ratio can then be compared to the Sharpe ratio of the simple benchmark market portfolio using Equation 18.2, using the average return and standard deviation of the market portfolio over the same time period.

In practice, the market portfolio used in measuring the performance of portfolio managers is a well-diversified portfolio of stocks rather than the true market portfolio of all risky assets. The simple benchmark strategy has been a difficult one to beat. Studies of the performance of managed equity mutual funds consistently find that the simple strategy outperforms around two-thirds of the funds. As a result, more households and pension funds have been adopting the passive investment strategy used as the performance benchmark. This type of strategy has come to be known as indexing, because the portfolio used as a proxy for the market portfolio often has the same weights as well-known stock market indexes such as the S&P 500. A number of mutual funds and exchange-traded funds offer investors the ability to invest directly in a fund that closely tracks such market indexes.

Another method commonly used to statistically measure the performance of investment strategies involves the SML and the CAPM equation. As we saw in Equation 18.5, the CAPM states that every security or portfolio of securities has a risk premium equal to its beta times the risk premium on the market portfolio. Thus, if a portfolio manager is adding performance beyond what the CAPM predicts, the risk premium the manager delivers should be *above* the portfolio's beta times the market risk premium. This additional return is known as alpha (α). Put differently, if you can find a portfolio manager with a positive alpha, you can beat the market (i.e., an indexing investment strategy).

Alpha can be found by taking the difference between a portfolio's expected return and what Equation 18.5 would predict the return to be:

$$\mathbb{E}[R_i] - r_f = \alpha + \beta_i \times \left[\mathbb{E}[R_M] - r_f\right],$$
$$\alpha = \left\{\mathbb{E}[R_i] - r_f\right\} - \left\{\beta_i \times \left[\mathbb{E}[R_M] - r_f\right]\right\}. \tag{18.8}$$

Thus, in Equation 18.8, $\left\{\mathbb{E}[R_i] - r_f\right\}$ represents the actual risk premium for asset i that is observed in the market, while $\left\{\beta_i \times \left[\mathbb{E}[R_M] - r_f\right]\right\}$ represents the *predicted* risk premium according to the CAPM. Figure 18.4 illustrates alpha using the security market line. A portfolio that produces an alpha lies above the SML, as illustrated by portfolio "Alpha." If the CAPM holds in reality, then the alpha on all portfolios should be zero—it should not be possible to achieve a positive alpha.

To illustrate, suppose that the market risk premium is 0.08, and Alpha's beta is 0.5. Then the CAPM would predict that the portfolio's risk premium would be (Equation 18.5):

$$\begin{aligned}\mathbb{E}[R_i] - r_f &= \beta_i \times \left[\mathbb{E}[R_M] - r_f\right] \\ &= 0.5 \times 0.08 \\ &= 0.04.\end{aligned}$$

Now suppose that Alpha portfolio's actual expected return is 0.06. Then its alpha would be (Equation 18.8):

$$\begin{aligned}\alpha &= \left\{\mathbb{E}[R_i] - r_f\right\} - \left\{\beta_i \times \left[\mathbb{E}[R_M] - r_f\right]\right\} \\ &= 0.06 - 0.04 \\ &= 0.02.\end{aligned}$$

Alpha portfolio thus produces an alpha of 0.02, meaning that it delivers an expected return above the riskless rate (risk premium) that is 2% above what the CAPM would predict it should.

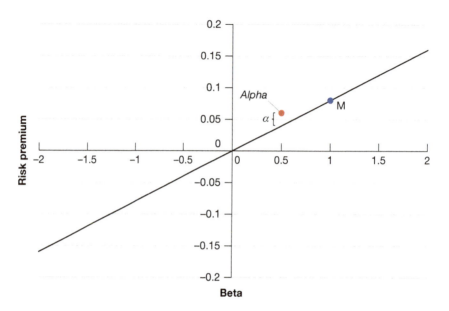

FIGURE 18.4 The security market line and Alpha portfolio. This figure illustrates an SML assuming a market risk premium of 0.08. Each point on the line represents some investment in the risk-free asset and the market portfolio. Point M represents an investment entirely in the market portfolio. Point *Alpha* represents an expected return–beta combination that produces a positive alpha, which is represented by the vertical distance between point *Alpha* and the SML.

QUICK CHECK 18.3 Suppose you are examining a stock that has a beta of 0.8. According to the CAPM, what should be its risk premium, given a market risk premium of 0.10? If the stock's risk premium is 0.10, what is the alpha of the stock?

Example 18.2 (Assessing Portfolios Using the CAPM): Consider a portfolio with a beta of 1.2 and a volatility (standard deviation) of 0.20. Suppose that the expected return on the market portfolio is 0.12, the volatility of the market portfolio is 0.10, and the risk-free interest rate is 0.03.

(a) What should the risk premium on the portfolio be, according to the CAPM?
(b) What is the Sharpe ratio on the portfolio and the market portfolio? Are these Sharpe ratios consistent with the CAPM?
(c) If the actual risk premium of the portfolio ended up being 0.12, what would be the portfolio's alpha?

Solution.

(a) To find the risk premium of the portfolio, we can apply the CAPM Equation 18.5, along with the given information on $\beta_i = 1.2$ for the portfolio, the market expected return $\mathbb{E}[R_M] = 0.12$, and the risk-free rate $r_f = 0.03$:

$$\mathbb{E}[R_i] - r_f = \beta_i \times \left[\mathbb{E}[R_M] - r_f\right]$$
$$= 1.2 \times \left[0.12 - 0.03\right]$$
$$= 0.108.$$

(b) We find the portfolio's Sharpe ratio by using Equation 17.9, using the risk premium we calculated above:

$$\text{Sharpe ratio} = \frac{\mathbb{E}[R_P] - r_f}{\sigma_P}$$

$$= \frac{0.108}{0.20}$$

$$= 0.54.$$

The Sharpe ratio on the market portfolio is given by (Equation 16.1):

$$\text{Sharpe ratio} = \frac{\mathbb{E}[R_M] - r_f}{\sigma_M}$$

$$= \frac{0.12 - 0.03}{0.10}$$

$$= 0.9.$$

The Sharpe ratio for the market portfolio is higher, which is consistent with the CAPM.

(c) If the portfolio's actual risk premium were 0.12, then the portfolio's alpha would be (Equation 18.8):

$$\alpha = \{\mathbb{E}[R_i] - r_f\} - \{\beta_i \times [\mathbb{E}[R_M] - r_f]\}$$

$$= 0.12 - 0.108$$

$$= 0.012.$$

18.2.2 Applying the CAPM Using Data

The CAPM provides a powerful model with a wide variety of applications, including providing guidance on the most effective investment strategies, calculating expected returns and measures of risk, and providing benchmarks for investment performance. Using the CAPM in reality, however, requires the use of data and estimation choices.

To understand this, recall the CAPM Equation 18.5:

$$\mathbb{E}[R_i] - r_f = \beta_i \times [\mathbb{E}[R_M] - r_f].$$

According to Equation 18.5, the risk premium on an asset i depends on its relation to the market risk premium. Thus, calculating the risk premium on an asset requires calculating the asset's beta, as well as determining the market risk premium. This in turn requires the following data:

- data on the risk-free interest rate r_f;
- data on the return on the market portfolio R_M; and
- data on the returns for asset i, R_i.

First, data on the risk-free rate can be found using the yields on Treasury bonds, as we covered in Chapter 17. There is a choice of Treasury bonds at different maturities for use as the risk-free rate: one-year T-bills, five-year Treasury bonds, ten-year Treasury bonds, etc. While the CAPM does not provide guidance to choose between these different bonds, in practice investment professionals typically will use the Treasury bond that corresponds to the investment horizon they are looking at.

Second, data on the returns of the market portfolio must be obtained. Theoretically, the market portfolio in the CAPM consists of *all* risky assets, including stocks, corporate and other bonds, derivatives, and other asset classes. As we mentioned, in practice a well-diversified portfolio of stocks, such as the S&P 500, is typically used as a proxy for the market portfolio. This is because data on such an index is more readily available, and furthermore, broader indexes do not usually offer substantially increased precision when applying the CAPM.

Third, return data for the asset i, R_i, is needed. Conceptually, the CAPM can be applied to *any* asset that return data can be obtained for. In practice, data availability can hinder the ability to use the CAPM. For example, applying the CAPM to a publicly traded company's stock may be relatively straightforward, as stock return data is readily available from a variety of sources. However, it may be difficult or impossible to collect such data for other types of assets such as corporate bonds or private company assets.

With this data in hand, the asset's beta can be calculated by applying Equation 18.4 after calculating the asset's standard deviation of returns, correlation with the market's returns, and standard deviation of the market's returns over some period of time in the past:

$$\beta_i = \rho_{i,M} \times \frac{\sigma_i}{\sigma_M}.$$

With the beta estimate in hand, you can then calculate the market risk premium, $\mathbb{E}[R_M] - r_f$, by taking the average market return minus the average risk-free rate over a time period. The risk premium for the asset is then obtained by multiplying the beta by that market risk premium, $\beta_i \times [\mathbb{E}[R_M] - r_f]$.

For example, suppose that you want to calculate the beta of a particular stock. To do so, you can collect the stock's daily returns over the past five years, and the daily returns of the S&P 500 over the past five years. You can also collect daily Treasury bond yields (say, for five-year maturity Treasuries) over this time period. You calculate that the correlation of the market returns with the stock's returns over the five years ($\rho_{i,M}$) is 0.6, the standard deviation of the stock's returns over the five years (σ_i) is 0.3, and the standard deviation of the market's returns over the five years (σ_M) is 0.1. Then the stock's beta would be given by (Equation 18.4):

$$\begin{aligned} \beta_i &= \rho_{i,M} \times \frac{\sigma_i}{\sigma_M} \\ &= 0.6 \times \frac{0.3}{0.1} \\ &= 1.8. \end{aligned}$$

To get an estimate of the risk premium of the stock according to the CAPM, you need to calculate the market risk premium, $\mathbb{E}[R_M] - r_f$. To do so, you can take the average return of the S&P 500 over a period time, say the same five years, and subtract the average return on Treasury bond yields over that same period of time.[2] Suppose that the market risk premium is $\mathbb{E}[R_M] - r_f = 0.08$. Then the risk premium of the stock, according to the CAPM, will be (Equation 18.5):

$$\begin{aligned} \mathbb{E}[R_i] - r_f &= \beta_i \times [\mathbb{E}[R_M] - r_f] \\ &= 1.8 \times 0.08 \\ &= 0.44. \end{aligned}$$

Box 18.1 explains how statistical software can be used to calculate these estimates.

In the previous example, note that we chose a period of five years with which to estimate the stock's beta and to calculate the market risk premium. The time periods for these calculations are additional choices when implementing the CAPM using data. For example, we could have chosen a period of ten years for both calculations, or five years when estimating the betas and ten years when estimating the market risk premium.

---

[2] If using returns that are not at an annual frequency, at this step it is typical to annualize the returns.

There is a trade-off when it comes to the choice of time period. On the one hand, a longer time window allows better statistical accuracy—for example, it becomes less likely that estimates are affected by temporary movements in stock returns. On the other hand, a longer time window runs the risk of including the influence of past periods that no longer reflect the state of the company or market today. A company may be very different today from how it was ten years ago, and including those returns may skew the picture when calculating the beta of the company's stock. Along similar lines, calculating the market risk premium using the average market return over the past 40 years may capture market events that are not representative of current economic conditions (such as crises, wars, periods of inflation, etc.). Sometimes a number of different choices may make logical sense when performing calculations with the CAPM.

In the end, it is important to consider how different choices, such as with estimation windows, can affect the final calculations and conclusions you arrive at when using the CAPM. The process of repeating calculations under different assumptions or choices is known as sensitivity analysis. If answers differ substantially under different scenarios when performing sensitivity analysis, then it may be a sign to be cautious when using the CAPM. This reinforces the fact that the CAPM is a model, and therefore one should keep in mind **Principle 4**: *Every model is an incomplete, simplified description of a complex reality.* As we will discuss in Section 18.4, in some cases there may be other models that provide a more complete view of reality and are better suited for certain applications than the CAPM.

> **QUICK CHECK 18.4** Go to a website such as Yahoo! Finance and choose a stock. Find the beta for the stock. If the market risk premium were 10%, what is your estimate of the risk premium for the stock?

Box 18.1 Excel in Practice: CAPM Calculations

Programs that can perform statistical calculations, such as Excel, can be used as a convenient way to apply the CAPM to data. Suppose that you obtain data on a stock's returns, the market's returns (proxied by the S&P 500), and the riskless rate (Treasury yields). The stock's beta can be calculated via Equation 18.3 by using the =STDEV.S and =CORREL functions:

	A	B	C	D
1	Date	Stock Returns	S&P500 Returns	Riskless Rate
2	1	5%	9%	1%
3	2	7%	8%	1%
4	3	9%	0%	1%
5	4	-15%	-2%	1%
6	5	-3%	15%	1%
7	6	8%	-1%	1%
8				
9	Beta	=CORREL(B2:B7,C2:C7)*STDEV.S(B2:B7)/STDEV.S(C2:C7)		

This provides a beta estimate, which can be used in combination with a calculation of the market risk premium (the average of the S&P 500 returns minus the average of the riskless rate) to calculate the risk premium of the stock:

578 18 CAPITAL MARKET EQUILIBRIUM

	A	B	C	D
1	Date	Stock Returns	S&P500 Returns	Riskless Rate
2	1	5%	9%	1%
3	2	7%	8%	1%
4	3	9%	0%	1%
5	4	-15%	-2%	1%
6	5	-3%	15%	1%
7	6	8%	-1%	1%
8				
9	Beta		0.11	
10	Market Risk Premium	=AVERAGE(C2:C7)-AVERAGE(D2:D7)		

This provides the stock's risk premium:

9	Beta	0.11
10	Market Risk Premium	3.8%
11	Stock Risk Premium	=B9*B10

9	Beta	0.11
10	Market Risk Premium	3.8%
11	Stock Risk Premium	0.4%

An alternative way to calculate the beta of an asset is through regression analysis. Note that beta in Equation 18.4 can be estimated by a regression using the asset's risk premium as the dependent (Y) variable, and the market risk premium as the independent (X) variable. The resulting coefficient on the market risk premium would thus be the estimate of beta. There are two ways to do this in Excel. The first is through the =SLOPE function. We first calculate the stock and market risk premiums by subtracting the riskless rate from the returns, and then use the =SLOPE function, first identifying the stock risk premium cells as the Y variables and the S&P 500 risk premium cells as the X variables:

	A	B	C	D	E	F
1	Date	Stock Returns	S&P500 Returns	Riskless Rate	Stock Risk Premium	S&P500 Risk Premium
2	1	5%	9%	1%	4%	8%
3	2	7%	8%	1%	6%	7%
4	3	9%	0%	1%	8%	-1%
5	4	-15%	-2%	1%	-16%	-3%
6	5	-3%	15%	1%	-4%	14%
7	6	8%	-1%	1%	7%	-2%
8						
9	Beta	=SLOPE(E2:E7,F2:F7)				

This leads to a value of:

9	Beta	0.11

The second method is through Excel's Regression tool. An advantage of this approach is that the intercept term of this regression will be an estimate of alpha, as in Equation 18.7. The statistical significance of the intercept term—and thus the asset's alpha—provides a test of whether the alpha is truly different from zero. To do so, we go to the *Data* tab, select *Data Analysis*, and finally select *Regression*. For the *Y* variables, we select the stock risk premium (cells E2:E7), while we select the market risk premium (cells F2:F7) as the *X* variables:

	E	F
	Stock Risk Premium	S&P500 Risk Premium
	4%	8%
	6%	7%
	8%	-1%
	-16%	-3%
	-4%	14%
	7%	-2%

This results in the following output:

16	Coefficients	Standard Error	t Stat	P-value
17 Intercept	0.00	0.05	0.09	0.94
18 X Variable 1	0.11	0.68	0.16	0.88

The regression coefficient for X Variable 1 is the coefficient for the market risk premium—that is, the beta estimate. The intercept term represents the alpha estimate. The regression indicates that the alpha in this case is zero, and is also statistically insignificant (with a *p*-value of 0.94).

18.3 Calculating Discount Rates Using the CAPM

As we have shown, the CAPM can provide an estimate of what investors should expect the rate of return to be on *any* asset. This lends the CAPM to another important application in practice—estimating the appropriate discount rate for discounted cash flow (DCF) calculations. Recall from Part II that the discount rate used to determine the present value of an investment depends on the rate of return that investors would expect from investing in an alternative with the same risk. Since the CAPM provides an estimate of expected rates of return, it can be used as a model to calculate discount rates used in DCF calculations. In Part II of the book, we used the DCF method to value projects and companies, but in our examples we often had to assume what the appropriate discount rate to use should be. The CAPM provides us with a tool that allows us to estimate this discount rate.

In this section we will look at how we can apply the CAPM to calculate a company's cost of capital, which is the discount rate used in valuing companies and projects.

18.3.1 Calculating Cost of Capital

In Part II we saw that the DCF model can be used to estimate the value of an entire company, the company's debt or equity, or a project the company is considering investing in. The cost of capital—the rate of return that investors expect in exchange for providing the company with funds—is an essential ingredient in any DCF model calculation.

To illustrate, consider how we calculated the value of an entire company, also known as the total value of the company, in Chapter 9. We saw that the total value of the company is given by the combination of the values of the company's debt and equity (Equation 18.9):

$$V = D + E. \tag{18.9}$$

To calculate V, we could discount the company's projected future cash flows (known as the free cash flows, or FCFs) by the company's overall cost of capital. Thus, suppose the company has free cash flows as follows:

Time t: $t=0$ $t=1$ $t=2$ $t=3$ $t=4$ $t=5$ ...

Free cash flow: FCF_1 FCF_2 FCF_3 FCF_4 FCF_5 ...

Then the total value of the company would be given by (Equation 18.10):

$$V = \frac{FCF_1}{1+r_A} + \frac{FCF_2}{(1+r_A)^2} + \frac{FCF_3}{(1+r_A)^3} + \frac{FCF_4}{(1+r_A)^4} + \frac{FCF_5}{(1+r_A)^5} + \cdots, \tag{18.10}$$

where r_A is the company's overall cost of capital.

How can we calculate r_A using the CAPM? For simplicity, suppose that there are no taxes or other frictions (and thus we are in the situation described by Modigliani and Miller, which we discussed in Chapter 13). Then, as we saw in Chapter 9, we can calculate the company's overall discount rate via the pre-tax weighted-average cost of capital (WACC). This incorporates an average of the rates of return that the company's equity and debt investors demand, denoted by r_E and r_D, respectively, weighted by the proportion of the company's market value composed of either debt or equity. The pre-tax WACC is as follows (Equation 18.11):

$$r_A = \text{WACC} = \left[\frac{E}{V} \times r_E\right] + \left[\frac{D}{V} \times r_D\right]. \tag{18.11}$$

We can use the CAPM to calculate the cost of equity r_E and the cost of debt r_D. First consider the cost of equity. If we can find the beta of the company's equity β_E, then we can use the CAPM Equation 18.5 to calculate r_E:

$$r_E = r_f + \beta_E \times \left[\mathbb{E}[R_M] - r_f\right]. \tag{18.12}$$

β_E in Equation 18.12 can be calculated as described in the previous section, using return data on the company's stock and data on the market's return and the risk-free rate. Note that Equation 18.12 also provides a method for calculating the discount rate used in valuation models to estimate the value of a firm's *equity E*, such as the dividend discount model and free cash flow to equity methods that we covered in Chapter 9.

Similarly, using the beta of the company's debt β_D, we can arrive at an estimate of the cost of debt:

$$r_D = r_f + \beta_D \times \left[\mathbb{E}[R_M] - r_f\right]. \tag{18.13}$$

Conceptually, we can calculate a debt beta in the same way as an equity beta: Use data on the returns of the company's bonds, and determine how it co-moves with the market's returns via Equation 18.4 or one of the other methods discussed in the previous section. The debt beta β_D for any given company will be lower than the company's equity beta, reflecting the fact that a company's equity is riskier than its debt (the debtholders must be paid first). The debt beta for a highly rated company (i.e., a company where the risk of default on its debt is low) will be low, often near zero. A debt beta of zero would imply that the debt for a company is risk-free (i.e., $r_D = r_f$).

With estimates for r_E and r_D in hand, we can plug them into Equation 18.11 and use the result as the discount rate in Equation 18.10. To illustrate, suppose that a firm expects free cash flows of $10 million next year and every year henceforth, so that the firm's FCFs form a perpetuity. Then, using the perpetuity formula, the total value of the firm becomes (Equations 9.4 and 2.15):

$$V = \frac{\$10}{1+r_A} + \frac{10}{(1+r_A)^2} + \frac{10}{(1+r_A)^3} + \frac{10}{(1+r_A)^4} + \frac{10}{(1+r_A)^5} + \cdots$$
$$= \frac{\$10}{r_A}.$$

Suppose the company's equity beta is 1.5 and its debt beta is 0.2. If the market risk premium is $\mathbb{E}[R_M] - r_f = 0.08$ and the riskless rate is $r_f = 0.01$, then the equity and debt costs of capital will be given by (Equations 18.12 and 18.13):

$$r_E = r_f + \beta_E \times \left[\mathbb{E}[R_M] - r_f\right]$$
$$= 0.01 + 1.5 \times 0.08$$
$$= 0.13,$$
$$r_D = r_f + \beta_D \times \left[\mathbb{E}[R_M] - r_f\right]$$
$$= 0.01 + 0.2 \times 0.08$$
$$= 0.026.$$

Let us assume that the firm is financed with 50% debt and 50% equity, so that $D/V = 0.5$ and $E/V = 0.5$. The WACC of the firm will then be (Equation 8.11):

$$r_A = \text{WACC} = \left[\frac{E}{V} \times r_E\right] + \left[\frac{D}{V} \times r_D\right]$$
$$= [0.5 \times 0.13] + [0.5 \times 0.026]$$
$$= 0.078.$$

Finally, plugging this in as the discount rate to the previous total firm value formula yields:

$$V = \frac{\$10}{1+r_A} + \frac{10}{(1+r_A)^2} + \frac{10}{(1+r_A)^3} + \frac{10}{(1+r_A)^4} + \frac{10}{(1+r_A)^5} + \cdots$$
$$= \frac{\$10}{0.078}$$
$$= \$128.205.$$

The total value of the company is thus $128.205 million.

Note that an alternative but equivalent way to calculate the cost of capital is through taking a weighted average of the betas that make up the firm's financing. In other words, we can calculate the beta for the entire company's assets, known as the asset beta, as an average of the debt and equity betas, weighted by the proportion of the company's market value composed of debt and equity. With this asset beta in hand, we can then apply the CAPM Equation 18.5.

In particular, the asset beta is calculated through the following formula:

$$\beta_A = \left[\frac{E}{V} \times \beta_E\right] + \left[\frac{D}{V} \times \beta_D\right]. \tag{18.14}$$

Thus, the asset beta of a company is calculated by taking the WACC equation, but replacing rates of return with betas. In this case, the asset beta is given by (Equation 18.14):

$$\beta_A = \left[\frac{E}{V} \times \beta_E\right] + \left[\frac{D}{V} \times \beta_D\right]$$
$$= [0.5 \times 1.5] + [0.5 \times 0.2]$$
$$= 0.85.$$

The logic behind this approach is the same as in Equation 18.6, which shows that the beta of a portfolio is the weighted average of its component betas, weighted by their proportion of the portfolio's value. It also highlights a useful property about betas: They are linear (i.e., we can take a weighted average of them to use in equations), as are rates of return. In the next section we explore this in more detail, connecting it to the insights on capital structure from Chapter 13.

With this asset beta, we can then use the CAPM Equation 18.5 to calculate the cost of capital for the firm:

$$r_A = r_f + \beta_A \times \left[\mathbb{E}[R_M] - r_f\right]$$
$$= 0.01 + 0.85 \times 0.08$$
$$= 0.078.$$

This gives us the same cost of capital as we calculated earlier. Note that this cost of capital would be appropriate for valuing the firm.

The CAPM thus provides a straightforward model with which to calculate discount rates for DCF calculations. However, although the CAPM may be straightforward theoretically, applying it to actual cost of capital calculations can be complicated, as it requires estimation choices such as those we discussed in Section 18.2.2. Box 18.2 discusses the various choices a finance practitioner may face when applying the CAPM in this way. This again reflects **Principle 4:** *Every model is an incomplete, simplified description of a complex reality.*

> **QUICK CHECK 18.5** Consider the firm discussed above, with expected free cash flows of $10 million next year and every year henceforth, and financed with 50% debt and 50% equity. Recalculate the total value of the firm, assuming that the firm's equity and debt betas were instead 1.0 and 0, respectively.

Example 18.3 (Calculating Cost of Capital Using the CAPM to Value a Company): Trek Technologies is a company you are trying to value. Its capital structure consists of 33% equity and 67% debt. You find that its equity beta is 1.3 and its debt beta is 0.1. The risk-free interest rate is 2%, and the market risk premium is 8%. The company currently projects free cash flows of $650,000 next year, and expects them to grow at a rate of 1% thereafter. What is the total value of Trek Technologies?

Solution. In order to calculate the total value of Trek, we need to discount its FCFs. To do so, we need to calculate the company's cost of capital. Since we are provided with equity and debt betas, we can use Equation 18.14 to calculate the company's asset beta:

$$\beta_A = \left[\frac{E}{V} \times \beta_E\right] + \left[\frac{D}{V} \times \beta_D\right]$$
$$= [0.33 \times 1.3] + [0.67 \times 0.1]$$
$$= 0.5.$$

Next, applying the CAPM Equation 18.5 gives us the cost of capital, which is:

$$r_A = r_f + \beta_A \times \left[\mathbb{E}[R_M] - r_f\right]$$
$$= 0.02 + 0.5 \times 0.08$$
$$= 0.06.$$

The company projects free cash flows of $0.75 million starting next year (year 1), expected to grow 1% thereafter. We can therefore apply the growing perpetuity formula (Equation 2.15) to value the company:

$$V = \frac{FCF_1}{r_A - g}$$
$$= \frac{0.75}{0.06 - 0.01}$$
$$= 15.$$

Thus, Trek Technologies should be worth $15 million.

Box 18.2 World of Business: Do You Know Your Cost of Capital?

Companies heavily rely on discounted cash flow (DCF) analysis when appraising potential projects to invest in. In a survey conducted by the Association for Financial Professionals (AFP), 80% of respondents used DCF analyses. Discounted cash flow analysis in turn critically depends on estimates of the cost of capital. For example, just a 1% drop in the cost of capital can lead to an increase in investments of $150 billion over three years. To estimate the cost of capital, about 90% of survey respondents use the CAPM.

However, when it came to choices in estimating the CAPM, the consensus ended as no question received the same answer from most survey respondents. Here are some of the differing choices that respondents provided:

- *Investment time horizon:* Respondents widely varied in terms of their forecast periods for cash flows, with under half estimating cash flows over five years, and others selecting different periods. While different industries may naturally have different investment horizons, there were also inconsistencies in terms of the method of calculating the terminal value.

- *Cost of debt:* The correct estimate of the cost of debt should be the cost the company faces on new debt issuance, yet most respondents used data on historical debt issuance. Furthermore, when incorporating the debt tax shield, only 29% used the marginal tax rate, considered the best approach by experts. Thus, the majority of companies are using the wrong cost of debt, wrong tax rate, or both.

- *The risk-free rate:* The risk-free rate is a critical component of the CAPM. Most investors, managers, and analysts use US Treasury rates to estimate the risk-free rate, but there are widespread differences on the maturity to use. Overall, 46% of respondents used the 10-year rate, 12% the 5-year rate, 11% the 30-year rate, and 16% the 3-month rate. The variation can be dramatic. For example, in 2012 the 90-day Treasury note yielded 0.05%, the 10-year 2.25%, and the 30-year roughly 3.25%. In 2022, the respective yields were 4.45%, 3.83%, and 3.92%.

- *Equity risk premium:* Another critical component of the CAPM is the equity risk premium,

$\mathbb{E}[R_M] - r_f$. In theory, estimates of this risk premium should be the same at any given time for all investors. However, estimates varied among respondents. About half used a risk premium of 5–6%, while others used one lower than 3% or above 7%.

- *Beta*: Most financial executives understand the concept of beta, but cannot agree on the time period over which it should be measured. For example, 41% used five years, 29% used one year, 15% used three years, and 13% used two years. Utilizing a time period which captures large changes in a company or market events can substantially affect the estimate of a company's beta.

- *Debt ratio*: In the calculation of cost of capital, the ratio of debt and equity to total company value (D/V and E/V) is important for calculating the overall cost of capital appropriate for evaluating company or project value. The correct way to measure the leverage ratio is to use market values for debt and equity. However, most respondents used book values to calculate the leverage ratio, which is incorrect as book values reflect past historical information. This can lead to a very different conclusion in calculations.

Trillions of dollars are at stake in project assessments, and thus it is critical for corporate directors and managers to closely look at their process for evaluating investments.

Source: Jacobs, M. T., and Shivdasani, A. (2012). Do you know your cost of capital? *Harvard Business Review* (July–August).

18.3.2 Capital Structure and Betas

In the previous section we saw that company betas can be used to calculate total company value, given a company's capital structure. However, it is also important to keep in mind that a company's betas are *affected* by the company's capital structure in the same way as a company's cost of capital is affected by its capital structure.

First, as we saw in Chapter 13, the more debt a company has, the riskier its cash flows to equity and thus the higher its equity cost of capital. The same conclusion applies to a company's equity beta—the more levered the company is, the higher its equity beta. It is for this reason that an equity beta is sometimes referred to as a levered beta. The fact that equity betas are affected by leverage means that equity betas cannot be directly compared across companies. Put differently, if a company has a higher equity beta than another company, it does not necessarily mean that its operations are more closely correlated with the market than the other company's operations. It could be the case that the two companies have *identical* operations with equal correlation to the market, but their equity betas are different because one has more leverage than the other: Their different betas result not from different levels of operational risk, but from different levels of financial risk.

Second, the beta of a company if it had no leverage is known as an unlevered beta, and is labeled as β_U. Since unlevered betas do not depend on the amount of debt a company has—they examine what the beta of a company would be without debt—unlevered betas can be directly compared across companies. Thus, two comparable companies with similar operations should have the same unlevered betas. In contrast, a company with operations more highly correlated with the market should have a higher unlevered beta than companies that are less exposed to market movements. This notion is very useful in performing net present value (NPV) calculations for projects that may be in a different business sector than a company normally operates in: Unlevered betas from companies that operate in the same business sector as the project can be used and then adjusted to calculate the project's discount rate. The formula often used to calculate unlevered betas is the same as Equation 18.14. The reason the formulas are the same is because, when there are no taxes, the asset beta of a company (i.e., the company's overall beta) will be the same as the unlevered beta of the company due to Modigliani–Miller: Capital structure does not affect the risk of the company (and thus the beta).

Third, when there are taxes and other frictions, the formula for calculating a company's asset beta will change, and the company's asset beta will be different from the company's unlevered beta. In particular, the formula for a company's asset beta will incorporate the tax rate, because having additional debt will lower the company's tax bill due to the debt tax shield, and thus lower the company's overall beta (as discussed in Chapter 13):

$$\beta_A = \left[\frac{E}{V} \times \beta_E\right] + \left[\frac{D}{V} \times \beta_D \times (1-\tau)\right]. \tag{18.15}$$

Since expected returns are a linear function of betas according to the CAPM, all the conclusions related to expected rates of return from Chapter 13 also apply directly to betas.

18.4 Alternatives to the CAPM

The CAPM holds substantial appeal and is widely used in financial practice for a number of reasons. First, it provides a simple and intuitive strategy for optimal investments from a risk–reward standpoint: Hold only the market portfolio and the risk-free asset. Second, it provides a way to measure the performance of a particular investment strategy. Third, it gives a straightforward way of calculating expected returns for assets, which affords a variety of applications, including calculating discount rates for present value calculations.

For these purposes, the appeal of the CAPM rests upon the assumption that the CAPM is a valid model that holds in reality. However, as with every model, we have emphasized **Principle 4:** *Every model is an incomplete, simplified description of a complex reality.* How well does the CAPM capture reality?

As early as the 1970s, researchers testing the empirical validity of the SML using the historical returns of common stocks in the United States found that it did not seem to fit the data well enough to fully explain the structure of expected returns on assets. Subsequent and still ongoing research formulated and tested a variety of enriched CAPM and alternative models using data from a variety of asset markets around the world. A consensus has emerged that the original simple version of the CAPM needs to be modified. Potential explanations for the apparent deviations from the CAPM fall into three categories. One is that the CAPM actually does hold, but the "market" portfolios used in the testing were incomplete and inadequate representations of the true market portfolio.[3] Another focuses on market imperfections—frictions—not contemplated in the CAPM, such as borrowing costs and constraints, short sale restrictions and costs, different tax treatments for various assets, and the nontradability of some important assets such as human capital. These elements are likely to change over time with changes in technology, institutional structures, and regulations.

A third approach has been to add greater realism to the modeling assumptions while maintaining the CAPM's basic methodology. This means retaining the fundamental assumption of the CAPM that investors (or their agents) follow the principles of optimal portfolio selection, and deriving the equilibrium implications of such optimizing behavior in the presence of additional complicating factors.

---

[3] For example, consider the situation (that holds in reality) in which some assets are traded and others are not. Note that it is *not* the case that a portfolio made up of the traded assets in proportion to their market values is the best mix of assets—that is, represents the market portfolio. Thus, the fact that we cannot measure the true market portfolio (we only observe *traded* assets) can account for the failure of the model empirically.

One such alternative CAPM model is the multifactor Intertemporal Capital Asset Pricing Model (ICAPM), which adds greater realism to the CAPM in a number of ways (Merton 1973b). The basic CAPM model is based on a single time period (i.e., agents make a single decision), but the ICAPM allows agents to make decisions over time (hence the term "intertemporal"), thus allowing them to respond to uncertain changes in the economy. This structure of the ICAPM, in addition to other elements, allows risk premiums on securities to come from several dimensions of risks—not only from a security's return sensitivity (i.e., beta) to the market portfolio, but also by its sensitivity to other systematic and thus nondiversifiable risks. In other words, there is no longer a single OCRA, and thus the market portfolio alone is not mean-variance efficient. These other systematic risks include changes in interest rates, expected returns on assets, and changes in consumption good prices. In this world, securities have a richer set of hedging roles in addition to their place in the market portfolio. These other dimensions of systematic risk—in addition to the market risk in each trading period—would each have their own risk premiums, which would be explicitly measured and considered to estimate expected returns.[4]

Another line of research has been to develop alternative theories to the CAPM with the goal of creating a model that is empirically more accurate and can be used in practice. The most prominent is the Arbitrage Pricing Theory (APT) (Ross 1976). According to the APT, a relation like the SML can exist even if investors are not mean-variance optimizers. If there are enough different securities to "diversify away" all but market risk, the APT shows that an expected return–beta relation will exist because of there being no arbitrage opportunities. Although the specific structure of asset risks in these models differs from the CAPM, the basic insights of the CAPM—that the risk premiums are related to broad systematic risk factors that matter to large segments of the population—still hold.

A form of the APT used in practice since the 1990s is the Fama and French three-factor model, conceived by Nobel Laureate Eugene Fama and financial economist Kenneth French (Fama and French 1992). In the Fama–French model, there are three broad systematic factors: the market (as in the CAPM), size, and value. Thus, the model predicts that investors will assign a risk premium to assets based on their correlation to the market and, in addition, will assign a higher risk premium to smaller versus larger firms, and to firms that have higher book values compared to their market values. The Fama–French model appears like the CAPM Equation 18.5:

$$\mathbb{E}[R_i] - r_f = \beta_{i,M} \times \left[\mathbb{E}[R_M] - r_f\right] + \beta_{i,size} \times size + \beta_{i,value} \times value. \tag{18.16}$$

In Equation 18.16, *size* is the size factor, which reflects the excess returns of smaller stocks compared to larger stocks, and *value* is the value factor, which reflects the excess returns of high book-to-market stocks compared to low ones. Estimating Equation 18.16 requires data on the returns of the asset in question, the market portfolio, the risk-free rate, and size and value factors. With this data in hand, the three betas are then estimated, as we described in the previous sections. This can be done through multiple regression analysis (as in the method described in Box 18.1 for the CAPM) using data on the returns of the factors.

The Fama–French three-factor model has been shown to be an improvement over the CAPM in terms of predicting expected returns. Additional systematic factors have been proposed and added to the model to improve estimates further, and research continues to further refine these models today.

---

[4] Thus, the resulting model will be *multi-dimensional* with respect to betas; put differently, there will be multiple betas that reflect the sensitivity to each risk factor, and furthermore incorporates the fact that risks and market conditions change over time. Such a model can be represented mathematically for any given asset as: $\mathbb{E}[R] = r_f + \sum_{k=1}^{m} \beta_k \times \left[\mathbb{E}[R_k] - r_f\right]$, where R_k is the return of the *k*th factor out of *m* possible factors.

Conclusion

Whether or not the CAPM is strictly true, it provides a rationale for having a significant component of every wealth management portfolio that is passive to achieve the benefits of diversification mentioned throughout this chapter. Such a strategy can be modified to include customized risks, insurance, diversification, and/or hedging to be optimal for the goals or risk preferences of the individual investor (or to take advantage of any "alphas"—the ability to generate returns above those predicted by market risk).

To construct the passive component of the portfolio, an investor can diversify holdings of risky assets according to the proportions of the market portfolio and mix this portfolio with the risk-free asset to achieve a desired risk–reward combination. In practice, because of the number of different asset classes available, this typically means holding a well-diversified portfolio with thousands of stocks globally weighted toward market capitalization.

The CAPM is used in portfolio management to establish a logical and convenient starting point in asset allocation and security selection, and as a benchmark for evaluating portfolio management ability on a risk-adjusted basis. In corporate finance, the CAPM is used to determine the appropriate risk-adjusted discount rate in valuation models of the firm and in capital budgeting decisions.

Today, few financial scholars or practitioners consider the CAPM in its simplest form to be an accurate enough model for fully explaining or predicting risk premiums on risky assets. However, modified versions of the model are still a central feature of the theory and practice of finance. The APT gives a rationale for the expected return–beta relation that relies on the condition that there be no arbitrage profit opportunities; the CAPM requires that investors be mean-variance portfolio optimizers. The APT and CAPM are not incompatible; rather, they complement each other.

This chapter connects with a number of topics we have covered thus far. First, it expands upon the insights about the optimal portfolio strategy for investors, developed in Chapter 17. Second, it provides a framework to define the types of risk that investors should consider, and thus that should be compensated for in the market. Finally, it connects to the DCF models introduced in Part I and extensively used in Part II, and provides a way of estimating the appropriate discount rate for an investment, project, or for valuing a company.

Takeaways

- The CAPM has three main implications:
  - In equilibrium, everyone's relative holdings of risky assets are the same as in the market portfolio.
  - The size of the risk premium of the market portfolio is determined by the risk aversion of investors and the volatility of the return.
  - The risk premium on any asset is equal to its beta times the risk premium on the market portfolio.
- The CAPM provides a rationale for passive investing and the growing popularity of index funds.
- The CAPM provides a model for estimating a company's cost of equity, of debt, and overall cost of capital that can be used as a discount rate in valuation models.
- Models that complement the CAPM and build on its foundations include the Arbitrage Pricing Theory and the Fama–French three-factor model.

Key Terms

Alpha 573
Arbitrage Pricing Theory (APT) 586
Asset beta 581
Benchmark 572
Beta 567
Capital Asset Pricing Model (CAPM) 562
Capital market line (CML) 564
Cost of capital 579
Idiosyncratic risk (or unsystematic risk) 566
Indexing 573
Intertemporal Capital Asset Pricing Model (ICAPM) 586
Levered beta 584
Market portfolio 563
Market risk premium 567
Pre-tax weighted-average cost of capital (WACC) 580
Security market line (SML) 567
Sensitivity analysis 577
Systematic risk 566
Unlevered beta 584

Key Equations

Portfolio weight	$w_i = \dfrac{MV_i}{MV_1 + MV_2 + \cdots + MV_N}$ $= \dfrac{MV_i}{\sum_{i=1}^{N} MV_i}$	Eq. 18.1
Sharpe ratio of market portfolio	Sharpe ratio $= \dfrac{\mathbb{E}[R_M] - r_f}{\sigma_M}$	Eq. 18.2
Capital market line (CML)	$\mathbb{E}[R] = r_f + \dfrac{\mathbb{E}[R_M] - r_f}{\sigma_M} \times \sigma$	Eq. 18.3
Beta of an asset	$\beta_i = \rho_{i,M} \times \dfrac{\sigma_i}{\sigma_M}$	Eq. 18.4
CAPM equation	$\mathbb{E}[R_i] - r_f = \beta_i \times \left[\mathbb{E}[R_M] - r_f\right]$	Eq. 18.5
Portfolio beta	$\beta_P = w_1 \times \beta_1 + w_2 \times \beta_2 + \cdots + w_N \times \beta_N$ $= \sum_{i=1}^{N} w_i \times \beta_i$	Eq. 18.6
Portfolio Sharpe ratio	Sharpe ratio $= \dfrac{\mathbb{E}[R_P] - r_f}{\sigma_P}$	Eq. 18.7
Alpha of an asset	$\mathbb{E}[R_i] - r_f = \alpha + \beta_i \times \left[\mathbb{E}[R_M] - r_f\right]$ $\alpha = \{\mathbb{E}[R_i] - r_f\} - \{\beta_i \times [\mathbb{E}[R_M] - r_f]\}$	Eq. 18.8

Total company value as a function of debt and equity	$V = D + E$	Eq. 18.9
Total value of a company (DCF)	$V = \dfrac{FCF_1}{1+r_A} + \dfrac{FCF_2}{(1+r_A)^2} + \dfrac{FCF_3}{(1+r_A)^3} + \dfrac{FCF_4}{(1+r_A)^4} + \dfrac{FCF_5}{(1+r_A)^5} + \cdots$	Eq. 18.10
(Pre-tax) WACC	$r_A = \text{WACC} = \left[\dfrac{E}{V} \times r_E\right] + \left[\dfrac{D}{V} \times r_D\right]$	Eq. 18.11
Equity cost of capital using CAPM	$r_E = r_f + \beta_E \times \left[\mathbb{E}[R_M] - r_f\right]$	Eq. 18.12
Debt cost of capital using CAPM	$r_D = r_f + \beta_D \times \left[\mathbb{E}[R_M] - r_f\right]$	Eq. 18.13
Asset beta	$\beta_A = \left[\dfrac{E}{V} \times \beta_E\right] + \left[\dfrac{D}{V} \times \beta_D\right]$	Eq. 18.14
Asset beta, incorporating tax shield	$\beta_A = \left[\dfrac{E}{V} \times \beta_E\right] + \left[\dfrac{D}{V} \times \beta_D \times (1-\tau)\right]$	Eq. 18.15
Fama–French model	$\mathbb{E}[R_i] - r_f = \beta_{i,M} \times \left[\mathbb{E}[R_M] - r_f\right] + \beta_{i,size} \times size + \beta_{i,value} \times value$	Eq. 18.16

Problems

1. Suppose there are only three risky assets, IAM stock, IBM stock, and ICM stock. The total market equity values of these companies at current prices are $150 million for IAM, $300 million for IBM, and $1,500 million for ICM. In addition, there is $50 million of riskless bonds in the market. What would the proportion of the riskless asset held in the aggregate market portfolio be?

2. Capital markets in Flatland exhibit trade in four securities, the stocks X, Y, and Z, and a riskless government security. Evaluated at current prices in US dollars, the total market values of these assets are, respectively, $24 billion, $36 billion, $24 billion, and $16 billion.
   (a) Determine the relative proportions of each asset in the market portfolio.
   (b) If an investor holds risky assets in proportion to their market values and divides their aggregate portfolio of $100,000, with $30,000 invested in the riskless asset, how much is invested in securities X, Y, and Z?

3. With a riskless rate of 0.06, an equity market premium of 0.05, and a capital market line of slope 0.75, what can we infer about the risk of the market portfolio?

4. If the Treasury bill rate is currently 0.04 and the expected return to the market portfolio over the same period is 0.12, determine the market risk premium. If the standard deviation of the return on the market is 0.20, what is the equation of the capital market line?

5. The riskless rate of interest is 0.06 per year, and the expected rate of return on the market portfolio is 0.15 per year.
   (a) According to the CAPM, what is the efficient way for an investor to achieve an expected rate of return of 0.10 per year?

(b) If the standard deviation of the rate of return on the market portfolio is 0.20, what is the standard deviation on the above portfolio?

(c) Plot the CML and locate the foregoing portfolio on the same graph.

(d) Plot the SML and locate the foregoing portfolio on the same graph.

6. If the CAPM is valid, which of the following situations is possible? Explain. Consider each situation independently.

(a)

Portfolio	Expected return	Beta
A	0.20	1.4
B	0.25	1.2

(b)

Portfolio	Expected return	Standard deviation
A	0.30	35%
B	0.40	25%

(c)

Portfolio	Expected return	Standard deviation
Risk-free	0.10	0%
Market	0.18	24%
A	0.16	12%

(d)

Portfolio	Expected return	Standard deviation
Risk-free	0.10	0%
Market	0.18	24%
A	0.20	22%

7. Consider two securities: Stock A has an expected return of 10% and a standard deviation of 20%, and stock B has an expected return of 10% and a standard deviation of 30%. Is such a situation possible according to the CAPM? Explain your answer.

8. Suppose the risk-free rate is 0.10 and a security with a beta of 1.0 has an equilibrium expected rate of return of 0.15. What is the equity market premium?

9. Suppose the equity market premium is 4% and a security with a beta of 1.25 has an equilibrium expected rate of return of 0.10. If the government wishes to issue risk-free zero-coupon bonds with a term to maturity of one period and a face value per bond of $100,000, how much can the government expect to receive per bond?

10. Consider a portfolio exhibiting an expected return of 0.20 in an economy in which the riskless interest rate is 0.08, the expected return to the market portfolio is 0.13, and the standard deviation of the return to the market portfolio is 0.25. Assuming this portfolio is efficient, determine:
    (a) its beta;
    (b) the standard deviation of its return; and
    (c) its correlation with the market return.

11. Consider the formula for beta, which is a function of a security's correlation with the market portfolio, standard deviation, and the standard deviation of the market portfolio. Based on these, what risk characteristics do securities with betas equal to 1 possess? Those with betas equal to 0?

12. If the return on the market portfolio is 0.12 and the riskless rate is 0.07, use the CAPM to determine if the following stocks are mispriced:

Stock	Expected return	Beta
M	0.115	0.8
M&M	0.135	1.2

13. The Suzuki Motor Company is contemplating issuing stock to finance investment in producing a new sports-utility vehicle, the Seiza. Financial analysts within Suzuki forecast that this investment will have precisely the same risk as the market portfolio, where the annual return to the market portfolio is expected to be 0.15 and the current risk-free interest rate is 0.05. The analysts further believe that the expected return to the Seiza project will be 0.20 annually. Derive the beta value that would induce Suzuki to issue the stock.

14. Suppose that the stock of the new cologne manufacturer, Eau de Rodman, Inc., has been forecast to have a return with standard deviation 0.30 and a correlation with the market portfolio of 0.9. If the standard deviation of the return on the market is 0.20, determine the relative holdings of the market portfolio and Eau de Rodman stock to form a portfolio with a beta of 1.8.

15. During the most recent five-year period, the Pizzaro mutual fund earned an average annualized rate of return of 0.15 and had an annualized standard deviation of 0.30. The average risk-free rate was 0.05 per year. The average rate of return in the market index over that same period was 0.10 per year and the standard deviation was 0.20. How well did Pizzaro perform on a risk-adjusted basis? Adjust the risk to be equal to that of the market portfolio by building a portfolio of Pizzaro and the riskless asset with the same level of risk as the market portfolio.

16. There are only two risky assets in the economy: stocks and real estate. Their relative supplies are 50% stocks and 50% real estate; thus, the market portfolio will be half stocks and half real estate. The standard deviations are 0.20 for stocks and 0.20 for real estate, and the correlation between them is zero. The market portfolio's expected return is 0.14. The riskless rate is 0.08 per year.
    (a) According to the CAPM, what must be the equilibrium risk premium on the market portfolio, on stocks, and on real estate?
    (b) What is the Sharpe ratio of the market portfolio?
    (c) Draw the capital market line (CML). What is its slope?
    (d.) Draw the security market line (SML). What is its formula?

17. Consider a market with only the following three risky assets:

	Expected return, %	Risk %, σ_i	Covariance with market, $\sigma_{i,m}$
Asset 1	2.03	2	1.12
Asset 2	1.79	1	0.90
Asset 3	1.49	1	0.62
Market portfolio		0.92	

    Note that the covariance between two assets is defined as the correlation between the assets multiplied by the standard deviation of each asset: $\sigma_{i,m} = \rho_{im} \times \sigma_1 \times \sigma_2$. Consider the market portfolio composed of 4% invested in Asset 1, 76% invested in Asset 2, and 20% invested in Asset 3. What is the expected return of this portfolio? What are the betas of the three risky assets? Suppose the riskless rate of interest is 0.8%. Are these three securities priced correctly? What is the beta of the market portfolio calculated as a weighted average of the betas of its components?

18. St. Petersburg Associates, a firm of financial analysts specializing in Russian financial markets, forecasts that the stock of the Siberian Drilling Company will be worth 1,000 rubles per share one year from today. If the riskless interest rate on Russian government securities is 0.10 and the expected return to the market portfolio is 0.18, determine how much you would pay for a share of Siberian Drilling stock today if:
    (a) the beta of Siberian Drilling is 3; and
    (b) the beta of Siberian Drilling is 0.5.
19. Suppose that you believe the price of a share of IBM stock one year from today will be equal to the sum of the price of a share of General Motors stock plus the price of a share of Exxon-Mobil. Further, you believe that the price of a share of IBM stock in one year will be $100, whereas the price of a share of General Motors today is $30. If the annualized yield on 91-day T-bills (the riskless rate you use) is 0.05, the expected return on the market is 0.15, the variance of the market portfolio is 1, and the beta of IBM is 2, what price would you be willing to pay for one share of Exxon-Mobil stock today?
20. The riskless rate of interest is 0.06 per year, and the expected rate of return on the market portfolio is 0.15 per year. Estimate the value of a stock with an expected dividend per share of $5 this coming year, an expected dividend growth rate of 0.04 per year forever, and a beta of 0.8.
21. Suppose a company's current dividend of $1.50 per share is expected to grow at a constant 0.05 rate into the indefinite future. In capital markets the market risk premium is 0.08 and the risk-free rate is 0.02. If the stable beta of the company's stock is 0.8, what is the estimated current stock price?
22. The Pure Blood Corporation, a home health supply company serving hemophiliacs, is considering purchasing a new delivery van that will increase the radius of its service area. For an initial outlay of $21,250 the van is estimated to produce the following incremental net after-tax cash flows:

Time period	ACF
1	$5,000
2	$6,000
3	$7,000
4	$6,000
5	$5,000

In capital markets the market risk premium is 0.10 and the risk-free rate is 0.04. If the beta of the company's stock is 1.25, what is the NPV of the investment using the estimated market capitalization rate?

23. Consider the results of Problem 22. How will a half of 1 percentage point increase in the expected return on the market portfolio impact the NPV of the investment?
24. Consider a company with projected FCFs of $10 million next year and continuing each year after that. The company pays no taxes. It has a debt beta of 0.1 and an equity beta of 1.5, and has a capital structure of 20% debt and 80% equity. If the expected return on the market portfolio is 15% and the risk-free interest rate is 3%, what is the total value of the company?
25. For Problem 24, suppose that the company faces a tax rate of 30%. What is your new estimate of the total value of the company?
26. Suppose we have a firm whose beta is 1.2. The market risk premium is 7%, the risk-free rate is 5%, the firm's pre-tax cost of debt is 7%, and the tax rate is 40%. The leverage ratio of the firm is 0.5. What is the total value of the firm if its cash flows are $60 million per year perpetually, starting next year?

27. Suppose we have a firm whose beta is 0.8. The market risk premium is 7%, the risk-free rate is 4%, the firm's pre-tax cost of debt is 5%, and the tax rate is 40%. The leverage ratio of the firm in market value terms at present is 0.6. What is the market value of the equity of this firm if its FCF next year is $600 million and expected to grow perpetually after that at 2% per year?

28. You are the CEO of a major conglomerate and are thinking of acquiring a tech company at the end of this year. You are wondering what price would be appropriate to offer. You take a look at the company's financial statements, and see that they expect the following accounting numbers for the next four years (in thousands of dollars):

	Next year	In 2 years	In 3 years	In 4 years
FCF	150	1,650	1,500	1,450

The current corporate tax rate is 35%. The market return is 10%, and the current risk-free interest rate is 4%. The company says that it will be able to sustain its cash flows at the year 4 level indefinitely after that.

(a) You see that the tech company operates with no debt, and is therefore all-equity financed. You look at the correlation between the market and the company's stock returns, and calculate that its stock beta is 0.9. What is the company's asset beta?
(b) What is the appropriate discount rate by which to discount the company's cash flows?
(c) What is the terminal value of the company as of 4 years from now? What is the present value of this terminal value?
(d) What is the total value of the company right now?

29. Firewall Technologies is a privately held developer of antivirus and network security software. As part of your growth strategy, you initiate discussions with Firewall's founder about the possibility of acquiring the business. You are trying to value Firewall using a DCF approach.

(a) To estimate Firewall's cost of capital, you obtain the following data on its closest publicly traded competitor. This competitor is also a developer of antivirus and network security software and has no other businesses:

Total debt market value	$400 million
Number of shares of common stock	80 million
Stock price per share	$15.00
Equity beta	1.10

The competitor's debt is highly rated and its debt beta is zero. Your contacts on Wall Street tell you that the expected return on the market portfolio is 10% for the foreseeable future. The current risk-free rate for long-term investments is 4%. Use the data provided to estimate the cost of capital to discount Firewall's FCFs. Assume that the CAPM holds.

(b) Suppose you forecast FCFs for Firewall of $30 million next year and $40 million the year after. In subsequent years you expect its FCFs to grow at a 5% rate forever. What is your estimate of Firewall's total company value as of this year?

19 DERIVATIVES

CHAPTER OVERVIEW

19.1	Types of Derivative Contracts	596
19.2	Derivative Markets	597
19.3	Options	598
19.4	Futures and Forwards	599
19.5	Swaps	611
19.6	Fundamentals of Pricing Derivatives	617

LEARNING OBJECTIVES

After reading this chapter, you will be able to:
- identify and describe the features and cash flows of the basic types of derivatives: options, futures, forwards, and swaps;
- describe how investors and companies can use forward and futures contracts and swaps to meet their financial goals through hedging, speculating, and arbitrage;
- explain the relations among spot, forward, and futures prices of commodities, currencies, and securities in order to better understand the characteristics of derivatives and how they may be affected by financial markets;
- demonstrate the fundamentals of pricing derivatives via replication in order to understand how much investors should be willing to pay for them.

EQUATIONS YOU KNOW

Call-option payoff	$C_T = \max(S_T - K, 0)$	Eq. 7.2
Put-option payoff	$P_T = \max(K - S_T, 0)$	Eq. 7.1

Black–Scholes–Merton Formula	$C_0 = S_0 \times N(d_1) - \dfrac{K}{e^{r_f \times T}} \times N(d_2)$ where $d_1 = \dfrac{\ln\left(\dfrac{S_0}{K}\right) + \left(r_f + \dfrac{\sigma^2}{2}\right) \times T}{\sigma \times \sqrt{T}}$ $d_2 = d_1 - \sigma \times \sqrt{T}$	Eq. 7.7

- You are planning to spend a year in Paris, one year from now. The apartment you have selected has an annual rent of €24,000. You are concerned that dollars will become more expensive to convert to euros in the future, and are going to sign a contract now to pay the apartment owner €24,000 one year from now. You want to pay in US dollars. What is the value of such a contract?

- You work for a pasta manufacturing company that requires wheat to produce its products. You are concerned that the price of wheat in the future may rise substantially and impact the company's costs. What financial contract can the company enter into to hedge against this?

- You are on the team managing the investments of a government, and some of the investments fund future retirement payouts. These investments have significant interest rate risk. What can you do to offset this?

- Your company has a contract with a Japanese company, and that company will pay out a certain amount of money each month in Japanese yen. You need to convert it to US dollars, but do not want to be exposed to currency risk. Is there a financial contract that your company can use to minimize this exposure?

- The new company you are working at purchased a number of forward contracts last year based on the price of wheat. You are in the financial division of the company, and you need to value these financial contracts in order to assess the company's assets. How can you determine the value of these contracts?

- You are working in the sales side of an investment bank, and the research team has constructed a new financial contract which pays the holder if oil prices either go up substantially or go down substantially. They believe that the product will be popular, given large recent swings in the price of oil. How can you determine the price to sell the contract for, and thus how much money the bank could make from it?

Introduction

In Chapter 5 we introduced derivatives, which are financial instruments whose price is based on (i.e., derived from) the value of one or more other assets called underlying assets. These underlying assets may be equity securities, fixed-income securities, foreign currencies, or commodities such as gold and silver. The value of a derivative is reliant on the movement of the value of the underlying asset; for example, a derivative might promise to pay you a specified amount of money if the price of another asset, such as a stock, goes above a certain level.

The most common types of derivatives are options (see Chapter 7), forward contracts (forwards), future contracts (futures), swap contracts (swaps), and asset-backed securities (ABS). Derivative instruments allow investors to tailor investments to their specific needs—for example, by allowing them to earn a rate of return on an asset without having to invest in the actual asset. They provide an effective way to hedge—that is, to offset or manage a specific risk.

In this chapter, we learn how commonly used derivative contracts work, why investors may purchase them, and how the pricing of such contracts works. We begin with an overview of common types of derivative contracts and describing derivative markets around the world. We then go into detail about how specific derivative contracts work and how we can understand their value, starting with a review of options, then moving on to futures and forwards contracts and swaps. We conclude the chapter with a general framework that can be applied to value *any* type of derivative contract, including new ones that are frequently created in financial markets.

19.1 Types of Derivative Contracts

Derivative contracts can be based on any underlying asset—not just financial assets—and can be constructed with customized terms and features. These underlying assets may be commodities such as gold, wheat, or oil, or may be financial assets such as shares of stock, financial indexes, or currencies of a particular country. While derivatives can take many forms, the common types of derivatives are options, forwards, futures, swaps, and asset-backed securities (ABS).

Options contracts give the holder a transaction choice in the future. A call option (or simply a call) gives its holder the right to buy some asset at a specified price on or before some specified expiration date. A put option gives its holder the right to sell some asset at a specified price on or before some specified expiration date, effectively insuring against a decrease in its price below the price specified on purchase of the put-option contract. Option contracts permit you to wait until after you know the asset's future price before deciding whether to buy or sell or do nothing.

Forward contracts are financial instruments that oblige one party to the contract to buy some asset and the other party to sell at a specified price on some specified date. They eliminate uncertainty about the future price at which the asset will be exchanged. Futures contracts function in the same way as forward contracts, except they are traded on financial exchanges, whereas forwards are traded between individual parties.

A swap is a financial contract that commits two parties to exchange—"swap"—the returns from one asset for the returns on another asset. One party "receives" the return on one asset and "pays" the return on the other asset, and the other does the reverse. Note that this definition applies to total return swaps as well as other types of swaps, but is not universal for every swap. For example, credit default swaps—discussed later in this chapter—may specify a one-time payment to one side upon a triggering event in exchange for that side paying regular fixed amounts of money.

The stream of potential payments is determined by a notional quantity and swap rate. The notional amount (or notional value) refers to the principal amount of money the contract is based upon, while the swap rate determines the calculation of the net cash flow that the two parties exchange. Swaps can be created based on returns from almost any kind of financial instrument, such as interest rates, foreign currency exchange rates, or stock markets. This exchange of returns allows for the efficient exchanging of risks. For example, a party that owns assets that are exposed to the risk of floating interest rates can enter into a swap exchanging those cash flows for cash flows based on a more stable, fixed interest rate. An asset-backed security (ABS) is a financial contract that provides cash flows to investors that are "backed" by an underlying asset such as mortgage loans, car loans, credit card loans, or some other asset that produces expected cash flows. For example, an ABS could be created by a bank that has extended a number of mortgages to individuals to buy a house (this is known as a mortgage-backed security [MBS]). The mortgage payments that the individuals make to the bank are the cash flows that are paid to the ABS investors.

19.2 Derivative Markets

Derivative contracts can be traded over-the-counter (OTC), which means that the contracts are created directly between two entities (e.g., a bank creates a contract directly with an investment fund); however, other derivative contracts may be exchange traded: They have standardized terms and can be freely traded between participants in financial markets. Derivatives markets feature active trading, and millions of contracts representing trillions of dollars of notional value are traded each year, both on exchanges and in OTC trading.

Figure 19.1 shows derivative trading activity over four decades. It shows the total notional value of OTC derivatives outstanding, by type of derivative. Of these, interest rate derivatives make up the largest portion of OTC derivatives. The figure shows that, since the mid 2000s, the total notional value of OTC derivatives outstanding has remained between $500 trillion and $700 trillion, six to seven times global GDP. While certainly a very large amount, as we will make clear in this chapter, the notional amount is not the *market value* of these contracts, but represents the value of the underlying assets whose risk is covered by these contracts. Nevertheless, the volume and size of these contracts indicates how important derivatives are in the global financial system and, as we will discuss in more detail, how they enable a great deal of efficient risk transfer.

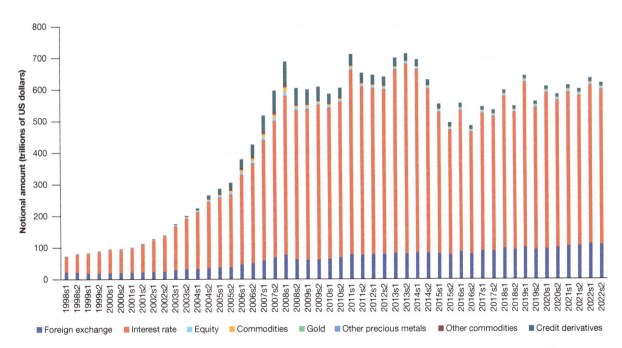

FIGURE 19.1 Size of derivatives markets. This figure shows the size of derivatives markets over time. The total notional amount of OTC derivatives, by type, from 1998 to 2021.
Source: Bank of International Settlements. Available at: https://data.bis.org/topics/OTC_DER.

19.3 Options

Options are a key type of derivative contract covered in detail in Chapter 7. In this section, we provide a brief review of how options work.

Options are financial contracts that allow the owner a choice in the future. Put options allow the choice to sell or not sell an underlying asset in the future, while call options allow the choice to buy or not buy an underlying asset in the future. The owner does not have to exercise the option in the future if it is not beneficial to them. Thus, option contracts embed *flexibility*: The option owner makes the decision after the market price of the underlying asset is observed.

Consider the example of a put option, a contract that allows you to sell a share of stock in one year for a price of $100. In one year, if, based on the market stock price, it is a good deal for you to sell the share of stock for $100 (e.g., if the price of the stock falls below $100), you can do so; otherwise (if the market price is above $100) you can simply let the contract expire. Now consider the example of a call option, which allows you to buy stock one year from now (but does not require you to do so), for a price of $100. If, in one year, the stock price goes above $100, then it is a good idea to purchase the stock for $100 and you will exercise the option. In contrast, if the stock price ends up being below $100, then it is not a good idea to buy it for $100, and you will let the contract expire. Figure 19.2 provides the payoff diagrams for the call and put options in this example, depicting what the payoffs to the holder of an option would be depending on the stock price at expiration.

As we saw in Chapter 7, we can mathematically represent the payoffs at expiration of a call and put option. In particular, we can represent the payoffs of a call option at expiration, which we will denote by C_T, mathematically as:

$$C_T = \max(S_T - K, 0), \tag{19.1}$$

where S_T is the price/value of the underlying asset (i.e., the stock price in our example) when the option expires at time T, and K is the pre-specified strike price ($100 in our example). Equation 19.1 thus states that, at expiration, you will choose whichever is larger—the payoff from exercising the option and buying the underlying asset for K, or leaving the option unexercised and getting a payoff of zero.

Similarly, we can represent the payoff of a put option at expiration, which we will denote by P_T, as:

$$P_T = \max(K - S_T, 0). \tag{19.2}$$

Equation 19.2 thus states that, at expiration, you will choose whichever is larger—the payoff from exercising the put option and selling the underlying asset for K (and paying S_T to buy the stock in the market), or leaving the option unexercised and getting a payoff of zero.

Options enable the flexibility to be able to make decisions after uncertainty is resolved, which takes away uncertainty (in general you must choose in advance). This flexibility of course has value, and in Chapter 7 we introduced tools for estimating this value. In this chapter we expand that set of tools. As we noted in Chapters 7 and 14, option pricing is foundational to decision making under uncertainty. Even beyond the fact that billions of option contracts are traded in financial markets each year, the applications of options concepts span well beyond financial markets and can be used to analyze and inform a wide array of decisions such as insurance, mortgages, corporate financing, and company projects.

19.4 FUTURES AND FORWARDS

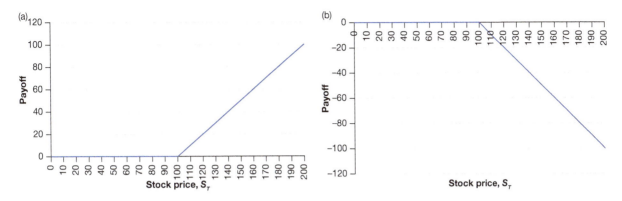

FIGURE 19.2 Payoff diagrams of long call or put options. (a) The payoff diagram of a long position in a call option with a strike price of $100; (b) the payoff diagram of a long position in a put option with a strike price of $100.

19.4 Futures and Forwards

Futures and forward contracts allow two parties to exchange an asset for a pre-specified price in the future. In this section, we will describe the mechanics of how futures and forwards work, and then discuss the institutional differences as well as how financial futures differ from commodity futures. We then consider how forwards and futures are priced, and end with a discussion of their economic functions.

19.4.1 How Futures and Forwards Work

Any time two parties agree to exchange some asset in the future at a prearranged price they are entering into a forward contract. A futures contract is conceptually the same as a forward contract, except that they are standardized and traded on an exchange, and thus have some differences in features. We discuss these differences in the next section; to describe the core functions of how these contracts work, in this section we use the example of a forward contract.

Often people enter into forward contracts without knowing that is what they are called. For example, you may be planning a trip from Boston to Tokyo one year from now. You make your flight reservations now, and the airline ticket booking website lets you either lock in a price of $1,000 now or lets you pay whatever the price may be on the day of your flight. In either case payment will not take place until the day of your flight. If you decide to lock in the $1,000 price, you have entered into a forward contract with the airline. By entering the forward contract, you eliminate the risk of the cost of your airfare going above $1,000. If the price of a ticket turns out to be $1,500 one year from now, you will be happy that you had the good sense to lock in a forward price of $1,000. On the other hand, if the price turns out to be $500 on the day of your flight, you will still have to pay the $1,000 forward price you agreed to. In that case, you will regret your decision.

With a forward contract, two parties agree to exchange some asset in the future at a price specified now. The agreed-upon date is known as the settlement date and is denoted by T, while the specified price is known as the forward price and is denoted by $F_{0,T}$.[1] With a forward contract, no money is paid by either party at time $t = 0$, which is when the contract is created. At the settlement date of the contract, time $t = T$, one party pays the forward price $F_{0,T}$ to the other party in exchange for the specified asset valued. We can denote the value of the underlying asset—known as the underlying price—at the settlement date T by S_T. The party who agrees to buy the specified item is said to take a long position, and the party who agrees to sell the item is said to take a short position. Thus, the long position receives a payoff worth $S_T - F_{0,T}$, and the short position receives a payoff worth $F_{0,T} - S_T$. We can represent the cash flows of the long position of the contract through a timeline, as shown in Figure 19.3.

From the timeline of cash flows, we can see that the end cash flow at the settlement date depends on the price of the underlying asset at that date T, S_T. If the price of the underlying asset ends up *above* the underlying price, the long position "wins"—they receive the asset, which is worth more than what they have to pay. In contrast, the short position "loses"—they must deliver the asset, which is worth more than what they receive in cash from the other party.

For example, consider a forward contract for the commodity—a physical asset such as raw materials, agricultural products, or resources—wheat. Suppose that a flour mill needs 100 bushels of wheat to make into flour in three months' time. The mill wants to make sure that the 100 bushels will be available when it is needed and is also concerned that the price of wheat will rise. The mill can therefore enter into a long position in a forward contract on wheat with wheat farmers, with a settlement date of three months. Suppose that the forward price agreed to is $10 per bushel. No money exchanges hands today. In three months, the mill will pay $10 × 100 = $1,000 to the farmer (the short position) and receive 100 bushels of wheat. Absent this contract, to lock in a price and the quantity needed, the mill would have to purchase the wheat now and store it for three months. Thus, one benefit of this contract is that the mill is eliminating the need for such storage, a point that we will return to as it factors into the forward price.

Since the only payoff occurs at the settlement date of the contract, we can also illustrate the positions using a payoff diagram that depicts the payoffs of both sides of the contract at the settlement date, depending on what the underlying price of the asset ends up being. Figure 19.4 shows this payoff diagram. The mill ends up benefiting from the contract (i.e., has a positive payoff) if the price of wheat ends up higher than $10 per bushel, but ends up taking a loss if the price of wheat ends up lower.

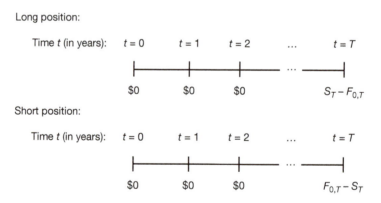

FIGURE 19.3 Timelines of the cash flows for a forward contract. The top timeline shows the cash flows for the long position of a forward contract with forward price $F_{0,T}$ and settlement date T, while the bottom timeline shows the cash flows for the short position.

---

[1] More precisely, the *forward price* is the delivery price that makes the value of the forward contract equal to zero at the time the contract is made.

19.4 FUTURES AND FORWARDS

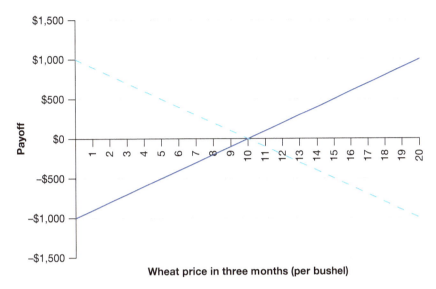

FIGURE 19.4 Payoff diagram for a forward contract. The figure shows a payoff diagram at settlement (in three months) for a forward contract on wheat based on a forward price of $10 per bushel and 100 bushels. The solid line depicts the long position, while the dashed line depicts the short position.

> **QUICK CHECK 19.1** Draw a timeline of cash flows and a payoff diagram from the perspective of both the long and short positions for a forward contract where the long position promises to purchase 100 barrels of oil in two years at a price of $80 per barrel.

19.4.2 The Difference between Forwards and Futures

Futures contracts are fundamentally the same as forward contracts, but differ in several respects, most importantly in how they are traded.

Forward contracts are negotiated between two parties (usually business firms and financial intermediaries) and can have unique specifications that depend on the demands of those parties. This "customization" is a disadvantage if one of the parties wants to terminate the contract before the delivery date because it makes the contract illiquid (i.e., difficult to trade freely with others). As with all contracts, there is always the issue of default risk between the parties, which can, however, be reduced by the posting of collateral.

Futures contracts are "standardized" forward contracts that are traded on an organized exchange. The exchange interposes itself between the buyer and the seller, so that each has a separate contract with the exchange. Standardization means that the terms of the futures contract are the same for all contracts. The exchange specifies the exact commodity, the contract size, and where and when delivery will be made. This makes futures more liquid than forward contracts and, therefore, makes it easier for parties to a futures contract to close out—that is, to terminate—their positions before the specified delivery date. Indeed, the vast majority of futures contracts are terminated before the final contract delivery date, since many times parties are interested in the financial aspect of the contracts—the changes in contract value based on the underlying asset—rather than taking possession of the underlying asset. Because futures contracts are traded on exchanges, they reduce the default risk that exists with forward contracts—the exchange requires participants to post an *initial margin*, a certain amount of money (i.e., collateral) when a participant enters into a position, and further money as *margin* each day to reduce the risk of a counterparty not fulfilling their end of the contract.

All future accounts are also *marked to market* each day based on that day's trading price, which means that money changes hands each day based on market price movements. For example, suppose that today you place an order to take a long position in a wheat futures contract for delivery of 5,000 bushels next month. The broker requires you to deposit money in your account to serve as collateral. On the next day, the futures price closes 2¼ cents per bushel lower (prices are frequently quoted in fractions of a cent). You have therefore lost 2¼ × 5,000 bushels = $112.50 that day. The broker will take that amount out of your account even though you may not have made any trades. The money is transferred to the futures exchange, which transfers it to the party who was on the short side of the contract.

If the margin in your account falls below a pre-specified level, you will receive a *margin call* from the broker asking you to add money. If you do not respond immediately, then the broker liquidates your position at the prevailing market price and returns any leftover collateral. This process of daily realization of gains and losses minimizes the possibility of contract default. Another consequence is that no matter how great the face value of a futures contract, its market value is always zero at the beginning of each day.

The use of mark to market establishes a uniform standard regarding the value of any given contract in trading. Furthermore, for a given underlying asset, there is only one contract and thus one futures price for a given delivery date; in contrast, with the OTC forward market, there are large numbers of contracts with different delivery prices. These features of futures contracts make them more homogenous and efficient for trading.

Because of their careful procedures to protect against the risk of contract default by requiring the posting of margin, futures markets are used by individuals and firms whose credit ratings may be costly to check. Forward contracts, on the other hand, tend to be used when the credit rating of the contracting parties is high and easy to verify—for example, between a bank and its corporate customers.

The pricing relations discussed later in this chapter that apply to forward prices apply with minor modification to futures prices. They may differ because of the daily marking-to-market feature of futures contracts. In practice, however, for most assets the futures and forward prices hardly differ at all.

> **QUICK CHECK 19.2** What will happen in your futures trading account if you take a long position in wheat futures, and instead of going down by 2¼ cents per bushel, the futures price went up by 7¼ cents per bushel?

19.4.3 Pricing of Commodity Forwards and Futures

At the onset of the forward contract, neither party exchanges money, but they agree upon the price that they will exchange the underlying asset for in the future. How is this price determined?

Forwards/futures represent an alternative way of exchanging the risk and return of their underlying asset without exchanging ownership. Commodity forward/futures contracts are frequently used to hedge against price movements in commodities by users exposed to such risks, and the commodities used as underlying assets range from specific crops (e.g., corn, wheat, soybeans) to energy (e.g., crude oil, heating oil, natural gas) to metals (e.g., iron ore, gold, silver). For example, consider two methods that will ensure that you will have a certain amount of wheat in the future: (1) you can physically purchase wheat for some price today and store it until the desired date; or (2) you can enter into a forward/futures contract that allows you to make that purchase on the desired date. The two methods produce equivalent results—giving you the same amount of wheat at the desired date—except for the potential benefits and costs of each. Thus, by **Principle 2**: *Equivalent assets that can be freely bought and sold will have the same market price*, the price of each method must be the same, adjusting for these benefits and costs.

What are the benefits and costs of each method? For commodities, physically purchasing the asset entails a storage cost; in our example, you would have to store the wheat in a silo or other facility. A forward/futures contract thus allows you to save on the costs of storage. This implies that the forward/futures price should embed a premium for avoiding this storage cost. However, there is also benefit to physically holding a commodity. If, before the settlement date, there is an unanticipated need to use the commodity (e.g., a shortage in the production process), then there is a benefit to having the physical commodity. We refer to this benefit of actually holding on to the physical commodity as a convenience. This convenience implies that the forward/futures price should embed a discount relative to the commodity price.

To illustrate, consider a forward contract for a barrel of oil with a settlement date of one year from now and a forward price of $90. Consider the cash flows for the forward contract compared to purchasing the asset outright. First, with the forward contract, there is no money exchanging hands at $t = 0$. At the settlement date of $t = 1$, you pay $90 and own the asset (the barrel of oil). Now consider the cash flows if you purchase the asset outright. Suppose that a barrel of oil costs $80 right now; to fund this purchase, you borrow money at a 5% interest rate. Suppose that the total storage costs for the barrel are $6. At the settlement date of $t = 1$, you pay back the borrowed amount, $80 \times 1.05 = 84, and also must pay the storage costs of $6. The actions for the two methods are illustrated in Table 9.1.

In this case, the cash flows at $t = 0$ for the two methods are the same, that is, zero. Also, the total cost at $t = 1$ for the two methods is the same. However, this *must* be approximately the case according to the law of one price (**Principle 2**: *Equivalent assets that can be freely bought and sold will have the same market price*), since both strategies are equivalent (although the costs may not be exactly the same due to transaction costs and other frictions). If this were not the case, there would be an

Table 19.1 **Cash flows for forward contract compared to outright purchase.** The top row of the table shows the cash flows that come from entering into a forward contract at $t = 0$ for a barrel of oil, with a forward price of $90 and settlement date at $t = 1$. The bottom row of the table shows the cash flows from borrowing money at a 5% interest rate at $t = 0$ to purchase the barrel for $80. Storage costs for oil are $6.

	Date		
	$t = 0$	$t = 1$	Total Cost at $t = 1$
Forward contract	Pay $0 for contract	Pay $90 forward price, own barrel	$90
Outright purchase	Borrow $80, pay $80 for barrel	Pay back $84, pay $6 storage costs, own barrel	$90

arbitrage, an opportunity to make free profits. To illustrate this point, suppose that the price of the forward contract was higher than the cost of the outright asset purchase (say $100). Then you could short the forward contract and purchase the asset. At $t = 1$, you would receive the forward price of $100 and would need to provide the asset to the long position (which you had already purchased). The total cost of the asset purchase is $90, resulting in a $10 total profit. Similarly, suppose that the price of the forward contract was only $75. Then you could go long the forward contract and short the asset now.

More generally, we can see that a forward/future price is directly linked to the spot price of the underlying asset it is based on. For the forward contract, suppose that the forward price as of now (time $t = 0$) for settlement at date T is $F_{0,T}$, while the spot price of the underlying asset at date t is S_t. Suppose that the (risk-free) interest rate is r_f. The forward contract will therefore cost $0 at initiation and pay off $F_{0,T}$ at the settlement date. The outright asset purchase requires borrowing S_0 at time $t = 0$ to pay for the asset—resulting in no net cash flow at the beginning—and then paying back the borrowed amount plus interest, $S_0 \times (1 + r_f)^T$ at time $t = T$. In addition, there are possible storage costs or convenience benefits associated with having the physical asset. Table 19.2 depicts these two situations.

From this, we get the following general relationship between forward prices and the spot prices of underlying assets based on the fact that the costs at $t = T$ must be the same between the methods:

$$F_{0,T} = S_0 \times (1 + r_f)^T + FV(\text{net storage costs}), \quad (19.3)$$

where the net storage costs include both storage costs and convenience benefits, and is the future value of those costs as of the settlement date T. Since the forward contract *de facto* "saves" money on storage costs, its price is increased relative to the underlying asset to reflect this value.

The convenience benefits and storage costs are often also expressed as a percentage of the price of the underlying asset. Let c represent the percentage storage costs each period. As we noted above, there is a disadvantage of having a forward/future contract rather than holding the physical commodity—in other words, holding the commodity affords a convenience. Convenience that one gives up from holding the financial contract is known as the convenience yield, and is quantified each period as y. We can then express Equation 19.3 equivalently as:

$$F_{0,T} = S_0 \times (1 + r_f + c - y)^T. \quad (19.4)$$

Table 19.2 Total costs for a forward/futures contract. This table provides the cash flows for a forward/futures contract for a contract start date of $t = 0$, a settlement date of T, an underlying asset price of S_t, a forward price of $F_{0,T}$, and an interest rate of r_f.

	Date		
	$t = 0$	$t = T$	Total cost at $t = T$
Forward contract	• Pay $0 for contract	• Pay $F_{0,T}$ forward price • Own asset	$F_{0,T}$
Outright purchase	• Borrow S_0 • Pay S_0 for asset	• Pay back $S_0 \times (1 + r_f)^T$ • Pay total storage costs • Incorporate convenience benefits • Own asset	$S_0 \times (1 + r_f)^T$ + net storage costs

19.4 FUTURES AND FORWARDS

Thus, the forward price accounts for the advantages of saving on storage costs (c) and the disadvantages of not having the asset before settlement (y). The net of storage costs and the convenience yield each period is often referred to as the cost of carry.

Example 19.1 (The Forward Price of Gold and Arbitrage): Suppose the spot price of gold is $300/ounce and storage costs are 2% per year. The riskless interest rate is 8%.

(a) What should the forward price of gold for delivery in one year be?
(b) Suppose instead that the forward price is actually $340/ounce. Construct an arbitrage strategy to take advantage of this mispricing.
(c) Suppose instead that the forward price is actually $320/ounce. Construct an arbitrage strategy to take advantage of this mispricing.

Solution.

(a) We can directly apply Equation 19.4 to determine the forward price, with $S_0 = \$300$, $r_f = 0.08$, and $c = 0.02$ (note that no convenience yield is provided, so we can assume that $y = 0$):

$$F_{0,T} = S_0 \times (1 + r_f + c)^T$$
$$= \$300 \times (1 + 0.08 + 0.02)$$
$$= \$330.$$

(b) If the forward price was actually $340 instead, then the forward price is too high relative to the actual commodity. Therefore, we can construct an arbitrage strategy by selling the overpriced forward (i.e., going short) and buying the actual gold commodity. To buy the gold, we can borrow money at the riskless interest rate. **Table 19.3** shows the cash flows for the arbitrage strategy. In **Table 19.3**, S_1 represents the price of gold at $t = 1$. By this strategy, shorting the forward requires delivery of the gold in one year. By buying gold, we are able to provide it for delivery in one year. After paying off the loan and storage costs one year from now, we would be left with $10 in arbitrage profits regardless of what the spot price turns out to be at that time.

(c) If the forward price was actually $320 instead, then the forward price is too low relative to the actual commodity. Therefore, we can construct an arbitrage strategy by buying the underpriced forward (i.e., going long) and selling (shorting) the actual gold commodity. We would invest the proceeds from the gold sale at the riskless interest rate. **Table 19.4** shows the cash flows for the arbitrage strategy. With this strategy, we short gold (and invest the proceeds), and then need to deliver the gold in a year by buying it then. However, by going long the forward contract, we purchase the gold in one year. We also receive the total invested proceeds and storage costs, which exceed the forward price for the gold. Note that

Table 19.3 Cash flow for an arbitrage strategy to take advantage of the mispricing for the forward price.

Position	$t = 0$	$t = 1$
Sell (short) forward contract	$0	$F_{0,T} - S_1 = \$340 - S_1$
Borrow $300	$300	$-\$300 \times 1.08 = -\$324$
Buy gold	-$300	S_1
Pay storage costs		$-\$300 \times 0.02 = -\$6$
Net cash flows	$0	$10

Table 19.4 Cash flow for an arbitrage strategy that buys the underprice forward and selling the commodity

Position	$t = 0$	$t = 1$
Buy (long) forward contract	$0	$S_1 - F_{0,T} = S_1 - \$320$
Sell gold	$300	$-S_1$
Invest gold proceeds	-$300	$\$300 \times 1.08 = \$324$
Receive storage costs		$\$300 \times 0.02 = \$6$
Net cash flows	$0	$10

we assume that we receive storage costs by short-selling gold, since we are in essence saving these costs from the person we borrow the gold from in order to short-sell. We would be left with $10 in arbitrage profits regardless of what the spot price turns out to be at that time.

QUICK CHECK 19.3 Suppose that, for an ounce of gold, $r_f = 0.06$, $S_0 = \$400$, and $c = 0.02$. What must the forward price of gold be? Explain how, if the actual forward price is different from this, there would be an arbitrage opportunity.

19.4.4 Extracting Information from Forward Prices

Forward prices can provide information about investor expectations for spot prices in the future—that is, the price that investors expect an asset to be at in the future. The reasoning is that the forward price reflects what investors expect the spot price to be at the contract delivery date and, therefore, indicate the likely future spot price.

To illustrate, let us consider a forward contract for wheat. What information can be extracted from the forward price of wheat in the contract? We must distinguish between two conditions: (a) no wheat is in storage and (b) wheat is in storage.

(a) If there is no wheat in storage—a condition called a stock out—then Equation 19.4 holds as a strict inequality, and the spot and forward prices are not linked precisely through an arbitrage-pricing relation. In this case, the forward price will provide information about the expected future spot price that is not extractable from the current spot price. The reason for this is that, with no wheat in storage, the price will be governed by supply and demand—it will be high enough so that the owners of wheat will want to sell all they can, and also so that no one will store wheat if they do not need it.[2]

---

[2] If there is a stock out, the spot price will be high enough that owners of wheat want to sell all the spot delivery wheat they can; once they emptied their silos (i.e., stock out) they would still want to sell more but they cannot physically create more wheat for delivery than all the wheat available (they also cannot "short sell" physical wheat because there is none being stored and so none to be lent for the short). Thus, the price must be whatever it takes so those who most need wheat immediately can get as much as they physically can, therefore implying that the price has to be "high enough" so that no one who does not need wheat stores it. Another part of the effect is that there is a risk that one might have to shut down businesses if one does not have the physical commodity available, and so storage of a commodity provides a "convenience" yield even when there is no formal return from holding it (or negative if storage is costly to do). But even in this case when it does provide information, the price is not necessarily an unbiased forecast of the future spot price.

(b) If wheat is being stored, then no further inference about the future expected spot price is possible beyond that extractable from the current spot price. The reason is that, by the force of arbitrage, Equation 19.4 must hold as an equality, as explained. Hence, the forward price is completely specified by knowing the spot price and the cost of carry, independently of what the assessments are about the future expected spot price. Therefore, if we observe that a commodity, an asset, or a security is being stored, then the forward price provides no additional information about the expected future spot price. This is in line with **Principle 5:** *The best estimate of an asset's value is usually its market price, which incorporates valuable information to guide the allocation of resources and risks.*

However, the forward price, when combined with the current spot price, can be used to extract an estimate of the cost of carry. If storage occurs and the forward and spot prices imply a negative cost of carry, then almost surely there are benefits to holding the physical commodity, asset, or security that are not being taken into account in the analysis (i.e., a convenience yield).

Beyond this, forward/future prices can also be used in order to derive implied interest rates in the economy. If we examine Equation 19.4, we can see that if we have information on the spot price, forward price, and net storage costs, then we can solve for what the interest rate should be based on the market prices.

19.4.5 Financial Forwards and Futures

In the previous examples we have focused on forward/futures contracts in which the underlying asset is a commodity. However, the underlying asset of forwards/futures need not be a physical commodity, but can be a financial asset. Unlike commodities such as wheat or gold, financial securities have no intrinsic value in the sense that they are not consumed, used as inputs to physical production, or held for their own sake. Rather, they represent claims to streams of payments in the future.

Consider a hypothetical stock called Z&T, which is a share in a mutual fund that invests in a broadly diversified portfolio of stocks. It reinvests all dividends received and pays no dividends. A forward contract on a share of Z&T is the promise to deliver a share at some specified delivery date at a specified delivery price. Let us denote this forward price by F. The party who is long the forward contract agrees to pay F dollars at the delivery date to the party who is short. The stock price on the delivery date is S_1. Rather than actually delivering the stock, the contract is usually settled in cash. This means that no delivery of stock takes place; only the difference between F and S_1 is paid at the contract maturity date. For example, suppose the forward price is $108 per share. Then if the stock price at the delivery date turns out to be $109, the party who is long receives $1 from the party who is short. However, if the spot price turns out to be $107, the party who is long must pay $1 to the party who is short.

Such a futures contract—where the underlying asset is an index or mutual fund—offers many advantages, as it allows an investor to receive the returns from an investment in an index/mutual fund without the need to purchase a share in the fund.

Another common type of financial future/forward involves the exchange of currencies, which allows firms that may be exposed to currency risk to be able to hedge that risk. For example, consider a forward contract on Japanese yen where the counterparties are a US-based firm and a Japanese firm. The US company is expecting to receive payment of ¥100 million one year from now. The Japanese company is expecting to receive US dollar revenue of $1 million one year from now. Both firms would like to eliminate their exposure to foreign currency risk—that is, the potential that one currency becomes more or less expensive to convert into another currency in the future. The two companies can enter a forward contract to deliver the Japanese yen for US dollars at a fixed forward price, ¥100 per dollar. The US company will therefore receive $1 million on the contract settlement date, and the Japanese counterparty will receive the ¥100 million, whatever the spot prices turn out to be.

19.4.6 Pricing of Financial Forwards and Futures

Determining the prices of financial forwards/futures follows the same principle as those for commodities: The total cost/benefit of purchasing the financial asset itself should equal that of entering into the forward/futures contract. For commodities, a difference between purchasing the asset and entering into the forward is the potential for storage/convenience costs. For financial assets, such storage costs are negligible—financial securities can be produced and stored at very low cost, and this is reflected in the relation between their spot and futures prices.

But a variation of these costs can be embedded in certain financial securities. In particular, the holder of a forward/futures contract on a financial asset that pays dividends will lose out on the dividend payments they would have otherwise gotten if they held the asset itself. To see this, consider a futures contract on a stock that pays a dividend. Let us denote the stock price at settlement date T (the date the dividend D is paid) as S_T, and the futures price of $F_{0,T}$. If we go long the futures contract for this stock, we will pay \$0 now and receive $S_T - F_{0,T}$ (the stock minus the futures price) at settlement. Now consider the stock itself. We can buy the stock for a price of S_0 now by borrowing that amount. At the settlement date T, we have the stock and also the dividend payment, D, but we also need to repay the initial borrowing, $S_0 \times (1 + r_f)^T$. We summarize this in Table 19.5.

Thus, comparing the two cases, we own the stock in both. But the cost in the case of the futures contract at settlement is $F_{0,T}$, while the cost in the case of the outright purchase of the stock is $S_0 \times (1 + r_f)^T - D$. By the same logic as before (i.e., the law of one price, Principle 2), it follows that the costs must be the same. Thus, for a futures/forward contract on a financial asset that pays dividends, we have the following relationship for the futures/forward price:

$$F_{0,T} = S_0 \times (1 + r_f)^T - FV(D). \tag{19.5}$$

We can equivalently express the dividends as dividend yield (i.e., as a percentage of the current stock price), which we can denote as d:

$$F_{0,T} = S_0 \times (1 + r_f - d)^T. \tag{19.6}$$

Another widely used type of financial forward contract is a *currency forward*, which allows a holder to lock in a fixed exchange rate at a future date. Such contracts thus offer a useful way to hedge against foreign currency risk. For example, a US company that imports microchips from Japan takes on the risk that the value of the Japanese yen will increase relative to the US dollar. Currency forwards specify that the holder will purchase the notional amount of a foreign currency for a fixed price of a reference currency.

To illustrate, consider a forward contract that specifies that the holder will receive ¥1 in exchange for paying a forward price in dollars of $F_{0,T}$. The forward contract costs nothing to enter into, and provides

Table 19.5 This table shows going long on the futures contract against the outright purchase of the stock.

	Date		Total cost at $t = T$
	$t = 0$	$t = T$	
Futures contract	• Pay \$0 for contract	• Pay $F_{0,T}$ futures price • Own stock	$F_{0,T}$
Outright purchase	• Borrow S_0 • Pay S_0 for stock	• Pay back $S_0 \times (1 + r_f)^T$ • Receive dividend D • Own stock	$S_0 \times (1 + r_f)^T - D$

¥1 in exchange for $F_{0,T}$ at time T. Purchasing ¥1 outright involves borrowing S_0–the spot price, in US dollars, for purchasing ¥1 based on the current exchange rate–and using the money to purchase ¥1. Note that this borrowing is in US dollars, and so at $t = T$, $S_0 \times (1 + r_\$)^T$ must be paid back based on the US dollar interest rate, $r_\$$. The ¥1 acquired at $t = 0$ would be invested at the yen interest rate (e.g., by purchasing a Japanese bond), and thus at $t = T$ would be the future value of ¥1: $¥1 \times (1 + r_¥)^T$. Thus, similar to our previous examples, both methods involve no cash flows at $t = 0$. At $t = T$, the outright purchase leaves us with $¥1 \times (1 + r_¥)^T$ yen. Note that while the forward contract leaves us with ¥1, if we scaled it up by $(1 + r_¥)^T$ (in other words, bought $(1 + r_¥)^T$ forward contracts, paying $F_{0,T} \times (1 + r_¥)^T$), this will provide us with $1¥ \times (1 + r_¥)^T$ yen as well. This scenario is depicted in Table 19.6.

By Principle 2, since both methods give us $¥1 \times (1 + r_¥)^T$ at $t = T$ for the same cash flows at $t = 0$, the costs at $t = T$ must be the same: $F_{0,T} \times (1 + r_¥)^T = S_0 \times (1 + r_\$)^T$. This provides us with a formula for understanding the relationship between currency forward prices, exchange rates, and interest rates:

$$F_{0,T} = S_0 \times \frac{(1+r_\$)^T}{(1+r_¥)^T}. \tag{19.7}$$

In Equation 19.7 the base currency is US dollars, and thus S_0 is the current (spot) exchange rate for purchasing one unit of a foreign currency (yen in the above formula) using US dollars.

Table 19.6 This table shows the forward contract against the outright purchase of the stock.

	Date		Total cost at $t = T$
	$t = 0$	$t = T$	
Forward contract	• Pay $0 for contract	• Pay $F_{0,T}$ forward price • Hold ¥1	$F_{0,T}$ per ¥1 $F_{0,T} \times (1+r_¥)^T$ total
Outright purchase	• Borrow S_0 • Pay S_0 for ¥1	• Pay back $S_0 \times (1+r_\$)^T$ • Hold $¥1 \times (1+r_¥)^T$	$S_0 \times (1+r_\$)^T$

Example 19.2 (Protecting against Exchange Rate Changes Using a Currency Forward): Suppose your US company is going to make a purchase in the UK in one year, paid for in British pounds. The purchase will be for £1 million. However, you are worried that the British pound will appreciate in value versus the US dollar—in other words, that it will take more US dollars to exchange for British pounds, and thus the purchase will be more expensive. You decide to enter into a forward contract to protect against this. Let the interest rate in the United States be $r_\$ = 3\%$, the interest rate in the UK be $r_£ = 2\%$, and the current exchange rate be $S = \$2.00 / £$.

(a) What are the details of the forward contract you should enter into in order to lock in an exchange rate? What would be the fair forward exchange rate on such a contract?

(b) Suppose that in one year the pound appreciates to $2.20 / £. At that time, how much would the purchase cost (in dollars) if you had not entered into the forward contract? Compare this to how much the purchase costs (in dollars) with the forward contract in place.

Solution.

(a) You will be purchasing £1 million in one year, so one way to lock in an exchange rate is to agree to buy £1 million in one year for a specified amount of dollars. In other words, you would want to enter into a currency forward where you forward *purchase* £1 million in one year, and you set the number of dollars you will pay for that right now. That number (which is the forward exchange rate) is given by:

$$F_{0,T} = S_0 \times \frac{1+r_\$}{1+r_\pounds}$$

$$= 2.00 \times \frac{1+0.03}{1+0.02}$$

$$= 2.02.$$

So our contract states that, in one year, we will buy £1 million for $2.02 \times \$1$ million $= \$2.02$ million. Note that a completely equivalent way to do this would be to forward sell US dollars for £1 million.

(b) Now the UK pound has done what we feared—it has increased in value versus the dollar. If we had not entered into the forward contract, then we would have had to first convert dollars into UK pounds to make the purchase. It would have thus cost us:

$$\pounds 1 \text{ million} \times \frac{\$2.20}{\pounds 1} = \$2.20 \text{ million}.$$

Overall, we saved $\$2.20 - \$2.02 = \$0.18$ million by using the forward contract than if we had not used it.

> **QUICK CHECK 19.4** Suppose that $r_\$ = 0.06$, $r_\yen = 0.03$, and $S_0 = \$0.01$. What must the forward price of ¥1 be?

19.4.7 The Economic Functions of Futures and Forwards Markets

As the previous examples illustrated, forward contracts are useful tools in risk management. A flour producer, concerned about a rise in wheat prices, was able to lock in a specific quantity and price for a future purchase (without needing to physically store the wheat). Forward and futures contracts can also be used as risk management tools to hedge against costs rising. For example, consider an airline that must purchase fuel for its planes. If concerned about the price of fuel possibly rising (thereby increasing operating costs), the airline could hedge against this risk by entering into a *short* forward contract on jet fuel. Thus, an increase in jet fuel prices will lead to a positive payoff at settlement, potentially offsetting any increase in fuel costs. Financial futures offer a similar hedging capability for firms exposed to risks related to currencies or other financial markets.

Forward and futures contracts also play an important informational role for producers, distributors, and consumers of commodities who must decide how much of a commodity to sell (or consume) now and how much to store for the future. By providing a means to hedge the price risk associated with storing a commodity, futures contracts make it possible to separate the decision of whether to physically store a commodity from the decision to have financial exposure to its price changes.

However, this method of risk management is not without uncertainty. As Figure 19.4 showed, if wheat prices had fallen, then the flour producer would end up paying more than the market price for wheat. Put differently, forward contracts—unlike options—do not offer the holder a choice; the exchange of assets and payments must go through at the settlement of the contract. Forwards therefore do not eliminate uncertainty as options do. However, as we also saw in Chapter 7, the elimination of uncertainty that comes with options has a price and therefore costs money to enter into, in line with **Principle 8:** *Flexibility in financial decisions has value, and the greater the uncertainty, the greater the value.* Forward contracts do not cost anything to enter into.

We have thus far focused on producers, distributors, and consumers of the underlying assets as the main users of forward and futures contracts; these are hedgers who use futures contracts to reduce risk. However, much of the trading of futures contracts is carried on by speculators, who take positions in the market based on their forecasts of the future spot price. Because speculators are not trying to reduce their risk exposure, their motivation for participating in the futures market is to make a profit on their futures trades. Speculators typically gather information to help them forecast prices, and then buy or sell futures contracts based on those forecasts. The same party can be both a hedger and a speculator. Indeed, if a farmer, baker, or distributor chooses not to hedge their price risk in the futures market, then they are speculating on the price of wheat.

Competition among active forecasters in the futures markets will encourage those who have comparative advantage in forecasting wheat prices to specialize in it. For example, suppose you are a wheat speculator. You gather information on all the supply and demand factors that determine the price of wheat, such as total acreage planted, rainfall, production plans of major baked goods producers, and so on, and come up with a forecast of next month's spot price for wheat. Say it is $2 per bushel. If the current futures price for delivery one month from now is less than $2 per bushel, you buy the futures contract (take a long position) because you expect to make a profit from it.

To see this, suppose the current futures price for wheat to be delivered one month from now is $1.50 per bushel. By taking a long position in this futures contract, you lock in a buying price of $1.50 per bushel for wheat to be delivered one month from now. Because you expect the spot price to be $2 at that time, your expected gain is $0.50 per bushel. On the other hand, suppose that the current futures price for delivery one month from now is greater than $2 per bushel (your forecast); say it is $2.50 per bushel. Then to earn an expected profit you sell the futures contract (take a short position). By taking a short position in this futures contract, you lock in a selling price of $2.50 per bushel for wheat to be delivered one month from now. You expect to be able to buy wheat at a spot price of $2 per bushel at that time. You, therefore, expect a gain of $0.50 per bushel.

As a speculator, you take whatever position gives you an expected profit. Of course, because you do not know for sure what the spot price will be one month from now, you could lose money on your futures contract. But you accept that risk in pursuit of what you believe to be expected profit.

Speculative activity in futures markets is sometimes perceived by critics as having no social value. Indeed, it is often portrayed as being the economic equivalent of gambling. However, there are at least two economic purposes served by the activity of speculators that differentiate it from gambling on sports or at the casino. First, commodity speculators who consistently succeed do so by correctly forecasting spot prices. Their activity, therefore, makes futures prices better predictors of the direction of change of spot prices. Second, speculators take the opposite side of a hedger's trade when other hedgers cannot readily be found to do so at the time of a desired trade. As seen, hedgers can be either buyers or sellers, but the demand by hedgers alone on each side may not balance. The activity of speculators as counterparties makes futures markets more liquid than they would otherwise be. Indeed, if only hedgers were permitted to buy and sell futures contracts, there might not be enough trading to support an organized futures exchange. Thus, the presence of speculators is often a necessary condition for the very existence of some futures markets.

19.5 Swaps

A swap is a derivative contract that is an agreement between two parties to exchange (or "swap") a series of cash flows at specified intervals over a specified period of time. The swap payments are based on an agreed principal amount (the notional amount). Like futures and forwards, there is no immediate payment of money and, hence, the swap agreement itself provides no new funds to either party. Functionally, swaps are back-to-back forward contracts, "married" together into one contract, which allows payments to be netted between them and thereby vastly reduces default risk for both parties while making the transactions more efficient. A swap facilitates the hedging of risks, one of the three main techniques of risk transfer (discussed in Chapter 6).

In principle, a swap contract could call for the exchange of anything. In addition to cash flows based on currencies and interest rates, many other items can be and are exchanged through swap agreements—for example, returns on different stock indexes, and even bushels of wheat for barrels of oil. The international swap market began in the early 1980s and has grown rapidly. Most swaps are traded over-the-counter (OTC), not on exchanges. As a result, counterparty risk must be considered with these instruments, and they are typically arranged through large firms such as investment banks and backed up with marked-to-market collateral, in a similar process to futures contracts.

In this section we provide an overview of the mechanics of four widely used types of swaps: interest rate swaps, total return swaps, currency swaps, and credit default swaps.

19.5.1 Interest Rate Swaps

A widely used type of swap is an interest rate swap, which specifies that cash flows between two parties be exchanged based on interest rates. As we showed in Section 19.2, interest rate derivatives comprise the bulk of the notional value of all derivatives. Interest rate swaps are useful instruments for hedging interest rate risk in portfolios, as well as for asset and liability management. For example, a state government that has promised retirement payments to individuals in 30 years may invest a large portion in fixed-income investments with long maturities; however, the value of such investments will likely fluctuate substantially when interest rates change.

In a typical interest rate swap (known sometimes as a "plain vanilla" swap), one side agrees to pay a percentage of the notional (principal) amount based on a *fixed* predetermined interest rate to the other, in exchange for receiving a percentage of the notional amount based on a floating interest rate that can change during a period. The rates that are used are based on various market instruments—for example, Treasury bond rates, the Federal Funds rate, or the Secured Overnight Financing Rate (SOFR).[3] The notional amount is not exchanged, thus allowing each participant to obtain a respective rate of return as if they had invested the notional amount, but without having to actually put in that capital. Such an exchange allows a user to "convert" cash flows that may be volatile, based on a floating rate, into fixed and predictable cash flows.

To illustrate, consider an interest rate swap with a $1 million notional value and a maturity date of three years, with annual payments. The fixed rate is 5% and the floating rate is SOFR plus 10 basis points (bps, i.e., 0.10%) or SOFR + 0.001. Right now ($t = 0$), there is no money that exchanges hands. Each year after that, the fixed payer will pay the other party 5% of the notional amount: $1 million $\times$ 0.05 = $50,000. The floating payer will pay the other party an amount based on whatever the SOFR rate ends up being. In one year at $t = 1$, suppose that the SOFR rate is 4%. Then the payment by the floating payer will be $1 million $\times$ (0.04 + 0.001) = $41,000. Suppose that at $t = 2$, SOFR goes up to 5%; the floating payment will be $1 million $\times$ (0.05 + 0.001) = $51,000. Finally, if SOFR drops to 4.5% at $t = 3$, the floating payment will be $1 million $\times$ (0.045 + 0.001) = $46,000. Figure 19.5 shows the cash flows for each side of the swap.

This example also reinforces the notion that swaps are functionally the same as two back-to-back forward contracts. One forward contract consists of payments based on SOFR (the floating payments)—the long position (fixed payer) receives a payoff based on what SOFR is in the future, while the short position (floating payer) pays that amount. The other forward contract consists of payments based on the fixed rate—the long position (floating payer) receives $50,000 each period in the future while the short position (fixed payer) pays that amount. Each forward has, by definition, a zero initial price/value, and so the swap overall has a zero initial price/value.

---

[3] SOFR is a broad measure of the cost of borrowing cash overnight that is collateralized by Treasury securities, based on actual trading. The rate has replaced the London Interbank Offered Rate (LIBOR) as a common reference rate for floating rate securities.

Time t (in years):	$t=0$	$t=1$	$t=2$	$t=3$
SOFR:		4%	5%	3%
Fixed payer				
Receives floating:	$0	$41,000	$51,000	$46,000
Pays fixed:	$0	−$50,000	$50,000	−$50,000
Net:	$0	−$9,000	$1,000	−$4,000
Floating payer:				
Receives fixed:	$0	$50,000	$50,000	$50,000
Pays floating:	$0	−$41,000	−$51,000	−$46,000
Net:	$0	$9,000	−$1,000	$4,000

FIGURE 19.5 Timeline of cash flows for an interest rate swap. The timeline shows the cash flows for an interest rate swap with a notional amount of $1 million, a fixed interest rate leg of 5%, and a floating rate leg based on SOFR + 10 bps.

The terms of customized interest rate swaps can vary substantially. For example, both sides can be based on a fixed rate or both sides on a floating rate, and the rate can be based on different horizons (e.g., one month, three months, six months, etc.). For example, a state government that has promised retirement payments to individuals in 30 years may invest a large portion in fixed-income investments with long maturities. The value of such investments will likely fluctuate substantially when interest rates change, and a swap based on a 30-year rate can help to hedge this risk. The notional amount can also be different among the periods covered by the swap. For example, consider a three-year real estate project financed by debt. The amount of debt outstanding can vary considerably over the life of the project. A swap used in conjunction with the project can set a different notional amount for different sub-periods of the three-year life of the swap.

> **QUICK CHECK 19.5** Draw the cash flows for both legs of a four-year interest rate swap with a notional amount of $2 million, a fixed rate of 3%, and a floating leg based on SOFR plus 50 basis points. Assume that SOFR is 3% in $t=1$, and increases by 1 percentage point each year after that.

19.5.2 Total Return Swaps

A *total return swap* allows a party to obtain cash flows based on some underlying asset's rate of return. For example, a common total return swap may be based on an equity index such as the S&P 500 index. The side that is long the index receives cash flows as if it had invested the notional amount in the S&P 500 index—thus, if the index goes up, the long position receives cash flows based on the notional amount and its return, including any dividends reinvested into the index (unlike the case with futures). In exchange, the long position pays a percentage of the notional based on an interest rate—this may be a fixed interest rate but is often a floating rate, such as SOFR plus a spread. As with interest rate swaps, the notional amount is not exchanged, thus allowing each participant to obtain a rate of return as if they had invested the notional amount but without having to put in that capital. Total return swaps may be used to hedge investments that are exposed to the underlying asset, or they may be used to gain exposure to that asset.

To illustrate, consider an equity total return swap based on the S&P 500 with a $1 million notional value and a maturity date of three years with annual payments. The position that is long the equity leg receives cash flows that are based on the percentage change in the S&P 500 applied to the notional amount. In exchange, that side pays SOFR plus 50 bps (i.e., 0.50%) of the notional amount each year. Suppose that at:

- $t = 0$, the S&P 500 is trading at 2,000;
- $t = 1$, SOFR is 4% and the S&P 500 is at 2,100;
- $t = 2$, SOFR is 5% and the S&P 500 is at 2,050; and
- $t = 3$, SOFR is 3% and the S&P 500 is at 1,900.

Right now $t = 0$ and no money exchanges hands. At:

- $t = 1$, the long equity leg will pay the floating rate cost of $1 million × (0.04 + 0.005) = $45,000, and receives/pays the percentage change in the S&P 500, (2,100 − 2,000) / 2,000 = 5%, applied to the notional amount: $1 million × 0.05 = $50,000.
- $t = 2$, with SOFR at 5% the long equity leg pays the floating rate cost of $1 million × (0.05 + 0.005) = $55,000, and receives/pays the percentage change in the S&P 500, (2,050 − 2,100) / 2,100 = −2.38%, applied to the notional amount: $1 million × −0.0238 = −$23,800.
- $t = 3$, with SOFR at 3% the long equity leg pays the floating rate cost of $1 million × (0.03 + 0.005) = $35,000, and receives/pays the percentage change in the S&P 500, (1,900 − 2,050) / 2,050 = −7.32%, applied to the notional amount: $1 million × −0.0732 = −$73,200.

This is shown in Figure 19.6.

In this case, the party that is long the equity leg of the swap loses money on net, because it pays the floating rate and also has to pay money in proportion to the drop in the S&P 500 index over this period.

The underlying asset of a total return swap can conceptually be anything that provides a rate of return—in practice, the underlying asset is commonly an equity index (such as the S&P 500, FTSE, Nikkei, etc.), but can also be bond indexes or other indexes. Furthermore, the other leg of the swap need not be based on a fixed income rate such as SOFR—for example, a swap might feature an exchange of cash flows based on the S&P 500 index on one side, and the FTSE 100 index on the other side.

Time t (in years):	$t = 0$	$t = 1$	$t = 2$	$t = 3$
SOFR:		4%	5%	3%
S&P 500 index level:	2,000	2,100	2,050	1,900
Long equity leg ($)				
Receives equity return:	0	50,000	−23,800	−73,200
Pays floating rate:	0	−45,000	−55,000	−35,000
Net:	0	5,000	−78,800	−108,200
Short equity($):				
Receives floating rate:	$0	$45,000	$55,000	$35,000
Pays equity return:	$0	−$50,000	$23,800	$73,200
Net:	$0	−$5,000	$78,800	$108,200

FIGURE 19.6 Timeline of cash flows for an equity total return swap. The timeline shows the cash flows for an interest rate swap with a notional amount of $1 million, a fixed interest rate leg of 5%, and a floating rate leg based on SOFR + 10 bps.

> **QUICK CHECK 19.6** Redraw the timeline of cash flows for both legs of the total return swap, but instead assuming that the level of the S&P 500 increases by 3% each period, and that the floating rate is based on SOFR plus 80 bps.

19.5.3 Currency Swaps

A currency swap involves exchanging cash flows based on two different currencies. It gives companies a useful way to hedge risk related to fluctuations in currency exchange rates.

For example, suppose that you have a computer software business in the United States, and a German company wants to acquire the right to produce and market your software in Germany. The German company agrees to pay you €100,000 each year for the next ten years for these rights. If you want to hedge the risk of fluctuations in the dollar value of your expected stream of revenues (due to fluctuations in the dollar–euro exchange rate), you can enter a currency swap now to exchange your future stream of euros for a future stream of dollars at a set of forward exchange rates specified now. This example also illustrates how the swap contract is equivalent to a series of forward contracts. The notional amount in the swap contract corresponds to the face value of the implied forward contracts.

To illustrate further with numbers, suppose the dollar–euro exchange rate is currently $1.30 per euro and that this exchange rate also applies to all forward contracts covering the next ten years. The notional amount in each swap contract is €100,000 per year. Each year on the settlement date you will receive (or pay) an amount of cash equal to €100,000 times the difference between the forward rate and the actual spot rate at that time. Thus, by entering the swap contract, you lock in a dollar revenue per year.

Suppose that one year from now on the settlement date, the spot rate of exchange is $1.20 per euro. Your counterparty (perhaps a European company in our example) in the swap is obliged to pay you €100,000 times the difference between the $1.30 per euro forward rate and the $1.20 per euro spot rate (i.e., €100,000 × ($1.30 / € − $1.20 / €) = $10,000). Without the swap contract, your cash revenues from the software license agreement would be $120,000 (= €100,000 × the spot rate of $1.20 per euro). But with the swap contract, your total revenues will be $130,000: You receive €100,000 from the German company, which you sell to get $120,000, and you receive another $10,000 from the counterparty to your swap contract.

Now suppose that in the second year on the settlement date, the spot rate of exchange is $1.40 per euro. You will be obliged to *pay* the counterparty to your swap agreement €100,000 times the difference between the $1.40 per euro spot rate and the $1.30 per euro forward rate (i.e., €100,000 × ($1.20 / € − $1.30 / €) = −$10,000). Without the swap contract your cash revenues from the software license agreement would be $140,000 (€100,000 times the spot rate of $1.40 per euro). But with the swap contract, your total revenues will be $130,000. Thus, in the second year, you will probably wish that you did not have the swap contract. But the possibility of giving up potential gains in order to eliminate potential losses is the essence of hedging.

As another example, consider a swap involving yen and dollars. Suppose the swap rate is ¥100 per dollar, and the notional quantity is ¥100 million per year for ten years. (Note that the notional quantity measured in dollars is $1 million.) Let us assume that the US firm is expecting ¥100 million in net revenue from sales in Japan, and the Japanese firm is expecting $1 million in net revenue from sales in the United States.

On each annual settlement date, if the actual spot exchange rate is equal to the swap rate, no money is exchanged between the counterparties. If the spot exchange rate turns out to be less than ¥100 per dollar on the annual settlement date—say ¥95 per dollar—then the Japanese firm pays the US firm enough to compensate for the loss in dollar value of the ¥100 million—that is, $50,000. The

US firm winds up getting compensated for the loss caused by the decline in the dollar value of the ¥100 million in its revenue from sales in Japan. It receives revenue of $950,000 from its operations and $50,000 from the swap contract. If the spot exchange rate turns out to be more than ¥100 per dollar, say ¥105 per dollar on a settlement date, the US firm pays the Japanese firm ¥50. Its total revenue winds up $1 million, consisting of operating revenue of $1.05 million less a loss of $50,000 on the swap. Both firms have used the swap to hedge their revenue against foreign exchange risk.

> **QUICK CHECK 19.7** Calculate the swap's cash flows for the dollar–euro example, assuming that the forward dollar–euro exchange rates are instead $1.05 each year.

19.5.4 Credit Default Swaps

Swaps can also be structured in a way that directly provides insurance to reduce risk. A widely used type of swap that does this is a credit default swap (CDS). In a typical CDS, one party pays a percentage (often based on the SOFR plus a spread) of the notional amount each period to the counterparty. In exchange, that party will receive the notional amount of the swap if there is a credit event for the underlying asset—that is, if the underlying asset triggers the event, such as by defaulting. Thus, CDSs are typically based on the bonds of companies and provide protection if that bond were to default. There is also an active CDS market for sovereign debt—that is, government bonds issued by countries which have the possibility of default. Such swaps can be useful for users that have bonds in their portfolio with some default risk, and want to insure against that risk.

To illustrate, suppose an investment manager has a portfolio that contains $1,000,000 in principal of JunkCo bonds. JunkCo is a company that many believe will go bankrupt in the coming years based on its poor performance—if this happens, the portfolio's value will take a big hit. The manager therefore decides to enter into a CDS contract based on JunkCo bonds, with a notional amount of $1,000,000. As part of the CDS, the manager will pay SOFR plus 450 bps each year.

Suppose, for simplicity, that SOFR ends up staying constant at 3%. Each year, the manager will pay a percentage (SOFR + 450 bps) of the notional: $1 million × (0.03 + 0.045) = $75,000. In each given year, if JunkCo's bonds do not default, then this will represent the only cash flow: The manager will pay $75,000 to the counterparty. However, if JunkCo goes bankrupt and its bonds default (let us assume for simplicity they expire worthless), the manager will receive the notional amount of $1 million. This insures against the loss of the JunkCo bonds in the manager's portfolio.

In practice, the amount paid is also based on the bond's recovery rate. In bankruptcy, a bond will often still pay some portion of the promised principal. The payout of the CDS is adjusted based on this amount. This will also correspond to the actual amount lost for a party using the CDS to insure against bonds that they hold. A contract can also be based on physical or cash settlement. Under physical settlement, the underlying bond is transferred to the CDS writer in exchange for the full notional. Under cash settlement, the writer pays the notional scaled by the recovery rate of the bond.

Credit default swaps provide insurance against credit events, and thus are valuable for risk management. Unlike swaps, the CDS buyer does not make additional payments if the value goes down. In that sense, CDS contracts are structurally more similar to an option contract than other types of swaps. Credit default swaps can be based on individual bonds, as in the above example, indexes of multiple bonds, or on other credit-based assets that have the potential to default. They are also used by speculators, who may enter into a position betting that the pricing of the swap does not properly reflect the probability that the underlying bond will default. The market for CDSs is large, and according to the Bank of International Settlements, as of the end of 2023 totaled more than $8.5 trillion in notional value globally.

19.5.5 Swap Contract Pricing

Swaps cost nothing to enter into, and therefore their price at inception is zero. However, in order for the zero net present value (NPV) to be a fair deal, the swap rate in the contract, which determines the exchange of cash flows in each period, must be set appropriately. The swap rate differs depending on the type of swap—for example, it can be the fixed interest rate versus the floating rate spread (for interest rate swaps), the spread over the specified interest rate (for total return swaps and CDSs), and the forward exchange rate (for currency swaps).

Since a swap can always be broken down into a series of forward contracts, the pricing of swap contracts is an extension of the principles for pricing forward contracts as already discussed in this chapter. For example, consider a yen–dollar currency swap. Suppose it is a contract extending over two years, with a notional principal of ¥100 million. At the end of each of the next two years, one of the two counterparties will have to pay the other the difference between the pre-specified rate of exchange and the actual spot rate of exchange at that time, multiplied by ¥100 million.

The one- and two-year forward rates of exchange between dollars and yen are observable in the forward market. For example, suppose that the one-year forward price of the yen is $0.01 and the two-year forward price is $0.0104. If instead of a swap the two counterparties entered a series of two forward contracts for delivery of ¥100 million each, we can compute the dollar amounts that would have to be paid in each year in exchange for ¥100 million. In the first year it is $1 million, and in the second it is $1.04 million.

But a currency swap calls for a single swap exchange rate to apply in both years. How can the swap rate be determined? Assume that the riskless dollar interest rate is 8% per year, and is the same for one- and two-year maturities. Let F be the swap rate in dollars per yen. The swap contract can be seen as the obligation for one of the counterparties to pay $100{,}000{,}000 \times F$ dollars this year and next year in return for a pre-specified quantity of yen in each of those years.

As we just saw, if the quantities to be paid were set in accordance with the separate one- and two-year forward prices of $0.01 per yen and $0.0104, then the amounts would be $1 million in the first year and $1.04 million in the second year. By Principle 2 (the law of one price), the present value of those payments discounted at the risk-free rate has to be the same as the present value of the payments under the actual swap agreement calling for a single swap rate of F. Thus, F is found by solving:

$$\frac{\$1 \text{ million}}{1.08} + \frac{\$1.04 \text{ million}}{1.08^2} = 100{,}000{,}000 \times F \times \left(\frac{1}{1.08} + \frac{1}{1.08^2}\right),$$

$$F = \frac{\dfrac{\$1 \text{ million}}{1.08} + \dfrac{\$1.04 \text{ million}}{1.08^2}}{100{,}000{,}000 \times \left(\dfrac{1}{1.08} + \dfrac{1}{1.08^2}\right)},$$

$$= \$0.010192307 \text{ per yen}.$$

In the next section, we discuss the general principles that underlie the pricing of all types of derivatives.

19.6 Fundamentals of Pricing Derivatives

To use derivatives, you need to understand how they are valued. We have touched upon how the pricing of certain derivatives works; however, there are many different types, including ones that combine features of more than one type. In this section, we cover the fundamentals of valuing all types of derivatives.

The core principle that underlies the pricing of derivatives is **Principle 2:** *Equivalent assets that can be freely bought and sold will have the same market price.* In particular, a financial asset such as a derivative can be priced by determining what combination of known assets with observable prices will reproduce or replicate the cash flows of the derivative contracts. By Principle 2, the value of that combination of assets must be the same as the value of the derivative, since they produce the same cash flows. Indeed, this was the basis of the forward pricing examples we covered in Section 19.4.

This general approach is referred to as replication. While some derivatives—those with linear payoffs that are simple functions of the known assets that we have prices for—can be replicated by just trading once and holding on to the positions of the known assets, a process known as static replication, the payoffs of many derivatives are not linear, and the replicating positions must change over time. The position in the known assets must change at each point in time by buying and selling them in different amounts to replicate the derivative's payoffs. This process is known as dynamic replication.

The general principle of dynamic replication gives rise to explicit formulas that can be used to value derivatives. To begin, we illustrate how this concept works with options—specifically, how dynamic replication provides the basis for the Black–Scholes–Merton (BSM) formula for pricing options. To show how dynamic replication works, we then introduce the binomial model for pricing options. We conclude with a discussion of how the methodology can be applied to derivatives in general.

19.6.1 Dynamic Replication and the BSM Options Pricing Model

Dynamic replication was originally used to derive the Black–Scholes–Merton (BSM) model (discussed in Chapter 7) for valuing options contracts, which provides a price of an option based on:

- the current price of the underlying asset (i.e., at time $t = 0$), S_0;
- the strike price of the option, K;
- the time to maturity (expiration date) of the option in years, T;
- a measure of the risk of the underlying asset: the standard deviation of its rate of return, σ; and
- the riskless interest rate, r_f.

Note that σ is the standard deviation of the annualized continuously compounded rate of return of the stock. By the same token, the riskless rate r_f is the annualized continuously compounded rate on a safe asset with the same maturity as the option. Given these inputs, the price of a call option can be computed as follows:

$$C_0 = S_0 \times N(d_1) - \frac{K}{e^{r_f \times T}} \times N(d_2), \tag{19.8}$$

where

$$d_1 = \frac{\ln\left(\frac{S_0}{K}\right) + \left(r_f + \frac{\sigma^2}{2}\right) \times T}{\sigma \times \sqrt{T}},$$

$$d_2 = d_1 - \sigma \times \sqrt{T}.$$

In Equation 19.8, note that ln is the natural logarithm, e is the base of the natural log function (approximately 2.7728) to reflect the fact that interest is continuously compounded, and $N(d)$ is the probability that a random draw from a standard normal distribution will be less than d.

The BSM model prescribes a trading strategy to dynamically replicate the payoff of an option based on trading in the underlying asset and a riskless bond. Put differently, one can construct a synthetic call using only an asset and riskless borrowing. By Principle 2 (the law of one price), we know that the price of the call must equal the cost of the synthetic call that we have constructed.

While the BSM model uses an underlying stock and a riskless bond to replicate the payoff of the option, it is important to note that there is no static replicating position over the life of the option. An investor cannot simply buy/sell a stock or riskless bond once and hold on to those positions over the life of the option—since the payoff of the option is nonlinear (it will be either zero or equal to $S_t - K$ in the case of a call), when the underlying stock's price changes then what is expected from the option's payoff changes as well. This means that the replicating position must be adjusted more frequently over time through dynamic trading. The BSM model takes this approach, and assumes continuous trading at every possible point in time. Indeed, this has become a more realistic assumption given that stock trading is open almost all the time (24/7) and today high-frequency trading intervals are measured in milliseconds or microseconds.

The formal mathematics for deriving the BSM model is beyond the scope of this textbook. However, in the following sections we introduce what is known as the binomial model for pricing options to show how dynamic hedging works.

19.6.2 The Binomial Model and Replication: Pricing Options

To begin, we will demonstrate the notion of replication by showing how an option's payoffs can be replicated using two assets: a stock and a riskless asset. We will first do so in a simplified setting with one period (thus using static replication), and in the next section expand to a setting with multiple periods to better illustrate dynamic replication.

The one-period binomial model assumes that the price of stock in the next period can take one of two different values. The model then determines the price of an option based on that stock by using a method of constructing a synthetic call that replicates the call option payoffs, using only stocks and riskless borrowing. As we will show, by the law of one price (**Principle 2**: *Equivalent assets that can be freely bought and sold will have the same market price*), we know that the price of the call must equal the cost of the synthetic call that we construct.

To illustrate, consider a one-year call option with an exercise price of $100. The underlying stock price is now $100 and it can either rise or fall by 20% during the year. Thus, at the option expiration date one year from now, the stock price can be either $120 or $80. If the stock price ends up being $120, the call option would be exercised, resulting in a payoff of $\max(S_T - K, 0) = \max(120 - 100, 0) = 20$ (Equation 19.1). If the stock price ends up being $80, then the call option would not be exercised, resulting in a payoff of $\max(S_T - K, 0) = \max(80 - 100, 0) = 0$. The payoffs to the stock and to the call can be described by the following "tree":

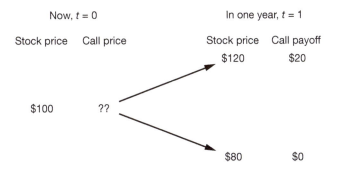

Suppose that the riskless interest rate is 5% per year. Now consider the following portfolio strategy: Buy one share of the stock and borrow money at the riskless rate (i.e., sell a bond) such that you must pay back $80 in one year. The payoff of this portfolio in one year is:

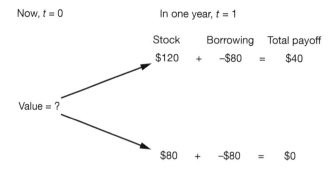

Notice that this portfolio gives a total payoff that is exactly double the payoff of the call option. That implies that if we take *half* of the portfolio, we will match exactly match the payoffs of the call option (and is thus equivalent). By the law of one price (Principle 2), this means that if we find (half of) the *cost* of the portfolio, we will also have found the cost (i.e., price) of the call option.

To find the cost of the portfolio, note that the value of the stock now (at $t = 0$) is $100, and thus the cash flow to buy the stock would be −$100. The borrowed money requires that $80 be paid back in one year, and thus the amount borrowed is the present value of that: $80 / 1.05 = $76.190, a cash inflow. The cash flow to create the portfolio is therefore: −$100 + $76.190 = −$23.810. Since the call is equivalent to half of this portfolio, the cost of the call option would therefore be $23.810 / 2 = $11.905. Put differently, we found that buying half of the portfolio, which is half of a share of stock and borrowing $40 (half of $80), is equivalent to purchasing the call option. We summarize this strategy in Table 19.7.

More generally, if we know the possible future values of the stock in the binomial model, we can calculate the number of shares of stock we need to buy and the amount we need to borrow (i.e., amount of riskless bonds) in order to replicate a call option and determine its value.

Suppose that a stock is worth S_0 right now ($t = 0$), and in one year ($t = 1$) it can either increase to $u \times S_0$ or decrease to $d \times S_0$. Now consider a call option that matures at $t = 1$ with a strike price of K. Let us denote the payoff of the call option if the stock increases to $u \times S_0$ as C_u (mathematically, by Equation 19.1 this will be $\max\left((u \times S_0) - K, 0\right)$. Let us also denote the payoff of the call option if the stock decreases to $d \times S_0$ as C_d. We then will have the following payoffs for the stock and the call option:

Table 19.7 Creating a synthetic call through replication. This table shows the strategy for replicating the payoffs of a call option using a stock and borrowing a riskless bond.

Position	Cash flow $t = 0$	Cash flow, $t = 1$ If $S_T = 120	If $S_T = 80
Call option	?	$20	0
Replicating portfolio (synthetic call):			
Buy half share of stock	−$50	$60	$40
Borrow $38.095	$38.095	−$40	−$40
Total portfolio	−$11.905	$20	0

19.6 FUNDAMENTALS OF PRICING DERIVATIVES

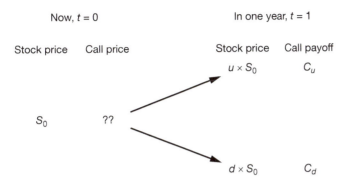

Let Δ denote the number of shares of stock we need to buy and let B denote the present value of any borrowing cash flows (i.e., bond cash flows) that will occur at $t = 1$ (thus $(1 + r_f) \times B$ in one year) that are needed in order to replicate the payoffs of the call option. Put differently, we want to solve for Δ and B such that the call option payoffs equal the payoffs of the portfolio of the stock and borrowing (bond):

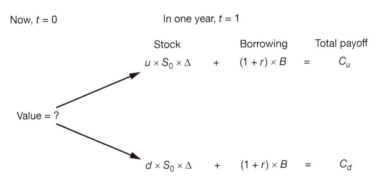

Since the number of shares of stock Δ and the current value of the bond payments B perfectly match the payoffs of the call option, it follows that the value of the stock (the stock price times number of shares Δ) combined with the value of the borrowing payments B will equal the price of the call option:

$$C_0 = S_0 \times \Delta + B. \tag{19.9}$$

We can calculate the values for the number of shares of stock, Δ, as well as the number of bonds, B, that will satisfy the above:

$$\Delta = \frac{C_u - C_d}{(u - d) \times S_0}. \tag{19.10}$$

The fraction of shares of stock needed to replicate the option's payoffs, Δ, is also known as the hedge ratio, and is the range of potential option values divided by the range of potential stock values. For the bond, we have:

$$B = \frac{(u \times C_d) - (d \times C_u)}{(u - d) \times (1 + r_f)}. \tag{19.11}$$

We can then plug these values for Δ and B into Equation 19.9, giving a general formula for the value of a call option in the binomial model:

19 DERIVATIVES

$$C_0 = S_0 \times \Delta + B$$
$$= \frac{1}{1+r} \times \left[\frac{(1+r_f) - d}{u - d} \times C_u + \frac{u - (1+r_f)}{u - d} \times C_d \right]. \tag{19.12}$$

It is important to note that, while this analysis uses an option on a share of stock, the underlying asset of an option need not be a share of stock, but can be *any* traded asset. Thus, the same methodology can be used to price any type of option, using a trading strategy based on the underlying asset that the option is based upon.

> **QUICK CHECK 19.8** Suppose that the underlying stock is more volatile than in the previous example, and it can rise or fall by 30% during the year. Use the binomial model to derive the price of the option.

Example 19.3 (Pricing a Call Option Using the Binomial Model): Suppose that a stock is worth $80 today, and could either increase by 10% or decrease by 10% one year from today. The riskless interest rate is 2%. What is the price of a call option on that stock with a strike price of $82, that matures in one year?

Solution. We can apply the binomial pricing model and formulas above. Note that the fact that the stock may increase or decrease by 10% implies that $u = 1.1$ and $d = 0.9$, and thus the stock price may go up to $u \times S_0 = 1.1 \times \$80 = \$88$ or down to $d \times S_0 = 0.9 \times \$80 = \$72$. This, in turn, means that the payoff of the call option will be (Equation 7.1) $C_u = \max(\$88 - 82, 0) = \$6$ when the stock goes up in value, and will be $C_d = \max(\$72 - 82, 0) = \$0$ when the stock goes down in value. We can now calculate the hedge ratio and value of the bond using Equations 19.9 and 19.10:

$$\Delta = \frac{C_u - C_d}{(u - d) \times S_0}$$
$$= \frac{6 - 0}{(1.1 - 0.9) \times 80}$$
$$= 0.375,$$

$$B = \frac{u \times C_d - d \times C_u}{(u - d) \times (1 + r_f)}$$
$$= \frac{1.1 \times 0 - 0.9 \times 6}{(1.1 - 0.9) \times 1.02}$$
$$= -26.471.$$

Thus, the call option can be replicated via 0.375 shares of stock and borrowing of 26.471 at the riskless rate. The value of the call option is therefore (Equation 19.9):

$$C_0 = S_0 \times \Delta + B = 80 \times 0.375 - 26.471 = 3.529.$$

Note that we could have alternatively used Equation 19.12 directly to solve for the value of the call option:

$$C_0 = \frac{1}{1+r_f} \times \left[\frac{(1+r_f) - d}{u - d} \times C_u + \frac{u - (1+r_f)}{u - d} \times C_d \right]$$
$$= \frac{1}{1.02} \times \left[\frac{1.02 - 0.9}{1.1 - 0.9} \times 6 + \frac{1.1 - 1.02}{1.1 - 0.9} \times 0 \right]$$
$$= 3.529.$$

19.6.3 Dynamic Replication: Pricing Options

The assumption that there are only two possible prices that the stock can have one year from now and that there are no trading opportunities during the year is clearly not realistic—there are many different prices a stock can end up at, and investors can trade many times within the year. To consider a more realistic situation, we can assume that the time interval between successive openings of the market for trading, the *trading interval*, is much shorter than the time until expiration of the option. In fact, we can subdivide the one-year period until expiration into smaller trading intervals, and assume that the stock price can either go up or down by some amount each period. As we assume shorter and shorter trading intervals, the cumulative number of possible values that the stock can attain at the end of the year will increase. This is known as the *multi-period binomial model*, and it permits a dynamic replicating strategy where the number of stocks/bonds traded is adjusted at each time period.

To illustrate, suppose the one-year period is divided into two six-month sub-periods, and assume that the stock price can either go up or down by $10 over each sub-period. Thus, the maximum amount the price can change during the year is $20 up or down. There will now be three possible stock prices at the end of the year—$120, $100, or $80—and the corresponding payoffs for the one-year call option with the strike price of $100 at the end of the year are $20, 0, and 0, respectively (i.e., using Equation 19.1, $C_T = \max(S_T - 100, 0)$, since you would exercise the call option when the stock price is $120, but not when the stock price is either $100 or $80). Figure 19.7 shows the possible values of the stock and option payoffs in the form of a *decision tree*.

For simplicity, assume that the riskless interest rate is 0%. We want to determine the value of the call option now (at $t = 0$). As for the one-period case, we will create a trading strategy using the stock and a bond (i.e., borrowing at the riskless rate) that will perfectly copy the payoffs of the call option. The value of that strategy right now ($t = 0$) will therefore be the value of the call option. To do so, we will work backward from $t = 2$. First, we need to determine how many shares of the stock and how

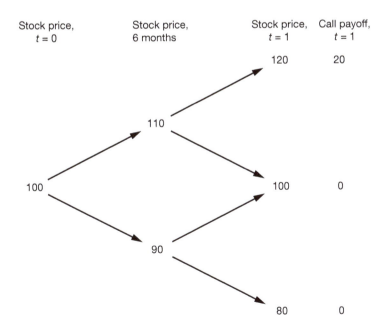

FIGURE 19.7 Decision tree for stock and call option. This figure provides a decision tree showing the price of a stock over time, assuming that it can rise or fall by $10 in each period, and the payoff of a call option with an expiration of one year and a strike price of $100.

much borrowing we need to do to copy the payoffs of the call option in the top-right branch of the tree. This boils down to the same type of problem that we had in the one-period case:

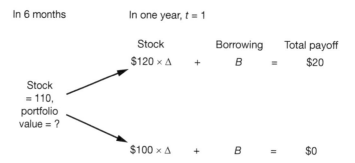

The values for Δ and B above will replicate the payoff of the call option. We therefore have the following equations:

$$120 \times \Delta + B = 20,$$
$$100 \times \Delta + B = 0.$$

Solving for Δ in the above equation yields $\Delta = 1$, and plugging that back into one of the equations and solving for B gives $B = -100$. Thus, by buying one share of stock and borrowing $100 in six months when the stock goes to $110, we will end up in a position where we will match the payoffs of the call option at $t = 1$. The value of this portfolio in six months (when the stock price is $110) will be the value of the call option at that time. This is the product of the stock price and the number of shares, plus the bond borrowing:

$$\text{Value of call in 6 months when } S \text{ is } 110 = 110 \times \Delta + B$$
$$= 110 \times 1 - 100$$
$$= 10.$$

Now consider the bottom-right branch of the tree that connects to when the stock price goes to $90 in six months. The situation here is:

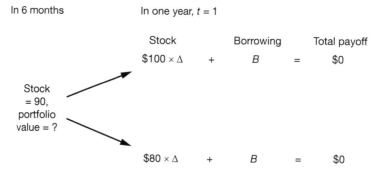

Again, the values for Δ and B above will replicate the payoff of the call option. We therefore have the following equations:

$$100 \times \Delta + B = 0,$$
$$80 \times \Delta + B = 0.$$

Solving for Δ in the above equation yields $\Delta = 0$ and $B = 0$. Thus, when the stock goes to $90, we will end up in a position where we will match the payoffs of the call option at $t = 1$ if we do not buy any shares of stock or borrow any money. The value of this portfolio in six months (when the stock price is $90) will be zero, and this is the value of the call option at that time.

Now, consider the final step in solving for the value of the call option: the actions we would take now (at $t = 0$). The situation here sets the payoffs of the portfolio equal to the potential values of the call option as of six months:

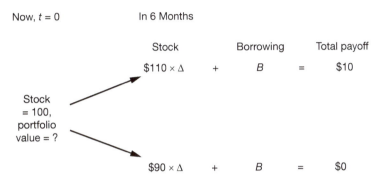

As before, the values for Δ and B above will replicate the value of the call option in six months. We therefore have the following equations:

$$110 \times \Delta + B = 10,$$
$$90 \times \Delta + B = 0.$$

Solving for Δ in the above equation yields $\Delta = 0.5$, and plugging that back into one of the equations and solving for B gives $B = -45$. Thus, by buying half a share of stock and borrowing $45 now (at $t = 0$), we will end up in a position where we will match the payoffs of the call option in six months. The present value of this is the stock price now ($100) times the number of shares, minus the present value of the borrowing amount:

$$\text{Value of call at } t = 0 = 100 \times \Delta + B$$
$$= 100 \times 0.5 - 45$$
$$= 5.$$

Thus, the value of the call option (by the law of one price) must be $5.

Note that the strategy is a *dynamic* one that calls for adjusting the number of shares of stock and the amount of borrowing after six months according to the stock price that materializes at that time. To see this, consider Figure 19.8. The stock price starts out at $100 (point A). Initially, you buy half a share of stock for $50, borrowing $45. Your net cash outlay is, therefore, $5. At the end of the first sixth-month sub-period, the stock price is either $110 (point B) or $90 (point C). If you find yourself at point B, you borrow $55 (to borrow a total of $100) more to buy another half share of stock. If, however, you are at point C, you sell your half share of stock and pay off your debt of $45 with the proceeds. This strategy produces exactly the same payoffs at the end of the year as does the option. Also note that this strategy is completely self-financing subsequent to the original cash outlay—any additional cash needed to fund the strategy is produced by selling stock held in the portfolio. That is, no additional funds are added or withdrawn prior to the option expiration date by the investor.

Greater realism and accuracy can be achieved with this binomial model by subdividing the one-year period into shorter and shorter time intervals. For example, adding a large number of increments and considering moves in the stock price of, say, $0.01 will produce a large decision tree and many possible values of the stock price, and a scenario closer to reality. Binomial option pricing models are widely used in practice. The number of time intervals used depends on the degree of accuracy required in any particular application.

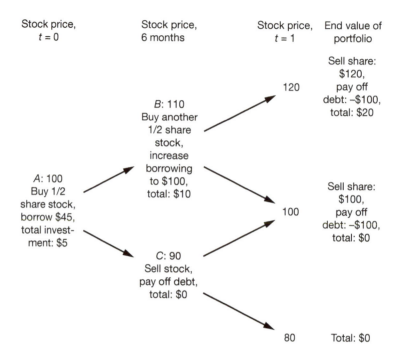

FIGURE 19.8 Decision tree for dynamic replication of call option. This figure shows the trading strategy needed at each point in time in order to replicate the call option with the stock and borrowing.

As the number of trading periods in a fixed calendar time period in the binomial model grows very large, representing movements in the stock price that correspond to fractions or a second or nanoseconds, then the binomial model is the Black–Scholes–Merton (BSM) model. In other words, the BSM model can be derived as a limiting case of the binomial model, and this provides an intuition for the BSM model: The model derives the price of an option by determining the portfolio of the underlying stock and a bond—that is, amounts of the stock and the bond—that are needed to replicate the payoffs of the option at any given moment. The binomial model is thus often used as a numerical methodological tool for solving the BSM model.

> QUICK CHECK 19.9 Suppose in the dynamic replication exercise in this section that the call option had a strike price of $80, and furthermore that the stock price increases or decreases by $20 each period instead of $10. Calculate the price of the call option.

19.6.4 Pricing Any Derivative

The dynamic replication strategy can be used to price any derivative (Merton 1977). To do so, we first determine the payoffs of the derivative, then determine the appropriate replicating portfolio using known assets—which could be a stock and bond or other assets entirely—in order to match the payoffs of the derivative. As noted, the number of periods of the binomial model can be expanded to account for movements in the value of the underlying asset that occur each second or fraction of a second, thus expanding the branches of the decision tree. This can move the model toward greater realism, but also can make the pricing calculations more difficult. For many derivatives, a formula along the lines of the BSM formula can be derived using the underlying intuition of the binomial model in order to calculate the price.

Conclusion

In this chapter we introduced derivative contracts and their more common uses. Options provide the ability to buy (a call option) or sell (a put option) an underlying asset in the future at a preset price. Forward/futures contracts are instruments that oblige one party to the contract to buy, and the other party to sell, a specified asset at a specified price on a specified date. Swaps are financial contracts that commit two parties to exchange the cash flows that come from two different financial assets.

We discussed the mechanics of each of these derivatives, and also discussed some fundamentals of how they are priced. We then introduced a general method of pricing derivatives—replication—that underlies the pricing of all derivatives. We focused on pricing options to illustrate how replication works, and also discussed the application of the methodology to futures/forwards, as well as other derivatives.

In the next chapter we discuss the financial system more broadly. However, we note that financial contracts such as derivatives serve important functions, such as the transfer of risk, and that such contracts can be implemented on a wide scale, even by governments.

Takeaways

- Derivative contracts are financial instruments whose values and payoffs are based on some underlying asset. The most common types of derivatives are options, forwards, futures, and swaps.
- Options are financial contracts that allow the owner a choice in the future. Put options allow the choice to sell an underlying asset in the future, while call options allow the choice to buy an underlying asset in the future (the expiration date).
- Futures and forward contracts allow two parties to exchange an asset for a pre-specified price in the future. With a forward contract, two parties agree to exchange some asset in the future at a price that is specified now. No money is exchanged at the start of the contract. The agreed-upon date is known as the settlement date, while the specified price is known as the forward price.
- Futures contracts are standardized forward contracts that are traded on organized exchanges. The exchange interposes itself between the buyer and the seller, so that each has a separate contract with the exchange, which enhances liquidity and reduces counterparty risk.
- Forward/future prices must be the same as physically buying and storing an asset or commodity, accounting for any storage costs, convenience yields, or dividends that are related to the underlying asset.
- A swap is a type of contract that facilitates the hedging of risks, and consists of two parties exchanging (or "swapping") a series of cash flows at specified intervals over a specified period of time. The swap payments are based on an agreed-upon principal amount (the notional amount). Like futures and forwards, there is no immediate payment of money and, hence, the swap agreement itself provides no new funds to either party.
- There are four widely used types of swaps: interest rate swaps, total return swaps, currency swaps, and credit default swaps.
- The principle of replication can be used to price options and other derivatives, and relies on **Principle 2:** *Equivalent assets that can be freely bought and sold will have the same market price.* Replication works by determining what combination of known assets with observable prices will reproduce or replicate the cash flows of the derivative contracts.
- The single-period binomial model is one method of static replication to price derivatives. The multi-period binomial model is a model of dynamic replication to price derivatives.

Key Terms

Asset-backed security (ABS) 596
Close out 601
Commodity 600
Commodity futures 599
Convenience 603
Convenience yield 604
Cost of carry 605
Credit default swap (CDS) 616
Credit event 616
Currency forward 608
Currency swap 615
Decision tree 623
Derivatives 595
Derivatives market 597
Dynamic replication 618
Dynamic trading 619
Exchange traded 597
Financial futures 599
Floating 596
Forward contracts 596
Forward price 599
Futures contracts 596
Hedge ratio 621
Hedgers 610
Illiquid 601
Initial margin 602
Interest rate swap 612
Long position 599
Margin 602
Margin call 602
Marked to market 602
Multi-period binomial model 623
Notional amount (or notional value) 596
One-period binomial model 619
Options contracts 596
Over-the-counter (OTC) 597
Payoff diagram 600
Replicate 618
Replication 618
Secured Overnight Financing Rate (SOFR) 612
Self-financing 625
Settlement date 599
Short position 599
Speculators 611
Spot price 604
Static replication 618
Stock out 606
Swap 611
Swap rate 617
Total return swap 613
Trading interval 623
Underlying assets 595
Underlying price 599

Key Equations

Call-option payoff	$C_T = \max(S_T - K, 0)$	Eq. 19.1
Put-option payoff	$P_T = \max(K - S_T, 0)$	Eq. 19.2
Relationship between forward and spot prices	$F_{0,T} = S_0 \times (1 + r_f)^T + FV(\text{net storage costs})$	Eq. 19.3
Forward price	$F_{0,T} = S_0 \times (1 + r_f + c - y)^T$	Eq. 19.4
Forward price, dividend-paying asset	$F_{0,T} = S_0 \times (1 + r_f)^T - FV(D)$	Eq. 19.5
Forward price, dividend-paying asset	$F_{0,T} = S_0 \times (1 + r_f - d)^T$	Eq. 19.6

Forward price, currencies	$F_{0,T} = S_0 \times \dfrac{(1+r_\$)^T}{(1+r_¥)^T}$	Eq. 19.7
Black–Scholes–Merton formula	$C_0 = S_0 \times N(d_1) - \dfrac{K}{e^{r_f \times T}} \times N(d_2)$ where $d_1 = \dfrac{\ln\left(\dfrac{S_0}{K}\right) + \left(r_f + \dfrac{\sigma^2}{2}\right) \times T}{\sigma \times \sqrt{T}}$ $d_2 = d_1 - \sigma \times \sqrt{T}$	Eq. 19.8
Call option price, binomial model	$C_0 = S_0 \times \Delta + B$	Eq. 19.9
Hedge ratio, binomial model	$\Delta = \dfrac{C_u - C_d}{(u-d) \times S_0}$	Eq. 19.10
Bonds, binomial model	$B = \dfrac{(u \times C_d) - (d \times C_u)}{(u-d) \times (1+r_f)}$	Eq. 19.11
Value of a call option, binomial model	$C_0 = S_0 \times \Delta + B$ $= \dfrac{1}{1+r_f} \times \left[\dfrac{(1+r_f)-d}{u-d} \times C_u + \dfrac{u-(1+r_f)}{u-d} \times C_d\right]$	Eq. 19.12

Problems

1. Explain why an investor might take an illiquid position in a forward contract rather than using an exchange-traded futures contract.
2. Explain in detail what is meant by a "speculator taking a short position in Australian dollar futures."
3. Suppose you are the manager of a municipal electric company that buys electricity on the wholesale market and distributes it to residential customers and charges by passing on the price of the electricity plus operating costs. Without a fixed-price supply contract, what futures market position could you undertake to hedge the residents' exposure to higher cooling bills this summer if an electricity shortage were to develop?
4. Draw a timeline of cash flows and a payoff diagram from the perspective of both the long and short positions for the following:
    (a) A forward contract where the long position promises to purchase 50 ounces of gold in two years at a price of $100/ounce.
    (b) A forward contract where the long position promises to purchase 100 barrels of oil in one year at a price of $90/barrel.
    (c) A forward contract where the long position promises to purchase one share of stock in one year at a price of $50.

5. Suppose you are a distributor of canola seed and you observe the spot price of canola to be $7.45 per bushel while the futures price for delivery one month from today is $7.60. Assuming a $0.10 per bushel storage cost, what would you do to hedge your price uncertainty?
6. As a speculator observing the futures price for hogs to be delivered in six months, you see a price of $14 per hundred weight while you believe the spot price for hogs will be $15 in six months. Explain what position you should take and how much profit you expect to make. What are the expected cash flows from this position?
7. Suppose that the *Wall Street Journal* gives the following futures prices for gold on September 6, 2025:

Maturity	Oct 25	Dec 25	Jun 26	Dec 26
Futures price ($/oz)	635.60	641.80	660.60	678.70

and the spot price of gold is 633.50/oz. Assume that there is no storage cost or convenience yield. Compute the annual interest rate implied by the futures prices for the corresponding maturities.

8. You are a dealer in kryptonite and are contemplating a trade in a forward contract. You observe that the current spot price per ounce of kryptonite is $180.00, the forward price for delivery of 1 oz of kryptonite in one year is $205.20, and annual carrying costs of the metal are 4% of the current spot price.
   (a) Can you infer the annual return on a riskless zero-coupon security implied by Principle 2 (the law of one price)?
   (b) Can you describe a trading strategy that would generate arbitrage profits for you if the annual return on the riskless security is only 5%? What would your arbitrage profit be, per ounce of kryptonite?
9. Suppose that you buy ten oil futures contracts at a price of $100/barrel. Each contract represents ten barrels. Suppose that the initial margin is 10%, and that in one year the futures price is $90/barrel. How much initial margin did you deposit? What is your gain/loss after one year?
10. Infer the spot price of an ounce of gold if you observe the price of one ounce of gold for forward delivery in three months is $435.00, the interest rate on a 91-day Treasury bill is 1%, and the quarterly carrying cost as a percentage of the spot price is 0.2%.
11. Calculate the implied net storage cost per ounce of gold if the current spot price of gold per ounce is $425.00, the forward price of an ounce of gold for delivery in 273 days is $460.00, the yield over 91 days on a zero-coupon Treasury bill is 2%, and the term structure of interest rates is flat.
12. How would your answer to Problem 11 change if the stock is expected to pay a $1 dividend at the end of the coming year?
13. Suppose the spot price of gold is $200/oz and storage costs are 1% per ounce. The riskless interest rate is 3%.
   (a) What should the forward price of gold for delivery in one year be?
   (b) Suppose instead that the forward price is actually $220/oz. Construct an arbitrage strategy to take advantage of this mispricing.
   (c) Suppose instead that the forward price is actually $180/oz. Construct an arbitrage strategy to take advantage of this mispricing.
14. The forward price for a share of stock to be delivered in 182 days is $410.00, whereas the current yield on a 91-day Treasury bill is 2%. If the term structure of interest rates is flat, what spot price for the stock is implied by Principle 2 (the law of one price)?
15. On your first day of trading in Vietnamese forward contracts, you observe that the share price of Giap Industries is currently 54,000 dong, whereas the one-year forward price is 60,000 dong. If

the yield on a one-year riskless security is 15%, are arbitrage profits possible in this market? If not, explain why not. If so, devise an appropriate trading strategy.

16. Suppose there is a stock that currently trades at $30. Thirty days from now it pays a dividend of $2. A forward contract is trading right now, with a settlement/maturity date of one year from now. The risk-free (annual) rate is 5%. What is the forward price?

17. Suppose the current spot price of a riskless zero-coupon bond with one year to maturity is $94.34 per $100 of face value. If a nondividend-paying stock is currently selling for $37.50 per share:
    (a) What is implied about its forward price for delivery in one year?
    (b) Suppose the actual forward price of the stock for delivery in one year is $40. What arbitrage opportunity exists? Demonstrate the cash flows from the strategy.

18. You observe that the one-year forward price of a share of stock in Kramer, Inc., a New York tour-bus company and purveyor of fine clothing, is $45.00, whereas the spot price of a share is $41.00. If the riskless yield on a one-year zero-coupon government bond is 5%:
    (a) What is the forward price implied by the law of one price?
    (b) Can you devise a trading strategy to generate arbitrage profits? How much would you earn per share?

19. The share price of Ivanov and Associates, a financial consultancy in Moscow, is currently 10,000 rubles, whereas the forward price for delivery of a share in 182 days is 11,000 rubles. If the yield on a riskless zero-coupon security with term to maturity of 182 days is 15%, infer the expected dividend to be paid by Ivanov and Associates over the next six months.

20. The S&P portfolio pays an annual dividend yield of 3%. Its current price is 1,350. The risk-free rate is 5%.
    (a) Suppose you observe a one-year S&P futures price of 1,380. Construct an arbitrage strategy and show that your profit in one year equals the mispricing in the futures market.
    (b) Suppose you observe a one-year S&P futures price of 1,360. Construct an arbitrage strategy and show that your profit in one year equals the mispricing in the futures market.

21. Infer the yield on a 273-day, zero-coupon Japanese government security if the spot price of a share of nondividend-paying stock in Mifune and Associates is ¥4,750, whereas the forward price for delivery of a share in 273 days is ¥5,000.

22. Suppose that the S&P 500 index currently is at 2,000. An investor holds $5,000 in an S&P 500 ETF. The ETF pays dividends of $30 over the year. Suppose that the futures price for a one-year contract on the S&P 500 is 2,100, and the risk-free interest rate is 3%. Construct an arbitrage strategy.

23. A stock has a spot price of $100; the riskless interest rate is 7% per year (compounded annually), and the expected dividend on the stock is $3, to be received one year from now.
    (a) What should be the one-year futures price?
    (b) If the futures price is $1 higher than your answer to part (a), what might that imply about the expected dividend?

24. Your US-based company has negotiated a contract to install an enterprise resource planning (ERP) system for a British firm. The customer has agreed to pay $1 million for the system in exactly 12 months, when the installation will be complete. However, the customer insists on paying in British pounds (GBP). You are worried about the exchange rate risk and want to lock in your US dollar revenues in advance. Assume that the current spot exchange rate for the British pound is $1.8975/GBP. The one-year interest rate in the United States is 5.15%, and the one-year interest rate in Great Britain is 3.55%.
    (a) What type of contract should you enter today in order to lock in your dollar revenues?
    (b) What is the one-year forward exchange rate that is consistent with no arbitrage? Ignore transaction costs for this calculation.

(c) How many British pounds (to be paid in 12 months) do you need to charge the customer to guarantee your company a revenue of $1 million?

25. The spot rate of exchange of Japanese yen for Canadian dollars is currently 113 yen per dollar, but the one-year forward rate is 110 yen per dollar. Determine the yield on a one-year zero-coupon Canadian government security if the corresponding yield on a Japanese government security is 2.21%.

26. Assume the current spot price of South African rand is $0.0995 and the one-year forward price is $0.0997. If the riskless annual dollar interest rate is 5%, what is the implied riskless annual rand interest rate?

27. Suppose that you are planning a trip to England. The trip is one year from now, and you have reserved a hotel room in London at a price of £50 per day. You do not have to pay for the room in advance. The exchange rate is currently $1.50 to the pound sterling.
    (a) Explain some possible ways that you could completely hedge the exchange rate risk in this situation.
    (b) Suppose that $r_£ = 0.12$ and $r_\$ = 0.08$. Because $S = \$1.50$, what must the forward price of the pound be?
    (c) Show that if F is $0.10 higher than in your answer to part (b), there would be an arbitrage opportunity.

28. In the forward market, the one-year and two-year forward prices of the euro are $0.901 and $0.903, respectively. A two-year swap with a notional principal of €1 million is priced when the dollar riskless rate is 5% per year. What is the agreed swap rate?

29. Draw the cash flows for both legs of a five-year interest rate swap with a notional amount of $1 million, a fixed rate of 2%, and a floating leg based on SOFR plus 75 basis points. Assume that SOFR is 1% in $t = 1$, and increases by 0.5 percentage points each year after that.

30. Draw the timeline of cash flows for both legs of a five-year total return swap on the S&P 500 index, assuming that the level of the S&P 500 is currently 2,000 and increases by 5% each year. Assume that the floating rate is based on SOFR plus 80 bps, and that SOFR is flat at 3% each year.

31. Johan works as a systems engineer. In order to finance the purchase of a new house, Johan plans to sell all of his stock in the company he works for in exactly three months. Johan currently owns 10,000 shares of stock and it is currently at $50 per share. Johan needs to put at least half a million dollars into his new $5 million house. After reading many analyst reports, he feels that the stock may go up over the next three months. He thinks that it can either go up to $65 dollars per share or go down further to $40 per share. The current risk-free rate is 4% quarterly APR (meaning 1% over the three months). (For this problem, assume that there are only two possible outcomes for the stock in three months.)
    (a) Johan is quite worried about how he will be able to come up with the money to put down for his house should the stock drop to $40 per share. Johan could take out his money now and save the money for three months. How much money will he have for the house in three months?
    (b) If instead Johan decides to purchase options as insurance for the price of Ericsson stock at $50, what type of option should he purchase? (Be specific—give the maturity, strike, type, and quantity needed.)
    (c) What is the price of the option described in your answer to part (b)?

32. Assume that the future possible paths for the dollar value of a share of XYZ Corp. are accurately described by the binomial model over the next two years shown in Figure 19.9. The riskless rate is zero.

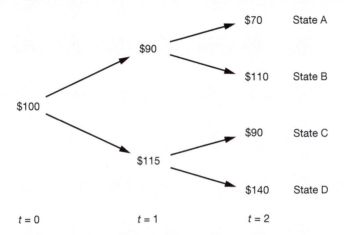

FIGURE 19.9 The binomial model for XYZ Corp.

(a) What is the price of a two-year call option to buy 1,000 shares of XYZ Corp. for $100 per share?
(b) An investment bank is introducing a new derivative called a "Squiggle." Using the replication method, price Squiggle AAA. Squiggle AAA pays $1,000,000 in State A, $500,000 in State B, $100,000 in State C, and $2,000,000 in State D. What are its risk characteristics (i.e., combination of stock and risk-free asset) at $t = 0$ and $t = 1$? Show all of your working.

33. Suppose that the riskless interest rate is 1%. Consider the stock shown in Figure 19.10.

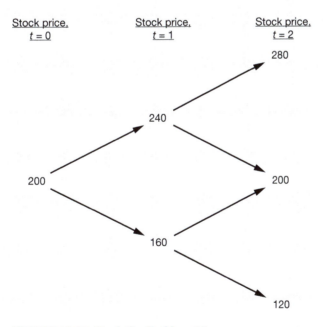

FIGURE 19.10 Stock for Problem 33.

(a) Determine the price of a put option expiring at $t = 2$ with a strike price of $220.
(b) Determine the price of a call option expiring at $t = 2$ with a strike price of $180.
(c) Determine the price, and show the replicating strategy, for a two-year forward contract on the stock with a forward price of $200.

20 THE FINANCIAL SYSTEM AND ITS FUNCTIONS

CHAPTER OVERVIEW

20.1 The Financial System — 636
20.2 Institutions and the Financial System — 637
20.3 The Functional Perspective and the Financial System — 644
20.4 Financial Innovation — 653
20.5 Trust and the Financial System — 656

LEARNING OBJECTIVES

After reading this chapter, you will be able to:

- understand the core functions performed by the financial system;
- explain why financial institutions such as banks, mutual funds, and insurance companies exist and matter;
- better understand the financial system through a unified framework based on the functions that financial institutions perform;
- analyze changes in the financial system over time and across areas, including future financial innovations;
- describe the role of trust in the functioning of financial markets, and understand how possible alternatives to trust may still allow investors and companies to participate in financial markets.

+ You want to work in finance, but a job at a bank doesn't sound interesting to you. Your friend tells you that there are many other types of institutions in the financial system. What are they and what do they do?

+ You have deposited your hard-earned savings in a bank. Your neighbor saw a social media post that lots of people are lining up to get money out of the bank, and warns you that you'll lose all of your money. Does your neighbor have a point? Should you be worried?

- You are a portfolio manager, and your colleague at work tells you in an excited voice about a new financial product that the designer says will change the world and replace traditional stock and bond investments, making them "old news." Your friend says that you should consider allocating a large portion of your portfolio's investments into this new product. How can you assess and understand this new product and whether your friend's suggestion is a good idea?

- You are an investment advisor working with clients to manage their life savings. A new client comes to you and says she wants to work with you because she heard from family that you are trustworthy. Why is this important in the financial industry, and how does it help your business?

- You are in need of a loan to purchase a new car. The car dealership offers you a loan, but your sister says that you should get one from your local bank. Your friend excitedly says that you could use a new online individual-to-individual lending service. Is there a difference to you between these options, and why might the institution you choose matter?

Introduction

In this chapter we explore the global financial system, which encompasses the institutions that carry out the financial decisions of households, firms, and governments. Up to this point in the book, we have presented principles, concepts, models, and analytical tools that are valid no matter what the institutional structure. In most cases the exact details of the institutions did not matter—for example, whether a company borrowed money from a small regional bank or a large international bank. However, in practice, the institutional structure does matter and you need to understand why and how in order to know what tools are best for financial decision making. There is a wide variety of different financial institutions across the globe that make up the financial system, and the nature and details of these institutions vary across different countries and also change over time. How can we understand why there are so many different financial institutions and the roles they play, when they are constantly changing?

The basis for answering this question is **Principle 10:** *The basic functions of a financial system are essentially the same in all economies all over the world, past, present, and future, but the institutions used to perform these functions differ across geopolitical borders and over time.* We begin by providing a high-level overview of how the financial system works, and then go over the key functions that it serves. A critical point is that the specific institutions that comprise the financial system do not matter if there are no frictions, which are forces that prevent "perfect" decision making. These include costs or market imperfections such as taxes, transaction costs, differences in information between participants, and agency costs (we covered the effects of some of these frictions on corporate decision making in Chapters 11 and 13), or behavioral biases—systematic behaviors that people tend to exhibit that can lead to suboptimal decisions (see Chapter 4). Put differently, in the absence of such costs—which has been the implicit assumption in much of the book—financial decisions can be analyzed without the need to consider many of the real-world institutions and limitations people must deal with.

However, when there are frictions, behavioral biases, or other costs, institutional design and the design of products and services can be very relevant. We will see that an understanding of these costs rationalizes the specific institutions we see in the financial system, and we provide a number of examples to illustrate. We then introduce a unified framework, known as the functional perspective, which allows an analysis of both existing products and institutions as well as *new* financial innovations based on the core economic functions they serve. This provides a powerful tool for understanding and forecasting *new* products and institutions that are constantly introduced while economic conditions rapidly change.

20.1 The Financial System

The financial system encompasses the markets, intermediaries, service firms, and other institutions used to carry out the financial decisions of households, business firms, and governments. Financial intermediaries are defined as firms whose primary business is to provide financial services and products. Examples are banks, investment companies, and insurance companies. Their products include checking accounts, commercial loans, mortgages, mutual funds, and a wide range of insurance contracts.

Today's financial system is global in scope. Financial markets and intermediaries are constantly linked, so that the transfer of payments and the trading of securities can go on around the clock. If a large corporation based in Germany wants to finance a major new investment, for instance, it will consider a range of international possibilities, including issuing stock and selling it on the New York or London Stock Exchanges or borrowing from a Japanese pension fund. If it chooses to borrow from the Japanese pension fund, the loan might be denominated in euros, in Japanese yen, or even in US dollars.

The flow of funds is the process of how funds move from one entity to another. The interactions among the various players in the financial system, in terms of how funds flow between each, are shown in Figure 20.1. Funds flow through the financial system from entities that have a surplus of funds (the box on the left) to those that have a deficit (the box on the right), thus allowing claims (such as loans or other financing arrangements) in which the funds from entities with a surplus move to entities with a deficit. For example, a household that is saving a portion of its current income for retirement has a surplus of funds, whereas another household seeking to buy a house and needing a loan to do so has a deficit. A firm with profits in excess of its need for new investment spending is a surplus unit, whereas another firm that needs to finance an expansion and does not have enough cash is a deficit unit. The figure shows that some funds flow from the surplus units to the deficit units through financial intermediaries, such as banks (the lower route in Figure 20.1), whereas some funds flow through the financial markets without going through a financial intermediary (the upper route).

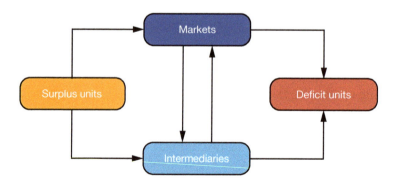

FIGURE 20.1 The flow of funds in the financial system. This figure shows how funds flow through the financial system or markets and intermediaries from entities that have a surplus of funds (the box on the left) to those that have a deficit of funds (the box on the right). Funds also move back and forth between intermediaries and the markets.

To illustrate the flow of funds along the upper route via the markets, an investor (surplus unit) may buy shares of stock directly from a firm (deficit unit) that issues them without using a broker. In most cases, however, a financial intermediary such as a broker or a dealer is involved in the flow of funds, collecting the money from the investor and transferring it to the issuing firm. Most of the funds flowing through the financial system never flow through markets, they go from the surplus units to the deficit units through financial intermediaries.

To illustrate the flow of funds through intermediaries, suppose you (surplus unit) deposit your savings in an account at a bank (intermediary), and the bank uses the funds to make a loan to a business firm (deficit unit). In this case, you do not own a direct claim on the borrowing firm; instead, you have a deposit at the bank. The bank has a claim on the borrowing firm. Your bank deposit has different risk and liquidity characteristics from the loan to the business firm, which is now an asset of the bank. Your deposit is safe and liquid (i.e., you can withdraw the full amount at any time), whereas the loan held as an asset by the bank has some default risk and may be illiquid. Thus, when funds flow from surplus units to deficit units through a bank, the risk and liquidity of the financial instruments created along the way can be substantially altered. But someone has to absorb the risk of the loans—either the bank's owners or the government entity that insures the bank's deposits.

Intermediaries often channel funds into the financial markets, as shown in Figure 20.1. For example, a middle-aged couple saving for retirement (surplus unit) may invest their savings in an insurance company account (intermediary), which then invests its funds in stocks and bonds (markets). Through the insurance company, the couple indirectly provides funds to the firms (deficit units) issuing the stocks and bonds. In addition to channeling funds into the financial markets, some intermediaries obtain funds from the financial markets. A finance company that makes loans to households might, for instance, raise those funds by issuing stocks and bonds in the markets for those securities.

Just as funds are transferred through the financial system, so are risks. For example, insurance companies are financial intermediaries that specialize in the activity of risk diversification and transfer. They collect premiums from customers who want to reduce their risks and transfer it to investors who are willing to pay the claims and bear the risk in return for some reward. Often, funds and risks are "bundled" together and transferred simultaneously through the financial system, so the flow of funds illustrated in Figure 20.1 can also characterize the flow of risks.

> **QUICK CHECK 20.1** A depositor puts $5,000 into a bank account and you take a $5,000 student loan from the bank. Use Figure 20.1 to explain the process of this flow of funds.

20.2 Institutions and the Financial System

In our description of the financial system, institutions "do not matter" because prices and the allocation of resources are unaffected by specific institutional structures. As long as markets are frictionless, we can use almost any convenient financial system and the end result, in terms of prices and risk allocations, will be the same in models with more complex financial systems. This is similar to capital structure choice of firms discussed in Chapter 13—in the absence of frictions, the Modigliani-Miller (M-M) Proposition stated that the choice between debt or equity did not affect overall firm value or risk. Consider a scenario: You want to get a loan to buy a new car and you are deciding what type of institution to get the loan from. There are many different types of institutions that can provide such a loan: the car dealership, your local bank, a loan from a credit card company, an individual-to-individual marketplace, etc. Since each of these institutions are doing the same thing—providing credit for purchasing a car—in the absence of frictions the choice does not matter.

However, in practice, there are many frictions that individuals are exposed to, and these in turn can rationalize the choice of many institutional structures. These may include costs from operating in markets, behavioral biases, or sociological forces. In the example above, you may choose to get the loan from the car dealership because it saves you time and effort. In this section we provide an overview of these frictions, and examples of how various institutional structures can matter given these frictions.

20.2.1 Market Costs and the Design of Institutions

Frictions may include costs that emanate from features of markets, such as contract law, regulations, transaction costs, taxes, differences in information, moral hazard, and transaction costs. We covered many of these in Chapters 11 and 13.

As an example, consider transaction costs, which are the fees and time needed for individuals to conduct transactions in marketplaces. As we discussed in Chapter 17, the theory of portfolio selection tells us that in the absence of transaction costs, fully informed individuals would not have a preference between picking individual assets or picking a prepackaged optimized portfolio. But in practice individuals often lack the expertise and time to perform the necessary portfolio calculations. Thus, the division of such labor—delegating these tasks to intermediaries—can be optimal for individuals. In Chapter 17 we discussed how intermediaries can efficiently perform such a task by offering a "menu" of risk and expected return combinations to customers and letting them choose, without needing to know specific customer preferences.

This insight justifies the existence of mutual funds, the investment intermediaries that specialize in producing optimized portfolios by gathering the information needed (expected returns, standard deviations, and correlations among the full set of risky assets) and combining them in the right proportions (the efficient portfolio frontier) to offer to customers. Because of economies of scale in gathering information, processing it, and trading securities, the transaction costs for mutual funds are significantly lower than for individuals, so individuals tend to diversify by holding mutual funds rather than trading in the individual securities themselves.

This addresses the issue of expectations in the Capital Asset Pricing Model (CAPM), discussed in Chapter 18, by offering a justifying interpretation for its standard assumption of homogenous beliefs: namely, investors in mutual funds in effect "agree to agree" with the estimates of means, variances, and covariances of the professionals who manage those funds. Since professional investors tend to use similar data sets and methods of statistical analysis, their estimates may be more homogenous than would otherwise be the case if individuals were gathering data and making forecasts directly for themselves. If this view is correct, then as transaction costs continue to decline, financial intermediaries will produce more complicated-to-produce products that combine features of investments and insurance. They will be customized to provide easy-to-understand solutions to complex risk management needs of households.

20.2.2 Behavioral Biases and the Design of Institutions

Even in the absence of costs that come from features in marketplaces, we often see that, in the real world, people do *not* make the decisions that are deemed "correct." Sometimes these decisions stem from cognitive mistakes—mistakes that result from a lack of knowledge or faulty logics. Such mistakes can be corrected through education or technology. However, sometimes even when our analysis tells us the logical course of action, we may not do it. Consider the issue of increasing fitness through exercise—that is, regularly going to the gym. People spend lots of money to learn how to improve their physical health. They know that lack of exercise is unhealthy, they sign up for a gym membership, and then never find the time to go even though they know they should. So rational thinking leads to the right conclusion, but many of us do not manage to implement it. An example of a common financial behavior pattern that is almost surely not rational is borrowing at high interest rates on credit cards when cheaper sources of credit are available. These factors—often called behavioral biases—are the subject matter of behavioral science, the study of how real people actually behave and make choices, which includes the disciplines of psychology and sociology. Thus, even when finance theory identifies the optimal decision to be made, an individual may steer away from the optimal decision. Institutional design can reduce costs and steer people toward the optimal decisions that financial models predict rational people should make.

To illustrate how institutional design can influence optimal decisions, consider the example of the design of retirement plans for employees. When an employee joins a company and is eligible to get retirement benefits, the employee typically has to choose whether and how to participate. In companies that have a voluntary retirement savings plan, employees have a choice about whether to participate (opt in) or not (opt out). The default option is what happens if an individual decides *not* to make a choice—that is, if an employee does not make a decision, whether the employee automatically opts in or opts out. From a rational finance perspective, the default options should *not* matter and are entirely equivalent. However, in practice, it makes a big difference what is the default—having the default option being to opt in results in substantially higher participation rates.

This example illustrates the concept of framing and how it can affect financial decisions. Framing of decisions refers to how the choice problem is presented and what alternatives are presented to individuals. It has been well documented through studies that how one presents logically equivalent choices can have a powerful influence on the choices that are actually made, even though there is no logical reason the presentation should do so.

There are many different types of financial decisions where framing can have an effect, beyond the previous example of default options. For example, academic research has shown that *how* information about past mutual fund performance is presented—such as the format of performance and whether information about funds is provided individually or in the context of an investor's existing portfolio—can affect the choice of mutual funds to invest in. For example, suppose that a mutual fund has historically had a high annual rate of return of 30%, but also a high annualized volatility of returns of 70%. Presenting an individual first with information about the high rate of return and then the volatility may push them toward viewing the fund more favorably (as a "high-return" fund), whereas presenting information on the high volatility first may push them toward viewing the fund less favorably (as a "high-risk" fund).

As another example of framing, consider the following situation. Suppose you are investing some cash for the next year and choosing between two (insured and thus risk-free) accounts offering fixed interest rates. The first account offers a fixed nominal interest rate of 5%, and the second offers a fixed real interest rate (i.e., adjusting for inflation) of 2%. Let us call the second account an inflation-linked (IL) account. Suppose that there is a lot of uncertainty about the rate of inflation over the next 12 months, but you expect that it will be 3%. There is an important financial difference between these two accounts: The first is risk-free in nominal terms, and therefore it is risky in terms of consumption—put differently, although you are guaranteed to have a certain amount of money in one year ($1.05 for every dollar invested), that amount may allow you to purchase *fewer* goods than before if the inflation rate is higher than 5%. The IL account is risk-free in terms of consumption—it will allow you to purchase the equivalent of $1.02 of today's goods—but it is risky in terms of dollars since the amount of cash you will get will depend on what the inflation rate actually ends up being. Put differently, the IL account is a perfect inflation hedge, while the unhedged nominal account is exposed to the risk of inflation. How should the choice between these two accounts be framed? Should it be presented in consumption units or in dollars? This is an accounting question, which is logically distinct from the question of whether or not to hedge the risk (which depends on your individual investment goals and risk preferences). Yet in practice the accounting frame heavily influences the actual choice.

Institutional design can help to correct some of the pitfalls of framing. In the example of retirement savings, making participation be the default option can be a solution to low participation rates.

However, financial decisions often require an active choice by the individual, and it may not be possible to set an optimal choice as a default option. For example, beyond default participation in a retirement savings plan, individuals typically have the choice of savings plan to choose from—that is, different mutual funds or other types of investments. The optimal choice depends on the individual's own personal risk preferences or life cycle goals, and thus it is difficult to choose a default option which is right for everyone. In such cases, the sheer amount of information available can overwhelm individuals, leading to choices based on heuristics or biases. In other cases, a *menu* of a limited number of choices, say ten different mutual funds, is provided. In such cases, due to framing, the specific information provided and choices can be critical for allowing the individual to make an informed or "optimal" choice of mutual fund. Box 20.1 discusses this issue and how one can think about the appropriate design of such a system.

> **QUICK CHECK 20.2** Suppose a company you have invested in experiences a drop in its stock price. Your investment advisor explains why this happened. How might this drop be framed in a way that makes your investment's performance seem either good or bad?

Box 20.1 Simple for the Individual: A Learning-by-Doing User Interface That Never Changes

The choice between individual and financial retirement plans and services is an important one for lifetime financial planning, but it can be a difficult choice for individuals to make. For an individual to make the "optimal" decision can be costly—it requires processing a vast amount of information and solving a complex optimization problem. The design of products and management of information provided to individuals can help to reduce these costs. As forecast by Robert Merton in 2012, improvements in technology and the introduction of new financial products have helped individuals with low knowledge or interest in finance succeed in their retirement goals.

In a "keep it simple for the individual" system, all the individual sees is a single page on a screen with choices and the necessary information to make those choices. All they need is the person's target income per year, which is the amount that allows them to achieve the goal of a proper retirement. A good interface will also provide a measure of the chance of reaching that goal conveyed in a simple, intuitive fashion—for example, as a speedometer or dial—and a minimum income (a floor) that may be guaranteed. The only other pieces of information needed on the individual's page are the contribution rate, how much is being saved, and the individual's retirement date. While other information, such as rates of return, are important factors in achieving success, they are not provided because they are not meaningful information for the individual's choice. When this kind of interface functions correctly for an individual, they can see if their target income and actions in three areas can improve their lot—save more, work longer, or take more risk in investments (to achieve a higher rate of return, at the cost of a potentially lower chance of reaching their goal). Those are thus the only three decisions the individual needs to think about in the context of retirement. And they are meaningful choices because if the individual increases their savings, their paycheck is going to be smaller. If they decide to work longer, they are going to have to keep working longer than planned.

Of course, making the product simple does not mean that it should be at the cost of doing an effective job. If complexity is needed for the functioning of the product, then that is fine;

however, this complexity should be with the producer (or professionals), and not be a burden to the customer. A useful design principle is that the product or service only requires what the user *already knows* in order to use it. In that case there is no need for financial education of the individual.

Retirement products are being designed and sold to individuals with these principles in mind (see, e.g., Muralidhar and Merton 2020). An example is a "retirement security bond" (RSB). An RSB is a government bond that mimics the pattern of payments of a pension—payments are deferred until a specified starting date and made until a specified ending date. The payouts are indexed to overall per-capita consumption, which protects the holder against risks related to changes in the standard of living. The RSBs are issued as a series with different annual starting dates, which individuals can purchase directly from the government based on traded prices. An online system makes it very straightforward for an individual to determine how many RSBs are needed to meet their goal, and also how close they are to their goal. Overall, RSBs exemplify the design principles described above: It is simple for the customer to use, requires only two inputs from the customer (which RSB to buy based on the date of retirement, and how many to buy based on the goal for retirement), is based on sound financial principles, and does not require financial literacy. An RSB called the RendA+ was officially implemented by the government of Brazil in 2023 as an alternative retirement solution for individuals.

However, whereas provision of simple answers to these important questions may be what the individual wants, providing those answers is not simple for either the producer or the regulator. The internal systems are complex and they continue to evolve, but in order to ensure nonexperts can still use the financial systems available for retirement success, it is important to maintain a clear and familiar face for investors.

Sources: Merton, R. C. (2012). Observations on financial education and consumer financial protection (corrected January 2013). In Bodie, Z., Siegel, L. B., and Stanton, L. (Eds.), *Life-Cycle Investing: Financial Education and Consumer Protection.* Charlottesville, VA: CFA Institute. Merton, R. C. (n.d.). Notes, 15.466 Functional and Strategic Finance. Course Notes. Muralidhar, A., and Merton, R. C. (2020). Selfies: a new pension bond and currency for retirement. *Journal of Financial Transformation*, 51: 8–20.

20.2.3 Sociological Effects and the Design of Institutions

The previous section described various individual psychological effects, and how they can influence choices in financial decision making and generate inefficient outcomes. In this section we describe an important sociological effect that can potentially create inefficient outcomes. An important sociological concept that has wide applicability in financial decisions is known as the self-fulfilling prophecy. The self-fulfilling prophecy was coined and popularized by American sociologist Robert K. Merton (see Merton 1948), and refers to a publicly expressed prediction or prophesy that would be false and not occur in its absence, but which ends up being true or fulfilled as a consequence of the prophecy. Put differently, the public prophecy itself induces people to act in a way that ends up causing it to be realized, when it would otherwise not have been realized. The difference between this sociological effect and the previous psychological effects is that collective action can lead to inefficient outcomes even if each and every individual behaves in a manner that their available information implies is completely rational.

A prime example of the power of the self-fulfilling prophecy in finance is bank runs. A bank run occurs when many people simultaneously try to withdraw their money from a bank, resulting in

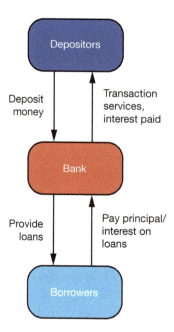

FIGURE 20.2 A simple model of a bank. This figure shows the basic model of how a bank works. Depositors put their money into a bank through checking and savings accounts, and the bank provides loans to borrowers with a portion of that money.

there not being enough money left in the bank for everyone to withdraw what they are owed. To understand how this works, consider a basic model of how a bank operates, presented in Figure 20.2. Banks receive money from depositors—that is, people putting money into either checking or savings accounts at the bank. However, banks do not simply keep all of the money that is deposited in cash (or "liquid" assets which can be rapidly converted to cash). They keep some portion of the money at the bank to meet typical withdrawal demands from bank accounts, but then will lend the rest of the money out to borrowers via loans, in exchange for interest/principal payments in the future.[1] Loans are assets of the bank but cannot be converted into immediate cash, and the bank must wait until the scheduled payments of interest and principal are made to receive cash.

To illustrate a bank run, suppose that your local bank has $1,000,000 in total deposits, but it is known that it only keeps $100,000 in cash on hand because that has been more than enough to meet the deposit needs it has experienced before. Importantly, the bank itself is "healthy" and solvent—the value of its assets exceeds the value of its liabilities by a material margin—and the individuals who use the bank also know that it is solvent. Suppose one day an anonymous post is publicly made on social media saying "the bank is out of money!" How might the individuals that use the bank react?

---

[1] The loans, because they represent promised repayments by borrowers, are assets of the bank. However, while loans can potentially be sold for equal or more than the amount of cash demanded, they may be "illiquid," which means that they cannot be easily or readily sold in the market (in contrast to "liquid" assets), or if they can be sold, it may not be possible to sell them for their full value. An example of such a circumstance is a "fire sale," which is a situation in which an illiquid asset has to be sold immediately or too quickly, and the price as a result becomes materially lower than what one would receive with adequate time to find appropriate buyers. Having to sell an asset quickly will thus result in receiving a materially lower price, and thus it is also possible for a bank with "adequate" assets (i.e., "solvent") to meet its promised payments to suddenly become insolvent.

Table 20.1 **Decisions of individuals leading up to a bank run.** This table provides the decisions that you face relative to the other individual, and the outcomes based on those choices.

		Other individual	
		Don't pull out money	*Pull out money*
You	*Don't pull out money*	Bank survives	You lose your money, other saves their money
	Pull out money	You save your money, other loses their money	You and others (maybe) get money; bank run

Even if all individuals are completely rational and know for certain that the post is erroneous and the bank is solvent, they will still get in line to pull out their money from the bank. Table 20.1 depicts the choices rational individuals face in this situation. Suppose for simplicity that there are just you and one other individual. If neither person pulls out their money, then the bank will be completely fine (top-left quadrant). But if you decide to not pull out your money and the other person does (top-right quadrant), you will be last in line—the bank will not have enough money left to give you what you are owed, and your savings will go down the drain! The other rational individual faces the exact same situation (bottom-left quadrant)—if they don't pull out their money and you do, they will be left without anything. As a result, it is a dominant strategy—a strategy that is better than other strategies no matter how others react—to pull out your money. Each and every individual will get into line and take out their money, and in so doing help to ensure that the bank will fail—the erroneous prophecy, which would not have otherwise occurred, thus becomes fulfilled, leading to a bank failure in which depositors will not receive what they were promised. Note that this outcome obtains even when each individual is totally rational—it does not depend on any behavior dysfunctions, and furthermore does not depend on individual knowledge or information (indeed, in this example each individual knows that the bank is in good financial health).

The social outcome of a bank run can be catastrophic, as it can cause banks to fail, resulting in sharp reductions in lending to individuals and businesses and people losing their savings. (Furthermore, individual customers of a bank will lose valuable services such as check-writing, financial advice, the ability to use ATMs, etc.; see Merton and Thakor 2019). Bank runs have occurred at various points in time during significant economic events around the world, such as the Great Depression and the 2008–2009 global financial crisis. Well-known examples of bank runs include the Toyokawa Shinkin Bank in Japan in the 1970s, widespread bank withdrawals (precipitating a reform known as Corralito) in Argentina in 2001, Northern Rock in the UK in 2007, and Silicon Valley Bank in the United States in 2023. The importance of the self-fulfilling prophecy in the case of a bank run is that it becomes rational for an individual to take out their money even if they are fully informed and there is nothing actually wrong with the bank. After all, you can always put your money back into the bank later at no penalty if somehow the bank run does not occur. The bank run in this case would not have happened without the effect of the public prophecy that it would fail. Indeed, with bank runs, the triggering event may be something *completely* unrelated to the financial health of the bank.

The prevalence of self-fulfilling prophecies in finance provides a role for institutional design to prevent some of their deleterious consequences. In the case of bank runs, governments can provide a means for coordinating collective action. The governments in many countries provide deposit insurance, which is a guarantee that the government will step in and cover any shortfall if a bank is unable to meet deposit claims. In the United States, deposit insurance is provided by a government entity known as the Federal Deposit Insurance Corporation (FDIC), which guarantees that the federal government will provide money to depositors, up to $250,000, that they would otherwise lose in their deposit accounts due to a bank failing. The deposit insurance agency goes by other names in different countries, such as the Financial Claims Scheme (FCS) in Australia, the Deposit Insurance Corporation of Japan, and the Corporation for Deposit Insurance (CODI) in South Africa. This guarantee by the federal government helps solve the problem of bank runs because depositors understand that they need not hurry to the bank to withdraw their money "just in case" for fear of losing it—the government will provide that money in the worst-case scenario. A guarantee such as deposit insurance has significant value not only in terms of promoting the stability of the financial system but also to individuals, and helps to reduce the uncertainty that can be introduced by self-fulfilling prophecies. Because of this, they can be analyzed as a put option—the government pays money in the event that the bank becomes insolvent. Thus, the value and effects of such guarantees can be analyzed using the option tools we introduced in Chapter 7, and this further reinforces **Principle 8:** *Flexibility in financial decisions has value, and the greater the uncertainty, the greater the value.*

Deposit insurance and related guarantees by government agencies have been shown to help prevent bank runs and are an example of how institutional design can solve some of the negative effects of behavioral biases. Other types of institutional features have been implemented and proposed to help with related issues. For example, there are many other types of bank regulations—stress tests by regulators, asset-holding requirements, risk requirements, and others—that are designed to keep banks healthy and prevent them from being in a situation that is vulnerable to bank runs. In addition, governments often monitor financial markets for potential bubbles, and may act if they feel that particular markets are in a bubble in order to avoid sudden price crashes. For example, central banks—institutions that are responsible for setting interest rates and managing the money supply of a country, such as the US Federal Reserve, Bank of Japan, and Swiss National Bank—increase interest rates through monetary policy in order to "cool down" growth in asset prices, and government agencies have the ability to affect prices and supply/demand in particular markets such as the housing market.

> **QUICK CHECK 20.3** Suppose you are invested in the stock of a tech company, and you observe a group of investors selling the stock. How might this lead to a self-fulfilling prophecy?

It should be noted that while the above discussion of runs focuses on a specific institution—banks—runs can also occur against any institution which promises a payment or service in the future. These can include pension funds, mutual funds, and insurance companies, among others. This highlights that the concepts described above are not specific to a particular institution.

20.3 The Functional Perspective and the Financial System

There are a wide range of different frictions that individuals are exposed to. Since institutions matter when there are frictions, we can expect to see many different types of institutions in financial markets to alleviate the impact of these frictions. In practice, financial institutions generally differ across geopolitical borders, and also change over time in response to changing frictions. Even when the names of institutions are the same, the functions they perform often differ dramatically. For example, banks in the United States today are very different from what they were in 1928 or in 1958, and banks in the United States today are different from institutions called banks in the Middle East or in Asia. The wide variety of differences between institutions—and the fact that they are constantly changing—provides a challenge for understanding the financial system.

In this section we will examine a unifying conceptual framework for understanding how and why financial institutions differ across geopolitical borders and change over time (Principle 10). The key element in the framework is its focus on functions—core economic goals or purposes that a product or institution aims to address—rather than on institutions as the conceptual "anchor." Hence, we call it the functional perspective (Merton 1993, 1995; Bodie and Merton 1995). It rests on two basic premises:

- Financial functions are more stable than financial institutions—that is, functions do not change and are the same everywhere and over time, while institutions do change substantially and frequently.
- Institutional form follows function—that is, innovation and competition among institutions ultimately result in greater efficiency in the performance of financial system functions.

The power of the functional perspective is that we can use it to analyze and understand the rationale for new financial innovations that have not been introduced yet. Put differently, rather than a focus on the details of financial innovations—which may be "new" or unfamiliar—the focus is on core functions that do not change, and how the innovations serve those functions.

To better understand the functional perspective, we begin by describing exactly what the functions are that the financial system performs. We then discuss how the functional perspective can be used to analyze specific components of the financial system, ranging from a broad financial ecosystem to individual financial products.

20.3.1 Functions of the Financial System

There are six basic or core functions of the financial system:

1. To provide ways to *transfer economic resources* through time, across borders, and among industries.
2. To provide ways of *managing risk*.
3. To provide ways of *clearing and settling payments* to facilitate trade.
4. To provide a mechanism for the *pooling of resources* and for the *subdividing* of ownership in various enterprises (i.e., shares).
5. To provide *price information* to help coordinate decentralized decision making in various sectors of the economy.
6. To provide ways of *dealing with the incentive problems* created when one party to a transaction has information that the other party does not or when one party acts as agent for another.

Function 1: Transferring Economic Resources across Time and Places

A financial system provides ways to transfer economic resources through time, across geographic regions, and among industries. Many of the funds flows shown in Figure 20.1 involve giving up something now in order to get something in the future, or vice versa. Student loans, borrowing to buy a house, saving for retirement, and investing in production facilities are all actions that shift resources from one point in time to another. The financial system facilitates such transfers of resources over time.

Without the opportunity to take out a student loan, for example, many young people whose families do not have the means to send them to college might have to forgo a higher education. Similarly, without the ability to raise capital from investors, many businesses might never get started.

In addition to facilitating the shifting of resources through time, the financial system plays an important role in shifting resources from one place to another. At times the capital resources available to perform an activity are located far from where they are most efficiently employed. Households in Germany, for example, may be generating capital through saving that could be more efficiently employed in China. The financial system provides a variety of mechanisms for facilitating the transfer of capital resources from Germany to China. One way is for German citizens to invest in shares issued by firms located in China. Another is for German banks to make loans to those firms.

The more complex the economy, the more important is the role of the financial system in providing an efficient means for shifting resources across time and place. Thus, in today's global financial system, a complex network of markets and intermediaries makes it possible for the retirement savings of Japanese workers to be used to finance the house purchased by a young couple in the United States.

Innovation that allows scarce resources to be shifted over time or place from a use with a relatively low benefit to a use offering a higher benefit improves efficiency. For example, suppose that all families were constrained to invest their savings only within the family. In that case, Family A could earn a rate of return of 2% per year on its savings, at the same time that Family B has opportunities to earn a rate of return of 20%. Efficiency is increased by creating an investment company to collect Family A's savings and lend them to Family B.

Function 2: Managing Risk

A financial system provides ways to manage risk. Just as funds are transferred through the financial system, so are risks. For example, insurance companies are financial intermediaries that specialize in the activity of risk transfer. They collect premiums from customers who want to reduce their risks and transfer it to investors who are willing to pay the claims and bear the risk in return for some reward.

Often funds and risks are "bundled" together and transferred simultaneously through the financial system so that the flow of funds illustrated in Figure 20.1 can also characterize the flow of risks. Figure 20.3 shows this. For example, suppose you want to start a business and need $100,000 to do so. You have no savings of your own, so you are a deficit unit. Let us assume that you convince a private investor (a surplus unit) to directly provide you with $70,000 in equity capital in return for a 75% share of the profits of the business, and you convince a bank (a financial intermediary) to lend you the other $30,000 at an interest rate of 6% per year. This flow of $100,000 would appear as a flow of funds from others to you. (For simplicity, we leave markets out of the picture since the investor is directly providing funds, although in reality all participants would interact with financial markets.)

What about the risk of business failure? In general, it is the equity investors who absorb the risk of business failure. Thus, if your business venture goes sour, the private investor may get none of their $70,000 back. However, the bank may also face some risk that it will not get all of its principal and interest. For example, suppose that at the end of a year the business has a value of only $20,000. Then the

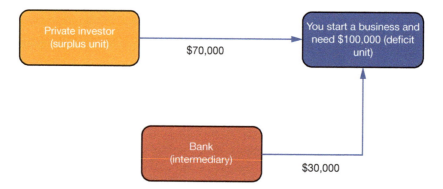

FIGURE 20.3 The flow of risk through the financial system. You want to start a business and need $100,000 (deficit unit, top-right). A private investor directly provides you with $70,000 in capital (surplus unit, top-left). A financial intermediary lends you the other $30,000 (bottom).

equity investors lose all of their investment of $70,000, and the bank loses $10,000 of the $30,000 it has lent to you. Thus, lenders share some of the business risk of the firm along with the equity investors.

Although funds and risks often come bundled together, they can be "unbundled." For example, consider the $30,000 loan from the bank to your business. Suppose the bank requires that you get other members of your family to guarantee the loan. The bank thereby transfers the risk of default from itself to your relatives. The bank is now providing you with $30,000 in funds at minimal risk to itself, and the risk of the loan has been transferred to your relatives.

Many of the financial contracts that we observe in the world of finance serve to transfer risks without transferring funds. This is the case with most insurance contracts and guarantees, and it is also the case with derivatives that we covered in previous chapters, such as futures, swaps, and options. The structure of even simple contracts like Treasury bonds can change in response to addressing the function of managing risk, as described in Box 20.2.

Box 20.2 The Return of the 30-Year Treasury

We often take for granted the current set of financial securities that are available to us as investors. But even common securities that investors are used to being able to buy and sell were not always around, and had to be introduced. Indeed, in the future there will certainly be financial securities that are widely traded that are not around today. It is therefore informative to understand how and why now-common financial securities came to be, which has potentially important implications for understanding future financial innovation.

Take US Treasury bonds with a 30-year maturity, for example. The US government, as with many governments, has a substantial amount of debt (over $33 trillion as of 2023). Since the 2000s, the US government's debt has been rising consistently, but in the second half of the 1990s and into 2001 the debt was actually falling. During that period the federal government's budget surplus prompted the US Treasury's decision to stop issuing 30-year Treasury bonds in October 2001. The vacation didn't last long: As the government quickly returned to fiscal deficits the 30-year bond was called back into service less than five years later.

The maturity structure of the government's debt can have interesting implications. On the one hand, long-term bonds allow the government to lock in a particular interest rate and avoid the costs associated with reissuing debt. With interest rates at historically low levels, and long-term rates only slightly higher than short-term rates, long-term borrowing has been particularly appealing in recent years. On the other hand, the government's motivations interact with the needs of the private sector. Government debt competes with private debt for available funds. At the same time, Treasury bonds act as a liquid, risk-free benchmark to the bond market, aiding in the pricing of private sector issues.

Certain investors, especially pension funds, may have benefited the most from the return of the 30-year Treasury. Pension funds had been holding two-thirds of their assets in equities. Since their liabilities, corresponding to the benefits they are obliged to pay retirees, are more closely aligned with long-term debt, pension funds can reduce their risk exposure by reallocating their asset portfolios to the new long-term bonds. The government is expected to encourage pension funds to do exactly that. Pension plans nationwide are estimated to be insolvent by nearly half a trillion dollars, a burden that could fall on the Pension Benefit Guaranty Corporation, a federal entity that insures pensions.

The size of the public debt matters, but its structure also has important implications for bond markets and the private sector.

Source: The Economist (2006). Long ranger. 2 Feb. www.economist.com.

Function 3: Clearing and Settling Payments

An important function of the financial system is to provide an efficient way for people and businesses to make payments to each other when they wish to buy goods or services. Suppose you live in the United States and are planning a trip around the world. You believe that $5,000 should be enough money to cover your expenses while traveling. In what form should you take the funds? How will you pay for things?

Some hotels, youth hostels, and restaurants will accept US dollars as payment, but others will not. You might be able to pay for everything with a credit card or a payment service like Apple Pay, but some places you're interested in visiting might not accept these forms of payment. Contemplation of your trip perhaps leads you to think how convenient it would be if every seller in every country were willing to accept the same means of payment.

Imagine instead that you are a wealthy person living in a country whose government limits your access to foreign currency and that you want to travel around the world. Inside your country you can buy whatever you want using the local currency, but outside your country no one will accept that currency as a means of payment. What can you do?

One possibility is to buy transportable goods (such as furs or jewelry) in your home country, pack them all in a suitcase, and try to use them to pay for your food and lodging abroad. In other words, you could engage in barter, the process of exchanging goods without using money. Needless to say, this would not be a convenient way to see the world. You would need to bring vast amounts of luggage, and instead of enjoying the sights, much of your time and energy would be spent in finding a hotel or restaurant that accepts furs or jewelry in exchange for a room or a meal.

As these examples suggest, an important function of the financial system is to provide an efficient payments system, so that households and businesses do not have to waste time and resources in implementing their purchases. The replacement of gold with paper currency as a means of payment is an example of a change that increases efficiency of the payments system. Gold is a scarce resource that is used in medicine and in the production of jewelry. Paper money serves as a superior means of payment. Compared with gold, paper currency is easier to verify (harder to counterfeit) and more convenient to carry around in one's pocket. It doesn't cost as much to make and print currency as it does to mine, refine, and mint gold. The subsequent development of checks, credit cards, electronic funds transfer, and app-based payment systems as alternative means of payment to paper currency has further increased efficiency.

Function 4: Pooling Resources and Subdividing Shares

A financial system provides a mechanism for the pooling of funds to undertake large-scale indivisible enterprise or for the subdividing of shares in large enterprises with many owners.

In modern economies, the minimum investment required to run a business is often beyond the means of an individual or even a large family. The financial system provides a variety of mechanisms (such as the stock market or banks) to pool or aggregate the wealth of households into larger masses of capital for use by business firms.

From the investor's perspective, the financial system provides opportunities for individual households to participate in investments that require large lump sums of money by pooling their funds and then subdividing shares in the investment. For example, suppose you want to invest in a racehorse that costs $100,000, but you only have $10,000 to invest. If there were a way of physically dividing the horse into ten pieces, then you could buy one piece. However, in this case the whole is surely worth more than the sum of its parts! A physical splitting of the horse will not do the trick. The financial system solves the problem of how to divide the horse without destroying it. By creating an investment pool and distributing shares to the investors, the $100,000 investment can be divided into $10,000 economic "pieces" without actually cutting up the horse. Any money the horse earns in race winnings or stud fees would, after training and upkeep expenses are taken out, be divided among all the shareholders.

As another example, consider money market mutual funds. Suppose you want to invest in the most secure and liquid dollar-denominated asset, US Treasury bills (T-bills). The minimum denomination is $10,000, and you have only $1,000 to invest. Therefore, the only way you can invest in T-bills is by pooling resources with other investors. In the 1970s, mutual funds that hold US T-bills were developed to facilitate this process. In a mutual fund, investors' money is pooled, and they are given accounts representing their proportional shares in the fund. The mutual fund frequently posts the price of a share and allows its customers to add or withdraw money at almost any time in almost any amount. Thus, if the price of a share is now $11 and you invest $1,000, the fund will credit your account with 1,000/11, or 90.91 shares. US T-bill mutual funds thus improve the performance of Function 4 by transforming large-denomination T-bills into almost infinitely divisible securities.

Function 5: Providing Information

A financial system provides price information that helps coordinate decision making across various sectors of the economy.

Every day, stock prices and interest rates are announced. Of the millions of people who see this information, relatively few actually buy and sell securities, but do use it to make other types of decisions. For example, deciding how much of their current income to save and how to invest it, households make use of information about interest rates and security prices.

For example, suppose that you are 30 years old, just got married, and want to buy a house for $100,000. Your local bank will make you a mortgage loan for $80,000 or 80% of the purchase price of the house at an interest rate of 8% per year, but you need to pay 20% down (i.e., $20,000). Your 45-year-old sister has an account at a savings bank with $20,000 in it—just enough for your down payment. She is saving the money for her retirement, which is far in the future, and is currently earning 6% per year. If your sister is willing to lend you her retirement savings for your down payment, how do you decide what a "fair" rate of interest is? Clearly, it is useful to know current market interest rates. You already know that your sister is earning 6% per year on her savings account and that your local bank will charge you 8% per year on the mortgage loan.

Similarly, knowledge of market prices of assets can be helpful for decision making within families. For example, suppose you and your sister inherit a house or a family business, and it is to be divided equally between you. You don't want to sell it because one of you wants to live in it or continue to operate it. How much should the other sibling receive? Clearly, it would be useful to know the market prices of similar assets to settle on a reasonable price for the inheritance.

Asset prices and interest rates provide critical signals to managers of firms in their selection of investment projects and financing arrangements. Managers of firms with no anticipated need to transact in the financial markets routinely use those markets to provide information for decisions. For example, a firm earns $10 million in profits in a good year and is faced with deciding whether to reinvest it in the business, pay it out in cash dividends to shareholders, or use it to buy back its own shares. Knowledge of its own and other firms' share prices as well as market interest rates will surely help in deciding what to do.

Whenever a new financial instrument is introduced, new possibilities for information extraction are created as a by-product. For example, the development of trading standardized option contracts on exchanges since 1973 has greatly increased the amount of quantitative information available about the riskiness of economic and financial variables. This information is particularly useful in making risk management decisions.

Function 6: Dealing with Incentive Problems

A financial system provides ways to deal with the incentive problems when one party to a financial transaction has information that the other party does not, or when one party is an agent that makes decisions for another. We discussed many of the consequences of these problems for firms in Chapter 11. Incentive problems arise because parties to contracts often cannot easily monitor or control one another. Incentive problems take a variety of forms—among them, moral hazard and agency problems.

An example of the moral hazard problem is when having insurance against some risk causes the insured party to take greater risk or to take less care in preventing the event that gives rise to the loss. Moral hazard can lead to unwillingness on the part of insurance companies to insure against certain types of risk. For example, if a warehouse owner buys fire insurance, the existence of the insurance reduces his incentive to spend money to prevent a fire. Failure to take the same precautions makes a warehouse fire a more likely occurrence. In an extreme case, the owner may be tempted to actually start a fire in order to collect the insurance money if the coverage exceeds the market value of the warehouse. Because of this potential moral hazard, insurance companies may limit the amount they will insure or simply refuse to sell fire insurance under certain circumstances.

Another example of a moral hazard problem is getting a loan from a bank. You are perhaps a little uncomfortable about discussing the details of your business plans with the bank loan officer, who is a complete stranger. She might disclose your plans to another customer, who could be a competitor. But even if you can resolve your concerns about the bank, there is the other side. The loan officer is reluctant to lend you the money you want because she knows that you have no incentive to disclose the pitfalls in your plans unless you have to. Thus, there is an imbalance or asymmetry in the exchange of information about the business opportunity: You know more about it than the loan officer. Moreover, the loan officer knows that she is a stranger to you and that the bank is just an impersonal institution to you. Therefore, if the going gets rough, you will not necessarily work as hard to turn it around as you would for your family and friends. Instead, you may decide to walk away from the business and not repay your loan. The reduced incentive for you to work hard when part of the risk of the enterprise has been transferred to an entity whose welfare you do not care much about (such as a bank or an insurance company) is, thus, an example of the problem of moral hazard.

A well-functioning financial system facilitates the resolution of the problems that arise from incentive problems so that the other benefits of the financial system, such as pooling, risk sharing, and specialization, can be achieved. For example, collateralization of loans, which means giving the lender the right to seize specific business assets in the event of default, is a widely used device for reducing the incentive problems associated with lending. Collateralization reduces the costs to the lender of monitoring the behavior of the borrower. The lender need only be concerned that the market value of the assets serving as collateral is sufficient to repay the principal and interest due on the loan. Over time, advances in technology have lowered the costs of tracking and valuing certain types of business assets that can serve as collateral—such as goods in inventory—and thereby broadened the range of situations in which collateralized loan agreements are feasible to implement.

20.3.2 Levels of Analysis

With an understanding of the functions that a financial system seeks to address, the functional perspective can be used to analyze specific components of the financial system. This analysis can be at several levels: system level, institution level, activity level, and product level. We provide examples of each of these in this section, and how the functional perspective can be used to analyze them.

Level of the System

The functional perspective offers a useful frame of reference for analyzing a country's entire financial system.

A number of countries with well-developed free markets for nonfinancial goods and services have centralized government control of their financial systems. With control over both the banking and pension systems and restrictions on cross-border capital flows, these governments collect savings of the household sector and allocate capital to the business sector. And even among countries such as the United States, with highly developed private sector financial markets and institutions, important changes in the way governments regulate the system are actively being debated. An example would be the system of financing retirement income. In general, such analyses begin with a description of the functions served by the pension system and a determination of how they are currently performed. From this base, the analysis then continues by examining alternative institutional arrangements used at other times and in other countries. It is unlikely that solutions developed in one country or group of countries cannot be improved upon. Functional analysis seeks new institutional arrangements or new combinations of existing ones that might improve the performance of the functions, given the specific local economic, political, and cultural circumstances.

Level of an Institution

Application of the functional perspective is not limited to analyses at the macro level of the financial system. A functional perspective is also useful in the study of a particular micro institutional form. Examples are savings and loan associations (S&Ls) in the United States (similar institutions include trustee savings banks in the United Kingdom), commercial banks, and financial technology (fintech) lenders that emerged during the 2010s.

Take S&Ls (or thrift banks) as an example. Evolving as specialized institutions in the United States during the first half of the twentieth century, S&Ls came to have two core economic functions: to provide long-term financing for residential homeowners at fixed interest rates; and to provide a riskless, liquid, short-term savings vehicle for large numbers of small savers. These are separable functions that need not be performed by the same intermediary. In the 1970s and 1980s, interest rates increased substantially in response to inflation, leading to financial trouble for S&Ls—the value of the mortgages they carried declined, while savers withdrew funds as the interest rates S&Ls were allowed to pay on deposits were capped. The US public policy response to the difficulties faced by S&Ls was to try to find ways of making them healthy again. The S&L problem was thus framed in terms of taking the existing institutions as a given (i.e., maintaining the institutional structure) and asking what changes could be made to improve the thrifts' competitive position. It is difficult to rationalize the public policy toward the thrifts during the 1980s unless preservation of existing financial institutions was a primary objective of that policy.

Ironically, while the government was struggling at great cost to save the thrifts during the 1980s, both of the thrifts' principal economic functions were being taken over by other institutional mechanisms. The creation of securitized mortgage instruments, ostensibly to help the thrifts, led to the creation of a national mortgage market that allowed mutual funds and pension funds to become major funding alternatives to the thrifts. These funding markets also allowed entry by agent-like institutions such as investment banks and mortgage brokers to compete with the traditional principal-like thrifts for the origination and servicing fees on loans and mortgages. The institutions that serve functions such as the origination of loans and mortgages continue to change. In the 2010s, financial technology (fintech) companies began taking a significant share of mortgage originations away from traditional financial institutions such as banks, increasing the processing speed of applications and allowing mortgage applications to be more automated.

Level of an Activity

To illustrate an application of the functional perspective to a financial activity, consider lending. Lending is often treated as a homogenous activity in both private sector and public sector decision making. But from a functional perspective, lending in general is multifunctional, involving two of the six basic functions of the financial system.

Lending in its purest form is free of default risk, so it falls under a single basic functional category: the intertemporal transfer of resources. But, of course, with few exceptions, payments promised in loan agreements are subject to some degree of default risk. Lending therefore also involves a second basic functional category: risk management. When a loan is made, an implicit guarantee of that loan (a form of insurance) is involved.

To see this, consider the fundamental identity, which holds in both a functional and a valuation sense:

$$\text{Risky loan} + \text{loan guarantee} = \text{default-free loan}, \tag{20.1}$$

$$\text{Risky loan} - \text{default-free loan} = \text{loan guarantee}. \tag{20.2}$$

Thus, whenever lenders make dollar-denominated loans to anyone other than the US government, they are implicitly also selling loan guarantees. The lending activity therefore consists of two functionally distinct activities: pure default-free lending (the intertemporal transfer function) and the sale of default risk insurance by the lender to the borrower (an example of the risk management function).

The relative weighting of these two functions varies considerably across the various debt instruments. A high-grade bond (rated AAA) is almost all default-free loan with a very small guarantee component. A below-investment-grade or "junk" bond, on the other hand, typically has a large guarantee component.

Level of a Product

To see an application of the functional perspective at the level of an individual financial product, consider municipal bond insurance. Municipal bonds are bonds that are issued by local and state governments. There are specialized insurance companies that sell insurance contracts that guarantee interest and principal payments on municipal bonds against default by the issuer. The policies are typically sold to the issuer, which "attaches" them to the bonds to give them an AAA credit rating. To succeed as a guarantor, the insurance company itself must be seen as a very strong credit.

In evaluating the firm's competitive standing, a manager with an institutional perspective would focus on other insurance companies as competitors. A manager with a functional perspective would instead focus on the best institutional structure to perform the function, which may not be an insurance company.

Consider as one alternative an option exchange that creates a market for put options on municipal bonds. In such a market, investors could achieve the same protection against loss by buying an uninsured municipal bond and a put option on that bond. The put option on the bond thus serves as a put option on the assets of the borrower, which is a local government in this case. Note that both structures serve the same function for investors—protection against loss from default—but the institutions are entirely different: an options exchange is not an insurance company. Furthermore, the put option traded on the exchange is a different product from the insurance guarantee. Although the products and institutions that provide them are both quite different, the economic function they serve is the same.

In certain environments it is surely possible that an options exchange with marked-to-market collateral and a clearing corporation could be a "better credit" than an insurance company and thereby be a superior institutional structure as the guarantor. In such environments, the institutionally oriented manager (who focuses only on the type of institution currently performing the function) may miss recognizing the firm's prime competitor. Regulatory bodies for financial services are almost exclusively organized along institutional lines, so they face similar problems. Because options are not insurance products, and exchanges are not insurance companies, insurance regulators would have no control over the option exchange even though its product is a perfect substitute for an insurance product.

20.4 Financial Innovation

In this section we apply the functional perspective to understand new financial innovations that are continuously introduced into the financial system.

20.4.1 Financial Innovation and Market Forces

Generally, financial innovations are not planned by any central authority but arise from the individual actions of entrepreneurs and firms. The fundamental economic forces behind financial innovation are essentially the same as for innovation in general. As the classical economist Adam Smith (1776) observed in *The Wealth of Nations*:

> Every individual endeavors to employ his capital so that its produce may be of greatest value. He generally neither intends to promote the public interest, nor knows how much he is promoting it. He intends only his own security, only his own gain. And he is in this led by an invisible hand to promote an end which was no part of his intention. By pursuing his own interest he frequently promotes that of society more effectually than when he really intends to promote it.

To illustrate, compare the situation faced by a college graduate traveling around the world 60 years ago with the one faced by a college graduate undertaking such a journey today. Back then you had the constant worry that you would run out of money in some place where no one could speak your language. If you ran out, then you had to wire home and try to arrange a wire transfer of money from a bank back home to a local bank. The process was costly and time-consuming. Prearranged lines of credit were available only to the wealthiest travelers.

But now, you can pay for almost anything you buy almost anywhere with a credit card or payment app. Credit cards like Visa, MasterCard, American Express, and payment apps like Apple Pay, Google Pay, and Alipay, are accepted virtually everywhere on the globe. To pay your hotel bill, you simply give the clerk your card or use the payment app, and within seconds they have verified that your credit is good (i.e., that the credit provider will guarantee payment), and you can be on your way to your next destination. Moreover, you need not worry about your money being lost or stolen. If you cannot find your credit card, you can contact the credit card company to cancel the missing card (so no one else can use it) and get another. If your phone is stolen, security credentials prevent someone else from using your payment apps.

Clearly, world travel has become less costly and more convenient as a result of such technology. Their invention and dissemination has made millions of people better off and contributed to the democratization of finance. But how has this happened? Let us use the example of credit cards to trace the key factors in the development of a financial innovation.

Technology is an important factor. Credit cards depend on a complex network of communications and information processing hardware and software. The same goes for app-based payment systems, which require smartphones that are advanced enough to utilize such technology. But for credit cards and apps to become an important part of the contemporary economic scene, financial service firms looking for profit opportunities had to employ the advanced technology in offering these services, and households and businesses had to buy them.

It is not uncommon in the history of innovations (financial or otherwise) that the firm that pioneers a commercially successful innovative idea is not the one to profit the most from it. And so it is here with the credit card. The first firm to offer credit cards to global travelers was Diners Club, which was formed just after World War II. The initial success of Diners Club led two other firms, American Express and Carte Blanche, to offer similar credit card programs.

Firms in the credit card business earn their revenues from fees paid to them by retailers on credit card purchases (usually a percentage of the purchase price) and from interest paid on loans to credit card customers (on their unpaid balances). Major costs stem from transactions processing, stolen cards, and loan defaults by cardholders. When commercial banks first tried to enter the credit card business in the 1950s, they found that they could not compete with the established firms because bank operating costs were too high. In the late 1960s, however, advances in computer technology lowered their costs to the point at which they could compete successfully.

This last observation leads us to another basic point about financial innovation. Analysis of individual preferences and the forces of competition among financial service providers helps one to make predictions about future changes in the financial system. For example, in light of the advantages of credit cards payment systems as a method of making payments, the use of traveler's checks has steadily declined. Many people now mainly rely on app-based payment in lieu of credit cards, given the convenience of having a method of payment incorporated into their phones. Are credit cards destined for the same fate as the slide rule after the invention of the smartphone?

Credit cards and app-based payment systems are only one of a wide array of new financial products developed over the past 40 years that have changed the way we carry on economic activities. Collectively, these innovations have greatly improved the opportunities for people to receive efficient risk–return trade-offs in their personal investments and more effective tailoring to their individual needs over the entire life cycle, including accumulation during the work years and distribution in retirement.

In assessing any innovation, it is important to be able to identify the function that it performs, and it can then be assessed in terms of its effectiveness in performing that function. The 2010s and 2020s have witnessed a variety of different "innovations" in financial markets, which include fintech products and services as well as assets such as cryptocurrencies. Many have commented that such innovations are so new and different that we do not have the means to properly analyze them and how they will affect financial markets. However, by focusing on the economic functions they perform—and whether they perform those functions better than existing products—we gain the means of analyzing such innovations.

For example, consider obtaining a loan from a fintech platform compared to obtaining a loan from your local bank branch. The key difference between banks and fintech loan platforms is thus not that they perform fundamentally different functions—the core economic function is lending—but rather that the institutional details (data processing, exposure to regulation) may permit that function to perhaps be performed more efficiently and at a lower cost. In other cases, it may not be at all clear what core function is served by innovations that may be popular or hyped-up.

For example, cryptocurrencies have gained popularity among some investors in the 2010s and 2020s. When first introduced, proponents of cryptocurrencies touted the assets as a replacement for traditional currencies (as the name implies). If the intended function of such assets is to act as a currency, then the assets must perform the functions of money. However, legal tender fiat currencies have intrinsic value because they can be used to settle government obligations of taxes and fees; in contrast, fiat digital currencies that are not legal tender do not have such intrinsic value. Furthermore, the viability of any currency depends on collective trust by its user, and thus the lack of any material intrinsic value is a prime source of instability. Governments also have the power to effectively ban the holding of any legal tender currency surrogate. Finally, cryptocurrencies have had considerably greater volatility than other traditional assets that are used as a store of value. These features raise the question of how cryptocurrencies outperform the functions of government legal tender currency.

Others have claimed that other forms of "crypto" assets may become a dominant asset class replacing "traditional" financial investments. In assessing such claims, it is again important to ask: What functions do such assets serve, and in what way do they serve those functions better than existing assets? In other words, what risks can it be used to manage and better distribute for society, since such assets produce no cash flows or have no other tangible uses? Do these assets provide improved diversification of necessary risks that must be borne by society? If so, which ones?

20.4.2 The Financial Innovation Spiral

The evolution of retirement systems, and indeed the financial system as a whole, can be viewed as a financial innovation spiral, in which organized markets and intermediaries compete with each other in a static sense and complement each other in a dynamic sense (see Figure 20.4). That intermediaries and markets compete to be the providers of financial products is widely recognized. Improving technology and a decline in transactions costs has added to the intensity of that competition. Extensive histories of innovative financial products suggest a pattern in which products offered initially by intermediaries ultimately move to markets. For example:

- The development of liquid markets for money instruments such as commercial paper allowed money market mutual funds to compete with banks and thrifts for household savings.
- The creation of "high-yield" and medium-term note markets, which made it possible for mutual funds, pension funds, and individual investors to service those corporate issuers who had historically depended on banks as their source of debt financing.
- The creation of a national mortgage market allowed mutual funds and pension funds to become major funding alternatives to thrift institutions for residential mortgages.
- Creation of these funding markets also made it possible for investment banks and mortgage brokers to compete with the thrift institutions for the origination and servicing fees on loans and mortgages.
- Securitization of auto loans, credit card receivables, and leases on consumer and producer durables has intensified the competition between banks and finance companies as sources of funds for these purposes.

This pattern implies that successful new products will inevitably migrate from intermediaries to markets. That is, once a successful product becomes familiar, and perhaps after some incentive problems are resolved, it will become a commodity traded in a market. Some see this process as disintermediation—destroying the value of intermediaries. However, this is a consequence of the functional role of intermediaries and is not dysfunctional. Just as venture-capital firms that provide financing for startup businesses expect to lose their successful creations to capital market sources of funding, so do the intermediaries that create new financial products expect to lose their successful and scalable ones to markets. Intermediaries continue to prosper by finding new successful products and the institutional means to perform financial functions more effectively than the existing ones, all made possible by the commoditization of existing products and services.

Thus, exclusive focus on the time path of individual products can be misleading. Financial markets tend to be efficient institutional alternatives to intermediaries when the products have standardized terms, can serve a large number of customers, and are well-enough understood for transactors to be comfortable in assessing their prices. Intermediaries are better suited for low-volume customized products.

As products such as futures, options, swaps, and securitized loans become standardized and move from intermediaries to markets, the proliferation of new trading markets in those

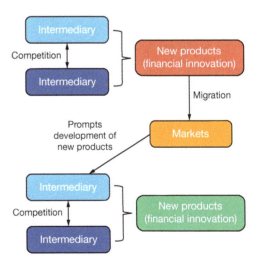

FIGURE 20.4 The financial innovation spiral. This figure illustrates the process behind the financial innovation spiral. Intermediaries first compete with each other and create new financial products. These products become successful and more widely adopted, moving into financial markets. To continue to prosper, intermediaries again compete and create new products, which continues the cycle.

instruments makes feasible the creation of new custom-designed financial products that improve "market completeness." To hedge their exposures on those products, the producers (typically, financial intermediaries) trade in these new markets and volume expands; increased volume reduces marginal transaction costs and thereby makes possible further implementation of more new products and trading strategies by intermediaries, which in turn leads to still more volume. Success of these trading markets and custom products encourages investment in creating additional markets and products, and so on it goes, spiraling toward the theoretically limiting case of zero marginal transactions costs and "dynamically complete markets" (Merton 1992b: 12–22).

20.5 Trust and the Financial System

A concept that is critical to many financial transactions is trust between agents. Trust is central to understanding various aspects of the financial system. The interaction of institutional features of various financial entities with their incentives to develop trust can yield a number of important insights. The importance of trust to finance is highlighted by the fact that it makes up **Principle 9**: *Transparency, verification, and trust are all important to the proper functioning of the financial system.*

20.5.1 Trust and Financial Markets

Trust can be viewed as having two dimensions: trustworthiness and competence. Trustworthiness is about intent; in other words, your belief that a person or system will do what is promised. In contrast, competence is about skills—a completely trustworthy but incompetent firm can make decisions that are just as bad as those of an untrustworthy firm. For example, you may trust someone as an individual but would not trust that person to perform surgery on you if the person was not a medical doctor trained in that type of surgery. Similarly, a person may be competent but you may not transact with them if they are not trustworthy.

For individuals and firms operating in financial markets, a general insight is that a trusted institution will be able to raise financing at a lower cost than one that is not trusted—investors will have much more confidence that any money you are raising will be put to productive use. This cost of capital advantage can be a powerful asset when competing with other institutions that perform similar functions, thus making trust a valuable asset to have. Indeed, for some financial transactions, trust is essential for them to take place. For example, recent years have seen the entry of new financial technology solutions to marketplaces that are inherently opaque in terms of how they work, such as automated financial advice, digital currencies, complex integrated financial products, and financial technology (fintech) lending. With such new technologies, trust may be necessary for them to be successful, given their complex and opaque natures. We discuss this point in more detail in the next section.

Another area where trust plays a critical role is wealth management. Trust has been recognized as being important for enabling clients to delegate the management of their wealth to financial advisors (Gennaioli et al. 2015: 91–114). First, a client and an advisor share the objective that their relationship last a long time, but there is a threshold of poor performance at which a client may leave. The greater the degree of trust that the client has in the advisor, the higher this threshold will be. Trust is therefore a valuable asset for a financial advisor to retain clients against competition, and it can help to create growth opportunities in expanding an advisor's client base (Thakor and Merton forthcoming). Second, however, trust can be lost, and when lost can be difficult or take a very long time to regain. One implication of this is that financial advisors and institutions with business strategies based on maintaining/restoring trust by minimizing conflicts of interest—such as fee-only independent advisors—will disrupt traditional product-based wealth management models. Finally, regulation can be used to cultivate and strengthen trust. For example, a fiduciary duty responsibility for financial advisors (if provided with enough clarity regarding what a client's "best interests" are) can be a means for strengthening trust. Government agencies, such as the Consumer Financial Protection Bureau (CFPB) in the United States, the Financial Conduct Authority (FCA) in the UK, and the Dubai Financial Services Authority (DFSA) in the UAE, have been created due to calls for better consumer protection with financial services and products, and can also help to generate trust.

> **QUICK CHECK 20.4** When you purchase a company's stock, in what way are you trusting the management running the company? What are some possible ways they can increase the trust of investors like yourself?

20.5.2 Building Trust and Substitutes for Trust

For firms and individuals that have trust—built up through a good reputation over time—it is a valuable asset. However, not everyone has the trust asset—for example, new financial advisors or startup firms do not have an established track record and thus have not yet built up trust. A natural question is whether there is something that can substitute for trust.

To the extent that the information is not inherently opaque or complex, transparency—providing additional information—can possibly be used to substitute for trust. For example, some information can be readily communicated, such as the financial information and investment decisions that a firm has made, or the specific stocks that the manager of a mutual fund decides to invest in. Institutional design can also play a role in creating transparency—for example, mandated disclosures can also be used to encourage transparency, avoid conflicts of interest, and foster trust. However, additional transparency may have costs as well. For example, any information that a firm provides also is seen by its product-market competitors, which can put the firm at a competitive disadvantage. As another example, stress tests of banks reveal information to regulators that is not in the public domain, and there is an active debate about how much of it should be disclosed. The downside of more disclosure is that poor results might erode confidence in these banks, hamper liquidity, and cause bank runs. Furthermore, transparency can have limited benefit with regard to complex information or "black box" technologies, where consumers and investors may not be able to understand the information even when disclosed.

Another possible substitute for trust is verification, which can be particularly valuable in cases where transparency is not feasible or too costly. For example, financial technology (fintech) payment systems like Alipay and WeChat Pay are clearly not transparent to users, but are widely used. Why? The answer is verification: A friend, co-worker, or family member tries it and it works, and thus you are willing to use it (Thakor and Merton 2023). Such verification is ubiquitous—examples include inspections with real estate transactions and public audits of firms' financial statements.

Conclusion

In this chapter we explored the financial system, which is composed of the institutions that carry out the financial decisions of individuals, companies, and governments. Throughout this book, we presented principles, concepts, models, and tools that are valid no matter what the institutional structure. However, in reality, there are many types of institutions in the financial system, and the design of these institutions does matter due to the effects—such as costs, behavioral biases, and sociological effects—that individuals are exposed to.

The functional perspective introduced in this chapter does not focus on the institutions that make up the financial system, but rather the core functions the financial system aims to address—which do not change over time and are constant across the world. We reviewed the six basic functions of the financial system with examples of how different institutions have come about to address those functions. The functional perspective provides a valuable lens through which to understand new developments in the ever-changing financial system. Financial innovations have been developed over time to address different functions for individuals and new financial innovations will continue to be developed. The functional perspective provides a powerful framework that can be applied to understand as-of-yet-unseen innovations.

Finally, a fundamental concept necessary to the proper functioning of the financial system is trust. There are many reasons why trust is important for financial markets to function, and transparency and verification are possible substitutes that can serve the same role.

Takeaways

- Financial intermediaries such as banks, insurance companies, and mutual funds exist because individuals transacting directly in markets cannot efficiently provide all the kinds of products that retail customers desire: deposits, insurance policies, diversified portfolios.
- Without frictions, institutional design does not matter, and multiple alternative institutional structures are possible to support the financial system.
- Behavioral considerations are very important in determining the institutional ways that financial functions are performed.
- Financial functions are more stable than financial institutions—that is, functions change less over time and vary less across geopolitical borders. The functional perspective analyzes the financial system through the lens of the functions that are performed.
- Institutional form follows function—that is, innovation and competition among institutions ultimately result in greater efficiency in the performance of financial system functions.
- The functional perspective is useful at several levels of analysis: system level, institution level, activity level, and product level.
- As technology progresses and transaction costs continue to fall, finance theory is likely to provide increasingly accurate predictions and prescriptions for future product innovations.

Key Terms

Agency problems 650
Bank run 641
Behavioral biases 635
Central banks 644
Deposit insurance 643
Disintermediation 655
Dominant strategy 643
Financial innovation spiral 655
Financial intermediaries 636
Financial system 635
Flow of funds 636
Framing 639
Frictions 635

Functional perspective 635
Functions 645
Moral hazard 650
Municipal bond insurance. 652
Municipal bonds 652
Mutual funds 638
Savings and loan associations (S&Ls) 651
Self-fulfilling prophecy 641
Thrift banks 651
Transaction costs 638
Transparency 657
Trust 656
Verification 657

Key Equations

| Default-free loan | Risky loan + loan guarantee = default-free loan | Eq. 20.1 |
| Loan guarantee | Risky loan − default-free loan = loan guarantee | Eq. 20.2 |

Problems

1. Suppose your great-uncle decides to take this month's savings and purchase a bond issued by Dell to finance an increase in computer components in their new factory. Describe how this exchange can be analyzed in the flow-of-funds framework.
2. Give an example of a new business that would not be able to get financing if insurance against risk were not available.
3. Suppose you invest in a real estate development deal. The total investment is $100,000. You invest $20,000 of your own money and borrow the other $80,000 from the bank. Who bears the risk of this venture and why?
4. Give an example of how the problem of moral hazard might prevent you from getting financing for something you want to do. Can you think of a way of overcoming this problem?
5. Give an example of how each of the six functions of the financial system are performed more efficiently today than they were in the time of Adam Smith (1776).
6. Describe your country's system for financing higher education. What are the roles played by households, voluntary nonprofit organizations, businesses, and government?
7. Describe your country's system for financing residential housing. What are the roles played by households, businesses, and government?
8. Describe your country's system for financing new enterprises. What are the roles played by households, businesses, and government?
9. Payments made by apps have increased in popularity in recent years. Explain the functions that these serve.
10. Explain how a drop in a company's stock price can lead to a severe crash in its price due to the self-fulfilling prophecy, even though the company is fundamentally sound.
11. Explain why a bank run might occur, and steps that can be taken to prevent one.
12. You observe that a lot of your friends on social media are pulling money out of the bank you use. Should you be worried? Explain.
13. You observe that a company's stock price increased over the past year. Explain how this can be framed in either a positive or a negative way.
14. Give an example of a financial transaction where trust is essential for it to occur.
15. Give an example of a financial transaction where one party is not trusted, but the transaction still occurs due to transparency or verification.

ANSWERS TO QUICK CHECK QUESTIONS

2 Basics of Valuation: The Time Value of Money

Quick Check 2.1 Your friend asks to borrow $100 from you, which she will pay back in three years. In the meantime, she will pay you a 10% interest rate each year for the use of your money. Construct two timelines to illustrate this situation for you (the lender) and for your friend (the borrower).

Answer. The timelines would be as follows:

You (lender) lend $100 at an interest rate r of 10%:

Time t (in years):	$t=0$	$t=1$	$t=2$	$t=3$
Cash flows:	−$100	10	10	110

Your friend (borrower) borrows $100 at an interest rate of 10%:

Time t (in years):	$t=0$	$t=1$	$t=2$	$t=3$
Cash flows:	$100	−10	−10	−110

Quick Check 2.2 What is the future value of $1,000 one year from now at an interest rate of 20%?

Answer. The future value can be calculated as:

$$\begin{aligned} FV &= \$1{,}000 \times (1+r) \\ &= \$1{,}000 \times (1+0.20) \\ &= \$1{,}200. \end{aligned}$$

Quick Check 2.3 Solve for the future value of $1,000 ten years from today at an interest rate of 5%.

Answer. Using our future value Equation 2.1, we get:

$$FV_T = \$PV \times (1+r)^T = \$1{,}000 \times 1.05^{10} = \$1{,}628.90.$$

Quick Check 2.4 If you take out a loan at an APR of 12% with monthly compounding, what is the EAR on your loan?

Answer. We can directly use the EAR Equation 2.4, with $m = 12$ given that we have monthly compounding:

$$EAR = \left(1 + \frac{APR}{m}\right)^m - 1 = \left(1 + \frac{0.12}{12}\right)^{12} - 1 = 0.1268.$$

Quick Check 2.5 Suppose that the one-year interest rate right now is 2%. The one-year interest rate one year from now (i.e., from year 1 to year 2) is expected to be 3%, and two years from now the one-year interest rate (i.e., from year 2 to year 3) is expected to be 3.5%. Assuming these expected interest rates hold, what is the value in three years of $1,000 invested at these rates?

Answer. The information given means that (in the notation of Equation 2.6) $r_1 = 0.02$, $r_2 = 0.03$, and $r_3 = 0.035$. We can then use Equation 2.6 to calculate the future value of the $1,000:

$$FV_{T=3} = \$PV \times (1+r_1) \times (1+r_2) \times (1+r_3)$$
$$= \$100 \times (1+0.02) \times (1+0.03) \times (1+0.035)$$
$$= \$100 \times 1.02 \times 1.03 \times 1.035$$
$$= \$108.74.$$

Quick Check 2.6 Solve for the present value of $1,000 one year from today at an interest rate of 5%. Is the present value higher or lower than when the interest rate is 10%? Why?

Answer. At an interest rate of 5%, the present value of $1,000 in a year is (using Equation 2.7):

$$PV = \frac{FV}{1+r} = \frac{\$1,000}{1.05} = \$952.38.$$

This is higher than when the interest rate is 10% (present value in that case was $909.09), which reflects the fact that lower interest rates mean that money in the future is worth more.

Quick Check 2.7 What is the present value of $100 to be received each year over the next four years at an interest rate of 6% per year?

Answer. The present value is calculated by discounting the $100 back four years (Equation 2.8):

$$PV = \frac{\$100}{1.06^4} = \$79.21.$$

Quick Check 2.8 You are promised $10,000 in five years. The current interest rate is 10% APR with monthly compounding. What is this promised amount worth to you now?

Answer. With monthly compounding, we can make use of Equation 2.10 with $m = 12$ in order to calculate the present value of the promised amount:

$$PV = \frac{CF_t}{\left(1+\frac{APR}{m}\right)^{m \times t}} = \frac{\$10,000}{\left(1+\frac{0.10}{12}\right)^{12 \times 5}} = \$6,077.89.$$

Quick Check 2.9 Consider the previous savings bond example: You are looking at a $100 savings bond maturing in five years and selling for a price of $75. Instead of your opportunity cost of capital (next best alternative) being a savings account paying 8% interest per year, suppose the savings account is paying only 2%. What is the NPV of the savings bond? What is the NPV of the savings account? What investment should you make?

Answer. Repeating our previous calculations using a discount rate of 2% gives (Equation 2.12):

$$NPV = -PV(\text{cash outflows}) + PV(\text{cash inflows})$$
$$= -\$75 + \frac{\$100}{1.02^5}$$
$$= -\$75 + \$90.57$$
$$= \$15.57.$$

The NPV in this case becomes positive, making the savings bond a good investment. The lower discount rate increases the value of the positive cash inflows in the future.

Quick Check 2.10 Calculate the present value of an annuity that pays $100 each year for ten years. The interest rate is 10%.

Answer. The cash flows for the annuity start next year, so we can straightforwardly apply the annuity formula (Equation 2.14):

$$PV = \frac{\$CF}{r} \times \left[1 - \frac{1}{(1+r)^T}\right] = \frac{\$100}{0.10} \times \left[1 - \frac{1}{(1+0.10)^{10}}\right] = \$614.46.$$

Quick Check 2.11 Calculate the present value of an annuity that pays $100 each year (starting next year) for ten years, but grows at a rate of 2% per year after the first year. The interest rate is 10%.

Answer. This annuity pays $100 next year, and then starts growing. It is therefore a growing annuity, and the present value can be solved using the growing annuity formula (Equation 2.15) with $g = 0.02$:

$$PV = \frac{\$CF_1}{r-g} \times \left[1 - \left(\frac{1+g}{1+r}\right)^T\right] = \frac{\$100}{0.10 - 0.02} \times \left[1 - \left(\frac{1.02}{1.10}\right)^{10}\right] = \$662.53.$$

Notice that this is larger than the previous quick check answer due to the higher growth rate.

Quick Check 2.12 What is the present value of a perpetuity that provides a cash flow of $1,000 each year (starting next year), with an interest rate of 5%?

Answer. Applying our perpetuity formula (Equation 2.17):

$$PV = \frac{\$CF}{r} = \frac{\$1,000}{0.05} = \$20,000.$$

Quick Check 2.13 What is the present value of a growing perpetuity that gives $1,000 each year (starting next year), and grows at a rate of 2% per year after that, with an interest rate of 5%?

Answer. Applying our growing perpetuity formula (Equation 2.18):

$$PV = \frac{\$CF_1}{r-g} = \frac{\$1,000}{0.05 - 0.02} = \$33,333.33.$$

Quick Check 2.14 In this section we calculated the real future value of $100 assuming a nominal interest rate of 8% and an inflation rate of 5%. Now let's assume that the nominal interest rate is instead 6%. How does this affect the real future value calculations?

Answer. As covered in the section, there are two alternative ways of doing this. First, we can calculate the real interest rate using Equation 2.20:

$$\begin{aligned} r_{real} &= \frac{r_{nominal} - \text{rate of inflation}}{1 + \text{rate of inflation}} \\ &= \frac{0.06 - 0.05}{1.05} \\ &= 0.01. \end{aligned}$$

The real future value is then given by the present value of $100, using this real interest rate for 45 years:

$$\text{Real } FV_T = \$PV \times (1 + 0.01)^T$$
$$= \$100 \times (1 + 0.01)^{45}$$
$$= \$156.48.$$

The other way of doing this is to first compute the nominal future value, and then adjust for the price level (inflation).

Quick Check 2.15 In the example presented in this section, you planned to buy a car four years from now and wanted to save enough money now to pay for it. The kind of car you had in mind costs $10,000 now. Recalculate the amount you would need to invest now for the car in four years, assuming a nominal interest rate of 6% and an inflation rate of 5% per year.

Answer. There are again two equivalent ways to take inflation into account. We can use the first: Take the present value of $10,000 in four years using the real interest rate. The real interest rate is (Equation 2.20):

$$r_{real} = \frac{r_{nominal} - \text{rate of inflation}}{1 + \text{rate of inflation}}$$
$$= \frac{0.06 - 0.05}{1.05}$$
$$= 0.01.$$

The present value is then:

$$PV = \frac{\$10,000}{1.01^4} = \$9,609.80.$$

3 Personal Finance

Quick Check 3.1 Georgette is currently 30 years old, plans to retire at age 65, and to live to age 85. Her labor income is $25,000 per year, and she intends to maintain a constant level of real consumption spending over the next 55 years. Assume no taxes, no growth in real salary, and a real interest rate of 3% per year.

- What is the value of Georgette's human capital?
- What is her sustainable consumption?

Answer. Using the present value of an annuity formula (Equation 2.14) we solve for the current level of human capital as:

$$PV = \frac{C}{r} \times \left[1 - \frac{1}{(1+r)^T}\right]$$
$$= \frac{\$25,000}{0.03} \times \left[1 - \frac{1}{(1.03)^{35}}\right]$$
$$= \$537,180.50.$$

Next we solve for the payment C that is needed to set the present value to this:

$$PV_{t=30} = \frac{C}{r} \times \left[1 - \frac{1}{(1+r)^T}\right]$$

$$\$537{,}180.50 = \frac{C}{0.03} \times \left[1 - \frac{1}{(1.03)^{55}}\right]$$

$$= \$20{,}063.19.$$

Quick Check 3.2 Suppose that the consumer tax rate is 30% instead of 20%. How large would be the advantage of tax deferral compared to our example with a 20% tax rate?

Answer. As in the example in the text, your total before-tax amount accumulated at retirement will still be $\$1{,}000 \times 1.08^{30} = \$10{,}062.65$. You will have to pay taxes at the rate of 30% on the entire amount, so your taxes will be $0.3 \times \$10{,}062.65 = \$3{,}018.80$, and you will be left with $\$7{,}043.85$ after taxes. If, instead, you choose not to participate in the retirement plan and invest in an ordinary savings plan, you have to pay 30% of the $\$1{,}000$, or $\$300$, immediately in additional taxes. The remaining $\$700$ will go into the ordinary savings plan and interest earnings on the $\$700$ will be taxed each year. The after-tax interest rate earned is, therefore, $(1 - 0.3) \times 8\%$, or 5.6%. The amount accumulated at retirement from this ordinary savings plan is $\$700 \times 1.056^{30} = \$3{,}589.35$.

Quick Check 3.3 Suppose that Jo is 30 years old instead of 20. If all the other assumptions remain the same, does the investment in the graduate degree still have a positive NPV?

Answer. As in the example in the text, Jo must give up $\$45{,}000$ (tuition plus forgone earnings) in each of the next two years in order to increase her earnings by $\$5{,}000$ per year over her remaining career. Jo is now 30 years old and expects to retire at age 65. The relevant cash flows for this investment are incremental outflows of $\$45{,}000$ in each of the next two years and then incremental inflows of $\$5{,}000$ in each of the succeeding 33 years. The present value of the outflows is $\$86{,}106$; the present value of the inflows is $\$97{,}869$. The NPV of the investment in human capital is, therefore, $\$11{,}763$, meaning it is still worthwhile.

4 Principles of Valuation

Quick Check 4.1 You win a contest, and the prize is a choice between a ticket to an opera and a ticket to a ball game. The opera ticket has a price of $\$100$ and the ticket to the ball game has a price of $\$25$. Assuming you prefer ball games to opera, which ticket should you choose?

Answer. Provided the cost to you of taking the time and trouble to exchange the tickets does not exceed the $\$75$ difference in the price of the tickets, you should take the opera ticket. Even if you prefer the ball game to the opera, you can exchange it for $\$100$, buy a ticket to the ball game for $\$25$, and pocket the $\$75$ difference.

Quick Check 4.2 If the price of silver is $\$20$ per ounce in Chicago and the total transaction costs of shipping silver to New York are $\$1$ per ounce, what can we say about the price of silver in New York?

Answer. The price of silver in New York must be within $\$1$ per ounce of its price in Chicago. Thus, the price of silver in New York must be between $\$19$ and $\$21$ per ounce.

Quick Check 4.3 Under what circumstances might two 25-cent coins have different values?

Answer. One of them might be a rare coin that is especially valuable to collectors. Alternatively, one of them might be slightly worn, so that a soda machine will reject it. To a thirsty person, the nonworn coin is more valuable.

Quick Check 4.4 Can you offer the assessor a way to alter her valuation model so that it accounts for the specific neighborhood the house is located in?

Answer. One way to take account of the neighborhood effect in the valuation model would be to calculate average price changes by *neighborhood*. Then the assessor could apply neighborhood price changes to estimating price changes for individual houses.

Quick Check 4.5 A firm's earnings per share are $5, and the industry average price/earnings multiple is 10. What would be an estimate of the value of a share of the firm's stock?

Answer. An estimate of the value is $50:

$$\text{XYZ earnings per share} \times \frac{\text{price}}{\text{earnings}} \text{ of comparables} = \$5 \times 10 = \$50.$$

Quick Check 4.6 If two assets have the same expected cash flows but different discount rates, can their prices be the same according to the law of one price?

Answer. No, the prices must be different to be consistent with the law of one price. If we discount the cash flows of the two assets, with different discount rates their prices will be different. If they are the same, we would have an arbitrage opportunity, where we could sell the more expensive one and buy the cheaper one, guaranteeing us a profit.

Quick Check 4.7 Suppose you can borrow money at a yearly interest rate of 3%. At the same time, Treasury bonds sell in the marketplace for a price of $1,000 and promise to pay interest of 5% per year. What is the arbitrage opportunity that you face?

Answer. You could borrow money at the 3% interest rate, and then use the money to invest in Treasury bonds—you would make "free" money this way. For example, suppose you borrowed $1,000 and you bought a Treasury bond. In one year you would owe 3% × $1,000 = $30 in interest. However, the Treasury bond would pay you 5% × $1,000 = $50 in interest, giving you a profit of $20. Note that we are not explicitly considering the principal amounts (i.e., what the Treasury bond pays at maturity and when your loan is due), but you could set the maturity of the loan to be the same as that of the Treasury bond, thus using the money the bond pays you to pay off the principal of the loan.

Quick Check 4.8 The DEF Corporation announces that over the next few years it will spend several billion dollars on developing a new product. The firm's stock price falls dramatically after the announcement. According to the EMH, what is the reason for the drop in price? If you were the president of DEF Corporation, what conclusions would you draw from the decline in your firm's stock price?

Answer. According to the EMH, the price drop reflects a predominant view in the marketplace that DEF Corporation's proposed new product is not worth developing. If you were CEO and believed that the market analysts had as much information as you did, you might reconsider the desirability of developing the new product. However, if you had superior information about the new product that the market analysts were not aware of, then you might go ahead with the product development despite market opinion. Alternatively, you might make the information you have public in order to gauge the reaction of the market to this new piece of information.

5 Financial Instruments and Rates of Return

Quick Check 5.1 Provide an example of a debt security, an equity security, and a derivative security and explain the goals they allow buyers and sellers to achieve.

Answer. An example of a debt security is a bond that a company issues that you can purchase as an investor. The bond is the company's promise to pay you interest and principal. An example of an equity security would be stock that the company issues which an investor can purchase. The purchaser of an equity security owns part of the company issuing the stock. An example of a derivative security would be an option contract (sold by, say, a bank), where the purchaser then has the right to buy the company's stock in the future (a call option).

Quick Check 5.2 Go to treasury.gov and discover what the level and shape of the US Treasury yield curve is.

Answer. You can see the yields for different maturity treasuries from one month to 30 years, and graph these. This yield curve is from 2 Jan. 2020:

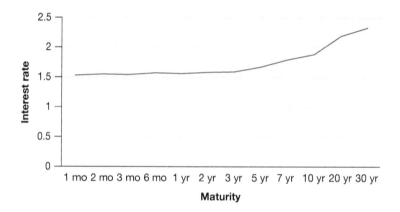

Quick Check 5.3 From the discussion of the pound–yen exchange rate, recalculate the realized yen rate of return if the current yen–pound exchange rate were instead ¥140 to £1.

Answer. Using the numbers from Section 5.2.3 and the new exchange rate, the realized yen rate of return is:

$$\text{Yen rate of return} = \frac{(£109 \times \text{future yen price of a pound (¥/£))} - (£100 \times \text{current yen price of a pound (¥/£))}}{¥15{,}000}$$

$$= \frac{(£109 \times 140) - (£100 \times 140)}{¥15{,}000}$$

$$= 0.084 \text{ or } 8.4\%.$$

The realized yen rate of return is thus 8.4% in this case, higher than the 3% risk-free yen interest rate for one-year Japanese bonds.

Quick Check 5.4 Go to the St. Louis Federal Reserve Economic Research website (https://fred.stlouisfed.org) and find information on Aaa corporate bond yields relative to ten-year Treasury bonds. What does this data series represent? Do you see any noticeable patterns?

Answer. You can view data on the "Moody's Seasoned Aaa Corporate Bond Yield Relative to Yield on 10-Year Treasury Constant Maturity," which gives the yield spread on typical highly rated (Aaa) corporate bonds compared to ten-year Treasury bonds. In 2020 there was a large spike in the spread at the beginning of the COVID-19 pandemic. This reflects the uncertainty regarding the financial health of many companies at the time, which translated to higher yields for corporate bonds relative to treasuries due to this financial risk.

Quick Check 5.5 Suppose the risk-free nominal interest rate on a one-year US Treasury bill is 6% per year and the expected rate of inflation is 3% per year. What is the expected real rate of return on the Treasury bill? Why is the Treasury bill risky in real terms?

Answer. Using Equation 5.1 and plugging in these new numbers:

$$\text{Real rate of return} = \frac{\text{nominal interest rate} - \text{rate of inflation}}{1 + \text{rate of inflation}}$$

$$= \frac{0.06 - 0.03}{1 + 0.03}$$

$$= 0.02913 \text{ or } 2.913\%.$$

Because the actual inflation rate is not known when the nominal interest rate is set, investors can never know for certain what their real return will be (it will depend on what inflation actually turns out to be).

Quick Check 5.6 You invest in a stock costing $50. It pays a cash dividend during the year of $1, and you expect its price to be $60 at year's end. What is your expected rate of return? If the stock's price is actually $40 at year's end, what is your realized rate of return?

Answer. Making use of Equation 5.2, the expected rate of return is:

$$\text{Rate of return} = \frac{\text{ending price of a share} - \text{beginning price} + \text{cash dividend}}{\text{beginning price}}$$

$$= \frac{\$60 - \$50 + 1}{\$50}$$

$$= 0.22 \text{ or } 22\%.$$

Now, if it actually ends up at $40 at year's end, the rate of return you actually realize is:

$$\text{Rate of return} = \frac{\text{ending price of a share} - \text{beginning price} + \text{cash dividend}}{\text{beginning price}}$$

$$= \frac{\$40 - \$50 + 1}{\$50}$$

$$= 0.18 \text{ or } 18\%.$$

Quick Check 5.7 What are the advantages of putting your money in a mutual fund, rather than investing individually in a few stocks?

Answer. Mutual funds allow investors to more easily track or benchmark against indexes like the S&P 500, or more easily allow indexing. Mutual funds also potentially have lower transaction costs for investors. Finally, mutual funds allow investors to benefit from diversification.

Quick Check 5.8 What are the fundamental determinants of rates of return? Which of the Ten Principles of Finance are these determinants an example of?

Answer. The four main factors that determine rates of return in a market economy are:

1. productivity of capital goods (Principle 5);
2. degree of uncertainty regarding the productivity of capital goods (Principle 6);
3. time preferences of people—the preference of people for consumption now versus consumption in the future (Principle 1), possibly due to uncertainty (Principle 6); and
4. risk aversion—the amount people are willing to give up in order to reduce their exposure to risk (Principles 6 and 7).

Quick Check 5.9 What are the arithmetic and geometric average returns for a stock that posted returns of 5%, 20%, and −5% in three consecutive years?

Answer. For the arithmetic average return, we can make use of Equation 5.4:

$$\text{Arithmetic average return} = \frac{R_1 + R_2 + R_3}{3} = \frac{5\% + 20\% - 5\%}{3} = 6.67\%.$$

The geometric average return comes from Equation 5.5:

$$\left((1+R_1) \times (1+R_2) \times (1+R_3)\right)^{\frac{1}{3}} - 1$$
$$= (1.05 \times 1.20 \times 0.95)^{\frac{1}{3}} - 1$$
$$= 0.062 \text{ or } 6.2\%.$$

6 Principles of Risk Management

Quick Check 6.1 Suppose there are two investments: (1) a riskless bond that sells for a price of $100 and promises to pay you $105 in a year; and (2) a stock that sells for a price of $100 and has a 50–50 chance of either going up in value to $110 or staying at $100. What is the expected return of each investment? Which would a risk-averse investor choose?

Answer. For the riskless bond, there is only one possible return, which is the same as its expected return:

$$\mathbb{E}[R] = \frac{P_{t=1} - P_{t=0}}{P_{t=0}} = \frac{\$105 - \$100}{\$100} = 0.05.$$

The return is therefore 5%. The stock will give either a return of $P_{t=1} - P_{t=0}/P_{t=0} = \$110 - \$100/\$100 = 0.10$ or a return of $P_{t=1} - P_{t=0}/P_{t=0} = \$100 - \$100/\$100 = 0$. The expected return for the stock is therefore (using Equation 6.1):

$$\mathbb{E}[R] = p_1 \times R_1 + p_2 \times R_2 = 0.50 \times 10\% + 0.50 \times 0\% = 5\%.$$

The expected return for both investments is the same (5%). But the riskless investment has no risk. A risk-averse investor would choose the risk-free investment given that the returns are the same.

Quick Check 6.2 Suppose that XYZ stock's rate of return can take three possible values: −50%, 50%, and 100%, each with equal probability. What is XYZ's expected rate of return and its standard deviation?

Answer. Each possible value has a probability of 1/3, and we can therefore directly apply our expected return (Equation 6.1) and standard deviation (Equation 6.2) formulas:

$$\mathbb{E}[R] = p_1 \times R_1 + p_2 \times R_2 + p_3 \times R_3$$
$$= \frac{1}{3} \times -50\% + \frac{1}{3} \times 50\% + \frac{1}{3} \times 100\%$$
$$= 33.33\%,$$

$$\sigma = \sqrt{\sum_{i=1}^{n} p_i \times (R_i - \mathbb{E}[R])^2}$$
$$= \sqrt{p_1 \times (R_1 - \mathbb{E}[R])^2 + p_2 \times (R_2 - \mathbb{E}[R])^2 + p_3 \times (R_3 - \mathbb{E}[R])^2}$$
$$= \sqrt{\frac{1}{3} \times (-50\% - 33.33\%)^2 + \frac{1}{3} \times (50\% - 33.33\%)^2 + \frac{1}{3} \times (100\% - 33.33\%)^2}$$
$$= 0.6236 \text{ or } 62.36\%.$$

Quick Check 6.3 Think of a fast-food restaurant. What risks is such a business exposed to, and who bears them?

Answer. The major risks that such a restaurant would be exposed to include:

- risk that ovens will break down;
- risk that raw materials will not arrive on time;
- risk that employees will be late or absent;
- risk of new competition in the area; and
- risk that raw material prices will increase unpredictably.

A number of different people may bear these risks. If the restaurant is owned by a single person, then that person would bear these risks because they could negatively affect revenues and the value of the business. Similarly, if shareholders own the business, then they would bear the bulk of the risks since they impact the business's value. In some cases, customers might bear these risks. If there are not good substitutes for the restaurant (for example, your child simply will not eat elsewhere), then a rise in material prices may translate to a rise in food prices, making the customers bear the cost.

Quick Check 6.4 Identify a major risk in your life and describe the steps you take to manage it.

Answer. A sample answer might include major risks of:

- sickness (hospitalization);
- unemployment (difficulty finding a job); and
- liability risk (car accident).

Some risk management techniques for these include:

- purchasing health insurance;
- investing in higher education to increase the likelihood of getting a job; and
- purchasing liability insurance (usually with an auto-insurance policy).

Quick Check 6.5 How might farmers reduce their exposure to risks of crop failure through diversification?

Answer. Farmers could plant several different types of crops instead of just one. In addition, they could own plots of land in several locations rather than own the same amount of land in just one location.

Quick Check 6.6 In the example of drug investment, suppose instead that Drug 2 pays off $100,000 if it is successful. What is the expected return and standard deviation of Drug 2 now? Recalculate the expected return and standard deviation of the combined investment.

Answer. Drug 2 now provides a return of $100,000 − $50,000/$50,000 = 100% if it "succeeds," and −100% if it fails. The expected return (Equation 6.1) and standard deviation (Equation 6.2) of it are now therefore:

$$\begin{aligned} \mathbb{E}[R] &= p_1 \times R_1 + p_2 \times R_2 \\ &= 0.5 \times 100\% + 0.5 \times -100\% \\ &= 0\%, \end{aligned}$$

$$\begin{aligned} \sigma &= \sqrt{\sum_{i=1}^{n} p_i \times (R_i - \mathbb{E}[R])^2} \\ &= \sqrt{p_1 \times (R_1 - \mathbb{E}[R])^2 + p_2 \times (R_2 - \mathbb{E}[R])^2} \\ &= \sqrt{0.5 \times (100\% - 0\%)^2 + 0.5 \times (-100\% - 0\%)^2} \\ &= 100\%. \end{aligned}$$

There are four possible outcomes for the combined investment (each equally likely with a 25% chance):

1. Both drugs succeed, and you receive $300,000. This gives a return of ($300,000 − $100,000) / $100,000 = 200% based off the initial $100,000 investment.
2. Drug 1 succeeds and Drug 2 doesn't, so you receive $200,000. This gives a return of ($200,000 − $100,000) / $100,000 = 100%.
3. Drug 2 succeeds and Drug 1 doesn't, so you receive $100,000. This gives a return of ($100,000 − $100,000) / $100,000 = 0%.
4. Both drugs fail, and you receive nothing. This gives a return of ($0 − $100,000) / $100,000 = −100%.

We can now calculate the expected return (Equation 6.1) and standard deviation (Equation 6.2) of the combined investment:

$$\begin{aligned} \mathbb{E}[R] &= p_1 \times R_1 + p_2 \times R_2 + p_3 \times R_3 + p_4 \times R_4 \\ &= 0.25 \times 200\% + 0.25 \times 100\% + 0.25 \times 0\% + 0.25 \times -100\% \\ &= 50\%, \end{aligned}$$

$$\sigma = \sqrt{\sum_{i=1}^{n} p_i \times \left(R_i - \mathrm{E}[R]\right)^2}$$

$$= \sqrt{p_1 \times \left(R_1 - \mathrm{E}[R]\right)^2 + p_2 \times \left(R_2 - \mathrm{E}[R]\right)^2 + p_3 \times \left(R_3 - \mathrm{E}[R]\right)^2 + p_4 \times \left(R_4 - \mathrm{E}[R]\right)^2}$$

$$= \sqrt{\begin{array}{c} 0.25 \times (200\% - 50\%)^2 + 0.25 \times (100\% - 50\%)^2 + 0.25 \times (0\% - 50\%)^2 \\ + 0.25 \times (-100\% - 50\%)^2 \end{array}}$$

$$= 111.80\%$$

Quick Check 6.7 A restaurant that serves dishes made out of corn is exposed to the risk of corn prices going up. If the restaurant wants to hedge against this risk, what could it do?

Answer. For the restaurant, the price of corn going up means higher food input costs, which would reduce its profits. The restaurant could hedge this risk by investing in corn. The investment value would go up when costs go up, thus providing the restaurant money (if it sells the investment) at a time when costs are high. As with hedges, the investment value also goes down when corn costs go down.

7 Analyzing Uncertainty: Options

Quick Check 7.1 Create a payoff diagram for a long position in a put option on a share of stock with a strike price of $200. What is the maximum payoff from the long position, and at what stock price does that happen? Create payoff and profit diagrams for the long and short positions, assuming that the option is bought at a price of $40.

Answer. Table 7.12 shows the position.

Table 7.12

Stock price, S_T	Exercise decision	Put option payoff, P_T
$0	Exercise	$200
50	Exercise	150
100	Exercise	100
150	Exercise	50
200	Indifferent	0
250	Do not exercise	0

The maximum payoff is $200 at a stock price of $0. The resulting payoff diagrams for the long position are (profit diagram is the dashed line):

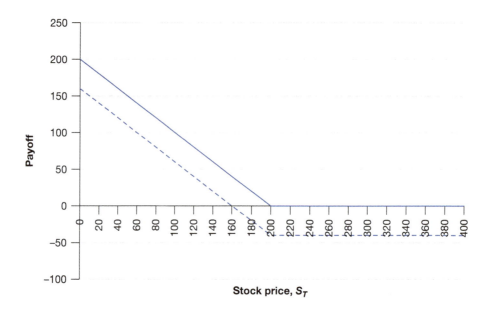

The payoff diagram for the short position is:

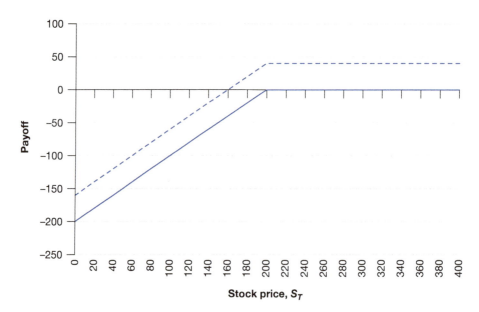

Quick Check 7.2 Create a payoff diagram at expiration for a long position in a call option on a share of stock, with a strike price of $200. Create a payoff diagram for the long and short positions. Also create net payoff diagrams for the long and short positions, assuming that the option was bought at a price of $40.

Answer. Table 7.13 shows the long position.

Table 7.13

Stock price, S_T	Exercise decision	Call option payoff, C_T
$0	Do not exercise	$0
50	Do not exercise	0
100	Do not exercise	0
150	Do not exercise	0
200	Indifferent	0
250	Exercise	50

The payoff (net payoff as dashed line) diagram for the long position is:

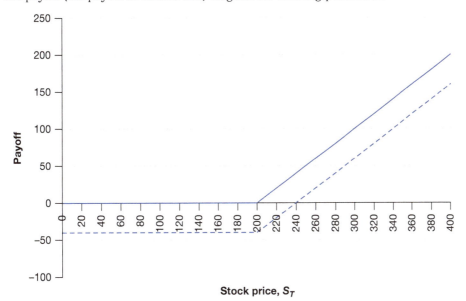

The payoff diagram for the short position is:

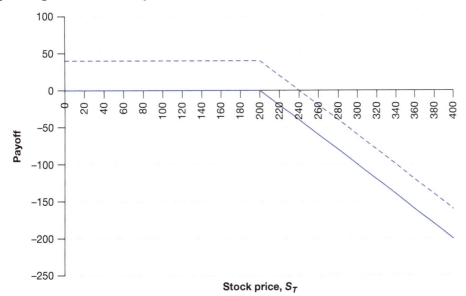

Quick Check 7.3 If the price of the call option with a strike price of 80 and a maturity of two years is 30.328, the price of the put option is 8.752, and the risk-free interest rate is 1% per year, what must be the price of the underlying stock?

Answer. We can use Equation 7.6, based on the put–call parity formula, to deduce the value of the stock:

$$\begin{aligned} S_0 &= C_0 - P_0 + \frac{K}{(1+r_f)^T} \\ &= 30.328 - 8.752 + \frac{80}{(1.01)^2} \\ &= 100.00. \end{aligned}$$

Quick Check 7.4 Using Table 7.6, compute the intrinsic value and the time value of the August HD 37.50 call. Do the same for the put.

Answer. The intrinsic value of a call option is the payoff of the call if it was expiring immediately. The HD stock price is 36.64, thus the intrinsic value of the call with a strike price of 37.50 is zero, since the stock price is less than the strike price. The difference between the option's price and the intrinsic value is the time value, which in this case is 1.40 since the price is 1.40. For the put, the intrinsic value is 37.50 − 36.64 = 0.86, and the time value given a put price of 1.65 is 1.65 − 0.86 = 0.79.

Quick Check 7.5 Suppose there is another strategy to invest $96,000 in the riskless asset and $4,000 in call options. What is the minimum guaranteed rate of return? Draw the graph (payoff diagram) of this strategy's return depending on what the stock's price is in one year.

Answer. The payoff diagram of the return is below. The minimum guaranteed rate of return is 0%.

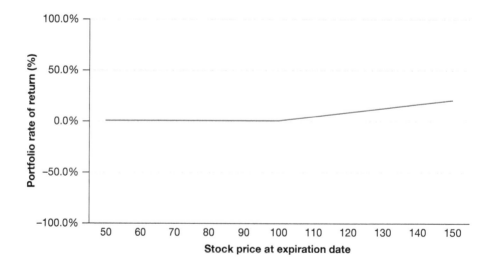

Quick Check 7.6 Choosing to deploy a straddle investment strategy, suppose that the put option had a strike price of $50 and the call option had a strike price of $80. This is also called a "strangle." Draw the payoff and profit diagram of the straddle.

Answer. Table 7.14 can be used to create the payoff diagram.

Table 7.14

Stock price, S_T	Long put option payoff	Long call option payoff	Combined payoff
$0	$50	$0	$50
50	0	0	0
80	0	0	0
100	0	20	20
120	0	40	40

The resulting payoff diagram is:

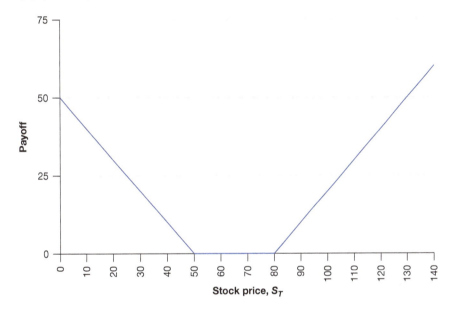

Quick Check 7.7 Suppose that the volatility of the underlying stock is 0.3. With a stock price of $100 (equal to the present value of the strike price), a strike price of $108.33, a maturity of one year, the riskless interest rate is 8%. What is the approximate and exact price of the call and put option?

Answer. The approximate price of the call can be derived using Equation 7.9:

$$\frac{C_0}{S_0} \approx 0.4 \times \sigma \times \sqrt{T}$$
$$= 0.4 \times 0.3 \times \sqrt{1}$$
$$= 0.12.$$

Multiplying by the stock price of $100 gives C_0, the price of the call: $0.12 \times 100 = 12$. The exact price of the call can be calculated using the BSM model (through the Excel app), and is 11.91. The approximate and exact prices of the put can be calculated using the put–call parity formula (Equation 7.8). Starting with the approximate price:

$$P_0 = C_0 - S_0 + \frac{K}{e^{r \times T}}$$
$$= 12 - 100 + \frac{108.33}{e^{0.08}}$$
$$= 12.00.$$

The exact price of the put is:

$$P_0 = C_0 - S_0 + \frac{K}{e^{r \times T}}$$

$$= 11.91 - 100 + \frac{108.33}{e^{0.08}}$$

$$= 11.91.$$

Quick Check 7.8 Suppose that there is a stock with a current price of $100 and an annual volatility of 20%. What is the price of a call option with a strike price of $100 and a maturity of one year if the riskless rate is 2%? Compare this to the price of the call when the stock's volatility is instead 30%.

Answer. Using the Excel app and inputting the relevant numbers, the call price is 8.92. When the volatility increases to 30%, the price increases to 12.82.

8 Financial Statements: Analyzing and Forecasting

Quick Check 8.1 What difference would it have made to the end-of-year balance sheet if GCP had issued an additional $50 million in long-term debt during 2025 and added that amount to its holdings in cash and marketable securities?

Answer. On the balance sheet, GCP's total liabilities and equity would have increased by $50 million, due to the increase in long-term debt. Total assets would also have to increase by $50 million to keep in balance. This increase would be reflected in an increase of $50 million in cash and marketable securities because GCP gets cash by issuing the debt (i.e., borrowing money).

Quick Check 8.2 What difference would it have made to the income statement if GCP instead had SG&A expenses of $50 million?

Answer. GCP would have had operating income or EBIT of $40 million, which would lead to taxable income of $19 million. Because GCP is taxed at a rate of 40%, its income taxes will now be $7.6 million, leading to a net income of $19 − 7.6 = $11.4 million.

Quick Check 8.3 What difference would it have made to the cash flow statement if GCP had retained all of its net income instead of paying out cash dividends of $10 million?

Answer. If GCP had not paid a cash dividend of $10 million, the cash flow statement would have showed no dividends paid. The total cash flow from financing activities would have been +$94.6 million, leading to a new total change in cash and equivalents of: +$25.4 − 90.0 + 94.6 = $30.0 million.

Quick Check 8.4 What potentially important information about a firm can be found in the footnotes to its financial statements?

Answer. A variety of information, including:

- an explanation of accounting methods used;
- greater detail regarding certain assets or liabilities;
- information regarding the firm's equity structure;
- documentation of changes in operations; and
- off-balance-sheet items.

Quick Check 8.5 Why does the market price of a firm's stock usually differ from its book value?

Answer. The book value does not include all of a firm's assets and liabilities (e.g., intangible assets). The assets and liabilities included on a firm's official balance sheet are not marked to market, meaning that book values are based on past information that does not necessarily reflect the current state of the company.

Quick Check 8.6 In 2025, X7 VGI corporation reported earnings per share of $5 and paid a cash dividend to shareholders of $3.00 per share. Its beginning-of-year book value per share was $30, and its market price was $40. At the end of the year, the book value per share was $32 and the market price was $35. Compare VGI's total shareholders' returns and ROE.

Answer. Using Equation 8.1, the total shareholders' returns are:

$$r = \frac{\text{ending share price} - \text{beginning share price} + \text{dividends}}{\text{beginning share price}}$$

$$= \frac{35 - 40 + 3}{40}$$

$$= -5\%.$$

Using Equation 8.2, the ROE is:

$$\text{ROE} = \frac{\text{net income}}{\text{shareholders' equity from previous year}}$$

$$= \frac{5}{30}$$

$$= 16.67\%.$$

Quick Check 8.7 What are the five types of financial ratios used to analyze a company's performance?

Answer. The five types of ratios are: profitability, activity, financial leverage, liquidity, and market price ratios.

Quick Check 8.8 Suppose you see two companies in the same industry with the same EBITDA. If Company A has a higher EV/EBITDA ratio than Company B, what does that tell you about the growth prospects of the two companies? Which company would you expect to have a higher enterprise value?

Answer. A higher EV/EBITDA generally indicates that the market's assessment of the firm's future growth prospects is higher. Thus, we can infer that the market views Company A as having better growth prospects than Company B. We know that we can estimate the enterprise value by multiplying the EBITDA by the EV/EBITDA multiple. Because the EBITDAs of the two companies are the same, a higher EV/EBITDA ratio for company A will lead to a higher estimated enterprise value.

Quick Check 8.9 How can a firm reduce its need for working capital?

Answer. It can reduce its inventories, speed up collection of accounts receivable, or delay payment of its own bills.

9 Company Valuation

Quick Check 9.1 Suppose you want to value a furniture company, and you see that a typical one has a stock price that is 12 times its earnings per share. If the company you aim to value has earnings per share of $1.50, what is an estimate of its stock price?

Answer. We can use the price–earnings valuation multiple as in Equation 9.3:

$$\text{Stock price} = EPS \times \left(\frac{P}{E}\right)_{comparable}$$
$$= \$1.50 \times 12$$
$$= \$18.$$

Quick Check 9.2 What are the different components of free cash flow? How would a typical company estimate the level of each of these components in the future?

Answer. The different components consist of the following:

- *EBIT:* Companies can use projected sales and projected cost growth rates.
- *Depreciation:* When companies make capital purchases, they choose a depreciation schedule to depreciate the value of the capital purchase over time.
- *CapEx:* Companies typically have plans for large capital investments in the short run.
- *ΔNWC:* Expected changes in inventory, accounts payable, and accounts receivable translate to expected changes in NWC. Companies also engage in working capital management.
- *Taxes:* Companies can estimate their expected tax rate based on their current operations.

Quick Check 9.3 Recalculate the total value in the example given in Section 9.3.2, with a growth rate g of 4%.

Answer. The terminal value becomes (Equation 9.9):

$$TV_3 = \frac{FCF_4}{r_A - g} = \frac{FCF_3 \times (1+g)}{r_A - g} = \frac{\$30 \times 1.04}{0.10 - 0.04} = 520.$$

This gives a total value of (Equation 9.6):

$$V = \frac{FCF_1}{1+r_A} + \frac{FCF_2}{(1+r_A)^2} + \frac{FCF_3}{(1+r_A)^3} + \frac{FCF_4}{(1+r_A)^4} + \frac{FCF_5}{(1+r_A)^5} \cdots$$

$$= \frac{FCF_1}{1+r_A} + \frac{FCF_2}{(1+r_A)^2} + \frac{FCF_3}{(1+r_A)^3} + \frac{TV_3}{(1+r_A)^3}$$

$$= \frac{\$10}{1+0.10} + \frac{\$20}{(1+0.10)^2} + \frac{\$30}{(1+0.10)^3} + \frac{520}{(1+0.10)^3}$$

$$= \$438.843.$$

Quick Check 9.4 Recalculate the total company value in the example using $r_E = 0.20$ and $r_D = 0.07$.

Answer. The cost of capital (after-tax WACC) will instead be (Equation 9.11):

$$r_A^{\text{after-tax}} = \text{after-tax WACC} = \left[\frac{E}{V} \times r_E\right] + \left[\frac{D}{V} \times r_D \times (1-\tau)\right]$$

$$= [0.50 \times 0.20] + [0.50 \times 0.07 \times (1-0.30)]$$

$$= 0.1245.$$

This gives a terminal value of (Equation 9.9):

$$TV_3 = \frac{FCF_4}{r_A - g} = \frac{FCF_3 \times (1+g)}{r_A - g} = \frac{\$30 \times 1.01}{0.1245 - 0.01} = \$264.629.$$

Finally, the total value with these new numbers will be (Equation 9.6):

$$\begin{aligned} V &= \frac{FCF_1}{1+r_A} + \frac{FCF_2}{(1+r_A)^2} + \frac{FCF_3}{(1+r_A)^3} + \frac{FCF_4}{(1+r_A)^4} + \frac{FCF_5}{(1+r_A)^5} \cdots \\ &= \frac{FCF_1}{1+r_A} + \frac{FCF_2}{(1+r_A)^2} + \frac{FCF_3}{(1+r_A)^3} + \frac{TV_3}{(1+r_A)^3} \\ &= \frac{\$10}{1+0.1245} + \frac{\$20}{(1+0.1245)^2} + \frac{\$30}{(1+0.1245)^3} + \frac{264.629}{(1+0.1245)^3} \\ &= \$231.913. \end{aligned}$$

10 Capital Budgeting

Quick Check 10.1 Where do you think new project ideas come from in the movie business?

Answer. Some sources of new project ideas in the movie business are:
- sequels to successful movies (e.g., Star Wars, Transformers, Frozen, etc.);
- best-selling novels; and
- ideas based on popular current trends.

Quick Check 10.2 Suppose that the Protojeans project is expected to have a year 3 cash flow of only $10,000 instead of $30,000. If all other cash flows are the same and the discount rate is still 8% per year, what would be its NPV?

Answer. The new cash flow timeline for the Protojeans project is:

Time t:	$t=0$	$t=1$	$t=2$	$t=3$
Net cash flow CF_t (\$ thousands):	−100	50	40	10

The NPV then becomes:

$$\begin{aligned} NPV &= -100 + \frac{50}{1.08} + \frac{40}{1.08^2} + \frac{10}{1.08^3} \\ &= -\$11.472. \end{aligned}$$

Quick Check 10.3 What would be the NPV of the UV1000 project if the production equipment cost $3 million instead of $2.8 million?

Answer. First note that the initial cash outlay will now be $3 + $2.2 = $5.2 million, which will be a negative cash flow at time 0. Note that this will also change depreciation each year, which will now be $3 / 7 = $0.429 million each year. The cash flow for each of the next seven years will change to:

$$\text{Cash flow} = \text{revenue} - \text{total expenses} - \text{taxes} + \text{noncash expenses}$$
$$= \$20 - \$18.5 - \$0.6 + \$0.429$$
$$= \$1.329 \text{ million.}$$

With these new cash flows, the NPV will be given by:

$$NPV = -5.2 + \frac{1.329}{1.15} + \frac{1.329}{1.15^2} + \frac{1.329}{1.15^3} + \frac{1.329}{1.15^4} + \frac{1.329}{1.15^5} + \frac{1.329}{1.15^6} + \frac{1.329 + 2.2}{1.15^7}$$
$$= \$1.156 \text{ million.}$$

Quick Check 10.4 Suppose that investing in the equipment would reduce labor costs by $650,000 per year instead of $700,000. Would the investment still be worthwhile?

Answer. Let us first show what the incremental after-tax cash flow is (Table 10.7).

Table 10.7

	Without investment (1)	With investment (2)	Difference due to investment (3)
Revenue	$5,000,000	$5,000,000	0
Labor costs	1,000,000	350,000	−$650,000
Other cash expenses	2,000,000	2,000,000	0
Depreciation	1,000,000	1,400,000	$400,000
Pretax profit	1,000,000	1,250,000	$250,000
Income taxes (at 33⅓%)	333,333	416,667	$83,334
After-tax profit	666,667	833,333	$166,666
Net cash flow (after-tax profit + depreciation)	$1,666,667	$2,233,333	$566,666

Thus, if the labor cost saving is only $650,000 per year, the incremental net cash flow in years 1–5 is only $566,666 instead of $600,000. In other words, the incremental net cash flow falls by $33,333. The project's NPV falls but still remains positive:

$$NPV = -2,000,000 + \frac{566,666}{1.10} + \frac{566,666}{1.10^2} + \frac{566,666}{1.10^3} + \frac{566,666}{1.10^4} + \frac{566,666}{1.10^5}$$
$$= \$148,110.$$

Quick Check 10.5 Suppose that the average cost of capital for AirCleaners' existing mix of businesses is 12% per year. Explain why this might not be the right discount rate to use in computing the NPV of the UV1000 project.

Answer. AirCleaners Corporation's existing lines of business may have a different risk than the risk of the UV1000 business.

Quick Check 10.6 Assuming its initial outlay is equal to its annual cash flow, what would the scale of the parking project have to be to make its NPV equal to the office building's NPV? The cost of capital remains at 15%.

Answer. The parking facility project has an NPV of $56,667 for an investment of $10,000, and the office building project has an NPV of $869,565. To find the scale at which the parking facility has an NPV of $869,565, we calculate:

$$\text{Scale} = \$869{,}565 / \$56{,}667 = 15.345.$$

Thus, at a cost of capital of 15% per year, the scale of the parking facility project has to increase by a factor of more than 15 to make its NPV greater than that of the office building project.

Quick Check 10.7 What are the disadvantages of the payback criterion?

Answer. The disadvantages are:

- the payback period ignores the time value of money (discounting); and
- the payback period disregards potentially large cash flows in the future.

Quick Check 10.8 Consider the same project as before, which requires an initial outlay of $2 million, and, in the absence of inflation, is expected to produce an annual after-tax cash flow of $600,000 for five years with a cost of capital of 10% per year. Analyze the same project assuming an expected rate of inflation of 8% per year instead of 6%.

Answer. The cash flow timeline will now be:

Time t:	$t=0$	$t=1$	$t=2$	$t=3$	$t=4$	$t=5$
Real cash flow:		600,000	600,000	600,000	600,000	600,000
Nominal cash flow: (8% inflation)		648,000	699,840	755,827	816,293	881,597

The nominal cost of capital will now be:

$$\begin{aligned}\text{Nominal rate} &= (1+\text{real rate})\times(1+\text{expected inflation})-1 \\ &= 1.1\times 1.08 - 1 = 0.188 \text{ or } 18.8\%.\end{aligned}$$

With this, we can discount the nominal cash flows by the nominal cost of capital:

$$\begin{aligned}NPV &= -2{,}000{,}000 + \frac{636{,}000}{1.188} + \frac{699{,}840}{1.188^2} + \frac{755{,}827}{1.188^3} + \frac{816{,}293}{1.188^4} + \frac{881{,}597}{1.188^5} \\ &= \$274{,}472.\end{aligned}$$

The NPV remains unchanged since the real cash flows and real cost of capital are unchanged, in line with the wealth of shareholders being unaffected by the unit of account.

11 Agency Costs and Governance

Quick Check 11.1 A corporation owned by a single person is not a sole proprietorship. Why?

Answer. In a corporation the liability of the single shareholder would be limited to the assets of the corporation.

Quick Check 11.2 What are the main reasons for having a separation of ownership and management of firms?

Answer. There are five reasons:

- Professional managers may be found who have a superior ability to run the business.
- The ability to access capital to achieve the efficient scale of a business may require many investors.
- In an uncertain economic environment, owners will want to diversify their risks across many firms. Such efficient diversification is difficult to achieve without separation of ownership and management.
- It can achieve savings in the costs of gathering information.
- The "learning curve" or "going-concern" effect: When the owner is also the manager, it is harder to ensure continuity of the business if the owner/manager decides to discontinue in either role.

Quick Check 11.3 Briefly describe the four main groups of stakeholders that own and control corporations. Why would each group usually take actions that are good for the company?

Answer. The four groups are:

- Shareholders: They own stock, and want the value of the stock to go up.
- Debtholders: They own debt, such as bonds, and the company doing well means they are more likely to be paid back.
- Managers: They run the company, and the company doing well means they continue to be paid, and if they are paid in stock this increases the amount they are paid.
- Board of directors: Their role is to oversee the proper functioning of the company.

Quick Check 11.4 Briefly describe how there may be agency problems associated with the different stakeholders that own and control corporations.

Answer. There may be the following agency problems:

- Conflicts between shareholders and bondholders: Shareholders may be concerned with dilution of their value, and may block additional stock from being issued. Shareholders may have an incentive to approve risky actions, since the bondholders will bear the cost. Debtholders may not lend in the first place if they are concerned by this.
- Managerial conflicts of interest: Managers may invest in projects that provide private benefits to themselves, or may be tempted to make bad investments if they can easily do so if the firm has a lot of cash.
- Board of directors: Members of the board may be inattentive and not spend enough time on issues related to the company. There is also the possibility of a captured board that just "rubber stamps" the CEO's recommendations.

Quick Check 11.5 What is corporate governance, and how can it help to solve agency problems?

Answer. Corporate governance is the systems that prevent or reduce agency problems. It includes pay and contracts, shareholder voting, financial policy, and voluntary disclosure, as well as external governance like laws and regulations and market discipline. Corporate governance works by either banning certain practices directly, or by providing incentives so that the stakeholders within a company do not take actions that harm company value.

Quick Check 11.6 How does the threat of a takeover serve as a mechanism to deal with the conflict of interest between owners and managers of a corporation?

Answer. The threat of a takeover is credible, and the possibility that the management will be replaced provides a strong incentive for current managers (acting in their self-interest) to act in the interests of the firm by maximizing market value.

12 Payout Policy

Quick Check 12.1 What do stockholders receive from dividends and repurchases?

Answer. Through dividends, stockholders receive cash payments. Through repurchases, participating stockholders receive cash; other stockholders may receive share price appreciation.

Quick Check 12.2 Recreate Table 12.1, assuming that GCP paid a dividend of $4 per share.

Answer. See below:

Original situation: 500,000 shares outstanding:

Assets		Debt and equity	
Cash	$2 million	Debt, D	$2 million
Other assets	$10 million	Equity, E	$10 million
Total	$12 million	Total, V	$12 million
		Price per share: $20	

After cash dividend paid using cash reserves; dividends paid = 500,000 × $4 = $2 million:

Assets		Debt and equity	
Cash	$0 million	Debt, D	$2 million
Other assets	$10 million	Equity, E	$8 million
Total	$10 million	Total, V	$10 million
		Price per share: $16; Cash per share: $4	

After cash dividend paid by raising debt:

Assets		Debt and equity	
Cash	$2 million	Debt, D	$4 million
Other assets	$10 million	Equity, E	$8 million
Total	$12 million	Total, V	$12 million
		Price per share: $16 Cash per share: $4	

Quick Check 12.3 Suppose GCP instead decided to repurchase 100,000 shares. Recreate Table 12.2 for this scenario.

Answer. Repurchasing 100,000 shares at $20 per share requires spending $2 million. See below:

Original situation:

Assets		Debt and equity	
Cash	$2 million	Debt, D	$2 million
Other assets	$10 million	Equity, E	$10 million
Total	$12 million	Total, V	$12 million
		Price per share: $20 Shares outstanding: 500,000	

After repurchase funded using cash reserves:

Assets		Debt and equity	
Cash	$0 million	Debt, D	$2 million
Other assets	$10 million	Equity, E	$8 million
Total	$10 million	Total, V	$10 million

Price per share: $20
Shares outstanding: 400,000

After repurchase funded by raising debt:

Assets		Debt and Equity	
Cash	$2 million	Debt, D	$4 million
Other assets	$10 million	Equity, E	$8 million
Total	$12 million	Total, V	$12 million

Price per share: $20
Shares outstanding: 400,000

Quick Check 12.4 Explain how a firm's stock price might increase when it begins paying dividends or does a repurchase.

Answer. When a firm begins paying dividends, it signals to the market that it has good cash flow prospects and is likely to be able to continue paying the dividends. Its stock price may rise after incorporating this information. With a repurchase, a firm is signaling to the market that it believes that it is undervalued, and the stock price may rise as a result of incorporating this.

Quick Check 12.5 Explain how dividends and repurchases can help to reduce agency problems.

Answer. Paying dividends or repurchases uses up cash, which helps to reduce the free cash flow problem. Repurchases can also increase a manager's ownership stake in a company, thus better aligning incentives. The inflexibility of dividends can cause a company to continue to reduce its cash holdings, and can impose discipline on managers.

Quick Check 12.6 What are some potential disadvantages of funding dividends or repurchases with debt?

Answer. Additional debt can potentially reduce value through costs of financial distress and distorted investment incentives like risk shifting and debt overhang.

Quick Check 12.7 Why may tax considerations and regulations favor the use of repurchases over dividends?

Answer. If the tax rate on capital gains is lower than the applicable tax rate for dividends, then shareholders will prefer repurchases. Regulations help enforce the relative flexibility of repurchases compared to dividends, since repurchases can't be used regularly in the same way as dividends.

Quick Check 12.8 What would be the effect of GCP paying a 20% stock dividend?

Answer. GCP would then have 600,000 shares outstanding, and with the total equity value unchanged the price per share would change to: $10 million / 600,000 = $16.67:

	Assets		Debt and equity
Cash	$2 million	Debt, D	$2 million
Other assets	$10 million	Equity, E	$10 million
Total	$12 million	Total, V	$12 million
	Price per share: $16.67		
	Shares outstanding: 600,000		

13 Capital Structure

Quick Check 13.1 How does the need for external financing impose market discipline on a corporation?

Answer. Outside providers of funds are likely to want to see detailed plans for the use of the funds, and will want to be convinced that proposed investments will produce sufficient future cash to justify the expenditure.

Quick Check 13.2 If GCP were to announce an issue of $50 million of debt to be used to repurchase and retire common stock, what would be the effect on its total company value and equity value?

Answer. GCP's total value would remain at $100 million, according to M-M Proposition 1. However, GCP would then have $50 million in debt, and therefore the total value of its outstanding equity will be $50 million.

Quick Check 13.3 Consider a company that decides to go from a leverage ratio (D/V) of 70% of firm value to 50% of firm value. If the assumptions of M-M hold (i.e., there are no frictions), explain how you expect this to affect the firm's overall cost of capital, its cost of equity, and its cost of debt.

Answer. If M-M holds, there will be no change to the overall cost of capital. Both the cost of equity and the cost of debt will decrease.

Quick Check 13.4 Suppose LGCP were instead composed of $50 million of debt and $50 million of equity. Would its equity cost of capital be higher or lower than what we calculated? Recalculate its equity cost of capital (assume that the cost of debt remains unchanged).

Answer. From Equation 13.4, LGCP's equity cost of capital was 19.67%. It had $40 million in debt and $60 million in equity, and thus increasing the proportion of debt to 50% of company value will cause the equity cost of capital to increase. We can recalculate it as follows (noting that the unlevered cost of capital will remain unchanged):

$$\begin{aligned} r_E^{LGCP} &= r_U + \frac{D^{LGCP}}{E^{LGCP}} \times \left(r_U - r_D^{LGCP}\right) \\ &= 0.15 + \frac{50}{50} \times (0.15 - 0.08) \\ &= 0.22. \end{aligned}$$

Quick Check 13.5 Recalculate the expected rate of return on debt in Example 13.3 assuming that there is a 10% chance the company's bonds will default.

Answer. For the pet food company's bonds, $y = 0.0205$, $p = 0.10$, and $L = 0.10$. Applying Equation 13.6, we have:

$$r_D = y - p \times L$$
$$= 0.0205 - 0.1 \times 0.10$$
$$= 0.0105.$$

Quick Check 13.6 With taxes, why is firm value changed when a firm changes its capital structure?

Answer. With taxes, firms that make interest payments because they have debt receive a tax deduction. Thus, a firm's tax bill is lower when it has more debt, which increases the value of the firm.

Quick Check 13.7 Recalculate the value of LGCP if it instead held 30% debt and 70% equity. Assume that the cost of debt remains at 8%. Compare your value to that calculated in the chapter.

Answer. We first recalculate r_E with the new capital structure:

$$r_E^{LGCP} = r_U + \frac{D}{E} \times (r_U - r_D) \times (1 - \tau)$$
$$= 0.10 + \frac{0.30}{0.70} \times (0.10 - 0.08) \times (1 - 0.40)$$
$$= 0.105.$$

The new after-tax WACC becomes:

$$r_A^{LGCP} = \left[\frac{E}{V} \times r_E\right] + \left[\frac{D}{V} \times r_D \times (1 - \tau)\right]$$
$$= [0.7 \times 0.105] + [0.3 \times 0.08 \times (1 - 0.40)]$$
$$= 0.088.$$

Finally, LGCP's firm value will be:

$$V^{LGCP} = \frac{FCF}{r_A^{LGCP}}$$
$$= \frac{6}{0.088}$$
$$= \$68.182 \text{ million.}$$

The number is lower than that in the chapter example because LGCP has a lower leverage ratio and thus a smaller tax shield.

Quick Check 13.8 Suppose instead that LGCP chose to change its leverage ratio to 50% starting in year 2. Recalculate LGCP's firm value.

Answer. The timeline will now look like this:

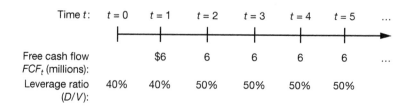

We would now apply the perpetuity formula using the WACC of 7% (given a 50% D/V) to calculate firm value as of $t = 2$:

$$V_{t=2}^{LGCP} = \frac{FCF_3}{r_{A,t=2}^{LGCP}}$$

$$= \frac{\$6}{r_{A,t=2}^{LGCP}}$$

$$= \frac{6}{0.07}$$

$$= \$85.714 \text{ million.}$$

The next step is to discount this value and the $t = 2$ cash flow back one year to $t = 1$. The rate that applies for discounting from $t = 2$ back to $t = 1$ is the 8.2% WACC using the leverage ratio of 40%; this WACC will also apply for discounting from $t = 1$ to $t = 0$, so $r_{A,t=0}^{LGCP} = r_{A,t=1}^{LGCP} = 0.082$. First we discount $V_{t=2}^{LGCP}$ and the $6 million cash flow occurring at $t = 2$ back one year:

$$V_{t=1}^{LGCP} = \frac{\$6}{1+r_{A,t=1}^{LGCP}} + \frac{V_{t=2}^{LGCP}}{1+r_{A,t=1}^{LGCP}}$$

$$= \frac{6}{1.082} + \frac{85.714}{1.082}$$

$$= \$84.763 \text{ million.}$$

This gives us the value of the firm as of $t = 1$. Next, we discount $V_{t=1}^{LGCP}$ and the $t = 1$ cash flow back one year to $t = 0$:

$$V_{t=0}^{LGCP} = \frac{\$6}{1+r_{A,t=0}^{LGCP}} + \frac{V_{t=1}^{LGCP}}{1+r_{A,t=0}^{LGCP}}$$

$$= \frac{6}{1.082} + \frac{84.763}{1.082}$$

$$= \$83.885 \text{ million.}$$

Quick Check 13.9 What are the steps involved in calculating the value of a firm using the APV method?

Answer. To calculate with the APV method:

1. Calculate unlevered firm value V_U.
2. Calculate the present value of the debt tax shield.
3. Sum the unlevered value of the firm and the present value of the debt tax shield.

Quick Check 13.10 As in the discussion above, suppose that your aircraft manufacturing company is considering building a new electric car. The electric car project costs $10 million now, and will generate $5 million in cash flows each year for the next three years. Your company currently has 50% debt and 50% equity in its capital structure, and it will continue to have this capital structure after issuing financing for the project. The unlevered cost of capital for electric car manufacturers is 15%. Your company's cost of debt is 5%, and the tax rate is 35%. What is the appropriate discount rate and NPV of the project?

Answer. First, the discount rate of the electric car can be calculated by first calculating the cost of equity (using the unlevered cost of capital for electric car manufacturers), and then the after-tax WACC for your company:

$$r_E = r_U + \frac{D}{E} \times (r_U - r_D) \times (1 - \tau)$$
$$= 0.15 + \frac{0.50}{0.50} \times (0.15 - 0.05) \times (1 - 0.35)$$
$$= 0.215,$$

$$r_A^{after\text{-}tax} = \left[\frac{E}{V} \times r_E\right] + \left[\frac{D}{V} \times r_D \times (1 - \tau)\right]$$
$$= [0.50 \times 0.215] + [0.50 \times 0.05 \times (1 - 0.35)]$$
$$= 0.124.$$

The NPV of the electric car project will be:

$$NPV = -10 + \frac{5}{1.124} + \frac{5}{1.124^2} + \frac{5}{1.124^3}$$
$$= 1.927.$$

Quick Check 13.11 How would a decrease in the costs of financial distress affect corporate capital structure?

Answer. Corporations would make greater use of debt financing.

Quick Check 13.12 How might conflicts between shareholders and creditors affect a company's investments?

Answer. These conflicts may result in firms investing in excessively risky and potentially negative-NPV projects (risk shifting), or in firms not investing in positive-NPV projects (debt overhang).

Quick Check 13.13 What are the advantages to a firm of having debt?

Answer. The required cash payments needed to pay off interest and principal can reduce free cash flow problems, impose discipline on managers, and provide a positive signal to investors about the firm's prospects.

Quick Check 13.14 Suppose a firm expects good news to happen in the future. Why might the firm's management decide to not issue stock?

Answer. Management could simply wait for the good news to break, and then issue stock to raise even more money. Managers (and shareholders) will gain even more if they do not dilute their shares of stock before the stock price increases when the good news breaks.

Quick Check 13.15 What is debt seniority and maturity?

Answer. Debt seniority refers to the legal priority that different types of debt have in terms of repayment. Debt maturity refers to when the principal of debt is due.

14 A Unified Approach to the Valuation of Corporate Assets and Capital Structure

Quick Check 14.1 Recreate Table 14.1 and Figure 14.1 for equity assuming that the firm's debt matures in two years and the total face value of the debt is $120 million.

Answer. See Table 14.5 and Figure 14.8.

Table 14.5 Answer to Quick Check 4.1.

Total company value in one year, V_1	Debt payoff in two years	Equity payoff in two years
$0	$0	$0
40	40	0
80	80	0
120	120	0
160	120	40
200	120	80
240	120	120

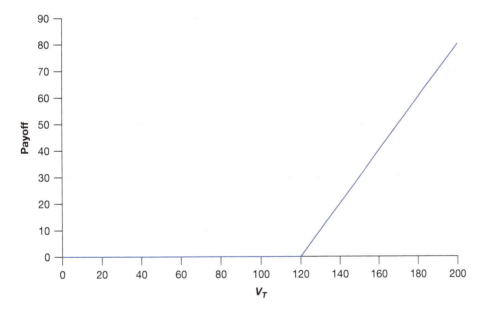

FIGURE 14.8 Answer to Quick Check 4.1.

Quick Check 14.2 Recreate Table 14.2 and Figure 14.2 for debt, assuming that the firm's debt matures in two years and the total face value of the debt is $120 million.

Answer. See Table 14.6 and Figure 14.9.

Table 14.6 Answer to Quick Check 14.2.

Total company value in one year, V_1	Riskless bond, par = $120 million	Write a put option, K = $120 million	Combined	Landco debt payoffs
$0	$120	−$120	$0	$0
40	120	−80	40	40
80	120	−40	80	80
120	120	0	120	120
160	120	0	120	120
200	120	0	120	120
240	120	0	120	120

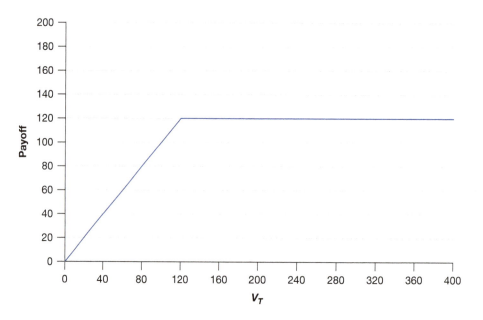

FIGURE 14.9 Answer to Quick Check 14.2.

Quick Check 14.3 Calculate the value of Landco's debt and equity assuming instead that the firm's debt matures in two years and the total face value of the debt is $120 million. Assume that the other characteristics of the firm remain the same as above.

Answer. Landco's equity can be calculated by determining the value of the call option. We have the same firm characteristics, except that the maturity date of the debt (and thus the expiration date of the option) is two years and the total face value (and thus the strike price of the option) is $120 million. Using the BSM formula via the Excel app, the new call option price (and thus the value of the equity) is $15.88 million. For the value of the debt, the put option value is 18.14 from the BSM calculator. The PV of the riskless bond is:

$$PV \text{ (riskless bond)} = \frac{120}{e^{2 \times 0.08}}$$
$$= 102.26.$$

Thus, the value of the debt is:

$$D = \text{riskless debt} - \text{put option}$$
$$= 102.26 - 18.14$$
$$= 84.12.$$

Quick Check 14.4 In the Landco example in this section, suppose instead that the project reduces the volatility of Landco to $\sigma = 0.1$. Recalculate Landco's equity value assuming the project is undertaken. Explain why the equity value changes in the way it does.

Answer. Landco's equity value was originally $28.24 million. With a new volatility of 0.1, the equity value (using the BSM calculator in the Excel app) becomes $26.15 million, which is lower. A lower risk (volatility) lowers the value of the call option, and thus makes the equity value lower. Intuitively, the downside remains the same for the equity holders but there is less of a potential upside.

Quick Check 14.5 Considering Landco with senior and junior debt, suppose instead that the principal amounts for the senior and junior debt were $40 million each. What would be the values of the senior and junior debts in this case?

Answer. A combination to replicate the senior and junior debt is:

- senior debt = riskless bond with principal $40 million − put option with K = $40 million;
- junior debt = long call with K = $40 million − call with K = $80 million.

Using the BSM calculator with Landco's inputs, the value of a call option with K = $40 million is $63.08 million, a put option with K = $40 million is $0.00, and a call option with K = $80 million is 28.24 million. PV (riskless bond) = $40 / e^{0.08}$ = 36.92. Thus, we have that:

- senior debt = $36.92 million − $0.00 = $36.92 million;
- junior debt = $63.08 million − $28.24 million = $34.84 million.

Quick Check 14.6 In the example in this section, if Bullseye's stock volatility increases to 30%, what happens to the value of the option to Rader? Explain why this is the case.

Answer. Since the real option is a call option, the value of the option goes up. Specifically, the value of the option goes up from $8 million to $12 million. The reason is that the option is to buy the shares for a fixed price; the increase in volatility means that there is more upside potential for the stock price to go even higher.

Quick Check 14.7 What is the option value of the Electro Utility investment project if the volatility of the power-generating plant is 0.3 instead of 0.2?

Answer. Using the BSM calculator from the Excel app and changing the volatility to 30%, we find an option value of $12 million. Subtracting the initial outlay of $6 million gives an NPV of $6 million instead.

15 Financing over a Firm's Life

Quick Check 15.1 What are the features of banks that enhance their ability to lend to firms?

Answer. Banks engage in qualitative asset transformation and are able to use deposits as a source of funding for loans, which is a relatively less-expensive funding source compared to other external funding. Banks also engage in relationship lending, which reduces asymmetric information and enables banks to lend more and at lower rates.

Quick Check 15.2 What are the reasons why entrepreneurs would want to seek venture capital funding? Why would venture capitalists want to provide money to entrepreneurs?

Answer. Entrepreneurs may have difficulty getting larger amounts of capital from other sources, or may find such sources unattractive, such as with bank loans and the potential for financial distress costs. Entrepreneurs can also benefit from the advice and connections that venture capitalists provide. Venture capitalists gain the potential for high investment returns if they sell their ownership stake after the company has become successful.

Quick Check 15.3 What are the reasons why a firm may do an initial public offering?

Answer. An IPO allows firms to access equity capital markets, which allows the firm to initially raise a large amount of money, and then subsequent amounts through seasoned equity offerings. This can allow a firm to invest and grow, and more effectively compete against other firms. Being a publicly traded company can also encourage management to focus on value creation due to stock market pressures. It can also help build positive employee compensation incentives, and credibility with customers and employees.

Quick Check 15.4 What is a leveraged buyout? Why is it common for PE firms to acquire companies in this manner?

Answer. An LBO is when a PE firm acquires a company and finances the purchase through significant amounts of debt. The debt is collateralized with the assets of the target firm, and debt payments are made via the cash flows of the target firm's operations. Using an LBO allows the PE firm to take advantage of the benefits of debt, like the debt tax shield. PE firms may also benefit from such a transaction due to risk shifting.

Quick Check 15.5 Consider the DCF valuation model in Equation 15.5. How might overestimating synergies affect the inputs into calculating the model?

Answer. An acquiring firm may overestimate projected improvements in sales, resulting in too high free cash flows. The acquiring firm could also anticipate that synergies will increase the long-run growth rate of free cash flows, g, by too much. An acquiring firm may also believe that synergies may reduce the cost of capital through effects such as reducing agency problems, when in reality such problems are exacerbated through effects such as cultural mismatch.

Quick Check 15.6 What is the difference between chapter 7 and chapter 11 bankruptcy for a business?

Answer. Chapter 7 bankruptcy aims to liquidate the business—sell off the business's assets in order to pay back debtors and other claimants. Chapter 11 bankruptcy seeks to reorganize the firm and renegotiate contracts and terms in order to allow the firm to successfully emerge from bankruptcy and continue to operate.

16 The Term Structure of Interest Rates

Quick Check 16.1 Suppose that interest rates in the economy are 0.5% instead. Recalculate the prices of the one-year bill and the two-year bond.

Answer. The prices will be as follows:

$$\text{Price of bill} = \frac{\$1{,}000}{1+r} = \frac{\$1{,}000}{1.005} = \$995.02,$$

$$\text{Price of bond} = \frac{\$1{,}000}{(1+r)^2} = \frac{\$1{,}000}{1.005^2} = \$990.07.$$

Quick Check 16.2 Suppose that $r_1 = 2\%$ and $r_2 = 1\%$. Recalculate the prices of the bill and the bond. What would be your rate of return if you sold the bond at $t = 1$?

Answer. The prices will be:

$$\text{Price of bill} = \frac{\$1,000}{1+r_1} = \frac{\$1,000}{1.02} = \$980.39,$$

$$\text{Price of bond} = \frac{\$1,000}{(1+r_2)^2} = \frac{\$1,000}{1.01^2} = \$980.30.$$

If sold at $t = 1$, the value of the bond would be $\$980.30 \times 1.02 = \$999.91$. The rate of return for the bond would therefore be $\$999.91 / \$980.30 - 1 \approx 0.02$ or 2%, which is the one-year interest rate.

Quick Check 16.3 Using the yields from Table 16.1, recalculate the value of the contract from the section that has a maturity of three years and pays a sure amount of $\$5,000$ at $t = 1$, $\$7,000$ at $t = 2$, and $\$9,000$ at $t = 3$.

Answer. Using the yields from the table as discount rates, we have:

$$\begin{aligned}\text{Price} &= \frac{\$5,000}{1+r_1} + \frac{\$7,000}{(1+r_2)^2} + \frac{\$9,000}{(1+r_3)^3} \\ &= \frac{\$5,000}{1.010} + \frac{\$7,000}{(1.011)^2} + \frac{\$9,000}{(1.012)^3} \\ &= \$20,482.62.\end{aligned}$$

Quick Check 16.4 Create a timeline of cash flows for a five-year bond with a face value of $\$1,000$ and a coupon rate of 8%.

Answer. The timeline is:

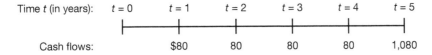

Quick Check 16.5 In the example of the 20-year maturity bond, suppose when the bond has one year remaining before it matures the interest rate on one-year bonds is instead 11% per year. What is the price of the bond now? Is it a discount, premium, or par bond?

Answer. The price of the bond is:

$$\begin{aligned}P &= \frac{\$1,100}{1.11} \\ &= \$990.99.\end{aligned}$$

The price is lower than the face value of $\$1,000$, and therefore the bond is now a discount bond.

Quick Check 16.6 Suppose that the one-year interest rate (r_1) is 4%, the two-year interest rate (r_2) is 5%, and the three-year interest rate (r_3) is 6%. What would be the price and YTM of a three-year coupon bond with a face value of $\$1,000$ and a coupon rate of 4% per year?

Answer. The timeline of cash flows for the bond is:

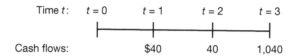

The price of this bond would be (Equation 16.5):

$$P = \frac{C}{1+r_1} + \frac{C}{(1+r_2)^2} + \frac{C+PAR}{(1+r_3)^3}$$

$$= \frac{\$40}{1.04} + \frac{40}{1.05^2} + \frac{1{,}040}{1.06^3}$$

$$= \$947.95.$$

The YTM of this bond will be given by Equation 16.7, given this price (which can be solved for via Excel or a financial calculator):

$$\$947.95 = \frac{\$40}{1+y} + \frac{40}{(1+y)^2} + \frac{1{,}040}{(1+y)^3}$$

$$y = 0.0595 \text{ or } 5.95\%.$$

Quick Check 16.7 Suppose that the two-year interest rate was the same as the one-year interest rate: 1%. What would the one-year forward interest rate be for $t = 1$?

Answer. Utilizing Equation 16.1 with $r_1 = r_2 = 0.01$, we have:

$$f_{1,2} = \frac{(1+r_2)^2}{1+r_1} - 1 = \frac{(1.01)^2}{1.01} - 1 = 0.01.$$

The forward rate will be 1%, consistent with the term structure of spot interest rates not changing for one- and two-year horizons.

Quick Check 16.8 Calculate the modified duration of the three-year zero-coupon bond which had a face value of $1,000 and a price of $863.84.

Answer. The bond is a zero-coupon bond, and thus its Macaulay duration will be three years, the same as its maturity. Its YTM is given by:

$$P = \frac{\$1{,}000}{(1+y)^3} = \$863.84$$

$$y = 0.05.$$

We can therefore solve for its modified duration (Equation 16.11):

$$\text{Modified duration} = \frac{\text{Macaulay duration}}{\left(1 + \frac{y}{T}\right)}$$

$$= \frac{3}{\left(1 + \frac{0.05}{3}\right)}$$

$$= 2.95.$$

Thus, the bond's price will go down by 2.95% when interest rates increase by 1%.

Quick Check 16.9 Between a five-year zero-coupon bond and a ten-year zero-coupon bond, which would you anticipate convexity would matter more for when ascertaining interest rate sensitivity?

Answer. Convexity will matter more for the ten-year bond, since it has a longer maturity and its value is thus more affected by changes in interest rates.

17 Portfolio Theory

Quick Check 17.1 How would the investment portfolio that is best for a young person with a secure job differ from the one that is best for a retired person whose only source of income is an investment portfolio?

Answer. The young person with a secure job can look forward to a long period of earning a salary that will probably increase with the rate of inflation. For her, investment in stocks would not be as risky as for the older person who needs to ensure a steady source of income for the rest of his life. The young person is somewhat protected against inflation but the older person is not, and may have to try to find insurance against price increases.

Quick Check 17.2 What is your current planning horizon? How might your planning horizon change in the future?

Answer. Answers will vary.

Quick Check 17.3 Do you think that risk tolerance increases with a person's wealth? Why?

Answer. A wealthier individual may be willing to take more risks than someone with less wealth because their capacity to take bigger gambles and lose is higher. That is, they may still be quite wealthy after taking losses.

Quick Check 17.4 What is the riskless asset if the unit of account is the euro and the length of the decision horizon is one week?

Answer. A euro-denominated, one-week, riskless zero-coupon bond.

Quick Check 17.5 Locate the point corresponding to portfolio J in Figure 17.1. Consult Table 17.2 for the portfolio's composition, its expected rate of return, and standard deviation. How much of your $100,000 would be invested in the risky asset if you chose portfolio J?

Answer. The proportion invested in the risky asset for portfolio J is 75%, so you would have invested 75% × $100,000 = $75,000.

Quick Check 17.6 Suppose that the risk-free rate was instead 0.03 per year and the expected rate of return on the risky asset was 0.10 per year. Recreate Table 17.2 with these new numbers. If you wanted to create a portfolio with a target expected return of 0.05 per year, what portion of your money would need to be invested in the risky asset?

Answer. With a risk-free rate of 0.03 and expected return on the risky asset of 0.10, we would get Table 17.7.

Table 17.7 Answer to Quick Check 17.6.

Portfolio	Proportion invested in risky asset, w	Proportion invested in riskless asset, 1 − w	Expected rate of return, $\mathbb{E}[R_P]$	Standard deviation (volatility), σ_P
(1)	(2)	(3)	(4)	(5)
F	0%	100%	0.03	0.00
G	25%	75%	0.05	0.05
H	50%	50%	0.07	0.10
J	75%	25%	0.08	0.15
S	100%	0%	0.10	0.20

At a target expected return of 5%, you would be investing 25% of your money in the risky asset and 75% in the riskless asset (Portfolio G).

Quick Check 17.7 If an investor wanted to achieve a target expected return of 0.20, what position would the investor need to take?

Answer. To determine the position, we can solve for w in Equation 17.4 with an expected return of 0.20:

$$\mathbb{E}[R_P] = r_f + w \times [\mathbb{E}[R_S] - r_f],$$
$$0.20 = 0.02 + w \times [0.14 - 0.02],$$
$$w = 1.5.$$

The investor would therefore invest 150% of their wealth in the risky asset (therefore borrowing at the riskless rate).

Quick Check 17.8 What are the mean and standard deviation of a portfolio that is 60% Risky Asset 1 and 40% Risky Asset 2, if the correlation coefficient is 0.1?

Answer. To calculate the mean return (expected return), we can use Equation 17.7 with $w = 0.6$, given that the expected return of Asset 1 is 0.14 and the expected return of Asset 2 is 0.08:

$$\begin{aligned}\mathbb{E}[R_P] &= w \times \mathbb{E}[R_1] + (1 - w) \times \mathbb{E}[R_2] \\ &= 0.6 \times 0.14 + 0.4 \times 0.08 \\ &= 0.116.\end{aligned}$$

The standard deviation can be calculated from Equation 17.8, with $\rho_{1,2} = 0.10$ and given that $\sigma_1 = 0.20$ and $\sigma_2 = 0.15$:

$$\sigma_P^2 = w^2 \times \sigma_1^2 + (1-w)^2 \times \sigma_2^2 + 2 \times w \times (1-w) \times \rho_{1,2} \times \sigma_1 \times \sigma_2$$
$$= 0.6^2 \times 0.20^2 + 0.4^2 \times 0.15^2 + 2 \times 0.4 \times 0.6 \times 0.1 \times 0.20 \times 0.15$$
$$= 0.01944,$$
$$\sigma_P = \sqrt{0.01944} = 0.139.$$

Quick Check 17.9 Recalculate the optimal combination of Risky Asset 1 and Risky Asset 2 assuming a correlation between the two of 0.50. What is the Sharpe ratio of this optimal combination?

Answer. Risky Asset 1 has an expected return of 0.14 and a standard deviation of 0.20. Risky Asset 2 has an expected return of 0.08 and a standard deviation of 0.15. The riskless rate is 0.02. Using Equation 17.10, we can recalculate the optimal combination:

$$w = \frac{\left[\mathbb{E}[R_1] - r_f\right] \times \sigma_2^2 - \left[\mathbb{E}[R_2] - r_f\right] \times \rho_{1,2} \times \sigma_1 \times \sigma_2}{\left[\mathbb{E}[R_1] - r_f\right] \times \sigma_2^2 + \left[\mathbb{E}[R_2] - r_f\right] \times \sigma_1^2 - \left[\mathbb{E}[R_1] - r_f + \mathbb{E}[R_2] - r_f\right] \times \rho_{1,2} \times \sigma_1 \times \sigma_2}$$

$$= \frac{[0.14 - 0.02] \times 0.15^2 - [0.08 - 0.02] \times 0.50 \times 0.20 \times 0.15}{[0.14 - 0.02] \times 0.15^2 + [0.08 - 0.02] \times 0.20^2 - [0.14 - 0.02 + 0.08 - 0.02] \times 0.15 \times 0.20 \times 0.15}$$

$$= 0.75.$$

To calculate the Sharpe ratio, we need to know the portfolio expected return and standard deviation. Using Equations 17.7 and 17.8:

$$\mathbb{E}[R_P] = w \times \mathbb{E}[R_1] + (1-w) \times \mathbb{E}[R_2]$$
$$= 0.75 \times 0.14 + 0.25 \times 0.08$$
$$= 0.125,$$

$$\sigma_P^2 = w^2 \times \sigma_1^2 + (1-w)^2 \times \sigma_2^2 + 2 \times w \times (1-w) \times \rho_{1,2} \times \sigma_1 \times \sigma_2$$
$$= 0.75^2 \times 0.20^2 + (1-0.75)^2 \times 0.15^2 + 2 \times 0.75 \times (1-0.75) \times 0.50 \times 0.20 \times 0.15$$
$$= 0.030,$$
$$\sigma_P = \sqrt{0.030} = 0.172.$$

The Sharpe ratio of this portfolio is therefore (Equation 17.9):

$$\text{Sharpe ratio} = \frac{\mathbb{E}[R_P] - r_f}{\sigma_P}$$
$$= \frac{0.125 - 0.02}{0.172}$$
$$= 0.61.$$

Quick Check 17.10 Suppose an investor chooses to invest 75% of their wealth in the tangency portfolio and 25% in the riskless asset. What is the expected rate of return and standard deviation of this portfolio? If the investor has $100,000, how much will they invest in each of the three assets?

Answer. The tangency portfolio has an expected return of 0.112 and a standard deviation of 0.127. The riskless return is 0.02. We can use Equations 17.3 and 17.4 to calculate the expected return and standard deviation of the portfolio, given that $w = 0.75$:

$$\mathbb{E}[R_P] = w_T \times \mathbb{E}[R_T] + (1 - w_T) \times r_f$$
$$= 0.75 \times 0.112 + 0.25 \times 0.02$$
$$= 0.089,$$

$$\sigma_P = w_T \times \sigma_T$$
$$= 0.75 \times 0.127$$
$$= 0.09525.$$

If the investor has \$100,000, this means that the investor is putting $75\% \times \$100,000 = \$75,000$ in the tangency portfolio and \$25,000 in the riskless asset. The tangency portfolio is composed of the two risky assets, with a weight of $w = 0.529$ in Risky Asset 1 and $1 - w = 0.471$ in Risky Asset 2. This means that out of the \$75,000, $\$75,000 \times 0.529 = \$39,675$ is invested in Risky Asset 1, and $\$75,000 - \$39,675 = \$35,325$ in Risky Asset 2.

18 Capital Market Equilibrium

Quick Check 18.1 Investor 3 has a \$100,000 portfolio with nothing invested in the risk-free asset. How much is invested in GM and how much in Toyota?

Answer. In the example, for any money put into risky assets, 75% should go into GM stock and 25% into Toyota stock. Thus, Investor 3 should put $75\% \times \$100,000 = \$75,000$ into GM stock and $25\% \times \$100,000 = \$25,000$ into Toyota stock.

Quick Check 18.2 Suppose you are examining a stock that has a beta of 0.8. According to the CAPM, what should be its risk premium, given a market risk premium of 0.08?

Answer. The risk premium of the stock is its expected return beyond the risk-free rate of return, and is given by Equation 18.5:

$$\mathbb{E}[R_i] - r_f = \beta_i \times [\mathbb{E}[R_M] - r_f]$$
$$= 0.8 \times 0.08$$
$$= 0.064.$$

Quick Check 18.3 Suppose you are examining a stock that has a beta of 0.8. According to the CAPM, what should be its risk premium, given a market risk premium of 0.10? If the stock's risk premium is 0.10, what is the alpha of the stock?

Answer. The risk premium can be calculated via Equation 18.5:

$$\mathbb{E}[R_i] - r_f = \beta_i \times [\mathbb{E}[R_M] - r_f]$$
$$= 0.8 \times 0.10$$
$$= 0.08.$$

If the stock's risk premium is 0.10, we can use Equation 18.8 to calculate the alpha:

$$\alpha = \{\mathbb{E}[R_i] - r_f\} - \{\beta_i \times [\mathbb{E}[R_M] - r_f]\}$$
$$= 0.10 - 0.08$$
$$= 0.02.$$

Quick Check 18.4 Go to a website such as Yahoo! Finance and choose a stock. Find the beta for the stock. If the market risk premium were 10%, what is your estimate of the risk premium for the stock?

Answer. Solutions will vary depending on the stock picked. In Yahoo! Finance, the beta is shown under "Summary." The risk premium for the stock would be found by multiplying that beta by 0.10.

Quick Check 18.5 Consider the firm discussed above, with expected free cash flows of $10 million next year and every year henceforth, and financed with 50% debt and 50% equity. Recalculate the total value of the firm, assuming that the firm's equity and debt betas were instead 1.0 and 0, respectively.

Answer. We can recalculate the asset beta using Equation 18.14 with the new numbers:

$$\beta_A = \left[\frac{E}{V} \times \beta_E\right] + \left[\frac{D}{V} \times \beta_D\right]$$
$$= [0.5 \times 1.0] + [0.5 \times 0]$$
$$= 0.5.$$

The CAPM Equation 18.5 allows us to calculate the firm's cost of capital, given the market risk premium of 0.08 and risk-free rate of 0.01:

$$r_A = r_f + \beta_A \times [\mathbb{E}[R_M] - r_f]$$
$$= 0.01 + 0.5 \times 0.08$$
$$= 0.05.$$

Finally, the total value can be calculated using the perpetuity formula and this cost of capital:

$$V = \frac{\$10}{1+r_A} + \frac{10}{(1+r_A)^2} + \frac{10}{(1+r_A)^3} + \frac{10}{(1+r_A)^4} + \frac{10}{(1+r_A)^5} + \cdots$$
$$= \frac{\$10}{0.05}$$
$$= \$200 \text{ million.}$$

19 Derivatives

Quick Check 19.1 Draw a timeline of cash flows and a payoff diagram from the perspective of both the long and short positions for a forward contract where the long position promises to purchase 100 barrels of oil in two years at a price of $80 per barrel.

Answer.

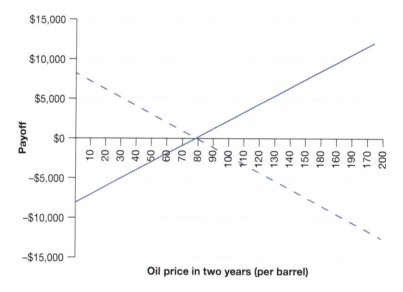

The payoff diagram for the position is:

Quick Check 19.2 What will happen in your futures trading account if you take a long position in wheat futures, and instead of going down by 2¼ cents per bushel, the futures price went up by 7¼ cents per bushel?

Answer. Assuming 5,000 bushels as part of the contract, you would gain 0.0725 × 5,000 bushels = $362.50.

Quick Check 19.3 Suppose that, for an ounce of gold, $r_f = 0.06$, $S_0 = \$400$, and $c = 0.02$. What must the forward price of gold be? Explain how, if the actual forward price is different from this.

Answer. Using Equation 19.4, the forward price must be:

$$F_{0,T} = S_0 \times (1 + r_f + c - y)^T$$
$$= \$400 \times (1 + 0.06 + 0.02)^1$$
$$= 432.$$

If the actual forward price is higher than this, then one could construct an arbitrage strategy by going long the forward contract and shorting gold. If the actual forward price is lower than this, then one could construct an arbitrage strategy by shorting the forward contract and buying gold.

Quick Check 19.4 Suppose that $r_\$ = 0.06$, $r_¥ = 0.03$, and $S_0 = \$0.01$. What must the forward price of ¥1 be?

Answer. Using Equation 19.7:

$$F_{0,T} = S_0 \times \frac{1+r_\$}{1+r_¥}$$

$$= 0.01 \times \frac{1+0.06}{1+0.03}$$

$$= 0.0103.$$

Quick Check 19.5 Draw the cash flows for both legs of a four-year interest rate swap with a notional amount of $2 million, a fixed rate of 3%, and a floating leg based on SOFR plus 50 basis points. Assume that SOFR is 3% in $t = 1$, and increases by 1 percentage point each year after that.

Time t (in years):	$t = 0$	$t = 1$	$t = 2$	$t = 3$	$t = 4$
SOFR:		3%	4%	5%	6%
Fixed payer					
Receives floating:	$0	$70,000	$90,000	$110,000	$130,000
Pays fixed:	$0	–$60,000	–$60,000	–$60,000	–$60,000
Net:	$0	$10,000	$30,000	$50,000	$70,000
Floating payer:					
Receives fixed:	$0	$60,000	$60,000	$60,000	$60,000
Pays floating:	$0	–$70,000	–$90,000	–$110,000	–$130,000
Net:	$0	–$10,000	–$30,000	–$50,000	–$70,000

Answer.

Quick Check 19.6 Redraw the timeline of cash flows for both legs of the total return swap, but instead assuming that the level of the S&P 500 increases by 3% each period, and that the floating rate is based on SOFR + 80 bps.

Answer. With a notional amount of $1 million, we have:

Time t (in years):	$t=0$	$t=1$	$t=2$	$t=3$
SOFR:		4%	5%	3%
S&P 500 index level:	2,000	2,060	2,121.80	2,185.45
Long equity leg ($)				
Receives equity return:	0	30,000	30,000	30,000
Pays floating rate:	0	−48,000	−58,000	−38,000
Net:	0	−18,000	−28,000	−8,000
Short equity ($):				
Receives floating rate:	$0	$48,000	$58,000	$38,000
Pays equity return:	$0	−$30,000	−$30,000	−$30,000
Net:	$0	$18,000	$28,000	$8,000

Quick Check 19.7 Calculate the swap's cash flows for the dollar–euro example, assuming that the forward dollar–euro exchange rates are instead $1.05 each year.

Answer. In the example, the exchange rate started at $1.30 per euro. In the first year, your counterparty in the swap is obliged to pay you €100,000 times the difference between the $1.30 per euro forward rate and the $1.05 per euro spot rate (i.e., €100,000 × ($1.30/€ − $1.05/€) = $25,000). In the second year, you will be obliged to *pay* the counterparty to your swap agreement €100,000 times the difference between the $1.05 per euro spot rate and the $1.30 per euro forward rate (i.e., €100,000 × ($1.05/€ − $1.30/€) = −$25,000).

Quick Check 19.8 Suppose that the underlying stock is more volatile than in the previous example, and it can rise or fall by 30% during the year. Use the binomial model to derive the price of the option.

Answer. If the stock can rise or fall by 30%, this means that $u = 1.3$ and $d = 0.7$. With a stock price of $100 right now, this means the price of the stock will be either $130 or $70. The call option payoff in each case will therefore be (with a strike price of $100) $30 or $0, respectively. The riskless rate was 5%, so in this case we can apply Equation 19.12 directly to get the call option price:

$$C_0 = \frac{1}{1+r_f} \times \left[\frac{(1+r_f)-d}{u-d} \times C_u + \frac{u-(1+r_f)}{u-d} \times C_d \right]$$

$$= \frac{1}{1.05} \times \left[\frac{1.05 - 0.7}{1.3 - 0.7} \times \$30 + \frac{1.3 - 1.05}{1.3 - 0.7} \times 0 \right]$$

$$= 16.667.$$

Quick Check 19.9 Suppose in the dynamic replication exercise in this section that the call option had a strike price of $80, and furthermore that the stock price increases or decreases by $20 each period instead of $10. Calculate the price of the call option.

Answer. The tree will look like:

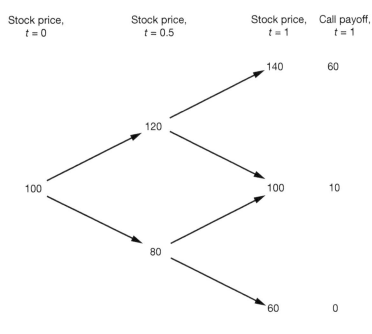

We then construct the replicating strategy for the option in each branch. Starting with the top-right section:
$$140 \times \Delta + B = 60,$$
$$100 \times \Delta + B = 10.$$

Solving for Δ in the above equation yields $\Delta = 1.25$, and plugging that back into one of the equations and solving for B gives $B = -115$. This gives:
$$\text{Value of call in six months when } S \text{ is } 120 = 120 \times \Delta + B$$
$$= 120 \times 1.25 - 115$$
$$= 35.$$

The bottom-right branch of the tree lets us set up the following equations:
$$110 \times \Delta + B = 10,$$
$$60 \times \Delta + B = 0.$$

Solving for Δ in the above equation yields $\Delta = 0.2$, and $B = -12$. This gives:
$$\text{Value of call in six months when } S \text{ is } 80 = 80 \times \Delta + B$$
$$= 80 \times 0.2 - 12$$
$$= 4.$$

The final step considers the branch at $t = 0$:
$$120 \times \Delta + B = 35,$$
$$80 \times \Delta + B = 4.$$

Solving for Δ in the above equation yields Δ = 0.775 and B = −58. Finally, the value of the call can be calculated as:

$$\text{Value of call at } t = 0 = 100 \times \Delta + B$$
$$= 100 \times 0.775 - 58$$
$$= 19.5.$$

20 The Financial System and its Functions

Quick Check 20.1 A depositor puts $5,000 into a bank account and you take a $5,000 student loan from the bank. Use Figure 20.1 to explain the process of this flow of funds.

Answer. The funds flow from the depositor (a surplus unit) to a financial intermediary, and then from the intermediary to you (a deficit unit).

Quick Check 20.2 Suppose a company you have invested in experiences a drop in its stock price. Your investment advisor explains why this happened. How might this drop be framed in a way that makes your investment's performance seem either good or bad?

Answer. One way it could be framed is in the context of other stock price changes. If you are shown other times when stocks have dropped even further in price, then the price drop of your stock may not seem as bad in comparison. In contrast, if you have been shown that the stock historically has done well, the drop may seem especially bad.

Quick Check 20.3 Suppose you are invested in the stock of a tech company, and you observe a group of investors selling the stock. How might this lead to a self-fulfilling prophecy?

Answer. The investors may be selling the stock for a variety of reasons. For example, they may have a portfolio in which they have too much weight in tech stocks, and thus need to sell. But if other investors take this to imply that the tech company's stock will do poorly, they may sell. If many investors sell the stock, then the price will fall, leading to a self-fulfilling prophecy.

Quick Check 20.4 When you purchase a company's stock, in what way are you trusting the management running the company? What are some possible ways they can increase the trust of investors like yourself?

Answer. You are trusting that the management will run the company properly, and not simply run away with the money that investors have provided (or use that money for things such as perks and pet projects). Management can increase trust by establishing a track record of good behavior or by transparency—doing things like communicating information to investors and filing thorough and accurate financial and operating reports. Verification by a third party, such as an auditing firm, can also possibly be a substitute for trust or can help to build trust.

GLOSSARY

acquired company the company that is purchased as part of a merger, takeover, or acquisition

acquiring company the company that buys the acquired company as part of a merger, takeover, or acquisition

acquisition when a company buys another firm to gain their assets

acquisition premium in a merger, the excess of the offer price over the current market price

actively managed an investment strategy that involves frequently buying and selling securities

activist shareholders individuals that own large numbers of shares of a company—and thus wield substantial influence—and are also outspoken to other shareholders and the media regarding their views on company policy

Adaptive Market Hypothesis the hypothesis that posits that rational investors may exhibit behavioral anomalies within efficient markets in an attempt to adapt to changing conditions.

adjusted present value (APV) method a discounted cash flow valuation model that accounts for the tax shield of debt as a cash flow; in contrast, the PV model accounts for the tax shield of debt by adjusting the discount rate

adverse selection a behavioral phenomenon where information asymmetry encourages riskier behavior—for example, those who purchase insurance are more likely than the general population to be at risk

after-tax cost of debt capital a company's cost of debt capital adjusted for the tax shield created by borrowing, since (for businesses) interest expense is tax deductible

after-tax WACC method a discounted cash flow valuation model that accounts for the tax shield of debt through the version of the weighted-average cost of capital (WACC) that uses the after-tax cost of debt, adjusting for the tax savings created when interest payments are tax deductible for a company

agency cost when agency problems reduce a company's value

agency problems incentive problems that arise when there is a conflict of interest between the different stakeholders of a company: One stakeholder is expected to work in the best interest of the other stakeholders (making that stakeholder an "agent" of the others), but may be more motivated to act in its own, conflicting interests

agents in a corporation, those who act on behalf of shareholders (i.e., principals), such as managers, employees, etc.

alpha excess return is traditionally designated as alpha (the Greek letter α)

American option a variation of a European option, a contract that gives a party the right but not the obligation to buy or sell an asset at a specified price and time. An American option may be exercised at the specified price any time prior to maturity

angel investors high-net-worth individuals that invest an equity stake in a privately held company, typically in an early-stage startup

annual percentage rate (APR) interest rates on loans and savings accounts are usually stated in the form of an annual percentage rate APR (e.g., 6% per year), which makes comparisons and calculations of interest consistent across loans, although it does not incorporate interest that is compounded over time

annuity a stream of cash flows that lasts for a defined period of time, with each cash flow being the same amount and occurring at regular intervals.

arbitrage the purchase and sale of equivalent assets in order to earn a riskless (and potentially unlimited) profit from a difference in their prices

arbitrage pricing theory (APT) a model of expected returns that expands on the CAPM, including multiple systemic risk factors in addition to or instead of sensitivity to the market's returns

arbitrageurs market participants that seek to profit from price discrepancies between equivalent assets

arithmetic average return or arithmetic mean rate of return a simple mean, calculated as the sum of a group of return observations divided by the number of return observations in the group

asset anything that has economic value

asset-backed security (ABS) a financial contract that passes through to investors the cash flows generated by a bundle of underlying assets such as mortgage loans, car loans, or credit card receivables

asset beta the broad measure of the sensitivity of the return on a company's assets to the market's return; since assets = debt + equity, it is also a measure of the sensitivity of a company's total financing return to the market's return

asset turnover ratio a measure of a firm's ability to use its assets productively to create revenue. Asset turnover = sales/(average total assets)

asset valuation the process of estimating how much an asset is worth

assets resources that a company uses to generate profits—that is, what it has to work with

asymmetric information asymmetric information exists when one party has access to more information than the other—for example, managers and other insiders know more about the company's operations and future prospects than investors and other outsiders

balance sheet a reported financial statement, prepared in compliance with accounting standards, that lists the values of a company's assets, liabilities, and equity on a given date

balance sheet date the point in time at which the firm's balance sheet shows its assets, liabilities, and equity

balloon payment lump sum payment that repays the principal balance on a loan, typically when the loan matures

bank financial institution that holds and lends money to individuals and businesses, and also facilitates cash transactions

bank loans a form of debt financing from a bank, widely used by individuals as well as companies, both privately and publicly traded

bank run happens when a significant number of bank depositors attempt to withdraw funds at one time, overwhelming the bank's reserves and capacity to meet their demands

bankruptcy a legal process to reorganize a company's operations and financing or to distribute the value of a company's assets to its creditors and shareholders if the company cannot meet its financial obligations

basis points (bps) basis points, known as bps or "bips," are used to describe percentage change in value. One basis point is equivalent to 0.01% (1/100th of a percent) or 0.0001 in decimal form

behavioral biases systematic but irrational behaviors that people tend to exhibit that can lead to suboptimal decisions. Behavioral biases such as overconfidence, confirmation bias, and regret/loss aversion are well-documented psychological phenomena that also apply to investors and corporate decision makers

behavioral finance a subfield of finance that examines why individuals may not behave rationally, and explores the implications of this

benchmark a comparison against which to measure the performance of an investment

beta the symbol of a measure of an asset's sensitivity to the market's behavior—that is, its systemic risk

bills a short-term debt obligation, usually with a maturity of up to one year

Black–Scholes–Merton (BSM) formula a mathematical equation that estimates the theoretical value of derivative instruments. The BSM was the first model to provide a practical way to price actively traded derivatives, opening the door to the active derivative markets of modern finance

blockholders a blockholder is the owner of a large number (or block) of the company's shares; commonly at least 5% of the outstanding shares of the company

board inattention when board members do not devote enough time or effort in their oversight of a company

board of directors a group of individuals elected by shareholders to oversee the proper functioning of a company

bond a debt contract representing a loan sold to investors. Investors purchasing the bond are lending money to bond issuers such as governments and corporate entities, which in turn promise to repay the loan amount in the future

bond rating a grade for individual bond issues based on the borrower's probable ability to repay the loan. A bond rating is issued by a ratings agency and is often used to determine the borrower's cost of debt

book values the reported values on financial statements, which may or may not reflect market values

bootstrap sampling or bootstrapping a method of simulating returns that generates a return for each period based on randomly selected actual past returns

breakeven rent the rent at which a renter would be indifferent between buying and renting

bullet payment a lump sum payment that repays the principal balance on a loan, typically when the loan matures

call option a contract that gives its owner the right, but not the obligation, to buy an asset at a specified price on or before some specified expiration date

callability a feature of financial instruments such as debt, in which the instrument has an embedded call option so that the borrower may redeem it at a pre-specified price (i.e., "call it back" from the owner) before the final maturity date. For example, a callable bond may be redeemed before maturity under specific circumstances

callable bond a bond that gives the issuer of the bond the right to redeem it at a pre-specified price

CAPE ratio (cyclically adjusted price earnings ratio, aka Shiller P/E ratio) created by Nobel Prize-winning economist Robert Shiller, which calculates a price to earnings ratio for the S&P 500 market index using average earnings over the past ten years (adjusted for inflation)

capital asset pricing model (CAPM) a financial model that estimates an asset's expected return, based on the risk-free interest rate, the market's risk premium, and the asset's sensitivity to market risk

capital budgeting the process of analyzing capital investment decisions

capital gain or capital loss a gain (or loss) created by a change in an asset's market value from its original cost

capital market the broad term for the conceptual market where financial transactions take place

capital market line (CML) the linear model of risk–reward trade-off facing each investor, given the market's risk premium

capital structure the mix of financing sources that a firm uses to fund its operations, growth, and investment projects

caps limits placed on compensation for particular losses covered under an insurance contract

captured board refers to a board of directors that is unlikely to disagree with the CEO's agenda

cash budget a forecast of cash outflows and inflows

cash cycle time the number of days between the date the firm must start to pay cash to its suppliers and the date it begins to receive cash from its customers. For the average sale, calculated using its receivables, inventory, and payables turnover ratios. Cash cycle time = inventory period + receivables period − days payables period

cash dividend a cash payment delivered directly to shareholders as a distribution

cash flow from operating activities (or cash flow from operations) the cash received from the regular business of a firm (i.e., selling the firm's products), less the cash paid for expenses (such as materials and labor to produce the products)

cash flows cash that flows into (i.e., a cash inflow) or out of (i.e., a cash outflow) a business or investment

cash flows from financing activities the cash that the company either receives from or pays out to its investors

cash flows from investing activities the cash used to make investments for the company, such as buying machinery, equipment, buildings, and so on

cash settlement settlement of a transaction by an exchange of cash, instead of an exchange of assets

central bank a financial institution designated by a government to be responsible for managing the money supply, interest rates, and other asset prices in the economy

Chapter 11 bankruptcy based on the US bankruptcy code, a form of bankruptcy that involves the reorganization of a debtor's operations, debts, and assets, which allows the company to continue to operate

Chapter 7 bankruptcy based on the US bankruptcy code, a form of bankruptcy where the company's assets are liquidated, and the proceeds distributed to creditors. The company ceases to operate or exist

close out to terminate an investment position before maturity

collateral assets promised to a creditor in case of loan default

commercial loan rate the rate charged by banks on loans made to businesses

commodity a physical asset such as raw materials, agricultural products, or resources

commodity future a publicly traded contract to buy or sell an amount of a commodity for a specific price at a specific date in the future

common stock equity shares of a company that represents a residual claim on a company's value

company value or total value the combined value of a company's assets, which is also the combined value of its debt and equity. Also referred to as enterprise value

comparable companies companies that are similar in many respects—they operate in the same industry, sell similar products, are roughly the same size, and so forth, such that they can be used for comparison with a company being evaluated or analyzed

compound interest interest earned on interest already paid—that is, "interest on interest"

compound options complex investment projects, which are typically organized in stages with critical decisions at the end of each stage, can be analyzed as investments with embedded options

compounding earning a return (i.e., interest) on an amount that has already earned interest

conflicts between shareholders a conflict of interest that occurs when a group of shareholders act to prioritize the value of their holdings at the expense of other shareholders and the company

consumption smoothing approach to planning for financial comfort over your lifetime

continuation value (aka equity terminal value or exit price) the estimated value of a company's equity at the end of the investment horizon or holding period, usually based on its discounted expected future cash flows at that time

continuous compounding interest is compounded continuously—not just every hour, every minute, or every second, but at the smallest time intervals imaginable

convenience the value of holding and thus being able to use a physical commodity

convenience yield the equivalent return one gives up from holding a financial contract instead of a physical commodity and the convenience afforded from being able to access that commodity at any time

conversion fee the fee a bond investor pays to convert a bond into a predetermined number of shares of stock

convertibility a feature of a financial instrument, such as a bond, that gives the owner the right to convert it into a pre-specified amount of another financial instrument, such as stock

convertible bond a bond that can be converted to a specified amount of equity in the future

convexity the amount by which a bond's price sensitivity to interest rates changes as interest rates change

copayment an insured party's share of payment

corporate governance systems put in place in order to encourage optimal functioning of a corporation and to correct agency costs

corporation a business structure that is a legal entity distinct from its owners, such that it provides the owners with limited liability for the business's liabilities

cost of capital the rate of return that investors expect in exchange for providing the company with funds

cost of carry the net of storage costs and the convenience yield each period for a forward/futures contract

cost of goods sold (COGS) the expenses incurred in producing or purchasing products sold, including materials and labor used in a manufacturing process

coupon bond a bond that pays a coupon or interest payment at regular intervals

coupon rate the interest rate applied to the bond's face value to compute the coupon payment

coupons (coupon payments) an interest payment on a bond, usually paid at regular intervals

covenants restrictions placed on a borrower as a condition of obtaining a loan, which aims to ensure the borrower does not take actions that will put it in a position where it cannot pay back the debt

credit default swap (CDS) a type of financial contract that pays out when there is a credit default, and is used to offset or hedge the risk of a credit default

credit event an event that triggers a credit default or a condition of settlement on a credit derivative

credit risk the risk that the borrower on a debt contract will default

crowdfunding very early-stage financing, where many different contributors provide small amounts of money

currency forward type of financial forward contract; a privately traded contract to buy or sell currency in the future at a specified price

currency swap exchanging cash flows based on two different currencies

current assets short-term assets a company owns that are either currently cash or will be converted into cash within one year

current liabilities items a company owes that must be paid off within a year

current ratio a measure of how well a company's short-term assets can support its short-term liabilities, it is calculated as the ratio of current assets to current liabilities

current yield a bond's annual coupon as a percentage of its price. Current yield = C/P

debt default the inability of a borrower to meet the commitments of its debt

debt overhang when a firm has debt that is so large, it cannot take on additional financing for investment

debt ratio (leverage ratio) a company's debt as a proportion of its total assets, a measure of how much debt a company has compared to the assets it owns, which, in turn, can be an indicator of its solvency and risk

debt securities financial instruments created to transact debt

debt tax shield the tax savings created by the interest deductibility of debt

debtholders (creditors) investors who provide debt financing by lending money to the company

debt-to-equity ratio the ratio of a company's debt to its equity, used as an indicator of the firm's broad capital structure, its use of leverage, and its solvency

decision horizon the length of time between the points in time when a portfolio owner decides to revise the portfolio

decision tree a graphic model that plots the progression of decisions and events over time, based on a diagram of a tree

deductible an amount of money that the insured party must pay out of their own resources before receiving any compensation from the insurer

default when a borrower does not meet the conditions of its debt by not paying interest or principal on time or by violating the conditions of the loan

default risk the risk that an issuer will not make its promised debt payments and/or meet the conditions of its debt

deferral option the option to postpone the beginning of an investment project

deposit insurance a guarantee made to bank depositors that they will not lose funds in the event of a bank failure, usually provided by a government agency

depreciation expense the amount that assets such as equipment depreciated in value during the year, applied as an accounting expense

derivatives financial instruments whose value is derived from the prices of one or more other assets such as stocks, bonds, foreign currencies, or commodities such as gold and silver

derivatives markets active trading of millions of derivative contracts representing trillions of dollars of notional value, both on exchanges and in over-the-counter (OTC) trading

dilute to issue additional shares of stock that makes current shares less valuable and reduces the voting influence of current shareholders

direct costs of financial distress the costs that firms incur if they enter into bankruptcy proceedings

discipline the effect of debt imposed on managers to ensure their decisions are for the benefit of the firm

disclosure voluntary release of information

discount bond a bond that trades at a price less than its par value—that is, face value

discount factor a number that, when multiplied by a future value, turns that value into a present value. Defined as $1/1 + r$, where r is the discount rate

discount function the prices (per $1 of par) of pure discount bonds

discount rate in present value calculations, the discount rate is the rate at which time affects value, due to risk and opportunity cost. In practice, the discount rate used is often a comparable rate of return or interest rate

discounted cash flow estimates of the value right now of future cash flows using a discount rate

discounted cash flow (DCF) analysis the calculation of the present value(s) of a future cash flow or stream of future cash flows that is used to value an asset or investment

discounted cash flow (DCF) model valuation based on discounting estimates of future cash flows using a discount rate

discounted payback period a method of analyzing capital budgeting projects that measures when the initial investment is "paid back" with discounted cash flows

discounting accounting for the time value of money by calculating present value

disintermediation a market development whereby the role of intermediaries is diminished as products are sold directly to consumers

diversifiable risk risk that can be diversified, such as the risk attributable to a particular company

diversification investing in an array of investments with different risks and different risk sensitivity in order to minimize overall exposure to risk

dividend discount model a model used to value a company's equity using the discounted value of its expected future dividends, based on the idea that dividends are the cash flows that a company provides to shareholders

dividends distribution of cash to shareholders

dividends paid cash paid as distributions to shareholders; reported on a company's cash flow statement

dominant strategy a strategy that is better than other strategies no matter how others react

downward-sloping yield curve a yield curve is a graphical depiction of currently expected interest rates for different maturities; when it is downward-sloping (i.e., negatively sloped), it indicates that longer-term interest rates are expected to be less than shorter-term interest rates

Du Pont Identity (or the DuPont model) ratio analysis used to show a company's return on equity (ROE) as a product of three broad factors: profit margin, total asset turnover, and equity multiplier. Each factor can be further defined by its contributing factors

duration a measure of the sensitivity of bond value to interest rate changes. The greater a bond's duration, the more sensitive its value is to changes in interest rates

dynamic replication a strategy used in derivatives trading that creates a position designed to replicate the payoffs of an existing position. The replicating position must be adjusted as the features of the replicated position change over time

dynamic trading a trading strategy that frequently adjusts the portfolio's asset allocation to achieve a goal such as replicating a position

early stage a "youthful" stage in a company's life cycle often characterized by high growth but low or no profits; the company is typically financed using privately supplied capital

earnings before interest and taxes (EBIT) the operating profit, before deducting interest and tax expense

effective annual rate (EAR) the stated annual rate of interest that reflects the frequency of compounding throughout the year

efficient frontier the set of portfolios that produces the highest possible expected rate of return for any given level of risk

efficient markets hypothesis (EMH) proposition that an asset's current price reflects all available information about future economic fundamentals affecting the asset's value

efficient portfolio the portfolio that offers the investor the highest possible expected rate of return at a specified level of risk

enterprise value the total value of a company's assets

enterprise value to EBITDA (EV/EBITDA) ratio a market valuation ratio calculated by dividing a company's enterprise value by its earnings before interest, taxes, depreciation, and amortization

entrenchment management making decisions and taking actions that make it more difficult for the company to do without them, thus increasing their own job security

environmental, social, and governance (ESG) objectives a firm may have to benefit the environment or achieve social goals

equity a financial instrument issued by a company that makes the purchaser of the instrument a partial owner of the firm. More broadly refers to a residual ownership claim in a company after all obligations have been paid. Also refers to the section of the balance sheet where such capital is listed

European option a contract that gives a party the right but not the obligation to buy or sell an asset at a specified price and time

exchange rate an exchange rate is a rate at which one currency will be exchanged for another, reflecting the relative purchasing power of each currency, as well as each country's risk-free interest rate

exchange-traded assets traded on organized exchanges

exchange-traded fund (ETF) investment funds that are traded on exchanges—just as stocks are—allowing any investor to buy a share of the fund

exchange-traded options exchange-traded options have standard contract terms defined by the options exchange. The exchange matches buyers and sellers and guarantees payment in the event of default by either party

exclusions losses that might seem to meet the conditions for coverage under the insurance contract but are specifically excluded

ex-dividend price share price immediately after a dividend has been paid

exercised when the decision for an option is made to buy (for a call option) or sell (for a put option) the underlying asset for the exercise price

exit strategy in private equity or venture capital investing, refers to the planned divestment of a portfolio company

expectations theory theory of the term structure of interest rates in which forward rates are often assumed to be forecasts of what investors expect future interest rates to be

expected rate of return (E[R]) a weighted-average expectation of the return on an asset, weighted by probability

expense ratio fund management fees as a percentage of money invested

expiration or maturity date the date that an investment with a finite life, such as an option or bond, ends

external financing funding generated from outside the firm from lenders or investors

external governance refers broadly to forces outside the company that align the incentives of managers and other stakeholders with those of the firm

face value (aka par value or principal amount) the principal amount borrowed when a bond is issued, which must be repaid in full at or before maturity

financial distress imminent danger of default on debt obligations

financial futures exchange-traded contracts to buy or sell financial assets for a specified price and at a specified time in the future

financial guarantee a guarantor's promise to step in and pay what is owed if one party in a financial agreement is not able to

financial innovation spiral a situation in which organized markets and intermediaries compete with each other in a static sense and complement each other in a dynamic sense, resulting in financial products being produced by intermediaries and then moving to markets

financial instruments financial assets such as a contract or security exchanged between two parties that has some monetary value

financial intermediaries the institutions, such as banks and insurance companies, that act as agents for buyers or sellers or both in financial transactions

financial leverage ratios a measure of the proportion of capital attained through debt and the relative burden of that debt placed on the firm's assets and/or earnings

financial markets organized marketplaces in which financial assets or instruments are bought and sold

financial planning the continual process of making plans for an investor's profitability and growth, implementing those plans, and revising them as actual results are known

financial ratios measures of company performance or condition based on its reported results and used in analysis of company strategy or valuation

financial service firms firms that help people and other firms understand and navigate the various parts of the financial system, such as tax preparers and financial advisors

financial statements reports published by businesses and other organizations that are prepared in compliance with accounting standards and provide investors and other stakeholders with information about a firm's assets, liabilities, existing and potential earnings and cash flows, and so on

financial system the markets and institutions used to carry out the decisions that households, business firms, and governments make about managing their money and other financial assets

financial technology (fintech) a broad term that refers to new technology or new applications of technology that seeks to improve and automate the delivery and use of financial services—for example, specialized software and algorithms that are used on computers and smartphones

fintech lenders financial companies that lend money but do not fund themselves with deposits (unlike banks)

fixed and perpetual debt where a company chooses to keep the same amount of debt on its balance sheet indefinitely going forward

fixed income describes a bond that offers a fixed coupon (i.e., interest) rate and payment, and thus provides a "fixed income" for the bondholder. Typically, the coupon rate (and thus payment) is fixed at the time the bond is issued and remains constant until the bond's maturity date; bond investments are often referred to as fixed-income investments

flat term structure of interest rates indicates an environment where longer-term interest rates are expected to be the same as current shorter-term interest rates, producing a flat yield curve

flat yield curve a graphical depiction of currently expected interest rates for different maturities; when it is flat, it indicates that longer-term interest rates are expected to be the same as shorter-term interest rates

flow of funds the process of how funds move from one entity to another

forward contracts similar to futures contracts, forwards are contractual agreements to buy or sell a specified amount of an asset at a specified price on a specified date. Unlike futures, forwards do not trade on an exchange but are privately traded

forward price the specified price in a forward contract

forward rate of interest the expected interest rate t periods from now (e.g., what the one-year spot interest rate will be t years from now) is known as the t-year forward rate of interest

framing how a choice problem is presented and what alternatives are presented to individuals, which can in turn affect decision making

free cash flow (FCF) estimate of the company's future projected cash flows that flow to investors and owners after expenses and projected obligations have been paid

free cash flow problem when managers have discretion about how to allocate a firm's cash flows, it may create an agency issue as there is a temptation to use the cash to invest in projects that do not increase the wealth of shareholders, but benefit management

free cash flows to equity (FCFE) the free cash flows that accrue specifically to equityholders

free cash flows to equity (FCFE) model a valuation model that discounts the portion of a company's expected cash flows that flow to equityholders

flows to equity (FTE) model a valuation model that discounts the portion of a company's expected cash flows that flow to equityholders and debtholders

frictionless environment (or market) an environment in which there are no market imperfections like taxes, transaction costs, information asymmetries, agency costs, etc., and no other inefficiencies

frictions imperfections that prevent markets from functioning perfectly efficiently and prevent "perfect" decision making, such as taxes, transaction costs, information asymmetries, and agency costs

functional perspective a unified framework which analyses both existing products and institutions, as well as new financial innovations based on the core economic functions they serve

fundamental value an estimate of value based on analysis rather than market price, also known as intrinsic value

future value (FV) the value at some point in the future of an equivalent amount today, given the effects of time on value

futures contract similar to forward contracts, futures are contractual agreements to buy or sell a specified amount of an asset at a specified price on a specified date. Unlike forwards, futures trade on an exchange and therefore are standardized contracts

general partner (GP) an equity owner in a partnership who has unlimited liability for the debts of the firm and makes the day-to-day business decisions

generally accepted accounting principles (GAAP) accounting standards created by the Financial Accounting Standards Board that specify requirements and best practices for financial reporting

geometric average rate of return (or average compound rate of return) an average annual rate of return that accounts for compounding

go private when a group of shareholders purchases the majority of a company's outstanding shares and make it so that the company is no longer publicly traded on a stock exchange

golden parachute a large payment made to an executive if they are forced to leave that position—for example, when there is a change of control in the company, such as a merger or acquisition

goodwill an intangible asset that results when one firm acquires another firm at a price greater than its book value

Greeks letters from the Greek alphabet used to model an option's sensitivity to a change in an option valuation factor such as the underlying asset's price or its price volatility. The "Greeks" are used to assess option valuation, for example, in the BSM model

greenmail a takeover tactic, when an acquirer purchases a large portion of the target company's shares, and threatens to purchase additional shares unless the company agrees to buy out the acquirer's shares at a premium (leaving the acquirer with a large profit)

gross margin the difference between revenues and cost of goods sold

growing annuity an annuity, a series of cash flows with equal payments at equal intervals that end at a defined time period, whose cash flows increase by some rate with each period

growth perpetuity or growing perpetuity a perpetuity, a series of cash flows with equal payments at equal intervals that does not end, whose cash flows increase by some rate with each period

guarantees implicit or explicit promises that an entity will step in and pay what is owed if one party in a financial agreement is not able to

hedge ratio when referring to options, the fraction of the number of shares of stock needed to replicate the option's payoffs

hedgers people who hope to preserve their wealth by investing in assets that decrease their exposure to certain risks posed by their existing investments

hedging (hedge) a position that reduces an investor's exposure to a loss (while simultaneously eliminating the investor's exposure to a gain)

holdup problems where agency issues create conflict between the venture capital (VC) fund and the entrepreneurs, causing investments to not be made

hostile takeover when a company (the target) is acquired by another company or individual (the acquirer) against the wishes of the target firm's management, as opposed to a friendly merger with amicable and negotiated terms

household one or more people, related or not, who live together in a dwelling (house, apartment, etc.)

human capital an intangible asset that represents the value of human knowledge, experience, and behavior as it contributes to a company's earning potential. Although an "asset," it cannot be listed on a firm's balance sheet

hurdle rate a minimum rate of return that a company requires from a capital investment

hybrid securities financial instruments that have features of both debt and equity—for example, convertible bonds

idiosyncratic risk (or unsystematic risk) the risk specific to a given investment—that is, not due to systematic factors such as market exposure

illiquid not easily converted to cash

illiquidity the characteristic of not being easily converted to cash (i.e., traded)

immediate annuity an annuity, a series of cash flows with equal payments at equal intervals, where the cash flows occur at the beginning of each period

implied volatility the volatility of an asset's return that is inferred from a model, typically an option-pricing model. For example, the value of σ that makes the observed market price of an option equal to the value computed using the Black-Scholes-Merton option pricing formula

incentive problems problems that arise when there is a conflict of interest between the different stakeholders of a company: A stakeholder may be more motivated to act in its own interest, conflicting with others or the firm's interests

income statement or statement of earnings or the statement of profit and loss (P&L) a reported statement that provides information about a company's profitability—that is, its ability to generate revenue and its cost to do so—over a period of time. An income statement is prepared in compliance with accounting standards

income taxes taxes based on income or earnings and paid to the government

index fund a special type of mutual or exchange-traded fund that aims to match the performance of a specific stock index

index options options where the underlying asset is a financial index such as a stock market index

indexing an investment strategy that seeks to match the investment returns of a specified stock market index, typically by holding a diversified portfolio of securities in the same relative proportions of value as in a broad market index such as the S&P 500

index-linked bonds bonds that have their interest linked to inflation using an index such as the consumer price index (CPI)

indirect costs of financial distress costs that arise when a firm is close to defaulting

inflation a general increase in prices over time that erodes the purchasing power of the currency

initial margin a certain amount of an investor's money (i.e., not borrowed funds) that must be invested when the investor enters into a position such as a derivative

insider trading when someone trades on nonpublic information—for example, where an individual working for or with a company trades knowing details about the company's future actions that other (outside) investors do not and uses that knowledge to create profitable positions

insuring when a person or entity enters into a contract that provides protection against risks by giving payments in specific cases of loss

intangible assets assets that a company can use to create revenue, but which are not physical assets, such as brand recognition and intellectual property

interest the cost of borrowing, periodic amounts that a borrower pays a lender in addition to the total amount owed

interest expense the periodic cost of interest

interest rate the cost of borrowing as a percentage of the amount borrowed that will be paid each period. Equivalently, the rate of return to a lender in exchange for lending money

interest rate arbitrage borrowing at a lower interest rate and lending at a higher interest rate

interest rate risk the risk that a change in interest rates will affect asset values

interest rate sensitivity how much an investment's value changes when interest rates change; duration is a widely used measure of interest rate sensitivity

interest rate swap a financial contract (derivative) which specifies that cash flows between two parties be exchanged based on interest rates

internal financing funding for an investment that comes from cash generated from the operations of the firm

internal rate of return (IRR) the average rate of return that a project is expected to provide. Mathematically defined as the rate of return that produces a net present value (NPV) of zero

intertemporal capital asset pricing model (ICAPM) a variation on the CAPM that accounts for investment decisions over multiple periods, thus allowing them to respond to uncertain changes in the economy

intrinsic or fundamental value an estimate of value based on analysis, often produced by a model, rather than market price

inventory turnover ratio examines how fast a company is able to sell its inventory on average, which in turn indicates how efficiently a company is using its inventory and turning it into revenue

IPO (initial public offering) when a private company issues shares of stock to public shareholders for the first time

issuer the company or other entity issuing (i.e., creating) the security to be traded

junior debt in the hierarchy of repayment to lenders, junior debt refers to debt that will be paid off last and thus has greatest risk of default

law of one price the economic theory that asserts that, in a well-functioning market, equivalent assets must have the same market price

leverage references the use of debt financing in an investment or company

leveraged buyout (LBO) when a private equity firm funds the purchase of a company using significant amounts of debt

leveraged position a position established in part with debt

levered beta the measure of sensitivity to market risk for a firm that uses debt in its capital structure

levered firm value the value of a firm with debt in its capital structure

levered financed in part with leverage; indicating the use of leverage

liabilities what a firm owes, reported on its balance sheet, along with assets and equity

limited liability a legal arrangement where equity owners are not legally liable for a firm's liabilities, used in corporations and limited partnerships: creditors cannot seek money from the common stockholders or limited partners to satisfy debt claims

limited partners (LP) equity investors in a partnership with no liability for the partnership's debts but also no authority to make day-to-day business decisions of the partnership

liquidate when a firm ceases all operations and sells off any remaining assets, often as a consequence of bankruptcy

liquidation value the value of the firm's assets when all of the assets are sold separately (i.e., the value obtained by selling off its component parts)

liquidity relative ease, cost, and speed with which an asset can be converted into cash; also refers to a company's ability to make immediate payments, either for a purchase or to pay off debt

liquidity ratios measures of the ability of a firm to meet its short-term obligations, such as paying its bills and meeting its debt obligations

long position buying and owning an asset or investment; the party who buys an asset is said to take a long position in that asset

long-term usually used to indicate a period of more than one year

loss given default the loss incurred by bondholders when a bond defaults, calculated as the difference between the actual amount bondholders receive in default compared to the promised payment on the bond

Macaulay duration a measure of a bond value's interest rate sensitivity based on the bond's cash flows and time to maturity

managers people who make decisions in a firm

margin call a request for additional funds to "cover" the margin requirement if an investment's value falls significantly

margin often refers to money put into an account to reduce the risk of a counterparty not fulfilling their end of the contract. Can also refer to borrowing used to make an investment

marked to market when investments are updated to current market values

market anomalies the observation of market price behavior that contradicts the efficient markets hypothesis

market portfolio a portfolio that holds all assets traded in a market in proportion to their market values

market risk premium the excess return or reward that investors can expect from investing in the market compared to the riskless rate of return

market to book (M/B) ratio the ratio of a company's market value per share (i.e., stock price) to its book value per share

market value balance sheet reports assets and liabilities at estimated market values rather than book (i.e., accounting) values

market value or fair value the current economic value of a firm based on its share price

market value ratios ratios that compare a firm's book (i.e., accounting) values to its market values and help to understand the market's view of the company's future growth prospects

market-force dominance the idea that multiple market participants will enforce the law of one price, even when individual participants have limited ability to arbitrage, such that markets will force any price discrepancy to converge to one price

marking to market updating values to current market values

mature for a company to grow larger and more established

maturity the end of the term of a financial asset, such as a bond, option, forward, future, or swap. Typically, all obligations of the instrument must be settled at or by maturity

maturity matching a strategy of matching the maturity of an investment with the investor's investment goals and/or horizon

mean-variance optimization the strategy of choosing a portfolio that provides the greatest expected return, measured by its mean return, for the least risk, measured by its return variance

merger and acquisition (M&A) transaction when two companies combine to form one entity; typically one company is the acquirer and the other is the target

mezzanine debt debt that is often in the middle of the repayment priority for debt, above junior debt but below senior debt

microfinance refers broadly to financial services such as loans, insurance, savings, or fund transfers that offer smaller amounts of financing to small businesses or individuals that do not have access to traditional banking services

minimum variance portfolio a portfolio formed to provide the lowest possible variance given the assets that comprise the portfolio

modified duration a measure of bond interest rate risk that shows the percentage change in bond price for a change in interest rates

Modigliani–Miller (M-M) theorem a proposition that states that, given efficient markets with no taxes or transaction costs, a company's market value and cost of capital are independent of its capital structure. That is, it is irrelevant whether a company finances itself through debt or equity

Modigliani–Miller (M-M) Proposition 1 capital structure is irrelevant to overall firm value (the combined value of debt and equity), but does affect the individual components of firm value

Modigliani–Miller (M-M) Proposition 2 specifies the relationship between capital structure and the risk (and thus expected return) of equity: $r_E = r_U + D/E \times (r_U - r_D)$, where r_U is the unlevered cost of capital and D/E is the debt-to-equity ratio

money market the market for short-term debt (which matures in less than one year)

Monte Carlo simulation an analytical technique that uses existing data to demonstrate possible outcomes, based on probabilities, that could occur in the future

moral hazard an agency conflict where the one who takes on risk does not bear its consequences, and so is encouraged to take actions with adverse consequences for others. For example, when those who buy auto insurance then drive more recklessly

mortgage rate the interest rate that homebuyers pay on the loans they take to finance their homes

multi-period binomial model a model that assumes two possible periodic results over multiple periods: either upward or downward movement of a specific variable—for example, a dynamic replicating strategy where the number of stocks/bonds traded is adjusted at each time period

multiple a ratio that shows a measure of value (e.g., price) as a multiple of a measure of company performance (e.g., earnings or book value) and that can be used to estimate the current value or forecast the future value of a company or investment

municipal bond insurance insurance bought by municipal bond issuers to guarantee payment of all interest and principal, which enhances the bond issue's credit rating and attracts investors

municipal bonds bonds issued by local and state governments

mutual fund a portfolio run by a professional money manager that takes investors' money and invests it into a range of investments, sometimes including both stocks and bonds

mutual fund separation the idea that intermediaries can create a variety of portfolios on the minimum variance frontier and investors can choose depending on individual preferences

mutually exclusive two cases that cannot both occur (e.g., a firm must choose one project or the other)

negative signal when management actions are perceived to signal negative performance or future outcomes—for example, a dividend cut that signals a decrease in earnings or cash flows

net income a company's earnings, calculated as revenues less expenses

net payoff/profit in options trading, the option payoff less (net of) its price

net present value (NPV) the difference between the present value of a project's cash inflows (revenues) and the present value of the project's cash outflows (initial investment and costs). In capital budgeting, used as a measure of project value

net present value (NPV) rule rule that states that a project with a positive NPV, if undertaken, would increase the firm's value. If choosing between projects with positive NPV, the project(s) with the largest total NPV should be chosen

net working capital (NWC) the difference between a firm's current assets and its current liabilities (current assets – current liabilities)

net worth or shareholders' equity the difference between the values of assets and liabilities

no-arbitrage condition a situation where the law of one price holds such that equivalent assets trade at the same price and therefore no arbitrage is possible

nominal interest rate the stated interest rate on an investment, not accounting for the effects of inflation

nominal prices prices stated in a given currency but not accounting for the effects of inflation

noncurrent assets or long-term assets or fixed assets assets that a company owns that are either not expected to be or cannot easily be sold (i.e., liquidated) in the short term

noncurrent liabilities long-term debt that a company is obligated to pay in more than one year

nondiversifiable risk risks that affect a market and thus all assets traded in that market, such as macroeconomic risks, also known as market or systematic risk

notes to financial statements addenda or footnotes to a financial statement that provide additional, often important, details

notional amount (or notional value) the principal amount of money that a financial contract is based upon

OCRA (optimal combination of risky assets) the portfolio combination consisting of risky assets that provides the best risk–reward trade-off

one-period binomial model a model that assumes two possible periodic results over one period: either upward or downward movement of a specific variable

open-market repurchase when a company purchases its own stock on a stock exchange

operating income a measure of a firm's overall profits that are generated from its operational activities

opportunity cost of capital a rate that money could earn somewhere else if it was not invested in the project or company under evaluation. This is often used as the discount rate for an investment, since investing cash into one investment precludes its use to fund any other

optimal capital structure the mix of debt and equity financing that maximizes a company's market value

option a financial contract which provides the investor with the opportunity but not the obligation to either buy (call) or sell (put) an asset at a specified price and time

optionality the potential to make a decision in the future that affects some aspect of a contract or project in response to observed changes; an example is having additional optional investment opportunities after having made an initial investment

option to abandon the ability to make a choice to abandon a project

option to rescale the ability to choose to rescale a project, which can be expanded or contracted for some fixed price

ordinary annuity a series of cash flows with equal payments at equal intervals that lasts a specified amount of time, where the cash flows occur at the end of each period beginning at the end of the current period

outside directors member of the board of directors who are unaffiliated with the company itself (i.e., not management)

over-the-counter (OTC) when derivative contracts are created directly between two entities and not traded on a public exchange

over-the-counter markets global electronic networks linking those that buy and sell financial assets

paid-in capital a component of shareholders' equity on the balance sheet that consists of the amount raised in the past by issuing common stock

par amount the promised amount (also called the principal or the face value) of a bond or loan, which must be repaid by or at maturity

par bond a bond with a price equal to its face value

partnership a firm with two or more owners, called the partners, who share the equity in the business

payback constraint an approach to capital budgeting that involves first filtering out projects that have payback periods that are too long, and then applying decision rules (such as the NPV rule or IRR hurdles) to the remaining projects

payback decision rule in capital budgeting, a decision rule for evaluating projects based on their payback periods

payback period in capital budgeting analysis, the length of time it takes for the future cash flows to "pay back" the initial investment

payoff the value of an option or other financial contract at expiration

payoff diagram a diagram depicting the payoffs of all sides of a contract at the settlement date

payoff-probability (or payoff-density) function a function showing the likelihood that various payoffs may be achieved

payout a distribution of funds from a company to investors (e.g., cash dividend or share repurchase)

payout policy the various ways a company can choose to distribute funds back to stockholders—for example, by paying a dividend or repurchasing shares

pecking order theory a theory of capital structure when there is asymmetric information, which predicts that firms should optimally first use internal funds, then debt, and then equity

percent-of-sales method a method of forecasting an income statement by assuming expenses will be a certain percentage of sales

perpetual annuity or perpetuity a stream of cash flows with no set maturity—that is, that lasts forever

personal investing investing done by individuals or retail investors to increase personal wealth

planning horizon the total length of time planned for in formulating a portfolio strategy

point of tangency in minimum variance portfolio analysis, where the curve representing all possible portfolio combinations meets the risk–reward trade-off line

poison pill a contingency built into a corporate charter that, in the event of a takeover attempt, a company's outstanding shares experience an automatic dilution or other shareholders are enabled to purchase shares at a discount, thus devaluing the firm

portfolio a set of financial assets invested in by an investor

portfolio selection the process through which people choose assets to invest in

portfolio weight the proportion of the value of a portfolio that is invested in a particular asset

positive signal when management actions are perceived to signal future positive performance—for example, a dividend increase that signals an increase in earnings or cash flows

preferred dividends dividends paid on preferred stock, and a company must prioritize these payments over payments to common stockholders

preferred stock shares of stock that offer a fixed dividend that the issuing firm must pay before paying any dividend payments to common stockholders

premium bond a bond that has a price which is greater than its face value

premium (insurance) the cost of insurance coverage, typically paid in advance

present value (PV) the value today of cash flows that occur in the future

pre-tax weighted-average cost of capital (WACC) the overall discount rate (i.e., cost of capital) for a company before accounting for taxes. Computed as the weighted average of the cost of each kind of capital in a firm's capital structure, weighted by its proportion of the total capital based on market values

price/earnings multiple or ratio the ratio of a stock's price per share to its earnings per share; this is a relative valuation measure often used to assess a company's value

principal the amount deposited, borrowed, or invested. For a bond, the larger lump-sum amount owed at maturity

principals owners of firms, that often delegate decision making authority to others (agents)

private companies/corporations companies whose shares are not publicly traded; usually owned by a small number of individuals or investors, and do not have access to public capital markets—stock and bond markets—to raise money

private equity (PE) firm a financial firm that raises money from investors, and invests that money in private companies through equity stakes, with an exit strategy in mind and the goal of maximizing profits from the investment

pro forma forecasted, refers to financial statements. For example, a pro forma income statement may be derived to forecast earnings

probability distribution a set of all possible outcomes and their probabilities, often displayed graphically

productivity of capital goods The expected rates of return of capital goods, goods produced in an economy that can be used to produce other goods. Measures how efficiently good such as mines, dams, roads, bridges, factories, machinery, and inventories contribute to output

profitability ratios various measures that indicate how well a firm is earning profits

protective put a position created by combining a stock and a put option that hedges the investment in the stock to limit potential loss should the stock price decline

public companies companies with shares issued and traded on a public exchange

publicly traded corporations (public corporations) corporations with shares issued and traded on a public exchange (i.e., public companies)

pure discount bonds or zero-coupon bonds bonds that offer no coupon, such that there is one payment: the principal repayment at maturity

put option (put) an option that gives its holder the right but not the obligation to sell an underlying asset at a specified price on or before some specified expiration date

put–call parity the observation that the prices of a call and a put option on the same underlying asset are related, since a call option can be replicated by a position that combines a put option, shares of the underlying asset, and risk-free bond(s)

qualitative asset transformation the process by which banks take money from bank deposits made by their account holders and turn it into loans, transforming the liability (deposits) into an asset (loans receivable)

quick ratio or acid test the ratio of the most liquid assets, usually cash, marketable securities, and accounts receivable, to near-term liabilities, which is a measure of firm liquidity

rate of return on capital the productivity of capital to create earnings, expressed as a percentage

ratio decomposition an analytical tool that breaks down financial ratios into their component factors

rational in investing, the assumption that investors act based on all relevant information to maximize their profits

real interest rate the nominal interest rate adjusted for inflation (i.e., changes in purchasing power)

real options application of option theory to physical/non-financial projects to consider changes in strategy over time

real prices prices adjusted for inflation in order to make meaningful comparisons across time

regular dividends scheduled cash dividend payments that happen at a regular frequency, often quarterly

regulators the various governmental, economic, industrial, and business groups that set and enforce the rules for participants in the financial system

relationship lending financing through bank loans that allows banks to develop familiarity with borrowers over time. When a bank knows a borrower through a previous loan, there can be less asymmetric information about the borrower; as a result the bank can lend more and charge a relatively lower interest rate

re-levering adding back the effect of leverage—using the target company's capital structure information (proportion of value composed of debt). This is usually applied to cost of capital calculations, and is used in the process of comparing companies with different capital structures

replicate to price a financial asset such as a derivative by determining what combination of known assets with observable prices will reproduce or replicate the cash flows of the derivative contracts

required rate of return the rate of return that investors demand given the amount of risk they face

residual claim the last claim on the company's assets, fulfilled only after all other claims have been satisfied. This is usually the claim of common shareholders, who follow all creditors and preferred shareholders

residual claimants stakeholders who receive payment of residual claims (i.e., common shareholders)

restricted stock stock that cannot be sold for a certain period of time

restructuring when a company reorganizes its operations and capital structure, usually as a part of the bankruptcy process, in order to make the company viable as a going concern; laws (and terms) vary across countries

retained earnings an equity account that records the cumulative amount of past earnings that have been kept as cash in the business

return on assets (ROA) a measure of how well the company turns its assets into profits; it compares profits (from the income statement) to the accounting value of a company's average total assets (from the firm's balance sheet)

return on equity (ROE) a measure of profitability based on a firm's equity; defined as the ratio of net income (i.e., profit) to the book value of shareholders' equity

return on sales (ROS) profits based on sales generated, measured by operating income (earnings before interest and taxes) divided by sales

risk uncertainty that matters to someone because it affects their welfare

risk assessment the quantification of the costs associated with the risks; in risk modeling, this is often identified in the first step of the risk management process

risk aversion the general preference of individuals to minimize or avoid risk, all else being equal

risk exposure action or behavior that makes one subject to risk

risk-free (or riskless) an investment or cash flow that does not have any risk or uncertainty regarding what it will pay in the future–for example, a bond without the probability of default

risk-free asset an asset without default risk or other risks; commonly refers to a US Treasury bond

risk-free interest rate the rate of return for borrowing when there is no probability of default; commonly refers to the rate of return on a US Treasury bond. In financial models, this often represents the time value of money (i.e., opportunity cost)

risk-free rate of return (risk-free rate) the rate of return on a risk-free asset; commonly refers to the rate of return on a US Treasury bond. In financial models, this often represents the time value of money (i.e., opportunity cost)

risk identification identifying the risk exposure(s) of a behavior or position

risk management the practices used for mitigating risk exposure or costs–for example, purchasing insurance is a risk management strategy that transfers risk from the insured to the insurer

risk management process the systematic attempt to identify, analyze, and mitigate risks

risk management techniques methods used by firms to handle risk (risk avoidance, loss prevention and control, risk retention, and risk transfer)

risk premium the excess return expected to compensate for risk. Expressed as a rate of return in excess of the riskless rate of return

risk-reward trade-off line the line depicting the expected return and standard deviation for various combinations of a risky asset and a riskless asset

risk shifting when managers (acting in the interests of shareholders) may choose to undertake volatile investments that have the potential to increase the wealth of shareholders at the expense of debtholders. This is due to the misalignment of incentives between stakeholders, and can result in negative-NPV investments being undertaken

risk tolerance the amount of risk investors or firms are willing to bear

riskless asset an asset without default risk or other risks; commonly refers to a US Treasury bond. Another term for a risk-free asset

riskless rate the rate of return on a risk-free/riskless asset; commonly refers to the rate of return on a US Treasury bond. In financial models, this often represents the time value of money (i.e., opportunity cost). Another term for the risk-free rate

risky assets assets that do not offer a certain return, and are thus not riskless/risk-free

risky in finance, an investment with an uncertain return or uncertain future cash flows

risky asset portfolio portfolio composed of risky assets

rolling over to reinvest or reborrow when an investment/loan matures/comes due, effectively extending maturity

sales revenue the total amount of proceeds generated from sales of goods or services

sales, general, and administrative (SG&A) expenses a broad category of expenses which includes the expenses incurred in managing the firm, such as salaries, advertising, and distributing costs for the products produced during the year, rent, and other general overhead costs

savings and loan associations (S&Ls) specialized financial institutions that perform two core economic functions: to provide long-term financing for residential homeowners at fixed interest rates; and to provide a riskless, liquid, short-term savings vehicle for large numbers of small savers. Also called thrift banks or thrifts

scenario analysis the process of repeating calculations under a different set of assumptions that replicate different possible scenarios to help determine a range of possible outcomes

seasoned equity offering (SEO) additional shares sold to investors by an existing publicly traded corporation

secured overnight financing rate (SOFR) a broad measure of the cost of borrowing cash overnight that is collateralized by Treasury securities, based on actual trading; often used as the reference rate for floating-rate loans

security any kind of tradable financial instrument

security market line (SML) the graph of the linear relationship between the risk premium of an asset and its sensitivity to systematic risk as measured by beta

self-financing an investment strategy that requires no additional funds to be added or withdrawn by the investor during the life of the investment

self-fulfilling prophecy a publicly expressed prediction that would be false and not occur in its absence, but which ends up being true or fulfilled as a consequence of the prophecy

semi-strong-form market efficiency the form of market efficiency where prices reflect all past price information and all public information (but not private information)

senior debt refers to debt with a senior claim to repayment—that is, that will be repaid before other forms of debt and thus is more likely to be repaid

seniority in finance, financial claim on assets with superior priority compared to other claims

sensitivity analysis the process of repeating calculations under a different set of assumptions that replicate different possible scenarios to help determine a range of possible outcomes. Also called scenario analysis

separated structure a form of business organization in many firms, where the owners do not manage the business, and instead delegate that responsibility to professional managers who do not own any part of it.

settlement date the future date when all obligations of a contract are fulfilled and all cash flows have been exchanged

share a unit of ownership; in a corporation, refers to a share of stock

shareholders those who own shares of stock

shareholders' equity a part of a firm's balance sheet representing the residual value of a firm's assets that may be paid to the firm's owners (i.e., its shareholders) once its liabilities have been paid

shark repellent policies explicit defenses against hostile takeovers

Sharpe ratio a measure of risk-adjusted return: the ratio of expected excess return (expected return above the riskless rate of return) to risk (as measured by the asset's standard deviation)

short position a position that obligates the investor to deliver an asset in the future; this may be created through borrowing an asset and selling it or engaging in the "short" side of a future, forward, or option position by selling (or "writing") the future, forward, or option

shortfall broadly refers to when an obligation exceeds the amount of funds available or the value of an investment. In the context of guarantees, the shortfall is the difference between the promised payment on the guaranteed contract and the price received from the sale of the assets that are available from the issuer as collateral

short-term a loan or investment that lasts one year or less

signal an action taken that conveys information to others, often about future outcomes

simple interest interest on the original principal of a loan

sole proprietorship a firm owned by an individual; the assets and liabilities of the firm are the personal assets and liabilities of the proprietor

special dividends one-time cash payments made to shareholders, which a company might not repeat in the future

special purpose acquisition companies (SPACs) also called "blank-check" companies, these are shell companies set up by (typically experienced) investors (PE firms, hedge funds) which do not contain any assets and exist solely for the purpose of acquiring another company

speculators investors who are not trying to reduce their risk exposure and take positions in the market based on their forecasts of the future price. Their motivation for participating in the futures market is to make a profit on their futures trades

spot interest rates market interest rates at any given point in time

spot price the market price at any given point in time

staged financing investments where not all the money is provided at once but invested in stages over time. These investments are typical of venture capital

standard deviation, σ (sigma) a measure of probable deviation from the mean (i.e., average) outcome; in finance or investing, the standard deviation is widely used as a measure of return risk

statement of cash flows a reported financial statement that tracks the actual cash that has flowed in and out of the firm during a period of time

static replication creating a replicating position that is not adjusted over time

stock token of ownership in a corporation, usually apportioned as shares

stock dividend a distribution to shareholders consisting of additional shares of stock

stock index a theoretical portfolio indicating the overall price level of a collection of stocks in a given industry, region, or exchange

stock market an organized exchange for buying and selling corporate shares

stock out a situation that may occur with a commodity forward contract where there is no further amount of the commodity in storage or generally available

stock repurchase (or stock buyback) when the company buys shares of its outstanding stock back from shareholders, decreasing the number of shares outstanding

stock split a company splits each existing share outstanding into multiple shares such that the number of outstanding shares increases

straddle an option position using a combination of options to hedge against the risk of greater volatility, that consists of buying both a call option and a put option on the same underlying asset

strategy a plan that takes account of future decisions in making current decisions

strike price (exercise price) the specified price that an option allows the owner to buy (in the case of a call) or sell (in the case of a put) the underlying asset at in the future

STRIPS zero-coupon bonds issued by the US Treasury, stands for Separate Trading of Registered Interest and Principal of Securities

strong-form market efficiency as defined by the efficient markets hypothesis, the form of market efficiency that states that market prices reflect all available information in the economy, even information that is privately held by individuals

subordinated debt debt that is paid only after senior debt claims are satisfied, and thus is less likely to be repaid than more priority claims

sunk costs prior costs associated with a project that have already occurred

surplus (deficit) unit a surplus unit is a firm or organization with profits in excess of its need for new investment spending. A deficit unit is a firm or organization that needs to finance an expansion and does not have enough cash

swap a financial contract that commits two parties to exchange the cash flows that come from two different financial assets

swap rate determines the calculation of the net cash flow that the two parties exchange under a swap contract

switching options a choice to change operating or production modes, discussed in the context of real options in capital budgeting decisions

synergy the value derived from the benefits of combining operating or administrative structures

systematic risk the risk that affects all assets traded in a market; broad risks that cannot be diversified

tangency portfolio as defined by minimum variance analysis, the portfolio consisting of the optimal combination of risky assets. It is the portfolio where the curve representing all possible portfolio combinations meets the risk-reward trade-off line

target company the company taken over by the acquirer in a corporate takeover or acquisition

target expected return a level of desired expected return

target risk a level of desired risk

taxable income income that creates a tax obligation

T-bill a short-term debt obligation issued by the US government, usually with a maturity of up to one year

tender offer repurchase a company goes to the shareholders directly and offers to buy back a predetermined number of shares at a certain price; this is an alternative to repurchasing shares in the open market

term structure of implied volatility the implied volatility of options with various maturities

term structure of interest rates market interest rates for borrowing over different maturities

terminal growth rate or long-run growth rate for discounted cash flow models of valuation, a growth rate applied to all cash flows after a future date, in which the cash flows after that date are assumed to grow at a constant rate in perpetuity

terminal value for discounted cash flow models of valuation, the value of the company (or investment) as of a future date (usually the date up to which cash flows are projected). After this date, cash flows are often assumed to stay the same or grow in perpetuity

terminal wealth expected investment value at the end of the investment horizon

terminal wealth ratio the amount that each dollar of an investment is expected to grow to by the end of the investment horizon

three dimensions of risk transfer three methods of transferring risks: diversifying, hedging, and insuring

thrifts another name for banks that operate as savings and loan institutions. Specialized financial institutions that perform two core economic functions: to provide long-term financing for residential homeowners at fixed interest rates; and to provide a riskless, liquid, short-term savings vehicle for large numbers of small savers

time horizon length of time into the future that is considered in an analysis

time pattern of promised payments when referencing debt, the schedule for repayment, which varies with debt instrument and maturity

time value when referring to an option, the difference between an option's price and its intrinsic value at any point in time prior to expiration

time value of money the principle that an amount of money in the present or closer to the present is worth more than the same amount further in the future

timeline a linear representation of cash outflows and inflows over a period of time

times interest earned ratio estimates how easily a company can pay the interest on its debt (interest expense) given how much it earns (EBIT). Both of these numbers come from a firm's income statement

total change in cash and equivalents a line item on the cash flow statement that sums the cash flows from operating, investing, and financing activities to show how a company's cash flow has changed over the year

total return swap a swap that allows a party to obtain cash flows based on some underlying asset's rate of return in exchange for cash flows based on some interest rate

total shareholder return the total return from a stock that comes from any gain (loss) in the share price plus any cash dividends

trade-off theory of capital structure a theory which predicts that firms will choose an optimal level of debt, trading off the tax benefits and financial distress costs of debt

trading horizon the minimum time interval over which investors can revise their portfolios

trading interval the time interval between successive openings of the market for trading

tranched an asset with cash flows that have been decomposed into separate claims, and then sold separately to investors with different repayment needs. For example, deconstruction of a debt security into separate debt securities, differentiated by their payment streams

transaction costs costs, both in terms of money and time/effort, associated with transactions. For financial transactions, these are typically brokerage fees and research costs

transparency the extent to which all parties to a financial transaction have available to them all the relevant information they need to make an informed decision

treasury stock stock that had been issued but is no longer outstanding, and can be reissued in the future. Alternatively, shares no longer outstanding may be retired

trust the belief that someone or something is reliable, truthful, and capable

underlying asset for a derivative security (e.g., option, swap, forward, future), the asset that its value derives from

underlying price the value of the underlying asset

underwriter a financial intermediary such as an investment bank, which facilitates the issuance of shares or bonds

unified general valuation framework a single framework that can be applied to analyze and value any type of capital structure that a company may have

unit of account the medium in which payments are denominated

unlevered without debt in its capital structure

unlevered beta the beta of a company if it had no leverage in its capital structure

unlevered cost of capital the cost of capital for the firm if it had no debt in its capital structure

unlevered firm value the value of the firm if it had no debt in its capital structure

unlimited liability if an organization is structured with unlimited liability, then the owner(s) are liable for the firm's debts—for example, owners' personal assets can be seized to satisfy the demands of the firm's creditors

upward-sloping yield curve a yield curve is a graphical depiction of expected interest rates for different maturities; when it is upward-sloping (i.e., positively sloped), it indicates that longer-term interest rates are expected to be greater than shorter-term interest rates

valuation the process of determining or estimating the value of an asset

valuation by comparables a method of valuation that uses relevant information about comparable–ideally identical–companies

valuation by multiples the method of using financial ratios and accounting earnings to estimate the market value of a company, often incorporating information from comparable companies

valuation model a quantitative method used to infer an asset's value

value how much something is worth; in finance, usually refers to market value unless explicitly defined as another model of value, such as intrinsic value

variance a measure of deviation from the mean or expected value, based on the probabilities of returns

VC funds investment funds run by venture capital firms, which pool investor money to invest in exchange for ownership (equity) stakes and control rights

venture capital (VC) a type of financing for entrepreneurs and companies where money is provided by financial firms (venture capital firms) directly (i.e., not through a public market transaction) in exchange for equity stakes and control rights

verification third-party examination and certification of information supplied to a customer

vesting periods a "waiting period" that is a condition of realizing value, often used in compensation. For example, if a manager is paid in stock with a vesting period, the manager cannot sell the stock until the vesting period ends

volatility the characterization of how widely an asset's value has moved or is expected to move. Often measured using the standard deviation of an asset's returns

voting/shareholder meetings meeting held periodically for shareholders to exercise their ownership and control rights by voting on important decisions for a company

weak-form market efficiency the version of market efficiency that posits that market prices reflect only past price information

wealth or net worth the value of a household's assets less liabilities

weighted-average cost of capital (WACC) the overall cost of capital for a company, computed as the weighted average of the cost of each kind of capital in a firm's capital structure, weighted by its proportion of the total capital and based on market values. This is used as the discount rate for the overall company in discounted cash flow (DCF) analysis

working capital the difference between current assets and current liabilities

working capital management managing operations to ensure that working capital will meet a firm's short-term funding needs, while paying attention to how these needs might change in the future

writing (selling) an option creating an option contract and selling to a counterparty. Taking the short position creates an obligation to buy the underlying asset from the put option holder or sell to the call option holder should the option be exercised

yield curve a graphical description of the term structure of interest rates, which represent interest rates for borrowing over different debt maturities

yield spread difference in yields, often used to determine a risk premium for a bond compared to another bond, such as the difference between the yield of a corporate bond and the yield of a Treasury bond

yield to maturity (YTM or yield) the annualized rate of return earned from a bond if held until maturity and the bond pays what it promised. Used as a measure of the internal rate of return of a bond, mathematically defined by the discount rate that sets the present value of the bond's payments equal to its price

zero-coupon bonds bonds issued with a coupon rate of zero, such that the bond pays no interest and the payment of all of the principal occurs at maturity

BIBLIOGRAPHY

Aghamolla, C., Jain, J., & Thakor, R. T. (2023). When private equity comes to town: The local economic consequences of rising healthcare costs. Available at: https://papers.ssrn.com/sol3/papers.cfm?abstract_id=4491104.

Aghamolla, C., Karaca-Mandic, P., Li, X., & Thakor, R. T. (2024). Merchants of death: The effect of credit supply shocks on hospital outcomes. *American Economic Review*, 114(11), 3623-3668.

Aghamolla, C., & Thakor, R. T. (2022a). Do mandatory disclosure requirements for private firms increase the propensity of going public? *Journal of Accounting Research*, 60(3): 755–804.

Aghamolla, C., & Thakor, R. T. (2022b). IPO peer effects. *Journal of Financial Economics*, 144(1): 206–226.

Almeida, H., and Philippon, T. (2007). The risk-adjusted cost of financial distress. *The Journal of Finance*, 62(6): 2557–2586.

Andrade, G., and Kaplan, S. N. (1998). How costly is financial (not economic) distress? Evidence from highly leveraged transactions that became distressed. *The Journal of Finance*, 53(5):1443–1493.

Asquith, P., and Mullins, D. W. Jr. (1983). The impact of initiating dividend payments on shareholders' wealth. *Journal of Business*, 56: 77–96.

Baer, J., and Lim, D. (2021). The hedge-fund manager who did battle with Exxon—and won. *Wall Street Journal*. Available at: www.wsj.com/articles/the-hedge-fund-manager-who-did-battle-with-exxonand-won-11623470420.

Bain & Company (2023). *Global Private Equity Report 2023*. Boston: Bain & Company.

Baird (2014). The truth about top-performing money managers. Available at: https://bit.ly/3JoRVkv.

Baker, S. R., Bloom, N., Davis, S. J. et al. (2020). The unprecedented stock-market reaction to COVID-19. Kellogg Insight. Available at: https://bit.ly/3VZ4JWr.

Bass, D. (2016). Microsoft plans another $40 billion buyback, boosts dividend. Bloomberg.com. Available at: www.bloomberg.com/news/articles/2016-09-20/microsoft-plans-to-repurchase-up-to-another-40-billion-in-stock?embedded-checkout=true.

Bereskin, F., Byun, S. K., Officer, M. S., & Oh, J. M. (2018). The effect of cultural similarity on mergers and acquisitions: evidence from corporate social responsibility. *Journal of Financial and Quantitative Analysis*, 53(5): 1995–2039.

Bernstein, S., and Sheen, A. (2016). The operational consequences of private equity buyouts: evidence from the restaurant industry. *The Review of Financial Studies*, 29(9): 2387–2418.

Big 4 Accounting Firms (2024). The best hedge fund managers of all time. Available at: https://bit.ly/4aY0ZIX.

Black, F., & Scholes, M. (1973). The pricing of options and corporate liabilities. *Journal of Political Economy*, 81(3): 637–654.

Bodie, Z. (1995). On the risk of stocks in the long run. *Financial Analysts Journal*, 51(3): 18–22.

Bodie, Z., Kaplan, R. S., and Merton, R. C. (2003). For the last time: stock options are an expense. *Harvard Business Review*, 81(3): 62–71.

Bradt, G. (2019). The root cause of every merger's success or failure: culture. *Forbes*. Available at: www.forbes.com/sites/georgebradt/2015/06/29/the-root-cause-of-every-mergers-success-or-failure-culture/?sh=a83a905d305b.

Bruner, R. F. (2017). Walt Disney Productions, June 1984. *Darden Business Publishing Cases*. Available at: https://store.darden.virginia.edu/walt-disney-productions-june-1984.

Burnett, J., and Schill, M. J. (1998). Ebay Inc. Available at: https://ssrn.com/abstract=162829.

Cameron, K. S., and Mora, C. M. (2003). Corporate culture and financial success of mergers and acquisitions. Working paper, University of Michigan Business School.

Convergences (2023). *Impact Finance Barometer*, 3rd edition. Available at: www.convergences.org/en/barometre-de-la-finance-a-impact.

Corkery, M. (2018). Toys 'R' Us case is test of private equity in age of Amazon. *New York Times*. Available at: www.nytimes.com/2018/03/15/business/toys-r-us-bankruptcy.html.

Cox, J. C., Ross, S. A., and Rubinstein, M. (1979). Option pricing: a simplified approach. *Journal of Financial Economics*, 7(3): 229–263.

Crockett, Z. (2020). Shark Tank deep dive: a data analysis of all 10 seasons. *The Hustle*. Available at: https://bit.ly/3QXjmq3.

Deeb, G. (2013). Comparing 'Shark Tank' to venture capital reality. *Forbes*. Available at: www.forbes.com/sites/georgedeeb/2013/10/09/comparing-shark-tank-to-venture-capital-reality/?sh=7cfc84111260.

De Vynck, G. (2022). LinkedIn, Candy Crush and Minecraft: Microsoft's empire goes far beyond Windows and Word. *The Washington Post*, 18 Jan. Available at: https://bit.ly/3JAKGWS.

Diacon, S., and Hasseldine, J. (2007). Framing effects and risk perception: the effect of prior performance presentation format on investment fund choice. *Journal of Economic Psychology*, 28(1): 31–52.

Dimson, E., Marsh, P., and Staunton, M. (2002). *Triumph of the Optimists: 101 Years of Global Investment Returns*. Princeton, NJ: Princeton University Press.

Dimson, E., Marsh, P., and Staunton, M. (2023) *Global Investment Returns Yearbook 2022*. Zurich: Credit Suisse Research Institute.

Eaton, C., Howell, S. T., and Yannelis, C. (2020). When investor incentives and consumer interests diverge: private equity in higher education. *The Review of Financial Studies*, 33(9): 4024–4060.

Eller, C. (1993). Movie deal on unwritten Grisham book sets record: film: Universal will pay $3.75 million for rights to next legal thriller by best-selling author of "The Firm." *Los Angeles Times*, 17 July. Available at: https://bit.ly/3wpIOND.

Fama, E. F., and French, K. R. (1992). The cross-section of expected stock returns. *Journal of Finance*, 47: 427–465.

Fama, E. F., and French, K. R. (2001). Disappearing dividends: changing firm characteristics or lower propensity to pay? *Journal of Financial Economics*, 60(1): 3–43.

Federal Deposit Insurance Corporation (2024). FDIC: regulations & examinations. Available at: www.fdic.gov/regulations.

Fernandez, J.-M., Stein, R. M., and Lo, A. W. (2012). Commercializing biomedical research through securitization techniques. *Nature Biotechnology*, 30(10): 964–975.

Fuster, A., Plosser, M., Schnabl, P., and Vickery, J. (2019). The role of technology in mortgage lending. *The Review of Financial Studies*, 32(5): 1854–1899.

Gennaioli, N., Shleifer, A., and Vishny, R. (2015). Money doctors. *The Journal of Finance*, 70(1): 91–114.

Gillan, S. L., Koch, A., & Starks, L. T. (2021). Firms and social responsibility: a review of ESG and CSR research in corporate finance. *Journal of Corporate Finance*, 66, 101889.

Gompers, P. A., Gornall, W., Kaplan, S. N., and Strebulaev, I. A. (2020). How do venture capitalists make decisions? *Journal of Financial Economics*, 135(1): 169–190.

Gornall, W., and Strebulaev, I. A. (2015). The economic impact of venture capital: evidence from public companies. Available at: https://papers.ssrn.com/sol3/papers.cfm?abstract_id=2681841.

Graham, J. R. (2000). How big are the tax benefits of debt? *The Journal of Finance*, 55(5): 1901–1941.

Graham, J. R. (2022) Presidential address: corporate finance and reality. *The Journal of Finance*, 77(4): 1975–2049.

Graham, J. R., and Harvey, C. R. (2001). The theory and practice of corporate finance: evidence from the field. *Journal of Financial Economics*, 60(2–3): 187–243.

Gupta, A., Howell, S. T., Yannelis, C., & Gupta, A. (2024). Owner incentives and performance in healthcare: private equity investment in nursing homes. *The Review of Financial Studies*, 37(4): 1029–1077.

Gustin, S. (2012). Raiders of the lost stream: Netflix fight with Carl Icahn escalates over "poison pill." *Time*. Available at: https://business.time.com/2012/11/06/raiders-of-the-lost-stream-netflix-fight-with-carl-icahn-escalates-over-poison-pill/#ixzz2BYWoNID1.

Jacobs, M. T., and Shivdasani, A. (2012). Do you know your cost of capital? *Harvard Business Review*. Available at: https://hbr.org/2012/07/do-you-know-your-cost-of-capital.

Jensen, M. C., (1986). Agency cost of free cash flow, corporate finance, and takeovers. *American Economic Review*, 76(2): 323–329.

Kamar, E., Karaca-Mandic, P., and Talley, E. (2009). Going-private decisions and the Sarbanes–Oxley Act of 2002: a cross-country analysis. *The Journal of Law Economics & Organization*, 25(1): 107–133.

Kilincarslan, E. (2022). Demystifying the "dividend puzzle" and making sense of government regulations in times of pandemics. LSE Blog. Available at: https://bit.ly/4do9qza.

King, I. (2023). Intel slashing CEO, managers' pay in a bid to preserve cash. *Bloomberg News*. Available at: https://bit.ly/3QsokL7.

Knight, F. H. (1921). *Risk, Uncertainty and Profit*, volume 31. Boston: Houghton Mifflin.

KPMG (2019). Q4'19 Venture Pulse report – United States. Available at: https://kpmg.com/xx/en/home/campaigns/2020/01/q4-venture-pulse-report-united-states.html.

Krieger, J. L., Li, X., and Thakor, R. T. (2022). Find and replace: R&D investment following the erosion of existing products. *Management Science*, 68(9): 6552–6571.

Lefley, F. (1996). The payback method of investment appraisal: a review and synthesis. *International Journal of Production Economics*, 44(3): 207–224.

Leuz, C., Triantis, A., and Yue Wang, T. (2008). Why do firms go dark? Causes and economic consequences of voluntary SEC deregistrations. *Journal of Accounting and Economics*, 45(2–3): 181–208.

Lewis, A. (2019). The inverted yield curve explained and what it means for your money. *CNBC*. Available at: www.cnbc.com/2019/08/14/the-inverted-yield-curve-explained-and-what-it-means-for-your-money.html.

Lo, A. W., & Thakor, R. T. (2022). Financing biomedical innovation. *Annual Review of Financial Economics*, 14: 231–270.

Lo, A. W., and Thakor, R. T. (2023). Financial intermediation and the funding of biomedical innovation: a review. *Journal of Financial Intermediation*, 54, 101028.

London, S. (2005). Why cash has become king once again. *Financial Times*. Available at: www.ft.com/content/5d781fa8-7df0-11d9-ac22-00000e2511c8.

Long, K. (2022). The rise of activist investors in Japan. *The Banker*. Available at: https://bit.ly/4b4sG2S.

Maloney, M. T., and Mulherin, J. H. (2003). The complexity of price discovery in an efficient market: the stock-market reaction to the Challenger crash. *Journal of Corporate Finance*, 9(4): 453–479.

MarketWatch (2020). Market action a century ago suggests worst could be over for stocks, if not for the coronavirus pandemic. Available at: https://bit.ly/3Q9pCKC.

Matthews, C. M. (2021). Activist likely to gain third seat on Exxon board. *Wall Street Journal*. Available at: www.wsj.com/articles/activist-likely-to-gain-third-seat-on-exxon-board-11622664757.

McAtamney, E. (2023). New retirement gap looms as people underestimate life expectancy. Canada Life UK. Available at: www.canadalife.co.uk/news/new-retirement-gap-looms-as-people-underestimate-life-expectancy.

Merton, R. C. (1969). Lifetime portfolio selection under uncertainty: the continuous-time case. *The Review of Economics and Statistics*, 51: 247–257.

Merton, R. C. (1971). Optimum consumption and portfolio rules in a continuous-time model. *Journal of Economic Theory*, 3: 373–413.

Merton, R. C. (1972). An analytic derivation of the efficient portfolio frontier. *The Journal of Financial and Quantitative Analysis*, 7: 1851–1872.

Merton, R. C. (1973a). The relationship between put and call option prices: comment. *The Journal of Finance*, 28(1): 183–184.

Merton, R. C. (1973b). Theory of rational option pricing. *The Bell Journal of Economics and Management Science*, 4(1): 141–183.

Merton, R. C. (1973c). An intertemporal capital asset pricing model. *Econometrica: Journal of the Econometric Society*, 41: 867–887.

Merton, R. C. (1977). On the pricing of contingent claims and the Modigliani–Miller theorem. *Journal of Financial Economics*, 5: 241–249.

Merton, R. C. (1981). On market timing and investment performance part I: an equilibrium theory of value for market forecasts. *Journal of Business*, 54(3): 363–406.

Merton, R. C. (1992a). *Continuous-Time Finance*. Chichester: Wiley-Blackwell.

Merton, R. C. (1992b). Financial innovation and economic performance. *Journal of Applied Corporate Finance*, 4: 12–22.

Merton, R. C. (1993). Operation and regulation in financial intermediation: a functional perspective. In: Englund, P. (Ed.), *Operation and Regulation of Financial Markets*. Stockholm: The Economic Council.

Merton, R. C. (1995). A functional perspective of financial intermediation. *Financial Management*, 24(2): 23–41.

Merton, R. C. (2012). Observations on financial education and consumer financial protection. In: Bodie, Z., Siegel, L. and Stanton, L. (Eds.), *Life Cycle Investing: Financial Education and Consumer Protection*. Charlottesville, VA: CFA Institute.

Merton, R. C. (2022a). Emergence of financial engineering from financial science: an MIT story. Killian Lecture, MIT, 28 Mar.

Merton, R. C. (2022b). On the emergence of financial engineering from financial science to improve sustainable economic growth and stability: history and future. Lecture at the 11th World Congress of Bachelier Finance Society, 13 June.

Merton, R. C. (n.d.). Notes, 15.466 Functional and Strategic Finance. Course Notes.

Merton, R. C., and Bodie, Z. (1995). A conceptual framework for analyzing the financial environment. In: Crane, D. B., Froot, K. A., Mason, S. P., et al. (Eds.), *The Global Financial System: A Functional Perspective*. Boston, MA: Harvard Business School Press.

Merton, R. C., and Bodie, Z. (2005). Design of financial systems: towards a synthesis of function and structure. *Journal of Investment Management*, 3(1): 1–23.

Merton, R. C., and Thakor, R. T. (2019). Customers and investors: a framework for understanding the evolution of financial institutions. *Journal of Financial Intermediation*, 39: 4–18.

Merton, R. K. (1948). The self-fulfilling prophecy. *The Antioch Review*, 8(2): 193–210.

Meyers, J. (2022). New report finds almost 80% of active fund managers are falling behind the major indexes. *CNBC*. Available at: www.cnbc.com/2022/03/27/new-report-finds-almost-80percent-of-active-fund-managers-are-falling-behind.html.

Michaely, R., and Moin, A. (2022). Disappearing and reappearing dividends. *Journal of Financial Economics*, 143(1): 207–226.

Miller, M. H. (1977). Debt and taxes. *The Journal of Finance*, 32(2): 261–275.

Miller, M. H., & Modigliani, F. (1961). Dividend policy, growth, and the valuation of shares. *The Journal of Business*, 34(4): 411–433.

Modigliani, F., and Miller, M. H. (1958). The cost of capital, corporation finance and the theory of investment. *The American Economic Review*, 48(3): 261–297.

Moody's (2009). Corporate defaults and recovery rates, 1920–2008. Report.

Muralidhar, A., and Merton, R. (2020). Selfies: a new pension bond and currency for retirement. *Journal of Financial Transformation*, 51: 8–20.

Myers, S. C. (1977). Determinants of corporate borrowing. *Journal of Financial Economics*, 5(2): 147–175.

Nichols, N. A. (1994). Scientific management at Merck: an interview with CFO Judy Lewent. *Harvard Business Review*. Available at: https://bit.ly/3JNV4up.

PBS News Hour (2023). Analysis: why Silicon Valley Bank and Signature Bank failed so fast. Available at: https://bit.ly/3w1a5G4.

Peregrine, M. W. (2021). The lasting, positive impact of Sarbanes–Oxley. Available at: https://bit.ly/3WkJTAS.

Peterdy, K. (n.d.). Government guarantee. Available at: https://bit.ly/44sA8m6.

Pitchbook.com (2021). Q1 2021 US PE Middle Market report. Available at: https://pitchbook.com/news/reports/q1-2021-us-pe-middle-market-report.

Potter, S. B. (2021). U.S. IPO market: SPACs drive 2020 IPOs to a new record. Factset.com. Available at: https://insight.factset.com/u.s.-ipo-market-spacs-drive-2020-ipos-to-a-new-record.

Prowse, S. (1998). Angel investors and the market for angel investments. *Journal of Banking & Finance*, 22(6–8): 785–792.

Ritter, J. R. (various years). IPO data. Warrington College of Business. Available at: https://site.warrington.ufl.edu/ritter/ipo-data.

Ross, S. A. (1976). The arbitrage theory of capital asset pricing. *Journal of Economic Theory*, 13(3): 341–360.

Schall, E. (2021). "The Godfather": how Paramount got the Mario Puzo bestseller for $12,500. *Showbiz CheatSheet*, 14 May. Available at: https://bit.ly/3y6COKh.

Schmidt, L., Timmermann, A., and Wermers, R. (2016). Runs on money market mutual funds. *American Economic Review*, 106(9): 2625–2657.

Shen. M., (2018). China eases restrictions on company share buy-backs: Xinhua. *Reuters*. Available at: https://bit.ly/4dodbEI.

Small, R. C. (2014). Buybacks around the world. Harvard Law School Forum on Corporate Governance. Available at: https://bit.ly/3UpTTGq.

Smith, A., (1977 [1776]). *An Inquiry into the Nature and Causes of the Wealth of Nations*. Chicago, IL: University of Chicago Press.

Social Security Administration (2020a). 2020 period life table. Available at: https://bit.ly/4bNhJDl.

Social Security Administration. (2020b). Actuarial life table. Available at: www.ssa.gov/oact/STATS/table4c6.html.

Statista. (2018). APAC: average private equity deal size. Available at: www.statista.com/statistics/983733/apac-average-private-equity-deal-size.

Statista. (2023). IPOs in the U.S. – statistics & facts. Available at: www.statista.com/topics/1272/ipos/#topicOverview.

Statista. (2024). Value of credit of U.S. commercial banks 2024. Available at: www.statista.com/statistics/214283/bank-credit-of-all-commercial-banks-in-the-united-states-monthly.

Thakor, A. V. (2020). Fintech and banking: what do we know? *Journal of Financial Intermediation*, 41: 100833.

Thakor, R. T. (2021). Short-termism, managerial talent, and firm value. *The Review of Corporate Finance Studies*, 10(3): 473–512.

Thakor, R. T., and Merton, R. C. (2023). Trust, transparency, and complexity. *The Review of Financial Studies*, 36(8): 3213–3256.

Thakor, R. T, and Merton, R. C. (forthcoming). Trust in lending. *The Review of Economics and Statistics*.

The Economist (2006a). Dismal science, dismal sentence. *The Economist*, 7 Sept.

The Economist (2006b). Long ranger. 2 Feb. Available at: https://bit.ly/3WJWvlh.

Trefis & Great Speculations. (2016). A look at Petrobras' capital structure. *Forbes*. Available at: www.forbes.com/sites/greatspeculations/2016/11/25/a-look-at-petrobras-capital-structure/?sh=1e0dea3c9fc0.

Tversky, A., and Kahneman, D. (1981). The framing of decisions and the psychology of choice. *Science*, 211: 453–458.

van Duyn, A. (2007). Automatic news makes headlines and money. *Financial Times*, 15 Apr.

Vipond, T. (n.d.). Terminal growth rate. Available at: https://bit.ly/3xMzeop.

Vishnoi, A. (2022). India overhauls stock buyback mechanism to aid small investors. *Bloomberg*. Available at: https://bit.ly/3UmWuRt.

Wessel, D., and Kovalski, M. A. (2018). The Hutchings Center explains: the yield curve–what it is, and why it matters. Brookings Institution. Available at: https://bit.ly/4bqQPAF.

Williams, S. (2020). 6 reasons Warren Buffett is such a successful investor. Nasdaq.com. Available at: www.nasdaq.com/articles/6-reasons-warren-buffett-is-such-a-successful-investor-2020-12-05.

Williamson, S. K., Babcock, A. F., and He, A. (2020). The dangers of buybacks: mitigating common pitfalls. Harvard Law School Forum on Corporate Governance. Available at: https://bit.ly/3wriBy6.

Wouters, O. J., McKee, M., and Luyten, J. (2020). Estimated research and development investment needed to bring a new medicine to market, 2009–2018. *JAMA*, 323(9): 844–853.

Yamazaki, M. (2022) Toshiba board gains two directors from activist funds in historic shift. *Reuters*, 28 June. Available at: www.reuters.com/business/toshiba-board-gains-two-directors-activist-hedge-funds-2022-06-28.

INDEX

accounting balance sheets, 58–59
accounting book value
    accounting conventions, 221–222
    for a company, 262
    difference from market values, 213, 221–224
    market value ratios, 231–232
accounting methods
    calculating returns with market and book values, 223–224
    disclosure requirements, 324
    limitations of financial ratios, 240
    notes to financial statements, 220
    why market and book values differ, 221–222
    see also financial statements
accounts payable, 213, 218
accounts receivable, 218, 230
acid test see quick ratio
acquisition premium, 456
acquisitions, 290–291
    activist shareholders, 328
    financing over a firm's life, 456–460
    hostile takeovers, 325–327
    hostile takeovers, preventing, 328
    manager conflicts of interest, 321
    real options, 430
    Special Purpose Acquisition Companies, 452–453
actively managed, 119
activist shareholders, 327–328, 329
actuaries, 151–152, 517
adaptive market hypothesis, 96
adjusted present value (APV) method, 382–387
adverse selection, 164
after-tax interest rate, 64
after-tax WACC
    capital structure, 374–378, 385
    with a changing capital structure, 379–382
    company value, 275
agency costs, 313
agency problems, 313, 319
    and capital structure, 391, 396–397
    the challenge of multiple objectives, 329–330
    conflicts of interest and the board of directors, 321
    conflicts with shareholders and debtholders, 319–320

    corporate governance and strategies, 322–324
    managerial conflicts of interest, 320–321
    payout policy, 343
    regulation and market discipline, 324–328
agents (firm ownership), 313
agricultural loan guarantees, 423
alpha portfolio, 573
ambiguity, and uncertainty, 142
American option, 174, 427
amortization, 215
    EBITDA, 232, 239, 263
angel investors, 449
annual percentage rate (APR), 21–23
annuities
    key equations, 50–51
    perpetual, 41–44
    valuing, 37–41
annuity due, 37–38
antitrust laws, 326
Apple, share repurchase and dividend program, 344
arbitrage
    capital structure, 360
    interest-rate arbitrage, 88
    law of one price, 79–80, 97
    limits to, 79–80
    market-force dominance, 82
    no-arbitrage condition, 81
    options payoff, 185
Arbitrage Pricing Theory (APT), 586
arbitrageurs, 80
arithmetic average return/mean rate of return, 123–124
    historical equity and bond returns across the world, 128–130
    volatility, 124–126
asset-backed securities (ABS), 106, 596–597
asset beta, 581–582
asset management, 546–549
    see also portfolio selection
asset turnover ratio (ATO), 227–228, 235–237
asset value
    crucial role of market prices, 77–78
    derivatives, 106
    efficient markets hypothesis, 93–94
    equivalent assets, 83, 86

    fundamental value, 83
    law of one price: arbitrage, 79–80
    law of one price: financial asset prices, 80–82
    law of one price: valuation models, 82–87
    Principle 2: law of one price, 7
    Principle 5: market price, 8
    use of options, 171–172, 174–179
    see also pricing
assets
    accounting methods, 221–222
    balance sheet, 211–212, 213
    betas, 566–569, 577–579
    financial statement notes, 220
    hedging risk, 160
    household balance sheets, 58–59
    measuring financial risk, 145–149
    return on assets (ROA), 226
    risk-free vs. risky, 143–144
    using options to modify payoff patterns, 189–191
Association for Financial Professionals (AFP), 583–584
asymmetric information, 340–341, 393–394
average compound rate of return see geometric average rate of return

balance sheet, 211–214
    accounting and economic, 58–59
    financial ratio analysis, 225–235
    household, 57–59
    limitations of, 217
    Silicon Valley Bank (SVB) failure, 223
    why market and book values differ, 221–222
balloon payment, 482
bank loans, 443–445
bank runs, 223, 641–644
bankruptcy, 368–372, 461
    see also defaults (on debt); liquidating a firm
banks
    the banking system, 445
    central banks, 480, 491, 644
    functional perspective, 644–652
    institutional details, 444–445
    thrift banks, 651
basis points (bps), 499

INDEX

behavioral finance
- behavioral biases, 96, 635–636, 638–641
- efficient markets hypothesis, 96
- rationality and the efficient markets hypothesis, 96

benchmarks, 118–119, 572

betas
- assets, 566–569, 577–579
- and capital structure, 584–585
- cost of capital, 581–582
- in Excel, 577–579
- and expected returns, 566–569
- time horizons, 584

bills, 470

binomial model
- multi-period, 623
- one-period, 619–622
- and replication, 619–622

Black, Fischer, 195–196
- *see also* Black–Scholes–Merton model

Black–Scholes–Merton model
- BSM formula, 196–197
- Greeks, 199–200
- implied volatility, 202–204
- option pricing, 172, 195–204, 413–414, 415, 618–619
- real options, 430–432
- volatility and pricing, 200–201

blockholders, 323

board inattention, 321

the board of directors, 317–318
- company structure, 316–318
- conflicts of interest, 321

bond pricing relationships, 488–490

bond ratings, 114, 370, 652

bonds
- callable, 425, 491
- convertible, 424–425, 491
- convexity, 501–505
- debt security, 104–105
- defaults, 114, 369
- duration, 496–501
- history of rates of return, 123–130
- interest rates, 87–88
- option pricing analysis, 408–410
- par, 110, 483, 484–485, 488–490
- payoff diagrams, 180–184
- premium, 483–484, 488–490
- time pattern of promised payments, 107–110
- unit of account, 111–112
- yield spread, 114
- *see also* capital structure; coupon bonds; discount bonds; zero-coupon bonds

book value *see* accounting book value

bootstrap sampling, 131

brands, intangible assets, 213

breakeven rent, 68

BSM *see* Black–Scholes–Merton model

Buffett, Warren, 130

bullet payment, 482

business
- firm growth, 239–240, 241–248, 269–273
- life of a firm, 441–442
- reasons to study finance, 4
- *see also* financing over a firm's life

business risk, 151
- diversification, 153
- hedging, 158–160
- risk assessment, 151–152
- risk identification, 150–151

buybacks *see* stock repurchase/buyback

call options, 106, 177–179
- accounting rules, 216
- corporate equity, 426–432
- how options work, 174
- investment strategies, 189–195
- option pricing analysis, 414
- put-call parity relation, 180–186
- volatility and pricing, 200–201

callable bonds, 425, 491

CAPE Ratio (cyclically adjusted price earnings ratio), 240

CapEx, 267–268

Capital Asset Pricing Model (CAPM), 460, 561–564
- alternatives to, 585–586
- applying in practice, 571–579
- betas and expected returns, 566–569
- calculating discount rates using, 579–585
- capital market line, 564–566
- CML vs. SML, 571
- design of institutions, 638
- security market line, 567–568

capital budgeting, 289
- and capital structure, 387–388
- choosing between investment projects, 289–291
- and inflation, 305–306
- internal rate of return, 298–302
- manager conflicts of interest, 320–321
- net present value investment rule, 292–298, 304
- payback period, 303–304

capital gain/loss, 117, 120, 338–339, 386–387

capital gains tax, 345

capital goods, 121
- expected rate of return, 121–122
- risk-free rate of return, 121–122
- uncertainty in rate of return, 122

capital market equilibrium, 561–564

capital market line (CML), 564–566
- vs. security market line (SML), 571

capital markets
- debt securities, 105
- understanding the financial system, 5

capital structure, 262
- and betas, 584–585
- with default/bankruptcy risk, 368–372
- financing decision, 355
- with frictions: other, 388–396
- with frictions: taxes, 373–388
- guarantees and other securities, 422–425
- internal and external financing, 356
- Modigliani-Miller (M-M) propositions, 357–368
- optimal, 355, 388–389, 396–397
- option pricing analysis, 416–417
- payout policy, 344
- unified general valuation framework, 407

caps, insurance, 162

captured board, 321

careers in finance, 4

cash budget, 248

cash cycle time, 247

cash dividends
- frictionless financial environment, 336–338
- as payout, 334–335
- tax on, 348–349

cash flow
- estimating for capital investment, 293–295
- inflation, 44–49
- total (company) value, 261–262
- using timelines to analyze, 14–15
- valuing annuities, 37–41
- valuing cash flows over multiple periods, 15–16
- valuing perpetuities, 41–44
- *see also* discounted cash flow analysis; free cash flows

cash flow from financing activities, 219

INDEX

cash flow from investing activities, 219
cash flow from operating activities, 218
cash flow statements, 217–219
   total change in cash and equivalents, 219
cash flow timeline, 14–15
cash settlement, 188–189
central banks, 480, 491, 644
CEOs
   captured board, 321
   golden parachute, 322
   pay and contracts, 322–323
   shareholder voting, 323
Challenger space shuttle disaster, 93
Chicago Board Options Exchange (CBOE), 172, 187
clearing payments, 648, 653–654
close out, 601–602
collateral, 423–424
collateralization, 650
commodity futures, 600, 602–605
common stock, 105, 316–317
company growth *see* firm growth
company organization *see* organization structure
company ownership
   going public or staying private, 450–455
   organization structure, 314–315
   principals, 313
   separation of ownership and control, 315–316
   shareholders, debtholders, managers, and the board of directors, 316–318
   see also private corporations; publicly traded corporations
company value, 261–262
   calculating equity value, 278–280
   definitions, 261–262
   discounted cash flow analysis, 265–278
   irrelevance of capital structure to, 357–360
   Modigliani-Miller (M-M) propositions, 357–368
   valuation by comparables, 263–264
comparable companies
   capital structure, 364
   company value, 263–264, 448
   stock value, 84–85
   unlevered beta, 584–585
   see also valuation by comparables
compensation *see* pay

competition *see* comparable companies; market competitors
compound interest, 16–17, 32–33
compound options, 427
compounding
   compared to simple interest, 16–17
   and discounting, 30–31
   frequency of, 21–23
   future value, 15–24
   investments with quarterly and continuous, 32–33
conflicts of interest, 313
   the board of directors, 321
   managerial, 320–321
   shareholders and debtholders, 319–320
   see also agency problems
consumer-durable asset risk, 150
consumer price index for urban consumers (CPI-U), 113
consumer product-obsolescence insurance, 173
consumption
   discounted cash flow model, 59–62
   household balance sheets, 57–59
   time preferences of people, 122
consumption smoothing, 59
continuation value, 280
continuous compounding, 32–33
contracts
   corporate governance, 322–323
   features of insurance contracts, 161–162
   types of derivative contract, 596–597
   see also forward contracts; futures contracts
convenience, forwards and futures, 603, 604–605
convenience yield, 604–605
conversion fees (bonds), 425
convertible bonds, 424–425, 491
convexity, 501–505
copayments, insurance, 162
corporate culture, 460
corporate governance, 322–324
   financial policy, 323
   pay and contracts, 322–323
   shareholder voting and board composition, 323
   voluntary disclosure, 323–324
corporate taxes, 374
corporations
   advantages of, 314–315
   organization structure, 314

separation of ownership and control, 315–316
shareholders, debtholders, managers, and the board of directors, 316–318
see also company ownership
cost of capital, 265
   after-tax WACC, 374–378
   after-tax WACC with a changing capital structure, 379–382
   calculating with CAPM, 579–584
   calculating with DCF model, 363–365, 387–388
   capital structure and the M-M propositions, 360–365
   inflation and capital budgeting, 305–306
   nominal vs. real, 305–306
   risk-adjusted discount rate, 297–298
   unlevered, 363–364, 365
cost of carry, 604–605
cost of debt
   after-tax WACC, 374–378
   bankruptcy risk, 369–370
   Capital Asset Pricing Model, 583
   changes in capital structure, 371–372
   debt tax shield, 275, 375
cost of goods sold (COGS), 215, 227
cost-saving projects, 296–297
country *see* national context
coupon bonds
   discounting, 483
   pricing, 482–484
   term structure of interest rates, 481–491
   yields, 485–491
   see also zero-coupon bonds
coupon payments, 104, 481–482, 484–485
coupon rate, 481–482
covenants, 317
COVID-19 pandemic, efficient markets hypothesis, 90
credit cards, history of, 653–654
credit default swap (CDS), 616
credit event, 616
credit guarantees, 162, 422–424
credit ratings, 114, 370, 652
credit risk
   changes in capital structure, 371–372
   financial guarantees, 162, 422–424
creditors *see* debtholders
crowdfunding, 449–450

cryptocurrencies, 654
culture, relevance to mergers and acquisitions, 460
currency forward, 608
currency risk, 607
currency swaps, 615–616
current assets, 213, 246–248
current liabilities, 213, 246–248
current ratio, 229–230
current yield, 485–486, 490

death, risk of, 150
debt
  advantages of, 393
  capital structure, 355, 357–368
  capital structure effects, 344, 371–372
  corporate debt structure, 416–421
  default/bankruptcy risk, 107, 113–114, 368–372, 652
  financial instruments, 104–105
  financial statement notes, 220
  interest rates, 107
  maturity, 395–396, 410–413
  maturity structure of the government's debt, 647
  option pricing analysis, 410–413, 414
  seniority, 395–396, 418–421
  time pattern of promised payments, 107–110
  use in corporate governance, 323
debt overhang, 393, 417
debt ratio, 228–229
  Capital Asset Pricing Model, 584
  capital structure, 362, 372, 385
  cost of capital, 375
debt tax shield
  after-tax WACC, 275
  cost of debt, 275, 375
  interest tax deduction, 374
  merger and acquisition transaction, 458
  personal taxes, 385–386
debt-to-equity ratio, 363–364
  see also capital structure
debtholders, 317
  capital structure conflicts, 391–392
  company structure, 316–318
  conflicts of interest, 319–320
  disciplining and monitoring, 323
  firm in bankruptcy, 461
decision horizon, 516
decision making *see* capital budgeting; financial decisions
decision trees, 623, 626

deductibles, insurance, 162
default/bankruptcy risk, 107, 113–114, 368–372, 652
defaults (on debt)
  bonds, 114, 369
  capital structure, 368–372
  credit default swap, 616
  debtholders, 317
  financial distress–direct costs, 389–391
  financial distress–indirect costs, 389–390
  option pricing analysis, 407–415
  see also liquidating a firm
deferral option, 427
degree courses, investing in, 64–66
deposit insurance, 172, 643–644
deposits, 444
depreciation
  accounting categories, 215, 218
  EBITDA, 232, 239, 263
  financial statements, 244–245
  free cash flows, 266–267
  project cash flows, 293–294, 296–297
depreciation expense, 215, 244–245
derivatives, 595–596
  derivative markets, 597
  fundamentals of pricing, 617–626
  swaps, 596, 611–617
  as type of financial instrument, 106
  types of derivative contract, 596–597
  see also forward contracts; futures contracts; options
Dimson, Elroy, 128–130
direct costs of financial distress, 389–391
disability, risk of, 150
discipline (imposed on managers)
  debt and capital structure, 393, 396–397
  hostile takeovers, 325–327
  payout policy, 343, 344
  publicly traded corporations, 451
disclosure
  legal requirements, 324
  voluntary, 323–324
discount bonds
  bond pricing relationships, 488–490
  meaning of, 483–484
  see also zero-coupon bonds (also known as pure discount bonds)
discount factor, 27

discount function, 477–479
discounted cash flow (DCF) analysis, 27
  buying vs. renting a house, 66–69
  calculating company discount rates, 274–276
  Capital Asset Pricing Model, 579–585
  capital structure, 372
  company growth rates, 272–273
  company value, 265–278
  comparison to options-based approach, 433–434
  cost of capital, 363–365, 387–388, 583–584
  equity value, 278–280
  and inflation, 44–49
  lifetime labor and consumption, 59–62
  merger and acquisition deal, 457–458
  and risk, 144
  valuation using, 85–87
  venture capital, 448
discounted payback period, 303
discounting
  Capital Asset Pricing Model, 579–585
  and capital structure, 387–388
  company value, 274–276
  coupon bonds, 482–484
  net present value rule, 34–37, 300–301
  present value, 26–34
  risk-adjusted discount rate, 297–298
disintermediation, 655
diversifiable risk, 155–156
diversification, portfolio selection, 528, 529
diversifying, risk transfer by, 153–156
dividend discount model, 86, 279
dividends, 105
  calculating returns with market and book values, 223–224
  capital structure effects, 344
  flexibility and firm life cycles, 346
  frictionless financial environment, 336–338
  how payout policy can add value, 340–346
  personal taxes, 385–386
  preferred, 335
  regular, 335
  signaling with, 342–343
  special, 335

stock dividends, 117, 335, 346–349
transaction costs and tax, 344–345
dominant strategy, 643
Dow Jones Industrial Index (DJI), 120–121
downward-sloping yield curve
predicting recessions, 479–481
zero-coupon bonds, 477–479
drugs development example, 158, 163–164
duration (bonds), 496–501
dynamic replication, 618–619, 623–626
dynamic trading, 619

early-stage companies
alternative financing, 449–450
life of a firm and financing sources, 441–442
small business loans, 422–423
sources of external private firm financing, 443–450
earnings
consumption smoothing, 59
price/earnings multiple, 84–85
see also EBIT; EBITDA
eBay's IPO example, 453
EBIT (earnings before interest and taxes)
accounting categories, 215
free cash flows, 266–267
profitability ratios, 225–226
times interest earned ratio, 229
EBITDA (earnings before interest, taxes, depreciation, and amortization)
calculating from the income statement, 232
comparables, 239, 263
see also enterprise value to EBITDA (EV/EBITDA) ratio
economic balance sheets, 58–59
economic efficiency, and risk transfer, 162–164
see also efficient markets hypothesis
education, investing in a professional degree, 64–66
effective annual rate (EAR), 22–23
efficiency frontier, 545–546
efficient markets hypothesis, 90
behavioral finance, 96
Challenger space shuttle disaster, 93
COVID-19 pandemic, 90

extracting information from market prices, 96–97
instantaneous trading on the news, 94–95
law of one price, 97
in the legal world, 95
market liquidity, 348
stock value, 90–92
and valuation, 93–94
efficient portfolio, 527–528
empire building, 321
employee stock options, 173, 216
employment, careers in finance, 4
enterprise value, 261–262
enterprise value to EBITDA (EV/EBITDA) ratio, 232, 238
comparable companies, 263, 264
firm growth, 239–240
terminal values, 273
venture capital, 448
entertainment industry
real options, 427
separation of ownership and control, 315–316
entrenchment, 321
entrepreneurs
contributing personal wealth, 441
life of a firm, 441–442
small business loans, 422–423
venture capital, 449
environmental, social, and governance (ESG) objectives, 329–330
equity
capital structure, 355, 357–368
capital structure and asymmetric information, 393–394
as component of company value, 262
financial instruments, 105
historical equity and bond returns across the world, 128–130
option pricing analysis, 408–410, 413–414
private equity firms, 453–455
return on, 223–224, 226, 235–237, 241
equity risk premium, 584
equity structure, 220
equity terminal value see continuation value
equity value
calculating using DCF, 278–280
calculating using options analysis, 416–417
dividend discount model, 279
flows to equity model, 280

equity holders
corporate debt structure, 418
flows to equity (FTE) model, 280
equivalent assets, 83, 86
ethics
capital structure, 391
incentive problems, 164, 650
moral hazard and risk, 164
option pricing analysis, 416–417
risk sharing, 164
European option, 174, 180–186, 188
European Union (EU) regulations, 314–315, 324
ex-dividend price, 336–337
Excel spreadsheets
Capital Asset Pricing Model, 577–579
duration, 499–500
effective annual rate, 24
future value, 18–19
minimum variance portfolio, 557–559
personal lifetime financial plan, 61–62
portfolio calculation, 538–540
present value, 31–32
sensitivity analysis, 277–278
yield to maturity (YTM), 487–488
exchange rate
currency swaps, 615–616
on government bonds, 111–112
exchange-traded funds (ETFs), 119–120, 573
exchange-traded options, 187–189
exclusions, insurance, 161–162
exercise price, 174
exit price see continuation value
exit strategy, 447
expectations theory, term structure of interest rates, 493
expected rate of return
achieving a target, 524
Capital Asset Pricing Model, 562–564, 566–569
forming portfolios, 518–525
fundamental determinants of, 121
productivity of capital goods, 121–122
and risk, 143–144
risky assets, 519–523, 528–532
Ten Principles of Finance, 8–9
expense ratio, 118–119
expenses
accounting rules, 216
in the income statement, 215–216
expiration date, 174, 192

external financing, 356
  see also capital structure
external governance *see* governance, external
external private firm financing
  going public or staying private, 450–455
  sources of, 443–450
  see also financing over a firm's life
Exxon-Mobil governance example, 329

face value, 474–475
fair value *see* market value
Fama-French three-factor model, 586
finance
  meaning of, 3
  reasons to study, 4–5
finance, Ten Principles of, 6, 11
  Principle 1: time value of money, 6, 7, 13, 27, 49, 56, 107, 122, 172, 165, 291, 303, 306, 496, 498
  Principle 2: law of one price, 6, 7, 77, 81, 97, 107, 110, 173, 180, 184–185, 196, 262–263, 360, 407, 410, 413, 419, 471, 473, 475, 489, 491, 493, 603, 608, 609, 617–620, 627
  Principle 3: everything has a cost, 6, 7, 81, 171, 185
  Principle 4: models as incomplete descriptions, 6, 8, 84, 98, 110, 143, 222, 238, 262, 279, 371, 372, 374, 385, 397, 434, 448, 449, 457, 577, 582, 585
  Principle 5: market price, 6, 8, 89, 93, 96, 98, 122, 203, 238, 264, 348, 375, 451, 457, 607, 668
  Principle 6: risk as universal, 6, 8, 9, 113, 122, 130, 135, 140, 145, 149, 162, 165, 171, 204, 292, 406, 426, 496, 514, 518, 562, 563, 567, 668
  Principle 7: risk and expected return, 6, 8, 144, 145, 191, 406, 414, 479, 514, 515, 519, 523, 533, 562, 563, 566
  Principle 8: flexibility in financial decisions has value, 6, 9, 172, 180, 201, 204, 216, 406, 426, 447, 610, 644,
  Principle 9: transparency, verification, and trust, 6, 9, 313, 324, 443, 449, 656
  Principle 10: systems and institutions, 6, 10, 635, 645

Financial Accounting Standards Board (FASB), 216
financial-asset risk, 150
financial assets
  debt as type of, 104–105
  derivatives as type of, 106
  equity as type of, 105
  law of one price, 80–82
  as part of financial markets, 104
financial calculators
  future value, 18
  yield to maturity, 486
  see also Excel spreadsheets
financial decisions
  behavioral biases, 96, 635–636, 638–641
  as different to other types of resource management decisions, 3
  option theory, 406–407
  Principle 6: risk as universal, 8
  Principle 7: risk and expected return, 8–9
  Principle 8: flexibility in financial decisions has value, 9
  Principle 10: systems and institutions, 10
  risk and uncertainty, 3, 140, 142–149
  scenarios for consideration, 2–3
  sociological effects, 641–644
  time value of money, 13
  use of options, 171–173
  using net present value, 34–37
  value maximization, 78
  see also personal financial decisions
financial distress
  direct costs of, 389–391
  indirect costs of, 389–390
  see also defaults (on debt)
financial guarantees, 162, 422–424
financial innovation spiral, 655–656
financial instruments, 103–106
  see also debt; derivatives; equity
financial intermediaries, 5, 103, 636–637
financial leverage ratios, 228–229
financial literacy, 56–57
  see also personal financial decisions
Financial Literacy and Education Commission (FLEC), 57
financial markets, 103
  fundamental determinants of rates of return, 121–122

history of stock and bond returns, 123–130
  and instruments, 103–104
  interest rates, 107–116
  Monte Carlo simulation of future stock market performance, 131–134
  stocks and funds, 116–120
financial models
  Black-Scholes-Merton model, 172
  choice of, 83–84
  law of one price and valuation models, 82–87
  Monte Carlo simulation of future stock market performance, 131–134
  Principle 4: models as incomplete descriptions, 8
  see also discounted cash flow (DCF) analysis
financial planning, 241
  annual cycle, 241–242
  and financial statements, 211, 241–248
  learning-by-doing user interface, 640–641
  shape of the yield curve and recessions, 479–481
  using financial statements, 241–248
financial policy, 323
financial ratios
  analysis and types of, 225–235
  company value, 263
  information about performance, 235–237
  limitations, 240–241
  market valuation, 237–240
  summary of, 233–234
financial service firms, 5, 103
financial statements, 210–211
  balance sheet, 211–214
  difference between market values and accounting book values, 213, 221–224
  financial ratio analysis, 225–235
  functions of, 210–211
  future financial planning and projections, 211, 241–248
  income statement, 214–216
  notes to, 220
  statement of cash flows, 217–219
financial system, 635–637
  components of, 103
  definition, 5
  functional perspective, 635–636, 644–652

functions of, 5–6, 645
and institutions, 637–644
institutions of, 5
levels of analysis, 650–652
new financial innovations,
    653–656
Ten Principles of Finance, 10
trust, 656–657
financial technology lenders (fintech
    lenders), 450
financing activities, cash flow from,
    219
financing decision, 355
    internal and external financing,
        356
    see also capital structure
financing over a firm's life, 440–441
    bankruptcy and liquidation, 461
    going public or staying private,
        450–455
    mergers and acquisitions, 456–460
    sources of, 441–442
    sources of external private firm
        financing, 443–450
fintech, 654, 657
firm growth
    financial ratios, 239–240
    future financial planning and
        projections, 241–248
    long-run, 269–273
    see also business risk
firm value see company value
firm's life see financing over a firm's
    life
fixed and perpetual debt, 384
fixed assets see noncurrent assets
fixed-income instruments, 105
    compared to risky assets, 116–117,
        492
    default risk, 107
    and discount bonds, 474–479
    interest rates, 111–112
    real and nominal rates, 116
    underlying asset, 595–596
fixed-income investments, 482
flat term structure of interest rates, 470
flat yield curve
    predicting recessions, 479–481
    zero-coupon bonds, 477–479
flexibility
    options, 598
    Principle 8: flexibility in financial
        decisions has value, 9
floating interest rates, 612
flow of funds, 636–637
flows to equity (FTE) model, 280
forward contracts, 106, 596

distinction from futures, 599–600,
    601–602
economic functions of, 610–611
extracting information from
    forward prices, 606–607
for financial assets, 607–609
pricing commodities, 602–605
pricing financial forwards,
    608–609
forward price, 599
forward rates of interest, 492–495
framing decisions, 639–640
free cash flow problem, 320–321, 323
    advantages of debt, 393
    payout policy, 343
free cash flow to equity (FCFE)
    model see flows to equity (FTE)
    model
free cash flows (FCF), 265–266
    capital structure, 360–363
    long-run growth rates, 269–273
    merger and acquisition deal, 458
    venture capital, 448
"free lunch", 7–8, 171–172
frictionless financial environment,
    357
    capital structure, 355
    institutions in the financial
        system, 635, 637–644
    Modigliani-Miller (M-M)
        propositions, 336–340, 357–368
    payout, 336–340
frictions, 336
    see also payout policy
functional perspective, the financial
    system, 5–6, 635–636, 644–652
fundamental value see intrinsic
    value
funds
    exchange-traded funds, 119–120,
        573
    financial market rates, 116–120
    index funds, 119
    mutual funds, 118–119, 573, 638
    see also cash flow; payout policy
future planning see financial
    planning
future value
    annuities, 38–39
    calculating, 18–19
    change in interest rate over time,
        24
    and compounding, 15–24
    and discounting, 26–34
    estimating a project's cash flows,
        293–295
    financial ratios, 239–240

inflation, 45–47
interest rates and the law of one
    price, 87–88
key equations, 50–51
long-run growth rates, 269–273
Monte Carlo simulation of future
    stock market performance,
    131–134
negative interest rates, 33–34
options, 171–173
risk, 144–145
sensitivity analysis, 277–278
shape of the yield curve and
    recessions, 479–481
valuing cash flows over multiple
    periods, 15–16
future value factor, 17
future value rule, 35–36
futures contracts, 106, 596
    distinction from forward contracts,
        599–600, 601–602
    economic functions of, 610–611
    extracting information from
        forward prices, 606–607
    for financial assets, 607–609
    pricing commodities, 602–605
    pricing financial futures,
        608–609

general partners, 314, 446
Generally Accepted Accounting
    Principles (GAAP), 211–212
geometric average rate of return, 124
    historical equity and bond returns
        across the world, 128–130
    volatility, 124–126
global financial system, 635–636
global travel, 648, 653–656
going-concern effect, 316
golden parachute, 322
goodwill, 213
governance, external
    activist shareholders, 327–328
    the challenge of multiple
        objectives, 329–330
    hostile takeovers, 325–327
    regulations, 324
governance, internal
    the challenge of multiple
        objectives, 329–330
    corporate governance systems,
        322–324
    financial policy, 323
    pay and contracts, 322–323
    shareholder voting and board
        composition, 323
    voluntary disclosure, 323–324

government decisions, option pricing analysis, 433
government guarantees, 172, 422–424, 643–644
Greeks, 199–200
greenmail, 326–327
gross margin, 215
growing annuities, 40–41
growing perpetuities, 43–44
growth *see* firm growth
guarantees
  capital structure, 422–425
  deposit insurance, 172, 643–644
  financial, 162, 422–424
  real interest rates, 506

health
  drugs development example, 158
  option pricing analysis, 433
  risk of poor health, 150
health insurance, 161–162, 173
hedge ratio, 621
hedgers, 142, 610–611
hedging
  binomial model and replication, 619–622
  risk transfer by, 158–160
heuristics, limitations of financial ratios, 240–241
holdup problems, 447
home ownership, compared to renting, 66–69
  see also mortgages
hostile takeovers, 325–327
household balance sheets, 57–59
households
  real options, 432–433
  risk identification, 150
  see also personal financial decisions
HPQ (Hewlett-Packard Company), 120
human capital
  investing in a professional degree, 64–66
  personal lifetime financial plan, 62
  portfolio selection, 515
  real options, 432–433
hurdle rate, 299
hybrid securities, 105, 424–425

IBM (International Business Machines), 120
idiosyncratic risk, 566–569
illiquidity, 248, 601
immediate annuity, 37–38

implied volatility, 202–204
incentive problems
  agency problems, 313, 319
  and capital structure, 391, 396–397
  the challenge of multiple objectives, 329–330
  conflicts of interest and the board of directors, 321
  conflicts with shareholders and debtholders, 319–320
  corporate governance and strategies, 322–324
  managerial conflicts of interest, 320–321
  payout policy, 343
  regulation and market discipline, 324–328
  risk management, 164
  role of the financial system, 650
income statement, 214–216
  financial ratio analysis, 225–235
  limitations of, 217
income taxes, 216
increase in accounts payable, 218
increase in accounts receivable, 218
increase in inventories, 218
index funds, 119
index options, 188–189
indexing
  Capital Asset Pricing Model, 573
  index-linked gilts, 506
  mutual funds, 118–119
  stock indexes, 118–119, 120–121
  theoretical justification for, 562
  total return swaps, 613–614
indirect costs of financial distress, 389–390
individual retirement accounts (IRAs), 64
inflation
  and capital budgeting, 305–306
  discounted cash flow analysis, 44–49
  effect on interest rates, 115–116
  real vs. nominal interest rates, 505–506
inflation risk, 151
information
  capital structure and asymmetric information, 393–394
  extracting information from forward prices, 606–607
  and market prices, 89–97
  payout with asymmetric information, 340–341

role of the financial system, 649
initial margin, 601–602
initial public offerings (IPOs), 447, 450–453
innovation, the financial system, 653–656
insider trading, 324
institutions
  behavioral biases, 638–641
  the financial system, 5, 637–644
  functional perspective, 644–652
  government guarantees, 422–423
  levels of analysis, 651
  market costs, 638
  sociological effects, 641–644
  Ten Principles of Finance, 10
insurance
  for deposits, 173, 643–644
  features of insurance contracts, 161–162
  financial guarantees, 162
  healthcare, 161–162, 173
  hedging risk, 160
  incentive problems, 164
  life, 515–516
  municipal bonds, 652
  against obsolescence, 173
  premiums, 161
  risk transfer by insuring, 161–162
  role of actuaries, 151–152
intangible assets, 213, 221–222
intellectual property, 213, 327
interest expense, 215
interest payments, 104
interest rate arbitrage, 88
interest rate risk, 151, 496
interest rate sensitivity, 496–501
interest rate swaps, 612–613
interest rates
  after-tax, 64
  APR vs. EAR, 21–23
  buying vs. renting a house, 68–69
  cash flows, 14–15
  certain and constant, 470–472
  changes over time, 24
  compound and simple, 16–17, 32–33
  financial market rates, 107–116
  inflation and discounted cash flow analysis, 44–49
  key equations, 50–51
  law of one price, 87–88
  negative, 33–34
  nominal vs. real, 45
  term structure, 108

see also rates of return; term structure of interest rates
interest tax shield see debt tax shield
internal financing, 356
   see also capital structure
internal governance see governance, internal
internal rate of return (IRR), 298–302, 304
International Financial Reporting Standards (IFRS), 211–212
International Network on Financial Education (INFE), 57
Intertemporal Capital Asset Pricing Model (ICAPM), 586
intrinsic value, 83
   options, 188
   risk, 145
inventories, 218
inventory turnover ratio, 227
investing activities, cash flow from, 219
investment
   allowing more investments through risk transfer, 163–164
   change in interest rate over time, 24
   compound interest, 16–17, 32–33
   cost-saving projects, 289–291
   diversification of risk, 153–157
   hedging risk, 158–160
   in human capital, 64–66
   inflation, 48–49
   more than your entire wealth, 525
   and risk, 143–144
   risk identification, 149–151
   risk redistribution, 163
   role of the financial system, 648–649
   strategies with options, 189–195
   successful investment management, 130
   time value of money, 13
   uncertainty in interest rates, 491–492
   using net present value, 34–37
   yields on bonds, 490
   see also portfolio selection
investment projects
   capital budgeting to choose between, 289–291
   manager conflicts of interest, 320–321
   option pricing analysis, 416–417, 426–432
investment risk, 151
investors

alternative financing, 449–450
forming portfolios, 518–525
personal portfolio selection, 515–518
personal taxes, 385–386
portfolios of multiple risky assets, 527–546
trading horizon, 516
venture capital, 446–449
issuers, 103–104

junior debt, 395, 418–421

Knight, Frank, 142

labor, discounted cash flow model, 59–62
land, investment example, 36
law of one price
   arbitrage, 79–80, 97
   efficient markets hypothesis, 97
   financial asset prices, 80–82
   interest rates, 87–88
   Ten Principles of Finance, 7
   valuation models, 82–87
learning curve effect, 316
legal context
   disclosure requirements, 324
   hostile takeovers and antitrust laws, 326
   laws applying only to corporations, 314–315
   payout policy, 345–346
leverage, 358–360
leverage ratio see debt ratio
leveraged buyout (LBO), 455
leveraged position, 189–191
levered beta, 584
levered firm value, 374
liabilities
   accounting methods, 221–222
   balance sheet, 211–212
   financial statement notes, 220
   hedging risk, 160
   personal resources, 58
   Silicon Valley Bank (SVB) failure, 223
liability risk, 150
life cycle see financing over a firm's life
life expectancy, 517
life insurance, 515–516
lifetime financial planning process, 515
limited liability, 105
   in corporations, 314–315

shareholder conflicts of interest, 319–320
limited partners, 314, 446
liquidating a firm
   hostile takeovers, 325–326, 327
   liquidation proceedings, 461
liquidation value, 456
liquidity
   exchange-traded funds, 119–120
   stock splits and stock dividends, 347–349
   working capital management, 248
liquidity ratios, 229–230
liquidity risk, 151
Lo, Andrew, 158
loan guarantees, 173
loans
   cost to pay back, 20
   default risk, 107, 113–114, 652
   external private firm financing, 443–445
   financial guarantees, 162
   future value, 36–37
   government guarantees, 422–423
long position, 177–179, 525, 599–600
long run
   company growth rates, 269–273
   Monte Carlo simulation of future stock market performance, 131–134
long-term assets, 213
long-term debt, 395
loss given default, 369
losses
   capital gain/loss, 117, 120, 338–339, 386–387
   in the income statement, 214–216
   loss prevention/control, 152

Macaulay duration, 497–500
managers, 317
   capital structure, 393–394
   company structure, 316–318
   conflicts of interest, 320–321
   free cash flow problem, 320–321, 323
   pay and contracts, 322–323
   payout policy, 343
   preventing hostile takeovers, 326, 328
   separation of ownership and control, 315
   threat of being fired, 321
margin, 601–602

margin call, 602
marked to market, 602
market anomalies, 96
market capitalization rate *see* opportunity cost of capital
market competitors, 290, 657
market costs, 638
market discipline
  activist shareholders, 327–328
  hostile takeovers, 325–327
  laws and regulations, 324
market efficiency *see* efficient markets hypothesis
market force dominance, 82
market indexes, 118–119
market liquidity *see* liquidity
market portfolio, 563–569
market prices
  crucial role in asset valuation, 77–78
  information and the efficient markets hypothesis, 89–97
  Ten Principles of Finance, 8
  see also valuation
market risk premium, 567
market to book (M/B) ratio, 231–232, 240
market value
  for a company, 262
  cost of capital, 375
  difference from accounting book values, 213, 221–224
  financial ratios, 237–240
  irrelevance of capital structure to, 357–360
  option pricing, 216
market value balance sheet, 222
market value ratios, 230–235
marketplace option trading, 187–189
marking to market, 222
Markowitz, Harry, 562
Marsh, Paul, 128–130
matching strategy (maturities), 492
mature firms (life of a firm), 441–442
maturity (bonds)
  continuous compounding, 32–33
  duration, 496–501
  price of bonds, 484–485
  the return of the 30-year Treasury, 647
  term structure of implied volatility, 203–204
  term structure of interest rates, 472–474
  yield spread, 114
  zero-coupon bonds, 474–479

maturity date, 174, 192
maturity (debt)
  option pricing analysis, 410–413
  structure of debt, 395–396
maturity matching, 492
mean variance analysis, 546–549
mean variance optimization, 547, 548
medical insurance *see* health insurance
merger and acquisition (M&A) transaction, 456–460
  see also acquisitions
Merton, Robert C., 195–196, 640–641
  see also Black–Scholes–Merton model
Merton, Robert K., 641
mezzanine debt, 395, 418–421
microfinance, 442, 450
Microsoft
  acquisitions as means to expand, 290–291
  share repurchase and dividend programs, 344
Miller, Merton, 357
  see also Modigliani–Miller (M-M) propositions
minimum variance portfolio, 532, 556–557
models *see* financial models
modified duration, 499
Modigliani, Franco, 357
  see also Modigliani–Miller (M-M) propositions
Modigliani–Miller (M-M) propositions
  capital structure, 357–368
  dividends, 336–340
  impact of adding in frictions, 373–388
  institutions in the financial system, 637
money market, 105, 649
money, time value of, 7
  see also pricing
Monte Carlo simulation of future stock market performance, 131–134
moral hazard
  capital structure, 391
  incentive problems, 164, 650
  option pricing analysis, 416–417
Morgan Stanley index, 562
mortality rate, 517
mortgages
  buying vs. renting, 66–69
  government guarantees, 423

  as an ordinary annuity, 37–38
  present value, 40
multi-period binomial model, 623
multiple cash flows, 30
multiples, valuation by, 238–239, 263
municipal bonds, 652
mutual fund separation, 547
mutual funds, 118–119, 573, 638
mutually exclusive projects, 292

national context
  historical equity and bond returns across the world, 128–130
  Principle 10: systems and institutions, 10
negative interest rates, 33–34
negative signal (payout), 341
net income, 216, 218, 223–224
net payoff, 175
net present value (NPV), 34–37
  calculating, 292–293
  capital budgeting, 292–298, 300–301
  capital budgeting in practice, 304
  capital structure, 391–392
  investment rule, 292–298, 304
  option pricing analysis, 431–432
  shareholder conflicts, 319
net working capital (NWC), 213
  free cash flows, 266–267
net worth
  balance sheet, 211–212
  personal resources, 58–59
Netflix, 328
New York Stock Exchange (NYSE), 119, 131–134
no-arbitrage condition, 81
nominal cost of capital, 305–306
nominal interest rates
  and inflation, 115, 505–506
  vs. real, 45, 505–506
nominal prices, 115
noncurrent assets, 213
noncurrent liabilities, 213
nondiversifiable risk, 155–156
notional amount/value, 596–597

obsolescence insurance, 173
off-balance-sheet items, 220
off-exchange markets *see* over-the-counter markets
one-period binomial model, 619–622
open-market repurchase, 335
operating activities, cash flow from, 218
operating income, 215

opportunity cost of capital, 35
  and risk, 144
optimal capital structure, 355,
    388–389, 396–397
optimal combination of risky assets
    (OCRA), 535–536, 547–548
optimal portfolio, 533–536
option pricing analysis, 406–407
  applications of real options
    outside firms, 432–433
  binomial model and replication,
    619–622
  comparison to DCF, 433–434
  corporate debt structure, 416–421
  corporate equity and debt, 407–415
  guarantees and other securities,
    422–425
  project valuation using real
    options, 426–432
option to abandon, 427
option to rescale, 427
optionality, 426
options, 106, 598
  accounting for, 216
  Black-Scholes-Merton model,
    172, 195–204
  in corporate finance decisions,
    406–407
  how options work, 174
  investment strategies with,
    189–195
  payoff diagrams, 180–184,
    192–195, 598
  Principle 8: flexibility in financial
    decisions has value, 9
  put-call parity relation, 180–186
  resolving uncertainty via,
    171–173
  trading in markets, 187–189
  see also call options; put options
ordinary annuities, 37–38
Organization for Economic
    Cooperation and Development
    (OECD), 57
organization structure
  the challenge of multiple
    objectives, 329–330
  conflicts of interest and the board
    of directors, 321
  conflicts with shareholders and
    debtholders, 319–320
  corporate governance and
    strategies, 322–324
  managerial conflicts of interest,
    320–321
  regulation and market discipline,
    324–328

separation of ownership and
    control, 315–316
  shareholders, debtholders,
    managers, and the board of
    directors, 316–318
  supporting decision making, 313
  types of, 314–315
organizational culture, 460
outside directors, 323
over-the-counter (OTC) markets, 104,
    597
over-the-counter (OTC) options,
    187–189
ownership *see* company ownership

paid-in capital, 213–214
par, 104
par bonds, 110, 483, 484–485,
    488–490
par value, 474–477
partners, 314
partnerships, 314
  advantages of, 314
pay
  accounting categories, 215
  corporate governance, 322–323
payables period, 247
payback constraint, 303
payback decision rule, 303
payback period, 303–304
payment services, 648, 653–654
payoff, 192–195, 619–622
payoff diagrams
  forward contracts, 600
  options, 180–184, 192–195, 598
  stocks and riskless bonds, 180–184
payoff probability/payoff density
    charts, 200
payout, 334
  forms of, 334–336
  in a frictionless environment,
    336–340
payout policy, 334
  agency frictions, 343
  asymmetric information and
    signaling, 340–341
  capital structure, 344
  flexibility and firm life cycles, 346
  free cash flow problem, 323
  how payout policy can add value,
    340–346
  stock dividends and splits,
    346–349
  transaction costs and tax, 344–345
  see also dividends; repurchases
pecking order theory, 394
percent-of-sales method, 243–244

performance guarantees, 407
performance monitoring, financial
    planning, 241–242
perpetual debt *see* fixed and
    perpetual debt
perpetuities
  key equations, 50–51
  valuing, 41–44
personal financial decisions, 56
  behavioral biases, 96, 635–636,
    638–641
  buying vs. renting a house, 66–69
  deferring taxes through voluntary
    retirement plans, 64
  discounted cash flow model of
    lifetime labor and consumption,
    59–62
  financial literacy, 56–57
  household balance sheets, 57–59
  human capital investments, 64–66
  portfolio selection, 515–518
  reasons to study finance, 4
  risk identification, 150
  risk tolerance, 518
  savings bonds, 113
  value maximization, 78
  see also investment
personal investing, 58
personal taxes, 385–386
Petrobras capital structure, 393
planning horizon, 516–517
point of tangency, 536
poison pill, 326, 328
pooling resources, 648–649
portfolio efficiency, 527–528
portfolio selection, 515
  betas, 566–569
  Capital Asset Pricing Model, 562,
    563–564, 571–579
  diversification, 528, 529
  personal circumstances, 515–516
  risk tolerance, 518
  time horizons, 516–517
portfolio theory, 514–515
  mean variance analysis and asset
    management, 546–549
  personal portfolio selection,
    515–518
  portfolios of multiple risky assets,
    527–546
  the trade-off between expected
    return and risk, 518–525
portfolio weight, 521
positive signal (payout), 340–341
pre-tax weighted-average cost of
    capital (WACC), 361, 580
preferred dividends, 335

preferred stock, 105, 317
premium, insurance, 161
premium bonds, 483–484, 488–490
present value
  adjusted present value method, 382–387
  annuities, 38–41
  buying vs. renting a house, 66–69
  company value, 265
  discounting, 26–34
  inflation, 47–48
  investment decisions using net present value, 34–37
  key equations, 50–51
  perpetuities, 41–44
  see also net present value
price/earnings multiple, 84–85
price risk of inputs, 150
price risk of outputs, 150
price to earnings (P/E) ratio, 230–231
  comparable companies, 263
  firm growth, 239–240
pricing
  commodity forwards and futures, 602–605
  coupon bonds, 482–484
  derivatives, 617–626
  financial forwards and futures, 608–609
  market price, 8, 77–78, 89–97
  Principle 1: time value of money, 7
  Principle 2: law of one price, 7
  Principle 3: everything has a cost, 7–8
  Principle 5: market price, 8
  see also law of one price; valuation
principal amount, 474–475
principals
  company ownership, 313
  separation of ownership and control, 315–316
private benefits, manager conflicts of interest, 321
private corporations, 314–315
  going public or staying private, 450–455
  ownership, 442
  sources of finance, 443–450
  see also financing over a firm's life
private equity (PE) firms, 453–455
pro forma financial statements, 241, 242–246
product development, capital budgeting, 289–291, 293–295

production risk, 150
productivity, of capital goods, 121–122
professional degrees/qualifications, investing in, 64–66
profit
  in the income statement, 214–216
  net payoff, 175
profitability ratios, 225–227
property, plant, and equipment (PP&E), 213
protective put, 181
psychology see behavioral finance; financial decisions
public choices, reasons to study finance, 4
publicly traded corporations (also known as public corporations)
  financing, 442
  legal context, 314–315
pure discount bonds see zero-coupon bonds
put options, 106, 174–177
  how options work, 174
  investment strategies, 192–195
  option pricing analysis, 414
  payoff diagrams, 598
  put–call parity relation, 180–186
  volatility and pricing, 200–201
putable equity, 425

qualifications, investing in, 64–66
qualitative asset transformation, 444
quick ratio, 230

rates of return
  average returns, 123–124
  on capital, 121–122
  exchange rates and government bonds, 111–112
  forming portfolios, 518–525
  fundamental determinants of, 121–122
  history of stock and bond returns, 123–130
  and inflation, 115–116
  internal (IRR), 298–302, 304
  Monte Carlo simulation of future stock market performance, 131–134
  promised vs. uncertain, 116–117
  and risk, 143–144, 145–149
  yields on bonds, 490
  see also expected rate of return; risk-free rate of return
ratings agencies, 370

rationality, the efficient markets hypothesis, 96
  see also behavioral finance
ratios see financial ratios
re-levering, 364
real cost of capital, 305–306
real interest rates
  and inflation, 115, 505–506
  vs. nominal, 45, 505–506
real options, 173, 407
  applications outside firms, 432–433
  in practice, 429–430
  project valuation using, 426–432
  types of, 427–429
  value of, 430–432
real prices, 115
recessions, shape of the yield curve, 479–481
regular dividends, 335
regulations
  disclosure requirements, 324
  hostile takeovers and antitrust laws, 326
  laws applying only to corporations, 314–315
  payout policy, 345–346
regulators
  checking company disclosures, 324
  understanding the financial system, 5, 103
relationship lending, 443–444
renting a house
  breakeven rent, 68
  compared to buying, 66–69
replication, 617–626
  binomial model, 619–622
  dynamic, 618–619, 623–626
  static, 618
repurchase, 334, 335
  capital structure effects, 344
  flexibility and firm life cycles, 346
  frictionless financial environment, 338–340
  global tech companies example, 344
  legal context, 345–346
required rate of return, 145
research and development (R&D), 290
residual claims, 105, 408
restricted stock, 316–317
restructuring, 461
retained earnings, 213–214
retirement planning

deferring taxes through voluntary retirement plans, 64
discounted cash flow model of lifetime labor and consumption, 59–62
future value, 20
learning-by-doing user interface, 640–641
retirement security bond (RSB), 641
return *see* rates of return
return on assets (ROA), 226, 235–237
return on equity (ROE)
  as accounting measure, 223–224
  calculating, 226
  information about performance, 235–237
  limitations of, 241
return on sales (ROS), 225–226, 235–237
revenues, in the income statement,
risk, 140–142
  capital structure, 360–363, 391–392
  exchange rates and government bonds, 111–112
  in financial decisions, 3, 140, 142–149
  forming portfolios, 518–525
  Knight's concept of, 142
  limitations of financial ratios, 241
  measuring interest rate risk, 496–505
  net present value analysis, 292–293
  option pricing analysis, 410–413
  Principle 3: everything has a cost, 7–8
  Principle 6: risk as universal, 8, 140–141, 171, 292
  Principle 7: risk and expected return, 8–9
  separation of ownership and control, 315–316
  and valuation, 144–145
risk-adjusted discount rate, 297–298
risk aversion, 122
risk avoidance, 152
risk exposure, 141–142
  diversification of risk, 153–156
  hedging, 158–160
  insuring, 161–162
risk-free assets, 143–144
  binomial model and replication, 619–622

Capital Asset Pricing Model, 561–564, 566
combining a riskless asset and a single risky asset, 520–523
how options work, 180–184
mean variance analysis and asset management, 546–549
portfolio optimization, 518
portfolio selection, 518–519, 540–544
terminology, 114
uncertainty in interest rates, 491–495
risk-free debt, 368–369
risk-free interest rate, 114
  cash flow, 479
  determinants of rates of return, 121–122
  fallacy of time diversification, 532–533
  flat term structure, 470–471
risk-free rate of return
  Capital Asset Pricing Model, 563–564, 575–577, 583–584
  capital goods, 121–122
  fundamental determinants of, 121
  history of STRIPS, 111
  Modigliani–Miller (M-M) propositions, 359
  optimal portfolio, 534
  portfolio selection, 519, 523
  types of, 114
  see also risk-free assets
risk management
  the financial system, 646–647
  forwards and futures, 610–611
risk-management process, 149–153
  implementation of techniques, 152
  incentive problems, 164
  in practice, 164
  review of outcomes, 153
  risk assessment, 151–152
  risk identification, 149–151
  selection of techniques, 152
  see also risk transfer
risk premium, 492–495, 523
  Capital Asset Pricing Model, 573, 575–577, 584
risk retention, 152
risk-reward trade-off line, 523, 534–536, 564–566, 572
risk shifting, 391–392, 416–417
risk tolerance, 518
risk transfer, 152, 153
  by diversifying, 153–156
  and economic efficiency, 162–164

by hedging, 158–160
by insuring, 161–162
riskless assets *see* risk-free assets
riskless rate *see* risk-free rate of return
risky assets, 143
  combining a riskless asset and a single risky asset, 520–523
  expected rate of return, 519–523, 528–532
  fallacy of time diversification, 532–533
  hedging risk, 158–160
  measuring financial risk, 145–149
  minimum variance portfolio, 556–557
  optimal combination, 533–536
  portfolio selection, 540–544
  portfolios of multiple risky assets, 527–546
  portfolios of two risky assets, 528–532
rolling over, 492
Rule of 72, 19

salaries *see* pay
sales, general, and administrative (SG&A) expenses, 215, 216
sales revenue, 214, 225–226
Sarbanes-Oxley Act, 325, 453
savings
  discounted cash flow model of lifetime labor and consumption, 59–62
  future value, 20
  household balance sheets, 57–59
  net present value rule, 34–37
  personal savings bonds, 113
savings and loan associations (S&Ls), 651
scenario analysis *see* sensitivity analysis
Scholes, Myron, 195–196
  see also Black–Scholes–Merton model
seasoned equity offering (SEO), 450–451
Secured Overnight Financing Rate (SOFR), 612
securities, 103–104
  30-year maturity example, 647
  capital structure, 422–425
  debt as, 104–105
Securities and Exchange Commission (SEC), 151, 211–212

security market line (SML), 567–568
  alpha portfolio, 573
  vs. capital market line (CML), 571
self-financing, 625
self-fulfilling prophecy, 641–644
semi-strong market efficiency, 94
seniority (debt), 395–396, 418–421
sensitivity analysis, 277–278
  buying vs. renting a house, 68–69
  Capital Asset Pricing Model, 577
  capital budgeting projects, 298, 304
separated structure, 315–316
settlement date, 599
settling payments, 648, 653–654
shareholder meetings, 316
shareholder voting, 316, 319
  board composition, 323
  captured board, 321
shareholders, 105
  activist, 327–328, 329
  calculating returns with market and book values, 223–224
  capital structure conflicts, 391–392
  company structure, 316–318
  conflicts of interest, 319–320
  in corporations, 314–315
  see also payout policy
shareholders' equity, 213–214
shares of stock, 105
shark repellent policies, 326
Shark Tank, 449
Sharpe ratio, 534, 541, 564–566, 572–573
Sharpe, William F., 562
Shiller P/E ratio, 240
short position, 176, 177–179, 525, 599–600
short-term debt, 213, 395
shortfall, 423–424
sickness, risk of, 150
signaling, 340–341, 393
Silicon Valley Bank (SVB), failure of, 223
simple interest, 16–17
small business loans, 422–423
Smith, Adam, 320, 653
social goals, as part of ESG objectives, 329–330
sociological effects, 641–644
sole proprietorship, 314
  advantages of, 314
special dividends, 335
Special Purpose Acquisition Companies (SPACs), 452–453
speculators, 142, 611

spot exchange rate, 615–616
spot interest rate
  forward rates of interest, 493, 495
  term structure, 108, 472–473
spot price, 106, 604–607, 608–609
spreadsheets *see* Excel spreadsheets
staged financing, 447
Standard and Poor's 500 (S&P 500), 120–121
standard deviation
  diversification of risk, 156–157
  measuring financial risk, 145–149
  rates of return, 124–126
standard of living
  financial literacy, 56–57
  portfolio decisions, 516–517
  saving to maintain, 59–61
  see also personal financial decisions
startups
  alternative financing, 449–450
  life of a firm, 441–442
  small business loans, 422–423
  sources of external private firm financing, 443–450
statement of cash flows, 217–219
  see also financial statements
statement of earnings *see* income statement
statement of profit and loss (P&L) *see* income statement
static replication, 618
Staunton, Mike, 128–130
Steinberg, Saul, 327
stock dividends, 117, 335, 346–349
stock indexes, 118–119
  major stock indexes around the world, 118
  types of, 120–121
stock markets
  efficient markets hypothesis, 90–92, 93–94
  Monte Carlo simulation of future stock market performance, 131–134
  publicly traded corporations, 314–315
  reactions to COVID-19, 90
  terminology, 105
  valuation by comparables, 237–239
stock out, 606
stock repurchase/buyback, 334, 335
  capital structure effects, 344
  flexibility and firm life cycles, 346

frictionless financial environment, 338–340
  global tech companies example, 344
  legal context, 345–346
stock splits, 335, 346–349
stock value
  balance sheet, 211–212
  comparable companies, 84–85
  efficient markets hypothesis, 90–92
  financial market rates, 116–120
  how payout policy can add value, 340–346
  instantaneous trading on the news, 94–95
  measuring financial risk, 145–149
  Monte Carlo simulation of future stock market performance, 131–134
  using comparables, 237–239
  vesting period, 322
stocks
  equity securities, 105
  history of rates of return, 123–130
  how options work, 174–179, 180–184
  option pricing analysis, 408–410
  shareholder ownership, 316–317, 319
  sources of return, 117
  using options to modify payoff patterns, 189–191
straddle (options), 192
strike price (options), 174, 175, 176–177, 188
STRIPS (Separate Trading of Registered Interest and Principal of Securities), 108–109
  history of, 111
  yield curve, 109–110
strong market efficiency, 93–94
student loans, 645
subdividing shares, 648–649
subordinated debt (*also known as* junior debt), 395, 418–421
sunk costs, 293–294
swap contract pricing, 617
swap rate, 596–597
swaps, 106, 596, 611–617
switching options, 427
synergy (acquisitions), 456, 457
system *see* financial system
systemic risk, 566–569

takeovers *see* acquisitions
tangency portfolio, 536, 540-542, 564-566
tangible value *see* intrinsic value
target company, 456
target expected return, 524
target risk, 524
tax shield
  adjusted present value method, 382-387
  after-tax WACC, 275, 374-378, 385
  after-tax WACC with a changing capital structure, 379-382
  company value, 374
  personal taxes, 385-386
  trade-off theory of capital structure, 390-391
taxable income, 215
taxation
  and capital structure, 373-388
  corporate taxes, 374
  debt tax shield, 275
  deferring taxes through voluntary retirement plans, 64
  EBITDA, 232, 239, 263
  income taxes, 216
  payout policy, 344-345, 346
technological innovation, 653-656
Ten Principles of Finance *see under* finance
tender-offer repurchase, 335
term structure of implied volatility, 203-204
term structure of interest rates, 108, 469-470
  certain and constant, 470-472
  coupon bonds, 481-491
  determining from pure discount bonds, 474-479
  maturity, 472-474
  measuring interest rate risk, 496-505
  real versus nominal, 505-506
  shape of the yield curve and recessions, 479-481
  uncertainty, 491-495
terminal values, 269-273
terminal wealth, 123
terminal wealth ratio, 123, 124, 126-128
thrift banks, 651
time
  consumption preferences, 122
  in financial decisions, 3
  instantaneous trading on the news, 94-95

time diversification, 532-533
time horizons
  Capital Asset Pricing Model, 577, 583
  par bonds, 110
  portfolio selection, 516-517
  present value, 28-29
time pattern of promised payments, 107-110
time value of money, 13
  future value and compounding, 15-24
  inflation and discounted cash flow analysis, 44-49
  investment decisions using net present value, 34-37
  personal resources, 56
  present value and discounting, 26-34
  Ten Principles of Finance, 7, 49
  using timelines to analyze cash flows, 14-15
  valuing annuities, 37-41
  valuing perpetuities, 41-44
time value (options), 188
timelines, cash flow, 14-15
times interest earned ratio, 229
total cash flow from operations, 218
total change in cash and equivalents, 219
total (company) value, 261-262
total return swaps, 613-614
Toys 'R' Us, 389
trade-off theory of capital structure, 390-391
trading horizon, 516
trading interval, 623
tranched securities, 407
transaction costs, 79-80
  design of institutions, 638
  payout policy, 344-345
  risk management, 164
  stock indexes, 118-119
transparency
  building trust, 657
  Ten Principles of Finance, 9-10
  voluntary disclosure, 323-324
Treasury Inflation Protected Securities (TIPS), 116, 506
treasury stock, 335
trust
  building trust and substitutes for, 657
  and the financial system, 656-657
  relationship lending, 443-444

  Ten Principles of Finance, 9-10
  using agencies, 313
turnover ratios, 227-228

uncertainty
  effect on valuation and decision making, 140
  interest rates, 491-495, 496-505
  investment risk, 151
  Knight's concept of, 142
  as part of risk, 140-142
  Principle 6: risk as universal, 8
  Principle 7: risk and expected return, 8-9
  Principle 8: flexibility in financial decisions has value, 9
  rate of return on capital, 122
  resolving via options, 171-173
underlying asset
  asset-backed securities, 106
  Black-Scholes-Merton model, 195-204
  options, 171, 174, 188-189
underwriters, 451-452, 453
unemployment risk, 150
unified general valuation framework, 407
  analyzing corporate equity and debt, 407-415
  applications of real options outside firms, 432-433
  corporate debt structure, 416-421
  guarantees and other securities, 422-425
  project valuation using real options, 426-432
unit of account, 107
  effect on interest rates, 111-112
  and inflation, 115-116, 306
  maturity matching, 492
  riskless assets, 519
university degrees, investing in, 64-66
unlevered, 358
  see also leverage
unlevered beta, 584-585
unlevered cost of capital, 363-364, 365
unlevered firm value, 374, 382-387
unlimited liability
  partners, 314
  sole proprietorship, 314
unsystematic risk, 566
upward-sloping yield curve
  predicting recessions, 479-481
  zero-coupon bonds, 477-479

valuation, 76–77
  crucial role of market prices, 77–78
  efficient markets hypothesis, 93–94
  financial ratios, 237–240
  financial statements, 211
  interest rates and the law of one price, 87–88
  law of one price and arbitrage, 79–80
  law of one price and efficient markets, 97
  law of one price and financial asset prices, 80–82
  market prices and information, 89–97
  by multiples, 238–239
  real options, 430–432
  and risk, 144–145
  uncertainty in interest rates, 491–495
  value maximization and financial decisions, 78
  see also company value; market value; time value of money; unified general valuation framework
valuation by comparables, 84–85, 89
  company value, 263–264
  financial ratios, 237–239
  limitations of financial ratios, 240
  venture capital, 448
valuation models
  adjusted present value method, 382–387
  after-tax WACC, 374–378
  after-tax WACC with a changing capital structure, 379–382
  law of one price, 82–87
  merger and acquisition (M&A) deal, 457–458

option pricing analysis, 406–407
unified general valuation framework, 407
see also discounted cash flow analysis; valuation by comparables
value see future value; present value
value maximization, 78
variance, portfolio selection, 529, 532
  see also minimum variance portfolio
VC funds, 446–449
venture capital, 446–449
verification, 9–10, 657
vesting period, 322
volatility
  history of rates of return, 124–126
  implied, 202–204
  measuring financial risk, 145–149
  option pricing, 200–201
  risky assets, 520, 521–522
volatility risk, 151
voluntary disclosure, 323–324
voting see shareholder voting

Walt Disney, hostile takeover attempt, 327
weak market efficiency, 94
wealth
  accounting and economic balance sheets, 58–59
  financial literacy, 56–57
  investing more than your entire wealth, 525
  personal portfolio selection, 515–518
  risk tolerance, 518
  trust and wealth management, 656–657
  see also investment; personal financial decisions

wealth ratio
  Monte Carlo simulation of future stock market performance, 131–134
  terminal wealth ratio, 123, 124, 126–128
weighted-average cost of capital (WACC), 275
  Capital Asset Pricing Model, 580
  capital structure, 361
  merger and acquisition (M&A) deal, 458
  see also after-tax WACC; pre-tax WACC
welfare, risk redistribution, 163
working capital, 246–248
world travel, 648, 653–656
writing (options), 176

yield curve
  forward rates of interest, 494–495
  interest rate change, 109–110
  shape of the yield curve and recessions, 479–481
  zero-coupon bonds, 477–479
yield spread, 114
yield to maturity (YTM), 109
  coupon bonds, 486–490
  different maturities, 471–472, 473
  zero-coupon bonds, 475–477
young companies see startups

zero-coupon bonds (also known as pure discount bonds), 108
  determining interest rates, 474–479
  discounting, 482–484
  forward rates of interest, 494
  measuring interest rate risk, 496–505
  option pricing analysis, 408–410
  options payoff, 180–181
zero-coupon yield curve, 109–110

For EU product safety concerns, contact us at Calle de José Abascal, 56–1°,
28003 Madrid, Spain or eugpsr@cambridge.org.

www.ingramcontent.com/pod-product-compliance
Ingram Content Group UK Ltd.
Pitfield, Milton Keynes, MK11 3LW, UK
UKHW052252100325
456030UK00004B/9